BUSINESS LAW IN CANADA

Ninth Edition

RICHARD A. YATES
SIMON FRASER UNIVERSITY

TERESA BEREZNICKI-KOROL
NORTHERN ALBERTA INSTITUTE OF TECHNOLOGY

TREVOR CLARKE
SAIT POLYTECHNIC

Pearson Canada
Toronto

Library and Archives Canada Cataloguing in Publication

Yates, Richard
      Business law in Canada / Richard A. Yates, Teresa Bereznicki-Korol,
Trevor Clarke. — 9th ed.

Includes bibliographical references and index.
ISBN 978-0-13-505177-1

      1. Commercial law—Canada. I. Bereznicki-Korol, Teresa, 1957– II.
Clarke, Trevor, 1952– III. Title.

KE919.Y376 2011   346.7107   C2009-905544-9
KF889.Y383 2011

ISBN 978-0-13-505177-1

Vice President, Editorial Director: Gary Bennett
Acquisitions Editor: Karen Elliott
Sponsoring Editor: Alexandra Dyer
Marketing Manager: Leigh-Anne Graham
Developmental Editor: John Lewis
Production Editor: Kevin Leung
Copy Editor: Catharine Haggert
Proofreaders: Strong Finish, Laurel Sparrow
Production Manager: Tracy Bordian
Permissions Research: Sandy Cooke
Composition: Christine Velakis
Art Director: Julia Hall
Cover Design: Miguel Acevedo
Cover Image: istock

Statistics Canada information is used with the permission of Statistics Canada. Users are
forbidden to copy the data and redisseminate them, in an original or modified form, for
commercial purposes, without permission from Statistics Canada. Information on the
availability of the wide range of data from Statistics Canada can be obtained from
Statistics Canada's Regional Offices, its World Wide Web site at http://www.statcan.gc.ca,
and its toll-free access number 1-800-263-1136.

2 3 4 5   14 13 12 11

Printed and bound in the United States of America.

Brief Contents

Contents

Preface

In order to ensure that *Business Law in Canada* continues to be a valuable resource to post-secondary instructors and students, the ninth edition has undergone a thorough revision and reorganization. The new edition reflects the most current developments in business law, as well as the increasing importance of information technology, the internet, intellectual property, and legal issues concerning small businesses. It also incorporates the large amount of feedback and many thoughtful suggestions provided by users of the eighth edition.

Changes to the Ninth Edition

The table of contents has been reorganized in the following ways:

1. Part 2 of the eighth edition, "The Fundamentals," has been divided into two separate parts, one for torts and one for contracts.
2. The material about real, personal, and intellectual property has been combined into one chapter (Chapter 13).
3. There is a chapter (Chapter 14) devoted to information technology and the internet.
4. Part 3 of the eighth edition, "Commercial Transactions," has become Part 5, the final part of the ninth edition.

In addition, the following pedagogical changes have been made to the ninth edition:

1. The Chapter Highlights have been changed to Chapter Objectives, which will facilitate the integration of the textbook with the new MyBusLawLab. The MyBusLawLab is an exciting new online learning tool for both students and instructors (see below under "Supplements" for more information).
2. The ninth edition introduces a new small business-based perspective for the textbook. A "Small Business Perspective" feature has been added to some of the Case Summaries. These features draw on the case material to highlight important legal issues, ideas, and precedents relevant to small business owners.
3. Other Case Summaries remain accompanied by Discussion Questions. These questions involve students with the subject matter, requiring them to critically consider the implications of the decisions for the everyday practice of business in Canada.
4. Many of the Case Summaries, Reducing Risk boxes, Cases for Discussion, and Discussion Questions have been replaced, reflecting recent legislative and judicial developments.
5. Changes have been made to facilitate use of the new MyBusLawLab. The cases at the end of each chapter have been updated and the MyBusLawLab provides links for more of them, either to a summary of the court judgment or to the text of the judgment itself. Students can then determine the outcome of the cases on their own. Strategically located provincial icons in the textbook indicate the presence of relevant material on the MyBusLawLab.

The key changes for each chapter are listed below:

Chapter 1: Managing Your Legal Affairs—Short discussions about solicitor-client privilege and the licensing of paralegals in Ontario have been added, pursuant to requests by reviewers of the chapter. The material was updated; reference has been made to the cases involving Martin Wirick, the Vancouver lawyer convicted of defrauding clients and lenders of nearly $40 million, and Bernard Madoff, who defrauded investors of as much as $65 billion.

Chapter 2: Introduction to the Legal System—This material was updated in light of recent political events and judicial decisions. Prime Minister Harper's request to prorogue Parliament provided an opportunity to examine the role convention continues to play in Canada. The *Chatterjee* case, where a university student recently challenged the constitutional validity of a provincial law, is examined. Several recent *Charter* cases are also discussed, including the *Fraser v. Ontario* decision and *Mounted Police Association of Ontario v. Canada* decision, dealing with laws restricting collective bargaining.

Chapter 3: The Resolution of Disputes—The Courts and Alternatives to Litigation—Reference is made to the recent changes in the court system, including the introduction of "mental health courts" and "Aboriginal courts." A short discussion regarding the change, in some jurisdictions, to the limitations of legislation which involves a discovery period and an ultimate limitation period, has been added. A short description of online dispute resolution has been included in the material dealing with alternative dispute resolution.

Chapter 4: Intentional Torts and Torts Impacting Business—The division of tort law into two chapters was well received by reviewers and users of the text, and was therefore maintained in this edition. Discussion of the torts of trespass to chattels, conversion, and detinue has been pooled. Recent case law concerning defamation over the internet, and whether defamation law violates freedom of expression (*WeGo Kayaking* case and *WIC Radio v. Simpson*) is presented. The evolution of defamation law, including the Court's recognition of the public interest responsible journalism defence in the *Cusson v. Quan* case is examined. Finally, the Courts' willingness to expand tort law to compensate victims of invasion of privacy is discussed.

Chapter 5: Negligence, Professional Liability and Insurance—Policy considerations evidently play a large role when the Courts are called upon to recognize a new duty of care. This is evident in several recent decisions discussed in the text, including *Dobson v. Dobson*, *Childs v. Desormeaux*, and *D'Amato v. Badger*. Insurance and tort law issues often arise simultaneously, as is evident in the recent cases concerning whether an insurer will need to pay when commission of the tort is severable from operation of the insured motor vehicle, as discussed in the recent *Vytlingam*, *Lubermen's Mutual*, and *Hannah* cases.

Chapter 6: Formation of Contracts—Several of the Case Summaries and Cases for Discussion have been updated to reflect recent judicial decisions. In addition, some of the Discussion Questions have been replaced by comments and questions from the Small Business Perspective.

Chapter 7: Formation of Contracts (Continued)—Chapter 7 continues the discussion started in the eighth edition, about how the Courts will handle cases involving the contractual element of "legality." A summary of a recent Supreme Court of Canada case which outlines the appropriate judicial approach to restrictive covenants in employment contracts, and in purchase and sale agreements, is included.

Chapter 8: Factors Affecting the Contractual Relationship—The case law concerning contracts is examined from the perspective of a small business. Pitfalls to avoid, such as failing to read a contract before signing it or making unsubstantiated representations that later damage a contract's enforceability, are highlighted.

Chapter 9: The End of the Contractual Relationship—Case summaries have been updated concerning anticipatory breach, the enforceability of deposit clauses, and the duty of good faith.

Chapter 10: Employment—The updating of the material includes reference to three recent Supreme Court of Canada decisions. The first case concerns the damages to be awarded in a wrongful dismissal case for the manner of dismissal. The second case examines the issue of whether there is a general duty on employees not to compete with their former employer. The third case relates to the constitutional right of employees to bargain collectively.

Chapter 11: Agency and Partnership—Several of the Case Summaries are new, as are some of the Cases for Discussion at the end of the chapter. As in other chapters, the Discussion Questions have often been recast as comments from the Small Business Perspective.

Chapter 12: Corporations—Some of the Case Summaries and Cases for Discussion have been revised to include recent jurisprudence involving the separate legal entity principle, the personal liability of corporate promoters, the extent of the fiduciary duty of shareholders and of directors, and the remedies available to shareholders and others.

Chapter 13: Real, Personal and Intellectual Property—The material concerning property and the laws pertaining to its ownership and use have been reorganized. Real property is now examined first. As this chapter examines such a breadth of topics, the topic of mortgage and foreclosure law has been removed. The examination of intellectual property law necessarily precedes the study of laws addressing the internet and its use.

Chapter 14: Information Technology and the Internet—Chapter 14 addresses a rapidly changing body of law—that concerning information technology and the internet. Several contemporary issues are examined, including employers' monitoring of computer use by employees; establishing jurisdiction when litigation concerns misuse of the internet; and cybersquatting and the steps taken to combat it, amongst others.

Chapter 15: Sales and Consumer Protection—The consumer protection material in Chapter 15 has been reorganized. It now begins with a discussion of the federal legislation, with an emphasis on the *Competition Act*. Provincial consumer protection legislation is then reviewed. This section includes a new discussion on some of the laws dealing with gift cards that have recently been introduced. Recent legislative changes dealing with payday loans are also reviewed.

Chapter 16: Priority of Creditors—A summary of a recent Supreme Court of Canada case which discusses how the *Bankruptcy and Insolvency Act* and the *Personal Property Security Act* will be interpreted by the courts has been added to Chapter 16. Recent amendments to the *Bankruptcy and Insolvency Act* that are now in force have been incorporated into the material.

We believe that the changes noted above have significantly improved the textbook. In addition, all of the material has been appropriately researched and updated, and the provincial material included in the new MyBusLawLab ensures that students will learn how to access legal information online. This knowledge will be of practical benefit to them in managing their future legal affairs.

With all of the revisions explained above, the updates reflecting recent changes to the relevant legislation and case law, and the interconnection with computer technology, the ninth edition of Business Law in Canada will continue to be an invaluable resource for instructors and students alike.

Features

You will find the following text features in the ninth edition:

Chapter Objectives provide an overview of the chapter content.

Diagrams illustrate cases with complex fact patterns.

"Reducing Risk" boxes are highlighted throughout the text.

Case Summaries appear throughout each chapter. They are used to introduce topics and to provide concrete examples that help students understand key legal issues. Many of the Case Summaries also include Discussion Questions, which help promote a more thorough understanding of the relevant issues, or Small Business Perspectives, which identify the relevant legal issues facing small business owners.

Key legal terms appear in bold and full definitions appear in the Glossary.

Marginal notes summarize adjacent paragraphs and highlight key points.

Provincial icons direct students to additional information in provincial supplements on the Pearson MyBusLawLab.

Summaries in point-form promote quick review and reference.

Finally, we remind all who use this text that it is designed as a tool for learning business law and not as an authoritative source of legal advice. When faced with a specific legal problem, the reader is advised to seek the assistance of a lawyer.

Supplements

Business Law in Canada, Ninth Edition, is accompanied by a complete supplements package.

www.pearsoned.ca/mybuslawlab

MyBusLawLab. We have introduced MyBusLawLab, an online study tool for students and an online homework and assessment tool for faculty. An access code to MyBusLawLab at **www.pearsoned.ca/mybuslawlab** is included with this textbook. MyBusLawLab provides students with an assortment of tools to help enrich the learning experience, including

- pre- and post-tests with study plan,
- mini-cases with assessment questions,
- provincial material,
- audio summaries and videos with assessment questions, and
- a Pearson eText electronic version of the textbook.

Pearson eText gives students access to the text whenever and wherever they have access to the internet. eText pages look exactly like the printed text, offering powerful new functionality for students and instructors. Users can create notes, highlight text in different colours, create bookmarks, zoom, click hyperlinked words and phrases to view definitions, and view in single-page or two-page view. Pearson eText allows for quick navigation to key parts of the eText using a table of contents and provides full-text search.

Instructor's Resource Manual. This supplement contains summaries of each chapter; answers to the questions found at the end of each chapter in the text; and solutions to the cases, plus their full citations. The Instructor's Resource Manual is available for download from Pearson Education Canada's online catalogue at **http://vig.pearsoned.ca** and on the Instructor's Resource CD-ROM that accompanies this textbook.

MyTest/TestGen. This computerized testbank contains over 2000 multiple choice, true/false, and short essay questions with answers. Each question has been checked for accuracy and is available in the latest version of TestGen software. This software package allows instructors to custom design, generate, and save classroom tests. The test program permits instructors to edit, add, or delete questions from the test bank; edit existing graphics and create new ones; analyze test results; and organize a database of tests and student results. This software allows for greater flexibility and ease of use. It provides many options for organizing and displaying tests, along with search and sort features. The TestGen testbank for *Business Law in Canada* is available for download from Pearson Education Canada's online catalogue at **http://vig.pearsoned.ca** and on the Instructor's Resource CD-ROM.

PowerPoint Presentations. Over 400 slides highlighting key concepts featured in the text are available for download from Pearson Education Canada's online catalogue at **http://vig.pearsoned.ca** and on the Instructor's Resource CD-ROM.

Instructor's Resource CD-ROM. This supplement includes electronic files for the complete Instructor's Resource Manual; the TestGen testbank; and the PowerPoint Presentations. The materials are provided as MS Word and PowerPoint files, as well as PDF files, allowing the instructor to customize portions and provide them to students as appropriate.

CBC Video Cases. Current information from CBC programs complements the text and enhances learning by bringing practical applications and issues to life. These videos are available in DVD format. An accompanying Video Guide can be downloaded in pdf format from Pearson Education Canada's online catalogue at **http://vig.pearsoned.ca.**

Study Guide and Workbook This supplement provides a list of learning objectives for each chapter; chapter-by-chapter outlines; matching quizzes of the key terms from each chapter; review questions with an accompanying answer key; Web activities; group study activities; and guidelines for conducting legal research and briefing a law report.

CourseSmart. CourseSmart goes beyond traditional expectations—providing instant, online access to the textbooks and course materials at a lower cost for students (average savings of 50%). With instant access from any computer and the ability to search the text, students will find the content they need quickly, no matter where they are. And with online tools like highlighting and note-taking, students can save time and study efficiently.

Instructors can save time and hassle with a digital eTextbook that allows them to search for the most relevant content at the very moment they need it. Whether it's evaluating textbooks or creating lecture notes to help students with difficult concepts, CourseSmart can make life a little easier. See all the benefits at **www.coursesmart.com/instructors** or **www.coursesmart.com/students**.

Technology Specialists. Pearson's Technology Specialists work with faculty and campus course designers to ensure that Pearson technology products, assessment tools, and online course materials are tailored to meet your specific needs. This highly qualified team is dedicated to helping schools take full advantage of a wide range of educational resources by assisting in the integration of a variety of instructional materials and media formats. Your local Pearson Canada sales representative can provide you with more details on this service program.

Acknowledgments

As has been the case in every new edition of *Business Law in Canada*, reviewers have played an important role in correcting, reshaping, and updating the book and we would like to acknowledge their invaluable contribution. In addition to providing encouragement and insight into what instructors want and need, they provide an important connection to the people this book is designed to serve.

We thank all those who have patiently gone over the text and made suggestions for revision, including Josje Andmore, Camosun College; Bernie Aron, Humber College; Joe Bateman; Douglas H. Beatty, Lambton College; Connie Carter, Royal Roads University; Dana H. Chamberlain, Vancouver Island University; Odette Coccola, Camosun College; David Coulson, Kwantlen Polytechnic University; Marshall Garnick; Andrew Hladyshevsky, Fraser Milner Casgrain LLP; N. Garth Maguire, Okanagan College; Glen W. McCann, Sullivan Mahoney LLP; Panayota Papadeas, St. Clair College of Applied Arts & Technology; Jim Silovs, Mount Royal College; Patti Ann Sullivan, Centennial College.

The writing and publishing of a textbook requires a coordinated effort by many people. We were fortunate; Pearson Education Canada provided us with a team of enthusiastic and knowledgeable people, all of whom willingly helped us, in many ways. We are extremely grateful for, and appreciative of, the assistance and support we received from everyone at Pearson Education Canada, including Alexandra Dyer, Don Thompson, Leigh-Anne Graham, John Lewis, and Kevin Leung.

Writing a currrent law text that addresses a breadth of legal topics can best be achieved through drawing on the expertise of others and building on earlier research. I would like to acknowledge the past contributions of Richard Yates, our former co-author, as well as Jennifer Flynn and Kelley Tees, researchers for earlier editions. I would also like to acknowledge the support received from the staff at the JR Shaw School of Business at NAIT, including the insightful contributions of the "legal team": Douglas Kennedy, Donna Groves, and Craig Grubisich.

—*Teresa Bereznicki-Korol, BA, LLB*

One of the biggest challenges in writing a business law textbook is ensuring that the legislation and the case law are up-to-date. This requires time-consuming, detailed research. I was very lucky that a former student of mine, Larissa Svekla, BMgt, LLB, agreed to assist me with the research needed on the chapters for which I was responsible. I was also fortunate to have Cristina Dahl as my Executive Assistant for most of the time during which I was writing the textbook. I would not have been able to do it without Larissa's excellent research and Cristina's exceptional support. Thank you very much, Larissa and Cristina!

—Trevor Clarke, BSc, MBA, LLB

Dedication

Writing a business law textbook is a huge undertaking. It requires commitment and sacrifice, not just by the authors, but also by their families. This edition of *Business Law in Canada*, like all of the previous editions, would not have been possible without the total and unwavering support of our families. We would again like to thank them for their patience, tolerance, and loyalty. We both realize how lucky we are to have such forgiving families!

Chapter 1

Managing Your Legal Affairs

1. Explain the meaning of "sophisticated client"
2. Describe the role of the lawyer
3. Identify when to hire a lawyer and when to represent yourself
4. Explain how to find a good lawyer
5. Describe legal aid
6. Explain how lawyers bill their clients
7. Outline the procedure to follow to complain about your lawyer
8. Discuss the ethics of lawyers and of clients
9. Describe a code of business conduct

Have you heard about the lawyers' word processor?
No matter what font you select, everything comes out in fine print.

Lawyers constantly hear lawyer jokes at parties and receive them via email. Some business law students tell lawyer jokes in class. This is often a humorous attempt to embarrass the lawyer who is teaching the class.

Students tell lawyer jokes...

"I THINK I NEED LEGAL ADVICE..."

Sometimes a student who has told a lawyer joke in class (or a friend or relative of the student) becomes involved in a "legal situation" during the semester. She may have been charged with a criminal offence. She may have become eligible to apply for a pardon for a crime for which she was previously convicted. She may have received a traffic ticket, or been charged with a drinking-and-driving offence. She may have been involved in a car accident and be facing charges, or be having difficulty dealing with the insurance company in obtaining benefits. She may not have received her damage deposit from her former landlord, or be in some sort of dispute with her landlord. She may be unable to collect from someone to whom she lent money. She may have been involved in a house deal that has collapsed. She may be involved in divorce proceedings, or a custody dispute. She may have been served with a restraining order. She may have a business idea involving a product she has invented. She may have written a song, or a software program for a computer game. She may be thinking of setting up a business with one of her friends or relatives.

All of the above situations (and many more) have been experienced by students of the authors of this textbook during recent semesters. (Some of these situations have in fact been going on for extended periods of time.) In every case, the involved student approached her business law instructor to ask for advice. That is, while the typical student may publicly participate in the criticism of lawyers, when faced with a personal problem involving legal aspects, she will unashamedly seek advice from a lawyer.

But will seek advice from lawyer when necessary

The student often approaches the instructor because she has suddenly realized that the situation in which the student (or her friend or relative) is involved relates to legal issues, or requires decisions that require legal input if they are to be dealt with appropriately. The student often says, "My parents don't know that I am speaking to you about this issue." Alternatively, she may say, "My friend heard me talking about the business law course I'm taking and asked me to ask you about this issue."

This usually indicates that the student has been listening during her business law classes and has been reading the relevant course materials. She has begun to realize that many decisions in today's world involve legal issues and that good decisions can be made only if appropriate attention is paid to the relevant legal advice. She therefore puts aside the bias against lawyers with which she started the course and approaches a lawyer (her business law instructor) to obtain the relevant legal advice.

This textbook attempts to help the student develop the attitude that it is often best to obtain legal advice before making business decisions. Obtaining relevant legal advice on a timely basis requires putting aside the usual derision and public mistrust of lawyers and, instead, building a good long-term relationship with a lawyer. We will refer to someone who understands the importance of the solicitor–client relationship and who knows how to form and utilize such a relationship to make good business decisions as a "sophisticated client." This textbook will try to help business law students become sophisticated clients, so that they can manage their legal affairs more efficiently and effectively.

Meaning of "sophisticated client"

Objective to help students become sophisticated clients

BECOMING A SOPHISTICATED CLIENT

The first step in becoming what is known as a "sophisticated client" is to understand what is meant by the phrase. The dictionary meaning of "sophisticated"[1] would suggest that a sophisticated client is confident, knowledgeable, and very up-to-date. A **sophisticated client** understands the role of the lawyer and of the client. A sophisticated client knows when to represent herself, when to hire a lawyer, and how to hire a lawyer. She understands the costs associated with hiring a lawyer. A sophisticated client also knows what can be done if she is dissatisfied with the conduct of her lawyer. All these topics will be discussed later in this chapter.

Taking a business law course often helps students understand the significance of becoming a sophisticated client. It also marks the beginning of their

---

[1.] Encarta World English Dictionary, online: encarta.msn.com/dictionary_/sophisticated.html.

development into sophisticated clients. One of the authors of this textbook asked the question "Explain the meaning of 'sophisticated client' and discuss whether the objective of helping you develop into a sophisticated client has been achieved during the course" on the final exam for a law course. The following is the answer to the question provided by J.D., one of the students in the class:

> My wife and I bought our first house last winter. When we met with the owners prior to making an offer, we asked, "What is hiding under the snow?" Their answer was what we expected: "A few perennials, tulips, and shrubs."
>
> Three months later, after the snow melted and the grass turned green, my wife and I were frustrated to find 18 horrific fairy rings![2] The only salvation to this unmanageable fungus required a backhoe, 10 dump-truck loads of dirt, and 7 pallets of new grass.
>
> This just didn't feel right. Why should we have to pay to correct the problem? Sure, the sellers told us most of what was under the snow, but they didn't mention the fairy rings. I knew that there must be something I could do.
>
> I sent a carefully worded letter to the sellers, advising them of the problem and reminding them of our question and their answer. I sent the letter to our address, hoping that the mail forward would catch it. It did. We soon received a cheque from the sellers for the amount it cost us to correct the problem.
>
> So, am I a sophisticated client? Maybe. But I'm sure that I have learned three major points:
>
> 1. The law will protect you from people who try to take advantage of you.
> 2. The law is sophisticated.
> 3. So, too, must you be.
>
> I am certain that I can identify when I'm in a situation where the law might be able to help. I'm not talking about going to court, or immediately hiring a lawyer. I'm referring to knowing how to use the law to get justice without going to court.
>
> •   Get advice from a professional or others in a similar circumstance.
> •   Send a persuasive and professional letter.
> •   Apply various pressures, such as follow-up telephone calls.
>
> You define a sophisticated client as one who approaches the law very carefully, takes nothing for granted, and makes suitable decisions given his specific circumstances.
>
> Yeah, I suppose I am sophisticated. Thank you, again.

Many other business law students have expressed similar thoughts. A business law course, with its practical emphasis on general legal principles as they apply to many different areas of business, often works as a catalyst in the development of students. It provides a spark that results in a sense of empowerment. Students come to realize that business decisions are made all of the time, and that these

---

[2.] Fairy rings are dark green or brown circular bands, sometimes including mushrooms, that appear in lawns during spring and summer months. The rings result from fungi. They are very difficult to control, often requiring expensive remedial measures.

decisions usually have serious consequences. They begin to understand that it is therefore critical that good decisions be made.

The business law course also makes it obvious that good business decisions cannot be made without consideration of the appropriate laws. The students start to appreciate that sometimes, through their own research, they can find the legal information required to enable them to make sound business decisions, but that sometimes the necessary information must be obtained from a lawyer. This understanding of the importance of having a good lawyer on your team is a critical component of being a sophisticated client.

Need a lawyer on team

A useful example illustrating how students come to understand the advantages of considering the relevant laws when making business decisions involves the importance of evidence. Students learn that the burden of proof borne by the plaintiff in a civil lawsuit is that he must prove his case on a balance of probabilities. The students see that evidence is introduced during the trial through the testimony of witnesses, on direct examination, cross-examination, and re-examination. They learn that the evidence can be a tangible object ("the bloody knife"), a piece of documentation ("the contract"), or simply an eyewitness account. They learn that hearsay (second-hand) evidence is not admissible. Once the students learn about the importance of evidence in satisfying the relevant burden of proof, and the different types of admissible evidence, their behaviour changes. They will take pictures after a car accident, for example, and get the names and telephone numbers of any witnesses. They will also understand the significance of having a written contract for a business transaction. They know that they may not win a case based on a verbal contract, when the evidence will consist of their word against the word of the other party. They then realize that the lawyer is not advising her clients to "Get it in writing!" simply to generate legal work for which the lawyer will be paid. They will instead understand that the lawyer has provided legal advice to facilitate the making of good business decisions. They are now approaching the situations that they encounter as sophisticated clients.

THE ROLE OF THE LAWYER

mybuslawlab
www.pearsoned.ca/mybuslawlab

BC AB SK MB ON

Client is decision-maker

One of the reasons for the general lack of respect for lawyers is that many people do not understand the role of the lawyer in the solicitor–client relationship. This misunderstanding is shown by the student who, after consulting with a lawyer, claims, "My lawyer told me to do this." This statement implies that the decision-maker in the relationship is the lawyer, not the client.

The better approach is to see the client as the decision-maker. She has encountered a problem and must make a decision. She needs to collect certain information before she can make an informed decision. In this regard, she consults her "experts," namely, her accountant, marketing manager, human resources officer... anyone who can provide relevant information. She gathers all of the useful information, which she then takes into consideration when she makes her decision.

Lawyer is expert providing advice

The lawyer is simply one of the experts the businessperson consults. The lawyer provides legal advice relevant to the client's situation. The client is, of course, free to ignore the legal advice she receives, just as she is free to ignore any other advice she receives. Sometimes it would be unwise to ignore the lawyer's advice. ("If you do this, then you will be committing a crime for which you will go to jail if you are convicted.") But the businessperson makes her decisions in light of all of the relevant factors. She may therefore choose to accept some legal risk because she deems some other business factors to be of greater importance.

A clear understanding of the nature of the solicitor–client relationship will demystify the role of lawyers. While they typically are experts in their area of practice and can provide invaluable assistance to their clients, lawyers are simply providers of advice. They are hired by the client, who provides them with instructions. The lawyer is bound to follow these instructions, provided that they are lawful.

There is one aspect of this relationship that must be emphasized. A lawyer's advice to his client will not be of any value unless the client has provided all relevant information to the lawyer. If the client does not have confidence that her information will be kept confidential, she may not divulge all of the relevant information to the lawyer. **"Solicitor–client privilege"** refers to the duty of the lawyer to keep the information provided by the client confidential. Solicitor–client privilege is therefore fundamental to our legal system as without it the access to justice would be significantly reduced. Most lawyers will advise their clients about solicitor–client privilege and encourage their clients to disclose all relevant information. A sophisticated client will understand that the value of the legal advice provided will vary directly with the completeness of the information provided to the lawyer.

> A client's information must be kept confidential.

CASE SUMMARY 1.1

Can Solicitor–Client Privilege Be Ignored? *Canada (Privacy Commissioner) v. Blood Tribe Department of Health*[3]

The Privacy Commissioner requested records from an employer, with respect to an employee requesting access to her personal employment information. The employee, who had been dismissed, suspected that the employer had improperly collected inaccurate information and used it to discredit her before its board of directors. At the time of dismissal, the employer had sought legal advice from its lawyers. The employer claimed solicitor–client privilege for certain records and refused to provide them. The Federal Court ordered that these records be provided to the Privacy Commissioner, so that she could fulfill her statutory investigative role. The Federal Court of Appeal reversed this decision and ordered that the records did not have to be provided. The Supreme Court of Canada upheld this decision on the basis that the relevant legislation did not expressly allow the Privacy Commissioner to "pierce" the solicitor–client privilege. Given the fundamental importance of the privilege, clear and explicit language is required to allow it to be breached.

SMALL BUSINESS PERSPECTIVE

A businessperson seeking legal advice must be completely honest with her lawyer or the legal advice provided by the lawyer will not be appropriate for her situation. The client need not worry that the information she provides will be made public, as the lawyer is obligated to maintain confidentiality, by the solicitor–client privilege. Are there any exceptions to the general rule that solicitor–client privilege attaches to all communications between a client and her lawyer?

[3.]   *Canada (Privacy Commissioner) v. Blood Tribe Department of Health*, 2008 SCC 44.

It is useful to examine the solicitor–client relationship in the context of a small business. From start-up to the selling of the business, the owner has many decisions to make. As a sophisticated client, when should the small business owner consult his lawyer for advice?[4]

Business owners make many different decisions

www.pearsoned.ca/mybuslawlab

BC AB SK MB ON

When to Hire a Lawyer

The first thing the owner should do is consider how he will organize his business. Will he operate as a sole proprietor? Will he have a partner? Should he incorporate? Will the business be operated as a franchise? The decision as to the form of business organization is very significant, with many implications (including liability, income taxes, and estate planning). The lawyer can provide information and advice that will help the owner make decisions appropriate for achieving his objectives.

If the owner is buying an existing business, the lawyer can provide advice and information that will enable the owner to minimize his potential risk and liability. What if the current owner has unsatisfied judgments against her? What if the assets of the current business have mortgages registered against them? Can the owner make good business decisions in these situations without receiving appropriate legal advice?

Anyone starting a business should ensure that all relevant laws will be complied with. How will the owner of the business determine which laws are relevant to his business? Can he understand the laws and whether his business plan will result in compliance with these laws? The lawyer can, of course, determine the relevant municipal, provincial, and federal laws that are relevant to the business and provide advice as to what is required to ensure compliance with them. This could cover everything from obtaining a business licence, to complying with municipal noise bylaws, to satisfying provincial and federal environmental standards.

Most businesses require a physical location, which usually means that there will be a lease to be negotiated. As is the case with all contracts, the owner should read the form of lease provided by the landlord. What if the owner doesn't understand various clauses of the document? Should he just sign the lease anyway, or should he consult his lawyer as to the meaning of the clauses before he signs?

The same questions apply to the documents provided by the bank or other lending institution. The owner of a small business usually must finance the start-up of the business or the purchase of an existing business. In particular, the extent of the personal liability of the owner for losses incurred by the business should always be carefully analyzed and understood by the owner before he signs the relevant documentation. This may require the provision of legal advice by the owner's lawyer.

There are other contracts that may need to be prepared in connection with the business. Examples include contracts with employees, suppliers, and customers. Can the owner of the business draft these documents himself? Would he be wise to do so without obtaining legal advice from his lawyer?

Most businesses today have intellectual property issues. These vary from the naming of the business, to the protection of the business's intellectual property such as patents, trade-marks, and copyrights, to ensuring that the business is not infringing on someone else's property rights. This is a very complicated area,

---

4. This approach was used in Glenna Erikson, "Pay Me Now or Pay More Later," *LawNow* (March 1993) 19.

which is changing rapidly. Is it prudent for the business owner to make decisions involving intellectual property without obtaining relevant legal advice?

Even when selling his business, the owner may need to seek legal advice from his lawyer. Should the sale involve the assets of the business, or the shares of the corporation that owns the assets? What are the income tax implications? Is there any potential future liability for the seller to consider? How does the seller ensure that he will get paid? It is clear that there are many issues for which a seller should consult his lawyer to ensure that he makes good business decisions, even when he is selling his business.

Legal advice will enable better decisions

mybuslawlab
www.pearsoned.ca/mybuslawlab

BC AB SK MB ON

When to Represent Yourself

The above section suggests that a good approach to understanding the solicitor–client relationship is to view the client as the decision-maker. The lawyer is one of the "experts" that the client approaches in her efforts to collect the information necessary for her to make good business decisions. This approach assumes that good business decisions will be based, at least in part, on relevant legal information and advice.

It is not, of course, necessary (or desirable) for the client to seek legal advice for every decision she must make. To do so would not only be prohibitively expensive, but it would also result in delays in the client's decision-making. The crucial question, then, is "When should you hire a lawyer?"

Not always necessary to retain lawyer

If you need to make a business decision, and you do not retain a lawyer, then you will either not be considering relevant legal information when you are making your decision or you will be obtaining the legal information yourself. For small, insignificant decisions, it may be appropriate to proceed without taking the time to find the relevant legal information. But, in most cases, it would be prudent to proceed only after completing some research of the relevant law.

A sophisticated client will understand this and will know how to find the relevant information. This is facilitated, of course, by the availability of legal information online. In the past, lawyers were "the keepers" of legal information. It was necessary to consult a lawyer to access legal information. This added to the "mystique" of (and the resentment against!) lawyers. This has recently changed, as anyone with a computer and access to the internet can find legal information online. A sophisticated client will capitalize on this; she will do her own legal research whenever she requires legal information to make a business decision and it is not appropriate to hire a lawyer to find the necessary information.

Sophisticated client may be able to find legal information

This textbook will help students realize that legal information is readily accessible and will assist them in overcoming their fear of the law. It will also serve as a valuable resource, with many references to online legal information and specific legal websites. The MyBusLawLab that accompanies this textbook (**www.pearsoned.ca/yates**) also emphasizes the availability of online legal information by providing relevant provincial law and legal information as well as direct links to significant legal websites.

For sophisticated clients, the availability of an abundance of easily accessible legal information is a positive development. Not only do they understand the need for legal input when business decisions are being made, but they know how to access relevant legal information. This is an important aspect of the empowerment experienced by business law students as they start to develop into sophisticated clients. It is important, however, that they develop an understanding and appreciation that not all online information is correct or complete, and that their research may be incomplete if, for example, they do not consider a relevant issue.

The question asked earlier in this chapter, "When should you hire a lawyer?" is therefore more difficult to answer than it was in the past. As always, the businessperson must consider the time and the cost that will be incurred if a lawyer is consulted for assistance in making a particular business decision. But there is now another alternative, namely, the businessperson's doing her own research and finding the relevant legal information herself.[5] If this approach is used, the time it takes to find the information must be considered. Furthermore, if the businessperson is unable to find the relevant information, or if she is unable to understand the information she did find, then she should call her lawyer for advice. This is an important attribute of a sophisticated client, being able to know when it is necessary to consult her lawyer.

One example that illustrates the above discussion involves small claims court litigation. Each of the provinces has set a monetary jurisdiction for small claims court. (The limit in several provinces has been increased to $25 000.) A sophisticated client will understand that any litigation involving an amount greater than the small claims court maximum limit will take place in a superior court, and that a lawyer should therefore be retained.[6] A sophisticated client, however, will also appreciate that while a case may involve an amount of money less than the monetary jurisdiction of small claims court, a lawyer may still need to be retained because of the complexity of the case.

Another example showing how a sophisticated client will manage his legal affairs in an appropriate manner involves the collection of accounts receivable. Assume that all of the accounts involve amounts less than the monetary jurisdiction of small claims court. One form of contract is used for all credit sales. A sophisticated client would realize that it is not necessary to retain a lawyer to secure judgment against customers who don't pay their accounts. The client, or one of his employees, can go to small claims court on behalf of the business. The client could hire a lawyer to train him, or his employee, with respect to how to conduct a trial in small claims court. The lawyer can be consulted if there are any complications on any particular collection file.

There is one issue that always needs to be considered when someone is deciding whether to represent herself. If you break the law, and harm someone else, there will likely be two different legal proceedings. First, there will be a criminal prosecution in which you will be charged by the government with committing a crime. If you are convicted, you will be punished and you will have a criminal record. Given this, it is wise to always retain legal counsel when you are facing criminal charges.

If the person you harmed sues you, you may be liable for damages, whether you were convicted of a crime or not. The civil litigation may take place in small claims court; in most of these cases you could represent yourself. If the litigation involves an amount of money greater than the monetary jurisdiction of small claims court, then you should hire a lawyer to represent you, as the trial will take

But if she can't, or if she can't understand it, then she should seek legal advice

Best to retain counsel for criminal charges

May be liable even if not convicted of crime

---

5. There now appears to be a third alternative, at least in some jurisdictions. Ontario, for example, has recently allowed the licensing of paralegals. Like lawyers, they are regulated by the Law Society of Upper Canada. Licensed paralegals are authorized to represent clients in the small claims court, the provincial offences court, the summary conviction courts, and before various administrative tribunals.

6. This is subject to the abandonment of small amounts over the limit.

place in a superior court. Given the growing complexity of the law and the resulting specialization of lawyers, you may even have two lawyers, one to represent you in your criminal trial and the other to represent you in your civil trial.

Reducing Risk

This textbook will try to help students become sophisticated clients, so that they can better manage their legal affairs. Such management involves managing legal risk, which is therefore a primary focus of this textbook. This emphasis will be highlighted by the inclusion of "Reducing Risk" boxes throughout the textbook. These boxes will contain suggestions as to how legal risk can be successfully managed.

Sophisticated clients understand that success ultimately depends on making good business decisions, and that good business decisions can only be made if they are based upon appropriate information. One type of information required for good decision-making is legal information. Sophisticated clients have the skills and the confidence that enable them to find basic legal information. Sophisticated clients will, however, understand that there will be situations in which it will be necessary to retain a lawyer to obtain the required legal information. Sophisticated clients will not be afraid to request legal advice from a lawyer in such situations. They will then incorporate the legal advice received in their decision-making process, thereby reducing their legal risk.

HOW TO FIND A GOOD LAWYER

mybuslawlab
www.pearsoned.ca/mybuslawlab

Assume that you are going to start a small business. You have decided that you need to retain a lawyer to help you. How do you find a good lawyer?

This question deals with an important issue, but it is not worded correctly. It would be better to ask, "How do you find an appropriate lawyer?" This emphasizes that a lawyer may be very knowledgeable and successful, but may not be appropriate for you. What, then, makes a lawyer "appropriate" for a particular client?

Make list of possible lawyers

The first step in finding an appropriate lawyer is to make a list of lawyers. There are many possible sources of lawyers' names. The first source most students think of is the telephone book, specifically, the *Yellow Pages.* This source can be overwhelming. For example, on 8 November 2008 there were 1550 lawyers listed on YellowPages.ca for Edmonton! It is possible to tell where a lawyer's office is located, and perhaps what type of law the lawyer practises, but there is definitely not sufficient information in the *Yellow Pages* advertisements to help you decide whether a particular lawyer is appropriate for you. The same limitation applies to any advertisement, regardless of the media used.

Another important source of lawyers' names involves getting referrals from friends or relatives. It is important that the referral be given by someone whose judgment you trust. Also, it is important that the referral be provided by someone who had the same type of legal problem that you are now facing. Being referred to a highly recommended real estate lawyer is not much help to you if you have just been charged for committing a serious crime. If you are considering setting up a small business, then you want a referral from someone who operates a small business and is willing to recommend the lawyer who has provided legal advice to him in this context.

Another possible source of lawyers' names is the provincial law society. These organizations are self-governing bodies for lawyers. Their mandate usually involves regulating the legal profession in the public interest.[7]

Some of the provincial law societies (such as the Law Society of Alberta and the Law Society of Upper Canada) offer a lawyer referral service. These services provide the names and phone numbers of lawyers who practise in the relevant area of law. In Alberta, this service is offered by the Law Society free of charge, while in Ontario there is a fee of $6. In both provinces, the lawyers who are referred will provide up to 30 minutes of free consultation.

In British Columbia, the Legal Referral Service is operated by the B.C. Branch of the Canadian Bar Association (CBA).[8] The CBA is a professional organization that represents judges and lawyers. One of its purposes is to enhance the profession and the commercial interests of its members. The Lawyer Referral Service is offered by the B.C. Branch free of charge. The lawyer to whom you are referred will charge you $25 for up to the first 30 minutes of consultation.

The website of the Law Society of British Columbia contains the following warning:

> Members of the public should exercise caution when seeking referrals from lawyer referral services or lawyer directory websites that are not sponsored by the Canadian Bar Association or a provincial law society. The Law Society has received a report of an online lawyer referral website that was charging a fee for referrals but not providing appropriate services.[9]

Call for initial consultation

Once you have the name of a lawyer near you who practises the type of law relevant to your situation, you should set up a meeting for an initial consultation. It is best to confirm the cost (if any) of this meeting when you are setting it up. You do not want any unpleasant surprises, such as receiving an unexpected bill from the lawyer after the meeting.

The primary purpose of the initial consultation is for you to decide whether to retain the lawyer. At the same time, the lawyer will decide whether to agree to represent you. Both of these decisions should be made on the basis of trust, as the solicitor–client relationship will not function as it should unless there is mutual **Mutual trust is key** trust between the lawyer and the client. Unfortunately, there are no objective criteria to measure "trust." Both you and the lawyer must use your instincts in deciding whether to form a solicitor–client relationship. Relevant factors may include whether you believe you can work with the lawyer; whether you feel comfortable discussing all relevant information, no matter how personal or sensitive, with her; and whether you want that particular lawyer to negotiate on your behalf or represent you in court. The lawyer will be concerned about whether the client will be honest and disclose all relevant information.

With respect to someone who is setting up a small business, the best approach to follow is to assume that the lawyer you choose to assist you in the start-up of the business will continue to represent you even after the business has been set up

---

7. This discussion will refer to three of the provincial law societies, the Law Society of Alberta (www.lawsocietyalberta.com/), the Law Society of British Columbia (www.lawsociety.bc.ca/) and the Law Society of Upper Canada (www.lsuc.on.ca/index_en.html). All of the information in the textbook referring to these law societies may be accessed through these websites.

8. www.cba.org/BC/Initiatives/main/lawyer_referral.aspx.

9. *Supra* note 7 at www.lawsociety.bc.ca/public/finding_lawyer.html.

and commences operating. There are several advantages to maintaining an ongoing relationship with your lawyer. She will know and understand you and your business, which will enable her to provide you with her legal advice more efficiently, reducing your legal costs. It will also enable her to customize her legal advice, so that it will be even more useful to you when you are making your decisions. As you are her client, she will give you, and your requests for legal advice, priority. This can be very important when you are facing matters that must be dealt with urgently. Finally, the more you deal with your lawyer, the more comfortable you will become, which means that you are more likely to call her when you require legal advice.

mybuslawlab
www.pearsoned.ca/mybuslawlab

LEGAL AID

You may be eligible for **legal aid** if you have a legal problem and you can't afford a lawyer. The provision of legal aid varies from province to province. If you believe that you are eligible for legal aid, it is best to check the website of the organization in your province that administers the legal aid program.[10]

Legal aid may be available

In British Columbia, for example, the Legal Services Society (LSS), an independent, non-profit organization, provides legal aid for people with low income.[11] LSS may pay for a lawyer if the client has a legal problem involving criminal charges, mental health and prison issues, serious family problems, child protection matters, or immigration problems. To receive legal aid, a client must meet certain financial guidelines involving household income and assets. If the client doesn't qualify for legal representation but meets other financial guidelines involving household income, he may be eligible to receive legal advice. Anyone can obtain legal information, provided by a toll-free telephone service, LSS publications, a family law website, and links to other sources identified as reliable.

It must be emphasized that not everyone qualifies for legal aid, and that even some of those who do qualify may have to pay some of the legal costs incurred. Furthermore, if you collect money as a result of a settlement or judgment, you will probably have to repay some or all of the benefits you received from legal aid. Finally, not all types of cases are covered by legal aid. Legal Aid Ontario, for example, states that legal aid will cover most criminal matters, family matters, immigration matters, and mental health issues.[12] All other matters will not be covered, including speeding charges, parking tickets, most provincial offences, and uncontested family matters. It is clear that the owner of a small business will usually not be able to receive legal aid with respect to the legal issues involving the business.

But usually not for owners of a small business

There is one aspect of legal aid that deserves special mention. **Duty counsel** are court lawyers who assist individuals who are not represented by a lawyer. Duty counsel may be available in criminal courts, family courts, or immigration courts, as well as for hearings before housing tribunals or in psychiatric facilities.

In British Columbia, the assistance of duty counsel is considered **legal advice**, not **legal representation**. In criminal court, duty counsel may provide advice to an

---

10. In Alberta, legal aid is administered by Legal Aid Alberta, www.legalaid.ab.ca/. In Ontario, legal aid is administered by Legal Aid Ontario, www.legalaid.on.ca/en/.

11. www.lss.bc.ca/.

12. *Supra* note 10, at www.legalaid.on.ca/en/getting/covered_not-covered.asp.

accused about the charges he faces, the relevant court procedures, and his legal rights. Financial eligibility tests do not need to be satisfied to receive duty counsel services but, as the LSS website states,

> Duty counsel can give you advice and speak on your behalf in court on simple matters. However, they will not take on your whole case and will not represent you at a trial.[13]

This statement is generally also true with respect to duty counsel in other provinces.

www.pearsoned.ca/mybuslawlab

HOW LAWYERS BILL THEIR CLIENTS

One of the reasons people don't retain lawyers even when they clearly require legal advice is that they are afraid of the cost. While the provision of legal services is not cheap, an understanding of how lawyers bill their clients will help someone determine whether to retain a lawyer. In this regard, the issue of fees should be discussed during the initial consultation with the lawyer.

Discuss fees with lawyer

Every legal problem is unique. Also, there are many factors a lawyer will consider when calculating the fee to charge a client. It is therefore important that the client understand from the very beginning exactly how the lawyer will bill him for providing assistance with his particular problem. It is prudent to confirm this understanding in a fee agreement with the lawyer.

Lawyer may bill on basis of fixed fee

Each of the provincial law societies provides online information on lawyers' fees.[14] It appears that there are three main ways that lawyers calculate their fees. First, the lawyer may charge a fixed fee for the work required, regardless of the time involved. This method of billing is often used for specific tasks, such as preparing a will, purchasing a house, or incorporating a business.

or on basis of time spent and hourly rate

Second, the lawyer may bill the client for all of the time she spends working on his file, using her hourly rate. Hourly rates usually vary with the number of years that the lawyer has been practising law. A senior lawyer may have a higher hourly rate than a junior lawyer, but the experience of the senior lawyer may enable her to complete the required legal work more efficiently, perhaps resulting in a fee lower than that charged by the relatively inefficient junior lawyer, who will be learning as she does the work.

or as a contingency fee

Third, the lawyer may receive a percentage of the amount the client collects, either through a settlement or a court judgment. If the client does not collect anything, then the lawyer does not receive anything. This is a contingency fee agreement, which is often appropriate in personal injury claims, or product liability cases, when the client does not have any funds to pay the lawyer at the beginning of the case. The provincial law societies may restrict the use of contingency fee agreements, or set a maximum contingency fee for certain types of cases. The Law Society of British Columbia, for example, does not permit contingency fee agreements for family cases involving child custody or access. The maximum contingency fee allowed in claims for personal injury or wrongful death resulting from a

---

13. *Supra* note 11 at www.lss.bc.ca/legal_aid/familyDutyCounsel.asp.

14. See the Law Society of Alberta, *supra* note 7 at www.lawsocietyalberta.com/LSA_Archives/index.cfm?page=arclawyerfees_iRQG4U.cfm; the Law Society of British Columbia, *supra* note 7 at www.lawsociety.bc.ca/public/lawyers_fees/types_fees.html; and the Law Society of Upper Canada, *supra* note 7 at www.lsuc.on.ca/public/a/faqs-finding-a-lawyer/index.cfm#8.

motor vehicle accident is one-third of the amount received; for all other personal injury or wrongful death cases, the limit is 40 percent of the amount received.[15]

The client is also responsible for paying the out-of-pocket costs incurred by the lawyer on the client's behalf. These costs are called **disbursements**. Disbursements usually include costs such as the court fees for filing documents, long distance telephone charges, courier charges, the fee charged by an expert for testifying or preparing a report, and photocopying costs.

If a client decides to hire a lawyer, and the lawyer agrees to represent the client, the lawyer will usually request that a **retainer** be paid before she commences work on the matter. A retainer works as a deposit. The amount paid by the client is deposited into a trust account, to the credit of the client. When the lawyer bills the client, the amount owed will be paid from the retainer. The lawyer may require the client to "top up" the retainer as funds are withdrawn from the trust account.

HOW TO COMPLAIN ABOUT YOUR LAWYER

As indicated above, the provincial law societies are self-governing bodies for lawyers. Their mandate involves regulating the legal profession. Part of this regulation involves dealing with complaints regarding a lawyer's conduct.

In general, the law societies do not assist clients with complaints about the fees being charged by their lawyers. In such cases, the client is usually advised to first discuss his concern about the fee with his lawyer. Some law societies offer a fee mediation service.[16] Participation in such a program is voluntary. These programs usually involve a neutral mediator who tries to facilitate a mutually acceptable resolution of the dispute.

If the client cannot resolve the fee dispute directly with the lawyer, and if any mediation is unsuccessful, then the client can have his lawyer's bill reviewed by a court official. In Alberta, for example, the review is conducted by a Taxation Officer of the Court of Queen's Bench.[17] In Ontario, the review is conducted by an Assessment Officer of the Superior Court of Justice.[18] Court officials, such as taxation officers and assessment officers, have the power to decide that the lawyer's bill is fair and does not need to be changed. Alternatively, they can decide that the bill is too high, and reduce it accordingly.

For complaints regarding a lawyer's conduct other than fee disputes, each of the law societies has a complaint-resolution process.[19] This process usually begins with an attempt at mediating the dispute between the client and the lawyer. If mediation fails, and the law society decides that the complaint is valid, then there will usually be a more formal investigation. This could result in a hearing before a panel. This hearing will involve the testimony of witnesses, the entering of other evidence, and submissions by the legal counsel for the lawyer and for the law

Client responsible for disbursements

Retainer is a deposit

www.pearsoned.ca/mybuslawlab

Fee mediation may be available

Lawyer's bill can be reviewed by court official

Complaints may be investigated

And there may be a hearing

---

15. *Ibid.*

16. One that does is the Law Society of British Columbia, *supra* note 7 at www.lawsociety.bc.ca/public/lawyers_fees/resolving_disagreements.html.

17. See James Christensen and Joe Morin, "Taxation of a Lawyer's Bill" (April 2006), www.albertacourts.ab.ca/cs/taxoffice/TaxationofaLawyers-.pdf.

18. See the Law Society of Upper Canada, *supra* note 7 at www.lsuc.on.ca/public/a/complaints/your-lawyers-bill—-too-high/.

19. See the Law Society of Alberta, *supra* note 7 at www.lawsocietyalberta.com/publicservices/complaintsprocesspublic.cfm, the Law Society of British Columbia, *supra* note 7 at www.lawsociety.bc.ca/public/lawyer_conduct.html, and the Law Society of Upper Canada, *supra* note 7 at www.lsuc.on.ca/public/a/complaints/.

society. If the panel finds the lawyer guilty of misconduct, the penalty could include a reprimand, fine, suspension, disbarment (termination of membership in the law society), and costs of the hearing.

Complainant does not receive compensation

It is important to note that the complaint resolution process does not result in compensation being paid to the client who made the complaint. If the client believes that he has suffered a financial loss because of his lawyer's misconduct (negligent or deliberate), it is necessary for the client to take other steps, such as commencing legal action against the lawyer. (All lawyers are required to purchase professional liability insurance to protect them if they are found liable for negligence or deliberate misconduct.) This may require the client to seek legal advice from another lawyer. Clients should not procrastinate with respect to these matters, as limitation periods may exist, meaning that they may not be able to pursue their claims after a certain period of time.

ETHICS

Ethics of Lawyers

www.pearsoned.ca/mybuslawlab

While understanding how to complain about a lawyer is important, it is equally important to know when to complain about a lawyer. In this regard, the website for the Law Society of British Columbia contains the following statement:

> High ethical standards are a hallmark of the legal profession—and a reason that people place their confidence and trust in lawyers. The Law Society sets standards of professional responsibility for BC lawyers and articled students and upholds those standards through a complaints and discipline process.[20]

Lawyers have ethical obligations

All of the provincial law societies have mandates to govern the conduct of lawyers in the public interest. The professional and ethical obligations of lawyers are set out in rules of professional conduct.[21] Lawyers who fail to satisfy these obligations will be subject to the complaint resolution procedure, as discussed in the previous section. As the rules of professional conduct consistently emphasize the need for ethical behaviour, it is important to know what is meant by ethics and ethical behaviour.

Difference between law and ethics

Law provides a set of rules for behaviour. If these rules are not complied with, the person breaking the rules will be punished. Law therefore tells us what we must do. Ethics, on the other hand, tells us what we should do. When a person breaks the law, he has also acted unethically. However, if a person acts unethically, he may not have broken the law. Ethical behaviour therefore implies integrity, honesty, and professionalism. This is illustrated by a dictionary definition of "ethics" as "a system of moral principles governing the appropriate conduct for a person or a group."[22] Ethics thus relates to issues of right and wrong; these depend on a person's conscience, rather than on what the law says.

---

[20] See the Law Society of British Columbia, *supra* note 7 at www.lawsociety.bc.ca/regulation_insurance/conduct.html.

[21] See the Law Society of Alberta, *supra* note 7 at www.lawsocietyalberta.com/files/Code.pdf; the Law Society of British Columbia, *supra* note 7 at www.lawsociety.bc.ca/publications_forms/handbook/handbook_toc.html; and the Law Society of Upper Canada, *supra* note 7 at www.lsuc.on.ca/regulation/a/profconduct/.

[22] *Encarta World English Dictionary*, http://encarta.msn.com/dictionary_/ethics.html.

Referring back to the lawyer joke at the beginning of this chapter, and how many people tell lawyer jokes to deride lawyers, it seems that many people today do not trust or have confidence in lawyers because they do not appear to meet the standards of professional responsibility set by their governing bodies. A review of the website for the Law Society of Alberta, for example, shows that between August 27 and November 11 of 2008 there were three suspensions and five disbarments of Alberta lawyers.[23] The reasons for these penalties include:

- failing to maintain the books and records of a trust account
- failing to reconcile trust accounts
- failing to comply with accounting rules
- collecting GST and taking the funds for personal use
- collecting retainers from clients and taking the funds before they are earned
- disguising the receipt of income to avoid a garnishee on a general account
- being involved in fraudulent real estate financing scheme
- failing to cooperate fully with a Law Society investigation and failing to respond to the Law Society
- misinforming a client
- lying to a client, the Taxation Officer, and the Law Society
- being convicted and sentenced to a term of imprisonment for criminal offences

Other common reasons for the suspension and disbarment of lawyers include failing to serve a client in a timely fashion, failing to respond to a client, failing to disclose to a judge that another judge has previously refused the same application, and swearing a false affidavit. The Law Society is required to refer these cases to the Minister of Justice and the Attorney General whenever there are reasonable and probable grounds to believe that a lawyer has committed a criminal offence.

While the vast majority of lawyers are completely honest and ethical, it only takes a few well-publicized cases involving lawyers being penalized for unethical behaviour to taint the reputation of the entire profession. The case involving Martin Wirick is a good example. Wirick was a Vancouver lawyer who, along with one of his clients, defrauded clients and lenders of close to $40 million. This amount was covered by the lawyers in British Columbia through their Special Compensation Fund. Wirick was disbarred in December 2002. Criminal charges were laid against Wirick and his client in August 2008; at the time of writing this, the trial had not yet taken place. Needless to say, this case has damaged the image of lawyers, even though the Law Society of British Columbia and its members took responsibility for Wirick's actions.[24]

For sophisticated clients, there are a few important points to keep in mind. First, lawyers operate under strict rules governing their professional and ethical obligations. You can therefore place your confidence and trust in your lawyer. But, second, there are some lawyers who unfortunately do not meet the standards of the profession. It is necessary therefore to understand the types of behaviour

[23] See the Law Society of Alberta, *supra* note 7 at www.lawsocietyalberta.com/lawyerregulation/notices/.

[24] See the Law Society of British Columbia, *supra* note 7 at: www.lawsociety.bc.ca/publications_forms/bulletin/2008/08-10-14_feature-wirick.html.

Clients should watch their lawyers and take action when appropriate

that are unacceptable, and the steps that can be taken if your lawyer violates your trust and confidence by breaching the professional standards. Third, as is the case with all professionals, it is necessary to be vigilant with respect to your lawyer and, if he breaks the rules he should be following, to take whatever action is appropriate, on a timely basis.

Ethics of Clients

No code of conduct for businesspeople

The discussion on the ethical behaviour of lawyers emphasized the need for lawyers to comply with the relevant rules of professional conduct. Unfortunately, there is not an equivalent set of rules for businesspeople. That is, there is not a "Code of Professional Conduct" for businesspeople in Canada, or even in any of the provinces.

Many businesspeople not making good ethical choices

There have been many recent cases involving influential and powerful people being charged with and, in some cases, convicted of crimes relating to the ownership and operation of businesses. The situations involving WorldCom,[25] Enron,[26] Martha Stewart,[27] and Conrad Black[28] are four well-known examples. There have been several other recent high-profile cases involving businesspeople who have been entangled in questionable situations:

- Madonna was found liable for plagiarizing the words of a song she wrote.[29]

- The CEO of RadioShack resigned after admitting he "misstated" his academic records on his resumé.[30]

- A Calgary stockbroker was fired for soliciting a prostitute and taking her back to the office, after hours.[31]

- The Chinese government ordered the execution of the Director of the State Food and Drug Administration for approving untested medicine in exchange for cash.[32]

- The mayor of Detroit was sentenced to four months in jail and five years of probation after pleading guilty to obstruction of justice charges. He denied having an affair with his aide.[33]

[25.] For an interesting timeline showing the significant events of the WorldCom saga, see "The WorldCom Story," CBC News Online, www.cbc.ca/news/background/worldcom/.

[26.] For a timeline of the interesting developments of the Enron story, see "Timeline," CBC News Online, www.cbc.ca/news/background/enron/.

[27.] For a timeline of the events that took place after Martha Stewart sold her shares in ImClone Inc. in 2001, see "Timeline," CBC News Online, www.cbc.ca/news/background/stewart_martha/timeline.html.

[28.] For a timeline of the events that led to Conrad Black going to prison, see "Timeline," CBC News Online, www.cbc.ca/news/background/black_conrad/timeline.html.

[29.] "Madonna Guilty of Plagiarism, Belgian Judge Rules", 18 November 2005, CBC News Online, www.cbc.ca/arts/story/2005/11/18/madonna_051118.html.

[30.] "RadioShack CEO Quits in Resume Scandal," 20 February 2006, CBC News Online,www.cbc.ca/money/story/2006/02/20/shack-060220.html.

[31.] "Disgraced banker loses fight with former employer" 6 June 2006 CBC News Online, www.cbc.ca/canada/edmonton/story/2006/06/06/ca-bankerloses-20060606.html.

[32.] "China Executes Former FDA Chief Amid Product Safety Crisis," 10 July 2007, CBC News Online, www.cbc.ca/world/story/2007/07/10/china-tainted-products.html."Disgraced Banker Was Living Double Life," 24 March 2006, CBC News Online, www.cbc.ca/edmonton/story/ed-whitehouse20060324.html.

[33.] "Embattled Detroit Mayor Pleads Guilty, Resigns," 4 September 2008, CBC News Online, www.cbc.ca/world/story/2008/09/04/detroit-mayor.html.

- A member of Prime Minister Stephen Harper's staff resigned after admitting he had plagiarized from a speech given by the Australian Prime Minister.[34]
- Bernard Madoff pleaded guilty to 11 charges (including securities, wire, and mail fraud, money laundering, and perjury) with respect to a "Ponzi" scheme (in which existing investors were paid with the money of new investors) involving as much as $65 billion.[35]

The increasing occurrence of cases such as these caused Gwyn Morgan, former CEO of EnCana Corp., to cite the 2005 Transparency International Survey, which showed that Canada ranked 14th among countries perceived as free of corruption.[36]

Mr. Morgan made the following statement:

> There can be nothing more crucial to the integrity and prosperity of our country than to protect Canada from the proliferation and acceptance of corruption.... When it comes to business and government, there is an especially heavy responsibility that comes with leadership.... It's up to Canadian business leaders to act as role models with strong ethical values.... If you don't have a moral compass, haven't got the discipline to steer in a direction of strong values, it doesn't matter whether you're rich or poor, you're still going to act unethically.[37]

Code of Business Conduct

For a sophisticated client who is starting a business, the best approach would appear to be to make a commitment to ethical behaviour. This would involve being a role model for employees, showing them, by example, the type of behaviour that is expected of all employees. As Dempsey said:

Commitment to ethical behaviour

> A more proactive approach for public sector, private, and non-profit organizations is to foster internal cultures that make ethical values, individual and collective accountability, integrity, and trust explicit priorities... As demonstrated by the transgressions that have shaken the corporate world and these lessons being learned with the public sector, an organization's continued good reputation and respectability depends on building and maintaining a culture founded on ethical values, integrity, and trust.[38]

A tangible step that can be taken in this regard is to prepare, and communicate to employees, a statement of values and principles of ethical conduct. Such statements are usually referred to as a "Code of Conduct" or a "Code of Ethics." In

Prepare a code of conduct for business and its employees

---

34. "Harper Staffer Quits over Plagiarized 2003 Speech on Iraq," 30 September 2008, CBC News Online, www.cbc.ca/news/canadavotes/story/2008/09/30/rae-harper.html.

35. "Bernard Madoff to Remain Jailed," 20 March 2009, CBC News Online, www.cbc.ca/money/story/2009/03/20/madoff-bail-appeal.html.

36. "Canada Is Now Is Now Ranked 9th on Corruption Perception Index," www.transparency.org/content/download/36521/574535 and www.transparency.org/policy_research/surveys_indices/cpi/2008/regional_highlights_factsheets.

37. "Corruption Threatens Our Values, EnCana Exec Says," 2 March 2006, *Business Edge News Magazine*, www.businessedge.ca/printArticle.cfm/newsID/12066.cfm.

38. Alison L. Dempsey, "Build an Ethical Organizational Culture Before the Whistle Blows," *LawNow*, February/March 2005, 9 at 10.

a recent article, Julie Walsh provides an overview of codes of conduct and ways to make them effective.[39] She states:

> A code of business conduct is a formal statement adopted by a company that sets out its values and standard of business practices. It essentially codifies a company's organizational values and establishes procedural norms and standards of expected behaviour for all employees, officers, and directors involved with that particular company. There is no prescribed format—it can be a short mission statement or a sophisticated declaration of business practices with articulated values, standards, and compliance required as a term of employment.

Even a sophisticated client starting a small business can follow this approach. In fact, this is probably the best way to ensure the long-term adoption of ethical behaviour by employees of the business. The organizations whose top management practises ethical behaviour are those that are most likely to experience compliance with a code of ethics.

Ethical values and principles

Walsh goes on to suggest that at least the following issues (taken from a policy proposed by the Canadian Securities Administrators) should be included in a code of ethics:[40]

- conflicts of interest;
- protection and proper use of corporate assets and opportunities;
- confidentiality of corporate information;
- fair dealing with the issuer's security holders, customers, suppliers, competitors, and employees;
- compliance with laws, rules, and regulations; and
- the reporting of any illegal or unethical behaviour.

The remaining question is to determine the content of the code of ethics. What should such a code say, for example, about the proper use of corporate assets and opportunities? While these sorts of decisions are very personal, the Josephson Institute for Ethics identified six core values and their supporting ethical principles shown in Table 1.1.[41]

Table 1.1 Core Values and Ethical Principles

Core Ethical Values	Supporting Ethical Principle
Trustworthiness	truthfulness, sincerity, candor, integrity, promise keeping, loyalty, honesty
Respect	respect, autonomy, courtesy, self-determination
Responsibility	responsibility, diligence, continuous improvement, self-restraint
Fairness	justice, fairness, impartiality, equity
Caring	caring, kindness, compassion
Citizenship	citizenship, philanthropy, voting

[39.] Julie Walsh, "Setting the Tone at the Top," *LawNow* (February/March 2005), 16 at 16.

[40.] *Ibid.* at 17.

[41.] Keith Seel, "Values, Ethics and Civil Society," *LawNow* (April/May 2005) 9 at 9.

These core values are fundamental to the relationships that individuals have with the people with whom they come into contact. It is apparent that they could form the basis of a code of conduct for a small business. It would therefore appear that a sophisticated client who starts a small business could enhance the success of the business by personally adopting these core values and then incorporating them into a code of conduct for the business.

SUMMARY

Becoming a sophisticated client

- Knowledgeable, confident, up-to-date
- Understands role of lawyer and of client

Role of lawyer

- Client is decision-maker
- Lawyer is expert who provides legal advice
- Information provided to lawyer must be kept confidential
- Small businesses face many issues lawyer can advise on

When to represent yourself

- Client makes many business decisions without consulting lawyer (time, cost)
- Sophisticated client can find relevant legal information
- Sophisticated client knows when to retain lawyer (e.g., criminal law)

How to find a good lawyer

- Many sources of lawyers' names
- Initial consultation
- Importance of mutual trust

Legal aid

- Available for certain types of legal problems
- Client eligible if meets financial requirements
- Even if client qualifies for legal aid, may have to pay some or all of legal costs

How lawyers bill their clients

- Fixed fee
- Time spent and hourly rate
- Contingency fee
- Disbursements must be reimbursed by client
- Retainer is a deposit

How to complain about your lawyer

- Mediation may be available to resolve fee disputes
- Lawyer's bill can be reviewed by court official
- Other complaints made to law society
- Investigation may be followed by hearing
- Penalties range from reprimand to disbarment

Ethics

- Rules of professional conduct contain professional and ethical obligations of lawyers
- If rules broken, lawyer may be penalized

- Many recent cases involving legal/ethical situations
- Sophisticated client will make commitment to ethical behaviour
- May prepare code of conduct for business
- Should be based on ethical values and principles

QUESTIONS

1. Explain the meaning of "sophisticated client."

2. Why should the owner of a small business have a lawyer on "the team"?

3. Distinguish the role of the client from the role of the lawyer.

4. "The elimination of 'solicitor–client privilege' would significantly undermine the integrity of the Canadian legal system." True or false? Explain your answer.

5. What are some examples of the decisions that owners of small businesses make? What role can a lawyer play with respect to the making of these decisions?

6. What role has the computer played with respect to the solicitor–client relationship?

7. "It is a good idea to hire a lawyer when you have been charged with a crime." True or false? Explain your answer.

8. When you are trying to find a lawyer to help you, what are some sources of lawyers' names?

9. What is the primary purpose of an initial consultation with a lawyer?

10. "Legal aid is available to anybody with a legal problem." True or false? Explain your answer.

11. Briefly explain three ways lawyers bill their clients. Which of the three is most commonly used?

12. What can a client do if she is unhappy with the bill she received from her lawyer?

13. "If a client loses money because of the carelessness of his lawyer, he will be compensated for his losses if he makes a complaint to the law society." True or false? Explain your answer.

14. When will a lawyer be disbarred?

15. "When a person acts unethically, she will also have broken the law." True or false? Explain your answer.

16. What is a code of business conduct? Should such a code be used by a small business?

Chapter 2

Introduction to the Legal System

1. Determine a functional definition of "law"
2. Identify the types of law that exist in Canada
3. Distinguish between common law and civil law
4. Identify the sources of Canadian law
5. Identify the three elements of Canada's Constitution
6. Explain how legislative power is divided in the Constitution
7. Detail how legislation is created in the parliamentary system
8. Describe the rights and freedoms protected by the *Charter of Rights and Freedoms*

WHAT IS LAW?

Most of us recognize the rules and regulations that are considered law and understand that law plays an important role in ordering society, but knowing that does not make it easy to come up with a satisfactory, all-inclusive definition. Philosophers have been trying for centuries to determine just what "law" means, and their theories have profoundly affected the development of our legal system. Law has been defined in moral terms, where only good rules are considered law (natural law theorists). Others have defined law by looking at its source, stipulating that only the rules enacted by those with authority to do so qualify as law (*legal positivists*). And some have defined law in practical terms, suggesting that only those rules that the courts are willing to enforce qualify as law (*legal realists*). Legal positivism helped shape the concept of law in Canada, where parliamentary supremacy requires that we look to the enactments of the federal parliament or provincial legislatures as the primary source of law. In the United States, however, a more pragmatic approach to law based on legal realism has been adopted. It allows judges to factor in current social and economic realities when they make their decisions.

No wholly satisfactory definition of law

For our purposes, the following simplified definition is helpful, if we remember that it is not universally applicable. **Law is the body of rules made by government that can be enforced by the courts or by other government agencies.** In our

Definition

daily activities, we are exposed to many rules that do not qualify as law. Courtesy demands that we do not interrupt when someone is speaking. Social convention determines that it is inappropriate to enter a restaurant shirtless or shoeless. Universities and colleges often establish rules of conduct for their students and faculty. These rules do not fall into our definition of law because the courts do not enforce them. But when there is a disagreement over who is responsible for an accident, a question as to whether a crime has been committed, or a difference of opinion about the terms of a contract or a will, the participants may find themselves before a judge. Rules that can be enforced by the courts govern these situations; thus, they are laws within the definition presented here.

Government agencies also enforce the law

A person dealing with government agencies, such as labour relations boards, workers' compensation boards, or city and municipal councils, must recognize that these bodies are also able to render decisions in matters that come before them. The rules enforced by these bodies are also laws within this definition. The unique problems associated with government agencies and regulatory bodies will be discussed in Chapter 3 under the heading of "Dealing with Regulatory Bodies."

Do not confuse law and morality

While the definition of law as enforceable rules has practical value, it does not suggest what is just or moral. We must not assume that so long as we obey the law we are acting morally. As discussed in Chapter 1, legal compliance and ethical behaviour are two different things, and people must decide for themselves what standard they will adhere to. Many choose to live by a personal code of conduct demanding adherence to more stringent rules than those set out in the law, while others disregard even these basic requirements. Some think that moral values have no place in the business world, but in fact the opposite is true. As was pointed out in Chapter 1, there is now an expectation of high ethical standards in business activities, and it is hoped that those who study the law as it relates to business will appreciate and adhere to those higher standards. We must at least understand that whether we are motivated by divine law, conscience, moral indifference, or avarice, serious consequences may follow from non-compliance with the body of rules we call law.

CATEGORIES OF LAW

Substantive law includes public and private law

Law consists of rules with different but intersecting functions. The primary categories are substantive and procedural laws. **Substantive law** establishes not only the rights an individual has in society but also the limits on his or her conduct. The rights to travel, to vote, and to own property are guaranteed by substantive law. Prohibitions against theft and murder as well as other actions that harm our neighbours are also examples of substantive law. **Procedural law** determines how the substantive laws will be enforced. The rules governing arrest, investigation, and pre-trial and court processes in both criminal and civil cases are examples. Law can also be distinguished by its public or private function. **Public law** includes constitutional law that determines how the country is governed and the laws that affect an individual's relationship with government, including criminal law and the regulations created by government agencies. **Private law** involves the rules that govern our personal, social, and business relations, which are enforced by one person suing another in a private or civil action. Knowing the law and how it functions allows us to structure our lives as productive and accepted members of the community and to predict the consequences of our conduct. Business students study law because it defines the environment of rules within which business functions. In order to play the game, we must know the rules.

ORIGINS OF LAW

Nine of the ten Canadian provinces and the three territories have adopted the common law legal system developed over the last millennium in England. For private matters, Quebec has adopted a system based on the *French Civil Code*. Although this text focuses on common law, understanding it may be assisted by briefly examining the basic differences between the common law and civil law legal systems. It is important to note that the term *civil law* has two distinct meanings. The following discussion is about the **civil law legal system** developed in Europe and now used in many jurisdictions, including Quebec. The terms *civil court*, *civil action*, and *civil law* are also used within our common law legal system to describe private law matters and should not be confused with the *Civil Code* or civil law as used in Quebec.

Quebec civil law; all other provinces common law

Civil Law Legal System

Modern civil law traces its origins to the Emperor Justinian, who had Roman law codified for use throughout the Roman Empire. This codification became the foundation of the legal system in continental Europe. Its most significant modification occurred early in the 19th century, when Napoleon revised it. The *Napoleonic Code* was adopted throughout Europe and most of the European colonies. Today, variations of the *Civil Code* are used in all of continental Europe, South America, most of Africa, and many other parts of the world, including Quebec. The most important feature of French civil law is its central *Code*—a list of rules stated as broad principles of law that judges apply to the cases that come before them. Under this system, people wanting to know their legal rights or obligations refer to the *Civil Code*.

Civil Code used throughout much of the world

Quebec courts rely on the rules set out in the *Code* to resolve private disputes in that province. While civil law judges are influenced by decisions made in other cases, and lawyers will take great pains to point out what other judges have done in similar situations, the key to understanding the *Civil Code* system is to recognize that ultimately the *Code* determines the principle to be applied. Prior decisions do not constitute binding precedents in a civil law jurisdiction. The most recent Quebec *Civil Code* came into effect on 1 January 1994.[1] One-quarter of the 1994 *Code* is new law, making its introduction a significant event in the evolution of the law of Quebec.

Civil Code provides predictability

One of the effects of the new *Code* was to make the doctrine of good faith (recently developed in common law and discussed in Chapter 7) part of Quebec's contract law. Prior to this, the law was similar to the common law, where the obligation to act in good faith toward the person you are dealing with applied only when special relationships existed. Article 1375 of the new *Code* states that contracting parties "shall conduct themselves in good faith both at the time the obligation is created and at the time it is performed or extinguished."[2] This means that the parties can no longer withhold important information or fail to correct

Quebec uses Civil Code to resolve private disputes

[1.] *Civil Code of Quebec*, S.Q. 1991, c. 64.*Civil Code of Quebec*, S.Q. 1991, c. 64.

[2.] *Ibid.*, Art. 1375.

Civil Code recognizes doctrine of good faith

erroneous assumptions that they know have been made by the other side without exposing themselves to an action for violating this obligation of good faith.

To illustrate how the law is applied in a civil law legal system as opposed to a common law legal system, consider the situation involving a person suffering injury because of the careless act of another. If a person was seriously burned in Quebec, as a result of being served overly hot coffee in a pliable paper cup at a fast-food restaurant drive-through, the victim would turn to the Quebec *Civil Code* to determine his or her rights. Articles 1457 and 1463 of the most recent *Code* state the following:

Civil Code also applied to tort cases

> 1457. Every person has a duty to abide by the rules of conduct which lie upon him, according to the circumstances, usage or law, so as not to cause injury to another. Where he is endowed with reason and fails in this duty, he is responsible for any injury he causes to another person and is liable to reparation for the injury, whether it be bodily, moral, or material in nature.
>
> He is also liable, in certain cases, to reparation for injury caused to another by the act or fault of another person or by the act of things in his custody.
>
> 1463. The principal is liable to reparation for injury caused by the fault of his agents and servants in the performance of their duties; nevertheless, he retains his recourses against them.

Thus, applying article 1457, the server may be held liable to the customer. But if in a subsequent identical case, the Court applied both articles 1457 and 1463, the employer could be held liable in addition to the employee, increasing the likelihood that the customer would actually recover any damages awarded by the court. Since the courts in a civil law jurisdiction are not required to follow each other's decisions, two very similar cases may be decided differently. The end result is shaped by the specific "law" or article of the *Code* that is applied to the facts of a case.

Consistency is reduced where preceding court decisions can be ignored

In a common law jurisdiction, liability may also be imposed on both the employer and the employee who caused injury due to the application of the principles of negligence and vicarious liability (see Chapter 5). But in a common law jurisdiction, the doctrine of following precedent would demand that the courts look to similar cases for the principles to be applied. Thus, if a litigant can point to a case similar to her own, where a superior court imposed liability on both the employee (server) and the employer (restaurant), it is likely that a similar decision will be delivered in her case.

Following precedent increases consistency and predictability

There are many important differences between civil law and the principles of common law. In this text, we have limited the discussion to common law—while there are many similarities, care should be taken not to assume that the same principles apply to Quebec or other civil law jurisdictions.

Common Law Legal System

Common law grew from struggle for power

As Roman civil law was taking hold in Europe, relations between the existing English and French kingdoms were frequently strained. It has been suggested that this strain is the reason England maintained its unique common law system of justice rather than adopting the more widely accepted Roman civil law. The early Norman kings established a strong feudal system in England that centralized power in their hands. As long as they remained strong, they maintained their power; but when weak kings were on the throne, power was surrendered to the nobles. The growth of the common law legal system was much affected by this ongoing struggle for power between kings and nobles and later between kings and parliament.

During times when power was decentralized, the administration of justice fell to the local lords, barons, or sheriffs, who would hold court as part of their feudal responsibility. Their courts commonly resorted to such practices as trial by battle or ordeal. Trial by battle involved armed combat between the litigants or their champions, and trial by ordeal involved some physical test. The assumption was made that God would intervene on behalf of the righteous party. Strong kings, especially Henry II, enhanced their power by establishing travelling courts, which provided a more attractive method of resolving disputes. As more people used the king's courts, their power base broadened, and their strength increased. The fairer the royal judges, the more litigants they attracted. Eventually, the courts of the nobles fell into disuse. The function of the royal courts was not to impose any particular set of laws but to be as fair and impartial as possible. To this end, they did not make new rules but enforced the customs and traditions they found already in place in the towns and villages they visited. The judges also began to look to each other for rules to apply when faced with new situations.

Henry II established travelling courts

Common law principles came from the common people— their traditions and customs

STARE DECISIS

Gradually, a system of justice developed in which the judges were required to follow each other's decisions. This process is called *stare decisis*, or "following precedent." Another factor that affected the development of *stare decisis* was the creation of appeal courts. Although the process of appeal at this time was rudimentary, trial judges would try to avoid the embarrassment of having their decisions overturned and declared in error. Eventually, the practice of following precedent became institutionalized. The most significant feature of our legal system today is that the decision of a judge at one level is binding on all judges in the court hierarchy who function in a court of lower rank, provided the facts in the two cases are similar.[3] Thus, a judge today hearing a case in the Court of Queen's Bench for Alberta would be required to follow a similar decision laid down in the Court of Appeal for Alberta or the Supreme Court of Canada, but would not have to follow a decision involving an identical case from the Court of Appeal for Manitoba.[4] Such a decision would be merely persuasive, since it came from a different jurisdiction. Because the Supreme Court of Canada is the highest court in the land, its decisions are binding on all Canadian courts.

Judges follow decisions—if made within that court's hierarchy

The role *stare decisis* plays in the English common law legal system is similar to the role the *Civil Code* plays in the French system. It allows the parties to predict

---

[3.] See *Toronto Star Newspapers Ltd. v. The Queen,*[2007]84 O.R. (3d) 766 (Ont. H.C.J.), where the applicants argued that the court could depart from an earlier 1984 decision of the Ontario Court of Appeal, which upheld mandatory publication bans. The judge declared that "the question put to the Court of Appeal in Global is indistinguishable from the one I am asked to consider. I find I have no authority to reconsider Global. Until such time as the Court of Appeal or the Supreme Court of Canada finds that Global was wrongly decided, it remains the law in Ontario."

[4.] Strictly speaking, a judge is not bound to follow decisions made by other judges in a court at the same level in that province. However, the practical effect is the same, since these judges must follow their colleagues' decisions "in the absence of strong reason to the contrary." *R. v. Morris*, [1942] O.W.N. 447 (Ont. H.C.J.).

CASE SUMMARY 2.1

Inconsistent Interpretations—Significance of Having a Supreme Court: *R. v. Keegstra*[5] and *R. v. Andrews*[6]

Each province in Canada has its own hierarchy of courts, thus a ruling from the highest court in one province may conflict with decisions from other courts. Consider the dilemma faced by the police in enforcing Canada's *Criminal Code* following the decisions in the *Keegstra* and *Andrews* cases. Both cases involved charges laid under section 319(2) of the *Code*, prohibiting wilful promotion of hatred against identifiable groups.

Keegstra had been teaching students in Eckville, Alberta, that the holocaust was a hoax. Andrews was also spreading anti-semitic, white supremacist hate literature. In the *Keegstra* case, the charges were set aside when the Alberta Court of Appeal declared the legislation to be unconstitutional. Keegstra successfully argued that the *Criminal Code* prohibition violated his freedom of expression as guaranteed by the *Charter of Rights and Freedoms*. But in the *Andrews* case, the Ontario Court of Appeal upheld the constitutionality of the same charges even though it had the benefit of the Alberta decision. It simply chose not to follow it.

Courts from different provinces are not bound to follow each other's decisions. Consequently, Canadians may face situations where charges cannot be laid in one province, whereas similar conduct will result in criminal prosecution in others. The police could not pursue hate crimes in Alberta because the Alberta Court of Appeal had ruled the law unconstitutional. Yet in Ontario, similar conduct drew charges.

The Supreme Court of Canada ruled on the *Keegstra* and *Andrews* appeals simultaneously. It declared section 319 constitutional, finding that although freedom of expression is violated by the *Code*, these infringements are justifiable under section 1 of the *Charter*. Prohibiting communications that are hateful and harmful was found to be justifiable, even if freedom of expression is thus curtailed, for the good of society as a whole. Charges for inciting hatred were thus tried against Keegstra and he was eventually convicted.

SMALL BUSINESS PERSPECTIVE

These cases demonstrate that one law may be interpreted and enforced differently from province to province. A sophisticated businessperson cannot assume that laws will receive similar interpretation across the country.

Stare decisis **provides predictability**

Results in an inflexible system

the outcome of the litigation and thus avoid going to court. However, a significant disadvantage of following precedent is that a judge must follow another judge's decision even though social attitudes may have changed. The system is anchored to the past, with only limited capacity to make corrections or to adapt and change to meet modern needs. Opposing legal representatives present a judge with several precedents that support their side of the argument. The judge's job is to analyze the facts of the precedent cases and compare them with the case at hand. Since no two cases are ever exactly alike, the judge has some flexibility in deciding whether or not to apply a particular precedent. Judges try to avoid applying prece-

---

5. [1988] A.J. No. 501 (C.A.), rev'd [1990] 3 S.C.R. 870.

6. [1988] O.J. No. 1222 (C.A.); [1990] 3 S.C.R. 870.

dent decisions by finding essential differences between the facts of the two cases if they feel that the prior decision will create an injustice in the present case. This process is referred to as **distinguishing the facts** of opposing precedents. Still, judges cannot stray very far from the established line of precedents.

A judge must choose among precedents

CASE SUMMARY 2.2

Lower Court Judge Must Follow Decision of Higher Court: *R. v. Clough*[7]

Ms. Clough was convicted in a B.C. Provincial Court of possession of cocaine for the purposes of trafficking and also for possession of a small amount of marijuana. At the time of sentencing, the provincial court judge had to decide whether this was an appropriate case to impose a conditional sentence on Ms. Clough or a harsher sentence involving a jail term. He was asked to take into consideration the Supreme Court of Canada decision in *R. v. Proulx*,[8] setting out certain guidelines for sentencing in these circumstances, and the British Columbia Court of Appeal decision in *R. v. Kozma*,[9] which upheld the imposition of a conditional sentence in a similar matter.

The B.C.C.A. had considered the *Proulx* judgment before reaching its decision in the *Kozma* matter. But the Provincial Court Judge in this case stated that the B.C.C.A. had wrongly decided the *R. v. Kozma* case and refused to follow it. He imposed a sentence of eight months on Ms. Clough, and that decision was appealed to the B.C.C.A.

The Court of Appeal stated that the Provincial Court Judge had the authority to find that the facts in this case were different and not apply the *Kozma* decision for that reason, but it was not within his power to refuse to follow the decision of a senior court on the basis that the case had been wrongly decided. "That was not for him to say." The Court of Appeal stated in its judgment that the Provincial Court Judge "was bound by the rule of *stare decisis* to accept the decisions of this court to the extent that they may apply to the case before him." Thus, the Court of Appeal overturned his decision, removed the eight-month jail term, and substituted a conditional sentence on Ms. Clough.

This case nicely illustrates how *stare decisis* works today. The Supreme Court of Canada made a decision in the *R. v. Proulx* case, and the British Columbia Court of Appeal interpreted and applied that decision in *R. v. Kozma*. Whereas the Supreme Court of Canada could declare the *Kozma* decision erroneous and refuse to apply it (or even overturn it on appeal), the Provincial Court of British Columbia was required to follow the *Kozma* decision, it being from a superior court.

DISCUSSION QUESTIONS

Should a lower court be required to follow the decision of a higher court that it believes has been wrongly decided? What about the requirement of following a precedent when the reason for it has long since disappeared? Consider the arguments for and against the application of *stare decisis*.

---

7. [2001] B.C.J. No. 2336 (C.A.).

8. *R. v. Proulx*, [2000] 1 S.C.R. 61.

9. [2000] B.C.J. No. 1595 (C.A.).

SOURCES OF LAW

Common Law

At an early stage in the development of common law, three great courts were created: the court of common pleas, the court of king's bench, and the exchequer court, referred to collectively as the **common law courts**. The rules developed in the courts were called "common law" because the judges, at least in theory, did not create law but merely discovered it in the customs and traditions of the people to whom it was to be applied. However, the foundation for a complete legal system could not be supplied by local custom and tradition alone, so common law judges borrowed legal principles from many different sources. Common law borrows from **Roman civil law**, which gave us our concepts of property and possessions. **Canon** or **church law** contributed law in relation to families and estates. Another important European system that had an impact on common law was called the **law merchant**. Trading between nations was performed by merchants who were members of guilds (similar to modern trade unions or professional organizations), which developed their own rules to deal with disputes between members. As the strength of the guilds declined, common law judges found themselves dealing increasingly with disputes between merchants. The law merchant was then adopted as part of the English common law, and it included laws relating to negotiable instruments, such as cheques and promissory notes.

Customs and traditions major source of common law

Common law borrows from:
- **Roman civil law**
- **Canon law**
- **Law merchant**

Equity

Common law courts had some serious limitations. Parties seeking justice before them found it difficult to obtain fair and proper redress for the grievances they had suffered. Because of the rigidity of the process, the inflexibility of the rules applied, and the limited scope of the remedies available, people often went directly to the king for satisfaction and relief. The burden of this process made it necessary for the king to delegate the responsibility to the chancellor, who, in turn, appointed several vice-chancellors. This body eventually became known as the **Court of Chancery**, sometimes referred to as the **Court of Equity**. It dealt with matters that, for various reasons, could not be handled adequately or fairly by the common law courts. The Court of Chancery did not hear appeals from the common law courts; rather, it provided an alternative forum. If people seeking relief knew that the common law courts could provide no remedy or that the remedy was inadequate, they would go to the Court of Chancery instead. Initially, the Court of Chancery was unhampered by the rules of precedence and the rigidity that permeated the common law courts, and could decide a case on its merits. The system of law developed by the Court of Chancery became known as the **law of equity**. This flexibility, which was the most significant asset of equity, was also its greatest drawback. Each decision of the Court of Chancery appeared arbitrary; there was no uniformity within the system; and it was difficult to predict the outcome of a given case. This caused friction between the chancery and the common law judges, which was solved, to some extent, by the chancery's adopting *stare decisis*. This caused the same problems found in the common law courts. The chancery courts eventually became as formal and rigid as the common law courts. Finally, the two separate court systems were amalgamated by the *Judicature Acts of 1873–1875*.[10] This merger happened in Canada as well, and today there is only one court system in each of the provinces.

Common law rigid

Courts of Chancery provided relief

Resulting in the law of equity

Conflict resulted in rigidity in chancery as well

[10.] *Judicature Acts* (1873–1875) 31 Geo. III.

Although the two court systems merged, the bodies of law they had created did not, and it is best still to think of common law and equity as two distinct bodies of rules. Originally, the rules of equity may have been based on fairness and justice, but when a person today asks a judge to apply equity, they are not asking for fairness: they are asking that the rules developed by the courts of chancery be applied to the case. Equity should be viewed as a supplement to, rather than a replacement of, common law. Common law is complete—albeit somewhat unsatisfactory—without equity, but equity would be nothing without common law. The courts of chancery were instrumental in developing such principles in law as the trust (in which one party holds property for another), and also provided several alternative remedies, such as injunction and specific performance, that will be examined later in the text.

> **Equity today does not simply mean fairness**

> **Equity supplements the common law**

The common law provinces in Canada administer both common law and equity, and judges treat matters differently when proceeding under equity as opposed to common law rules. Of course, judges must always be alert to the fact that any applicable parliamentary statute will override both.

Statutes

In many situations, justice was not available in either the common law or chancery courts, and another method was needed to correct these inadequacies. The English Civil War of the 17th century firmly established the principle that Parliament, rather than the king, was supreme, and from that time, Parliament handled any major modification to the law. Parliamentary enactments are referred to as statutes or legislation and take precedence over judge-made law based on either common law or equity. Throughout the text, reference will be made to the MyBusLawLab, where statute details and provincial variations between them will be available.

mybuslawlab
www.pearsoned.ca/mybuslawlab

> **Statutes and regulations override judge-made law**

It is important to remember that government has several distinct functions: legislative, judicial, and administrative. Parliament legislates or creates the law, as do each of the provincial legislatures; the judicial branch is the court system, and the judiciary interprets legislation and makes case law; the executive branch and its agencies administer and implement that law. Organizations such as the RCMP, the Employment Insurance Commission, and the military are part of the executive branch of government. Often, legislation creating such bodies (the enabling statute) delegates power to them to create regulations (the subordinate legislation). Through those regulations, government agencies implement and accomplish the goals of the enabling statute and enforce its terms. Similarly, municipal bylaws operate as subordinate legislation. A provincial statute, such as *Ontario's Municipal Act, 2001*,[11] may enable municipalities to pass bylaws, but only with regard to matters stipulated in the *Act*.

For the businessperson, these statutes and regulations have become all-important, setting out the specific rules governing business activities in all jurisdictions. Although judge-made law still forms the foundation of our legal system, it is statutes and regulations that control and restrict what we can do and determine what we must do to carry on business in Canada today. See Table 2.1 for a summary of the sources of law in Canada.

[11.] S.O. 2001, c. 25.

Table 2.1 Sources of Law in Canada

Branch of Government	Legislative	Executive	Judicial
Who fills these positions?	Federally: Parliament	Prime Minister and Cabinet Ministers together with each department's civil servants/ bureaucrats	Judges appointed by the various provinces and federally appointed justices
	Provincially: Legislative Assemblies	Premier and the Cabinet together with each department's civil servants/bureaucrats	
Type of law made	Statute law (legislation)	Subordinate legislation • regulations made by order-in-council or as authorized by legislation • bylaws made by municipal governments	Case law
Examples	(Federal) • *Immigration and Refugee Protection Act* • *Criminal Code*	(Federal) Immigration and Refugee Protection Regulations	(Federal) The decision of the Supreme Court of Canada in *R. v. Keegstra*
	(Provincial) • *Workers' Compensation Act* • *Traffic Safety Act* • *Business Corporations Act*	(Provincial) Workers' Compensation Regulations	(Provincial) The decision of the Ontario Court of Appeal in *Haig v. Canada*

LAW IN CANADA

Confederation

Canada came into existence in 1867, with the federation of Upper and Lower Canada, Nova Scotia, and New Brunswick. Other provinces followed, with Newfoundland being the most recent to join Confederation. Every jurisdiction except Quebec adopted the English common law legal system. Quebec elected to retain the use of the French civil law legal system for private matters falling within provincial jurisdiction.

Confederation was accomplished when the British Parliament passed the *British North America Act* (*BNA Act*), now renamed the *Constitution Act, 1867*.[12] The *BNA Act*'s primary significance is that it created the Dominion of Canada, divided power between the legislative, executive, and judicial branches of government, and determined the functions and powers of the provincial and federal levels of government. The preamble to the *BNA Act* says that Canada has a constitution "similar in principle to that of the United Kingdom"; that is, we claim as part of

BNA Act created Canada and divided powers

---

12. *Constitution Act, 1867* (U.K.), 30 & 31 Vict., c. 3, reprinted in R.S.C. 1985, App. II, No. 5 (formerly the *British North America Act, 1867*).

our constitution all the great constitutional institutions of the United Kingdom, such as the *Magna Carta* and the *English Bill of Rights*. Also included are such unwritten conventions as the **rule of law**, which recognizes that although Parliament is supreme and can create any law considered appropriate, citizens are protected from the arbitrary actions of the government. All actions of government and government agencies must be authorized by valid legislation. In addition, our constitution includes those acts passed by both the British and Canadian Parliaments subsequent to the *Constitution Act, 1867* that have status beyond mere statutes, such as the *Statute of Westminster* (1931) and the *Constitution Act, 1982*,[13] which includes the *Charter of Rights and Freedoms*. The most recent addition to the constitutional statutes is the *Constitution Act, 1999* (Nunavut).[14]

More to Canadian Constitution than *BNA Act* and *Charter*

Canada's Constitution is, in essence, the "rulebook" that government must follow. It is comprised of three elements: (1) statutes, such as the *Constitution Act, 1982* and the statutes creating various provinces; (2) conventions, which are unwritten rules dictating how the government is to operate and include the rule of law; and (3) case law on Constitution issues, such as whether the federal or provincial government has jurisdiction to create certain statutes.

CASE SUMMARY 2.3

The Power to Prorogue Parliament[15]

Within two months of the October 2008 federal election, Canadians were facing the prospect of going to the polls again. The decision of whether to prorogue (adjourn) Parliament or not rested with the Governor General, Michaelle Jean. Canadians learned that reserve powers, vested in the head of state (the Queen, as represented by the Governor General and Lieutenant-Governors), are protected by unwritten constitutional conventions. These reserve powers include the power to dismiss a Prime Minister, to dissolve Parliament (or not), and to delay or refuse royal assent to legislation.

Since the King-Byng affair in 1926, the convention (unwritten rule) has been that the Governor General is expected to take the advice of the sitting Prime Minister. This convention arose on the heels of the then Governor General's (Lord Byng's) decision to ignore the wishes of the Prime Minister (McKenzie King) to dissolve Parliament. Instead the Governor General called upon the Leader of the Opposition to lead Parliament, which proved to be futile since the opposition did not have the support of the House of Commons. The minority government was soon defeated and an election had to be called anyway.

In December 2008, the leaders of the Liberal and New Democratic parties formed a coalition and, with the support of the Bloc Québécois, planned to defeat Harper's Conservatives during the first sitting of Parliament. Harper thus asked the Governor General to prorogue Parliament until a new budget could be presented. In deciding to prorogue Parliament, the Governor General essentially dealt a death-blow to the coalition and allowed the Conservatives a chance to win back the confidence of the House.[16]

[13.] *Constitution Act, 1982,* being Schedule B to the *Canada Act 1982* (U.K.), 1982, c. 11.

[14.] S.C. 1998, c. 15, Part II; (in force 1 April 1999).

[15] For more information on this Constitutional spectacle, see online: http://www.cbc.ca/canada/story/2008/12/02/f-governor-general.html (accessed May, 2009).

[16.] See "The Delicate Role of the Governor General," http://www.cbc.ca/canada/story/2008/12/02/f-governor-general.html. To view a video clip summarizing the King-Byng affair, see http://archives.cbc.ca/politics/federal_politics/clips/11688/, May 13, 2009).

For the person in business, it must be remembered that the effect of Confederation was not simply to create one country, with one set of rules. Each province was given the power to establish rules in those areas over which it had jurisdiction. As a consequence, businesses operating within and between provinces must comply with federal, provincial, and municipal regulations. In spite of the opportunity for great divergence among the provinces, it is encouraging to see how similar the controls and restrictions are in the different jurisdictions.

Constitution and Division of Powers

www.pearsoned.ca/mybuslawlab

| BC | AB | SK | MB | ON |

Constitution Act and **Charter** limit power of federal and provincial governments

Constitution Act (1867) divides powers between federal and provincial governments

Federal powers set out in sec. 91

Provincial powers set out in sec. 92

In Canada, as in Britain, Parliament is supreme and traditionally has had the power to make laws that cannot be overruled by any other body and are subject only to the realities of the political system in which they function. In addition, the *Constitution Act, 1867* and the *Charter of Rights and Freedoms* place some limitations on this supremacy. Unlike the United Kingdom, Canada has a federal form of government with 11 different legislative bodies, each claiming the supreme powers of Parliament. Refer to the MyBusLawLab for links to the federal and various provincial government sites for current legislation.

The *Constitution Act, 1867* assigned different legislative powers to the federal and provincial governments. The powers of the federal government are set out primarily in section 91 of the *Constitution Act, 1867,* and those of the provincial governments in section 92. The federal government has power over such matters as banking, currency, the postal service, criminal law (although not its enforcement), and the appointment of judges in the federal and higher-level provincial courts. The federal government passes considerable legislation affecting such matters as the regulation of all import and export activities, taxation, environmental concerns, money and banking, interprovincial and international transportation, as well as important areas of intellectual property, such as copyrights, patents, and trademarks. The provinces have jurisdiction over such matters as hospitals, education, the administration of the courts, and commercial activities carried on at the provincial level.

Thus, most business activities that are carried on within the province are governed by provincial legislation or municipal bylaws, including statutes dealing with the sale of goods, consumer protection, employment, workers' compensation, collective bargaining, secured transactions, incorporation, real estate, and licensing. For industries that fall within federal jurisdiction, such as banking and the railways, there are corresponding federal statutes, such as collective bargaining and incorporation legislation. Under the "Peace, Order, and Good Government" (P.O.G.G.) clause (found in the introduction to section 91), the federal government has residual power to make law with respect to things not listed in the *Constitution Act, 1867,* such as broadcasting and air transportation.

Under section 92(16), the provinces are given broad powers to make law with respect to all matters of a local or private nature. It is important to note that these assigned areas of jurisdiction are concerned with the nature of the legislation being passed, rather than the individuals or things affected. Thus, the federal government's power to pass banking legislation allows it to control anything to do with banking, including interest rates, deposits, and how those deposits are invested. The division of powers accomplished by sections 91 and 92 of the *Constitution Act, 1867* has been very important in the development of Canada as a nation and, until the recent entrenchment of the *Charter*, was the main consideration of courts when faced with constitutional questions. In these jurisdictional disputes between governments, where competing governments claim to control a particular activity, the courts are called upon to act as a referee. See Table 2.2 for a summary of the division of powers.

Sections 91 and 92 deal with types of legislation, not things

Table 2.2 Division of Powers

Federal—Section 91	Provincial—Section 92
Trade and commerce	Municipal institutions
Employment insurance	Hospitals (and health care)
Raising monies by any mode of taxation	Direct taxation within the province
Criminal law (although not its enforcement)	Administration of justice within the province
Banking, currency, postal service	Property and civil rights
Residual power under the "P.O.G.G." clause	Generally, matters of a local or private nature

CASE SUMMARY 2.3

Challenging Provincial Forfeiture Laws: *Chatterjee v. Ontario (Attorney General)*[17]

Chatterjee, a university student, was being arrested for breach of probation when the police coincidentally found $29 000 in cash and items associated with drug trafficking in his car, but no drugs. No charges were laid relating to the money, nor was Chatterjee charged with any drug-related activity. Nonetheless, the Attorney General applied for and obtained an order allowing the Crown to keep the money and equipment, as proceeds of unlawful activity under Ontario's *Remedies for Organized Crime and Other Unlawful Activities Act*, also known as the *Civil Remedies Act (CRA)*. Chatterjee challenged the constitutional validity of the *CRA*, arguing that the province did not have the right to seize proceeds of crime since criminal law is a matter of federal, not provincial, jurisdiction.

The Supreme Court of Canada unanimously upheld the provincial law, since the dominant feature related to "property and civil rights," is a provincial matter. While its provisions may incidentally overlap with criminal law, "the fact that the CRA aims to deter federal offences as well as provincial offences, and indeed, offences outside of Canada, is not fatal to its validity."

---

[17] 2009 SCC 19.

As stated by Binnie, J. for the Court: "The CRA was enacted to deter crime and to compensate its victims. The former purpose is broad enough that both the federal government (in relation to criminal law) and the provincial governments (in relation to property and civil rights) can validly pursue it. The latter purpose falls squarely within provincial competence. Crime imposes substantial costs on provincial treasuries. Those costs impact many provincial interests, including health, policing resources, community stability and family welfare. It would be out of step with modern realities to conclude that a province must shoulder the costs to the community of criminal behaviour but cannot use deterrence to suppress it."

SMALL BUSINESS PERSPECTIVE

This case is interesting because the party raising the constitutional challenge was not a government, but rather, an individual. Thus if one finds oneself objecting to a particular law, one might solve the issue by challenging the constitutional validity of the enactment!

Courts examine the essence of laws in constitutional challenges

When determining the constitutional validity of legislation, the courts often resolve the issue by looking at the "pith and substance" of the challenged law. In other words, what is the main purpose of the law and does the government which enacted the law have the constitutional jurisdiction to regulate that concern. Such was the approach taken in the *Reference re Firearms Act* (Can.) case.[18] In 1995, Parliament amended the *Criminal Code* by enacting the *Firearms Act*.[19] The amendments require all holders of firearms to obtain licences and register their guns. Alberta, backed by Ontario, Saskatchewan, Manitoba, and the territories, challenged the law, arguing it was a brazen intrusion on private property and civil rights, a provincial power according to section 92(13) of the *Constitution Act, 1867*. The opponents argued that the new law would do no more to control gun crimes than registering vehicles does to stop traffic offences.

Laws upheld if interference with another jurisdiction's power is incidental

The Supreme Court of Canada upheld the *Firearms Act* as **intra vires** Parliament, meaning that it was within its power. It found that the *Act* constitutes a valid exercise of Parliament's jurisdiction over criminal law because its "pith and substance" is directed to enhancing public safety by controlling access to firearms. Because guns are dangerous and pose a risk to public safety, their control and their regulation as dangerous products were regarded as valid purposes for criminal law. In essence, the law was determined to be criminal in focus. The *Act* impacted provincial jurisdiction over property and civil rights only incidentally. Accordingly, the *Firearms Act* was upheld as a valid exercise of federal power under section 91(27) of the *Constitution Act, 1867*.

Conflicting Powers

On occasion, one level of government passes legislation that may infringe on the powers of another. For example, municipal governments have tried to control prostitution or pornography, using their zoning or licensing power, when in fact

---

18. [2000] 1 S.C.R. 783.

19. S.C. 1995, c. 39.

these matters are controlled by criminal law, a federal area.[20] Such bylaws have been struck down as ***ultra vires*** (beyond one's jurisdiction or power) by the courts, as veiled attempts to control moral conduct, matters to be dealt with under criminal jurisdiction. Municipalities sometimes try to dramatically increase the licensing fee charged to a business to accomplish the same purpose, often with the same result.

Validity of statute determined by its true nature

One level of government cannot invade the area given to another by trying to make it look like the legislation is of a different kind. This is called colourable legislation and the court simply looks at the substance of what the governing body is trying to do, as opposed to what it claims to be doing, and asks whether or not it has that power.

CASE SUMMARY 2.5

Municipal Bylaw to Ensure Covering of Breasts: *Maple Ridge (District) v. Meyer*[21]

A quiet B.C. community was shocked to see Ms. Meyer bare her breasts at a public swimming pool—after all, she was no longer a child! The response was an amendment to the Maple Ridge Park bylaw, making it an offence punishable by a fine of $2000 and six months' imprisonment to appear in a park unclothed. "Clothed" was defined to require females over the age of eight years to fully cover their nipples and areolae with opaque apparel. The Court determined that the amendment to the bylaw was motivated by complaints regarding morality, modesty, and embarrassment. The bylaw created a stricter standard regarding nudity than that found in the *Criminal Code*. It imposed strict liability whereas under the *Code* defences were available; further, it criminalized the conduct of girls as young as nine years old. The Court struck the bylaw down as *ultra vires* the legislative competence of Maple Ridge, finding it a "colourable attempt to regulate morality and thus displace the federal jurisdiction in respect of criminal law."

DISCUSSION QUESTIONS

In light of the division of powers, can you think of other laws that may be characterized as colourable legislation? Who can challenge such legislation and how is this done?

The powers of the federal and provincial governments can overlap considerably. When overlap does take place, the principle of **paramountcy** may require that the federal legislation be operative and that the provincial legislation go into abeyance and no longer apply. If the overlap between provincial and federal legislations is merely incidental, both are valid, and both are operative. An individual must obey both by adhering to the higher standard, whether provincial or federal. It is only when the laws are such that only one can be obeyed that a true conflict exists, and then the federal provision will prevail.

When provincial and federal laws conflict, follow federal

[20.] *R. v. Westendorp*, [1983] 1 S.C.R. 43.

[21.] [2000] B.C.J. No. 1154 (B.C.S.C.).

Another Challenge Goes Up in Smoke: *Rothmans, Benson & Hedges Inc. v. Saskatchewan*[22]

The Federal *Tobacco Act* permitted manufacturers and retailers to display tobacco products and to post signs setting out availability and prices. Saskatchewan passed the *Tobacco Control Act* prohibiting all advertising, display, and promotion of tobacco products in any location where they might be seen by someone under 18. The provincial statute was challenged by Rothmans, Benson & Hedges Inc. on the basis that it was in conflict with the federal *Act*, and because of the principle of paramountcy it could not stand. It was clearly established that the federal legislation was valid and within the competency of the federal government under its criminal law power described in section 91(27) of the *Constitution Act, 1867*. The provincial legislation was presumably valid under the provincial powers set out in section 92 of the *Constitution Act, 1867*. The problem was to determine whether the provincial *Act* could stand given the federal intrusion into the area.

The Supreme Court of Canada concluded that the federal *Tobacco Act* didn't actually permit advertising in those areas prohibited by the provincial legislation; its restrictions were simply not as broad as those covered by the provincial *Act*. The Court found that the two statutes were not in conflict; one simply went further than the other. It was possible for the retailers and manufactures to obey them both by following the higher standard set out in the provincial *Act*. Thus if young people were prohibited from coming into a place where there was such advertising, such as a bar or pub, the merchant would be in compliance with both the federal and the provincial *Acts*. Further the court determined that since the purpose of the federal *Act* was to promote public health and restrict the use of tobacco products, the provincial legislation did not frustrate the purpose. Thus, finding no conflict, the court found the provincial *Act* valid and binding.

The case not only illustrates that when there is a true conflict between valid federal and valid provincial legislation, the federal act will prevail, but also shows that often what appears to be a conflict is not. Generally, when it is possible to obey both statutes, there is no conflict and both are valid.

SMALL BUSINESS PERSPECTIVE

The above case demonstrates an interesting tactic—if a particular law restricts the profitability of one's business, one may be able to challenge its constitutionality. If the challenge is successful, the courts can strike the law down, resolving the problem for you

Delegation of Powers

Direct delegation prohibited

Since neither the federal nor the provincial levels of government are considered inferior legislative bodies, both are supreme parliaments in their assigned areas. Over the years, for various reasons, these bodies have sometimes found it necessary to transfer the powers given to them to other levels of government. However, direct delegation between the federal and provincial governments is prohibited. For example, during the Depression of the 1930s, it became clear that a national

---

22. [2005] 1 S.C.R. 188.

system of unemployment insurance was needed. The provinces, having jurisdiction in this area, attempted to delegate their power to the federal government. The Supreme Court held that they could not do so, as it was an "abdication" of the "exclusive powers" given to the provinces under the *Constitution Act, 1867*. To make unemployment insurance an area of federal responsibility, the British Parliament needed to amend the constitution. This amendment is now incorporated in section 91, subsection (2A) of the *Constitution Act, 1867*.

Indirect delegation permitted

Although direct delegation is prohibited, it is possible for the federal and provincial governments to delegate their powers to inferior bodies, such as boards and individual civil servants; in fact, this is usually the only way that governmental bodies can conduct their business. It is thus possible for the federal government to delegate its power in a particular area to a provincial board or a provincial civil servant. Similarly, a province can give powers to federal boards, since these are also inferior bodies. In this way, governments overcome the prohibition against delegation.

Agreements to Share Powers

Another means used to circumvent the constitutional rigidity created by the 1867 division of powers is by federal and provincial government agreements to share powers. These agreements may consist of *transfer-payment schemes*, or conditional grants under which the transfer of funds from the federal government is tied to conditions on how the money is to be spent. Through such schemes, the federal government can exercise some say as to how a provincial government operates programs that fall under the province's constitutional area of control. The federal government may set certain national standards to which the funding is tied and in this fashion ensure that all Canadians have access to similar levels of service.

Transfer-payment schemes in the areas of health, social programs, and education are examples of provincial areas where the federal government provides considerable funding along with the imposition of national standards or other conditions on the provinces. At the time of Confederation, government spending on these services was minuscule. Now these areas may account for two-thirds of all government spending. The provinces, with their restricted taxing powers, would have difficulty providing these services without federal funding. In the fairly recent past the federal government dramatically cut payments to support health and social programs in the provinces, but more recently these transfer payments have been at least partially restored.

Legislation

Legislation is introduced to the parliamentary process in the form of a **bill**, which goes through a sequence of introduction, debate, modification, and approval that is referred to as first, second, and third readings. When a bill is finally enacted, it has the status of a statute (although it may still be referred to as a bill or an act). Such a statute does not have the status of law until it receives the approval (signature) of the Governor General at the federal level or the Lieutenant-Governor in a province, a process referred to as receiving **royal assent**. The Governor General and the Lieutenant-Governors are the Queen's representatives in Canada and can sign on behalf of the Crown. Current convention (practice) in Canada directs the Queen's representatives to sign as the government in power directs them, and such approval is therefore usually a formality. The government may use this

mybuslawlab
www.pearsoned.ca/mybuslawlab

Statutes must receive royal assent

requirement to delay the coming into effect of legislation, and care should therefore be taken when examining an act to make sure that it has received royal assent. The statute itself may have provisions for different parts of it to come into force at different times. There are many examples where whole acts, or portions of them, have no legal effect for these reasons. See Figure 2.1 for a summary of the traditional process for passing bills.

The Government of Canada publishes a compilation of these statutes annually; the collection can be found in most libraries, under *Statutes of Canada*. The federal government has summarized and published all current statutes in the *Revised Statutes of Canada* in 1985, cited as R.S.C. (1985). It is not necessary to go back any earlier than this compilation to find current legislation. Indexes and guides are provided to assist in the process of finding the federal statutes and subsequent amendments. Refer to the MyBusLawLab for links to these statutes.

Federal and provincial statutes compiled and published

Similarly, each province annually publishes the statutes passed by its legislative assembly and provides a compilation in the form of revised statutes. Unfortunately, there is no uniformity in the timing of the revisions, and each province has revised and compiled its statutes in a different year. Most jurisdictions provide official or unofficial consolidated updates of their statutes online as an ongoing service. These statutes, along with useful commentary about new legislation, are currently available on the internet at their respective government's website. The Access to Justice Network provides easy access to the laws across the country (see its website at **www.acjnet.org**) as does the Canadian Legal Information Institute (**www.canlii.org**).The MyBusLawLab (**www.pearsoned.ca/yates**) will also provide important information with respect to relevant statutes and other material as they are discussed throughout the text.

Regulations also published

Statutes often empower government agencies to create further rules to carry out their functions. As long as these regulations meet the terms of the statute, they have the effect of law. They are also published and are available to the public as *Regulations of Canada* or of the respective provinces. Cities and municipalities pass bylaws under their statutory authority in the same way, and these too are published and made available by those jurisdictions. Statutes passed within the power of the respective governments as set out in the *Constitution Act, 1867* and other constitutional provisions override any previous law in place, whether judge-made law (common law or equity) or prior legislation.

Judges interpret and apply statutes

A trial judge required to deal with a statute must first determine what it means. This task is not always easy, since it is difficult for those drafting the law to anticipate all of the situations in which it will be applied. The judge must then determine whether, under the *Constitution Act, 1867* and other constitutional provisions, the legislative body that passed the statute in question had the power to do so. When a judge interprets and applies a statute, that decision becomes a precedent, and henceforth the statute must be interpreted in the same way by courts lower in the court hierarchy.

Decisions create precedents

PROTECTION OF RIGHTS AND FREEDOMS

As noted earlier in this chapter, the preamble of the *Constitution Act, 1867* states that Canada will have "a Constitution similar in principle to that of the United Kingdom." The courts have interpreted that phrase as importing into Canada the unwritten conventions and traditions of government developed in the United

Figure 2.1 Traditional Passage of Bills

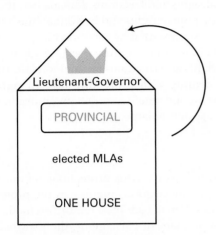

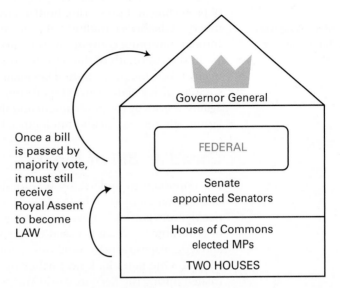

Once a bill is passed by majority vote, it must still receive Royal Assent to become LAW

First Reading—Bill is introduced in the Legislative Assembly. Customarily passes first reading without debate.

Second Reading—Bill is read again. Now debated. After approval, it may go to Committee of the Whole for review and amendment.
Committee of the Whole must approve all bills before they can receive a third reading.

Third Reading—Bill is read again. Final debate. **VOTE** held.

If passed

If defeated

To Lt.-Governor for Royal Assent

DIES

Assented to

Assent refused (RARE)

DIES

Effective immediately

OR

Effective on proclamation

First Reading—Introduction (by government, by private member, or possibly by all-party committee*¹).
Bill is printed.
May go to all-party committee after approval.*²

Second Reading—Bill is debated.
After approval in principle, the Bill goes to all-party committee, which may recommend amendments.

Third Reading—Final debate and **VOTE**.

If passed

If defeated

DIES

To Senate
First Reading
Second Reading   as above
Third Reading

VOTE

If passed

If defeated ⟶ DIES

To Governor General for Royal Assent

Assented to

Assent refused ⟶ DIES (RARE)

Effective immediately

OR

Effective on proclamation

The Federal Government now allows for two variations from the "traditional" passage of bills.*¹ A motion may be tabled for a Committee to prepare and introduce a bill.*² Bills may now be referred to Committee *before* second reading. In any event, a bill goes to Committee only *once*.

Kingdom over the centuries. Among those unwritten conventions are the practices of protecting and preserving fundamental rights and freedoms. Canada has, thus, inherited the British tradition of protecting human rights and individual freedoms through unwritten conventions (practices) as supported by common law.

In the aftermath of the Second World War, concern arose over the adequacy of entrusting the protection of personal rights and freedoms to common law. Two streams of legislation developed, one dealing with protecting human rights against abuses by the government and the second aimed at protecting individuals against discrimination and intolerance by society at large.

Rights and freedoms were historically protected by convention

Canadian Bill of Rights

It is important to understand that the basic human rights protections set out in ordinary statutes passed by the federal or provincial governments may not protect people from abuses by government. Because Canada adopted the British method of government, which is based on the supremacy of Parliament, the provincial and federal governments were free to interfere at will with civil rights through legislation. One need look no further than the way the Japanese Canadians were treated during the Second World War to conclude that it could be dangerous for Canadians to leave the protection of their basic rights to the political process.

The first attempt at limiting the federal government's power to pass legislation that violates basic human rights was the passage (in 1960) of the *Canadian Bill of Rights*.[23] Because it was not entrenched in the Constitution, the courts viewed the *Bill of Rights* as just another statute that could be repealed, amended, or simply overridden by any subsequent federal statute. Furthermore, when asked to apply the *Bill of Rights*, the courts approached its provisions in the same narrow, restrictive way that they did any other legislation, thus significantly limiting its scope and effect. For example, when federal legislation passed subsequently was found to be in conflict with the provisions of the *Bill of Rights*, instead of applying the *Bill of Rights* and limiting the operation of the new statute, the courts would treat the new legislation as overriding the old and would disregard the provisions that conflicted with the new legislation. This, of course, effectively defeated the purpose of the *Bill of Rights*, and while it is still considered law in Canada, its effectiveness is extremely limited. Something more was needed.

Bill of Rights just another statute

Charter of Rights and Freedoms

A constitutional guarantee of basic rights and freedoms arose in 1982 following a series of constitutional conferences. *The Constitution Act, 1982*[24] was simultaneously enacted in Canada and the United Kingdom. In the latter, it was contained in a statute called the *Canada Act 1982*.[25] One effect of these enactments was to make a very significant addition to the Canadian Constitution in the form of the Canadian *Charter of Rights and Freedoms*.

The effect of including the *Charter* in our Constitution is twofold. First, neither the federal government nor the provinces have the power to modify or otherwise interfere with the basic rights set out in the *Charter* except through constitutional amendment. Ordinary legislation will not override the *Charter* simply because it is

mybuslawlab
www.pearsoned.ca/mybuslawlab

BC AB SK MB ON

[23.] S.C. 1960, c. 44.

[24.] Schedule B to the *Canada Act 1982* (U.K.) 1982, c. 11.

[25.] *Canada Act 1982*, (U.K.) 1982, c. 11.

passed after the *Charter*. The provisions are said to be entrenched in the Constitution and are, as declared in section 52 of the *Constitution Act, 1982*, "the supreme law of Canada." The section goes on to state: "Any law that is inconsistent with the provisions of the Constitution is, to the extent of that inconsistency, of no force or effect." In other words, the *Charter* and the rights protected by it come first.

Second, the burden of protecting those rights has shifted from the politicians to the judges. Now, an individual who feels that his or her rights have been interfered with by legislation or other forms of government action can seek redress from the courts, relying on the provisions of the *Charter*. The courts can remedy a violation of rights by excluding evidence improperly secured and can grant any remedy deemed just in the circumstances.[26] The courts can even strike down statutes that infringe on those rights. Hence, the doctrine of parliamentary supremacy has been to some extent limited, the courts now being able to check the power of Parliament and the legislatures in those areas covered by the *Charter*.

The Constitution includes the *Charter*

Constitution including the *Charter* is the supreme law of Canada

Courts are empowered to strike down offending statutes

LIMITATIONS

There are three important limitations on the entrenchment of these basic rights. Section 1 of the *Charter of Rights and Freedoms* allows "reasonable limits" on those rights and freedoms when limiting them can be "demonstrably justified in a free and democratic society." This gives the courts the power to interpret the provisions of the *Charter* to avoid an unreasonable result. The rights and freedoms set out in the *Charter* are, therefore, not absolute. For example, the *Charter* guarantees freedom of expression, but there would be little dispute that libel, slander, or hardcore pornography must be controlled.

The Supreme Court was asked in *Hill v. Church of Scientology of Toronto* (1995)[27] to give effect to the freedom of expression provision of the *Charter* by dismissing a defamation action against the Church and its representative, especially where the remarks were directed at a government official or Crown prosecutor. The Court found that the laws of defamation were, under section 1, a reasonable limitation on the operation of the freedom of expression clause of the *Charter*, thus confirming the lower court's finding of defamation and the highest defamation award up to that time in Canada.

Government cannot interfere with basic rights and freedoms except if reasonable to do so

The interests of the public are considered when applying section 1. Nonetheless, a law that restricts *Charter* rights, though apparently justified, will be rejected if it goes too far. For example, section 1 of the *Charter* was used to justify the imposition of reasonable limits on the rights of prisoners; prisoners serving two years or more in jail could not vote in federal elections. The Federal Court of Appeal found that the voting bans violated section 3 of the *Charter* but were justifiable in light of the objectives of the amended *Canada Elections Act*, specifically the fostering of civic responsibility and respect for the rule of law.[28] These objectives were important enough to warrant (in some cases) a compromise of *Charter* rights. But on further appeal, the Supreme Court of Canada overturned this decision, reasserting prisoners' right to vote. (See Case Summary 2.10 later in this chapter.)

---

26. *Canadian Charter of Rights and Freedoms*, s. 24, Part I of the *Constitution Act 1982*, being Schedule B to the *Canada Act 1982 (U.K.)*, 1982, c.11.

27. [1995] 2 S.C.R. 1130.

28. *Sauvé v. Canada (Chief Electoral Officer)*, [2002] 2 F.C. 119 (C.A.), rev'd [2002] S.C.J. No. 66.

Government Reneges on Agreement: *Newfoundland (Treasury Board) v. Newfoundland and Labrador Association of Public and Private Employees*[29]

In this case a significant pay inequity had been identified between female health-care workers and their male counterparts in Newfoundland. The government of Newfoundland and Labrador had entered into an agreement to correct the problem in 1988, including the making of substantial payments to address this pay inequity. The agreement was not implemented, and in 1991 the government brought in legislation, the *Public Sector Restraint Act (Nfld.)*, which contained provisions to delay the imposition of the increases meant to correct the imbalance and to eliminate the accumulated arrears altogether. Essentially, the government wiped out $24 million it owed to its employees to correct the imbalance under the agreement. The union took this to arbitration, and the arbitration board decided in the union's favour, finding that the employees' section 15 equality rights under the *Charter* had been infringed. The government appealed and the matter eventually came before the Supreme Court of Canada. The Supreme Court agreed that the section 15 equality rights of the female employees had been infringed. There was a clear case of gender discrimination here. The agreement was designed to correct a historical discrimination, which the government itself acknowledged existed. But the Court also held that because of the serious financial crisis then being experienced by the government of Newfoundland and Labrador, their actions in refusing to pay and delaying the increases was a reasonable limitation "prescribed by law as can be demonstrably justified in a free and democratic society" under section 1 of the *Charter*. This case illustrates how section 1 of the *Charter* can be used to justify some pretty serious deviations from the basic rights and freedoms set out in the *Charter*.

DISCUSSION QUESTIONS

Should the rights and freedoms listed in the *Charter* be absolute or are the exceptions listed under sections 1 and 33 acceptable given the requirements of efficient government and justice?

The second limitation is contained in section 33, and is referred to as the "notwithstanding clause." It allows each of the provinces and the federal government to override the basic rights contained in section 2 and sections 7 through 15 of the *Charter* simply by stating that the new legislation operates "notwithstanding" (regardless of) the *Charter*. The sections that can be overridden in this way include **fundamental freedoms** (such provisions as freedom of conscience and religion, of thought and belief, of opinion and expression, and of assembly and association); **legal rights** (the right of life, liberty, and security of person; security against unreasonable search and seizure, arbitrary imprisonment and detention); and **equality rights** (the right not to be discriminated against on the basis of gender, age, religion, race, or colour; and the guarantee of equality before the law).

It would appear that section 33 weakens the *Charter of Rights and Freedoms* considerably. The supremacy of Parliament appears to have been restored, at least in

---

[29.] [2004] 3 S.C.R. 381.

relation to the designated sections. It was originally hoped that most provinces would find the political cost too great to override the *Charter* in this way and, as a result, would refrain from doing so; for the most part, this has been the case. Quebec, however, used the notwithstanding clause to support language legislation restricting the use of English on business signs in that province. This legislation clearly violates the *Charter's* guarantee of freedom of expression, but the Quebec government gambled that the majority of the electorate would favour such protection of the French language. Refer to the MyBusLawLab for details. There are very few other examples of the clause's being used, and Alberta's experiments with invoking the clause have been controversial.[30] The notwithstanding clause does not apply to the sections guaranteeing democratic rights (the right to vote, to elect members to Parliament and the legislative assemblies), mobility rights (the right to enter and leave Canada), or language rights (the right to use both official languages). In addition, the rights of aboriginal people and the rights guaranteed to both genders cannot be overridden by the federal or provincial governments.

A "sunset clause" is applied to the operation of section 33. If the notwithstanding clause is invoked, the statute must be re-enacted by that legislative body every five years. This forces a re-examination of the decision to override the *Charter*, after the intervening event of an election where the use of the notwithstanding clause can be made an issue. New legislators may not be as willing to pay the political cost of using the notwithstanding clause.

The third limitation is the restriction of the operation of the *Charter* to government and government-related activities. Section 32(1)(a) declares that the *Charter* applies only to matters falling within the authority of "the Parliament and Government of Canada" and the territories, and section 32(1)(b) makes the *Charter* apply "to the legislature and government of each province." A serious problem facing the courts is determining just where government stops and government institutions acting in a private capacity start. Are government institutions—universities, schools, hospitals, and Crown corporations such as the CBC—affected?

While there are still many questions, it does seem clear that when such institutions are acting as an arm of government, the *Charter* applies. Certainly the *Charter* applies to the legislation creating these institutions and to the services provided directly by government departments, including the police and military. When government agencies act in their private capacity (for example, in employee relations), the appropriate federal or provincial human rights legislation applies; such legislation must, in turn, comply with the provisions of the *Charter*. If a section of a statute is in conflict with the provisions of the *Charter*, the offending section will be void, or an appropriate section will be added. In the *Vriend* case[31] (discussed in Case Summary 2.16), the Supreme Court of Canada showed its willingness to interpret into the Alberta statute a provision prohibiting discrimination on the basis of sexual orientation, rather than overturning the statute. Occasionally, the courts have declared legislation invalid but have stayed (held in abeyance) their decision to give the legislators an opportunity to amend the statutes themselves.[32]

Use of notwithstanding clause may be a political gamble

Sunset clause

Charter **applies only to the government—but where does government stop?**

---

[30] Alberta had used the notwithstanding clause to override equality rights when it passed the *Marriage Act* provisions restricting marriage to a man and a woman. The clause was used to deny same sex couples the ability to marry. The sunset clause caused that override to expire in 2005. See *Marriage Act*, R.S.A. 2000, c. M-5, s. 2.

[31] *Vriend v. Alberta*, [1998] 1 S.C.R. 493.

[32] See *Haig v. Canada* (1992), 9 O.R. (3d) 495 (Ont. C.A.).

While the *Charter* directly affects an individual's relationship with government, it only indirectly affects the relationships between individuals and between individuals and private institutions. Human rights legislation impacts these latter relationships, but these federal and provincial human rights codes must comply with the *Charter*. It is also important to remember that the provisions of the *Charter* apply not only to the regulations and enactments of these government bodies and institutions but also to the conduct of government officials employed by them. These officials derive their authority from provincial or federal enactments. If they are acting in a way that violates the provisions of the *Charter*, either they are not acting within their authority, or the statute authorizing their conduct is itself in violation of the *Charter*. In either case, such offending conduct can be challenged under the *Charter*.

mybuslawlab
www.pearsoned.ca/mybuslawlab

BC AB SK MB ON

Charter Provisions

A brief summary of the types of rights and freedoms Canadians now enjoy because of the *Charter of Rights and Freedoms* follows. The *Charter* sets out several rights that are available in some cases only to citizens of Canada and in other cases to everyone in the nation. The extent of these rights and freedoms, their meaning, and the limitations on those rights are still being defined by court decisions. Recourse is available through the courts if the declared rights are interfered with by laws or by the acts of government agents. The courts have been empowered under section 24 of the *Charter* to "provide such remedies as the court considers appropriate and just in the circumstances." These powers are in addition to the inherent power of the court to declare that the offending legislation or conduct is of no effect. This provision allows the courts to award damages, injunctions, and other remedies, when otherwise they would have had no power to do so. Section 24 also gives a judge the power in a criminal matter to exclude evidence that has been obtained in a way that violates the *Charter* rights of the accused, if its admission "would bring the administration of justice into disrepute."

FUNDAMENTAL FREEDOMS

Section 2 of the *Charter* declares certain underlying fundamental freedoms available to everyone in Canada. These are freedom of conscience and religion,[33] freedom of belief, opinion, and expression; and freedom of assembly and association. The *Charter* protects the right to believe in whatever we wish, to express that belief, and to carry on activities associated with it free from interference. When the expression of those freedoms or the activities associated with them interferes with the freedoms of others, the courts may restrict those freedoms by applying section 1 of the *Charter*.

Freedom of expression, which includes freedom of the press, is an extremely important provision for preserving the democratic nature of Canada, and our courts are very careful to uphold these freedoms. Still, there are many limitations on them, such as the laws of defamation and obscenity.

[33.] See *R. v. Hutterian Brethren of Wilson Colony*, [2007] A.J. No. 518 C.A., wherea regulatory amendment, which required that all drivers' licences include a photo of the licence, violated the respondents' rights of freedom of religion and equality under the *Charter* and was not justified under s. 1. The appeal to the Supreme Court of Canada was heard and reserved October 7, 2008. [2007] S.C.C.A. No. 397.

CASE SUMMARY 2.8

Sunday Shopping: Does It Prevent Corporations from Going to Church? *R. v. Big M Drug Mart Ltd.*[34]

Big M Drug Mart Ltd. was charged with violation of the *Lord's Day Act*, which required that all such businesses be closed on Sunday. This statute was enacted by the federal government under its criminal law power long before the enactment of the *Charter*. It compelled the observance of a religious duty by means of prohibitions and penalties. This matter went to the Supreme Court of Canada, which held that the *Lord's Day Act* was invalid and of no effect because it interfered with the right of freedom of conscience and religion. It did not matter that the applicant was a corporation incapable of having a conscience or beliefs. Any accused, whether corporate or individual, may defend a criminal charge by arguing that the law under which the charge is brought is constitutionally invalid.

Compare this to the decision in *London Drugs Ltd. v. Red Deer (City)*,[35] which involved a similar requirement that businesses close one day a week. In that case, however, the bylaw was upheld. It simply required the business to be closed one day a week. The bylaw specified Sunday as a default, but allowed the business to specify another day if it wished. That made it secular rather than religious with the object of simply giving the employees one day in the week free of work. This treated all businesses equally since they had a choice as to when to close.

SMALL BUSINESS PERSPECTIVE

Apparently, it is open to governments to impose restrictions upon business hours by just avoiding any reference to religion. Just as the *Charter* can be used to challenge legislation, legislators are free to achieve desired ends, so long as rights and freedoms are not violated in the process.

CASE SUMMARY 2.9

The Signs of the Times: *Vann Niagara Ltd. v. The Corporation of the Town of Oakville*[36]

The corporation of the town of Oakville, Ontario, had passed a bylaw in 1994 that prohibited the erecting of billboards in the municipality, except those that advertised an activity taking place on the premises where the sign was located. Vann Niagara Ltd. applied for permission to erect 86 billboards in the industrial part of the town, but this was turned down because of the bylaw. Vann Niagara challenged that decision, claiming that it violated the company's rights under the freedom of expression provision (section 2b) of the *Charter of Rights and Freedoms*.

[34.] [1985] 1 S.C.R. 295.

[35.] [1987] A.J. No. 815 (Q.B.); appeal dismissed [1988] A.J. No. 701 (C.A.); leave to appeal to S.C.C. refused [1988] S.C.C.A. No. 246.

[36.] [2002] O.J. No. 2323 (C.A.).

The Ontario Court of Appeal held in this case that indeed the company's rights to freedom of expression had been infringed. The *Charter* protects freedom of expression whether it relates to political, social, or commercial expression. Although Vann Niagara was a commercial entity and the expression was for a commercial purpose, its right to do so was still protected under section 2b of the *Charter*. The Court also found that this infringement was not justifiable under section 1 of the *Charter*. The stated objective of the bylaw, to preserve the small-town character of the municipality, did not justify the total ban on billboards. The Court could not agree that such signs erected in an industrial area as requested would have a negative effect on the character of the town and so the bylaw went too far. Note that the implementation of the decision was suspended for six months for the municipality to bring the bylaw into compliance with the *Charter*.

Compare this to the *R. v. Bryan* case,[37] where the Canada Elections Act prohibited the publication of election results from other parts of the country in British Columbia before the polls closed on election night. The objective here was to make sure that the B.C. electors had the opportunity to make their own decisions unaffected by what was happening in the rest of the country. This was also clearly an infringement of the right of freedom of expression as guaranteed in the Charter, but in this case the Court held that the Act was a reasonable limitation under section 1 considering the importance of ensuring voting unaffected by outside interference, and that the Act went no further than was necessary to accomplish that objective. The conviction stood.

These two cases illustrate not only the protection of freedom of expression under the *Charter* but also the limitation provisions under section 1. The issue for the Courts is deciding when the limitation provisions will come into operation and when they won't.

The Supreme Court of Canada has stated that collective bargaining is the "most significant collective activity through which freedom of association is expressed in the labour context."[38] Laws that restrict collective bargaining rights are thus subject to *Charter* scrutiny. Accordingly, in *Fraser v. Ontario (Attorney General)*[39] the Court of Appeal unanimously supported the agricultural workers whose collective bargaining rights were inadequately protected by the *Agricultural Employees Protection Act*. Whereas this legislation enabled agricultural workers to form associations that could make representations to employers about working conditions, it did not allow them to bargain collectively. Further, employers were under no obligation to listen in good faith and the law contained no dispute resolution mechanism. The Court declared the law unconstitutional, but gave the Ontario government 12 months to draft a new *Act*.

Similarly, members of the RCMP successfully challenged the regulations to the *Public Service Labour Relations Act*, which excluded the RCMP from collective bargaining. In *Mounted Police Assn. of Ontario v. Canada (Attorney General)*,[40] Justice MacDonnell found that the RCMP Staff Relations Representation Program (SRRP) was not an independent association formed by or chosen by the police officers. It merely was a mechanism for consultation. Essentially, the Program was

---

[37] [2007] S.C.J. No. 12.

[38] *Health Services and Support—Facilities Subsector Bargaining Assn. v. British Columbia*, [2007] S.C.J. No. 27, at p. 66.

[39] [2008] O.J. No. 4543; Notice of Appeal to S.C.C. filed May 2009, [2009] S.C.C.A. No. 9.

[40] [2009] O.J. No. 1352 (Sup.Ct.J.).

an entity created by management to avoid unionization. Since the regulations blocked collective bargaining rights of RCMP members, they were unconstitutional. This declaration was suspended for 18 months to give Parliament a chance to provide a statutory framework for collective bargaining.

When employer rights are interfered with by inappropriate trade union activity, limits may be imposed on the right to peaceful assembly. The rights to peaceful assembly and freedom of association have likewise been limited when riots may occur.

Note that section 2 is one of the areas of the *Charter* that can be overridden by the use of the notwithstanding clause (section 33).

DEMOCRATIC RIGHTS

Sections 3, 4, and 5 protect our rights to vote and to qualify to be elected to the House of Commons or the provincial legislative assemblies. Reasonable limitations can be put on the right to vote, restricting those who are underage and, most likely, the mentally incompetent. But the abuses of the past, where racial groups were denied the vote, are now prohibited. These rights were protected in the past by constitutional convention, but now they are enshrined in the *Charter*. Section 4 ensures that there will be an election at least every five years, except in times of war, and section 5 requires that the elected body be called into session at least once every 12 months. The government in power still has the right to decide when to call an election within that five-year period and also whether to call the session into sitting more often than the "once every 12 months" minimum. The government also has the power to determine what that session will consist of, which also gives some potential for abuse. These sections cannot be overridden by the notwithstanding clause (section 33), a distinction of which the courts have taken notice (see Case Summary 2.10).

Maximum duration is five years unless crises loom

Right to vote, to be elected, duty to have government sit annually

---

CASE SUMMARY 2.10

Ballot Boxes in Jails: *Sauvé v. Canada (Chief Electoral Officer)*[41]

All prison inmates were prohibited from voting in federal elections by the former provisions of the Canada Elections Act. That Act was held unconstitutional as an unjustified denial of the right to vote, guaranteed by section 3 of the *Charter in Sauvé v. Canada (Attorney General)*.[42] Parliament responded to this litigation by changing the Act, denying the right to vote to a smaller group—those inmates serving sentences of two years or more. The issue in this case was whether the new provisions were likewise unconstitutional. It was argued that they violated the right to vote (section 3) and equality rights as protected by section 15. The Crown conceded that the Act contravened section 3 of the Charter. The key issue was thus whether this restriction could be demonstrably justified under section 1.

---

41. [2002] 2 F.C. 119 (C.A.), rev'd [2002] S.C.J. No. 66.

42. [1993] 2 S.C.R. 438.

The Court decided that the violation was not justified. As stated by Chief Justice McLachlin: "The right to vote, which lies at the heart of Canadian democracy, can only be trammeled for good reason. Here the reasons do not suffice... Charter rights are not a matter of privilege or merit, but a function of membership in the Canadian polity that cannot be lightly set aside. This is manifestly true of the right to vote, the cornerstone of democracy, exempt from the incursion permitted on other rights through s. 33 override."

DISCUSSION QUESTIONS

The fact that the notwithstanding clause cannot be used to override democratic rights was emphasized in the above decision. What does this suggest about the inviolability of mobility rights and language rights?

MOBILITY RIGHTS

Citizens enjoy right to enter and leave Canada

Section 6 of the *Charter* ensures that Canadians can travel and live anywhere within the geographic limitations of Canada as well as enter and leave the country at will. It also ensures that all Canadians have the right to earn a livelihood in any part of Canada. But again these assurances are qualified. Programs that are of general application in a province or region can be valid even though they appear to interfere with these rights. In the field of employment, for instance, provincial licensing and educational requirements may prevent people trained and licensed in other parts of the country from carrying on their chosen profession without requalifying in that province. Section 6(4) specifically allows for programs that are designed to better the condition of those "who are socially or economically disadvantaged," even when those programs interfere with the mobility rights of other Canadians who might want to take advantage of the programs but are prohibited from doing so.

CASE SUMMARY 2.11

Resident Non-Resident Asserts the Right to Earn a Living: *Basile v. Attorney General of Nova Scotia*[43]

Under the Direct Sellers' Licensing and Regulation Act,[44] anyone involved in the activity of direct selling (door-to-door sales) in Nova Scotia had to be a resident of that province. Mr. Basile was a bookseller and a resident of Quebec. He applied for a licence to sell in Nova Scotia and was refused because he was not a permanent resident, as required by the statute. He challenged this decision as a violation of his mobility rights under the *Charter of Rights and Freedoms*. This was clearly an infringement of the mobility rights under the Charter, which gave any Canadian the right to travel to and earn a living in any part of the country. The main difficulty was to decide whether this fell into one of the exceptions set out in either section 6(3)(a) (laws of general application) or the reasonable limitation clause in section 1 of the Charter. The Court held that this did not qualify as a

---

[43.] [1984] N.S.J. No. 337 N.S.S.C. (App.Div.).

[44.] S.N.S. 1975, c. 9.

law of general application, since it was directed at one specific group—non-residents. Further, since no evidence had been presented that would support the argument that this was a reasonable limitation as required under section 1 of the Charter, Mr. Basile was successful, and the offending section was declared by the Court to be "of no force and effect."

SMALL BUSINESS PERSPECTIVE

Mr. Basile was successful in asserting his mobility rights and in having the restricting legislation struck down. But would a business or corporation be able to raise a similar argument? Consider to whom mobility rights are extended.

LEGAL RIGHTS

The rights listed under this heading are intended to protect individuals from unreasonable interference from the government or its agents and to ensure that when there is interference, it is done in a way that is both procedurally fair and consistent with basic principles of fundamental justice. It is important to note that the protection provided in this section does not extend to interference with property rights. There is no specific reference to property rights in the *Charter*.

Section 7 states that we have the right to life, liberty, and the security of person and the right not to have these rights taken away, except in accordance with the "principles of fundamental justice." In the *Baker* case, where the Supreme Court examined the procedure followed at deportation hearings, Justice L'Heureux-Dubé summarized what is required by the principles of procedural fairness. "The values underlying the duty of procedural fairness relate to the principle that the individual or individuals affected should have the opportunity to present their case fully and fairly, and have decisions affecting their rights, interests, or privileges made using a fair, impartial, and open process, appropriate to the statutory, institutional, and social context of the decision."[45] The requirements of fundamental justice include procedural fairness but go further. Certain underlying principles considered basic to our legal system would also be included. An example would be the rule of law discussed above.

> **Everyone has a right to life, liberty, and security of person**

> **Everyone is entitled to procedural fairness**

CASE SUMMARY 2.12

Duty to Assist Citizens: *Khadr v. Canada (Prime Minister)*[46]

In April 2009, almost seven years after Omar Khadr was arrested (at age 15) in Afghanistan for allegedly throwing a grenade that caused the death of a U.S. soldier, the Federal Court required the Canadian government to request that Khadr be repatriated. Khadr had been detained at Guantanamo Bay in Cuba, and the Canadian government had refused to intervene in his behalf. At issue was whether Khadr's *Charter* rights under

---

45. *Baker v. Canada (Minister of Citizenship and Immigration)*, [1999] 2 S.C.R. 817, at 841.

46. 2009 FC 405; note: Leave to appeal to the S.C.C. granted on 4 September 2009.

section 7 were violated by his continued detention, as the legal regime at Guantanamo violated Geneva Conventions.

Justice O'Reilly noted that when a person's life, liberty, and security are at stake, the *Charter* requires Canadian officials to respect principles of fundamental justice. In doing so, officials should consider factors specific to the claimant, such as his age, his need for medical attention, his presence in an unfamiliar, remote, and isolated prison with no family contact, as well as his lack of education. Justice O'Reilly ruled: "I find that the Government of Canada is required by s. 7 of the *Charter* to request Mr. Khadr's repatriation to Canada in order to comply with a principle of fundamental justice, namely, the duty to protect persons in Mr. Khadr's circumstances by taking steps to ensure that their fundamental rights, recognized in widely-accepted international instruments such as the Convention on the Rights of the Child, are respected. The respondents did not offer any basis for concluding that the violation of Mr. Khadr's rights was justified under s. 1 of the *Charter*.

"The ongoing refusal of Canada to request Mr. Khadr's repatriation to Canada offends a principle of fundamental justice and violates Mr. Khadr's rights under s. 7 of the *Charter*. To mitigate the effect of that violation, Canada must present a request to the United States for Mr. Khadr's repatriation to Canada as soon as practicable."

DISCUSSION QUESTIONS

The Court has recognized that the Crown has a *duty* to protect its citizens. Do you find the above ruling reassuring? Note that the federal government's subsequent appeal to the Federal Court of Appeal was unsuccessful. It remains to be seen whether a further appeal will be brought.

Everyone to be secure from unreasonable search, seizure, detention, or imprisonment

Sections 8 and 9 prohibit such activities as unreasonable search and seizure and arbitrary imprisonment. Subsequent sections provide for the right to be informed of the reason for an arrest, the right to retain counsel, the right to be tried within a reasonable time, the presumption of innocence, the right not to be tried twice for the same offence, and the right not to be subjected to any cruel or unusual punishment. The common theme here is to protect people from abusive, arbitrary, or unequal application of police and prosecutorial power. Not only is the individual protected in the event of such an abuse, but the provisions also serve to discourage the police and prosecutors from acting outside the law. The powers given to the courts further help to persuade the law-enforcement community to act properly by allowing the court to exclude evidence obtained in violation of these provisions, where not to do so "would bring the administration of justice into disrepute" (see section 24(2)). These basic legal rights can be overridden by the invocation of the notwithstanding clause.

CASE SUMMARY 2.13

A Right to Die? *Rodriguez v. British Columbia (Attorney General)*[47]

Does the right to life as guaranteed by section 7 of the *Charter* also protect the right to die? Sue Rodriguez, a terminally ill patient, sought the assistance of a physician to commit suicide. The *Criminal Code of Canada*, however, prohibits aiding a person to commit suicide, so Rodriguez argued that this violated her rights under sections 7, 12, and 15(1) of the *Charter*. Rodriguez also argued that the guarantee of security of person found in section 7 protected her right to decide what would happen to her body. Control over one's body would be violated if she could not choose to die. She claimed that as her health deteriorated, she would no longer be able to end her own life. The *Code*, to the extent that it bars a terminally ill person from a "physician assisted suicide," in effect creates inequality. It prevents persons physically unable to end their lives unassisted from choosing suicide, when that option is, in principle, available to other members of the public without contravening the law (since commission of suicide is not a punishable offence or crime). Finally, Rodriguez claimed that forcing her to live in a degenerated body would be cruel and unusual treatment.

In a split decision, the Supreme Court of Canada determined that the right to security of person also had to be viewed in light of the sanctity of life, the right to life also being specifically guaranteed under section 7. Section 12 was not violated by the *Code*, as a prohibition of assisted suicide is not a form of "treatment" by the state. Finally, the majority determined that if equality rights were violated by the *Code*, this violation would be justifiable under section 1. Criminalizing assisted suicide was to protect the sanctity of life and prevent abuses. Out of concern that decriminalization of euthanasia might lead to abuses, the Court was not prepared to go down the path toward it. "Active euthanasia," or doctor-assisted suicide, remains illegal in Canada.

DISCUSSION QUESTIONS

The basic question here goes beyond the *Charter*, requiring us to think about the sanctity of human life in our society. Should someone be allowed to assist another to end life? Will the plea of terminally ill patients pressure politicians to legislate guidelines for doctor-assisted suicide? What do you think?

EQUALITY RIGHTS

The equality rights set out in section 15 of the *Charter* prohibit discrimination in the application of the law on the basis of gender, religion, race, age, or national origin and ensure that all people in Canada have the same claim to the protection and benefits of the law. This means that the various provisions of the federal and provincial laws must be applied equally to all. Any time a distinction is made in any provincial or federal law or by a government official on the basis of one of these categories, it can be challenged as unconstitutional. Even where the discrimination relates to a category not listed, there is a general prohibition against such discrimination, and so victims will be protected.[48] The courts tend to interpret the Constitution and its provisions broadly. Thus, even though section 15

Every person is to be equal before and under the law

---

47. [1993] 3 S.C.R. 519.

48. See *Morrow v. Zhang*, [2008] A.J. No. 125, where two motorists who had suffered soft tissue injuries as a result of motor vehicle collisions succeeded in challenging the validity of Alberta's Minor Injury Regulations. The regulations, which restricted the right to sue a tortfeasor to $4000 (for damages for pain and suffering) was struck down as a violation of their rights under ss. 7 and 15(1). In stark contrast, the Nova Scotia Supreme Court essentially ruled the opposite in *Hartling v. Nova Scotia (Attorney General)* 2009 NSSC 38. The appeal on the *Morrow* case resulted in the Alberta Court of Appeal concluding that *Charter* rights had not been infringed. [2009] A.J. No. 621 (C.A.). Further appeals are anticipated.

makes no reference to sexual preference, the courts have had no difficulty in concluding that a denial of benefits to same-sex couples is prohibited because it discriminates against applicants on the basis of their sexual orientation. See the MyBusLawLab for details.

CASE SUMMARY 2.14

Courts Prompt Significant Legislative Changes: *M. v. H.*[49]; *Halpern v. Canada (Attorney General)*[50]

Two women cohabited in a same-sex relationship for 10 years. When their relationship broke down, M. applied for spousal support under Ontario's *Family Law Act*. She argued that the opposite-sex definition of spouse was discriminatory and unconstitutional, as it included married persons and heterosexual couples who had cohabited without marrying, but failed to include same-sex couples. The Courts found the definition violated section 15(1) of the *Charter* as it formally distinguished between M. and others on the basis of sexual orientation. The lower courts favoured "reading in" a non-discriminatory definition of spouse to the legislation, to enable same-sex couples to claim spousal support. The Supreme Court of Canada, however, dismissed the appeal, and chose to sever the offending section from the legislation. It suspended its declaration for six months to allow the government time to amend the legislation. This would mean that if the government didn't create new legislation, the Supreme Court's decision would result in no spousal benefits being available to either heterosexual or homosexual unmarried couples. In response to this case, the Ontario government amended 67 statutes to extend similar benefits to non-married couples, regardless of their sexual orientation.

In the *Halpern* case, the Ontario Court of Appeal took a different approach when asked to review the common law definition of marriage. It declared the definition of marriage as "one man and one woman" to be invalid as it offends equality rights. It reformulated the definition to the "voluntary union for life of two people to the exclusion of all others" and declared this definition to have immediate effect. Consequently, numerous same-sex couples rushed to secure marriage licences. The federal government responded by referring a proposed bill on same-sex marriages to the Supreme Court of Canada for review.[51] After the Supreme Court affirmed the validity of the proposed legislation and the authority of the federal parliament to define marriage, Parliament proceeded to redefine marriage to include same-sex couples.[52]

DISCUSSION QUESTIONS

Parliament remains supreme in Canada, so long as it does not violate the Constitution. Knowing what you do about the *Charter*, what steps could Parliament have taken if it wished to preserve the traditional definition of marriage?

---

49. [1999] 2 S.C.R. 3.

50. [2003] O.J. No. 2268 (C.A.).

51. *Reference re: Same-Sex Marriage*, [2004] 3 S.C.R. 698.

52. *Civil Marriage Act*, S.C. 2005, c. 33.

It is important to note that section 15(2) provides for affirmative-action programs. When a provision is intentionally introduced that has the effect of discriminating against one group of people, it may still be allowed if its purpose is to correct an imbalance that has occurred through discrimination in the past. Thus, the government may intentionally set out to hire women or specific ethnic minorities to get a better balance in the civil service. This is permissible even though it will have the effect of preventing people of other groups, such as Caucasian men, from having an equal opportunity to obtain those same jobs. Universities often have similar programs to encourage minorities to enter faculties or professions to correct historical imbalances.

In addition to the provisions set out in section 15, there are other provisions in the *Charter* setting out equality rights. Section 28 guarantees that the provisions of the *Charter* apply equally to males and females. Equality rights (protected by section 15) can be overridden by the operation of the notwithstanding clause, but section 28 cannot be overridden.

Section 35 states that the *Charter* in no way affects the aboriginal and treaty rights of the native people of Canada. Although this last provision may have the effect of preserving inequality rather than eliminating it, the object of this section was to ensure that during the process of treaty negotiations and land claim disputes between the provincial governments and the native groups of Canada nothing in the *Charter* would interfere with the special-status rights associated with that group. Section 33 cannot be used to override the protection given to the position of the aboriginal people of Canada.

Although these *Charter* provisions apply only in our dealings with government, it is important for businesspeople to remember that these equality provisions are the essence of most provincial and federal human rights legislation. Since those statutes must comply with the *Charter* provisions, the *Charter* indirectly controls business practices (see Case Summary 2.16, which discusses *Vriend v. Alberta*). In addition, there are many examples of provincial and federal legislation that require all those working on government-funded projects to comply with special federal and provincial programs aimed at correcting past injustices. These special requirements may range from fair-wage policies (where non-union businesses must pay wages comparable with union-negotiated wages) to programs requiring the hiring or promotion of disadvantaged minorities or the correction of gender imbalances in the workforce.[53]

LANGUAGE RIGHTS

The part of the *Charter* headed "Official Languages of Canada" outlined in sections 16 to 22 ensures that French and English have equal status and that the rights of minorities to use those languages are protected.[54] Of the Canadian provinces, only New Brunswick is officially bilingual, and so section 16 of the *Charter* declares that English and French are the official languages of Canada (federally) and of New Brunswick. All federal government activities, including

---

[54] For an example, see *R. v. Beaulac*, [1999] 1 S.C.R. 768, where the accused succeeded in appealing his conviction on murder charges and a new trial was ordered because the trial judge refused his request for a trial before a bilingual judge and jury. The trial arose in the province of British Columbia, and although the accused could express himself in English, his own official language was French.

[53] See, for example, the federal *Employment Equity Act*, S.C. 1995, c. 44.

French and English have
equal status—Canada and
New Brunswick

court proceedings, publications, and other services where numbers warrant, must be available in both official languages. Similar rules are established for New Brunswick. Note that some language rights are set out in the *Constitution Act, 1867*. For example, section 3 requires that Quebec provide court services in English as well as French. *The Constitution Act (1867)* also requires that Manitoba provide many government services in both English and French.

CASE SUMMARY 2.15

Traffic Ticket Challenge May Require Translation of Alberta's Laws: *R. v. Caron*[55]

It is amazing what fighting a traffic ticket might lead to. Gilles Caron, a francophone truck driver, challenged the $54 traffic ticket, arguing that his constitutional right to a hearing in French was violated. Alberta's 1988 *Languages Act* revoked French language rights, but Caron argued this law was unconstitutional.

Expert testimony was introduced, revealing that a key piece of historical evidence was missing when the *Languages Act* was passed. Records established that Rupert's Land (from which Alberta was carved) agreed to join Canada only if French language rights were protected. Judge Wenden ruled the *Languages Act* unconstitutional and Caron was found not guilty of the traffic violation.

The ruling could mean that Alberta's laws must be translated to French.

DISCUSSION QUESTIONS

Who should bear the cost of *Charter* challenges? Note that Caron obtained an order directing the Crown to provide approximately $94 000 to him for legal costs incurred during the trial. While the traffic ticket charges were minor, the trial occupied more than 80 days because the respondent raised the issue of French language rights. The government appealed the funding order, but lost.[56] Leave to appeal to the Supreme Court of Canada on this issue was granted in 2009.[57]

Minority-language educational rights, outlined in section 23, are guaranteed for the citizens of Canada, ensuring that those whose first language is English or French and who received their primary education in English or French, or have had one of their children educated in English or French, have the right to have their other children educated in that language. People who are immigrants to Canada have no such rights, no matter what their native language may be. Note that the right to be educated in English or French applies only where community numbers warrant the expense of setting up such a program. Language rights and minority-language educational rights cannot be overridden by section 33 of the *Charter*.

[55.] 2008 A.B.P.C. 232.

[56.] [2008] A.J. No. 268 (C.A.); see also [2009] A.J. No. 70 (C.A.).

[57.] [2009] S.C.C.A. No. 128.

SECTION 52

The Constitution Act, 1982 makes other important changes to Canada's Constitution. In addition to declaring that the Constitution is the "supreme law of Canada," section 52 also sets out all the statutes that have constitutional status in an attached schedule. Important amendments are also made to the *Constitution Act, 1867,* creating section 92A, which expands the power of the provinces to make law with respect to non-renewable natural resources, including the generation of electric power and forestry resources.

The Importance of the Changes

The significance of the 1982 additions to the Constitution cannot be overemphasized. The *Charter of Rights and Freedoms* will continue to affect the development of Canadian law over the next century. Traditionally, Canadian courts had adopted the position that their function was to apply the law as it existed. If the law needed to be changed, the judiciary left the job to Parliament and the legislative assemblies. It is clear that the courts have been forced to play a more active role and create new law through their interpretation and application of the provisions of the *Charter.* The broad, generalized nature of the *Charter* provisions contributes to this more expansive role of the courts. Statutes have traditionally been interpreted in a very narrow way, and because of this they are always very carefully and precisely worded. But the *Charter* provisions are generalizations, and the courts must therefore interpret these broad statements, filling in the gaps and thus making new law.

The *Constitution Act, 1982* also eliminated the requirement that any major change involving Canada's Constitution had to be made by an act of the Parliament of Great Britain. Because the original *BNA Act* was an act of the British Parliament, any changes to it had to be made by that body. When the provinces and the federal government agreed on a formula for amending the Constitution, the British Parliament passed the *Canada Act,*[58] making Canada completely independent of Britain. It should be emphasized that although Canada's ties to the British Parliament have been severed, our relationship with the monarch remains. The Queen remains the Queen of Canada, just as she is the Queen of the United Kingdom, Australia, New Zealand, and other independent nations.

Quebec, however, did not assent to this document. Subsequently, another important agreement that attempted to change this amending formula was drawn up; this agreement was known as the Meech Lake Accord. However, the Accord did not receive the required unanimous approval by the provinces within the specified time limit. Its failure and the failure of the subsequent Charlottetown Accord (which went to a national referendum) have created a constitutional crisis in Canada, with Quebec seeking independence. The pro-separatist government in Quebec took the question of sovereignty to a provincial referendum in 1996, which failed by a margin of only 1 percent. Thereafter, the federal government submitted a Reference to the Supreme Court of Canada[59] to determine whether Quebec could unilaterally secede from Canada. Discussions regarding granting

mybuslawlab
www.pearsoned.ca/mybuslawlab

BC AB SK MB ON

Quebec did not agree with patriating the Constitution

---

59. *Reference Re Secession of Quebec,* [1998] 2 S.C.R. 217.

58. *Canada Act 1982* (U.K.) 1982, c. 11.

Quebec distinct status in Canada have occasioned much debate and dissension within the federation. The question of whether Quebec will remain in Canada continues to be an important and troubling issue for Canada.

Human Rights Legislation

www.pearsoned.ca/mybuslawlab

Human rights legislation prohibits discrimination on certain grounds

Whereas the *Canadian Bill of Rights* and the *Charter* address protecting individuals' rights from abuses by government, various federal and provincial statutes have been enacted with the aim of protecting an individual's rights from abuse by other members of the public. Initially, human rights legislation was designed to stop discrimination against identifiable minority groups in specific areas, such as hotels and restaurants. (See *Racial Discrimination Act, 1944* of Ontario.[60]) Today's statutes are broader in scope, protecting individuals against human rights violations by the public at large, in a variety of settings. The *CanadianHuman Rights Act*[61] is one example. Refer to the MyBusLawLab for details and provincial variations.

The *Canadian Human Rights Act (CHRA)* applies to abuses in sectors regulated by federal legislation, such as the broadcast and telecommunication industries; similar provincial statutes apply only in areas controlled by provincial legislation.[62] For example, if one is employed by a bank, any human rights complaints concerning activities at work would be brought before the Canadian Human Rights Commission (CHRC), as banks are federally regulated; whereas if one was employed by a provincially regulated retailer, those human rights complaints would be addressed by the provincial human rights commission. These statutes aim at ensuring that individuals will have access to employment (including membership in professional organizations and unions) without facing barriers created through discrimination. Access to facilities and services customarily available to the public, as well as to accommodation (tenancies), is likewise addressed.

These acts prohibit discrimination relating to gender, religion, ethnic origin, race, age, disabilities, and various other prohibited grounds. The *CHRA* now specifically protects against discrimination on the grounds of sexual orientation and pardoned criminal conviction; not all provincial legislation goes so far. Where protection against discrimination on the basis of sexual orientation has been left out of human rights legislation, the courts have shown a willingness to imply the existence of this protection. The principle applied is that under the *Charter of Rights and Freedoms*, every individual is entitled to the "equal protection and equal benefit of the law"; therefore, such rights ought to have been included. In the process, the courts are effectively rewriting statutes.

[60.] S.O. 1944, c. 51.

[61.] R.S.C. 1985, c. H-6.

[62.] See: *Human Rights Code*, R.S.O. 1990, c. H-19; *Charter of Human Rights and Freedoms*, R.S.Q. c. C-12; *Alberta Human Rights Act, R.S.A. 2000, c. 25-5*; *Human Rights Code*, R.S.B.C. 1996, c. 210; *Saskatchewan Human Rights Code*, S.S. 1979, c. S-24.1; *The Human Rights Code*, S.M. 1987–88, c. 45, C.C.S.M. c. H175; *Human Rights Act*, R.S.N.B. 1973, c. H-11; *Human Rights Code*, R.S.N.L. 1990, c. H-14; *Human Rights Act*, R.S.N.S. 1989, c. 214; *Human Rights Act*, R.S.P.E.I. 1988, c. H-12; *Consolidation of Fair Practices Act*, R.S.N.W.T. 1988, c. F-2 (as duplicated for Nunavut by s. 29 of the *Nunavut Act*, S.C. 1993, c. 28); *Human* Rights Act, R.S.Y. 1986, c.11.

CASE SUMMARY 2.16

Equality Issues Resolved by the Courts: *Vriend v. Alberta*[63]

In 1987, Delwin Vriend was employed by a private religious school in Alberta. His job performance was not in question, but he was dismissed after he "disclosed his homosexuality." He complained under the Alberta *Individual's Rights Protection Act (IRPA)* to the Alberta Human Rights Commission, claiming that he had been discriminated against because of his sexual orientation. He was told that he could not make such a complaint because the *Act* did not provide protection against discrimination due to sexual orientation.

This case went to the Supreme Court of Canada, which agreed with the trial court that the protections given by the *Act* were under-inclusive, protecting some but not all from discrimination. The Supreme Court rewrote the provincial statute so that it complied with section 15 of the *Charter of Rights and Freedoms*. It read sexual orientation into the impugned provisions of the *IRPA*, reasoning that this was the most appropriate way of remedying the under-inclusiveness. In light of the *Act's* preamble and stated purpose, if the legislature had the choice of having no human rights statute or having one that extended protection to those historically facing discrimination—such as homosexuals—the latter option would be chosen.

This case is interesting because it raises the issue of how far the courts can go in shaping the law. Here the Supreme Court has effectively rewritten provincial legislation it found to have violated *Charter* rights.

DISCUSSION QUESTIONS

What do you think? Is "judicial legislating" proper under Canada's Constitution? Or should the courts merely declare whether legislation is constitutional or not, and then allow the legislators time to amend any contravening legislation?

It is interesting to reflect upon the evolution of human rights protection. Three decades ago, discrimination based on sexual orientation was not specifically prohibited. Passage of the *Charter* enabled individuals to challenge laws that denied equal treatment. Cases like the *Vriend* decision brought the issue of discrimination based on sexual orientation to the attention of the public. As public sensitivity increased, the protection given to same-sex relationships expanded. The denial of marriage licences was held to be unconstitutional; eventually, the federal government was pressured to redefine marriage and sought the Supreme Court's input in the *Reference re: Same-Sex Marriage* case.[64] Now the protections extended to same-sex marriages equal those extended to traditional marriages. See the MyBusLawLab for details.

Both the federal and the provincial governments have set up special human rights tribunals authorized to hear complaints of human rights violations, to investigate, and, where appropriate, to impose significant sanctions and remedies.

Human rights commissions hear complaints

---

63. [1998] 1 S.C.R. 493 (S.C.C.).

64. [2004] 3 S.C.R. 698.

There are time limits to consider: a complaint before the CHRC, for example, must be filed within 12 months of the alleged incident. The Commission then proceeds to attempt settlement of the complaint through conciliation and investigation. If all else fails, a panel hearing is convened.

An issue that has arisen since the adoption of the *Charter of Rights and Freedoms* is whether these human rights acts go far enough. The protections extend only to certain areas as identified by the specific federal or provincial legislation—typically, employment, tenancies, public facilities and services, and public signs and notices. Private clubs can still discriminate as to who they will admit as members because discrimination by private facilities is not prohibited by the legislation. This explains why some golf clubs, for example, do not have female members.

Another area addressed by human rights legislation is harassment. The offending conduct in question usually involves the misuse of a position of power or authority to obtain a sexual or some other advantage. Protection against sexual harassment exists because sexual harassment is regarded as a form of discrimination on the basis of gender. Protection against other forms of harassment, although not specifically addressed by legislation, is now being addressed by employers in their policy manuals and in collective agreements. Commission decisions recognize that when there is discrimination in the workplace or where public services are provided, there is a duty not to discriminate and also a duty to take reasonable steps to accommodate any person who may be discriminated against. This may require anything from creating wider spaces between workstations to accommodate a wheelchair to providing a digital reader for a blind person. Failure to accommodate religious beliefs may result in the employer's being required to take reasonable steps to rearrange work schedules so that employees are not obligated to work on their day of worship. The field of employment is impacted significantly by human rights legislation. This will be treated as a specific topic in Chapter 10.

CASE SUMMARY 2.17

Duty to Accommodate Those Facing Discrimination: *Ontario Human Rights Commission et al. v. Simpsons-Sears Ltd.*[65]

The clerks employed at a particular branch of Simpsons-Sears Ltd. were required to work some Friday nights and two out of every three Saturdays. Mrs. O'Malley, who was a clerk at Sears for three years before joining the Seventh-day Adventist Church, informed her manager that she could no longer work on their Sabbath day (Friday night to Saturday night). Her employment was terminated, and she was hired back part-time to accommodate these restrictions. She wanted to continue working full-time and laid a complaint with the Ontario Human Rights Commission on the basis of discrimination against her because of her creed. The matter went all the way to the Supreme Court of Canada, which held that discrimination had, in fact, taken place. It was not necessary to show that there was an intention to discriminate, only that there was discrimination in fact. Even

---

[65] *[1985] S.C.J. No. 74.*

where the rule or practice was initiated for sound economic and business reasons, it could still amount to discrimination. The employer was required to take reasonable steps to try to accommodate the religious practices of this employee, short of creating undue hardship on the business. The business had failed to show any evidence of accommodation or that to accommodate would have created undue hardship, and so the complaint was upheld. Simpsons-Sears was required to pay Mrs. O'Malley the difference in wages between what she had made as a part-time employee and what she would have made as a full-time employee.

SMALL BUSINESS PERSPECTIVE

Human rights legislation forces employers to be sensitive to the diverse needs of employees and accommodate their differences. Employers may complain about this added inconvenience or added obligation, but if employees are treated respectfully, they may respond in kind. Greater loyalty from the workforce may well offset any additional costs borne by the employer. This case highlights the necessity of being familiar with human rights legislation as an employer or provider of services or accommodation. Failure to take reasonable steps to accommodate the different needs of different people may lead to a finding of unlawful discrimination. The consequences may be costly.

Part of the mandate of human rights commissions is to promote knowledge of human rights and to encourage people to follow principles of equality. The prohibition of discriminatory signs and notices assists in that end. The federal *CHRA* goes even further and deems it a discriminatory practice to communicate hate messages "telephonically or by means of a telecommunication undertaking within the legislative authority of Parliament."[66] In 2002, Ernst Zundel's internet site was found to have contravened section 13 of the *Act*. This was Canada's first-ever human rights complaint involving an internet hate site. The Canadian Human Rights Tribunal concluded that the site created conditions that allow hatred to flourish.

Amendments to the *Canadian Human Rights Act (CHRA)* impacting the First Nations governments came into force in June 2008. Since 1977, the *CHRA* did not apply to the federal government and First Nations governments for decisions authorized by the *Indian Act*. Complaints arose largely from First Nations women who married non-status Indians and were thus exposed to discriminatory treatment; these women were not able to seek remedies under the *CHRA*.

This exemption from the *CHRA* was removed and gender equality stipulations were expressly protected.[67]

---

66. Canadian Human Rights Act, R.S. 1985, c. H-6, s. 13.

67. Section 67 of the Canadian Human Rights Act restricted the ability of First Nations people living on reserve to file a complaint against band councils or the federal government. It was repealed by Bill C-21 effective June 18, 2008.

CASE SUMMARY 2.18

Family Needs Require Support: *Health Sciences Association of British Columbia v. Campbell River and North Island Transition Society*[68]

Mrs. Howard worked as a child and youth support worker, working part-time regular hours between 8:30 a.m. and 3:00 p.m., Monday through Thursday. She also had a 13-year-old son who had severe behavioral problems requiring psychiatric supervision and treatment. After school Mrs. Howard looked after her son, but when her employer unilaterally changed her employment hours from 11:30 a.m. to 6:00 p.m., Monday through Thursday, she could no longer do this. Her union filed a grievance on her behalf, claiming that her rights under the *B.C. Human Rights Code* not to be discriminated against on the basis of family status had been violated. The Court had to decide whether the action of the employer in changing her work hours amounted to discrimination on the basis of family status in contravention of the *Code*. The Court decided that since there was a significant parental obligation to take care of her son in these circumstances, the action of the employer in changing her work hours was a significant interference with that obligation, and therefore constituted discrimination on the basis of family status and a violation of the *Code*.

SMALL BUSINESS PERSPECTIVE

Human rights legislation may actually go further in protecting basic rights than does the *Charter*. Even when the employer is the government, it may be more appropriate to turn to human rights mechanisms, rather than to the *Charter*, to redress discrimination in the workplace.

Although the *Charter of Rights and Freedoms* has justifiably been given a great deal of attention in recent times, for businesspeople, the human rights codes in force in the various provinces are of greater concern. These codes not only govern how employees are to be treated but also apply to the treatment of customers and those with whom business is conducted. In fact, a significant number of cases before human rights commissions deal with complaints arising from business interactions, usually because of questionable customer-relations practices. A nightclub, for example, that typically demands identification only from customers of certain racial backgrounds may be investigated on allegations of discriminating when granting access to a public facility.

! REDUCING RISK 2.1

Businesspeople are well advised to become familiar with the human rights legislation in place where they do business and to make sure that their activities comply with these laws. In addition to requiring offenders to pay compensation and damages to those aggrieved, human rights commissions often require public apologies when discriminatory practices have been condoned. The resulting damage to the goodwill and reputation of the business simply is too great to ignore.

---

[68] 2004 BCCA 260.

SUMMARY

A workable definition

- Law is the body of rules made by government that can be enforced by courts or government agencies

Categories of law

- Substantive law governs behaviour
- Procedural law regulates enforcement processes
- Public law comprises constitutional, criminal, and administrative laws
- Private law involves one person's suing another

Origins of law

- Codes in civil law jurisdictions
- Judge-made laws and precedents in common law jurisdictions

Sources of Canadian law

- Common law
- Equity from chancery courts
- Statutes—legislation of federal and provincial governments

Constitution of Canada

- *Constitution Act, 1867 (BNA Act)*
- *Constitution Act, 1982* including the *Charter of Rights and Freedoms*
- Various other statutes
- Various statutes that have Constitutional status
- Conventions and traditions
- Case law on constitutional issues

Constitution Act, 1867

- Created the Dominion of Canada and established its structures
- Divides power between federal and provincial governments
- Legislative powers are set out in sections 91 and 92
- Courts interpret and rule on constitutional issues

Charter of Rights and Freedoms

- All legislation must be compliant with the *Charter*
- Applies to relationships with government
- Limited by sections 1, 32, and 33

Human rights legislation

- Federal—provides protection against discrimination by businesses that fall under federal jurisdiction
- Provincial—protects individuals in private relationships; addresses discriminatory practices by parties under provincial regulation

QUESTIONS

1. Why is it difficult to come up with a satisfactory definition of law?

2. Where do we look to predict the outcome of a legal dispute:
   a. in a common law system?
   b. in a civil law system?

3. Explain how the use of previous decisions differs in civil law and common law jurisdictions.

4. Describe what is meant by the following statement: "Common law judges did not make the law, they found it."

5. Describe the advantages and the disadvantages of the system of *stare decisis*.

6. Describe the problems with the common law system that led to the development of the law of equity.

7. Detail what was accomplished by the *Judicature Acts of 1873–1875*.

8. Explain what is meant by the phrase "the supremacy of Parliament."

9. What effect will a properly passed statute have on inconsistent judge-made law (case law)?

10. Outline how a parliamentary bill becomes law.

11. Using the principles of *stare decisis*, explain how judges determine whether they are bound by another judge's decision in a similar case.

12. What is included in Canada's Constitution?

13. What is the effect of sections 91 and 92 of the *Constitution Act, 1867*, formerly the *British North America Act*?

14. How did the *Constitution Act, 1867* limit the power of the federal and provincial governments? How is it possible, given the division of powers, to have identical provisions in both federal and provincial legislations and have both be valid?

15. Explain what is meant by the doctrine of paramountcy. When does the doctrine apply?

16. Describe the limitations on the federal and provincial governments' powers to delegate their authority to make laws.

17. Identify the limitations of human rights legislation.

18. Explain how the *Constitution Act, 1982*, including the *Charter of Rights and Freedoms*, affects the doctrine of supremacy of Parliament.

19. Explain any limitations that apply to the rights and freedoms listed in the *Charter*.

20. Give examples of democratic rights, mobility rights, legal rights, and equality rights as protected under the *Charter*. Give examples of three other types of rights protected under the *Charter*.

21. How do human rights codes differ in their application from the *Charter of Rights and Freedoms*?

CASES AND DISCUSSION QUESTIONS

1. *R. v. Eurosport Auto Co.* [2003] B.C.J. No. 1108 (B.C.C.A.).

This case is an appeal from a conviction of the accused under section 42.1(2)(b) of the *Insurance (Motor Vehicle) Act* (British Columbia) of "making a statement or representation to the corporation (ICBC [the Insurance Corporation of British Columbia]) that the person knew or ought to have known was false or misleading in order to obtain payment for goods or services." This offence was subject to serious penalties that could include a significant fine and jail term. The defendants operated an auto repair business and had been found to have installed cheaper parts than billed for and to have billed ICBC for parts that had not been installed on vehicles. This charge amounted to fraud.

Considering the division of powers, explain the constitutional arguments that might be raised by the defendants and any answers to those arguments.

2. *B. (R.) v. Children's Aid Society of Metropolitan Toronto*, [1995] 1 S.C.R. 315 (or *H.(T.) v. Children's Aid Society of Metropolitan Toronto*).

In this case, the parents were Jehovah's Witnesses, and when their child was born prematurely with several physical ailments, they resisted the recommendations of the doctors to use blood transfusions. An application was made to a Provincial Court Judge to make the child a ward of the Court. This was done, and the transfusion was administered. The parents objected to this as an interference with their *Charter* rights.

Discuss what sections of the *Charter* they might use in these circumstances as well as the arguments that can be put forward to support the position of the authorities and the likely outcome. Do you think that the parents in these circumstances should have the right to make life-and-death decisions for their children based on their religious beliefs?

3. *R. v. Badesha*, [2008] O.J. No. 854 (C.J.)

Badesha was charged with failing to wear a helmet in violation of s. 104(1) of Ontario's *Highway Traffic Act*. He challenged the legislation arguing that it violated his rights under section 15(1) of the *Charter* [equality] and section 2(a) [freedom of religion]. Badesha is a Sikh and the law interferes with his religion as it prevents him from wearing a turban, a practice required by his faith.

Badesha's conviction was upheld. Explain what arguments the government may have made to defend its legislation.

This decision conflicts with that in *Dhillon v. Ministry of Transportation and Highways* (1999), 35 C.H.R.R.D./293, a decision of the B.C. Human Rights Tribunal. Explain how this is possible despite the doctrine of *stare decisis*.

4. *Dartmouth/Halifax (County) Regional Housing Authority v. Sparks* [1993] N.S.J. No. 97 (C.A.).

According to the *Residential Tenancies Act* in place in Nova Scotia, residents who have been renting premises for more than five years have security of tenure, which means that they can be given notice to leave only if they are in violation of their obligations under the lease. The *Act*, however, specifically excludes people who are living in public housing, and Mrs. Sparks, a single mother with two children, had been living in the public housing for 10 years when she was given one month's notice to leave.

What arguments might she raise to defeat this notice to vacate? How would it affect your answer to know that Mrs. Sparks was a black woman, and she was one of a group of black women on social assistance particularly hard hit by the legislation in question?

5. *Ontario (Human Rights Commission) v. Ontario*, [1994] O.J. No. 1732 (C.A.).

The Ministry of Health in Ontario started a program to assist disabled children by providing them with various types of devices. That program was gradually expanded to provide services to other disabled people. Part of this service was to assist in providing vision aids for the blind. In 1986, Mr. Roberts, who was legally blind, applied for financial assistance to purchase such a vision aid and was turned down. The reason given was that he was 71 years of age and therefore too old. Mr. Roberts purchased the device himself and filed a complaint under the *Human Rights Code of Ontario*.

Explain the likely outcome of that complaint. Consider the cost to the medical health system if everyone is to be treated equally, leaving the government no power to regulate and limit expenditures.

6. *R. v. Indoe* [2004] O.J. No. 4422 (Ont. S.C.J.).

Douglas Indoe was a passenger in a truck heading north with his friend on a hunting trip. They were stopped pursuant to a regular roadside check done under the provincial R.I.D.E. program searching for liquor, as authorized under the *Liquor Licence Act* of Ontario. The police found liquor in the car and charged the driver. They then conducted a further search and found a backpack owned by Mr. Indoe. Note that at the time of the search he had not been charged nor accused of any criminal activity. Without asking permission they searched the backpack and found a significant amount of hashish and cocaine. He was charged with possession and possession for the purpose of trafficking.

Explain any arguments that might be available to Mr. Indoe in his defence and the likely outcome of the case. Has our concern with protecting individual rights put so much of a burden on police that they are no longer able to do their jobs properly? What do you think?

7. *R. v. Spratt*, [2008] B.C.J. No. 1669 (B.C.C.A.)

Spratt and Watson were charged under ss. 2(1)(a) and 2(1)(b) of the provincial *Access to Abortion Services Act* as a result of their activities outside of a Vancouver Health Clinic. Signs stating "You shall not murder" and "Unborn Persons Have the Right to Live" were waived within a "bubble" or access zone outside the abortion clinic. The law aims to protect women from interference in this zone. The accused argued that the law violates their freedom of expression. Note: an application for leave to appeal to the Supreme Court of Canada was submitted on 19 May 2009, [2009] S.C.C.A. No. 97.

Whose rights should be paramount in cases such as this?

Be sure to visit the MyBusLawLab that accompanies this book at **www.pearsoned.ca/mybuslawlab.** You will find practice tests, a personalized study plan, province-specific material, and much more!

Chapter 3

The Resolution of Disputes— The Courts and Alternatives to Litigation

In addition to hearing criminal matters, the courts have been charged with the duty of adjudicating civil or private disputes, including assessing liability for injuries and awarding compensation when someone has been harmed by the actions of another. But having the court settle those claims can be an expensive and time-consuming process. While it is always a good idea for the parties to try to resolve their own disputes, when this is not possible they can turn to the courts to adjudicate a resolution. In this chapter, we examine the structure of the courts in Canada and then look at the litigation process, from the initial claim to the enforcement of a judgment. Also discussed in this chapter is the important area referred to as administrative law, which concerns itself with decisions made by an expanding government bureaucracy that affect businesses and individuals. These decision-making bodies often look like courts, though they are not, and their decision-making powers are sometimes abused. Restrictions on the powers of such decision makers and how those decisions must be made as well as what we can do when those restrictions are violated will be discussed in the second part of this chapter. The final part of this chapter outlines a variety of alternatives to the litigation process, along with a review of the reasons why businesspeople might choose negotiation, mediation, or arbitration over courts in resolving their disputes.

THE COURTS

Trials open to public

The process described below outlines the various procedures used at the trial level of the superior courts; students should note that the actual procedure may vary with the jurisdiction. Procedural laws ensure that the hearing will be fair, that all litigants have equal access to the courts, and that parties have notice of an action against them and an opportunity to reply.

As a general rule, Canadian courts are open to the public. The principle is that justice not only must be done but also must be seen to be done; no matter how prominent the citizen and no matter how scandalous the action, the procedures are open and available to the public and the press. There are, however, important exceptions to this rule. When the information coming out at a trial may be prejudicial to the security of the nation,[1] the courts may hold in-camera hearings, which are closed to the public. When children are involved, or in cases involving sexual assaults, the more common practice is to hold an open hearing but prohibit the publication of the names of the parties.[2]

Both criminal and civil functions

The courts in Canada preside over criminal prosecutions or adjudicate in civil disputes. While civil matters are the major concern of this text and criminal law is discussed only incidentally, it should be noted that there are some important differences between civil and criminal actions. In civil actions, two private persons use the court as a referee to adjudicate a dispute, and the judge (or, in some cases, the judge with a jury) chooses between the two positions presented. The decision will be made in favour of the side advocating the more probable position. The judge, in such circumstances, is said to be deciding the matter on the balance of probabilities, which requires the person making the claim to show the court sufficient proof so that there is greater than 50 percent likelihood that the events took place as claimed.

Civil test—balance of probabilities

Criminal prosecutions are quite different. When a crime has been committed, the offence is against the state and the victims of the crime are witnesses at the trial. The government pursues the matter and prosecutes the accused through a Crown prosecutor. Since the action is taken by the government (the Crown) against the accused, such cases are cited as, for example, "*R. v. Jones.*" (The R. stands for either Rex or Regina, depending on whether a king or queen is enthroned at the time of the prosecution.) While a civil dispute is decided on the balance of probabilities, in a criminal prosecution the judge (or judge and jury) must be convinced beyond a reasonable doubt of the guilt of the accused. This is a much more stringent test in that even when it is likely or probable that the accused committed the crime, the accused must be found "not guilty" if there is any reasonable doubt about guilt.

Criminal test—beyond reasonable doubt

As illustrated by Case Summary 3.1, a person might be faced with both a civil action and a criminal trial over the same conduct, and as occurred here, even though a person was acquitted at the criminal trial he may still be found liable in the civil action. While there may not be enough proof to establish beyond a reasonable doubt that the accused committed the crime, there may be enough evidence to show that he probably committed the wrong. Another recent example involves a woman in British Columbia who won a $50 000 civil judgment against the man she accused of raping her even after a criminal prosecution had acquitted him of the sexual assault.[3]

May face both criminal and civil trial for same matter

[1.] See *Ruby v. Canada (Solicitor General)* for a recent discussion of the issue of open courts.

[2.] *John Doe v. Smith* provides a concise summary of the law on this issue.

[3.] *J.L.L. v. Ambrose.* The criminal prosecution is unreported in case reports, but was reported in *The Vancouver Sun* (25 February 2000).

CASE SUMMARY 3.1

What Is the Appropriate Burden of Proof? *Rizzo v. Hanover Insurance Co.*[4]

Rizzo owned a restaurant that was seriously damaged by fire. When he made a claim under his insurance policy, the insurer refused to pay on the basis of its belief that Rizzo had started the fire himself. It was clear that the fire was intentionally set and that it was done with careful preparation. Because the restaurant business had not been doing well and Rizzo was in financial difficulties, the finger of blame was pointed at him. Other evidence damaged his credibility. The Ontario High Court in this case had to decide what burden of proof the insurer should meet. Because the conduct that Rizzo was being accused of was a crime, he argued that it should be proved "beyond a reasonable doubt." The Court held that because this was a civil action, it was necessary only that the insurer establish that Rizzo was responsible for setting the fire "on the balance of probabilities" and that it had satisfied that burden. "I have found on balance that it is more likely than not that the plaintiff did take part in the setting of the fire." As a result, Rizzo's action against the insurer was dismissed. Note that the fact that Rizzo had been acquitted of arson in a criminal proceeding was inadmissible in a civil proceeding as proof that he had not committed the arson.

DISCUSSION QUESTIONS

Should there be two different standards of proof? Wouldn't it be better to require the higher standard of proof even in civil matters? What effect would that have on the amount of civil litigation taking place in our courts?

Criminal law is restricted to the matters found in the *Criminal Code,* as well as certain drug control legislation and a few other areas under federal control that have been characterized as criminal matters by the courts. There is a much broader area of law that subjects people to fines and imprisonment but does not qualify as criminal law. This involves regulatory offences, sometimes referred to as quasi-criminal matters, and includes such areas as environmental, fishing, and employment offences as well as offences created under provincial jurisdiction, including motor vehicle, securities, and hunting offences. See the MyBusLawLab for examples.

Regulatory offences

The provincial and federal governments have authority to create enforcement provisions including fines and imprisonment for laws that have been enacted under the powers they have been given under the *Constitution Act, 1867.* These regulatory offences are manifestations of the exercise of that power. Only the federal government has the power to make criminal law, and although people may be punished with fines, and sometimes even imprisonment, for violations of these regulatory offences, the violations do not qualify as criminal acts. People charged under these provisions usually go through a process similar to prosecution of a summary conviction offence under the *Criminal Code.*[5]

[4.] (1993), 14 O.R. (3d) 98 (C.A.), leave to appeal to S.C.C. refused, [1993] S.C.C.A. No. 488.

[5.] To view a flowchart depicting the criminal justice process followed when adults are prosecuted for commission of a crime, go to "Overview of the Justice System: The Criminal Justice Process—Adults," www.justice.gov.ab.ca/criminal_pros/process_adults.aspx.

www.pearsoned.ca/mybuslawlab

| BC | AB | SK | MB | ON |

Lower and superior courts

Trial Courts of the Provinces

The nature and structure of the courts vary from province to province—see the MyBusLawLab to view the court structures in each province—but there are essentially four levels, including the Supreme Court of Canada. (Figure 3.1 provides an outline of Canada's court system.) At the lowest level are the Provincial Courts (their titles may be different in some provinces or territories). These courts have a criminal jurisdiction over the less serious criminal matters that are assigned to magistrates and judges under the *Criminal Code*. As a separate body, but usually as a division of the provincial courts, most jurisdictions also have small claims courts and family courts. Small claims courts deal with civil matters that involve relatively small amounts of money, no more than $5000 to $25 000 depending on the province.[6] Family courts handle family matters, such as custody issues that arise once the parents have separated. Enforcement of maintenance and alimony can also be dealt with by these courts, but they have no jurisdiction to issue divorces, which must be obtained in the superior trial court.[7] Some provinces maintain separate youth justice courts while others designate the family court to fulfill this function. These deal with offences under the *Youth Criminal Justice Act*.[8] In Canada, youth offenders aged 12 to 18 years are subject to the same *Criminal Code* provisions as adults, but are subject to a different level of punishment, and so the role of youth courts is very important.

The judges in the provincial courts are appointed and paid by the relevant provincial government. The mandatory age of retirement varies from province to province. For example, in Ontario, judges must retire upon reaching the age of 65; in Alberta, upon reaching the age of 70; and in New Brunswick, upon reaching the age of 75.[9]

The highest trial level court, referred to generally as the superior court of a province (the specific name varies with the jurisdiction), has an unlimited monetary jurisdiction in civil matters and deals with serious criminal matters. Some provinces have also retained specialized courts, referred to as **surrogate** or **probate courts**, dealing with the administration of wills and estates. In most jurisdictions, however, this is now just a specialized function of the superior court. Similarly, bankruptcy courts operate within the superior court system. These courts deal with the legal aspects of bankruptcy and must comply with the procedural rules set out in the *Bankruptcy and Insolvency Act*.[10]

It is before the trial courts that the disputing parties in a civil case first appear and testify, the witnesses give evidence, the lawyers present arguments, and judges make decisions. When both a judge and a jury are present, the judge makes findings of law, and the jury makes findings of fact. When the judge is acting alone, which is much more common, especially in civil matters, the judge decides both **Questions of law and fact** matters of fact and matters of law. Matters of fact are those regarding the details of

---

6. In Alberta, British Columbia, Nova Scotia, and the Yukon, the monetary jurisdiction of the small claims courts is $25 000, while in Saskatchewan and Newfoundland and Labrador, the jurisdiction is $5000. The monetary jurisdiction in Ontario is to change from $10 000 to $25 000 on 1 January 2010.

7. *Divorce Act*, R.S.C. 1985 (2nd Supp.), c. 3, s. 2(1).

8. S.C. 2002, c. 1. This legislation replaced the *Young Offenders Act* on 1 April 2003.

9. See *Courts of Justice Act*, R.S.O. 1990, c. 43, s. 47, *Provincial Court Act*, R.S.A. 2000, c. P-31, s. 9.22, and *Provincial Court Act*, R.S.N.B. 1973, c. P-21, s. 4.2. In Ontario and Alberta, judges can be reappointed for a term of one year, to the age of 75.

10. R.S.C. 1985, c. B-3.

Figure 3.1   Outline of Canada's Court System[11]

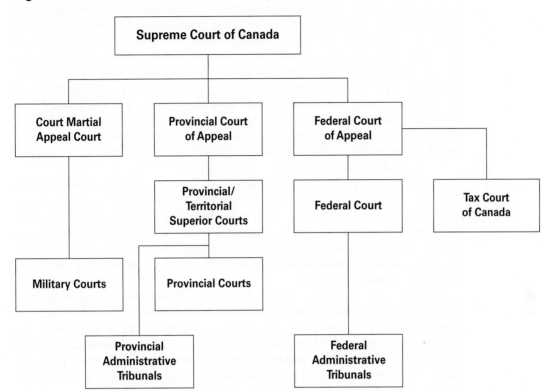

an event. For example, was Erasmus at the corner of Portage and Main in the city of Winnipeg at 7:00 a.m. on 5 March 2007? Did a portion of the building owned by Bereznicki fall on Erasmus? Was he paralyzed as a result of his injury? Was Bereznicki aware of the danger? Had she taken steps to correct it? Questions of law, on the other hand, concern the rules or laws that are to be applied in the situation. For example, was Bereznicki obliged to keep the outside of her building in good repair? Would this obligation be affected if Bereznicki were unaware of the danger? The trial itself is discussed in more detail under "The Process of Civil Litigation," below.

RECENT DEVELOPMENTS

Canada's system of courts is dynamic; it is constantly changing to reflect changes in Canadian society. For example, several innovations have recently been made by various governments. For a full understanding of the court system, it is necessary to review these innovations. The MyBusLawLab outlines regional differences.[12]

Court reforms dictate change

[11.] Department of Justice Canada, http://canada.justice.gc.ca/eng/dept-min/pub/ccs-ajc/page3.html. Note: The Federal Court Trial Division changed its name to Federal Court on 2 July 2003. See explanation on p. 72.

[12.] Inspiration and information for this section came from a series of articles included in "Feature on Evolution of the Courts," in *LawNow* 26:4 (February/March 2002), a series of articles included in "Feature Report on Specialized Courts," in *LawNow* 33:2 (November/December 2008), and Department of Justice Canada, "Canada's Court System," http://canada.justice.gc.ca/eng/dept-min/pub/ccs-ajc/page5.html.

Drug treatment courts have been established in several large Canadian cities. The emphasis in these courts is on the treatment of addicts, not incarceration. Non-violent offenders involved in minor drug offences agree to be bound by the terms of a structured outpatient program designed to reduce their dependence on drugs. They are released on bail, subject to random drug tests, and must appear regularly in court. If they demonstrate control of their addiction, the criminal charges are stayed, or the offender receives a non-custodial sentence. If they cannot demonstrate such control, they are sentenced in the normal way. Research appears to indicate that drug treatment courts are more successful in preventing addicts from re-offending than the traditional court system involving incarceration, and that the yearly cost per participant is far below what it costs per year to maintain an offender in jail.[13]

Domestic violence courts have been established in several provinces in Canada. Ontario has a Domestic Violence Court Program in each of the province's 54 court jurisdictions.[14] These courts deal with spousal, elder, and child abuse. While the structure and jurisdiction of these courts vary from province to province, most of them offer specialized investigations by police, counselling for first-time offenders, prosecution of repeat offenders by specialized prosecutors, and support services for victims.

Unified family courts have jurisdiction over all legal issues related to the family and do not deal with any other types of cases. Such courts have been created in several provinces. This simplifies the court process, which can be extremely complicated due to the overlapping jurisdiction of the federal government and the provincial governments. In addition, the court procedures and rules for family cases have been simplified. As is the case with all specialized courts, judges in unified family courts develop expertise in family law.

As health-care services involving mentally ill persons have declined in recent years, the criminal justice system has seen an increase in the number of accused persons with mental illnesses. As criminal courts are not designed to identify and address the mental health concerns of accused persons, several of the provinces have implemented "mental health courts." These are specialized courts that focus on the treatment and rehabilitation (rather than the punishment) of those who have committed criminal acts due to mental disorders. Judicially monitored programs involving a multidisciplinary team (judges, lawyers, psychologists, nurses, community caregivers) encourage voluntary treatment over punishment. This allows accused persons with mental disorders the opportunity to access appropriate resources and services while ensuring public safety.

The Nunavut Court of Justice, established in 1999, is Canada's first single-level court. Judges in this court are given the powers of both the superior trial courts and the territorial courts. These judges can, therefore, hear all of the cases that arise in the territory. The court is a "circuit court," which travels throughout the territory hearing cases.

Sentencing circles are found in several provinces and are used primarily at the provincial court level for cases involving aboriginal offenders and victims. Sentencing circles are not courts. They involve all interested persons meeting in a circle to discuss the offence, including sentencing options. The circle may suggest

---

13. "Canada's First Drug Court Breaks the Cycle of Drugs and Crime," *LawNow* 26:4 (February/March 2002), "Drug Treatment Court: Not a Free Ride," *LawNow* 33:2 (November/December 2008).

14. Ontario Ministry of the Attorney General, Domestic Violence Court (DVC) Program, www.attorneygeneral.jus.gov.on.ca/english/about/vw/dvc.asp.

restorative community sentences, including restitution to the victim and treatment or counselling of the accused. The judge is not bound to accept a circle sentence. A judge in Saskatchewan created controversy when he granted a sentencing circle in a recent high-profile case involving two young children who froze to death.[15]

Aboriginal persons have been over-represented in Canadian prisons in recent years. An initiative to try to remedy this involves the establishment of specialized courts dedicated to serving Aboriginals. In these courts, charges against aboriginal accused are heard such that cultural sensitivity and respect are incorporated into the criminal justice process. Alberta, British Columbia, Ontario, and Saskatchewan have established aboriginal courts.

It is clear that the Canadian court system will continue to evolve in an effort to improve its success in helping Canadians resolve their disputes fairly. These reforms are taking place with respect to the structure of the courts themselves, as well as the processes involved at both the criminal and civil level. It must be clearly understood, however, that many of the suggested reforms are strenuously resisted on the grounds that they threaten to damage a very effective system that is the envy of much of the world. Retired Supreme Court Justice Frank Iacobucci has urged caution before we embark on such reforms. "We must not take what we have for granted, and we must be particularly vigilant so that in our quest for improvement, we don't desert the values and procedures that have brought us to this level of excellence."[16]

Not all are in favour of reforms

Courts of Appeal of the Provinces

Each province's appellate court hears appeals from the lower courts of that province. They must hear a matter before it can go to the Supreme Court of Canada. In most cases, this is the court of last resort. When one of the parties is dissatisfied with the decision of a provincial trial court and an error in law or procedure is identified, the decision may be successfully appealed. As a general rule, an appeal court will consider a case only when questions of law are in dispute, not questions of fact. But many appeals are based upon questions of mixed law and fact, where the rules that are applied are inseparably connected to the facts that are found. Whether a person lived up to the standards of a reasonable person in a given situation would be an example of such a question of mixed law and fact. Refer to the MyBusLawLab to determine specific provincial structures and jurisdiction.

www.pearsoned.ca/mybuslawlab

Appellate courts

The court exercising an appellate jurisdiction does not hold a new trial. The assumption is that the judge (or judge and jury) who saw and heard all of the evidence presented at trial is (are) best qualified to determine questions of fact. The appeal court judges (usually three) read the transcript of the trial, as well as the trial judge's reasons for decision. They then deal with the specific objections to the trial judge's decision submitted by the appellant's lawyers, hearing the arguments of both the appellant and the respondent.

The judges who serve on provincial superior and appeal courts are appointed by the federal government from a list of candidates supplied by the provinces.[17] Once appointed, the judges have tenure until they retire (by age 75) or are appointed to new positions. They can be removed from the bench only for serious

---

15. "Father of Girls Who Froze to Death Gets Sentencing Circle" (7 January 2009), CBC News Online, www.cbc.ca/canada/saskatchewan/story/2009/01/07/pauchay-sentencing.html.

16. *Lawyers Weekly* 24:9 (2 July 2004.)

17. Part VII of the *Constitution Act, 1867*.

misconduct,[18] but not as the result of making an unpopular decision or one that is unfavourable to the government.

Courts at the Federal Level

Federal Court and Federal Court of Appeal

The Federal Court and Federal Court of Appeal serve a function similar to that of the provincial superior courts. Until 2 July 2003, the Federal Court of Canada had a trial division and an appellate division. On that date, the *Courts Administration Service Act*[19] came into effect, making the two divisions of the Federal Court separate courts. The Trial Division became the Federal Court, a trial court. It hears disputes that fall within the federal sphere of power, such as those concerning copyrights and patents, federal boards and commissions, federal lands or money, and federal government contracts. The Federal Court of Appeal kept its previous name; it is an appellate court. It hears appeals from the Federal Court. Both of the federal courts can hear appeals from decisions of federal regulatory bodies and administrative tribunals. The role of these quasi-judicial bodies will be discussed below under the heading "Administrative Law." An appeal from the Federal Court of Appeal goes directly to the Supreme Court of Canada.

The Tax Court of Canada is another very specialized court, which was established in 1983 to hear disputes concerning federal tax matters. This body hears appeals from assessment decisions made by various federal agencies enforcing taxation statutes, such as the *Income Tax Act*, the *Employment Insurance Act*, and the *Old Age Security Act*. Pursuant to the *Courts Administration Service Act*, the Tax Court of Canada became a superior court on 2 July 2003; its powers and jurisdiction did not change. The courts that hear cases involving the military are also specialized courts; a discussion of these courts is beyond the scope of this text.

Supreme Court of Canada

The Supreme Court of Canada is the highest court in the land. It has a strictly appellate function as far as private citizens are concerned. There are nine judges appointed by the Government of Canada, according to a pattern of regional representation.[20] A quorum consists of five judges, but most appeals are heard by a panel of seven or nine judges. There is no longer an automatic right of appeal to the Supreme Court of Canada (except in criminal cases where a judge in the appellate court dissented on a point of law, or when an appellate court sets aside an acquittal and enters a verdict of guilty).[21] In all other cases, leave to appeal must be obtained from the Supreme Court, and such leave will be granted only if a case has some national significance. The Supreme Court hears both criminal and civil cases. In addition, it is sometimes asked to rule directly on constitutional disputes involving federal and provincial governments. For example, the federal government submitted a Reference to the Supreme Court of Canada in February 1998, asking whether Quebec could unilaterally secede from Canada.[22] Decisions of the Supreme Court set binding precedents for all other courts in Canada.

Supreme Court decisions set binding precedents

---

18. *Judges Act*, R.S.C. 1985, c.J-1, s. 65(2).

19. S.C. 2002, c. 8.

20. Three of the judges must be from the province of Quebec, pursuant to the *Supreme Court Act*, R.S.C. 1985, c. S-26, s. 6.

21. *Criminal Code*, R.S.C. 1985, c. C-46, s. 691.

22. *Reference Re Secession of Quebec*, [1998] 2 S.C.R. 217. Another reference to the Supreme Court was submitted to determine whether the federal government had the power to authorize same-sex marriages. That positive decision was rendered 9 December 2004. *Reference Re Same-Sex Marriage*, [2004] S.C.J. No. 75, 2004 S.C.C. 79.

THE PROCESS OF CIVIL LITIGATION

Most of this text deals with matters of substantive law (that is, law that summarizes rights and obligations of the "you can" or "you can't" variety) rather than procedural law (that is, law that deals with the process by which we enforce those rights and obligations). But it is important to be familiar with the procedures involved in bringing a dispute to trial, if only to understand the function of lawyers and the reasons for the expense and delay involved. Before a decision is made to sue someone, all avenues for settling the dispute outside of litigation ought to be exhausted. Alternative methods for resolving legal disputes have been developed, including negotiation, mediation, and arbitration. Often the court requires the disputing parties to have tried these dispute-resolution mechanisms before a trial procedure will be instigated. The litigation procedures may vary somewhat from province to province, but they are substantially the same in all common law jurisdictions. They apply to most superior courts. (One of the distinguishing characteristics of small claims courts is that this involved procedure has been streamlined significantly, eliminating many of the steps described.) The discussion below is based on the procedure followed in British Columbia. Figure 3.2 sets out the process of civil litigation. Refer to the MyBusLawLab for procedures used in other provinces.

Limitation Periods

Whether to remove ongoing uncertainty or to ensure fairness when memories dim or witnesses become unavailable, court action must be brought within a relatively short time from the event giving rise to the complaint. This time is referred to as a **limitation period**. In most provinces, for example, a person who is owed money from a simple sale of goods transaction must bring an action against the debtor within six years of the failure to pay the debt.[23] The plaintiff must commence an action by filing the appropriate pleading (the writ of summons or the statement of claim) with the appropriate court. Failure to fulfill that step within the limitation period will result in the plaintiff being barred from pursuing the action. This time limitation will vary depending on the jurisdiction and the nature of the complaint involved, and may be embodied in several different statutes in a province. Refer to the MyBusLawLab.

With the expiry of the limitation period and the threat of court action removed, the potential defendant is not likely to settle out of court and the plaintiff is left with no recourse. For this reason, it is important for a person involved in a potential lawsuit to quickly get the advice of a lawyer regarding the relevant limitation period. Whether the limitation period had expired is the problem facing the court in the Canada's Wonderland case discussed in Case Summary 3.2. This case shows that a person not only has to sue for the right thing—in this case, negligence—but he also has to do so in a timely manner.

---

23. But in Alberta, the *Limitations Act* states that most lawsuits (including those for breach of contract and tort) must be commenced within two years of discovering the claim, or within 10 years from the date when the claim arose, whichever period expires first. Ontario has a similar system, except that the ultimate limitation period is 15, rather than 10, years, pursuant to the *Limitations Act, 2002*. Both the Alberta Act (ss. 8–9) and the Ontario legislation (s. 13) carry forward the rule that a written acknowledgment, or part payment, of a debt before a limitation period expires revives the limitation period, which begins again at the time of the acknowledgment or part payment. The Alberta legislation (s. 7) also allows the parties to extend a limitation period, by agreement. In British Columbia, no action may be brought after 30 years from the time the right to do so arose (*Limitation Act*, R.S.B.C. 1996, c. 266, s. 8(1)(c)).

Figure 3.2   Process of Civil Litigation

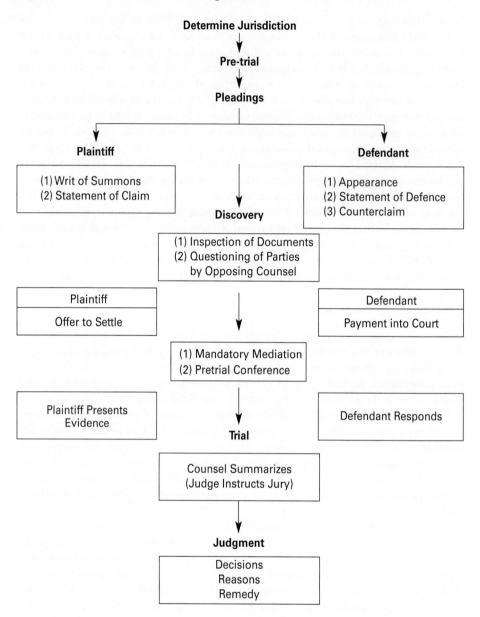

Jurisdiction

The first step when suing is to determine which court should hear the action. The proper geographic jurisdiction in which to bring an action can be a very difficult question, but generally the plaintiff or person bringing the action can choose a court in the area where the defendant resides or in the area where the matter complained about arose. If a traffic accident that happened in Alberta involved one driver from British Columbia and one from Ontario, the Ontario driver would have to sue in British Columbia or Alberta.

CASE SUMMARY 3.2

Does a Judge Have Discretion to Extend a Limitation Period? *Joseph v. Paramount Canada's Wonderland* [24]

Joseph suffered an injury at Paramount's amusement park. His lawyer prepared a statement of claim, but his assistant did not file it before the limitation period expired. She believed that the relevant limitation period was six years. However, in Ontario, the *Limitations Act, 2002* established a basic two-year limitation period and an ultimate limitation period of 15 years. (The basic limitation period runs from when the claim is discovered.) When the lawyer realized the error that had been made, he filed and served the statement of claim. The Defendant applied for a ruling that the action was barred, as the limitation period had expired. A Judge of the Superior Court of Justice held that the action was barred by the two-year limitation period provided by the new *Act*. The Judge also held, however, that he had discretion under the common law doctrine of special circumstances to extend the time to commence an action, as long as there was no prejudice to the defendant that could not be compensated for with either costs or an adjournment.

The Court of Appeal briefly discussed the aim of the new *Act* ("to balance the right of claimants to sue with the right of defendants to have some certainty and finality in managing their affairs"). It also discussed some of the reforms introduced by the new *Act,* such as the doctrine of discoverability. With respect to the special circumstances doctrine, the Court held that the Ontario legislature did not intend that the courts would continue to have discretion to extend the limitation periods under the new *Act*, which was intended to be comprehensive.

DISCUSSION QUESTIONS

If the special circumstances doctrine no longer applies, and a claim is not filed prior to the expiration of the limitation period because of a mistake by a lawyer's assistant, is the plaintiff out of luck? Is there anyone who could be held liable for the damages she may have recovered if her lawsuit had proceeded? If there is an ultimate limitation period, claims that have not been discovered prior to the expiration of the period can never be pursued. Is that fair?

The internet has complicated this to some extent since its messages are received in all jurisdictions. Where the internet is involved, a court is more likely to allow an action to proceed if there has been some sort of interaction or transaction over the internet with a resident of that province.[25] Still a court can refuse to hear a case if it believes that another jurisdiction would be more appropriate. There can also be serious jurisdictional problems when a successful litigant tries to enforce that judgment in another jurisdiction.

[24.] (2008), 90 Ont. R. (3d) 401 (C.A).

[25.] *Easthaven Ltd. v. Nutrisystem.com Inc.* (2001), 202 D.L.R. (4th) 560 (Ont. Sup. Ct.).

Once the province has been chosen, the plaintiff must then choose the court in which to commence the litigation. In a civil action, this is either the province's small claims court or superior court. The monetary jurisdiction of the small claims court varies from province to province, as discussed above. Although it is simpler and less expensive to bring an action in the small claims court, a disadvantage is that that court is restricted in the costs it can award. The costs incurred for representation by a lawyer usually cannot be recovered. On the other hand, the procedure followed at the small claims court has been significantly streamlined. It is designed to enable ordinary people to present their legal problems without the need to hire a lawyer. Hiring a lawyer, asking a friend to assist in court, or handling the action on one's own are all options.

Small claims court is simple but only minimal costs are recoverable

---

CASE SUMMARY 3.3

When Does a Court Have Jurisdiction? *UniNet Technologies Inc. v. Communications Services Inc.*[26]

1. Entered licence agreement

| UniNet | | ALA | | CSI |

3. Entered licence agreement

2. Terminated licence agreement

"ALA," a corporation formed in St. Vincent and the Grenadines, granted UniNet, a B.C. corporation, a 99-year licence to use a domain name for the development and operation of an online gambling licence. UniNet sublicensed the name to Poker.com, a Florida corporation. Communication Services Inc. (CSI) was incorporated, by the principals of ALA, in Samoa, a country with strong asset protection laws that would protect the assets of the directors and officers of CSI and ALA from foreign claims and judgments. UniNet claimed that ALA wrongfully terminated the licence agreement and then transferred the domain name to CSI. The issue was whether B.C. courts had jurisdiction over the court proceeding. The lower court held that the B.C. courts had such jurisdiction.

The licence agreement between ALA and UniNet indicated that it was to be interpreted by the laws of British Columbia and that the B.C. courts were to have jurisdiction over any relevant litigation. It also required that any dispute arising out of the licence agreement was to be resolved by arbitration under B.C. legislation. UniNet had commenced such arbitration with respect to the termination of the agreement.

The Court of Appeal held that the test as to whether a court has jurisdiction is "whether the plaintiff has established that there is a 'real and substantial connection between the court and either the defendant or the subject-matter of the litigation.'" The Court considered that the licence agreement was governed by the law of British Columbia, that the parties had agreed to the jurisdiction of B.C. courts, that the right to use and own the domain name was being determined in arbitration in British Columbia, that the licence agreement was entered into in British Columbia, and that the agreement may have been performed, at least in part, in British Columbia. CSI argued that it was not

---

26. (2005), 251 D.L.R. (4th) 464, (2005), 38 B.C.L.R. (4th) 366 (C.A.).

a party to the licence agreement. The Court held that the litigation was about whether CSI received the domain name from ALA in breach of its obligations under the licence agreement with UniNet, and was therefore a natural continuation of the arbitration being held in British Columbia. The Court ruled that the cumulative effect of all of these factors gave the B.C. courts jurisdiction over the litigation.

REDUCING RISK 3.1

To avoid problems, those doing business over the internet should specify what law is to apply to transactions entered into with customers and which courts are to have jurisdiction over relevant litigation. When business is solicited, it would also be wise to include disclaimers setting limits on the parties who can enter into such transactions. Such disclaimers would be similar to those contained in product warranties, namely: "Void where prohibited by law" or "Available only to residents of Canada." If a business creates a website and uses it to do business in other jurisdictions, not only will it be subject to the law of those jurisdictions, but also any resulting litigation may be conducted in the courts of those jurisdictions. See Chapter 14 for a more detailed discussion of this topic.

Pre-Trial Procedures

The traditional way to commence an action in a superior court was for the plaintiff to issue a **writ of summons** (this has been abandoned in most provinces but is still used in British Columbia). Where the writ of summons is still in use, if the defendant chooses to dispute the claim, he must promptly file an **appearance** with the court clerk. The second step (the first in provinces where the writ of summons is not used) requires a **statement of claim** to be served on the defendant. The statement of claim sets out in detail the plaintiff's allegations. It must be filed with the court clerk and served on the defendant. The defendant must then prepare and file a **statement of defence**, in which he provides answers to the claims of the plaintiff stating areas of agreement, disputed claims, and contrary allegations.

If the defendant believes that he is the real victim, he can also file a **counterclaim**. This is similar to a statement of claim. A counterclaim requires the filing of a statement of defence from the plaintiff in response.

The documents used to start and defend a lawsuit constitute the **pleadings**. The purpose of the pleadings is not to argue and justify positions; rather, the parties are merely stating the claims giving rise to the dispute and establishing the required elements of the legal action. If either party believes that the documents do not make the other party's position completely clear, she may ask for clarification or further information. Once the pleadings have closed, the parties have the right to apply to set a date for trial and begin the process of discovery. Throughout the pre-trial process, the parties have the right to—and often do—make applications to the court for direction regarding what details have to be disclosed, what questions have to be answered, and other matters that may arise.

www.pearsoned.ca/mybuslawlab

Writ of summons
Appearance
Statement of claim

Statement of defence

Counterclaim

The process of discovery has two distinct parts:

Documents may be used at trial

1. Discovery of documents. Each party has the right to inspect any document in the possession of the other party that may be used as evidence in the trial. This includes email and computer files on a disk or a hard drive.

2. Examination for discovery. The parties (with their lawyers) meet before a court reporter and, under oath, are asked detailed questions relevant to the problem to be tried. The parties are required to answer these questions fully

Statements made under oath may be used at trial

and truthfully. Everything said is recorded, and may be used later at the trial. This examination process generally applies to only the parties to the action, not to witnesses. When corporations are involved, a representative who has personal knowledge of the matter may be examined. As part of a general reform of the litigation process in some provinces and in an attempt to reduce the costs of an action, the examination for discovery has been eliminated in actions involving smaller amounts.[27] Other provinces have limited the amount of time given to the examination process.[28]

In most jurisdictions, a pre-trial conference must be scheduled. This is a meeting of the parties, their lawyers, and the judge. It is held to determine which issues remain to be tried and whether the parties can themselves resolve the dispute. In fact, most disputes are resolved by the parties during these pre-trial processes.

Offer to settle

Another tool often available to parties before a trial is an **offer to settle.** Either party can make an official offer to settle; if it is accepted, that ends the matter. If it is refused and the judgment at the trial is different from the offer made, the costs awarded are adjusted to punish the parties for failing to act more reasonably.

If Jones was claiming $200 000 against Smith for an automobile accident, Smith could make an offer to settle (a "payment into court") of $150 000. The judge would know nothing about such a payment. If the eventual judgment was for more than $150 000, costs would be awarded as normal, since Jones acted reasonably in refusing to accept the offer. But if the judgment was for less than $150 000, obviously Jones would have been better off accepting the payment. Because he

---

! REDUCING RISK 3.2

The discovery stage is an extremely important part of the litigation process; cases are often won or lost at this point. When parties testify under oath at discovery, they often make admissions or incorrect statements that come back to haunt them at the trial. Admissions of fact that may not seem important at the time may become crucial at the actual trial, and a party is bound by those admissions. A false claim can be investigated before trial, and the party can be forced to recant at the trial, bringing her credibility into question. This means that what is said at the discovery stage often determines the outcome of the case, compelling the parties to come to a settlement. For businesses, it is extremely important that the person who testifies at discovery not only be familiar with the matter, but also be well prepared and appreciate the importance of her testimony and its potential impact on the legal action.

[27.] Under Ontario's Simplified Procedure, for example, examination for discovery is not permitted for actions involving less than $50 000 (Ontario *Rules of Civil Procedure*, r. 76).

[28.] In Alberta, the Streamlined Procedure for cases involving $75 000 or less sets a six-hour limit for examinations for discovery (Alberta, *Rules of Court*, r. 662). In British Columbia, there is a two-hour limit on examinations for discovery for Fast Track Litigation (British Columbia, *Supreme Court Civil Rules*, r. 66). Rule 68, the "Expedited Litigation Project Rule," has been in force province-wide since 1 January 2008. It also allows for a two-hour examination for discovery. New civil rules are scheduled to be implemented on 1 July 2010. They will probably include new fast track litigation rules.

acted unreasonably in not doing so, he would be denied compensation for the legal expenses incurred from the time of his refusal of the offer. The plaintiff can also make an offer to settle, showing a willingness to take less than originally claimed. If this is unreasonably refused by the defendant, he will be required to pay greater costs due to his failure to accept a fair settlement.

RECENT INITIATIVES

While it is obvious that the purpose of this long, involved, and expensive pre-trial process is to encourage the parties to reach a settlement and thereby avoid a trial, it is also clear that such a process results in frustrating delays for the parties. For this reason, the provinces have implemented reforms to speed up the litigation process, especially when smaller amounts are involved. British Columbia and Alberta, for example, allow for Summary Trials, where evidence is adduced by **affidavit** instead of by the testimony of witnesses.[29] British Columbia also provides for Fast Track Litigation for trials that can be completed within two days;[30] Alberta's Streamlined Procedure applies to trials involving claims of $75 000 or less.[31] Ontario and Saskatchewan have a Simplified Procedure for claims of $50 000 or less,[32] New Brunswick[33] and Prince Edward Island[34] have procedures for Quick Rulings, and Manitoba has implemented Expedited Trials and Expedited Actions.[35] Some provinces, including Ontario and Saskatchewan, have introduced Mandatory Mediation.[36] Several provinces, including Ontario, have started mandatory case management, which involves judicial supervision of the specific steps in the litigation process.[37] Ontario now regulates paralegals, which provides people involved in disputes with an alternative to hiring lawyers.[38] The objectives of reducing costs and delay—and of making the justice system more accessible—have motivated all jurisdictions to create small claims courts where the procedures have been dramatically simplified and costs reduced accordingly. (Refer to the MyBusLawLab for provincial variations.) It is important for businesspeople to understand that these changes, and all of the other changes to the justice system discussed above, have provided them with increased opportunity to utilize the system when necessary.

Recent initiatives

Payment into court

The Trial

Because the burden of proof at trial rests with the plaintiff, the plaintiff's case and witnesses are presented first. The plaintiff's lawyer assists witnesses in their testimony by asking specific questions, but the types of questions that may be asked are very restricted. For example, the plaintiff's lawyer is prohibited from asking

mybuslawlab
www.pearsoned.ca/mybuslawlab

BC AB SK MB ON

---

29. British Columbia, *Supreme Court Civil Rules, ibid.* r. 18A, and Alberta, *Rules of Court,ibid.* Part 11.

30. British Columbia, *Supreme Court Civil Rules, ibid.* r. 66.

31. Alberta, *Rules of Court, supra* note 28, Part 48.

32. Ontario, *Rules of Civil Procedure, supra* note 27, r. 76, and Saskatchewan, *Queen's Bench Rules*, Part 40.

33. New Brunswick, *Rules of Court*, Rule 77.

34. Prince Edward Island, *Rules of Civil Procedure*, Rule 75.

35. Manitoba, *Court of Queen's Bench Rules*, Rule 20 and Rule 20A.

36. Ontario, *Rules of Civil Procedure, supra* note 26, r. 24.1, and Saskatchewan, *Queen's Bench Act, 1998*, S.S. 1998, c. Q-1.01, s. 42.

37. *Ibid.* r. 77.

38. Paralegals are regulated by the Law Society of Upper Canada. See the Paralegal Society of Ontario website at www.paralegalsociety.on.ca/. See the section on Paralegal Regulation on the LSUC website at: www.lsuc.on.ca/paralegals/.

Plaintiff presents its case first—defendant cross-examines

leading questions, in which the answer is suggested (such as, "You were there on Saturday, weren't you?"). When the plaintiff's lawyer completes this direct examination of the witness, the defendant's lawyer is given the opportunity to cross-examine the witness. In cross-examination, the defence has more latitude in the type of questions asked and so is permitted to ask leading questions. When the opposing lawyer believes that the lawyer questioning the witness is abusing the process by asking prohibited questions, she can object to the question. The judge rules on the objection, deciding whether to permit the question or order the lawyer to withdraw it. The rules governing the type of testimony that can be obtained from witnesses—and, indeed, all other types of evidence to be submitted at a trial—are referred to as the **rules of evidence**. (These rules are very complex and beyond the scope of this text.) If something new arises from the cross-examination, the plaintiff's lawyer re-examines the witnesses on those matters. When the plaintiff has completed presenting evidence, the lawyer for the defence will then present its case calling witnesses and presenting evidence that supports its side, and the plaintiff cross-examines. After both sides have finished calling witnesses, the plaintiff's lawyer and then the defendant's lawyer are allowed to summarize the evidence and make arguments to the court. Again, if anything new comes up, the other party is given a chance to respond to it.

When the plaintiff is finished, the defence then presents its case

Judgment

mybuslawlab

www.pearsoned.ca/mybuslawlab

BC | AB | SK | MB | ON

Juries determine questions of fact

If a jury is involved (which is not very common in civil cases), the judge will instruct it on matters of law. The jury then retires to consider the case and returns to announce its decision to the judge. The function of the jury is to decide questions of fact; the judge decides questions of law. Where the matter is heard by a judge alone, a decision may be delivered immediately; however, it is more common for the judge to hand down a judgment in writing some time later that includes reasons for the decision. These reasons can form the basis for an appeal.

COSTS

The cost of retaining a lawyer to sue someone is often prohibitive; some creditors may decide to write off a debt rather than incur this outlay. In small claims courts, the presence of a lawyer is the exception rather than the rule, mainly because the winning party usually will not recover the costs of obtaining the services of a lawyer from the losing party. In higher-level courts, lawyers are generally essential, although parties do have the right to represent themselves. Although legal fees are usually the greater part, other expenses are often incurred, such as the costs of obtaining transcripts from the discovery process and the fees paid to secure specialized reports from experts.

! REDUCING RISK 3.3

The delay and costs associated with litigation, as well as the lack of control over the process and outcome, have contributed to its decreasing popularity. For businesspeople, finding themselves in court should normally be viewed as a failure. Considerable care should be taken to avoid disputes, or to attempt to settle them before litigation becomes nec-

essary. When a settlement cannot be reached by the parties, and both parties are willing, it is sometimes advantageous to explore some of the alternatives to litigation that are available. (These are discussed below.) However, in some situations—especially when it may be necessary to enforce the court's decision—litigation may be the best option available.

Even the winning party must pay her own legal expenses. She may, however, obtain as part of the judgment an order for "costs." This means that the defendant will be required to compensate the successful plaintiff for at least a portion of her legal expenses. While a judge always has discretion when awarding costs, **party and party costs** are usually awarded to the victorious party in a civil action. Party and party costs are determined using a predetermined scale and normally fall short of the actual fees charged.[39] Consequently, the plaintiff will usually have to pay some legal expenses even when she is successful. There is, of course, always the risk that a party may lose the action and have to pay all of her own legal expenses as well as the winning party's costs. If the judge finds the conduct of the losing party objectionable (for example, if an action is "frivolous and vexatious"), then he may award the winning party the higher **solicitor and client costs**. Refer to the MyBusLawLab for the various provincial approaches.

> Losing party usually pays costs

> Legal expenses usually not completely recoverable

REMEDIES

One of the things that must be decided when a civil suit is begun is what the plaintiff will ask the court to do. The most common remedy requested in a court action is monetary payment in the form of **damages**, which are designed to compensate the victim for any loss suffered. **General damages** are based on estimates, such as when the court awards compensation to a litigant for pain and suffering or for future lost wages. **Special damages**, on the other hand, are calculated to reimburse the litigant for expenses or costs incurred before the trial. **Punitive** or **exemplary damages** are intended not to compensate the victim but rather to punish the wrongdoer for outrageous or extreme behaviour. This may result in a windfall for the victim. Punitive damages will be awarded only in very serious cases, such as a sadistic physical attack, or when an insurer pursued an unfounded allegation of arson against a vulnerable insured.[40]

> Damages involve payment of money

In rare cases, remedies other than damages may be awarded. The court can order money incorrectly paid to the defendant to be restored to the rightful owner. In some circumstances, it is also possible to obtain an **accounting**, which results in any profits derived from the defendant's wrongful conduct to be paid over to the victim. The court also has the power to order an **injunction** stopping wrongful conduct or correcting some continuing wrong. The court may compel proper performance of a legal obligation by **specific performance**. In some situations, it may be appropriate for the courts to simply make a **declaration** as to the law and the legal rights of the parties.

> Other remedies

Enforcement

Even when the litigation process is completed and judgment is obtained, there is no guarantee that the amount awarded will be paid. There may no longer be a dispute over liability, but if the **judgment debtor** refuses to pay, steps must be taken by the plaintiff, now the **judgment creditor**, to enforce the judgment. If the judgment debtor cannot pay and owns no assets (a "dry judgment"), it was likely unwise to have pursued the action in the first place. The successful plaintiff not only will get nothing from the defendant, but also will have to pay his own legal expenses. On the other

www.pearsoned.ca/mybuslawlab

> A judgment does not ensure payment

---

[39] In Alberta, for example, party and party costs are usually awarded for actions in the Court of Queen's Bench pursuant to Schedule C of the *Rules of Court*, *supra* note 28.

[40] *Whiten v. Pilot Insurance Co.*, [2002] 1 S.C.R. 595.

Is Specific Performance Always an Appropriate Remedy for Land Transactions? *Semelhago v. Paramadevan*[41]

Although damages or monetary compensation is the common remedy in a civil action, sometimes the court will order the equitable remedy of specific performance. In land transactions, it was thought that because all land is unique, specific performance would always be available—at least until this case was decided by the Supreme Court of Canada. Semelhago agreed to purchase from Paramadevan a house that was under construction, for $205 000. When it was time to perform the contract, Paramadevan refused, and this action was brought. Semelhago asked for the remedy of *specific performance*—or, as permitted by statute, damages in lieu of specific performance. At the trial he elected to receive damages, and the Court awarded him $125 000 damages in lieu of specific performance. The reason for this high award was that the market value of the house had risen from the $205 000 agreed upon at the time the contract was made to $325 000 at the time of trial. Paramadevan appealed the award, and the Appeal Court reduced it by the amount of the interest that Semelhago would have had to pay to finance the purchase of the house over the period from when the contract was entered into until the trial, saying that damages should reflect not only the increase in the value of the house from the time of the contract, but also the interest that would have been paid out had the deal closed as required by the contract. This reduced the damages to just less than $82 000.

The purpose of such damages is to put the victim in the position he would have been in had the contract been properly performed—and, so, the interest he would have had to pay should have been taken into consideration. The Supreme Court of Canada stated that specific performance should not always be considered the appropriate remedy in such land transaction disputes. It then refused to further reduce the award, and also refused to take into consideration the increased value of the house that Semelhago had intended to sell to acquire the one in question, but which he had instead retained. This case shows the factors that will be taken into consideration when assessing damages to be paid. An important statement that came out of the case was that it should no longer be thought that all land is unique, and that specific performance is therefore not always appropriate in a land transaction.

DISCUSSION QUESTIONS

Consider the remedies available to a court in a civil action. Here the Court refused to grant specific performance, but took into consideration the increasing values of the property and interest costs that would have been incurred when awarding damages. Were these appropriate considerations in the circumstances? Should remedies be limited to monetary compensation in most cases? Should damages always simply compensate or are there situations where punitive damages should be awarded?

hand, if the judgment debtor has prospects of owning future assets, the judgment does remain enforceable for several years and could be enforced in the future. The plaintiff must consider all of these factors—as well as the risk of losing the action—when deciding whether to proceed with an action against the defendant.

---

41. [1996] 2 S.C.R. 415.

ENFORCING JUDGMENT

The process to follow when enforcing a judgment is set out in Figure 3.3. Once judgment has been obtained, most provinces provide for a further hearing, sometimes called an **examination in aid of execution**[42] to determine the judgment debtor's assets and income that can be seized or garnished to satisfy the judgment. The plaintiff can question the judgment debtor (who is under oath) about her property, income, debts, recent property transfers, and present and future means of satisfying the judgment. At the conclusion of the process, the plaintiff can take appropriate steps to execute against particular property or income to recover the judgment.

Hearing to enforce judgment

SEIZURE OF PROPERTY

The execution process allows for the **seizure** and eventual sale of the debtor's property to satisfy the judgment. The property is seized by a government official (or in some provinces by a private business designated for that purpose[43]) who, after deducting a fee, sells it, usually through public auction. The proceeds are distributed first to **secured creditors**, then to preferred creditors and, finally, on a

Property may be seized and sold

Figure 3.3   Enforcement of Judgment

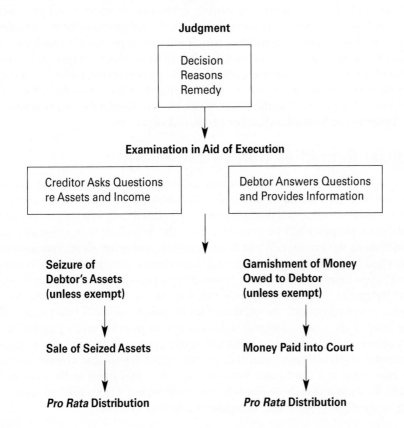

Judgment

Decision
Reasons
Remedy

Examination in Aid of Execution

| Creditor Asks Questions re Assets and Income | Debtor Answers Questions and Provides Information |

Seizure of Debtor's Assets (unless exempt)

Garnishment of Money Owed to Debtor (unless exempt)

Sale of Seized Assets

Money Paid into Court

Pro Rata Distribution

Pro Rata Distribution

---

42. In Alberta, this hearing is called an examination in aid of enforcement—*Rules of Court, supra* note 28, r. 371–372. Instead of conducting an examination, the plaintiff may attempt to determine the information by requiring the judgment debtor to complete a financial report, verified by statutory declaration (in Alberta *Rules of Court*, r. 370).

43. In Alberta, a "civil enforcement agency" pursuant to the *Civil Enforcement Act*, R.S.A. 2000, c. C-15.

Proceeds of sale shared by all creditors

pro rata or proportionate basis, to the remaining unsecured creditors. **Secured creditors** used the property in question as security for a loan or other indebtedness, and so they have first claim to the proceeds from its sale, up to the amount secured. **Preferred creditors** are those who, by legislation, must be paid before other unsecured creditors. Landlords, owed unpaid rent, and employees, owed unpaid wages (both for a limited number of months), are examples of preferred creditors.

Some properties are exempt from seizure

Not all property is subject to seizure. The "necessities of life" are exempt from seizure. Exempt assets vary from province to province, but generally include—within specified limits—food, clothing, household furnishings, tools or other personal property needed to earn income, motor vehicles, and medical and dental aids. It should be noted that real property (land and buildings) can be seized to satisfy a judgment, but that the method employed varies with the jurisdiction. Often, registering the judgment against the real property is enough to pressure the debtor to pay. But when this is not enough, the property can be sold to satisfy the judgment.

Funds owed to debtor can be garnished

Garnishment involves the interception of funds owed to the judgment debtor and the payment of those funds into court. A creditor may garnish funds such as wages earned by the debtor but not yet paid to him, or the balance of the debtor's bank account. The legislation governing garnishment varies from province to province. Typically, when wages are garnished, the judgment debtor is entitled to an employment earnings exemption, which will vary depending on such factors as the amount earned and the debtor's number of dependants.[44] Once the required documentation is served on the garnishee (the person owing money to the judgment debtor), she must pay the amount owing (less the employment earnings exemption, if applicable) to the court, which then disburses the funds to the creditors. Refer to the MyBusLawLab for provincial variations.

Judicial Remedies Before Judgment

mybuslawlab

www.pearsoned.ca/mybuslawlab

BC AB SK MB ON

Pre-judgment remedies limited

Although most methods of execution require that a judgment first be obtained, some judicial remedies may be available to a creditor even before judgment. These are extraordinary remedies that are normally granted only when there is risk that the debtor's property will be removed from the jurisdiction or otherwise made unavailable to the creditor. While bank accounts and other debts can sometimes be attached before judgment, garnishing wages before judgment is usually not permitted.[45] New Brunswick and Nova Scotia do not permit any form of garnishment before judgment. When property other than money is involved, and there is risk of its being removed or sold, the creditor may be able to obtain a court order allowing seizure. This is not a judgment, but rather an interim order granted by the court before the actual trial to ensure that the goods will be available to satisfy a judgment if one is ultimately granted. Another remedy available in some situations is an injunction to a third party from paying out money owed to the debtor. This remedy does not direct those funds to the creditor, but it does prevent them from going to the debtor—who may dissipate or abscond with them.[46]

[44.] In Ontario, for example, 80 percent of a person's wages are usually exempt from garnishment—*Wages Act*, R.S.O. 1990, c. W. 1, s. 7.

[45.] See, for example, s. 3(4) of the *Court Order Enforcement Act*, R.S.B.C. 1996, c. 78.

[46.] In Alberta, the *Civil Enforcement Act*, *supra* note 43, Part 3, enables claimants to apply for attachment orders, which can allow both seizure and garnishment before judgment is obtained.

DEALING WITH REGULATORY BODIES

Most people are aware of the significant growth of government regulation and bureaucracy over the last 50 years. Sometimes these government regulators abuse their positions or go beyond their authority when making decisions that affect individuals or businesses. This section deals with an examination of our rights before these regulatory bodies.

Government can be divided into three different functions: legislative, judicial, and executive. The legislative branch in Canada consists of the federal Parliament and its provincial counterparts. The judicial branch consists of the courts at both the federal and provincial levels. The executive branch includes the Prime Minister, the Premiers of the provinces, the Cabinet Ministers, and all of the civil servants in the various government departments. In Canada, the theoretical head of the executive branch is the Queen, and so this aspect of government is often referred to as "the Crown."

Civil servants, or the bureaucracy of the executive branch at both federal and provincial levels, assist people in their dealings with government. They provide service functions such as security, education, health, and welfare; they administer departments such as customs and revenue; and they manage government affairs generally. They also regulate such matters as human rights, the environment, and employment. Government agents exercise their powers directly through the enforcement of rules and the imposition of penalties, and indirectly through funding or education.

Government departments establish regulatory bodies or **administrative tribunals** such as labour relations boards, human rights commissions, and workers' compensation boards to implement and enforce their policies. These bodies may look and act like courts, but it is important to keep in mind that they are not part of the judicial branch and therefore not subject to the same regulations that govern the courts. Because administrative tribunals make decisions that profoundly impact businesses and individuals and have powers of enforcement that can be abused, the courts have some jurisdiction, albeit limited, to supervise their actions.

It is important to keep in mind that there are some significant advantages to administrative tribunals. Government employees who make up the decision-

mybuslawlab
www.pearsoned.ca/mybuslawlab

BC | AB | SK | MB | ON

Government consists of legislative branch, judicial branch, and executive branch

Executive branch also known as the Crown

Government objectives achieved through rule enforcement, economic incentives, and education

When powers are abused, judicial review available

REDUCING RISK 3.4

The process of collection and enforcement of judgments as described above may appear cumbersome, but it can be quite effective because of the diversity of options available. The process can be expensive, however, and may therefore not be justifiable economically depending on the amount of the debt and the likelihood of recovery. Note that when property has been used to secure a debt, and the security has been properly registered, the creditor has a right to seize the property upon default, without recourse to the courts. Bankruptcy will also affect the debtor's obligation to pay. (Secured transactions involving personal property as well as the bankruptcy process are dealt with in Chapter 15.)

A businessperson should consider the various ways to structure a transaction ("Should I take security or not?") before she enters into a business arrangement. This will require an analysis of whether the other party will be able to fulfill his obligations ("Is his business plan reasonable?"), and if not, whether it will be possible to collect any resulting shortfall through the litigation process ("What other assets does he own that could be used to satisfy the debt?"). An understanding of the process of collection and the enforcement of judgments will enable a prudent businessperson to make better decisions, thereby reducing the risk associated with her business arrangements.

making panels usually have specific expertise in the matter being decided and the tribunals generally have more discretion than a judge. This flexibility creates a more efficient, quicker, and less costly process. To protect the public interest, courts are empowered to review the process by which these decisions are made. When a decision is challenged, the court determines whether the decision maker acted within his authority and whether the procedure used to come to the decision was fair. It is a review, rather than an appeal, of the decision. In fact, the Supreme Court of Canada has established a standard that significantly restricts when the decision of such a body can be challenged. As long as the administrative decision maker acted within the authority granted, and any discretion was exercised in a fair and honest way so that the decision can be said to be reasonable, the decision will stand.[47]

Procedural Fairness in Tribunals

www.pearsoned.ca/mybuslawlab

BC   AB   SK   MB   **ON**

To determine our rights before such tribunals, there are several questions that must be addressed:

1. From where did the tribunal derive its authority?
2. Was the decision-making process fair?
3. What recourse is there if there has been a failure in jurisdiction or procedure?

1. THE AUTHORITY OF THE DECISION MAKER

Decision maker must have authority

Decision makers cannot act arbitrarily. They must be able to point to some statutory authority that empowers them to make a decision. Authority is granted by statute or by a regulation created pursuant to that statute. Both are considered legislation and can be the source of authority for the decision maker but the provisions must clearly authorize the conduct.

Rules of statutory interpretation

The statutes usually start out with a definition section, which must be used to interpret the terms used in the statute. Most jurisdictions provide a general **interpretation statute** to provide further guidance. Usually, the application of a little common sense with reliance on the statutory definitions and the rules of interpretation provided solves most difficulties. The words of a statute are read in their ordinary grammatical sense unless it is clear from the overall statute that a different meaning was intended. The words should then be read in such a way as to be in harmony with the objective and other provisions of the statute.

Statutes must be passed by appropriate level of government

Remember that the *Constitution Act, 1867* divides powers between the provincial and federal governments. If the statute goes beyond the powers of the level of government enacting it, whether federal or provincial, it will be void and will not support the actions of the decision maker who relied on it. Similarly, if the statute, the regulation, or the conduct of the decision maker is found to violate a provision of the *Charter of Rights and Freedoms*, the decision can be successfully challenged. A court may determine that a statute has the effect of discriminating on the basis of gender, religion, or ethnic origin, or that it restricted freedom of the press or religion, and is, therefore, invalid. And even where the statute is valid, if the decision maker in reaching that decision has violated a provision of the *Charter*, that decision can be set aside.

Statutes and regulations must comply with *Charter*

---

47. In *Dunsmuir v. New Brunswick*, the Supreme Court reconsidered the approach to judicial review and decided that there will be only two (instead of three) standards of review: correctness and reasonableness.

2. THE FAIRNESS OF THE PROCESS

Once it is determined that the decision maker acted under proper authority, the question to be considered is whether that authority was exercised properly. Essentially, the decision maker is required to act fairly when making a decision. What constitutes fair treatment will vary with the circumstances, but the minimum standards of procedural fairness, otherwise known as the **rules of natural justice**, set a basic standard. The first requirement is a fair hearing. The person affected by the decision must be notified that a decision was going to be made and he must be given an opportunity to respond.

Administrator must act fairly

There is no fair hearing without notice that includes the disclosure before the hearing of any evidence or information that will affect the decision so that an effective defence can be prepared. There must also be an opportunity to cross-examine witnesses presenting material evidence, to refute written declarations, and to present supporting evidence and arguments. But again, what constitutes fairness will be dictated by the circumstances. The strict rules of evidence need not be followed, nor is there a general right to be represented by a lawyer (unless provided for in legislation or where criminal charges can result). The decision maker is not required to give reasons for the decision unless required by the supporting statute. The test is reasonableness and in some cases the right to submit a letter for consideration by the decision maker is sufficient to satisfy the requirement of procedural fairness.

Notice must be given and all information must be disclosed

Another requirement of the rules of natural justice is that the decision be made by the persons hearing the evidence. If, for example, a panel of five is hearing a case and one member has to leave because of illness, that person cannot be replaced by another part way through the proceedings because the replacement would not have heard all of the evidence.

Decision must be made by persons hearing all evidence

A third requirement is that the decision makers must be impartial. As shown by Case Summary 3.5, any indication of **bias** will normally be sufficient grounds to have the decision overturned. Even the appearance of bias must be avoided, and any indication of hostility or bad feelings, or the involvement of a relative, friend, or business acquaintance of the decision maker, will taint the decision. Of course, when it can be demonstrated that the decision maker has an interest (especially a financial interest) in the matter being decided, or where he has already made his decision before the hearing, the decision can be challenged. Note, however, that in some types of panels a bias seems to be built in. For example, in labour matters such panels are often composed of three members, one with a union background, one from the business side, and a third (who normally becomes the chair) chosen by the two of them. Thus any appearance of bias is balanced by both sides being represented.

Decision maker must be free of bias

Sometimes these basic procedural standards will be modified by statute, either increasing or decreasing the requirements. Thus a statute will often require a written decision or set out specific procedural requirements and time limits that must be met. When a statute attempts to remove or significantly reduce these basic rights, certain requirements set out in the Canadian *Charter of Rights and Freedoms* may come into play. Section 7 of the *Charter* states that everyone has the right to "life, liberty, and the security of person," and it requires that all decisions depriving a person of them must be made "in accordance with the principles of fundamental justice." The **principles of fundamental justice** include the procedural fairness and natural justice rules set out above, but go further. Even when a proper hearing has taken place with appropriate notice and all other procedural requirements have been met, if the statute offends our basic concepts of justice such as offending the rule of law or requiring the imposition of retroactive penalties, it is likely to offend the principles of fundamental justice and be overturned.

CASE SUMMARY 3.5

Was There a Fair Hearing? *Baker v. Canada (Minister of Citizenship and Immigration)*[48]

A woman was ordered deported. She applied, on humanitarian and compassionate grounds, for an exemption from the rule that an application for permanent residency had to be made from outside of Canada. Her application was supported by letters about the availability of medical care in her home country and the effect of her departure on her Canadian-born children. An immigration officer refused her application by letter, without providing reasons for his decision.

The Supreme Court indicated that the duty of procedural fairness is flexible and variable. The extent of the duty depends on several factors, including the nature of the decision, the relevant legislation, the importance of the decision, and the procedure followed in making it. Here the claimant had to have an opportunity to present evidence and to have it fully and fairly considered. An oral hearing was not required; the chance to provide written documentation was sufficient. Written notes prepared by a junior officer that were provided to the claimant's lawyer were a sufficient explanation of the decision. The claimant was successful, however, as these notes gave rise to a reasonable apprehension of bias. The decision appeared to be based on the fact that the claimant was a single mother with several children and had been diagnosed with a psychiatric illness. This was inappropriate; decisions of this nature should instead be made impartially, based on the evidence. The Court ordered that another hearing be held, in front of a different immigration officer.

DISCUSSION QUESTIONS

Are the standards imposed on administrative tribunals too onerous? Should the courts ever have the power to interfere with the operation of statutory tribunals in the execution of their function? Should such tribunals remain unfettered from the restrictions of rules and procedures found in the court process? What do you think?

 REDUCING RISK 3.5

It is vital that businesspeople remember that challenging government regulators and administrators should be done only as a last resort. As with all litigation, an administrative proceeding can be a frustrating, costly, and often fruitless exercise that should be avoided if at all possible. Further, this is a specialized field in which the costs incurred may be even higher than the expense of litigation. The complainant must deal with officials who have access to government funds and who may be more than willing to spend those funds to save themselves the embarrassment of being found in the wrong.

3. REVIEWING A DECISION

Many statutes establishing administrative boards and panels provide for appeals of their decisions to another level of decision maker. The rights under any such appeal process must be exhausted before asking the courts to exercise their right to review the decision. Remember that judicial review is not an appeal on the

---

48. [1999] 2 S.C.R. 817.

CASE SUMMARY 3.6

Was There a Reasonable Apprehension of Bias? *Ahumada v. Canada (Minister of Citizenship and Immigration)*[49]

Ahumada applied for refugee status in Canada before the Convention Refugee Determination Division (CRDD) of the Immigration and Refugee Board, which dismissed his claim. A member of that panel was on temporary leave from her job with Citizenship and Immigration Canada (CIC) as an enforcement officer. In that job she appeared before the panel on behalf of the CIC on a regular basis. Ahumada challenged the decision, claiming the presence of the enforcement officer on the board gave rise to a reasonable apprehension of bias. The Federal Court, Trial Division, agreed and quashed the CRDD's decision, remitting the matter back to a differently constituted panel.

The Federal Court of Appeal dismissed the government's appeal. The test for bias in these circumstances is "whether a reasonable person, who is informed of the facts, viewing the matter realistically and practically... would think it more likely than not that the tribunal was biased." The Court held that a reasonable apprehension of bias arose because a panel member on temporary leave from her job as an enforcement officer might believe that when she returned to her duties with CIC she would be rewarded or punished, depending on whether her decisions on the panel had favoured the CIC or not. To eliminate this potential bias, CIC enforcement employees appointed to the CRDD must now relinquish their CIC employment.

DISCUSSION QUESTIONS

Is this too much interference in the operation of the Refugee Board? Was the minimal apprehension of bias here sufficient to disqualify her? Should the mere apprehension of bias be enough to justify a court's interference or should proof of actual bias be required? What do you think?

---

merits of the case, but instead refers to the court's right to supervise the process by which the decision was reached. For the courts to exercise their right of judicial review, one of the following must be present:

1. When the validity of the statute or regulation (or provision under it) relied on by the decision maker is in question. This usually relates to a challenge of the statute or regulation based on the *Charter of Rights and Freedoms* or the division of powers under the *Constitution Act, 1867*.

2. When the decision maker has acted outside his authority under the statute or regulation. Sometimes a decision maker will act beyond his jurisdiction in deciding to deal with the matter in the first place, or render a decision or impose a penalty not authorized under the statute.

3. When an **error of law** on the record has been made. The record consists of the decision and any documents associated with the process of reaching that decision. The courts will not tolerate such an error and will generally overturn a decision based on it.

> Judicial review can follow from
>
> • invalid statute or regulation
>
> • action outside prescribed jurisdiction
>
> • error of law on record

---

49. [2001] 3 F.C. 605 (C.A.).

• **failure to follow procedural fairness**

4. When the decision-making process itself has failed to follow the requirement of **procedural fairness** (the rules of natural justice), as discussed above.

• **abuse of discretionary power**

5. When there has been an **abuse of power** (including discretionary power) by the decision maker. Any decision directed by malice, dishonesty, or fraud is reviewable by the courts. A decision must not be made for an improper purpose and the exercise of any discretion must be a genuine exercise. For example, a decision maker in exercising discretionary power cannot merely follow the direction of a superior.

Methods of Judicial Review

Historically, the right to judicial review of the decision of one of these boards or tribunals involved obtaining a prerogative writ from the court. The three main ones are the writs of certiorari, prohibition, and mandamus. The writ of *certiorari* is an order declaring that the decision made by the tribunal is void and of no effect. The writ of prohibition is given before a hearing to the tribunal, ordering it not to proceed. An order of *mandamus* is given to a tribunal that is stalling, ordering it to get on with it and make a decision. In addition the courts always had the right to declare the law in these situations, making a **declaratory judgment** and then providing remedies such as damages or an injunction to enforce that declaration. Today many provinces have consolidated and simplified this procedure by statutory enactment.[50] Whether the person challenging the tribunal proceeds by statute or by writ, it must be kept in mind that any remedy provided by the court is completely discretionary when judicial review is involved. There is a reluctance to exercise this discretion except in situations in which the decisions can be demonstrated to be "incorrect" or "unreasonable."[51]

Governments are naturally reluctant to have the courts interfere with boards that they have empowered to make such decisions. To prevent such judicial review, they will include statutory provisions that are designed to stop the courts from reviewing the board's decision. **Privative clauses** take several different forms, but a typical example is found in the current *Ontario Labour Relations Act*:

Privative clauses

> No decision, order, direction, declaration or ruling of the Board shall be questioned or reviewed in any court, and no order shall be made or process entered, or proceedings taken in any court, whether by way of injunction, declaratory judgment, certiorari, mandamus, prohibition, quo warranto, or otherwise, to question, review, prohibit or restrain the Board or any of its proceedings. S.O. 1995, c. 1, Sch. A, s. 116.[52]

The intent of this kind of provision is obvious, but the courts interpret it to apply only when the Board is acting within its jurisdiction. Thus, the original question as to whether the administrator has jurisdiction is still open to review. In fact, the way the courts have interpreted this type of privative clause varies with circumstances. If the courts wish to review a decision, they will often find a way to do so, despite the presence of a privative clause. And, of course, such privative

---

50. See, for example, *Judicial Review Procedure Act*, R.S.B.C. 1996, c. 241, *Judicial Review Procedure Act*, R.S.O. 1990, c. J-1., Alberta, *Rules of Court*, *supra* note 43, Parts 56.1 and 60, and Saskatchewan, *Queen's Bench Rules*, *supra* note 32, Part 52.

51. As these words are explained in *Dunsmuir v. New Brunswick*, *supra* note 42.

52. S.O. 1995, c. 1, Sch. A, s. 116.

clauses cannot remove rights given under the *Charter of Rights and Freedoms* such as the right that the rules of fundamental justice be followed when a person's right to "life, liberty, and the security of person" is compromised.

It must be remembered that, because of recent Supreme Court of Canada decisions, courts today are generally reluctant to exercise their right of judicial review even when there is no privative clause involved. As stated by the Supreme Court of Canada, "Courts, while exercising their constitutional functions of judicial review, must be sensitive not only to the need to uphold the rule of law, but also to the necessity of avoiding undue interference with the discharge of administrative functions in respect of the matters delegated to administrative bodies by Parliament and legislatures."[53]

Finally, it must be emphasized that anyone adversely affected by the decision of an administrative board or tribunal should think long and hard before attempting to exercise any of the rights outlined above. It is generally very expensive to go through the process of judicial review and often the resulting remedy is hollow. For example, when an order of *certiorari* is obtained, quashing a board's decision, that board will often simply reconvene, making sure that it does everything right, and make the same decision again. The result of this approach is that the whole process of challenging a decision becomes futile. Also, when a government agency is involved, it can usually afford to pay the legal costs involved, and it may prefer to incur those costs rather than face an embarrassing court decision. There is more than a little truth in the old adage that, "You can't fight city hall." For these reasons, even when rights have been clearly violated, it is often more appropriate, especially when dealing with government, to turn to the alternative methods of dispute resolution that are described below.

> Courts resist operation of privative clauses

> Challenging administrative decisions may be futile and costly

> Alternative dispute resolution may provide better resolution

ALTERNATIVES TO COURT ACTION

Businesspeople involved in private disputes are well advised to avoid litigation whenever possible because of the high costs, long delays, and likelihood of dissatisfaction with the results. In this section, we will discuss the various alternatives that can be used instead of—or in conjunction with—the litigation process. Many jurisdictions are now questioning the efficiency of the present civil justice system and are looking for better alternatives. Compulsory mediation, for example, has been incorporated as part of the litigation system in several jurisdictions. (In Ontario, the mandatory mediation component of the case management system appears to have been successful in increasing the resolution rate of disputes before trial and in reducing costs to the parties.[54])

Alternative dispute resolution (ADR) and litigation can work hand in hand, with the threat of one encouraging the parties to take advantage of the other. (The "Collaborative Family Law Process" involves an ADR approach in which litigation cannot even be threatened.[55]) Even if the matter does go to court, negotiation and mediation can be used at any stage in the litigation process, including post-judgment, when the parties wish to avoid an appeal. Note that the comments below with respect to the value of ADR apply equally to processes before administrative tribunals and other government decision-making bodies.

mybuslawlab
www.pearsoned.ca/mybuslawlab

---

53. *Dunsmuir v. New Brunswick, supra* note 47 at 27.

54. See Helen Burnett, "Pilot Project Meets Many of its Goals" *Law Times*, (21 April 2008), www.lawtimesnews.com/200804213999/Headline-News/Pilot-project-meets-many-of-its-goals.

55. See the discussion at www.collaborativelaw.ca/right_choice.php.

WHAT IS ALTERNATIVE DISPUTE RESOLUTION?

Negotiation

Mediation

Arbitration

ADR leaves control in the hands of the parties

Less delay with ADR

Less distraction with ADR

Less expense with ADR

Risk of adverse judgment reduced

Any strategy that is used as a substitute for court action qualifies as a method of ADR, but there are three main approaches: (1) **Negotiation**—when the decision making is left in the hands of the disputing parties to work out for themselves; (2) **Mediation**—when a neutral third party assists the parties in coming to a resolution on their own; and (3) **Arbitration**—when a third party makes a binding decision in the matter under dispute.

Table 3.1 compares these methods with litigation. They are discussed in more detail later in this section.

ADVANTAGES OF ADR VERSUS LITIGATION

There are some significant advantages in choosing an alternative to litigation. One is the retention of control of the matter by the people most affected by it. Rarely does a court judgment compensate the parties for all their time, money, and personal and business resources expended. It is, therefore, vitally important that businesspeople maintain control over the problem-solving process and appreciate the disadvantages of placing the matter in the hands of lawyers and the court when doing so can be avoided.

Most of the delays in litigation occur because of the lengthy pre-trial process and the problems of scheduling court personnel and facilities. When other resolution processes are used, there are fewer procedural and scheduling delays because these matters are controlled by the parties themselves.

An ongoing court battle can be very distracting to a corporation's directors, managers, and employees. Key people may find themselves involved over a considerable period of time in overseeing the process, providing information, or preparing to testify. Much of this can be avoided by looking to an alternative method of resolving these disputes.

The fact that there is faster resolution of the matter with a simplified process involving fewer parties and fewer lawyers but with continued access to expert witnesses if needed contributes to a significant cost saving. Also, indirect considerations, such as the fact that the matter can be kept private, avoiding negative publicity and the disclosure of sensitive information, and the reduced risk of an adverse judgment, make an ADR approach more attractive.

An American case against fast-food chain McDonald's illustrates the risk of insisting on litigation. In that case, a woman was injured when a cup of extremely hot coffee spilled on her as she removed the lid to add sugar. She suffered serious

Table 3.1 Summary and Comparison of Litigation and ADR Methods

	Litigation	Arbitration	Mediation	Negotiation
Control	Low	Low	High	Highest
Delay	Lengthy	Moderate	Brief	Briefest
Cost	High	Moderate	Low	Low
Privacy	Low	Moderate	High	Complete
Flexibility	Low	Moderate	High	Highest
Good Will	Unlikely	Possible	Likely	Ensured
Predictability	High	Reasonable	Low	Low
Appealability	Usually	Moderate	None	None
Visibility	High	Moderate	None	None

burns and spent some time in hospital. She had asked for some small compensation from McDonald's and was rebuffed. When the matter went to trial, the jury awarded more than $2.7 million in punitive damages. (Note that the trial judge later reduced the punitive damages to $480 000; the $160 000 compensatory damages award remained intact.) This could have been avoided had the representatives of McDonald's simply negotiated reasonably with her in the first place.[56]

One of the costs of a protracted conflict is the breakdown in the relationship between the parties. Litigation—in which questioning the opposition's credibility and honesty is routine—is adversarial in nature, often resulting in bitterness and animosity between the parties, thereby poisoning any future business relationship. In contrast, a quick settlement using ADR techniques may actually strengthen the relationship.

Good relationship can be retained with ADR

Another attractive feature of ADR is its flexibility. The parties remain in control, allowing them to accommodate the needs of multiple parties and competing interests. Even cultural differences can be taken into consideration. ADR can even be used to resolve internal disputes within an organization, often in an informal atmosphere with a quick resolution that is satisfactory to all.

ADR provides more flexibility

It should also be noted that when international trade is involved, ADR methods are much more common, especially when dealing with businesses that are in a civil law jurisdiction. Organizations have been established throughout Canada to assist in the conduct of such processes.[57] Legislation enabling the enforcement of arbitrated awards strengthens their usefulness.[58]

ADR can resolve conflicts between businesses operating internationally

DISADVANTAGES OF ADR VERSUS LITIGATION

It must also be emphasized that there are many situations in which ADR should be avoided. The qualities of judicial fairness and impartiality associated with the litigation process are not always present in ADR. The court has no prior interest in the parties or their problems, but it does have extraordinary powers to extract information from the parties that do not exist outside the litigation process. A mediator cannot ensure that all relevant information has been brought forward. In the court system, there are safeguards and rules in place to ensure that each side gets a fair hearing. Because there are few rules or required procedures, ADR may not be able to provide this assurance. The court strives to balance the process so that neither side can take unfair advantage of the other, although this balance may be compromised when only one side can afford extensive legal help. If parties are using ADR, and there is a power imbalance, there is the danger that the stronger party will take advantage of the weaker. In contrast, the discovery process does much to level the playing field where such inequality exists.

ADR cannot ensure full disclosure

ADR does little to overcome a power imbalance

Other advantages of litigation are that the decision will be based on, or set a precedent, and that the decisions will normally be made public and thus be an effective deterrent to similar behaviour. (In fact, concern has been expressed by judges and academics that the case law will not develop because mediation and arbitration are becoming much more popular than litigation, and they are private.[59]) There are also effective tools available for enforcing the judgment as well as a right to appeal the decision.

ADR cannot ensure consistent outcomes

---

56. *Liebeck v. McDonald's Restaurants, P.T.S. Inc.*, 1995 WL 360309 (N.M. Dist. Ct. 1994).

57. For example, the British Columbia International Commercial Arbitration Centre at www.bcicac.com.

58. See, for example, *International Commercial Arbitration Act*, R.S.B.C. 1996, c. 233.

59. See Daryl-Lynn Carlson, "Family Lawyers Flocking to ADR" *Law Times* (11 June 2007), online: http://www.lawtimesnews.com/200706182260/Headline-News/Family-lawyers-flocking-to-ADR.

ADR agreements not enforceable or appealable

It must always be remembered that what is a disadvantage to one party may be the most attractive feature of the chosen process to another. As in all business decisions, sound, properly informed judgment is needed in deciding between ADR and litigation in any given situation.

ADR Mechanisms

www.pearsoned.ca/mybuslawlab

| BC | AB | SK | MB | ON |

Negotiation should be tried first

Upon concluding that ADR is a viable option, the businessperson must then decide which of the various strategies would be most effective in resolving the dispute.

NEGOTIATION

Negotiation should be the first recourse for people who find themselves in a disagreement—too often, it is the last. Negotiation involves the parties or their representatives meeting to discuss the problem to come to an agreement as to how it should be resolved. Both sides must be willing to enter into negotiations, and the goal must be to find a solution even if that means making concessions. Negotiation can be as simple as a phone conversation, an exchange of correspondence, or sitting down together in a private meeting; any meeting with the goal of resolving a dispute qualifies as a negotiation.

Because the process is cooperative and non-binding, either side can withdraw from the negotiations if the other is being unreasonable or intransigent; the parties may then elect to move on to some other means of dealing with the matter. An understanding of the law surrounding the dispute will help the parties recognize the consequences of a failure to settle as well as the relative strength or weakness of the position they are taking.

Negotiation requires cooperation and compromise

Successful negotiation requires an understanding of the issues and a willingness to cooperate and compromise. A competitive approach that tries to best the other party will likely not resolve underlying issues. Similarly, there is danger in being too willing to accommodate demands from the other side. It may not always be possible to reach a win–win solution, but satisfactory results often involve both sides cooperating to minimize their losses. Of course, there is always the danger of being subjected to unethical behaviour or coercion, and since not everyone can be a skilled negotiator, any decision to take this course of action must be made weighing all of the advantages and disadvantages.

Representatives may conduct negotiation

When there is a lack of skill or experience, or when one party is in a more powerful position, it is often wise to negotiate through a representative. While this involves extra costs and a certain amount of loss of control, it has the advantage of overcoming the lack of skill problem and creates a buffer between the parties so that a more powerful personality can be resisted. When lawyers are used, care must be exercised to choose one that is skilled in negotiation and not simply predisposed to litigation. There is a further advantage of the lawyer's better understanding the legal issues involved, and if the matter does proceed to litigation, the lawyer is already involved in the process. It should also be kept in mind that any legal concession, admission, or compromises made during these negotiations when made "**without prejudice**" will not hurt the parties if the negotiations fail and litigation results. And it may also be true that successful negotiation, when there has been concession and compromise between the parties, can actually improve the business relationship.

Relationship may be enhanced

MEDIATION

Mediation also has a long history in resolving disputes. Its use in labour relations has been mandated by statutes for most of the last century, and its use in family disputes is commonplace. Mediation has always played a role in commercial relations but has become much more vital in recent years. The main difference between negotiation and mediation is that mediation involves a neutral third party, hopefully properly trained, who assists the parties to come to an agreement. The **mediator** does not make decisions but facilitates the discussion, making sure that each side has the opportunity to put his side forward, eliciting information, finding areas of possible compromise, identifying potential problems and solutions, and encouraging settlement.

The mediation process can be very informal or it can be carefully structured with rules of procedure and a set timeframe. Often only a few meetings are necessary, with the main objective of the mediator being to find some common ground between the parties. The mediator will meet with both parties together and separately, using a variety of techniques to find some area of agreement and developing compromises between the parties, which can be used to encourage a settlement. It is this degree of flexibility and creativity that makes the process effective in the hands of a skilled mediator. Mediation has been so successful because the persuasiveness, skills, and neutrality of a trained third party are introduced, while control of the problem is retained by each party. While the parties are not bound by any solutions suggested by the mediator, once an agreement is reached it can be enforced just like any other contract.

Successful mediators require considerable specialized training. There are organizations that provide membership and certification, and that set recognized professional standards. The disputing parties will normally choose a mediator who is a member in good standing with such an organization. They may, in fact, choose a mediator from a list provided by the organization.[60]

In several situations, mediation has been mandated by statute—perhaps the highest-profile of these is in collective bargaining. In many jurisdictions, mediation is also compulsory in family disputes and in the litigation process itself.[61]

Disadvantages of Mediation

Mediation depends on cooperation and good will between the disputing parties. When there has been some wrongdoing involved, or blame is to be attached, it is unlikely that proper disclosure will be made, and crucial information may be withheld. Mediators have little power to compel parties to produce evidence and documentation when they are unwilling to do so.

Also, when one of the parties is weaker, mediation may just exacerbate that weakness. This can be a serious problem in family disputes, when the weakness of one of the parties—or his desire to accommodate—leads to an unbalanced result. Also, when one of the parties is suspected of acting in bad faith, mediation is simply inappropriate, because trust is such an important component of the mediation process.

Mediation does work well when highly confidential or sensitive information that should not be disclosed to the public is involved, a speedy resolution is vital, good ongoing relations must be maintained, there is some trust involved, or both parties are desirous of reaching a settlement.

Neutral third party facilitates communication

Mediator does not make decision

Mediator finds common ground

Mediation may be required

Mediation may be inappropriate

Successful mediation requires balance of power and willingness to act in good faith

---

60. One example of such an organization is the ADR Institute of Canada, www.adrcanada.ca/.

61. Ontario has introduced a Mandatory Mediation pilot project, which requires that a mediation session take place after a statement of defence has been filed. See *supra* note 36. In several provinces, including Alberta and British Columbia, parties involved in small claims litigation may be required to attempt mediation before a trial date will be fixed. See *Mediation Rules of the Provincial Court—Civil Division*, Alta. Reg. 271/1997 and *Small Claims Rules*, B.C. Reg. 261/93 Rule 7.2.

> ## ! REDUCING RISK 3.6
>
> There are a variety of circumstances in which mediation might be preferable to and more productive than other means of dispute resolution. One example would be when the benefits of a continuing relationship outweigh the benefits of securing a damage award. In the construction industry, for example, it may appear that a contractor is about to fail to complete the building on time or on budget, leading to a dispute with the owner. Rather than expending time, energy, and expense on litigation, with the likelihood of further delay of the project, it may be more reasonable to call in a mediator who has knowledge of the construction industry. This mediator could help the parties arrive at an understanding of the problems each has faced, such as unexpected illness, increased costs, or the unavailability of materials. This could lead to a solution acceptable to both sides, resulting in the completion of the building and the maintenance of the relationship. In fact, in the construction sector, it is reported that millions of dollars are saved annually in jurisdictions where the first recourse in the event of problems is to mediate rather than to litigate.

ARBITRATION

mybuslawlab

www.pearsoned.ca/mybuslawlab

BC AB SK MB **ON**

Arbitration involves third-party decision maker

The third major category of alternative dispute resolution involves surrendering the decision making to a third party. In most cases, arbitration is voluntary, but in some situations, such as labour relations, the parties are required by statute to agree to some arbitration mechanism as part of the collective agreement process.[62] In some instances, arbitration is agreed upon before any dispute has arisen by including, in the original contract, a requirement to arbitrate. Often, however, the parties agree to arbitrate after a dispute arises. Arbitration can be very effective when external disputes arise with creditors, suppliers, or customers, and even internally with employees and shareholders or between departments. Arbitration is commonly used in resolving disputes arising from international trade agreements.[63]

Arbitrators are chosen by parties

Arbitrators may be experts in the field

Typically, the **arbitrator** is chosen from a pool of trained and certified professionals, often with expertise in the subject matter of the dispute. Organizations of professional arbitrators have been established, and the members offer their services like any other professionals.[64] These organizations not only provide training and certification, but also set professional and ethical standards requiring that their members be properly trained, avoid conflicts of interest, be free of bias, and keep in strict confidence all information they obtain. In more formal instances, retired judges are hired to hold what is essentially a private trial, rendering a decision much like a court but without the attendant publicity or delay.

Procedure must be fair

Parties can stipulate in their contract the requirement for arbitration, how the arbitrator is to be chosen and, if they want, that provincial arbitration legislation apply to the process. The specific process to be followed may be left to the arbitrator or, alternatively, the procedure may be set out in the agreement,[65] but such procedures, whether determined by the parties or by the arbitrator, must be fair.

---

62. See, for example, s. 48 of Ontario's *Labour Relations Act, 1995,* S.O. 1995, c. 1, Sch. A.

63. See the discussion regarding International Commercial Arbitration, at www.bcicac.com/bcicac_ica.php.

64. One such organization is the ADR Institute of Canada, *supra* note 53.

65. The ADR Institute of Canada has published National Arbitration Rules, which the parties can agree to use to resolve their contractual disputes, www.adrcanada.ca/rules/arbitration.cfm.

Usually, before an arbitration hearing takes place, there is a requirement that information relating to the matter be disclosed by both sides. At the hearing itself, lawyers or other representatives of the parties usually examine witnesses, present documents, make arguments and summarize their cases. Formal rules of evidence need not be adhered to, nor is the arbitrator required to follow precedent in reaching the decision. When the process is mandated by statute, as in labour disputes, the requirements are much more stringent and more closely resemble an actual court hearing. An arbitrator's decision is binding on the parties and is generally not appealable, but it is important to remember that the courts still have the right to supervise and review the decision-making process as discussed above under the heading "Dealing with Regulatory Bodies."

Decision cannot be appealed but process may be reviewed by court

The unique feature of arbitration is that a third party makes the decision. To be effective, it is vital that the parties be required to honour that decision. Most jurisdictions provide that the decisions reached by arbitrators are binding and enforceable.[66] As a result, arbitration is usually an effective process.

Third party makes a decision that is binding

Arbitration is, however, still essentially adversarial in nature. In this sense, it is like litigation, with the attendant danger that bitterness and hard feelings may be aggravated. Arbitration is more costly than other forms of ADR, because it is more formal and involves more people, but it is still much less expensive than the litigation process.

Ideally, arbitration should be voluntary, but clauses requiring arbitration are finding their way into standard form contracts at an alarming rate. These contracts often cover consumer transactions, with the consumer unaware that he has surrendered the right to a court hearing until the dispute arises. Because the decision is binding and non-appealable, the disgruntled party may challenge the validity of the arbitration clause in court, compounding an already complex resolution procedure.

Arbitration may look much like litigation, but it is still private and still usually within the control of the parties. When expertise is important, an arbitrator with that expertise can be chosen. Arbitration is faster, less costly, and more private than litigation, but it also has disadvantages. Arbitration is still more costly and likely more time consuming than other forms of ADR. Also, there may be little certainty or predictability, as precedents are usually not binding and animosity between the parties may actually increase as a result of this adversarial process.

Arbitration is private

It should be noted that these ADR mechanisms are not mutually exclusive. Sometimes the tools of mediation and arbitration will be brought together when the outsider starts out as a mediator and, if it grows clear that the parties cannot reach a settlement even with the mediator's help, she becomes an arbitrator, making a decision that is binding on both parties. Of course, such a change of roles must be agreed upon by the parties.

Mediator may become an arbitrator

Finally, mediation and arbitration are becoming more common in resolving online disputes.[67] There are many advantages to using ADR in the context of e-commerce. Many internet transactions involve relatively small amounts of money, so litigation is not practical. Using ADR for online disputes overcomes geographical issues, reduces costs, and enables a quick resolution of disputes. Confidentiality is often important to online businesses, which do not want publicity about problems with their sites or security systems.

[66.] See, for example, *Arbitration Act*, 1991, S.O. 1991, c. 17, ss. 37, 50.

[67.] See Derek Hill, "ADR Picking up in Internet and E-commerce Law" *Law Times* (1 August 2008), www.lawtimesnews.com/200808014192/Headline-News/ADR-picking-up-in-internet-and-e-commerce-law.

Online dispute resolution (ODR) programs have been developed to help resolve disputes between parties.[68] Such programs will continue to improve and become more cost effective. Over time, this may enable businesses to impose mandatory ODR systems that would be effective and acceptable to consumers.[69]

REDUCING RISK 3.7

ADR services are now being offered online. Such services can be very helpful in attempting to mediate between corporations and their customers, when information, services, or products do not meet expectations, or when customers have not fulfilled their obligations. In addition, such intermediaries may serve to set standards, monitor compliance, and warn potential customers when problems exist. As there is little regulation controlling ADR generally, it is likely that there will be even less in the electronic environment. Businesspeople should ensure that the services are being offered by qualified professionals and be aware that they may have little recourse if things go wrong.

[68.] Glenn Kauth, "ODR in Canada Getting a Boost" *Law Times* (8 December 2008), www.lawtimes-news.com/200812084400/Headline-News/ODR-in-Canada-getting-a-boost.

[69.] See Gary Oakes, "Your Virtual Day in Court: How Online Dispute Resolution Is Transforming the Practice of ADR" *Lawyers Weekly* (16 January 2009), www.lawyersweekly.ca/index .php?section=article&articleid=737. This article indicates that ODR is "the next step to traditional ADR" and that "it's not just for commercial transactions." It can be used for small claims litigation, divorce actions, and even "in the context of world peace or interstate conflict"!

SUMMARY

The courts

- Procedural rules govern structure and function, which may vary with jurisdiction
- Open to the public, with some exceptions
- Both criminal and civil functions at trial and appellate levels
- All but lower-level provincial court judges are appointed by federal government

Provincial courts

- Handle less serious criminal offences, civil matters under a set amount, custody and maintenance in family divisions, youth offenders
- Provinces have recently created new specialized courts to deal with societal changes and problems

Superior courts

- Handle serious criminal offences, civil matters with unlimited monetary jurisdiction, divorce

Appellate courts

- Deal with appeals of law from trial courts, usually have three judges, do not rehear the facts, usually hold final hearing for most criminal and civil matters

Federal courts

- Tax Court hears cases involving federal tax matters
- Federal Court hears disputes within federal jurisdiction and appeals from some administrative tribunals
- Federal Court of Appeal hears appeals from Federal Court, Tax Court, and some administrative tribunals

Supreme Court of Canada

- Highest-level appeal court
- Deals primarily with Constitutional and *Charter* matters, as well as cases of national importance

Process of civil litigation

- Limitation periods
  - Set by statute
- Pre-trial
  - Plaintiff files writ of summons (if required) and statement of claim
  - Defendant responds with appearance (if required) and statement of defence
  - Discovery of documents and questioning of parties by opposing counsel
  - Payment into court or offer of settlement to encourage reasonable demands and offers
  - Purpose—to bring information to light and encourage settlement
- Trial
  - Examination of witnesses and presentation of evidence
  - Judgment
  - Jury decides questions of fact
  - Judge decides questions of law
  - Loser usually pays some legal costs

- Enforcement
  - Examination in aid of execution
  - Seizure of property
  - Garnishment
- Remedies
  - Damages—general, special, punitive
  - Accounting, injunction, specific performance, declaration

Dealing with regulatory bodies

- Decisions of government bureaucrats are reviewable by the courts

Administrative tribunals

- Enforce government policies and resolve disputes
- Act within the jurisdiction granted by the enabling statute
- Comply with the *Charter of Rights and Freedoms*
- Maintain a minimum standard of procedural fairness
- Rules of natural justice require
  - Fair hearing with adequate notice
  - Decision made by person who heard the evidence
  - Absence of bias in process
- Role of the courts
  - Courts can review administrative decisions when the administrative tribunal did not have jurisdiction or did not follow the rules of natural justice
  - Can issue prerogative writs including *certiorari*, *mandamus*, and prohibition
  - Can make a declaration or order an injunction
  - Privative clauses are statutory provisions that attempt to prevent judicial review, which sometimes are resisted by the courts

Alternative dispute resolution (ADR)

- Recent trend to avoid costs and delays associated with litigation
- Advantages
  - Control, timeliness, productivity, cost, privacy, good will, flexibility
- Disadvantages
  - Unpredictable, no precedents set, cannot deal with complex legal problems
  - Must be voluntary, must have a balance of power between the parties
  - Parties must cooperate to ensure agreement and resolution
- Methods
  - Negotiation—direct discussion between parties
  - Mediation—neutral third party facilitates discussion
  - Arbitration—neutral expert makes a binding decision

QUESTIONS

1. Describe the court hierarchy in Canada, including provincial and federal courts.

2. Distinguish between questions of law and questions of fact, and explain why this distinction is significant.

3. Who appoints provincial superior court judges? Provincial court judges?

4. How would the expiration of a limitation period affect the rights of parties to litigate a matter in dispute?

5. What are the pleadings used to commence an action in the superior trial court in your jurisdiction?

6. How does the discovery process take place, and what is its significance in civil litigation?

7. Explain how an offer to settle can affect the judgment award made by the court to the plaintiff.

8. Describe the recent initiatives taken in your jurisdiction to "speed up" the litigation process.

9. Explain the trial process.

10. Compare party–party costs with solicitor–client costs. To whom are these costs generally awarded?

11. Distinguish among the various remedies available to a successful plaintiff in a civil action.

12. Explain the role of the examination in aid of execution in enforcing those remedies (from Question 11), and indicate what methods are available to enforce a judgment against a debtor who is trying to avoid payment.

13. Explain the value of an injunction as a pre-judgment remedy. Discuss other pre-judgment remedies available to aid in the collection of debt.

14. Under what circumstances will the courts review a decision made by a government bureaucrat or administrative tribunal?

15. What must be examined to determine whether a decision maker has acted within her authority?

16. What are the requirements for a fair hearing and what is necessary to satisfy the rules of natural justice?

17. Distinguish between *certiorari*, prohibition, *mandamus*, and a declaration.

18. What is a privative clause? How do courts usually react to them?

19. List and describe the principal advantages of alternative dispute resolution.

20. Distinguish between negotiation, mediation, and arbitration, and discuss the advantages and disadvantages of each of them.

CASES AND DISCUSSION QUESTIONS

1. *T. v. T.*(2003), 63 O.R. (3d) 188 (Ont. S.C.J.).

A husband and wife were involved in matrimonial litigation. The husband asked the Court for an order that he and his wife be identified only by initials, and that the court documents be sealed. The husband said that the wife's allegations were malicious and false, and that embarrassing sexual matters were at issue. He also argued that his wife and children from his second and third marriages would be hurt by publication.

Should there be an open trial, or should the court documents remain sealed? Explain your reasoning. This is one aspect of the wider question as to whether trials and court procedures generally ought to be open to the public. Consider the arguments for giving the public access to such personal and private matters and explain your conclusions.

2. *Royal Trust Corp. of Canada v. Dunn*(1991), 6 O.R. (3d) 468 (Gen. Div.).

Royal Trust lent just over $200 000 to the four defendants, taking security in the form of a mortgage for the loan. They defaulted on the loan, and an action was commenced against them. The lawyers acting for Royal Trust served a copy of the statement of claim on the lawyer who had acted for the defendants when they had purchased the property, and that lawyer, in turn, forwarded it to the one defendant he had dealt with. None of the defendants responded to the statement of claim, and so Royal Trust obtained a default judgment against them.

In this action, the defendants are applying to have the judgment set aside. Explain the nature of their complaint and the likely outcome. In your answer consider the role of fairness in the administration of justice and whether practical requirements should be permitted to overrule this requirement of procedural fairness within court processes or when dealing with government tribunals.

3. *Canada (Attorney General) v. Lameman*, [2008] 1 S.C.R. 372.

In 1877, the Papaschase Indians were allotted a reserve in what is now southeast Edmonton. In 1886, most of the Band members surrendered their treaty rights and rights connected with the Reserve in exchange for cash. In 1889, the remaining members of the Band agreed to surrender their rights in the Reserve on the condition that the proceeds from the sale of the Reserve be held in trust and be paid to Band members and their descendants. In 2001, the plaintiffs, claiming to be descendants of the Papaschase Band members, commenced an action against the federal government, for breach of fiduciary duty, fraudulent and malicious behaviour, and breach of treaty. The Federal Government applied for summary dismissal of the claims. The lower court allowed the application, on the grounds that most of the claims did not show a genuine issue for trial, that the plaintiffs did not have standing to bring the action, and that the claims (except for the claim for an accounting of any proceeds of the sale of the Reserve that the Federal Government still had in its possession) were barred by the provisions of the *Alberta Limitation of Actions Act*.

While the Court of Appeal overruled the lower court, the Supreme Court restored its order. The Court ruled that even if the claims involved triable issues, and the Plaintiffs had standing, the limitation legislation applied and the claims were therefore barred. In the 1970s, an Edmonton lawyer had made inquiries of the Federal Government with respect to making a land claim on behalf of the descendants of the Papaschase Band members. A student had completed a master's thesis in 1979 that uncovered most of the facts forming the basis of the claims in the action. This meant that the causes of action became discoverable to the plaintiffs in the 1970s and that the claims were therefore statue-barred, with the exception of an accounting, a continuing action not caught by the legislation. The statute required that an action be brought within six years of the cause of action arising or being discovered.

What is the policy behind the existence of limitation periods? Is it fair that such a significant claim be struck out because anyone exercising due diligence could have uncovered the relevant facts in the 1970s?

4. *Fujitsu Consulting (Canada) Inc. v. Themis Program Management & Consulting Limited* (2007), 76 B.C.L.R. (4th) 160 (B.C.S.C.).

The defendants entered into a contract with the Government of Ontario, regarding the development of software. The defendants then entered into a subcontract with the plaintiff, requiring the plaintiff to provide staff and perform portions of the work. The Government terminated the contract, and the defendants terminated the subcontract. The plaintiff claimed payment for all of the work it had performed pursuant to the subcontract. The Government sued the defendant for breach of the contract, in Ontario. The defendant was going to add the plaintiff as a party to this litigation, which was eventually settled. All of the work was done in Ontario and most of the witnesses were in Ontario. The defendant claimed that the most appropriate place for a trial was Ontario.

Should the Court rule that the litigation involving the subcontract take place in Ontario or British Columbia? Explain your reasoning. What if the subcontract contained a clause indicating that it was to be governed and construed in accordance with the laws of British Columbia, and that the sole venue for legal actions related to the subcontract was the Supreme Court of British Columbia?

5. *Fidler v. Sun Life Assurance Co. of Canada*, [2006] 2 S.C.R. 3.

Fidler was an insured under a group policy that included long-term disability benefits. Due to illness, she could no longer perform her job. She began receiving benefits in January 1991. Under the terms of the policy, she was entitled to benefits for a maximum period of two years, after which payments would continue only if her condition was that she could not be employed. In May 1997 the insurer informed Fidler that her benefits would be terminated, on the basis of its conclusion (based on investigator reports) that she was capable of performing light or sedentary work. Opinions from Fidler's doctor and an independent physician stated that she couldn't do any work. One week before trial, the insurer offered to reinstate Fidler's benefits and to pay all arrears with interest. As a result, the only issue was Fidler's claim for damages.

Prior to this case, damages had never been awarded for metal distress for breach of contract. Should Fidler be entitled for damages for mental distress for the insurer's breach of the insurance policy? Should Fidler receive punitive damages? Should an insurer be liable for punitive damages whenever it incorrectly denies a claim? Explain your reasons.

6. *Parlee v. College of Psychologists of New Brunswick*, [2004] N.B.J. No. 191 (N.B.C.A.).

The College of Psychologists recommended revoking the licence of Cindy Parlee in 2002 on the basis of her professional misconduct. The primary complaint was that when working for the correctional services of the province she had failed to report and had in fact encouraged a colleague to engage in an inappropriate sexual relationship with an inmate. The warden had logged a complaint and the complaint committee of the College served proper notice and started to hear the complaint on 21 February 2002. But the hearing was not completed that day and was not resumed until 25 November 2002. The statute required that a committee of three members hear the complaint, but at the time of resumption of the hearing in November one of the members was incapable of participating. To avoid the costs of starting over, all parties including Ms. Parlee agreed in writing to allow the matter to proceed with only the remaining two members of the complaint committee hearing the rest of the evidence and arguments and making the decision. Ms. Parlee specifically agreed that she would submit to the jurisdiction of the two-member panel "as if the Committee met the quorum requirements of the Act and the Bylaws" and also that the lack of quorum "shall not form the basis of, or be included as a ground of appeal or judicial review of the decision of the Discipline Committee."

The committee found her guilty of professional misconduct and recommended that her licence be revoked and she never again be reinstated as a member of the college. Explain what recourse is available to Cindy Parlee, what arguments she might raise against the decision, and the likely outcome including what remedy she might expect if she is successful. Consider also whether requiring strict compliance with these rules of procedural fairness makes the process more or less efficient, especially as in this case where all the parties agreed to the deviation and to be bound by the decision despite the change.

7. *Bell Mobility Inc. v. MTS Allstream Inc.* (2008), 229 Man. R. (2d) 97 (Q.B.).
Bell entered into a mobility alliance agreement (MMA) with MTS. MTS issued a notice of arbitration with respect to a dispute between the parties, after it had filed a statement of claim and a notice of motion for interim and interlocutory injunctive relief. Bell claims that this was an election by MTS to have the dispute adjudicated in a court action and not by way of arbitration. Bell therefore asked the Court to strike out the notice of arbitration. The relevant portions of the MAA read, in part, as follows:

> 17.1 Subject to the exceptions listed in section 17.3 and to section 17.4, any claim, controversy, or dispute . . . that arises between the Parties with respect to this Agreement . . . must be subject to attempts to resolve the Dispute according to this Section and submission to arbitration is a condition precedent to the bringing of any court action. . . .]]

> 17.3 If the Presidents are unable to resolve the Dispute . . . it shall be resolved by arbitration . . . either Party may, by sending a written notice of arbitration . . . begin the arbitration process. . . . .The arbitrator's decision and award will be final and binding . . . The following matters shall be excluded from arbitration: (c) any claim for interim or interlocutory injunctive relief under Section 17.4. . . .]]

> 17.4 Notwithstanding the foregoing, the Parties agree... that injunctive relief may be the only effective relief for a breach of certain covenants. . . . Each Party agrees that the other Party will be entitled to seek . . . injunctive relief on an interim and interlocutory basis in any court . . . without first complying with the other dispute resolution procedures. . . .]]

Do these provisions mandate that all disputes between the parties must be resolved by arbitration? Do they instead provide the parties with an election to proceed by arbitration or by litigation? Do they require the parties to resolve all disputes through arbitration, except in limited cases, including interim and interlocutory relief? Should the court strike out the notice of arbitration or should it determine the interim and interlocutory claim, leaving the final determination of the dispute to arbitration? Explain your reasoning; note that a fundamental principle of contract interpretation is that the courts are to give effect to the intentions of the parties.

Chapter 4

Intentional Torts and Torts Impacting Business

CHAPTER OBJECTIVES

1. Describe the role of tort law
2. Distinguish torts from crimes and breaches of contract
3. Identify remedies awarded to redress torts
4. Explain vicarious liability indicating when it may be imposed
5. Distinguish the torts of assault, battery, and trespass to land, listing the relevant defences
6. Describe three torts that deal with wrongful interference with goods (chattels)
7. Contrast the torts of false imprisonment and malicious prosecution
8. Differentiate private from public nuisance
9. Compare defamation with the tort of injurious falsehood
10. Describe the following torts:
    - Inducing breach of contract
    - Interference with economic relations
    - Conspiracy to injure
    - Intimidation
    - Deceit (fraudulent misrepresentation)
    - Passing off
    - Misuse of confidential information
    - Invasion of privacy
11. Identify torts frequently committed in the online environment

The law of torts involves private disputes decided in the civil courts. When one person harms another, either intentionally or carelessly, a tort has likely been committed. An action can be brought seeking compensation for injuries suffered, from the person who committed the wrong. In this chapter, we examine the nature of tort law and discuss the distinctions between intentional torts and negligence, focusing primarily on intentional torts and their business counterparts. We also examine the defences that the person being sued may raise, and the conditions that must be met for the plaintiff to be awarded compensation.

A tort is a civil or social wrong

Tort law compensates victims and deters wrongful conduct

Crimes are wrongs that affect society as a whole

Torts differ from actions based on breach of contract

THE NATURE OF TORTS

When people engage in commercial activities, conflicting interests or simple interactions can sometimes lead to the commission of torts. It is difficult to find a wholly satisfactory definition for torts because of the different kinds of conduct that may be considered tortious. Some general principles, however, do apply. A **tort** is committed when one person causes injury to another, harming his or her person, property, or reputation. The right to sue for redress arises when the injurious conduct falls below a minimum social standard. In other words, a tort is a social or civil wrong that gives rise to the right to sue and to seek one of several remedies. Such remedies may include an injunction or even punitive damages but normally will be limited to a monetary award of damages intended to compensate the victim for the loss suffered. The role of tort law is multi-faceted. It aims to compensate victims, requiring the party at fault to bear the burden of the loss suffered. In so doing, it deters the occurrence of such wrongful behaviour and educates society by "making someone pay." Further, it serves a psychological function, in providing some appeasement to those injured by wrongful conduct.

The approach used in this text is to look at different categories of torts because different rules sometimes apply. Although this is convenient, students need to appreciate that the courts may find that a tort has been committed that does not conveniently fit into the identified categories. Tort law is continually evolving, with the courts declaring new torts to exist as the need arises. (See the discussion at the end of this chapter concerning invasion of privacy and spoliation). From a business perspective, it might be better to approach tort law as a body of law that aims to provide remedies wherever wrongful conduct is involved.

Crimes must be distinguished from torts. Harmful conduct that is so serious that it poses a threat to society generally is said to be criminal in nature. The prosecution for such acts is carried by the state in a criminal court where the goal is to punish the wrongdoer, not to compensate the victim. A tort is considered a private matter where the victim of the injurious conduct sues the person responsible for the injury. With many crimes, the victim has the right to sue for tort, even if the prosecution results in an acquittal. Thus, wrongful conduct is often both a crime and a tort. Most of the torts discussed in this chapter have a *Criminal Code* counterpart. For example, a driver racing, and thereby causing an accident resulting in injury, could be charged with criminal negligence and face a fine and imprisonment. But whether convicted or acquitted of the criminal charges, that driver could also be sued in a civil action for the tort of negligence and if found liable would be ordered to compensate the injured parties. It is much easier to successfully sue for tort, because the standard of proof is based on a "balance of probabilities" test. In a criminal action, the standard is "beyond a reasonable doubt," a much higher standard than required in a civil action. (See discussion under the heading "The Courts" in Chapter 3.)

A tort must also be distinguished from a **breach of contract**. An act that breaches a contract may not be inherently wrong, but the contractual relationship makes the violation of its terms unacceptable. A tort, on the other hand, is inherently wrongful conduct that is either deliberate or falls below a minimal social standard. When the victim sues, the court examines who was at fault, who caused the injury, and determines who should bear the loss for the injuries suffered. Ultimately, the court assesses the amount that should be paid to the victim.

There are two major categories of tortious activity: *intentional* (or deliberate) acts and *unintentional* (or careless) negligent acts. Businesspeople can find themselves liable for both intentional and unintentional torts, but the latter is by far the most important area of tort law for businesspeople and professionals to understand. One important difference between deliberate torts and negligence is in the remedies that the courts are willing to grant to the injured party. When the interference has been intentional, the courts may be persuaded to grant punitive damages in addition to the more common general and special damages. **General damages** compensate for estimated future losses, including both future pecuniary losses (such as loss of earning capacity) and non-pecuniary losses (such as pain and suffering). **Special damages** are awarded to cover actual expenses and calculable pretrial losses. **Punitive** or **exemplary damages** are designed to punish the wrongdoer and do not relate to the injury suffered. To avoid excessive awards, the Supreme Court of Canada has placed an upper limit of approximately $325 000 on damages that can be awarded to compensate for pain and suffering and loss of enjoyment of life.[1] Occasionally, the court will also order the return of property or grant an injunction to stop some offending activity.

Torts may involve intentional or inadvertent conduct

It is important for businesspeople to keep the concept of **vicarious liability** in mind while studying tort law. An employer can be held liable for the tortious act an employee commits while at work. This liability is limited to torts committed while carrying out employment duties. The employer will not be vicariously liable when the employee is off doing his or her own thing, even if done during working hours instead of doing the employer's business. The importance of vicarious liability in the business world cannot be overemphasized. A detailed examination of the master/servant (employer/employee) relationship and vicarious liability can be found in Chapter 10. Several provinces have imposed vicarious liability by statute on the owners of motor vehicles, making them liable for damage and injury caused by the people they allow to drive their cars. Refer to the MyBusLawLab for provincial variations.

Employer may be vicariously liable for employees' torts

REDUCING RISK 4.1

Perhaps the most valuable thing to gain from the study of tort law—or for that matter any of the rules discussed in this text—is the habit of mind that anticipates and avoids legal problems. This is called *risk avoidance* or *risk management*. Businesspeople have a responsibility to manage their legal affairs in the same way they manage the production, marketing, and distribution of their products. Too often, managers wait for something to go wrong, then put the matter into the hands of a lawyer and wait for the results of a lawsuit. Managing risk responsibly means avoiding the problem in the first place. As you learn about torts and other aspects of the law, you might observe the conditions and practices that pose a danger to the public, customers, suppliers, or employees, and decide how they should be corrected. This might be as simple as checking the creditworthiness of customers, keeping a record of emails, putting a warning sticker on a plate-glass window, or lighting a dark stairwell. Businesspeople should adopt an attitude of risk avoidance and promote the adoption of such an attitude throughout their organization. Holding risk evaluation meetings, ensuring adequate insurance coverage, developing policies, and providing incentives that encourage risk avoidance will have the effect of reducing exposure to costly and time-consuming legal actions.

---

[1] The Supreme Court of Canada established a cap of $100 000 for non-pecuniary damages for personal-injury actions in the 1978 "trilogy": *Andrews v. Grand & Toy Alberta Ltd.*, [1978] 2 S.C.R. 229; *Thornton v. Prince George School District No. 57*, [1978] 2 S.C.R. 267; *Arnold v. Teno*, [1978] 2 S.C.R. 287. Due to inflation, the amount is approximately $325 000 (as of 2009).

INTENTIONAL TORTS

Intentional physical interference

The following discussion is concerned with torts where the conduct involved was intended or deliberate, as opposed to the following chapter's discussion of negligence, where the conduct is inadvertent. The term *intentional* does not mean that the wrongdoer intended to do harm, only that the conduct itself was wilful as opposed to inadvertent. As with all forms of actionable torts, fault on the part of the wrongdoer must be demonstrated, but when we examine intentional torts as discussed here, that fault is embodied in the wilful act of the wrongdoer.

Trespass to Person: Assault and Battery

Actual contact—battery

Fear of contact—assault

Assault and battery (or **trespass to person**) involve the intentional physical interference with another person. These torts are a concern to businesses whose employees serve the public. Conduct that makes a person think he is about to be struck is an **assault**. If someone fakes a punch, points a gun, or picks up a stone to threaten another person, an assault has been committed. A **battery** takes place when someone intentionally makes unwanted physical contact with another person. Since battery almost invariably involves an assault, the term *assault* is often used to refer to both assault and battery. Assault and battery are actionable, even where there is no injury; "the least touching of another in anger is battery."[2] The purpose of the tort of trespass to the person is to recognize the right of each person to control his body and who touches it. Damages are awarded when this right is violated.

The test to determine whether an assault has taken place is to look to the victim and ask whether she was fearful or anticipated unwanted physical contact. If the defendant's conduct would cause a reasonable person to feel threatened with imminent harm or even simply unwanted contact, it constitutes an assault. In *Warman v. Grosvenor*,[3] for example, the defendant waged a "campaign of terror" against the plaintiff by posting threatening and intimidating messages on the internet and in personal emails. By virtue of their repetitiveness, their detail regarding the plaintiff's whereabouts, and their level of malevolence, the postings were more than empty threats and insults. Damages of $50 000 were awarded for assault and defamation.

Verbal threats (face-to-face, at a distance, or online) may constitute assault

Intent to harm not required

The anticipated contact might be anything from a physical blow, to unwanted medical treatment, to a kiss. The motive or goodwill of the person attacking is not relevant. The words are taken into consideration as well as the gestures and actions. The action of a person walking toward another can be an assault when accompanied by threatening words, whereas words such as "How nice to see you again" remove the threat.

CASE SUMMARY 4.1

Bouncers Beware! *Tardif v. Wiebe*[4]

There is no dispute that Tardif was drunk when he was refused further service and was asked to leave the hotel on the Friday night in question. He was not usually a fighter but did get obnoxious and rude when he was in an intoxicated state. In the process of leaving

---

2. *Cole v. Turner* (1704), 6 Mod. 149, 87 E.R. 907.

3. [2008] O.J. NO. 4462 (SUP. CT J.).

4. [1996] B.C.J. No. 2254

the bar with his girlfriend, he got into an altercation with a woman who made some offensive remarks about the two of them. This scuffle resulted in the hotel bouncers, Wiebe and Poburn, being called to intervene and eject Tardif. On the landing above the outside steps of the hotel, Poburn held Tardif while Wiebe struck him twice. As a result of the second blow, Tardif was thrown off the landing and fell down four steps onto the concrete sidewalk below causing serious injuries. Tardif has no recollection of this, but Poburn testified that his head "cracked like an egg."

While Poburn was a professional bouncer, Wiebe was untrained, and both were considerably larger than Tardif, who posed no threat to them. Excessive and unjustified force was clearly used against Tardif.

The bouncers may have had a right to eject Tardif with force if he had been refusing to leave, but that was not the case here. And even if it were, it would not have justified the bouncers using such forceful blows when Tardif was already outside the hotel. The Judge found that Tardif had done nothing to justify the bouncers' actions.

Because of considerable brain and nerve damage and other injuries, Mr. Tardif was unable to return to work. The award against the hotel and bouncers was more than $1 million. Because no malice was involved, there was no award for punitive damages.

SMALL BUSINESS PERSPECTIVE

This, and numerous cases like it, demonstrates the potential liability faced by businesses dealing with the public. Due to vicarious liability, investing in training one's staff will not totally eliminate the risk. The fact that the business has instructed employees not to use force does not operate as a defence. Do these principles in law expose the business to too much liability? Should employers always be liable for their employees' wrongdoing in these situations? Should bouncers face personal liability if they are just "doing their job"? What do you think?

DEFENCES

There are several defences that can be raised against an assault or battery claim. Normally, doctors escape liability for their actions when operating on or otherwise treating patients through the principle of consent. Essentially, a person who expressly or implicitly consents to conduct that would otherwise constitute an assault or battery loses the right to sue. This is the reason why injured boxers cannot sue their opponents.

Consent is a defence

It is important to remember that the level of interference cannot exceed the consent. Excessive violence in a sporting activity will constitute the tort of battery despite the consent. Mike Tyson faced liability after biting his opponent during a boxing match. Excessive violence may also be a crime, as Todd Bertuzzi discovered when he was charged and subsequently convicted of assault causing bodily harm for a vicious hit to the head of Steve Moore in an NHL game in 2004.[5] Also, the consent must be *informed consent;* people must know what they are consenting to.[6]

---

5. *R. v. Bertuzzi*, [2004] B.C.J. No. 2692, (B.C.P.C.). Note: a civil action has also been commenced by Moore. See: *Moore v. Bertuzzi*, [2008] O.J. No. 347, (Ont. S.C.J.) dealing with an interim application to add a claim against the owners of the Vancouver Canucks.

6. See *Halushka v. University of Saskatchewan et al.*, [1965] S.J. No. 208 (C.A.)where medical researchers were unable to establish that the consent was an informed one. The student had agreed to participate in a drug experiment in exchange for $50 but was not fully informed of the risk. His heart stopped when the drug was administered and he had to undergo emergency surgery to restart it. Halushka was paid $50 four days later when he regained consciousness. The battery action succeeded.

People may refuse or give only limited consent to medical treatment. In *Malette v. Shulman,*[7] the physician administered a blood transfusion, which likely saved the patient's life, and yet the plaintiff successfully sued for battery. The plaintiff had a card in her purse stating that, as a Jehovah's Witness, she refused consent to receive any blood products. If this refusal of consent is made clear to a doctor and the refused treatment is administered anyway, the doctor can be sued for the battery committed.[8] This is true even where the patient would die without the treatment, putting physicians in an unsettling position.[9]

Note that **consent** to conduct that would otherwise constitute a tort, when informed and voluntary, operates as an effective defence to any of the torts discussed in this chapter or the next.

Self-defence can also be raised to counteract an assault and battery accusation. The law entitles people who are being attacked to use necessary force to defend themselves. The test is reasonable force. An attack is not a licence to respond with unrestrained violence. Of course, the experience of the person being attacked will be taken into account in determining what is reasonable. Thus, a boxer is held to a higher standard than an ordinary person not accustomed to such violence. When a bouncer ejects an unruly patron from a bar, the same principle applies. If a patron refuses to leave when asked, he becomes a trespasser, and reasonable force can be used to eject him. But as seen in Case Summary 4.1, use of excessive force may result in liability on the part of the occupier of the premises.

Trespass to Land

Trespass to land involves going onto another person's property without having either the lawful right or the owner's permission to do so. Such a trespass is an actionable wrong, even when no damage or injury takes place, and even if the intruder does not know she is trespassing. Ignorance of the location of the property line is no excuse. Only if the intruder had no control of where she was would there be a defence. Thus, if she were struck by a car and thrown on the property, there would be no trespass. But if she were running away and went on the property to escape a threat, it is still a trespass and she would be responsible for any damage caused. A mere "bruising of the grass" is trespass; but if only nominal damages are likely, why sue? In some provinces, legislation has been passed enabling occupiers to have trespassers apprehended and fined.[10]

People acting in an official capacity, such as postal workers, meter readers, municipal inspectors, and the police, have the right to come on private property and are not trespassing. In shopping malls and other premises where the public is welcome, visitors have an implied right to be there even when they have not come to shop. Permission is also implied when visitors have been allowed on the property

Reasonable force permitted to defend self

Reasonable force permitted to eject trespasser

www.pearsoned.ca/mybuslawlab

BC AB SK MB ON

On land without authority

---

7. [1990] O.J. No. 450 (C.A.)

8. When for religious reasons parents refuse treatment needed to save the lives of their children, the courts are often willing to interfere by taking custody of the children away from the parents and ordering treatment. See *B. (R.) v. Children's Aid Society of Metropolitan Toronto,*[1988] O.J. No. 78 (C.A.).

9. Patients now can indicate what treatment they do and do not consent to by creating an advance directive in the form of a Personal Directive. See Alberta's *Personal Directives Act,* R.S.A. 2000. c. P-6, as an example of legislation validating these directives.

10. See Alberta's *Petty Trespass Act,* R.S.A. 2000, c. P-11, and *Trespass to Premises Act,* R.S.A. 2000, c. T-7, both of which enable the arrest without warrant of individuals caught trespassing. Fines range from $2000 to $5000 (for subsequent violations).

over time without steps being taken to remove them. If such visitors become unruly or dangerous to other patrons, they can be asked to leave. In fact, visitors can be required to leave even though they have done nothing wrong, so long as the reason does not violate human rights legislation (such as refusing entry to persons based on their race or religion).[11] If visitors refuse to leave, they become trespassers, and reasonable force can be used to eject them.

REDUCING RISK 4.2

The importance of careful training of employees with respect to how they interact with customers and the public cannot be overemphasized. To protect the business from the possibility of devastating lawsuits, employees must know what they can and cannot do when faced with shoplifting, fraud, and other improper conduct. The courts may be somewhat sympathetic to the plight of businesses when faced with the considerable losses caused by shoplifting, fraud, and other wrongs committed by customers, but people who have done nothing wrong must be protected from assault, intimidation, or improper restraint. The damages awarded are based not only on what the employee has done but also on the plaintiff's status in the community and any injury or humiliation suffered. For example, in the *Osz* case, a 16-year-old struck a city bus with a snowball, splattering the defendant driver with snow. The driver stopped the bus, confronted the teen, hit him twice in the face, breaking the teen's nose, and then kicked him. In addition to suffering a painful and debilitating injury, the plaintiff suffered the embarrassment and indignity of being throttled in the presence of his friends. He was awarded general, special, and punitive damages exceeding $10 000, for which the City of Calgary, as the driver's employer, was vicariously liable. Quite a price to pay for losing one's cool!

Trespass can also occur indirectly. When a person throws some item on another's property, or erects a sign without the occupier's permission, a trespass has taken place. Trespass can also involve a permanent incursion onto the property of another. This is referred to as a **continuing trespass** and can take the form of a building or other structure that encroaches on the property of another. The remedy requested would likely include an injunction. Where multi-storeyed buildings are involved, the costs of correcting the problem can be enormous. Of course, consent (in the form of permission to come onto the property or build the encroaching structure), if there has been full disclosure, will be a complete defence to an action for trespass.

Trespass can be indirect

CASE SUMMARY 4.2

Trespassers Present Without Lawful Right: *Costello v. Calgary (City)*[12]

The Costello family owned a property on which a 10-unit motel was situated. They applied for a development permit seeking to build a 40-unit motel on that site, but the application approval was delayed because the city wanted to expropriate the land for a roadway interchange. The subject lands were expropriated in 1972 and leased to a third party. The Costellos opposed the expropriation, and in 1983 the Supreme Court of

---

11. See *Russo v. Ontario Jockey Club*, [1987] O.J. No. 1105, where a private racetrack was able to exclude a gambler from the premises simply because she was very successful.

12. [1995] A.J. No. 27 (Q.B.), varied [1997] A.J. 888 (C.A.), leave to appeal refused, [1997] S.C.C.A. No. 566.

Canada ruled the expropriation illegal and invalid. The Costellos then commenced an action for trespass against the city.

The trial Court found the city liable and awarded damages. (The subsequent appeal was dismissed, and leave to appeal to the S.C.C. was refused.) The Court held that a trespass occurs if an authority takes possession of land pursuant to an expropriation that is subsequently determined to be invalid. The fact that the city did not intend to commit the tort was not a defence. Neither mistaken belief of fact or lawful authority, nor the absence of fault, operates as a defence in the trespass context.

The trial Judge correctly assessed damages on the basis that the Costellos would have developed a 40-unit motel on the property. Damages were calculated to place the plaintiffs in the position they would have enjoyed had the city not committed the wrong. Damages of $572 265 were awarded to reflect the profits the family would have earned from the proposed 40-unit motel. Additionally, $518 295 in interest plus solicitor and client costs were awarded. The case emphasizes the care that parties must exercise before taking possession of or entering another's property.

DISCUSSION QUESTION

In this case it was clear that neither the good intentions of the parties nor their understanding of the facts or the law amounted to an excuse. Do you think that these factors should be given more consideration in a trespass or other tort action?

Trespassers who cause damage while on private property bear responsibility for any injury or loss caused. This is the case whether injury was foreseeable or not. But what if the trespasser is the one injured? Under common law, the injured trespasser generally has no claim against the occupier. Provincial occupiers' liability legislation generally reiterates this rule, requiring only that the occupier of property not wilfully or recklessly cause harm to a trespasser or someone on the property for a criminal purpose. A greater duty is owed, however, to minors who trespass. If it is foreseeable that minors who trespass may be harmed, a duty may arise to take reasonable steps to ensure reasonable safety. Check the appropriate provincial statutes through the MyBusLawLab to determine the exact nature of the duties owed.

Occupiers' liability legislation

Trespass to Chattels, Conversion, and Detinue

There are three torts that deal with the wrongful interference with goods. The decision to assert one tort and not another may impact the remedies available. Any direct intentional interference causing damage to the goods of another is a **trespass to chattels**. Generally, the remedy for trespass to chattels is compensatory damages. When vandals smash the windshield of a car or kick the door in, they have committed trespass to chattels and are liable to pay compensation and possibly punitive damages to the victim. They may also face criminal charges.

Trespass to chattels actionable

Conversion involves one person's intentionally appropriating the goods of another person for her own purposes. In addition to being crimes, theft of goods or acquiring possession of goods through deceit are also actionable under the tort of conversion. Conversion takes place when someone sells or otherwise wrongfully disposes of goods belonging to someone else. When goods are damaged or destroyed to the extent that they are no longer of any value to the rightful owner, the wrongdoer should have to pay the market value at the time of the tort.

Conversion actionable

Conversion involves defendant treating plaintiff's goods as his own

In essence, conversion consists of interference with the plaintiff's chattels in such a way that a forced sale is justified. In such circumstances the person converting the goods is forced to purchase them. In exchange for payment, the defendant acquires the property. The courts also have the power to order the return of the goods if that is a more appropriate remedy.

Unfortunately for the unsophisticated buyer, if one purchases an item from someone other than the true owner, one may later be sued by the rightful owner for conversion. The court may require the buyer to return the goods to the rightful owner, or pay damages equal to the market value of the goods when misappropriated. In the end, the buyer may end up paying the price twice—once to the seller who misrepresented ownership, and secondly to the true owner.

The third tort involving wrongful interference with goods is called **detinue**. Like conversion, it involves the wrongful possession of someone else's goods. But where conversion requires wrongfully taking control of the goods through some intentional act, detinue deals with situations where the person is wrongfully retaining the goods. The defendant may have come into possession of them legally but is now, after a proper request, refusing to return them. As the name of the tort suggests, it is the wrongful detention that gives the plaintiff the ability to sue. For example, if Rick lends Henry his lawnmower and Henry refuses to return it, Rick could bring an action in detinue for compensation. Like conversion, the calculation of damages essentially amounts to a forced sale of the goods, but since detinue is a continuing tort, damages are calculated as at the date of the trial. This distinction proved to be very significant in the *Steiman* case, below.

Refusal to return goods enables owner to assert detinue

CASE SUMMARY 4.3

Expensive Selection of Cause of Action: *Steiman v. Steiman*[13]

In this dispute, the defendants were found liable in conversion for taking the plaintiffs' jewellery. Damages were assessed at $186 787 on the basis of the value of the jewellery at the time of trial. The defendants appealed, arguing that the proper date of valuation was 1976, as that was when the loss or taking occurred.

Since the action was framed in the tort of conversion, the plaintiffs were claiming the money value of the goods wrongfully taken. The Court determined that a wrongdoer who destroys a chattel is bound to pay only that amount which will cover the cost of replacing the chattel at the time of the tort (or a reasonable time thereafter) plus loss of use limited to the period of time required to find a replacement.

Had the plaintiffs claimed in detinue instead of conversion, the Court would have been able to order return of the goods or payment of their value at the time of trial. In detinue the plaintiff has a continuing cause of action arising out of the wrongful refusal of the defendant to deliver up the goods. However, in detinue, the plaintiff runs the risk of a falling market and of depreciation in value. In this case, however, the plaintiffs would have been better off to sue in detinue, as the value of the property had appreciated.

13. [1982] M.J. No. 21 (C.A.).

False Imprisonment

Restraint without lawful excuse—false imprisonment

Submission to authority can constitute imprisonment

False imprisonment, including false arrest, occurs when people are intentionally restrained against their will and the person doing the restraining has no lawful authority to do so. This may be in the form of complete imprisonment, where the person is held in a cell or room, or in the form of an arrest. In either case, the person's liberty to go where he pleases must be totally restrained. Even a person who submits to authority or threat can be considered imprisoned, since in his mind he has been restrained. The second requirement is that the restraint be unlawful. When a security guard arrests someone found shoplifting, there has been no false imprisonment. Generally, a private person has the power to make an arrest, but only when she finds someone in the process of actually committing a crime, such as shoplifting.

A citizen's powers of arrest are set out in section 494 of the *Criminal Code*.[14]

494. (1) Any one may arrest without warrant
(*a*) a person whom he finds committing an indictable offence; or
(*b*) a person who, on reasonable grounds, he believes
(i) has committed a criminal offence, and
(ii) is escaping from and freshly pursued by persons who have lawful authority to arrest that person.

(2) Any one who is
(*a*) the owner or a person in lawful possession of property, or
(*b*) a person authorized by the owner or by a person in lawful possession of property, may arrest without warrant a person whom he finds committing a criminal offence on or in relation to that property.

(3) Any one other than a peace officer who arrests a person without warrant shall forthwith deliver the person to a peace officer.

Damage awards for false imprisonment can be significant

A charge of false imprisonment is a significant risk for any business involved in serving the public. This risk is great when, either because of store policy or inexperienced staff, customers are detained whenever they are suspected of wrongdoing. If the customer has not in fact stolen any goods, there is no justification for holding him. A manager will often discourage their employees from apprehending shoplifters, since the potential loss from goods stolen is far outweighed by the danger of losing a false-imprisonment action. Of course, this may encourage more shoplifting. The answer is to carefully select and train security people to deal with these matters and have the other employees only inform the security people of what they observe. Case Summary 4.4 below demonstrates the difficulties a retail store or other business may encounter should its security guards be overzealous.

---

14. *R.S.C. 1985 c. C-46, s. 494.*

Employer Pays for Loss of Temper: *Chopra v. Eaton (T.) Co.*[15]

The plaintiff, Mr. Chopra, went to Eaton's department store seeking a refund. An argument ensued. Mr. Frauenfeld (from security) told Chopra that he would have to leave; Frauenfeld took Chopra's elbow and started to escort him out of the store. Chopra protested but did not create a disturbance. Near the doors, Chopra pushed Frauenfeld away, presumably wishing to go through the doors unassisted. Frauenfeld reacted quickly and violently, putting Chopra into a headlock. Chopra's glasses were knocked off and his lip was cut; he was handcuffed, detained in the security office, and subjected to racial slurs. Chopra asked to leave, asked to call his wife, and asked Frauenfeld to call the police; all of these requests were refused. After Chopra had been detained for four hours or more, the police arrived and charged Chopra with assaulting Frauenfeld and causing a disturbance. Chopra was subsequently acquitted of both charges.

Chopra's complaint to the Alberta Human Rights Commission and his civil action against Eaton's were both successful. The Court awarded damages totalling $38 000 against Frauenfeld and vicariously against Eaton's.

The Court found that once Chopra was told he would have to leave the store, he did not resist. Thus, Chopra never became a trespasser against whom reasonable force could be justified. But Chopra did push Frauenfeld, which constituted an assault, albeit a nominal one, contrary to section 265 of the *Criminal Code*. This offence gave lawful authority to the initial arrest and detention. But the failure to deliver the party arrested to the police forthwith transformed an initially lawful imprisonment into an unlawful one. In addition, the amount of force used by Frauenfeld in restraining Chopra was excessive, constituting an unjustified battery against Chopra. Since the arrest was made while Frauenfeld was acting within the scope of his employment, Eaton's was held vicariously liable for the damages awarded.

SMALL BUSINESS PERSPECTIVE

What instructions should businesses give to their security personnel in light of the tort of false imprisonment? If a cost benefit analysis is conducted, one might conclude that it only makes sense to detain a customer if one has solid proof that a crime has been committed.

Malicious Prosecution

Sometimes the criminal justice system is improperly used. When this happens, the victim may be able to sue for the tort of **malicious prosecution**. The defendant in the tort action must have initiated a criminal or quasi-criminal prosecution in which the accused was subsequently acquitted of the charge or the prosecution was abandoned. In addition, the plaintiff must establish that the prosecution was motivated by malice and that there were no reasonable grounds to proceed with the criminal action in the first place. Successful malicious prosecution actions

Malicious prosecution available where charges unjustifiably laid

---

15. (1999), 240 A.R. 201 (Q.B.).

may involve prosecutors who have chosen to ignore important evidence or complainants who have lied or manufactured evidence used to improperly support the charges.

An interesting example of a successful claim for malicious prosecution involved a patron at a restaurant who disputed his obligation to pay for liquor. He had been served the drinks but couldn't consume them before they had to be removed from the table under provincial liquor law.[16] The patron was detained and held for the police. When the police arrived he was arrested, charged under the *Criminal Code* with fraudulently obtaining food, and imprisoned. There was no basis for the criminal charge as this was at worst a civil dispute between the parties. The restaurant owner and police were liable for false arrest, but the restaurant owner was also liable for malicious prosecution. The complaint that led to the charge was initiated at his request. There was no basis for the charge, and it was dismissed for want of prosecution. The fact that threat of criminal charges was used to pressure the patron to pay for the drinks provided was enough to constitute malice. All the elements required for malicious prosecution were thus established.

CASE SUMMARY 4.5

Suppression of Evidence Establishes Malicious Prosecution: *McNeil v. Brewers Retail Inc.*[17]

The employer, Brewers Retail Inc. (BRI) fired McNeil from his job for allegedly stealing $160 from the till. BRI handed over surveillance tapes to the police that incriminated McNeil, but suppressed parts of the tapes that would have exonerated him. Initially McNeil was convicted, but these convictions were quashed on appeal. McNeil commenced a civil action and was awarded over two million dollars in aggravated and punitive damages.

The Court of Appeal upheld the award finding that all four elements of malicious prosecution were established, namely:

1. the proceedings must have been commenced by the defendant;
2. the criminal proceedings must have been terminated in favour of the plaintiff;
3. there must have been an absence of reasonable and probable cause; and
4. there must be malice (or a primary purpose other than that of carrying the law into effect).

SMALL BUSINESS PERSPECTIVE

The jury awarded $100 000 for general damages, $188 000 for aggravated damages $500 000 in punitive damages, $240 000 in pecuniary damages for future loss of income, and $308 000 in special damages for past loss of income and legal expenses. The Court of Appeal found that the award of damages, while generous, was not in error. Do awards such as this deter others from being less than honest with the police?

[16.] *Perry et al. v. Fried et* al. (1972), 32 D.L.R. (3d) 589 (N.S.S.C. Trial Div.). Also see *Bahner v. Marwest Hotel Co.* (1969), 6 D.L.R (3D) 322 (B.C.S.C.); aff'd (1970), 12 D.L.R. (3d) 646 (B.C.C.A.) where the facts were very similar. False imprisonment was established as against both the restaurant and the police.

[17.] [2008] O.J. No. 1990 (C.A.).

Private Nuisance

The tort of **private nuisance** is committed when an individual or business uses property in such a way that it interferes with a neighbour's use or enjoyment of her property. Such interference is usually ongoing and continuous. When a commercial building, such as a mill, is built near a residential neighbourhood, and the resulting odour and noise interfere with the neighbours' enjoyment of their yards, it is appropriate for them to sue for nuisance. Such an action is possible only where the property is being used in an unusual or unreasonable way and the problem caused is a direct consequence of this unusual activity. A person living in an industrial section of a city cannot complain when a factory begins operating in the neighbourhood and emits noise, smoke, and dust. Nor could the residents of a rural area complain about the normal odours associated with farming. But if the odours create a significant disturbance, far beyond what one would expect from farming operations, liability may follow. For example, in the *Pyke* case the plaintiff's complaint stemmed from odours emanating from the composting phase of the defendant's mushroom farm.[18] The odours were described in graphic terms, including: "nauseating and like rotten flesh," "worse than a pig farm," and "like an outhouse, ammonia, sour, putrid, rotten vegetables." The Court considered the proximity of the neighbours and the fact that the plaintiffs were there first. The degree and intensity of the disturbance exceeded that of a "normal farm practice" and thus damages exceeding $260 000 were awarded.

Normally, the properties would need to be in close proximity for private nuisance to apply and for a nuisance action to be brought. However, in an Alberta case a telephone was used to harass people on the other side of the city, interfering with the enjoyment of their property. The Court found this to be a private nuisance, even though the two parties were kilometres apart.[19]

For a private nuisance to be actionable, the consequences must be reasonably foreseeable to the defendant. Reasonable foreseeability will be discussed in the following chapter, but essentially it requires that an ordinary, prudent person, in the same circumstances, would have anticipated the risk. Because nuisance often involves offending substances, it is one of the few common law tools that can be used to enforce environmental protection. In *St. Lawrence Cement Inc. v. Barrette*,[20] the Supreme Court of Canada discussed the common law of environmental nuisance and held that the term *neighbour* must be construed liberally. Residents in the greater Quebec City area who endured dust, smoke, and noise pollution generated by the cement plant during the 1990s were awarded damages despite the fact that St. Lawrence Cement spent more than $8 million to collect the dust emitted by its plant. Liability was nonetheless imposed because neighbours had been exposed to excessive and abnormal annoyances, contrary to art. 976 of the *Civil Code of Quebec*.

> **Private nuisance—use of property interferes with neighbour**

> **Private nuisance at a distance**

---

[18] *Pyke v. TRI GRO Enterprises Ltd.* (2001), 55 O.R. (3d) 257 (Ont. C.A.), leave to appeal to S.C.C. refused, [2001] S.C.C.A. No. 493.

[19] *Motherwell v. Motherwell* (1976), 1 A.R. 47, 73 D.L.R. (3d) 62 (C.A.).

[20] [2008] S.C.J. No. 65.

CASE SUMMARY 4.6

Golf Balls Destroy Enjoyment of Property: *Carley v. Willow Park Golf Course Ltd.*[21]; *Cattell v. Great Plains Leaseholds Ltd.*[22]

The Carleys purchased their home, which was next to the Willow Park Golf Course, about 28 years after the golf course and driving range were constructed. Golf balls from the driving range regularly landed in their yard, making it impossible for them to use their backyard for fear of being hit. Over the years the golf course had taken steps to solve the problem, building several fences and placing nets to stop the balls, but the errant golf balls raining down on their property and those of their neighbours persisted.

They knew of the driving range when they bought their home but were also aware of a 90-foot net and assumed that kept any balls from falling on their property. While some errant golf balls had to be expected living next to a golf course, the Judge at one point characterized this as a "barrage."

The Court found that the driving range constituted a private nuisance. A private nuisance is present when property is used in such a way as to unreasonably interfere with a neighbour's interest in the beneficial use of his or her land. The "bombardment" of golf balls from the driving range constituted such an interference. "No use of property is reasonable which causes substantial discomfort to others or is a source of damage to their property."[23]

The Court ordered damages of $2500, but more importantly a permanent injunction was issued against the golf course ordering it to prevent people using the driving range from hitting balls onto the Carleys' property.

Similarly, in the *Cattell* case, a barrage of misdirected golf balls emanating from the ninth hole of the Emerald Park Golf Course created a nuisance for the plaintiff homeowners. At trial, a permanent injunction was granted, restraining the golf course, its members, their guests, or any other users of the golf course from hitting golf balls on the ninth hole of the course so that they landed anywhere on the plaintiffs' property! This time, the remedies were appealed. The injunction was replaced with an order allowing use of the ninth hole—with conditions.

SMALL BUSINESS PERSPECITVE

What remedy do you think might be more problematic? A one-time award of damages or an injunction preventing a particular use? Findings of private nuisance have been made in several cases with similar circumstances to these, where injunctions have likewise been granted. From the plaintiff's perspective, obtaining an order to stop the offending conduct may well be the preferred solution, but this could be problematic for the defendant.

---

[21] [2002] A.J. No. 1174 (Q.B.).

[22] [2008] S.J. No. 347 (Sask. C.A.).

[23] *Carley v. Willow Park Golf Course Ltd.,supran.* 21;para. 27, citing Lewis N. Klar, *Tort Law*, Carswell 2nd edition, at 535.

It should also be noted that private nuisance as discussed here is different from **public nuisance**. Only rarely is an action for public nuisance brought and then usually by the government. A public nuisance takes place when some public property is interfered with. Protesters blocking a road or park, or a mill polluting a river, would be examples. The Supreme Court of Canada found that such a public nuisance had occurred when a forest company in British Columbia allowed a controlled burn to escape.[24] The resulting forest fire caused damage to environmentally sensitive streams and the Attorney General of that province brought an action for public nuisance against the company. The Supreme Court adopted the language of an earlier decision, stating, "any activity which unreasonably interferes with the public's interest in questions of health, safety, morality, comfort or convenience" is capable of constituting a public nuisance.[25] Note that a private individual can bring an action of public nuisance only if able to show that the conduct harmed him or her particularly and more than other members of the general public.

www.pearsoned.ca/mybuslawlab

Defamation

Defamation is a published false statement that is to a person's detriment. It is a primary concern for businesses involved in media communications, but all commercial enterprises face some risk over defamation, even if it is only from a carelessly worded letter of reference. For the statement to be an actionable defamation, it must be derogatory, false, and published, and must refer to the plaintiff. If the false statement causes people to avoid or shun someone, it is derogatory. In the *Youssoupoff* case, Lord Justice Scrutton said that a statement was defamatory if it was "a false statement about a man to his discredit."[26] A complimentary statement about a person, even if it is false, is not defamation. Thus, if a manager were to say of an employee that he was the best worker in the plant, it would not be defamation even if false. Once the plaintiff establishes that the derogatory statement was made, he need not prove it was false. This is assumed, and it is up to the defendant to prove it true if he can. If the statement can be shown to be true, it is an absolute defence to a defamation action.[27]

For a statement to be actionable, it must be clear that it refers to the person suing. Thus, a general negative reference to a group,[28] such as the faculty or student body of a university, will not qualify. It is not possible to defame a dead person; however, it is possible to defame a corporation, which is a person in the eyes of the law, and it is possible to defame a product. (See the discussion of product defamation, trade slander, and injurious falsehood, below.)

Defamation: derogatory, false, and published

Member of group defamed may not be personally defamed

24. *British Columbia v. Canadian Forest Products Ltd.*, [2004] S.C.J. No. 33.

25. *Ryan v. Victoria (City)*, [1999] 1 S.C.R. 201 (S.C.C.), at para. 52.

26. *Youssoupoff v. Metro-Goldwyn-Mayer Pictures Ltd.* (1934), 50 T.L.R. 581 at 584 (C.A.).

27. *Elliott v. Freisen et al.* (1982), 136 D.L.R. (3d) 281 (Ont. H.C.) aff'd (1984), 6 D.L.R. (4th) 388 (Ont. C.A.); leave to appeal refused (1984), 6 D.L.R. (4th) 388 n (S.C.C.).

28. In *Diffusion Metromedia CMR inc. c. Bou Malhab*, [2008] J.Q. no 10048, the Quebec Court of Appeal dismissed a group defamation action brought against a shock radio host who made negative racist comments against taxi drivers of Arab and Haitian descent. The Court found that because the statements did not target any specific individuals, individual members could not claim their reputation had been damaged by comments aimed at large groups. A group defamed by racist comments may, however, file a complaint under human rights legislation.

Statement must be published

Further, the false statement must be published. In this sense, "to publish" means that the statement had to be communicated to a third party. Publication could have occurred in a newspaper, in the broadcast media, on the internet, or simply by word of mouth. It is sufficient publication if just one person other than the plaintiff hears or reads the defamatory statement.

In those situations where legislation does not specifically restrict damages payable, the damages for defamation can be substantial. The courts not only will compensate the victim for actual losses as well as for a damaged reputation, but will go further, awarding damages to rehabilitate the victim's reputation. For this reason, the Supreme Court of Canada upheld a decision to award a Crown prosecutor defamed by a church $1.6 million in damages—far in excess of what would be awarded for general damages in a normal tort action.[29] Justice Cory stated that, unlike non-pecuniary losses in personal injury cases, general damages in defamation are not capped.

Significant damages available

CASE SUMMARY 4.7

Pricey Condemnation: *WeGo Kayaking Ltd. v. Sewid*[30]

Imagine discovering that a competitor has posted defamatory statements about your businesses on the internet! WeGo Kayaking Ltd. and Northern Lights Expeditions Ltd. brought a defamation action against the defendant Sewid after reading statements posted on villageisland.com. The Plaintiffs offered kayak tours in the vicinity of Vancouver Island and relied heavily on the internet to attract customers. Sewid operated a water taxi service and had provided services for the guides and clients of the plaintiffs in 2003 and 2004. Following his termination, Sewid went into competition with the plaintiffs and posted the following on the web:

Bad Kayak Companies

These are the companies that arenot looked at favourably. They are ones that have done things to try and make First Nations become token Indians who are only needed as items of attraction or convenience. There may be some environmental concerns with their operating practices as well . . .

Fifteen businesses were rated as good kayak companies and the plaintiffs were among the three businesses listed as bad kayak companies. Sewid refused to remove the plaintiffs from the bad list and refused to apologize. He also claimed that the statements on the website were protected by the defence of fair comment. That defence failed because the statements were presented as facts rather than as comments based on true facts; further, the statements were motivated by malice. Evidence that Sewid had published the bad companies list to punish the plaintiffs for not continuing to do business with him, and evidence suggesting he also wanted to remove the competition, supported the finding of malice. WeGo was awarded general damages of $100 000; Northern Lights recovered general damages of $150 000. The Court determined that general damages were not sufficient, and awarded the plaintiffs punitive damages of $2500 and $5000, respectively.

---

29. *Hill v. Church of Scientology of Toronto*, [1995] 2 S.C.R. 1130.

30. [2007] B.C.J. No. 56 (B.C.S.C.)

SMALL BUSINESS PERSPECTIVE

This decision suggests that damage awards granted to corporations are getting larger. Earlier case law suggested that a corporation's reputation deserved less protection. *Jameel v. Wall Street Journal Europe SPRL*, [2006] UKHL 44, confirms that all plaintiffs, be they corporations or real persons, are to be treated equally in the assessment of damages.

Statements often contain **innuendo**, which is an implied or hidden meaning. A statement may appear perfectly innocent on the surface, but when combined with other information it may take on a more sinister meaning. It is no excuse to say that the person making the statement thought it was true or did not know of the special facts that created the innuendo. Such a mistake is no defence, and the offending party can be held liable for the defamatory remark. Innuendoes in the form of suggested inferences can be actionable, as the CBC discovered in the *Leenen* case. During a *Fifth Estate* episode, the CBC called into question the plaintiff doctor's honesty and integrity. The program implied that the doctor and research scientist was in a conflict of interest, receiving payoffs from a pharmaceutical company and prescribing "killer drugs." By presenting an unbalanced view of the issue, the audience was lead to draw negative inferences.

Innuendo

Mistake no excuse

mybuslawlab
www.pearsoned.ca/mybuslawlab

Libel and Slander

Defamation can be either **slander**, which is spoken defamation, or **libel**, which is usually written defamation. The significance of finding a defamatory remark to be libelous rather than slanderous is that libel is easier to prove because there is no requirement to show that special damages have been sustained. Libel is seen to be more deliberate, more premeditated, and also more permanent than slander, thus causing more harm. However, modern means of mass communication give slander a potentially huge audience, so the rationale for distinguishing between libel and slander is breaking down. In fact, this distinction has been eliminated altogether in some provinces, while in others, legislation has simply declared that all broadcast defamation will constitute libel whether spoken or written. Refer to MyBusLawLab for details.

Slander spoken/ Libel written

While defamation is primarily governed by common law, most provinces have passed statutes modifying those common law provisions in light of the needs of a modern society. Should defamation by the media occur, for example, legislation may reduce the damages plaintiffs can claim where material was published in good faith. If the publisher shows that the damage was done by mistake or misapprehension of the facts, and a full apology or retraction has been made, damages may be restricted to special damages (the actual losses and expenses incurred).[31]

Apology reduces damages

These statutes will need even more modification to take into account the new problems associated with defamation on the internet. It is often difficult to trace the original source of defamation in an internet message because it can be so easily copied and transferred by intermediate parties. Nevertheless, the injury caused

---

[31.] See, for example, Alberta's *Defamation Act*, R.S.A. 2000, c. D-7, s. 16, or New Brunswick's *Defamation Act*, S.N.B. c. D-5, s. 17.

by such transmission of defamatory information can be extensive. Another problem is that in a traditional communication environment there is usually a broadcaster or publisher that can be held responsible for the damaging words, but in online communication there is often no intermediary who checks and authorizes material, nor is there any clear way of determining just how far a message has been spread or even who wrote it in the first place. Refer to MyBusLawLab for provincial variations.

CASE SUMMARY 4.8

Is Posting a Link Publication? *Crookes v. Wikimedia Foundation Inc.*[32]

The plaintiffs claimed they had been defamed in a "smear campaign." A website known as "p2pnet" published an article examining the implication of defamation actions on those who operate internet forums. The author claimed to be interested in freedom of speech. His article contained hyperlinks to other sites, but the operator of p2pnet did not quote any of the alleged defamatory words from those other websites.

The Court concluded that although individuals who read an article containing a reference to another website may go there, this does not make the publisher of the first website the publisher of the material posted on the second site. Since the publisher of the first site did not reproduce any of the disputed content, nor make any comment on the linked material, he could not be deemed a publisher of the derogatory statements.

The issue in this case is not how accessible the website is, but rather, if anyone followed the hyperlinks posted on the p2pnet site. Without proof that persons other than the plaintiff visited the defendant's website, clicked on the hyperlinks, and read the articles complained of, there cannot be a finding of publication.

Justice Kelleher concluded: "In my view, the mere creation of a hyperlink in a website does not lead to a presumption that persons read the contents of the website and used the hyperlink to access the defamatory words." Accordingly, the action was dismissed.

DISCUSSION QUESTIONS

Might the Court have reached a different conclusion if the author of the article had commented on the material contained on the linked site? Justice Kelleher stated: "It is not my decision that hyperlinking can never make a person liable for the contents of the remote site." When might liability be imposed if mere reference to (or hyperlink to) an article containing defamatory content is insufficient to constitute republication?

DEFENCES

Truth is an absolute defence

Once it has been established that a defamatory statement has been made, several defences are available to the defendant. **Truth**, also called the defence of **justification**, is an absolute defence. But even when a statement is technically true, it can still be derogatory if it contains an innuendo or is capable of being interpreted as

---

32. [2008] B.C.J. No. 2012 (B.C.S.C.)

referring to another person about whom the statement is false. Note also that substantial truth is sufficient. If the defendant claimed that the plaintiff had stolen $300 000 when in fact he had stolen only $250 000, justification would still be an effective defence.

The second defence is called **absolute privilege**. Anything discussed as part of parliamentary debate on the floor of the legislature, Parliament, or in government committees, and statements made or documents used as part of a court procedure cannot give rise to a defamation action, no matter how malicious, scandalous, or derogatory they are.

The rationale for this defence is that there are certain forums where, for the good of society, people should be able to exercise freedom of expression without fear of being sued. For example, even statements made to an investigator in the context of a *Human Rights Act* investigation are privileged.[33] Absolute privilege has also been extended to documents used in the process of a complaint before the College of Physicians and Surgeons in British Columbia.[34]

The most significant defence for businesspeople is called **qualified privilege**. When a statement is made pursuant to a duty or special interest, there is no action for defamation so long as the statement was made honestly and without malice, and was circulated only to those having a right to know. A manager reporting to a superior about the performance of a worker or members of a professional organization describing the performance of an officer of that organization to other members would be instances protected by qualified privilege. When a manager sends a defamatory email specifically to someone with a shared interest in the matter, such as his superior or the particular group of employees he supervises, that may be protected by qualified privilege, but that privilege would be lost if the defamatory message were sent to a website available to everyone. Since anyone could access the website, the publication would be too broad and privilege could no longer be claimed. Thus, in *Egerton v. Finucan,* a community college professor's claim for wrongful dismissal was complicated by the fact that his supervisor sent a highly critical performance evaluation to all the professors in the institution via email. The Court found that the plaintiff had grounds for a defamation suit against his superior.[35] Note that when reporting on matters of public interest, newspapers and other media often claim this defence, but it is normally denied them on the grounds that although they claim that they have a duty to report and that the public has a right to know, there is no legal duty on them to report matters to the public and so no qualified privilege.

A further defence available in the field of defamation is the defence of **fair comment**. When people put their work before the public, as with movies, plays, artwork, books, and the like, they invite public criticism and run the risk that the opinions expressed may not be complimentary. Even when these opinions amount to a vicious attack and may be unreasonable, artists cannot sue for defamation. The defence raised here is fair comment. Public figures are also open to such criticism. To successfully use this defence, the critic or editorial writer must be able to show that what was said was a matter of opinion, drawn from true facts that were before the public, and was not motivated by malice or

Absolute privilege

Qualified privilege, requires duty

Fair comment

[33.] *Ayangma v. NAV Canada* (2001), 197 Nfld. & P.E.I.R. 83 (P.E.I.S.C. (A.D.)), leave to appeal to S.C.C. refused, [2001] S.C.C.A. No. 76.

[34.] *Schut v. Magee,* [2003] B.C.J. No. 1689 (B.C.C.A.).

[35.] *Egerton v. Finucan,* [1995] O.J. No. 1653 (Gen. Div.).

some ulterior motive. A food critic expressing a negative opinion of a restaurant[36] and a theatre critic attacking a play or movie are examples of fair comment. The same defence should apply where a play, photograph, or musical performance is put on the internet and made available to a wide audience.

CASE SUMMARY 4.9

Freedom of Expression Clashes with Defamation Law: *WIC Radio Ltd. v. Simpson*[37]

Rafe Mair, a sometimes controversial radio talk-show host, tackled Ms. Simpson on the airwaves. Simpson was a widely known social activist who opposed the introduction of materials dealing with homosexuality into public schools. During a WIC Radio editorial broadcast, Mair disagreed with Simpson's views and compared Simpson to Hitler, the Ku Klux Klan, and skinheads. Simpson commenced an action in defamation against Mair and the station.

Mair argued that the purpose of his words was to convey that Simpson was an intolerant bigot, not that she condoned violence against homosexuals as alleged. The Supreme Court of Canada, like the trial Judge, found Mair's editorial defamatory but allowed the defence of fair comment. The action was thus dismissed.

The Supreme Court considered that the evolution of the common law should be informed and guided by *Charter* values. Whereas the tort of defamation aims at protecting a person's reputation, there is also a need to accommodate the value of freedom of expression.

The fair comment defence is consistent with the values of freedom of expression and freedom of the press. Here there was a public debate about the inclusion of educational material on homosexuality in schools. The subject clearly engaged the public interest. The inflammatory words would most likely be understood as comment, rather than fact. Further, the comment satisfied the objective test regarding whether any person could honestly express that opinion on the proved facts. Having regard to the content of some of Simpson's speeches, the defamatory imputation that while Simpson would not engage in violence herself, she would condone violence by others, is an opinion that could honestly have been expressed. The fair comment defence could have been defeated if the comment was actuated by malice, but Simpson failed to establish malice.

DISCUSSION QUESTIONS

Freedom of opinion, freedom of expression, and freedom of the press all seem to conflict with defamation law. What is the appropriate balance to be struck between encouraging such freedoms and protecting one's good name?

Public interest responsible journalism defence

Canada's media may now be able to utilize a new defence, as the Ontario Court of Appeal recognized the public interest responsible journalism defence in *Cusson v. Quan*[38]. Cusson, an OPP constable, voluntarily went to New York City following the September 11 attack on the World Trade Center to assist with rescue

---

36. Fair comment was successfully raised in *Sara's Pyrohy Hut v. Brooker*, [1993] A.J. No. 185 (C.A.).

37. [2008] S.C.J. No. 41.

38. [2007] O.J. No. 4348 (C.A.).

operations. Initially, he was portrayed in the media as a hero, but a newspaper later published three negative articles about him. The Court of Appeal would not allow the public interest responsible journalism defence to be relied upon, since it had not been raised at trial. Nonetheless, it agreed that defamation ought to be subject to this defence, in light of freedom of expression. The Court adopted the rationale of the House of Lords in *Reynolds v. Times Newspapers Ltd.*[39], which identified ten factors that courts might consider in applying the public interest responsible journalism defence:

1. The seriousness of the allegation. The more serious the charge, the more the public is misinformed and the individual harmed, if the allegation is not true.

2. The nature of the information, and the extent to which the subject-matter is a matter of public concern.

3. The source of the information. Some informants have no direct knowledge of the events. Some have their own axes to grind, or are being paid for their stories.

4. The steps taken to verify the information.

5. The status of the information. The allegation may have already been the subject of an investigation that commands respect.

6. The urgency of the matter. News is often a perishable commodity.

7. Whether comment was sought from the plaintiff. He may have information others do not possess or have not disclosed. An approach to the plaintiff will not always be necessary.

8. Whether the article contained the gist of the plaintiff's side of the story.

9. The tone of the article. A newspaper can raise queries or call for an investigation. It need not adopt allegations as statements of fact.

10. The circumstances of the publication, including the timing.

This list is not exhaustive. The weight to be given to these and any other relevant factors will vary from case to case.

Thus the media may avoid liability if they act responsibly when reporting on matters of public interest. What remains to be seen, however, is whether non-traditional journalists, such as bloggers and others posting to websites, will be able to seek the benefit of this defence.

Product Defamation (Injurious Falsehood)

Is the goodwill associated with a product entitled to protection, much like the good reputation of a person or corporation? The tort of **injurious falsehood** addresses such a wrong. This tort takes place when one person attacks the reputation of another's product or business. When a person spreads a false rumour that the wine manufactured by a competitor is adulterated with some other substance, or that his business is about to become bankrupt, she has committed an injurious falsehood. Although this tort is often called **trade slander** or **product defamation**, it must be distinguished from the tort of defamation that involves injury to the

Injurious falsehood actionable

---

[39] [1999] 4 All ER 609, [2001] 2 AC 127 (H.L.); www.bailii.org/uk/cases/UKHL/1999/45.html. [2007] O.J. No. 4348 (C.A.).

personal reputation of the injured party. Injurious falsehood deals with the reputation and value of a person's property. It may reflect negatively on the quality of the product, or it may relate to title. When a person falsely claims that the seller does not own what he is selling or that the product is in violation of patent or copyright, he has uttered an actionable injurious falsehood.

CASE SUMMARY 4.10

Unfounded Accusations Can Be Costly: *Procor Ltd. v. U.S.W.A.*[40]

Procor Ltd., a manufacturer that exports much of its product to the United States, was involved in a serious and difficult labour dispute with its employees. In the air of hostility created by the labour dispute, members of the union accused the company of customs fraud, saying that it was exporting Japanese products into the United States (marked as products made in Canada) without disclosing the fact. This caused an intensive and disruptive investigation into the operations of the company, even stopping production for a time. In addition, there was considerable negative publicity. The investigation exonerated the company, showing the union members to be wrong and the accusations to be unfounded. Procor Ltd. then sued for injurious falsehood the union and the members who had made the accusations. These defendants knew, or should have known, that the statements they were making to customs agents were false, thus instigating the investigation.

In addition to the presence of a false statement made to a party causing damage, it is also necessary to establish malice to succeed in an injurious falsehood action. "Malice" is usually described as a dishonest or improper motive. While the Judge did not find that they lied outright, he did find that the union officials were "willfully blind to the truth" when they made these false statements to the customs officials. That was enough to establish malice. In addition, their motive was not to act as good citizens but to further their labour dispute and vent their frustrations and hostility toward the company. This was an improper purpose supporting the finding of malice. The Judge also found that the defendants had participated in a conspiracy to accomplish these goals and were, as a result, liable to pay $100 000 general damages and a further $100 000 punitive damages. In a society like ours, we have to be careful about what we say about others. This case is an example of the difficulties that a few misplaced words can cause.

DISCUSSION QUESTIONS

Is this sort of thing just what is to be expected in heated labour disputes? Do you think the prospect of tort action further aggravates hostilities between parties such as these?

Successfully Establishing a Tort Claim

When a plaintiff commences a tort action, he bears the burden of establishing each of the required elements or *ingredients* of that tort. Failure to prove an ingredient should result in the action's being dismissed. See Table 4.1 for a simplified list of ingredients for the torts examined thus far.

---

40. [1989] O.J. No. 2156 (H.C.J.).

Table 4.1 Simplified Ingredients for Torts

Assault	1) Deliberate threat creating fear of imminent harm 2) No consent
Battery	1) Deliberate physical interference (contact) with one's body 2) No consent
Trespass to Land	1) Deliberate interference with property 2) No consent/permission/lawful right to be there
Trespass to Chattels	1) Deliberate interference with goods of another 2) No consent
Conversion	1) Deliberate appropriation of the goods of another 2) In such a way that a forced sale is justified.
Detinue	1) Deliberate possession of another's goods 2) Wrongful refusal to return the goods to the owner
False Imprisonment	1) Deliberate restraint 2 Lack of lawful authority
Malicious Prosecution	1) Initiation of prosecution on criminal or quasi-criminal charges 2) Subsequent acquittal of the plaintiff 3) Prosecution was motivated by malice
Private Nuisance	1) Unusual use of property 2) Interference caused to neighbour's enjoyment/use of property 3) Foreseeable consequences
Defamation	1) False statements made 2) Derogatory to the plaintiff's reputation 3) Publication or communication to a third party
Injurious Falsehood (trade defamation)	1) False statements made 2) Derogatory to the reputation of the product or service 3) Publication or communication to a third party

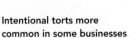

OTHER TORTS IMPACTING BUSINESS

People involved in business activities can find themselves faced with tortious liability for their conduct or the conduct of their employees and agents. Businesses that deal directly with the public, especially in the service industries, such as restaurants, hotels, and retailers, may find their employees becoming involved in altercations with customers in the course of their work. Vicarious liability for assault and battery, negligence, trespass, and even false imprisonment may follow. When business premises visited by customers or the public are involved, there can be actions for negligence based on occupiers' liability.

Intentional torts more common in some businesses

Negligence will be the primary focus of the following chapter. Those providing consulting services to businesses and private individuals, such as bankers, accountants, auditors, lawyers, financial advisers, engineers, and architects, are only a few of the professionals who find themselves increasingly vulnerable to damage actions for both tort and breach of contract.

In addition to the torts already discussed in this chapter, there are other unique torts that can be important to businesses: inducing breach of contract, interference with economic relations, intimidation, deceit, conspiracy, passing-off, breach of confidence, and invasion of privacy. Most of these are associated with unfair or overly aggressive competition.

Inducing breach of contract actionable

CASE SUMMARY 4.11

Cold and Calculated: *Polar Ice Express Inc. v. Arctic Glacier Inc.*[41]

The trial Judge found that the defendant, Arctic Glacier, ambitious to become the sole supplier of ice to many customers in area, used threats and bribery to get customers to stop doing business with the plaintiff, Polar Ice. Arctic Glacier had a virtual monopoly over ice sales in Alberta to grocery stores, liquor stores, service stations, small confectionary stores, and concrete supply companies. Polar Ice, a fledgling company, adduced evidence revealing that Arctic Ice threatened to refuse further delivery of ice to Inland Cement, at a critical time, unless Inland Cement stopped buying ice from Polar Ice. A bribe was also offered to Inland Cement's employee to secure an exclusive contract.

Arctic Glacier also made offers to match or undercut Polar's price, but only to the liquor outlets and Sobeys stores that Polar Ice supplied. These direct and deliberate attempts to induce those targeted businesses to breach their contracts with Polar Ice breached the *Competition Act* in addition to being actionable torts. Damages for inducing breach of contract were thus awarded.

To establish the tort of interference with economic relations, the plaintiff had to prove that: (1) the defendant had an intention to injure it; (2) the means employed by the defendant to accomplish this were unlawful; and (3) the plaintiff suffered economic loss or a related injury as a result. All three requirements were met and damages of $50 000 were awarded.

The Court of Appeal upheld the decision and found that the award of solicitor and client costs to the plaintiff was justified. The defendant's employee had lied under oath, which impeded earlier settlement of the action and necessitated a longer trial.

SMALL BUSINESS PERSPECTIVE

Competition is encouraged in Canada but within ethical guidelines. Businesses need to teach their employees that certain lines are not to be crossed to "make a deal."

Inducing Breach of Contract

There are several ways that one can interfere with the operation of another's business. **Inducing breach of contract** usually involves an employer persuading an employee of another business to leave that employment and work for him or her.

---

41. [2009] A.J. No. 19 (C.A.).

This practice is more common when that employee has special knowledge about trade secrets or customer lists or has a special relationship with customers, enabling him or her to bring them to the new job. If the employee is contractually committed to stay in that position of employment for a period of time or not to disclose secret information, he will breach that contractual obligation if he submits to the enticement to make the move and make the disclosure. A different employer that persuades someone else's employee to commit such a breach, usually with financial incentives, violates a duty not to intervene in that relationship. As a result, that employer may face the tort action of inducing breach of contract. For the victim to sue for inducing breach of contract, he must be able to establish that there was a contract that was breached and that the person being sued knew about the contract and intentionally induced the breach. The victim likely has the right to sue the employee for breach, but it is often preferable to sue the other employer because it tends to have "deeper pockets" (the funds to make the action worthwhile), and legal action may deter the defendant from luring other employees away and causing the plaintiff such losses again.

Inducing breach of contract can also be committed when one business induces severance of contractual relations with someone else, as when a supplier is persuaded to abandon one customer in favour of another or a customer is persuaded to breach its contract with a competing supplier. Another interesting application of this tort is to sue a director of a corporation for inducing the corporation to breach a contract it had with the plaintiff. See Case 6 (*369413 Alberta Ltd. v. Pocklington Holdings Inc.*) at the end of the chapter.

CASE SUMMARY 4.12

The Consequences of Inducing Breach: *Ahmad v. Ontario Hydro*[42]

Dr. Ahmad was an engineer working for Atomic Energy Canada Limited (AECL) as head of the Advanced Engineering Branch. He was working on a project to get the nuclear reactors to work at a higher efficiency, which was of great interest to Ontario Hydro, AECL's primary customer. Each percentage rise in efficiency would reap a reward of $20 million in income. Ahmad was working on a process that would lead to such results but stated in his report that further study was required. Ontario Hydro needed a more positive report to take before the controlling board, so it persuaded Ahmad's employer to transfer him and put someone more "supportive" in charge. Ontario Hydro threatened to withdraw from future joint research projects unless Ahmad was reassigned.

AECL complied, assigning Ahmad to a project where he was no longer in contact with Ontario Hydro. The result was that he could no longer work in his area of expertise and went from managing 24 employees to being in a one-person office with nothing to do. Ontario Hydro produced a press release stating that Ahmad was reassigned due to research delays and inadequate research, accusations that were repeated in *The Globe and Mail*. Ahmad sued Ontario Hydro, and when AECL failed to supply documents he needed for his action, he joined them in the action. As a result he was terminated. In this

---

42. [1993] O.J. No. 3104 (Gen. D.); [1997] O.J. No. 3047 (C.A.)

action Ahmad sought remedies against Ontario Hydro for defamation and inducing breach of contract.

This is a classic example of one company putting extensive pressure on another to breach its employment relationship with a long-term employee. The Court awarded $488 525 in damages against Ontario Hydro for inducing breach of contract and another $40 000 for defamation. The Court even awarded the plaintiff solicitor and client costs. It found that there had been a valid contract between AECL and Ahmad that Ontario Hydro was aware of, and that it had intentionally and wrongfully induced AECL to breach that contract, causing substantial damage to Ahmad. In a separate action, Ahmad was awarded $102 000 against AECL for wrongful dismissal.

SMALL BUSINESS PERSPECTIVE

Knowing that one can sue a third party for wrongfully causing a contract to be breached in effect doubles the potential for the relief following a breach of contract. More importantly, it allows one to pursue the wrongdoer who initiated the damage.

When one business intentionally interferes with the operation of a competitor, problems can develop. When this is done through ordinary competition there is no complaint, but sometimes that competition becomes unfair. Examples of improper interference in business and unfair competition include: one business seeking confidential information from the employees of another; intimidation to discourage someone from opening a business in an area; or one restaurant sending employees to the door of another to redirect customers to the first. Most of these kinds of problems are dealt with by the federal *Competition Act*,[43] and this will be discussed in Chapter 15.

Interference with Economic Relations

Interference with economic relations is also actionable where no breach of contract has taken place, but there must be some other unlawful conduct associated with the complaint, such as bribery or defamation. That unlawful conduct must have been intended to cause harm and, in fact, harm must have resulted. For example in the *Sagaz* case,[44] a company had supplied seat covers to a retailer for over 30 years when that business arrangement was abruptly terminated. A competitor bribed a key employee of the retailer with a 2 percent kickback for every seat cover the competitor supplied. The key employee accepted the bribe and arranged for the change in suppliers. The bribe was sufficient illegal activity to support the claim of illegal interference with the supplier's economic relations.

In *Barber v. Vrozos*,[45] the complaint related to the supply and sale of water at a Rolling Stones concert. The plaintiffs purchased for $100 000 what they thought was the exclusive right to supply and sell water at the concert from the defendant Vrozos, who in turn had acquired these rights through an oral contract with the

Interference with economic relations

[43.] R.S.C. 1985, c. C-34.

[44.] *671122 Ontario Ltd. v. Sagaz Industries Canada Inc.*, [2001] S.C.R. 983.

[45.] [2008] O.J. No. 2616 (Sup. Ct. J.); [2008] O.J. No. 3357 (Sup. Ct. J.) as to punitive damages; [2009] O.J. No. 865 (Sup. Ct. J.) ruling as to costs.

defendant, Molson, for $120 000. Molson proceeded to breach this contract by negotiating a deal with the defendant, GMIC, giving GMIC "exclusive" rights to onsite food and beverages sales. Vrozos also allowed the sale of water by other vendors in a barbecue area.

The plaintiffs ultimately were awarded damages in excess of $1.3 million—$531 616 for breach of contract and a further $180 000 in tort against Vrozos, and $632 000 against Molson for intentionally interfering with the plaintiffs' economic relations when it breached its exclusive water contract with Vrozos. Note that an additional $50 000 in punitive damages and costs of $481 185 were also awarded.

Intimidation

Even just the threat of violence or some other illegal activity, such as an illegal strike, can constitute the tort of **intimidation** where it forces the businessperson to do something that harms the business. For example, a trade union threatening an illegal strike if a particular employee was not terminated amounted to the tort of intimidation and was actionable in England.[46] Of course, if a union was in a legal strike position, the threat of such a strike would not amount to intimidation since the necessary element of a threat to do an illegal act would be missing. Such intimidation is often associated with the tort of unlawful interference with economic relations. In *Cheticamp Fisheries Co-operative Limited v. Canada,*[47] the Department of Fisheries instituted a fee on the fishers and fish processors at the dock to pay for the weighing and inspection of the catch to ensure that the quotas were being adhered to. This was not supported by statutory authority, and as an illegal fee it was held to be an unlawful interference with economic relations. The fishers also claimed that it amounted to intimidation, but the Judge found that since the unlawful interference had been established it was not necessary to determine whether intimidation was present as well. Note that a related tort of **intentional infliction of mental suffering** (or nervous shock) will often also be alleged where such threats and harassing behaviour is involved. Examples include harassing behaviour associated with wrongful dismissal, such as harassing an ill employee for justified absences after she has already been given notice of termination.[48] Another example involves the improper activities of a collection agency, including harassment and threat of physical violence, to encourage repayment of a loan.[49]

Intimidation

Intentional infliction of mental suffering

Deceit (Fraudulent Misrepresentation)

The tort of **deceit** involves the fraudulent and intentional misleading of another person, causing damage. This is where one person lies to another, causing loss.[50] It is an intentional tort and one of the few situations where the court will entertain an application for punitive damages. The case of *Derry v. Peek* [51] established that

Fraud or deceit actionable

---

46. *Tran v. Financial Debt Recovery Ltd.,* [2000] O.J. No. 4293 (Sup.Ct.J.).

47. *Rookes v. Barnard,* [1964] 1 All E.R. 367 (H. of L.).

48. [1995] N.S.J. No. 127 (N.S.C.A.); application for leave to S.C.C. dismissed, [1995] S.C.C.A. No. 202.

49. *Prinzo v. Baycrest Centre for Geriatric Care,* [2002] O.J. No. 2712 (C.A.).

50. (1889), 14 App. Cas. 337 at 374 (H.L.).

51. See *Usenik v. Sidorowicz,* [2008] O.J. No. 1049 (S.C.J.), where the plaintiffs purchased a home from the defendants after being assured there were no problems with moisture and flooding. These statements were untrue. The defendants were ordered to redress the water damages suffered.

deceit did not require actual knowledge that what was stated was incorrect. It was enough that the person making the statement did not believe it to be true. This is a common wrong committed in business and will be dealt with in Chapter 8 under "Fraudulent Misrepresentation."

Conspiracy

Conspiracy

A **conspiracy to injure** takes place where two or more persons act together using unlawful means to injure the business interests of another. For example, in the *Sagaz* case mentioned above, where the key employee was given kickbacks to change to a new supplier of seat covers, the actions of that employee and the supplier together also constituted a conspiracy. When a group of employees work together to get another employee fired, a conspiracy is involved. In *Meehan v. Tremblett*,[52] the plaintiff worked as a corrections officer. His immediate supervisor and the superintendent got together, creating a false performance evaluation report that led to the plaintiff's forced resignation. This conspiracy to injure involved the wrongful act of creating false and misleading documents and was thus an actionable tort. Not only were the parties to it liable, but due to vicarious liability, the New Brunswick government (as employer) was held liable as well. See also the *Procor* case discussed above (Case Summary 4.10).[53]

An interesting case where an insurer alleged conspiracy to injure is *Insurance Corp. of British Columbia v. Husseinian*.[54] The plaintiff (ICBC) alleged that the defendants staged motor vehicle accidents to obtain insurance monies for personal injuries and property damage. Most of the motor vehicle accidents involved a stolen car either rear-ending another vehicle or hitting a parked car. The driver of the stolen vehicle would flee the scene of the accident on foot without ever being caught. The insurer established that the defendants either knew each other or shared acquaintances. The Court concluded there was conspiracy to injure. Further, this extensive scheme to defraud an insurer of significant monies was the type of reprehensible conduct that warranted an award of punitive damages.

Passing Off

Passing-off actionable

A **passing-off** action is appropriate when a business or product is presented to the public in such a way as to lead the public to believe that the product is being provided by another. When imitation Rolex watches are sold as the real thing, or when a restaurant adopts the golden arches logo, leading the public to believe it is part of the McDonald's chain when it is not, the tort of passing-off has been committed. The court can award damages in these circumstances, but an injunction or an order that the offending product be delivered to the plaintiff for destruction may be a more appropriate remedy. This will be discussed in more detail in Chapter 13 under "Intellectual Property."

Misuse of Confidential Information

Misuse of confidential information actionable

Wrongful disclosure of **confidential information** will also be discussed more extensively in Chapter 16. A company's trade secrets and other forms of confi-

---

52. *Supra* n.40.

53. [1996] N.B.J. No. 142 (C.A.).

54. [2008] B.C.J. No. 333 (S.C.).

dential information, including customer lists and future plans, are some of the most important assets a business can have, and their improper disclosure to a competitor can do that business great harm. Key employees, agents, and others that do business with that company have a duty not to disclose its confidential information to others or to use it for their own purposes. Persons can be sued where they fail in that duty. As discussed above, an action can also be brought against anyone who induced them to breach that confidence. This duty to maintain confidentiality may be imposed through contract or may arise simply because the information has been provided in confidence. Often it exists because of the fiduciary relationship existing between the parties. A fiduciary duty arises when one party places a considerable amount of trust in another, making himself particularly vulnerable to any wrongful actions of that trusted party. A fiduciary duty may arise, for example, if a client puts his business affairs in an advisor's hands. Fiduciary duty will be one of the topics discussed under the heading of professional liability in the next chapter.

An example of the misuse of such confidential information is found in *Enterprise Excellence Corporation v. Royal Bank of Canada*.[55] The plaintiffs approached the bank with a promotional idea, including the sponsorship of a radio program and the use of the phrase "Today's Entrepreneur." The bank rejected their proposal and instead went ahead on its own using the phrase "Today's Entrepreneur" constantly over a one-year period while the promotion ran. The Court found that this was a misuse of information that had been given to the bank in confidence and awarded damages of over half a million dollars to the plaintiff. The Judge found that such a breach of confidence took place where (1) the information was of a confidential nature, (2) it was given in confidence, and (3) it was misused by the person to whom it was conveyed. In this case all three requirements had been met.

CASE SUMMARY 4.13

Cheaters Never Prosper: *Walter Stewart Realty Ltd. v. Traber*[56]

A 200-acre tract of undeveloped land beside a housing development was thought to be unserviceable—at least until the plaintiff, Walter Stewart, discovered a method to service it. He found that the land was available, making it very valuable for residential development. He approached Mr. Traber, a real estate developer, with his plan, disclosing it to him only after receiving a promise that the information would be kept secret and confidential and that he would receive 30 percent of the profits from the venture. The developer then acquired the property and developed it, but refused to give Stewart the funds promised. Stewart sued, claiming that the project amounted to a joint venture and that there had been a breach of confidentiality.

At trial the Judge found that the agreement for a joint venture, while discussed, had never been finalized. Nonetheless, the conduct of the developer amounted to a breach of confidentiality, and Stewart was awarded 15 percent of the profits. On appeal the

---

55. [2002] O.J. No. 3086 (Sup.Ct.J.).

56. [1995] A.J. No. 636 (C.A.); supplementary reasons [1995] A.J. No. 971 (C.A.).

Court agreed that there had been a breach of confidentiality but also held that the appropriate damages should be based on the original amount of 30 percent of the profits from the development, as originally agreed.

SMALL BUSINESS PERSPECTIVE

The case illustrates that a breach of confidence not only involves conveying that confidential information to someone else but also includes using it inappropriately for one's own purposes.

PRIVACY

Privacy protection initially found only in statutes

Invasion of a person's **privacy** may take the form of a physical intrusion, surveillance, misuse of an image or name, or access to information. Businesses often use information that people would like to keep private. They sometimes use images or likenesses to promote products without permission. Until very recently, there was no tort of invasion of privacy in common law, but several provinces made interfering with a person's privacy a statutory tort.[57] These statutes enabled claimants to sue if, for example, their likeness or voice was used without their consent. In *Heckert v. 5470 Investments Ltd.*[58] a tenant sued her landlord for invasion of privacy by video surveillance and was awarded $3500 in damages. British Columbia's *Privacy Act* was relied upon. In *L.A.M. v. J.E.L.I.*[59] the defendant videotaped the plaintiff and her daughter in the bathroom through a peephole; general and punitive damages were awarded.

Pursuant to these *Privacy Acts*, remedies ranging from damages to injunctions and accounting for profits may be awarded. Often, consent of the claimant operates as a defence.

CASE SUMMARY 4.14

Time to Recognize Invasion of Privacy as a Tort: *Somwar v. McDonald's Restaurants of Canada Ltd.*[60]

The plaintiff sued his employer for invasion of privacy after discoveringthat the employer conducted a credit check on him without his permission."

Can someone whose privacy has been violated by another person pursue a civil remedy in the courts of Ontario? Does our law recognize the tort of invasion of privacy?" The trial judgment begins by asking these two questions.

After reviewing the developing case law and legal commentary on this issue, the trial Judge concluded: "The traditional torts such as nuisance, trespass, and harassment may

---

57. [2008] B.C.J. No. 1854 (S.C.).

58. See *Privacy Act*, R.S.B.C. 1996, c. 373; *The Privacy Act*, R.S.S. 1978, c. P-24; *The Privacy Act*, C.C.S.M. c. P125. *Privacy Act*, R.S.N.L. 1990, c. P-22.

59. [2008] B.C.J. No. 1612 (S.C.).

60. [2006] O.J. No. 64 (Sup.Ct.J.).

not provide adequate protection against infringement of an individual's privacy interests. Protection of those privacy interests by providing a common law remedy for their violation would be consistent with *Charter* values and an 'incremental revision' and logical extension of the existing jurisprudence." . . . "Even if the plaintiff's claim for invasion of privacy were classified as 'novel' (which, in any event, is not a proper basis for dismissing it) the foregoing analysis leads me to conclude that the time has come to recognize invasion of privacy as a tort in its own right."

DISCUSSION QUESTIONS

Based on your understanding of *stare decisis*, does this case establish the tort of invasion of privacy across Canada? What level of judicial recognition is required before one can say with certainty that the tort of invasion of privacy exists in its own right?

With judicial recognition of the tort of invasion of privacy increasing, parties may soon be relieved of trying to "fit a square peg into a round hole." Because of the courts' reluctance to recognize invasion of privacy as a tort, parties have tried to characterize the action complained as another kind of tort. For example, where a business uses a person's image, name, or likeness to promote its product without permission, there is an innuendo communicated that the person has endorsed the product. That is a false statement and is actionable as defamation. Obviously, it would be much clearer if parties could simply sue for breach of privacy.

In the last decade, the number of problems arising from abuses with respect to the use of personal and private information, such as the misuse of health and medical records, has increased exponentially, largely as a result of ecommerce. Governments have taken steps to help protect consumers, but still face the challenge of enforcing new regulations in light of the borderless nature of the internet. The encouragement of self-regulation has not been overly successful. This is an area where international treaties may make an important contribution.

Internet poses new problems

Violations of privacy occur when private information is exchanged in a commercial transaction over the internet and then is used again without consent or is sold to another company for another purpose. Legislation has been enacted at both the federal and provincial levels to control the collection, use, and distribution of such personal information. The federal *Privacy Act*[61] gives people the right to access their personal information held by government and government agencies and severely restricts how that information can be disseminated to others. The *Personal Information Protection and Electronic Documents Act (PIPEDA)*[62] regulates the collection and use of personal information at both the federal and provincial level and applies to all organizations including private corporations. It requires them to account for their activities, identify the purposes for which the information is being collected, inform and get the consent of the individuals involved, and limits the use, disclosure, and retention of the information.

Collection and use of private information

The organization concerned must ensure the accuracy of the information, protect it with security safeguards, and be open about policies and practices relating to the management of the information. The *Act* requires that organizations

Requirement of notice and consent

---

[61] R.S.C. 1985, c. P-21.

[62] S.C. 2000, c. 5.

make available to individuals, upon request, the nature of the information and how it is being used. It also outlines how an individual would proceed to have a complaint reviewed and empowers a privacy commissioner to impose fines for violations.

Model Code approved as a national standard for privacy protection

PIPEDA has attached as its central core—and has given statutory standing to— the Code of the Canadian Standards Association (CSA). The CSA code, entitled the "Model Code for the Protection of Personal Information," was approved as a national standard by the Standards Council of Canada and was published in 1996. It sets out ten privacy-protection principles. The European Union enacted legislation to protect privacy in this area some time ago, and the passage of this *Act* provides similar protection here, removing a major barrier that threatened to interfere with international business.

The federal government's *PIPEDA* applies in all provinces except where legislation that provides for equivalent protection has been passed by the province. At the time of writing, Quebec, British Columbia, and Alberta have passed "substantially similar" legislation. It must also be emphasized that while the rights, obligations, and remedies set out in these statutes are important with respect to safeguarding private information, they do not create a general right to sue in tort for a violation of those provisions.

Limits on advanced encryption

Another problem relating to privacy is the unauthorized interception of communications between individuals. While most sites where important information is transferred have encryption devices, determined hackers can break those codes. If the codes become too sophisticated, then governments that make use of this information in their surveillance activities cannot decode the information and so are reluctant to allow advanced encryption. This creates a serious dilemma.

Another related problem is the widespread use of "cookies" and other related tools associated with internet communication. These are embedded devices that track a user's internet activities and allow others to read private information about their internet browsing. The information may simply be used by the user's internet service provider to improve its service, but it may also be sold to retailers for marketing purposes, or used to incriminate a person who has been downloading and inappropriately using sites.

Privacy and the internet

Businesses are often tempted to extract private information from their employees or even to use surveillance techniques to obtain information about them. Secret surveillance of computer users is a major problem, especially in the work environment, where it seems that employers have the right to read employees' emails and monitor their internet use on their office computers. Telephones and electronic mail are sometimes monitored. Medical information, political or religious affiliations, treatment for alcohol or drug-related problems, even mental conditions, all may be of considerable interest. Surveillance for detecting theft and monitoring other security concerns is also common. This is dangerous territory, as it may violate statutory rights to privacy in place in that jurisdiction. It may also be a violation of human rights legislation, depending on the kind of information being sought and the methods used to obtain it.

As stated at the beginning of this chapter, tort law is continually evolving, with the courts declaring new torts to exist as the need arises. The tort of spoliation, for example, is recognized in the United States and has been recently asserted in Canada. It would provide a remedy where one party has deliberately spoiled or destroyed the evidence needed by the plaintiff to establish a civil case. In *Spasic*

Estate v. Imperial Tobacco Ltd.[63] the Ontario Court of Appeal found that in the proper circumstances a trial judge might find that the tort of spoliation did exist; pre-trial dismissal of the action on the grounds that no cause of action was disclosed was therefore inappropriate. The Court stated at para. 22:

Tort of spoliation grants remedy where evidence has been destroyed

> If it is established that the conduct of the respondents resulted in harm to the plaintiff by making it impossible for her to prove her claim, then it will be for the trial judge, in the context of a complete record, to determine whether the plaintiff should have a remedy. This is how the progress of the common law is marked in cases of first impression, where the court has created a new cause of action where none had been recognized before... I can see no reason why the trial judge should be precluded from considering all possible remedies, including a separate tort, on the basis of the record that will be developed.

The evolution of tort law, with new torts being recognized as the need arises, certainly makes tort law interesting from an academic's perspective. From a businessperson's perspective, this constant evolution of law underscores the importance of having an ongoing relationship with a lawyer to keep abreast of changes in the law.

CASE SUMMARY 4.15

Torts in Cyberspace: *Braintech, Inc. v. Kostiuk*[64]

A case heard in British Columbia helps to clarify some of the problems regarding jurisdiction in internet-related disputes. In this case, a Vancouver firm sued a Vancouver investor for defamation over comments he made about the company in a chat room at Silicon Investor. The lawsuit was filed in a Texas court (even though both litigants were in Vancouver, and there was no active presence of the plaintiff in Texas) primarily because the court in that jurisdiction has a reputation for making huge damage awards. The defendant did not defend himself, believing that the court had no jurisdiction in the case. The plaintiff was awarded US$300 000 in damages. When the successful plaintiff took the judgment to the British Columbia Court to have it enforced, the defendant argued that the Texas court had no jurisdiction in the matter and was not the appropriate forum to hear the case. He lost at the trial level, but that decision was reversed on appeal.

It was argued that the case should have been heard where there was a "real and substantial connection" to the matter in dispute. Because of the nature of the internet, the only connection with Texas was that a Texas resident could have logged on to an out-of-state internet site and read the alleged libel. But that was true of any location in any country, and to allow any location to have such jurisdiction would have a "crippling effect" on the internet and freedom of expression. The danger is having several different parallel actions going on at the same time. The action should be brought according to American law in a jurisdiction where there was a "real and substantial presence," or according to Canadian law if that was the jurisdiction having a "real and substantial connection" to the case. The Court found that the connection was to British Columbia and not Texas. The Supreme Court of Canada refused leave to appeal. The decision is important

---

63. [2000] O.J. No. 2690 (C.A.).

64. [1999] B.C.J. No. 622 (C.A.); leave to appeal to S.C.C. refused, [1999] S.C.C.A. No. 236.

because it spells out under what conditions a given jurisdiction can rule on an internet dispute and, by extension, which set of laws ought to apply to cyberspace behaviour.

Note, however, that the use of the internet here was passive. An active use of the internet occurs where the parties use the internet to communicate while engaging in commercial transactions.

DISCUSSION QUESTIONS

In such circumstances, do you think the legal outcome ought to be different? Could several jurisdictions then have a "real and substantial" connection to the case? What impact would that have on the practice of business over the internet?

TORTS ONLINE

The popularity of the internet has given rise to new problems. Because the internet is uncontrolled, people can say whatever they want. All sorts of mischievous, defamatory, and obscene materials appear on the internet every day. Confidential information may easily be leaked, defamation and injurious falsehood may take place, privacy may be invaded, fraud may be perpetrated, and negligent misrepresentations made. What can victims do? The persons making the offending comments are liable for what they say, but litigation may be useless if it is not possible to determine who is responsible. Can the online service provider, the people who operate the internet server, or the operators of the particular website or chat room be sued for allowing their facilities to be used in this way? Arguably, the people who have direct control will have some responsibility, but the larger service providers have been treated more like telephone companies, escaping direct responsibility for the calls unless they have been asked to intervene. Canada's courts and legislators are now addressing these issues, and recent information on torts committed online can be found in Chapter 14 of this text

SUMMARY

Intentional torts

- Assault and battery involve deliberate interference with one's person—defences are consent or self-defence (reasonable force)
- Trespass—temporary or permanent intrusion on someone else's property, without lawful right or consent
- Trespass to chattels, conversion, and detinue—involve deliberate interference with another's goods
- False imprisonment—restraint of a person by someone without authority
- Malicious prosecution—pursuing criminal charges in the absence of evidence
- Private nuisance—unusual use of property causing foreseeable disturbance to neighbour
- Defamation—a false, published statement that discredits a person
  - Libel is written defamation; slander is spoken
  - Defences—truth, absolute privilege, qualified privilege, fair comment, and public interest responsible journalism
  - Injurious falsehood (product defamation or trade slander)—false, published statements that damage the goodwill associated with a product or business

Other business torts

- Inducing breach of contract—causing breach of a contract that exists between two other parties
- Interference with economic relations—using unlawful means to disrupt the business of another
- Intimidation—using threats to cause another to act against its interests
- Deceit—deliberately misleading another with false statements
- Conspiracy—acting in concert with others to damage a third party
- Passing-off—misleading the public to think one's goods or services are those of another
- Misuse of confidential information—wrongful use or disclosure of trade secrets and other confidential information
- Invasion of privacy—violation of a person's reasonable expectation of privacy
- Spoliation—destruction of evidence to hide proof of wrongdoing

Online torts

- Problems with jurisdiction and with enforcement

QUESTIONS

1. Explain what is meant by the statement "A tort is a civil wrong."
2. Distinguish between assault and battery.
3. How do doctors avoid liability for the tort of battery when operating on or otherwise treating patients?
4. What limitations are there on the right of self-defence when people are defending themselves against an attack?
5. Describe the situations in which battery may be justified.
6. What are the necessary elements that must be present for a person to be classified as a trespasser?
7. What may the proprietor of a business do when faced with an unruly patron?
8. Distinguish between trespass to chattels, conversion, and detinue.
9. Imprisonment can take the form of confinement, arrest, or submission to authority. Explain.
10. What must be established to sue successfully for false imprisonment?
11. How is malice typically established by a plaintiff who sues in malicious prosecution?
12. Distinguish between libel and slander, and explain the significance of the distinction.
13. Define the terms *innuendo* and *qualified privilege*.
14. Distinguish between defamation, trade slander, and deceit, indicating in what situations each would be used.
15. Explain the nature of the tort of inducing breach of contract and what circumstances would give rise to such an action.
16. How does the tort of interference with economic relations differ from the tort of inducing breach of contract?

17. Differentiate between conspiracy and intimidation.

18. List the remedies that may be appropriate to redress misuse of confidential information.

19. Privacy concerns are becoming more problematic in the technological age. What statutes protect the rights of individuals in this area?

20. How do the courts determine if they have jurisdiction over a tort action where the internet is the means of communicating a defamatory message?

CASES AND DISCUSSION QUESTIONS

1. *Babiuk v. Trann* (2005), 248 D.L.R. (4th) 530 (Sask. C.A.).
During a rugby game the defendant in this action punched the plaintiff (who was on the opposing team) in the face, breaking his jaw in two places.

Given the particularly violent nature of this game, consider the nature of any defence that might be available to the defendant and its likelihood of success. Would it make any difference to your answer to know that the punch was characterized by the plaintiff as a "sucker punch"?

How would it affect your answer to know that the defendant claimed that he was coming to the aid of a teammate who was on the ground with the plaintiff deliberately "stomping on his face"? There is considerable violence in some sports; if both parties are willing participants would it be better to leave matters like this to the governing sport body rather than involve the courts? Should there be exceptions?

2. *Kovacs v. Ontario Jockey Club* (1995), 126 D.L.R. (4th) 576 (Ont. (Gen. Div.)).
Kovacs tried to use a credit voucher that he had obtained from one racetrack at another, both owned and operated by the Ontario Jockey Club. Because of some misunderstanding, he was identified as a person who had committed a fraud on the racetrack. He was approached by two security guards and was asked to go to the office to discuss the matter. Kovacs felt that he had no choice, and he accompanied them. The matter was straightened out in about 20 minutes, and he went on his way. Kovacs sued.

What is the nature of his complaint and what will be the likely outcome? When the matter involves only a minor interference with a person's rights as in this case, wouldn't it be better to balance that against the need for the security guards to be free to do their jobs? Have we become such a litigious society that we threaten to paralyze retail and service businesses?

3. *Banfai v. Formula Fun Centre Inc.* (1984), 19 D.L.R. (4th) 683 (Ont. H.C.).
Ontario Hydro leased property to the defendant who ran a small racetrack operating scaled-down Grand Prix cars from 11 a.m. to 11 p.m. each day during the summer season. The noise generated from the motors and screeching tires seriously interfered with the plaintiffs' operation of their motel located adjacent to the amusement park.

Indicate the nature of the plaintiffs' complaint, the likelihood of success, and what would be an appropriate remedy if they were successful in their action. How would you balance the interests of the two businesses?

4. *Haight-Smith v. Neden* (2002), 211 D.L.R. (4th) 370 (B.C.C.A.).
Haight-Smith was a teacher in an elementary school in British Columbia for many years and during that time had a difficult relationship with her employer. At one stage she

filed a harassment charge and the person designated to investigate disclosed the allegations at a staff meeting. She felt this was a violation of her confidentiality rights and made some strong statements to that effect at that meeting. After receiving several complaints that those attending the meeting felt intimidated by her comments, the superintendent decided to investigate her conduct and suspended her from teaching pending the outcome of that investigation. The assistant superintendent interviewed a number of her fellow teachers and colleagues and it is the statements made during that investigation that she is claiming defamed her. She grieved this suspension and it was settled by her employer and union. She then sued a number of those fellow teachers and colleagues for defamation because of the things they had said about her.

Indicate what would be the most effective defence for those teachers in this situation and what would have to be established for that defence to be effective. Do you think the rules about defamation and privileges are sufficient to deal with the conflicting interests in this type of situation?

5. *Ha v. Harnois*, 2004 SKCA 172, 136 A.C.W.S. (3d) 773 (Sask. C.A.).

The defendant, Harnois, in this action alleged that Ha had inappropriately touched her buttocks and later her breast at a Tae Kwon Do Canada social event. Both parties were prominent figures in that organization. She sent a letter summarizing her complaint to the president of the organization, other grandmasters, and to a number of other officials in the Canadian chapter. She also sent copies to government sports agencies and to the international Tae Kwon Do associations. There were 28 copies sent in all. Ha sued for defamation. Explain what likely defences would be raised by Harnois and her likelihood of success.

How would it affect your answer to know that she had approached the president and grandmasters of the Canadian organization who had asked her not to report the incident? Consider also the objectives of encouraging free expression against the damage to a person's reputation that these defamation rules are intended to protect.

6. *369413 Alberta Ltd. v. Pocklington* (2000), 194 D.L.R. (4th) 109, 271 A.R. 280, (Alta. C.A.).

Gainers was an Alberta corporation beset with financial difficulties when its sole director, Peter Pocklington, signed a director's resolution transferring certain shares owned by Gainers (valued in the millions) to his own company, Pocklington Holdings Ltd., for $100. Gainers had earlier agreed not to sell or dispose of its assets without the prior written consent of its major creditor, the Alberta government. This transfer took place one day before Alberta gave notice of its intention to exercise its rights under their security agreement.

What is the nature of the creditor's complaint and what would be the appropriate remedy? Should any remedy be awarded in this type of situation or should this simply be treated as clever business practice?

7. *Myers v. Canadian Broadcasting Corp.* (2001), 54 O.R. (3d) 626 (C.A.), leave to appeal to S.C.C. refused, [2001] S.C.C.A. No. 433.

In an episode of *TheFifth Estate*, the CBC interviewed Dr. Myers on his views about a certain heart medication; Myers had conducted a study on behalf of Bayer concerning the drug. The broadcast clips from the interview distorted Myers's statements and conveyed the impression that Myers promoted the interests of pharmaceutical companies over the interests of patients. The innuendo suggested that Myers was dishonest, recommending medication he knew to be harmful.

Would the CBC be able to establish the defences of fair comment or qualified privilege with any success? Does the media have a duty to communicate such information?

Might the Court conclude that distortion of Dr. Myers's statements suggests malice on the part of the broadcaster? Will malice defeat these defences if proven?

8. *Reichmann v. Berlin*, [2002] O.J. No. 2732 (Sup. Ct. J.).

The internet provides direct and inexpensive access to a massive audience and with it the opportunity to defame. Who should be held liable for defamatory statements broadcast via the internet, the originator alone or the service provider as well? In the *Reichmann* case, defamatory statements published on the internet repeatedly asserted that Reichmann interfered with an estate by knowingly cheating an innocent man out of a multimillion-dollar inheritance. The statements were published over a three-and-a-half-year period, using seven different websites.

Should the courts order a service provider to disclose the identity of an originator once a *prima facie* case against the unknown originator is disclosed? Should the internet be subject to defamation laws? If the information can be viewed worldwide, whose laws should apply?

9. *Bahner v. Marwest Hotel Co.* (1969), 6 D.L.R. (3d) 322 (B.C.S.C.); aff'd (1970), 12 D.L.R. (3d) 646 (B.C.C.A.).

Bahner, unfamiliar with the provincial liquor laws, ordered and obtained a bottle of wine shortly before 11:30 p.m. When Bahner discovered just before midnight that he had to consume the opened but untouched wine in the few minutes remaining, he left it and refused to pay for it. He paid for the meal but not the wine. When he attempted to leave, he was detained by the manager and a security guard until the police arrived. Bahner was arrested and spent the night in jail.

Name the tort action that Bahner might commence. Against whom is the case likely to succeed? Why?

10. *Duke v. Puts* (2004), 21 C.C.L.T. (3d) 181, 241 Sask. R. 187, 313 W.A.C. 187, [2004] 6 W.W.R. 208 (Sask. C.A.).

Duke, a pharmacist, operated a successful pharmacy in Saskatchewan for 20 years. Dr. Puts developed a suspicion about Duke's association with a physician in another town; Puts accused Duke of conspiring with that physician to cheat the health care |system by claiming for false prescriptions and double billing. In a letter of complaint sent to the College of Physicians, Puts alleged professional misconduct against Duke. He told other people that Duke was a crook. These accusations greatly harmed the pharmacist's reputation and business, and caused him to sell his business at a reduced price.

Assuming all the allegations were false, what tort actions could Duke bring against Dr. Puts? What defences, if any, could the defendant assert?

Chapter 5

Negligence, Professional Liability, and Insurance

CHAPTER OBJECTIVES

1. Identify the four elements of a negligence claim
2. Define when a duty of care arises and explain how the courts determine whether it is owed
3. Describe a breach of the standard of care
4. Identify the test used to determine if a breach has occurred
5. Explain how both physical and legal causation are proven
6. Identify the types of damage or loss that the courts have recognized and deemed compensable
7. Distinguish the defences applicable to the tort of negligence
8. Describe the circumstances where professional liability may arise
9. Clarify when product liability may be imposed
10. Define the four types of insurance businesses commonly need
11. Identify when an insurable interest exists
12. Explain the significance of insurance being a contract of utmost good faith
13. Identify the duties imposed on the insured and insurer

The torts discussed in the previous chapter involved intentional conduct. The tortfeasor's deliberate or "intentional" acts established the required degree of fault necessary to constitute an actionable wrong or tort. In this chapter we will examine the law of negligence, which, unlike intentional torts, involves inadvertent conduct causing injury or damage to others. The required fault is found in the failure of the wrongdoer to live up to the degree of skill or care required in the circumstances. In this chapter we will also examine defences that can eliminate or reduce a tortfeasor's liability. Finally, product and professional liability are explored, two applications of the law of negligence that are of particular interest to businesspeople.

In the last part of this chapter, insurance will be discussed. While not related specifically to the subject of tort law, insurance is used primarily as a method of spreading the risk of injury or damages. Several different types of insurance will be discussed, including liability insurance, which is uniquely designed to provide insurance coverage for the liability that individuals or businesses may face when a tort action is brought against them.

CASE SUMMARY 5.1

Contestant Takes a Tumble: *Crocker v. Sundance Northwest Resorts Ltd.*[1]

Mr. Crocker went to Sundance resorts and participated in an inner tube competition run by the resort for the entertainment of its patrons. It consisted of going down a regular portion of the ski hill containing many moguls, which caused the inner tubes and participants to be bounced around like "rag dolls."

Crocker entered the competition by signing, but not reading, a document that contained a waiver absolving the ski hill of responsibility. He went down the hill the first time and won his heat but by the second heat it was clear he had been drinking and the operators suggested he not compete. He had consumed several drinks at the bar and some brandy given to him by the driver of the beer van. But Crocker insisted on continuing in the competition. He dropped one tube down the hill but the operators supplied him with another. On his second run he was thrown from the inner tube and seriously injured.

The Supreme Court of Canada found that the resort organized a dangerous competition for commercial gain. It owed a duty to be careful, especially to visibly intoxicated participants where the potential for injury was great—potentially more so than with sober individuals. Although Crocker was initially cautioned not to proceed with the second run, Sundance later supplied him with a replacement tube. The resort thus failed its duty to keep intoxicated contestants from competing and injuring themselves and because of its negligence, was liable for the injuries suffered.

Sundance asserted the defence that Crocker had voluntarily assumed the risk, pointing to the signed waiver. The Court rejected the *volenti non fit injuria* argument. By voluntarily participating in the race, Crocker had assumed only the physical risk, not the legal risk. The signed waiver didn't apply since he had not read it and insufficient steps were taken to alert Crocker of its presence in the entry form. However, Crocker had also been negligent. Because of his contributory negligence Crocker was held responsible for 25 percent of the loss.

The case illustrates the requirement of the existence of a duty of care and the use of the reasonable person test to determine whether sufficient care was exercised. It demonstrates the operation of contributory negligence in reducing the award of damages. It further illustrates the significant restriction on the defence of *volenti non fit injuria*, which can only be used where there is an assumption of both the legal risk and the physical risk.

DISCUSSION QUESTIONS

So what is an event organizer to do to eliminate its potential liability? Is it ever safe to rely solely on waivers? Is back-up protection in the form of insurance a virtual necessity?

---

1. [1998] 1 S.C.R. 1186

NEGLIGENCE

Negligence: Its A, B, C, and D

Negligence is by far the most important area of tort liability for businesspeople and professionals. It involves inadvertent or unintentionally careless conduct causing injury or damage to another person or his property. Four required elements or ingredients must be established by the plaintiff to succeed in a negligence action. Failure to establish any one of these four will lead to dismissal of the plaintiff's action. See Table 5.1, which sets out those ingredients and lists the tests used by the courts to determine whether these elements have in fact been proven

Table 5.1 Negligence: The Required Ingredients

Ingredients		Tests used
A	A duty of care is owed to the plaintiff	1. Foreseeable plaintiff test (reasonable foreseeability test)
		2. Policy considerations—may negate existence of a duty
B	Breach of that duty; breach of the standard of care	Reasonable person test
C	Causation	1. Physical: "but for" test
		2. Legal: remoteness test
D	Damage	Refer to precedents—has this type been recognized by courts as compensable?

A: A DUTY TO EXERCISE CARE MUST EXIST

Negligence involves a failure on someone's part to live up to a duty to be careful to someone else. We do not have a duty to be careful to everyone. The court must determine whether the defendant owed a duty of care to the plaintiff. The court uses the **reasonable foreseeability test**, also called the *foreseeable plaintiff test*, to determine the existence of such a duty. Based on the proximity of the parties, if it were reasonably foreseeable that the conduct complained of would cause harm to the plaintiff, a duty to be careful exists. It seems almost self-evident today that we should act carefully toward people who we can see are put at risk by our behaviour, but this was not always the case.

www.pearsoned.ca/mybuslawlab

Reasonable foreseeability test establishes duty

Foreseeable plaintiff test

(a) injury to plaintiff foreseeable

CASE SUMMARY 5.2

"Neighbours" Are Owed a Duty of Care: *Donoghue v. Stevenson*[2]

The reasonable foreseeability test was developed in *Donoghue v. Stevenson*, one of the most significant cases of the 20th century. Mrs. Donoghue went with a friend into a café,

---

2. [1932] A.C. 562 (H.L.).

where the friend ordered a bottle of ginger beer for her. After consuming some of it, Donoghue discovered part of a decomposed snail at the bottom of her bottle. She became very ill as a result of drinking the contaminated beverage. In the process of suing, she discovered that she had some serious problems. She could not successfully sue the café that had supplied the ginger beer for breach of contract; she had no contract with the establishment, as her friend had made the purchase. Similarly, she could not successfully sue the café for negligence, since it had done nothing wrong, the ginger beer having been bottled in an opaque container and served to her in the bottle. Her only recourse was to sue the manufacturer for negligence in producing the product, but the bottler claimed it owed her no duty to be careful. The Court had to determine whether a duty to be careful was owed by the manufacturer to the consumer of its product. In the process of finding that such a duty was owed, the House of Lords developed the reasonable foreseeability test. Lord Atkin, one of the Judges in the case, made the following classic statement when discussing how to determine to whom we owe a duty:

> The rule that you are to love your neighbour becomes in law, you must not injure your neighbour; and the lawyer's question "Who is my neighbour?" receives a restricted reply. You must take reasonable care to avoid acts or omissions which you can reasonably foresee would be likely to injure your neighbour. Who, then, in law, is my neighbour? The answer seems to be— persons who are so closely and directly affected by my act that I ought reasonably to have them in contemplation as being so affected when I am directing my mind to the acts or omissions which are called in question.[3]

SMALL BUSINESS PERSPECTIVE

Risk management involves asking whether one's actions put others at risk. If injury is foreseeable, then a duty to take care may be owed. Liability could follow unless reasonable precautions are taken to avoid causing harm.

(b) proximity between the parties

We owe a duty, then, to anyone whom we can reasonably anticipate might be harmed by our conduct. The reasonable foreseeability test has been further refined in the English *Anns* case.[4] The *Anns* case created a two-stage test for determining the existence of a duty of care. The first question to ask is whether there was a degree of neighbourhood or **proximity** between the parties such that if the person being sued had thought of it, he or she would have realized that his or her actions posed a risk of danger to the other. Essentially, this question restates the *Donoghue v. Stevenson* reasonable foreseeability test. Note that this test has two requirements. First that injury to the plaintiff was *reasonably foreseeable*, but also that there is a *relationship* between them such that the plaintiff was of a class of "persons who are so closely and directly affected by my act" that the defendant should have had them in mind when committing the act in question.

Policy aspect applies to new situations

The second set of questions probes deeper, providing for exceptions or modifications to the prime test. Was there any reason that the duty should not be imposed? Should the scope of the duty be reduced? Should the class to whom the duty is owed be limited, or should the damages be reduced? These questions

---

3. *Ibid.* at 580.

4. *Anns v. Merton, London Borough Council*, [1977] 2 All E.R. 492 (H.L.).

allow the court to consider social policy rather than strict legal rules when looking at special situations and relationships. Essentially, the courts try to avoid situations where a defendant may be exposed to "liability in an indeterminate amount for an indeterminate time to an indeterminate class."[5] The English have abandoned the principles set out in the *Anns* case, but the Supreme Court of Canada has made it clear that it is good law in Canada.[6] It is important to note, however, that this second policy aspect of the *Anns* test will only be applied to those new situations that don't fit into a category of negligence where a duty of care has already been recognized by the courts.

Only relevant where a duty of care has never been imposed in the past

In Canada, then, the existence of a duty of care is established, by the reasonable foreseeability test set out in the *Donoghue v. Stevenson* case; however in new situations or classes of cases where a duty of care has not already been established, the court can apply the second half of the *Anns* case test negating or modifying that duty on the basis of policy considerations.

Duty owed to anyone who could foreseeably be harmed

In many negligence cases, the existence of a duty is obvious and the court need not deal with the problem at length. Still, it is a required element in a negligence action and is important in those cases where the existence of a duty of care is brought into question.

Scope of duty can be reduced where apropriate

CASE SUMMARY 5.3

Is the Employer Owed a Duty of Care? *D'Amato v. Badger*[7]

Key issues that surfaced in the *D'Amato* case concerned to whom a duty of care is owed. If a corporation's key employee is injured, can the corporation recover its economic loss from the party at fault? It is conceivable that an employer corporation will suffer economically if its employee(s) are unable to work. But will the party who caused injury to an employee be held liable for the economic loss suffered by the employer?

D'Amato was injured in a motor vehicle accident. The respondent Badger was held liable for D'Amato's injuries. But D'Amato was also part owner of the appellant shop. Because D'Amato could no longer perform auto repairs, the appellant auto shop had to hire a replacement. The appellant claimed its economic loss from the defendant.

The Supreme Court, however, decided there was no relationship between the respondent and the shop. The injury to D'Amato occurred on the open road—not within the business premises of the appellant. Thus, there was insufficient proximity between the respondent's negligence and the economic loss suffered by the appellant shop to ground liability. Essentially, injury to the appellant was neither foreseeable nor sufficiently proximate to the act of negligence to warrant recovery.

Note that in this case the Court was being asked to recognize a new duty of care—as between a motorist and the employer of the one injured in a collision. Accordingly, policy considerations, as required by the second half of the *Anns* case, had to be considered. The Supreme Court indicated that even if there was sufficient proximity, there were policy reasons to prohibit recovery by employers for losses resulting from injuries to employees. Allowing such recovery could lead to indeterminate liability to an unlimited

5. *Canadian National Railway Co. v. Norsk Pacific Steamship Co.*, [1992] 1 S.C.R. 1021.

6. *Ultramares Corp. v. Touche* (1931), 174 N.E. 441 at 444 (N.Y.C.A.).

7. [1996] S.C.J. No. 84.

number of potential plaintiffs. The Court reasoned that employers/corporations could plan for the risk of physical injury to their employees/shareholders through insurance or other means. Essentially, the Supreme Court reasoned that it made more social sense to put this duty onto the shoulders of employers rather than to cause motorists and their insurers to bear this additional risk.

SMALL BUSINESS PERSPECTIVE

Since the Courts are reluctant to expand the duty of care to employers in such cases, purchasing insurance on the lives of key employees may be the only way to protect against economic loss that follows injury to key personnel. A cost-benefit analysis may well be called for.

The Supreme Court also dealt with this issue of expanding the duty of care to new situations in the case of *Cooper v. Hobart*.[8] Cooper, one of more than 3000 investors who suffered a loss after advancing funds to a registered mortgage broker, brought a class action, suing the Registrar of Mortgage Brokers, a statutory regulator. Cooper claimed that the Registrar, aware of serious violations of the B.C. *Mortgage Brokers Act* committed by the broker, failed to notify investors of the investigation and negligently failed to promptly suspend the broker's licence.

Again, the issue was whether a duty of care was owed—this time by the Registrar to the investors. The Court determined there was insufficient proximity between the Registrar and investors to found a duty of care. The Supreme Court further held that even if a *prima facie* duty were established, it would have been negated for overriding policy reasons. Imposing a duty would have effectively created an insurance scheme for investors, at great cost to the taxpaying public. This result, on policy grounds, was unacceptable to the Court. Admittedly, this approach of taking policy considerations into account before a duty of care is recognized in "new" situations, weakens the predictability of case law—but how else can "new" situations be adequately addressed?

CASE SUMMARY 5.4

"Policy Considerations" Negate Finding a Duty of Care: *Dobson v. Dobson*[9]; *Childs v. Desormeaux*[10]

Two further examples of the Court applying policy considerations in determining whether a new duty of care should be imposed arose in two cases involving negligent operation of vehicles. In the *Dobson* case, a pregnant mother drove a snowmobile negligently, crashed, and caused injury to her unborn child. The child was mentally and physically disabled and the child's grandfather sought recovery from the negligent parent (who was insured). The Court decided that the existence (or absence) of insurance was not to be a factor. Instead, the Court found that due to the proximity of the parties, the mother did owe her unborn child a duty of care. Injury to one's fetus is foreseeable if

---

8. [2001] 3 S.C.R. 537.
9. [1999] 2 S.C.R. 753.
10. [2006] 1 S.C.R. 643.

one drives without due care. However, the Supreme Court was loath to impose a new duty of care as between a pregnant mother and her fetus, for to do so would severely impair the mother–child relationship. The purpose of tort law—compensation and deterrence—would not be furthered if pregnant mothers could be liable to their children. Further, imposing such liability on pregnant women would involve severe intrusions into their bodily integrity, privacy, and autonomy rights, as it would subject every aspect of pregnant women to judicial scrutiny. Thus, on policy grounds, the action was dismissed.

In the second case, Childs was severely injured when a drunk driver struck her vehicle in the early hours of New Year's Day. Childs sought to add as defendants the social hosts who served alcohol to Desmormaux and then allowed him to drive while impaired. Again, applying the foreseeability test, hosts may owe a duty of care to their guests and to other users of the road that they might encounter. But on policy grounds, the Court rationed that Canadians were not ready for the imposition of social host liability. Insurance to protect against such liability was not yet readily available, if at all.

SMALL BUSINESS PERSPECTIVE

In the *Childs* case, the Court sent the signal that social host liability may become a reality in the future. Note that many insurers now provide this type of coverage. Businesses that rent out facilities for parties, weddings, and other social events where alcohol is to be served are well advised to require the host to purchase social host liability coverage. It may also be prudent to require that the facility owner be named as a co-insured!

Misfeasance and Nonfeasance

When discussing duty of care, it is also important to note that the law imposes a duty on people to carry out their activities carefully so as to not cause harm to others. This involves **misfeasance** or wrongful conduct. But the courts are very reluctant to provide a remedy in a case of **nonfeasance** (when a person fails to do something), unless it can be established that a particular relationship existed, such as in the case of a swimmer and a lifeguard, or a child and a guardian. People who see a child drowning have no duty in tort law to rescue that child, unless they happen to be lifeguards. Doctors have no legal duty to come to the aid of an accident victim when they pass a car crash. But once someone does start to help, he has an obligation to continue to do so in a reasonable way. Stopping midway may lead to a claim of abandonment, which can draw liability in itself. Also, when someone attempts to repair a car of a friend, he has no legal duty to help, but if he does he is responsible for any damage caused by his carelessness. These rules discourage people from coming to the aid of others. In an attempt to alleviate such harsh consequences, some jurisdictions have introduced legislation either creating a duty to assist or at least protecting rescuers from liability for injuries arising out of their rescue efforts.[11] Refer to the MyBusLawLab for details.

Unacceptable action—misfeasance

Failure to act—nonfeasance

Usually no duty in case of nonfeasance

Once starting help, person must take reasonable care

B: BREACH OF THE STANDARD OF CARE

In a negligence action, the court must first determine whether the defendant owed the plaintiff a duty to act with care in the first place; secondly, the court

---

11. *Emergency Medical Aid Act*, R.S.A. 2000, c. E-7; Good Samaritan Act, R.S.B.C. 1996, c. 172; Good Samaritan Act, 2001, S.O. 2001, c. 2.

Reasonable person test establishes standard

needs to ascertain whether the defendant demonstrated sufficient care. How careful need one be to avoid liability? The **reasonable person test** is used by the court in many areas of law to establish standards of socially acceptable behaviour. Faced with the problem of having to decide if certain conduct is socially acceptable, the courts ask, "What would a reasonably prudent person, in possession of all the facts of the case, have done in this situation?"

Reasonable care, not perfection, required

It is important to understand that the standard determined using the reasonable person test is not what would be expected of an average person. A reasonable person is expected to be "prudent" or particularly careful, demonstrating a level of behaviour considerably better than average. On the other hand, the conduct is not required to be perfect. If one draws an analogy to the concept of par in a golf game, a standard score, called *par*, is set for each hole on the course. If par for a particular hole is 3, the average golfer would likely score 4 or 5. On the other hand, 3 is not the best possible score. Rather, par is the score you would expect from a good golfer playing well. Similarly, the reasonable person test represents the standard of care expected from a prudent person who, in light of the circumstances, acts with reasonable care. To avoid liability for negligence, the standard of care is reasonableness as opposed to average or perfection. If the conduct of the defendant is found to have fallen below this standard, he is negligent and liable for any injury or loss thus caused.

Surrounding circumstances relevant to degree of care

What is reasonable conduct will vary with the circumstances. For example, the court will take into account the risk of loss. In *Blyth v. Birmingham Water Works, Co.*,[12] the plaintiff's home was flooded when a water main serving a fireplug froze and burst during a severe winter cold spell. The Court rejected the plaintiff's claim that the water works company was negligent for not having placed the pipes deeper. Considering the risk, one could not justify the great costs of digging the pipes in deeper. The risk was low—the system had been in place for 25 years and this was the coldest winter in 50 years. The Judge in the case said, "Negligence is the omission to do something which a reasonable man, guided upon those considerations which ordinarily regulate the conduct of human affairs, would do, or doing something which a prudent and reasonable man would not do."[13]

Risk of injury affects standard, as does cost

Similarly, a person driving a truck or car must be more careful than a person driving a hay wagon because of the increased risk of significant injury. A teacher must exercise greater vigilance in supervising students engaged in risky gymnastics exercises, especially if students are unfamiliar with the equipment.[14]

---

12. (1856), 156 E.R. 1047 (Ex. Ct.).

13. *Ibid.*, p. 1049.

14. See *MacCabe v. Westlock Roman Catholic Separate School District No. 110*, reversed in part (2001), 293 A.R. 41 (C.A.), where liability was imposed partly on the teacher for failing to adequately supervise a gym class at which the student was rendered quadriplegic.

CASE SUMMARY 5.5

Police Chase Found to Violate Standard of Care Required: *Burbank v. Bolton*[15]

The Attorney General of British Columbia appealed a finding of negligence on the part of one of its police officers. The officer had been chasing a stolen vehicle, driven by a suspected impaired driver, when it sped through a stop sign and collided with a third automobile. The collision claimed the life of one child; others were seriously injured. The trial Judge determined that in conducting the pursuit, the officer had breached the requisite standard of care. Although the impaired driver was found to be 85 percent at fault, the officer was also negligent and fault was assessed at 15 percent. The action against the officer personally was dismissed, as a police officer could not be held liable for other than gross negligence. But the Attorney General was nonetheless liable on behalf of the Government for the conduct of the officer.

The Court of Appeal affirmed the finding that the officer had breached the standard of care. In addressing whether the risk of pursuit was justified, the evidence revealed that the officer had no specific information that any serious offence had been committed. She had good reason to believe that the driver of the vehicle might be impaired, but there was no justification for pursuing a suspected impaired driver through a residential area where it was expected that there would be a high volume of pedestrian and vehicular traffic.

As to causation, the "but for" test required a finding of causation when it could be said that but for the impugned conduct, the injury that was the subject of the claim would not have been suffered. Here, the collision would not have occurred but for the pursuit by the police officer.

SMALL BUSINESS PERSPECTIVE

This case exemplifies that the amount of care is dependent upon and shaped by the risks inherent in the activity. As risk increases, so does the requisite amount of care.

Expenses or costs will also be taken into consideration in determining the required standard of care. It may be possible to design and build an automobile that would suffer minimal damage in a high-speed accident, but the costs involved would be prohibitive. No one could afford such a car; therefore, it would be unreasonable to hold a manufacturer to such a standard. But here, care must be taken because saving money will not excuse the production of a defective or dangerous product. A balance must be struck.

What constitutes reasonable behaviour will also vary with the expertise of the person being sued. A doctor is expected to function, at least as far as medical matters are concerned, at a higher level than a non-medical person, and so is held to a higher standard. The test asks: Was the person's conduct up to the standard expected of a reasonable person in the same circumstances? Did he or she conduct himself or herself as a reasonable doctor, reasonable lawyer, reasonable accountant, reasonable plumber, or reasonable driver? This has special implications for professionals and other experts as the standard is not lowered due to inexperience; the novice is required to perform at the same standard as the rea-

---

15. [2007] B.C.J. No. 752 (B.C.C.A.).

Standard depends on expertise

sonably prudent practitioner. Note also that the standard does not diminish in the case of an elderly person.[16]

Liability varies with age

The opposite is true when children are involved. The courts recognize that a 13-year-old cannot be expected to act at the same level of responsibility as an adult. Children are liable for their torts, but the standard required of them is the level of conduct that would be expected of a reasonable child of the same age. Thus, a small child playing with matches may not be liable for a resulting fire, whereas a teenager doing the same thing could very likely be held responsible. At this point, attention usually turns to the parents. Although many people do not realize it, parents are not, as a general rule, vicariously liable for the torts committed by their children. In the absence of a statute to the contrary (and these are becoming much more common[17]) parents are liable only if it can be established that they were negligent in their own right by failing to properly train, control, or supervise their children. Refer to the MyBusLawLab for information on the provinces that have passed such statutes.

! REDUCING RISK 5.1

It has been suggested that risk avoidance is the most appropriate course for businesspeople to reduce the likelihood of being sued. Professionals should examine not only the condition of their premises, tools, cars, and other physical objects used in the course of business, but also the habits and practices that may give rise to a complaint. Medical professionals such as doctors, nurses, podiatrists, chiropractors, and the like run some risk of being sued in tort for battery and negligence. Since the nature of their practice depends on physical contact with their clients and patients, securing proper consent is a vital component of risk management. If the nature of the contact is more invasive, as in performing surgery, the consent must be fully informed. Detailed explanations of the procedure, the risks attached, and the alternatives available must all be given to secure an informed consent. Problems may also arise when physical injury is caused by an error in judgment or a mistake in practice. People involved in sports, education, training, and recreational activities face such a risk. The main thing to remember is that the standard of care demanded of such experts is that of the reasonable person operating in similar circumstances. A keen eye should be focused on physical premises, practices, service, and advice to make sure that potential dangers and misinformation or misdirection can be anticipated and avoided.

Liability may be established by circumstantial evidence

It is not always necessary for the plaintiff to show that the defendant was careless. This can sometimes be implied from the surrounding circumstances. For example, if a piano were to fall into the street from a fourth-floor apartment, injuring a passerby, those facts by themselves seem to say more eloquently than anyone could that the people who were handling the piano were careless in the way they moved it. From the evidence of the falling piano, the court can conclude that the handlers were negligent.

This type of situation used to be dealt with under a special provision of the law of negligence called *res ipsa loquitur* ("the thing speaks for itself"), but the

---

16. See *McKee (Guardian ad litem of) v. McCoy* (2001), 9 C.C.L.T. (3d) 294 (B.C.S.C.), where the standard of care applicable for a driver was that of an ordinary driver, not that of a person whose capacities are reduced by age. (Initially the defendant was found 100% liable, but on appeal it was determined that the plaintiff was struck in an "unmarked crosswalk" so the matter was remitted to the trial judge to reconsider liability. The defendant's liability was reduced to 80% as the plaintiff was found partly at fault.)

17. See, for example, Manitoba's *Parental Responsibility Act*, S.M. 1996, c. 61, C.C.S.M. c. P8, B.C.'s *Parental Responsibility Act,* S.B.C. 2001, c. 45, s. 3 and Ontario's *Parental Responsibility Act, 2000*, S.O. 2000, c. 4, s. 2.

Supreme Court of Canada has said that it is better approached as a matter of circumstantial evidence.[18] The new approach is somewhat more flexible, but the effect is similar. The court can find that the circumstantial evidence establishes a *prima facie* ("on the face of it") case and then turn to the defendants to produce evidence that they were not negligent. Without such evidence from the defendants, the plaintiff will be successful.[19]

C AND D: CAUSATION AND DAMAGES

Unlike intentional torts, which may be actionable even without any specific damage, negligence requires that some sort of loss to person or property be suffered. When a customer slips and falls on a wet floor in a store but suffers no injury there is no right to sue, even though the store employees have been careless. However, if the customer breaks a leg, this would be a tangible, physical injury, which would provide grounds for an action. For example, in *Joslyn & Olsen Contracting Ltd. v. Bouey*[20] architects were sued by the school division because the architects made an error in determining how much earth had to be removed to match one floor of an existing school with the floor of a new addition. Had a correct measurement been made in the first place, the cost of removing the extra dirt would have been factored into the initial price and would have been borne earlier. As it turned out, the greater excavating cost was paid later—after the error was discovered. Regardless of the miscalculation, the school division would have to remove and pay for removal of the same amount of dirt—so in essence it suffered no damage. The case was dismissed because no loss had been incurred.

In the past, there had to be some actual physical damage or bodily injury for the plaintiff to successfully sue for negligence. Today, the courts are willing to provide a remedy even in cases of pure economic loss or where the negligence has caused a recognized mental disorder, such as depression. Some parents have even successfully sued physicians for the "wrongful birth" of their child. It is a matter of considerable controversy, but where a physician fails to advise parents of a potential genetic defect and the pregnancy is allowed to continue, the cost of raising a child born with severe defects may be awarded.[21]

Damage or injury must be present

Economic loss and mental distress recognized as compensable injuries

"But For" Test: Physical Causation
For negligence to apply, not only must there be damage, but also that damage must be a direct result of the careless conduct. If the operator of a motor vehicle knowingly drives at night without tail lights, the driver can be said to be careless. However, if the vehicle is involved in a head-on collision, the driver of the other car could not rely on the first driver's failure to have tail lights to support a negligence action. The test usually applied in such situations is called the **"but for" test**. The plaintiff must prove to the court's satisfaction that but for the conduct complained of, no injury would have resulted. In this illustration, the plaintiff cannot say that but for a failure to have properly functioning tail lights, no collision would have occurred.

Conduct must be cause of injury

---

18. See *Jordan v. Power*, [2002] A.J. No. 1080 (Q.B.), which held: (1) in discharging the plaintiff's primary burden of proving negligence, circumstantial evidence can be used with or without direct evidence; (2) to avoid liability, the defendant need only neutralize or negate the inference of negligence, with evidence explaining the occurrence of injury without the defendant's negligence.

19. *Fontaine v. British Columbia (Official Administrator)*, [1998] 1 S.C.R. 424.

20. (1976), 2 A.R. 18 (C.A.).

21. *Zhang v. Kan*, [2003] B.C.J. No. 164 (B.C.S.C.) and *Jones (Guardian ad litem of) v. Rostvig*, [2003] B.C.J. No. 1840 (B.C.S.C.).

The "but for" test is the general test for causation. Where this test is unworkable, as where multiple causes bring about a single harm, the courts will look for material causation (whether the conduct complained of materially contributed to the injury or loss). If the defendant is part of the cause of an injury, the defendant may be liable even though his act alone was insufficient to cause the injury. For example, with respect to tainted blood, the Red Cross was found negligent in employing certain donor screening procedures. Even though others, such as the blood donors, may have been part of the cause of the injury, the Red Cross was held liable because the Court found that its carelessness was a material cause of injury to the recipients of tainted blood.[22]

Remoteness Test—Legal Causation

Problem of remoteness

Once the plaintiff has established that the defendant owed a duty to be careful to the plaintiff, that the defendant's conduct fell below the standard of care required in the situation, and that the conduct complained of caused some injury or loss to the plaintiff, negligence is established. Problems sometimes arise, however, when the connection between the conduct complained of and the injury seems tenuous or where the nature of the injury suffered is unusual or unexpected. For example, if a careless driver were to damage a power pole, causing an interruption of power to a business and thereby resulting in considerable economic loss, should the driver be held responsible for such an unexpected result? The suggestion is that the connection between the conduct complained of and the actual damage suffered is too remote. In Canada today, our courts will impose liability only when the defendant could have reasonably anticipated the general nature of the injury or damage suffered. Liability is avoided if the injury is too remote, or too unforeseeable. As Justice Dickson in *Ontario v. Coté* explained it: "It is not necessary that one foresee the precise concatenation of events; it is enough to fix liability if one can foresee in a general way the class or character of injury which occurred."[23]

The **"remoteness" test** is often confused with the test to determine whether a duty of care exists, since both are based on reasonable foreseeability. However, with duty of care, the test is used to determine whether *danger to the plaintiff* should have been anticipated, whereas with remoteness it is the *type of injury* itself that must have been foreseen.

CASE SUMMARY 5.6

Fly Phobia Not Foreseeable: *Mustapha v. Culligan of Canada Ltd.*[24]

Mustapha was replacing an empty bottle of drinking water with a full one when he saw a dead fly and part of another dead fly in the unopened replacement bottle. His reaction was surprisingly severe. The incident caused him so much distress that he developed a major depressive disorder, phobia, and anxiety. At trial, he was awarded an amount that

---

22. *Walker Estate v. York-Finch General Hospital*, [2001] 1 S.C.R. 647.

23. [1976] 1 S.C.R. 595 at 604.

24. [2008] S.C.J. No. 27.

shocked many—$80 000 in general damages, $24 174 in special damages, and $237 600 in damages for loss of business.

On appeal, however, the Supreme Court of Canada agreed that there was a duty owed to Mustapha that had been breached. Injury had indeed been caused. But what Mustapha failed to show was that it was foreseeable that a person of ordinary fortitude would suffer injury from seeing flies in a bottle of drinking water he was about to install. Such an injury was too remote. Accordingly, the claim was dismissed.

SMALL BUSINESS PERSPECTIVE

The above decision indicates that unusual or excessive reactions to events caused by negligence are not reasonably foreseeable. If a *type* of injury is too unlikely or too remote to foresee, then even if such a loss is suffered, liability will not be imposed.

The problem of remoteness may arise twice in a negligence action. The proximity of the parties is considered when determining if a duty of care is owed. Further, when applying the second half of the *Anns* test, the courts ask: Was there any reason that the duty should not be imposed? Should the scope of the duty be reduced? Should the class to whom the duty is owed be limited, or should the damages be reduced? In addressing these issues the courts will sometimes be influenced by the remoteness of the injuries or damages suffered. Secondly, remoteness is a factor in determining causation.

Anns case applied to determine existence of duty

Nonetheless, where the *nature* or type of injury is foreseeable, but not the *extent* or gravity of a personal injury, the rule is clear. *We take our victims as we find them.* If personal injury is a foreseeable consequence of a motor vehicle collision, then one is liable for the full extent of injuries suffered. If a person has osteoporosis, brittle bones, or an "egg-shell thin skull," we cannot avoid responsibility by claiming that we could not reasonably be expected to foresee the special condition. If a person experiences greater injury from our conduct than would be expected because of a unique physical condition, there is nonetheless a responsibility to compensate for all consequences of the injury. This principle is often referred to as the **thin skull rule**. Thus, if through our negligence we cause a concert pianist to lose the use of his hand, we can't escape liability for the greater loss by claiming we could not have anticipated that the person we would hurt would be a concert pianist. But we must not take this principle too far. If the concert pianist had a deteriorating condition in his hand such as arthritis, and in a short time would have lost use of it anyway, we are not responsible for the lost career as those damages would have taken place in any case. This has been dubbed the **crumbling skull rule**, and must be used in conjunction with the thin skull rule.[25]

We take our victims as we find them

Not responsible for inevitable loss

When the Court applies the crumbling skull rule, it recognizes the pre-existing frailties and the award of damages aims at restoring the plaintiff to that (original) position.[26]

---

[25]. *Athey v. Leonati*, [1996] 3 S.C.R. 458.

[26]. For example, see *Whitfield v. Calhoun* (1999), 242 A.R. 201 (Q.B.), where the plaintiff developed antisocial, paranoid, and schizoid behaviour and depression as a result of a motor vehicle collision. His preexisting personality traits contributed to these psychological problems and the reduced damages reflected this original predisposition.

DEFENCES

Contributory Negligence

Historically, when a defendant could show that the plaintiff was also careless, contributing to his own loss, it was a complete bar to recovery. This was an all-or-nothing result and was clearly unfair. The courts then developed the **last clear chance doctrine**, which held the person who had the last opportunity to avoid the accident, and failed to do so, completely responsible. This wasn't much better and so most jurisdictions have since adopted a legislated compromise where both parties are held responsible.

The *Negligence Act* in Ontario[27] is one example; it abandons the all-or-nothing approach and permits the court to apportion responsibility between the two parties. Compensation must be paid in proportion to that assigned responsibility. If a collision is caused where one driver fails to stop at a light and the other is adjusting his radio and not paying attention, both have contributed to the accident. The courts in Ontario and the other provinces with similar legislation would assign a degree of fault to each party (for example 80 percent on one driver and 20 percent on the other) and liability would be apportioned accordingly. Refer to the MyBusLawLab for specific provincial details.

Voluntary Assumption of Risk

Historically, where a plaintiff voluntarily assumed the risk of injury, this operated as a complete bar to recovery of damages. An example might be knowingly getting into a car with a drunk driver. This is referred to as *volenti non fit injuria*. Today the principle is much more restrictive. To escape liability the defendant must show that the plaintiff not only assumed the physical risk but also the legal risk. That requires that the person assuming the risk make it clear that she is also completely absolving the other party of any responsibility. This is very difficult to do and so a successful claim of volenti is very rare today.

The courts now usually deal with such foolhardy behaviour under the heading of **contributory negligence**, which permits the courts to apportion the loss between the parties—a much more satisfactory result. This rejection of *volenti* in favour of contributory negligence was applied in *Crocker v. Sundance* discussed above (Case Summary 5.1).

Some jurisdictions have included provisions in their occupiers' liability acts (see below) absolving the occupier of responsibility where the visitor has voluntarily assumed the risk. Although the legislation does not say it, the Supreme Court of Canada has interpreted this in the same restrictive way, and so this provision will also absolve the occupier of responsibility only where it is clear that the visitor has assumed the legal risk as well as the physical risk.[28]

Legislation allows apportionment of responsibility

The law will not assist volunteers

But assumption of legal risk must be clear

---

[27] R.S.O. 1990, c. N.1; see also Alberta's *Contributory Negligence Act*, **R.S.A.** 2000, c. C-27.

[28] *Waldick v. Malcolm*, [1991] 2 S.C.R. 456.

REDUCING RISK 5.2

Businesses may require customers to sign waivers, counting on these waivers to prove that the customer voluntarily assumed the risks. As is evident from the case law, however, the onus is upon the party trying to claim protection under the waiver to show that the customer knew the physical risks and accepted them. Secondly, the customer must appreciate that he is releasing the business of legal liability. A waiver that is not brought to the customer's attention may not be worth the paper it's written on. To be effective, waivers should be brought to the customer's attention, explained, and assented to. Even then, if the customer does not fully appreciate the physical risks (as with novice students who are learning a new physical activity), the waiver will be insufficient. Insurance, to cover against liability to third parties, may be a necessary back-up.

What about a rescuer? If the rescuer gets hurt, can it be said that she voluntarily assumed the risk? A mother who is injured when she jumps in front of a train to save her child can hold the railway responsible for failing to have proper barriers. If the rescuer is injured, the author of the danger cannot escape liability by claiming the rescuer voluntarily assumed the risk. If the potential danger was reasonably foreseeable, so was the potential need for a rescue. The person who caused the danger must pay compensation to both the victim and the injured rescuer.[29] Similarly, the principle of *volenti* does not apply to work-related accidents, even if the work being performed is inherently dangerous.

Duty owed to rescuer

Illegality (Ex Turpi Causa)

Plaintiffs harmed while acting illegally or immorally may be denied recovery in tort law. The maxim "*ex turpi causa, non oritur actio*" suggests that "an action does not arise from a base cause." In simple terms, the courts should refuse to entertain a lawsuit brought by a party who engaged in unlawful activity. Generally, the illegal conduct must cause the loss of the plaintiff before the defence will operate.[30]

There is little judicial enthusiasm for this defence and cases where a tort action has been defeated by the *ex turpi causa* maxim have been rare. "In the vast majority of cases where the defence might have been employed, the claimant would have lost in any event on the basis of *volenti*. Moreover, if one were to re-examine the *volenti* cases carefully, one would discern a flavour to some of them, indicating that the courts are really relying on the defence of "illegality," while insisting that they are denying reparation because of *volenti*."[31]

CASE SUMMARY 5.7

Contributory Negligence Preferred over *Ex Turpi Causa* and *Volenti: Hall v. Hebert*[32]

Hebert owned a "souped-up muscle car." After consuming a large amount of alcohol with Hall, Hebert stalled that vehicle on an unlit gravel road and proceeded to lose the keys. Hebert suggested they attempt a rolling start and Hall asked to take the wheel.

---

29. *Videan v. British Transport Commission*, [1963] 2 All E.R. 860 (C.A.).

30. *Canada Cement Lafarge v. British Columbia Lightweight Aggregate Ltd.* [1983] S.C.J. No. 33.

31. See Linden and Feldthusen, *Canadian Tort Law* (Lexis Nexis Canada Inc. 2006) p. 523.

32. [1993] S.C.J. No. 51.

Both men were clearly drunk and in the process of rolling the car to start it, Hall lost control of the vehicle. It rolled over into a gravel pit and Hall was severely injured. Clearly, Hebert owed Hall a duty to be careful, which he breached by allowing his intoxicated friend to drive the car. The problem that the Supreme Court of Canada had to deal with was whether *volenti non fit injuria* or *ex turpi causa* would apply in this case and operate as a complete bar to recovery of damages.

For *volenti* to apply, the Court would have to find that it was clear to both parties that "the defendant assumed no responsibility to take care for the safety of the plaintiff and the plaintiff did not expect him to do so." The Court found that the plaintiff assumed the physical risk, but there was no indication that he had assumed the legal risk as well.

As to the application of *ex turpi causa*, McLachlin J., writing for the majority, stated:

> [T]here is a need in the law of tort for a principle which permits judges to deny recovery to a plaintiff on the ground that to do so would undermine the integrity of the justice system. The power is a limited one. Its use is justified where allowing the plaintiff's claim would introduce inconsistency into the fabric of the law, either permitting the plaintiff to profit from an illegal or wrongful act, or to evade a penalty prescribed by criminal law. Its use is not justified where the plaintiff's claim is merely for compensation for personal injuries sustained as a consequence of the negligence of the defendant.

Since neither *ex turpi causa* nor *volenti* applied, the Court was then free to apply the principle of contributory negligence and apportion the loss between the parties.

DISCUSSION QUESTIONS

The defences of *volenti* and *ex turpi causa* are rarely successful today. Instead, the courts demonstrate a preference towards apportioning the loss on the basis of contributory negligence. Is this a better approach or should people assume the whole loss when they are foolish enough to put themselves in harm's way?

mybuslawlab
www.pearsoned.ca/mybuslawlab

BC AB SK MB ON

Special Situations

LEGISLATION

Although the reasonable person standard discussed in the context of negligence is extremely important, there are many situations where this has been changed by statute. Examples are the occupiers' liability acts and innkeepers' acts discussed below. The motor vehicle acts of the provinces also create special categories of duty that make people responsible for the condition of their car even if they were not aware of a defect. As a general rule, however, these statutes do not create new categories of tort unless they specifically say so. Thus, human rights acts and privacy legislation may impose new obligations on people, but violations of these obligations do not amount to a tort unless the act says they do. Some jurisdictions have also changed tort law with respect to automobile collisions. Because of the devastating losses and injuries associated with this area, many provinces have turned to compulsory insurance schemes. Some jurisdictions have gone further, instituting **"no fault" programs** by which people are treated the same and compensated for their injuries whether they were at fault or not. Ontario, in the face

Modifications imposed by statute

The trend away from fault

of exploding settlements, has passed controversial legislation setting a threshold for physical injury that must be met before **non-pecuniary damages** (damages based on non-monetary factors) for such things as pain and suffering can be awarded. Refer to the MyBusLawLab to determine regional differences.

It is also possible to create a duty of care by statute where none existed before. At common law, a mother owes no duty of care to an unborn child, and this has caused tragic results when an unborn child was injured in an automobile accident caused by the negligence of the mother. Owing no duty to the unborn child, the mother was not at fault, and so no claim could be made against her insurance company, which would pay only where liability could be established against her. Alberta has recently passed legislation that overcomes this difficulty by creating a duty of care on the mother toward the unborn child where there is such insurance coverage.[33]

STRICT LIABILITY

Tort law generally requires the demonstration of fault, but there are some situations where liability will be imposed even where there is no fault on the part of the defendant who has acted completely reasonably. Note that this discussion of **strict liability** must be distinguished from those situations where fault is required, but the standard imposed is extremely high, such as where dangerous products, processes, or animals are involved. The liability of food handlers, for example, approaches strict liability because extreme care is demanded by law in light of the potential for illness or contamination.

The case of *Rylands v. Fletcher*,[34] however, established that strict liability arises in certain circumstances, where liability will be imposed regardless of absence of fault. The defendant had built a reservoir on his property, but under the surface there was a shaft from a coal mine leading to his neighbour's property. The water escaped, flooding his neighbour's mine. The defendant was in no way negligent, having no knowledge of the underground shaft. Still, the Court held him liable for the damage. The principle applied was that if a person brings something inherently dangerous, such as stored water or explosives, onto his property and it escapes, the occupier is liable for any damage.

When dangerous things escape

It must be noted that strict liability will not be imposed unless the use of the property is unusual. Today, electricity and plumbing are part of normal operations for modern buildings, and damage caused by these conveniences will normally not support a claim of strict liability. On the other hand, the escape of flammable gasses due to an unusual use of land can lead the court to impose strict liability.[35]

Must be unusual use of property

Vicarious liability is also a form of strict liability in that the employer is being held responsible for the wrongful acts of an employee even though the employer has done nothing wrong. The imposition of vicarious liability is limited to those situations where the employee is carrying out his employment responsibilities. Vicarious liability was introduced in the prior chapter and will be discussed in more depth in Chapter 10 under the heading "Liability of Employer."

Vicarious liability of employer

---

33. *Maternal Tort Liability Act*, S.A. 2005, c. M-7.5.

34. (1868), L.R. 3 H.L. 330.

35. See *Gertsen v. Toronto (Metro)*, [1973] O.J. No. 2223 (H.C.J.).

Occupiers' Liability

Occupiers owe special duty

In common law, people who occupy property have a special obligation to people who are injured on their property. Note that this obligation rests on the occupier, not the owner; thus, where the property is leased, the duty falls on the tenant, not the landlord.

The obligation to look out for the welfare of visitors varies with their status. A person coming on a property for a business purpose is referred to as an **invitee**. A person on the property with permission but for a non-business purpose is a **licensee**, and a person there without permission is a **trespasser**. At common law, the occupier must take reasonable steps to protect invitees from unusual dangers. This may extend to putting up a fence around an elevator shaft or providing a hard hat. The duty toward licensees is lower, requiring the occupier only to take reasonable steps to warn of hidden dangers on the property; here, a sign would suffice. The only duty to a trespasser is not to wilfully or recklessly cause him harm.

Invitee/licensee distinction may no longer be important

Most provinces have passed legislation eliminating the distinction between invitees and licensees, imposing an obligation on occupiers to take reasonable steps to protect all classes of visitors to their property. As for trespassers, most jurisdictions retain the common law minimum obligation not to wilfully or recklessly cause them injury. In some provinces, this minimal duty also applies to those visitors who voluntarily assume the risk of dangerous conditions on the property. But for trespassers who are children, the duty of care may well equate that extended to visitors. These rules vary from province to province, so refer to the MyBusLawLab of the text for provincial variations.

CASE SUMMARY 5.8

Liability to Recreational Users (Trespassers): *Houle v. Calgary (City)*[36]; *Skopnik v. BC Rail Ltd.*[37]

When will an occupier be liable to those who come onto its property to play? In the *Houle* case, Sean Houle, an eight-year-old child, was severely burned when he came into contact with a live wire. His arm had to be amputated. Houle had managed to climb up a power pole adjacent to a ten-foot fence and came into contact with the enclosed electrical transformer. The location of this transformer proved to be significant. It was situated in the parking lot of an abandoned supermarket, in the middle of a residential neighbourhood filled with children. The parking lot had essentially become a playground. The City, which had built the enclosure and had the only keys to it, was found to be the occupier. It should have realized that the live wire posed a substantial threat to the children playing in the parking lot. The Court applied section 13 of Alberta's *Occupiers' Liability Act*: "the occupier owes a duty to that child to take such care as in all the circumstances of the case is reasonable to see that the child will be reasonably safe from that danger." The city failed in this duty—the danger could have been eliminated by simply placing the pole inside the fence. Liability was thus imposed.

---

36. [1985] A.J. No. 1102 (C.A.).

37. [2008] B.C.J. No. 1603 (B.C.CA); leave to appeal dismissed,[2008] S.C.C.A. No. 452.

By contrast, liability was avoided when the Court of Appeal determined that the respondent was not a visitor but a trespasser in the *Skopnik* case. Skopnik was injured when the ATV he was riding became airborne after cresting an excavated area within a right of way. He sustained a critical spinal injury. The accident took place on a portion of the right of way maintained by appellant BC Rail. Much of it was left in its natural state. Although at trial the Court focused on the inspection procedures followed by the BC Rail, on appeal the standard of inspection was downplayed. The Court of Appeal found Skopnik to be a trespasser; as such, the appellant railway owed him just a minimal duty. As long as the appellant did not intentionally create a danger, or act with reckless disregard to his safety, the appellant could not be liable for the respondent Skopnik's injuries.

SMALL BUSINESS PERSPECTIVE

From these cases it is obvious that a business needs to ascertain what duties are owed to visitors and trespassers in each jurisdiction where property is held. There will be provincial variances, so knowledge of the law will help one ascertain what precautions must be taken to minimize risk.

An innkeeper at common law was in a unique position and was required to protect his guests from the wrongful acts of others, even when the innkeeper or servant was not at fault. Only when the damage or loss to a guest's property was caused by that guest's own negligence was the innkeeper relieved of responsibility. Again most jurisdictions have modified this obligation by statute and impose liability only when the innkeeper or his servants are negligent. Note that this reduction in liability is available only where the innkeeper has carefully complied with the statute by placing notices at designated locations. (Refer to the MyBusLawLab to review the specific legislation and note how it is applied.)

Special duties of innkeepers

A special problem arises when alcohol is served. The courts are willing to hold commercial dispensers of alcoholic beverages at least partially responsible when a patron becomes intoxicated and is injured or injures others, as the Supreme Court of Canada made clear in the *Crocker* case in Case Summary 5.1. Businesses supplying liquor at company activities have also been liable for subsequent drinking-related injuries,[38] but the Supreme Court of Canada has so far refused to extend this responsibility to social hosts holding private parties. In the *Childs v. Desormeaux*[39] case the Supreme Court of Canada found that there was no duty owed by social hosts for the damage caused by a guest who became drunk at their party and who subsequently caused an automobile accident that resulted in serious injuries. This was true even though the hosts were aware of the guest's propensity to get drunk. The Court decided, applying the second part of the *Anns* case test, that as a matter of social policy such social hosts owed no duty to the users of the public highways. It should be noted that the door is still open to a more compelling case, possibly where the hosts actually supplied the liquor to someone they knew was driving and they knew was getting drunk. For example, in *Kim v. Thammavong*,[40] a negligence action was brought against a twenty-year-old

---

38. *Jacobsen v. Nike Canada Ltd.* [1996] B.C.J. No. 363 (B.C.S.C.).

39. [2006] S.C.J. No. 18.

40. [2008] O.J. No. 4908 (Sup.C.J.).

who held a party in her parents' home while they were on vacation. One of the guests was injured by an intoxicated guest. The Court refused to dismiss the action summarily as against the host:

> In the case at bar, in terms of foreseeability and proximity, the relationship between the defendant Tracy and the plaintiff Mr. Kim is somewhat closer than the relationship between the parties in *Childs*, because Mr. Kim was a guest at the party and not a third party passenger in a car some distance away. In my opinion, whether there is "something more" in the circumstances of the party hosted by Tracy that led to the injuries suffered by Mr. Kim is a genuine issue for trial.

Canadians will have to await the trial decision to learn whether social host liability will be established in this case.

CASE SUMMARY 5.9

Serving Alcohol to Drivers Can Lead to Liability: *Holton v. MacKinnon*[41]

MacKinnon, Holton, and another friend had been drinking at an establishment in Whistler, British Columbia, known as the Crab Shack. All three were in an intoxicated state when they left in a car driven by MacKinnon and went to another establishment called Garfinkel's, where they consumed more alcohol. They then went to Holton's residence but left shortly afterward to go to a party. On the way there the car rolled over into a ditch and Holton was seriously injured. Holton sued the driver, MacKinnon, and also the two establishments that had served them alcohol.

The Court held that both establishments had a positive duty to see that Holton was not exposed to injury because of his intoxication or because of the intoxication of the driver MacKinnon. Since all three were drunk, the employees should have foreseen the risk that one of them would drive and should have taken steps to intervene. They should have at least asked them how they were getting home and if they were driving.

The Judge also found contributory negligence stating that when such a person drinks himself into a state of intoxication so that he can't take care of himself and gets into a car driven by someone obviously intoxicated, he must bear a considerable portion of the loss. The Court held the driver 40 percent liable, the plaintiff 30 percent liable, and the two commercial hosts each 15 percent liable.

DISCUSSION QUESTIONS

Although the Supreme Court of Canada has shown reluctance in the *Childs v. Desormeaux* case to impose liability on social hosts, the opposite is true for commercial hosts. Since commercial hosts have repeatedly been found liable for injuries suffered by those they serve liquor to, as well as those who are injured by the drunken guests, what precautions should those serving alcohol take?

---

41. [2005] B.C.J. No. 57 (B.C.S.C.)

REDUCING RISK 5.3

Even where there is no physical contact between the professional and the client, care should be taken to ensure that the premises are safe and secure. The best method of risk avoidance is to carefully inspect the premises and examine the practices of the business, anticipating what might go wrong and taking steps to correct the problems. A key aspect of this is to identify an individual or committee charged with the responsibility of finding such dangers or risks, removing these dangers, and providing training for staff and management in the area of risk awareness and avoidance.

PRODUCT LIABILITY

Manufactured products are often dangerous, either because of some inherent defect or because of their nature, such as in the case of chemicals, tools, or explosives. In the United States, it is often enough to show that the product was defective and that the defect caused the injury. This is a strict liability approach requiring no demonstration of fault on the part of the manufacturer. In Canada, however, it is still necessary to establish fault when suing manufacturers for some injury or loss caused by their product. Not only is it necessary to establish that there was a duty to be careful, it is also necessary to prove that there was a failure to live up to that duty. Either the manufacturer or an employee must be shown to have been negligent or careless.

Donoghue v. Stevenson, discussed in Case Summary 5.2, had a significant impact on product liability in tort law. Historically, if there was no privity of contract between the manufacturer and the party injured by the product, an action for breach of contract could not succeed. Further, because there were usually several intervening parties between the manufacturer and the ultimate consumer of a product, it was thought that the manufacturer owed no duty of care to the ultimate consumer. The *Donoghue* case established that if a product was designed in such a way as to get into the hands of the consumer without intervening inspection or modification, a duty of care did exist. Now, with the prevalence of prepackaged and complicated manufactured goods, there is even less likelihood that a problem will be disclosed by intermediate inspection. It is thus much more difficult for a manufacturer to deny the existence of a duty of care. This duty, if coupled with evidence of a breach of that duty, will impose liability on the producer of the product.

Over time, the obligation to exercise care has been extended, so that those repairing or assembling products, in addition to those manufacturing the product, may all owe a duty of care to the consumer. Further, it is not just the purchaser who is owed a duty of care. Where the purchaser buys the product for a third party, the Courts may regard the purchaser as the agent for the ultimate consumer. In this way, a child who eats a spoiled food item purchased by her parent can nonetheless maintain an action against the manufacturer. The parent will be regarded the child's agent in making the purchase.

The *Donoghue* case suggested that a duty is owed by the manufacturer to the consumer if a product was designed in such a way as to get into the hands of the consumer without intervening inspection or modification.[42] But what if there is opportunity for intervening inspection, or worse, for tampering? Does the onus fall on the consumer to prove that there was no tampering? It appears that the courts prefer to put the onus on the manufacturer to prove tampering or interference—if that party hopes to avoid liability.

> Breach of duty must be shown for product liability

---

42. [1932] A.C. 562, at 599.

On the other hand, where there has been intermediate inspection or modification of a product, it is unlikely that the courts will find that the manufacturer still owes a duty of care to the ultimate consumer. The rationale for this rebuttal of duty is that where intermediate inspection is contemplated and has occurred, it is no longer reasonably foreseeable that the product would be used and cause harm despite the discovery of a defect. If harm is not foreseeable, a duty does not arise.

CASE SUMMARY 5.10

Manufacturer Relieved of Duty Where Defect Discovered but Product Still Used: *Viridian Inc. v. Dresser Canada Inc.*[43]

Mainland Foundries was a manufacturer producing, among other products, cast iron diaphragms to be used as components in various products. Dresser Canada ordered 400 of these diaphragms and certain patterns for the manufacture of moulds for its use. There was no particular product that these diaphragms were intended for at the time of order; rather they were a stock item to be incorporated into several different products as needed. The arrangement between Mainland and Dresser was for Mainland to produce five as samples, which would then be inspected, and if these were approved, the rest would be produced and sent. This process was followed and a bulk order was eventually delivered.

The plaintiff Viridian operated an ammonia plant and contracted with Dresser to produce a high-pressure compressor valued at $1.7 million for use in that plant. Some of these diaphragms were incorporated into that compressor, which then failed. It was determined that the diaphragms were of insufficient strength and had contributed to the failure of the compressor. The compressor was repaired, and with Viridian's knowledge, again the deficient diaphragms were used. The compressor failed a second time, causing significant damage including the shutdown of the plant. It should be noted that Mainland had not been notified of the failure of the compressor or the attempts at repair.

Because recovery against Dresser was limited by contract, Viridian brought this action in negligence against Mainland, the manufacturer of the diaphragm. The Court found that no duty of care was owed by the manufacturer to the ultimate consumer. It was the clear intention of all parties that there was to be intermediate inspection of the product before use, and that inspection did, in fact, take place. Mainland was entitled to rely on that inspection and on the expertise of Dresser to ensure that the product was not defective for the intended use and was used properly. Thus Mainland owed no duty of care to Viridian in these circumstances.

SMALL BUSINESS PERSPECTIVE

The importance of this case is that it emphasizes the fact that where an intermediate inspection of manufactured goods should have disclosed a particular defect or problem, this removes any duty of care that the manufacturer may have had to the ultimate consumer of those goods. Since the consumer may only have recourse against those inspecting the product, businesses that carry out inspections had best be knowledgeable and vigilant in conducting any such inspections.

Recent cases demonstrate that the introduction of contributory negligence legislation has lead to the courts finding shared liability. Both the negligent manufacturer and the negligent inspector may be held jointly liable to the

---

43. [2002] A.J. No. 937 (C.A.).

injured consumer. Similarly, if it is the plaintiff who has failed to adequately inspect a product before its use, or uses a product despite an apparent defect, he may be held partly responsible. The courts seem to prefer this shared liability approach over finding that the plaintiff's failure to inspect negated the manufacturer's duty to exercise care.[44]

Defective products may cause manufacturers to be held liable; liability may also be imposed for negligent designs. The fact that a design defect only causes injury when coupled with the wrongdoing of the consumer does not preclude manufacturer liability. The onus rests with the manufacturer to post warnings, and these warnings must be reasonably communicated. The warning must also be adequate. The required explicitness of the warning will vary with the danger likely to be encountered. In assessing whether a warning was adequately worded and disseminated, the courts will give weight to the difference in knowledge and expertise of the parties.

CASE SUMMARY 5.11

Warning Inadequate in Light of Defective Design: *Nicholson v. John Deere Ltd.*[45]

The Nicholsons purchased a second-hand riding lawnmower manufactured by John Deere Ltd., and one day when filling it with gas, the gas cap rolled off the tank where it had been placed, hitting the exposed battery cable and causing a spark that ignited the gas fumes. The resulting fire burned down the plaintiffs' house.

This was not the first time such an explosion had happened, and John Deere had a program in place to correct the defective design and warn of the problem. The company had placed a warning decal on the gas tank and supplied a battery cover safety kit to owners to remove the danger. There were also several warnings in the operating manual about the danger, but the Nicholsons had purchased the mower used and had not received the manual or been told about the safety kit by the dealer when they had it serviced. The Court held that these efforts on the part of John Deere were inadequate. The manufacturer should have taken much more positive action to make sure the defects were corrected. In addition, the dealer, who had failed to tell the Nicholsons about the danger and the safety kit, was also liable for negligence. This case is interesting in that it shows the great responsibility placed on a manufacturer when such a defective and dangerous product is produced. Once it had been established that the design was defective and dangerous, it was very difficult, if not impossible, for the manufacturer to show that it was not negligent, despite its stringent efforts to correct the situation.

SMALL BUSINESS PERSPECTIVE

The duty to warn is a continuing one. Once a manufacturer learns of a defect, the duty to warn consumers arises and this includes both future and past purchasers. Product recalls can be very costly, but failure to take adequate steps to warn and otherwise protect consumers invites liability—and bad publicity.

---

44. See, for example, *Orlando Corp. v. Bothwell Accurate Co.*, [2001] O.J. No. 1946, (S.C.J.); aff'd [2003] O.J. No. 2036 (C.A.), where the defendant manufacturer and the plaintiff were both held liable for the cost of replacing corroded steel roofs. The plaintiff negligently failed to use a vapour barrier and the manufacturer negligently failed to warn of the likelihood of corrosion if moisture was present. Both partiers thus contributed to the loss.

45. [1986] O.J. No. 1320 (H.C.J.), varied [1989] O.J. No. 495 (C.A.).

A particularly difficult problem in product liability cases is to show that some-one was "careless" in the manufacturing process. In Canada, the courts are willing to draw, from the circumstantial evidence of the injury or loss, a conclusion that someone must have been negligent, leaving it to the defendant to then produce evidence to the contrary. As discussed above, this **"circumstantial evidence"** method replaces the *res ipsa loquitur* approach used in the past and also seems more appropriate for product liability cases.[46]

Since it is not easy for a consumer to prove negligent design or production, plaintiffs have often chosen to allege negligent warning as an additional basis for the action.

The manufacturer may find itself in a no-win situation. On the one hand, where policies and procedures are in place such that if followed no injury could happen, then they must not have been followed if injury did occur. On the other hand, if policies and procedures were followed and still injury occurred, this suggests the policies were not adequate. Either way, negligence is established. Once negligence has been inferred from the circumstances of the injury, it will be difficult for the manufacturer to avoid liability unless it can show that it was not careless. Even then, if injury has occurred despite the absence of negligence in its production, does the fact of injury alone suggest that the warning, if any, was inadequate? The figurative snail in the bottle will be enough for the court to draw an inference of negligence on the part of the defendant.

Where the products are inherently dangerous, as is the case with chemicals, explosives, tools, and pharmaceuticals, the requirements are more stringent. Manufacturers must do all that they can to make the products as safe as reasonably possible given the risks. They must also give appropriate warnings and instructions. In Canada, the courts thus examine whether the warnings and instructions were clear, as well as whether everything reasonably possible had been done to reduce the risk. Adding child-proof caps to pharmaceutical products is an example, as is the practice of adding a double-switching mechanism to power tools so they can't be turned on accidentally. Where this has been done effectively and sufficient warnings are included, the manufacturer will likely escape liability. It may be self-evident that the misuse of a knife or table saw might result in injury, but a wise manufacturer will still include warnings to that effect.

Manufacturers must warn
and act reasonably to make
dangerous products safer

It must be emphasized that liability for damage or injury caused by products may also be based on contract. When there is such a contract between the parties, there is no need to establish fault. Liability will follow simply by showing the contract has been breached through the sale of the defective product. Contracts will be the subject of the following four chapters. Note that some jurisdictions have passed legislation extending this contractual liability of the seller and manufacturer to injured consumers even where they were not the direct purchaser of the product. For a more complete discussion of contractual product liability, refer to "Consumer Protection Legislation" in Chapter 15. New Brunswick and Saskatchewan have gone even further, imposing strict liability for consumer loss upon manufacturers of defective products.[47]

---

[46] Fontaine, supra note 18.

[47] See *Consumer Product Warranty and Liability Act*, S.N.B. 1978, c. C-18.1, s. 27; *Consumer Protection Act*, S.S. 1996, c. C-30.1, s. 64.

LIABILITY OF PROFESSIONALS AND OTHER EXPERTS

For business students who are planning to enter professions or who intend to do consulting work, the subject of **professional liability** may be one of the most important covered in this text. Experts are simply people who hold themselves out to have some specialized knowledge or skill not generally available. Professionals are usually experts who belong to professional organizations and practise in a specific area of service. The definition is obviously imprecise and, for the purposes of this discussion, should be viewed as expansive rather than restrictive. Whether we are talking of doctors or accountants, interior designers or building contractors, litigation by clients injured as a result of their services or disgruntled over the quality of their work has had a major impact on professional practice. Not only have the occurrences of such malpractice actions increased dramatically, so too have the damages awarded by the courts. Today, an important consideration for many professionals is the amount of **liability insurance** they must obtain at a very high cost. The liability of professionals may be founded in contract law or based on fiduciary duty, but the recent expansion of liability has been in the area of tort law, specifically negligence. Professionals must also adhere to the rules and standards set by their governing bodies. Failure to comply with the rules, or unskilled or unprofessional conduct, may result in disciplinary action with the potential consequence of losing the right to practise.

> *Professional liability and insurance costs important aspects of business*

> *Liability must be based on contract, fiduciary duty, or tort*

Contract

In the past, the liability of accountants, bankers, lawyers, business consultants, and other professionals was based on the contract they had with their clients. Contracts will be discussed in the next chapters, but briefly, when professionals provide substandard service, they are liable for the losses resulting from the breach of the contract. The actual standard of service expected is normally implied; it is implied that the professional will provide a *reasonable level of performance* given his claimed expertise. Often professionals attempt to limit that liability with terms to that effect included in the contract.

> *Tort standard implied in contract, but note disclaimer*

Because professionals' liability is based on the contract with the client, their liability is also restricted to that client. An outsider has no rights under the agreement. Thus, an accountant's contractual liability for improperly prepared financial statements is limited to the company for which they were prepared. The shareholders and investors have no claim. But in tort law, the courts are willing to expand liability beyond these immediate (contractual) parties. This expansion of potential plaintiffs has had an important impact on the risks faced by accountants and other experts.

> *Tort liability extends beyond parties to contract*

Negligence

The expansion of tort liability has introduced considerable uncertainty into the area of professional liability. The standard of care expected of a professional is reasonably straightforward and will be discussed below. What has changed in recent times is who can sue. Expansion of the duty of care has increased the potential liability of most experts far beyond what it has been. Is an architect liable to a person injured in a collapsed building when errors are found in her designs? Is an accountant liable to shareholders or investors because of erroneous

> *Extension of tort liability to third parties*

financial statements prepared for a specific corporate client? The extension of liability to these third parties has greatly expanded the risks faced by professionals who provide these services. The discussion that follows will take a closer look at a professional's liability for negligence.

STANDARD OF CARE

The standard of care expected from an expert is a little different from that expected from a non-expert. Experts must live up to the standard of a reasonable person *in the circumstances*. There are two problems here: first, the level of skill they must have, and second, how they exercise that skill. Essentially, these people are required to have the skills and abilities that one would expect from an expert or professional in that field. If a person professes to be a medical doctor, he had better have the training and skills of a medical doctor. The same applies to a chartered accountant or investment counsellor: she has to have the training and skills expected of someone in that profession.

The accounting professions, for example, have established standards of practice for their members: GAAP (Generally Accepted Accounting Principles) and GAAS (Generally Accepted Auditing Standards). Where it can be shown that an accountant has failed to live up to these standards, that failure generally will be enough to establish negligence.

The second problem relates to how that skill is exercised. In assessing liability, the court determines what a reasonable person, possessed of the same skills and abilities as the defendant, would have done in the circumstances. For a doctor, the test is that of a reasonable doctor; for an accountant, a reasonable accountant; for a lawyer, a reasonable lawyer. Often, the degree of care to be exercised is described by others in one's profession who are called to testify as to what a reasonable, prudent professional would have done in the circumstances. The standard of care is thus defined by one's peers.

It must be emphasized that a client or patient is not required to tolerate ineptitude on the part of professionals because of inexperience. It may be true that a doctor or mechanic in the first month of employment is more likely to make a mistake, but these people have represented themselves as proficient members of their profession. They must, therefore, live up to the level of competence one would expect of a normal member of their profession functioning in a reasonably prudent manner.

It can be very helpful to the defendant to show that what he did was common practice among his colleagues. Such common practice in the profession is generally an indication of competent professional service. But this is not always the case. The test is that of a reasonable person, not an average person. Although one would hope that the average standard of practice in the skilled professions would coincide with the practice one would expect from a reasonable person, this is not always so. When it is obvious that the common practice is dangerous or careless, then such sloppy practice will not be tolerated. The court, in such circumstances, is not reluctant to declare that the common practice falls below the standard of a reasonable person and is, therefore, negligent. This principle has recently been reinforced by the Supreme Court of Canada in the *Waldick v. Malcolm* case, where Justice Iacobucci, quoting Professor Linden, states: "Tort courts have not abdicated their responsibility to evaluate customs, for negligent conduct cannot be countenanced, even when a large group is continually guilty of it." In short, no amount of general community compliance will render negligent conduct

---

Standard is that of a reasonable member of the profession

Common practice may not measure up to reasonable standard

"reasonable... in all the circumstances."[48] It is clear, however, that to find such negligence in the face of common practice in a profession would happen only in extraordinary circumstances.

CASE SUMMARY 5.12

Not Enough to Follow GAAP: *Kripps v. Touche Ross*[49]

The British Columbia Court of Appeal held that even where accountants follow GAAP (the standard used by the Canadian Institute of Chartered Accountants), they cannot be sure they are acting with sufficient care. In this case, the company Kripps raised funds from investors and then invested those funds in mortgages. In fact, more than $4 million of its mortgages (about one-third of the company's entire investment portfolio) were in default, and this was not disclosed in the 1983 financial statements, even though the auditors were aware of the situation. The unpaid interest on those mortgages was added to the principal, inflating the apparent value of the asset. The Court held that the investors were misled by the accounting statements, and the accountants were held liable even though they had carefully followed GAAP. They did not disclose this information (that the mortgages were in default) because the GAAP rules then in place did not require such disclosure. The Court said, in effect, that the accountants could not hide behind the GAAP standards to escape liability.

SMALL BUSINESS PERSPECTIVE

Following a standard practice, even one established by a professional body, will not act as a shield against liability. If a practice leads to deception or a misrepresentation of the facts, liability for misrepresentation may follow. This case emphasizes that poor excuses, such as abidance to common practice, will not suffice if in the end the courts conclude that parties were harmed by one's failure to be diligent and professional.

TO WHOM IS THE DUTY OWED? (THE PROBLEM WITH WORDS)

In the past, professionals and other experts faced liability to their clients only for shoddy work (based on contract law), and to their colleagues and clients on the basis of a breach of a fiduciary duty. Liability to strangers or third parties arose only where physical damage or bodily injuries resulted. For example, experts such as architects and engineers, whose services produced physical structures that would cause injury if they failed, might be subject to liability to strangers. On the other hand, if those injured were not immediate parties and their loss (whether caused by physical acts or words) was purely economic, there was considerable reluctance on the part of the courts to extend the professional's liability to them.

Today, however, accountants, bankers, lawyers, business consultants, and other professionals giving financial advice may be sued in tort even when their negligent words cause only economic loss. Only in the past few years have courts been willing to grant compensation for this kind of loss.

Modern standards recognize economic loss caused by negligent words

---

48. [2000] B.C.J. No. 390

49. (B.C.C.A.); leave to appeal dismissed

NEGLIGENT MISSTATEMENT

Negligent words may create liability

Until recently, liability for negligence was thought to be limited to *conduct* that fell below an acceptable standard of care. In 1963, the House of Lords in the United Kingdom indicated its willingness to expand this liability to *careless words* (or **negligent statements**) causing economic loss.[50]

Negligent words causing economic loss actionable

The Supreme Court of Canada adopted a similar approach in the case of *Haig v. Bamford.*[51] An accounting firm negligently prepared financial statements for a company, knowing that the statements would be used to entice potential investors to purchase shares. Haig relied on these statements in his decision to purchase a number of shares; later he found the company to be considerably less profitable than the incorrect financial statements had led him to believe. As a result, he suffered a financial loss and sued. The Court found that a duty was owed by the accounting firm to the victim, even though there was no direct contract relation between them. The services were contracted to the company; Haig was just a potential investor, but it was foreseeable that potential investors would rely upon the financial statements when making their decision to buy. Since they were "foreseeable plaintiffs," a duty of care was owed to anyone that fell within that class of claimants.

Liability even when conduct was reasonable

This opened the door to other claims of negligent misstatement and has had a great impact on the law of negligence in this country. This is especially true when it comes to experts such as accountants and lawyers, extending their liability for economic loss beyond the actual clients they serve. The liability of professionals and other experts will be discussed as a special topic below.

CASE SUMMARY 5.13

Bank Liable for Careless Words: *Keith Plumbing & Heating Co. v. Newport City Club Ltd., (Micron Construction Ltd. v. Hong Kong Bank of Canada)*[52]

In the process of converting a large office building to another use, the contractors approached the developer's bank for assurances that the developer had funding in place to support the project. The bank responded in writing and in a telephone conversation that the project was well financed and that there were no problems. In fact at the time of these assurances, the developers had failed to advance sufficient security to support the bank loan. Without the security there was no bank loan and the project failed, causing the plaintiff contractors considerable losses.

They sued the bank in question for negligent misrepresentation. The bank had included a disclaimer in its written letter of recommendation and relied on that disclaimer as its main defence. The Court found that it was reasonable for the plaintiffs to rely on the representations of the bank in this matter. They had no other source of information and the bank supported the project in a very positive manner. The disclaimer was held not to apply because it was reasonable for the contractors to rely on the very clear and explicit representation despite the disclaimer; further, the exact meaning of the disclaimer was

---

50. *Hedley Byrne & Co. v. Heller's Partners Ltd.,* [1963] 2 All E.R. 575 (H.L.).

51. [1977] 1 S.C.R. 466.

52. [2000] B.C.J. No. 390

not clear except to a banker. A second very important factor was that there was no disclaimer associated with the telephone conversation. Since reliance on the statements was found to be reasonable, a duty of care was owed to the contractors. Applying the second part of the *Anns* case test, the Court found that "no policy concerns arose to impede the assessment of liability." The Bank was aware of the developer's failure to provide sufficient securities at the time it made these representations, which it knew were being relied on by the plaintiffs. That conduct amounted to a failure to live up to the required standard of care in the circumstances. Accordingly, the Bank was held liable for its employee's negligent misrepresentation.

SMALL BUSINESS PERSPECTIVE

This case nicely illustrates the modern approach to negligent misrepresentation in commercial relationships. How thorough must one train employees if their careless statements can lead to liability?

The case of *Haig v. Bamford*[53] was the first in this country where accountants were found liable to third-party investors for their negligence in preparing audited financial statements. As a result of this precedent, accountants and other experts now find themselves responsible not only to their immediate clients but also to others who suffer loss because of their careless statements.

Liability may extend beyond immediate parties

Once the Court decided to provide liability for economic loss caused by such negligent words, it then had to decide just how far this liability would extend. The problem was that the reasonably foreseeable test as developed in *Donoghue v. Stevenson* was simply too broad when it came to negligent words. The argument was that words were much more volatile, and if that test for duty was used, it would expose professionals and other experts to considerably greater liability than would be appropriate.

In fact, the Judges in the *Haig* case stopped short of adopting the reasonable foreseeability test, but said that a duty of care was owed only when the person making the misleading statement actually knew it was to be used by an individual or a limited class of people. To determine the existence of a duty, the courts are now asking whether the plaintiff's reliance on these representations was reasonable, especially where the defendants may have tried to eliminate or reduce their liability by using disclaimers or exculpatory words. To determine if there was "reasonable reliance," courts may ask whether

Duty determined by reasonable foreseeability

1. The defendant had a direct or indirect financial interest in the transaction in respect of which the representation was made.

2. The defendant was a professional or someone who possessed a special skill, judgment, or knowledge.

3. The advice or information was provided in the course of the defendant's business.

---

53. [1977] 1 S.C.R. 466. [2000] S.C.C.A. No. 193. (B.C.C.A.); leave to appeal dismissed

4. The information or advice was given deliberately, and not on a social occasion.

5. The information or advice was given in response to a specific inquiry or request.

These indicators have been accepted as helping to distinguish those situations where reliance on a statement is reasonable from those when it is not. In the *Keith Plumbing (Micron)* case discussed above (Case Summary 5.13), the Court applied these five indicators; since four of the five were present, the Court concluded that there was "reasonable reliance" on the statements by the plaintiff, establishing that a duty of care did exist in these circumstances.

The *Hercules*[54] case illustrates a slightly different approach to establishing the existence of a duty of care. There, the shareholders of a company relied on incorrect financial statements to make further investments in that company. The shareholders were clearly a group that the accountants knew would rely on the statements, and so, using the *Haig* case, a duty was owed. But these financial statements were prepared not to encourage further investment but to evaluate the capabilities of the management team at the shareholders' meeting. Should accountants' liability extend beyond the purpose for which the statements are prepared? The Supreme Court of Canada found there was a *prima facie* duty owed by the accountants. But, applying the second part of the *Anns* case test, the Court also decided that the accountants' duty extended only to the purpose for which the financial statements were prepared, in this case to evaluate management and not to be used by shareholders for investment decisions. The accountants therefore escaped liability.

It seems clear that the *Anns* case remains important in Canadian law, allowing the courts to apply social policy to limit duty and liability where it seems appropriate to do so. From the point of view of professionals or any other persons professing expertise, it is vital to understand that a duty to be careful exists not only towards one's clients but also towards others who may reasonably rely on the advice or service given. This liability may result from careless conduct or careless words. In rare circumstances, that duty may be reduced or restricted by the application of the second test set out in the *Anns* case. The courts appear loath to allow indeterminate liability to an indeterminate class, but it is risky to count on the courts applying the *Anns* case test to excuse liability.

(margin notes)
but

Scope of duty may be reduced where appropriate

Tort liability of professionals extends beyond clients

! REDUCING RISK 5.4

Businesspeople often find themselves in the position of receiving tips or other forms of advice with respect to their business activities. This advice may come from friends, business associates, or professionals in that field. If the advice proves to be unsound, leading to losses, the persons relying on that advice may find it difficult to establish negligent misrepresentation, even though they clearly relied on the advice. It cannot be overemphasized that in business, people are expected to have a certain amount of business acumen. Simply relying on others may not be good enough. A sound risk management strategy requires careful evaluation of all such advice, no matter the source. When businesspeople are less than vigilant, they may find themselves responsible for at least a portion of their own losses.

---

54. *Hercules Management Ltd. v. Ernst & Young*, [1997] 2 S.C.R. 165.

Finally, it should be emphasized that to succeed in any negligence action, the plaintiff must show that the negligent conduct (or words) *caused* the loss. If the professional can show that the negligent words were not relied on, that the investment or action involved would have taken place in any case, there is no liability. Also, the liability of the defendant will be reduced by any contributory negligence that might be present on the part of the plaintiff.

Practices should be adapted to avoid risk

When an expert conveys erroneous information, carelessly causing economic loss, this constitutes negligent misrepresentation for which the professional can be held liable. Even disclaimers may not protect the professional from liability if the court determines that he or she should have been aware of the error. Where the expert knowingly makes a false statement, she can be sued for **deceit** and may have to pay, not only compensation to the victim, but punitive damages as well. In many cases a professional's insurance will not cover such intentional fraud.

mybuslawlab

www.pearsoned.ca/mybuslawlab

BC AB SK MB ON

Fiduciary Duty and Breach of Trust

Fiduciary duty extended

When a person places trust in a professional, the professional has a **fiduciary duty** to act in the client's best interests. In the past the principle was narrower, but now the Supreme Court in *Hodgkinson v. Simms* (Case Summary 5.14) seems to have extended this obligation to any situation where one person advises another and reliance is placed on that advice. This is, in effect, a relationship built on the trust placed in the professional by the client. The resulting duties of the fiduciary (the person being relied on) are significant. Loyalty and good faith on the part of the professional are demanded. Further, the fiduciary is required to act in the best interest of the client, putting the client's interests ahead of her own and avoiding any situation where her self-interest conflicts with that duty. Any opportunity to acquire property or some other business interest or benefit that arises as a result of that relationship belongs to the client. Even when taking advantage of the opportunity will not harm the client, the fiduciary should refrain from doing it. It would be risky to take advantage of the opportunity even with the client's consent; at a minimum, the fiduciary should insist that the client obtain independent legal advice before granting consent. Furthermore, any information coming to the fiduciary because of her position must remain confidential, must not be disclosed, and must not be used by the fiduciary for her own benefit.

CASE SUMMARY 5.14

Conflict of Interest: *Hodgkinson v. Simms*[55]

Perhaps the most difficult and common violation of a fiduciary duty is the conflict of interest. This case is a classic example, where an accountant advised a client to invest in a real estate development while also acting for the developers. Such a conflict would require the accountant to at least disclose his role in the development to the investors. The defendant's failure to disclose his financial interest in the investment to those putting their trust in him was a breach of fiduciary duty that resulted in a judgment against him for more than $350 000. Since the investor made his own decision to invest, the vulnerability normally present in fiduciary relationships was not present here. Still, the Supreme Court found that

---

55. [1994] 3 S.C.R. 377.

"the presence of loyalty, trust and confidence" were the identifying features of a fiduciary relationship; since they were present, a fiduciary duty was imposed.

DISCUSSION QUESTIONS

Should the existence of a conflict of interest be enough to draw liability? Or should liability be restricted to those situations where the fiduciary is shown to have acted in his own interest to the detriment of the person to whom that duty was owed? As to proving that the defendant acted out of self-interest, is it fair to put this onus on the injured client? Is this too onerous?

Fiduciary duty owed by directors and officers to company

Real estate agents, travel and insurance agents, professionals giving advice, bankers, and financial planners are all likely to find themselves in a fiduciary relationship. Even within organizations, **fiduciary duty** is common. Directors, officers, and managers owe a fiduciary duty to the company. Any situation where people put their affairs in the hands of a trusted adviser or employee can give rise to a fiduciary duty. Generally, ordinary employees are not fiduciaries, but a fiduciary duty may be imposed because of the function they assume. Even where no fiduciary duty exists, specific aspects of it, such as the obligation to keep information confidential, may rest on the employees.

People acting as agents sometimes have the opportunity to take a commission from both the seller and the buyer. This will constitute a breach of **fiduciary duty** unless disclosed to and permitted by both sides.

Trust funds

Often, funds from transactions or property are left in the hands of professionals for periods of time. Real estate agents, accountants, lawyers, and financial planners, for example, often find themselves in possession of large amounts of their clients' money. Any misuse of such property or funds is actionable as a breach of trust. Struggling professionals may be tempted to borrow from such funds, with every intention of paying the money back. No matter how sincere the intention, this is a very serious violation, and the professional not only is liable for any loss but also is subject to disciplinary action within his professional organization. Criminal penalties may also be imposed.

The fiduciary duty goes far beyond the avoidance of negligence and can be the greatest potential risk to a business if it is not taken seriously. The subject of fiduciary duty will be discussed again in the chapters devoted to employment, agency, and business organizations.

mybuslawlab
www.pearsoned.ca/mybuslawlab

BC AB SK MB **ON**

Problems have increased significantly

Professional insurance often required

Professional Insurance

Professional associations (such as the law society or society of chartered accountants) require their members to carry specialized liability insurance, sometimes called "errors and omissions" insurance. The premiums associated with such insurance can be a significant cost of carrying on business and some may be tempted to avoid the cost. Insurance is also required for professionals practising in limited liability partnerships (see Chapter 11 for more details).

Lawyers and accountants may require insurance as a condition of practice. Law societies often arrange for coverage for their members, and a lawyer cannot practise without it. Such liability insurance will normally cover negligence but will not cover **fraud** or **breach of trust**. This may cause serious problems for a professional being sued for the frauds committed by a partner. Another problem occurs when the policy covers only claims made during the period of coverage. If the coverage is allowed to lapse and claims are then made, even if for events that happened during the period of coverage, the insurer will likely not be required to pay.

An insurer will also normally provide legal representation for insured parties when they are sued. This is, of course, in the company's own self-interest since it will have to pay out on the policy if the court imposes liability. The courts have recently been stricter in their interpretation of the insurer's obligations. With the increased risk caused by the expansion of liability to third parties for negligent words and for economic loss, it is not surprising that the premiums have been rising.

Because of the significant costs of litigation, malpractice actions involving professionals require the commitment of significant resources, even if the professional wins. It has been suggested that professional malpractice is an ideal area to be handled by the mechanisms for alternative dispute resolution discussed in Chapter 3.

Some professional bodies exercise significant control

INSURANCE

A recurring theme of this text is to encourage risk management and to promote an attitude of risk avoidance. A sound strategy is to learn the law, recognize potential pitfalls, and correct them before any harm takes place. A second aspect of risk management is to reduce the effect of risk by acquiring appropriate personal and business insurance.

www.pearsoned.ca/mybuslawlab

www.pearsoned.ca/mybuslawlab

Insurance transfers the risk from the insured to the insurer. When property is insured against fire, for example, the risk of loss shifts from the insured to the insurer. The insurer calculates the risk and assesses premiums based on the amount of coverage and the amount of risk involved. As risk increases, so too should the premiums charged. In essence, insurance spreads the loss across a great number of parties in exchange for the payment of a premium.

Insurance transfers risk to the insurer

The industry is tightly regulated by the federal *Insurance Companies Act.*[56] This statute requires all non-provincial insurance corporations to be registered and sets out the amount of reserves that must be retained to cover eventual claims. All provincial jurisdictions have similar insurance legislation. These provincial and federal statutes can be viewed as a type of consumer protection legislation in the field of insurance.

Industry regulated by statutes

The Insurance Industry

Most insurance is purchased through an agent or a broker. Both are agents in the technical sense, but the broker operates an independent business, usually dealing with several different insurance companies in the course of finding the best deal for his client, the insured. Agents and brokers owe significant duties to the people they represent, and so it can be very important whether the person an insured individual is dealing with is acting for the insurance company or for the insured. While **insurance agents** owe important obligations to their principals (the insurance corporations), they also owe a duty of good faith to the customer; thus, agents will be held liable if they fail to provide the insurance coverage asked for, or otherwise fail to properly service the client's needs. The general topic of agency will be discussed in Chapter 11.

Insurance can be acquired through agents and brokers

---

56. S.C. 1991, c. 47.

Adjuster values the loss for the insurance company after the insured-against event takes place

Adjusters are employees or representatives of the insurance corporation charged with investigating and settling insurance claims against the corporation after the insured-against event takes place. It is important to remember when dealing with adjusters that they are normally looking after the interests of the insurance corporation rather than those of the person making the claim. Independent adjusters may also be engaged when problems arise with respect to claims.

Insurance companies often re-insure

Often businesses need the assistance of a broker to ensure adequate coverage. In the event of a large risk, a broker may further spread the risk by involving two or three insurance companies, each taking a percentage of the total. The primary company may take 60 percent, the second company 30 percent, and the third company the final 10 percent. Often one company will carry the risk on paper, but turn to the re-insurance market where the risk is divided among a larger number of secondary market companies. Many of these companies operate only behind the scenes so that the policyholder has to deal with only one adjuster in the event of a claim.

Types of Insurance

(A) LIABILITY INSURANCE

The insurance industry is divided between commercial and personal insurance, with the commercial line offering a variety of products. Liability insurance is the type of insurance most closely associated with torts. The main objective of tort law is to determine who should pay when wrongful conduct causes injury and loss, while the function of insurance is to spread that loss. It is important for businesspeople to maintain appropriate insurance coverage to avoid potentially devastating claims against them or their employees.

Liability insurance covers negligence by self or employees

Only to extent of coverage

Liability insurance is normally designed to cover not only a loss that could be reasonably expected, but legal defence and court costs as well. Should the policy holder purchase an insufficient amount of coverage, she will have to cover any shortfall. It is thus a good idea to follow a broker's advice and insure for an amount that will cover most eventualities. Note that liability insurance will not cover wilful acts, such as assault, theft, arson, or fraud. Nor will it provide coverage where the insured is not the one at fault. There must be negligence or some other basis for liability on the part of the insured for the insurer to pay out on the policy. Liability insurance takes many forms. Professionals, like lawyers and accountants, who exchange their expertise for money, should carry **professional liability insurance**. A contractor should have a **builder's risk policy** in place. Anyone shipping goods should carry insurance that protects the goods while they are in his care. A recent innovation in the industry is **umbrella liability** where several types of liability are bundled together, allowing the insured higher limits of coverage for a more economical premium.

Coverage only when insured is at fault

CASE SUMMARY 5.15

Policy's Terms Determine Coverage: *Omega Inn Ltd. v. Continental Insurance Co.*[57]

There was both fire insurance and business interruption insurance coverage on the Omega Inn when it burned down in 1985. Because the insurance company suspected arson, however, it refused to pay, and with no funds available the insured was not able to rebuild. Finally, after six months of investigation where no evidence of arson was discovered, Continental agreed to pay. The reconstruction took another four months, resulting in a total of 10 months' delay in the reopening of the business. The insurance company claimed that the policy obligated it to pay only for the four-month delay caused by the actual rebuilding. The policy stated that Omega was covered only for the length of time it was actually in the rebuilding process.

At trial the Court held that because the delay had not been caused by the insured, Continental had to pay for the whole 10-month period. But on appeal that decision was reversed.

The policy was clear and required payment only for the time the business would be interrupted while diligent effort was being made to rebuild. That obligation should not be affected by the fact that the insured did not have the funds to rebuild. As stated in the decision, "the impecuniosity of the plaintiff cannot be laid at the door of the insurer because it failed to pay more promptly. Its obligation and the full extent of its obligation, with respect to the business loss interruption coverage under the policy, was to pay for such length of time as would be required with the exercise of due diligence and dispatch to rebuild."[58]

SMALL BUSINESS PERSPECTIVE

Fire insurance and business interruption insurance usually go together, and this case demonstrates how they work. It also highlights the necessity to get back into business as soon as possible, despite any delays attributable to the insurer. The need to read one's policy, to be clear on what is covered and what is not, is likewise critical.

(B) PROPERTY INSURANCE

The predominant form of property insurance covers losses to buildings and their contents due to fire or other named perils. **Comprehensive policies** cover everything except what is specifically excluded. Typical exclusions are acts of war, riots, or illegal activity. Insurance companies often set limits on what the company will pay in the event of a loss or apply a higher deductible. Most insurance contracts require insured parties to maintain certain safety and security standards to protect themselves against the risk of fire and theft.

There are problems with arranging for more or less coverage than is needed. If you take out more insurance than required, you are wasting money since you can collect only on what is actually lost. Carrying too little insurance is also a problem since companies normally include **co-insurance clauses** in most property

---

[57.] (1988), 55 D.L.R. (4th) 766 (B.C.C.A.).

[58.] *Ibid.* at p. 768.

Co-insurance clause may reduce coverage

insurance policies requiring that the insured parties maintain a certain percentage of coverage or bear some of the risk of loss themselves. Thus, in a policy with an 80 percent co-insurance clause, if the policy coverage were for less than that portion of the actual potential loss (say, only $50 000 coverage on property worth $100 000), the insured would have to assume a portion of any covered loss that occurred. The formula is:

The amount of insurance carried, divided by the minimum coverage that should have been in place, times the actual loss.

In this example that would be expressed as

$$\frac{\$50\ 000}{(\$100\ 000 \times 0.8)} \times \$10\ 000 = \$6\ 250$$

Note that the minimum insurance that should have been carried is determined by the co-insurance clause.

REDUCING RISK 5.5

A business that has been categorized as high risk or undesirable because of a claims history, late payments, or generally poor practices may not be able to acquire insurance or may be forced to pay high premiums for limited coverage. Strategies should be developed to avoid such a consequence. Insurance companies and brokers may offer services to help a client identify ways to diminish or eliminate losses.

(C) BUSINESS INTERRUPTION INSURANCE

Business interruption insurance covers lost profits

Often, a business suffering a loss from a fire will have insurance to cover the property damage, but there will be nothing to cover the losses the business suffers during the period it is closed down for repairs. Business interruption insurance is designed to cover that gap, providing coverage not only for lost profits but also any additional expenses incurred to bring the business back into production. Comprehensive property insurance and business interruption insurance together are an attempt to put the insured in the same financial position it would have been in had the fire or other damage not occurred.

(D) LIFE AND HEALTH INSURANCE

Life insurance used in business to cover key personnel

Life insurance provides security for a family or business against the death of the insured. Death is inevitable, and so premiums are calculated on the basis of a prediction of how long a person of a certain age and health can be expected to live. Businesses often take out life insurance against the death of key personnel to cover losses incurred from any disruption that may result from the death or illness of an executive partner or key employee.

CASE SUMMARY 5.16

Consent Given—Insurable Interest Requirement Satisfied: *Chantiam v. Packall Packaging Inc.*[59]

Mr. Chantiam was working as the plant manager for Packall Packaging Inc. when he consented to the company's taking out an insurance policy on his life (called a "keyman" policy). Later he left the company and started another business in competition with it. When he discovered that the insurance policy on his life was still in place, he demanded that it be terminated or transferred to him; when his former employer refused, he brought this action against the company.

Like all forms of insurance there must be an insurable interest to support such a policy. There was no question that an insurable interest for the employer existed in Chantiam's life at the time the policy was taken out, but he argued that conditions had changed, the insurable interest had ended, and it was against the public interest for a business to maintain an insurance policy on the life of a competitor.

The trial Court agreed, ordering the policy to be cancelled. But on appeal the Court held that the appropriate time for determining whether an insurable interest existed or not was at the time the policy was taken out. Once that had been established and it was clear that an insurable interest existed at that time, the company was entitled to continue the policy even where the employment ended and where the subject of the policy became a competitor. Furthermore, the applicable legislation stipulated that where the insured consents in writing to the creation of the policy, as happened here, that satisfies the insurable interest requirement. Since there was an insurable interest at the time the policy was created, there were no grounds to challenge the continuation of the policy.

This case illustrates that with life insurance, the question of insurable interest relates only to when the policy is taken out. Note that Manitoba has changed its legislation, allowing a person to bring an application to the court to have the policy cancelled when that insurable interest is no longer present.[60] But in this case, Ontario (like other provinces) had no similar provision.

SMALL BUSINESS PERSPECTIVE

It is necessary to refer to the applicable provincial legislation for clarity as to when one has an insurable interest in the life of another. Having "something to lose" suggests that an insurable interest may exist. So would a business have an insurable interest in the life of a debtor? Should the size of the debt matter?

There are various forms of life insurance to meet the needs of different individuals. Term insurance provides only a benefit upon death, and the premiums are lower than whole life insurance, which provides coverage in the event of death as well as investment potential and retirement income. These are just two of several variations of life insurance available.

[59.] (1998), 38 O.R. (3d) 401 (C.A.), leave to appeal to S.C.C. refused, [1998] S.C.C.A. No. 358.

[60.] *Insurance Act*, R.S.M. 1987, c. I-40, s. 155(4).

Health and disability insurance provides coverage during the life of the insured and is designed to pay health care expenses and provide an income for a person who is unable to earn a living because of illness or accident. Medical insurance can be arranged individually or as part of group coverage. Health care services in Canada are funded through the government-sponsored medical system, which is often supplemented by plans providing extended coverage.

In most Canadian jurisdictions, disability insurance can be obtained on an individual basis with an insurance corporation, but it is more often acquired by large organizations as part of an employee benefits package. See the MyBusLawLab for provincial variations.

Sometimes, where the husband and wife are both working, there will be overlapping extended benefits coverage such as dental and disability. Usually, there is a deductible amount that must be paid or a limitation on the coverage. When there are two policies, often one can be used to cover the shortfall of the other but not to overpay. Today these policies often include a provision declaring them to be "excess coverage" when another policy is in place, with the result that the first policy will cover up to the deductible or the limit of the coverage and only then will the other kick in and pay the rest. Where both policies declare themselves to be excess coverage, the two insurers will split the cost of the coverage.[61]

> **Health and disability insurance usually part of group coverage**

> **Contract governs coverage but where conflict, both share equally**

Insurable Interest

mybuslawlab
www.pearsoned.ca/mybuslawlab

For insurance not to be considered a wager, the insured must be able to demonstrate an **insurable interest** in what is insured. That means that when the insured-against event happens, the insured must have suffered a loss for which the insurance payout provides compensation and no more. The contract for insurance is a contract of indemnity. Consequently, except in the case of life insurance, the insured can recover only what he or she has actually lost, up to the limit set out in the policy. When the payout becomes a windfall, the insurance agreement is void as an illegal contract.

The insurable interest, then, is the amount an insured stands to lose if the insured-against event takes place. If Flynn owned a half-interest in a painting worth $150 000, she would have an insurable interest of $75 000. If Flynn carried an insurance policy of $150 000 on the painting and it was stolen, she would be able to collect only $75 000 for herself, even though she had insured it for the higher amount. (Were the painting to be stolen, she would likely collect the entire $150 000 but be required to hold the other $75 000 in trust for the person who owned the other half interest in it.)

> **Must be insurable interest to avoid illegality**

CASE SUMMARY 5.17

Insurance Void Due to Lack of Insurable Interest: *Walton v. General Accident Insurance Co. of Canada*[62]

The Waltons had an insurance policy on their home with the defendant. Because of a dispute with the municipality they stopped making payments on their taxes and mortgage. Even though a final foreclosure order was made they were still living in the house when it

---

61. See *Family Insurance Corp. v. Lombard Canada Ltd.*[2002] 2 S.C.R. 695; [2002] S.C.J. No. 49.

62. (2001), 194 D.L.R. (4th) 570 (Sask. C. A.).

was destroyed by fire. They had continued to pay premiums and so claimed under the insurance policy, but the insurer refused to pay, saying they had no insurable interest in the property. At trial it was held that because the Court still had a right to reconvey the property to them, that was a sufficient insurable interest and the insurance company had to pay. But on appeal that decision was reversed.

The Saskatchewan Court of Appeal found that the Waltons had no right to the property and they were living in it illegally. True, they had a hope that the property would be reconveyed to them, but this was at best a strong expectation. In fact at the time of the destruction of the home they had no legal or equitable right to it and so had no insurable interest.

SMALL BUSINESS PERSPECTIVE

This case dramatically illustrates the nature of insurable interest. Sometimes, following incorporation of a family business, owners fail to distinguish between assets owned individually and assets now owned by the corporate entity. The importance of having the actual owner named as the insured cannot be overstated.

It should be noted that when life insurance is involved, people have an insurable interest in their own life and in the lives of their spouse and other close relatives. A loss, economic, emotional, and otherwise, is assumed if a close relation dies. Depending on the jurisdiction, where the lives of key business personnel are insured, the written consent of that person may be required as was the case in the *Packall* case discussed above (Case Summary 5.16). The value of that insurable interest will be the amount of insurance coverage contracted for.

In the past, it was thought that because a corporation was a separate legal entity, the shareholder had no insurable interest in the assets of the corporation. The Supreme Court of Canada, however, has decided that shareholders may have an insurable interest in those assets even though they don't have a direct legal claim to them. The fact that they would suffer a loss is enough.[63]

Shareholders now have insurance interests in assets of corporation

LIMITATION CLAUSES

Ambiguities Resolved in Favour of the Insured

Insurance contracts take a standard fixed form and often contain limitation clauses favouring the insurer. Where there is ambiguity in the meaning of such clauses the *contra proferentum* rule allows the court to choose an interpretation that favours the insured. Coverage will be broadly construed while exclusions will be narrowly interpreted. Thus courts will apply an interpretation that favours the insured since it was the insurer that chose the language to use.

Ambiguities in contract interpreted in favour of the insured

---

63. *Kosmopoulos v. Constitution Insurance Company of Canada Ltd.,* [1987] 1 S.C.R. 2, at para. 42: "if an insured can demonstrate, in Lawrence J.'s words, 'some relation to, or concern in the subject of the insurance, which relation or concern by the happening of the perils insured against may be so affected as to produce a damage, detriment, or prejudice to the person insuring', that insured should be held to have a sufficient interest."

CASE SUMMARY 5.18

Contra Proferentum Rule Applied: *Heitsman v. Canadian Premier Life Insurance Co.*[64]

The insured's widow sued for death benefits under a policy of accidental death and dismemberment insurance. The insured died after suffering a heart attack while trying to free himself from an overturned tractor-trailer following a motor vehicle accident. Medical experts testified that the heart attack was brought on by the stress, emotional and physical, resulting from the accident. The stress would not have been fatal were it not for the deceased's pre-existing heart problems. The Court determined that both the pre-existing condition and the stress caused by the accident contributed to the death. Neither one was the proximate cause. The insurance policy included an exclusion of liability for loss of life caused by sickness or disease. The Court found the clause ambiguous. It was not clear whether the parties had excluded payment for a death where one of its causes was accidental, the other a pre-existing disease. The *contra proferentum* rule was applied, and the exclusion was narrowly interpreted; thus, judgment was issued to the widow.

DISCUSSION QUESTIONS

This case illustrates that one's insurer may try to avoid payment, relying upon an "exclusion" to justify its actions. Do you think that this rule of interpretation is sufficient to protect the interests of the insured? What if the clause is clear but unfair?

www.pearsoned.ca/mybuslawlab

| BC | AB | SK | MB | ON |

Insured has duty to disclose changes in risk

Contract of Utmost Good Faith

A relationship of *trust* exists between the insured and insurer, creating an *obligation to act in good faith*. An important aspect of that obligation is the duty on the part of the insured to disclose pertinent information, especially where it affects the *risk* assumed by the insurer. After all, it is the insured that knows, has possession of, or has access to the information relevant to that risk. Even after the contract is made, there is often a duty to notify the insurance company when circumstances change, as when an occupied building becomes unoccupied for a length of time.[65]

CASE SUMMARY 5.19

Failure to Notify of Change Voids Policy: *Mueller v. Wawanesa Insurance Co.*[66]

The fire insurance policy in question was taken out by the landlord when the house was rented as a residential family dwelling. The "family" never moved in—instead, the building was occupied by three members of a motorcycle gang. Despite notice from the police that the property was being used as a clubhouse, the landlord did not terminate the

---

[64] (2002), 4 B.C.L.R. (4th) 124 (S.C.).

[65] See, for example, *528852 Ontario Inc. v. Royal Insurance Co.* (2000), 51 O.R. (3d) 470 (Sup. Ct. J.), where the insured's failure to disclose a change of use, namely that the premises were left unoccupied, was a material non-disclosure that entitled the insurer to deny coverage.

[66] [1995] O.J. No. 3807 (Ont. Ct. (Gen.Div.)).

lease. The rent cheques were kept current, so the landlord felt unable to terminate the lease. The property was eventually destroyed by fire and the police suspected arson at the hands of a rival gang.

The insurance company refused to honour the policy, and in this action the Court agreed, finding that the use of the house was not the residential use envisioned under the policy and that there had been a material change in risk. The failure to notify the insurer of the change voided the policy and the insurance company did not have to pay.

SMALL BUSINESS PERSPECTIVE

The case shows how important it is to inform the insurer of any material changes that take place. Could leaving a building vacant, even for a limited period of time, constitute a material change? To be on the safe side, advance notification of changes to risk should be given to the insurer and a written record of the notice should be retained.

When applying for property insurance, the insurer will want to know what the property will be used for, whether it is for a business, whether it will be vacant for extended periods, and what kind of security and safety equipment is in place. For life, disability, or medical insurance, any injury, disease, or other health problems that may affect that person's health must be disclosed.

These factors affect eligibility or the rates charged for insurance, and since the insurer usually has no way of determining this information by itself, it must depend on the honesty of the insured to disclose it. Failure to disclose information material to the loss may be misrepresentation and may result in the loss's being unrecoverable. Even where it is not relevant to the loss, if it is a material misrepresentation it may cause the entire policy to be void. Legislation in some provinces upholds the insurance where the misrepresentation was innocent; but even in those jurisdictions, the policy will be unenforceable if the misrepresentation or failure to disclose was done knowingly. An all too common misrepresentation involves representations as to who owns and who is driving an automobile. The insured may be tempted by potentially lower premiums to misrepresent who the primary driver will be. Such misrepresentations have enabled many insurers to avoid payment following collisions.[67] See the MyBusLawLab for provincial legislation and cases.

Insured must disclose relevant information

CASE SUMMARY 5.20

Perilous Non-Disclosure: *Agresso Corp. v. Temple Insurance Co.*[68]

Since insurance contracts are contracts of utmost good faith, parties must err on the side of caution when completing applications for coverage. The insured software company applied for Information Technology Errors and Omissions insurance from the defendant

---

[67.] See *Demontigny v. Insurance Corp. of British Columbia,*[1989] B.C.J. No. 2475;*Schoff v. Royal Insurance Company of Canada,*[2004] A.J. No. 592 (C.A.).

[68.] [2007] B.C.J. No. 2466 (B.C.C.A.).

insurers for the period of 28 February 2002 to 28 February 2003. Prior to that time, the insured had signed a software license, implementation, and maintenance agreement with the third party, pursuant to which maintenance was to continue until 2005. By 20 January 2003, the insured was aware that the third party was dissatisfied with the insured's progress on solving a major problem with the software. But when the insured applied for a second policy, it did not disclose that there was a potential claim from the third party to the defendant insurers. In April 2003, the third party abandoned the software agreement and retained legal counsel. The insured notified the insurers on 20 January 2004 of a potential claim.

The insurers took the position that the insured had no coverage due to non-disclosure of a potential claim in the application form of 21 February 2003. Questions in the application for insurance required the insured to attach a list and status of all "claims, disputes, suits or allegations of non-performance" made during the past five years against the insured. Further, the insured was asked to advise whether it was aware of any "facts, circumstances or situations that may reasonably give rise to a claim other than advised in the previous question". Negative answers to both of these questions were given.

The Court of Appeal concluded that the insured's failure to disclose a potential claim from the third party constituted a material non-disclosure. There was "ample" evidence that the insured had knowledge of a "dispute" and of "allegations of non-performance." Accordingly, the insurer was able to have the insurance policy set aside.

SMALL BUSINESS PERSPECTIVE

This case underlines the need to be open and forthright with one's insurer. The consequences of keeping silent or failing to disclose information relevant to risk can be disastrous.

Insurer's duty to process claims fairly

Just as the insured has a duty to be honest in its dealings with the insurer, the insurer has a duty to process claims fairly. Where insurers have withheld payments without justification, damages, punitive damages, and solicitor and client costs have been awarded to the aggrieved insured. In the *Fowler* case,[69] for example, the insurer cut off disability payments to the insured even in light of medical evidence supporting the claim. The insurer's actions further exacerbated the insured's condition, by adding to the stress he was already under. Similarly, in the *Whiten*[70] case, the insurer's rejection of proof of loss (without explanation) was regarded as a failure of its duty of good faith. The insured had fled their burning house in their nightclothes, suffering frostbite as they watched their house burn down. After paying their living expenses for only a brief time, the insurer abruptly cut off payments. It raised a weak claim of arson, which was wholly discredited at trial. Punitive damages of $1 million were awarded by the jury, which evidently regarded the insurer's conduct as reprehensible.

Duty to defend

Normally the insurer also has a duty to arrange for legal representation and a defence for the insured. One reason for purchasing liability insurance is to avoid such costs. But this duty does not extend to funding a defence where intentional or criminal acts are involved. In the *Scalera* case,[71] where the insured had a

---

69. *Whiten v. Pilot Insurance Co.*, [2002] 1 S.C.R. 595.

70. *Fowler v. Manufacturers Life Insurance Co.* (2002), 216 Nfld. & P.E.I.R. 132 (Nfld. S.C. (T.D.).

71. Non-Marine Underwriters, *Lloyd's of London v. Scalera*, [2000] 1 S.C.R. 551.

comprehensive general liability policy, the insurer was not required to defend the insured against charges of sexual assault. Also in *Hodgkinson v. Economical Mutual Insurance Company*[72] there was no obligation to provide a defence where the defendant was sued for defamation for making a deliberate verbal attack on the plaintiff on the internet.

Subrogation

The right of **subrogation** gives the insurance corporation, once it has paid out a claim, the right to take over the rights of the insured in relation to whoever caused the injury or loss. The insurer steps into the shoes of the insured and can then sue whoever caused the loss as if it were the insured. Thus, where a neighbour carelessly allows a bonfire to get out of control, causing Mrs. Kostachue's house to burn down, Mrs. Kostachue would normally claim on her insurance and receive compensation. Her insurance corporation would then sue the neighbour for negligence and recoup what it can. In fact, if the neighbour had liability insurance, it would likely be his insurer that would ultimately pay. You should not assume when you are involved in an accident that just because the other person has insurance, you are protected. If it is your fault, that person's insurance company will normally seek to recover its loss from you.

Right of subrogation

Insurance corporations will also normally have the choice to rebuild, repair, or replace what is damaged so that they can minimize their cost. They also have the right of **salvage**. If stolen goods are recovered, for example, insurers can sell those goods to recover their costs. When personal property has been lost, the insurer usually has to pay only the depreciated value of the goods, not the replacement cost, unless it has agreed otherwise. Most personal household insurance policies today provide for the replacement of destroyed or stolen goods at their full retail value. When a loss does take place, there is a general requirement on the part of the insured to report that loss to the insurance corporation right away so that the insurance corporation can take steps to minimize the damage. There might also be an obligation to report the matter to the police if a crime is involved or if the loss resulted from an automobile accident.

Basic rules of contract apply to agency contracts

Depreciated rather than replacement value

It should also be pointed out that the insured is not permitted to profit from his wilful misconduct. If the insured deliberately causes the loss, he will not be able to collect. Thus, if Fagan burns down his own house, killing his wife in the process, he will not be able to collect on the fire insurance and he will not be able to collect on his wife's life insurance, even where he is named as beneficiary. The **forfeiture rule** (that a criminal should not be permitted to profit from a crime) also extends to those who claim through the criminal's estate. In the above example, if Fagan were also to die in the house fire, his estate would not be able to collect on either policy.

Insured can't profit from wilful misconduct

Bonding

While insurance coverage is not generally available for intentionally wrongful acts, such as assault, many businesspeople insist on some protection against losses brought on by their employees or the people they deal with, who may act wrongfully, even wilfully so. Bonding is available in these circumstances, and it takes two forms. Usually, an employer will pay a fee to have an employee bonded against

---

72. *Hodgkinson v. Economical Mutual Insurance Company*, [2003] I.L.R. 1–4168, [2003] O.J. No. 151 (Ont. S.C.J.). *Non-Marine Underwriters, Lloyd's of London v. Scalera*, [2000] 1 S.C.R. 551.

Bonded parties still liable

that employee's own wrongful conduct (**fidelity bond**). If the employee steals from the employer or a customer, the bonding corporation will compensate the employer for that loss. It must be emphasized, however, that this does not relieve the bonded employee of responsibility. The bonding corporation can turn to the employee and collect from that party, which is what distinguishes bonding from normal insurance arrangements.

The second form of bonding, a **surety bond**, occurs when the bonding is designed to provide assurance that a party to a contract will perform its side of the contract. For example, in a large construction project, the corporation doing the foundation may be required to put up a performance bond that it will finish the job at a specified level of quality and by a certain time. If it fails to complete or does not complete on time, the bonding company will be required to pay compensation.

SUMMARY

Negligence

- Inadvertent conduct falling below an acceptable standard of behaviour
- Plaintiff must establish:
  - A duty of care was owed—using reasonable foreseeability test; in new situations, the court may also refer to policy considerations
  - Breach of duty—by conduct falling below the level expected from a reasonable person
  - Causation—"but for" test establishes physical link; remoteness test used to determine if the injury or damage was unforeseeable
  - Damage—must show that material damage resulted from the conduct
- Defences to negligence
  - If there is contributory negligence, courts may apportion the losses
  - If the plaintiff voluntarily assumed the legal risk, the defendant has a complete defence
  - If the plaintiff was hurt while engaged in illegal activity, he may be denied a remedy
- Special situations
  - Statutes—may impose a duty of care where none exists at common law, or may create liability in the absence of fault
  - Strict liability—liability will be imposed even where there is no fault on the part of the defendant
  - Vicarious liability—liability imposed on one party for the wrong committed by another; employers are held vicariously liable for torts committed by employees
  - Occupiers' liability—legislation imposes duty upon occupiers to people who are injured on their property
- Product liability
  - Unlike in the United States, strict liability is not imposed on manufacturers in Canada
  - Manufacturers owe a duty of care to consumers of their products, but the plaintiff consumer must establish breach of that duty, causation, and damage

Professional liability

- Also usually based on negligence
- Professionals may be liable for:
  - False or inaccurate information that causes economic loss
  - Breach of fiduciary duty or of contractual obligations

Insurance

- Designed to spread the risk of loss
- Liability, property, business interruption, life, and health are the primary forms of insurance available
- Insured must have an insurable interest in the subject matter. Recovery limited to the extent of that insurable interest
- *Contra proferentum* rule: policy's ambiguities interpreted in the insured's favour
- Insurance is a contract of utmost good faith
- Insured has a duty to act fairly, fully disclose material facts, and be honest
- Misrepresentation of material facts enables the insurer to have the insurance contract rescinded
- When a claim is paid, the insurance company has salvage rights and is subrogated to the rights of the insured

QUESTIONS

1. List and explain what a plaintiff must establish to succeed in a negligence action.

2. When a tort is committed intentionally, what remedies are available that may not be available when the conduct is unintentional?

3. Explain what is meant by the reasonable person test.

4. What test do courts use to determine whether the defendant owed to the plaintiff a duty to be careful?

5. Explain how the adoption of the *Anns* case test by the Supreme Court of Canada modified the approach to duty of care established by *Donoghue v. Stevenson*.

6. Distinguish between misfeasance and nonfeasance, and explain the significance of the difference in tort law.

7. Describe the test used in determining the appropriate standard of care demanded of the defendant in a negligence action.

8. How has an occupier's liability to persons using the property changed in recent years?

9. How does the "but for" test help to satisfy the requirements of causation?

10. Distinguish between the "thin skull rule" and the "crumbling skull rule" and explain how they relate to the question of remoteness.

11. Explain how the effect of contributory negligence has been modified in recent years.

12. Explain why the defence of *volenti non fit injuria* is difficult to establish.

13. Explain the obligations that are imposed on the producer of a product and to whom that obligation is owed.

14. Why is the case of *Haig v. Bamford* important in the development of tort law?

15. Describe how the *Anns* case test can impact the establishment of a duty of care in cases involving professional liability.

16. Identify the *Rylands v. Fletcher* principle. When it will be applied?

17. What is vicarious liability? Are there any restrictions on its availability?

18. How does the standard of care required from professionals or other experts differ from the standard of care required generally?

19. Explain the nature of a fiduciary duty and under what circumstances it arises.

20. Explain the source and nature of the powers of a professional organization. List the rights a member of that organization has when facing disciplinary proceedings.

21. Distinguish between business interruption insurance and fire insurance. Why might a businessperson want to have both forms of coverage?

22. What is meant by an insurable interest, and how does it apply to the various types of insurance discussed in the chapter?

23. What remedies does an insurer have if the insured misrepresented material facts when applying for insurance coverage?

24. Explain what is meant by the right of subrogation. How may subrogation affect not only the insured but also the person who has caused the injury or damage? Indicate what other means the insurance corporations have to keep their damages as low as possible.

CASES AND DISCUSSION QUESTIONS

1. *Roper v. Gosling*, [2002] 5 W.W.R. 79, (Alta. C.A.).
Roper and Jensen had consumed beer and smoked marijuana before going with Gosling for the evening to a bar, where they all consumed a considerable amount of alcohol. They were drunk when they left and got into Roper's car so that he could drive them home. A single-car accident caused by his impairment occurred in which Roper rolled the car and Gosling was seriously injured. She sued Roper for negligence.

Indicate what arguments can be raised in his defence and what factors the courts will take into consideration in determining liability. Would it make any difference to your answer if the court determined as a finding of fact that although a reasonable person would have been aware that Roper's ability to drive was impaired, Gosling wasn't in fact aware of this when she got into the vehicle with him? What if she didn't have any other way home? If she did know, should her conduct be a complete bar to recovery?

2. *Jetz v. Calgary Olympic Development Association*, 2002 ABQB 887, [2002] A.J. No. 1470 (Alta. Q.B.).
This accident happened at Calgary's Olympic Park (the legacy park left after the 1988 Calgary Winter Olympics). Jetz was a competitive cyclist who like others was in the habit of practising using the roadway in the park. The park was private with a gate to bar

entrance but the public normally was allowed to use the park and the gate was left open. A sign made it clear that the park and roadway were for use of park patrons only, but park officials were aware that others including cyclists regularly used the park roadways. The accident took place because the park officials, being concerned about excessive speeds of those using the park roads, erected a speed bump at the bottom of one of the curves in the road. This new addition was unknown to Jetz, who hit the speed bump at a considerable speed and was thrown from his bike and seriously injured. He sued the association for negligence.

Indicate what arguments can be raised by the Calgary Olympic Development Association in its defence and what factors will be taken into consideration by the court in determining liability. How would it affect your answer to know that a sign had been erected to notify about the new speed bump but that it was located at a point where it was unlikely to attract the attention of road users or that Jetz was not exceeding the posted speed limit of 30 km/h at the time of the accident. Consider the provisions of the *Occupier's Liability Act* in place in your jurisdiction and apply it to these facts. Does this lead to an appropriate outcome? What changes, if any, would you make to the statute?

3. *Dixon v. Deacon Morgan McEwan Easson* **(1989), 62 D.L.R. (4th) 175 (B.C.S.C.).**
Mr. Dixon was an investor who chose to invest $1.2 million in National Business Systems when the share price was $12.89 per share. These shares went up in price somewhat, but before he could sell, the Securities Commission suspended trading. When trading resumed, the shares sold at about $3 each. Dixon had invested on the strength of financial statements, including one marked "Consolidated Statements of Income and Retained Earnings (Audited)," which had been audited by the defendants. In fact, these statements were based on fraudulent information supplied by the management of National Business Systems to indicate annual profits of $14 million, when the company had in fact lost $33 million. There is no question that the accounting firms involved in the audit were negligent for not detecting the inaccuracy. Mr. Dixon sued the accounting firm for negligence. Nothing on the document indicated who the auditors were, and the statements had been prepared without the auditors' knowing that they would be used by an investor such as Mr. Dixon.

Did the auditors owe a duty to Mr. Dixon to be careful? If the auditors had known that the statements were being prepared to attract investors, would this affect your answer? Is this a just way of treating liability for professionals, or should they only be liable to their clients, the ones they have contracted with?

4. *Jacobsen v. Nike Canada Ltd.* **(1996), 133 D.L.R. (4th) 377 (B.C.S.C.).**
Mr. Jacobsen was an employee of Nike Canada and was working for the company setting up a display at a trade show in the B.C. Place Stadium. Because of the nature of the job, he was required to work for a long period of time. The employer, through its representative, supplied the workers with food and considerable amounts of beer, which they were allowed to drink while on the job. At 11:30 p.m., they finished working. Mr. Jacobsen, along with some of the other employees, went to two clubs where they consumed more beer. The plaintiff consumed about 10 beers while working and more at the clubs. Driving home that night, he was involved in a serious single-vehicle accident that left him a quadriplegic. Jacobson sued his employer.

Explain the basis of his action and any defences that the employer might be able to raise. Just how responsible should employers be for the stupidity of their employees? Consider company Christmas parties and other celebrations. How should a responsible employer handle these situations?

5. *Schoff v. Royal Insurance Company of Canada*, [2004] A.J. No. 592 (C.A.)

Charles Goyan, an underage driver, was driving his 1966 Malibu when he caused an accident injuring the driver and passenger in another car (the Schoffs). They successfully sued him, obtaining a judgment totalling almost $500 000. They then sought to collect this amount from the insurance company that had insured the Malibu. The insurance company refused to pay, claiming that it was not bound by the policy contract because of misrepresentations made when the policy was made. Goyan had transferred ownership of the vehicle to his mother at the time the policy was taken out, and on the application she claimed that she was the only licensed driver in her household and she would be the only person driving the Malibu. She also claimed that there had been no accidents in relation to any vehicle she owned in the past six years and that she owned three vehicles at the time of the policy. In fact, of her four sons living with her, three had valid driver's licences and the fourth had his suspended. Also, the three with licences were under the age of 25. She owned five vehicles, not the three claimed, and her accident record had also been incorrectly stated. Obviously, her son Charles was driving the Malibu.

Do you think that the insurance company should be required to pay the Schoffs? Would it affect your answer to know that the insurance company had learned that the statement she gave about having no accidents in the last six years was incorrect before it issued the policy, and it was issued anyway?

6. *Citadel General Assurance Co. v. Vytlingam*, [2007] S.C.J. No. 46; *Lumbermens Mutual Casualty Co. v. Herbison*, [2007] S.C.J. No. 47

The Supreme Court of Canada released its decisions in these two cases on the same day. In the Vytlingham case, the respondents' vehicle was struck by a large boulder dropped from an overpass by two tortfeasors, one of whom was the insured motorist. In the Lumbermens case, the insured motorist stopped his vehicle to shoot at what he thought was a deer. In fact he shot another member of the hunting party. In both cases, the issue was whether the insurer was required to compensate the injured third parties under the motor vehicle insurance carried by the respective tortfeasors.

When is operation of the vehicle severable from the commission of a tort by the insured driver? Consider also the decision in *Hannah v. John Doe*, [2008] B.C.J. No. 1580 (S.C.), where the plaintiff was injured when a van drove past her and the passenger reached out of the window and grabbed her purse strap. The plaintiff was pulled backwards, hit her head on the pavement, and was dragged a short distance before the purse ripped. Did the plaintiff's injuries arise out of the use or operation of a motor vehicle in this case? Should the insurer of this motorist be able to escape liability by asserting that the cause of the plaintiff's injuries was severable from operation of a motor vehicle?

Chapter 6

Formation of Contracts

Along with torts, the second area of private law affecting businesspeople—and by far the most important—is the law of contracts. The world of commerce and most business relationships are based on contracts. In this and the following three chapters, we will discuss how a contract is formed, various factors that affect those contracts, and how they can come to an end. This chapter introduces the first two of the five essential elements necessary for valid contracts. The other three elements will be discussed in the next chapter.

THE CONTRACTUAL RELATIONSHIP

Definition of Contract

Knowledge of contract law is vital to all businesspeople because most commercial transactions are built on contractual relationships. A good starting point would be a practical definition of a contract. We will define a **contract** as a voluntary exchange of promises, creating obligations that, if defaulted on, can be enforced and remedied by the courts.

Exchange of promises enforceable in court

It is important to understand that when agreeing to the terms of a contract, people are creating and defining their own rules and obligations. This differs from other areas of the law, such as torts, where rules and obligations are imposed on them. A valid contract creates a situation in which parties to the contract can predict, with some certainty, their future relationship because each party knows that the courts will hold them to their agreement.

While the courts will enforce a valid contract after it has been created, what the parties agree to in the first place is generally unrestricted. This approach is referred to as the *freedom of contract*. People can enter into almost any kind of contractual agreement they want to, as long as the contract meets the common law requirements that will be discussed in this and the following chapters. Although the law of contracts is found primarily in the common law, there are a number of specialized areas in which legislation that modifies, restricts, or replaces these common law principles has been enacted, thereby interfering with the freedom to contract. Examples include the sale of goods, consumer protection, employment, partnerships, corporations, and real property, which will be the subjects of later chapters.

When we study contract law, the focus is usually on the problems that can arise. It may therefore appear that most contractual relationships experience difficulties. In fact, most contracts are honoured or resolved to the mutual satisfaction of the parties. The courts become involved in a small proportion of contractual agreements, when an unresolvable dispute arises.

Elements of a Contract

Not all agreements are contracts. To qualify as a valid contract, an agreement must contain certain elements. They are:

1. **Consensus**. Parties to a contract must have reached a mutual agreement to commit themselves to a certain transaction. They are assumed to have negotiated the agreement from equal bargaining positions. The process by which the agreement is reached usually involves an offer and an acceptance, although consensus can be implied.

2. **Consideration**. There must be a commitment by each party to do something or to abstain from doing something. The consideration is the price each is willing to pay to participate in the contract.

3. **Capacity**. Parties to a contract must be legally capable of understanding and entering into the agreement. Limitations in contracting capacity have been placed on infants, insane or intoxicated persons, aliens (persons who are not Canadian citizens), and, in some instances, native people, and corporations.

4. **Legality**. The object and consideration involved in the agreement must be legal and not against public policy.

5. **Intention**. Both parties must be serious when making the agreement, and both must intend that legally enforceable obligations will result from it.

It should be noted that the general rule is that an agreement reached verbally between parties is every bit as binding as a written one. However, legislation (the *Statute of Frauds*) has been passed requiring that certain types of agreements be supported by evidence *in writing* before they will be enforced in the courts. For convenience, this limited requirement of writing will be discussed along with the five elements of a contract.

Important Terms and Definitions

Before addressing the elements of a contract in more detail, it is necessary to outline some basic terminology that is used in the discussion of contractual obligations.

FORMAL AND SIMPLE CONTRACTS

A formal contract is one that is sealed by the party to be bound. Traditionally, a seal involved making an impression in sealing wax. A modern seal normally consists of a paper wafer affixed to a document, but any mark or impression will do. Simple contracts, sometimes called **parol contracts**, may be verbal or written, but are not under seal.

The use of a seal

EXPRESS AND IMPLIED CONTRACTS

An **express contract** is one in which the parties have expressly stated their agreement, either verbally or in writing. An **implied contract** is inferred from the conduct of the parties. When people deposit coins in vending machines, it can be inferred that they intend to create a contractual relationship, and thus an implied contract is in force. Portions of an express contract may also be implied.

Contracts may be implied

VALID, VOID, AND VOIDABLE CONTRACTS

A **valid contract** is one that is legally binding on both parties. A **void contract** does not qualify as a legally binding contract because an essential element is missing. If the parties to a void contract thought they were bound and followed the agreement, the courts would try to put the parties back to their original positions. A **voidable contract** exists and has legal effect, but one of the parties has the option to end the contract.

A void contract is no contract

A voidable contract is valid but one party has the right to escape

The distinction between void and voidable can have important implications for outsiders to the contract who have acquired an interest in the subject matter of the contract. If the original contract is void, the goods must be returned to the seller. If the original contract is voidable, the outsider has acquired good title to the goods and can keep them.

UNENFORCEABLE AND ILLEGAL CONTRACTS

An example of an **unenforceable contract** is one that is required to be in writing under the *Statute of Frauds* and is not. It may be valid in all other respects, but the courts will not force a party to perform such a contract. As well, if an unenforceable contract has been performed, the courts will not help a party to escape the contract.

Court won't enforce unenforceable contract

An **illegal contract** is one that involves the performance of an unlawful act. An illegal contract is void. The parties to such an agreement cannot be required to perform it. If an illegal contract has been performed or partially performed, the court, because of the moral taint, normally will not assist the parties by returning them to their original positions. This would usually be done if the contract was void. For example, if there is an illegal contract, and a deposit has been paid, the court will not order its return. Neither will the court require property to be returned if the contract is illegal, even when one of the parties has been enriched at the other's expense. There is, however, an exception to this general approach:

Illegal contract is void

The courts will help a person who is innocent of any wrongdoing even when the contract is illegal.

BILATERAL AND UNILATERAL CONTRACTS

A **bilateral contract** is one in which both parties make commitments and assume obligations. There is no exchange of promises in a **unilateral contract**. This type of contract comes into effect when one party actually performs what has been requested by the other. For example, a person may offer a reward for the return of a lost item. It is not until the lost item is returned that the offer is accepted and the contract created. Thus, a bilateral contract involves an exchange of promises, whereas a unilateral contract involves a promise followed by an act.[1]

Consensus

A MEETING OF THE MINDS

The essence of a contract is, at least in theory, the *meeting of the minds* of the contracting parties. The two parties must have a common will in relation to the subject matter of their negotiations, and they must have reached an agreement. They must share an understanding of the bargain struck and be willing to commit themselves to the terms of that contract.

In practice, however, it is not necessary that both parties fully understand, or even have read, all the terms of the contract. Few people thoroughly read the major contracts they enter into, such as insurance policies, leases, and loan agreements. Of those who do, few fully understand the specific meaning of the documents. The law does not recognize the excuse that one of the contracting parties did not read the contract or that he did not understand it.

Both parties must have had an opportunity to read and understand the contract for it to be valid. The terms of the agreement must be clear and unambiguous. If the terms of the contract are ambiguous, then the court will decide that there has not been consensus between the parties and it will declare the contract void. Case Summary 6.1 provides an example of a court declaring a contract void because of a lack of consensus.

Unilateral contract—performance is acceptance

www.pearsoned.ca/mybuslawlab

BC **AB** SK MB ON

Agreement reached— bargain struck

Terms must be clear and unambiguous

No Consensus, No Contract! *Sussexinsuranceagency.com Inc. v. Insurance Corp. of British Columbia*[2]

Sussexinsuranceagency.com Inc. (Sussex.com) sued the Insurance Corp. of British Columbia (ICBC) for breach of an oral agreement. It claimed damages for loss of profits of between $26 million and $40 million, as well as punitive damages. Sussex.com claimed that ICBC had promised it an exclusive one-year pilot project to operate a call centre. Sussex.com also claimed that it relied on this promise and incurred significant

---

1. See *Speidel v. Paquette* (1979), 20 A.R. 586 (Q.B.), which involved a promise to convey title to a house if the other party moved into the house, looked after it, and paid rent for five years. The Court ruled that a unilateral contract was formed when the other party performed all of the stipulated terms.

2. [2005] B.C.S.C. 58.

costs. ICBC denied that a contract had been formed, as there was no intention to be bound and the parties had not agreed to the terms of the contract.

The Court held that the parties did not agree on the essential terms of a contract at their first meeting. There was simply an agreement to continue negotiations. While there was an agreement reached between the parties at their second meeting, the Court ruled that there was not an agreement as to the meaning of "a premium rate finder." In addition, the agreement that ICBC would provide client lists was based on a mistake of fact by ICBC. The Court therefore concluded that there was not a binding contract because of a lack of consensus between the parties.

SMALL BUSINESS PERSPECTIVE

Courts make their decisions based on the evidence presented to them. What types of evidence will a court consider in cases in which the existence of a contract is at issue? In light of this, what can parties involved in contractual negotiations do to ensure that a court will reach the correct decision as to whether there was a meeting of the minds of the parties?

Obviously, mistakes happen, and some very complex rules, which we will discuss later, have been developed to handle them. Nevertheless, contract law is based on the assumption that the culmination of the bargaining process occurs when one party states its position in the form of an offer in the expectation that the other party, through acceptance, will make a similar commitment to be bound by the terms of that offer. It should be stressed that a valid offer and an acceptance are not always obvious and yet, from the conduct of the parties or other factors, it is clear that the parties have a mutual understanding. In such circumstances, the courts are willing to imply the existence of a contract, and no evidence of a specific identifiable offer and acceptance is required.

Offer

A valid **offer** contains all of the terms to be included in the contract; all that is required of the other party is to give its consent or denial. The offer is a tentative promise on the part of one party to do whatever is set out, providing that the other party consents to do what is requested in return. When a sales person offers to sell a car to a customer for $5000, the offer is a tentative promise by the seller to deliver the car, contingent on the customer's willingness to pay the $5000. The process of making an offer is the communication of a willingness to be bound by the terms and conditions stated in that offer.

This aspect of the offer can be confusing to those involved in commercial activities. People often have documents placed before them and are asked to sign "the contract" (for example, in transactions involving insurance policies or leases). In fact, at that stage, the document is not a contract; it is merely an offer. Only after it is accepted and signed can it be said to be the "contract," and even then it is probably only the written evidence of the contractual relationship between the parties.

The offer must contain all significant terms of the proposed contract. The parties, the subject matter of the contract, any price to be paid, as well as any other important terms, should all be stated in the offer. The courts do have the power to imply into contracts the insignificant terms that the parties may not have

 mybuslawlab
www.pearsoned.ca/mybuslawlab

Offer—tentative promise

Offer—must include all important terms

considered, such as time of delivery, time of payment, and so on. Such terms must be incidental to the agreement, but consistent with the apparent intention of the parties. Courts will often turn to the common practice of the trade or industry for assistance in deciding which terms should be implied. As discussed in Chapter 15, when goods are sold, the *Sale of Goods Act* sets out the terms to be implied if they are not in the contract of sale. Sometimes, as mentioned above, it is even possible for the courts to imply the entire contract from the conduct of the parties, but if it is clear that important terms have been left out, or are to be negotiated later, the courts will rule that there is no contract.

Some terms can be implied

CASE SUMMARY 6.2

An Agreement to Enter into a Contract Is Not Good Enough: *Beacock v. Wetter*[3]

Wetter owned a house. She and Beacock discussed him renting the house for $950 per month and eventually buying it for $200 000. No written contract of purchase and sale was signed by the parties. Beacock moved into the house and paid rent of $950 per month. He made improvements to the house that were worth $23 000. During further discussions, Beacock increased his offer to $215 000. He could not obtain funding, and Wetter would not agree to take back a second mortgage. He filed a builder's lien for the cost of the improvements. Wetter served him with a notice to vacate the house. Beacock sued for specific performance of his agreement with Wetter or, in the alternative, damages for breach of contract. Wetter denied entering into an agreement to sell the house to Beacock.

The Court ruled that there was no consensus, or meeting of the minds, regarding the terms of the alleged agreement. The discussions between Wetter and Beacock resulted in "an agreement or intention to enter into a contract of purchase and sale at some unspecified date in the future." There was no definite offer that contained the specific terms of an agreement that could be accepted. The Court quoted from *Bawitko Investments Ltd. v. Kernels Popcorn Ltd.* (1991), 53 O.A.C. 314, at 327:

> [W]hen the original contract is incomplete because essential provisions intended to govern the contractual relationship have not been settled or agreed upon; or the contract is too general or uncertain to be valid in itself and is dependent on the making of a formal contract; or the understanding or intention of the parties, even if there is no uncertainty as to the terms of their agreement, is that their legal obligations are to be deferred until a formal contract has been approved and executed, the original or preliminary agreement cannot constitute an enforceable contract. In other words, in such circumstances, the "contract to make a contract" is not a contract at all.

The Court also held that there was no option to purchase agreement, as there was no consideration for such an agreement. Finally, the Court denied Beacock's claim for the cost of the improvements, as they had not been requested by Wetter and she did not accept them.

[3.] [2006] B.C.S.C. 951, aff'd [2008] B.C.C.A. 152.

Do you think that this is a fair result from Beacock's perspective? What about the expectations that were created? What should he have done to protect himself?

It must be emphasized that the parties can make it clear that, while they intend to put the agreement into a more formal document later, they intend to be bound before the contract is formalized, as long as all of the important terms have been agreed upon. An **interim agreement** (agreement of purchase and sale) in a real estate transaction is an example of such a contract. It is binding even though a more formal document will follow. A letter of intent will also be binding if all significant terms are included in it. If a person does not want to be bound by such a letter, she should clearly state this in the document.[4] A court will consider the common practice of a particular industry when determining whether a particular agreement constitutes a valid contract and at what stage it is considered binding.

> **Interim agreement binding**

It should also be noted that **"subject-to" clauses** often raise the same concerns. An offer may include a term making the contract conditional on some future event. A person may offer to purchase a house "subject to" the sale of her house. These types of provisions are not necessarily uncertain or ambiguous, unless the subject-to clause itself is uncertain. If the terms of the offer are clear, and nothing is left to be negotiated or agreed upon, the parties are bound to perform as agreed once the subject-to term has been satisfied.[5]

> **Contract not binding until condition satisfied**

Some types of contractual relationships, often referred to as **quasi-contracts**, must be viewed as exceptions to the rule that important terms must be clear. These contracts involve requests for goods and services. They will be discussed later in this chapter, with *quantum meruit,* under the heading "Request for Services."

> **Note exception for request for goods or services**

INVITATION TO TREAT

An offer is usually made to an individual or to a group of people, but it is also possible to make an offer to the world at large, such as by posting a notice offering a reward for information, or the return of a lost item. Most newspaper, radio, television, and internet advertisements, however, are just **invitations to treat**. They are simply invitations to potential customers to engage in the process of negotiation. As part of the pre-negotiation process, invitations to treat have no legal effect. The typical process to create a contract is illustrated in Figure 6.1.

[4.] For a case in which an enforceable contract was found, despite an argument that it had been a mere "agreement to agree," see *Knappett Construction Ltd. v. Axor Engineering Construction Group Inc.* (2003), 24 C.L.R. (3d) 120 (B.C.S.C.).

[5.] See *McIntyre v. Pietrobon*, [1987] B.C.J. No. 1571 (S.C.), in which a sale was made "subject to purchaser obtaining satisfactory personal financing." The Court held that the clause was vague, that there was therefore no contract, and that the deposit paid by the purchasers was to be repaid. This decision was distinguished in *Young v. Fleischeuer*, [2006] B.C.S.C. 1318, in which the condition precedent was "Subject to the Buyer . . . receiving . . . financing satisfactory to the Buyer." The Court held that this condition was not void for uncertainty.

Figure 6.1 Typical Process to Create a Contract

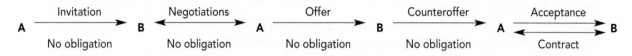

Invitation to treat not an offer

Goods displayed on a shelf an invitation only

It is sometimes difficult to distinguish between an offer and an invitation to treat. A newspaper advertisement stating, "Automobile tires for sale, two for the price of one" is not an offer. The advertisement is meant to encourage the reader to visit the store and then make an offer to purchase some tires. Catalogues and personal advertisements in the classified section of a newspaper are also invitations to treat. According to the famous English case *Pharmaceutical Society of Great Britain v. Boots Cash Chemists (Southern), Ltd.,*[6] goods displayed on the shelves of self-serve stores are also mere invitations to treat, even though the price of the items may be clearly marked.

With the display of such goods being merely an invitation to treat, a customer might be tempted to switch the prices on items displayed for sale in a store. To do so, however, is a crime.[7] The use of scanners and bar codes has made this crime more difficult to commit.

OFFER BY CONDUCT

Offer may be implied by conduct

A customer in a self-serve store takes the goods to be purchased to a cashier and places the goods and money on the counter. A person hails a cab by the gesture of raising a hand and calling, "Taxi!" These are both examples of offers being made by conduct. However, an auctioneer's comment "Do I hear $50?" is merely an invitation to the people in the audience to make an offer. When one of them raises a hand or makes some other acceptable gesture, that is an offer. The auctioneer is free to accept or reject it. A further question "Do I hear $60?" is another invitation for offers. The statement "Sold!" is an acceptance of a person's offer.

COMMUNICATION OF AN OFFER

Offer must be communicated

Before you can accept an offer, it must be communicated to you. You can accept only an offer that has been communicated to you as an individual, to you as a member of a group, or to the world at large. You can't accept an offer made to someone else, no matter how you learn about it. Also, you cannot accept an offer you did not know about. If you return a lost item unaware that a reward has been offered, you have no claim to the reward, because the offer was not communicated to you.

Even where two offers cross in the mail with both parties of the same mind, there is no contract. If one party sent a letter offering to sell, and the other, in

---

[6.] [1953] 1 All E.R. 482 (C.A.), aff'g [1952] 2 All E.R. 456 (Q.B.).

[7.] Obtaining goods by false pretences, *Criminal Code*, R.S.C. 1985, c. C-46, ss. 361, 362.

another letter sent at the same time, offered to buy, a particular car for $500, there would not be a contract. Neither letter could be an acceptance, since neither party was aware of the other's offer.

It is also important to note that, for a contract to be binding, all important terms must have been disclosed to the offeree. This is especially important with respect to exemption clauses. In contracts with customers, merchants will often include clauses that favour their own position, or limit their liability. There are usually signs disclaiming responsibility for theft or damage to cars or contents posted in parking lots. Tickets to athletic events, or for the use of sporting facilities, will often include terms disclaiming responsibility for injury, damages, or loss of personal property by theft. In cases such as these, an exemption clause will be binding only when it has been reasonably brought to the attention of the customer at the time the contract is made. For example, the sign in the parking lot must be placed in a well-lit location where the driver will see it before, or at the time, the contract is made; this is usually at the cashier's booth or vending machine, as well as at other strategic locations on the lot. When the clause is on the back of a ticket, there must be a reference to it on the front of the ticket for it to be binding. Also, the ticket must be given to the customer at the time the contract is made, not afterwards. Even if these precautions are taken, consumer protection legislation may restrict the effect of an exemption clause. This issue will be discussed in Chapter 15.

Important terms must be disclosed, especially exemption clauses

 REDUCING RISK 6.1

Whether terms are set out in signs or included in written agreements, it is vital that any that are at all unusual be reasonably brought to the attention of the other party, especially if they limit the liability of the first party. It is no longer good enough for the term to appear in small print in a document, or to put it on a receipt so that it can be seen only after the contract has been created. It is likely that those terms will simply not be considered part of the contract and therefore not binding on the other party.

Exemption clauses are also commonly found in written contracts. When people sign contracts, they are generally taken to have read the entire document. Even then, when an exemption clause is unusually restrictive, the court may hold that there was a requirement to specifically bring the clause to the attention of the other contracting party and that the obligation was not met. Even when the clause was brought to the attention of the other party, if the merchant's failure to perform amounts to a fundamental breach, she still may not be able to rely on the exemption clause for protection. The topic of fundamental breach will be discussed in Chapter 9.

Fundamental breach may avoid exemption clause

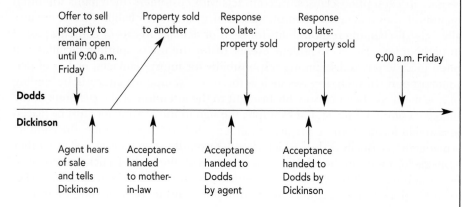

CASE SUMMARY 6.3

An Offer Can't Be Accepted After You Know the Offeror Has Changed His Mind: *Dickinson v. Dodds*[8]

Dickinson v. Dodds, an old case from the latter part of the 19th century, remains one of the best cases to illustrate how offer and acceptance work. Dodds made an offer to sell certain property to Dickinson for £800, stating, "This offer to be left over until Friday, 9:00 a.m." Before the expiration of that deadline, Dickinson learned through his agent that Dodds had been trying to sell, or had sold, the property to someone else.

He quickly went to Dodds's home and left a written acceptance with Dodds's mother-in-law. The next morning, Dickinson and the agent went down to the train station to intercept Dodds as he arrived in town. The agent found him first and handed him a written acceptance. Dodds replied that it was too late and that he had already sold the property. This scenario was repeated a few minutes later when Dickinson intercepted Dodds, with the same response—all before the stated deadline.

This case is important because it illustrates the nature of an offer. The offer is a tentative commitment on the part of the person making it. Until the other party accepts it, there is no obligation on the offeror. Dodds was free to withdraw his offer any time before it was accepted. Even though he had promised to hold the offer open, he was not obligated to do so. He could change his mind and sell the property to someone else, but he had to let the other party know he had changed his mind. In this case, Dodds was extremely lucky, because although he didn't tell Dickinson directly that he had changed his mind, Dickinson found out indirectly. He couldn't accept an offer he knew was no longer available. Had Dickinson not found out about the sale, his acceptance would have been valid and Dodds would have been bound in contract to sell the property to two different purchasers.

SMALL BUSINESS PERSPECTIVE

Do you think that Dodds should have been bound by his promise to hold the offer open? Should a sale to someone else automatically end the offer? Why would a businessperson want to keep her promise, even if she doesn't have to?

[8.] (1876), 2 Ch. D. 463 (C.A.).

THE END OF AN OFFER

For the acceptance of an offer to be effective, the offer must be in force at the time of the acceptance. There are several ways for an offer to come to an end before acceptance.

Offer ends

1. End of a specified time. The offer will end at the time stated in the offer. Note that the offeror is still free to revoke the offer before this time expires, unless an option has been purchased. Option agreements will be discussed below.

• when specified

2. Expiration of a reasonable time. If no time is specified in the offer, it will expire at the end of a reasonable time. What is reasonable depends on the circumstances. Thus, an offer to sell a ship would likely last longer than an offer to sell a load of ripe peaches.

• after a reasonable time

3. Death or **insanity** of offeror. The offer will end even if the offeree is unaware of the death or insanity.

• upon death or insanity of offeror

4. Revocation of offer. The offeror may revoke an offer any time before acceptance, but the revocation must be communicated to the offeree to be effective. (When letters are used, the revocation is effective only when received by the offeree.) Until the revocation is communicated to the offeree, the offeree can still accept the offer. The offeror should therefore not contract with another party until she is sure that the message that she has revoked the offer has been received by the offeree. While it is possible for the revocation to be communicated indirectly, as in *Dickinson v. Dodds* discussed above, reliance on such a method would be foolish in the extreme. Dodds was extremely lucky in that case.

• when revoked (revocation must be communicated)

5. Rejection and **counteroffer**. During the bargaining process, several different proposals may be put forward, rejected, and then followed by counterproposals. Each counteroffer or rejection ends the offer before it. For example, when a car is offered for sale for $5000 and the customer replies "I'll give you $4500," a counteroffer has been made, and the original offer is thereby ended. If the seller rejects the counteroffer, it is too late for the purchaser to reconsider and accept the original offer, as it no longer exists. Under such circumstances, an attempt to accept the original $5000 offer constitutes a new offer, which the seller is free to accept or reject.

• when rejected or counteroffer is made

Note that a simple request for information or clarification, such as an inquiry as to whether the sale of a car includes the stereo, does not constitute a counteroffer or a rejection. It therefore does not end the offer. On the other hand, a counteroffer that is worded like a question will end the offer (such as "Will you take $4500?").

Request for information is not a counteroffer

The existence of an offer can be affected by other factors as well. For example, the offer will be ended if the activity contemplated by the contracting parties becomes illegal before acceptance. Also, if the goods forming the subject matter of the contract are destroyed without the parties' being aware of it, the offer is ended.

OFFERS THAT CANNOT BE REVOKED

Often, businesspeople find the uncertainty associated with the offeror's right to revoke any time prior to the point of acceptance very inconvenient, especially when they are arranging their business affairs to take advantage of the offer.

For example, when assembling land, a land developer will get offers from several sellers. He will not accept any of them until he is sure that all of the required properties can be obtained. The right of each of the sellers to revoke is inconsistent with this process. The developer will therefore acquire an option on each property. An option is a subsidiary contract, with separate consideration given to the offeror in exchange for a commitment to keep the offer open for a specific length of time. The developer thereby gains the certainty necessary to accomplish his goal. Such arrangements are quite common; they are found in all areas of finance and business. (Options can also be put under seal; the use of the seal will be discussed below, under "Consideration.")

A similar problem exists when dealing with *tenders*, the normal practice in the construction industry. A purchaser issues a request for bids to get the best possible price on a required product or service. The request for bids is an invitation to treat, and each submitted bid is an offer. The problem is that normally there would be nothing to stop the offeror from withdrawing her offer if she realizes she has made a mistake or, if upon seeing the other bids, she realizes that hers is too low. The Supreme Court of Canada has decided that in some circumstances such tendered bids cannot be revoked.[9] When the original request for tenders made it clear that bids would be considered only when the offeror agreed that the offer could not be withdrawn once submitted, a subsidiary contract exists, and the offer then cannot be revoked. As above, the problem is also avoided when the tendered bid is made under seal.

Where option exists, offer cannot be revoked

It is likely that the same principle will apply in any situation in which a unilateral contract is involved and performance of the act requested has started. Thus, if an employer promises to give her business to an employee if he stays until she retires, the acceptance is made simply by the employee's staying on. With such an implied subsidiary contract, the employer could not wait until just before her retirement and then revoke the offer.

Unilateral offer can't be revoked once performance begins

Subsidiary contracts may be implied

CASE SUMMARY 6.4

The Tendering Process and the Duty to Be Fair: *Martel Building Ltd. v. Canada*[10]

The Department of Public Works issued a call for tenders, pursuant to which it did not have to accept the lowest bid. Martel submitted the lowest bid. However, the Department conducted a financial analysis of the bids and added certain costs to Martel's bid. The tender was then awarded to another bidder.

After reviewing the general principles of the law of tender, the Court stated that a call to tender is an offer to contract and a binding contract may arise when a bid is submitted. The Court held that the parties intended to include an implied term that all bids were to be treated fairly and equally. Pursuant to the call for tenders, the Department did have some discretion in evaluating the bids. It added fit-up costs to all of the bids, using the same approach. This was not a breach of the duty to act fairly. The Department was entitled to add another specific cost to Martel's bid, as this was an express requirement

---

9. *R. v. Ron Engineering & Construction* (Eastern) Ltd., [1981] 1 S.C.R. 111.

10. [2000] 2 S.C.R. 860.

to which all of the bidders had to comply. The Department did breach its duty to treat all bidders fairly and equally, by adding this cost only to Martel's bid. This addition did not, however, cause Martel to lose the tender. Martel's claim for damages was therefore dismissed.

DISCUSSION QUESTIONS

Given the duty to treat all bidders fairly, can a party calling for tenders protect itself simply by including, in the tender documents, a "privilege clause," stating that the lowest or any tender will not necessarily be accepted? Can a privilege clause be used to attach an undisclosed condition to the offer of the party calling for tenders?

STANDARD FORM CONTRACT

The law assumes that the two parties to an agreement are in equal bargaining positions and that both will negotiate the terms of the agreement until a consensus, which represents a fair bargain, is reached. In actual fact, most large businesses do not negotiate with their customers. Rather, they present an offer with fixed terms, which the customer is invited to accept. A passenger purchasing an airline ticket is an example. These are called **standard form contracts** and usually contain one-sided terms favouring the business. Exemption clauses, discussed above, that attempt to limit the liability of the business, are examples of such one-sided terms.

Bargaining difficult with standard form contract

In an effort to correct the imbalance in bargaining power, and to alleviate some of the unfairness, *consumer protection legislation* has been enacted in most jurisdictions, controlling the worst abuses. Consumer protection is covered in Chapter 15. Also, when the courts deal with exemption clauses, they interpret them strictly, so that any ambiguity is read in favour of the disadvantaged party. Thus, a business that includes in its contracts terms disclaiming responsibility for "damage" to goods left on the premises would still be held responsible for goods that were stolen. Even when exemption clauses are clear, the courts are showing a willingness to set them aside on the basis of fairness and good faith.[11]

Statutes and attitude of courts mitigate this

mybuslawlab
www.pearsoned.ca/mybuslawlab

    ON

Acceptance

At the heart of contract law are the concepts of consensus and mutual commitment. The manifestation of an intention to commit on the part of the offeror is found in the offer; the offeree's intention to commit is found in the acceptance. The contract is formed, and the parties are bound by it, at the point of acceptance. The key to understanding acceptance is that the commitment must be total. If a condition or qualification is put on the acceptance, it becomes a counteroffer, and is not an acceptance. If a salesperson offers to sell a car and a trailer to a customer for $5000 and $3000, respectively, and the response is "I accept, provided

---

[11.] For a good discussion of the duty of good faith in commercial contracts, see *Transamerica Life Canada Inc. v. ING Canada Inc. (2003)*, 68 O.R. (3d) 457 (C.A.). Unlike American courts, Canadian courts have not recognized a "stand-alone" duty of good faith in the performance or enforcement of commercial contracts. Canadian courts have implied only a duty of good faith that ensures that the parties do not act in a way that defeats the objectives of the agreement that they have entered into.

Acceptance must be complete and unconditional

you include new tires," that response is a counteroffer. Nor is it possible to accept only part of an offer. In this example the purchaser cannot say, "I accept your offer, but I want only the car." For an acceptance to be valid, it must be an all-or-nothing proposition.

A serious problem can arise when customers and suppliers exchange order forms. Sometimes, instead of filling in the supplier's order form, the customer simply sends her own, which may include different terms. This is not an acceptance, but a counteroffer. If the supplier simply sends the product in response, he has accepted and is bound by the new terms. Suppliers often do not realize the difference. Such a mistake is easily made, and care should be taken to watch for such substituted forms.

An incomplete offer cannot be accepted

Even a clear acceptance cannot correct an incomplete offer. When the wording of an offer is unclear, the courts will interpret the agreement to find the most reasonable construction. They will not, however, go so far as to strike a bargain on behalf of the parties. As mentioned, there is no such thing as a contract to enter into a contract.

CASE SUMMARY 6.5

An Incomplete Offer Can't Be Accepted: *Zynik Capital Corp. v. Faris*[12]

A Memorandum of Understanding was signed by Zynik and by Faris, who signed on behalf of a non-existent corporation, Intergulf Developments Ltd. The Memorandum provided that the parties would jointly acquire the Versatile Shipyards property. Zynik alleges that Intergulf repudiated the Memorandum, with the result that the property was purchased by a third party. Zynik claimed damages of $10 million, representing the profits it would have made if it had been able to develop the property.

The Court referred to the paragraph in the *Bawitko* case quoted in Case Summary 6.2. It held that the Memorandum was not a binding contract, as it was missing an essential term. There was no acquisition price for the property provided. Further, there was no evidence that the parties had agreed on an acceptable price. As there was not a binding contract, the action for damages was dismissed.

SMALL BUSINESS PERSPECTIVE

In this case, the offer was incomplete and therefore could not be accepted. No matter how definite the acceptance was, it could not overcome the defect of an incomplete offer. How can parties ensure that the agreements they enter into will be enforceable?

COMMUNICATION OF ACCEPTANCE

Offer may be accepted by conduct, where specified or implied

Acceptance of an agreement is usually accomplished by communicating it to the offeror. It is possible, however, for an offer to be accepted by conduct. If the offeror has indicated particular conduct to specify acceptance, the offeree must comply with that stipulation for it to be effective. Acceptance may also be implied from conduct as when, for example, a purchaser leaves a deposit on a car she has purchased.

[12.] (2007), 30 B.L.R. (4th) 32 (B.C.S.C.).

CASE SUMMARY 6.6

Communication of Acceptance May Be Indirect: *Lanca Contracting Ltd. v. Brant (County) Board of Education*[13]

The president of Lanca was present when the Board of Education passed a resolution to accept Lanca's bid for the construction of a new school. The members of the Board were aware of his presence. Several members of the Board, as well as its architect and controller, spoke at the meeting in terms that implied that Lanca was going to be building the school. Two days later, the Board rescinded its resolution and awarded the contract to someone else. The question facing the Court was whether notice of the acceptance had been given to Lanca sufficient to create a binding contract. The Court decided that it had been, and that the Board was liable for its breach of the contract.

DISCUSSION QUESTIONS

If acceptance can be implied from the conduct of the parties, is the law too subjective? Does it make the law too unpredictable? If acceptance can be implied from the offeror's conduct, it will be the courts that will make the determination as to whether the conduct in a particular case implies acceptance. Does this give the courts too much discretion? Would it be better if the law were that acceptance must be communicated to the offeror to be effective?

A **unilateral contract** is accepted by performance of the act specified in the offer.[14] If a prize were offered for the first human-powered flight across the English Channel, acceptance would be by making the flight. Starting the flight would not qualify; only the completion of the cross-Channel flight would constitute effective acceptance of the offer. But what if the offeror tried to revoke his offer when the flight was only partially performed? In theory, an offer can be revoked any time before acceptance. As discussed above, a Canadian court would likely follow the American example, and find a subsidiary contract requiring that once the performance starts the offer cannot be revoked. In any case in which acceptance is by conduct, there is no requirement to communicate the acceptance to the offeror, although there may still be a need to notify the offeror that the required conduct has taken place when this is not self-evident.

Unilateral contract accepted by completion of performance

Merchandisers often send unsolicited goods to people along with an invoice stating that if the goods are not returned within a specified time, the customer will have purchased them. But silence, as a general rule, does not constitute acceptance. When goods are supplied in this way, the customer can normally ignore them and just put them away. If the customer uses the goods, he is receiving a benefit and is deemed to have accepted the offer. Consumer protection legislation in many provinces outlaws "negative option practices," reinforcing the common law. Consumer protection legislation is discussed in Chapter 15.

Unsolicited offer not accepted by silence

An important exception to silence not being an acceptance occurs when there is an ongoing business relationship between the parties. It is quite common for a supplier to send materials used by a business on a regular basis, with the understanding that they will continue to be sent unless the supplier is informed

But silence can be acceptance if prior dealings

---

13. [1986] O.J. No. 234 (C.A.).

14. See *Speidel*, supra note 1, for an example of a case involving a unilateral contract.

otherwise. A relationship of trust has developed, and the purchaser now has a duty to inform the supplier when he changes his mind. When a person joins a book-of-the-month club, a similar duty is created, and return of the book is likely required to escape obligation. But such clubs sometimes continue to send products when there has not been a request, or even after they have been told to stop. As mentioned above, there is now consumer protection legislation in place in most provinces dealing with negative option practices in an attempt to prevent this kind of abuse.

Acceptance is effective when and where received

When acceptance is not by conduct, the general rule is that it is not effective until it has been communicated to the offeror, in the manner stipulated in the offer. The result of this general rule is that the contract is formed when and where the offeror learns of the acceptance. If a supplier of lumber products in Halifax makes an offer to a customer in Winnipeg, and the offeree accepts over the telephone, the contract comes into existence in Halifax, when the offeror hears the acceptance. Where the contract is formed can be an important factor in determining which court has jurisdiction and which jurisdiction's law will apply to the contract.

THE POSTBOX RULE

Mailed acceptance effective when and where dropped in postbox

Difficulties arise when parties deal with each other over long distances using non-instantaneous forms of communication. Because neither party can be absolutely sure of the other's state of mind at a given time, there can be no certainty of the contract's status. The **postbox rule** was developed to solve this problem. When use of the mail is reasonable, an acceptance is effective when and where it is deposited in the mailbox. This is a clear exception to the general rule discussed above, which states that an acceptance is not effective until the offeror learns of it. Figure 6.2 illustrates how the postbox rule works.

CASE SUMMARY 6.7

Should the Postbox Rule Be Extended? *R. v. Commercial Credit Corp.*[15]

This case dealt with whether a creditor had lost its priority by failing to properly register a security interest as required by Nova Scotia law. If the contract was formed within the province, the creditor would lose any claim to the assets because of the failure to register; if it was formed outside the province, the creditor would have a valid claim. The original offer had been sent by courier by Commercial, from its Nova Scotia office, to the offeree, which was outside of the province. The offer was accepted, and the acceptance was also sent by courier. The Court held that this communication was akin to using the mail and so the postbox rule applied. This meant that the acceptance was effective where sent, which was outside the province. Referring to the offeror, Commercial, the Court said that "They were the ones that chose the method of communication, and having done so on behalf of both parties, the mailbox doctrine was brought into play. Its extension to a courier service was sound in principle and, in my opinion, the contracts were therefore made outside of Nova Scotia when their acceptances were sent back to

---

[15] (1983), 4 D.L.R. (4th) 314 (N.S.C.A.).

Commercial Credit." This is one of the few cases in which the postbox rule has been extended beyond communication by mail or telegram. The case has not yet been followed in other jurisdictions in Canada.

DISCUSSION QUESTIONS

Is there any justification to extend the postbox rule to other forms of communication? Should it even be in effect today?

Figure 6.2 Postbox Rule

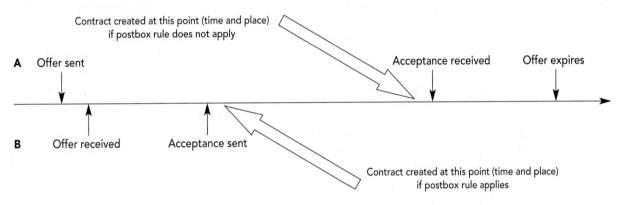

One problem—determining the point of consensus—is solved, but another is created. For a period of time, while the letter of acceptance is still in the mail, the offeror is bound in contract but unaware of that fact. Note that the offeror can avoid this problem by stipulating a different means of communication. When use of the mail is inappropriate, or if another method of acceptance was specified by the offeror, the acceptance will be effective only when received.

> **Applies only when response by mail appropriate**

Response by mail when an offer is sent by mail is normally reasonable. The problem arises when a means of communication other than mail is used to make the offer, but acceptance is then made by mail. This is illustrated in *Henthorne v. Fraser*.[16] Henthorne was handed an offer in Fraser's office, which was to remain open for 14 days. He took the offer home to think about it and, after several days, posted a letter of acceptance. In the meantime, Fraser sold the property to another party and wrote a letter to Henthorne revoking the offer. The two letters crossed in the mail. The Court decided that even though the offer had been handed to Henthorne, use of the post for acceptance was reasonable. The acceptance was therefore effective when sent. Note that the letter of revocation was not effective until Henthorne received it.

The question must also be asked whether the postbox rule applies to any other form of communication. The postbox rule has been extended to include telegrams. It has not been applied to instantaneous forms of communication, such as telex or fax.

> **Postbox rule extended to telegrams**

---

16. [1892] 2 Ch. 27 (Eng. Ch. D.).

CASE SUMMARY 6.8

Limitation of the Postbox Rule: *Entores Ltd. v. Miles Far East Corp.*[17]

Miles Far East Corp. — Acting through Dutch company

Dutch company — Offer made by telex

Acceptance by telex — **Entores**

An American company contracted with a British company through a Dutch subsidiary for the purchase of electronic components. The British company wanted to sue the American company in England, but the British courts would have jurisdiction only if the contract came into existence in the United Kingdom. It was argued that since the Dutch company sent the acceptance by telex (similar to a modern fax machine), the postbox rule should apply, meaning that the contract came into existence where the acceptance originated, in Holland. The Court rejected this argument. The Court found that because telex was instantaneous, like the telephone, there was no need to extend the postbox rule exception to that form of communication. Therefore, the general rule applied and the acceptance was effective in the United Kingdom, when and where it was received. The contract thus came into existence in the United Kingdom, and the courts there had jurisdiction.

DISCUSSION QUESTIONS

This case illustrates the operation of the postbox rule and its limitations. There is some question whether there is any justification for the postbox rule in this day of modern high-tech communication. Should the postbox rule be eliminated by legislation, so that it is not possible for a court to apply the rule to any contract, no matter how the acceptance is communicated?

Should postbox rule be extended?

Today, it is becoming much more common to use electronic means of communication, such as electronic mail and fax, rather than the postal service. The question arises whether the postbox rule will be extended to these methods of doing business. Since these new electronic communications are instantaneous, or near-instantaneous, it is not likely that the postbox rule will be extended to them. This conclusion was confirmed, at least with respect to communication by fax, in *Eastern Power Ltd. v. Azienda Comunale Energia and Ambiente*,[18] where it was decided that an acceptance sent by fax was effective only when it was received by the offeror. There is also a U.S. case indicating that an acceptance by email will not be effective until read by the offeree or offeror, which likely indicates the direction our courts will go.[19]

---

[17] [1955] 2 All E.R. 493 (C.A.).

[18] *Corinthian Pharmaceutical Systems Inc. v. Lederle Laboratories*(1984), 24 F. Supp. 605 (S.D. Ind.).

[19] (1999), O.A.C. 54, (1999), 50 B.L.R. (2d) 33, leave to appeal to S.C.C. refused, [1999] S.C.C.A. No. 542.

The applicability of the postbox rule to electronic communications is just one example of how the law of contracts must adapt to the rapid growth of internet transactions. All aspects of contract law will have to be reconsidered, as electronic transactions grow in importance. An advertisement, for example, is usually an invitation to treat, but an advertisement on the internet may be an offer if it can be accepted by clicking on an "I Accept" button.[20] The development of contract law in light of internet transactions is discussed in some detail in Chapter 14.[21]

Law of contracts must adapt to new technology

REDUCING RISK 6.2

People often make the mistake of thinking that, if they make an offer to sell something to several people and then sell it to one of them, their other offers are automatically ended. Normally you must notify the other parties that you have sold the item to revoke the offers. If you fail to do so, you face the risk of one of these parties accepting your offer. You would then be bound to sell the same item to two different people. To avoid the problem of being bound in contract without knowing it, because of the postbox rule, the offeror should be careful to specify the method of acceptance and to clearly state in the offer that it will not be considered accepted until the acceptance is actually received by the offeror. Of course, when a long-term business relationship is involved, this may not be a problem.

It should be noted that there are still significant advantages to using the mail. The use of the mail involves the exchange of a permanent tangible record of the transaction and its terms. Electronic communication, such as email, may be convenient, but it suffers from a lack of permanency or certainty. Such records can be lost through the crash of a system, or simply altered in an undetectable way, making written records and communications through the mail still—and likely to remain—an attractive option as a common aspect of future business transactions.

As mentioned above, where a contract is formed can also determine which law applies or whether a court has jurisdiction. These things may therefore be determined by the postbox rule. In the *Entores* case, the British court had jurisdiction because the postbox rule did not apply to an acceptance by telex and the contract was thus made in England. In the *Commercial Credit Corp.* case, the transaction was not subject to Nova Scotia law because the postbox rule was held to apply to a couriered acceptance, meaning that the contract was made outside the province.

Postbox rule can also determine what law applies to the contract

It must be stressed that the postbox rule is an exception to the requirement that an acceptance must be communicated to be effective. It does not apply to the offer or to a revocation of an offer. In the *Henthorne v. Fraser* case, discussed above, the postbox rule applied only to the letter of acceptance, and not to the letter of revocation, which had to be received before it could have any effect on the transaction.

Postbox rule does not apply to revocation of offer

www.pearsoned.ca/mybuslawlab

BC AB SK MB ON

CONSIDERATION

The Price One Is Willing to Pay

Central to contract law is the *bargaining process*, in which people trade promises for promises, and all parties derive some benefit from the deal. That benefit, essential

---

20. See, for example, *Electronic Transactions Act*, S.A. 2001, c. E-5.5, which was created to ensure that electronic transactions have the same validity and enforceability as traditional paper-based transactions.

21. See Martin P.J. Kratz, "So I Clicked 'I Agree'—Am I Bound?" *LawNow* (March/April 2008), in which the author notes that the courts apply traditional contract law principles in "clickwrap" cases.

Consideration—not necessarily money

to the existence of a contract, is called consideration, which is defined as the price one commits to pay for the promise of another. Consideration is not restricted to the exchange of money. A bargain may involve the exchange of anything the parties think is of value. For example, when Brown purchases a computer from Ace Computers Ltd. for $2000, there is valid consideration on both sides. The promise to deliver the computer is valid consideration, as is the promise to pay $2000. Note that before the parties actually exchange the computer for the cash, they are bound in contract, because the consideration given is the exchange of commitments or promises, and not the actual money or goods. If one of the parties fails to honour that commitment, the other can successfully sue for breach of contract.

Because it is sometimes difficult to determine the value a person is getting from a deal, it is often better to look at what the parties are giving or paying. For example, if a public-spirited business agrees to pay someone to clean up a public park, the commitment is still binding, even though it might have been made out of a sense of civic responsibility and may result in no actual benefit to the business. Both sides have exchanged promises or commitments. Normally, the promise to make a charitable donation is not enforceable, because it is a one-sided promise, or gift, but when the charity makes a commitment in return—such as a promise to name a building after the donor, or to use the money in a certain way—it has made a commitment, and both parties will be bound.

Promise of charitable donation usually not enforceable

Consideration can be benefit or detriment

Similarly, a contract is just as binding if the consideration involved is a commitment not to do something, as opposed to a promise to do something. For example, if a business promises to pay its employees $500 to quit smoking, such an arrangement is a valid, binding contract. The consideration on the one side is the promise to pay $500, and the consideration on the other side is the promise to refrain from doing something the party has a legal right to do (that is, smoke). Consideration is a benefit or a detriment flowing between the parties to an agreement as the result of the striking of a bargain (see Figure 6.3).

Figure 6.3 Consideration Involves the Exchange of Promises or Commitments

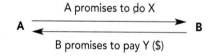

A promises to do X

A ⟶ B

B promises to pay Y ($)

Courts will not enforce gratuitous promise

If the agreement is one-sided, and only one of the parties is getting something from the deal, it is called a **gratuitous promise**, or a gift, and the courts will not enforce it. It may well be that such gratuitous promises ought to be honoured from an ethical point of view, but there is no legal obligation to do so. Once the gift has been given, however, the courts will not assist the giver in getting it back. Also, when services are performed gratuitously, there is still an obligation to do a proper job. If through the negligence of the person performing the gratuitous service, damage or injury results, he can be sued in tort. For example, if a skilled carpenter, out of the goodness of her heart, helps her neighbour repair a roof, and because of her negligence the roof leaks and causes damage to furniture and belongings, the neighbour will be successful in suing in tort for compensation.

CASE SUMMARY 6.9

Promise to Pay Was Gratuitous: *NAV Canada v. Greater Fredericton Airport Authority Inc.*[22]

NAV provided aviation services and equipment to the Authority. The Authority decided to extend one of its runways and requested that NAV relocate its instrument landing system. NAV decided that it made economic sense to replace part of the system rather than move it. The cost of the replacement part was $223 000. NAV asked the Authority to pay for the part. The Authority refused, saying it was not contractually bound to do so. Eventually, the Authority agreed to pay, to ensure that the extended runway became operational. The payment was made "under protest." NAV installed the part, but the Authority refused to pay for it. An arbitrator held that there was nothing in the Agreement between NAV and the Authority that required the Authority to pay for the cost of the part. He held, however, that the subsequent correspondence between the parties resulted in a contract, which required the Authority to pay.

The Court of Appeal held that the Authority was not required to pay for the part because the subsequent correspondence did not create a valid contract. It ruled that the variation of the existing Agreement between the parties was not supported by consideration. Performance of a pre-existing obligation does not qualify as valid consideration. NAV had not promised anything in return for the Authority's promise to pay for a part for which it was not legally obligated to pay.

DISCUSSION QUESTIONS

What step could NAV have taken to ensure that the Authority would be bound by its promise to pay for the part, even if the Court held that there was no consideration given by the Authority for its promise? Should a gratuitous promise to vary an existing contract be enforceable as long as it was not procured under economic duress? If that was the law, would the Court have held the Authority liable to pay for the part?

Adequacy of Consideration

Consideration need not be fair. The court will not interfere with the bargain struck, even when it is a bad deal for one of the parties. If a person agrees to sell someone a brand new Cadillac for $100, this becomes a valid, binding contract. When businesses deal with each other, the value of a particular deal to the parties is not always apparent, and the wisdom of the courts not reviewing the fairness of the consideration is clear. But when businesses deal with consumers, the courts are much more concerned with fairness. They are therefore sometimes willing to assist consumers who have been taken advantage of by merchants. They have developed such concepts as *unconscionability*, *fraud*, and *mistake* (to be discussed in Chapter 8), which give them power to review these transactions. The courts will also examine the fairness of consideration when insanity, drunkenness, or undue influence may have affected the transaction. This power to intervene is now also often found in legislation, such as consumer protection statutes.

The courts will not bargain for the parties

Inadequate consideration may indicate fraud, insanity, etc.

---

22. (2008), 229 N.B.R. (2d) 238 (C.A.).

CASE SUMMARY 6.10

Both Sides Must Make Commitments: *Gilbert Steel Ltd. v. University Construction Ltd.*[23]

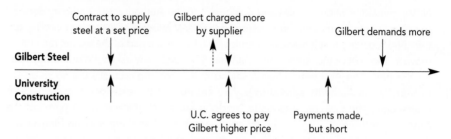

Gilbert had supplied construction steel to University for a number of its projects. For one particular project, it had a contract for a specified amount of steel to be provided at a set price. But Gilbert's costs for the steel increased, and it requested that University pay a higher price for the steel supplied for that project. University agreed to pay the higher price.

The steel was delivered, but the payments made were never enough to cover the increased price. When Gilbert demanded payment, University refused to pay the amount over the original price, claiming it didn't get anything in return for its promise to pay more. It had agreed to pay more, but Gilbert's position hadn't changed; it still had the same obligation to deliver steel that it had under the original agreement. Such a one-sided agreement was not a binding contract. For a contract to exist, there must be an exchange of promises or commitments between the parties—a one-sided agreement is not enforceable.

The lawyers for Gilbert argued that University received consideration in that Gilbert promised to give University a "good price" on a subsequent project. The Court found that this promise was not specific enough, and that there was no commitment involved. Gilbert also argued that because University did not have to pay for 60 days after the price went up, it was getting free credit, but the Court also rejected that argument. The Court therefore held that there was no bargain struck. Only one side made a commitment, and thus there was no obligation to pay the higher price even though there was a promise to do so. (Note that Gilbert also argued that there was *promissory estoppel* in this case, but this position was rejected by the Court. This aspect of the case will be discussed below.)

DISCUSSION QUESTIONS

What could Gilbert have done to ensure that the promise of University to pay more would be enforced by the Court?

Consideration
• need not be fair but must be specific

Although the consideration paid does not need to be fair, it must have some legal value. The promise of "love and affection" is not good enough, nor is a promise to stop "bothering" someone's father.[24] Whatever the parties have bargained for must have some material value for the courts to enforce the bargain.

---

23. (1976), 12 O.R. (2d) 19 (C.A.).

24. *White v. Bluett* (1853), 23 L.J. Ex. 36 (C.E.).

In addition, the parties must agree to a specific consideration or price. Suppose someone agrees to exchange a car for another's promise to "do some work around the house." Such a promise would not be enforceable because the work to be done is not specified. This was the problem in the *Gilbert Steel* case discussed in Case Summary 6.10, when Gilbert promised to give University a "good price" on a future project. This problem becomes acute whenever a monetary consideration is involved. It is not sufficient to promise to give "some money" as payment for the promise of another. Such a commitment must refer to a specific or calculable amount of money. When the parties agree to pay the "market value" of an item, or when some other objective method or formula for pricing a product at some time in the future is used, the consideration is calculable and is thus sufficiently specific to be binding, thus overcoming the problem. Even then, great care must be taken to make sure the price at that time will be clear.[25]

• particularly if money is involved

CASE SUMMARY 6.11

Without Notification, Continued Employment Not Consideration: *Churchill v. Stockgroup Media Inc.*[26]

Churchill was hired by Stockgroup as a sales representative. The employment contract provided that Stockgroup reserved the right "to change compensation and incentive plans at any time . . . " Three years later, Stockgroup provided Churchill with a revised compensation plan that gave it "the right to set targets to be achieved by you and to determine the territory to be covered by you." Churchill agreed to this plan, after some of its terms were changed in response to concerns she raised. Stockgroup assigned Churchill a new sales territory that resulted in her commission decreasing. Stockgroup then became concerned about Churchill's attitude and performance and placed her on probation. Churchill went on disability leave, but did not return to work. She sued, claiming constructive dismissal.

The Court held that Stockgroup was entitled to change the compensation and incentive plans. The change in Churchill's sales territory was, however, constructive dismissal. A fundamental term of the employment contract cannot be changed unless the employer provides the employee with consideration. There was no consideration for the change in the employment contract that entitled Stockgroup to change Churchill's sales territory.

SMALL BUSINESS PERSPECTIVE

Why it is important that employers use detailed employment contracts when hiring new employees?

Gratuitous Promises Are Not Consideration

EXISTING DUTY

Sometimes people enter agreements to do what they are already legally obligated to do. This raises a problem concerning the adequacy of consideration. For

---

25. *Foley v. Classique Coaches* (1934), 2 K.B. 1 (C.A.).

26. 2008 B.C.S.C. 578.

No consideration where extra pay to do same work

example, Olsen agreed to paint Chang's house for $1500. When the painting was three-quarters finished, Olsen demanded $500 more to finish the job on time. Even if Chang agreed, there would be no binding obligation because Chang got nothing in exchange for the promise to pay more. Olsen was obligated to finish painting the house before the promise to pay the extra $500 was made, and after the promise the obligation remained the same. Olsen's legal position did not change; therefore, there was no consideration. These types of problems often arise in the construction industry, when unforeseen factors may increase the costs significantly, as in the *Gilbert Steel* case discussed in Case Summary 6.10. This is just one more reason for the parties to take great care to predict all costs that are likely to arise and to build into their agreement provisions for resolving conflicts over these unexpected eventualities.

A new bargain requires new consideration

When a duty to act exists, but that duty is owed to a third party, a promise to do the same thing for someone else is enforceable. In the situation above, if Chang's tenant Adams promised to pay Olsen the extra $500 to ensure the job was finished on time, that agreement would be binding. Before Adams's promise to pay the extra $500, Olsen was legally obligated to Chang to finish painting the house. After the promise to Adams, Olsen is now legally obligated to Adams, as well as to Chang, to paint the house. Olsen's legal position has changed because Olsen now runs the risk of having to pay Adams' damages, as well as Chang's, if the contract is breached. There is valid consideration here, and the contract would be binding.

When a public duty is involved, a demand for further compensation will not be tolerated. A police officer, firefighter, or other public servant can't demand more money to do her job. A firefighter cannot arrive at a blaze and extract a promise from the victim to pay an extra $500 to put out the fire. Such a contract would be against public policy and void. But paying police personnel in their off-duty hours to provide security at a rock concert or celebration is valid, as they are on their own time and not otherwise obligated to help.

PAST CONSIDERATION

Past consideration is no consideration

There are situations in which there is no consideration even though it appears to be present. One of these is when the consideration was given in the past; that is, the bargain is struck after the price agreed on has been paid. An employer's promise to pay a bonus in recognition of good work already performed by the employee would not be binding: the work has already been done. Although it may appear that both parties have given something (the employer the promised bonus and the employee the good work), such a promise is not enforceable. The key to this problem is in the timing. When the promise to pay the bonus was made, the work had already been performed, so where is the bargain? In fact, the employee is in exactly the same legal position before the promise as afterward. Thus, it is often said, "Past consideration is no consideration."

Common law states that agreement to take less to satisfy debt is not binding

PAYING LESS TO SATISFY A DEBT

A creditor will often agree to take less in full satisfaction of a debt. Such agreements also raise problems with respect to consideration. A creditor who agrees, after a $5000 debt becomes due, to take $3000 from the debtor as full payment, has received no consideration for the reduction in the debt. In fact, the reduction of the debt is gratuitous. It is quite clear that, under the common law, such a one-sided promise is not binding, and that the debtor can therefore sue for the remaining $2000. Even if the partial payment is actually made, the creditor can still turn around and sue for the remainder.[27]

But, as a practical business matter, such an arrangement to accept less is often beneficial to the creditor as well as the debtor. The creditor might otherwise have to sue to recover, and then not collect anything. Many jurisdictions have passed legislation providing that when a creditor has agreed to take less in full satisfaction of a debt, and has actually received the lesser sum, the creditor is bound by the agreement and cannot sue for the difference.[28]

Legislation may overrule common law if there is payment of the lesser sum

When the creditor has agreed to take less, but none of the money has yet been paid, the creditor is still free to change her mind and insist on the entire amount being paid. Of course, when the debtor has agreed to pay the lesser amount early, or to do something in addition to the payment, such as pay a higher rate of interest, there is consideration on both sides to support the new arrangement. In cases like these, the creditor is bound by her promise to accept less.

ILLEGAL CONSIDERATION

There are some policy restrictions on what constitutes good consideration. For example, when illegal drugs are sold, the agreement is void because the consideration is illegal. Contracts between businesses to interfere with free competition and unduly restrain trade may also be void due to illegality.

Illegal or impossible consideration is no consideration

In addition, for consideration to be valid it must be possible to perform the consideration promised. An agreement to change lead into gold for a fee would also be void due to the impossibility of performance (at least at this time).

REDUCING RISK 6.3

The old adage that you cannot get something for nothing has been enshrined in the law of contract in the form of the requirement of consideration. In all contracts (with a couple of exceptions, discussed below) there must be a bargain in which both parties make a commitment to each other. The lack of such consideration is often difficult to see, especially in business deals in which pre-existing obligations are being modified. In such circumstances, we have to be especially vigilant in our dealings, to ensure that the deals we make are legally binding and not simply one-sided gratuitous agreements that can be ignored by the other party.

Examples of Valid Consideration

SETTLEMENT OUT OF COURT

When the parties to a dispute settle the matter outside of court, there is also valid consideration on both sides. When a litigant learns later that he would likely have won, it may look like there is no consideration. In fact, as both parties have given up their right to have the court determine the matter, there is consideration on both sides. As a result, the release signed in such situations is a binding contract.

Consideration exists in out-of-court settlements

---

27. *Foakes v. Beer* (1884), 9 App. Cas. 605 (H.L.).

28. See, for example, *Law and Equity Act*, R.S.B.C. 1996, c. 253, s. 43.

REQUEST FOR SERVICES

Must pay reasonable amount for services

When services are requested from providers, such as lawyers or mechanics, the parties often do not agree on a specific price before the service is performed. When you ask a lawyer for assistance in resolving a contractual dispute, or a mechanic to fix your car, you are often not given a firm price for the service. In these circumstances, the courts will impose an obligation to pay a reasonable price. This is an application of the principle of *quantum meruit*, sometimes called a quasi-contract. *Quantum meruit* means "as much as is deserved." The courts use this principle to impose an obligation to pay a reasonable price when services are requested. The requirement to pay a reasonable price when no specific price has been agreed upon has also been applied to the sale of goods by provincial statutes.[29]

The courts will also use *quantum meruit* to determine how much should be paid when a person providing the services is not allowed, by a breaching party, to finish the job. For example, when a person has agreed to paint a house and, before the job is finished and payment is due, the other party refuses to allow completion, the court will use the *quantum meruit* principle to require the breaching party to pay a reasonable price for the benefit he has received. The same is not true if the breaching party is the one seeking payment. In the example above, if the painter were the one who refused to finish the job, she could not demand partial payment for what she had done.

Exceptions to the General Rule

PROMISSORY ESTOPPEL

Another exception to the rule that a promise is enforceable only if consideration is present is based on the principle of **promissory estoppel**, sometimes referred to as *equitable estoppel*. The more common or ordinary use of the term *estoppel* involves statements of fact, which will be discussed in Chapter 11. Promissory estoppel, in contrast, deals with a person making a promise, or a commitment, to do something in the future. As we have discussed, an exchange of such promises or commitments constitutes consideration, and the result is a binding contract. But when the promise is one-sided, or gratuitous, it is normally not enforceable. (Figure 6.4 illustrates how promissory estoppel works.)

Gratuitous promises usually not enforceable

But sometimes the promisee, in anticipation of the promise being performed, incurs expenses or other obligations that otherwise could have been avoided. In the presence of such reliance, unique remedies have been developed to compensate for significant loss. In the United States, when such reliance is placed on a gratuitous promise and injury results, it is possible to sue for compensation. In the United Kingdom and Canada, however, such an unfulfilled promise can be used only as a defence to an action initiated by the person who made the promise.

In London, England, just before World War II, High Trees leased an apartment building from Property Trust under a 99-year lease, with the intention of renting out the individual flats in the building.[30] The two parties agreed to a set yearly rent of £2500. Because of the outbreak of the war, it soon became apparent that High Trees would not be able to rent out all of the flats. Therefore, in 1942, Property Trust agreed to lower the yearly rent to £1250. After the war, it changed its mind, and demanded payment of all of the rent owed under the original lease,

---

29. See, for example, *Sale of Goods Act*, R.S.A. 2000, c. S-2, s. 10.

30. *Central London Property Trust, Ltd. v. High Trees House, Ltd.*, [1947] 1 K.B. 130.

Figure 6.4 Promissory Estoppel

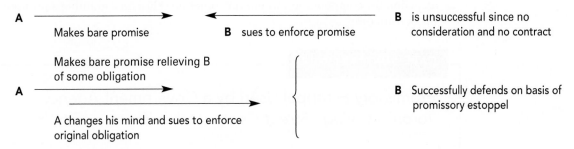

including back rent for the portion that had not been paid since 1942. It argued that the promise to take less rent was one-sided and, as a gratuitous promise, was not binding. The Court agreed that, for the period after the war, High Trees had to again pay the full rent. With respect to the back rent, however, Property Trust was bound by its promise to take the lower amount. The key to understanding this is to realize that High Trees was not suing to enforce the promise; rather, Property Trust was suing for the higher amount in spite of its promise. High Trees was using the plaintiff's promise as a defence to the plaintiff's claim. Thus, in the United Kingdom, the principle of *promissory estoppel* is remedial in nature. In *Combe v. Combe*, Lord Denning made it clear that "it does not create new causes of action where none existed before,"[31] and Lord Asquith, in his concurring judgment, said that promissory estoppel could be used only as "a shield but not as a sword."[32]

Canada has followed the English example, limiting the use of promissory estoppel to a defence. That is why, in the case of *Gilbert Steel* (discussed in Case Summary 6.10 above), the argument of promissory estoppel failed. Gilbert Steel argued that because University Construction promised to pay more and Gilbert Steel relied on the promise, it created an "estoppel" and University Construction should be required to pay the higher amount. But Gilbert Steel was not using the promise as a defence; it was suing, claiming payment on the basis of that promise. Since it was using the promise as a sword instead of a shield, it failed. Note that if University Construction had made the higher payments and then sued Gilbert Steel to get them back, promissory estoppel would have been available to Gilbert Steel, as a defence.

In fact, in almost every case where promissory estoppel has been successfully used as a defence, there was an existing legal relationship, usually contractual, that was modified by a promise. The promisor was attempting to enforce the original terms of the agreement, ignoring the relied-upon promise to alter the terms. The disappointed promisee was using the promise as a shield, or defence, to the action. To raise this defence successfully, the victim must demonstrate reliance on the promise and suffer an injury as a result of that reliance. That was another reason why the promissory estoppel argument raised in the *Gilbert Steel* case failed. True, it delivered the steel as required, but it was required to do so under the original contract in any case. It did only what it was required to do under the contract; it didn't take on any extra obligation, or incur any extra expense, that could have otherwise been avoided.

Promissory estoppel can be used only as a defence

There must also be reliance placed on the promise

---

31. [1951] 1 All E.R. 767 at 769 (C.A.).

32. *Ibid.* at 772.

Do you think we would do better to adopt the American approach and allow an action for compensation whenever someone relies on a gratuitous promise to his detriment?

CASE SUMMARY 6.12

Promissory Estoppel Used by a Government Agency: *Toronto College Street Centre Ltd. v. Toronto (City)*[33]

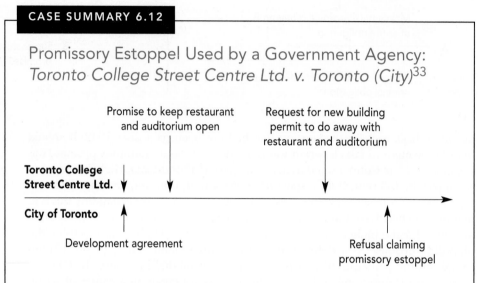

The use of promissory estoppel is not limited to contract. An example of the use of promissory estoppel in a non-contract case involved the owners of a building that was recognized as an important heritage site. The owners had been allowed to develop the building, but they had promised the City to retain a restaurant and auditorium on the seventh floor. When this proved uneconomical, the owners applied for a building permit to change the use of the seventh floor to rental units. The permit was refused, and that decision was challenged by way of judicial review of administrative action, as discussed in Chapter 3. The Court based its decision partly on promissory estoppel. The owners of the building had promised to maintain the seventh floor as a restaurant and auditorium, and the City had refused to grant a permit to do otherwise. The owners were estopped by their promise. Note that the promise of the owners of the property was being used as a defence by the City; it was clear that the City had relied on the promise when allowing them to do other things with the building. The case is interesting in that it involves the enforcement of the doctrine in a non-contract situation and to the benefit of a government entity rather than an individual.

SMALL BUSINESS PERSPECTIVE

In light of this case, businesspeople must be careful in making promises to government agencies while seeking government approval or permission. What should government agencies do to ensure that such promises will be enforced against the promisors?

SEALED DOCUMENTS

Sealed documents do not require consideration

The last major exception to the requirement of consideration involves the use of a seal. Seals were originally made by placing melted wax on a document and impressing a signet ring in it, thus lending authenticity or authority to the

---

33. (1986), 56 O.R. (2d) 522 (C.A.).

document. When the parties went to so much trouble to indicate they were serious, they were bound by their commitment. This practice—which predates modern contract law—has been retained; thus, when a seal is used, it is not necessary to show consideration for the contract to be binding. Today, instead of a wax impression, the seal normally takes the form of a paper wafer, although almost any form of marking on the document that the parties have identified as a seal can be used. A sealed contract is a formal contract, or a deed. The court will not entertain any suggestion that the promise contained in a formal contract is not supported by consideration. Although it is not necessary to look for consideration when a seal is present, the existence of the seal does not eliminate the need for the other elements of a valid contract.

To summarize, consideration (the price one is willing to pay for a promise) is one of the required elements of a contract. There must be some form of valid consideration in the form of a benefit or detriment flowing between the parties for a court to enforce a contract. Only when the document embodying the agreement is sealed, or on those rare occasions when the promise of the promisor is being raised as a defence by the promisee, will the court enforce an agreement without requiring consideration to be established.[34]

SUMMARY

The contractual relationship

- A contract is an exchange of promises enforceable in court
- There are five elements of a valid contract: consensus, consideration, capacity, legality, and intention
- There are many important terms and definitions relevant to the contractual relationship

Consensus

- A contract requires "a meeting of the minds"
- An offer is a tentative promise by the offeror contingent upon an acceptance by the offeree
- All the essential terms of the contract must be contained in the offer; non-essential terms will be implied by the courts
- An invitation to treat, or an invitation to negotiate, is not an offer
- An offer must be communicated to the offeree before it can be accepted
- An offer will end at a specified time, but it may be revoked earlier by notice to the offeree, unless an option agreement has been entered into
- If there is not a specified time limit, an offer will lapse after a reasonable time
- A counteroffer, a rejection of the offer, or the death or insanity of the offeror will also cause an offer to lapse
- A standard form contract is interpreted strictly against the party who drafted it
- An acceptance is an indication of a willingness to be bound; a contract is formed when an offer is accepted
- An acceptance must be complete and unconditional

---

[34]. See *Romaine Estate v. Romaine* (2001), 95 B.C.L.R. (3d) 95, (2001), 205 D.L.R. (4th) 320 (C.A.), in which gift documents with wafer seals were enforced as sealed contracts.

- An acceptance must be communicated in the manner required by the offer; it is effective when and where received
- Silence may be acceptance if there is an existing business relationship
- The postbox rule says that an acceptance by mail (when reasonable) is effective when and where it is dropped in the mailbox
- The postbox rule has been extended to telegrams, but not to instantaneous forms of communication

Consideration

- Consideration is the price paid for another party's promise and can be anything of value
- Both parties must have experienced some benefit; a gratuitous promise is not enforceable
- Consideration must be specific, but it need not be fair; courts will not review its adequacy
- A promise to do what you are already legally obligated to do is unenforceable
- Past consideration is no consideration
- An agreement to accept less in full satisfaction of a debt is unenforceable in common law, but may now be binding under legislation
- Illegal consideration and impossible consideration are not valid consideration
- An out-of-court settlement is enforceable, as there is valid consideration
- *Quantum meruit* is used when there is a request for services with no agreement as to the amount; a reasonable price must be paid
- Promissory estoppel enables a gratuitous promise to be used as a defence
- When a contract is sealed, consideration is not necessary

QUESTIONS

1. What is meant by "freedom of contract"? Explain the impact of this principle on the development of contract law. What are two types of restrictions on this principle?

2. List and explain the elements that must be present for an agreement to qualify as a valid contract.

3. Explain the difference between a formal contract and a parol contract.

4. Explain the difference between void and voidable. What is a practical result of this difference?

5. Distinguish between unenforceable contracts and illegal contracts.

6. Explain the difference between a bilateral contract and a unilateral contract.

7. What practical concepts does contract law use to determine if "a meeting of the minds" has happened?

8. At what stage in the process of forming a contract are the significant terms of the contract clearly set out?

9. Explain the role of implied terms in a contract. Who has the power to imply terms into a contract? When will the power be used?

10. Is an "agreement to agree" binding? Explain your answer.

11. Distinguish between an offer and an invitation to treat.

12. Can you accept an offer that was made to someone else? Explain your answer.

13. List and explain the various ways an offer can come to an end.

14. What is the effect of the offeror stating in an offer that the offer will remain open for acceptance until a specific date? What can an offeree do to protect herself from the offer being revoked?

15. What risks are faced when a person offers to sell certain goods to A and then sells them to B? How can this problem be avoided?

16. Explain the two types of contracts that result from the tendering process.

17. What do the courts do, when interpreting standard form contracts, to correct the imbalance in bargaining power between the parties?

18. What qualities must an acceptance demonstrate to be effective?

19. When is a contract formed?

20. When will silence be considered an acceptance of an offer?

21. What is the general rule regarding acceptance? What is a practical result of this rule?

22. Explain the effect of the postbox rule on the principles governing acceptance.

23. Discuss the role the postbox rule plays when modern communication methods are used.

24. Define consideration and explain what is meant by the term "the exchange of consideration."

25. Explain under what circumstances a person who fails to properly perform a gratuitous promise can be held legally liable for that failure.

26. Does consideration have to be fair? Explain your answer.

27. What difficulty might be faced by a person who has already agreed to do a specific job and then extracts a promise of more pay from the other party?

28. If a person who is rescued promises to pay the rescuer $1000 but doesn't pay, will the rescued person be successful in suing for breach of contract? Explain your answer.

29. "A creditor is bound by her promise to take less in full satisfaction of the debt." True or false? Explain your answer.

30. Explain why a contract dispute settled out of court is considered binding even though one party would have obtained more if the action had been taken to court.

31. Explain a person's obligation regarding payment when she has requested a service without specifying a particular fee.

32. Describe what is meant by promissory estoppel and the circumstances in which it will arise in contract disputes.

33. How does the presence of a seal affect the requirement that consideration must be present in a contract?

CASES AND DISCUSSION QUESTIONS

1. *Wembley Marketing Ltd. v. ITEX Corp.*, [2008] O.J. No. 5194 (S.C.).

Wembley claimed it did not receive goods and services from ITEX for which it had paid. ITEX argued that the action should not proceed, as the relevant contract said that any actions must be brought in California. Wembley had completed an Application, providing relevant information, two different times. The Application included the word *AGREEMENT* in bold letters. The section below that required a separate signature and referred to "the most recent Membership Agreement and Operating Rules." The Rules required that any action arising under the Agreement "shall lie only in the courts of Sacramento, California." A copy of the Agreement and Rules had been provided to Wembley; they were also available on ITEX's website. The person who signed the Application on behalf of Wembley testified that he would not have signed it had he read the Agreement and Rules. He admitted that he "did not bother to read the small print on the Application."

Was there a contract between Wembley and ITEX? Does it matter if the person who signed the contract did not read all of it? Would the clause giving jurisdiction to California courts be enforced?

2. *McCunn Estate v. Canadian Imperial Bank of Commerce* (2001), 53 O.R. (3d) 304, 140 O.A.C. 151.

McCunn had a line of credit with the Bank with insurance coverage that was to end at age 70. The Bank automatically deducted the premiums from her account every month. Unfortunately, after she turned 70, it simply continued to do so. McCunn was not aware of this, and the Bank obviously made these deductions in error. When she died more than a year later, a representative of her estate claimed that the insurance coverage had continued, or been renewed, and was therefore in effect when she passed away. This claim was based on the continuing deduction of the insurance premiums from her account. The Bank refused to pay the amount owing on the line of credit, claiming there was not continued insurance coverage. The Court had to decide whether a new contract had been created, giving McCunn the additional coverage.

Explain what arguments could be raised by both sides and the likely outcome.

3. *Vollmer v. Jones* (2007) 36 R.F.L. (6th) 340 (Ont. S.C.).

A husband and wife who were separated met with their lawyers to negotiate a settlement agreement. One of the lawyers typed the agreement on a laptop computer as it was negotiated during the meeting. The parties did not have time to review the agreement and sign it that day. The husband and wife, and their lawyers, shook hands, and the wife's lawyer asked both the husband and his lawyer whether "we have a deal" and they both confirmed that there was a deal, and that no one would "change their mind." The parties had agreed that there would be no need to attend a scheduled Trial Management Conference, as the signed agreement could be entered as a court order. The wife signed the agreement the next day, but the husband then refused to sign it. The wife asked the Court to enforce the terms of the settlement agreement.

Should the Court enforce the settlement agreement, or was there just an "agreement to agree"? Was there a complete and unconditional acceptance? Was it communicated? Was this a case in which the parties did not intend to be bound by their agreement until the written contract was signed by both of them?

4. *Force Construction Ltd. v. Queen Elizabeth II Health Sciences Centre* (2008), 269 N.S.R. (2d) 250 (S.C.).

The Hospital called for tenders for a construction project. Force submitted the lowest bid, but its labour unit prices were the highest of any bidder. The Manager for the Hospital wanted to discourage the practice of submitting high unit labour rates. The bids were therefore recalculated using a contingency overrun. Force's bid was then $1187 more than that of the second lowest bidder, which was awarded the job. Force sued the Hospital.

Did the Hospital have a contract with Force? If so, did it breach the contract? Would a "privilege clause " protect the Hospital if it did not treat Force fairly?

5. *Ayerswood Development Corp. v. Hydro One Networks Inc.*, [2004] O.J No. 4926 (S.C.).

Ontario Hydro published information about an incentive program designed to promote energy efficient initiatives. The stated deadline for applications was 31 March 1993. Just before this date, Ontario Hydro announced that the program was suspended. Ayerswood applied under the incentive program on 30 March 1993, but its application was not even processed. It therefore sued for the incentive payment that it would have been entitled to under the incentive program.

Should the Court order that the incentive payment be made? If there was a contract, what type was it?

6. *Pumphrey (c.o.b. Skeeter's Pet World) v. Carson* (2002), 206 N.S.R. (2d) 338 (S.C.).

Carson was a pet groomer who entered into an oral agreement with Pumphrey regarding the provision of pet grooming services. Pumphrey prepared a written document that included a non-competition clause. The terms of this document were discussed, but nothing was agreed to. Carson did not sign the document. Carson eventually left Pumphrey's business and set up her own pet grooming business, right across the street from Pumphrey's business! Pumphrey sued for enforcement of the non-competition clause in the written document.

Should the Court enforce the clause against Carson and order her to shut down her new business? Explain your answer.

7. *Earn v. Kohut* (2002), 164 Man. R. (2d) 50 (Q.B.), aff'd (2005), 192 Man. R. (2d) 65 (C.A.).

Kohut shot Earn after a graduation party. Kohut was convicted criminally. Just before his sentencing, Kohut's lawyer delivered a consent judgment to Earn's lawyer for an action that had not yet been commenced. This settlement was not accepted by Earn until more than two years later. Kohut claimed that the offer was not acceptable at that time, as the limitation period for an action for assault had expired.

Is there a settlement that the Court should enforce? Did the offer end in any way, so that it was not capable of being accepted? Was there consideration that would have been received by both parties?

8. *N.M. v. A.T.A.* (2003), 13 B.C.L.R. (4th) 73 (C.A.).

N.M. promised to pay the outstanding mortgage on A.T.A.'s home if she would leave England and move to Canada to live with him. A.T.A. gave up her job and moved to Canada. N.M. did not keep his promise and eventually evicted A.T.A. from his home. The trial Judge said that promissory estoppel did not apply, as there was no legal relationship between the parties.

Should the appeal Court overturn the trial Judge? If A.T.A. relied on N.M.'s promise, to her detriment, should there be an award of damages to A.T.A.? Would there have been a different decision if the case had been heard in an American court?

PEARSON
mybuslawlab™

Be sure to visit the MyBusLawLab that accompanies this book at **www.pearsoned.ca/mybuslawlab.** You will find practice tests, a personalized study plan, province-specific material, and much more!

Chapter 7

Formation of Contracts (Continued)

CHAPTER OBJECTIVES

1. Explain the capacity of minors
2. Compare the capacity of the insane and the drunk
3. Review the law for others of limited capacity
4. Discuss the law relating to contracts performed illegally
5. Discuss the law relating to contracts formed illegally
6. Review the contractual element of intention
7. Examine the requirement that contracts be in writing
8. Explain the principle of part performance

In addition to consensus and consideration (discussed in the previous chapter), contracting parties must have the capacity to contract, the contract must be legal and be performed legally, and both parties must have intended that legal consequences would follow from their agreement. Each of these elements will be discussed in this chapter. Although it is always a good idea to put a contract in writing, the general principle is that a verbal contract is as binding as a written one. There are several situations, however, for which contracts are required by statute to be evidenced in writing. These will also be discussed in this chapter.

CAPACITY

Lawmakers have always recognized that some people are more vulnerable than others and thus require special protection. Over the years, several categories of people have been identified as needing protection. These categories have been protected by having their freedom to enter into contracts limited, or in some cases eliminated completely.

Minors/Infants

The age of majority was 21 at common law, but it has been reduced by statute to 18 or 19, depending on the province. The general principle is that persons under

www.pearsoned.ca/mybuslawlab

Age of majority varies with provinces

Minors not bound by their contracts, but adults are

the age of majority, called *infants* or *minors,* are not bound by their agreements, but the adults with whom they contract are bound. The courts try to balance protecting the minor against the objective of not imposing undue hardship on the adult. It is important to distinguish between the actual incapacity of a child who is incapable of understanding what is happening, and the artificial incapacity imposed on a youth who is a functioning member of society.

Most problems relating to minors and contracts they have entered into arise in situations involving young people who are approaching the age of majority. The test for capacity is objective. When an adult deals with a person who is a minor, it does not matter if the adult was under the impression that the other person was an adult, or even that that person clearly understood the terms of the contract. The only question is whether the other person was under the statutory age of majority at the time the contract was created. As a general rule, whenever a minor enters into a contract with an adult, the adult is bound by the contract, but the minor can choose not to be bound by it.

Test for capacity is objective

For example, when a sales representative of a car dealership offers to sell a car for $2500 to a minor who accepts the offer, the dealership will be bound by the contract. If the young person has not yet taken delivery of the car, she has the choice as to whether to go through with the deal or not. If she takes delivery of the car and then chooses not to pay for it, she would have to return the car. She could not, however, be forced to pay or otherwise go through with the contract, even if she wrecks the car or it is stolen.

In most provinces, these principles are based on English and Canadian case law. British Columbia, however, has a unique *Infants Act*.[1] This legislation states that, in most cases, a contract made by a minor is unenforceable against him. The minor may, however, enforce the contract against an adult party to the contract. The result, then, is the same as in the provinces which rely on the common law. Other provinces may also have legislation dealing with the contractual capacity of minors. For example, the *Minors' Property Act*[2] allows a court to confirm a contract entered into by a minor if it believes it is in the best interests of the child to do so. See the MyBusLawLab for other relevant provincial legislation.

Legislation supplements common law

Special problems arise when dealing with contracts made online. The law with respect to capacity will be determined by the jurisdiction where the contract is created, which is sometimes not clear. Also, there is no way for online merchants to know the personal characteristics of the parties with whom they are dealing. It is important that such merchants include appropriate restrictions and disclaimers in their online contracts. The unique challenges arising from advances in technology and communications as they relate to the formation of contracts will be discussed in Chapter 14.

NECESSARIES AND BENEFICIAL CONTRACTS OF SERVICE

Except in British Columbia, minors are bound by contracts for the acquisition of necessaries and for contracts of service that benefit the minor. **Necessaries** are things required to function in society, such as food, clothing, lodging, and transportation. What constitutes a necessary will vary with the particular needs of a minor and her status. If the young person is purchasing clothing, but already has a sufficient supply, then that clothing will not be considered a necessary.

---

[1] S.A. 2004, c. M-18.1, s. 3.

[2] R.S.B.C. 1996, c. 223.

When a minor is married, or is living on his own, what constitutes a necessary will be broader than would be the case if he were single and dependent on his parents. The courts have held that medical, dental, and legal services, along with toiletries, uniforms, and even a house, will be considered as necessaries in different situations. It is unlikely, however, that they will find that a car qualifies as a necessary, since other alternative forms of transportation are generally available. Even when the subject of the contract is determined to be a necessary, it does not guarantee that the merchant will get paid full price, as the minor is obligated only to pay a reasonable price for such necessaries.[3]

Minors bound by contracts for necessaries

When a minor borrows money to buy necessaries, there is an obligation to repay the debt only if the funds advanced are actually used for necessaries. For this reason, a creditor cannot recover money loaned to a minor to pay for school tuition if it is used instead for gambling. Government student loans are exceptions, because they are supported by legislation requiring repayment regardless of what the money is used for and regardless of the age of the borrower.

Minors must repay money borrowed and used for necessaries

Contracts of employment, apprenticeship, or service are binding if it can be demonstrated that, taken as a whole, the contract is for the benefit of the minor. If it becomes apparent that the minor is being taken advantage of, or the contract is not in the minor's best interests, the minor will not be bound. Today, these kinds of relationships are usually controlled by legislation.[4]

Minors bound by contracts of service that substantially benefit them

Note that in British Columbia's *Infants Act,* all contracts, including contracts for necessaries and beneficial contracts of service, are unenforceable against an infant. Only contracts made specifically enforceable by legislation will be binding on infants.[5] An example of such a contract is a student loan agreement.[6]

Note B.C. exception

ON BECOMING AN ADULT

If a minor agrees to a contract (other than a contract for necessaries or a beneficial contract of service), she is not bound by it. If, however, she ratifies the contract after becoming an adult, she loses the right to avoid the contract. That is, ratifying the contract makes a voidable contract binding. For example, if a minor agrees to pay $5000 for an automobile in a series of instalment payments, she cannot be forced to pay. If, however, the minor, after becoming an adult, makes an instalment payment, or provides a written statement indicating that she intends to be bound, the contract will then be binding. Ratification can be in writing,[7] or it can be implied. Ratification must be complete; a minor cannot affirm the beneficial provisions of the contract and repudiate the rest.

Minor can ratify contract at age of majority

[3.] Some provinces have legislation dealing with the purchase of necessaries by minors. See, for example, the *Sale of Goods Act,* R.S.A. 2000, c. S-2, s. 4, which states that minors need only pay a reasonable price for necessaries, and that necessaries are goods suitable to the "condition in life" of the minor and to the minor's actual requirements.

[4.] See, for example, the *Apprenticeship and Industry Training Act,* R.S.A. 2000, c. A-42.

[5.] See, for example, the *Canada Student Loans Act,* R.S.C. 1985, c. S-23, s. 19, which states that a lender may recover a student loan made to a minor as if the minor "had been of full age at the time the loan was made."

[6.] *Supra* note 1, s. 19.

[7.] In some provinces, ratification must be in writing, and be signed by the minor, to be effective. See, for example, *Statute of Frauds,* R.S.N.S. 1989, c. 442, s. 9.

CASE SUMMARY 7.1

What Amounts to Ratification? *Bayview Credit Union Ltd. v. Daigle*[8]

Daigle was a minor when he borrowed a considerable sum from the Bayview Credit Union. He used his motorcycle as security for the loan. While still a minor, he stopped making payments, and hid the motorcycle. After reaching the age of majority, he disclosed the location of the motorcycle. The Credit Union repossessed and sold the motorcycle, but there was still $4100 owing on the loan. The Credit Union sued Daigle. It claimed that his disclosure of the location of the motorcycle when he was an adult amounted to ratification of the contract, making it enforceable against him.

The Court held that Daigle was not liable. His action was not ratification. He was merely assisting the Credit Union in realizing its security. The Court commented, "Surely the acts of the defendant here, in co-operating as he did to the benefit of the plaintiff, should not place him in a worse position than a person who would refuse co-operation to reduce the plaintiff's loss." The case illustrates the danger of businesspeople dealing with minors as if they were adults. It also shows the implications of a minor ratifying a contract after becoming an adult.

DISCUSSION QUESTIONS

Should a minor lose the protection of the law when, whether out of ignorance or a sense of obligation, he chooses to continue to pay, or acknowledges, a debt after becoming an adult?

Some contracts must be repudiated

There are certain contracts that a minor must repudiate within a reasonable time after becoming an adult to avoid obligations (or, as some cases suggest, a failure to repudiate can be evidence of ratification). These situations tend to involve contracts through which a minor acquires some interest of a permanent and continuous nature. The cases in this area tend to be very old, with little in the way of recent case law.[9] Specific examples of contracts that minors may need to repudiate to avoid being bound by them include those involving land, shares in corporations, partnerships, and marriage settlements.

Description of contractual relationships

Although these principles may seem reasonably straightforward, their application has created a good deal of confusion. To appreciate the reasons for this confusion, it is necessary to understand how the contractual relationship progresses through prescribed stages. At the first stage, when the parties have entered into the contract but the minor has not yet obtained any benefit from it, and has not yet paid, the minor is not bound by the contract. This is an **executory contract**. If the minor has received the goods, but has not yet paid for them, she is not necessarily bound by the contract. This is a **partially executed contract**. When the goods are in the minor's possession, she will be required to return them or pay for them, and upon return is entitled to a refund of any money already paid. If the

---

[8.] (1983), 3 D.L.R. (4th) 95 (N.B.Q.B.).

[9.] See, for example, *R. v. Rash* (1923), 53 O.L.R. 245, *Saunders v. Russell*, [1902] B.C.J. No. 65, 9 B.C.R. 321 (S.C.), *Lovell and Christmas v. Beauchamp*, [1894] A.C. 607 (H.L.), and *Edwards v. Carter*, [1893] A.C. 360 (H.L.).

minor has passed the goods on to a third party, or the goods have been destroyed, the merchant will not be entitled to payment, and the merchant also cannot insist that the party to whom the goods have been given return them.

Conflict may arise when the contract has been **executed**. Once minors have obtained the benefit under a contract, can they change their minds and insist on the return of their money? In Canadian law, the conclusion seems to be that minors are bound by the contract unless it can be demonstrated that what was received was of no value at all. That is, a minor can insist that payment be refunded if there is a total failure of consideration and the minor gained nothing from the deal. In general, if the contract is prejudicial to the interests of the minor, it is void.

When contract gives no benefit, minor can escape even executed contract

REDUCING RISK 7.1

Merchants run a great risk when they deal with even mature youths as if they were adults. Contracts cannot be enforced against them and, while security can be taken in goods, even that may not be much protection when the goods used as security are destroyed or otherwise made unavail-able, as illustrated by Case Summary 7.1. When dealing with minors, it is advisable not only to take security for the loan, but also to have the parents of the minor co-sign the contract, or to have them give a personal guarantee. Secured transactions will be discussed in Chapter 16.

PARENTS' LIABILITY

There is a popular misconception that liability will rest with the parents if a child fails to pay a debt. As a general rule, parents are not responsible for the torts of their children, nor are they responsible for the contractual obligations of their children, in the absence of specific legislation creating such a responsibility. If a minor enters into a contract, she alone is responsible to perform the contract. The adult contracting with the minor cannot turn to the parents if the minor does not perform as required by the contract.

Parents not responsible for minor's contracts

Many jurisdictions have passed legislation making parents liable for the torts, contracts, and even criminal activities of their children.[10] In the absence of such legislation, parents can be held liable for their children's contracts only under specific conditions. Parents can be liable when the minor is acting as an agent having the appropriate authority to bind the parent in contract. (Agency will be discussed in Chapter 11.) Parents will also be bound if they guarantee the minor's obligation at the time the contract is entered into. A guarantee is a written commitment whereby the guarantor agrees to pay the debt if the debtor does not. Since the very purpose of the guarantee is to encourage the merchant to enter the contract, these guarantees have been held to be binding on the parents. Also, because parents are responsible to provide for their minor children, they can be held responsible by the merchant for contracts their children enter into for necessaries.[11]

Parents may be responsible where there is agency or guarantee, or where goods are necessaries

---

10. Several provinces have enacted legislation to this effect. See, for example, the *Family Law Act,*R.S.O. 1990, c. F.3, s. 45(2).

11. See, for example, the Manitoba *Parental Responsibility Act,* C.C.S.M. c. P8, which makes parents liable if their child "deliberately takes, damages or destroys the property of another person." The parents' liability is limited to $10 000. The parents may avoid liability by showing that they were exercising reasonable supervision and that they made reasonable efforts to prevent or discourage the child from engaging in the kind of activity that resulted in the property loss. For a comment on proposed legislation in Nova Scotia, see "Parental Responsibility: Law Liable to Do Nothing," The *Chronicle Herald* online, 1 June 2009, http://thechronicleherald.ca/Editorials/1125097.html.

INFANTS' LIABILITY FOR TORTS

Minor may be liable in tort

A merchant will occasionally try to get around the protection given to a minor in contract law by suing in tort instead. Sometimes the act that constitutes the breach of contract will also qualify as negligence, or some other tort, as discussed in Chapters 4 and 5. It is a basic tenet of tort law that a minor is as liable as an adult for torts committed, although the standard of behaviour expected may differ. But the courts will not allow adults to bring a tort action just to get around the incapacity problem in contract law. If the minor used the subject matter of the contract in a way that would be expected under the contract, then the adult must sue in contract, not tort, despite the protection given to the minor by the law of contracts.

Adults cannot avoid protection given to minors under contract law by suing in tort

On the other hand, if the minor used the subject matter of the contract in a way that was not contemplated in the contract, carelessly causing injury or damage to those goods, the adult would be able to sue for negligence and the minor would not be protected by the defence of infancy. For example, if a minor rents a two-wheel-drive automobile and then damages it while off-roading, the merchant would be able to sue the minor for negligence because the use to which the automobile was put was outside what was anticipated in the contract.

Except when tort arises independent of contract

CASE SUMMARY 7.2

Minor Liable for Tortious Acts Not Contemplated by Contract: *Royal Bank of Canada v. Holoboff*[12]

Holoboff, a minor, entered into an agreement for a savings account with the Bank. He then sold his client card and his personal identification number (PIN) to a third party. The third party proceeded to defraud the Bank by making a "fake" deposit to Holoboff's account and then withdrawing money from the account. Holoboff was convicted of fraud. He was then sued by the Bank.

Holoboff claimed that he should not be found liable because of the common law that allows minors to avoid contracts that are not for necessaries. The Bank argued that the fraudulent use of the debit card by a third party with Holoboff's assistance was not contemplated by the terms of the contract. The Court found that the contract required Holoboff to keep his PIN confidential and to restrict the use of his debit card to his personal use only. Therefore, Holoboff's selling of his card, and revealing of his PIN, were outside the contemplation of the contract. The Court thus allowed the Bank's claim, and found Holoboff liable for the tort of conspiracy to commit fraud.

DISCUSSION QUESTIONS

Is the distinction between liability in tort and in contract artificial? Is it appropriate that an infant may be found liable in tort but not in contract? Should the law be made consistent, so that an infant cannot be found liable for any of her actions?

However, if the minor had an accident while driving the rented automobile on a highway, the adult could not sue in tort, even if the minor was clearly negligent, because that activity would be expected when a car is rented. In short, the adult

---

12. (1998), 221 A.R. 192 (Q.B.).

cannot circumvent the protection afforded to the minor in contract law by suing in tort instead. (This explains why car rental agencies will not rent to minors, but when a minor misrepresents himself as an adult and contracts to rent a vehicle, the agency may be able to get damages from the minor by suing for the tort of fraudulent misrepresentation.) Nor are the parents responsible, since parents are not liable for the torts of their children unless they can be said to have been negligent in their own right, or when there is a statute in place imposing such liability.

Insanity and Drunkenness

The law extends its protection to those incapacitated because of insanity or mental incompetence in a way similar to the protection given to minors. To qualify for this protection, it must be shown that the person could not understand the nature of the act being performed. To take an extreme example, if a man thinks that he is Napoleon and that he is selling his horse when, in fact, he is selling his car, he would be declared to lack the capacity to contract because he does not understand the nature of the transaction. The burden of proving incapacity on the basis of insanity or mental incompetence rests with the person claiming to be incapacitated. That person must lead evidence showing that he did not understand the consequences of his actions.

Insanity or mental incompetence applies if person did not understand

To escape contractual liability on the basis of insanity or mental incompetence, the person (or a representative) must prove not only insanity or mental incompetence, but also that the person he was dealing with knew, or ought to have known, of the incapacity. This is the point illustrated in the case in Case Summary 7.3.

and if other party knew or ought to have known of incapacity

CASE SUMMARY 7.3

Bank Must Know, or Ought to Have Known, of Insanity: *Canadian Imperial Bank of Commerce v. Milhomens*[13]

Milhomens executed a Visa Application Agreement in favour of CIBC and was issued a Visa card. He used the card and, eventually, had an outstanding balance owing of $18 104.29 plus interest at the rate of 18.5 percent. CIBC sued for non-payment of the debt. Milhomens claimed that "he was of unsound mind and incapable of appreciating or understanding the meaning and effect of the Visa Application Agreement when he signed it." The evidence showed that Milhomens had a long psychiatric history. There was no evidence showing that CIBC ever knew, or ought to have known, about his condition.

DISCUSSION QUESTIONS

Should CIBC be awarded judgment for the amount claimed? Is there an obligation on a bank to monitor the spending patterns of its credit card holders to determine if they change and, if they do, the reason for the change? Is there anything else Milhomens could have done with respect to the purchases he made with his Visa card?

---

13. [2004] S.K.Q.B. 168.

Provincial legislation applies to people who are mentally incompetent

A person may be declared mentally incompetent by a court. In such cases, a trustee will be appointed to handle that person's affairs. To understand the precise rights and obligations of a trustee, and the care and use of that person's property, the appropriate provincial legislation should be carefully examined.[14]

Drunkenness treated like insanity

People who lose their ability to reason through intoxication, whether from alcohol or drugs, are treated in the same way as people incapacitated by insanity or mental incompetence. As is the case with insanity, for the contract to be avoided, the person must have been so intoxicated that she didn't know what she was doing, and the other person must have known, or ought to have known, of the incapacity. The person trying to escape a contract on the basis of drunkenness must also be able to show that, on reaching sobriety, the contract was repudiated. For example, an intoxicated person who purchases shares is not permitted, on becoming sober, to wait and see whether the stocks go up or down before repudiating the contract. Hesitation to repudiate makes the contract binding. This requirement of **repudiation** also applies to insane people who regain their sanity. As with minors, the insane, mentally incompetent, or intoxicated person is also required to pay a reasonable price for necessaries.

Must repudiate upon becoming sober

A person who is of weakened intellect, or otherwise vulnerable, but not insane or mentally incompetent, is still to some extent protected. Unconscionable transactions, the legal principle providing this protection, will be discussed in Chapter 8.

www.pearsoned.ca/mybuslawlab

BC · AB · SK · MB · ON

Others of Limited Capacity

Corporate capacity—usually no longer a problem

Corporations have their capacity to contract determined by the legislation under which they are incorporated. In some jurisdictions, corporations can limit their capacity to contract by so stating in their incorporating documents. Otherwise, corporations incorporated under these general statutes have "all the power of a natural person" to contract. Even in those jurisdictions where the capacity of a corporation can be limited, people dealing with those corporations are affected by that limitation only if they have notice of it.

CASE SUMMARY 7.4

Unincorporated Business Has No Capacity: *Maple Engineering & Construction Ltd. v. 1373988 Ontario Inc.*[15]

Maple submitted a bid to be the general contractor of a project. One of the defendants, Bisson, was the director and sole shareholder of 1373988, which carried on business using the trade names "AC" and "ACI." Bisson submitted a bid to Maple for subcontract work, on behalf of ACI. After winning the contract for the project, Maple provided Bisson with plans and specifications of the project. Maple received a new bid from Bisson, also on the letterhead of ACI. It forwarded a formal contract to ACI for review. ACI eventually advised Maple that an agreement between them could not be reached. Maple entered into a contract with another subcontractor, and sued Bisson for the difference in price.

---

14. See, for example, the *Dependent Adults Act*, R.S.A. 2000, c. D-11.

15. [2004] O.J. No. 5025 (S.C.J.)

Maple did not know of the existence of 1373988. Maple argued that a contract between it and ACI came into existence when it accepted the second bid. The Court agreed. It held that an unconditional contract was formed when ACI submitted its second bid, and it was accepted by Maple. When ACI refused to perform, Maple lost profits by having to hire a second subcontractor, at a greater cost. Bisson was personally liable for the damages, as he had signed the bid on behalf of ACI, an unincorporated business, and had then induced Maple to enter into a contract by representing himself as an agent of ACI.

This case shows that it is important that businesspeople understand the status of the businesses they are representing. A corporation has the capacity to enter into contracts; an agent will therefore not incur personal liability if a contract is breached by the corporation. If a business is unincorporated, it does not have the capacity to enter into contracts and a person representing the business may thus be personally liable for breaches of any contracts entered into.

SMALL BUSINESS PERSPECTIVE

How can a person determine whether the business he is contracting with is incorporated? If it is, is there any way to ensure that the person representing the corporation will be held responsible for the liabilities of the corporation if it breaches the contract?

Other corporate bodies are created by special legislation. These include some private companies, Crown corporations, and other government bodies that have been created to accomplish particular government purposes. Business Development Bank, Canada Revenue Agency, Canada Mortgage and Housing Corporation, Canada Post Corporation, Canadian Air Transport Security Authority, and Canadian Tourism Commission are some examples. The capacity of these entities depends on the legislation creating them. Their power to contract is often limited by that legislation. If they have not been given the capacity to enter into a particular type of contract, any agreement of that type will be void. Outsiders dealing with these corporations or government bodies would be well advised to determine ahead of time the validity of any such dealings. This is especially true when the contract involved is unusual in any way.

Capacity of Crown corporations and government bodies limited by legislation

CASE SUMMARY 7.5

When a City Lacks Capacity: *Pacific National Investments Ltd. v. Victoria (City)*[16]

Pacific believed it had a contract with the City whereby the City had agreed not to rezone several lots Pacific was developing. When the property was "downzoned," Pacific sued. At trial, the City was held in breach of an implied contract. The Supreme Court of

---

16. [2000] 2 S.C.R. 919. Note that this case went to the Supreme Court a second time, with respect to Pacific's alternative claim of unjust enrichment. The claim was successful, as the Supreme Court found that the City had no right in equity to retain the benefits of the improvements without paying for them. See [2004] 3 S.C.R. 575.

Canada, upon examination of the *Municipal Act*, and its history and tradition, decided that the City did not have the power to bind itself with respect to rezoning. In other words, the City did not have the capacity to agree to the terms included in the contract.

SMALL BUSINESS PERSPECTIVE

This case illustrates how important it is to determine the power of incorporated bodies before dealing with them. How can a businessperson do this, when she is dealing with a government body? What should she do if she can't determine whether the government body she is dealing with has the power to enter into the contract that is being negotiated?

! REDUCING RISK 7.2

Since Crown corporations and government bodies acting under statutory authority may have their power to contract limited by legislation, businesspeople dealing with them should determine, before entering into the contract, whether any contemplated dealings are within their statutory power. If they are not, the contract will be void. This will usually result in the businessperson suffering a loss.

Capacity of enemy aliens limited in times of war

Dealing with aliens and representatives of foreign governments also gives rise to capacity issues. When at war, any contract with a resident of an enemy country is void if detrimental to Canada. If not detrimental, the contract is merely suspended for the duration of the hostilities. Note that the government usually passes special legislation covering this area whenever hostilities break out.

Contracts with foreign governments may or may not be enforceabl

Even in times of peace, contracts with foreign governments or their representatives were traditionally thought to be unenforceable because of that government's sovereign immunity. The principle is that the sovereignty of the foreign government would be lost if subjected to the jurisdiction of our courts. This provision was particularly important when dealing with matters of state that were of diplomatic importance. However, since foreign governments are now more frequently involved in simple commercial activities that have nothing to do with matters of state, the courts have been willing to treat them as any other party to commercial transactions. These principles are now embodied in legislation.[17]

Foreign diplomats have immunity

Representatives of foreign governments, such as ambassadors and their families, have traditionally been immune from prosecution in our criminal courts and continue to be. In civil matters, a court will not allow a lawsuit to proceed against such persons, and their property is immune from seizure. Of course, these representatives can waive this immunity, if they wish, but anyone dealing with persons who have diplomatic immunity ought to be aware of the protection they have been given.[18]

[17.] *State Immunity Act*, R.S.C., 1985, c. S-18.

[18.] To review the law relating to the privileges and immunities of foreign diplomats, see the *Foreign Missions and International Organizations Act*, S.C. 1991, c. 41.

A problem may also arise with respect to the capacity of trade unions. While they are not incorporated as such, it is likely safe to conclude that they at least have the capacity to enter into contracts that relate to their trade union activities. The capacity of trade unions is governed by legislation.[19]

Bankrupts also have their capacity to contract limited. A **bankrupt** is a person who has made an assignment in bankruptcy or been forced into bankruptcy through a court order obtained by a creditor, and who has not been discharged from bankruptcy. Bankruptcy will be discussed in Chapter 16.

Finally, the capacity of Indians is limited to some extent by the *Indian Act*.[20] Section 89, for example, says that the property of an Indian on a reserve "is not subject to charge, pledge, mortgage, attachment, levy, seizure, distress or execution in favour or at the instance of any person other than an Indian or a band." Although provisions such as these may seem discriminatory, they remain because section 35 of the *Constitution Act, 1982* recognizes and affirms existing aboriginal and treaty rights. Section 25 of the *Charter of Rights and Freedoms* states that the *Charter* should not be construed to abrogate or derogate from these rights. Businesspeople contracting with Indians must therefore be aware of their limited contractual capacity.

> **Trade unions have capacity to contract for union activities**

> **Indians protected under *Indian Act***

REDUCING RISK 7.3

As a general rule, the capacity to enter into contracts is not a problem facing most businesspeople. Still, it is important to be aware of the problem, and to be alert to the possibility that the law may protect the person being dealt with, so that appropriate steps can be taken. For example, the difficulty in dealing with minors can be avoided through the use of cash, without the extension of credit.

LEGALITY

An agreement must be legal and not contrary to public interest to qualify as a binding contract. It is easy to understand that a contract to commit a crime would be void. But contracts involving activities that, while not illegal, are considered immoral or contrary to public interest may also be void. The courts have taken several different approaches when faced with the problem of illegal or immoral contracts.

Contracts Performed Illegally

When discussing legality, it is necessary to distinguish between illegality as to formation of the contract (the contract itself is illegal) and illegality as to performance (the contract is performed in an illegal way). The Supreme Court of Canada explained this distinction in a case in which a man died when a cocaine-filled condom burst in his stomach.[21] The beneficiaries of his life insurance policy were

my buslawlab
www.pearsoned.ca/mybuslawlab

> **Difference between contracts formed illegally and contracts performed illegally**

---

19. See, for example, s. 25 of the *Labour Relations Code*, R.S.A. 2000, c. L-1, which states, "For the purposes of this Act, a trade union is capable of (a) prosecuting and being prosecuted, and (b) suing and being sued."

20. R.S.C. 1985, c. I-5.

21. *Ibid.* at para. 54.

Lawful contracts performed illegally may be enforced

found to be entitled to the proceeds of the policy. The Court held that the insurance policy was lawful and that the innocent beneficiaries should not be disentitled to the insurance benefits because the insured accidentally died while committing a criminal act. The Court stated: "If the insurance contract purported to cover an illegal activity, the contract would be unlawful and could not be enforced."[22] But, as the case involved a lawful contract that was performed in an illegal manner, the Court enforced the contract. There was no **public policy** reason to prevent the beneficiaries from receiving the insurance proceeds.

The response of the courts to the illegal performance of a lawful contract will vary. In making their decisions, the courts will consider many factors, such as the intent of the parties, the actions of the parties, and public policy. The case discussed in the previous paragraph shows that in such situations the court may enforce the contract, in appropriate circumstances.

The illegal performance of a lawful contract often involves a breach of legislation that is regulatory in nature. Such legislation may contain provisions declaring that a breach of the legislation will result in the relevant contract being void, or other specified consequences. The courts will apply these statutorily mandated outcomes whenever a contract is performed contrary to the legislation.

Several possible results when performance breaches regulatory legislation

Sometimes, however, regulatory legislation does not indicate the result of a violation of the legislation. In such cases, the courts may make a variety of decisions. They may treat the contract as void but not illegal. They will then restore the parties to their original positions, ordering the return of any deposits advanced and property that has been transferred. If the illegal performance can be separated from the rest of the performance of the contract, then they may rule that only that part of the contract is void. If the violation of the legislation is more one of procedure than of substance, the courts may enforce the contract. The current judicial approach is illustrated by Case Summary 7.6.

CASE SUMMARY 7.6

Renovation Contract Void Because of Illegality: *Chung v. Idan*[23]

This case involved what the Court referred to as "renovation hell." The plaintiffs made a claim for payment for extra goods and services relating to a home renovation contract. The defendants denied liability for the amount claimed. The Court dismissed the plaintiffs' claim for several reasons, including their failure to provide required goods and services, their supply of items with deficiencies, their charges for goods and services for which there was no agreement, their charges for goods and services that were within the scope of the initial contract, and because "they supplied goods and services illegally."

With respect to the illegality, one of the plaintiffs did the renovation work without being licensed as required, and without insisting that a required building permit be obtained. The Court referred to older case authorities that held that a building contract contrary to a statutory provision is illegal and unenforceable as a matter of public policy.

---

22. *Oldfield v. Transamerica Life Insurance Co. of Canada*, [2002] 1 S.C.R. 742.

23. 2006 CanLII 2048 (On. S.C.), aff'd 2007 ON C.A. 544.

The Court, however, adopted the approach of more recent authorities stating that a renovation contract may be enforceable notwithstanding a breach of the relevant legislation. The Court stated that

> the recent cases adopt a sophisticated approach to illegality that considers such factors as: (a) the purpose of the statute; (b) the enforcement mechanisms within the statute; (c) whether the statute makes the contract inherently illegal or only illegal if performed without compliance with the provisions of the statute; (d) whether the violation of the statute was only a technical non-compliance because the party intended to comply with the statute and could have done so; and (e) whether the illegality can be severed from the balance of the contract.[24]

The Court held that the plaintiffs made no effort to comply with the licensing and permit requirements. The statutory violations were not just technical, they were "advertent." The Court therefore did not allow the plaintiffs' claim, as it was "tainted by illegality."

DISCUSSION QUESTIONS

Is the modern approach, which may result in enforcement of an illegal renovation contract, appropriate? Does this introduce uncertainty into the law? Would it be better to follow the traditional approach, which makes all illegal renovation contracts unenforceable? Wouldn't this encourage the parties to comply with all relevant laws?

Contracts Formed Illegally

As discussed above, the Supreme Court has distinguished between illegality as to formation of the contract (the contract itself is illegal) and illegality as to performance (the contract is performed in an illegal way). A reference to an "illegal contract" is to a contract that is illegal at the time it was formed. As the Supreme Court observed, an illegal contract will not be enforced; it is void. Usually, when faced with a void contract, the court will restore the parties to their original position, ordering them to return any deposits advanced and property that had been transferred. But an illegal contract involves unacceptable or immoral conduct. Under such circumstances, while the contract is void, the courts will not assist the parties by restoring them to their original position unless one of them is innocent of any wrongdoing.

Illegal contracts are illegal when formed

Illegal contracts are void and courts will not assist parties

An illegal contract usually involves the commission of some prohibited conduct, such as the sale of a controlled substance, or the commission of some violent or antisocial act. The conduct may be identified as wrongful and specifically prohibited by the *Criminal Code* or some other statute, or it may simply be inconsistent with the provisions of such a statute. The common law, however, goes even further, and assumes that some types of immoral conduct are unacceptable and against public policy. Even though the immoral conduct is not a crime, or does not result in a violation of a statute, when people make agreements involving such conduct, the agreements are treated like illegal contracts. One example involves an agreement with a prostitute; prostitution is not illegal, but it is considered immoral and against public policy.

An agreement involving immoral conduct is an illegal contract

---

24. *Ibid.* at para. 53.

CASE SUMMARY 7.7

Contracts with Criminal Rates of Interest—An Exception to the Rule? *Transport North American Express Inc. v. New Solutions Financial Corp.*[25]

The parties entered into a credit agreement that included many payments other than the principal and interest: a monthly monitoring fee, a standby fee, royalty payments, payment of legal and other fees, and a commitment fee. The trial Judge held that the agreement contained an interest component greater than the 60 percent allowed by section 347 of the *Criminal Code*. He applied "notional severance" to reduce the effective annual interest rate to 60 percent. The Court of Appeal allowed the appeal and struck out the interest clause, leaving in place the other payments, which amounted to an effective annual rate of 30.8 percent when computed as interest.

The Supreme Court of Canada overturned the Court of Appeal decision. It held that all of the various payments under the agreement were "interest" under section 347. The Court stated, "There is broad consensus that the traditional rule that contracts in violation of statutory enactments are void *ab* initio is not the approach courts should necessarily take in cases of statutory illegality involving section 347 of the Code. Instead, judicial discretion should be employed in cases in which section 347 has been violated in order to provide remedies that are tailored to the contractual context involved."[26]

These remedies range from declaring the contract void if it is very objectionable, to severing the illegal clause if the contract is otherwise unobjectionable. The courts should consider "the specific contractual context" and the illegality involved when determining an appropriate remedy.

The Supreme Court ruled that notional severance was appropriate in this case. It therefore affirmed the decision of the trial Judge. The Court outlined four factors to be considered when deciding whether to declare an illegal contract void, or to partially enforce it, and cited the following:

> In Thomson, at p. 8, Blair J.A. considered the following four factors in deciding between partial enforcement and declaring a contract void ab initio: (i) whether the purpose or the policy of s. 347 would be subverted by severance; (ii) whether the parties entered into the agreement for an illegal purpose or with an evil intention; (iii) the relative bargaining positions of the parties and their conduct in reaching the agreement; and (iv) whether the debtor would be given an unjustified windfall. He did not foreclose the possibility of applying other considerations in other cases, however, and remarked (at p. 12) that whether "a contract tainted by illegality is completely unenforceable depends upon all the circumstances surrounding the contract and the balancing of the considerations discussed above and, in appropriate cases, other considerations."[27]

---

25. [2004] 1 S.C.R. 249.

26. *Ibid.* para. 4.

27. *Ibid.* para. 24.

It appears that the approach followed in the *Transport* case applies in all cases, not just those involving section 347 of the *Criminal Code*. The classic approach of declaring every illegal contract void was viewed as harsh and inequitable, as it could result in a windfall to one of the parties. The modern approach means that an illegal contract may be partially enforceable. The courts may sever the illegal provisions of the contract, leaving the balance of the contract enforceable. In the *Transport* case, the Supreme Court said that the severance can even be "notional," meaning that the courts can, in effect, rewrite part of the contract.

New judicial approach to illegal contracts

EXAMPLES

The following is a list of some of the types of contracts that have been determined to be illegal. The list includes contracts that are in violation of legislation, as well as contracts that are against public policy.

Examples of illegal contracts

1. **Contracts to commit a crime.** Agreements involving murder, drug dealing, or even charging a high rate of interest are contrary to the *Criminal Code* and are therefore illegal contracts.

2. **Contracts to commit a tort.** If Mullins offers Nowak $100 to falsely claim that Abercromby did a poor job of repairing his house, that would be defamation. The contract to pay Nowak to defame Abercromby would be illegal.

3. **Contracts involving immoral acts.** As indicated above, prostitution is not illegal in Canada. However, a prostitute could not expect the courts to enforce an agreement made with a client. Prostitution is considered immoral, and the contract would therefore be illegal.

4. **Contracts that are bets and wagers.** Historically, the courts would not enforce contracts related to gambling activities, as they were against public policy. Now this area is covered by statute, and the rules vary from province to province. The statutory provisions are designed primarily to limit and regulate gambling activities. The courts will enforce only contracts for which the activities have statutory approval or are licensed.

Insurance is like a wager. A person owning property pays for insurance to insure against the destruction of the property. If the property is destroyed, the insurer compensates the owner for the loss. This requirement of loss is called an insurable interest. It must be present for the insurance contract to be valid. Insurance is discussed in Chapter 5.

Insurance contract is valid when there is an insurable interest

Contracts for the sale of shares have the same difficulty. If the contract merely requires the parties to pay each other the difference if the share price goes up or down, it is void as a wager. To avoid this problem, the contract must provide that the share will actually change hands. Commodities traded in a similar fashion suffer the same problem.

5. **Contracts in restraint of marriage, or in favour of divorce.** Any contract that has as its object the prevention or dissolution of marriage is against public policy. An agreement to pay someone $100 000 in return for a promise never to marry would be an illegal contract.

6. **Contracts that promote litigation.** An agreement in which one person, to satisfy some ulterior motive, pays another to sue a third would be an illegal contract and therefore void, because it promotes litigation. An exception is a lawyer's contingency fee. In such an agreement, the lawyer agrees to proceed with an action without payment, in return for a share of the judgment (often amounting to 30 percent or 40 percent). This agreement appears to be permissible because it does not promote litigation, and it serves to make the courts more accessible to those who normally could not afford to proceed.[28]

7. **Contracts that obstruct justice.** If the effect of a contract is to interfere with the judicial process, it is against public policy. An agreement that encourages criminal activity by providing to pay a person a salary whenever he is in jail would involve such an obstruction of justice.

Contingency fee agreements permissible because they make courts accessible

---

CASE SUMMARY 7.8

An Agreement Made to Avoid Prosecution Is Void: *Newell v. Royal Bank of Canada*[29]

A woman forged her husband's signature on 40 cheques totalling more than $58 000. He tried to protect her from prosecution by signing a letter prepared by the Bank agreeing to assume "all liability and responsibility" for the forged cheques. The Court found that this was "an agreement to stifle a criminal prosecution which is an illegal contract and unenforceable." Because the contract was illegal, the husband's agreement to accept responsibility for the cheques was void. He was therefore entitled to get his money back. A merchant may find an arrangement such as the husband's letter very appealing. Such an agreement, however, smacks of blackmail and tries to cover up a criminal act. It may even be considered an obstruction of justice. Any such agreement will therefore be an illegal contract and void.

DISCUSSION QUESTIONS

Was the Court's decision appropriate? Should the parties be free to make their own arrangements in these circumstances? Explain your reasoning.

---

28. For a case in which a contingency fee agreement that allowed an arbitrator to resolve any disputes was held to not be contrary to public policy, see *Jean Estate v. Wires Jolley LLP*, 2009 ON C.A. 339.

29. (1997), 156 N.S.R. (2d) 347 (C.A.).

8.   **Contracts that injure the state.** An example is a contract to sell secret military information.

9.   **Contracts that injure public service.** Bribing a public official to vote a certain way is an example of an illegal contract.

10.   **Contracts between businesses to fix prices or otherwise reduce competition.** These types of contracts are controlled by the federal *Competition Act*.[30] This statute specifically prohibits agreements that have the "undue" restriction of competition as their primary purpose or objective:

> 45. (1) Everyone who conspires, combines, agrees, or arranges with another person... (c) to prevent or lessen, unduly, competition in the production, manufacture, purchase, barter, sale, storage, rental, transportation, or supply of a product, or in the price of insurance upon persons or property, or (d) to otherwise restrain or injure competition unduly, is guilty of an indictable offence and is liable to imprisonment for a term not exceeding five years or to a fine not exceeding ten million dollars or both.

Undue restriction of competition prohibited

Thus, if two merchants agreed not to sell a particular commodity below a certain price, or not to open up branches that would compete with each other in specified communities, and they were the only ones selling the products in that community, such agreements would likely be illegal contracts and void. Such a conspiracy may also be punishable as a criminal act. This is another example of a contract in restraint of trade. The *Competition Act* prohibits a number of other unacceptable business practices, some of which will be discussed in Chapter 15.

11.   **Contracts that unduly restrain trade.** When a business is sold, the contract often includes a clause prohibiting the seller from opening another business in competition with the business she is selling. If such a provision is reasonable, and necessary to protect the interests of the parties, it is enforceable. If the provision is unreasonably restrictive, or against public interest, it will be void. An agreement is against the public interest when it interferes with free trade, drives up prices, decreases service, or has any other effect whereby the public may be harmed.

Restrictive covenants must be reasonable

For example, assume Fiona purchases a barbershop from Ahmed for $50 000. A considerable portion of the purchase price may be for the customer relations established by Ahmed. This is called *goodwill*. If Ahmed opens another barbershop next door to the business he sold Fiona, it would destroy the goodwill value of the contract. It would be reasonable for the buyer to include a provision in the contract prohibiting the seller from carrying on a similar business for a specified time (for example, three years) and within a specified geographical area (for example, five kilometres). If the time and distance restrictions agreed to are not excessive, the agreement would be considered a reasonable restraint of trade. The contract would be valid.

[30.] R.S.C. 1985, c. C-34.

CASE SUMMARY 7.9

Helping Business Owned by Daughter-in-Law a Breach of Sale of Goodwill Agreement and Non-Competition Agreement: *Ascent Financial Services Ltd. v. Blythman*[31]

Carolyn and Don Beveridge agreed to combine their financial services business with that of Anna and Art Blythman. Carolyn and Don were told that Anna and Art's son, Brad, and his wife, Marilyn, were not entering the financial services business. Ascent was incorporated; Anna, Art, Carolyn, and Don were its directors and shareholders. Anna and Art sold the goodwill in their business to Ascent. They were to retire over the next five to ten years, with Carolyn and Don taking over the business. Anna and Art signed a non-competition agreement that required that they not compete with the business nor solicit any suppliers or customers of the business.

The relationship between the couples broke down quickly. Carolyn and Don exercised their right to purchase Anna and Art's shares. Art was upset. He asked clients to pick up their files instead of giving them to Carolyn and Don. He encouraged clients to transfer their business to Lifestyle, a new financial services corporation owned by Marilyn. Art also provided client information to Marilyn. Carolyn and Don sued for breach of the sale of goodwill agreement and the non-competition agreement.

The Court decided that Anna and Art were in breach of both the sale of goodwill agreement and the non-competition agreement, as well as their fiduciary duty, because they did not do what they could have to have the clients stay with the business. The Court assessed damages at $150 000, based on a decrease in the book value of the clients' portfolios transferred from Ascent to Lifestyle.

DISCUSSION QUESTIONS

In cases such as this, who has the burden of proof? What presumption do the courts make in cases involving restrictive covenants? Which party has to rebut this presumption to be successful in litigation regarding the enforceability of restrictive covenants?

Restrictive covenants will be void if too broad

When a restriction is excessive and is deemed to be an unreasonable restraint of trade, normally only that provision will be void. It will be severed and the rest of the agreement will be enforced. The effect would be that the purchase price and all other terms of the agreement would be the same, but the seller would have no restrictions at all. He would be free to open a similar business anywhere, at any-time. In the example above, if the provision in the contract for the purchase of the barbershop prohibited Ahmed from opening another shop anywhere in Canada, or imposed an unreasonably long period of time, such as 10 years, the provision would likely be void. Ahmed would then be free to open a new barber-shop wherever and whenever he wanted. Great care must therefore be taken to avoid the purchaser's normal inclination to make the restriction on competition as broad as possible. It is best that such a clause go no further than necessary to protect the interests of the purchaser.

[31.] (2006), 276 Sask. R. 23 (Q.B.), aff'd (2002), 302 Sask. R. 118 (C.A.).

CASE SUMMARY 7.10

When Can Severance Be Used with Restrictive Covenants? *Shafron v. KRG Insurance Brokers (Western) Inc.*[32]

Shafron sold his insurance agency to KRG in 1988. Shafron agreed to be employed by KRG to provide management and insurance brokerage services until 1991. He also agreed to stay out of the insurance brokerage business in the "Metropolitan City of Vancouver" for three years after leaving employment with KRG. In 1991 Shafron agreed to become KRG's president and director and to manage its operations. He also agreed to a restrictive covenant very similar to the one he agreed to in 1988. Intercity purchased KRG's shares in 1991. Shafron's employment contract was subsequently renewed a couple of times. In 2000 Shafron advised Intercity that he would not renew his contract again. Shafron then started working with another insurer; a number of his former customers followed him. KRG sued to enforce the restrictive covenant.

The trial Judge found the restrictive covenant to be unreasonable, unclear, uncertain, and too broad. The Court of Appeal allowed the appeal. It held that the restrictive covenant was reasonable and that to not enforce it would give Shafron a windfall. The Court interpreted "Metropolitan City of Vancouver" to mean Vancouver and the municipalities directly contiguous to it.

The Supreme Court of Canada allowed the appeal. It held that the phrase "Metropolitan City of Vancouver" was uncertain and ambiguous. There was no mutual understanding as to the geographic area the restrictive covenant covered. The Court refused to rewrite the restrictive covenant. The headnote of the case contains the following passage:

> Restrictive covenants generally are restraints of trade and contrary to public policy. Freedom to contract, however, requires an exception for reasonable restrictive covenants. Normally, the reasonableness of a covenant will be determined by its geographic and temporal scope as well as the extent of the activity sought to be prohibited. Reasonableness cannot be determined if a covenant is ambiguous in the sense that what is prohibited is not clear as to activity, time, or geography. An ambiguous restrictive covenant is by definition, *prima facie*, unreasonable and unenforceable. The onus is on the party seeking to enforce the restrictive covenant to show that it is reasonable and a party seeking to enforce an ambiguous covenant will be unable to demonstrate reasonableness. Restrictive covenants in employment contracts are scrutinized more rigorously than restrictive covenants in a sale of a business because there is often an imbalance in power between employees and employers and because a sale of a business often involves a payment for goodwill whereas no similar payment is made to an employee leaving his or her employment. In this case, the restrictive covenant arises in an employment contract and attracts the higher standard of scrutiny.

[32.] 2009 SCC 6.

The Court went on to say that notional severance (reading down a contractual provision to make it legal and enforceable) is not appropriate to apply to an unreasonable restrictive covenant. This approach would encourage employers to draft overly broad restrictive covenants. "Blue-pencil" severance (removing part of the restrictive covenant) may be used when part of the restrictive covenant is severable, trivial, and not part of the main purpose of the restrictive covenant. It is not appropriate with respect to the phrase "Metropolitan City of Vancouver."

SMALL BUSINESS PERSPECTIVE

What should the owner of a small business do to ensure that a restrictive covenant in an employment contract that has been signed by an employee will not be struck down by the courts? Is it a good idea to simply draft the provision as broadly as possible?

Law applies to employers as well

An employer will often impose a similar restrictive covenant requiring employees to promise not to compete during, or after, their employment. Although the same test of reasonableness is used, the courts are much more reluctant to find such restrictive covenants valid. It is only when the employee is in a unique position to harm the company (for example, by having special access to customers or secret information) that these provisions will be enforced. This will be discussed in more detail in Chapter 10.

! REDUCING RISK 7.4

There is a great temptation for a purchaser of a business, or an employer, to protect herself from competition. Purchasers of a business and employers are particularly vulnerable to unreasonable competition. They can therefore include terms in their contracts that restrict that competition, but such provisions must not go too far. There is a tendency for the person who is advantaged by such a clause to make it much broader than is necessary to prevent unfair competition. Such clauses, however, must be reasonable in the circumstances and must not be against the public interest. They must go no further than is necessary to prevent unfair competition. They should have a geographical limit and a time limit to their operation. A clause restricting competition within a 500-kilometre radius, when 50 kilometres would be sufficient, is void. A clause with a five-year restriction, when one year would be enough, is also void. Great care should be exercised in negotiating these non-competition clauses. Legal advice should be obtained to make sure that resulting clause will be enforceable.

List of illegal contracts will continue to grow

The list above describes some of the types of contracts restricted by statute or held to be against public policy. This list is neither complete nor exhaustive. It may well be that new types of activities made possible by changing technology could also be controlled by statute or be declared as being against public policy in the future. Special care should be directed to activities on the internet. Gambling and pornography account for a large portion of internet use; the validity of the activity depends on the jurisdiction involved, which often is not clear. Several jurisdictions have passed or will soon enact statutes controlling these activities. Great care should be taken, by both businesses and consumers who become involved in such activities, to determine the legality of that involvement.

INTENTION

Not all agreements are contracts. Often, people enter into arrangements or undertakings never intending that legal consequences will flow from them. For example, if a person invited a friend over for dinner and the friend failed to show up for some reason, the delinquent guest would probably be quite surprised if the would-be host were to sue for breach of contract. The law requires that for an agreement to be a binding contract, the parties must have intended that legal obligations and rights would flow from it. Since neither the host nor the guest intended to create a legal obligation, the host's legal action would fail.

When determining intention, the courts do not look to the state of mind of the person making the promise. Rather, they look to the reasonable expectations of the promisee. The test is objective. Would a reasonable person have thought that the person making the promise was serious and that the agreement was legally binding? If so, it is not going to help the person making the promise to say, "I was only kidding."

Parties must have intended legal consequences from agreements

Courts will enforce reasonable expectations

CASE SUMMARY 7.11

When Friends Fall Out Over Money: *Osorio v. Cardona*[33]

Osorio and Cardona went to the horse races together and bought tickets on the "Sweep Six" (betting on six races where they had to predict all six winners). After the third race, they discovered that both their tickets were still eligible to win. They made an agreement that if either of them won, they would split the winnings. Cardona went on to win $735 403 but refused to honour the deal. Because of the odds involved, Osorio was entitled to $147 000. Cardona refused to pay, offering Osorio "$60 000 or nothing." Osorio took the $60 000 and then sued for the remainder. The Court held that the agreement was not a bet or a wager; rather, it was an agreement to pool the winnings, so there was no problem regarding legality. The Court then decided that there was an intention to be bound and thus a valid contract. The fact that they had adjusted the split to reflect the odds indicated that they were serious. Cardona had always acted toward Osorio in a way that led Osorio to believe that he was serious and that he intended the agreement to be in force. Note that because there were threats involved, the agreement to take $60 000 was held to be unconscionable and not binding as a settlement. Osorio was able to collect the other $87 000.

This case illustrates not only the requirement of intention, but also that the test whereby the court seeks to determine the intention of the parties is objective.

DISCUSSION QUESTIONS

When friends enter a contest and agree to divide the prize if they win, and they in fact do win the contest, and then they disagree as to the division of the prize, who will have to convince the court that there was an intention to be bound by the agreement? What is the most convincing evidence to use in this regard? What advice would you therefore give to friends who are entering a contest together?

[33.] (1984), 15 D.L.R. (4th) 619 (B.C.S.C.).

The following examples illustrate situations in which the issue of intention arises and indicate the courts' probable responses.

1. **Stated intention of the parties.** If the parties clearly state that they do not wish to be legally bound by their agreement, or that their agreement is not to be enforceable in any court, that instruction will be honoured. Such a statement must be embodied in the terms of the contract and be very clear as to the intention not to be bound. Often, in commercial relationships, the parties will make agreements that are convenient, but which they don't want to be legally binding. Sometimes, the parties are in pre-contract negotiations and are not yet ready to be bound. "Letters of intention" are examples of such communications; they clearly do not create legal obligations for the parties.

2. **Commercial relations.** If the relationship between the contracting parties is primarily commercial in nature, the courts will presume that the parties intended to be legally bound by their agreement. The contract will be binding on them in the absence of any evidence or clear instructions to the contrary.

3. **Domestic and social relations.** When an agreement is between members of a family, or friends involved in domestic (non-business) activities, there is a presumption that the parties do not intend legal consequences to flow from their agreement. For example, if members of a family informally agree to make payments to each other, such as a child agreeing to pay room and board, or parents to pay an allowance, the courts would assume that there is no intention to be legally bound and would therefore not enforce the agreement. However, if the parties had gone to the trouble of having a lawyer draw up a formal contract, then the courts would be satisfied that the parties did intend that legal consequences would flow from their agreement and so they would enforce the contract. The presumption of no intention would have been rebutted.

4. **Social and business relations.** Problems arise when the relationship involved is a mixture of social and commercial relations. Such an example arises when friends jointly enter a contest and then disagree on the distribution of the prize. This problem could become more common in Canada with the increase in the number of lotteries with large prizes. In such cases, the courts must judge each situation on its individual merits. The courts use the reasonable person test to determine whether it is reasonable for the parties trying to enforce the agreement to think that a legally binding contract had been created.

5. **Exaggerated claims.** Merchants often exaggerate the qualities of their products in advertisements or when they talk to customers. They may, for example, claim that their product is "the biggest" or "the best." To some extent, this enthusiasm is expected, and is not taken seriously by the customers or the courts. The problem is where to draw the line, and the courts again apply the reasonable person test to determine whether, in the circumstances, the customer should have taken the exaggerated claim seriously. Note, however, that even when the exaggeration is obvious, it may still be prohibited by statute, as misleading advertising or an unfair trade practice. Such consumer protection legislation will be discussed in Chapter 15.

Courts will enforce stated intention

Courts will presume intention in commercial transactions

Courts will presume no intention in domestic and social relations

Reasonable person test applied when social and business relations mix

Reasonable person test also applied when dealing with exaggerated claims

CASE SUMMARY 7.12

Are Businesses Permitted to Exaggerate? *Carlill v. Carbolic Smoke Ball Company*[34]

The defendants manufactured a product that they claimed would protect users from influenza. They offered £100 to anyone who used their product as prescribed and still contracted influenza. They stated, in an advertisement, that £1000 had been deposited in the Alliance Bank, Regent Street, and that this showed their sincerity in the matter.

Carlill used the product, got influenza, and claimed the money. The company refused to pay, stating that the advertisement was an advertising puff that merely indicated enthusiasm for the product, and that it was not meant to be taken seriously by the public. The Court held that depositing money to back up the claim had taken it out of the category of an advertising puff. It was determined that a reasonable person would have thought that the advertisement was serious, so there was intention. The offer was held to be valid, and Carlill's use of the product and contracting of the illness were appropriate forms of acceptance. There was therefore a valid contract.

Misleading advertising has become a serious problem and is now controlled by consumer protection legislation, which will be discussed in Chapter 15.

DISCUSSION QUESTIONS

Should merchants ever be allowed to make exaggerated claims about their products?

FORM OF THE CONTRACT

mybuslawlab
www.pearsoned.ca/mybuslawlab

We have established that the essential elements of contracts are consensus, consideration, capacity, legality, and intention (as summarized in Table 7.1 on p. 253). Next we will examine the form of the contract.

The Requirement of Writing

Historically, the form of the contract was very important. Promises were enforceable because they were contained in sealed documents, called *deeds*. Today, there is no general rule that a contract must take a certain form, although most jurisdictions have statutory requirements regarding the transfer of land.[35] Contracts may be in writing, they may be under seal, they may simply be verbal, or they may even be implied from the conduct of the parties.

People are often surprised to discover that most verbal agreements have the same legal status as written ones, provided they meet the requirements described in this and the previous chapter.

---

34. [1893] 1 Q.B. 256 (C.A.).

35. See, for example, s. 155 of the *Land Titles Act*, R.S.A. 2000, c. L-4, which requires a Transfer of Land to be signed in front of a witness, who must swear an Affidavit of Attestation of an Instrument.

The importance of a written contract is practical, not theoretical. It is always a good idea to put the terms of an agreement in writing, so that if a dispute arises there is something permanent that establishes the terms to which the parties agreed. In the absence of such a document, it is surprising how differently even well-intentioned people remember the terms of their agreement. If a dispute between the parties does end in litigation, each of the parties will be in a better position to prove her case if she can produce written evidence to support her claim. We can expect changes to what will be required to prove the existence of a valid contract as we move away from a paper-based economy to an electronic one. The effect of developments in technology and communications as they relate to the formation of contracts will be discussed in Chapter 14.

Verbal contracts binding but writing advised

www.pearsoned.ca/mybuslawlab

| BC | AB | SK | MB | ON |

Statute of Frauds requires writing for enforcement of some contracts

Statute of Frauds in force in some provinces

WHEN WRITING IS REQUIRED

In some limited circumstances, a contract is required by statute to be evidenced in writing to be enforceable. These requirements for writing are found primarily in the *Statute of Frauds*. There are also, however, some other statutes that set out similar requirements.

The first *Statute of Frauds* was enacted in England in the 17th century. It was adopted with some variation by the Canadian provinces. The *Statute* requires that certain types of contracts be evidenced in writing to be enforceable. The *Statute* has been criticized as causing as much abuse as it was intended to prevent. As a result, many important changes have been made by the provinces to the *Statute*. Manitoba[36] and British Columbia have repealed the *Statute* altogether, although British Columbia retains some of its provisions in its *Law and Equity Act*. [37]

CASE SUMMARY 7.13

Writing Still Needed in Manitoba: *Megill Stephenson Co. v. Woo*[38]

Two parties negotiated by telephone. At the conclusion of their conversation, an agreement was reached regarding the purchase and sale of a parcel of land. However, before any documents were prepared, the vendor changed his mind. The purchaser sued. The Court held that, despite the fact that the *Statute of Frauds* had been repealed in Manitoba, there was the usual expectation of the parties that a contract dealing with the sale of land would not be effective until it was put into writing. The Court honoured that expectation and refused to enforce the agreement.

Note that the Court first had to find that an agreement had been reached. It can be argued that by this decision the vendor was allowed to take advantage of the purchaser for his own profit. It was this type of fraud that led to the adoption of the *Statute of Frauds*.

DISCUSSION QUESTION

Should the requirement of writing therefore be retained for important transactions such as the purchase and sale of land?

---

36. See *An Act to Repeal the Statute of Frauds*, C.C.S.M. c. F158.

37. *R.S.B.C. 1996, c. 253, s. 59.*

38. (1989) 59 D.L.R. (4th) 146 (Man. C.A.).

The following is a discussion of the types of contracts generally included under the *Statute of Frauds* in Canada. The actual wording varies among provinces.

1.   **Contracts not to be performed within one year.** When the terms of the agreement make it impossible to perform the contract within one full year from the time the contract is entered into, there must be evidence in writing for it to be enforceable. For example, if Sasaki Explosives Ltd. agrees in March 2010 to provide a fireworks display at the 1 July celebrations in Halifax in the summer of 2011, that contract must be evidenced by writing to be enforceable. Failure to have evidence in writing will make it no less a contract, but the courts will refuse to enforce it. Some provinces, including British Columbia (which has repealed the *Statute of Frauds*) and Ontario,[39] have eliminated the requirement of writing in this area. Note that even when it is impossible for one party to complete performance within the year, written evidence is not required when it is clear in the contract that the other party is expected to perform within that year.

> When contract cannot be performed within one year

2.   **Land dealings.** Any contract that affects a party's interest in land must be evidenced in writing to be enforceable. It is often difficult to determine what types of contracts affect interest (or ownership) in land and what types do not. Any sale of land (or part of it, such as the creation of a joint tenancy in land) must be evidenced in writing. Any creation of an easement, right of way, or estate (such as a life estate), is also covered by the *Statute of Frauds*. But contracts for services to the land that do not affect the interest in the land itself are not covered. For example, if a carpenter agrees to build a house, such an agreement may affect the value of the land, but not the interest in the land itself. It therefore need not be evidenced in writing to be enforceable. This provision of the *Statute of Frauds* has also been modified in some jurisdictions. For example, in British Columbia[40] and Ontario,[41] a lease for three years or less is exempt from the legislation, but longer leases are treated just like any other interest in land and must be evidenced in writing to be enforceable.

> When an interest in land is involved

3.   **Guarantees and indemnities.** When creditors are not satisfied with the creditworthiness of a debtor, they may insist that someone else also assume responsibility for the debt. This can be done by using a guarantee or an indemnity. If the third party incurs a secondary liability for the debt, he has given a guarantee. A guarantor promises that, if the debtor fails to pay the debt, he will assume responsibility and pay it. Note that in this type of transaction, the obligation is secondary, or contingent; there is no obligation on the guarantor until the debtor actually fails to pay the debt.

> When guarantee is involved

An **indemnity** describes a relationship in which a third party assumes a primary obligation for the repayment of the debt along with the debtor. As a result, both owe the debt, and the creditor can look to either for repayment. When a third party says, "I'll see that you get paid," there is an assumption of a primary obligation, and the promise is an indemnity.

> But not an indemnity

39.   See the *Statute of Frauds*, R.S.O. 1990, c. S.19.

40.   *Supra* note 39, s. 3.

41.   *Supra* note 37, s. 59(2)(b).

The distinction between a guarantee and an indemnity is important, because in most provinces the *Statute of Frauds* requires that a guarantee be in writing, but not an indemnity. If the court classifies the nature of a third-party agreement as an indemnity, there is no requirement of writing. The distinction can be vital when a person has made only a verbal commitment to pay the outstanding loan to the debtor.[42] In British Columbia, the Law and Equity Act requires that both indemnities and guarantees be evidenced in writing to be enforceable.[43]

4. **Others.** The original *Statute of Frauds* required that whenever the purchase price of goods sold exceeded a specified minimum, there had to be evidence in writing for the sale to be enforceable. This provision has been included in the *Sale of Goods Act* in many jurisdictions in Canada.[44] It is usually sufficient evidence in writing if a receipt or sales slip has been given. The definition of goods and the sale of goods generally will be discussed in Chapter 15.

Parliament and the provincial legislatures have passed many statutes that require certain transactions to be in writing to be valid. Some examples are the *Bills of Exchange Act,* insurance legislation, consumer protection legislation, some of the legislation dealing with employment relations, and the carriage of goods and passengers. For example, while there does not seem to be a provision in the Ontario *Sale of Goods Act*[45] requiring that certain transactions be evidenced in writing, other legislation requires certain types of consumer contracts to be in writing.[46] In many jurisdictions, the *Statute of Frauds* also requires the promises of executors (to be responsible personally for the debts of an estate),[47] and promises made in consideration of marriage,[48] to be evidenced in writing to be enforceable.

WHAT CONSTITUTES EVIDENCE IN WRITING

Note that it is not the whole agreement that must be in writing to satisfy the *Statute of Frauds*. There need be evidence in writing supporting only the essential terms of the agreement. The essential terms are normally an indication of the parties, the subject matter of the contract, and the consideration to be paid. Other terms may become essential, however, depending on the nature of the contract. The evidence in writing can take the form of the actual agreement itself, or simply a receipt, or note, or email. It can even come into existence after the creation of the contract referring to it. The writing can be a single document, or a collection of documents, which taken together provide the required evidence. The document(s) must also be signed, or initialed, but only by the person denying the existence of the contract.

[42.] For a good discussion of guarantees and indemnities, see *MacNeill v. Fero Waste and Recycling Inc.* (2003), 213 N.S.R. (2d) 254 (C.A.).

[43.] See, for example, s. 6 of the *Sale of Goods Act,supra* note 3, which sets a minimum value of $50.

[44.] *Supra* note 37, s. 59(6).

[45.] See the *Consumer Protection Act, 2002,* S.O. 2002, c. 30, Sch. A., which requires future performance agreements, time share agreements, personal development services agreements, direct agreements, and other consumer agreements to be in writing.

[46.] R.S.O. 1990, c. S.1.

[47.] See Ontario's *Statute of Frauds, supra* note 39, s. 4.

[48.] In Alberta, this provision is now subject to the *Matrimonial Property Act,* R.S.A. 2000, c. M-8, s. 37, which deals with pre-nuptial agreements.

Note that important adaptations have been necessitated because of changing technology. As electronic records and communications become more common, and paper plays less of a role, the traditional requirements of writing and signatures are becoming obsolete. One solution is to give digital records and electronic signatures the status of written documents. Legislation to allow this is now in place in several jurisdictions.[49] The problems brought about by computers and electronic communications, and some of the legislative solutions, will be discussed in Chapter 14.

EFFECT OF THE STATUTE OF FRAUDS

It is vital to remember that if a contract is not evidenced in writing this does not make it void under the *Statute of Frauds;* it is merely unenforceable. The contract is binding on the parties, but the courts will not assist them in enforcing it. If the parties have already performed, or if there is some other remedy available that does not require the court's involvement, the contract will still be binding. The courts will not assist a person who has performed to get out of the contract. Nor will the court order the return of any money paid (see Figure 7.1). In effect, the party has only done what was required under the contract. Similarly, when there is a lien (a right to seize property), or when there is a right to set off a debt against the obligations created by the contract, the parties themselves may be able to enforce the contract, without the help of the courts. In that sense, such a contract is binding, even though there is no evidence in writing, and it won't be enforced by the courts.

Contract valid when no writing, but unenforceable

Figure 7.1 Effect of *Statute of Frauds*

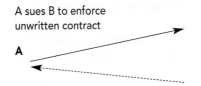

A sues B to enforce unwritten contract

A

B Contract is valid but unenforceable; B can't be forced to perform.

B But if B performs he can't change his mind to get $ back, since contract is valid.

! REDUCING RISK 7.5

There are only a few situations in which evidence in writing is required to ensure that a contract is enforceable. However, from a practical business point of view, contractual arrangements should always be put into writing (or, as technology develops, some other permanent form). Even people with the best of intentions will remember things differently as time passes. It is vital, therefore, to have a permanent record that can be referred to later, so that the terms are certain and the good will between the parties is retained. When relations have broken down, there is nothing better than a written document to resolve a dispute that arises over a business transaction that has gone bad. The existence of the document may, by itself, prevent litigation. If it does not, at least there is evidence as to what the parties agreed to that can be used in the lawsuit. So, while in law it may be true that a verbal contract is as binding as a written one, it is poor practice indeed to rely on verbal agreements in business.

49. See, for example, the *Electronic Transactions Act*, S.A. 2001, c. E-5.5.

PART PERFORMANCE

The court will waive the requirement of writing if the parties can produce evidence to show that a contract dealing with an interest in land has been partially performed. There are some important limitations to this principle. The part performance must be evidence of the existence of the contract and consistent only with the existence of the contract. The payment of money owed under the contract will therefore not usually be acceptable as proof of part performance, as the payment of money is consistent with any number of different obligations. In British Columbia, however, the payment of a deposit is sufficient part performance with respect to land transactions to make such contracts enforceable.[50] A good example of acceptable part performance when land has been sold is the start of construction. The permission to enter onto the land and start building is consistent with the sale of the land, and so the courts will accept the part performance as sufficient evidence to support the contract.

CASE SUMMARY 7.14

Part Performance Satisfies Statute: *Hill v. Nova Scotia (Attorney General)*[51]

Land was expropriated to build a highway, but the provincial government agreed to allow the owner of the land to move people, livestock, and equipment across the highway. A government department helped the owner by producing fencing and ramps to enable the movement across the highway. This arrangement continued for 27 years. The result was that the owner of the property acquired a right of way (an equitable interest) across the highway.

The Court held that even though the *Statute of Frauds* required evidence in writing, that was not necessary in this case. The 27 years of crossing the highway with the help of the government constituted part performance.

The *Statute of Frauds* was passed originally to prevent fraudulent transactions. The doctrine of part performance provides an exception to the requirement of writing.

DISCUSSION QUESTIONS

Does adoption of the doctrine of part performance therefore increase the likelihood of fraud being committed with respect to transactions involving interests in land?

---

50. *Supra* note 37, s. 59(4).

51. [1997] 1 S.C.R. 69.

Table 7.1 summarizes the elements required to make a contract valid and enforceable.

Table 7.1   Summary of Contract Formation

No consensus	Contract void	But must pay for requested services
No consideration	Contract void	But note promissory estoppel, gift, and seal
No capacity	Contract voidable	But infants can enforce contracts with adults
		But infants bound by contracts for necessaries and beneficial contracts of service
	Contract void	But insane persons must show the others knew of insanity
Illegal	Contract void	But depends on statute
No intention	Contract void	Note presumptions
No writing	Valid	But note *Statute of Frauds* exceptions

SUMMARY

Capacity

- For a contract to be binding, each of the parties must have legal capacity
- In most provinces, contracts with minors are not binding on them, except for contracts for necessaries and beneficial contracts of service
- In British Columbia, all contracts with minors are unenforceable, except those that are specifically made enforceable by legislation, such as government student loans
- The test for the capacity of minors is objective
- Parents are not liable for the torts or contractual obligations of their children unless there is legislation making them liable
- A contract with someone who is insane or drunk will be rendered invalid only when the person was so incapacitated as to not know what he was doing, and the other contracting party knew, or ought to have known, of that incapacity
- Corporations, enemy aliens in times of war, trade unions, Crown corporations and government bodies, bankrupts, and Indians have their capacity to enter into contracts limited to some extent

Legality

- To be binding, a contact must be legal and be performed legally
- If a lawful contract is performed illegally, the courts may rule that the contract is illegal and void, or just void, or they may enforce some, or all, of the contract
- An illegal contract is illegal at the time it is formed. Illegal contracts include contracts that violate legislation and contracts that are against public policy
- The courts may rule that an illegal contract is illegal and void, or just void, or they may enforce some, or all, of the contract
- There are many types of contracts that are illegal because they violate legislation or are against public policy
- One example is contracts that unduly restrain trade, which are usually illegal, but contracts in which one party agrees not to carry on business in competition with another are legal, if they can be shown to be reasonable in terms of the interests of the parties and the public

Intention

- For a contract to be binding, each of the parties must intend to be bound by it
- The courts will enforce the stated intention of the parties
- In family and other social relationships, there is a presumption of no intention. This presumption can be challenged by evidence that shows an intent to be bound
- In commercial relationships, intention is presumed. This can also be rebutted
- In other situations, the courts use the reasonable person test to determine intention

Form of the contract

- Most verbal contracts are valid, if they contain the essential elements of a contract
- Under the *Statute of Frauds,* certain contracts must be evidenced in writing to be enforceable
- The *Statute of Frauds* has been repealed or modified in many jurisdictions
- Most jurisdictions now have legislation requiring certain types of contracts to be in writing
- When part performance is established, verbal agreements dealing with interests in land are also enforceable

---

QUESTIONS

1. "In determining whether a child has contractual capacity, the court will attempt to determine if she actually understood the transaction." True or false? Explain your answer.

2. Explain the circumstances in which a minor may escape liability for a contract and the circumstances in which a minor is bound by a contract.

3. What is the significance of a minor's contract being designated as a beneficial contract of service?

4. In addition to debts incurred for necessaries, when will a minor be liable for a debt he incurred?

5. What are the three stages of a contractual relationship? Describe the legal situation of a minor in each of these stages.

6. If there is no relevant legislation, when will the parents of a minor be responsible for the minor's contracts? When will they be liable for the torts of the minor?

7. When can an adult sue a minor in tort even though there is a contract between them?

8. What must an insane or drunk person establish to escape liability under a contract?

9. Explain what care businesspeople must exercise when entering into contracts with government corporations or bodies.

10. Explain four other situations where businesspeople must be careful that those they deal with have the capacity to contract.

11. Explain the difference between a contract that is performed illegally and an illegal contract.

12. What decisions can a court make if performance of a contract violates a regulatory statute?

13. What are the two reasons that can cause contracts to be illegal?

14. How has the law regarding the judicial treatment of illegal contracts changed?

15. Give five examples of contracts deemed by the courts to be against public policy, and describe the effect of such a designation.

16. "All contracts that restrain trade are illegal." True or false? Explain your answer.

17. Describe the test the court will use in determining whether the parties had an intention to be bound when they made an agreement.

18. With respect to the element of intention, explain how the courts' treatment of domestic agreements differs from their treatment of commercial transactions.

19. How will a court determine if there was contractual intention when there is a dispute between a brother and his sister over how to operate their business?

20. What is the significance of a written document in contractual relations?

21. Explain why some people have suggested that the *Statute of Frauds* has led to more frauds than it has prevented.

22. Give examples of the types of contracts currently included under the *Statute of Frauds.*

23. What "evidence in writing" is required to satisfy the requirements of the *Statute of Frauds*?

24. "A contract that does not satisfy the *Statute of Frauds* is void." True or false? Explain your answer.

25. Under what circumstances will a contract falling under the jurisdiction of the *Statute of Frauds* be enforceable even though it is not evidenced by writing?

CASES AND DISCUSSION QUESTIONS

1. *Williams v. Condon*, [2007] O.J. No. 1683 (Sup. Ct.).

Williams was hit by a vehicle when he was walking in a parking lot. He sued for damages relating to his injuries. He signed a Release. His injuries turned out to be much more serious than he believed they were. He then claimed that the Release was void, and of no force and effect, because he was intoxicated when he signed it. He claimed that he had consumed five or six cans of beer and a couple of painkillers (as he did every day after his injury) before he met with the insurer's representative to sign the Release. He said that he did not read the documentation before signing the Release. He then had two days to change his mind about accepting the settlement but did not do so. The insurer's representative said she explained the documentation to Williams in detail. She did not smell alcohol on his breath and did not believe that he was impaired. She testified that he did not have any difficulty communicating with her.

Should Williams be bound by the Release he signed? Besides a defence based on intoxication, is there any other basis on which he could claim that the Release should be set aside?

2. *Graham v. Capital Cabs Ltd.,* [2005] N.W.T.T.C. 6.

In July 2004, a group of people, including Graham, decided to set up a taxi-cab business. Graham agreed to assist however she could in setting up the business, by doing such things as arranging telephone hookups and applying for licences. It was agreed that she would be the Office Manager for the business. It was also agreed that Graham would receive a share in the corporation that was to be set up in return for the work she was doing and for agreeing to work for a reduced salary for the first year the business operated. The Corporation (the Defendant) was incorporated on 6 August 2004. A meeting was held the next day, and it was agreed that Graham would be paid $2000 for the work she had done, and would continue to do, in setting up the business. There was also an agreement that Graham would receive a share in the Corporation only if she invested $5000 in it and provided a car to be used in the business. The business opened on 1 September 2004. Graham resigned on September 3 because the working conditions had deteriorated very quickly. She sued for the $2000, for reimbursement of the expenses she had paid on behalf of the Corporation, and for a share in the Corporation.

What, if anything, is Graham entitled to judgment for, against the Corporation?

3. *Nova Scotia Union of Public Employees v. Halifax Regional School Board (2001),* 195 N.S.R. (2d) 97 (C.A.).

The provincial government enacted legislation prohibiting increases in pay raises during a certain period. The Union and the Board entered into a collective agreement, which provided that increases that were to have been paid during the period would be paid as a lump sum at the end of the period. The Board then refused to make the payment, claiming that it would contravene the legislation.

Assuming that the collective agreement was contrary to the legislation, should the Court order the Board to make the payment? Would it make a difference if the legislation specified that any provision contravening the legislation was to be of no force or effect?

4. *Eha v. Genge (2007),* 68 B.C.L.R. (4th) 7 (C.A.).

Eha lent Genge $32 000 at an interest rate of 10 percent per month, a rate that both parties charged their customers in their pawnbroking businesses. Genge did not repay the amount owing, so Eha sued, claiming a total of approximately $100 000, representing principle and interest. During the trial, Eha's lawyer agreed that the amount owing was only $60 000 if interest was calculated at the maximum permissible rate. The trial Judge dismissed Eha's claim, as the agreement was illegal because the interest rate was much higher than 60 percent per year, the maximum permitted rate. Eha appealed.

Should the appeal succeed and, if so, how much should Genge be ordered to pay Eha?

5. *Bursey v. Bursey (1999),* 174 Nfld. & P.E.I.R. 291 (Nfld. C.A.).

This case involves the enforcement of a separation agreement between a husband and wife. The husband operated a business. He brought in a considerable amount of equipment from outside the province. He did not pay the sales tax on the equipment. When he and his wife separated, a term of the separation agreement required his wife to pay half of the unpaid sales tax if the husband was eventually required to pay it. The husband was eventually required to pay $54 000 in unpaid sales tax. He brought this action to enforce the separation agreement and thereby recover from his wife half of the sales tax he had paid.

Should his wife have to pay?

6. *Duncan v. Sherman*, [2006] B.C.C.A. 14 (CanLII).

The appellants purchased a property from Duncan, who created an easement over the property in favour of the owner (Duncan) of an adjoining lot. The contract of purchase and sale included an addendum prepared by the real estate agent. The addendum contained a copy of the easement, as it was registered at the Land Titles Office, along with certain handwritten markings. Duncan built an eight-foot, solid cedar fence along the boundary of the easement. The appellants objected, arguing about the interpretation of the addendum. Duncan claimed that the addendum had no contractual effect, because he had not communicated with either of the appellants. He did, however, sign the contract to which the addendum was attached.

Is Duncan bound by the addendum? Did he intend to be bound by it? What problem will Duncan face in trying to convince the Court that he should not be bound?

7. *Zukiwski v. Yakmac Investments Ltd. (1999)*, [2000] 244 A.R. 136 (C.A.).

The plaintiffs, father and son, worked for the defendant during the construction of condominiums and a hotel. There were notes such as the following:

> TO WHOM IT MAY CONCERN
>
> I, [Nick M. Zukiwski], hereby agree to transfer all my profits from the sale of the St. Lawrence Court Condominium and Henday Village to [Archway Inns Corp.] which own the motel. The profits are to be used as the down payment on the purchase of the motel.

Each of the plaintiffs signed such a note, but it was not clear what interest each was to buy. Archway Inns Corp. was never the owner of the hotel. The price to be paid was not mentioned in the notes. When the notes were signed, the hotel was not built. Neither the closing date nor the financing was specified. The owner of the defendant did sign a note, but there was no indication that he signed it on behalf of the defendant.

Should the Court grant the plaintiffs an order for specific performance?

8. *McKnight v. Grant*, [2009] N.B.C.A. 4.

Grant executed documents to sell her cottage to her nephew. Six months later, she commenced an action requesting that the transaction be set aside because of misrepresentation and undue influence. The nephew decided to re-convey the cottage to Grant. Her lawyer talked to her nephew a couple of times, and an agreement was made that the cottage would be conveyed if Grant repaid the nephew the deposit he had made and the legal fees he had incurred. They agreed that the lawyers were to "paper" the settlement agreement. Two days later, the nephew changed his mind and advised that he did not want to settle the action. The trial Judge found that there was a binding settlement agreement. The nephew appealed, on the basis that the *Statute of Frauds* applied, and that the settlement agreement should therefore not be enforceable.

Was the agreement to re-convey the cottage subject to the *Statute of Frauds*?

Chapter 8

Factors Affecting the Contractual Relationship

The two previous chapters examined the process of forming contracts. This chapter examines what happens when the parties disagree as to the nature and effect of the contract. The obligations and the extent of the responsibilities of the original parties to an agreement are also discussed, together with how those obligations are affected when an innocent third party, or a stranger to the contract, becomes involved.

www.pearsoned.ca/mybuslawlab

MISTAKE

Misunderstanding that destroys consensus results in void contract

In limited circumstances, the courts will provide a remedy where one or both of the parties have made a mistake with respect to a contract. Where it is clear that because of the mistake, the parties have failed to reach a consensus, the contract is void; there is no complete agreement between them. It must be made clear at the outset that the court will not interfere when the parties have simply made a bad bargain: this is an error in judgment and the person who made it must live with it.

Mistake must go to the very root of the contract

Reviewable mistakes in contract involve a person's mind being at odds with the terms, surrounding circumstances, or other factors relating to the contract. Such a mistake can relate to the terms of the contract, including the identity of the parties. It can relate to an assumption upon which the contract is based, whether as to a matter of fact, some future event, or the law surrounding the contract. And it can also concern an expected result or consequence of the agreement. The mistake can be made by only one of the parties or by both. Where both parties are making a mistake, it can be a *shared mistake*, where both are making the same mistake, or it can be a *misunderstanding*, where each party has a different idea as to the meaning of the terms of the contract. This is a complex and difficult area of contract law to understand. It will help to keep in mind that the guiding principle seems to be that the courts will try to do what is necessary to give effect to the reasonable expectations of the parties.

Courts will try to give effect to the reasonable expectations of the parties

---

CASE SUMMARY 8.1

Bad Advice Does Not Void Contract Made Based on It: *Works v. Works*[1]

The husband had agreed to transfer his interest in the matrimonial home to the wife in settlement of a claim for spousal support. Later, the husband discovered that he had received incorrect tax advice as to the consequences of this settlement and he tried to avoid signing the formal Minutes of Settlement. He now claimed to have entered a contract based on a mistake. The Court held that a consensus had been reached. The husband knew he was transferring his interest in the home for a release from spousal support. The fact that he had made a "bad deal" because the tax advice given to him was erroneous, did not void the agreement itself.

The issue of tax deductibility was not discussed between counsel, and the wife's counsel had no reason to believe the agreement was based on that assumption. The court concluded that where only one party is mistaken about something significant in a contract, the court will exercise its discretion to set aside the contract only if satisfied that, in light of the circumstances, it would be unfair or unjust to enforce the contract. The issue of a tax saving was never a central issue; thus the deal was deemed fair.

SMALL BUSINESS PERSPECTIVE

If there are certain assumptions upon which parties are acting, would it be wise to state those assumptions in the contract itself? This decision suggests that would be prudent.

When the mistake relates to the terms of the agreement itself, such as the identity of the parties or the subject matter of the agreement, the courts are more willing to provide a remedy. The courts also will not interfere with contractual obligations unless the demonstrated mistake is significant or material with respect to the agreement. If a person ordering a new car is delivered one that is a slightly different colour than the one he had in mind when he chose it, that will not be enough to allow him to avoid the contract. Finally, where the mistake is caused by the negligence of one of the parties, that party will normally be held responsible for the error.

Mistake must be serious

Careless party responsible when mistake is result of negligence

It should also be noted that if the mistake is one about the facts involved, as opposed to a mistake based on an interpretation of the law or its effect, the court will be more likely to provide a remedy. On the other hand, where one party stands to make a windfall at the expense of the other, the courts likely will review the transaction—whether the mistake is one of law or of fact. For example, when one party receives a payment she is not entitled to because the other has misunderstood his legal obligation, the court will likely order those funds returned on the basis of **unjust enrichment**.

The courts are less likely to remedy a mistake in law

[1.] (2002), 206 N.S.R. (2d) 292 (S.C.).

The area of mistake in contract law is evolving; it has not been uncommon over the years for the courts to reverse or modify their position. The discussion below is an attempt to summarize the important aspects of the law in this area. The approach taken concentrates on three different ways that a mistake can be made. It should be remembered that if a contract is found to be *void* it is not a contract at all; if it is *voidable* the contract does exist, but one of the parties has the option of getting out of it. Consequently, when an innocent third party has acquired goods that are the subject of a voidable contract, that party gets to keep the goods; but if the previous contract was void—that is, there never was a contract—the person who sold the goods to the third party never had title to them, and those goods must be returned to the original owner.

Fundamental shared mistake about subject matter—void

Shared Mistake

A **shared mistake** occurs when the two parties are in complete agreement but they have both made the same mistake regarding some aspect of the contract. The courts will review the transaction only where the mistake relates to some fundamental aspect of the subject matter of the contract. The most common example of such a shared mistake resulting in a void contract is where the subject matter of the contract no longer exists at the time the contract is made. Thus, where the parties enter into an agreement for the sale and purchase of the cargo of a ship, without knowing that the ship and cargo were destroyed the night before, the contract is void because of the shared mistake. The courts have also found a contract void because of a shared mistake when, unknown to the parties, the property being sold was already owned by the purchaser. In both these instances, the parties have together made the same significant mistake with respect to a factual aspect of the agreement that has destroyed the basis of the contract. As a result, the contract is void for lack of consensus.

When the shared mistake relates only to the value of what they are dealing with, it normally will not affect the enforceability of the contract. For example, if both vendor and purchaser think that they are dealing with an ordinary violin when, in fact, they are dealing with a rare and valuable Stradivarius, the contract would be binding nevertheless.

RECTIFICATION

If the written document does not reflect the common intention of the parties to the contract, the courts are willing to correct or **rectify** the document. For example, if two parties had agreed to the sale of land for $500 000 and a clerical error made the document read $50 000, the court would add the missing zero and require the parties to perform the corrected agreement. The courts will do this only where it is clear that both understood what they were agreeing to and what was written was different from that understanding.[2]

---

2. See *Pacific Petroleums Ltd. v. Concordia Propane Gas Marketers Ltd.* (1977), 5 A.R. 421 (T.D.), where the contract referred to Canadian gallons instead of American gallons, as agreed. Rectification was ordered.

CASE SUMMARY 8.2

Damages Awarded as Rectification Not Possible: *Sylvan Lake Golf & Tennis Club Ltd. v. Performance Industries Ltd.*[3]

A verbal agreement had been reached between the parties concerning the purchase and operation of a golf course. One of the terms discussed was the future residential development of lands adjacent to the eighteenth hole. The agreement was reduced to writing by a lawyer acting on instructions from the defendant. The plaintiff proved, beyond any reasonable doubt, that he signed the agreement of 21 December 1989 under a unilateral mistake as to the dimensions of the development property and further that the defendant knew he had signed that agreement by mistake.

The preconditions to obtaining the equitable remedy of rectification of the contract were met: (1) The plaintiff established the existence and content of the prior oral agreement. There was a definite project in a definite location to which both parties had given their definite assent. (2) It was found that the defendant had fraudulently misrepresented the written document as accurately reflecting the terms of the prior oral contract. (3) The precise terms of rectification were readily ascertained. All that was required was to change the word *feet* in the phrase "one hundred ten (110) feet in width" to "yards." (4) There was convincing proof of the plaintiff's unilateral mistake and the defendant's knowledge of that mistake. The plaintiff's version of the oral agreement was sufficiently corroborated on significant points by other witnesses and documents.

The court held that the defendant's conduct in attempting to take advantage of the plaintiff's mistake was equivalent to a fraud—or a misrepresentation amounting to fraud—or sharp practice. It would thus be unjust and unconscionable for the court not to offer redress to the plaintiff in the face of that conduct. Rectification itself was no longer a real option as the lands had been developed by the defendant. Accordingly, damages in lieu of rectification were awarded, compensating the plaintiff for the loss of the opportunity to profit from developing residential lots around the 18th hole.

SMALL BUSINESS PERSPECTIVE

The importance of thoroughly reading and comprehending the terms of contract prior to signing it cannot be overstated. The courts are reluctant to rectify contracts where there was a lack of due diligence on the part of the mistaken party. Here, the Court overlooked this lack of care because the defendant's fraud was the greater evil.

It is important to remember that the courts are not rewriting the agreement during rectification. They are simply correcting a written document so that it corresponds to the demonstrated intention of the two parties.[4]

Rectification of the contract may be available as a remedy in other situations as well, such as where one person makes a mistake caused by the fraud by the other party.

Courts will correct an improperly recorded agreement

3. [2002] 1 S.C.R. 678.

4. For a recent case in which the court rectified minutes of a family settlement, see *Mills v. Mills*, [2004] O.J. No. 3169 (S.C.J.). Both parties had miscalculated what the sale proceeds from their home would be. They believed it would be $65 824, whereas only $22 408 was available for distribution. Nonetheless, the Court found that there was consensus to split the balance equally, so the amounts were rectified but the balance itself was split equally.

CASE SUMMARY 8.3

The Case of the Million-Dollar Comma: *AMJ Campbell v. Kord Products Inc.*[5]

This case involved AMJ Campbell's selling the assets of a subsidiary to the defendant, Kord. The transaction included the sale of a significant inventory of plant containers with the value determined by calculating the "average sales price" over the prior eight months. This was to be calculated "net of taxes, freight rebates and discounts," but the solicitors for Kord changed that by inserting a comma between the words *freight* and *rebates*. This change, along with some others, was made to the final contract. Before the change only freight rebates would be deducted from the average price, but with the insertion of the comma all of the freight costs as well as any rebates would also be deducted. This resulted in a saving to Kord of more than $759 000 (hence the million-dollar comma).

AMJ Campbell, claiming mistake, asked the Court to rectify the contract by removing the comma. The Court refused, saying that for rectification to take place it had to be clear that both parties had intended the document to read the other way. Here the solicitors for Kord had intentionally inserted the comma and intended that any freight costs be deducted from the purchase price. Only AMJ Campbell had made a mistake by agreeing to the change—and that is not good enough for rectification.

SMALL BUSINESS PERSPECTIVE

This case demonstrates the limited power of the Court to rectify. In light of the restricted situations where rectification can be used, what should a party do before concluding a contract?

Misunderstanding

Court will enforce reasonable interpretation

A different type of mistake occurs when the parties have a misunderstanding about the terms of the agreement itself and neither party is aware of the other's different understanding. When one party to an agreement thinks that the agreement is to do something else, the courts will usually apply the reasonable person test to determine which interpretation of the contract is more reasonable. The court will then adopt the more reasonable position as the correct interpretation of the contract. This point is discussed below in more detail under the heading "Rules of Interpretation." Only if the error is a serious one and the court cannot choose between the two positions because both are equally reasonable will the contract be declared void.

Where equally reasonable and error serious—void

The case of *Raffles v. Wichelhaus*[6] is a good example of such a dilemma. In this case, the contract concerned a cargo being transported on a ship called *The Peerless*. It happened that there were two ships by this name, both leaving the same port but at different times. The seller intended one of these two ships, and the purchaser had in mind the other. The reasonable person test could not resolve this case, and since the disagreement was fundamental there was no consensus between the parties and the contract was void.

[5.] [2003] O.J. No. 329 (Ont. S.C.J.).

[6.] (1864), 2 H. & C. 906, 159 E.R. 375 (E.D.).

CASE SUMMARY 8.4

Misunderstanding Leads Court to Conclude No Consensus Had Been Reached: *British Columbia (Minister of Transportation and Highways) v. Reon Management Services Inc.*[7]

When the Ministry of Transportation expropriated Reon's land, it offered Reon $75 000 plus interest. Reon countered at $100 000 plus interest calculated under section 46 of the *Expropriation Act*. Section 46(1) provided for regular interest, whereas section 46(4) provided for penalty interest where the expropriating party failed to pay within 90 days of the due date. Reon claimed that its counteroffer had been accepted and that the Ministry had agreed to pay all section 46 interest including any penalty interest.

Counsel for the Ministry had responded to Reon's counteroffer thus: . . . "I am instructed to accept the offer contained therein. I have attached the interest calculation from August 3.1990 to April 7, 2000 on $100,000.00. The total amount payable by month, exclusive of costs, will be $204,324.51...."

Evidently, the Ministry's calculation was based on regular interest, whereas Reon's counteroffer was for a settlement based on regular plus penalty interest.

The Court of Appeal concluded that there was no consensus between the parties. No agreement had been reached as to an essential term, namely the price to be paid. Accordingly the settlement was declared void.

SMALL BUSINESS PERSPECTIVE

It may save parties time (and expense) in the long run to spend a little extra time carefully reviewing every term in a contract before leaving the bargaining table.

One-Sided Mistake

A one-sided or **unilateral mistake** takes place where only one of the parties to the contract is making a mistake with respect to the contract. This was the situation in *Moss v. Chin* in Case Summary 8.5. As a general rule, there is no recourse for a person who makes such a one-sided mistake. Thus, when the manager of a business buys a computer by name and model thinking it will do a specific job, and it turns out that it does not have the required capacity, a mistake has been made by the purchaser but there will likely be no remedy. This is a one-sided mistake, and if there were no reliance placed on the salesperson and no misrepresentation or misleading information supplied in the documentation and brochures, there will be no remedy. In effect, the purchaser has misled himself, and the principle of *caveat emptor* ("Let the buyer beware") applies.

One-sided mistake—"Let the buyer beware"

---

7. [2001] B.C.J. No. 2500.

Unilateral Mistake MAY lead to Rescission of Contract: Moss v. Chin;[8] *Hodder Estate v. Insurance Corporation of Newfoundland Limited*[9]

Mrs. Moss was left unconscious after being struck by a car driven by Mr. Chin. Her representative, the public trustee, started a legal action and negotiated with the driver's insurer, ICBC. ICBC made an offer to settle, but Moss died before it was accepted. The public trustee accepted the offer, on behalf of Moss, without informing ICBC of her death. When ICBC found out what had happened, it applied to have the settlement set aside.

This was a unilateral mistake on the part of ICBC, and normally it would not affect the rights of the other parties. But in this situation, rather than this being a matter of ICBC's misleading itself, the public trustee deliberately set out to make sure ICBC did not discover a mistake. The Court accordingly ordered that the contract be rescinded.

Contrast this decision with the judgment in the *Hodder* case. Marie Hodder died in a motor vehicle accident in January 2001. Four months later, Hodder's widower was diagnosed with terminal cancer. No estimate of life expectancy was given. When counsel for the Hodder family put forward a claim for Marie Hodder's death, he did not disclose that Mr. Hodder had terminal cancer. Several months later, on instructions from the Hodder family, counsel requested a reply to his claim letter. Numerous telephone conversations followed, and Hodder's lawyer was asked why his clients were so anxious to settle the claim. Counsel responded that they just wanted to get it behind them. The insurers thus offered to settle the claim for $35 000, which was accepted. Shortly thereafter, Mr. Hodder died. The insurer submitted that there could be no settlement because Hodder's lawyer failed to disclose this material change in circumstances. But the court concluded there was a binding settlement agreement for $35 000.

There was no duty to disclose the illness or imminent death of Mr. Hodder to the insurers. There was no fundamental change in the nature of the claim prior to the settlement being concluded. There was nothing to indicate that the settlement amount was inequitable or should be set aside for fraud or mutual mistake. Hodder's lawyer had not been untruthful. He had a duty to his client to conduct the litigation according to instructions. While he had a duty to disclose information to the opposing parties as required by law, he had no duty to assist his adversary or volunteer information otherwise.

SMALL BUSINESS PERSPECTIVE

These two cases, when read together, suggest that the courts will be more willing to rescind a contract based on unilateral mistake, where that mistake or error has been contributed to or caused by wrongful behaviour on the part of the other party. Otherwise, the courts are reluctant to set aside an agreement.

It should be noted, however, that when the offeror makes an obvious error in relation to his or her offer, the purchaser will not be allowed to take advantage of this obvious error and snap up the offer. Thus, if the merchant selling the

---

8. (1994), 120 D.L.R. (4th) 406 (B.C.S.C.).

9. [2002] N.J. No. 47 (Nfld. & L. S.C.).

computer misquoted it, agreeing to sell it at $25 instead of the $2500 normal price, the purchaser would not be able to ignore such an obvious error and "snap it up" at the bargain price.[10]

When a one-sided mistake takes place, the person making the mistake usually has a remedy only when he or she has been misled, and then the normal course of action is to claim for misrepresentation with its associated remedies. There are some situations, however, where the one-sided mistake is so fundamental as to destroy consensus between the parties. The lack of consensus may be important to establish even where misrepresentation is involved, since the contract would then be void, providing even broader remedies. For example, if the subject goods are later resold to an innocent third party, the remedy of rescission for misrepresentation would not be available to the mistaken party. However, if a mistake sufficient to destroy consensus takes place, the contract would be void, allowing recovery of the goods involved even from an innocent purchaser.

For consensus to be destroyed, the one-sided mistake must be profound. Such a one-sided mistake can occur when there is incorrect identification of one of the parties to a contract. If the person claiming that a mistake has taken place actually thought the deal was with someone else and can demonstrate that identity was an important aspect of the agreement, the court can declare the contract to be void. However, if the error was only about some attribute of the other party, such as her wealth, this will not affect the existence of the contract. The first party has to have thought he was dealing with another person, not just that the person he was dealing with was wealthy.[11]

Snapping up an offer—contract is rescinded

If mistake goes to identity—void contract

CASE SUMMARY 8.6

Read the Contract or Live with It: *978011 Ontario Ltd. v. Cornell Engineering Co.*[12]

When is it fair to set aside a contract where only one party suffers a mistake? Apparently, the courts will not exercise their discretion to grant rectification or rescission where the mistaken party is to blame, or as in this case, where the mistaken party contributed to his own mistake.

The shares in Cornell Engineering Co. (Cornell) were owned by Stevens and Bimboga. Bimboga sought to sell his interest and Stevens suggested that Macdonald, whom Stevens had mentored, buy the shares. Negotiations were held and eventually the parties agreed that Macdonald would enter a service agreement and demonstrate to Bimboga that Macdonald was capable of carrying on Cornell's business.

Stevens asked Macdonald to prepare the agreement; Macdonald amended a standard form agreement and presented it to Stevens, asking him to read it. The agreement provided for compensation to be paid to Macdonald in the event of termination of his services. Stevens read only the first page, where salary was laid out, and signed the eleven page contract on Cornell's behalf. Later, when Cornell terminated the service

---

10. See *City of Ottawa Non-Profit Housing Corp. v. Canvar Construction (1991) Inc.* [2000] O.J. No. 1078 (C.A.) for a case involving a tender error. Since the error was evident on the face of the tender, the tenderer was not obligated to perform the construction job at the erroneous tender price.

11. *Cundy v. Lindsay* (1878), 3 App. Cas. 459 (H.L.).

12. (2001), 53 O.R. (3d) 783 (C.A.), leave to appeal to S.C.C. refused, [2001] S.C.C.A. No. 315.

agreement, Macdonald claimed compensation pursuant to the termination clause. Stevens took the position that Macdonald should have brought the alteration to the standard contract, specifically the termination clause, to his attention. The trial Judge held that since termination had not been discussed by the parties during their negotiations, Macdonald had a duty to draw the termination clause to Stevens' attention. The Court thus rectified the contract by striking out the termination clause entirely.

On appeal, however, no such duty was found to exist. Stevens was a sophisticated businessperson. Macdonald had put no pressure on Stevens to sign without reading the contract; in fact, he had asked Stevens to read the contract. The Court thus refused to grant an equitable remedy to correct a mistake that Stevens had allowed, through oversight, to occur.

SMALL BUSINESS PERSPECTIVE

Clearly, the message is "Read before you sign!"

NON EST FACTUM

Where one of the parties is unaware of the nature of the document being signed, the courts will, in rare circumstances, declare the agreement to be void on the basis of **non est factum** ("It is not my act"). If a person were led to believe he was guaranteeing a note and was, in fact, signing a mortgage agreement on his home, he could argue that there was no consensus between the parties and no contract. This might be a valid defence even against an innocent third party who had acquired rights under the agreement. For this defence to succeed and the contract to be void, it must be shown that the mistake about the document went to the very nature of that document rather than merely to its terms. In this example, if the mistake went only to the rates, with the mortgagor thinking he was to pay 10 percent interest when the document actually required 15 percent, he would still be bound, as the mistake only concerned some aspect of the document and not the document itself. Today, negligence, such as failure to read the document before signing, can defeat the defence of *non est factum* and as a result, successful claims of *non est factum* are quite rare.

If mistake goes to nature of document signed—void

• but not where negligence present

CASE SUMMARY 8.7

Non Est Factum Not Available for Pension Waiver: *Deraps v. Coia*[13]

Mr. Deraps was a labourer who had paid into a pension fund for 20 years when he discovered he had lung cancer. He spoke to his union representative, Mr. Hickey, about a disability pension. Hickey explained to the Derapses that they would receive a higher pension if Mrs. Deraps signed a waiver of spousal benefits. Mrs. Deraps signed the waiver; within a year, Mr. Deraps died. His widow claimed that when she signed the

---

13. (1998), 173 D.L.R. (4th) 717 (Ont. Ct. Gen. Div.); rev'd on other grounds (1999), 179 D.L.R. (4th) 168 (C.A.).

waiver she didn't understand that when her husband died she would be left with nothing. She applied to the Court to have the waiver declared void on the basis of *non est factum*. The trial Court held in her favour, but this ruling was overturned on appeal. The effect of the waiver was clear and it had been explained to her in as simple terms as possible. Also, she read and wrote English and the document she signed was not fundamentally different from what she thought she was signing. In addition, the fact that she did not bother to read the document before signing disqualified her from claiming *non est factum*. In the end the Ontario Court of Appeal did decide in her favour, but on the basis of negligent misrepresentation. The Derapses were dependent on Hickey, who had a duty to supply all material information. His failure to do so was just as misleading as a positive misstatement. Damages were awarded on the basis of what Mrs. Deraps would have received had she not signed the waiver.

DISCUSSION QUESTIONS

This case shows how difficult it now is to succeed in claims for *non est factum*.[14] Fortunately for Mrs. Deraps, she was able to succeed on other grounds. Have we gone too far in limiting the application of *non est factum*? Or do you take the position that individuals should bear more responsibility for their own mistakes?

Rules of Interpretation

The test to determine whether a mistake has taken place is objective. The courts are not concerned with what the parties thought they were agreeing to but rather with what the parties should have been aware of and expected when they made the agreement. In such instances, the courts use the reasonable person test. Instead of declaring the contract void because one of the parties has made a mistake about the meaning of a term, the courts will look at the wording to determine what a reasonable person would have understood the term to mean. Only in those rare circumstances in which there is no reasonable interpretation of the agreement, or the positions taken by the two parties are equally reasonable, will the courts declare the contract to be void.[15]

> **Reasonable person test applies when there is a misunderstanding**

Whenever there is a dispute involving the meaning of a specific term, the courts have a choice of applying the literal meaning of the term or adopting a more liberal approach by trying to determine the parties' intent. Usually, the courts will apply the literal meaning of the wording chosen by the parties if there is no ambiguity. If the term is ambiguous, the court will look at what was behind the agreement and apply the most reasonable meaning of the term to the contract.

> **Courts apply literal meaning to specific wording**
>
> **Ambiguous wording interpreted liberally**

Determining the literal meaning of the words is not as simple as it might first appear. Even dictionaries often have several different meanings for particular words. Determining the intention of the parties may also be difficult because of the conflicting positions taken by the parties to the dispute. The court will often look at how the terms are normally used in the particular industry involved. The

---

14. For a case where the defence of *non est factum* failed, see *McCoy Brothers Group v. Wilson* (1993), 12 Alta. L.R. (3d) 32. For a case where the defence succeeded, see *Bank of Montreal v. Barath*, [2000] A.J. No. 352.

15. *Raffles v. Wichelhaus*, *supra* note 6; *British Columbia (Minister of Transportation and Highways) v. Reon Management Services Inc.*, *supra* note 7.

court will also look at past dealings between the parties as well as their dealings at the time the contract was formed to determine what they intended by the words they used. The key to the court's approach to such ambiguous terms in an agreement is to choose the most reasonable interpretation. Another rule courts use in these situations is the **parol evidence rule**. Where the terms used in an agreement are clear and unambiguous, the courts will not allow other outside evidence to be introduced to show a different meaning was intended: "What you see is what you get." If you state in your agreement that the contract is for the sale of a "2008 Honda Civic automobile," you cannot later try to introduce evidence that a Honda motorcycle was intended. Of course, if the contract only referred to a "2008 Honda," this term is ambiguous, and evidence then could be introduced to show that a car or a motorbike was intended.

Several exceptions to the parol evidence rule have developed over the years. The courts will override the parol evidence rule when the evidence to be introduced is of a *fraud* or some other problem associated with the formation of the contract, such as *duress or undue influence* (see below). Other exceptions include evidence of a *condition precedent* (a condition that has to be met before the obligations set out in the contract are in force); evidence of a **collateral contract** (a separate contractual obligation that can stand alone, independent of the written one); evidence of a *subsequent agreement* entered into by the parties after the written one; or the *absence of an intention* that all of the contract would be embodied in the written document. When the evidence contradicting the terms of the agreement falls into one of these categories, the court can be persuaded to hear it, despite the parol evidence rule.

Courts will not permit outside evidence to contradict clear wording

Exceptions to the parol evidence rule

Courts will imply terms, where appropriate

CASE SUMMARY 8.8

Judgment Set Aside Due to Incorrect Use of Parol Evidence: *Gainers Inc. v. Pocklington Financial Corporation*[16]

While Peter Pocklington controlled Gainers, a meat-packing company, it had numerous financial dealings and agreements with some of his other companies. Gainers later defaulted on its loans and the government effectively became the owner. Gainers then sued several of its related companies for unpaid debts and for unjust enrichment.

The trial Judge admitted and made repeated use of large amounts of parol evidence about the understanding, intent, and knowledge of Pocklington and his lawyer at various steps in the drama. He found additional agreements created by conduct, and even used the evidence to redefine a number of the terms in the written contracts.

The written contracts were long and detailed, obviously drafted by lawyers. Both sides had legal advice. The Court of Appeal could not find ambiguity or significant lack of clarity in the relevant parts of the written agreements. Yet the trial Judge referred to parol evidence not just to clarify ambiguities, but even to flatly contradict some of the express terms of the contract.

The Court of Appeal outlined its position on use of parol evidence thus: "When the deal is complete in the written contracts, and not subject to an escrow, other evidence

---

16. [2000] A.J. No. 626 (C.A.).

(parol evidence) is inadmissible to vary or contradict a clear written contract" . . . "Even earlier promises or representations, otherwise having legal effects, may be wiped out by suitable contractual clauses . . . There is such a "whole contract" clause here. Such a clause may also bar side oral contracts". . . . "Similarly, the parties may validly contract, as they did here, that oral modifications of the contract will be ineffective, and that amendments must be written." . . . "The power to imply terms is to be used cautiously, and no implied term can be inconsistent with or contrary to the express terms of the contract" . . . "Nor can the court find a collateral parol contract inconsistent with the express written contract." . . . "Collateral contracts are viewed suspiciously and must be proved strictly, along with clear intent to contract." . . . "The intent of the parties is to be determined from the words which they put in their written contract; their subjective intent is irrelevant . . . . Subjective intent cannot even be used to interpret the written words, if they are clear."

The Court of Appeal thus concluded: "It is apparent that an incorrect use of parol evidence and a misconception of fundamental company law principles underlie almost all of the trial judgment in this suit. The whole approach at trial was misconceived, and the judgment cannot stand."

SMALL BUSINESS PERSPECTIVE

The *Pocklington* judgment illustrates that admission of and reliance upon parol evidence is to be severely restricted. All the more reason to read and fully understand any written contract before signing it!

The courts are willing to imply terms into an agreement when necessary. It does not occur to most contracting parties to provide terms in their agreement for every possible eventuality, and the courts are willing to supply these missing terms. Where the parties agree to the purchase of a car, for example, they might not specify the time of delivery or when the price is to be paid. The courts will imply what is reasonable in the circumstances, likely that delivery must take place within a reasonable time determined by the nature of the goods, and that the price is to be paid upon delivery. What is reasonable will often be determined by looking at past dealings between the parties or the normal practices and traditions found within that specific industry or trade. Some terms may be implied automatically by statute. The *Sale of Goods Act* has set down, in rule form, the terms that are implied in a contract for the sale of goods when the parties have not addressed them. As well, some consumer protection legislation imposes terms in contracts whether or not the parties have agreed to them. (See Chapter 15.) The courts have also been known to impose contract terms on the parties and modify obligations, using the principle of fairness[17] and unconscionability discussed below.

Statutes may imply terms into contract

[17.] *Cooper v. Phibbs* (1867), L.R. 2 H.L. 149 (H.L.).

REDUCING RISK 8.1

The interpretation of contracts often leads to confrontation; businesspeople would be wise to review their practices. A deal made on a handshake involves a lot of trust, but this examination of mistake and misrepresentation shows the danger of failing to review contracts carefully. Even the most sincere businessperson can forget just what she has agreed to, or two parties may recall the terms quite differently even when they had the same understanding of the terms of the agreement in the first place. And that does not even consider the instances of wilful blindness and convenient memory loss. Putting an agreement into some permanent form, such as writing, is only the first step. Great care should be taken to ensure that the words used are clear and unambiguous so that there can be no question later of what has been agreed upon. This type of approach will usually contribute to the good will between businesspeople rather than threaten it. Conflict is reduced and confidence increased on the basis of good business practices.

CASE SUMMARY 8.9

Terms Are Sometimes Implied into Contracts: *Dansway International Transport Ltd. v. Lesway and Sons Inc.*[18]

Following the theft of one of its 53-foot trailers, the plaintiff agreed to buy two trailers from the defendant for $100 000. A deposit was paid. No time for payment or delivery was stipulated. The plaintiff contacted the defendant 10 days later, requesting an extension, advising that it was still waiting for insurance proceeds to close the deal. One month later the plaintiff called the defendant to arrange delivery and was told by the defendant that the deal was off.

Since time was not expressed to be of the essence, and since time of payment and delivery were not stipulated, the Court had to determine what would be a reasonable time for payment. One month was found to be reasonable, but the plaintiff was in breach through effluence of time. Nonetheless, where a seller believes the buyer is not taking delivery within a reasonable period of time, the seller must give *notice* requiring the buyer to take delivery, before the contract can be treated as terminated. The defendant failed to give such notice, so the plaintiff's action succeeded. Damages were restricted, however, to loss of profit for one month, that being the time required to buy alternative trailers.

SMALL BUSINESS PERSPECTIVE

This case illustrates that the courts will imply certain terms if the parties fail to do so themselves. Rather than face future clashes with customers, businesses are well advised to anticipate problems and design contracts that deal with contentious issues up front.

---

mybuslawlab

www.pearsoned.ca/mybuslawlab

MISREPRESENTATION

During pre-contract negotiations, people often say things that are designed to persuade the other party to make the deal but that never become part of the contract. When these statements are false, misleading the other party and inducing it to enter into the contract, an actionable misrepresentation has taken place.

---

18. [2001] O.J. No. 4594 (S.C.J.).

Misrepresentation is a false statement of fact that persuades someone to enter into a contract. The false statement can be made fraudulently, when the person making the statement knew it was false; negligently, when the person should have known the statement was false; or completely innocently, when the misrepresentation is made without fault.

Misrepresentation is a misleading statement that induces a contract

---

CASE SUMMARY 8.10

Evidence of Fraud Opens Door to Extrinsic Evidence: *Metropolitan Stores of Canada Ltd. v. Nova Construction Co.*[19]

Nova, upon taking over ownership of the Antigonish Mall, tried to evict Metropolitan, resulting in litigation between the two parties. In the process of attempting to reach a settlement, a new lease was negotiated for a 20-year term. The lease contained a non-competition clause, such that no stores in competition with Metropolitan would be allowed to be located in the mall. However, the non-competition clause would not apply if there was any expansion to the existing shopping centre.

When questioned about this exception (or exemption clause) the representative of Nova explained that the only expansion that would take place would be within the present boundaries of the mall and that another clause in the agreement protected Metropolitan from competition within those boundaries. The representative knew that this was false. Seven years later, Nova purchased surrounding property, expanded into that area, and leased property to another department store. It claimed that the exemption clause permitted this.

In the original lease agreement between Metropolitan and Nova, the area of the present mall was specifically covered by the non-competition clause. So when Metropolitan was told that any expansion was going to take place within the present boundaries of the mall, it did not worry about a competing department store moving in. In effect, Metropolitan was tricked into signing a lease that did not protect it the way it thought it would.

The Court found that a fraudulent misrepresentation had taken place, which induced Metropolitan to enter into the contract. Although the parol evidence rule restricts consideration of any outside extrinsic evidence that conflicts with the plain meaning and unambiguous wording of the contract, there are several exceptions. An exception arises if there is evidence of fraud inducing the parties to enter into the contract. Such fraud was found in these circumstances.

This case is unusual because the normal remedies for misrepresentation are rescission or, when fraud is present, rescission and/or damages. In this case, however, Metropolitan asked for rectification of the contract, that is, for the contract to be rewritten to include the terms as it understood it, making the expansion with the inclusion of the rival department store a breach of its lease. The trial Judge thought this was going too far, but the Court of Appeal was willing to rectify the agreement; it added the appropriate words to the lease, and declared Nova in breach of that lease. Rectification, the rewriting of a contract on behalf of one of the parties at the expense of the other, is a drastic remedy, but because of the fraud, it was deemed appropriate.

[19.] (1988), 50 D.L.R. (4th) 508 (N.S.C.A.).

Allegation of Fact

The statement that forms the basis of the misrepresentation must be an allegation of fact. Only statements made about the current state of things that prove to be incorrect can be considered misrepresentation. "This car has a new motor" is a statement of fact. "I will have the car inspected next year" is not a statement of fact, but a promise to do something in the future. A promise to do something in the future will qualify as a misrepresentation only when it can be clearly shown that the person making the promise had no intention of honouring that promise at the time it was made. Such promises of future conduct have to be enforced under general contract law, and the buyer should take care to ensure that this commitment is included as a term of the contract. Where the misleading statement being complained of was an expression of opinion rather than fact, it too is not actionable, unless the person making the statement was an expert. When a person declares that the car he is selling is a "good car" or a "good deal" he is entitled to have that opinion, and the statement is not actionable if the car later breaks down. But if a mechanic makes the same statement, and it proves false, it can be actionable as misrepresentation because he is an expert.

Misrepresentation must be fact, not opinion or promise

Opinion by expert may be misrepresentation

CASE SUMMARY 8.11

Representation Made by "Expert" Was Relied Upon: *Whighton v. Integrity Inspections Inc.*[20]

The Whightons made an offer to buy a home in Stony Plain, Alberta, and retained the services of an inspector to check the condition of the building. The inspector assured them that the home was in good condition and that the cost of any needed repairs would not exceed $6000. Confident with this information, the purchasers closed the deal and moved in. They then discovered major problems including leaking, corrosion of the sewage pump, water damage, and deterioration of cedar siding and shingles. They sought damages in excess of $100 000. The inspector pointed to an exculpatory clause in the contract, which he claimed limited liability to $10 000.

The Court determined that negligent representations had been made both as to the condition of the building, and beyond that, as to the cost of repairs. This latter representation clearly went beyond the services contracted for. These representations were reasonably relied upon by the purchasers, so in addition to breaching the contract by

---

20. [2007] A.J. No. 330 (Q.B.).

failing to adequately inspect the property, the inspector was also liable in tort law. The exculpatory clause did not apply to limit damages for misrepresentation. Further, the Court found the defendant had fundamentally breached the contract by failing to adequately inspect the property, so again the exculpatory clause could not be relied upon to limit damages. The plaintiffs could only produce proof of cost of repairs for approximately $40 000 so damages for that sum were awarded.

SMALL BUSINESS PERSPECTIVE

Clearly if businesspeople give assurances and make representations knowing that the recipient may be swayed by them, extra care must be invested. Those making the statements better be sure the representations are accurate or are made only after due diligence is exercised.

Silence or Non-Disclosure

For a misrepresentation to take place, there also must be some actual communication of information. Silence or non-disclosure by itself is not usually actionable. There are, however, some special situations where the person contracting is required to disclose certain information. For example, insurance contracts require the parties acquiring insurance to disclose a great deal of personal information that affects the policy. People who apply for life insurance are required to disclose if they have had heart attacks or other medical problems. The sale of new shares involves a similar obligation of disclosure to an investor in a prospectus. If the terms require that the parties disclose all information to each other as a condition of the agreement, the contract can be rescinded if they fail to do so. Professionals also have an obligation to disclose certain information at their disposal that might affect the actions of their clients. These are often referred to as **utmost good faith** contracts. This requirement of good faith is being expanded, and it is now much more common for the courts to find that a misrepresentation has taken place where one party withholds information from the other.

Where a person actively attempts to hide information that would be important to the other contracting party, this also might qualify as misrepresentation. A person anxious to sell a car might be tempted to hide a noisy transmission by using a heavier grade of oil, and such an act might well invite a claim of misrepresentation. It is not necessary that the statement be written or verbal; misrepresentation can occur even if the method of communicating it is a gesture, such as a nod of the head.

Generally, misrepresentation is available as a cause of action only when an actual representation has been made. When individuals mislead themselves, *caveat emptor* applies, and there is no cause for complaint. In *Hoy v. Lozanovski,*[21] the home Mr. Hoy purchased from the Lozanovskis proved to be infested with termites. Hoy sought rescission of contract, alleging misrepresentation, but the Judge determined that since the Lozanovskis did not know of the termites when they sold the house, there was no fraudulent misrepresentation. Also, they had remained silent, so no representation had been made. Finally, since Hoy had had

mybuslawlab
www.pearsoned.ca/mybuslawlab

Silence not misrepresentation, unless there is duty to disclose

Misrepresentation must have misled the victim

---

21. (1987), 43 R.P.R. 296 (Ont. Dist. Ct.).

the house inspected, he had not relied on any representations from the vendors. In effect, Hoy misled himself about the condition of the building. Accordingly, no remedy against the Lozanovskis was available to Hoy.

False Statement

Partial disclosure may be misrepresentation

It is necessary to demonstrate not only that the misleading comment qualifies as an allegation of fact, but also that the statement is incorrect and untrue. Even when a person technically tells the truth but withholds information that would have created an entirely different impression, this can amount to misrepresentation. For example, if a used car salesperson tells a potential purchaser that the transmission of a particular car has just been replaced but fails to say it was replaced with a used transmission, this partial truth can be misrepresentation if it leads the purchaser to believe a new or rebuilt transmission was installed.

Statement Must Be Inducement

A victim of misrepresentation must show that he or she was induced into entering a contract by a false statement. If the victim knew that the statement was false and entered into the agreement anyway, either because he or she did not believe the statement or believed that the statement did not make any difference, the misrepresentation is not actionable. Similarly, if the person thought the statement was true but would have entered into the contract even if he or she had known it was false, there is no remedy. For there to be an actionable misrepresentation, the false statement must affect the outcome of the agreement, and the victim must have been misled into doing something that she otherwise would not have done. In *Hoy v. Lozanovski*, even if the Court had found that the Lozanovskis had made a misleading statement it likely would not have qualified as an actionable misrepresentation because the purchaser did not rely on it. We know this because Hoy was careful to have the house inspected before it was purchased.

CASE SUMMARY 8.12

False Information Induces Purchase: *Yourside Club Consulting Solution Ltd. v. Exfone Exchange Inc.*[22]

The plaintiff company was in the business of selling long-distance telephone services. The defendant company, through its agent Liang, represented it had a product that would allow customers to place long-distance calls over the internet using an ordinary telephone. This system would be cheaper than using land-line phones. Liang assured the plaintiff orally and in writing that the defendant had a product ready for market and had commitments for $10 million from investors. Based on these representations, the plaintiff invested $200 000 in Exfone in return for 5 percent of the company and 500 000 warrants at $2 each.

In fact, the product was not market ready. It was still in a testing phase.

The plaintiff thus sued seeking its money back. Much of the case rested on the credibility of the parties as to the contents of the oral representations, but the written

---

22. [2006] B.C.J. No. 1231 (S.C.).

business plan clearly suggested that the company had a unique product for which it had patents. The Court found that merely having a prototype that works does not mean the product is market ready. Accordingly, based on this material misrepresentation, the plaintiff company was granted rescission of the contract.

SMALL BUSINESS PERSPECTIVE

Especially when launching a new product or service, businesspeople must temper enthusiasm with caution. Care should be taken not to make unsubstantiated claims in the heat of zealous marketing. If one is reluctant to put representations in writing, that in itself should serve as a warning!

As a Term of the Contract

The law of misrepresentation discussed here applies where the misleading statement induced or persuaded the victim to enter into a contract. Special remedies are needed because the misleading statement usually does not become a term of the agreement itself. If the misleading statement complained of has become a term of the agreement, the normal rules of breach of contract apply, providing much broader remedies that are easier to obtain. If Mills agreed to sell Boothe a used Nissan automobile, which in the contract was described as a 2005 Nissan Murano with a rebuilt transmission, Boothe could sue for breach of contract if the vehicle turned out to be a 2003 Murano and the transmission was used, not rebuilt. But if Mills bought a particular property because the vendor Boothe said that the municipal council had voted to build a new access road nearby, rarely would such a provision be inserted as a term of the agreement. Because the statement is an inducement to buy, not a term of the contract, the victim must rely on the rules of misrepresentation to obtain a remedy. The remedies available will depend on whether the statement was made inadvertently, fraudulently, or negligently.

Even so, the courts today are more open to the suggestion that such representations have become terms of the contract. Even statements in advertisements now can be taken to be part of the contract. Many provincial consumer protection statutes contain provisions controlling misleading and deceptive trade practices; several specifically state that representations of salespeople are made part of the contract. Refer to the MyBusLawLab for particulars. The topic of consumer protection legislation will be discussed in Chapter 15.

Innocent Misrepresentation

An **innocent misrepresentation** is a false statement, made honestly and without carelessness, by a person who believed it to be true. Where a heavy-duty equipment supplier sells a truck claiming it can haul five tonnes of gravel but its actual capacity is only three tonnes, this is misrepresentation even where the seller believes what he said was true. If the person making the misrepresentation is in no way at fault, the misrepresentation is innocent, and the remedies are limited. The only recourse available to the victim is to ask for the equitable remedy of rescission. As soon as the victim realizes what has happened, he or she can either choose to ignore the misrepresentation and affirm the contract, or refute the contract and seek rescission.

mybuslawlab
www.pearsoned.ca/mybuslawlab

BC   AB   SK   MB   ON

Breach of contract action may be appropriate if misleading term inserted in contract

Innocent misrepresentation—remedy is rescission

RESCISSION

Property returned along with
monetary benefit minus
expenses

Rescission attempts to return both parties to their original positions; the subject matter of the contract must be returned to the original owner, and any monies paid under the contract must also be returned. The courts will also require the party who is returning the subject matter of the contract to return any benefit derived from the property while it was in his or her possession. Similarly, a person can be compensated for any expenses incurred. Damages are not available as a remedy, because both parties are innocent. Although rescission is an important remedy, because it is equitable, it is quite restricted in its application. Rescission is not available in the following situations:

Rescission not available in
certain circumstances

• if contract affirmed

1.   **Affirmation.** Victims of misrepresentation who have affirmed the contract are bound by the affirmation and cannot later insist on rescission. Thus, where a person uses the proceeds of a contract knowing of the misrepresentation, he has affirmed the contract.

• if restoration impossible

2.   **Impossibility of restoring.** The remedy of rescission is not available if the parties cannot be returned to their original positions because the subject matter of the contract has been destroyed or damaged. Since neither party is at fault with innocent misrepresentation, the court will not impose a burden on either one of them but will simply deny a remedy.

• if it will affect third party

3.   **Third-party involvement.** Rescission will not be granted if it will adversely affect the position of a third party. When the subject matter of the contract has been resold by the purchaser to a third party who has no knowledge of the misrepresentation and otherwise comes to the transaction with "clean hands," the courts will not interfere with that person's possession and title to the goods.

• if plaintiff is not
blameless—does not have
clean hands

4.   **Failure on the part of the victim.** Where the victim comes without clean hands, rescission will not be available. Where the victim has also misled or cheated, rescission will be denied. Where the victim has caused unreasonable delay, rescission will be denied. These principles apply to all equitable remedies, and these will be discussed in the next chapter.

Note, as discussed above, that in those few situations where the misrepresentation causes the victim to make a fundamental mistake about the nature of the contract, the agreement may be void due to failure to reach a consensus. When this happens, there is no contract and the victim can recover money or goods supplied despite the effect on third parties or the presence of affirmation.

Fraudulent Misrepresentation

Rescission and/or damages
for torts for intentional
misrepresentation

If a misrepresentation of fact is intentional and induces another person to enter into a contract, the victim of the fraud can sue for damages under the tort of deceit in addition to or instead of the contractual remedy of rescission. According to the 1889 decision in *Derry v. Peek*, fraud is established when the false statement was made "(1) knowingly, (2) without belief in its truth, or (3) recklessly, careless whether it be true or false."[23] Essentially, it is fraud if it can be demonstrated that the person who made the false statement did not honestly believe it to be true. The person making the statement cannot avoid responsibility by claiming she did not

---

23.   (1889), 14 App. Cas. 337 (H.L.) at 374.

know for sure that what she said was false, or because she did not bother to find out the truth. Fraud exists even if the victim of the misrepresentation could have found out the truth easily, but relied instead on the statement of the defendant.

CASE SUMMARY 8.13

Disguising Used Goods as New: *Kellogg Brown & Root Inc. v. Aerotech Herman Nelson Inc.*[24]

The plaintiff purchased 282 portable heaters from the defendant, Aerotech. Immediately after delivery, it became apparent that the heaters were not new. The plaintiff made some use of the heaters before deciding to discontinue its attempts to service or use them further. It notified Aerotech that the contract was being rescinded and demanded reimbursement. The Court found an obvious intent to mislead the purchaser. Aerotech tried to disguise the used heaters as new by altering hour meters, repainting, cleaning, re-serializing, and changing the manufacturer's plates on the units. The fact that the plaintiff had tried to repair the heaters to make them useable did not operate as a bar to rescission. Victims of fraud do not, as soon as there is an inkling of a misrepresentation, have to make up their minds whether to rescind or not. The plaintiff was found to have repudiated the contract within a reasonable period of time and the cost of the heaters ($1 359 571) and the cost of shipping ($321 905) *plus* punitive damages ($50 000) were awarded.

SMALL BUSINESS PERSPECTIVE

If one reflects upon all the additional costs incurred—the loss of the sale, the cost of shipping, the punitive damages, and the legal costs—it was hardly a sound business decision to mislead the purchaser just to get a better initial price.

When a person innocently makes a false statement and later discovers the mistake, he must inform the other person of the misrepresentation without delay. Failure to do so will turn an innocent misrepresentation into a fraud. If during the process of negotiating the terms of a contract, a person makes a statement that was true but later becomes false because of changing circumstances, she must correct the statement upon finding out the truth.

> **Failure to correct turns innocent misrepresentation into fraud**

Once it has been established that the false statement was intentional and thus fraudulent, the courts can award rescission or damages:

1. **Rescission or avoidance.** The victim of fraudulent misrepresentation retains the right to have the parties to the contract returned to their original positions and to be reimbursed for any out-of-pocket expenses.

> **Rescission**

2. **Damages for deceit.** The victim of fraudulent misrepresentation can seek monetary compensation as well as rescission for any loss incurred as a result of the fraud. The damages are awarded for the tort of deceit. Note that to obtain damages there is no obligation to return property, nor is the court attempting to return both parties to their original positions, as with rescission. Rather, the courts require financial compensation to be paid to the victim by the person at

> **Damages**

---

24. [2004] M.J. No. 181 (C.A.), leave to appeal to S.C.C. refused, [2004] S.C.C.A. No. 344.

fault. A victim of fraud can seek damages even where rescission is not available. The victim does not lose the right to demand monetary compensation by affirming the contract or where the goods have been resold to a third party. The victim of a fraudulent misrepresentation can also seek punitive damages, that is, damages intended to punish the wrongdoer rather than compensate the victim.

The major problem with fraudulent misrepresentation is the need to establish that the person being sued knowingly misled the victim. This is often difficult to do and is not necessary if only rescission is sought.

Negligent Misrepresentation

Damages for negligence may be available in cases of misrepresentation

An important recent development in tort law is the granting of the remedy of damages for negligent misrepresentation (sometimes called negligent misstatement, as discussed in Chapter 5). Today, if it can be shown that the parties should have known what they said was false, even though they honestly believed it was true, the remedies of damages as well as rescission will be available. Even when the negligent statement becomes a term of the contract or arises out of a contractual relationship, the plaintiff may have a choice about whether to sue in contract or sue in tort for negligence. The Supreme Court of Canada made it clear that such "concurrent liability" may exist, subject to limitations that may be included in the contract.[25] Thus, whether the plaintiff can circumvent the protection provided in an exemption clause by suing in tort instead depends on the wording and breadth of the exemption clause.

As stated by Justices La Forest and McLachlin in *BG Checo International Ltd. v. British Columbia Hydro and Power Authority*.[26]

> In our view, the general rule emerging from this Court's decision in *Central Trust Co. v. Rafuse*, [1986] 2 S.C.R. 147, is that where a given wrong *prima facie* supports an action in contract and in tort, the party may sue in either or both, except where the contract indicates that the parties intended to limit or negative the right to sue in tort. This limitation on the general rule of concurrency arises because it is always open to parties to limit or waive the duties which the common law would impose on them for negligence. This principle is of great importance in preserving a sphere of individual liberty and commercial flexibility . . . . So a plaintiff may sue either in contract or in tort, subject to any limit the parties themselves have placed on that right by their contract. The mere fact that the parties have dealt with a matter expressly in their contract does not mean that they intended to exclude the right to sue in tort. It all depends on how they have dealt with it.

---

25. *Central Trust Co. v. Rafuse*, [1986] 2 S.C.R. 147.

26. [1993] S.C.J. No. 1, at para.15.

Damages are available as a remedy where the misrepresentation has become a term of the contract that is breached, where the misrepresentation is fraudulent, and where there is negligence.[27]

Thus, it appears that only when the misrepresentation is truly innocent and without fault is the victim restricted to the remedy of rescission.

DURESS AND UNDUE INFLUENCE

Duress

When people are forced or pressured to enter into contracts against their will by threats of violence or imprisonment, the contract can be challenged on the basis of duress. Today, duress includes not only threats of violence and imprisonment but also threats of criminal prosecution and threats to disclose embarrassing or scandalous information.[28]

In Canada, duress also includes threats to a person's goods or property. If O'Rourke threatened to vandalize Tong's store unless Tong agreed to purchase his vegetables from O'Rourke, this would qualify as duress and Tong would have recourse against O'Rourke. To succeed, it is necessary to show that the threat was the main inducement for entering into the agreement.

Even though the threat of loss of employment and other financial losses can amount to economic duress and be actionable,[29] it is important not to mistake the normal predicaments in which we all find ourselves for improper pressure or duress. If a person has no choice except to use a particular taxi because it is the only one on the street, or has to deal with the only airline or telephone company that services a particular area, these accepted conditions of the marketplace do not amount to duress. Likewise, where a person has to pay a high rate of interest because no one else will loan money at a lower rate, it is not duress. Even the threat of suing when the person doing so has a legitimate right to sue is not duress. Rather, it is the legitimate exercise of the rights of that person.

Note that duress only causes a contract to be voidable, thus a third party's position cannot be jeopardized if the victim of duress seeks a remedy. If someone is forced to sell a gold watch by threat of violence and the watch is then resold to an innocent third party, the watch cannot be retrieved. Because a voidable contract is still a contract, the title has passed on to the third party. Had the watch been stolen from the original owner and then sold to an innocent third party, the original owner would not have given up title to the watch and could, therefore, retrieve it.

> Duress involves threats of violence or imprisonment—contract voidable

> Economic disadvantage not enough

> Voidable contracts cannot affect third parties

[27.] *Beaufort Realties v. Chomedey Aluminum Co.*, [1980] 2 S.C.R. 718.

[28.] See, for example, *Byle v. Byle*, (1990), 65 D.L.R. (4th) 641 (B.C.C.A.), where one son threatened physical harm to a sibling. The parents, fearing that threat, conveyed some land and gave other advantages to the aggressor son. The trial judge declared the transactions void on the basis of duress, but the Court of Appeal reversed this decision, finding the contract to be only voidable. A void contract is no contract and nothing can save it, but a voidable contract could be revived later by affirmation and be binding on the parties.

[29.] For a recent case dealing with economic duress, see *1239745 Ontario Ltd. v. Bank of America Canada*, [2005] O.J. No. 920 (C.A.). The debtors sought to have a restructuring agreement set aside, alleging it was signed under economic duress.

Vendor's Threats Fail to Amount to Duress: *Braut v. Stec*[30]

Braut brought an action seeking to enforce an equity sharing agreement allegedly made with Stec. Stec defended the action arguing that Braut, literally, put a gun to Stec's head to force him to sign the agreement.

Braut offered to sell certain properties to Stec, and offered to arrange the financing. Since Stec was impecunious, they falsely reported his income to lenders. and Braut arranged for further financing to be advanced by his friend. After the transfers were complete, Braut presented the equity sharing agreement to Stec, who refused to sign it. Stec consulted with a lawyer, who also advised Stec not to sign. The agreement imposed significant obligations upon Stec and required that he bear all of the risks related to the property.

Duress under gunpoint is a serious allegation and the trial judge stated the amount of proof needed would approach the criminal standard. Such proof was not established. However, the judge had no doubt that Braut threatened Stec, warning he would expose the fact that Stec had lied on the applications for the mortgages (which Braut had completed). Braut also threatened to have his friend demand repayment of the second mortgages.

Braut, a sophisticated businessperson, evidently sought to dupe Stec, an uneducated immigrant. The equity sharing agreement imposed considerable obligations upon Stec but no obligations upon Braut. Stec was to bear all of the risks related to the property. Stec was required to expend considerable work and labour on the properties and to obtain Braut's prior consent before making expenditures on the property. Stec was required to share any income and ultimate gains from sales of the properties, but if losses ensued, Braut was not required to bear any share. Stec was required to give notice to Braut if he intended to sell any property and Braut had an option of first refusal to buy. Braut was to receive half of the profits from the enterprise. The equity sharing agreement was found to be unconscionable.

Reference was made to *Harry v. Kreutziger* (1978), 9 B.C.L.R. 166 (C.A.), where McIntyre J.A. said: "Where a claim is made that a bargain is unconscionable, it must be shown for success that there was inequality in the position of the parties due to the ignorance, need or distress of the weaker, which would leave him in the power of the stronger, coupled with proof of substantial unfairness in the bargain. When this has been shown a presumption of fraud is raised and the stronger must show, in order to preserve his bargain, that it was fair and reasonable." Since inequality existed yet Braut failed to rebut the presumption of fraud, the Court refused to enforce the equity sharing bargain.

SMALL BUSINESS PERSPECTIVE

A presumption of fraud is difficult to dispel. Where the agreement in question is blatantly unfair or one-sided, courts are drawn to conclude that the deal is unconscionable and thus unenforceable.

---

30. *Braut v. Stec*, [2005] B.C.J. No. 2318 (B.C.C.A.), appeal to S.C.C. dismissed without reasons, [2005] S.C.C.A. No. 559.

Undue Influence

The types of pressure brought to bear upon people are often more subtle than those described by duress. When pressure from a dominant, trusted person makes it impossible to bargain freely, it is regarded as **undue influence**, and the resulting contract is also voidable.

In the case of *Allcard v. Skinner*,[31] a woman entered a religious order and gave it all her property. The court determined that there had been undue influence when the gift was given, even though there was clear evidence that there had been no overt attempt on the part of the religious order to influence this woman. The court would have set the gift aside, except that she had affirmed it after leaving the relationship.

www.pearsoned.ca/mybuslawlab

BC AB SK MB ON

CASE SUMMARY 8.15

Undue Influence Presumed: *Rochdale Credit Union Ltd. v. Barney*[32]

Mr. Barney was a friend and client of John Farlow, a solicitor. He reluctantly guaranteed Farlow's $50 000 loan from Rochdale Credit Union. Farlow died, and the credit union demanded payment from Barney. The Ontario Court of Appeal found undue influence on the part of Farlow, in persuading his client to guarantee the loan. Because Farlow represented both the lender and the guarantor, the credit union was also held responsible for that undue influence. Barney thus did not have to pay the debt.

The relationship of solicitor/client leads to a presumption of undue influence. Unless that presumption is overturned with evidence that the contract was freely entered, the contract may be set aside. It is interesting that the credit union was also affected by that presumption.

SMALL BUSINESS PERSPECTIVE

Depending on the line of work one's business is engaged in, a presumption of undue influence may arise particularly when contracts are made with clients. To preserve the enforceability of such contracts, extra precautions need to be taken, including a requirement that the client seek independent legal advice.

> Undue influence presumed in certain relationships

The court may find undue influence in the following situations:

1. **Presumption based on a special relationship.** In certain categories of relationships the courts will presume the presence of undue influence, and if the presumption is not rebutted the contract will be set aside. Some examples of such relationships are

- professionals such as doctors or lawyers contracting with their patients or clients and the green para is part of the first nl item as well

- parents or guardians contracting with infant children in their care

> Where undue influence must be proven

---

31. (1887), 36 Ch.D. 145 (C.A.).

32. (1984), 14 D.L.R. (4th) 116 (Ont. C.A.); leave to appeal refused (1985), 8 O.A.C. 320 (S.C.C.).

- adult children contracting with mentally impaired parents
- trustees contracting with beneficiaries
- religious advisers contracting with parishioners (as in *Allcard v. Skinner*, discussed above).

Note that in contracts between parents and adult children and between spouses, undue influence is not automatically presumed but may be established upon consideration of special circumstances.

Undue pressure from circumstances

2. **Presumption based on unique circumstances.** If the relationship involved does not fall into one of the protected classes listed above, there still can be a presumption of undue influence on the basis of unique circumstances. The courts then attempt to determine whether one person was in a position to dominate the will of another, in which case the court may still presume undue influence where it is just and reasonable to do so. A husband or a wife signing a guarantee for a spouse's indebtedness might constitute such a situation. If the court makes that presumption, it falls on the party trying to enforce the contract to show that there was no domination or unfair advantage taken of the other party. In *Bank of Montreal v. Duguid*,[33] for example, the issue was whether an automatic presumption of undue influence arises when one spouse guarantees a loan for the other. Although the bank was concerned about the wisdom of the investment, it did not send Mrs. Duguid to get independent legal advice. The Court held that a presumption might arise in a marriage where one partner is unaware of and not involved in financial decisions. In this case, however, the wife was a sophisticated real estate agent who knew what she was doing, and so no such presumption of undue influence evolved. Evidently, for the presumption to arise, there has to be more than just a close relationship; the guarantor has to be vulnerable and the bank has to know of that vulnerability.

3. **Undue influence determined from facts.** In the absence of a relationship that gives rise to the presumption, it is still possible for a victim to produce actual evidence to satisfy the court that undue influence was, in fact, exerted and that there was coercion. This can be difficult to prove, since the victim must show that a relationship of trust developed and that this trust was abused. When it can be shown that the person trying to enforce the contract took advantage of the fact that he or she was being relied on for advice, the courts may find that there was undue influence.

Even when undue influence is presumed, the contract will be binding if the person trying to enforce the contract can show that the undue influence was overcome and that the victim either affirmed the contract, which was the situation in the *Allcard* case, or did nothing to rescind it after escaping the relationship. The courts may also refuse a remedy if the person trying to escape the contract is not altogether innocent of wrongdoing.

Of course, if the party accused of undue influence can convince the court that in fact there was no such influence, any presumption is rebutted and the contract is binding. It is advisable, therefore, for contracting parties who are concerned about this problem to ensure that the other party secure independent legal

---

33. (2000), 185 D.L.R. (4th) 458 (Ont. C.A.).

advice before entering into an agreement. This is especially true for professionals who are contracting with clients for matters outside that professional relationship. When it can be demonstrated that the potential victim followed independent legal advice, it is very likely that the courts will enforce the agreement. It must be stressed that the terms of the agreement must be reasonable in such circumstances. The courts will resist enforcing a contract that conveys great advantage to one of the parties, whether or not independent legal advice has been taken.

Independent legal advice desirable, but contract must be fair

mybuslawlab
www.pearsoned.ca/mybuslawlab

BC   AB   SK   MB   ON

Unconscionable Transactions

The concept of **unconscionable transactions** has received a greater acceptance by the courts in recent years. This is an equitable doctrine that permits the court to set aside a contract in which one party has been taken advantage of because of such factors as desperation caused by poverty and intellectual impairment that falls short of incapacity. To escape from such a contract, it must be shown that the bargaining positions of the parties were unequal, that one party dominated and took advantage of the other, and that the consideration involved was grossly unfair.

CASE SUMMARY 8.16

Insurance Settlements Set Aside When Unconscionable: *Woods v. Hubley;*[34] *Gindis v. Brisbourne*[35]

Woods suffered back and neck pain resulting from a car accident caused by the negligent driving of Hubley. A week before her spinal surgery, the insurance adjuster contacted her by telephone offering her a $3500 settlement. "Take it or leave it." She agreed, signed a release, and was paid the $3500. Unfortunately, even after the operation, her condition got worse and she brought an application to the court to have the release set aside. This was done, and she was awarded damages of more than $500 000, but the amount was reduced to $150 000 on appeal.

Woods had been taken advantage of and the original settlement was set aside on the basis of unconscionability. The insurance adjuster had deceived and misled her and "effectively dissuaded her from seeking the services of a lawyer, thereby taking advantage of her ignorance and her need." A transaction can be set aside as unconscionable where the evidence shows that (1) there is an inequality in the bargaining positions of the parties arising out of ignorance, need, or distress of the weaker party; (2) the stronger party has consciously used the position of power to achieve an advantage; and (3) the agreement reached is substantially unfair to the weaker party. The presence of these elements in this case warranted the setting aside of the settlement agreement.

Contrast the *Woods* decision with that in *Gindis v. Brisbourne*, which also involved settlement of a personal injury claim. Brisbourne's insurer offered Gindis $25 000 for a release of his claim and Gindis accepted. Initially, he succeeded in having the settlement set aside and damages were assessed at $249 189. But on appeal, the Court determined that the release was not obtained in an unconscionable manner—especially in light of the

---

34. (1995), 130 D.L.R. (4th) 119 (C.A.); leave to appeal refused (1996), 136 D.L.R. (4th) vii (note) (S.C.C.).

35. (2000), 72 B.C.L.R. (3d) 19 (C.A.).

fact that the insurer had a duty to the insured to ensure that the settlement was not overly generous or extreme. If a contract is reasonable in light of all the risks and contingencies, it is not unconscionable.

DISCUSSION QUESTIONS

When comparing the above two decisions, one differentiating factor was the deception employed by the insurance agent in the *Woods* case. In light of the dim view the Court took of such behaviour, how should businesses train their employees to conduct themselves? Will one-sided bargains be upheld to favour those who act unethically?

Simple economic advantage does not, in itself, qualify a transaction as unconscionable. If a person having limited assets cannot get a loan from anyone else and must pay 20 percent interest, that alone will not make the contract unconscionable. There must be evidence that the debtor was taken advantage of because of some problem, such as lack of sophistication, age, or desperation, and then it must be shown that the resulting deal was not reasonable. If the 20 percent interest charged was reasonable given the risk, the contract is not unconscionable.

Both common law and statute

There is some overlap in the principles of unconscionable transactions and undue influence. Although legislation has been passed in most common law provinces prohibiting unconscionable transactions,[36] in most instances the statutory provisions are limited to loan transactions.[37] The recent acceptance of this equitable doctrine makes the defence of unconscionability available even when the contracts in question do not involve the loan of money. Of course, as with other equitable remedies, the court will not grant a remedy based on undue influence or unconscionability where a third party is negatively affected or where the victim also has unclean hands.

CASE SUMMARY 8.17

When Is Legal Advice Independent? *Bertolo v. Bank of Montreal*[38]

When Mr. Bertolo borrowed money from the Bank of Montreal to open a restaurant, he needed his mother to mortgage her home as added security. The mother was not fluent in English and didn't really understand what was going on other than that she was helping her son, so the bank sent her to obtain independent legal advice. The bank referred her to the bank's lawyer, who was also Mr. Bertolo's lawyer, and he had his partner advise her of her legal position. There was no actual evidence of just what advice she did

---

36. See, for example, the *Unconscionable Transactions Act*, R.S.A. 2000, c. U-2.

37. See B.C.'s new *Business Practices and Consumer Protection Act*, S.B.C. 2004, c. 2, particularly Part 2 (Unfair Practices) and Ontario's new *Consumer Protection Act, 2002*, S.O. 2002, c. 30 (in force 30 July 2005), especially Part III (Unfair Practices).

38. (1986), 33 D.L.R. (4th) 610 (Ont. C.A.).

receive, but before leaving, the bank's lawyer assured her that she should not worry and that all would be fine. The bank manager later gave her similar assurances.

The Court held that both the lawyer for the bank and his partner were in a conflict of interest position and as a result the advice given was not independent. They should have known better. The manager knew the bank had to provide Bertolo's mother with independent legal advice, and its failure to do so caused the mortgage to be set aside on the basis of being unconscionable. This was a failure on the part of the lawyers as well as the bank manager.

DISCUSSION QUESTIONS

When dealing with vulnerable people, what precautions should thus be taken to ensure that there is no undue influence? If the courts determine that the vulnerable party has been taken advantage of, what is the likely consequence?

REDUCING RISK 8.2

Businesspeople—especially professionals in service industries, such as lawyers, bankers, and accountants—should be careful when dealing with their clients to avoid situations where an accusation of undue influence or unconscionability can arise. Business arrangements outside of those related to the profession should be avoided, and even those related to the profession should be guarded so that conflicts of interest do not arise. When in doubt, the transaction should be avoided. Insisting that the client obtain independent legal advice is another option. If the deal goes well, chances are no one will complain; but if a loss occurs, the client may have grounds to seek compensation from the professional to cover those losses.

PRIVITY OF CONTRACT AND ASSIGNMENT

Privity

When two parties enter into a contract, they create a world of law unto themselves. Contracting is a bargaining process, and only those participating in the bargain can be affected by it (see Figure 8.1). It is a fundamental principle of contract law that the parties to a contract do not have the power to impose benefits or obligations on third parties or outsiders who are not parties to the contract. The contracting parties have created a private agreement, and outsiders to it can neither enforce it nor be bound to perform its terms. This principle is called **privity of contract**.

Contract binds only parties to it

The case of *Donoghue v. Stevenson*[39] referred to in Case Summary 5.2 illustrates the application of the privity principle. In that case, a woman bought her friend a bottle of ginger beer, which contained a decomposed snail. The friend, who consumed the contaminated drink, could not sue the owner of the café for breach of contract because she was not the person who bought it. There was no contract between them. Under normal circumstances, merchants can be sued by the purchaser for breach of contract for selling faulty products, even though they are

---

39. [1932] A.C. 562 (H.L.).

Figure 8.1

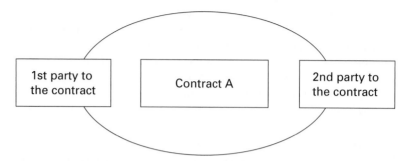

Only the parties to the contract can enforce it, even if outsiders are to benefit from it.

unaware of the problem. But if there is no contract between the merchant and the individual harmed, the victim can normally sue only the manufacturer in tort.

EXCEPTIONS

There are several exceptions and apparent exceptions to the operation of the privity rule. First, it must be emphasized that while a third party designated to receive a benefit cannot enforce the contract, the original parties still have the right to insist on performance. Thus, if Currah, who operates a landscaping company, contracts with Bermark to mow Kicia's lawn, Kicia cannot enforce the agreement but Bermark certainly can. The court may provide either damages or money compensation calculated on the basis of what it would cost to have somebody else mow the lawn.

Original party to contract can enforce it where benefit to be bestowed on outsider

Where land is involved, the rights of the parties are said to run with the land. If a person leases a suite in a house and the owner sells the house, the new owner must honour the lease, even though the lessee was not a party to the contract of sale.

Where interest in land involved, rights run with the land

When an agent acts on behalf of a principal in contracting with a third party, the actions of that agent are binding on the principal. When a clerk in a store sells a magazine to a customer, the storeowner is bound. This may seem inconsistent with privity, but in fact the contract is between the storeowner and the customer; the clerk is merely acting as a go-between. Agency will be discussed in detail in Chapter 11.

Agents create contract between principal and third party

The concept of the **trust** is a little more complicated. This involves one person's transferring her property to a second person who in turn is obligated to use it to the benefit of a third. This is often done in estate planning, the beneficiaries being the family of the person creating the trust. For this to work, the third-party beneficiary must be able to enforce the contract between the original parties. Since the person creating the trust is often dead and unable to enforce the original contract, it would be an affront to allow the trustee to ignore the obligations set out in the agreement and take the benefits for himself. The Courts of Chancery developed the equitable principle of the trust to overcome this problem, and the beneficiary now can enforce the terms of the original trust agreement even though he is not a party to it.

Trust allows a third party to benefit from the property of another

Beneficiary can enforce trust agreement against trustee

Insurance is handled in a similar fashion, with the beneficiary of an insurance contract having the power to enforce it after the death of the insured. Sometimes, when a contract bestows a benefit on a third party, the courts will infer a trust, even though parties did not specifically create one. This is called a **constructive trust** and provides an important method for the third party to obtain the benefit promised.

Beneficiary can enforce insurance contract

Finally, when the parties to a contract agree to substitute someone new for one of the original parties, there is also no problem with privity so long as all three parties agree to the change. This is called a **novation** (see Figure 8.2). If Jones has a contract to provide janitorial services to a college and he sells his business to Brown, there is no problem with Brown taking over that service contract, provided the college agrees. A new contract has been substituted for the old one, and no privity problem arises since all parties have agreed to the change.

Novation involves new agreement

In fact, there are signs that the doctrine of privity may be breaking down. The Law Reform Commission of Nova Scotia, for example, recommended reform of the law pertaining to privity, particularly as it relates to third party rights in contract.[40] One of its recommendations is that privity be relaxed by statute, to allow third-party beneficiaries to enforce their rights under contracts.

Contracting parties often protect themselves from contract and tort liability by including exemption clauses in contracts that limit that liability. In the case of *London Drugs Ltd. v. Kuehne & Nagel International Ltd.*,[41] Kuehn & Nagel contracted to store a large and valuable transformer for London Drugs. The contract between them limited a "warehouseman's" liability for damage to only $40. Unfortunately, two employees were careless in their handling of the transformer, causing significant damage, and London Drugs sued. However, instead of suing Kuehne & Nagel for breach of contract, it sued the employees in tort for negligence. By doing this London Drugs thought to avoid the protection of the

Figure 8.2

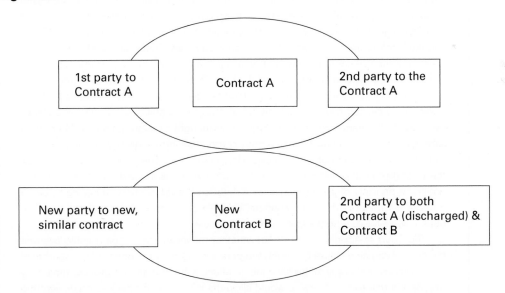

Novation: If the 2nd party agrees to the substitution of the new party, a new contract is formed and Contract A is discharged, replaced by the new Contract B.

---

40. See online: www.lawreform.ns.ca/Downloads/Privity_FIN.pdf.

41. [1992] 3 S.C.R. 299.

exemption clause limiting any claim to $40, the theory being that the employees were not privy to the contract and therefore not protected by it. The Supreme Court, however, found that the protection of the exemption clause extended to the employees, even though they were not party to the contract; the Court created a "principled exception" to the common law doctrine of privity. The rationale underlying this decision is that the employees were third-party beneficiaries under the exemption clause. Obviously, if an employer was exempted from liability for negligence by the exemption clause, employees who would actively be doing the storing of the goods were intended to be included under that exemption as third-party beneficiaries. In essence, the protection from liability given to the warehouseman extended not just to the employer that signed the contract, but to its employees who performed the tasks contemplated by the contract as well. The Court held that in circumstances where the traditional exceptions (such as trust or agency) do not apply, the Court should examine whether the doctrine of privity should be relaxed in the given circumstances. The departure of the Supreme Court from the privity rule in this case indicates a willingness to do so in other circumstances as well.

Employees protected by exemption clauses

CASE SUMMARY 8.18

Exception to Privity Rule Applied: *Tony and Jim's Holdings Ltd. v. Silva*[42]

Norman Silva was the primary shareholder and president of Mamma Mia Pizza (Kingston) Ltd., which operated from a strip mall. The tenancy agreement required that the tenant (Mamma Mia Pizza) pay the premiums for the insurance that was to be purchased by the landlord. The landlord took out insurance on the premises with the Canadian General Insurance Company. Silva caused a fire on the premises when he negligently left a pot of butter on a gas fire while he went next door for a coffee. Considerable damage occurred, and the landlord made a claim to the insurance company. That claim was honoured, but when an insurance company pays out on a claim, it normally takes over the right of the claimant to sue the person who caused the loss. This is called the right of subrogation.

Once the insurance company paid out on the claim, it assumed the right to sue the person who caused the loss, namely Silva. The policy, however, contained a clause whereby the insurance company had given up its right to subrogation: "[A]ll rights of subrogation are hereby waived against any corporation, firm, individual, or other interest with respect to which insurance is provided by this policy." The insurance company took the position that this was a contractual right between its insured and itself and that, under the principle of privity, the clause did not and could not bestow any rights on an outsider (Silva) not party to the contract. Because of privity, it claimed to still have the right to sue Silva despite the non-subrogation clause.

The Court of Appeal had to decide whether the insurance company could override the non-subrogation clause by raising the principle of privity of contract. The Court held that privity did not apply in this situation. In effect, it created an exception to the privity rule, saying that to do otherwise would allow the insurance company to circumvent the provision of the contract. The waiver of the right to subrogate had to be enforced, even to the benefit of the third party (Silva), to give effect to the reasonable expectation of the parties to the insurance contract.

---

42. (1999), 170 D.L.R. (4th) 193 (Ont. C.A.).

A critical case from the Supreme Court of Canada on the doctrine of privity and third-party beneficiaries is *Fraser River Pile & Dredge Ltd. v. Can-Dive Services Ltd.*[43] There the owner of a barge insured it. The policy extended coverage to "charterers" and contained a waiver of subrogation, such that the insurer waived its right to sue charterers. The barge sank while chartered to the respondent and the insurer paid the owner under the policy. But the insurer had the owner waive the "waiver of subrogation clause," and the insurer sued the charterer for the loss of the barge. The issue was whether the charterer could use the "waiver of subrogation" as contained in the insurance policy, as a defence, even though the charterer was not a party to the policy. The Court held in favour of the charterer on the basis of a principled exception to the privity of contract doctrine.

Essentially, where two contracting parties intend to extend the benefit to a third party, who relies on that contractual provision (here the policy stated that coverage was extended to charterers and the waiver of subrogation also applied to charterers) and the activities performed by the third party are the very activities contemplated as coming within the scope of the contract (here the charterer used the barge in stormy weather and it sank), a principled exception to the doctrine of privity applies. The third party will be allowed to raise clauses in the contract, which admittedly it was not a party to, in its defence. The insurer's action against the charterer thus failed.

Another area where the rule of privity of contract may be weakening is in the field of product liability. In *Donoghue v. Stevenson*,[44] the consumer of the ginger beer could not sue the merchant for breach of contract because she was not the one who purchased it. Some provinces have passed legislation allowing the consumer of defective products to sue the seller in contract law, even when the injured person is not the purchaser and not party to the contract. The courts have also extended the right to sue in contract law in product liability cases by finding collateral contracts created by advertising brochures, giving the purchaser a right to seek redress in contract law past the retailer back to the manufacturer. These topics will be discussed in Chapter 15 under "Consumer Protection Legislation."

mybuslawlab

www.pearsoned.ca/mybuslawlab

Assignment

Just as a person buying goods under a contract is then free to resell them, so can a person entitled to receive a benefit under a contract transfer that benefit to a third party (see Figure 8.3). This is called the **assignment** of contractual rights, and the benefit transferred is known as a **chose in action**. While the practice of transferring such rights was originally not permitted because of privity, it is now an essential aspect of doing business. The principle is that a person who has

Contracting parties can assign rights

[43.] [1999] 3 S.C.R. 108.

[44.] *Supra*, footnote 39.

Figure 8.3

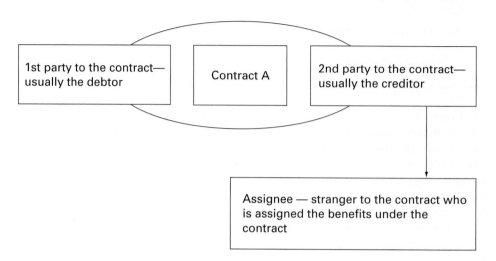

acquired a right or a benefit under a contract has the right to assign that benefit to another. Where Schmidtke does carpentry work for Nehring and is owed money for those services, Schmidtke is free to assign (sell) that claim (or account receivable) to Green. Schmidtke is referred to as the *assignor,* a party to the original contract, and Green as the *assignee,* a stranger to it. It is common for businesses to assign their accounts receivable (money they are owed by their customers) outright to obtain immediate cash or to make a conditional assignment to a creditor to secure a loan.

Only benefits can be assigned

The ability to make such assignments has become a vital component of our commercial world. There are, however, some important qualifications to keep in mind. First, only a benefit can be assigned, not an obligation. In the example above, if Schmidtke has done poor work or failed to do the job, he is still obligated to Nehring, despite the assignment. Schmidtke cannot say that it is no longer his problem, as he has assigned the contract to Green. Schmidtke has assigned only the benefits, not the obligations.

Assignee in no better position than assignor

Of course, if Green tried to collect those benefits (the money owed) in face of the defaulted contract, he would fail. While it is true that the assignment of the benefits of the contract between Schmidtke and his client Nehring was valid, Green can be in no better position to collect that benefit than was Schmidtke, and Schmidtke has no claim since he has defaulted; Schmidtke cannot sell something he doesn't have. The principle is that an assignee is "subject to the equities" between the original parties, meaning that the assignee can be in no better position than was the assignor. Schmidtke transferred only what claim he had against Nehring to Green, and that claim was tainted. If the debtor, then, has a good defence against the assignor, he also has a good defence against the assignee.

CASE SUMMARY 8.19

The Vulnerability of an Assignee: *First City Capital Ltd. v. Petrosar Ltd.*[45]

TDC graphics was to supply specialized computers to Petrosar Limited. For financing purposes, TDC graphics sold the computers to Casselman Financial Underwriters Limited (CFUL), which in turn leased them to Petrosar. An important term of the agreement gave Petrosar the right to terminate the lease at the end of one year and either return the computers or purchase them for "the residual amount left owing." This term was not set out in the lease agreement itself (it was contained in a purchase order and a schedule attached to the lease), but was found by the Court to be an essential part of the lease agreement. When CFUL assigned this lease agreement to First City Capital Ltd. it failed to inform First City of Petrosar's right to terminate at the end of the first year.

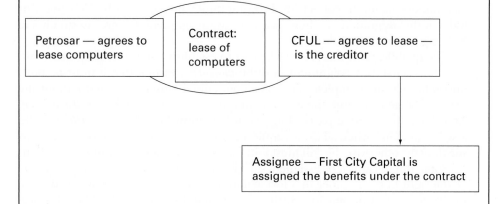

At the end of one year Petrosar opted to purchase the computers, but when a price couldn't be agreed on, Petrosar simply stopped paying and put the computers in storage. First City sued, and the main problem for the Court was to determine whether First City was bound by Petrosar's right to purchase or to terminate. The Court held that, as the assignee, First City could be in no better position than the person who assigned the lease to it. Whether it knew of the provision or not, First City took it "subject to the equities." What First City got was only what CFUL had to give, and that was a lease subject to this right to purchase or terminate. First City's failure to convey the computers to Petrosar for "the residual amount owing" as agreed, entitled Petrosar to stop paying.

SMALL BUSINESS PERSPECTIVE

This case illustrates how an assignee gets only what the assignor has to give. It also shows how careful parties have to be in arranging these kinds of transactions.

[45.] (1987), 42 D.L.R. (4th) 738 (Ont. H.C.)

Although only the benefits can be assigned, that does not mean the original party to the contract always has to be the one to perform. Often, it is understood that the actual work or service involved will be performed by an employee or subcontractor. This is called **vicarious performance**. The point is that the original party to the contract remains responsible for the work no matter who does it. But in many cases, the service must be performed by the person so contracting. If a famous artist agreed to paint a portrait, it is likely that the customer would not be satisfied if the actual painting were subcontracted to another.

Contractual obligations can be performed by others

Because of the restrictions of privity, it was left to the courts of chancery to develop an "equitable" method to enforce assignments. This involved the assignee's bringing an action against the original contracting party through the assignor and is referred to as "joining" the assignor in the action. Joining can be a cumbersome process, and it has since been modified by statute.[46] If the assignment meets certain qualifications, it qualifies as a **statutory assignment** and the assignee can enforce the claim directly without involving the assignor. In the example above, in the past Green would have had to bring an action in Schmidtke's name, to collect funds owing under the contract by Nehring. But today, if the assignment qualifies as a statutory assignment, Green can simply sue Nehring for the money directly.

Qualifications for statutory assignment

The qualifications that have to be met to establish a statutory assignment are as follows: First, the assignment must be *absolute*, meaning that it must be both unconditional and complete. The full amount owed must be assigned without any strings attached. Second, the assignment must be *in writing, signed by the assignor*. And third, the original party obligated to pay must be *notified in writing* of the assignment. Only when all these requirements are met will the assignee be able to sue directly; otherwise, he still must join the assignor in any attempt at collection.

Some things cannot be assigned

Some things cannot be assigned, such as the right to collect support payments or the right to sue another in a tort action. Certain statutes, such as the *Workers' Compensation Act* (in some jurisdictions)[47] prohibit the assignment of benefits provided under the statute. Note, however, that although the right to sue cannot be assigned, there is no such restriction on the assignment of the proceeds from such a lawsuit once awarded.

Debtor must pay first assignee who gives notice of assignment

Sometimes, an assignor may be tempted to assign the same claim to two assignees. This, of course, is fraud, and the victim has the right to seek redress from the assignor. Often, however, that assignor has fled or has no funds. The original debtor against whom the assignment is made is obligated to pay only once, and one of the two assignees will be out of luck. In such circumstances, it is the first assignee to give the debtor notice of the assignment who will collect. The other assignee will be left to seek remedies against the assignor, which may be worthless. It is, therefore, vital in business to take such assignments with care and then to *immediately notify* the debtor. It is only when the debtor makes the mistake of ignoring such notice and paying either the wrong assignee or insisting on paying the original assignor that it may have to pay twice.[48]

The principles discussed so far relate to voluntary assignments. There are some circumstances in which the assignment of rights can take place involuntar-

---

[46.] See, for example, Alberta's *Judicature Act*, R.S.A. 2000, c. J-2, s. 20.

[47.] See, for example, Alberta's *Workers' Compensation Act*, R.S.A. 2000, c. W-15, s. 141, which says that benefits may not be assigned without the approval of the Workers' Compensation Board.

[48.] Rights of an assignee and the consequences of notice are also dealt with in provincial legislation. See, for example, the *Personal Property Security Act*, R.S.A. 2000, c. P-7, s. 41.

ily. For example, rights and obligations are automatically transferred to the administrator or executor of the estate when a person dies. This representative steps into the deceased's shoes and is not restricted by the privity of contract rule, unless the terms of the contract require personal performance by the deceased. The second situation of **involuntary assignment** occurs when a party to a contract goes bankrupt. Under bankruptcy legislation, the bankrupt's assets are transferred to a trustee, called the *receiver*, who will then distribute them to pay the creditors as much as possible. Bankruptcy will be discussed in Chapter 16.

Involuntary assignment in cases of death and bankruptcy

REDUCING RISK 8.3

Businesspeople should never ignore a notice of assignment and continue paying the original party. There is no problem so long as the payment is passed on, but you cannot be sure that this will be done. Also, businesspeople often assume that once they have assigned the debt they no longer have anything to do with the transaction. If a product has been sold and the financing arrangements have been assigned to a finance company, the merchant vendor is still responsible with respect to the performance of the product. If it is defective or dangerous, causing injury or loss, it is the vendor that is responsible, not the finance company. One can assign only the benefits, not one's obligations under such a contract..

Negotiable Instruments

Another exception to the privity of contract rule recognizes the commercial realities of modern business. As commerce developed it became necessary to devise a method to freely exchange and pass on claims for debt that had been incurred in the process of business. When these claims met certain qualifications, they were defined as **negotiable instruments**, and through them unique rights were bestowed on the parties. Cheques, promissory notes, and bills of exchange (commonly called drafts) are examples of negotiable instruments. While the use of cheques as a method of payment has significantly decreased as credit and debit cards have gained popularity, cheques are still an important method of transferring funds in business. Promissory notes retain their popularity where credit is involved because of the unique advantages they bestow.

Negotiable instruments true exceptions to privity

Briefly, a negotiable instrument can be freely passed from one person to another, conveying with it all the rights associated with the original agreement between the parties, and no notice of the transfer is required. This flexibility is completely inconsistent with the doctrine of privity of contract and the law of assignment discussed above. The most significant innovation of negotiable instruments was that better rights or claims than those held by the initial parties could be passed on. As discussed under "Assignment," it is clear that even when it is possible to assign contractual rights, the assignee can be in no better position than was the assignor. Thus, if a defence such as deceit or breach of contract was available against the original party to the contract (the assignor), it was available against the assignee as well. This is not the case with negotiable instruments. When you give a cheque or promissory note to someone (who has deceived or cheated you) once that instrument gets into the hands of an innocent third party who satisfies the qualifications to be a "holder in due course," you can be required to pay despite the existence of the fraud. In other words, if Nehring pays Schmidtke by cheque and then Schmidtke endorses the cheque and delivers it to Carter, Carter is entitled to cash the cheque despite any complaints Nehring might later have with regards to the quality of the work done by Schmidtke.

Negotiable instruments give better rights to holder than is the case with assignment

SUMMARY

Mistake

- Must go to the nature of the agreement or the existence of the subject matter, not just to the effect of the agreement when performed

Types	Remedies
- Both parties making a common error	- If serious, there is no contract
- An error in recording the terms	- Can be corrected by rectification
- A misunderstanding between the parties	- Most reasonable interpretation of the contract is enforced
- A one-sided mistake	- *Caveat emptor* applies unless the mistake is so fundamental as to destroy consensus or there is fraud

Misrepresentation

- A false statement that induces a person to enter a contract

Types	Remedies
- Innocent misrepresentation	- Rescission is the only remedy
- Fraudulent misrepresentation	- Damages (and possibly punitive damages) for the tort of deceit and/or rescission
- Negligence	- Damages and/or rescission

Duress, undue influence, or unconscionability

Types	Remedies
- Duress; contract made involuntarily	- Contract is voidable—rescission
- Undue influence	- Contract is voidable—rescission
- Unconscionable contract	- Court may rescind or modify the contract

Privity of contract

- Only the original parties to the contract are bound. Any benefit going to a third party must be enforced by the original party to the agreement
- The trust is a true exception to the privity rule because the beneficiary can enforce it even though he or she is not a party to the original agreement
- Other exceptions include real estate transactions, contracts of insurance, and various principled exceptions as defined by the courts

Assignment

- Only the benefits, not the obligations, in a contract can be sold (assigned) to a third party, and those benefits are to be enforced through the original contracting party, the assignor
- But when an assignment qualifies as a statutory assignment, the assignee can enforce the assigned rights directly, in its own name

Negotiable instruments

- Negotiable instruments may be enforced by third parties without notification to the original drawer (the party who writes and signed the cheque) of the instrument
- Negotiable instruments sometimes convey better rights than existed between the original parties

QUESTIONS

1. A mistake may result in a contract being declared void or voidable. What difference does it make if a contract is merely voidable?

2. When will a misunderstanding as to the terms of a contract cause that contract to be void?

3. Distinguish among shared mistakes, misunderstandings, and one-sided mistakes.

4. What approach will the courts usually take when the mistake involves disagreement about the meaning of the contract?

5. What must a party to a contract show to obtain rectification of a document?

6. How will the courts respond to ambiguous wording in a contract?

7. Explain what is meant by *caveat emptor*. What is the significance of this principle in relation to a one-sided mistake?

8. Under what circumstances would a person raise a claim of *non est factum*? What restrictions are there on its availability?

9. Explain the parol evidence rule.

10. What happens when a misrepresentation becomes a term of the contract?

11. Explain how fraudulent, negligent, and innocent misrepresentations differ. Identify the remedies that are available for each type of misrepresentation.

12. Under what circumstances can silence or a statement of opinion become misrepresentation?

13. What factors may affect the availability of the remedy of rescission?

14. Describe the relationship between misrepresentation and mistake.

15. Distinguish among duress, undue influence, and unconscionability and give examples of each.

16. What is meant by privity of contract?

17. Explain what is meant by the term *novation*.

18. Explain the relationship of the privity principle to land transactions, agency, trusts, and assignment. With regard to third-party beneficiaries under a contract, what direction does the law appear to be taking?

19. What qualifications must be realized before there can be a statutory assignment?

20. What limitations are placed on the rights and obligations of the assignee when a contract is assigned?

21. What is meant by "the assignee takes subject to the equities"?

22. Can a "holder in due course" obtain better rights than an assignee? Explain.

CASES AND DISCUSSION QUESTIONS

1. *White v. E.B.F. Manufacturing Ltd.*, [2005] N.S.C.A. 167.

This dispute centres mainly upon the method of calculating royalties payable to White on sales of products derived from an invention of his called ElectroBraid. White created a braided polyester rope interwoven with conductive copper wire which, when electrified, could be used to fence animals and keep them from escaping their pens. As holder of the patent, he was to receive a royalty from EBF Manufacturing Limited (EBF), the company that manufactured the braided electrical fencing. That royalty was determined by the "Company's gross revenues." ElectroBraid Fence Limited ("Fence") was incorporated to market and sell EBF's product.

Initially Bryson, White, and White's wife were all shareholders in EBF. These three were also the shareholders in Fence. White granted EBF an irrevocable and exclusive licence to all patents related to the manufacture of "braided electrical fencing." Subsequently, Bryson bought all of the shares held by White and his wife in EBF. White commenced an action against EBF, claiming unpaid royalties. The trial Judge awarded royalties based on the sales of both Fence and EBF. It was this decision to include Fence sales in determining gross revenues that Bryson appealed.

Did the trial Judge err in finding that in calculating the royalty payments owed to White by EBF, the gross revenue of Fence was to be included? If the Court simply enforced the licence agreement as worded, only sales by EBF would be factored into the equation. However, this would allow EBF to sell at a minimal price to Fence, and Fence could then earn revenue on the sale of product to third parties, without paying any royalty on the actual retail price.

What approach should the court take in light of these commercial realities? Should a literal interpretation prevail? Is "the Company's gross revenues" an ambiguous term?

2. *Carranza v. Dhaliwal Ventures Ltd. (c.o.b. G&G Auto Sales)*, [2006] A.J. No. 183.

The purchasers of a vehicle that turned out to be defective brought an action against the dealership where the vehicle was sold. The dealership claimed it wasn't the owner or the vendor of the vehicle in question. The plaintiffs had bought a 1997 Dodge Caravan on the lot of a used car dealership, G & G Auto Sales, a business owned and operated by the defendant, Dhaliwal Ventures Ltd. When Luis Carranza first visited the car lot, he was greeted by Gurverinder Dhaliwal, president of Dhaliwal Ventures Ltd. But a person by the name of Steve Simpkins intervened, saying, "I'll look after this guy." Simpkins appeared to the plaintiff to be one of Dhaliwal Ventures Ltd.'s salespeople. Unfortunately Simpkins was not an employee, agent, or salesperson for Dhaliwal Ventures Ltd. He simply had that defendant's permission to sell cars from the premises. The vehicle sold was actually owned by Simpson's company, Autostar Financing and Leasing Inc. A written contract of purchase and sale was entered into in the form of an "offer to purchase from the above-named dealer," later identified as Autostar Finance and Leasing Inc. Mr. S. Simpkins, described as the "manager" of the dealership, signed the "Dealer Acceptance."

The plaintiffs argue that Dhaliwal Ventures Ltd. misled them into believing that it was the vendor. Based on these facts, will an action against the defendant Dhaliwal Ventures Ltd. succeed? Was a misrepresentation made? How and by whom?

3. *RF Real Estate Inc. v. Rogers Telecom Holdings Inc.* [2008] O.J. No. 3314 (Ont. S.C.J.)(2001), 52 O.R. (3d) 97 (Ont. C.A.).

The plaintiff real estate brokerage firm brought an action seeking $1.6 million as its commission. It submitted that it had completed four of five stages of a commercial lease project that never came to fruition. Had the project been completed, its commission would have equaled $2 million. The defendant submitted that commission was payable only on a completed deal. (Note: Sprint had been sold to the defendant, Rogers Telecom, after the subject agreement had been made). The issue before the court was whether the agreement between the parties was ambiguous, thereby justifying consideration of extrinsic evidence, such as industry norms, by the courts. Rogers argued that real estate commissions were typically payable only once a deal was concluded.

The agreement stipulated: "For purposes of clarification, Sprint may not cancel this agreement arbitrarily. In the event that Sprint terminates RF, Sprint will pay RF a percentage payment based on work completed at the date of termination."

Is the clause ambiguous? Is the termination clause to be given a literal interpretation? Explain how a court would deal with this problem and the likely outcome.

4. *Pettit v. Foster Wheeler Ltd.,* [1950] 2 D.L.R. 42 (Ont. H.C.).

Roderick Ashley Ltd. was supplying materials for Foster Wheeler Ltd. at a project at the University of Alberta in Edmonton. Mr. Pettit had supplied financing worth $14 000 to Roderick Ashley Ltd. Pursuant to that agreement, Pettit took an assignment of all accounts of Roderick Ashley. Notice of this assignment was given to Foster Wheeler Ltd., which was told to make all payments to Mr. Johnston, Pettit's lawyer, who would hold the money in trust for him. Some payments were made, but on 27 December the Bank of Nova Scotia sent a letter to Foster Wheeler Ltd. stating that it had received a general assignment of book debts of Roderick Ashley as collateral security for a debt and that any payments to be made to Roderick Ashley should now be paid to the Bank of Nova Scotia. Accordingly, Foster Wheeler Ltd. immediately paid the $7345 outstanding to the Bank of Nova Scotia instead of paying it to Pettit and Johnston. Pettit and Johnston then sued Foster Wheeler Ltd. for this amount, claiming that it should have been paid to them.

What impact does receipt of a second notice of assignment have? Who should Foster Wheeler have paid? Explain the likely outcome of this case.

5. *Re Royal Bank of Canada and Gill et al.* (1988), 47 D.L.R. (4th) 466 (B.C.C.A.).

The younger Mr. Gill was fluent in English and a sophisticated businessperson. He had worked in a credit union for a number of years and had managed his father's berry farm. To take advantage of a business opportunity, he arranged with the Royal Bank to borrow $87 000. During the negotiations, it became clear that he could get a more favourable rate of interest if his father guaranteed the loan. In fact, the son had done a considerable amount of banking on behalf of his father, who was also a customer of the same bank. The elder Gill could not read, write, or speak English and relied on his son in all his business dealings. The documents were prepared, and the son brought his father to the bank to sign. At no time did he explain to his father that he was signing a personal guarantee, and the evidence is clear that the father had no idea what he was signing other than that it was a document associated with a loan transaction. Gill, Sr., had implicit faith in his son's handling of his business affairs. Gill, Jr., on the other hand, was so excited about the deal that he apparently never explained the nature of the documents to his father. It is clear in this situation that at no time was there any misrepresentation to the father or the son on the part of the bank. When the son defaulted on the loan, the bank turned to the father for payment.

Should Gill, Sr., be held responsible for this debt? What precautions should the bank have taken? Identify the best arguments of the father. What arguments should the bank advance?

6. *MacCosham Inc. v. Deck*, [2005] A.J. No. 1702 (Prov. Ct.).

Deck was employed as a driver by MacCosham, which supplied Deck with a cellular telephone for which Deck was required to accept full responsibility. The telephone was accidentally destroyed. MacCosham claimed the cost of replacement under a signed acknowledgment, which Deck says was obtained under duress on threat of loss of employment. The acknowledgment reads: "I understand that the [cell telephone is] provided to me in confidence and in good working order and that it is my responsibility to care for and ensure that [it is] returned upon my completion of work with MacCosham or whenever requested. Lost, broken or unreturned items will become the sole expense of myself."

MacCosham was concerned that employees "accept responsibility." It thus created the form to ensure that drivers take "due care and caution." Drivers, including Deck, were not expressly threatened with job loss for failure to sign but believed that would be the result. In fact, none of the drivers refused to sign but the court determined that had a driver done so, that driver would have been fired.

Based on these facts, should Deck now be able to have the acknowledgement set aside on the grounds of duress? Was the acknowledgment an unconscionable transaction that could be set aside on that basis? Or was the agreement reasonable and thus enforceable?

7. *Kassian v. Hill* (2002), 305 A.R. 148 (Q.B.).

Mrs. Kassian was injured in an automobile accident, and two days later the insurance adjuster persuaded her to sign a waiver of any claim for bodily injury in exchange for a $2000 settlement. She didn't read the document before signing. Note that prior to the accident she was taking Prozac and Ativan as treatment for depression and distress, but she couldn't recall whether she was taking the medication at the time she signed the waiver. Kassian didn't cash the cheque, and upon getting legal advice she brought this action for damages for the accident. The insurance company relied on the waiver, but Kassian asked that the waiver be set aside on the basis of either *non est factum* or unconscionability.

Explain the factors the Court would consider and the likely outcome of the action. How would it affect your answer to know that Kassian had a good education, she had been in a similar accident in the past and had signed a similar waiver, and the judge found that the amount of the settlement was reasonable given her injuries?

The End of the Contractual Relationship

1. Outline how a contract is discharged by performance
2. Describe when a breach of contract will be sufficient to relieve the opposite party from its obligations
3. Explain how a contract may be discharged by agreement
4. Illustrate the consequences flowing from frustration of contract
5. Detail the remedies available for a breach of contract

Contracts can come to an end or be discharged by performance, breach, agreement between the parties to end or modify, or frustration. This chapter examines each of these and ends with a discussion of remedies for breach of contract.

PERFORMANCE

Contractual obligations are discharged and a contract is ended when both parties have satisfactorily completed their obligations under the contract. Often parties perform their obligations simultaneously. The closing of a sale requires the purchaser to tender the price in exchange for the transfer of title. The purchaser hands over the cash and the seller hands over the goods. With most bilateral contracts, however, one party must complete its side before the other is required to perform. In employment contracts, the employee must perform the work before the employer is obliged to pay wages. If the employee fails to report for a shift, the employer has no obligation to pay the hourly wage. It becomes vitally important, then, to determine whether one party has properly performed its side, thereby obligating the other party to perform in turn. The question that must be asked is: Will anything short of exact performance satisfy the requirement?

In fact, there are two situations where something short of exact performance of the contract will still be considered proper performance. Contracts usually consist of major terms (called **conditions**) and minor terms (called **warranties**)—see the section "Conditions and Warranties" below. When the failure to perform is relatively insignificant, or where failure to perform involves only a warranty or a

Where warranty breached, contract still considered performed

minor term, that party is regarded as having performed his side of the agreement. The other party will be required to perform, subject to a claim for compensation for whatever loss was caused by the breach of warranty. Thus, if the new car is delivered, but without the ordered fog lights, a minor term or warranty has been breached; but the purchaser will still be required to take delivery and pay for the car minus the cost of the fog lights.

But some contracts must be performed exactly

On the other hand, where the breach is significant, as when a condition or major term of the contract is breached, the contract is normally considered discharged and the other party is relieved of performing her obligations under it. Still, when the condition is breached in some minor, inconsequential way, the court will usually treat it like a breach of warranty, requiring the other party to perform subject to a claim for the loss caused by the shortfall. This is called **substantial performance**. For example, if a farmer is required to deliver 2000 kilograms of potatoes and delivers only 1987 kilograms, the contract would be considered substantially performed. The farmer would be discharged from further performance and the purchaser would have to pay for the potatoes that were delivered. Of course, exact performance will be required where only exact performance will do. If a contract with a driller requires a producing well and 25 dry holes are drilled, there has been no substantial performance and there is no obligation to pay.

Contract discharged when contract substantially performed

CASE SUMMARY 9.1

Minor Breach Will Not Discharge Contract: *Sail Labrador Ltd. v. Challenger One (The)*[1]

Sail Labrador Ltd. leased a ship from Navimar Corp. Ltd. with an option to purchase, but only if every payment was properly made. The contract required cash, but the parties agreed to payment through a series of post-dated cheques. One cheque was dishonoured because of a bank error, and despite immediate correction, the owner took the position that the option was no longer available because of this failure.

The Supreme Court of Canada decided that the owners had assumed this kind of risk when they agreed to take post-dated cheques. Since the error was inconsequential and immediately corrected, the contract had been substantially performed and the option was still available. This case illustrates not only the nature of an option but also the doctrine of substantial performance. Here the contract was properly performed except for some minor variation and the owners then had to honour their contractual obligations.

SMALL BUSINESS PERSPECTIVE

Does it strike you as fair that a contract that is substantially performed be enforced despite imperfect performance? If the prospect of incomplete performance is troubling, one might build in penalty provisions for incomplete performance, or bonus provisions for early performance, to encourage the opposite party to perform in a timely and exact manner.

[1.] [1999] 1 S.C.R. 265.

Tender

The general rule in common law is that when a person has tendered performance of a contract, it counts as if the contract had been performed. **Tender of performance** means that if a person is ready, willing, and able to perform a contractual obligation and attempts to do so, but the other party refuses to accept it or prevents it, the first party is taken to have completed its obligation and the other party is then required to perform. If it fails to do so then it is in breach, not the party who has tendered performance.

Where goods and services are involved and tender of performance is refused, the tendering party has no further obligation and can sue immediately. If Chan's Renovation Service contracted with Smith to install new gutters on his house, and when Chan shows up to do the job on the specified day he is refused entrance, he has discharged his obligation and can sue. It is no excuse for Smith to claim that the work was not done.

Tender of performance ends obligation

The effect of tendering proper payment of debt is different. It does not extinguish the debt but simply relieves the debtor of the normal obligation to seek out the creditor to make payment. Once proper payment has been tendered and refused, the debtor can just wait for the creditor to collect the debt. Any costs associated with that process will then be borne by the creditor.

Where debt owed and money refused—money still owed, but creditor bears expense

Proper payment of a debt requires legal tender. Cheques, even certified cheques, are acceptable only when the parties have agreed to allow cheques to be used to pay debts. This may be an actual agreement between the parties, or it may be implied from accepted business practice.

If there is any question about the acceptable form of payment, it is advisable to present cash and then only the exact amount in proper legal tender. Under the *Currency Act*[2] creditors can refuse to take more than a limited amount in coins, as set out below.

When being paid in coins of this denomination	No more than this need be taken
$2	$40
$1	$25
10, 25, 50 cents	$10
5 cents	$5
1 cent	25 cents

There is no limit on what qualifies as legal tender when paper money is offered, as long as official Canadian bank notes are used. To avoid problems, especially as we move toward a cashless society, the parties should specify the appropriate method of payment in their agreement.

Payment must be in legal tender

When not specifically addressed in the contract, the tendering of performance must be done at a reasonable time and place.[3] Usually, this means during normal business hours at a person's place of business. Thus, if Aronyk has a contract to deliver five tonnes of ripe grapes to Demers by 10 July, Aronyk would be

Delivery must be as specified or at a reasonable time and place

---

2. R.S.C. 1985, c. C-52.

3. See the *Sale of Goods Act*, R.S.A. 2000, c. S-2, s.29, for example.

expected to make that delivery to Demers's winery rather than to her home or office. The delivery should also take place during the usual working day. Demers would not be obligated to accept delivery at 6:00 p.m. on Saturday, unless such a time was permitted in the contract.

When the parties do specify a time for performance in the contract, the court will have to determine whether it is an important term or not. Where the parties specify (or the court determines) that "time is of the essence," it must be strictly adhered to. Even just a few seconds can make a difference. This was the case in *Smith Bros. & Wilson (B.C.) Ltd. v. British Columbia Hydro and Power Authority*,[4] where a bid was submitted for a job just a few minutes late. Tenders were to be submitted no later than 11:00 a.m. The bid was submitted at 11:01, but could not be considered.

When the contract has been properly performed by both parties, there may still be some continuing obligations. For example, where a product is sold and the purchase price has been paid, title has transferred to the purchaser. Even then, if the product is dangerous or fails to meet the specifications of the agreement, the purchaser can turn back to the seller and seek compensation for the breach. This continuing obligation is imposed, in the case of sales of goods, by legislation. Provincial *Sale of Goods Acts* impose certain implied warranties of fitness and merchantability upon sellers. Breach of these implied warranties can lead to an award of damages. This topic is examined further in Chapter 15.

Some obligations continue after discharge

BREACH

Breach of contract involves the failure of the breaching party to properly perform its contractual obligations. Such a breach can take place in two ways: (1) by improper or incomplete performance of the obligations set out in the agreement, and (2) by refusal to perform.

Breach may involve failure to perform or repudiation

Allegations of improper or incomplete performance are quite common. In the *Olson v. Beaulieu* case,[5] for example, a seamstress performed alterations on a wedding gown so poorly that the bride-to-be was distraught. The hem and bustle were uneven, the sleeves bulged and beads kept falling off. The plaintiff (bride) sued, claiming the cost of the dress and damages for emotional distress. The Court found that the defendant had breached the contract, but limited damages to the cost of having further alterations done in another town, plus travel costs.

CASE SUMMARY 9.2

When Is a Breach Enough to Discharge a Contract? *Baid v. Aliments Rinag Foods Inc.*[6]

It is often difficult to determine just how serious a breach must be to discharge a contract. In the *Baid* case, the father of the groom arranged to have the reception catered. The caterer failed to show and the father hastily arranged to have the reception hall supply food and drinks—at nearly twice the cost. The caterer's truck had broken down and its

---

[4.] (1997), 30 B.C.L.R. (3d) 334 (S.C.).

[5.] [2002] S.J. No. 779 (Prov. Ct.).

[6.] [2003] O.J. No. 2153 (S.C.J.).

cell phone wouldn't work, so the wedding party was not notified. When the caterer finally arrived five hours late, it served food that hadn't been properly warmed. The father sued for breach of contract, claiming the extra costs, plus damages for emotional distress. The caterer counterclaimed, demanding payment of the balance of their unpaid account. Whereas in some situations a five-hour delay in performance would not justify treating the contract as discharged, here the Court determined that the failure to perform was significant. Accordingly, the plaintiff was relieved of paying for the poorly performed task, and the defendant had to pay for the costs that flowed from the breach.

SMALL BUSINESS PERSPECTIVE

Examine the consequences flowing from the above breach. Not only was the defendant caterer unable to get paid, it also had to compensate the plaintiff his costs in hiring a third party to supply the food and drinks. A costly lesson, indeed!

Breach, by refusal to perform, can also lead to discharge of the contract. Refusal to perform will be addressed under the heading "Repudiation," below.

Conditions and Warranties

Conditions are terms essential to the substantial performance of a contract; **warranties** are minor, insignificant terms or terms that are peripheral to the central obligation of the contract. A breach of warranty will not relieve the other party of the obligation to fulfill her side of the agreement. The victim of such a breach of warranty has the right to sue the other party for whatever it costs to overcome the deficiency in performance but still must perform her part of the agreement. However, when a condition or important term is breached, so that the victim of the breach is deprived of the major benefit of the contract, the other party can usually treat his or her obligation as ended and sue for breach of contract. It must be stressed that the breach of condition must be a serious impairment of the performance of the contract. A minor breach of even an important term will not generally allow the victim of the breach to discharge the contract. A common example of this occurs when goods are to be delivered in instalments. A single missed instalment usually will not be enough to discharge the agreement, even though it is the breach of an important term.

Breach of warranty—performance required

Breach of condition—party relieved

Although the breach of a condition normally allows the victim of the breach to treat the contract as discharged, she can elect or choose to treat the contract as still binding. In fact, if the non-breaching party has received some significant benefit under the agreement, she loses the right to discharge and must perform her obligations subject to a claim for compensation for the breach.

It may be tempting for one party to breach a condition of the contract so as to relieve herself of any further obligation to perform. But the breaching party can't choose how the breach will be treated. It takes both parties to end a contract. If Willoughby provided a sculpture of a moose instead of the flying geese agreed to for the foyer of Kubicki's new office building in Regina, this would normally be a breach of a condition, and Kubicki would not have to pay. However, if Kubicki liked the moose sculpture he could keep it, but he would have to pay for it—albeit at a reduced value. Thus, when a breach of condition in a contract has been accepted by the other party, it is treated as a breach of warranty.

What is important to one person might seem unimportant to another. Therefore, terms can be designated as either conditions or warranties in the agreement. Normally, when a person orders a new car, the particular shade of red ordered would be a minor term, and if a car of a slightly different shade were delivered the purchaser would still have to take it. But where the exact shade is important to the purchaser, which might be the case where it is used as a trademark for a business, it can designate the required shade to be a condition and refuse to take the car if a car of any other shade of red is delivered. Similarly, the person supplying goods or services will often designate as a warranty a term that would normally be a condition in the agreement. The B.C. *Sale of Goods Act* states that in transactions governed by the *Act* the court has the option of treating a term as a condition although it is specified as a warranty in the contract.[7]

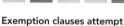

Exemption Clauses

Exemption clauses are an attempt by a party to significantly limit or eliminate its liability under an agreement. The courts will generally enforce exemption clauses because the object of contract law is to carry out whatever the parties have freely bargained to do. But they do so reluctantly, especially where the parties are not in an equal bargaining position. If there is any ambiguity in the terms of the exemption clause, the narrow or restrictive meaning will be used.

If a restaurant has a sign above the cloakroom stating that it is "Not responsible for lost or stolen clothing," by bringing this term to the customer's attention, the restaurant would make it part of the contract for care of the goods, or bailment. If clothes left were damaged by fire or water, the proprietor would not be protected, as that kind of loss was not specified on the sign. Similarly, if a briefcase were stolen, the exemption clause would not apply because it was a briefcase and not "clothing" that was stolen.

Exemption clauses are intricate and involved because the people who draft them try to cover all possible eventualities, knowing that the courts will take a restrictive approach in their interpretation. Such clauses usually form a part of the written document, but they could be included in a sign or notice. In any case, the terms cannot be unilaterally imposed and must be brought to the attention of the customer at the time the contract is made. If the clause is on the back of the ticket or receipt, there must be a reference on the front directing the holder to read the back. Where a sign limiting liability is involved, as at a car park or bus depot, it must be in clear view so that a reasonable person would notice it when entering the premises or undertaking a contractual obligation. Even when the exemption clause is part of a written contract, if it is in any way unique or unusual it must be brought to the attention of the other contracting party. If it is buried in other insignificant writing, or so small it cannot be read, it is doubtful that it will have any legal effect.[8]

When goods or services are sold in consumer transactions, these exemption clauses are usually embodied in terms referred to as "limited warranties." The

---

7. R.S.B.C. 1996, c. 410, s. 15.

8. In *Boutcev v. DHL International Express Ltd.* (2001), 283 A.R. 19 (Q.B.) the defendant was unable to rely on an exclusion (exemption) clause despite the fact that the front of the waybill directed parties' attention to provisions that were printed on the back of the form. The Court found that the exclusion clause was illegible and incomprehensible.

term is misleading and causes confusion, since these are major terms of the contract or conditions, not minor ones. The courts are likely to be much more sympathetic to the plight of a customer in a consumer transaction who has not read the exemption clause than to the more sophisticated parties in a business transaction. It is important to note that under the *Sale of Goods Act* or other consumer protection legislation, the sellers' rights to restrict their obligations in such sales may be extremely limited. Consumer protection and the sale of goods will be discussed in Chapter 15.

Effect of legislation

CASE SUMMARY 9.3

Exemption Clauses Strictly Interpreted: *Meditek Laboratory Services Ltd. v. Purolator Courier Ltd;*[9] *Zhu v. Merrill Lynch HSBC*[10]

A Purolator employee delivered an expensive medical machine meant for Meditek to the wrong address. To make matters worse, the delivery sheets showing where the goods were delivered had been falsified and the goods could not be traced. After a long delay the goods were found, but Meditek had in the meantime obtained a replacement machine. It refused delivery and sued Purolator for damages. Purolator relied on an exemption clause in the contract limiting its liability "whether or not from negligence or gross negligence." But the act of the employee in falsifying the documents had been wilful, not negligent, and the Court found that Purolator was not protected by the clause.

In the *Zhu* case, Zhu used Merrill Lynch's internet trading facility to trade shares from his registered retirement savings account. He cancelled the trade immediately afterwards and shortly thereafter attempted to make the trade a second time. A problem arose because the first cancellation had not been completed, which resulted in a duplicate trade and a short position in Zhu's account. Merrill Lynch then insisted that Zhu buy back the shares—at a higher price. Zhu argued that he relied on the notation on his computer screen that the trade had been cancelled. Merrill Lynch tried to assert a limitation of liability clause, warning that clients had to confirm cancellations, but the Court would not allow that. The disclaimer was deemed unenforceable, for Merrill Lynch could have made it clear that the cancellation was not complete, but it had failed to do so. After all, who would expect one had to telephone to confirm a cancellation, where the entire transaction had been conducted online?

SMALL BUSINESS PERSPECTIVE

In light of the restrictive approach taken by the courts when asked to enforce exemption clauses, a party who wishes to limit its liability should realize that simply inserting an exemption clause may not be enough. Steps should be taken to evidence that the clause was brought to the other party's attention, explained, and assented to.

[9.] (1995), 102 Man.R. (2d) 85 (C.A.), leave to appeal to S.C.C. refused, [1995] S.C.C.A. No. 405.

[10.] [2002] B.C.J. No. 2883 (Prov. Ct.).

Exemption clauses usually ineffective in cases of fundamental breach

Fundamental Breach

Contracting parties often try to limit their liability as much as possible, and sometimes they try to contract out of all obligations and responsibilities. The Supreme Court of Canada, in Hunter Engineering,[11] has made it clear that a properly worded exemption clause can overcome even a **fundamental breach**—particularly where sophisticated businesspeople are involved on both sides. Because of the parties' freedom to contract, the courts may enforce an exemption clause that protects the breaching party even in the face of such a fundamental breach. It must be absolutely clear, however, that the parties understood the exemption clause would cover such a basic failure to perform. In most cases it is unlikely that one party would knowingly exempt the other from such basic obligations, and so the courts usually have no difficulty finding that such an exemption clause, even a carefully worded one, does not apply. The Ontario Court of Appeal has taken the position that it will not enforce exemption clauses where, given a fundamental breach, it would be unconscionable, unfair, or unreasonable to do so.[12]

But in the *Fraser Jewellers* case, where the defendant alarm company was negligent in failing to promptly call the police, thereby allowing the thieves to escape with $50 000 of property, the exemption of liability clause was nonetheless enforced! The Court determined that failing to respond appropriately to the alarm was negligent, but could not be equated to a fundamental breach. More significantly, however, the clause was not unconscionable. The provision was reasonable in the commercial context of this case, the contract was clear and unambiguous, and the clause was evidently drawn to the plaintiff's attention as it was highlighted in bold black letters. Accordingly, company was only liable in the amount of $890.

 REDUCING RISK 9.1

In business dealings, people may assume that the courts will enforce all the clauses found in their contracts. This is not necessarily so, especially if terms are oppressive or unconscionable. Furthermore, the courts may even take an expansive role, by implying obligations that may not be stated. The duty to act in good faith toward the other contracting party is such a commonly implied obligation. Whereas lawyers may be familiar with the manner in which courts interpret and enforce contracts, most laypeople are not. Getting legal advice on the enforceability of one's standard form contracts is evidently a good business practice.

---

11. *Hunter Engineering Co. v. Syncrude Canada Ltd.*, [1989] 1 S.C.R. 426; see also *Beaufort Realties v. Chomedey Aluminum Co. Ltd.*, [1980] 2 S.C.R. 718.

12. *Fraser Jewellers (1982) Ltd. v. Dominion Electric Protection Co.* (1997), 148 D.L.R. (4th) 496 (Ont. C.A.).

CASE SUMMARY 9.4

Franchisor Had a Duty of Good Faith to the Franchisee: *Shelanu Inc. v. Print Three Franchising Corporation*[13]

The franchise agreement in question dealt with the operation of print and copy stores in Toronto. BCD bought one store franchise in 1987 and subsequently, its sole shareholder purchased two further stores through Shelanu Inc. The franchise agreement contained three exclusionary clauses, including one stating that the "written agreement constituted the entire agreement between the parties."

One store was closed in 1991; later a second location was closed. Operations were relocated to the sole remaining store. In 1995, Print Three (the franchisor) and the franchisee orally agreed to cancel the first franchise agreement (made with BCD). Shelanu began reporting its sales as a single franchise, which entitled it to a greater royalty rebate under the franchise agreement than was the case when sales were divided between BCD and Shelanu. Print Three failed to pay the greater royalty rebate, thus Shelanu purported to terminate the franchise agreement and commenced an action against Print Three for damages. Despite the litigation, Shelanu continued to pay royalty remittances—on the basis of one franchise—and continued to use the Print Three name on its store. The issue at trial was whether Print Three had breached its contractual obligations. Shelanu argued that Print Three owed it a duty of good faith, which it breached: (1) by attempting to rescind the agreement; (2) by unilaterally changing the terms of an Air Miles program; (3) by its failures to make royalty payments; and (4) by allowing the establishment of Le Print Express franchise (a new franchise that located in close proximity to Shelanu and competed with it). The trial Judge held that the breach entitled Shelanu to terminate the franchise agreement. Print Three appealed. The Court of Appeal held that the trial Judge was correct in concluding that Print Three had breached a duty of good faith. A duty of good faith may arise out of the nature of the relationship. In *Wallace v. United Grain Growers Ltd.*,[14] the Supreme Court of Canada held that a duty of good faith was found to exist in employment contracts, where there typically is a power imbalance between employer and employee. The situation for franchisees was found to be similar.

A franchisee (such as Shelanu) rarely has bargaining power equal to the franchisor. The franchisee is dependent on the franchisor for information and for training. Courts have thus recognized that a duty of good faith exists at common law in the context of a franchisor–franchisee relationship.

SMALL BUSINESS PERSPECTIVE

Evidently, in light obligations that may be implied or determined by the courts to exist, parties must refrain from acting underhandedly or in bad faith. So when does acting out of self-interest cross the line?

[13.] [2003] O.J. No. 1919, (C.A.).

[14.] [1997] 3 S.C.R. 701.

Repudiation

Repudiation is refusal to perform

Repudiation occurs when one of the parties to a contract indicates to the other "an intimation or an intention to abandon and altogether to refuse performance of the contract."[15] Repudiation that takes place after performance is due is just one more way that a contract can be breached; but if this refusal occurs before performance is due, it is called **anticipatory breach** and is treated somewhat differently.

CASE SUMMARY 9.5

Anticipating a Breach: *Driver v. Hrabok (c.o.b. Creative Glass and Mirror)*[16]

Driver entered into an agreement with the defendant, Hrabok, carrying on business as Creative Glass and Mirror, to have a granite countertop installed in her newly renovated kitchen. Driver selected the granite and paid half of the quoted price. When Hrabok arrived to take measurements, he indicated that several cabinets and appliances were not in the right place. He left without completing the measuring, stating he could not go ahead unless several changes were made. The kitchen had been carefully designed and in Driver's view, Hrabok's suggestion to relocate the cabinetry would impede walkways. Further, the changes would cost over $2000.

Believing Hrabok was unable or unwilling to complete the job unless the kitchen was modified, Driver cancelled the job. She hired another contractor who installed a granite counter on the cabinets without difficulty. Driver sought return of her down payment which Hrabok disputed, claiming he suffered a loss as a result of the cancellation of the contract. The Judge stated the issues thus:

- Is Hrabok responsible to refund any or all of the down payment in the amount of $3806.80?
- Is Hrabok entitled to any set off for materials or work he completed on Driver's behalf?

Cases dating back to the turn of the century have determined that if a party states or implies in advance that he will not be able to perform the very thing which is intended by the contract, the other party will be entitled to end the obligation if the threatened non-performance would have the effect of depriving her of substantially the whole benefit under the contract. If a party has acted in such a way as to lead a reasonable person to the conclusion that he does not intend to fulfill his part of the contract, there has been an anticipatory breach.

Accordingly, Driver was entitled to terminate the contract based on anticipatory breach. Hrabok was ordered to repay the down payment and Hrabok's claim for compensation (for his labour and the costs incurred in reserving the granite) was dismissed.

SMALL BUSINESS PERSPECTIVE

Evidently, if through words or actions a party gives the impression that it will not be able to fulfill its primary obligation under the contract, the other party may terminate the contract and go elsewhere.

---

[15] Comment of Lord Coleridge, C.J. in *Freeth v. Burr* (1874), L.R. 9 C.P. 208 (Crt. C.P.).

[16] [2008] S.J. No. 309 (Prov. Ct.)

In the face of an anticipatory breach, victims have a choice. Victims can choose to immediately treat the contract as breached, refuse to go through with any further performance on their part, and sue. However, the repudiation must relate to an important term of the contract and be a clear refusal to perform, not just a disagreement as to the nature of the contractual obligations. Alternatively, the victim of the repudiation can ignore the breach, demand performance, and continue to perform its side of the agreement. If the repudiating party still fails to perform, the innocent party can then sue for breach of contract, and the party repudiating will be held responsible for damages incurred even after the repudiation.

Once made, the choice is binding. This can have serious consequences, for if the victim chooses to insist on performance and then in turn cannot perform, she is then in breach herself, as happened in the *Vanderwal* case discussed in Case Summary 9.6.

Victim is discharged and can sue if repudiation occurs before due date—or demand performance and wait

Victim is bound by choice

CASE SUMMARY 9.6

Bound by Choice When Faced with Anticipatory Breach: *Vanderwal v. Anderson*[17]

Mrs. Anderson agreed to purchase property from the Vanderwals conditional on the purchaser's selling her house. This condition precedent was subsequently removed. Anderson's obligation to purchase was thus unconditional when she explained to the vendors, through her lawyer, that she didn't understand what she had done and didn't have the money to complete the transaction. She asked that the condition be reinstated and the time extended. The vendors refused, insisting that the contract was binding on her unconditionally. The vendor then sold the property to another purchaser and sued Anderson for breach. The Appeal Court found that the purchaser's claim of insufficient funds and plea for an extension amounted to an anticipatory breach. The vendors had a choice to ignore the breach and insist on performance or treat the contract as discharged. By insisting that the contract was binding unconditionally, they made their choice to reject the repudiation and insist on performance. When they sold the property they abandoned the contract—so they were in breach, and not the purchaser.

SMALL BUSINESS PERSPECTIVE
When the event of anticipatory breach occurs, the innocent party has a right to demand performance or to sue for breach. But if that party demands performance, it had better be prepared to perform its side of the agreement. It would be prudent to seek legal advice before one responds to an apparent breach of contract.

Repudiation can be expressed or implied from the conduct of the parties. Where the goods to be sold are sold to someone else, such repudiation will be implied. Also, repudiation may be implied from the failure to properly perform a term of the agreement. For example, failure to deliver an important instalment

Repudiation may be implied from conduct

17. [1999] O.J. No. 2646 (Div. Ct.).

can lead to repudiation being implied. Missing just one delivery will normally not be serious enough, but if non-delivery is serious enough to cast doubt on the proper performance of the rest of the agreement, repudiation may be implied. Thus, if Chan agreed to deliver 10 loads of gravel to Singh's building site and failed to deliver the first two on the specified days, this might well be considered a repudiation of the contract. Singh could then look for another source. See Table 9.1 for a summary of the results of a failure to perform.

Table 9.1 Result of Failure to Perform

Breach of minor term		Other party must perform but can seek damages	
Repudiation	Major refusal	Victim chooses to perform	Contract binding on both
		Victim chooses to discharge	Contract ends but victim can seek damages
Breach of major term	Major failure		Other party can treat contract as discharged and sue for bre--h
	Minor failure	Substantial performance	Other party must perform but can seek damages

DISCHARGE BY AGREEMENT

Just as the parties to a contract can agree to create contractual obligations, they can also agree to end or modify those obligations. This is referred to as **discharge by agreement**. Whether the intention of the parties is to merely modify the old agreement or to end it and substitute a new one, all the ingredients necessary to form a contract, including consensus and consideration, must be present.

CASE SUMMARY 9.7

Must Be Consideration to Support Change: *Gregorio v. Intrans-Corp.*[18]

Gregorio ordered a truck from Intrans conditional upon financing, which was arranged on 3 July 1984. The only condition was thus removed, creating a binding contract. When the truck was delivered on 2 August, Gregorio was required to sign a one-year limited warranty that excluded all other implied warranties and other liability for consequential damages for failure to perform.

The truck turned out to be a lemon, and when the company couldn't fix it, Gregorio sued to get his money back. It was now 1987. The company claimed to be protected by the limited warranty, but the Court held that this warranty was a modification of the original 12 May agreement. Since Gregorio had received no consideration for the change, he

---

18. (1994), 18 O.R. (3d) 527 (C.A.), additional reasons, [1994] O.J. No. 2834 (C.A.).

was not bound by it. Thus, the statutory protections set out in the *Sale of Goods Act* still applied to the purchase, and Gregorio was entitled to his money back as the truck was defective. (The *Sale of Goods Act* will be discussed in Chapter 15.)

DISCUSSION QUESTIONS

A contract can be modified by agreement, but it is vitally important that all the elements be present. In this case, consideration was missing and Gregorio was not affected by the changes. Would prior legal advice as to the enforceability of the one-year limited warranty have been beneficial to Intrans? How could Intrans have ensured that the limitation would be effective?

If both parties have something left to do under the original contract and the agreement to modify relieves them of their respective obligations, there is valid consideration on both sides to support the change. This is called **bilateral discharge** or mutual release. The problem arises where the discharge or modification is one-sided. Where one party performs its side, yet allows the other out of all or part of its obligations, the discharge, being unilateral, may not be binding because of lack of consideration. The original contract may still be enforceable. When a significant change is introduced that favours only one party, there may also be a problem with consideration. Lack of new consideration was the reason the limited warranty provision, agreed to later, did not bind Gregorio in Case Summary 9.7 discussed above. Of course, the consideration problem can be avoided by putting the agreement under seal. Note, however, that even when the discharge is entirely one-sided, the person being relieved of his obligation may be able to raise the defence of promissory estoppel if sued under the original agreement. In fact, a prime example where the principle of promissory estoppel arises is in the context of such one-sided discharges or modifications of contracts.

Modifications—must have consideration

Where the party benefiting from a modification agrees to do something extra to support the change (or discharge) of the contract, this is called **accord and satisfaction**. The accord refers to the agreement to change (or end) the old contract and the satisfaction is the extra consideration to be supplied by the party benefiting from the change (or discharge). For example, if Groves was renovating her house and paid Grubisich in advance to paint it, there would be a problem with lack of consideration if she simply allowed Grubisich to abandon the contract. But if Grubisich were to agree to do something extra, such as paint Groves' garage instead, there would be a new agreement (an accord) with added consideration (satisfaction), and the new arrangement would be binding.

Accord and satisfaction overcomes consideration problem

Sometimes the old contract is discharged by agreement and a new contract is substituted for it. This is often mistaken for a simple modification of the old contract. Whether a new agreement has been created or the old one modified will be determined by looking at the intention of the parties and what has been changed. The more important the provision changed, the more likely it is that a new agreement has been substituted for the old one. The difference can be important since it may affect whether various terms from the old agreement, such as exemption and penalty clauses, are carried over to the new one. If the original agreement was merely modified (and not discharged and substituted) then the clauses found in the original agreement continue to apply.

When the new agreement involves a new party being substituted for one of the original parties to the agreement, it is called a *novation*. Naturally, both parties

Novation involves new party but all must agree to the change

must agree to the substitution of one party for there to be a consensus. One party cannot unilaterally impose substitution of a party. It may be tempting to cancel a deal when a better one comes along, but if there is a binding contract it must be honoured even when the job has not yet been started.

When a debt is assumed by a new debtor, an issue that can arise is whether the original debtor is still liable if the new debtor fails to repay the indebtedness. When one sells one's home and the new purchaser assumes the mortgage, is the original debtor still indebted to the mortgagee? Or has novation occurred, thereby extinguishing the original debtor's obligation to pay? Madame Justice Wilson explains:

> [T]he burden of establishing novation is not easily met. The courts have established a three part test for determining if novation has occurred. It is set out in *Poulson v. Wuffsohn* (1890), 2 B.C.R. 39 as follows:
>
> 1. The new debtor must assume the complete liability;
> 2. The creditor must accept the new debtor as principal debtor and not merely as guarantor; and
> 3. The creditor must accept the new contract in full satisfaction and substitution for the old contract.[19]

Novation cancels the old contract, substituting it with the new

Must have consensus

It must be emphasized that whether the terms of the agreement or the parties to it are being changed, or the contract is being discharged, there must be complete agreement among all the parties before the new agreement becomes binding.

CASE SUMMARY 9.8

Accord and Satisfaction Can Overcome Significant Defects: *Vandekerkhove v. Litchfield*[20]

Mr. Litchfield borrowed $150 000 from Mr. Vandekerkhove. The agreement required payment of interest and a bonus, which, unknown to them, constituted a criminal rate of interest. Litchfield borrowed a further $145 000, and eventually these two loans plus the unpaid interest were consolidated into one loan for $318 250 at 12.5 percent interest secured by a mortgage on Litchfield's house.

Vandekerkhove subsequently tried to enforce the original bonus but couldn't because it was part of an illegal contract. This prompted the debtor, Litchfield, to bring this action to recover $23 250 of the consolidated loan since it represented the unpaid interest portion of that illegal contract. The trial Judge agreed, but on appeal the Court held that since the parties had renegotiated in good faith not being aware of the illegality, the new agreement was binding on them. There was an exchange of consideration on both sides supporting the modification, and the new interest rate was fair and reasonable.

SMALL BUSINESS PERSPECTIVE

This is an example of the principle of accord and satisfaction with consideration on both sides supporting a renegotiated contract. Especially when loans are being consolidated or the creditor is forgiving part of a loan, the debtor best ensure that some new consideration is being given to the creditor. Otherwise the original contract and original debt may still be payable.

---

19. *National Trust Co. v. Mead*, [1990] 2 S.C.R. 410 at pp. 431–432.

20. (1995), 1 B.C.L.R. (3d) 70 (C.A.), leave to appeal to S.C.C. refused, [1995] S.C.C.A. No. 131.

Contractual Terms

Most contracts, by their nature, will end upon proper performance. However, sometimes they involve an ongoing relationship, with no provision to bring that relationship to an end. In these circumstances, the parties can usually terminate the contract simply by giving the other reasonable notice. Often, the contract will provide for its own termination, usually by specifying a particular period of notice that must be given, and that provision will be binding subject to contrary legislation. In employment relationships and residential tenancy arrangements, for example, such termination provisions must comply with the governing statutes.

    When the contract itself specifies that some event or requirement must be satisfied before the parties are bound by it, this is properly referred to as a **condition precedent** but is more commonly called a *"subject to" clause.* For example, if Nishiama were to agree to buy Fafara's house, subject to the sale of her own house, the contract is conditional on that event. Thus, if Nishiama fails to sell her house, she is not obligated to go through with any agreement for the purchase of Fafara's house. When such a condition precedent is not satisfied, there is no contractual obligation.

    A **condition subsequent** is a term that brings the obligations of the parties to an end upon some event or condition taking place. Whereas conditions precedent determine when the obligations between the parties begin, conditions subsequent determine when they end. For example, if Halford agreed to pay Perron $400 per month for custodial services "until Perron ceases to be a full-time student," this term is a condition subsequent. Halford will be obligated to pay only until Perron finishes school.

    Sometimes the contract anticipates some catastrophic event, such as a riot, invasion, earthquake, or flood that will interfere with the performance of the contract. This is referred to as a *force majeure* **clause**. Such terms might set out the consequences—such as which party will bear the risk of loss—alternatively, they may provide for discharge of the contract. When catastrophic events take place and are not anticipated in the contract, they will likely cause the contract to be discharged by frustration, as discussed below.

    Of course, when such terms are not included in the contract, the parties can always agree to end, modify, or substitute obligations with a new agreement, as discussed above. Contracts can also end by operation of law, as would be the case when one of the parties dies, becomes insane, or is declared bankrupt. Bankruptcy will be discussed in Chapter 16.

> **Contract may provide for its own discharge**

> **Conditions precedent determine when obligations to perform contract begins**

> **Conditions subsequent determine when contractual obligations end**

mybuslawlab
www.pearsoned.ca/mybuslawlab

FRUSTRATION

Sometimes some unexpected event (out of the control of the parties) makes performance of the contract impossible. For example, where a construction firm agrees to repair a bridge but the bridge is destroyed in a storm before the repair work begins, performance has become impossible. In such circumstances, the contract is considered discharged through frustration. **Frustration** occurs when some unforeseen, outside event (out of the control of either party) interferes with the performance of the contract, making the basic object of the agreement unobtainable.

    It is easy to understand frustration when performance of the contract is made impossible, such as when a person agrees to paint a house that is destroyed in a fire before the job can be performed. Difficulties arise because the courts have

> **Frustrating event may end contract**

expanded the principle to also cover situations where the foundation of the contract is destroyed. Performance may still be technically possible, but the whole nature of the relationship has changed, making performance something essentially different from what the parties anticipated.

In the case of *Krell v. Henry*,[21] the parties agreed to the rental of an apartment from which the tenant could view the coronation parade of Edward VII. A small deposit was paid at the time the contract was entered into, but because of the King's sudden illness, the coronation parade was cancelled before the balance was paid. It was still possible to occupy the flat, but to require the tenant to do so with no coronation parade to watch would be something essentially different from what the parties had in mind when they entered into the contract. Although performance of the contract was possible in a literal sense, it was no longer possible to obtain the purpose or object of the contract itself. Thus, the contract was discharged through frustration.

Even injury, causing an employee to be unable to perform her work, can be a frustrating event, as was determined by the Court in the *Demuynck* case.[22] Having benefits such as long term disability coverage is a safeguard that employees should seek to secure, for damages for wrongful dismissal may be denied if one is terminated following an injury that prevents one from performing the job. (Note, however, that human rights legislation may offer some relief as employers have a duty to accommodate disabilities, to some extent.)

CASE SUMMARY 9.9

Contract Is Frustrated Even Though Performance Still Possible: *KBK No. 138 Ventures Ltd. v. Canada Safeway Ltd.*[23]

Canada Safeway entered an agreement to sell property to KBK. At the time, the property was zoned for high-density development. But when the city rezoned the property to a much lower density, this destroyed KBK's plans for redevelopment. KBK demanded the return of the $150 000 deposit paid, claiming frustration. Safeway argued that the essential nature of the contract was for the purchase of the property and that remained intact, but the Court found frustration and ordered the return of the deposit. In this case the whole substance of the contract had been radically altered by the unanticipated intervention of the city in rezoning the property. The change struck at the root of the contract, fundamentally changing its nature and thus frustrating it.

SMALL BUSINESS PERSPECTIVE

If certain factors are crucial to one's participation in a contract (such as the zoning in the above the case) parties can make performance conditional upon those factors being present. These key terms should be brought to the attention of the lawyer drafting the contract.

---

21. [1903] 2 K.B. 740 (C.A.).

22. *Demuynck v. Agentis Information Services Inc.*, [2003] B.C.J. No. 113 (S.C.).

23. (2000), 185 D.L.R. (4th) 650 (B.C.C.A.).

Care should be taken not to confuse frustration with shared mistake, discussed in the preceding chapter. With shared mistake, there is no contract because the subject matter had been destroyed before the contract was entered into. Frustration deals with situations where the problems arise after the formation of the contract. If a ship that is the subject of a contract is destroyed before the contract is made, the parties are making a mistake assuming the ship to still be functioning. But if the ship is destroyed after the contract is made, the contract is discharged through frustration.

Shared mistake not the same as frustration

Frustration commonly arises in the following circumstances:

Circumstances constituting frustration

1. Performance of a contract becomes impossible because the subject matter of the agreement is destroyed or is otherwise unusable. Contracts may be frustrated when a person who has agreed to supply personal services becomes ill or dies, or when the specific article that formed the object of the contract is destroyed before the agreement can be performed.

In the case of *Taylor v. Caldwell*,[24] there was an agreement between the parties to rent out a music hall. The hall burned down six days before the performance was to take place. The Court held that the contract was discharged through frustration.

2. An event that forms the basis of a contract fails to take place. An example is the cancellation of the coronation parade in *Krell v. Henry* cited earlier.

3. Acts of the government interfere with performance. Government policy can interfere with the performance of a contract in several different ways. A contract with someone in another country may become unlawful or impossible to perform because of a declaration of war; contracts involving the manufacture and production of particular drugs or foodstuffs may become illegal by statute. A contract may anticipate the acquisition of a licence or permit that the government does not grant. Note as well that all levels of government have the power to expropriate the property that may form the basis of a contract.

The above is not intended to be a complete list, but most of the frustrating events that do take place fall into one of these three categories.

Circumstances Not Constituting Frustration

Self-induced frustration involves one of the parties causing—or, if it is within his control, failing to prevent—the frustrating event. It may appear to be frustration, but self-induced frustration is simply treated as a breach of contract. For example, if Moser has a contract to build an apartment building for Wu but the city refuses to grant Moser a building permit, we would expect the contract to be frustrated. However, if the building permit is refused because Moser failed to submit the appropriate plans as required by city bylaw, the frustration is self-induced. Moser is responsible for the misfortune and the refusal of the city to grant a permit will not provide an excuse for Moser's failure to perform the contract.

Self-induced frustration is breach

Secondly, where the parties have anticipated the frustrating event or have provided for one of the parties to bear the risk of such an eventuality, these contractual terms (often called *force majeure* clauses) will prevail. The parties will not be able to claim that their agreement has been frustrated. It is only when the event is an unforeseen interference, not caused by either party, that the courts are willing

Must be unanticipated to be frustration

---

24. (1863) 3 B. & S. 826 (Q.B.).

to find frustration. In *Naylor Group v. Ellis-Don Construction*,[25] for example, the doctrine of frustration was found not to apply because the parties had made specific provision for the supervening circumstances. The defendant contractor had inserted a clause in the contract stipulating it could object to awarding the subcontract to Naylor if it had a good reason. When it failed to utilize that option and awarded the contract to Naylor (despite Naylor's obligation to hire employees from a union other than the IBEW) it could no longer claim that Naylor's inability to hire IBEW workers was a frustrating event.

Finally, the contract is not frustrated if the unforeseen outside event only makes the performance of the contract more costly or more difficult. If a farmer agrees to sell 50 boxes of Golden Delicious apples to a buyer and then his crop is destroyed by hail, this is not frustration unless the terms of the contract specifically stated that the apples were to come from his trees. If the source of the apples is not a term of the contract, the farmer can simply obtain them from another farmer and thus fulfill his contractual obligation, albeit at a higher cost.

In the case of *Tsakiroglou Co. v. Noblee & Thorl G.m.b.H.*,[26] delivery of a cargo from a port in the Sudan on the east coast of Africa to Germany became more onerous when the Suez War closed the canal. The seller claimed that the contract was frustrated. The Court, however, found the seller liable for breach, holding that although it was more difficult and costly to ship the cargo around Africa, the essential nature of the contract remained intact and frustration did not apply. Note that the result would likely have been different had the parties specified delivery through the Suez Canal, since using that route was now impossible.

Increased difficulty is not frustration

Increased cost is not frustration

CASE SUMMARY 9.10

Frustrating Event to Be Unforeseen and Outside of Parties' Control: *Dinicola v. Huang & Danczkay Properties*[27]

Huang & Danczkay Properties sold certain condominiums before they were built, in fact, even before they had finalized the purchase of the property. In the sales contracts there was a clause providing that if municipal approval was not obtained, the developers could terminate the agreement and return deposits paid without further liability up to 30 June 1988. Although things looked as if they were going well, negotiations deteriorated, and the permit to build was eventually refused. This action for damages was brought by a number of the purchasers against the developers for breach of contract. The developers argued that the contract was discharged by frustration because of the failure of the municipality to grant the permit to build.

This position was rejected by the Courts for two reasons. The parties anticipated the possibility that the development might not be approved and provided for an escape for the developer, at least until June 30. Frustration must be an outside event that was not anticipated by either party. Here, the developers not only anticipated that this might take place but provided for it in the contract.

---

25. [2001] 2 S.C.R. 943.

26. [1962] A.C. 93 (H.L.).

27. (1998) 29 O.R. (3d) 161 (Ont. C.A.); aff'g (1996), 29 O.R. (3d) 161 (Ont. Ct. G.D.).

> Secondly, the developers had caused the situation that led to the refusal of the permit. In the final stages of the negotiations, the developers' representative wrote to the municipal council declaring that they would not negotiate further. As a result, the permit was refused. Because the letter precipitated the refusal, the Court found that this was an example of self-induced frustration.

To find frustration, performance must be impossible or the foundation or purpose of the contract must be fundamentally or radically changed. Lack of profits or funding will not frustrate a contract. Thus in the *Korol v. Saskatchewan Federation of Police Officers* case,[28] the federation's inability to pay wages did not frustrate the contract. Lack of financial ability alone will not establish frustration and so, the employer was held liable for wrongful dismissal when it terminated Korol on that basis.

Effect of Frustration

The major problem associated with frustration is to determine who shall suffer the loss when the contract is discharged. Under common law, the general principle was "Let the loss lie where it falls." In other words, the party who had done work or provided services before the frustrating event would bear the loss and could not seek compensation from the other party. Similarly, money already paid was lost. Note, however, that where payment was due before the frustrating event, that payment still had to be paid. This is illustrated by *Chandler v. Webster*,[29] a case that also involved the rental of a flat for viewing King Edward VII's coronation parade. But in this case the entire rent of just over £141 was due and payable in advance, but only £100 had actually been paid. Because the principle was that the loss should lie where it fell when a contract was frustrated, the tenant could not get his money back. In addition, because the sum not yet paid was owed before the frustrating event, that sum had to be paid as well.

This position was considered unsatisfactory and the House of Lords made a significant change in the *Fibrosa* case,[30] which required the return of a deposit paid by a Polish company to a British manufacturer after the outbreak of war frustrated their contract. Because the Polish company had received no benefit under the contract, it was entitled to the return of its deposit. This represents the common law position today but still leads to some unsatisfactory results. The whole deposit or nothing has to be returned, depending on whether any benefit was received.

Where a benefit has been obtained by one party prior to the frustrating event, legislation in most jurisdictions in the form of the *Frustrated Contracts Act*[31] now permits the court to order that party to pay the other for it.

Where a deposit has been paid, the legislation usually allows the court to take into consideration the costs that have been incurred in preparation to perform the contract, whether or not the other party has received a benefit. The court can now apportion that deposit on the basis of the costs incurred and the benefits

mybuslawlab
www.pearsoned.ca/mybuslawlab

    ON

Problems with deposits

Legislation allows deposits to be split

[28.] (2000), 198 Sask. R. 181 (Q.B.).

[29.] [1904] 1 K.B. 493 (C.A.).

[30.] *Fibrosa Spolka Akeyjna v. Fairbairn Lawson Combe Barbouk Ltd.*, [1943] A.C. 32 (H.L.).

[31.] Such legislation exists in all common law provinces with the exception of Nova Scotia.

received (see Table 9.2). In British Columbia and the Yukon, such costs can be apportioned between the parties whether or not a deposit is involved.

Table 9.2 Effect of *Frustrated Contracts Act*

	Impact on Agent's Actual Authority	Impact on Agent's Apparent Authority
Frustrated contract	No deposit paid or payable With deposit	–Contract discharged –Deposit used to pay for benefit received & contract discharged –Deposit split to cover expenses & contract discharged –No benefit received / costs incurred, deposit returned & contract discharged

Other statutes also modify the common law application of the frustration principle. In common law, frustration does not apply to leases, but most jurisdictions have clearly stated that frustration applies to residential leases.[32] British Columbia extends the application of frustration to commercial leases as well.

CASE SUMMARY 9.11

Reimbursement for Expenses Where Contract Frustrated: *Can-Truck Transportation Ltd. v. Fenton's Auto Paint Shop Ltd.*[33]

The plaintiff's truck was sent to the defendant for repairs after an accident. Repairs worth some $28 000 were completed when a fire destroyed both the shop and the truck, thus frustrating the repair contract. The Ontario *Frustrated Contracts Act* provided that when funds were paid (as with a deposit) or were payable before the frustrating event took place, they could be used to reimburse for expenses incurred. The Court found that payment for repairs was payable prior to the fire, thus the plaintiff had to reimburse the company for the expenses it had incurred in repairing the vehicle even though it had been destroyed.

DISCUSSION QUESTIONS

Here the plaintiff ended up with a destroyed truck, but still had to pay for repairs notwithstanding that it received no benefit from those repairs. Is there a better method for dealing with unforeseen events?

---

32. See, for example, Alberta's *Residential Tenancies Act,*R.S.A. 2000 c. R-17.1, s. 40.

33. (1993), 101 D.L.R. (4th) 562 (Ont. C.A.).

When goods are being sold, the *Sale of Goods Act* provides that if the goods, through no fault of the parties, perish before the risk passes to the purchaser, the contract is voided. The effect is that the contract is not binding on the purchaser, and any moneys paid have to be returned.

REMEDIES FOR BREACH OF CONTRACT

Several examples of remedies provided to parties involved in contractual disputes have already been discussed. *Rescission* deals with problems with the formation of a contract and focuses on restoring the parties to their original position. *Rectification* interprets and corrects the terms of contracts, whereas *damages* compensate a victim who has been misled or pressured into the contract. The following discussion looks at remedies available where a party has failed to properly perform its obligations under the contract.

Damages

The most common remedy for a breach of contract is an order that the breaching party pay damages. Damages are amounts of money assessed by the court and designed to compensate victims for their losses.[34] The object is to put the victim, as near as monetary compensation can, into the position he would have been in had the contract been properly performed. Thus, in contract law, damages look forward, whereas in tort actions, damages look backward and try to put the victim in the position he would have been in had the tort never taken place. For example, in a contract action, if a person bought defective paint from a supplier that blistered when put on the walls, necessitating repainting, the court would not only award the cost of the paint as damage. The court would also take into consideration the amount it would cost for a painter to scrape the blistered paint off and repaint the house. The court would then order the vendor to pay a sum sufficient to put the purchaser in the position he would have been in if the paint had not been defective.

mybuslawlab
www.pearsoned.ca/mybuslawlab

BC **AB** SK MB ON

Damages in contract law designed to compensate

Victim of breach compensated as if contract had been properly performed

---

CASE SUMMARY 9.12

Damages to Look Forward, Not Backward: *Ed Learn Ford Sales Ltd. v. Giovannone*[35]

Giovannone traded his Lincoln car in for a truck at Ed Learn Ford Sales Ltd., receiving a $9200 trade-in allowance. The dealer resold the car before it discovered the car had been stolen before Giovannone acquired it. The dealer paid $6175.50 to the insurance company to cover what had been paid to the legitimate owner on the original loss. The dealer then sued Giovannone for the $9200 trade-in allowance. But the Court awarded the dealer only the $6175.50 paid to the insurance company. The Judge quoted from *Wertheim v. Chicoutimi Pulp Co.*:"[I]t is the general intention of the law that, in giving

---

34. See *Hamilton v. Open Window Bakery Ltd.*, [2004] 1 S.C.R. 303, which confirms that where a party who has breached a contract had a variety of ways of fulfilling its obligations, damages will be based on the least expensive method of performance.

35. (1990), 74 D.L.R. (4th) 761 (Ont. Gen. Div.).

damages for breach of contract, the party complaining should, so far as it can be done by money, be placed in the same position as he would have been in if the contract had been performed."[36]

DISCUSSION QUESTIONS

What steps could the dealer have taken to prevent this situation? Even though the dealer recovered the amount paid to the insurance company, it still had to pursue legal action to recover that sum.

When the damages awarded are to cover specific costs and expenses, they are called *special damages*, but when the funds awarded are an estimate of what has been lost or what will be lost, they are called *general damages*. The calculation of damages may be based on the shortfall from what was expected from proper performance, but sometimes damages are designed to cover what has been lost because reliance was placed on the performance of the contract. Only in rare circumstances involving particularly vexatious conduct will courts award punitive damages for breach of contract.[37] Punitive damages are intended to punish the offending party rather than compensate the injured and may result in a considerably higher award.

> **Damages awarded may be special, general, or punitive**

Limitations on Recoverable Damages

Although damages are designed to compensate a person for injuries suffered, not all losses are recoverable. Remoteness and mitigation are two limitations on the recoverability of damages. As well, the parties are free to place terms in the contract itself limiting the damages recoverable or specifying other courses of action in the event of breach.

> **Not all losses can be recovered**

REMOTENESS

The important case of *Hadley v. Baxendale*[38] involved the shipping of a broken crankshaft from a steam engine to be used as a pattern for the manufacture of a new one. The shipper was asked to send it quickly but failed to do so. Unknown to the shipper, the plaintiff's entire plant was shut down while waiting for the crankshaft. This caused great expense to the plaintiff, who sued the shipper for lost profits. The shipper claimed that he could not be responsible for the unusual loss because he had no knowledge of it. The Court used the reasonable person test to determine the extent of the shipper's responsibility for damages and held that the shipper was responsible only for the usual damages that could be expected if the contract were breached. The shipper was thus not liable for the plaintiff's lost profits.

The principle that has developed from this and other cases is essentially that a breaching party is responsible only for those damages that, at the time the

---

36. [1911] A.C. 301 at 307 (P.C.).

37. *Whiten v. Pilot Insurance Co.*, [2002] 1 S.C.R. 595, has become a leading authority on punitive damages. In contract cases, punitive damages should not be awarded in the absence of an independent actionable wrong.

38. (1854), 156 E.R. 145 (Ex. Ct.).

contract was entered into, seem a likely outcome if the contract were breached. Thus, the breaching party is responsible not only for the normally expected damages that flow from a breach, but also for any unusual damages resulting from special circumstances that were communicated to it at the time of the contract. In short, the breaching party is responsible in contract law for any damages that can be reasonably foreseen at the time the contract is entered into.

One area where the problem of remoteness often arises is in a claim for damages to compensate for lost profits. Applying this principle, the breaching party will be responsible only for the loss of ordinary profits that could have been expected given his knowledge of the business. In *Horne v. Midland Ry*[39] the defendants were one day late in the delivery of a shipment of shoes, causing the merchant to lose an opportunity to sell the shoes at an exceptionally high price. The shipper knew only that the merchant would have to take the shoes back if they were late, not that an exceptional profit would be lost. The defendants were not responsible for the unusually high lost profit since they were not aware of those special circumstances, and such a loss was not reasonably foreseeable.

> **Must pay reasonably anticipated losses**

When a contract is breached, damages are awarded to compensate for economic losses. Courts have only recently shown a willingness to award monetary compensation for mental distress. These situations are generally limited to cases where some non-monetary benefit was the subject matter of the contract, such as a disrupted vacation or cruise.[40]

> **General damages compensate for**
> • economic loss
> • even mental distress (recently)

MITIGATION

Victims of a breach are sometimes tempted to do nothing when a contract is breached, allowing damages to accumulate on the assumption that they are the responsibility of—and therefore will be paid by—the breaching party. This is bad practice for several reasons. Victims of breach have a duty to **mitigate** the damages, meaning they must do what they can to keep those damages as low as possible. Also, if they fail to mitigate or minimize losses, courts may actually make a deduction from damages equal to the amount attributable to the failure to mitigate.

> **Victims must mitigate their losses**

The failure to mitigate is a common problem in wrongful-dismissal actions. A person who has been wrongfully dismissed has a right to sue but must make a reasonable effort to find other employment. Damages in such actions are based on the difference between how much notice the employee should have been given as opposed to how much he actually received. If the employer can show that the dismissed employee failed to look for another job, the damages will be reduced by the amount he should have earned during that notice period. For example, if the court concludes that the employee could have found a job, had he looked, after three months, he will recover damages equal to three months' pay notwithstanding that the reasonable notice period was nine months long.

> **Failure to mitigate may result in damages**

Note also that the obligation to mitigate means simply that the victim of the breach must take all reasonable steps to minimize losses suffered. That person is not required to take personal risks or to incur unreasonable expense in the process. Reasonable costs associated with mitigation, such as the cost of flying to another city to attend an interview, can be recovered from the breaching party.

> **Reasonable costs associated with mitigation are recoverable**

---

[39]. (1873), L.R. 8 C.P. 131 (C.P.).

[40]. *Jarvis v. Swan Tours Ltd.*, [1973] 1 All E.R. 71 (C.A.). Here, the vacationer was awarded compensation for the loss of the enjoyment he had been promised. Awards in the travel industry are normally limited to the cost of the holiday, or a portion thereof.

CONTRACTUAL LIMITATIONS

Remedies set out in contract

It is possible for a contract to set out the consequences in the event of breach. The consequences may be quite varied. The contract may call for mediation or arbitration to resolve disputes and determine compensation. The contract might state the maximum amount of compensation to be paid by the breaching party. Businesses often post signs indicating that they are not responsible for losses over a specified amount. Failure to make an instalment payment will often trigger an **acceleration clause**, which makes the entire outstanding debt due and payable immediately. Where the contract involves a consumer transaction, the operation of acceleration clauses are often restricted by consumer protection legislation,[41] which will be further examined in the Chapter 15.

Liquidated damages are specified in contract

When the contract specifies the damages to be paid, they are called **liquidated damages**, and the courts will normally enforce such terms once liability has been determined. Where the amount is actually prepaid with the provision that the funds are to be forfeited in the event of a breach, it is called a **deposit**. For example, to secure the purchase of an automobile, the vendor will usually require the buyer to pay a substantial deposit when ordering. If the purchaser fails to go through with the deal when the car arrives, the vendor can retain the deposit.

Deposit is forfeited—down payment is not

It is important to distinguish between deposits and down payments. Deposits are to be forfeited in the event of a breach, whereas a **down payment** is just the first payment and may have to be returned. Of course, from a practical point of view, once a down payment is made, it may be used as a lever to force performance. But if the matter comes to trial, the court will order the return of the down payment, usually setting off the actual damages to be paid against it. Regardless of what the term is called, it is the provision requiring the forfeiture of the prepayment that will cause the court to treat it as a deposit.

---

41. See, for example, Alberta's *Fair Trading Act,* R.S.A. 2000, c. F-2, s. 71, which requires written notice of a default to be served on a borrower, and the passage of 10 days from such service, before the acceleration clause takes effect.

A $1000 deposit on a new car might be fair in view of the cost of advertising, the time lost, the extra interest payments, and so on. But a $10 000 deposit on a $15 000 car is no longer an attempt to compensate for possible loss or injury, but becomes an attempt to punish the breaching party for failure to go through with the contract. A penalty clause, if excessive, is unconscionable and void. Such a penalty would have to be returned subject to an action to establish the actual loss. Thus, demanding too large a deposit defeats itself. Even when no prepayment is involved, a liquidated damages clause may be challenged if the amount involved is exorbitant and the object is to unreasonably punish rather than to compensate.

Deposit must be reasonable

CASE SUMMARY 9.13

Liquidated Damages Must Be Reasonable: *Meunier v. Cloutier*[42]

When Cloutier returned to Timmins with his wife, he purchased a hotel only a block away from the one he had sold to Meunier four years earlier. In doing so, he violated a non-competition clause prohibiting him from participating in the hotel business in Timmins for five years following the sale to Meunier. The original contract required him to pay $50 000 for such a breach as liquidated damages, and Meunier brought this action to recover that amount.

The Court determined that on its face, the clause was not a penalty; the amount, time, and geographical area were all reasonable from the point of view of when it was made. Nor was the public interest offended. But, following the Supreme Court of Canada precedent in *H.F. Clarke Ltd. v. Thermidaire Corp. Ltd.*,[43] the Court held that when such a lump sum was involved, it had to be satisfied that the amount was "reasonable in the circumstances." Given the minor nature of the breach and absence of evidence that the plaintiff suffered any damage, requiring Cloutier to pay the $50 000 in these circumstances would be unconscionable. Therefore the non-competition clause was a penalty and unenforceable.

DISCUSSION QUESTIONS

While the courts may be willing to enforce predetermined damages, if the amount is unreasonable, the clause will be characterized a penalty clause and be deemed unenforceable. In this case, the non-competition clause was valid; it was the damages portion of that provision that was unacceptable. Should restraint thus be exercised when imposing penalties in the form of liquidated damages? Would legal advice be beneficial in determining an appropriate sum?

Equitable Remedies

The following are examples of remedies that have been developed by the Courts of Chancery to deal with special situations in which the ordinary remedy of

---

42. (1984), 46 O.R. (2d) 188 (H.C.J.).

43. [1976] 1 S.C.R. 319.

damages would not be adequate. Note that these remedies are discretionary and will be granted only when the judge thinks it right and fair to do so.

SPECIFIC PERFORMANCE

Court orders defaulting party to perform its obligations

Specific performance occurs when the court orders the defaulting party to live up to the terms of the contract. Where a developer signs up agreements to buy several adjacent properties, and one property owner refuses to go through with the deal, it would be appropriate to obtain a court order for specific performance. The developer won't be assisted by an award of damages if its goal is to build a shopping centre on the total parcel; it wants the court to order that property owner to transfer the property at the agreed-upon price. But if the same developer ordered a number of new trucks from a dealer who then refused to deliver them, specific performance would not be appropriate as equivalent vehicles could be obtained elsewhere. The appropriate remedy would be damages, and they would be assessed on the basis of the extra cost of getting the vehicles from another dealer. Only if the trucks were unique and not available from some other source might specific performance be available.

Courts will not force performance of contracts for personal services

The courts will not order the defaulting party to perform a contract that requires personal service. If the above developer were to contract with a famous performer to sing at a concert celebrating the opening of the shopping mall and the performer then refused to perform, the court would not order specific performance. Similarly, the courts will not award specific performance as a remedy in any situation that would require close supervision to ensure that the contract is properly performed. Nor will specific performance be available where it would hurt a third party.

Specific performance only available if damages are inappropriate

On the theory that all land is unique, the courts in the past have been willing to award specific performance whenever the parties to the purchase of land breached their contract. The Supreme Court of Canada has indicated, however, that contracts dealing with the purchase of land will now be treated like any other contract, limiting the availability of specific performance to those situations where damages are inappropriate.[44]

CASE SUMMARY 9.14

Specific Performance Ordered Despite Presence of Deposit Clauses: *Romfo v. 1216393 Ontario Inc.*[45]

The vendors of several lots appealed an order of specific performance, which demanded that the sales proceed. The prices of these lots had increased substantially, and the vendors made deals with new purchasers to sell the lots at the higher prices. The vendors argued that since the initial contracts contained deposit clauses, stipulating that if a party breached the contract the deposit would be forfeited, the purchasers would have to be content with the return of their respective deposits. In other words, the vendors argued damages were limited by these "liquidated damages" clauses to the deposits paid earlier.

---

44. *Semelhago v. Paramadevan*, [1996] 2 S.C.R. 415 (S.C.C.).

45. [2008] B.C.J. No. 745 (B.C.C.A.).

The Court of Appeal, however, dismissed the appeal. The parties to the contract could not have intended the deposit clauses to apply where the vendors deliberately deceived the purchasers, by holding onto the deposits while they applied for development approval and then breaching the contracts once approval was granted. The deposit clauses were severed and the contracts were enforced. The vendors were required to transfer the lots to the initial purchasers at the initial price.

SMALL BUSINESS PERSPECTIVE

Here the vendors fundamentally breached the contracts for self-serving reasons. In light of the vendors' questionable conduct, the purchasers were not restricted to seeking damages. This case demonstrates that equitable remedies may be granted to parties who come to the courts with "clean hands."

INJUNCTION

Specific performance involves a court order to do something (to perform the contract) whereas an injunction usually involves an order to refrain from some offensive conduct. In the above example involving personal service by a singer, the court would not order the performer to fulfill the contract by singing at the concert; but the aggrieved party may be able to secure an injunction preventing the performer from performing somewhere else on the day she was to sing at the shopping mall's concert. The injunction is not limited to contractual disputes; it may be available in any situation in which wrongful conduct is involved.

In rare circumstances, the courts may issue a mandatory injunction when a person does something to violate a contractual term and thereby creates an ongoing problem. Striking workers involved in an illegal work stoppage are often ordered to stop breaching their contract and return to work. Another example might involve a shopping centre that erects signs exceeding the permitted height limit set out in a restrictive covenant or a municipal bylaw. The courts may order the shopping centre to remove the sign or reduce it to the permitted height. Such mandatory injunctions are not common.

As with specific performance, there are many instances in which the courts will refuse to issue an injunction. The courts are reluctant to order an injunction that would make it impossible for the person defaulting on the contractual agreement to earn a living. A court might well enforce, by injunction, a term requiring an employee not to work for a competitor for three years upon leaving, but would not enforce a term preventing that employee from working for anyone for three years. Similarly, the courts will not issue an injunction when damages provide a sufficient remedy. An injunction is designed not to punish someone for breaching a contract, but to prevent further injury. An injunction will also not be awarded where it will cause harm to a third party.

An injunction is sometimes ordered even before there has been a trial on the issues. If an employee leaves and works for a competitor, it is important to get an injunction right away and sort out the merits of the dispute later. This is called an **interlocutory injunction**, and is issued by the court when some ongoing injury will increase the damage done to the person seeking the interlocutory injunction. When waiting for the trial to determine the matter is unacceptable, granting an interlocutory injunction becomes the preferable alternative.

Courts may order breaching conduct to stop

• but not where a person can no longer earn a living

• but not where damages are more appropriate

• but not where it would hurt a third party

Interlocutory injunction issued before the trial

ACCOUNTING

Court may order accounting and require profits to be paid over

It is often difficult for the victim of the breach to determine just what kind of injuries he or she has suffered, especially when the offending party has taken advantage of some opportunities or rights belonging to the victim. This can happen when there is a fiduciary relationship between the contracting parties, that is, a relationship in which the person breaching the contract has a duty to act in the best interests of the other party. In these circumstances, the court can order that the defaulting party disclose all financial dealings and records so that the injured party can determine what he or she is entitled to claim. In some circumstances the court will then order the offending party to pay over to the injured party all or a portion of the profits made from the wrongful conduct. So the court, instead of awarding damages on the basis of what has been lost by the victim, awards damages on the basis of what has been wrongfully obtained by the breaching party.

QUANTUM MERUIT

Court may order payment for part performance

In some situations, the contract is breached when only part of the work has been done and before the amount agreed to in the contract is due and payable to the injured party. In these circumstances, the courts have the power to award compensation for the value of work that has been done on the basis of *quantum meruit.* As discussed in Chapter 6, *quantum meruit* is the principle that allows the supplier of a service to collect a reasonable fee, even when no price had been agreed upon. Note that only the victim of the breach can claim compensation on the basis of *quantum meruit.* The courts are extremely reluctant to grant any compensation for the breaching party's partial performance of the agreement, unless the contractual obligations have been substantially performed. Sometimes partial payment is payable before completion, and in that case, even the breaching party can collect.

If a contractor has agreed to build a house with payment due upon completion of the job and refuses to continue after completing half, he will not be successful in claiming compensation for what he has done. He should finish the job. But if he has finished half the project and the owner of the property with whom he has contracted refuses to let him continue, the contractor, being the innocent party, will be able to claim compensation for the work that has been done under the principle of *quantum meruit.* Only where the contract called for partial payments at different stages of completion will the breaching party be able to collect those payments due before the breach.

Equitable remedies are discretionary

• unavailable if hardship caused

• only available if claimant applies with clean hands

• unavailable if claim unduly delayed

Some general requirements must be met before the courts will grant an equitable remedy. If there has been **laches**, an undue delay on the part of the person seeking the equitable remedy, the courts can refuse to grant the remedy. The plaintiff will still be able to pursue any common law remedy, such as damages, without penalty for delay—provided the action is brought within the limitation period. The courts can also refuse to award an equitable remedy in any situation in which it would cause undue hardship to the parties or to some other person or would be inappropriate for any other reason. A person seeking equity must come to the court with **clean hands**, meaning the remedy will be denied when the person seeking the equitable remedy is also guilty of some wrongdoing. These requirements apply to all equitable remedies.

CASE SUMMARY 9.15

Equitable Remedies Are Not Always Available: *Island Properties Ltd. v. Entertainment Enterprises Ltd.*[46]

Entertainment Enterprises Limited and Denis Galway made arrangements to sell property through one real estate agent and then made similar arrangements with another. Two different purchasers acting through the two different agents accepted the offer to sell. The Court found that both were valid and that the property had been sold to both purchasers. The property was transferred to Pegasus; Island Property, which had accepted first, sued for specific performance.

At trial, the Judge ordered that the property be returned by Pegasus and transferred to Island Properties. But the Appeal Court ordered that the property be returned to Pegasus. Pegasus was a completely innocent third party, and an equitable remedy cannot be given where it will cause harm to such an innocent party. Because the property had been conveyed to the innocent Pegasus, it could not be taken back. Island Properties was limited to a remedy of damages for breach.

SMALL BUSINESS PERSPECTIVE

This case illustrates the limitations placed on equitable remedies. Even when one's action is successful, the preferred remedy may not be available.

Another factor that may affect the right of the victim of a breach of contract to obtain any remedy is the limitations legislation discussed in Chapter 3. The limitation periods outlined in these statutes apply to any action brought to court including contract claims, with the result that once the limitation period has expired, none of the remedies discussed in this chapter will be available to the victim of the breach.

Time limits

Finally, it should be noted that when a judgment or an equitable remedy has been awarded and a defendant refuses to comply, the defendant may be held in contempt of court and can be jailed for contempt, although this is extremely unlikely. The remedies to enforce a judgment, outlined generally in Chapter 3, are available to the victim of a breach of contract as well.

Contempt

[46.] (1986), 58 Nfld. & P.E.I.R. 151 (C.A.).

SUMMARY

Discharge of contracts

- Can come to an end through performance, breach, agreement, or frustration

Performance

- When properly tendered but refused, contract may be discharged
- When payment is tendered but refused, the creditor must bear the cost of its collection

Breach

- Breached condition—the victim may treat the contract as discharged and sue
- Breached warranty—contract is still binding but the victim can sue for damages
- Anticipatory breach—victim can treat the contract as discharged immediately or wait for performance (and later sue) but is bound by choice

Agreement

- Contract may provide for its own end; the agreed-upon method for termination is effective in ending the contract
- Condition precedent—obligations to perform arise if the condition is fulfilled
- Condition subsequent—obligations exist and continue until condition is fulfilled
- Liquidated damages—parties may agree in advance as to sum payable in event of breach
- Deposit, if forfeitable, regarded as liquidated damages

Frustration

- Performance impossible or fundamentally changed
- Monies advanced may be apportioned to compensate for expenses or losses incurred
- Self-induced frustration is breach of contract

Remedies

- Damages paid to compensate the victim
- Damages limited to what was reasonably foreseeable
- Damages must be reduced or mitigated by victim
- Deposits or liquidated damages set out in contract must be reasonable, or treated as a penalty provision—courts do not enforce penalty clauses
- Specific performance requires the breaching party to fulfill agreement
- Injunction—a court order to stop conduct that breaches the contract
- Accounting—requires disclosure of information so other party can assess extent of damages
- *Quantum meruit*—an equitable remedy requiring payment of a fair sum, equal to what the goods or services are reasonably worth

QUESTIONS

1. Describe the various ways in which a contractual relationship can come to an end.

2. Under what circumstances would a breaching party who had partially performed the terms of the contract be entitled to receive part payment?

3. Describe the differences between a condition and a warranty. Why is the distinction significant?

4. When might the victim of a breach of a condition lose the right to treat the contract as discharged?

5. What constitutes adequate tender of performance?

6. What recourse is available to one party to a contract when performance is made impossible by the other party's conduct?

7. What options are available to the victim of an anticipatory breach? Explain the advantages, disadvantages, and risks associated with these options.

8. What is an exemption clause? When might an exemption clause be unenforceable?

9. What is meant by fundamental breach? What remedy is available to the victim of a fundamental breach of contract?

10. Assume the defendant claims that the contract was discharged or modified by agreement; the plaintiff challenges this conclusion and seeks to enforce the original contract. What will the defendant need to prove to avoid having the initial contract enforced?

11. Explain what happens when a creditor agrees to take less than is owed to settle a debt.

12. How do conditions precedent differ from conditions subsequent?

13. Define frustration. List three ways in which frustration can take place.

14. What is the significance of a court's determination that a contract was frustrated through the fault of one of the parties?

15. Explain how the *Fibrosa* case and subsequent statute law have modified the previously accepted common law rule on the obligations of the parties in the face of a frustrating event.

16. Distinguish between a deposit and a down payment. What is the significance of this distinction?

17. What must be shown for the court to conclude that money paid ought to be categorized as a deposit?

18. In light of the decision in *Hadley v. Baxendale*, how is the recovery of damages limited?

19. Describe what is meant by mitigation. Explain how the obligation to mitigate damages limits the ability of the victim of a breach to obtain damages.

20. Distinguish between specific performance and injunction. Explain the restrictions on their availability.

CASES AND DISCUSSION QUESTIONS

1. *Sumpter v. Hedges*, [1898] 1 Q.B. 673 (C.A.).
The plaintiff agreed to erect certain buildings for the defendant for a lump-sum payment to be made upon completion. The plaintiff failed to finish the work and asked for reimbursement for the amount he had done. The defendant refused. The plaintiff then sued for payment for the work he had done.

What factors would the court need to determine before it decided the case? Explain the likely outcome.

2. *Betker v. Williams* [1991] B.C.J. No. 3724 (C.A.).
Mrs. Williams owned property in Cranbrook and listed the property for sale with Mr. Klinkhammer, a real estate agent. It was advertised as a residential lot in the local newspaper, with a clear indication that a house could be built on it. Mr. Betker bought the property after specifically asking Klinkhammer if it would be appropriate for a solar home and receiving a positive reply. Four years after the sale, the Betkers discovered that a house could not be built on the property because it was too small for a septic tank and had no access to the city sewer line.

It turned out that neither Williams nor the real estate agents were aware of this problem. The Betkers brought an action against the agents and Williams. There was a term in the agreement stating that there were no representations other than those contained on the written agreement itself, but this provision had not been specifically brought to the attention of the purchasers.

Explain the arguments available to both parties. Were representations made that were subsequently relied upon? Must a party who wishes to limit its liability have to bring those limitations to the attention of the opposite party? What remedies might be sought by the purchaser in this case?

3. *Trio Roofing Systems Inc. v. Atlas Corp.* [2004] O.J. No. 707 (S.C.J.).
Trio Roofing Systems Inc., a roofing subcontractor, agreed to complete the roofing on two schools being built by Atlas Corp. Trio completed the first job, but Atlas failed to pay it in full. Trio claimed that this failure to pay created an anticipatory breach of the second roofing contract. It refused to begin work on the second roof. Atlas took the position that Trio had abandoned the second contract. Atlas hired another roofer and sought to set off against the money still owed to Trio on the first contract, the extra amount it had to pay the second roofing subcontractor.

Did Atlas's failure to pay on the first contract give Trio grounds to claim anticipatory breach of the second? What is the significance of a failure to pay? Was there an abandonment on Trio's part that entitled Atlas to damages under the second contract?. What would you expect the court's ruling to be?

4. *Teleflex Inc. v. I.M.P. Group Ltd.* **(1996), 149 N.S.R. (2d) 355.**

Teleflex Inc. (Teleflex), an American company manufacturing aircraft components, knew that I.M.P. Group Ltd. (I.M.P.) was negotiating with the Brazilian government to carry out a program for the turbinization of its Tracker aircraft fleet. Teleflex offered to supply necessary parts, to which proposal I.M.P. responded with a purchase order for 13 quadrant assembly sets at $27 500 each. The shipping schedule was to commence in March 1990. Included was a provision whereby I.M.P. could order a suspension of the work with a reasonable price adjustment, and a further provision whereby I.M.P. could terminate the order with payment to Teleflex for both completed and uncompleted work, according to a formula that factored in lost profits. Thereafter, Teleflex commenced manufacturing the quadrant assembly units.

In September 1989, Teleflex received the first of a series of notices from I.M.P. requesting postponement of delivery of the units. Teleflex acknowledged receipt of these stop-work letters, advising that in the event of termination, its termination liability schedule "attached to our original proposal will apply." I.M.P. continued to experience difficulties in closing the deal with the Brazilian government and finally, in 1994, indicated it would not be requiring fulfillment of the purchase order.

Teleflex treated this as a termination notice and advised I.M.P. that it would submit a termination claim based on work performed to date. The claim amounted to US$229 576 for materials, overhead, and profit. I.M.P. countered that no monies were payable because the contract had been frustrated by the Brazilian government, and further, no quadrant assembly units were ever delivered by Teleflex.

Based on these facts, was the contract frustrated? Is any money payable to Teleflex? What factors affect your conclusion?

5. *Rinn v. Parent Seeds Ltd.* **(2001), 156 Man. R. (2d) 191 (C.A.).**

Rinn had a contract to supply a quantity of black beans and white beans to Parent Seeds Ltd. Unfortunately, Rinn's crop was damaged by frost and he couldn't deliver the beans from his farm. He then made arrangements to obtain the beans from another source and Parent accepted the alternative white beans supplied, not knowing Rinn didn't grow them. Parent refused to take delivery of the black beans, claiming that the contract had been frustrated.

Explain the arguments that could be advanced by both parties. How would it affect your answer to learn that the contract required the delivery of specific black beans grown by Rinn with seed supplied by Parent?

6. *Computer Workshops v. Banner Capital Market Brokers* **(1988), 64 O.R. (2d) 266 (H.C.J.), affirmed (1990), 1 O.R. (3d) 398 (C.A.).**

Banner, the defendant in this action, was in the brokerage industry and was developing a computer software network to handle his business. The plaintiff, Computer Workshops, entered into an agreement with Banner to provide him with the necessary hardware and software equipment to do the job. After 25 of the 100 computers agreed to were delivered, Banner discovered that Computer Workshops was negotiating with Banner's competition to provide that company with a similar system with similar capabilities. Banner learned that in those discussions, certain confidential information that he had given to Computer Workshops had been disclosed to its competitor. Banner refused to take the rest of the computers. Computer Workshops sued for breach.

Explain the arguments on both sides and any defence that might be available to Banner in these circumstances.

7. *968703 Ontario Limited v. Vernon* (2002), 58 O.R. (3d) 215 (C.A.).

Vernon contracted with an auctioneer company to sell the equipment located at his gravel pit. The proceeds were to be deposited in a joint bank account and then split between the parties in specified proportions. But when the auctioneer refused to deposit the first $100 000 as required, Vernon refused to allow it back on the property to complete the sale. Vernon also uncovered that the auctioneer had attempted to make a secret profit by attempting to sell Vernon's assets at a reduced price to three related companies controlled by the auctioneer.

Was Vernon justified in refusing to continue performance? The auctioneer had brought in $100 000 in sales and expected to bring in more.

8. *652013 B.C. Ltd. v. Kim*, [2006] O.J. No. 423 (Ont. S.C.J.).

The defendant rented six illuminated signs from the plaintiff. Upset that one of the signs was illuminated only sporadically, the defendant stopped payment. Later the defendant also complained that one of the signs was obstructed by trees. After repeated demands for payment, the plaintiff sued. The lease agreement contained an acceleration clause, so the plaintiff claimed the accelerated amount owing under the lease. The plaintiff established that the cause for the interrupted illumination was beyond its control—the power supply was not its responsibility. The acceleration clause, when applied, resulted in an effective rate of interest of 26.8 percent.

Should the plaintiff recover judgment for the accelerated amount? What facts are relevant and what further facts would one need to predict the outcome of this case?

PEARSON
mybuslawlab™

Be sure to visit the MyBusLawLab that accompanies this book at **www.pearsoned.ca/mybuslawlab.** You will find practice tests, a personalized study plan, province-specific material, and much more!

Chapter 10

Employment

A contract for employment is one of the most important contracts in which a person will become involved. This chapter is devoted to exploring the legal ramifications of the employment relationship.

WHAT IS EMPLOYMENT?

Employment involves one person doing work for another, but not all such relationships are classed as employment. The work of independent contractors, such as doctors, lawyers, and plumbers, must be distinguished from employment. Such independent contractors work for themselves and act independently, providing a specific service for the person they contract with, whereas an employee is said to be in a master–servant relationship, acting under the direction of the master.

Agency is a third type of business relationship, in which one person acts as a go-between in relationships between others. Agency will be discussed in detail in the next chapter. Each of these relationships imposes different legal rights and obligations on the parties; understanding which body of rights and obligations governs a particular relationship can be of vital importance.

The Control Test

The traditional method of determining whether an employment relationship exists is to assess the degree of control exercised by the person paying for the service. A person who is told not only what to do but also how to do it is classed as an employee. But if the person doing the work is free to decide how the job should be done, the position is more likely that of an independent contractor. For example, if Fong hires Kirk to paint a house, Kirk could be either an independent contractor

mybuslawlab
www.pearsoned.ca/mybuslawlab

Not all work is employment

Employee controlled by employer

or an employee. If Fong tells Kirk which tools to use, when to work, and how to perform the job, then Kirk is probably an employee. If Kirk supplies the tools and determines what time to start work and the best way to perform the job, then he is probably an independent contractor. Whether the person is paid a wage or salary, or is paid by the job, is also taken into consideration in determining if an employment relationship exists. Courts will also look at who owns the tools used and who profits or runs the risk of loss from the work performed.

Independent contractor works independently

The employment relationship involves a contract in which the employee agrees generally to serve the employer, who has the right to supervise and direct. On the other hand, an independent contractor agrees to do a particular job, not to enter into a general service relationship. In other words, employees work for their employer, whereas independent contractors work for themselves. In Case Summary 10.1, it was clear to the court that Ms. Samuda was working for the employer and not for herself.

CASE SUMMARY 10.1

Control Suggests Employment—But It's Not the Only Test: Samuda v. Recipco Corp;[1] *Algoma Taxicab Management Ltd. v. M.N.R.*[2]

Ms. Samuda initially provided consulting services through her company, pursuant to an oral agreement. She then signed an employment contract with Recipco for the position of Senior Vice-President of Legal and Business Affairs. She was eventually dismissed from this position. She therefore brought an action for wrongful termination and breach of an employment contract. The defendants argued that Samuda was a "consultant," that the relationship was governed by the oral agreement, and that Samuda voluntarily terminated the relationship.

The Court referred to a Supreme Court of Canada ruling in which Justice Major listed a number of factors that should be considered in determining whether a person is an employee or an independent contractor:

> [T]he central question is whether the person who has been engaged to perform the services is performing them as a person in business on his own account. In making this determination, the level of control the employer has over the worker's activities will always be a factor. However, other factors to consider include whether the worker provides his or her own equipment, whether the worker hires his or her own helpers, the degree of financial risk taken by the worker, the degree of responsibility for investment and management held by the worker, and the worker's opportunity for profit in the performance of his or her tasks.[3]

The Court held that the oral agreement between the parties was superseded by the written agreement, which clearly stated that the status of Samuda was that of an employee. Furthermore, Samuda did not maintain her own office premises but instead used offices at Recipco's premises, Recipco paid for her laptop computer, her expenses

---

1. [2007] B.C.S.C. 1013 (CanLII), additional reasons at [2008] B.C.S.C. 192 (CanLII).

2. (2006), 60 D.T.C. 2497 (T.C.C.).

3. 671122 Ontario Ltd. v. Sagaz Industries Canada Inc., [2001] 2 S.C.R. 983, at para. 47–48.

were reimbursed by Recipco, she did not hire her own assistants, her activities were subject to the control and direction of Recipco's Board of Directors, and she did not undertake any financial risk. The fact that her salary was paid to her consulting company was immaterial.

Contrast this with the *Algoma* case, in which Brouillard worked as a taxi driver for Algoma. The contract between Algoma and its drivers entitled the drivers to use a vehicle and Algoma's dispatch services. Algoma paid for the vehicle insurance, as well as the maintenance, fuel, oil, and other supplies for the vehicles. The drivers paid a rental fee that varied from 62 percent to 70 percent of their gross receipts. Algoma did not assign drivers to work at particular times, on particular days, or in specific geographical areas. Drivers could request a vehicle for a specific date and time. Drivers were not required to work any minimum period. They did not have to be consistently available during a shift. Drivers could have customers call them directly rather than calling the dispatcher.

The Court indicated that the central question is whether the person is performing the services as a person in business on his own account. The level of control the employer has over the worker's activities will always be a factor, although other factors will also be considered. In this case, the Court concluded that all of Algoma's drivers, including Brouillard, were performing services as independent contractors.

SMALL BUSINESS PERSPECTIVE

The determination as to whether a worker is an employee or an independent contractor is often important with respect to the applicability of government legislation, such as the Canada Pension Plan or the *Employment Insurance Act*, or in determining whether a terminated worker is entitled to severance pay. Courts consider the level of control the worker is subject to, as well as other factors, when classifying the worker. Should the contract between the parties be the sole determinant of the nature of the relationship? Should the courts defer to the agreement between the parties? What about the imbalance of power between those parties?

The Organization Test

In recent years, the courts have supplemented the control test with the organization test. Even if there is little direct control, when the individual is an integral part of the organization, working only for that corporation and subject to group control, that person is likely an employee.[4]

Organization test supplements control test

On the other hand, if that person is free to offer services to others and bears the risks of profit or loss if work is not completed in a timely manner, she may be an independent contractor.

It is important to note that, at least for the purposes of establishing vicarious liability, a person can be an independent contractor for most purposes but an employee or a servant in some specific instances.[5] This ruling has prompted the courts to find employment relationships in areas that were traditionally considered purely independent. Jones could be a plumber acting as an independent contractor for Smith for most of the job, but while digging a drainage ditch at Smith's direction he could be considered an employee for that purpose. If someone was

Definition of employment broadened

---

4. John G. Fleming, *The Law of Torts*, 8th ed. (Sydney: The Law Book Co. Ltd., 1992), p. 372.

5. *Cooperators Insurance Association. v. Kearney*, [1965] S.C.R. 106.

hurt, Smith could be found vicariously liable for Jones's careless conduct in digging that ditch.

Individual statutes may provide a definition of employment for the purposes of that statute, but there is no general legislated definition. When a court is dealing with vicarious liability or wrongful dismissal, it must therefore turn to the principles enunciated in precedents to determine whether an employment relationship exists.

An employee can be an agent

It is also important to note that while a person normally cannot be an independent contractor and an employee at the same time, the same is not true of an agent. **Agents** can be independent contractors or employees. A sales clerk in a store is both an employee and an agent; a person selling insurance is likely an independent contractor but is also functioning as an agent for her client. It's important to keep these categories separate, as the liability of the parties will likely be determined by the relationship between them.

An agent can be independent

The legal principles governing the independent contractor are embodied in the general rules of contract law already covered in Chapters 6 through 9. This chapter will examine the law of master and servant, the relevant federal and provincial legislation, the trade union movement, and collective bargaining.

THE LAW OF MASTER AND SERVANT

Over the years, the common law courts developed special rules to deal with the unique problems associated with employment, which was then referred to as a master–servant relationship. Today, employment law is governed primarily by the general provisions of contract law, supplemented by these special rules as well as by a number of statutes that further define the responsibilities and obligations of the parties.

The Employment Contract

Obligations of employer include
• payment of wages or salary
• safe working conditions

The main responsibility of the employer, in addition to payment of wages, is to provide a safe workplace and good working conditions for the employee. Some types of jobs are inherently dangerous, such as construction, and the employer is obligated to minimize the danger, usually by promoting safe work practices; erecting protective fences, barriers, and nets; and requiring the use of proper safety equipment. The employer must hire competent people. If it can be shown that the employer hired a careless or incompetent worker who caused injury to others, the employer may be held accountable. For example, when an inexperienced crane operator caused the crane to topple, injuring other workers, the employer was responsible because of its failure to ensure that only a competent and experienced worker operated the crane.[6] Job-site health and safety requirements, and injuries caused by other workers, are specialized areas covered by occupational health and safety legislation and workers' compensation legislation; both are discussed below.

The contract of employment usually includes a commitment by the employer to pay a specific wage or salary. That agreement will often also set out bonus arrangements, benefit packages, and promises to repay any reasonable expenses incurred.

The employee also has obligations to fulfill. The employee must possess the skills claimed and exercise them in a reasonably competent and careful manner.

[6.] R. v. A. W. Leil Cranes & Equipment (1986) Ltd., [2003] N.S.J. No. 524.

The employee has an obligation to follow any reasonable order pertaining to the employment and must treat the property of the employer carefully. The employee must be honest, loyal, and courteous; an employee who does the work required but acts in an insubordinate or disloyal way can be fired. Similarly, an employee must be punctual and work for the time specified in the contract. If the employee uses the employer's time or facilities without permission, he may be disciplined. With some types of jobs, there may also be an obligation to generally act in the best interests of the employer. This is referred to as a fiduciary obligation and is usually imposed only on senior-level employees. For normal employees, unless the employment contract provides otherwise, their obligations to the employer end when that employment is terminated. But for those senior level employees who have a fiduciary duty, that duty may continue after the employment ends.

Obligations of employee:
• **competent work**
• **honesty and loyalty**
• **punctuality**
• **action in employer's best interests**
• **fiduciary obligations in some cases**

An employee who is also a fiduciary is automatically subject to certain obligations toward an employer. These include a duty to act in good faith, make full disclosure, and not take corporate opportunities for one's own benefit. For example, in the *Felker* case,[7] when the employee secretly engaged in negotiations to become the sales agent for a second company and did not advise or offer his employer the opportunity to represent the second company, the Court found just cause for that employee's dismissal. Failure to disclose this activity and to secure prior consent justified the dismissal.

Employment contracts are often not formal or written documents. It is, however, a good idea to put the contract in writing, clearly stating the provisions that are important for the parties. Such provisions may include the rate of pay, the hours of work, and a description of what services are required and for what period. As with other contracts, all the ingredients necessary for a contract to exist must be present. Employers often try to impose new, one-sided employment contracts on their employees after the commencement of employment. These contracts often include terms adverse to the employee, such as restrictive covenants or terms limiting the period of notice to be given upon termination. When imposed after the fact, these provisions are often not binding because of a failure of consideration. The employment contract is illustrated in Figure 10.1.

Restrictive covenants must be reasonable

General contract law applies to employment

When **restrictive covenants** are included in the original contract, committing the employee not to work in a particular geographic area or in a particular industry after leaving the position, they have to specify a reasonable time and area. If they are too broad, the covenants will not be enforced. Further, such covenants must be the most appropriate way of protecting the employer's interests, and not be against the public interest. For example, if an employer invents a special production method, the secrecy of which could be maintained only by requiring that

Figure 10.1 The Employment Contract

Employer: Promises to pay wages, provide safe workplace,...

→

Employment contract

←

Employee:

Promises to be honest, loyal, punctual, competent,...

| Breach of these major terms may enable opposite party to treat contract as discharged |

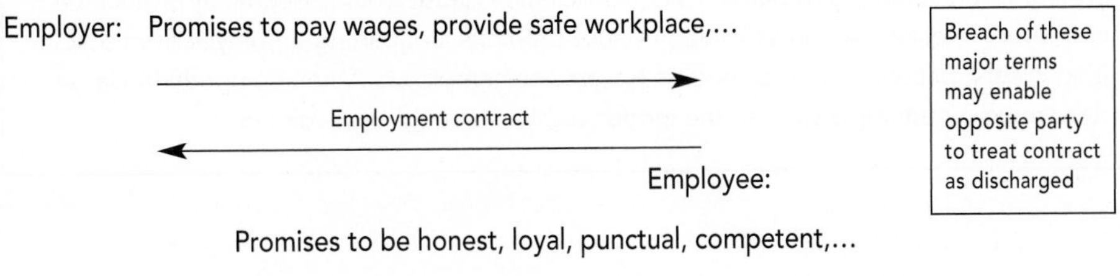

7. *Felker v. Cunningham* (2000), 191 D.L.R. (4th) 734 (Ont. C.A.), leave to appeal to S.C.C. refused, [2000] S.C.C.A. No. 538.

the employees commit themselves not to work in a similar industry for a reasonable period of time, a restrictive covenant in the contract of employment to that effect would likely be valid. But, in general, there is some reluctance on the part of the courts to enforce restrictive covenants in employment contracts because of the danger of denying the employee the ability to earn a livelihood and because of the normally weaker bargaining position of employees.

CASE SUMMARY 10.2

Injunctions Sought to Enforce Promises Not to Compete: *Herff Jones Canada Inc. v. Todd;*[8] *Lyons v. Multari*[9]

Todd entered into a sales-representative agreement with the respondent whereby he agreed to solicit schools and colleges for the purpose of selling class rings, medals, awards, and yearbooks supplied by the respondent. After six years, Todd severed the relationship and went to work for a competitor, Jostens. By doing so, he breached a promise that he would not compete with his former employer for four years. The respondent sought and obtained an injunction from the trial Judge, preventing Todd from "soliciting or contacting directly or indirectly any of those schools or accounts who were customers" of the respondent as of 20 May 1994, for a period of four years.

Todd appealed, arguing that the trial Judge erred in deciding that the restrictive covenant in the sales representative agreement was valid. Prohibiting an employee from working for a competitor for four years does, at first glance, appear excessive. The Court of Appeal, however, found the trial Judge had applied the correct tests: (1) The covenant was reasonable as between the parties. Its duration, four years, was reasonable in light of the fact that Todd would have been entitled to a split commission for three years after leaving the respondent had he not breached the restrictive covenant. Further, Todd had developed a special relationship with the customers, so the proprietary interest of the respondent would be jeopardized if Todd could approach them on the competitor's behalf. Nor did the covenant cover too large a geographical area. Todd had simply promised not to compete in the area formerly serviced by him on behalf of the respondent. (2) The covenant was also reasonable with regard to public interest.

Contrast the above with the *Lyons* case, in which the plaintiff oral surgeon hired a new associate. They signed a short, handwritten contract containing a non-competition clause. The defendant therein agreed not to compete for three years within a five-mile area. After 17 months, he gave the agreed 6 months' notice and opened his own oral surgery practice, in the same city. The Court of Appeal determined that it was not appropriate to enforce a non-competition clause if a non-solicitation clause would adequately protect the employer's interests. A non-solicitation clause prohibits a departing employee from soliciting clients, patients, or customers of his previous employer. A non-competition clause does more—it attempts to keep the former employee out of the business.

---

8. (1996), 181 A.R. 236 (C.A.).

9. (2000), 50 O.R. (3d) 526 (C.A.), leave to appeal to S.C.C. refused, [2000] S.C.C.A. No. 567.

These cases suggest that not only must the non-competition clause be reasonable as between the parties (not overly broad geographically or in terms of time), but the party trying to enforce the same must show that the clause is necessary to protect some proprietary interest. Otherwise, the court might regard the clause as being too restrictive or unnecessary and simply refuse to enforce it.

SMALL BUSINESS PERSPECTIVE

The question again arises, should the parties to such agreements be required to honour them? Remember that the compensation and benefits would have been calculated on what the parties thought their obligations were under the contract of employment. Should the courts be able to disregard what the parties have agreed to, on the basis that they consider the agreement to be too restrictive or unreasonable?

mybuslawlab
www.pearsoned.ca/mybuslawlab

Termination

An employment contract may provide for its own discharge (as when the contract is for a fixed term, say one year, and that term expires), or the parties can mutually agree to bring it to an end. However, most contracts of employment are for an indefinite period of time with no reference to notice requirements. In general, such contracts of employment can be terminated by either party giving reasonable notice, by the employer giving the compensation that should have been earned in that notice period (pay in lieu of notice), or immediately with just cause.

> Contract may stipulate amount of notice to be given
>
> • Otherwise, reasonable notice of termination required of both employer and employee

Just as the employee is not bound to the job and can leave after giving reasonable notice, so too is the employer free to terminate the employment relationship for no specific reason as long as sufficient notice is given. Note, however, that the employer's right to terminate even with proper notice is restricted somewhat by provincial and federal human rights legislation and by the *Charter of Rights and Freedoms*, which prohibit such action when it amounts to discrimination on the basis of gender, religion, colour, physical disability, or other protected ground.[10]

> • But note human rights violations

REASONABLE NOTICE

The problem for employers is that reasonable notice, especially when long-term employees are involved, can be quite significant. The courts impose notice periods on the basis of such factors as length of service, the type of job, the employee's age, experience, training and qualifications, and the availability of similar employment.[11] In some cases involving long-term senior managers, the required notice period may even exceed two years.

> What constitutes reasonable notice varies with circumstances
> Courts consider
> • length of service
> • type of job
> • age of employee
> • qualifications
> • availability of similar employment
> • bad-faith conduct

---

10. *Canadian Charter of Rights and Freedoms*, ss. 15 and 28, Part I of the *Constitution Act, 1982*, being Schedule B to the *Canada Act 1982*(U.K.), 1982, c. 11, and, for example, *Human Rights Code*,R.S.O. 1990, c. H.19, s. 5.

11. *Honda Canada Inc. v. Keays*, 2008 SCC 39.

CASE SUMMARY 10.3

Bad Faith of Employer May Add Significant Damages: *Honda Canada Inc. v. Keays*[12]

Keays had worked for Honda for 14 years but was persistently absent due to chronic fatigue syndrome. He went on long-term disability for a period, but that was terminated (wrongfully, as later determined by the Court) and he had to return to work. There followed a considerable amount of absenteeism caused by his illness. Honda required him to submit to its doctor, and when he followed his lawyer's advice and refused "pending clarification of the purpose, methodology and the parameters of the assessment," his employment was terminated.

He sued for wrongful dismissal. At trial, the Judge found that Honda had a culture of "lean operation" and production efficiency, which led it to hound Keays because of his absences. It was also clear to the Judge that Honda thought his condition was "bogus." The Judge also determined that the request to see Honda's doctor was not made in good faith but as a pretext to fire him. There was also an internal meeting during which the Honda representatives tried to persuade Keays to reject the advice of his own lawyer. Because of the deceit and insensitive method of termination amounting to bad faith on the part of the employer, the normal notice period was extended by 9 months, from 15 to 24 months. This amounted to an award of $150 000 for wrongful dismissal.

The Judge also found that the harassment and discrimination Keays experienced and the denial of his disability benefits constituted a separate wrong. The Court found that the employer had been guilty of a "protracted corporate conspiracy" and awarded Keays a further $500 000 in punitive damages. This was the largest award of punitive damages in a wrongful dismissal action thus far in Canada.

On appeal, the Court of Appeal upheld the finding of wrongful dismissal and the awarding of the extra damages because of the manner of dismissal. The Court did, however, reduce the punitive damages from $500 000 to $100 000.

The Supreme Court of Canada set aside the damages for the manner of dismissal. It also set aside the punitive damages and reduced the costs awarded to a regular level. The Court indicated that damages for wrongful dismissal do not usually include damages for the actual loss of a job or for pain and distress suffered as a result of being terminated. Damages for the manner of dismissal will only be available if the employer has acted, during the course of the dismissal, in a manner that is (para. 57) "unfair or is in bad faith by being, for example, untruthful, misleading or unduly insensitive." Such damages should be awarded through an award that reflects actual damages, not by extending the notice period.

The Court ruled that the trial Judge had made an error of fact and that Honda's conduct was not deserving of an award of damages for misconduct in dismissal. Punitive damages are awarded for deliberate wrongful acts that are malicious and outrageous. The Court ruled that Honda's behaviour was not deserving of punitive damages.

---

12. *Ibid.*

While the sympathy of the lower courts was with the dismissed employee, the Supreme Court took a much more balanced view. As long as an employer's conduct is not untruthful, misleading, or unduly insensitive, the employee will not receive damages for the manner of the dismissal. Aggravated or punitive damages will only be awarded if the employer acts maliciously or outrageously. In a time of recession, does the Supreme Court decision give too much of an advantage to employers who would like to terminate the employment of employees?

Even seasonal employees who are fired at the end of a season and then repeatedly re-hired may be entitled to reasonable notice if not recalled.[13] Short-term or probationary employees may be entitled to extended notice periods if the employee has not been informed of the basis on which his performance will be evaluated, or if he was persuaded to leave another job but is then terminated after a short time. Similarly, if an employer fosters employee loyalty by promising job security, that employer may be required to provide even greater notice of termination to its employees than would otherwise be the case.[14] Trade unions generally include terms in their collective agreements as to when an employee can be terminated and what notice is required. Also, minimum statutory notice periods are set out in employment standards statutes and will be discussed below.

REDUCING RISK 10.1

What the foregoing highlights is that legal advice should be sought if an employer wishes to terminate an employee without cause. In such a situation, adequate notice must be given. If the amount of notice has not been agreed upon by the parties, either in the employment contract or through subsequent mutual agreement, then reasonable notice must be given. If the employer has concerns about the employee's continuing to work during the notice period, pay in lieu of notice (a severance package) can be given instead. A lawyer can advise as to the length of the required notice, and costly litigation may thus be avoided.

JUST CAUSE

When there is just cause, there is no requirement for an employer to give any notice. An employee can be dismissed without notice for things such as serious absenteeism, consistent tardiness, open disobedience, habitual negligence, incompetence, harassing other employees, drinking on the job, or immoral conduct on or off the job that reflects badly on the employer. Even swearing at the employer

Notice not required when there is just cause

[13.] See *Levy v. Ken-Wo Country Club* (2001), 194 N.S.R. (2d) 213 (N.S.S.C.), in which the golf course groundskeeper was not recalled after 24 seasons with that employer.

[14.] *Singh v. BC Hydro and Power Authority* (2001), 95 B.C.L.R. (3d) 238 (C.A.), leave to appeal refused, [2002] S.C.C.A. No. 45.

has been determined to be serious misconduct sufficient to justify dismissal. Such conduct may be used to defend a wrongful dismissal action, even if it is discovered after the employee has been dismissed. In the *Dowling* case in Case Summary 10.4 below, it was the employee's dishonesty that justified the dismissal. Such dishonesty need not be tolerated by the employer, regardless the plight of the employee.

When dismissing employees for dishonesty or behaviour such as fraud or theft, great care must be taken to ensure that the accusations are accurate and the evidence firm. The courts have awarded significant damages for wrongful dismissal, augmented by punitive damages, when such charges have not been substantiated.[15]

Also, care should be taken to ensure that when a person is dismissed, the real reason for the termination is not discrimination. The human rights tribunals of the various jurisdictions are very active in prosecuting such violations.

A final word: In rare instances, even dishonesty will not constitute just cause for dismissal when other mitigating factors are present. For example, when a bank clerk was found to have stolen $2500 from her employer and then lied about it, her dismissal was overturned by an arbitrator who substituted a 22-month suspension. This decision was upheld when appealed to a Quebec court.[16] The clerk had an unblemished record of 25 years' employment with the bank. She stole the money because of a pathological addiction to video poker. There was great remorse, along with expert testimony of the family and personal problems she had faced because of the addiction. These factors led the arbitrator, supported later by the court, to decide that dismissal was too harsh in this instance. Proportionality between the offence and the punishment is the key in such decisions.

CASE SUMMARY 10.4

Honesty Is Still the Best Policy: *Dowling v. Ontario (Workplace Safety and Insurance Board)*[17]

Dowling was a manager of an office of the Workplace Safety and Insurance Board. He had worked for that organization for 25 years. He was terminated for cause, with the employer claiming that he had purchased a computer from one of its clients (an account he supervised), receiving a discount in the process and giving an advantage in return. It was also claimed that he had accepted a payment of $1000 on another occasion from the same client. His employer conducted an investigation and, in the process, Dowling made misrepresentations and provided false documents.

At trial, the Judge found that the dishonest conduct was not enough to justify Dowling's termination. On appeal, however, the Court of Appeal found that the receipt of the $1000 payment and the discount with respect to the computers amounted to a conflict of interest. The Court also went on to find that the conduct of Dowling during the investigation in which he lied and presented false documents constituted dishonesty and misconduct sufficient to result in a breakdown of the employment relationship. This

---

[15] See *Clenndenning v. Lowndes Lambert (B.C.) Ltd.* (1998), 41 C.C.E.L. (2d) 58 (B.C.S.C.), varied (2000), 4 C.C7L. (3d) 238 (B.C.C.A.), in which the trial Court awarded an additional 36 months' salary as damages for the bad faith of the employer. On appeal, this award was reduced as the employer's honest belief that it had cause for dismissal negated bad faith.

[16] *Banque Laurentienne du Canada c. Lussier,* [2003] J.Q. No. 1468.

[17] (2005), 246 D.L.R. (4th) 65 (Ont. C.A.).

amounted to cause for termination and was characterized by the Court as giving rise to a fundamental breach of his employment relationship. In the words of Justice Gillese, "It was indispensable to the parties' employment relationship that Mr. Dowling exercise the powers of his position with honesty and impartiality, and exclusively in the interests of the Board and the public. The underpinnings of faith and confidence, necessary to the parties' employment relationship, were destroyed by Mr. Dowling's misconduct. When the various acts of misconduct are considered in the context of Mr. Dowling's position, the degree of trust reposed in him and the public nature of the Board's responsibility, it is clear that summary dismissal was a proportionate response."

DISCUSSION QUESTIONS

What do you think? Should even minor instances of dishonesty associated with the business justify termination? What if that dishonesty is not associated with the business but relates to some private aspect of the employee's life?

DISABLED WORKERS

In the past, employees who became seriously ill, even though not "at fault," could be discharged without notice if they could no longer perform their job. The employer did not have to pay for work not done. There was no suggestion of fault here. The employment contract was considered to be frustrated. Even today, when the employee can't work, termination is justified. However, there is a legislated duty to accommodate disabled workers who are still able to work. Human rights commissions are very willing to rule against employers who too quickly fire workers because of illness or disability. The employer must take great care to accommodate such disabled workers and to otherwise comply with the provisions of both the applicable human rights legislation and the workers' compensation legislation, which are designed to protect disabled or injured workers.

> *Illness may constitute frustration of contract*

Disability is a prohibited ground. In enforcing the prohibition of discrimination against the disabled, the courts have ruled that employers have a legal duty to take reasonable steps to accommodate an employee's individual needs. This legal duty does not apply, however, if the only way to resolve the problem will cause the employer *undue hardship*, that is, hardship that is substantial in nature. To deal with this problem, most businesses offer some form of illness and long-term disability insurance or policy as part of their benefits package.

DISOBEDIENCE AND INCOMPETENCE

Although an employee is entitled to refuse to work because of dangerous working conditions, failure to perform a reasonable order is also grounds for dismissal without notice. Disobedience justifies dismissal. Incompetence is also just cause for dismissal; however, employers are well advised to let employees know when the level of performance is unacceptable as soon as it becomes apparent, and provide an opportunity for improvement. It may appear to be easier to let the matter go, but the employer may then be faced with the argument that the employer's conduct and acceptance of the employee's performance led that employee to believe that the level of performance was appropriate. This argument will be especially difficult to overcome if bonuses or wage increases were given to the employee in the past despite the poor performance.

> *Problem when incompetence tolerated*

LAYOFFS

Layoff or termination

When an employer simply runs out of work for the employee to do, or runs into financial difficulties, that is not just cause for termination, and reasonable notice is still required. Even when the layoff is only temporary, the employee may be entitled to treat it as termination and demand the appropriate notice and compensation. In the absence of such reasonable notice or just cause, the employee can sue the employer for wrongful dismissal. Provisions in collective agreements often cover layoffs and recalls, and several provinces have included provisions covering temporary layoffs in their employment standards legislation.

For example, Ontario's *Employment Standards Act*[18] stipulates that if an employee has been laid off for a period longer than the defined "temporary layoff" (generally 13 weeks) employment terminates, and the employer must pay the employee termination pay. However, if wages or other payments are made to, or for the benefit of, the employee during the layoff, the length of the temporary layoff can be extended to 35 weeks. (Each province will have different rules in this area; refer to the MyBusLawLab to determine the specific provincial or federal law in effect where the employee is working.)

WRONGFUL LEAVING

Employees are also required to give reasonable notice upon leaving, although what constitutes reasonable notice is usually considerably less. Unless the employee is in a key position, such as senior executive or salesperson, it is usually not worth the effort to sue when an employee leaves without giving proper notice. But key employees may be required to give substantial notice just like employers.

Employees can leave without notice if contract breached by employer first

When there is a serious breach of the employment contract by the employer, however, the employees are entitled to leave without notice. If the employer gives an unreasonable or dangerous order, if the working conditions are dangerous and the employer refuses to correct them, or if the employer involves the employee in illegal or immoral activities, the employee may be entitled to "quit."

Employees may be sued for breach of duty

If former employees are sued, it is usually for breach of fiduciary duty or for disclosing confidential information. Ordinary employees do not have a fiduciary duty and, unless there is a valid restrictive covenant in their employment contract preventing them from doing so, they are free to compete with their former employer as soon as they leave.[19] That competition, however, must start after they leave. Employees cannot gather information, copy customer lists, or solicit customers before termination. If they do, they can be sued. Similarly, if the departing employee takes confidential information and misuses it, that conduct is also actionable.[20] As managers and other executives owe a fiduciary duty to their employer, they may find themselves somewhat restricted in what they can do even after they leave their employment. It is much preferable for the employer to set out such restrictions clearly in the original employment contract.

---

18. S.O. 2000, c. 41, s. 56.

19. See *Gertz v. Meda Ltd.* (2002), 16 C.C.E.L. (3d) 79 (Ont. Sup. Ct. J.), in which Gertz's wrongful dismissal action succeeded whereas the employer's claims of breach of fiduciary duty and of confidentiality were dismissed. Gertz took certain knowledge about the industry and client needs with him, but the Court held that a mere employee's duty of fidelity to the employer ceases with termination of employment.

20. See *CRC-Evans Canada Ltd. v. Pettifer* (1997), 197 A.R. 24 (Q.B.); aff'd (1998), 216 A.R. 192 (C.A.), in which two former key employees set up a competing corporation and used confidential information from the former employer in bidding against that party. They were ordered to pay $305 507.72 in damages for breaching their duty to serve their employer honestly and faithfully, and for breach of their fiduciary duty.

CASE SUMMARY 10.5

No General Duty Not to Compete with Former Employer: *RBC Dominion Securities Inc. v. Merrill Lynch*[21]

Virtually all of the investment advisers at the Cranbrook RBC branch left without notice. They went to the branch of a competitor, Merrill Lynch. Delamont, the RBC branch manager, orchestrated the move. RBC sued Delamont and the investment advisers, as well as Merrill Lynch and its manager. The trial Judge held that: (1) Delamont and the investment advisers were not fiduciary employees; (2) the investment advisers breached the implied terms of their employment contracts requiring reasonable notice (which was held to be 2.5 weeks) and prohibiting unfair competition with RBC; and (3) Delamont had breached his contractual duty by organizing the departure.

Damages were assessed against the investment advisers and Delamont; Merrill Lynch and its manager were found jointly and severally liable, as the manager had induced the breach of the duty not to compete unfairly. The Court of Appeal overturned the award of damages against the investment advisers and Merrill Lynch and its manager. It also set aside the award against Delamont for breach of a contractual duty of good faith.

The Supreme Court of Canada reinstated the award of the trial Judge except for the damages payable by the investment advisers for losses due to unfair competition based on their actions during the notice period. The Court ruled that damages arising in respect of an employment contract should, as for all contracts, be such as arise naturally, or as may reasonably be supposed to have been in the contemplation of both parties, at the time they made the contract, as the probable result of a breach. The Court decided that an implied term of Delamont's employment contract was the retention of RBC's employees under his supervision. Delamont therefore breached his contractual duty of good faith by organizing the departure of the investment advisers.

The Court also held that an employee who has terminated employment is not prevented from competing with his employer during the notice period. The employer is restricted to damages for the employee's failure to give reasonable notice. The employee could be liable for damages for such things as improper use of confidential information during the notice period. The award of damages by the trial Judge for the investment advisers competing against their former employer was therefore wrong in law. Given the loss of profits award made against Delamont, it was inappropriate to award damages against the investment advisers for loss of profits based on their improper use of confidential information.

DISCUSSION QUESTIONS

In Canada, the required notice periods with respect to termination can be very lengthy compared to those in other countries. Consider the effect of such lengthy notice periods imposed on employers and employees with respect to the flexibility of the labour market and the efficient operation of an employer's business.

[21.] 2008 SCC 54.

CONSTRUCTIVE DISMISSAL

When an employer demotes the employee or otherwise unilaterally changes the nature of the job, this may constitute constructive dismissal, and the employee may be able to sue for wrongful dismissal. Sometimes the employer does this inadvertently; sometimes she does it to humiliate or to make an employee uncomfortable so that the employee will voluntarily leave. From a contractual perspective, one party cannot simply impose a change in the terms of a contract without first securing the consent or agreement of the other party. In essence, the employer is simply refusing to perform the original contract when it demotes an employee.

As with harassment or sexual harassment, even when the problems are caused by other employees, the employer is still responsible. For example, in the *Stamos* case, in which an employee suffered stress-related health issues as a result of another employee and resigned, the Court found that the employer's failure to defuse the hostile work environment constituted constructive dismissal.[22] When there is constructive dismissal, the employee has an obligation to mitigate, possibly to the extent of accepting a new position offered by the employer. The employee is not, of course, obligated to accept such a position when it would cause undue humiliation or otherwise create an impossible working situation, especially if bad relations have been created because of the way the termination took place.

Promoting one employee is fine, but demoting another without cause may prompt a costly lawsuit. An employee may be constructively dismissed even when offered a comparable position. Consider the *Weselan* case, in which an employee was relocated and given a similar position.[23] The new job, however, involved a substantial daily commute at the cost of time and approximately $34 000 per year. This meant that the employee's working conditions and net remuneration would be substantially different, so he was constructively dismissed. The law simply requires reasonable steps to be taken to mitigate damage. One does not have to suffer a substantial loss to mitigate damages.

CASE SUMMARY 10.6

Employment Contracts Are Binding: *Hilton v. Norampac Inc.;*[24] *Weselan v. Totten Sims Hubicki Associates (1997) Ltd.*[25]

Hilton had worked for Norampac as a mill worker for 15 years when his conditions of employment were unilaterally changed by the employer. He was working as a foreman when the employer demanded that he, along with other foremen, was required to be on call for extensive periods including weekends without any extra pay. He explained that he couldn't do this as it required him to be available on the weekends when his wife worked and he had to look after his young children. He offered to be on call during the

---

22. *Stamos v. Annuity Research & Marketing Service Ltd.* (2002), 18 C.C.E.L. (3d) 117 (Ont. Sup. Ct. J.).

23. *Weselan v. Totten Sims Hubicki Associates (1997) Ltd.* (2001), 16 C.C.E.L. (3d) 184 (Ont. C.A.), varied on issue of costs, [2001] O.J. No. 5145 (Ont. C.A.).

24. (2003), 26 C.C.E.L. (3d) 179, (2003), 176 O.A.C. 309 (O.C.A.).

25. [2003] O.J. No. 1242 (On. S.C.).

week, or to be demoted to a union position, but these offers were rejected and his employment was terminated for cause based on his refusal to obey proper instruction. He sued for wrongful dismissal. The trial Court and the Appeal Court found that this was a material change in his terms of employment, which amounted to constructive dismissal. He was therefore successful in his wrongful dismissal action.

The enforcement of the employment contract does not always favour the employee. Weselan had been working for his employer for more than 10 years, and had been associated with the firm as an independent engineer for much longer than that, when his employment was terminated. The Court found that if the common law prevailed he would have been entitled to 24 months' notice, or $147 400 in lieu of that notice. Unfortunately for Weselan, his original contract of employment contained a provision requiring only 90 days' notice if dismissed without cause. Since this provision was greater than the statutory minimum, it prevailed, and the damage award was limited to only $18 925, representing that 90-day entitlement.

SMALL BUSINESS PERSPECTIVE

Does the ruling against Norampac impose too much restriction on the employer's operation of its business? In light of the law of constructive dismissal, should an employer's employment contracts be very specific as to the duties of the employees, or should they be very broad, outlining the duties of the employees in a general sense?

REMEDIES FOR WRONGFUL DISMISSAL

In a wrongful dismissal action, the damages awarded are usually based on what the employee would have received had proper notice been given. If a person is fired and is given only one month's notice when he should have received five months' notice, he will be awarded the difference, including any benefits and pension rights to which he would have been entitled. The employee does, however, have an obligation to mitigate. He must try to find another job.[26] Any damages awarded will be reduced by what is earned from that other employment.[27]

Compensation based on notice that should have been given

Obligation to mitigate losses

In rare circumstances, the court will also take into account a person's damaged reputation or mental distress, and sometimes will even award punitive damages where appropriate.[28] It is normally the employer, often a corporation, that is sued for wrongful dismissal, but the individual manager implementing the decision may also be sued when defamation or some other actionable wrong has taken place.

It is evident that great care must be exercised when dismissing an employee for incompetence or misconduct. An employer must have clear evidence of the misconduct or incompetence and, with the latter, must demonstrate that the employee has been given a reasonable opportunity to improve. Failure to substantiate just cause will likely result in a successful action by the employee for wrongful dismissal.

Employer must have clear evidence of misconduct

26. But see *E.C. & M. Electric Ltd. v. Alberta (Employment Standards Code)* (1994), 7 C.C.E.L. (2d) 235 (Alta. Prov. Ct.). While a duty to mitigate exists under common law, no such duty is imposed on the employee under Alberta's *Employment Standards Code*. Money earned from other employment need not be deducted from the statutory severance pay.

27. Efforts to mitigate damages need only be those expected of a reasonable person. See *Bradbury v. Newfoundland (Attorney General)*(2001), 207 Nfld. & P.E.I.R. 181 (Nfld. C.A.).

28. See *Honda Canada Inc. v. Keays, supra* note 11.

REDUCING RISK 10.2

Employers are often surprised to learn of the lengthy notice requirements for termination in Canada. Including specified notice entitlements in the contract of employment will go a long way to solving the problem. But if this is done, it is vital not to make the contracted notice period less than the minimum specified in the relevant employment standards legislation. If it is, the contract clause may be void, and the employer may be required to pay a much higher amount based on the common law notice period.

Employers must avoid the temptation to manufacture reasons to justify dismissal without notice or to make an employee so uncomfortable that he will quit. Courts are now willing to find constructive dismissal, and assess higher damages, if there is evidence of false statements, defamation, a poisoned work environment, or damage to the employee's reputation. The sensible way to approach the problem is to negotiate with the employee. Typically, the employee will settle for less when he realizes that he will thereby avoid the significant legal costs of a wrongful dismissal lawsuit.

Damages are the appropriate remedy for wrongful dismissal. It is rare for a court to order that an employee be given back the job. Reinstatement is more common if collective agreements are involved, when the decision is made by an arbitrator rather than a judge. Some statutes, such as the *Canada Labour Code*,[29] provide for reinstatement in non-union situations. Still, in general, reinstatement is rare.

Liability of Employer

Although not directly at fault, an employer can be held liable for torts committed by an employee during the course of employment. This is the principle of vicarious liability that was discussed in Chapters 4 and 5. Because the employer benefits from the work of the employee, the employer is held responsible for losses caused by the employee. The employer's liability is limited to those activities that take place during the course of employment. This includes not only incidents arising during working hours, but also any conduct that takes place as part of the employment activity. If Pawluk, while delivering a letter to his employer's client on his way home, injures a pedestrian, both Pawluk and his employer would likely be liable. The negligent act occurred during the course of employment, even though it did not happen during working hours. But if Pawluk injures the pedestrian when he goes out to do his personal banking during working hours, the employer would not be liable. In this case, Pawluk is "on a frolic of his own," and the injury did not take place in the course of his employment.

As a general rule, there must be an employment relationship for vicarious liability to apply. This is one reason why the tests discussed above for determining whether an employment relationship exists are so important. (Some exceptions to this requirement will be discussed in the next chapter.) Several jurisdictions have legislated vicarious liability in special situations. For example, in Alberta, British Columbia, and some other provinces, the owner of a motor vehicle is vicariously liable for any torts committed by the person driving the vehicle with the

mybuslawlab
www.pearsoned.ca/mybuslawlab

BC AB SK MB ON

Employer liable for torts committed by employee while on the job

Vicarious liability and motor vehicle

---

[29] R.S.C. 1985, c. L-2.

owner's consent. The driver is deemed to be "the agent or employee of the owner of the motor vehicle, employed as the agent or employee of the motor vehicle, and driving the motor vehicle in the course of that person's employment."[30]

This section actually expands the potential liability of an employer that allows its employees to drive its vehicles beyond the normal scope of vicarious liability. Under vicarious liability, the employer escapes liability if the employee negligently hurts the plaintiff while "on a frolic of his own." The statute, on the other hand, deems the driver to be driving in the course of his employment, whether he's driving for a job-related purpose or not. For example, in the *Morad* case, the employer was held liable when an employee borrowed the company vehicle and then deliberately ran over some third party who owed him money![31] Other provinces, such as Ontario, simply make an owner liable for any damage negligently caused by a person driving his car with consent without reference to an employment or agency relationship.[32] Refer to the MyBusLawLab for provincial variations on this issue.

Although the employer has the right to turn to the employee for compensation when it is found vicariously liable, this is usually a hollow remedy, the employee typically being in no financial position to pay such compensation.

Employers often try to separate portions of their operations from the actual business they conduct. Cleaning and office management, as well as sales and product service, may be contracted out. This is done to reduce the number of employees, thereby reducing administrative costs, leaving the organization free to concentrate on what it does best. It may also reduce the risk of the employer being found vicariously liable when injuries take place. Avoiding vicarious liability is more likely when great care has been taken to make sure the people doing those jobs are truly independent. But even then, the courts may still find a sufficiently close relationship to impose vicarious liability on the employer for the wrongful acts committed by these supposedly independent workers. The risk of such liability should be planned for in the operation of the business. Liability insurance is typically advisable.

Legislation

As a consequence of the relatively weak position of individual employees in the employment relationship, employees have tended to band together to exert greater pressure on the employer. Such collective action is now governed by legislation and will be discussed under "Collective Bargaining" later in this chapter.

A considerable amount of legislation has also been passed that is designed to protect employees, whether unionized or not, by setting minimum standards of safety, remuneration, hours of work, and other benefits. Conditions of employment normally fall under provincial jurisdiction. Most provinces have concentrated their employee welfare legislation into one statute, generally called the *Employment Standards Act*, or *Labour Standards Act*, which sets minimum standards in connection with

- wages
- overtime, work hours, and rest periods

mybuslawlab
www.pearsoned.ca/mybuslawlab

BC AB SK MB ON

Provincial legislation applies

---

30. *Traffic Safety Act*, R.S.A. 2000, c. T-6, s. 187. See also *Motor Vehicle Act*, R.S.B.C. 1996, c. 318, s. 86.
31. *Morad v. Emmanouel* (1993), 9 Alta. L.R. (3d) 378 (Q.B.).
32. *Highway Traffic Act*, R.S.O. 1990, c. H-8, s. 192(2).

- vacation and holiday entitlements
- maternity and parental leave
- termination and severance pay.

Some also provide for bereavement and sick leave.

There are substantial differences in the details. For example, the general minimum wage in Alberta in April 2009 was set at $8.80 per hour, whereas in neighbouring British Columbia it was $8.00 ($6.00 for employees newly entering the workforce). Employment standards legislation varies with each jurisdiction. Refer to the MyBusLawLab for specific information relevant to your particular jurisdiction.

Federal legislation also may apply

There are, however, a number of activities, such as banking, the military, activities on aboriginal reserves, the post office, telephone and broadcast companies, and airlines, railroads, and steamships that fall under federal jurisdiction. The employment relationship in those sectors is governed by the federal *Canada Labour Code*,[33] Part III sets out employment standards. Since it applies across the country, its provisions will be reviewed here to illustrate employment standards.

EMPLOYMENT STANDARDS

Statutes set out minimum standards

Notice periods less than the common law standard can be set out in employment contracts, and as long as they are greater than the minimum statutory requirement, they will prevail. This was illustrated in the *Weselan* case (second part of Case Summary 10.6 above). If a notice period is shorter than the statutory minimum, it will be void and the employer will then have to comply with the longer "reasonable notice" provisions found in common law. The statutory provisions set a minimum standard, thus agreements that waive the protections or remedies available under the legislation may likewise be declared void. When the parties have agreed to a higher standard, or when a higher standard is imposed by common law, that higher standard will normally prevail.[34] But even the minimum statutory provisions do not treat all employees equally. The government may exempt, or modify certain provisions in respect of, certain types of employment. In other words, employers may, for example, be excused from paying minimum wage to managers or students, and overtime may be calculated differently for persons engaged in different lines of work. (Note that details as to payment of wages, minimum wage, deductions from pay, hours of work and overtime, vacation and holiday entitlements, maternity and parental benefits, employment of minors, and bereavement and sick leave can be obtained from the MyBusLawLab.)

[33.] *Supra* note 29.

[34.] *Ibid.*, s. 168. Note that similar provisions are found in provincial acts.

CASE SUMMARY 10.7

Statutory Notice May Not Suffice: *Machtinger v. HOJ Industries Ltd.*[35]

This case involves two employees who were terminated from their employment with only four weeks' notice, despite the fact that they both had been employed for a number of years. The employees each brought a wrongful dismissal action against the employer, demanding compensation. The issue was whether the four weeks' notice was enough. This notice corresponded with the statutory minimum under the *Employment Standards Act*. The employment contracts required even less notice to be given. If common law applied, each employee would be entitled to more than seven months' notice.

The Supreme Court of Canada held that any contractual term that did not comply with the minimum standards set out in the *Act* was a nullity. The minimal notice provisions found in the contract were therefore void. The Court then observed that, although the notice given satisfied the requirements of the legislation, that was merely a minimum standard. Since common law required more than seven months' notice in such circumstances, that longer notice requirement prevailed. Complying with the statutory minimum was not good enough in this case.

SMALL BUSINESS PERSPECIVE

This case illustrates the confusion and inconsistency involved in enforcing the terms agreed to in the contract, applying the statutory minimums, or requiring the much more lengthy common law notice period to be followed. Because of this complexity, it is important for a small business owner to obtain legal advice with respect to the preparation of employment contracts for employees. Should governments attempt to simplify the law relating to the employment relationship?

TERMINATION

As under common law, the *Canada Labour Code* recognizes that no notice is required when the dismissal is for cause; otherwise, notice of termination is necessary.[36] Where the *Code* and common law differ is in the remedies available for wrongful dismissal. When determining adequate notice and severance pay, the *Code* does not consider the nature of the employment, only its length. Employees who have completed three months or more of continuous employment are to receive two weeks' notice of termination (except when the dismissal is for cause). Additionally, employees who have been employed for more than 12 months are entitled to severance pay of two days' wages for each completed year of service, plus five days' wages. The *Code* also provides that when a person has been laid off for a period longer than three months, he may be able to treat this layoff as a termination and claim termination pay and severance pay. (There are exceptions, as when payments are made to the employee during the layoff.)

Termination entitlements determined by length of service

Layoffs may trigger termination pay

---

35. [1992] 1 S.C.R. 986.

36. *Supra* note 29, ss. 230–237.

Most jurisdictions have passed similar legislation, but the provisions vary substantially; it is thus necessary to review the provisions of the relevant statute to determine the entitlements of a particular employee.

ISSUE ESTOPPEL

Choosing to file complaint may preclude suing later

Employees who face termination have a real concern. Case law makes it imperative that employees seek legal advice before filing a complaint under employment standards legislation. By simply applying for these minimal legislative benefits, an employee may lose the ability to later sue for damages for wrongful dismissal based on common law. If an employment standards officer determines that the complainant was terminated for cause, not only will the complainant's claim for termination pay under the statute fail, but if the employee later tries to sue for damages for wrongful dismissal, the court may decide that the issue was already settled.[37] This is because the employment standards officer has already decided that the termination was not wrongful. **Issue estoppel** may cause the court to dismiss the wrongful dismissal suit altogether, without even hearing the details. Such were the results in the *Fayant* and *Wong* cases,[38] where the pleadings were struck out after issue estoppel was successfully raised.

COMPLAINTS

Employment standards legislation allows employees to file a complaint with a government board; the investigation and determination is then made by civil servants.[39] This process enables the employee to avoid the costs of litigation. Note that time limitations vary between employment standards statutes and may well be as short as a few months. Under the federal legislation, the inspector may dismiss the complaint if it is unfounded, but this determination may be appealed. If the inspector determines that earnings are due to the employee, she may order payment to be made. If the employer is a corporation, the individual directors may be liable personally for up to six months' wages per employee.

HUMAN RIGHTS

Federal and provincial human rights legislation prohibit most forms of discrimination in employment

An area of employment law that is becoming much more significant is the protection of employee rights. With the passage of the *Charter of Rights and Freedoms*, as well as federal and provincial human rights legislation, employers are required not only to ensure that they do not discriminate in their hiring and employment practices, but that they take active steps to ensure that these basic rights are protected. Although the *Charter* does not apply directly to most employment situations, it does have an important indirect effect, since federal and provincial human rights statutes must be consistent with the provisions of the *Charter*. Indeed, as mentioned in Chapter 2, the courts have gone as far as to read into human rights statutes protection for homosexual persons, where no such provision was originally included.[40] Human rights legislation has an impact on employment

---

[37.] *Fayant v. Campbell's Maple Village Ltd.* (1993), 146 A.R. 175 (Q.B.); *Wong v. Shell Canada*(1995), 174 A.R. 287 (C.A.), leave to appeal to S.C.C. refused, [1995] S.C.C.A. No. 551.

[38.] *Rasanen v. Rosemount Instruments Ltd.* (1994), 17 O.R. (3d) 267 (C.A.), leave to appeal to S.C.C. refused, [1994] S.C.C.A. No. 152.

[39.] *Supra* note 29, ss. 249–251.

[40.] *Vriend v. Alberta*, [1998] 1 S.C.R. 493.

by prohibiting discrimination on the basis of race, national or ethnic origin, colour, religion, gender, sexual orientation, and, in some cases, age, marital status, family status, physical or mental disability, and pardoned criminal convictions.

CASE SUMMARY 10.8

Family Needs Must Be Accommodated: *Health Sciences Assoc. of B.C. v. Campbell River and North Island Transition Society*[41]

Howard was a part-time employee working as a child and youth support counsellor at a women's safe house. She worked between 8:30 a.m. and 3 p.m., giving her time to look after her own son who suffered from ADHD and Tourette's syndrome and who needed special care after school because of these conditions. Her employer decided to change her hours, requiring her to work until 6 p.m. Unfortunately, this interfered with her ability to provide the necessary care of her own son after school. She grieved the decision.

The employer's reason for the change was based on business considerations requiring her to be available so she could spend more time counselling school-aged children. Even after her request and a doctor's letter asking that the decision be reconsidered, the employer refused. The grievance was argued on the basis that the employer's decision amounted to discrimination against Howard on the basis of family status, which was prohibited under the B.C. *Human Rights Code*. The employer argued that the *Code* did not stipulate that employers had an obligation to accommodate an employee's child care needs. The Court held that because this was a change that caused a serious interference with a substantial parental or family duty, a prima facie case of discrimination on the basis of family status had been established. There was a duty to accommodate as long as doing so didn't impose undue hardship on the employer.

DISCUSSION QUESTIONS

Do you think we have taken human rights enforcement too far?

Human rights tribunals have been established to hear complaints about violations of human rights legislation. These tribunals have the power to investigate, levy fines, and even order reinstatement of employees if they find that the employees have been terminated in violation of some human rights provision, or forced to quit because of harassment.

Tribunals hear complaints

The *Canadian Human Rights Act*, for example, prohibits discrimination with regard to any term or condition of employment on the basis of a person's race, religion, and so on. It specifically prohibits the refusal to hire, or the firing of, any person on the basis of one of the prohibited grounds.[42]

For example, to discriminate against a woman because of pregnancy would constitute gender discrimination. Employers cannot, therefore, fire or demote an

---

41. (2004), 240 D.L.R. (4th) 479, 28 B.C.L.R. (4th) 292 (B.C.C.A.).

42. *Canadian Human Rights Act*, R.S.C. 1985, c. H-6, s. 7.

employee because of pregnancy. Also, an employer's refusal to permit an employee to breastfeed in the workplace may constitute discrimination on the basis of gender.[43] Furthermore, employers must refrain from asking women at job interviews whether they are pregnant, or plan to have children, for the legislation also addresses discrimination during pre-employment inquiries.

Job advertisements and application forms must not directly or indirectly express a limitation or preference based on race, colour, gender, or other prohibited ground. The forms used cannot require applicants to furnish information concerning their gender, age, marital status, and so on. Accordingly, unless a bona fide occupational requirement exists that would justify such an inquiry, employers must refrain from requesting photographs or that the applicant's gender, previous name, marital status, date of birth, or religion be provided in the application form.

Harassment also covered

Harassment is a form of discrimination that occurs when one subjects another person to unwelcome verbal or physical conduct because of his or her colour, gender, age, or other characteristic. Unwanted physical contact, jokes, or insults are harassment when they negatively affect the working environment. Note that interaction between a supervisor and her subordinates, even outside the workplace, can be employment-related harassment. If the supervisor's conduct creates a perception that continued employment is dependent on sexual interaction with that person, then that supervisor has engaged in harassment.[44] Sexual harassment is just one example of harassment. When harassment is committed by an employee, the employer can be held responsible if it has failed to take adequate steps to protect the employee who was harassed. It is, therefore, vital for employers to be proactive and to take positive steps to develop anti-harassment and anti-discrimination policies, clarifying that such conduct will not be tolerated. These policies should also spell out what disciplinary steps might be taken if one employee harasses, or discriminates against, another employee.

CASE SUMMARY 10.9

Should the Employer Be Liable? *Robichaud v. Canada (Treasury Board)*[45]

The Supreme Court of Canada had to determine whether the employer was responsible for the sexual harassment committed by an employee. Robichaud worked as a lead hand in a cleaning operation for the Department of National Defence. A supervisor subjected her to unwanted sexual attention. Such behaviour amounts to discrimination on the basis of gender because it differentiates adversely against an employee on the basis of her gender. The Court held that the employer, under the *Canadian Human Rights Act*, was liable for the discriminatory acts of its employees that were committed in the course of their employment, much like vicarious liability in common law. The case indicates the approach taken by courts when faced with sexual harassment.

---

43. *Re Carewest and H.S.A.A. (Degagne)* (2001), 93 L.A.C. (4th) 129 (Alta.).

44. *Simpson v. Consumers' Association of Canada* (2001), 57 O.R. (3d) 351 (C.A.), leave to appeal to S.C.C. refused, [2002] S.C.C.A. No. 83.

45. [1987] 2 S.C.R. 84.

In fact, this precedent has been followed when applying provincial legislation to instances of sexual harassment. In the *Katsiris* case,[46] the corporation owning the restaurant was held liable for the harassment committed by its employee. That case also addressed whether the CEO of the corporation should be personally liable. Since it was not shown that he knew of the sexual harassment, liability was not imposed on him personally.

SMALL BUSINESS PERSPECTIVE

What factors should the court consider in determining whether to hold the employer liable for the wrongful conduct of its employee in these circumstances? What can an employer do to minimize its potential liability (and the liability of the directors, if the employer is a corporation) for the actions of its employees?

This positive obligation on the employer to protect vulnerable employees in the workplace has been taken further. As mentioned above, employers now have an obligation to take steps to accommodate employees with disabilities and special needs. This may extend to changing the physical work environment to accommodate visually impaired people or wheelchair users. It includes allowing workers with chronic illness, such as AIDS, or partial disability, to do lighter work or to work only part-time.[47] Schedules may require adjustment to accommodate different religious holidays, as long as the request does not cause the employer undue hardship.[48]

Duty to accommodate

Employers may find their rules being challenged as discriminatory. Rules requiring employees to be of a certain stature may, for example, discriminate against certain racial groups. Rules requiring uniforms or hard hats to be worn may discriminate against certain religious groups. These rules may, however, be saved if the employer establishes them to be bona fide (genuine) occupational requirements. The hard-hat rule may prevail, even if it violates a religious right to wear a turban, if safety concerns justify its use. But for the requirement to be a bona fide one, it must relate to a necessary part of the job. Also, when a rule adversely affects a particular group, the employer must take reasonable steps to accommodate the disadvantaged group.

CASE SUMMARY 10.10

Effect Duty to Accommodate and Adverse-Effect Discrimination: *Meiorin*[49]

This is a leading case for determining whether a particular occupational requirement is reasonable and justifiable. Meiorin, who worked as a firefighter, failed a running test designed to measure aerobic fitness. She was therefore terminated after three years of

---

46. *Katsiris v. Isaac* (2001), 204 Sask. R. 52 (Q.B.).

47. See *Ontario (Human Rights Commission) v. Roosma* (2002), 21 C.C.E.L. (3d) 112 (Ont. Sup. Ct. J.), in which it was held that releasing employees from Friday night shifts to accommodate their religious beliefs would cause undue hardship. Such accommodation was therefore waived.

48. See the updated Canadian Human Rights Commission Policy on HIV/AIDS, Canadian Human Rights Commission, www.chrc-ccdp.ca/legislation_policies/aids-en.asp.

49. *British Columbia (Public Service Employee Relations Commission) v. British Columbia Government and Service Employees' Union (B.C.G.S.E.U.)*, [1999] 3 S.C.R. 3.

service. Minimum fitness standards for firefighters had been introduced by the government. The issue before the arbitrator was whether the running test component was discriminatory on the basis of gender. It measured aerobic capacity and women generally have lower aerobic capacity than men. It was argued that this amounted to *adverse-effect discrimination* against Meiorin. This type of discrimination involves a *generally applicable rule* that has a *particular adverse effect* on one group (women) because of a prohibited ground (their gender). In these circumstances, when a rule is shown to have a discriminatory effect, the employer can continue to apply the rule only if it is justifiable as a *bona fide* occupational requirement.

The Supreme Court of Canada stated that the categorization of discrimination as adverse effect or direct effect was no longer appropriate. The Court enunciated a three-part test to evaluate whether an occupational requirement (meeting the fitness standard) is justified. Once the complainant shows that the standard is discriminatory, the employer must prove

1. That there is a rational connection between the test and performance of the job;

2. That the test was adopted under an honest and good-faith belief that the standard was necessary; and

3. That the standard is reasonably necessary to accomplish the employer's legitimate purpose.

The third point implies that the employer may need to show that it cannot accommodate the employee without suffering undue hardship.

The test requires employers to accommodate different members' capabilities before adopting a "standard" or occupational requirement. Before setting the aerobic standard, and setting it so high that most women cannot attain it, it must be shown that such a level of aerobic capacity is necessary to do the job. If it is unnecessary, then the standard cannot be saved as a genuine or bona fide occupational requirement.

No credible evidence was shown to establish that the prescribed aerobic capacity was necessary for either men or women to perform the work of a forest firefighter. The employer also failed to show that it would experience undue hardship if a different standard were used. Accordingly, reinstatement of the claimant was ordered, and she was compensated for her lost benefits and wages. This case underscores the need to be vigilant in setting occupational standards or requirements, for they may be challenged if they have a discriminatory impact on a particular individual or group.

DISCUSSION QUESTIONS

What do you think? Does the Supreme Court's approach result in a lowering of the standards that employers can enforce?

Pay equity

Some jurisdictions have passed **pay equity** statutes requiring equal pay for work of equal value.[50] These provisions usually benefit women, who have traditionally been paid less than men for similar jobs, but they may place considerable hardship on the organization that must bear the extra expense. Most notably, in the *Public Service Alliance of Canada* case, the federal government was required to pay more than $3.3 billion to some 230 000 current and former employees for

---

[50.] *Canada (Attorney General) v. Public Service Alliance of Canada*, [2000] 1 F.C. 146 (T.D.).

13 years' back pay with interest![51] The Canadian Human Rights Tribunal ruled that the federal government had failed to abide by section 11 of the *Canadian Human Rights Act* by allowing a wage gap between men and women doing clerical work—work of equal value. Note that this must be contrasted to a Newfoundland case where the government refused to honour such a back pay order on the grounds that it was experiencing a financial crisis. This was challenged under the *Charter* and the Supreme Court of Canada held that such a financial crisis was a valid reason justifiable under section 1 to continue the inequity.[52] Discrimination in the workplace has prompted the passage of various **employment equity** acts as well.[53] Organizations may be required to take steps to correct employment situations where there has been a tradition of racial or gender imbalance, such as in nursing and engineering. This usually means giving preferential treatment to those job applicants or candidates who belong to underrepresented minority groups. The resulting **reverse discrimination** directed at individuals in the overrepresented group is also distasteful to many. Programs that are intended to correct these historical imbalances in the workplace are specifically authorized under section 15(2) of the *Charter of Rights and Freedoms*. They are sometimes referred to using the American terminology "**affirmative action.**"

Mandatory retirement also raises human rights issues. Forced retirement at 65 years is often justified as good social policy, opening up new jobs for youth. But from the point of view of the retiree, it can be a disaster. Although discrimination in employment on the basis of age is usually prohibited, retirement at 65 years is generally exempted in provincial employment standards or human rights statutes. Where "age" is defined as being 18 or older and less than 65, one who faces age discrimination in the form of forced retirement at age 65 may have no remedy. The Supreme Court of Canada has held that where such a mandatory retirement policy is allowed under provincial human rights legislation, it does not violate the provisions of the *Charter of Rights and Freedoms*, being a reasonable exception under section 1.[54] But if an employer tries to impose a retirement policy commencing at a younger age (for example, 60 for firefighters) it can be saved only if the employer establishes the policy as being justifiable in the circumstances of its workplace.[55]

Note that while forced retirement policies may be tolerated in most jurisdictions, there is nothing requiring an employer to have such a policy. Many employers find that keeping older employees on the job after 65 has a positive impact on their business.

As the rules with respect to discrimination in employment change, employers should be particularly vigilant in developing policies that avoid unjust discrimination against same-sex couples, that accommodate disabled workers, and that prevent the various forms of harassment that can take place in the workplace.

Correction of past imbalance

Mandatory retirement at 65 permitted

[51.] See, for example, *Canadian Human Rights Act, supra* note 42, s.11.

[52.] *Newfoundland (Treasury Board) v. N.A.P.E.*, 2004 S.C.C. 66, 2004 C.L.L.C. 230–035, 244 D.L.R. (4th) 294 (S.C.C.).

[53.] See, for example, *Employment Equity Act*, S.C. 1995, c. 44.

[54.] See "Policy on Discrimination Against Older Persons Because of Age," Ontario Human Rights Commission, http://www.ohrc.on.ca/en/resources/Policies/agepolicyen/pdf.

[55.] *Dickason v. University of Alberta*, [1992] 2 S.C.R. 1103.

WORKERS' COMPENSATION

Worker's compensation—compulsory insurance coverage

Common law was often unable to provide an appropriate remedy for an employee injured on the job. This was especially true when the accident resulted from the employee's own carelessness. All provinces and the federal government have enacted workers' compensation legislation that provides a compulsory insurance program covering accidents that take place on the job.[56] The legislation sets rates of compensation to be paid for different types of injuries and establishes a board that hears and adjudicates the claims of injured employees. The system is essentially a no-fault insurance scheme, in which benefits are paid to injured workers, or to their families in the event of death. Careless conduct on the part of the worker will not disqualify an injured employee from receiving compensation. The program is financed by assessments levied by the provincial workers' compensation boards against the employers; the amount levied varies with the risks associated with the industry involved. Some employees, such as casual workers, farmers, and small business employees, are often excluded. British Columbia has, however, extended workers' compensation coverage to almost all workers in the province. Refer to the MyBusLawLab for provincial variations.[57]

Worker gives up right to any other compensation and cannot sue

A significant aspect of workers' compensation legislation in most jurisdictions is that the worker gives up the right to any other compensation. The worker can no longer sue the employer (or the party who caused the injury, if he also contributed to the plan), being limited to the benefits bestowed by the workers' compensation system. When the injury is caused by someone other than the employer or another employee, the plans usually give the injured worker the choice of receiving workers' compensation benefits or pursuing a civil action.

Compensation is also limited to injury or disease that arises in the course of the employment. This can sometimes be a problem when it is difficult to establish that a disease, such as emphysema or a heart condition, was caused by the work of the employee. Compensation is typically paid to the employee, but when an employee dies as a result of injuries sustained on the job, payments are then made to her dependants,[58] which may include same-sex partners.[59]

HEALTH AND SAFETY

Provision of safe workplace

Related to workers' compensation legislation, in that they work to reduce compensation claims, are statutes controlling health and safety conditions in the workplace. Health and safety requirements are sometimes embodied in general labour statutes, as in the *Canada Labour Code*.[60] Some jurisdictions deal with health and safety in a separate statute, as in Ontario's *Occupational Health and Safety Act*.[61]

[56.] Further information on workers' compensation in Canada is available through the Association of Workers' Compensation Boards of Canada, www.awcbc.org.

[57.] See, for example, Alberta's *Workers' Compensation Act*, R.S.A. 2000, c. W-15, and *Workers' Compensation Regulation*, Alta. Reg. 325/2002. The federal legislation is entitled the *Government Employees Compensation Act*, R.S.C. 1985, c. G-5.

[58.] *Government Employees Compensation Act*, R.S.C. 1985, c. G-5, s. 4.

[59.] For example, see *Workplace Safety and Insurance Act, 1997*, S.O. 1997, c. 16, s. 22.

[60.] R.S.O. 1990, c. O.1.

[61.] *Supra* note 29, Part II.

The main thrust of these statutes and their related regulations[62] is to

1. provide safer working conditions, by requiring fencing of hazardous areas, safety netting, proper shielding of equipment, environmental control, and so on

2. ensure safe employment practices, such as requiring the supply and use of hard hats, goggles, and protective clothing

3. establish programs to educate both the employer and the employee on how to create a safer working environment for all concerned.

These objectives are facilitated through the establishment of a board with the power to hear complaints and enforce correction. Officers are empowered to enter the workplace without a warrant. When such officers encounter dangerous conditions (such as lack of fencing or shielding), poor safety practices (such as failure to use hard hats or safety lines), or environmental contamination (caused by hazardous chemicals, fumes, or dust), they can order the problem corrected or, in serious cases, they can shut the job site down. The offending business can be prosecuted for violations, especially when injury or death results. These provisions are effective only if the fines are significant. Ontario, for example, has increased the maximum fines levied and extended liability to make directors of corporations personally responsible for harmful and dangerous practices. Other provincial variations are available on the MyBusLawLab.

Safety boards ensure regulations are adhered to

EMPLOYMENT INSURANCE

The federal government was given jurisdiction over insurance coverage for unemployed workers by an amendment to the *Constitution Act, 1867* in 1940.[63] Under the *Employment Insurance Act,*[64] both employers and employees pay into a government-supplemented fund. Laid-off employees are entitled to receive payments for a specific period of time. This is not a fund from which the employee is entitled to get back what he has contributed. Rather, the payments are insurance premiums, and an employee is entitled to receive only what is set out in the statute and regulations. This amount is based on the number of weeks worked before the claim and the amount of wages received. Workers who voluntarily leave their employment, or are involved in a strike or lockout, are generally not entitled to receive employment insurance benefits. Those who cannot work because others are on strike will receive benefits, provided they otherwise qualify. A severance package from the employer will also limit eligibility, and no benefits will be paid until the severance period is over. Benefits are also paid under the *Employment Insurance Act* to those who are unable to work because of illness, disability, pregnancy, or adoption. Workers may appeal any decisions made, such as entitlement to benefits, to an administrative body set up under the legislation. The rights of individuals before such administrative tribunals were discussed in Chapter 3.

Employment insurance is federal jurisdiction

Employee must meet qualifications to receive benefits

---

62. These statutes are supplemented by numerous regulations, such as Ontario's *Confined Spaces Regulation*, O. Reg. 632/05, *Training Program Regulation*, O. Reg. 780/94, and *X-ray Safety Regulation*, R.R.O. 1990, Reg. 861.

63. S.C. 1996, c. 23.

64. *Constitution Act, 1940*, 3–4 Geo. VI, c. 36 (U.K.).

REDUCING RISK 10.3

Adhering to the employment standards legislation and dealing with government regulatory bodies can impose considerable hardship on employers, straining their management resources. Health and safety and workers' compensation issues are a fact of life, and enforcement provisions usually put enough pressure on the employer so that there is adherence with the legislative requirements. The same is true with respect to employment insurance and taxation. But human rights standards, including provisions against direct and indirect discrimination and harassment, as well as employment standards, such as minimum wage, hours of work, overtime, holidays, maternity leave, and so on, are usually enforced only when someone makes a complaint. Employees who want to keep their jobs usually do not make such complaints. These complaints therefore usually come after the fact, often after the employee, or a group of employees, has been working in those condi-

tions, sometimes for years. Penalties imposed can be significant.

Ideally, the employer will develop carefully crafted policies and develop training for all, especially those in key decision-making positions, to make sure that the many pitfalls are avoided. When jobs are advertised and potential employees interviewed, great care should be taken to avoid stating qualifications or asking questions that could be construed as discriminatory. Questions relating to a person's place of birth, race, religion, age, language, arrest history, gender, sexual preference, child care arrangements, marital status, or medications being taken should be avoided. Care should also be taken to avoid practices that could be considered discriminatory in promotions, benefits, and bonuses. Clear policies, designed to prevent harassment or discrimination by other employees, should be designed and implemented, with the policy and penalties being made clear to all.

OTHER LEGISLATION

Many other statutes affect the employment relationship. Most jurisdictions have legislation controlling the apprenticeship process and trade schools.[65] Pension benefits are controlled by legislation. Some jurisdictions have legislation controlling the licensing of private employment agencies and restricting the types of payments they can receive from their clients. And, as will be discussed in Chapter 16, legislation such as the *Bankruptcy and Insolvency Act,* the *Wage Earner Protection Program Act,* and the mechanics' or builders' lien acts provide security to the worker in the payment of wages. All jurisdictions have legislation dealing with special categories of employees, such as teachers and public servants.

COLLECTIVE BARGAINING

Consequence of weaker unions

A significant portion of the legislation affecting employment relates to the collective bargaining process. But because the percentage of unionized workers in Canada has declined over the past few decades, those laws have changed in response to the diminished political strength of the unions. Trade unions today are fighting to hold on to what they have gained and are resisting the further weakening of their position. Since the time of the industrial revolution in the United Kingdom, workers have banded together in an attempt to overcome poor working conditions and low wages. A considerable amount of confrontation and violence flared up between unions and employers, especially when unions first

---

[65.] See, for example, Alberta's *Apprenticeship and Industry Training Act,* R.S.A. 2000, c. A-42 and Ontario's *Apprenticeship and Certification Act 1998,* S.O. 1998, c. 22.

attempted to organize or unionize the workforce. In North America, earlier governments and courts treated efforts to organize workers as criminal conspiracies, and the activists were severely punished.

Over the years, trade unions gained grudging acceptance, if not respectability, and legislation passed in the first half of the 20th century allowed them to play an increasingly significant role in the economy. The first example of important modern legislation was passed by the United States Congress in 1935 and was known as the *National Labor Relations Act* or the *Wagner Act*.[66]

This *Act* reduced conflict by recognizing an employee's right to be a member of a union and eliminating the employer's power to interfere in any way with the organizational process. A trade union successful in persuading more than 50 percent of the employees to join was recognized as the official bargaining agent for all the employees in that workforce. The employer was then required to negotiate with the trade union in good faith. The primary objectives of the *Wagner Act* were to promote labour peace and to give some stability and structure to the field of labour relations in the United States.

Legislation designed to reduce conflict

Legislation

After a considerable amount of labour strife in Canada, the federal government passed the *Wartime Labour Relations Regulations* by an order-in-council.[67] This order incorporated most of the provisions set out in the *Wagner Act* and, after the war, most Canadian provinces added the provisions of this federal regulation to their provincial statutes. The Canadian legislation, in addition to controlling **recognition disputes** (disputes arising between unions and employers during the organization process), included provisions that reduced conflict in interest disputes and rights disputes. An **interest dispute** is a disagreement between the union and employer about what terms to include in their collective agreement. A **rights dispute** is a disagreement over the meaning or interpretation of a provision included in a collective agreement that is in force. Another type of dispute that can arise is a **jurisdictional dispute**, which is a dispute between two unions over which one should represent a particular group of employees or over which union members ought to do a particular job. For example, should carpenters or steel workers put up metal-stud walls in an office building? The employer is usually caught in the middle in jurisdictional disputes and has little power to affect the situation.

The federal collective bargaining legislation is embodied in the *Canada Labour Code*.[68] This legislation covers those industries over which the federal government has jurisdiction, such as railroads, shipping, air transportation, broadcasting, and dock work. Each provincial government has passed collective bargaining legislation covering sectors over which it has jurisdiction. These acts are variously called the *Labour Code*, *Labour Relations Code*, *Trade Union Act*, *Labour Relations Act*, *Industrial Relations Act*, and *Labour Act*. The statutes cover most labour relations situations arising within the jurisdiction of the provinces as set out in section 92 of the *Constitution Act, 1867*. Some types of activities, such as public services, schools, and hospitals, have unique federal or provincial legislation specifically designed

Canada followed example of American legislation

Types of disputes— recognition, interest, rights, jurisdiction

Both federal and provincial legislation covers collective bargaining

---

66. (1935), 49 Stat. 449.

67. 1944, P.C. 1003. (Because of the war emergency, the federal government had the power to pass general legislation for Canada.)

68. *Supra* note 29.

to cover labour relations within that industry.[69] Refer to the MyBusLawLab for particulars.

Labour tribunals regulate process

In all jurisdictions, labour relations boards have been established to deal with disputes associated with the collective bargaining process. These boards take the place of courts. It is important to remember that although they quite often look and act like courts, they are not. They are part of the executive branch of government and, as such, they can be used as an instrument of government policy. Labour relations boards have the advantage of expertise in labour matters. Resolution of disputes by such tribunals is usually accomplished more quickly than would be the case in the courts. Administrative tribunals are discussed in more detail in Chapter 3.

No constitutional right to belong to a union

Important questions arise with respect to union membership, collective bargaining, and the *Charter of Rights and Freedoms*. Is there a constitutional right to belong to a union, to strike, or even to bargain collectively? Earlier, the Supreme Court of Canada held that there was not. These rights had been created by statute, and the limitations imposed by government were held not to have violated section 2(d) of the *Charter* guaranteeing freedom of association. However, recent case law suggests a different direction by the Court. See the Supreme Court of Canada decision in Case Summary 10.11.

CASE SUMMARY 10.11

Constitutional Right to Bargain Collectively? Health Services and Support—Facilities Subsector Bargaining Assn. v. British Columbia[70]

Several unions and some of their members challenged the constitutional validity of the *Health and Social Services Delivery Improvement Act* (the Act), claiming it violated the guarantees of freedom of association (s. 2(d)) and equality (s. 15) set out in the *Charter of Rights and Freedoms*. The Act was passed by the B. C. government to deal with problems in the provincial health care system. Costs had increased significantly and it was becoming more difficult for the provincial government to provide health care services. The legislation was designed to resolve both of these issues.

The *Act* came into force three days after it received first reading. There was no meaningful consultation with the affected unions. The legal challenge related to the provisions dealing with changes to transfers and multi-worksite assignment rights, contracting out, job security programs, and layoffs and bumping rights. These provisions gave health care employers greater flexibility in dealing with employees. In some cases, they could do so in ways contrary to existing collective agreements and without consultation or notice. The legislation not only over-ruled existing agreements, it eliminated the need for meaningful collective bargaining on a number of issues. Section 10 of the *Act* said that "Part 2 prevails over collective agreements."

The trial Court and the Court of Appeal both ruled that the *Act* was constitutional. Neither recognized a right to collective bargaining under section 2(d) of the *Charter*, as the Supreme Court had not previously explicitly done so. The Supreme Court, however,

---

69. See, for example, Alberta's *Public Service Employee Relations Act*, R.S.A. 2000, c. P-43.

70. 2007 SCC 27, [2007] 2 S.C.R. 391.

held that section 2(d) protects the capacity of union members "to engage, in association, in collective bargaining on fundamental workplace issues." The Court explained that this protects the right of employees to associate in a process of collective action to achieve workplace goals. The Court was careful to note that this does not guarantee any particular outcomes in labour disputes. If the government substantially interferes with that right, it would be in violation of section 2(d).

The Court based its decision on the historic recognition in Canada of the importance of collective bargaining to freedom of association. Collective bargaining is also an integral component of freedom of association in international law. Canada has ratified international human rights documents that have recognized a right to collective bargaining. Finally, interpreting section 2(d) as including a right to collective bargaining is consistent with, and promotes, other *Charter* rights, freedoms, and values, including dignity, personal autonomy, equality, and democracy.

The Court ruled that the violation of section 2(d) by the *Act* was not reasonable and justifiable under section 1 of the *Charter*. The B. C. government had passed an important piece of labour legislation very quickly and without any meaningful consultation with the unions. The government had not considered achieving its goal by less intrusive measures and the violation of the employees' section 2(d) right of collective bargaining was significant.

DISCUSSION QUESTIONS

Does this decision restrict the power of the government too much? Conversely, does it enhance the power of unions beyond what it should be?

Labour rights have been gained politically and political action must be relied on to retain them. But there is now a constitutional right to bargain collectively. This decision may ensure the continued existence of unions, whose power and influence has dwindled in recent years.

Canadian labour statutes vary considerably from jurisdiction to jurisdiction. Reference herein will generally be made to the federal legislation that has application across the country. Province-specific information is available in the MyBusLawLab.

Organization of Employees

CERTIFICATION

While in some Canadian jurisdictions it is possible for employers to voluntarily recognize a trade union as the bargaining agent for their employees, the most common method of union recognition in Canada results from the certification process adopted from the *Wagner Act* of 1935. For a union to obtain certification as the bargaining agent for a group of employees, referred to as the bargaining unit, it must apply to the appropriate labour relations board for certification and satisfy the board that a certain percentage of the workforce are members of the union. The particular requirements vary with the jurisdiction.

Under the Canada Labour Code, Division III, if the applicant can show that 50 percent of the workforce has joined the union, it can apply for and receive certification. If the union has less than 50 percent support, but more than 35 percent, a representation vote will be held, and to obtain certification it must receive the

mybuslawlab
www.pearsoned.ca/mybuslawlab

Certification of bargaining unit adopted from *Wagner Act*

Majority of workers must be members of union

support of a majority of those that vote and over 35 percent of the workforce must have participated in that vote. Note that the granting of certification without a vote is unusual. In most provinces, a vote must be taken no matter how much support is included in the initial application. Even in the case of the *Canada Labour Code*, the Canada Industrial Relations Board has the option to order a vote even when the union has over 50 percent support.

BARGAINING AGENT

Once certified, the trade union has exclusive bargaining authority for the employees it represents. A unionized employee loses the right to negotiate personally with the employer, hence the term collective bargaining. The resulting contract between union and employer is binding on all the employees in the designated unit. It is important, therefore, to determine whether the workforce the trade union intends to represent is an appropriate bargaining unit before certification is granted. Labour relations boards discourage bargaining units that are either too small or too large, or that contain groups of employees with conflicting interests. Management employees are, thus, excluded. Also, to obtain certification, the trade union cannot be guilty of any discriminatory practices. A union that has applied for certification and has failed must wait a specified period before trying again.[71]

Only union has right to bargain for employees

UNFAIR LABOUR PRACTICES

The primary objective of labour legislation is to create an orderly process for the organization and recognition of trade unions, eliminating the conflict that often takes place in such circumstances. Prohibited unfair labour practices include threats or coercion of employees by either the union or management. For example, in the *Convergys* case,[72] the employer implemented a policy prohibiting disclosure of employee contact information to union organizers, and threatened dismissal for violating this policy. Surveillance cameras, positioned near the entry to the workplace, enabled the employer to monitor union organizers' activities. Further, a security guard was posted at the entrance whenever union officials appeared to hand out leaflets. The employer was ordered to stop these unfair labour practices and to schedule paid staff meetings where the union could meet with staff, without employer surveillance.

Rules of conduct reduce conflict

Threats, coercion, dismissal—unfair labour practices

The employer cannot threaten dismissal for joining a trade union or require that an employee refrain from joining a trade union as a condition of employment. Once the organization process has begun in most provinces, the employer cannot change conditions or terms of employment to influence the bargaining process. In some jurisdictions, in the face of such an unfair labour practice, if the labour relations board concludes that a vote would not reflect the true feelings of the employees, it can grant certification without a vote. This is rarely done and will take place only when there is clear evidence of intimidation interfering with the reliability of the voting process. What constitutes an unfair labour practice can also vary with the jurisdiction. Refer to the MyBusLawLab for jurisdiction-specific details.

In some provinces, unfair labour practices can result in certification without vote

---

71. Each jurisdiction may specify a different waiting period. In Alberta, for example, the period is 90 days. See *Labour Relations Code*, R.S.A. 2000, c. L-1, s. 57.

72. *Re Convergys Customer Management Canada Inc.*, [2003] B.C. L.R.B.D. No. 62 (B.C.L.R.B.).

Requiring that an employer not coerce or intimidate employees does not eliminate the employer's right to state his or her views during the electioneering process that precedes a certification vote. Freedom of expression as set out in the *Charter of Rights and Freedoms* requires that, as long as such statements are merely statements of opinion or fact, and do not amount to threat or coercion, they are permitted. But it is an unfair labour practice for an employer to participate in, or interfere with, the formation or administration of a labour union. Consequently, employers cannot contribute financially or otherwise provide support to a labour union, undermining the independence of the union. Note that many of these unfair labour practices are also crimes under the *Criminal Code* of Canada. For example, when an employer fires, refuses to hire, or threatens an employee with demotion or dismissal because of his union activities, that is a crime punishable with a significant fine and/or imprisonment.[73]

Trade unions, even in the process of organizing the workers, do not have the right to trespass on the employer's property, or to organize during the employees' work time. However, employers will sometimes allow this so that they can at least know what is going on. Once the trade union has successfully completed the certification process, it becomes the certified bargaining agent for all the employees in the bargaining unit. The employer must recognize it as such and bargain with it. The trade union can then serve notice on the employer requiring the commencement of collective bargaining. Employers often wish to join together to bargain collectively with a trade union. In some jurisdictions, such **employers' organizations** can also be certified (or designated to be the "employer" authorized to bargain with the union),[74] creating bargaining agents that are stronger and better able to negotiate with large unions on behalf of their members. These employers' organizations are usually found where there are a number of small employers, such as in the construction industry. In a similar fashion, local trade union organizations are often affiliated with much larger, parent unions, which strengthen the local bargaining units by providing funds to support a prolonged strike and making available research and other expertise to assist in negotiations.

Unfair labour practices are not limited to the organization process. It remains vitally important to ensure that the union remains independent from employer domination even after certification and to ensure that it can carry on its union activities free from harassment by the employer.

mybuslawlab
www.pearsoned.ca/mybuslawlab

Bargaining

COLLECTIVE AGREEMENTS

Once a union is certified as the bargaining agent for the bargaining unit, it has exclusive authority to bargain on behalf of the employees in the unit. Employees can no longer negotiate "their own deal" with the employer. In a recent Ontario decision,[75] the Arbitration Board found that an employer program, designed to reward good performance by awarding non-cash gifts, violated the collective agreement (compensation above scheduled wage) and breached the requirement

---

73. *Criminal Code*, R.S.C. 1985, c. C-46, s. 425.

74. *Canada Labour Code*, *supra* note 29, s. 33.

75. *Re Toronto Hydro and Canadian Union of Public Employees, Local 1* (2002), 103 L.A.C. (4th) 289 (On. L.A.).

that the employer recognize the union as the exclusive bargaining agent. By unilaterally implementing this program, the employer was compensating select employees above the wage scales set in the collective agreement. This interfered with the union's exclusive right to negotiate matters of wages, benefits, and other terms of employment.

Any time after a trade union is certified, either party can give notice, requiring bargaining to commence, usually within 10 to 20 days, depending on the jurisdiction.[76] When the union has been certified for some time and a collective agreement is already in place, this notice cannot be given until shortly before the expiration of the old agreement, usually three to four months.[77]

Once this notice has been given, the parties are required to bargain or negotiate with each other, and in most jurisdictions, the bargaining must be "**in good faith**." Whatever the term means, the parties must at least meet with a willingness to explore compromises and to try to find an area of agreement. It does not mean that either party has to agree to the other's terms. Some provinces have adopted the wording used in the federal legislation, requiring the parties to make "every reasonable effort" to reach an agreement.[78]

Either party can give notice to commence collective bargaining

Parties must bargain in good faith

CASE SUMMARY 10.12

Employer Must Bargain in Good Faith: *Royal Oak Mines Inc. v. Canada (Labour Relations Board)*[79]

The employer operated a mine in the Northwest Territories. It put forward an offer to contract with its unionized employees. The offer was rejected. A bitter 18-month strike followed in which a number of replacement workers died. Some employees were dismissed, and the employer, when pressured to at least provide for due process in the dismissals, steadfastly refused. After attempts at mediation, an industrial inquiry commission and intervention by the Minister of Labour, there was still no settlement to the strike. The union went to the Canadian Labour Relations Board, complaining that the employer had failed to bargain in good faith. The Board agreed. It ordered the employer to renew the original offer made before the strike. The employer refused and appealed the Board's decision. The Supreme Court of Canada upheld the Labour Relations Board's right to find that the employer had not bargained in good faith and upheld its right to impose the settlement.

DISCUSSION QUESTIONS

While this may constitute interference in the bargaining process to the disadvantage of the employer, the Supreme Court of Canada held that if there is a requisite nexus or connection between the terms imposed and the breach of the duty to bargain in good faith, specific terms can be so imposed. Do you agree with this approach?

---

76. Twenty days under federal legislation, *Canadian Labour Code, supra*note 29, s. 50.

77. Four months under federal legislation, *ibid.*, s. 49.

78. *Ibid.*, s. 50.

79. [1996] 1 S.C.R. 369. See also *Allsco Building Products Ltd. v. United Food and Commercial Workers International Union, Local 1288P* (1998), 207 N.B.R. (2d) 102 (C.A.), which followed this decision.

RATIFICATION

Once a bargain has been reached, it is presented to the union membership and, when appropriate, to the employer's board, or to an employer's organization, for ratification. If both sides ratify, there is a binding collective agreement. The agreement is a contract but, because of the modifying legislation, it must be viewed as a special form of contract with unique features, such as the method of its enforcement. In most jurisdictions, while bargaining is ongoing, the employer is not permitted to change the terms and conditions of the employment, such as wages, benefits, or hours of work.[80] When it is clear that the parties cannot reach an agreement, it is possible in some jurisdictions for the Labour Relations Board to impose a first contract, although this option is seldom used.[81]

Agreement must be ratified

MEDIATION (CONCILIATION)

Mediation, sometimes called conciliation, has been provided for in the various Canadian jurisdictions. The subjects of mediation and arbitration were introduced in Chapter 3 as part of the discussion on alternate dispute resolution. When negotiations begin to break down, either party has the right to apply to the appropriate government agency for the appointment of a **conciliator** or *mediator*.[82] This person then meets with the two parties and assists them in their negotiations. The hope is that communications between the two parties will be greatly facilitated by this third-person go-between. The parties are prohibited from taking more drastic forms of action, such as strike or lockout, as long as a conciliator/mediator is involved in the negotiations.

Some provinces provide for a two-tiered process of conciliation with, first, a single officer and, subsequently, a conciliation board consisting of three mediators, but the function is essentially the same. Federally, the Minister must choose among a conciliation officer, a conciliation commissioner, and a conciliation board.[83] It is only after the officer, commissioner, or board has checked out of the dispute and filed a report that the parties are allowed to proceed to strike or lockout. In some jurisdictions, conciliation is a prerequisite to strike or lockout.[84] Although conciliators have no authority to bind the parties, they do have the power to make recommendations that will be embarrassing to an unreasonable party. Note that, in many jurisdictions, conciliation can be imposed on the parties by the Labour Relations Board, even when neither party has requested it.[85] These provisions vary considerably between jurisdictions; see the MyBusLawLab for details.

Mediation assists negotiation process

Arbitrators can also play a role in the bargaining process. Arbitration differs from conciliation in that an arbitrator is authorized to make a decision, which is binding on the parties. Under federal legislation, the parties can choose to voluntarily submit any matter respecting renewal, revision, or the entry into a new collective agreement to an arbitrator for a binding decision.[86] Alternatively,

---

[80]. *Ibid.*, s. 80; *Labour Relations Code*, R.S.B.C. 1996, c. 244, s. 55; *Labour Relations Act, 1995*, S.O. 1995, c. 1, s. 43.

[81]. *Canada Labour Code*, *supra* note 29, s. 50(b).

[82]. *Canada Labour Code*, *ibid.*, s. 71.

[83]. *Ibid.*, s. 72.

[84]. *Ibid.*, s. 89.

[85]. *Ibid.*, s. 72(2).

[86]. *Ibid.*, s. 79.

Contract must be for at least
one year

legislation may empower labour relations boards to impose a first contract when
the parties themselves cannot reach an agreement.[87]

Terms of Collective Agreements

The completed collective agreement must satisfy certain requirements, such as
having a term of at least one year. If the parties have placed no time limit on the
agreement, it will be deemed to be for one year.[88] Federally, when the labour relations board has imposed a collective agreement on the parties, its term will be for
two years.[89] Collective agreements may have an automatic renewal clause so that if
no notice to bargain is given at the appropriate time, the contract will automatically be renewed, usually for another year. Retroactivity is generally a matter to be
negotiated by the parties; if the new collective agreement is to apply retroactively,
any changes in terms (such as a new rate of pay) will take effect from the date the
old agreement expired. The parties often do not reach an agreement until well
after the old collective agreement expires. If the new one then takes effect
retroactively, even with this one-year minimum requirement in effect, the new
contract will last only a few months. It can be readily seen why every province has
taken the approach that any agreement for a period shorter than one year is
unworkable.

ARBITRATION

Interpretation of contract
disputes to be arbitrated
through grievance process

All collective agreements must contain provisions for the settlement of disputes
arising under the agreement. This is usually accomplished through a **grievance
process** that ultimately leads to arbitration. The contract will set out a process
involving a series of structured meetings during which the parties can negotiate a
settlement. If a settlement is not reached, the matter is submitted to an arbitrator
(or panel of arbitrators), who will hold a hearing and make a decision that is binding on both parties. This grievance process is used to resolve disputes not only
over the interpretation of the contract provisions, but also as a response to individual employees' complaints of violations of their rights by the employer.

Decision of arbitrator
binding

While both arbitration and mediation/conciliation involve the intervention of
an outside third party, the distinction is that the parties are not required to follow
the recommendations of a mediator/conciliator, but the decision of an arbitrator
is binding. Arbitration, therefore, is a substitute for court action. Each party is
given an opportunity to put forth its position and present its evidence before the
arbitrator makes a decision. Arbitrators are not required to follow the stringent
rules of evidence that normally surround judicial proceedings, and their decisions can, in some jurisdictions, be appealed to the Labour Relations Board or to
the courts. Some provinces, on the other hand, do not permit appeals, so that the
decision of the arbitrator is final. In all jurisdictions, an arbitrator's decision is
subject to judicial review when the arbitrator has exceeded the authority given, or
when the decision is unreasonable. The collective agreement replaces any individual contract that may have existed previously between the employer and
employee, so all disputes between the parties relating to the workplace must be

---

87. *Ibid.,* s. 80.

88. *Ibid.,* s. 80(4).

89. *Ibid.,* s. 67.

handled by the grievance procedure. This method of dispute resolution is compulsory. It is not permissible for the parties to indulge in strikes or lockouts, or to use the courts, to resolve a dispute over the terms of the contract once a collective agreement is in force.

No strike when contract is in force

CASE SUMMARY 10.13

There Is a Time to Grieve and a Time to Sue: *Goudie v. Ottawa (City)*[90]

A number of unionized animal control officers were transferred from the police force to the City of Ottawa. They were to be covered by a new collective agreement. In the process, their work week increased and other provisions of their employment were changed, to their disadvantage. They claimed that they were promised prior to their transfer that the terms and conditions of their employment would not change as a result of the transfer. In this action they were claiming breach of that contract and negligent or fraudulent misrepresentation.

At the first level of hearing, the dispute was dismissed. The Judge ruled that this was a matter dealing with the collective agreement and that the grievance process should therefore have been used and the matter arbitrated. The case went to the Supreme Court of Canada, which overturned that decision. The Court allowed the animal control officers to bring a civil action on the basis that the dispute arose from a pre-employment contract rather than a labour dispute based on a collective agreement. The Court relied upon a principle developed in an earlier case stating that

> If a dispute between the parties in its "essential character" arises from the interpretation, application, administration or violation of the collective agreement, it must be determined via a grievance procedure by an arbitrator appointed in accordance with the collective agreement, and not by the courts.

DISCUSSION QUESTIONS

In this case, the dispute arose over the terms of a promise or agreement that had been made before these animal control officers became employees of the City of Ottawa. A civil action to determine the matter was thus appropriate. Consider the reasons for restricting a person's right to sue civilly over a collective agreement matter. Do you agree with such restrictions and, if so, was the Court correct in allowing an exception in this case?

OTHER TERMS

In addition to the terms specifically relating to conditions of work, rates of pay, vacations, termination, and the like (which are the main object of the collective bargaining process), there are various other terms that often appear in collective agreements. The federal government and some provinces have passed legislation requiring collective agreements to cover how technological changes in the industry will be handled.[91] Throughout Canada, the parties can agree to terms

Agreement must provide for technological change

---

90. [2003] 1 S.C.R. 141, 2003 S.C.C. 14.

91. *Canada Labour Code, supra* note 29, ss. 51–55.

Union shop and closed shop provisions

that provide for union security. One example is the **union shop** clause, which requires that new employees join the union within a specified period of time. A second arrangement, used particularly in such industries as construction or long-shoring, requires that the employee be a member of the union before getting a job. This is a **closed shop** clause. A third option enables employees to retain the right not to join a union, but they must still pay union dues. This arrangement is referred to as the **Rand Formula**, or an **agency shop**. Fourthly, the collective agreement may contain a **check-off provision**, which means that the parties have agreed that the employer will deduct union dues from the payroll. A fifth option, **maintenance of membership**, requires those who are already union members to pay dues and to maintain their membership, though new employees need not join the union.

Agency shop, check-off, and maintenance of membership provisions

Strikes and Lockouts

Job action may involve lockout, strike, work to rule

Some sort of job action will probably result if the parties cannot agree on what terms to include in the collective agreement. A **lockout** is action taken by the employer to prevent employees from working and earning wages. A **strike** is the withdrawal of services by employees. Although a strike usually consists of refusing to come to work, or intentional slowdowns, other forms of interference with production may also be classified as strikes. For example, postal employees announced just before Christmas 1983 that they would process Christmas cards with 10-cent stamps on them despite the fact that the appropriate rate was 32 cents per letter. This action was taken to draw attention to the fact that certain commercial users of the postal system got a preferential bulk rate not available to the public. The courts declared that the action was a strike. Since a strike would have been illegal under the circumstances, the union reversed its position. Employees can pressure an employer by strictly adhering to the terms of their agreement, or by doing no more than is minimally required. This behaviour is called **work to rule** and will often prompt a lockout. Strikes and lockouts are both **work stoppages**. The lockout is imposed by the employer, while the strike involves the employees' withdrawing their services.

CASE SUMMARY 10.14

There Is No Guaranteed Right to Strike: *Ontario Hospital Assn. v. Ontario Public Service Employees Union*[92]

Health workers in Ontario had been without a contract for over 300 days when they decided to hold a day of protest. On this day, the employees would not work, but would hold rallies and do other things to bring their plight to the public's attention, including picketing at various health-related institutional locations. The employer claimed this was an illegal strike, as health employees in Ontario were prohibited from striking under the *Hospital Labour Disputes Arbitration Act*. The union claimed that this was a political protest rather than a strike, and that its right to strike and to picket was protected under

---

92. [2003] O.L.R.D. No. 1545.

the *Charter of Rights and Freedoms*. The Board held that this was indeed an illegal withdrawal of services amounting to a prohibited strike. While the union's political communications were protected under section 2(b) of the *Charter* (freedom of expression), its right to strike was not. Any restriction on its freedom of expression in connection with the prohibition of strike action was also supported as a reasonable exception to its freedom of expression under section 1 of the Charter.

DISCUSSION QUESTIONS

This case illustrates the principle that there is no guaranteed right to strike under the *Charter* and that even the right to freely express opinions can be curtailed when associated with a violation of a prohibition against striking. Do you think there should be such a right to strike? Should it be included in the *Charter*? Would the result of this case be different in light of the Supreme Court decision discussed in Case Summary 10.11?

Since the main objective of modern collective bargaining legislation is to reduce conflict, the right to strike and the right to lock out have been severely limited. It is unlawful for a strike or lockout to occur while an agreement is in force. Strikes and lockouts can take place only after an agreement has expired and before the next one comes into effect.[93] Any strike or lockout associated with the recognition process, or involving jurisdictional disputes between two unions, is also illegal and must be dealt with through the certification process described above. Only when the old collective agreement has expired, and the dispute is part of an interest dispute involving the negotiation of the terms to be included in a new collective agreement, is a strike or lockout legal.

> Strike or lockout can occur only between contracts in an interest dispute

If a collective agreement is in place and a dispute arises as to the terms (a rights dispute), it must be resolved through the grievance and arbitration process described above. Any strike associated with such a dispute is illegal.

Even when a dispute concerns what will go into the new agreement (an interest dispute), there are still some limitations on strike action. The old contract must have expired and the parties must have attempted to bargain in good faith. A vote authorizing strike action must have been taken, and a specified period of notice must have been given, for example, 72 hours in Alberta, in British Columbia, and under the *Canada Labour Code*.[94] The employer must give the same notice to the employees when a lockout is about to take place. No strike or lockout can take place until a specified period of time has passed after a mediator/conciliator has made a report to the relevant cabinet minister. Even then, in some areas, a further cooling-off period may be imposed. In some jurisdictions, the employer is prohibited from hiring replacement workers during a strike. This restriction puts considerably greater pressure on the employer to settle the dispute and goes some way in reducing the violence associated with such labour–management confrontation. The federal government has amended the *Canada Labour Code* to partially prohibit the use of such replacement workers.[95]

> Must bargain in good faith first and vote before strike

> Proper strike notice must be given

---

93. *Canada Labour Code, supra* note 29, ss. 88–89.

94. *Supra* note 29, s. 94 (2.1).

95. *Labour Relations Code* (Alberta), *supra* note 71, s. 78, *Labour Relations Code* (British Columbia), *supra* note 81, *Canada Labour Code, ibid.*, s. 87.2.

Picketing

Right to picket limited by legislation

Once a strike or lockout is underway, one of the most effective techniques available to trade unions is picketing. As with striking, the use of picketing is severely limited and controlled. Picketing involves strikers standing near, or marching around, a place of business, trying to dissuade people from doing business there. Picketing is permissible only when a lawful strike or lockout is in progress. Employees who picket before proper notice has been given, or somewhere not permitted under the labour legislation, are in violation of the law. A picketer responsible for communicating false information to those who might cross the picket line can be sued for defamation.

When the information communicated does not try to discourage people from crossing the picket line, or dealing with the employer, the action may not qualify as picketing.

CASE SUMMARY 10.15

Leafleting and Picketing Distinguished: *United Food and Commercial Workers, Local 1518 (U.F.C.W.) v. KMart Canada Ltd.*[96]

The UFCW represented employees who were locked out from the KMart department stores in Campbell River and Port Alberni. It decided to escalate the dispute by handing out leaflets to customers in KMart stores in the Vancouver and Victoria areas, explaining the nature of their complaints against the company and encouraging them not to shop at KMart. In British Columbia, the legislation prohibits secondary picketing (picketing at a location other than where the employees work). The issue was whether this leafleting qualified as prohibited secondary picketing. The Supreme Court of Canada held that it did not. The Court determined that "the distribution of leaflets did not interfere with employees at the secondary sites, nor was there any indication that it interfered with the delivery of supplies. The activity was carried out peacefully, and it did not impede public access to the stores. Neither was there any evidence of verbal or physical intimidation." Some customers may have been persuaded not to deal with the stores, but this was a consequence of leafleting rather than picketing.

The court distinguished between picketing and leafleting. It held that leafleting was an expression of free speech and as such was protected by section 2 of the Charter of Rights and Freedoms. Because the B.C. *Labour Relations Code's* definition of picketing was overly broad, including leafleting, it was struck down. The prohibition against secondary picketing was also an interference with free speech, but it was justified under section 1 because of its interference in commercial relations. Note that even leafleting is not permitted when the activity involves trespassing on a company's parking lot ordinarily not used by the public.[97]

DISCUSSION QUESTIONS

Consider the delicate balance of power between trade unions and employers that labour relations legislation tries to maintain and whether allowing leafleting or secondary picketing upsets that balance.

[96.] [1999] 2 S.C.R. 1083.

[97.] *RMH Teleservices v. BCGEU* (2003), 223 D.L.R. (4th) 750.

Picketing must be peaceful and merely communicate information. Violence will not be tolerated. A tort action for trespass may follow the violation of private property. If violence erupts, the assaulting party may face criminal and civil court actions. When picketing goes beyond the narrow bounds permitted in common law and legislation, the employer can resort to the courts or labour relations boards to get an injunction to limit or prohibit the picketing. Using an excessive number of picketers, as with mass picketing, goes beyond simple information communication and becomes intimidation. The employer can then apply to have the number of picketers restricted.

Violence not permitted

Although picketing limited in this way may seem to be an ineffectual weapon, there is an extremely strong tradition among union members and many others never to cross a picket line. Others simply wish to avoid the unpleasantness of a confrontation. Employers must deal with other businesses that employ union members, and these workers generally will not cross the picket line. It eventually becomes very difficult for an employer to continue in business surrounded by a picket line.

Strong tradition of union solidarity makes picketing effective

Which locations can be legally picketed varies with the jurisdiction. Employees in every jurisdiction can picket the plant or factory where they work. In some jurisdictions, such as New Brunswick,[98] **secondary picketing** is allowed, and striking employees are able to picket not just their own workplace, but also other locations where the employer carries on business. In any case, unrelated businesses cannot legally be picketed, even if they are located on the same premises as the one struck, as might be the case, for example, in a shopping mall. Of course, whether the picketing is directed toward such an unrelated business in a given dispute is a question for the court or board to decide. The more extensive the picketing, the more effective the economic pressure placed on the employer. There is some variation with respect to the specific rules relating to picketing; reference should be made to the MyBusLawLab to determine what is allowed in the various jurisdictions.

Some provinces permit secondary picketing

Anyone has the legal right to cross a picket line. Customers are free to continue doing business with an employer involved in a strike or lockout; suppliers are free to continue supplying goods and services to the employer if they can persuade their employees to cross the picket line; and the employer has the right to continue normal business activities. Unfortunately, picketers can lose sight of these basic rights when they think that their picket line is not being effective. As a result, a considerable amount of intimidation, coercion, violence, and injury still takes place, despite all of the precautions that have been introduced into the labour relations system in Canada.

No legal obligation to honour picket line

www.pearsoned.ca/mybuslawlab

    ON

Public Sector and Essential Services

The discussion thus far relates to people employed in private industry. Many people, however, are employed either as part of the public sector, or in service industries that are considered essential to society, such as hospitals, and police and fire departments. Employees falling into these categories are treated differently than those employed in private industry, and special legislation governs their activities. Although labour issues and disputes in these occupations are virtually the same as those in the private sector, the government and the public regard the position of

Public-sector employees have limited rights to job action

---

98. *Industrial Relations Act*, R.S.N.B. 1973, c. I-4, s. 104.

public service employees as quite different. Strikes by police, firefighters, hospital workers, schoolteachers, and other public servants are usually considered inappropriate by members of the public.

Every province has special legislation to deal with these groups. Most provinces permit collective bargaining to some extent, but only a few allow public-sector employees to participate in strikes and picketing, the others substituting some form of compulsory arbitration of disputes.[99] Of course, in all labour disputes, including private ones, the government retains the right, either by existing statute, or by the passage of a specific bill, to impose a settlement, or an alternative method of resolving the dispute, such as compulsory arbitration.

! REDUCING RISK 10.4

Some employers will feel threatened by the prospect of a union organizing its workforce. Often emotional rather than economic factors come into play, with employers not wanting to give up their right to manage, or to surrender any control to trade unions. This is true especially at the organizational stage and is the main reason the employer's role at that level has been minimized. The certification process, supervised by government, has reduced conflict at that stage. Employers are well advised to exercise care, especially in a newly unionized situation, to avoid unfair labour practices and other situations that poison the atmosphere because of ill-thought-out tactics and strategies.

Union Organization

Unions can expel for misbehaviour

Trade unions are democratic organizations in which policy is established by vote. Executives and officers are elected. Members can be expelled or disciplined for misbehaviour, such as crossing picket lines after being instructed not to by the union executive. Expulsion can be devastating for a worker, since many collective agreements provide for a union shop in which all employees must be members of the union. Some jurisdictions have passed legislation stipulating that a person who loses her union membership for reasons other than failure to pay dues will be able to retain employment.[100] There are some employees whose religious beliefs prevent them from joining or contributing to such organizations as trade unions, which presents a real dilemma in a union shop situation. Some governments have passed legislation exempting such individuals from joining unions; dues are still deducted but are paid to a registered charity. The other terms of the collective agreement still apply.[101]

Trade unions are subject to human rights legislation. In some jurisdictions, the labour legislation provides that they can be denied certification, or lose their status, as a trade union, if they discriminate.[102] Unions have an obligation to represent all their members fairly.[103] Employees who feel unfairly treated by the union, or who feel that the union is not properly representing them in disputes with employers, can lodge complaints with the Labour Relations Board. The union may find itself required to compensate the wronged employees.

---

99. See, for example, *ibid.*, s. 80.

100. *Ibid.*, s. 70(2).

101. *Canada Labour Code, supra* note 29, s. 95(e).

102. *Ibid.*, s. 25(2).

103. *Ibid.*, s. 37.

Trade unions were once considered illegal organizations with no status separate from their membership and therefore no corporate identity. Most provinces have passed legislation giving a recognized trade union the right to sue or be sued on its own behalf, at least for the purposes outlined in the labour legislation.[104]

Trade unions overseen by labour relations boards and courts

CASE SUMMARY 10.16

Union Has Duty of Fair Representation: *Dezentje v. Warchow*[105]

The employer usually gave employees extended leaves of absence rather than layoffs. In this case, three employees were laid off by the employer while other employees were given leaves of absence. The three workers went to their union representative for advice about filing a grievance. The union did not help them very much. Eventually, they were told that they had a negligible chance of success. They filed a complaint against the union under a provision that imposed a duty of fair representation on the union.

The Labour Relations Board found that they had a modest chance of success, and that the union had an obligation to represent them and to help them pursue the grievance. In refusing to do so, it had failed its obligation of fair representation. Damages were awarded based on the modest chance of success. One employee was awarded higher damages because the employer had offered to rehire him, and the union had failed to convey the offer to him.

An application for judicial review was made to the Court of Queen's Bench, which overturned the decision. On further appeal to the Court of Appeal the original decision was restored. The Board had dealt with matters within its area of expertise and had done so reasonably. There was evidence that the union representatives had not acted with honesty, or good faith, and that the remedies imposed had been appropriate.

DISCUSSION QUESTIONS

Do you think that giving union members this kind of power puts too many restrictions on the union's ability to effectively maneuver in its relations with the employer?

---

104. See, for example, *Labour Relations Code*(Alberta),*supra*note 71, s. 25.

105. 2002 ABCA 249, [2002] Alta. L.R.B.R. 305, 220 D.L.R. (4th) 566, 25 Alta. L.R. (4th) 249 (Alta. C.A.).

SUMMARY

What is employment?

- Must distinguish employees, independent contractors, and agents
- Control and organization tests used to determine if employment relationship

The law of master and servant

- Employment law governed by contract law, common law, and legislation
- Both employers and employees have obligations to fulfill
- Restrictive covenants will be enforced if not too broad and are reasonable
- Employment contracts can be terminated by the giving of reasonable notice, pay in lieu of notice, or by just cause
- Just cause includes disobedience, dishonesty, incompetence, and absenteeism
- Reasonable accommodation must be provided to disabled workers
- Damages awarded for wrongful dismissal (including constructive dismissal)
- Employer vicariously liable for the acts of the employee during the course of employment
- Employment standards legislation sets minimum standards to protect employees
- Human rights legislation prohibits discrimination and harassment in workplace
- Many other types of legislation affecting the employment relationship now exist

Collective bargaining

- All Canadian jurisdictions now have collective bargaining legislation
- The legislation governs certification of unions to represent a group of employees
- Unions have exclusive authority to bargain on behalf of employees
- Collective agreements must be ratified by union members
- Mediation and arbitration can be used if negotiations break down
- Legislation requires that certain terms be included in collective agreements, including a grievance process
- Strikes and lockouts cannot take place while a collective agreement is in force
- Picketing can only take place during a strike or lockout
- Public-sector and essential service employees not allowed to strike or picket
- Unions are democratic organizations with a duty to represent all members fairly

QUESTIONS

1. Distinguish among an employee, an independent contractor, and an agent.

2. Explain how a court will determine whether a person is an employee rather than an independent contractor.

3. Summarize the employer's obligations to the employee, and the employee's obligations to the employer, under common law.

4. Explain what is meant by a restrictive covenant and what factors determine whether it is enforceable.

5. What is the proper way to terminate an employment contract that is for an indefinite period of time?

6. How is the appropriate notice period to terminate an employment relationship determined?

7. Under what circumstances can an employee be dismissed without notice? When can an employee leave employment without giving notice?

8. What risk does an employer face who ignores an employee's incompetence over a period of time?

9. What is "constructive dismissal"? Be sure to explain it using a contractual perspective.

10. What factors will a court take into consideration when determining compensation in a wrongful dismissal action? Indicate the various types of remedies that may be available to the plaintiff.

11. Explain what is meant by "vicarious liability." Describe the limitations on its application.

12. Describe how the employment standards legislation protects basic workers' rights.

13. Explain how human rights legislation applies to areas of employment.

14. Explain what is meant by a "duty to accommodate" in the field of human rights and how it can affect employers.

15. Explain the object and purpose of workers' compensation legislation and how those objectives are accomplished. If a worker is injured on the job and is not covered by workers' compensation, what course of action need he take to secure a remedy?

16. What is the significance of the *National Labor Relations Act (Wagner Act)* in Canada?

17. Compare and contrast recognition disputes, jurisdiction disputes, interest disputes, and rights disputes.

18. Once a collective agreement is in place, what effect will it have on the individual rights of employees? How will it affect the employer?

19. Explain the difference between mediation/conciliation and arbitration. Describe how these tools are used in Canadian labour disputes.

20. Distinguish among a union shop, a closed shop, and an agency shop.

21. Distinguish between a strike and a lockout. What kind of disputes are strikes and lockouts limited to? How are the other types of disputes between union and employer dealt with?

22. Explain what steps must take place before a strike or lockout is legal.

23. Explain what is meant by "picketing," when it can take place, and the limitations that have been placed on picketing in different jurisdictions.

24. What is the legal position of a person who wishes to cross a picket line?

25. How is collective bargaining for public-sector and essential service employees different from that for people employed in private industry?

CASES AND DISCUSSION QUESTIONS

1. *Paso Services Ltd. v. Ratz*, [2008] S.K.Q.B. 356.
Ratz was employed as a sales representative by Paso, which sold promotional products in the Saskatoon area. Ratz signed a "sales representative agreement," which included non-disclosure and non-competition clauses. The latter stated, in part, that Ratz could not "engage, either directly or indirectly, including as an employee . . . in any business or undertaking at any place in Saskatoon which is in competition with the business of the Corporation." Ratz commenced employment with a competitor four days after resigning from Paso. Paso sued, claiming Ratz was in breach of the non-disclosure and non-competition clauses, as well as his common-law fiduciary duty not to use Paso's confidential information for the benefit of a competitor.

Did the Court find Ratz to be liable? Was the non-competition clause binding on Ratz? Is it contrary to public policy? Was Ratz in a fiduciary position?

2. *Chambers v. Axia Netmedia Corp.* (2004), 220 N.S.R. (2d) 338; (2004), 30 C.C.E.L. (3d) 243 (S.C.N.S.).
Chambers had worked for Axia for 14 years in sales when he was informed that he was being put on probation for a year. He was told that he had to improve his sales performance and, if he didn't meet his increased sales targets, he could be terminated any time during that year. Also, instead of a salary, his remuneration in the future would be based on commissions from sales. Chambers quit and sued for wrongful dismissal. He then looked for a new job, but his search was limited to searching on the internet.

Explain the likely outcome of his wrongful dismissal action and what remedy he is likely to receive. In your answer, consider any arguments the employer might have for treating its employee in this manner. What requirements did the employee have to satisfy in these circumstances to mitigate his losses?

3. *Evans v. Teamsters Local Union No. 31*, [2008] S.C.C. 20.
Evans worked for the union in Whitehorse for 23 years. He was dismissed by a letter faxed to him by the newly elected president. Evans offered to accept 24 months' notice; 12 months of employment, followed by 12 months' salary. Negotiations continued; Evans continued to be paid. Four months later, the union asked Evans to return to his employment for the balance of the 24-month notice period. Evans refused, and the union treated his refusal as just cause. The trial Judge awarded Evans 22 months' pay for wrongful dismissal. The Court of Appeal set aside the award, ruling that Evan's refusal to accept the union's offer meant that he failed to mitigate his damages.

The Supreme Court found in favour of the union, holding that a dismissed employee may have to mitigate his damages by returning to work for the same employer. Is this fair to the employee? What factors should a court consider when deciding whether an employee should return to work for the employer who dismissed him?

4. *Brazeau v. International Brotherhood of Electrical Workers* (2005), 248 D.L.R. (4th) 76 (B.C.C.A.).
Brazeau worked as a senior union representative for the union for 25 years. Shortly after his marriage ended, he encouraged a female acquaintance 25 years younger to apply for a job as a union representative and supported her in that application. They went out to dinner, but she thought of him as a mentor. She had no idea that he had

sexual interest in her until he sent her cards expressing love for her and bought her gifts. She became uncomfortable and rejected further advances. As a result, Brazeau made negative remarks about her to others, which had a harmful impact on her work. She complained to the union, which had a policy against sexual harassment. When Brazeau refused to retire, he was fired on the basis of the sexual harassment of a co-worker. He brought an action for wrongful dismissal.

Explain the arguments on both sides and the likely outcome. Have we gone too far in protecting human rights in employment relations? What is the justification for holding the employer responsible when one employee harasses another in situations like these? If he is successful in his wrongful dismissal action, what course of action should the employer have taken instead?

5. *Alberta (Human Rights and Citizenship Commission) v. Kellogg Brown & Root (Canada) Company*, [2007] A.B.C.A. 426, leave to appeal to S.C.C. refused, May 28, 2008, No. 32505.

Chaisson was offered a position by Kellogg to work on an oil sands project. He was required to take a pre-employment drug test, which was administered to all Kellogg employees, whether they were in a safety-sensitive position or not. He failed the test, as he had used marijuana five days before the test. He was immediately terminated by Kellogg. He filed a complaint with the Human Rights Commission, claiming discrimination on the grounds of a physical disability. The Panel rejected his claim, but the lower court ruled that he had been discriminated against, based on Kellogg's perception that he was a drug addict. There was no evidence that he was a drug addict.

The Court of Appeal supported the position of the Panel. This decision means that Kellogg's pre-employment drug test was not discriminatory. Why did the Court make this decision?

6. *Emerald Foods Ltd. (c.o.b. Bird's Hill Garden Market IGA) v. United Food and Commercial Workers' Union, Local 832* 177 Man. R. (2d) 163, 92 C.L.R.B.R. (2d) 286, 2004 C.L.L.C. 220–011 (Man. C.A.).

In Manitoba, the employees of Emerald were in the process of applying for certification when, on the day before the certification vote was to be taken, the president of the company wrote a threatening letter to the employees, hinting that unionization would prevent the implementation of planned wage increases. Only 60 of the 83 employees voted, and they split 30/30 as to supporting certification. The union claimed that the letter intimidated the employees so that the vote actually taken wasn't a true reflection of the employees' feelings. The union made application to the Labour Board.

Indicate the arguments available to both sides, the likely outcome and what the union could expect if it was successful. Note the restrictions put on an employer in the collective bargaining process and consider whether the statutes in place have allowed unions to become too powerful, placing unfair restrictions on the employers in dealings with such unionized employees.

7. *Loyalist College of Applied Arts and Technology v. Ontario Public Service Employees Union* (2003), 63 O.R. (3d) 641, (2003), 225 D.L.R. (4th) 123 (Ont. C.A.).

Bergman was hired by Loyalist College to a teaching position, but her employment was made conditional on her pursuing graduate studies in her field. Her first year of teaching was probationary. After 10 months of teaching she still had not enrolled in a graduate program, and her employment was terminated. There was a collective agreement in place and her union launched a grievance over her dismissal.

Indicate the basis for the union's complaint, the arguments on both sides, the likely outcome and the appropriate remedy if any. Do you think the collective agreement and presence of a trade union should override any special pre-employment commitment she might have made?

8. *United Food and Commercial Workers Union, Local 401 v. Westfair Foods Ltd. (The Real Canadian Superstore)*, [2008] A.B.C.A. 335.
Westfair adopted a policy prohibiting all visible body piercings. A grievance was filed. The Arbitrator found the total ban to be unreasonable. He ordered the parties to try to negotiate a policy. The parties could not agree, so the Arbitrator imposed a policy that permitted discreet nose piercings. Westfair applied to have the policy struck down as being unreasonable. The lower court granted the application.

Should the Court of Appeal reinstate the Arbitrator's policy? The Arbitrator had relied on an opinion survey that found that "nose studs were viewed more positively (or less negatively) than other forms of facial piercings." The survey concluded that Westfair's policy of banning all visible piercings was warranted.

Be sure to visit the MyBusLawLab that accompanies this book at **www.pearsoned.ca/mybuslawlab.** You will find practice tests, a personalized study plan, province-specific material, and much more!

Chapter 11

Agency and Partnership

CHAPTER OBJECTIVES

1. Describe the agency relationship, a relationship of utmost good faith, outlining the rights and responsibilities of agents and principals

2. Distinguish between actual authority and apparent authority of agents

3. List the characteristics of a sole proprietorship and explain why sole proprietors face unlimited liability

4. Distinguish the three types of partnerships used in Canada, focusing on the method of creation and the rights and obligations of partners specific to each type

5. Outline the advantages and disadvantages of operating a business through a partnership and describe the processes of dissolving partnerships

INTRODUCTION

The subject of agency is a vital component in any discussion of business law. The legal consequences that stem from an agency relationship are of utmost concern to businesspeople because at least one of the parties in most commercial transactions is functioning as an agent. Agency law is the basis of the law of partnership, and an understanding of it is essential for coming to terms with corporate law. Agency and partnership are dealt with in this chapter and corporations will be the topic of the following chapter.

Agent represents and acts for principal

An agent's function is to represent and act on behalf of a principal in dealings with third parties. Although by far the most common example of agents representing principals is in the creation of contracts, agents also find themselves involved in other types of legal relationships. Real estate agents do not usually have the authority to enter into contracts on behalf of vendors, but they function as agents nonetheless because they participate in the negotiations and act as go-betweens. Other professionals, such as lawyers and accountants, may make representations or act on behalf of their clients or principals. The term **agency** refers to the service an agent performs on behalf of the principal. This service may be performed as an employee, as an independent agent, or gratuitously. When an agent is acting independently, the business performing the service is often called an agency, such as a travel agency, employment agency, or real estate agency.

Agency refers to service performed by an agent

> ## CASE SUMMARY 11.1
>
> ### Vicariously Liable for Fraud: *Steinman v. Snarey*[1]
>
> Mr. Snarey was a "well-respected agent" working for the Mutual Life Assurance Company of Canada when he was approached by a customer who wanted to take advantage of one of the investment opportunities offered by the company. Snarey persuaded the customer to part with $16 000 by way of a cheque made out to the agent. The customer was told that his money was going into an "investment vehicle offered to the public by Mutual Life." Actually, the company did not offer this kind of investment plan and never had. This was simply a scheme used by Snarey to cheat a trusting customer out of a considerable amount of money. When the customer discovered the fraud, he turned to the Mutual Life Assurance Company for compensation. In the resulting action, it was determined that Snarey had devised and conducted a fraudulent scheme. Because he was an agent of Mutual Life with the actual authority to enter into this general type of transaction with the company's customer, the company was vicariously liable for his conduct and had to pay compensation to the client.
>
> ---
>
> #### DISCUSSION QUESTIONS
>
> Evidently, it is critical to retain agents that are well trained, ethical, and trustworthy. Does it place too great a burden on a principal to hold it liable for an agent's fraud that it had nothing to do with? Should such vicarious liability be limited to situations where the agent is an employee as well? Should some degree of wrongdoing, such as negligence on the part of the principal, be required before imposing vicarious liability?

What follows focuses on the law of agency generally, and in most cases no distinction will be made between people functioning as agents as part of an employment contract and those acting independently. Note that where employees also act as agents of the employer, their duties and obligations as agents go far beyond the employment relationship and must be understood as a separate function or set of obligations.

THE AGENCY RELATIONSHIP

The agency relationship can be created by an express or implied contract, by estoppel, by ratification, or gratuitously, the key element being the granting of **authority**.

Formation by Contract

mybuslawlab
www.pearsoned.ca/mybuslawlab

BC AB SK MB ON

Agency relationship usually created through contract

Usually, an agency relationship is created through a contract, called an **agency agreement**, between the agent and the principal; thus, general contract rules apply. This should not be confused with the contracts agents enter into on behalf of their principals. The agency contract can cover such things as the authority of the agent, the duties to be performed, and the nature of payment to be received (Figure 11.1). It may be imbedded in a contract of employment or the contract

---

1. [1987] O.J. No. 2400 (Dist. Ct.); aff'd [1988] O.J. No. 2917 (H.C.J.).

Figure 11.1 The Agency Agreement

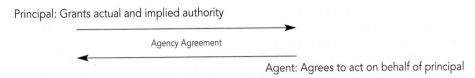

Principal: Grants actual and implied authority

Agency Agreement

Agent: Agrees to act on behalf of principal

may create a more independent relationship between principal and agent. Generally, there are no additional formal requirements for the creation of such a contract. Thus, although it is a wise practice to put the agency agreement in writing, doing so is not necessary except in those jurisdictions where required by the *Statute of Frauds* or other statute. Under the *Bills of Exchange Act*,[2] where the agent is to sign cheques or other negotiable instruments, the granting of the agent's authority must also be in writing. Although there may be other advantages in doing so, it is not necessary that the agency agreement be under seal, unless the agent will be sealing documents on behalf of the principal as part of his or her agency function. An agency agreement in writing and under seal is called a **power of attorney**. Most provinces have powers of attorney acts.[3] Refer to the MyBusLawLab for details. Enduring powers of attorney will be discussed below.

All the elements of a contract, such as consensus, consideration, legality, intention to be bound, and capacity on the part of both parties, must be present for an agency agreement to be binding. The lack of any one of these elements may void the agency contract, but that will not affect the binding nature of any agreement the agent enters into on behalf of the principal. Thus, if Clarke is underage and acts as Drinkwater's agent in the sale of Drinkwater's car to Skoye, the agency contract between Clarke and Drinkwater may be voidable because of the incapacity of Clarke. But the contract between Drinkwater and Skoye for the purchase of the car is still binding. Only when agents are so young, drunk, insane, or otherwise incapacitated that they do not understand what they are doing does the contract between the principal and third party become doubtful on the basis of incapacity or lack of consensus.

> Basic rules of contract apply to agency contracts

The actions of an agent may be binding on the principal even when the agent is acting gratuitously. Only consent is necessary, which explains why, in the above example, the contract for the purchase of the car is binding between Drinkwater and Skoye despite the infancy of the agent, Clarke. Still, most agency relationships are based on contract, either expressly entered into by the parties or implied from their conduct. Often, these are simply employment contracts.

> Consent only essential requirement of agency

AUTHORITY OF AGENTS

Most disputes that arise in agency relate to the extent of the authority of the agent in dealing with third parties. An agent's authority can be derived from the principal in several ways.

---

2. R.S.C. 1985, c. B-4.

3. For example, the *Powers of Attorney Act*, R.S.O. 1990, c. P.20.

Actual Authority

The authority specifically given by the principal to the agent and usually set out in the agency agreement is called the agent's **actual authority**. This actual authority may be **expressly** stated by the principal or **implied** from the circumstances, such as from the position the agent has been given. In Case Summary 11.1, the contract entered into by Mr. Snarey was just the kind of contract he was authorized to conclude with his clients. Because of this actual authority, the principal was liable for his fraud. A person who is hired as a purchasing agent has the authority to carry out the customary and traditional responsibilities of purchasing agents as well as the duties necessarily incidental to that function. Of course, if the principal has specifically stated that the agent does not have certain powers, no such authority is implied. Still, even where actual (express or implied) authority is absent, there may be apparent authority.

Any written agency agreement should carefully set out the authority of the agent, eliminating, as far as possible, the need for any implied authority. An agent who exceeds this actual authority may be liable to the principal for any injury caused by his conduct. But no matter how much care is used in drafting an agent's actual authority, the principal may still be bound by the agent's conduct that falls within his apparent authority.

Apparent Authority—Authority Created by Estoppel

When a principal does something by conduct or words to lead a third party to believe that an agent has authority, the principal is bound by the agent's actions, regardless of whether there is or is not actual authority. Even when the principal has specifically prohibited the agent from doing what he did, the principal will be bound because of the agent's **apparent authority**. This is an application of the principle of estoppel. **Estoppel** is an equitable remedy that stops a party from trying to establish a position or deny something that, if allowed, would create an injustice. It would not be fair if a principal could say to a third party, "George has authority to act for me," and then later to be able to deny it and escape liability for George's actions. In these circumstances estoppel applies. If the principal has held out the agent to have authority even if no such authority has been granted, the principal is bound. If a third party has relied on this representation, the principal cannot then claim that the agent had no authority.

CASE SUMMARY 11.2

Apparent Authority of a Sibling: *Willoughby Residential Development Corp. v. Bradley*[14]

The parents of the brother and sister defendants in this action bought property in 1975, which they owned jointly with their daughter, Dawne. When property is owned jointly, the whole property passes to the survivor. After both parents died, the daughter was registered as the sole owner of the property. But her brother had the same first name as the father and claimed that he was the one who had purchased the property in 1975 with his mother. This claim was supported by evidence of contributions he had made toward the

---

4. [2002] B.C.J. No. 1103 (C.A.).

purchase price. Allegedly, the brother had not raised the issue of ownership earlier as he had been convicted of importing narcotics and did not want his name on the title. Instead he allowed his sister to reside in the house and to become registered as the sole owner of it. But when she tried to sell the house in 1996, he brought an application to stop the sale.

This action was brought by the purchaser who had bought the property in good faith from the sister. By the time of trial the property had increased considerably in value, but the purchaser was granted an order of specific performance forcing sale of the property at the original price. The Court held that as the registered owner, the sister had a right to sell the property. Philip Bradley had allowed his sister to act as the manager of the property and to be the registered owner, and as such she had apparent authority to contract on his behalf as his agent. Even if he was an actual owner of the property, he was bound by the contract entered into by his agent sister.

This case illustrates the nature of apparent authority and the danger of allowing someone to be held out as your representative when they are not. Bradley was estopped from denying that his sister had the authority to act as his agent. It also introduces some important concepts of real property law, which will be expanded on in Chapter 13.

DISCUSSION QUESTIONS

Should liability for an agent's actions be limited to those situations where the agent has been given actual authority? Does the doctrine of apparent authority impose too great a burden on a principal?

The most important example of the application of estoppel is in the field of agency. It is important not to confuse this principle of estoppel with equitable or promissory estoppel, as described in Chapter 6. **Equitable estoppel** involves a promise or commitment to do something in the future. Here, we are dealing not with a promise but with a claim or a statement of fact made by the principal.

Although the principal may look to the agent for compensation, so long as that agent has acted within his apparent authority, the principal is still bound in contract with the third party. If Pedersen employed Mohammed as sales manager of his used car dealership, it would be reasonable for customers to assume that Mohammed had the authority of a normal manager to sell cars and to take trade-ins. If after receiving instructions from Pedersen not to accept trades over $2000 without his express approval, Mohammed were to give Kim a $5000 trade-in for a 1995 Mercedes, Pedersen would still be bound by the deal. Pedersen put Mohammed in that position and led Kim to believe that Mohammed had the ordinary authority and power of a sales manager. The agent acted within his apparent authority, and the contract was binding on the principal. If, however, the agent had sold Kim the entire car lot, this would be beyond both his actual and apparent authority and would not be binding on Pedersen.

Agent acting on apparent authority will bind principal

A principal can also be bound by the actions of an agent that would normally be beyond the agent's authority if the principal has sanctioned similar actions in the past. Kim's chauffeur, Green, would not normally be expected to have the authority to purchase automobiles on behalf of his principal. But if he had done so several times in the past and Kim honoured the deals, the dealer, Pederson, would be entitled to assume that the next purchase was authorized as well and Green had apparent authority. Even if Kim specifically told Green not to buy any

Previous acceptance of agent's actions

Actions of principal create apparent authority

more cars, and Green in violation of those instructions purchased another car from Pederson, the contract would be binding on Kim because of apparent authority. The existence of this apparent authority is based on the statements and conduct of the principal, not the agent. When the misleading indication of authority comes from the agent rather than the principal, and the action is otherwise unauthorized, the third party will have no claim against the principal.

Reasonable person test used to determine existence of authority

The **reasonable person test** has a significant role to play in determining the existence of apparent authority. The usual authority associated with the position in which an agent has been placed is based on this test. The reasonable person test is also used to determine whether the third party should have been misled into believing that the agent had authority by the statements and conduct of the principal.

CASE SUMMARY 11.3

When Is It Reasonable to Conclude Authority Exists?
Gooderham v. Bank of Nova Scotia;[5] *LeRuyet v. Stenner*[6]

The first case demonstrates how apparent authority can result in a principal's being bound by the actions of its agent. Mrs. Gooderham and her husband (now deceased) went to the Bank of Nova Scotia for a $55 000 mortgage. The Bank's representative, Braun, provided them with an application for mortgage life insurance supplied by the insurer Canada Life. They properly filled in the form, but the Bank failed to forward it to Canada Life. Had the Bank done so, Canada Life would have denied coverage because of Mr. Gooderham's poor health. The Bank negligently conveyed premium information to the Gooderhams and collected premiums for several months. Mr. Gooderham died and Canada Life denied coverage, claiming the Bank was not its agent and they were not bound by the Bank's actions.

The Court awarded judgment to the Gooderhams, concluding that Braun had apparent authority to represent Canada Life. The Bank had the application forms supplied by Canada Life and supplied them to the Gooderhams. The Bank generally, on behalf of Canada Life, sought out "prospective policy holders," assisted in completing the application for insurance, possessed and supplied rate information, accepted money for premiums, forwarded the money and forms to Canada Life, and was paid for this service by Canada Life. Given these factors it was reasonable for the Gooderhams to assume that the Bank had authority to represent the insurer.

Compare the first case with *LeRuyet v. Stenner*, where the Court found that there was no apparent authority and no agency relationship. LeRuyet approached Stenner seeking assistance with investments. In accordance with Stenner's recommendations, LeRuyet gave Stenner $130 000 to purchase a Great West annuity. Stenner defrauded LeRuyet, showing him false documents and failing to actually purchase the annuity. Stenner was convicted and LeRuyet turned to Great Life to recover his loss, claiming they were vicariously liable for Stenner's fraud. The Court found that although there was a Great Life logo on some of the documents Stenner had been shown, there was no other connection between the two. Stenner did not have Great West business cards, did not work out of

---

5. [2000] O.J. No. 890 (Sup. Ct. J.).

6. [2001] B.C.J. No. 1669 (S.C.).

Great West's premises, nor did he display any connection to Great West. There being no representations made by Great West that would lead a reasonable person to assume that Stenner acted as an agent of Great West, the Court dismissed the claim of apparent authority.

DISCUSSION QUESTIONS

Do you think that Stenner's claim that he was acting for Great Life should have been enough to impose liability on it?

As illustrated by Case Summary 11.3, when a principal puts an agent in a position so that it appears to others that they have authority to make certain commitments, they have that authority, even though it has not actually been given. This is the very nature of apparent authority. It shows how important it is, for public and private institutions alike, to carefully define the authority of those acting for them and then take steps to ensure that their agents act within those boundaries.

To determine whether a principal is bound in contract with a third party by the actions of an agent, a person must first ask, "Was the agent acting within the actual authority given by the principal?" If the answer is yes, then there is a contract, provided all the other elements are present. If the answer is no, then the question to ask is "Did the principal do anything to lead the third party to believe that the agent had the authority to act?" In other words, was the agent acting with apparent authority? If the answer is yes and the third party relied on that apparent authority, there is a contract between the principal and the third party. It is only when the answer to both these questions is no that there is no contract, and the third party must look to the agent for redress.

Most people find it difficult to understand the difference between implied and apparent authority, and in most cases the distinction is not important. But to clarify, when a principal has specifically stated that the agent does not have authority, no authority can be implied. In spite of such a declaration, however, there may still be apparent authority because of the principal's comments or conduct in relation to the third party. The principal has then led the third party to believe that the agent has authority; now, because of the principle of estoppel, the principal cannot deny that fact.

Ratification

A principal can still ratify a contract even if the agent has acted beyond both actual and apparent authority. The first time Kim's chauffeur bought a car on Kim's behalf, there would likely have been no apparent authority, since this is not normally a chauffeur's job. If Kim liked the car, however, he could ratify the contract and the deal would be binding on the dealer. The effect of such ratification is to give the agent authority to act on behalf of the principal retroactive to the time of the sale. The result can seem unfair because the principal is not bound when an agent goes beyond the authority given, but if the principal chooses to ratify, the third party is bound and can do nothing to change that.

Was the action of the agent authorized by principal?

mybuslawlab
www.pearsoned.ca/mybuslawlab

 BC AB SK MB ON

If principal ratifies unauthorized contract, it is binding

In fact, the power of the principal to ratify must meet the following qualifications:

Third party can set time for ratification

1. The third party has the right to set a reasonable time limit within which the ratification must take place. In the case of a chauffeur buying a car without authority, the dealer cannot simply repudiate the contract but could give the principal a short time to ratify by saying, for example, "You have until noon tomorrow to decide." In the United States, once the third party repudiates, it is too late for the principal to ratify. This may indicate the future direction in Canada, but the courts have not adopted this approach as of yet.

Agent must have been acting for a specific principal

2. The agent must have been acting for the specific principal who is now trying to ratify. A person cannot enter into a contract with a third party while purporting to be an agent and then search for a principal to ratify. The customer would be free to repudiate the purchase, since the would-be agent did not have a particular principal in mind when entering into the contract. There is no one to ratify the agreement.

Principal must be capable of entering into contract
• when it is entered into

3. The principal has to be fully capable of entering into the contract at the time the agent was claiming to act on his or her behalf. A principal who did not have the capacity to enter into the original deal because of drunkenness or insanity does not have the power to ratify upon becoming sober or sane. This requirement of capacity can be a problem where pre-incorporation contracts are involved. Often, promoters who are planning incorporation will enter into contracts, such as the purchase of property on behalf of the proposed corporation, assuming that once the corporation is formed it will ratify the agreements. But because there is no corporation at the time the contract is entered into, there can be no ratification, leaving the promoter personally liable for any losses suffered by the third party. Legislation in some jurisdictions has modified this principle to allow a corporation to ratify such pre-incorporation contracts.[7]

• when it is ratified

4. The parties must still be able to perform the object of the contract at the time of the ratification. For example, if an agent enters into a contract on behalf of a principal to insure a building against fire, the principal cannot ratify the agreement after a fire. There is no building to insure when ratification is attempted, so there can be no contract. Furthermore, the contract the agent enters into must not make any reference to the need for ratification. If the contract includes such terms as "subject to principal's approval" or "subject to ratification," it becomes merely an agreement to enter into an agreement. The contractual requirement of consensus is not satisfied, and there is no contract.

Ratification can take place inadvertently

Ratification can work against the principal in other ways. The principal can inadvertently ratify by knowingly accepting some sort of benefit under the agreement. If Kim's chauffeur bought a new Rolls-Royce on Kim's behalf without the actual or apparent authority to do so, Kim would normally not be bound by such a contract. However, if Kim were to use that car in some way, such as driving it to work before returning it to the dealer, Kim would have accepted some benefit under the contract and thus ratified it by his conduct. Kim would be bound to go through with the purchase of the automobile, provided that at the time he received the benefit, Kim knew that the purchase was made on his behalf.

---

7. For example, the Canada *Business Corporations Act*, R.S.C. 1985, c. C-44, s. 14.

CASE SUMMARY 11.4

Delay in Repudiating Unauthorized Act Treated as Ratification: *Community Savings Credit Union v. United Association of Journeymen and Apprentices of the Plumbing and Pipefitting Industry of the United States and Canada, Local 324*[8]

A credit union needed additional supporting security to finance a building project and approached several members for assistance. Mr. Crossett, the business manager of the defendant union local, acted without authority when he pledged, in the form of an indemnity, $80 000 of the local's funds to that purpose. Later he informed the union's governing board that he had made the pledge on the behalf of the local, but they did nothing about it and did not inform the credit union that Crossett's action was not authorized. Still later when the project ran into difficulty, Crossett acting as business manager of the local, informed the credit union that the union had disavowed further financial responsibility for financing the project. Subsequently, when the project failed, the credit union demanded payment from the union under the indemnity agreement. But the union local took the position that the pledge (indemnity agreement) was invalid as it was entered into without authority. The Court of Appeal found that although the business manager acted without actual authority, the failure of the Board to notify the credit union of that fact once they had knowledge of the unauthorized acts was sufficient to constitute ratification. The pledge was thus enforceable against the union.

DISCUSSION QUESTIONS SMALL BUSINESS PERSPECTIVE

When should a failure to act be taken as ratification? This case demonstrates that one's silence may be regarded as acquiescence. The union's Board had opportunities to notify the credit union as to its position regarding the indemnity once it learned of the transaction but it chose not to do so. This was sufficient to constitute ratification.

Agency by Necessity

Without authority (apparent or actual) or ratification, the principal cannot be bound. In the past, when communications were less reliable, authority was sometimes implied on the basis of **agency by necessity**. For example, an agent might have to sell deteriorating goods to preserve some value for the principal. If the cargo of a ship might get wet, the shipper may be required to have it sold en route, often without getting authorization from the principal. In these circumstances, authority arises on the basis of necessity. Today, with instantaneous forms of communication, it will be rare indeed for an agency by necessity to arise.

But where it does, there must be some duty or responsibility placed on the agent to care for those goods. Merely finding another person's property in danger does not, in and of itself, create an agency-by-necessity relationship.

Agency by necessity rarely used today

---

8. [2002] B.C.J. No. 654 (C.A.).

EXCEPTION IN FAMILY RELATIONSHIPS

It is common for one spouse to have the actual or even apparent authority to act on behalf of the other when dealing with merchants, especially for the purchase of necessities and other household goods. When the marriage breaks down, those merchants who, because of past dealings, have been led to believe a person has authority to act for a spouse may rely on that apparent authority. In the absence of notice to the contrary, the authority continues, even when the spouse has been specifically prohibited from making such purchases.

In some circumstances, authority can be implied by operation of law against the will of the other party. A wife who is deserted by her husband is presumed to have the authority to bind him to contracts with third parties for the purchase of necessities. But this must be viewed in the light of modern family law legislation. In Ontario, spouses and same-sex partners can be held liable for the purchases of necessities made by the other partner, so long as the purchases were made during cohabitation and the spouse or same-sex partner has not notified the third party that this authority has been withdrawn.[9] In some jurisdictions, this principle has been abolished altogether.[10] For example, in Alberta, a wife's common law right to pledge her husband's credit for necessaries after separation was recently abolished. So too was the common law presumption of implied agency of a wife to render her husband liable for necessaries supplied by a third party.[11]

REDUCING RISK 11.1

A businessperson who deals through an agent runs a risk of that agent's entering into contracts that are not authorized. Whether this is done by mistake or intentionally, the effect on the businessperson can be significant. To avoid the problem, the principal should make the limits of that authority absolutely clear to the agent. Those limitations should be stip-ulated in a written agency agreement. The principal should also, where practical, make the limits of the agent's authority clear to the customers or third parties with whom that agent will deal. Customers should also be notified immediately upon the termination of that agent's authority, otherwise it will continue because of the principle of apparent authority.

THE RIGHTS AND RESPONSIBILITIES OF THE PARTIES

www.pearsoned.ca/mybuslawlab

The Agent's Duties

THE CONTRACT

When an agency agreement has been created by contract, the agent has an obli-gation to act within the actual authority given in that agreement. An agent violat-ing the contract but exercising apparent authority can be sued for breach and will have to compensate the principal for any losses suffered. Failure on the part of the agent to fulfill any other obligation set out in the agreement will also consti-tute an actionable breach of contract unless the specified act is illegal or against public policy.

---

9. *Family Law Act,* R.S.O. 1990, c. F.-3, s. 45.

10. See Saskatchewan's *Equality of Status of Married Persons Act,* S.S. 1984–85–86, c. E-10.3, s. 5.

11. *Family Law Act,* S.A. 2003 c.F-4.5, ss. 105, 106.

An agent owes a **duty of care** to the principal. The agent must not only have the skills and expertise claimed but also must exercise that skill in a reasonable manner. For example, if Khan hires Gamboa to purchase property on which to build an apartment building, Gamboa must not only stay within the authority given but also must exercise the degree of care and skill one would expect from a person claiming to be qualified to do that type of job. If Gamboa buys a property for Khan and it turns out to be zoned for single-family dwellings, such a mistake would be below the standard of reasonable performance one would expect from someone in this type of business, and Gamboa would be liable to compensate Khan for any loss.

Agent owes duty of reasonable care

Agents often have considerable discretion in carrying out agency responsibilities as long as they act to the benefit of the principal. However, an agent cannot go against the specific instructions received, even if it might be in the principal's best interests to do so. If a stockbroker is instructed to sell shares when they reach a specific price, the broker must do so, even though waiting would bring the principal a better price.

Agent must perform as required by principal

Agents also have a duty to act in the best interests of their principals.

CASE SUMMARY 11.5

Failure to Follow Instructions Can Be Costly: *Volkers et al. v. Midland Doherty Ltd.*[12]

Mr. Volkers, a knowledgeable investor, was assured by the representatives of Midland that he could give instructions to Mr. Hill, or any other trader, and they would be followed. On 28 February, Hill, following instruction from Volkers, purchased on his behalf a substantial number of shares in Breakwater Resources Ltd. Later that day, Volkers phoned and, since Hill had left for the day, gave instructions to Mr. Gurney to purchase additional shares in that company first thing the next morning.

Gurney arrived at 7:00 a.m. but, because of some doubts about the wisdom of the trade, delayed making the purchase until Hill arrived about two hours later. Unfortunately, trading in Breakwater shares had been stopped before Hill's arrival, and when it came back on the market, it had doubled in price. Volkers suffered substantial loss and sued.

It was argued that Gurney had a duty to act in the best interests of his client, and since this was what he was doing, there should be no liability. But the Appeal Court held Gurney had been given specific instructions to purchase the Breakwater shares first thing in the morning, and his duty was to do so, or to tell Volkers that he did not, so that Volkers could make other arrangements. Although the agent was obligated to do what he thought was best for the client, the agent bore an even greater obligation to keep Volkers informed. Volkers was the one to make the decision, not Gurney.

DISCUSSION QUESTIONS

This case illustrates that it is an important aspect of the agent's duty to the principal to follow instructions. Do you think this obligation should apply where it is clear the agent was acting in what he thought was the best interests of the principal?

---

12. [1985] B.C.J. No. 2163 (C.A.); leave to appeal to S.C.C. refused, [1985] S.C.C.A. No. 121.

DELEGATION

Agent cannot delegate responsibility

Generally, the agent has an obligation to perform the agency agreement personally. An agent is not permitted to delegate responsibility to another party unless there is consent to such delegation, either express or implied by the customs and traditions of the industry. Even then the primary agent has the responsibility to see that the terms of the agency agreement are fulfilled. The authority of an agent is commonly delegated to sub-agents, when that agent is a corporation or large business organization, such as a law firm, bank, real estate agency, or trust company.

ACCOUNTING

Agent must turn money over to principal

Agent must account for funds

The agent must turn over any monies earned pursuant to the agency function to the principal. If the agent acquires property, goods, or money on behalf of the principal, there is no entitlement to retain any of it other than the authorized commission. Even when the agent has some claim against the funds, he cannot keep them. If the third party owes money to the agent and pays money to the agent intended for the principal, the agent cannot intercept those funds on his own behalf but must pay over any money collected to the principal. To facilitate this process, the agent also has an obligation to keep accurate records of all agency transactions.

FIDUCIARY DUTY

One may be sympathetic with the position of Mrs. Forbes in Case Summary 11.6 below. She paid over part of her commission to Mr. Halbauer only to preserve the deal. But who was she acting for? If she did not reduce her commission, the property may have been sold by another real estate agent to somebody else, and she would have received nothing. Thus, it is clear that she was acting in her own self-interest above the interest of the principal. This case strongly illustrates the nature of fiduciary duty: a person owing that duty must submerge personal interests in favour of the interests of the principal he or she represents.

CASE SUMMARY 11.6

Conflicting Interests: *Ocean City Realty Ltd. v. A & M Holdings Ltd.*[13]

Mrs. Forbes was a licensed real estate salesperson working for Ocean City Realty Ltd. She was approached by Mr. Halbauer to find a commercial building in downtown Victoria. After some investigation, Forbes approached the owners of a building to determine whether it might be for sale. The owner of the property, A & M Holdings Ltd., entered into an arrangement with her, whereby they agreed to pay a commission of 1.75 percent if she acted as their agent in selling the building. After some negotiations the sale was concluded for $5.2 million, but unknown to the seller, Forbes had agreed to pay back half her commission to the purchaser, Halbauer. When A & M discovered the secret deal between Forbes and Halbauer, they refused to pay any commission.

[13.] [1987] B.C.J. No. 593 (C.A.).

Forbes had a fiduciary obligation to act in the best interests of her principal, A & M, but she argued that A & M got what it expected and her sacrifice only ensured that the deal went through. That did not hurt A & M but helped it. The Court held, however, that one of the key elements in the duty of a fiduciary is to disclose all pertinent information with respect to the transaction that would be considered important by the principal. In this case, the knowledge that she was paying part of her commission back to Halbauer was important to A & M, and it may have determined whether it would go through with the deal or not. In effect, A & M thought that Halbauer was paying one price, when, in fact, he was paying less for the property. A & M was entitled to this information, and it may have influenced its decision. Therefore, the fiduciary obligation of the agent had been breached, and the agent was entitled to no commission at all.

DISCUSSION QUESTIONS

Is this too harsh an application of fiduciary duty? Should the agent be penalized where the agent was just helping to make the deal go through? On the other hand, is a principal not entitled to have all the relevant information brought to its attention? When an agent profits from a breach of the duty to disclose, the Court's reaction is stern and uncompromising.

Agents owe their principal a positive duty of **full disclosure**. The agent cannot arbitrarily decide what would likely influence the conduct of the principal and what would not. For example, in the *Krasniuk* case,[14] the real estate agent assumed, incorrectly, that she was obligated to forward only written offers to the vendor. She unilaterally turned down the verbal offers for $135 000 and $137 500. Later, when the same purchasers submitted a written offer for $130 000, the vendor, unaware of the earlier offers, accepted it. The agent had breached its fiduciary duty by failing to disclose this information, so no commission was payable. Had the vendors been aware of the earlier offers, they may have accepted them or at least countered the subsequent written offer. Similarly, in the *Skinner* case,[15] the realtors' failure to fully disclose all offers that were made resulted in the Court declining its commission. A listing agent has a duty to ensure that all serious offers communicated to him are presented to the vendor for consideration, whether they are verbal offers or written offers.

> **Agent must disclose information**

Because the principal puts trust in the agent, the principal may be vulnerable; accordingly, the law imposes a fiduciary duty obliging the agent to act only in the best interests of the principal. The relationship is often referred to as an *utmost good faith* relationship, in which the agent has an obligation to

- keep in strict confidence any communications that come through the agency function
- act in the best interests of the principal, even if the agent may lose some personal benefit
- not take advantage of any personal opportunity that may come to his or her knowledge through the agency relationship
- disclose to the principal any personal benefit the agent stands to gain. Only with the informed consent of the principal can the agent retain any benefit.

---

14. *Krasniuk v. Gabbs* [2002] M.J. No. 13 (Q.B.).

15. *D.E.M. Corp. (c.o.b. ReMax Charlottetown Realty) v. Skinner*, [2004] P.E.I.J. No. 90 (S.C. T.D.).

If there is a failure to disclose, the principal can seek an accounting and have any funds gained by the agent in such a way paid over to the principal.

Agent cannot act for both principal and third party without consent of both

An agent cannot act for both a principal and a third party at the same time. It would be very difficult for an agent to extract the best possible price from a third party on behalf of a principal when the third party is also paying the agent. The common practice of agents accepting gifts, such as holidays, tickets to sporting events, and liquor, is an example of the same problem. If the principal discovers the agent accepting payment from the third party, the principal is entitled to an accounting and the receipt of all such funds and will likely have just cause to terminate the relationship. Only where full disclosure has been made at the outset and permission given can the agent profit personally in this way.

In real estate transactions, the agent usually acts for the seller. This can cause problems for purchasers, who often do not realize this and expect the agent to protect their interests as well. In some western provinces, this difficulty is largely overcome by requiring the purchasers to have their own agent acting for them and splitting the commission.

Agent must not profit at principal's expense

Another problem sometimes arises where an agent who is hired to purchase goods or property sells to the principal property actually owned by the agent as if it came from some third party. This is a violation of the agent's fiduciary duty; even if that property fully satisfies the principal's requirements, there must be full disclosure.[16] The reverse is also a breach, where the agent buys for himself what he has been hired to sell to others. An example would be where a real estate agent hired to sell a house recognizes it as a good deal and purchases it for himself, perhaps through a partner or a corporation. The agent then has the advantage of a good price, knowing how low the principal will go, and getting the commission as well. This is not acting in the best interests of the principal, and the agent would be required to pay back both profits and commission to the vendor of the property.

Agent must not compete with principal

It also follows that the agent must not operate his own business in competition with the principal, especially if a service is being offered. Nor can the agent also represent another principal selling a similar product without full disclosure. Finally, the agent must not collect any profits or commissions that are hidden from the principal, but must pay over all the benefit resulting from the performance of the agency agreement. Such a breach of fiduciary duty by an agent who is also an employee will likely constitute just cause for dismissal. Note that with senior employees this duty will probably continue after termination of the employment, but for ordinary employees any duty owed ends when they leave.

! REDUCING RISK 11.2

When professionals or independent businesses offer their service to others, a relationship of trust is created that leaves a client vulnerable, so a fiduciary duty is owed. The person providing the service must put the interests of the client ahead of his or her own and follow the instructions given. It is sometimes difficult to keep personal interests and the interests of customers and clients separate, but failure to do so is asking for trouble. It is vitally important that professionals or businesspeople in such a position learn the nature of their fiduciary duty and make sure they honour it.

---

16. *G.L. Black Holdings Ltd. v. Peddle* [1998] A.J. No. 1488 (Q.B.), aff'd [1999] A.J. No. 1083 (C.A.).

The Principal's Duties

THE CONTRACT

The principal's primary obligation to the agent is to honour the terms of the contract by which the agent was hired. If the contract is silent as to payment, an obligation to pay a reasonable amount can be implied on the basis of the amount of effort put forth by the agent, as well as the customs and traditions of the industry. If the agreement provides for payment only on completion, there is no implied obligation to pay for part performance. Thus, if an agent is to receive a commission upon the sale of a house, even if the agent puts considerable effort into promoting a sale, there is generally no entitlement to commission if no sale occurs. Unless there is agreement to the contrary, or a different custom in the industry, the agent is normally entitled to compensation for reasonable expenses, such as phone bills and car expenses.

Principal must honour terms of contract and pay reasonable amount for services

Principal must reimburse agent's expenses

If the agency agreement is vague about the extent of the agent's authority, the courts will usually favour an interpretation that gives the agent the broadest possible power. Thus, if Jones is hired as a sales manager for a manufacturing business and is given authority to enter into all sales related to the business, a court will likely interpret it to include authority to sell large blocks of product but no authority to sell the plant itself. When the power to borrow money is involved, however, the courts take a much narrower approach. Thus, if Klassen were hired as a purchasing agent with "all the authority necessary" to carry out that function and he found it necessary to borrow money to make the purchases, the courts would not imply an authority to borrow without getting additional approval from the principal. It is necessary for an agent to be given specific authority to borrow money on the principal's behalf in order to proceed.

*Ambiguous authority will be interpreted broadly
• except when power to borrow money is in question*

Undisclosed Principals

In some transactions principals attempt to conceal their identity from the third parties they are dealing with. These are referred to as an undisclosed principal relationship and might be used, for example, when a well-known company is assembling land for a new project. Agents approach property owners in the area to obtain options on their properties. The options are exercised only if a sufficient number of property owners are willing to sell at a reasonable price. The undisclosed principal approach is used to discourage people from holding out for higher prices once they find out who is really buying the property.

In these circumstances the agent will usually declare that they are acting for a principal whose identity will remain confidential. Sometimes, however, the agent will simply sign in such a way as to be consistent with them being principal or agent or will actually sign as if he or she were the principal contracting party. The rights and obligations of the parties are different in each case. When the agent makes it clear they are acting as agent for an undisclosed principal, the agent has no liability to the third party and only the principal can enforce the agreement. If the would-be agent acts as if he were the principal, only he can be sued by the third party and only he can enforce the contract.

Where agent makes it clear she is acting as agent for undisclosed principal, the third party cannot sue or be sued by the agent

Where agent acts as principal, only the agent can sue or be sued by the third party

CASE SUMMARY 11.7

No Liability under Contract When Agent Makes It Clear He Is Acting as Agent: *Q.N.S. Paper Co. v. Chartwell Shipping Ltd.;*[17] *Logistec Stevedoring Inc. v. Amican Navigation Inc.*[18]

Chartwell provided stevedoring services for Q.N.S., which operated a chartered ship. Although Chartwell never mentioned specifically who it was acting for, Chartwell made it clear at all times that it was acting as an agent on behalf of others in their dealings with Q.N.S. The deal fell through. Q.N.S. sued Chartwell. The Supreme Court of Canada had to decide whether this was an undisclosed principal situation where the agent could be successfully sued. The Court held that because Chartwell had made it clear at all times that it was functioning as an agent, there was no personal liability for that agent on the contract. Chartwell consistently emphasized that its sole responsibility was as an agent. It identified itself as "Managing Operators for the Charterers" or "acting on behalf of principals" or signed "as agent only." Thus the only option open to Q.N.S. was to sue the principal.

In a subsequent case, *Logistec v. Amican*, Amican also claimed it had acted as agent but in this case didn't make it clear. It signed as an agent on only a few occasions, but this was not done consistently and on several occasions it had acted as if it were the principal party. The Federal Court held that to escape liability the agent acting for an undisclosed principal had to make it clear that it was acting as an agent and this it had failed to do. Thus it could not escape liability, and both principal and agent were liable.

SMALL BUSINESS PERSPECTIVE

In several industries, businesses are engaged as agents. If personal liability is to be avoided, it is necessary to make it clear that one is acting in a representative capacity.

Where agent acts ambiguously as to whether principal or agent, third party can also be sued by either

Where agent acts ambiguously as to whether principal or agent, third party can sue either

Apparent authority does not apply where principal undisclosed

Where the agent acted ambiguously so that it is not clear whether he was acting as agent or the principal party, the third party has a choice. He can choose to sue the agent or when the identity of the principal is determined he can end that action and commence an action against the principal instead. Once the choice is made, however, he is bound by it. For example, when the agent signs a purchase order in a way consistent with being an agent for the purchaser or the actual person purchasing the goods, if the contract is breached the third party/seller can sue either the agent or, upon learning the identity, can sue the principal instead. The injured party cannot sue both; once the choice is made, the third party is bound by it. The converse is also true in that the agent can enforce the contract against the third party unless the principal chooses to take over and enforce the contract himself.

There are some types of transactions done on behalf of an undisclosed principal that are not binding on the parties. The undisclosed principal is liable only when the agent has acted within his actual authority. Apparent authority applies only when the principal has held out the agent to have authority, and since the

---

17. [1989] 2 S.C.R. 683.

18. [2001] F.C.J. No. 1009 (T.D.).

principal is unknown there can be no holding out and no apparent authority. For the same reason an undisclosed principal cannot ratify since the agent must be claiming to be acting on behalf of a specific principal in those dealings with the third party for such a ratification to be valid. Where the agent has made no such claim there can be no ratification of it. Finally an undisclosed principal contract cannot be enforced where the identity of the parties is important to the third party. In a contract involving personal services, for example, the third party would be able to repudiate upon discovering that the deal had been made with an agent rather than with the principal. Similarly, in the case of *Said v. Butt,*[19] a theatre refused to sell a ticket to someone on opening night because he had caused a disturbance in the past. That person arranged for a friend to acquire the ticket on his behalf but was refused admittance even though he had a ticket. He sued for breach, but the Court held that in this situation, the identity of the party was obviously important, and the Court did not enforce the contract.

> **Undisclosed principal cannot ratify**

> **Third party can repudiate when identity of undisclosed principal important**

To further complicate matters, where the contract is made under seal (sealed by the agent) the undisclosed principal cannot be sued. Only parties to a sealed document can have rights or obligations under it.

As can be seen, the responsibilities of the parties in undisclosed principal situations can become very complicated. To avoid the problem of an undisclosed principal, persons acting as agents should be extremely careful to make it clear that they are acting in an agency capacity. This is normally done by writing "per" immediately before the signature of the agent. For example, if Sam Jones were acting for Ace Finance Company, he would be well advised to sign:

Ace Finance Company per
Sam Jones.

The Third Party

When an agent does not have the authority claimed, either actual or apparent, that agent may be sued by the third party for breach of "warranty of authority." This action is founded in contract law and is the most common example of an agent being sued directly by the third party. Also, an agent who intentionally misleads the third party into believing that she has authority when she does not may be sued by the third party for the tort of deceit. Furthermore, agents who inadvertently exceed their authority can be sued for negligence.

> **Third party can sue agent for unauthorized acts**

CASE SUMMARY 11.8

Misrepresentation or Breach of Warranty of Authority: *Alvin's Auto Service Ltd. v. Clew Holdings Ltd.*[20]

The plaintiff was approached by a realtor about making an offer to purchase a building. The plaintiff indeed submitted an offer to purchase and the defendant bank was named as the vendor. A counteroffer was remitted to the plaintiff and again the bank was identified as the vendor.

---

19. [1920] 3 K.B. 497.

20. [1997] S.J. No. 387 (Q.B.).

In fact, the registered owner was Clew Holdings Ltd., (Clew) an insolvent corporation that had defaulted in payment of its mortgage to the defendant bank. Clew had earlier instructed the bank to find a buyer for its commercial premises.

Over two weeks, the bank and plaintiff exchanged offers until they finally agreed on a price. However, before the bank approached Clew about approving the deal, the bank received an offer from a third party for much more money than the bank had originally asked. Clew accepted the third party offer and executed the agreement as vendor.

The plaintiff was forced to purchase another building, which required renovations. Consequently, its business relocation was delayed by a month and a half.

An action for damages for breach of warranty of authority and negligent misrepresentation was commenced. Judgment was granted to the plaintiff. The bank's conduct clearly gave the impression that it was Clew's agent for the purpose of negotiating the sale of the building; it was thus liable for breach of warranty of authority. Further, the bank owed a duty of care to disclose that it did not have the authority to negotiate a binding sale. By conducting itself otherwise, it made a negligent misrepresentation, which the plaintiff reasonably relied upon to its detriment. The plaintiff was entitled to compensation for economic loss suffered in locating and securing an equivalent property for its business expansion.

SMALL BUSINESS PERSPECTIVE

Officers and other employees of corporations often negotiate contracts on behalf of the company. If they do not have actual authority to bind their principal to contracts yet act as though they do, they run the risk of later being sued for breach of warranty of authority, misrepresentation, or both.

Remedies in tort available for fraud or negligence

It is important to distinguish between the tortious liability of the agent based on fraud or negligence and a contract action based on breach of warranty of authority. Where a breach of warranty of authority action is brought, the damages will be limited to those that were reasonably foreseeable at the time the contract was entered into or those that flow naturally from the breach (that is, the damages awarded for breach of contract). If, unknown to the agent, the goods were to be resold at an unusually high profit that was lost because of the breach of warranty of authority, the agent would not be liable for those losses, since they were not reasonably foreseeable. However, if the third party could establish the agent's fraud or negligence, the lost profits might be recovered from the agent because they are the direct consequence of the tortious conduct—and in tort law, damages are awarded to compensate for the loss caused.

www.pearsoned.ca/mybuslawlab

Liability for Agent's Tortious Conduct

Vicarious liability limited to employment

As discussed in Chapters 4 and 10, an employer is vicariously liable for the acts an employee commits during the course of employment. When an agent is also an employee of the principal, the principal is vicariously liable for any tortious acts committed by the agent in the course of that employment. The difficulty arises when the agent is not an employee but acts independently. In 1938, the Supreme Court of Canada held that the principle of vicarious liability is restricted to those situations in which a master–servant relationship can be demonstrated.[21] This position was reaffirmed in 2001 in the *Sagaz* case[22] when Major J. of the Supreme Court said, "Based on policy considerations, the relationship between an employer and independent contractor does not typically give rise to a claim in vicarious liability."

The courts have been expanding the definition of employment. Fleming points out that "the employment of a servant may be limited to a single occasion, or extend over a long period; it may even be gratuitous."[23] Even if the relationship involves a person who is essentially an independent agent, that agent may be functioning as an employee or servant in a given situation; thus, the courts may impose vicarious liability on the principal by simply asserting that the agent is also an employee. With such a broad definition of employment, judges will have little difficulty imposing vicarious liability on principals when the circumstances warrant. Still it is only in rare cases that a principal will be found vicariously liable for the acts of an independent agent. Of course, the principal can then look to the agent for compensation for any losses incurred.

There are some situations in which vicarious liability will apply even if the agent is acting independently. The courts appear willing to hold the principal responsible for theft or fraudulent misrepresentation by an agent, even when no employment exists. In Case Summary 11.1, it made no difference whether Mr. Snarey was an employee or was acting as an independent agent; because fraud was involved, the principal was liable for the agent's wrongful conduct. It does appear, however, that vicarious liability for the acts of independent agents is limited to those situations where the acts complained of are actually committed in the process of the exercise of that agency function. In the *Thiessen* case[24] the B.C. Court of Appeal grappled with the problem of whether vicarious liability ought to be imposed on the principal where the agent was clearly an independent contractor. In that case Mr. Carey Dennis diverted funds to be invested with Mutual Life Insurance and instead put them into his own account. The insurance company had made every effort to ensure that the agent, Carey Dennis, was an independent contractor, even defining him as such in their contract. But the Court found that because he represented only Mutual Life and could sell another company's products only with Mutual Life's permission, and because that company intended that a relationship of trust would be developed between their customers and Dennis, he had apparent authority to represent Mutual in the offending transaction. The act of taking the client's investment funds was the very exercise of that apparent authority and as a result Mutual was vicariously liable for his fraud. Although this was a decision of the B.C. Court of Appeal, it should be noted that an application for appeal to the Supreme Court of Canada was rejected.

• but definition of employment may be broadened

Vicarious liability where independent agent deceitful

---

21. *T.G. Bright and Company v. Kerr*, [1939] S.C.R. 63.

22. *671122 Ontario Ltd. v. Sagaz Industries Canada Inc.*, [2001] 2 S.C.R. 983 at para.3.

23. John G. Fleming, *The Law of Torts*, 8th ed. (Sydney: The Law Book Co. Ltd., 1990) at 371.

24. *Thiessen v. Mutual Life Assurance Co. of Canada*,[2002] B.C.J. No. 2041 (C.A.); leave to appeal dismissed, [2002] S.C.C.A. No. 454.

CASE SUMMARY 11.9

Even Innocent Principals Can Be Liable for an Agent's Negligence: *Betker v. Williams*[25]

The Williamses owned land in Cranbrook, British Columbia, and entered into a listing agreement with a realtor to sell it. The realtor advertised it for sale as a building site and, when asked, indicated that it was suitable for building a residential home.

The property was purchased by the Betkers, and several years later when they decided to build, they discovered a problem. In fact the city bylaws required that such residential building lots either be accessible to city sewers or be more than 2 1/2 acres in size to accommodate a septic filter field. This property satisfied neither requirement and so could not be used as a residential building site. The Betkers sued, and the question in this case was whether the Williamses could be held liable for the negligence of their agent. Also the remedy sought was the rescission of the contract and the return of the purchase price. Linda Williams, in turn, sued the agent in a third-party action.

Although the mistake was entirely that of the agent, the Court found that because of the principle of vicarious liability, the vendors of the property (that is, the Williamses), who had profited from the sale, were responsible. They had to pay significant damages for the negligent misrepresentation of their agent. It is interesting to note that the remedy of rescission was rejected because of the delay in bringing the action. Also, Linda Williams was successful in her third-party action. The Judge ordered the agent to reimburse her for any losses suffered due to their vicarious liability to the Betkers for the agent's wrongful conduct.

SMALL BUSINESS PERSPECTIVE

Many businesses interact with customers through agents. This case illustrates the potential liability principals bear for the wrongful actions of their agents. Even though the principal may be entitled to compensation from the agent, this in itself may be problematic. If the agent is impecunious, securing compensation from the agent may be difficult.

Direct liability if principal is origin of fraud

A principal can also be found directly liable for his own tortious conduct. If the principal has requested the act complained of, has told the agent to make a particular statement that turns out to be defamatory or misleading, or is negligent in allowing the agent to make the particular statements complained of, the principal may be directly liable. In the case of *Junkin v. Bedard*,[26] Junkin owned a motel that was sold to a third party through an agent. Junkin provided false information regarding the profitability of the motel to the agent, knowing that the agent would pass it on to the purchaser, Bedard. The agent did so, and Bedard bought the property. Bedard later discovered the falsification and sued Junkin for fraud. Because the agent had innocently passed the information on to Bedard, Junkin alone had committed the fraud, even though the agent had communicated the information. Here, the principal was directly liable for his own fraud. If the agent

---

25. [1991] B.C.J. No. 3724 (C.A.).

26. [1957] S.C.J. No. 67.

had fabricated the false information, the principal would have been vicariously liable for the agent's fraud.

As is the case with employment law, vicarious liability makes the principal responsible, but it does not relieve the agent of liability for his own tortious conduct. Both can be sued, but the principal can then seek compensation from the agent.

Vicarious liability—both parties liable

Termination of Agency

Since the right of an agent to act for a principal is based on the principal's consent, as soon as the agent is notified of the withdrawal of that consent, that authority ends. When the agent is an employee, the relationship is usually ended with appropriate notice, as discussed in Chapter 10. But even where employment may continue, the authority to act as an agent will end immediately upon notification of the agent to that effect. Sometimes, the agency agreement will set out when the agent's authority will end. If the agency relationship was created for a specific length of time, the authority of the agent automatically terminates at the end of that period. Similarly, if the agency contract created the relationship for the duration of a particular project or event, for example, "for the duration of the 2010 Olympic Games," the authority ends when the project or event ends.

Termination as per agreement

Requirement of notification

REDUCING RISK 11.3

Since most business is done through agents, businesspeople must take care to understand the exposure they have to liability for their agents' conduct. That liability may be based in contract or tort, and both are derived from the duties and authority given. Whether the agent is independent or an employee, care should be taken to carefully define his or her authority and to make sure that the agent stays within those specified parameters. Even then, liability may be incurred when agents do in a careless manner what they are authorized to do. The key here is to minimize exposure, not to eliminate it. In the end, the best practice is to ensure that agents are reliable, trustworthy, and well trained.

When the principal wants to end the agent's authority to act, simple notification is usually sufficient, for there is no requirement that the notice be reasonable, only that it be communicated to the agent. This applies to the termination of authority to enter into new contracts on the principal's behalf, not necessarily to the right to continued payment, which may be based on other contractual considerations. If the activities the agent is engaged to perform become impossible or essentially different from what the parties anticipated, then the contractual doctrine of frustration may apply, terminating the agent's authority. Similarly, an agent's authority to act on behalf of a principal is terminated when the actions the agent is engaged to perform become illegal. If Cantello agreed to act as Jasper's agent to sell products in a pyramid sales scheme, that authority would have been terminated automatically upon passage of the *Criminal Code* provision prohibiting such activities.[27]

Frustration may terminate agency, as will requests to perform illegal tasks

An agent's authority to act on behalf of a principal can be terminated in several other ways, as Table 11.1 shows. The death or insanity of a principal will automatically end the authority of an agent. When the principal is a corporation, its dissolution will have a similar effect. An agent will lose authority when a principal

Death, insanity, or bankruptcy will terminate agency

---

27. *Criminal Code*, R.S.C. 1985, c. C-46, s. 206.

becomes bankrupt, although other people may assume such authority under the direction of the trustee. How third parties are affected by termination of agency varies. Certainly, as far as termination of authority on the basis of agreement is concerned, unless the principal notifies the third party of such termination, the actions of the agent may still be binding on the principal on the basis of apparent authority. Though it is not entirely clear, this may also be the case when the principal becomes insane. However, in the case of bankruptcy or death of the principal, or dissolution of the principal corporation, the agent's actual and apparent authority ceases. Because of the lingering effect of apparent authority, it is vitally important for a principal to take steps to notify current and potential customers, as well as other people and businesses that they may have dealings with, regarding the termination of the agent's authority.

Table 11.1 Other Ways to Terminate an Agent's Authority

	Impact on Agent's Actual Authority	Impact on Agent's Apparent Authority
Death of principal	Ceases	Ceases
Bankruptcy of principal	Ceases[1]	Ceases
Dissolution of principal corporation	Ceases	Ceases
Insanity of principal	Ceases	Unclear—possibly continues[2]
By mutual agreement	Ceases	Continues until the third party is notified of termination[2]

[1] Other people may assume this authority under the direction of the Trustee.

[2] Since apparent authority continues, the principal must actively notify third parties that the agent's authority has been terminated. Only then does apparent authority cease.

Enduring Powers of Attorney

www.pearsoned.ca/mybuslawlab

BC AB SK MB ON

As stated above, loss of sanity on the part of the principal will terminate an agency; consequently, authority to act under a power of attorney terminates when the principal loses capacity. This is problematic, especially where society is aging and many individuals may desire to appoint someone as their agent or decision maker with power to act in the principal's stead after the principal loses capacity. In the past, it was necessary for family members (or others) to apply to the courts for an order appointing them as the trustee of the person who had lost capacity. These applications could be expensive and time-consuming, especially if the family was divided as to who should act as trustee. The process could also be a humiliating one for the principal involved, whose loss of mental capacity would be openly examined in a public setting.

To remedy some of these difficulties, provinces have passed legislation to allow individuals to execute **enduring powers of attorney**,[28] vesting powers similar to those given to trustees to the person chosen to act as one's attorney. These powers typically are exercisable after the principal loses mental capacity. The attorney generally can make all financial decisions on behalf of the donor. Through use of an enduring power of attorney, a person can decide, in advance,

---

[28] See for example B.C.'s *Power of Attorney Act,* R.S.B.C. 1996 c. 370 and Ontario's *Powers of Attorney Act,* R.S.O. 1990 c. P.20.

who to entrust with the future handling of his financial affairs. It is now also possible for individuals to exercise some control over who will make health care decisions and similar personal decisions for them.[29] Refer to the MyBusLawLab for provincial variations.

Specialized Agency Relationships

Many examples of specialized services offered to businesses and the public are essentially agencies in nature, such as those of travel agents, real estate agents, lawyers, accountants, stockbrokers, financial advisers, and insurance representatives. Some of these agents do not enter into contracts on behalf of their clients but negotiate and act on their clients' behalf in other ways. For example, a real estate agent neither offers nor accepts on behalf of a client. In fact, the client is usually the vendor of a property, and the agent's job is to take care of the preliminary matters and bring the purchaser and vendor together so they can enter into a contract directly. Nonetheless, few would dispute that these real estate agents are carrying out essentially an agency function and thus have a fiduciary obligation to their clients. The important thing to remember is that the general provisions set out above also apply to these special agency relationships, although there may be some exceptions. For example, in most of these specialized service professions, the rule that an agent cannot delegate usually does not apply. The very nature of these businesses requires that employees of the firm, not the firm itself, will act on behalf of the client.

General principles apply to specialized agencies as well

Special statutes and professional organizations

Most of these specialized agencies are fulfilling a service function and are governed by special statutes and professional organizations. For example, the real estate industries in each province have legislation in place that creates commissions or boards that govern the industry. The commissions require that anyone acting for another in the sale of property be licensed or be in the employ of a licensed real estate agent. Bodies that license their members often provide training, and discipline them when required. It is beyond the scope of this text to examine these professional bodies in detail; students are encouraged to examine the controlling legislation, as well as to seek information directly from the governing professional bodies. Most of them are concerned about their public image and are happy to cooperate.

Often, agencies perform a service to their customers that involves not only representing those customers but also giving them advice. Because of the specialized expertise provided, customers are particularly vulnerable to abuse should such agencies try to take advantage of them. The governing bodies hear complaints and go a long way toward regulating the industry and preventing such abuses. But abuses still occur, and victims should know that they have recourse based on the fiduciary duty principles set out here as well as remedies in contract and tort discussed before. Such fiduciary duties, in fact, may be imposed on other professional advisers, even when their duties do not extend to being agents.[30]

[29.] See, for example, Alberta's *Personal Directives Act*, R.S.A. 2000, c. P-6.

[30.] See *Hodgkinson v. Simms*, [1994] 3 S.C.R. 377, where the Supreme Court held that the relationship of broker and client is not necessarily a fiduciary relationship. However, where the elements of trust and confidence and reliance on skill, knowledge, and advice are present, the relationship is fiduciary and the obligations that attach are fiduciary. It thus remains a question of fact as to whether the parties' relationship was such as to give rise to a fiduciary duty on the part of the adviser.

TYPES OF BUSINESS ORGANIZATION

The law of agency discussed above is of particular importance when discussing different methods of carrying on business. These business organizations almost always conduct their business through representatives or agents.

Sole proprietorship involves one person

There are essentially three major types of business organization (see Figure 11.2). The first, the **sole proprietorship**, involves an individual carrying on business alone. Employees may be hired and business may be carried on through the services of an agent, but the business is the sole responsibility of one person, the owner. A second method of carrying on business is called a **partnership**,

Partners share responsibilities

where ownership and responsibilities, along with both profits and losses, are shared by two or more partners. As was the case with the sole proprietorship, the partnership may also employ others and act through agents. Also each partner acts as an agent for the other partners and has a fiduciary duty to them. The third type of business organization is the incorporated company. Any type of business

Corporation is a separate legal entity

organization involving more than one person can be called a company; a **corporation**, however, is a legal entity. By statute, it has been given an identity separate from the individual members who make it up. Thus, contracts with a corporation are dealings with the corporation itself as if it were a person in its own right. And because the corporation is a fiction, it must conduct all of its affairs through employees and agents.

Societies are separate legal entities, but obligations differ

There are other ways for people to work together to carry on a commercial activity. For example, a **non-profit society** can be set up under legislation such as the Nova Scotia *Societies Act*.[31] This also creates a separate legal entity, but the procedure of incorporation and the obligations of those involved are quite different. There are also several ways in which these various types of business organizations can be combined. A **holding corporation** holds shares in other corporations. A **joint venture** involves several different incorporated corporations that band together to accomplish a major project. They may form a separate corporation or a partnership. The discussion in this chapter will be limited to an examination of sole proprietorship and partnership, while Chapter 12 will deal with corporations.

Figure 11.2 Types of Business Organization

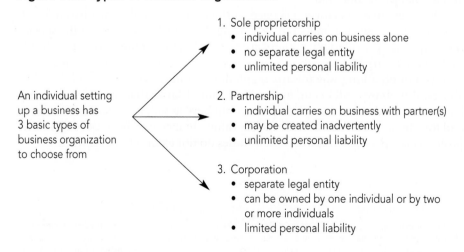

An individual setting up a business has 3 basic types of business organization to choose from

1. Sole proprietorship
   - individual carries on business alone
   - no separate legal entity
   - unlimited personal liability

2. Partnership
   - individual carries on business with partner(s)
   - may be created inadvertently
   - unlimited personal liability

3. Corporation
   - separate legal entity
   - can be owned by one individual or by two or more individuals
   - limited personal liability

[31.] R.S.N.S. 1989, c. 435.

THE SOLE PROPRIETORSHIP

The sole proprietorship is simply an individual carrying on a business activity on her own. The sole proprietor makes all the decisions associated with the business and is the only one entitled to the benefits derived from the business. A sole proprietor also bears full responsibility for all the costs, losses, and obligations incurred in the business activity. Thus, there is no distinction between the personal assets of the sole proprietor and those of the business. They are all the assets of the proprietor and are available to creditors if things go wrong.

Sole proprietorship carries on business in own right

mybuslawlab
www.pearsoned.ca/mybuslawlab

BC AB SK MB ON

Government Regulations

The sole proprietor, like all other types of business organizations, must satisfy many federal, provincial, and municipal requirements to carry on business. Usually, the name of the business must be registered if it is different from the sole proprietor's name,[32] and a licence to operate must be obtained from the appropriate level of government. This licensing process is used to control or restrict certain types of businesses, such as door-to-door sales, credit information services, moneylenders, hotels, and cabarets. When the handling of food or dangerous commodities is involved, there are further provincial and federal regulations that must be obeyed. Sole proprietors must also satisfy local zoning bylaws, and if they have employees they are subject to employment legislation, such as workers' compensation, employment insurance, and income tax regulations. They are also required to remit Goods and Services Tax if the business income is more than $30 000 per year.

Must adhere to licensing and governing regulations

As a general rule, sole proprietors are subject to fewer government regulations than partnerships and corporations. Only minimal records need be kept, and sole proprietors are usually not required to disclose information about the business to others. They must keep sufficient records to satisfy government agencies, such as the Canada Revenue Agency. In essence, the sole proprietor has complete control and complete responsibility for the business activity.

Sole proprietor relatively free of outside interference

Liability

Sole proprietors do not have accountability to others and alone are responsible for making important business decisions. They can look only to their own resources to finance the business operation; they cannot sell shares and are restricted to their own credit standing when borrowing money to finance the business. The sole proprietor owns all the assets, receives all the profits of the business, and is responsible for all its debts and liabilities. This **unlimited liability** can be the most significant disadvantage of the sole proprietorship. When liability is incurred for breached contracts or torts, or where there is insurmountable debt, the whole burden falls on the sole proprietor. Under the principle of *vicarious liability*, the sole proprietor is responsible for any tort committed by an employee during the course of employment. Although the sole proprietor's entire personal fortune is at risk, much of this risk can be offset by carrying adequate insurance. Any profit derived from a sole proprietorship is subject to personal income tax, while some tax advantages available to partnerships and corporations are not available to sole proprietors. These factors alone are often enough to encourage the businessperson to incorporate.

Sole proprietor has unlimited liability but can purchase insurance

---

[32.] See, for example, *Business Names Act*, R.S.O. 1990, c. B. 17, s. 2(2).

In most jurisdictions, professional individuals such as doctors, dentists, lawyers, and accountants cannot incorporate their practice, and they derive little advantage from doing so in those jurisdictions where professional incorporations are permitted.[33] They carry on business as sole proprietors or band together in a group as partners. (Note that in some jurisdictions, limited protection can now be obtained as limited liability partners discussed below.) These professionals must join the appropriate professional organization, such as the law society or medical association of the province. Note that it is only the practice of the professional service that cannot be incorporated, and so these professionals obtain many of the advantages of incorporation by establishing companies that supply them with management services and equipment, own the building, and employ the office staff.

Professionals bound by certain rules

PARTNERSHIP

Partnership—carrying on business together for profit

A partnership is the simplest form of business in which people pool their resources and carry on business together with the object of making profit. This relationship is based on contract, and so basic contract law applies, with special provisions to deal with this unique relationship. Unlike a corporation, a partnership is not a separate legal personality from those making it up. However, it is possible for the firm to enter into legal relationships so that it is not necessary to contract with each partner individually. This allows the partnership the convenience of functioning as a single business unit. It can own land, contract with others, and sue or be sued in its own name.

Partnership governed by contract law

www.pearsoned.ca/mybuslawlab

Legislation

In 1890, as part of a similar trend in other areas of law in the United Kingdom, the vast body of case law governing partnership was summarized into one statute, the *Partnership Act*.[34] This legislation was adopted in all the common law provinces of Canada, where it has remained in place to the present day, with only a few alterations, such as the creation of limited liability partners. With some minor variations province to province, the law of partnership is basically consistent across Canada. For convenience, this chapter will refer to the Ontario legislation, the *Partnerships Act*, and the sections discussed will refer to that statute.[35]

Partnership Act still used today

[33.] See, for example, the *Regulated Accounting Profession Act*, R.S.A. 2000, c. R-12, which, in s. 38, provides that a shareholder or professional corporation is liable as if the business were carried on as a partnership or a sole proprietorship, and that the liability of an accountant is not affected if the practice is carried on by the individual as an employee and on behalf of a professional corporation.

[34.] (1890), 53 & 54 Vict., c. 39 (U.K.).

[35.] *Partnerships Act*, R.S.O. 1990, c. P. 5. Note that Ontario is the only province for which the name of the partnership legislation is in the plural; all of the other provinces have a "Partnership Act."

Creation of the Partnership

CASE SUMMARY 11.10

What Are the Damages for Breach of Fiduciary Duty?
Olson v. Gullo[36]

Mr. Gullo entered into a verbal agreement with Mr. Olson to purchase and develop a 1000-acre (405-hectare) tract of land as an industrial park. They were both to contribute equal funding and their special skills—Gullo in real estate speculation and Olson in marketing and promotion. The pair had difficulty purchasing the designated land from the owners and eventually abandoned the project.

As it turned out, however, Gullo was able to maintain part of the deal by purchasing one 90-acre (36-hectare) parcel for himself, which he then sold at a $2.5-million profit. Olson, who was an employee of Gullo, found out about the deal, quit his job, and sued. It is interesting to note that Gullo died before the trial, but not before trying to have Olson murdered. Gullo's son carried on the defence of this action.

The first problem for the Court was to decide whether a partnership existed between the parties. The Court determined that there was an oral agreement between the parties whereby each was to contribute an equal share of the funds needed to acquire the land; that Gullo was to negotiate the purchases; and that Olson was to find interested investors and prepare promotional material. Thus, as they were carrying on business together with a view to making profits, their relationship was one of partnership. Gullo then had a fiduciary obligation to act in the best interests of his partner. When he secretly purchased the 90-acre parcel for himself, he did so in breach of that obligation.

The trial Judge held that because of his breach of fiduciary duty, Gullo should surrender all profit made on the transaction, but the Appeal Court overturned this and determined that despite his bad behaviour, he was entitled to half the profits because the sharing of such profits was the essential nature of a partnership.

SMALL BUSINESS PERSPECTIVE

The case illustrates not only what is necessary for a partnership to exist and the essential nature of that partnership, but also the fiduciary obligation or duty between the partners to act in the best interests of each other. Unless one is prepared to accept the obligation to act in the best interests of others, care should be taken to avoid creation of a partnership.

A partnership is not always created by formal agreement between the partners. The *Partnerships Act* provides that a partnership is created when two or more people carry on business in common with a view toward profits.[37] A profit does not actually have to be made, only that profit is the object of the exercise. It should be noted that the sharing of gross returns from a business activity does not in itself create a partnership. It is the sharing of the net proceeds after expenses have been

Partnership created by agreement or inadvertently

---

36. [1994] O.J. No. 587 (C.A.); leave to appeal refused, [1994] S.C.C.A. No. 248.

37. *Supra* note 35, s. 2.

deducted (the profits) from the enterprise that gives rise to the presumption of a partnership. The splitting of the commission on a sale by two real estate agents does not create a partnership, but when they split what is left after expenses the presumption of a partnership will arise.

The *Partnerships Act* sets out a number of other circumstances, which, though they involve the sharing of income, by themselves will not establish a partnership.[38]

1. Owning property in common, even when it is rented out for profit.

Partnerships Act lists exceptions—refer to MyBusLawLab for specific provincial wording

2. When a debt is repaid by the creditors' taking a share of the debtor's profits. For example, Pallas owes Clegg $10 000, and Clegg agrees to let Pallas pay it back by paying 20 percent of the profits of Pallas's furniture store per month until repaid.

3. When the payment of an employee is based on a share of sales or profits, such as commission selling or profit-sharing schemes.

4. When the beneficiary of a deceased partner receives the deceased partner's share of the profits.

5. When a loan is made in relation to a business and payment of interest varies with the profit. For example, Pallas loans Clegg $10 000 to start a furniture business, and Clegg pays interest on that $10 000 principal by paying 10 percent of the store's profits per month.

6. When a business is sold and the payment of the goodwill portion varies with the profitability of the business. For example, Pallas sells Clegg a furniture business for $10 000 for the assets and 50 percent of the first year's profits for goodwill.

When partnership presumed

The question remains: What constitutes carrying on business together with a view to profit? When evidence indicates that there has been one of the following, a partnership will be presumed:

- joint contribution of capital to establish a business
- intention to share expenses, profits, or losses
- joint participation in the management of a business.

Partnership must carry on continuing business

If two people operate a restaurant together by sharing the work and expenses and jointly making decisions, and the business has not been incorporated, the relationship is a partnership. It should be further noted that the *Partnerships Act* requires that the parties carry on a continuing business together. A single joint project, for example a school dance put on by two university students who combine their resources, would probably not be classed as a partnership. (If the students put on several dances, they would be in the "business" of providing this type of entertainment and, thus, would be in legal partnership, whether they looked at it that way or not.) Whether a business relationship is held to be a partnership will always depend on the circumstances.

---

[38]. *Ibid.*, s. 3.

CASE SUMMARY 11.11

Failure to Establish Partnership Means "No Team": *Blue Line Hockey Acquisition Co., Inc. v. Orca Bay Hockey Limited Partnership*[39]

Gaglardi, Beedie, and Aquilini, three experienced and prominent businesspersons, agreed to work together to acquire an ownership interest in the Vancouver Canucks hockey team. The Canucks were owned by the Orca Bay companies. The purchase was to occur through a tax-efficient entity to be created at a later date. Aquilini subsequently left the group but later asked to rejoin it. This request was rejected by the plaintiffs. The plaintiffs continued to negotiate an agreement to purchase the Canucks, but no agreement was reached.

Aquilini began negotiating the purchase on his own and eventually acquired the team. The plaintiffs sued Aquilini, alleging that a partnership had been formed among the three individuals and that Aquilini misappropriated a business opportunity belonging to the partnership by acquiring the Canucks on his own behalf. A breach of fiduciary duty by Aquilini was also alleged.

The action was dismissed. There was a common understanding among the parties that each member of the group was free to leave at any time. This finding was consistent with the fact that neither Gaglardi nor Beedie objected when Aquilini withdrew from the group. The plaintiffs failed to establish that the parties shared an "intention to carry on business in common with a view to profit." They were careful not to commit to anything except to the payment of their lawyer's fees in equal shares. They refrained from entering into any other obligations to third parties and did not make any actual offer to Orca Bay but simply advanced "expressions of interest." Since the parties could withdraw at any time from the talks without legal consequences, the claim that they intended to carry on business together failed.

As to the breach of fiduciary duty, the Court concluded that there was no expectation that the three men would forward each other's best interests. All were experienced businesspersons who were familiar with partnerships and partnership agreements. No evidence was submitted indicating that they discussed or assumed that each of them would act in the others' best interest. Aquilini was as entitled as the others to pursue the acquisition on his own. Further, since there was no intent to form a partnership, the claim of misappropriation of a business opportunity also failed.

SMALL BUSINESS PERSPECTIVE

The courts are often called upon to determine whether parties intended to "carry on a business" or simply to create an agreement for the regulation of their rights and obligations. Evidently, more than a mere common pursuit to purchase an opportunity must exist to found a partnership.

---

[39] [2008] B.C.J. No. 24 (S.C.); aff'd [2009] B.C.J. No. 136 (C.A.).

CREATION BY INADVERTENCE

It is important to realize that the existence of a partnership relationship is a question of fact that a court can imply from the conduct of the parties. A partnership can therefore be created inadvertently. Because of the liability of one partner for the contracts and misdeeds of other partners, the finding of such a relationship can have significant consequences for that person. This must be a consideration whenever someone is involved in any kind of business activity with another. Failure to appreciate this possibility can have disastrous financial consequences when one partner incurs liability to a third party.

The partnership relationship is primarily one of contract, usually created by agreement, but this agreement often does not take a written form. The *Olson v. Gullo* case summarized above is an instance where a court found that a partnership had been created by an oral agreement.

In addition to setting out the responsibilities of partners to third parties, the *Partnerships Act* also sets out the rights and obligations of the partners to each other. But like the *Sale of Goods Act*, the *Partnerships Act* provisions, at least as far as the rights between the partners themselves are concerned, can be modified by the partnership agreement. It is important for the partners to enter into an agreement, preferably in writing, setting out the exact nature of the relationship between them.

> **Partnership can be created by conduct**

> **But should be created by agreement**

CASE SUMMARY 11.12

Does Co-owning Property Create a Partnership? *A. E. LePage Ltd. v. Kamex Developments Ltd.*[40]

A number of people owned an apartment building together under the name of one of them, "M. Kalmykow in trust"; that is, in trust with the other owners as well. A corporation, called Kamex Developments Ltd., was created to control the property. The co-owners met monthly to discuss the property and what should be done including the possibility of sale. One of these parties, Mr. March, took it upon himself to list the property for sale under an exclusive listing agreement. He was not authorized to do so by the others. The property was eventually sold by a different agent, and A. E. LePage claimed their commission of $45 000 on the basis that March was in partnership with the rest and therefore bound the partnership to the exclusive listing agreement. Looking at the nature of the agreement, the Court found that although all these people owned the property together, this was not enough to constitute a partnership, and so the others were not liable for the commission.

SMALL BUSINESS PERSPECTIVE

When parties own property together with others they run the risk of being identified as "partners." The courts may be called upon to determine whether the intention of the co-owners was to "carry on a business" or simply to create an agreement for the regulation of their rights and obligations as co-owners of a property. The determination that a partnership exists will impact not just the "partners'" rights, but also those who do business with the group.

---

40. [1977] O.J. No. 2273 (C.A.); aff'd [1979] S.C.J. No. 38.

CREATION BY CONTRACT

As is the case with most business relationships, it is best to create the partnership through contract, preferably in writing, setting out the rights and obligations of the partners. But the terms of that contract are not always conclusive of the relationship. Even where the parties clearly state they are acting in partnership, this may not be enough to create such a partnership. See the *Backman* case set out in Case Summary 11.13 below. On the other hand a court may find that a partnership exists even where the parties clearly state in their agreement that they are not partners.[41]

Written contract not always conclusive proof of a partnership

---

CASE SUMMARY 11.13

Intention to Create Partnership Is Not Enough: *Backman v. Canada*[42]

Some Canadian investors took an assignment of the interests of the American partners in a limited partnership established in Texas to build an apartment building. The project failed, and the day after acquiring the interests the new owners resold the apartment building back to the original American owners at a significant loss. Each of the new Canadian partners then claimed that loss to be used against their Canadian taxes as was permitted of a Canadian partnership experiencing losses in another country. But this claim was rejected and the partners' taxes were reassessed on the basis that this was not a valid partnership. The would-be partners appealed first to the Tax Court, then to the Federal Court of Appeal, and finally to the Supreme Court of Canada.

From the documentation it was clear that the parties involved intended to create a partnership but that was not good enough. The partnership had been formed not to make a profit; instead it was formed with the predominant motive of acquiring a tax loss. A further problem was that there was no ongoing business relationship. The object of the transaction was to acquire the apartment building and sell it the next day, not to create or continue an ongoing business. And so no partnership was created.

SMALL BUSINESS PERSPECTIVE

For the partners to obtain the benefit of carrying on business as a partnership they must do more than simply call themselves partners. They must create an ongoing business relationship where they carry on business in common with a view of sharing any profits they make from that ongoing business.

A partnership agreement should deal with all of the matters important to the partnership, such as

- the duties of each partner
- what type of work or talent each is expected to contribute

Rights and obligations of partners can be modified by agreement

---

41. *See Foothills Dental Laboratory Ltd. v. Naik (c.o.b. Apple Dental Group)*[1996] A.J. No. 583, (Prov. Ct.). The court determined a partnership existed despite the contract, which stated "It shall be an express term of this agreement that the Association herein provided for shall, under no circumstances, be deemed to create an employer and employee or partnership relationship between Naik and Goldstein respectively."

42. [2001] 1 S.C.R. 367.

- the amount of time to be committed to the business
- how the profits are to be shared and how the capital is to be distributed
- any limitations on the powers or authority of each partner
- methods of resolving any disputes between the partners
- the circumstances in which the partnership will be dissolved.

It must be remembered that the rights of outsiders dealing with the partnership are, without notice, unaffected by any agreement between the partners. Outsiders' rights are determined by the provisions of the *Partnerships Act* and partnership law generally.

Partnership can be imposed by the principle of estoppel

It should also be noted that a partnership relationship can arise because of estoppel. If one of the parties represents to a third party, either by words or by conduct, that another person is a partner and that representation is relied on, the existence of a partnership cannot be denied, even if it can be clearly demonstrated that the two were not carrying on a business together. The principle of estoppel applies to partnership just as it does to agency.

CASE SUMMARY 11.14

Does Holding Someone Out as a Partner Create a Partnership? *Brown Economic Assessments Inc. v. Stevenson*[43]

Cara Brown provided consulting services to Mr. Stevenson and his law firm and submitted a bill for $23 242.59, which was never paid. Since bankruptcy overtook Stevenson in this action, Brown sued the other members of the law firm for what was owed. The other members of the law firm claimed that there was no partnership. The claim was that they were not partners with Stevenson or with each other, and therefore they were not liable for the claimed amount.

When Brown first met with Stevenson, he introduced himself as "senior litigator and partner" in the firm, presenting her with a business card with the name of the firm listed as "Stevenson, Gillis, Hjelte, Tangjerd, Barristers and Solicitors." She also received correspondence from time to time on a letterhead containing that name.

The Court found that although there was no actual partnership, because the defendant lawyers had allowed themselves to be held out as partners and that holding out had been relied on by the plaintiff, they were estopped from denying that they were partners and were liable to pay the amount owing.

SMALL BUSINESS PERSPECTIVE

This case shows how dangerous it is to hold yourself out as a partner or even to allow yourself to be held out as a partner because it is not likely that you will be allowed to deny that fact later.

---

43. [2004] S.J. No. 377 (C.A.).

The Partner as an Agent

Every partner is the agent of the other partners and so has the power to bind them in contract as long as the contract involves the business of the partnership.[44] To properly understand the law of partnership, this discussion must be read in conjunction with the material above on agency. Even where the authority of a partner has been limited and the partner exceeds the power given, that contract will be binding if the third party is unaware of the limitation and the contract relates to the partnership business.[45] Assume Akbari and Carlson operated a shoe store in partnership, and Akbari, while visiting his regular supplier in Toronto, purchased 500 pairs of yellow patent-leather oxfords he was unable to resist for $5000. That contract would be binding on Carlson, even if the partnership agreement specifically set out that neither partner could make any purchase over $1000 without the other's approval. However, if Akbari bought a new boat during his trip to Toronto, this purchase would not be binding on his partner because the purchase could not be said to be made pursuant to the partnership business of selling shoes.

Laws of agency apply to partnership

Vicarious Liability

All partners are also vicariously liable in tort for both careless and intentional conduct of their partners in all business-related activities, including personal injury. Thus, if Agostino and Paradis were partners selling firewood, and Agostino negligently dropped a load of wood on a passing pedestrian, both Agostino and Paradis would be liable to pay compensation for the injury. There are many cases showing vicarious liability for intentional wrongs, such as an Ontario case in which the partners of a lawyer, even though they were completely innocent, were required to make good the loss when that lawyer fraudulently acquired $60 000 from his client by forging a cheque.[46]

Partners liable for each other's acts

Partners liable for breach of trust

Partners can also be held responsible for the breach of trust of their partners, such as the misuse of their clients' money. In such situations, all the partners are responsible for compensating the victim's loss. Note, however, that under the *Partnerships Act* the other partners are liable only if they have notice of the breach of trust.[47]

Since a partnership can employ individuals, the principles set out in Chapter 10 on employment law apply. Partners are vicariously liable for the misdeeds of their employees committed in the course of their employment. They must also adhere to government regulations on workers' compensation, employment insurance, and income tax.

Partners liable for wrongful acts of employees

---

44. *Partnerships Act, supra* note 35, ss. 6, 7.

45. *Ibid.,* ss. 6, 9.

46. *Victoria & Grey Trust Company v. Crawford* (1986), 57 O.R. (2d) 484 (H.C.J.).

47. *Partnerships Act, supra* note 35, s. 14.

REDUCING RISK 11.4

For a businessperson, a serious risk associated with the law of partnership is the danger of becoming a partner inadvertently. This can come about by carrying on business together without realizing that a partnership has been created, or by allowing oneself to be held out as a partner by someone else. The danger is the liability imposed by such a partnership both in tort, on the basis of vicarious liability, and in contract, on the basis of each partner being an agent. This unlimited liability means a partner's entire fortune is at risk, and can lead to devastating results. Care should be taken to avoid the risk that an inadvertent partnership can create.

 mybuslawlab
www.pearsoned.ca/mybuslawlab

Partners share losses equally or proportionally by agreement

Third party can collect from any partner regardless of agreement

Unlimited Liability

Like that of a sole proprietor, a partner's liability is unlimited, and her personal fortune is at risk to satisfy the claims of an injured party. With partners, however, they are liable not only for their own wrongful acts and those of their employees but also for the conduct of their partners. If the assets of a partnership are not sufficient to satisfy the claims of the creditors, the partners must make up the difference out of their own personal assets. This is typically done in the same proportion that they share the profits. Thus, if a partnership agreement provides that a senior partner gets 40 percent of the profits and each of the three junior partners gets 20 percent of the profits, the senior partner will bear 40 percent of the loss and the junior partners will each bear 20 percent of the loss. But it is possible for the partners to agree to a different sharing of losses or profits if so stipulated in their agreement.[48]

Note that such a provision in the partnership agreement will affect only the relations between the partners. An outsider is not affected by any term in the partnership agreement that limits the liability of one of the partners and can collect all of what is owed from any partner. If one partner is particularly well off and the other partners have few personal assets, the injured party will look to the partner with significant assets for compensation once the assets of the partnership have been exhausted. That partner can seek contributions from the other partners on the basis of the partnership agreement if they have anything left to contribute.

In most provinces, partners are only **jointly liable** for the debts and obligations of the partnership, as opposed to jointly and **severally liable**.[49] This means that for someone to seek a remedy against all the partners, they all must be included in the original action, as there is only one cause of action. Thus, if only two of the three partners are sued and it later turns out that they do not have enough assets to satisfy the judgment, it is then too late to sue the third. It must be emphasized, however, that when liability arises because of wrongful conduct (tort) or because of breach of trust, this liability is both joint and several.[50] This means that it is possible for the injured party to sue one partner and still maintain the right to sue the other partners if the claim is not satisfied. In any case, when an action is brought against the partnership in the partnership name, the plaintiff will be able to enforce the judgment against any of the partners. The result of this vicarious liability is that all the partners are personally responsible for the injuries incurred to

---

[48]. *Partnerships Act, supra* note 35, s. 24.

[49]. *Ibid.*, s. 10.

[50]. *Ibid.*, ss. 12, 13.

the extent of their entire personal fortunes. The liability of partners for each other's conduct is one area where there are some provincial differences. Refer to the MyBusLawLab for further information.

All personal assets at risk

A retiring partner remains liable for any wrongs committed or liability incurred during the partnership period. This liability also continues for acts committed after the dissolution of the partnership or the retirement of the partner, unless the third party has been given notice that the retiring party has left the firm. The remaining partners or a new partner coming in can agree to take over these obligations in the partnership agreement, but the new partner is not automatically liable for them.[51] This is why such care is taken to notify colleagues and customers when the membership of a partnership changes.

Retiring partner remains responsible

CASE SUMMARY 11.15

Was the Loss Incurred in the Normal Course of Business? *McDonic v. Hetherington (Litigation Guardian of)*[52]

In 1985, two elderly sisters, Ms. McDonic and Ms. Cooper, on the advice of Cooper's son-in-law, retained Mr. Watt, a solicitor, to advise them on investments. Watt invested a considerable sum of money for them but failed to properly secure those investments. The result was that McDonic lost more than $230 000 and Cooper lost more than $10 000. Watt was successfully sued on the basis that he failed in his fiduciary duty to these clients. The problem here was for the Court to determine whether his partners were also liable for these losses on the basis of vicarious liability. The partners denied liability, claiming that this was misconduct on the part of Watt outside the scope of the business, as Watt was acting as an investment adviser, not a lawyer, in these transactions. The lower Court agreed. However, the Ontario Court of Appeal decided that the partners were liable for the losses caused by their partner because Watt did what he did as a partner in the normal course of that partnership's business. The money went into a partnership trust account. It was dealt with like all other accounts, and the other partners actually dealt with those funds as well. In addition, he was liable as an agent acting within the apparent authority given by the other partners.

It is true that the transactions were not expressly authorized by the partners, but it is clear that he was acting within his apparent authority and, as such, made the other partners liable for his conduct. His office was part of the firm's offices, he used the firm's letterhead, and in making the investments for the sisters he used the facilities of the law office as well as the firm's accounts in the normal course of the firm's business.

SMALL BUSINESS PERSPECTIVE

This case emphasizes the need to be vigilant in knowing what dealings partners are engaging in. Evidently a great deal of trust is required between partners as well as a thorough understanding of partnership law.

---

51. *Ibid.,* s. 18.
52. [1997] O.J. No. 51 (C.A.); leave to appeal dismissed, [1997] S.C.C.A. No. 119.

www.pearsoned.ca/mybuslawlab

Registration

Registration usually required

Most provinces require that a partnership be registered. Some provinces, such as British Columbia[53] and New Brunswick,[54] require registration only when the partnerships involve trading, manufacturing, and mining. Alberta also requires registration of partnerships involving contracting.[55] Ontario prohibits partners from carrying on business or identifying themselves to the public unless the firm name has been registered.[56] Registration may also be required when the partners are in limited partnerships or limited liability partnerships, as discussed below. See the MyBusLawLab for individual provincial requirements.

REDUCING RISK 11.5

All partners are liable to the extent of their personal fortune for the wrongful acts and mistakes of their partners. Case Summary 11.15 deals with the misuse of trust money in a law firm, but this is just one of the many examples that could be used where one partner's liability for the acts of another is present. We must use great care in choosing our partners and even then we face great risk of loss. This is one reason that incorporation has become much more popular as a method of doing business.

Failure to register properly can result in the imposition of a fine[57] but typically will prevent the unregistered partnership from maintaining an action[58] and cause joint liability to become joint and several liability.[59] Note that an unregistered partnership can still be sued, and so there are pressing reasons to register and no advantage in not doing so.

Rights and Obligations of the Parties

FIDUCIARY DUTY

Fiduciary duty exists between partners

Partners must account for any profits or use of property

Each partner has a fiduciary duty to act in the best interests of the other partners. This duty imposes an obligation to account for any profits that have been made or for any partnership funds or property used. A partner who uses partnership property for personal benefit without the consent of the other partners must pay over any profit made and reimburse the partnership for any deterioration of the property. Property brought into a partnership for the purposes of the business becomes the property of the partnership, even though the title documents might not reflect this ownership. The partner with title is said to hold the property in trust for the partnership. This was the situation in *Olson v. Gullo*, discussed in Case Summary 11.10, and why Olson had the right to one-half of the profits from the

---

53. *Partnership Act*, R.S.B.C. 1996, c. 348, s. 81.

54. *Partnerships and Business Names Registration Act*, R.S.N.B. 1973, c. P-5, s. 3.

55. *Partnership Act*, R.S.A. 2000, c. P-3, s. 106.

56. *Business Names Act*, S.O. 1990, c. B.17, s. 2.

57. In Alberta, for example, a fine not exceeding $500 can be imposed on each partner who fails to register. See *Partnership Act*, *supra* note 55, s. 112.

58. *Ibid.*, s. 113.

59. *Ibid.*, s. 115.

sale of the property that Gullo had secretly purchased. It also underlines why the Appeal Court found it necessary to reverse the lower Court's decision to award all the profits to Olson. This was inconsistent with the true nature of the partnership where they shared the ownership of the property and thus the rights to the profits.

If a partner operates a similar business without consent, he will be required to pay over any profits made to the partnership, which will then be distributed normally to all the partners. That partner, however, will not be reimbursed for losses. If a partner in a restaurant in Vancouver were to open another in Victoria without consent, any profits made from the Victoria operation would have to be paid over to the partnership and then be distributed equally among them. However, any losses sustained would be borne by that partner alone.

Partners cannot compete with partnership

Any information obtained through a person's position as partner must be used to the benefit of the partnership, not for personal use. If Grubisich came across a deal for some mining claims because of his position as a partner in a mining partnership, he would be required to inform his partners about the opportunity. If he bought the claims for himself without his partner's consent, he would have to turn over any profits earned to the partnership but suffer any losses himself. In effect, the information he used was the property of the partnership.

Information must be disclosed

CASE SUMMARY 11.16

Partner Must Account for Income from Other Sources: *McKnight v. Hutchison*[60]

McKnight and the defendant, Hutchison, were partners in a law firm. The partnership agreement stipulated that partners were allowed to conduct business other than the practice of law, provided that notice was given to the other partners and that the business did not compromise the law practice. Hutchison became a director of a corporation that was a client of the partnership and accepted an honorarium as well as company shares that subsequently returned substantial dividends. McKnight contends that Hutchison breached a fiduciary duty to disclose the activities giving rise to these and other subsequently revealed privately retained earnings.

Hutchison advised his partners of his directorship, but he did not disclose that he was retaining the honorarium and dividends privately. The parties had entered a partnership agreement that expressly incorporated provisions of the *Partnership Act*, thus sections 22–33 of the *Act* were binding on the parties:

> 22(1) A partner must act with the utmost fairness and good faith towards the other members of the firm in the business of the firm.

> 31 Partners are bound to render true accounts and full information of all things affecting the partnership to any partner or his or her legal representatives.

> 32(1) A partner must account to the firm for any benefit derived by the partner without the consent of the other partners from any transaction concerning the partnership, or from any use by the partner of the partnership property, name or business connection.

---

60. [2002] B.C.J. No. 2211 (S.C.).

33 If a partner, without the consent of the other partners, carries on any business of the same nature as and competing with that of the firm, the partner must account for and pay over to the firm all profits made by him or her in that business.

The Court held that Hutchison owed his partner duties of disclosure, loyalty, utmost good faith, and avoidance of conflict and self-interest. While Hutchison's acceptance of the directorship and his activities of directorship did not place him in a position of conflict with his partner, his entitlement to the shares and stock options, however, should have been disclosed. Hutchison's silence and his failure to account for the payments received was in breach of his duties. The Court determined that Hutchison's partner was thus entitled to an accounting of these benefits.

SMALL BUSINESS PERSPECTIVE

Again, we see just how important fiduciary duty is. It is present when there is a relationship where one party places trust in another and is vulnerable if that trust is not honoured.

PROVISIONS OF THE *PARTNERSHIPS ACT*

See the MyBusLawLab for provincial variations

The rights and obligations of partners to each other are set out in the *Partnerships Act,* and these provisions apply except where modified by the partnership agreement.[61] Some of the provisions of the *Act* are as follows:[62]

Profits and losses shared equally or modified by agreement

1.   The partners will share profits equally between them. Similarly, any losses incurred are shared equally between the partners. This provision is often modified by a partnership agreement, but outside third parties will not be affected by any agreement, as they can recover losses from any partner who has assets. That partner may then look to the other partners for reimbursement.

Partners' expenses reimbursed

2.   The partners are entitled to reimbursement for any expenses they incur in the process of the partnership business. They are also entitled to be reimbursed for any money other than capital they have advanced to the partnership, before the other partners can claim a share of the profits. In addition, the partner advancing such funds is entitled to the payment of interest on that money.

Partners participate in management

3.   All partners have the right to take part in management. This provision is often modified by partnership agreements, which create different classes of partners, particularly in firms with a large number of partners.

No salaries paid to partners

4.   A partner is not an employee and is not entitled to wages or other remuneration for work done, only to a share of the profits. To provide partners with a steady stream of cash flow, the firm may pay partners a monthly draw against the yet-to-be-calculated profits of the partnership.

Unanimous agreement needed for major changes

5.   No major changes can be made to the partnership business without the unanimous agreement of all the partners. No new partner can be brought

---

61. *Partnerships Act, supra* note 35, s. 20.

62. *Ibid.,* s. 24.

into the partnership, nor can a partner be excluded from the firm without the unanimous consent of all the partners.[63] However, for the ordinary matters of the firm a simple majority vote is sufficient, unless the partnership agreement states otherwise.

6.   Partners do not have the right to assign their partnership status to some other party without the consent of the other partners. The benefits can be assigned, but the assignee will not be a partner and will not have the right to interfere in the management or administration of the partnership business.[64]

Assignment requires consent of other partners

7.   The business records of the partnership must be kept at the partnership office, and all the partners have the right to inspect them.

Partners must have access to records

As can be seen from this summary, the general principle governing a partnership relationship is that the partners function as a unit and have a considerable responsibility to look after each other's interests.

Advantages of Partnership

Although the problems associated with a partnership may appear overwhelming, many of these difficulties can be overcome by proper insurance coverage. It should also be noted that a disadvantage to one person may be an advantage to another. For example, the unanimous consent required for important changes in a partnership may appear to interfere with effective management, but it does provide considerable protection to the individual partner. Such an individual partner cannot be outvoted by the majority, as is the case with a minority shareholder in a corporation. Similarly, the right of the individual partner to inspect all records of the business confers advantages not shared by minority shareholders in corporations to the same extent.

Insurance coverage important

Unanimous consent protection

It may be less expensive to set up a partnership than a corporation and less costly to operate a partnership because there are few formal requirements once the business has been established. For example, a corporation must keep certain types of accounting records and file annual reports with the appropriate government agency. A partnership, on the other hand, has only the needs of the partners to satisfy in this regard. But, as with sole proprietorships and corporations, there are other government regulatory bodies that require records, such as the Canada Revenue Agency, the Workers' Compensation Board, and the Employment Insurance Commission.

Partnership less costly to form and operate

 REDUCING RISK 11.6

Businesspeople should not be too quick to discard partnership as a valuable method of carrying on business with others. From the individual's point of view, all partners have an equal say, and in all important matters there must be unanimity. This eliminates the "tyranny of the majority" problem usually associated with corporations. The disadvantages, such as unlimited liability, can be overcome, to a large extent, by obtaining appropriate insurance. Before a decision is made to incorporate, consideration should therefore be given to the pros and cons of using a partnership to carry on the business instead.

---

63.   *Ibid.*, ss. 24, 25.

64.   *Ibid.*, s. 31.

It should not automatically be assumed that, because of the unlimited liability and unwieldy management structure of partnerships, incorporation is a better way of carrying on business. For a small business operating in a "low-risk" industry, for example, it may be advantageous to start up and then carry on business as a partnership until the business becomes profitable. This would enable the partners to personally take advantage of the business losses for tax purposes.

Dissolution of a Partnership

Dissolution by notice

Usually, a partnership is easy to dissolve, requiring only notice to that effect by one of the partners.[65] Such notice can be implied, as in the case where a partnership was terminated when Mr. Singh, one of two partners driving a shared taxi cab, stopped driving.[66] While it is an advantage to the leaving partner to be able to dissolve the partnership simply by giving notice to the other partners, it can be a considerable disadvantage to the others, requiring the sale of the partnership assets and distribution of the proceeds to the partners. Usually, this is overcome by providing in the partnership agreement a mechanism whereby one partner can leave without causing the remainder of the partnership to dissolve.

Dissolution by death, bankruptcy, or insolvency

Subject to the partnership agreement, a partnership is dissolved by the death or insolvency of any partner.[67] This provision varies slightly from province to province.[68] Dissolution can give rise to significant problems in ongoing, long-term partnerships of professional groups. Therefore, professionals will typically set out in partnership agreements that the death or insolvency of one partner will not dissolve the partnership and that, instead, the partner's share will be made available to the heir or creditor of the partner. Insurance coverage is often taken out to cover such a contingency.

British Columbia's partnership legislation is unique because it establishes that, when more than two partners are involved, the partnership will be dissolved only in relation to the partner who has died or become bankrupt. This provision can be modified by agreement, but its unique feature is that the death or bankruptcy of one partner will not bring to an end the whole partnership relationship in the absence of an agreement among the partners.[69]

Partnership established for specified time will end at expiry

A partnership that has been entered into for a fixed term is dissolved by the expiration of that term.[70] Similarly, a partnership that is entered into for a single venture or undertaking is dissolved by the termination of that venture or undertaking.[71] A partnership is automatically dissolved if the business engaged in by the partnership becomes illegal.[72] In addition, a partner can apply to the court to dissolve the partnership if any of the following factors are present:[73]

Partnership can be dissolved by request to the court

---

[65] *Ibid.,* s. 32.

[66] *Singh v. Taggarh,* [2000] M.J. No. 237 (Q.B.).

[67] *Partnerships Act, supra* note 35, s. 33.

[68] In Alberta, for example, a partnership is dissolved by the death or bankruptcy of a partner, or by an assignment of a partner's property in trust for the benefit of his creditors. See s. 37 of the *Partnership Act, supra* note 51.

[69] *Partnership Act, supra* note 53, s. 36(1)(b).

[70] *Partnerships Act, supra* note 35, s. 32(a).

[71] *Ibid.,* s. 32(b).

[72] *Ibid.,* s. 34.

[73] *Ibid.,* s. 35.

1. One of the partners has become mentally incompetent, or otherwise incapable of performing partnership responsibilities.

2. The conduct of one partner is prejudicial to the partnership relationship, or the partner is otherwise in breach of the partnership agreement.

3. It is clear that the partnership business can be carried on only at a loss.

4. It is just and equitable that the partnership be dissolved.

The effect of dissolution is to end the partnership relationship, oblige the partners to wind up the business, liquidate the assets to pay off any obligations to creditors, and then distribute any remaining assets and funds to the former partners. Individual partners should take care to give public notice of dissolution.[74] The law may require that such notice be filed with the partnership registration office or registrar of corporations, depending on the jurisdiction. For further protection, such notice should be sent to all regular customers of the business. Failure to do so may render each partner liable for the acts of the other partners even after dissolution. Note that although dissolution takes place, the partners still have the authority to act as partners and bind the firm by their actions in doing whatever is necessary to wind up the affairs of the partnership.[75]

Public notice may prevent liability

Distribution of Assets and Liabilities

Subject to the partnership agreement, when dissolving a partnership the debts must be paid first out of profits and, if they are insufficient, out of the capital the partners originally invested. If there is still not enough money to pay the debts, the creditors can then turn to the partners themselves, who are liable in the proportion in which they were entitled to share profits. On the other hand, once all creditors have been paid and the other obligations of the partnership satisfied, any assets still remaining are applied first to pay back the partners for advances and then to pay back the original capital investment. Any remaining funds are divided among the partners on the established basis for sharing profits.[76]

Debts paid out of profits first, then capital, then personal assets of partners

The dissolution of the partnership and the distribution of assets may be a problem, especially when some of the partners want to continue the business in a new partnership. To avoid this problem, the partners often agree in the partnership agreement to a different process than that described above. It should be noted that if one partner owes a debt to an outside creditor that has nothing to do with the partnership business, that creditor can claim against only the assets of that partner, including his or her share of the partnership assets left after all other claims against the partnership are settled.

mybuslawlab
www.pearsoned.ca/mybuslawlab

BC AB SK MB ON

Limited Partnerships

Additions to the legislation governing partnership in every province provide for the creation of limited partnerships.[77] This measure gives some of the advantages

74. *Ibid.*, s. 37.

75. *Ibid.*, s. 38.

76. See *Partnerships Act, supra* note 35, s. 44, for the rules governing the distribution of assets on final settlement of accounts.

77. These additions vary from province to province. In Ontario, see the *Limited Partnerships Act*, R.S.O. 1990, c. L.16. In Alberta, see the *Partnership Act, supra* note 55, ss. 49–80. The discussion in the text refers to the Ontario legislation.

Limited partners liable only to the extent of their investment

of incorporation to partnerships. But partners can lose their status as limited partners if they fail to carefully adhere to all the requirements of the governing legislation, with the result that they are then deemed to be general partners with all the consequences inherent in that designation. The main advantage of a limited partnership is that it allows the partners so designated to invest money in a partnership but to avoid the unlimited liability that goes with being a general partner. The only loss a limited partner can incur is the original investment.[78]

If Gingras and Gitter were general partners with Leopold, a limited partner, and Gingras were to negligently injure a customer to the extent of $300 000 damages, Leopold would lose only his investment in the firm. Both Gingras and Gitter would be liable for the entire $300 000, but Leopold's liability would be limited to the amount he invested, even if the combined assets of Gingras and Gitter were not enough to cover the loss.

Unfortunately, it is relatively easy for the limited partner to lose that special status, thus becoming a general partner with unlimited liability. In the preceding example, if Leopold had allowed himself to be represented as a partner in the business, taken part in the control of the business, allowed his surname to be used in the name of the business, or contributed services to the partnership, he would have become a general partner and would have been required to pay along with Gingras and Gitter, with no limitation on his liability.

Registration required to become a limited partner

To form a limited partnership, it is necessary to file a declaration at the appropriate government registry. This declaration will set out information such as the term of the agreement, the amount of cash and other property contributed, and the way profits are to be shared.[79] The name used by the limited partnership can contain the name of the general partners, but the surname of a limited partner cannot be included in the firm name unless it is also the surname of one of the general partners. It is not possible to form a partnership with only limited partners; there must be at least one general partner in the firm.

! REDUCING RISK 11.7

Limited partnerships may be attractive to people because of favourable tax implications. To obtain these tax benefits, limited liability may have to be sacrificed to a considerable extent through modifications set out in the partnership agreement. Often, these changes are not brought to the attention of prospective investors. Great care should be taken before entering into investment vehicles structured as limited partnerships, to ensure that one understands exactly what one is getting into.

Limited partners cannot take part in control of the business

A limited partner can contribute money and other property to the business, but not services. A limited partner cannot take part in the control of the business, without becoming a general partner. The limited partner is not prohibited from giving the other partners advice as to the management of the business, but since it is often difficult to determine where advice stops and control of the business starts, there is a considerable risk in doing so. When a business starts to fail, there

78. *Limited Partnerships Act, Ibid.*, s. 9.

79. In Ontario, the specifics of what is to be included in the declaration are prescribed by the *Limited Partnerships Act* General Regulation, R.R.O. 1990, Reg. 713.

is a great temptation for the limited partner to jump in to preserve the investment, but doing so raises the risk of becoming a general partner and should be avoided.

Limited Liability Partnerships

Historically, professionals have not been allowed to incorporate their businesses and have therefore carried on business using partnerships. This has caused increased concern as the size of professional partnerships has grown and the number and size of liability claims against professionals have increased significantly. Ontario addressed this issue in 1998, by introducing the limited liability partnership (LLP).[80] At the time of writing, all provinces except Newfoundland and Labrador and Prince Edward Island have enacted provisions for limited liability partnerships.

An LLP is formed when two or more persons enter into a written agreement that designates the partnership as an LLP and states that the agreement is governed by the *Partnerships Act*.[81] Only professionals belonging to professional organizations permitted to do so in legislation and requiring their members to carry a minimum amount of professional liability insurance coverage[82] can practise their profession through LLPs. They must include "LLP" or "L.L.P." or "Limited Liability Partnership" (or the French equivalent) in their name[83] and be registered as a limited liability partnership.[84] Initially, lawyers and accountants took steps to form LLPs in most jurisdictions. It is likely that other professions will follow suit. Eligible professions include accountants, chiropractors, dentists, lawyers, optometrists, and physicians.

The main advantage to professionals carrying on business in an LLP is that potential liability is limited. A limited liability partner is not liable for the liability of the partnership arising from the negligent acts or omissions of another partner, or an employee, agent, or representative of the partnership.[85] This does not apply to liability caused by the partner's own negligence, or the negligence of a person under the partner's direct supervision or control.[86] The result of these provisions appears to be that the partnership's assets are at risk with respect to liability caused by negligent acts or omissions of partners, employees, agents, or representatives of the LLP, but the victim of the negligence may not pursue the individual assets of non-negligent partners.

These provisions apply, however, only to negligence. They do not apply to actions for other torts, breaches of contract, or breaches of trust. While one partner may not be liable for another partner's negligence, the innocent partner will not be protected from losing her share in the partnership's assets, and all partners, including "innocent partners," will be liable for the ordinary debts of the

mybuslawlab
www.pearsoned.ca/mybuslawlab

BC   AB   SK   MB   ON

Limited liability partners
must be professionals
authorized by statute,
maintain minimum insurance
coverage, be registered with
LLP in name

LLP has unlimited liability
only for own negligent acts
and for those they supervise

---

80. The general provisions regarding LLPs are found in the *Partnerships Act, supra* note 35, ss. 44.1–44.4.

81. *Partnerships Act, supra* note 35, s. 44.1. LLP legislation varies from province to province. The discussion in the text is based primarily on the Ontario legislation.

82. *Ibid.*, s. 44.2.

83. *Ibid.*, s. 44.3(3).

84. *Ibid.*, s. 44.3(1).

85. *Ibid.*, s. 10 (2).

86. *Ibid.*, s. 10(3).

partnership. Of course, insurance coverage will be available to satisfy any claims against the negligent partners, who will also be personally responsible for any shortfall.

Note that there are some differences between jurisdictions. (See the MyBusLawLab for specifics.) While in Ontario a partner will be liable for the negligent acts or omissions of someone he supervises, in Alberta that personal liability will only be imposed where the partner failed to provide adequate supervision.[87] The Saskatchewan legislation states that limited liability partners are liable for any partnership obligation for which they would be liable if the partnership were a corporation of which they were directors.[88]

Keep in mind the distinction between a limited partnership and the more recent limited liability partnership. A limited partner is in effect an investor who does not participate in the partnership business. His liability is limited to losing what he has invested, whereas a limited liability partner is an active professional who practises his profession with other partners and who is liable for his own negligent acts and for those committed by others under his supervision.

Refer to Table 11.2 for a comparative summary of the different types of business organizations.

Table 11.2 Comparison of Different Types of Business Organizations

Type of Business Organization	Created by Registration?	Number of Participants?	Separate Legal Entity?	Unlimited Personal Liability?	Vicarious Liability?
Sole proprietorship	No, but registration of business name is usually required	1	No	Yes	Yes, for employees
Partnership	No; can even be created inadvertently	2 or more	No	Yes	Yes, for employees and partners
Limited partnership	Yes	2 or more; must be at least one general partner	No	Only general partner	General partners for employees and other general partners
Limited liability partnership	Yes	2 or more members of eligible profession	No	No, except for own negligence	No except for those supervised

---

[87]. *Ibid.*, s. 12(2).

[88]. *Partnership Act*, R.S.S. 1978, c. P-3, ss. 80, 81.

SUMMARY

Agency

- Exists with consent from the principal
- Agents act for a principal in dealings with third parties
- Authority
  - Actual authority is defined in the contract
  - Apparent authority arises from the position of the agent or from the conduct of the principal
    - When the principal has done something to lead the third party to believe that the agent has authority, even when such authority has been specifically withheld
  - Even when the agent has exceeded both the actual and apparent authority, the principal may ratify the agreement
  - When the agent acts beyond all authority he or she can be sued (breach of warranty of authority)
- Agent's duties
  - Involve performing terms of contract, providing an accounting of funds, and fiduciary duty
  - Cannot be delegated
- Principal's duties
  - To honour terms of contract and reimburse agent's expenses
- Undisclosed principal
  - Third party's recourse is against agent if existence of principal is not disclosed
  - Third party has a choice to sue the agent or the undisclosed principal to enforce the contract, once existence of the principal is revealed
  - Undisclosed principal cannot ratify contracts
- Vicarious liability
  - In the absence of an employment relationship, the principal may escape vicarious liability for the acts of the agent, except when fraud is involved
  - Principal may be vicariously liable if misconduct of agent applies to acts within agent's actual or apparent authority
- Fiduciary relationship
  - Exists between the agent and the principal
  - Agent has obligation to act in the best interests of the principal
  - Full disclosure by the agent is required
- Termination
  - The agency relationship is typically terminated by simple notification or as agreed in the agency contract
  - Bankruptcy, death, or insanity of the principal or, when the principal is a corporation, the dissolution of that corporation, will also terminate the agent's authority

Sole proprietors

- An individual, carrying on business independently, without co-owners
- Must nonetheless deal with some government regulation
- Have unlimited liability for their debts and obligations

Partnership

- Involves two or more partners carrying on business together with a view to profits
- Controlled by partnership legislation and by specific agreement of the partners
- Can be created by agreement but often comes into existence by inadvertence when people work together in concert in a business activity
- Partners' duties
  - Each partner is an agent for the partnership, and all partners are liable for the contracts and torts of the other partners and employees. That liability is unlimited, and all the assets of the partners, including personal assets, are at risk to satisfy such debts and obligations
  - Fiduciary duty—partners must act in the best interests of the partnership
  - Unanimous agreement required to effect major changes, offering partners control over firm's direction
- Dissolution
  - Unless the partners have agreed otherwise in their partnership agreement, dissolution occurs:
    - Upon notice to that effect from a partner
    - Upon death or bankruptcy of one of the partners
- Limited and limited liability partnerships
  - Limited partnerships involve general and limited partners
  - Limited partners are liable only to the extent of the investment made in the business, but must be careful to protect that limited liability status
  - Limited liability partnerships now available for professionals who cannot incorporate their businesses
  - Qualifying professions include accountants, lawyers, doctors, dentists and others as identified by legislation

QUESTIONS

1. What is the agent's function? Why is it important to understand the law of agency in business?

2. Explain what effect an agent's limited capacity will have on the contractual obligations created between a principal and a third party. What effect would the incapacity of the principal have on this relationship?

3. Distinguish between an agent's actual, implied, and apparent authority. Explain why this distinction can be important from the agent's point of view.

4. Explain the role estoppel plays in agency law.

5. Explain what is meant by "ratification" and describe the limitations on a principal's right to ratify the actions of his or her agent. How can the principle of ratification be as dangerous to the principal as it is to the third party?

6. What effect does it have on the relationship between the principal and the third party when an agent writes on an agreement "subject to ratification"?

7. Agents owe a fiduciary duty to their principals. What are the requirements of that duty?

8. What options are open to a third party who has been dealing with an undisclosed principal if the contract is breached? Does an undisclosed principal have the right to ratify an agent's unauthorized act?

9. Explain how the doctrine of vicarious liability applies in a principal–agent relationship.

10. Distinguish among a sole proprietorship, a partnership, and a corporation.

11. What advantages and disadvantages are associated with carrying on business as a sole proprietorship? As a partnership?

12. Distinguish between sharing profits and sharing revenues.

13. If two people enter into a business together with the object of making money but lose it instead, can the business still be a partnership?

14. Why must a person understand the law of agency to understand the law of partnership?

15. What danger exists when a third party is led to believe that two people are partners when, in fact, they are not? What legal principle is applied in this situation?

16. What is the significance of the existence of a partnership agreement for outsiders dealing with the partnership? What is the advantage of entering into a formal agreement?

17. Explain the different ways in which a person can become responsible for the acts of his or her partner and describe the limitations on this responsibility. Describe the liability of retiring and new partners.

18. Partners have fiduciary obligations to each other. Explain what this means and give examples.

19. What events may bring about the end of a partnership prematurely? Under what circumstances might it be necessary to get a court order to end a partnership?

20. What will the normal effect be on a partnership when a partner dies or becomes insolvent? How is the law of British Columbia significantly different?

21. When a partnership is being dissolved and does not have sufficient assets to pay its debts, how is the responsibility for these debts distributed? How are excess assets distributed?

22. What must a person do to qualify as a limited partner? What happens when a limited partner fails to meet one of these qualifications?

23. What is the main advantage of limited liability partnerships? In light of this, what does the law require to protect those who suffer losses through the actions of a partner or an employee of a limited liability partnership?

CASES AND DISCUSSION QUESTIONS

1. *N.A.I.T. Academic Staff Association v. N.A.I.T.* [2002] A.J. No. 1013 (Q.B.).

The Northern Alberta Institute of Technology arranged a group insurance policy with an insurer for its employees. Because of a change in policy (demutualization) the insurer reimbursed over $1 million back to the insured. N.A.I.T. took this money as its own, but the employees claimed that they were entitled to the funds.

Explain who was entitled to these funds and why. In your answer consider the arguments supporting the positions taken by both sides. Is it appropriate to find an agency relationship in such a formal arrangement unless clearly stated?

2. *Saima Avandero S.p.A. v. Coppley Noyes & Randall Ltd.*, [2000] O.J. No. 2841 (Ont. Sup. Ct.).

Saima was in the freighting business and shipped goods to Jomar Traffic Services (a freight forwarder) for further shipment to the defendant, Coppley. Coppley paid Jomar; then Jomar went out of business without paying Saima. Saima therefore sued Coppley for payment. Coppley was not even aware that Saima or anyone else was involved in the transaction.

Explain the arguments on both sides and who would likely win this action. Should an agency ever be imposed on a principal without their intention or approval?

3. *Canadian Pacific Forest Products Ltd. v. Termar Navigation Co.*, [1998] 2 F.C. 328 (F.C.T.D.), aff'd [2000] F.C.J. 450 (F.C.A.).

The ship carrying the defendant's lumber was struck by a large wave, causing the load to shift. The ship thus had to stop in Portugal to have the lumber discharged and re-stowed before it could be delivered at its destination in England. The shipper claimed that the costs of discharging and restowing the lumber were incurred on behalf of, and were thus payable by, Canadian Pacific Forest Products Ltd.

After examining the arguments on both sides, indicate who you think should have to pay and why. Should agency ever be imposed today where obtaining authority to act is simply a phone call away?

4. *Lampert Plumbing (Danforth) Ltd. v. Agathos*, [1972] 3 O.R. 11 (Co. Ct.).

Magoulas, the sole owner of Alpha Omega Construction Company, signed a contract for advertising with Agathos, the owner of a Toronto radio station. Magoulas was unable to pay, but Agathos continued to give him advertising in hopes that the business would get going to the point that he would be able to pay. Agathos also helped Magoulas out in his business, signed many contracts, and performed other acts on behalf of Magoulas, including writing cheques on his personal account.

In January 1971, Kreizman, president of the plaintiff corporation, entered into a contract to supply the Alpha Omega Construction Company with certain plumbing and heating equipment. This contract was entered into at the construction company's premises yet the person Kreizman dealt with was Agathos. Kreizman thought he was dealing with the owner of the business, and Agathos did nothing to dissuade him of this notion. In all the many subsequent dealings between these two parties, Kreizman continued to think that Agathos was the principal of the construction company. It is clear that there was no partnership agreement or arrangement between Agathos and

Magoulas; Agathos was helping Magoulas out gratuitously, hoping for eventual payment under the advertising contract.

Magoulas only partially paid for the supply and installation of the plumbing equipment. Lampert Plumbing sued Agathos as a partner for the unpaid funds. Explain the arguments available to both sides and the likely outcome.

5. *3464920 Canada Inc. v. Strother,* [2005] B.C.J. No. 1655 (C.A.).

A lawyer advised his client (Monarch) that they could no longer participate in a certain business because of changes to the tax laws. He then secretly took advantage of an exception provision in those tax laws to start up his own business doing the same thing. He failed to advise his client of that exception and kept his own participation in the business a secret while continuing to act as their lawyer. When the client found out, he sued both the lawyer and his partners in the law firm.

Explain the nature of the complaint and the appropriate remedy in these circumstances. Should the innocent partners also be liable for the loss?

6. *Kent v. Oliver,* [2000] B.C.J. No. 1558 (S.C.).

Waldock, a solicitor, had acted for the plaintiff in a personal injury claim that resulted in a mistrial. A dispute arose between the plaintiff and Waldock with respect to Waldock's claim for a share of the settlement. In the action that followed, the plaintiff was successful and was awarded costs against Waldock. Waldock declared bankruptcy before the plaintiff could recover on this award. During this time Waldock had shared office space in a legal partnership consisting of Oliver, Chester, and Donaldson. There was no partnership between Waldock and this firm; they kept separate funds and separate accounts, and Waldock's name was not used in conjunction with the partnership name. The plaintiff sued the firm for the costs owed by Waldock.

Indicate the arguments on both sides and the likelihood of success. How far should the principles of apparent authority and estoppel be applied to partnerships?

7. *Rochwerg v. Truster* [2002] O.J. No. 1230 (C.A.)

The parties were chartered accountants who practised together in a partnership. There was no written partnership agreement. One of the partners, Rochwerg, became a director of a corporation that was a client of the partnership. Rochwerg advised his partners of his directorship, but he did not disclose information regarding the shares and stock options to which he had become entitled.

Indicate whether Rochwerg's partners have a cause of action against him. What remedies might be available to Rochwerg's partners?

Chapter 12

Corporations

CHAPTER OBJECTIVES

1. Describe the process of incorporation
2. Understand the separate legal entity principle
3. Explain the funding of a corporation
4. Describe the duties of corporate officers
5. Outline the advantages and disadvantages of incorporation
6. Explain the termination of a corporation

Much of the previous chapter dealt with the simpler methods of carrying on business, sole proprietorship, and partnership. This chapter will examine the third method, the incorporated company. Since incorporation is, by far, the most common means of setting up a large business organization, exposure to the concepts and forms that regulate this important aspect of the commercial world is a vital part of the study of business law. In this chapter we will examine the process and effect of incorporation, some features of incorporated bodies, and the rights and responsibilities of the various parties involved.

mybuslawlab
www.pearsoned.ca/mybuslawlab

    ON

Corporation is a separate legal entity

THE PROCESS OF INCORPORATION

The concept of an incorporated company was developed in response to the need to finance large economic projects without the limitations associated with sole proprietorships and partnerships. What was needed was to have a large number of people participate financially in a venture without playing active roles in it. The incorporated company was the means to accomplish this end. The most significant feature of an incorporated company is that it has a separate legal personality from the people who own shares in it. The shares that represent an individual's interest in the incorporated company can be bought and sold; thus, the shareholders can be continually changing, while the company itself remains intact. This structure provides considerably more flexibility in meeting the needs of owners and directors, and is a much more effective method of attracting capital.

An early example of incorporation was the monarch's grant of a royal charter to a town or university, thereby creating a separate legal personality. It was a natural step to extend that practice to commercial ventures. The Hudson's Bay Company was one of the earliest English commercial companies created by royal charter. Parliament also got involved by creating "special-act companies" when ventures were considered important enough to be incorporated by their own special legislation.

At this stage, ordinary citizens could not incorporate. They created their own unofficial companies through contracts called **deeds of settlement**. Parliament eventually permitted incorporation for private business activities, but in the process it also had to accommodate the numerous voluntary contractual associations that were already in existence. The resulting legislation gave these companies formal status and the advantages of incorporation by allowing them to register at the appropriate government office and pay a fee.

Canada adopted many of the features of the British approach to incorporation. Both the federal and provincial governments have created many companies through their power to pass special statutes. For example, the Canadian Broadcasting Corporation (CBC) and the Canadian Pacific Railroad (CPR) were created by special acts of Parliament. Some Canadian jurisdictions adopted the British practice of incorporation through **registration**. Other jurisdictions developed their incorporation process from the royal charter approach and created incorporated bodies through the granting of **letters patent**. A third approach, which was borrowed from the United States, is based on the filing of **articles of incorporation**. Although there are technical differences between these three methods of incorporation, it is important to understand that the practical effect of each system is the same. Each method is described in more detail below. Refer to the MyBusLawLab for specific provincial variations.

In Canada, it is possible to incorporate a corporation at the federal level or in each province. The choice should be made on the basis of what the corporation will be doing and where it will be done. If the activity is to be confined to a local area, it is likely that incorporation under the provincial legislation would be appropriate. A business created to operate a restaurant would therefore be provincially incorporated. When the activity involves something that will be carried on in several provinces, such as a chain of restaurants, or generally across Canada, as with some service provided on the internet, the federal option might be preferable. Cost will be a major consideration. It is possible, even after choosing to incorporate provincially, to carry on business in other provinces as well, but the corporation will have to be registered in all of the provinces in which it does business, with corresponding fees paid in each jurisdiction. If a corporation has been federally incorporated, it can carry on business in any part of the country, although it must go through the formality of registering extra-provincially in each province. Another factor might be the nature of the particular statute involved. For example, Quebec investors might choose to incorporate under the *Canada Business Corporations Act,* which has more favourable shareholder protection and remedies than does the Quebec *Companies Act.*[1]

Royal charters created early corporations

Special-act companies were corporations

Three general methods of incorporation in Canada

Federal and provincial corporations

[1.] Luis Millan, "Quebec Rulings, Laws Seen as Improving Shareholders' Rights," *Lawyers Weekly* Vol. 24 No. 22, 15 October 2004.

Registration accomplished by filing memorandum and articles

Memorandum is like a constitution

Operational rules in articles

Use of letters patent method declining

Registration

Incorporation through registration recognizes the contractual relationship between its members and grants them corporate status. Nova Scotia is the only jurisdiction in Canada still using the registration system of incorporation. The process involves registering a "memorandum of association" and "articles of association" with the appropriate government agency, and paying the required fee. The British Columbia government introduced new corporate legislation[2] moving away from the previous registration system, but retaining significant aspects of it and creating a process of incorporation unique to that province.

The memorandum of association serves the same function as a constitution in that it sets out important matters, such as the name of the company, the authorized share capital (the total value of shares that can be sold), and, when appropriate, the objects of the incorporation.

These objects are a list of the purposes for which the company is created. The memorandum can also set out any restriction on those objects. Historically, these objects were very important since they limited the capacity of the corporation to contract but today, since the corporation has all of the powers and capacity of a natural person,[3] the only ones affected by these objects and any restriction are those that have specific notice of them. Care should be taken in crafting the memorandum of association, since it is difficult to alter once it has been registered.

The internal procedural regulations for governing the ordinary operation of the company are contained in the articles of association (not to be confused with the articles of incorporation used in other jurisdictions, discussed below). These articles deal with such matters as how shares are to be issued and transferred, requirements for meetings of the board of directors and of shareholders, voting procedures at those meetings, regulations covering borrowing, powers of directors and other officers, requirements dealing with dividends, regulations concerning company records, and how notice will be given to shareholders. The articles also set out the procedures for altering the articles, so there is considerably less difficulty in changing them than in changing the memorandum of association. But because the articles of association are filed along with the other incorporating documents, subsequent changes are more difficult to make than in the jurisdictions where the corresponding bylaws are considered internal documents and need not be filed.

Because this method of incorporation is accomplished by registration only, the registrar has no discretionary right to refuse incorporation except when the requirements set out in the legislation are not complied with. But because of the requirement to file both the memorandum of association and the articles of association in the registration process, there is less flexibility in amending the internal procedures for managing the company.

Letters Patent

The letters patent method of incorporation is based on the practice of the monarch granting a royal charter. The process involves an applicant petitioning

---

[2.] *Business Corporations Act*, S.B.C. 2002, c. 57.

[3.] *Companies Act*, R.S.N.S. 1989, c. 81, s. 26 (8).

the appropriate government body for the granting of the letters patent. The government representative, acting by statute, grants a charter of incorporation to applicants who meet certain qualifications. Today, only Quebec and Prince Edward Island use this method of incorporation.

The letters patent set out the constitution of the new company and contain information such as the purpose for which the company is formed, the name to be used, the share structure, any restrictions on the transferability of shares, and the rights and obligations of the parties. The rules governing the ordinary operation of the company are set out in separate bylaws. In letters patent jurisdictions, companies have always had all the powers of a natural person to enter into contracts.

Articles of Incorporation

The other provinces and the federal government have adopted a system of incorporation, developed in the United States, based on the filing of articles of incorporation and the granting of a certificate of incorporation. The articles of incorporation method has features of both the letters patent and the registration methods. As with letters patent companies, corporations under this system are primarily the creations of government rather than being based on contract. The articles that are filed are similar to a constitution or statute controlling the activities of the parties rather than a binding agreement between them. A corporation is granted a certificate of incorporation by filing the articles of incorporation and paying the appropriate fee. The articles of incorporation serve the same function and contain the same types of information as the memorandum of association and the letters patent in the other systems. The day-to-day operation is controlled through bylaws similar to the bylaws in a letters patent system or the articles of association in a registration system. It is not necessary to file these bylaws when applying for incorporation. It is also important to note that in an articles of incorporation system, the government body assigned to grant certificates of incorporation has no general discretion to refuse a request for incorporation. British Columbia made significant changes to its incorporation legislation in 2002, moving much closer to this approach. But it retained some aspects of its old registration system, creating a process of incorporation that is unique to that province. Refer to the MyBusLawLab for a more detailed outline of the B.C. changes.

A considerable amount of confusion is caused by the use of the term *articles*. The articles of association used in a registration system are similar to the bylaws in articles of incorporation or letters patent jurisdictions. The "articles" in an articles of incorporation jurisdiction is the main incorporating document and so corresponds most closely to the letters patent in that system or the memorandum of association in a registration jurisdiction. To make matters worse, British Columbia, in reforming its legislation now accomplishes incorporation through the filing of a "notice of articles." Separate articles have to be kept, but not filed, and so correspond to the bylaws in those other jurisdictions. Table 12.1 will provide assistance in keeping these differences straight.

Other Incorporated Bodies

Cities, universities, and other public institutions are incorporated legal entities that can sue or be sued in their own right. Under both federal and provincial

mybuslawlab
www.pearsoned.ca/mybuslawlab

BC   AB   SK   MB   ON

Incorporation accomplished through granting certificate of incorporation

Articles of incorporation method borrows features from each

Societies also incorporated

legislation,[4] it is also possible to establish (incorporate) non-profit bodies, sometimes called "societies," or non-share capital corporations. These bodies are primarily cultural, social, charitable, and religious organizations, such as the B.C. Society for the Prevention of Cruelty to Animals (SPCA), the Canadian Red Cross Society, and the Canadian National Institute for the Blind (CNIB). The one thing these bodies have in common is the non-profit nature of their activities. The legal obligations and technicalities associated with these bodies are much simpler and more straightforward than those associated with corporations generally. Businesspeople often deal with such bodies and so should be aware of them and the statutes by which they are regulated. An examination of these non-profit organizations is beyond the scope of this text.

mybuslawlab
www.pearsoned.ca/mybuslawlab

    ON

Table 12.1 Other Ways to Terminate an Agent's Authority

Jurisdiction	Charter Documents	Bylaws
Nova Scotia	Memorandum	Articles (filed)
Quebec and P.E.I.	Letters patent	Bylaws (not filed)
British Columbia	Notice of articles	Articles (not filed)
Other provinces & federal	Articles of incorporation	Bylaws (not filed)

SEPARATE LEGAL ENTITY

CASE SUMMARY 12.1

Is a Corporation a Separate Legal Entity? *Salomon v. Salomon & Co.*[5]

Salomon ran a successful shoe manufacturing business that he decided to incorporate. He set up a company in which he owned almost all the shares. He then sold the business to that company. Since the company had no assets to pay for the business, he loaned the company enough money to purchase the business from himself, securing the loan with a debenture similar to a mortgage on the company's assets. In short, Salomon loaned the company he "owned" enough money to purchase the business from him and had a mortgage on the assets of the business created to secure the loan.

When the business failed because of labour problems, the creditors turned to Salomon for payment. Not only did he refuse to pay, but as a secured creditor he had first claim on the assets of the company, leaving nothing for the unpaid creditors. In fact, the creditors had dealt only with Salomon and blamed him for their problems. They sued, claiming that he should not only be prevented from claiming ahead of them, but he should also be responsible for paying them if the company's assets were not enough.

The Court decided that since the company was a separate legal entity, it had a separate legal existence apart from Salomon and the debts were those of the company, not Salomon. There was nothing to prevent Salomon from selling his assets to the company and taking security back. The end result was that Salomon was a secured creditor who

---

4. See, for example, the *Societies Act*, R.S.A. 2000, c. S-12.

5. [1897] A.C. 22 (H.L.).

stood in line ahead of the other unsecured creditors. He thus had first claim on the assets of the corporation and no responsibility for its debts.

This case graphically illustrates not only what is meant by a company or corporation being a separate legal entity, but also the consequences of limited liability on the part of the shareholder. This chapter will discuss the concept of the corporate entity and the legal benefits and responsibilities that result from the creation of a corporation.

SMALL BUSINESS PERSPECTIVE

Do you agree with this result? Should a major shareholder be able to escape liability for a company's debt in this way? Should a major shareholder be able to acquire priority over other creditors as was done in this case?

The *Salomon* case in Case Summary 12.1 is still cited as an important authority for the existence of the company or corporation as a separate legal entity. The case recognized the separate legal existence of even a "one-man company." The decision emphasized that, when the incorporation process is completed, there are two legal persons: the shareholder and an incorporated company. Although the corporation does not exist except on paper and is only a "legal fiction," all the forces of law assume that it does exist as a legal entity separate from the shareholder, and that it can function in the commercial world. Shareholders often have difficulty understanding that they do not actually own the assets of the business and that the corporation they have incorporated does. Shares held in a corporation bestow the rights of control, but give the right to share in the liquidation of the assets (the right to participate in capital) only when the corporation is wound up. See Figure 12.1 for an illustration of the separate legal entity concept.

The problem is the opposite when dealing with a large corporation. It is difficult to think of either Sears Canada Inc. or Imperial Oil Limited as a fiction or myth. It is easy to make the mistake of thinking of the corporation's assets, its warehouses and stores, or its shareholders as the entity. But just as Vandenberg's car is not Vandenberg, but an asset owned and used by her, so, too, is Sears Canada Inc. separate from its stores or shareholders. The large corporation, just like the small one, is a legal fiction, which is often referred to as the corporate myth.

It is also important to recognize that the status of separate legal entity for a corporation is a flimsy one. Businesspeople are often shocked to see the courts cast aside this aspect of the law governing corporations to get at the principals of that corporation. For example, the tax department will often deem several different corporations to be one person for tax purposes. Similarly, when the object of incorporation is to get around some government regulation, or commit a fraud, the courts will ignore the separate legal entity aspect of the corporation, and "lift

Corporation a separate legal entity

Courts will sometimes ignore separate legal entity

Figure 12.1 Separate Legal Entity

```
              buy shares                buys assets
Shareholders ───────────▶ Corporation ───────────▶ Assets
                          (a separate legal entity)
```

The shareholders own the shares of the corporation. The corporation (not the shareholders!) owns the assets it purchases.

the corporate veil" to get at the directors, shareholders, or officers committing the fraud. The case discussed in Case Summary 12.2 illustrates a situation where the courts were willing to lift the corporate veil.

Limited liability derived from separate legal entity

Nevertheless, the separate legal entity aspect of a corporation is tremendously important for commercial activities. It allows for the acquisition of capital without involving the shareholders in the operation of the corporation. It also allows the purchase and sale of their shares without interfering with the ongoing operation of the business. Like sole proprietorships and partnerships, a corporation is responsible for contracts made on its behalf, and for the torts of its employees, under the principle of vicarious liability. The corporation can even be convicted and fined for the commission of a crime. But it is the corporation itself that is liable, not the shareholders, who have limited liability. They can lose only their initial investment. It is this principle that protected Mr. Salomon in Case Summary 12.1. As a shareholder, he was not liable for the debts of the company. He was even able to claim ahead of the others, as a secured creditor of the company.

❗ REDUCING RISK 12.1

Unfortunately, businesspeople often act as if the corporation is a real person. Managers often make decisions they find repugnant and which they would not otherwise make because they think that the corporation they serve is real. They draw a distinction in their minds between the corporate entity and themselves, as managers. While it is true that the legal duty of directors and officers is owed to the corporation, it must also be remembered that the corporation itself is merely a fiction. It has no mind or personality, and its existence cannot be used as an excuse for immoral conduct.

Today, creditors can protect themselves by requiring directors or shareholders to sign a personal guarantee and become liable for the debt along with the corporation. A significant advantage of incorporation—that of **limited liability**—is, to a large extent, thereby lost. Furthermore, there are examples, such as the case discussed in Case Summary 12.2, where the courts are willing to lift the corporate veil. But, in most cases, the status of the corporation as a separate legal entity will be respected. This is an important institution in our commercial world, although it is important that businesspeople not take it completely for granted.

CASE SUMMARY 12.2

When Will the Court Lift the Corporate Veil in the Event of Fraud? *Parkland Plumbing & Heating Ltd. v. Minaki Lodge Resort 2002 Inc.*[6]

Archer incorporated Minaki Inc. for the purpose of acquiring and developing Minaki Lodge. Archer was the president, chief operating officer, and a director of Minaki Inc., while his wife was the sole shareholder and a director. Minaki Inc. purchased Minaki Lodge for $1.95 million. A $1 million first mortgage was registered against the title, in favour of Celestine Mortgage Corporation. Archer was the president, chief operating officer, and sole shareholder and director of Celestine.

---

6. 209 ON C.A. 256.

Parkland registered a lien against Minaki Lodge as it was not paid for services and materials it provided to Minaki Inc. Minaki Lodge was then destroyed by fire. There was no fire insurance in place. Parkland sued Minaki Inc. and Celestine for the amount of its lien. The issue was whether Celestine was an "owner" of Minaki Lodge. If it was, it had priority over Parkland with respect to the proceeds from the sale of the remains of Minaki Lodge.

The trial Judge held that Archer had complete control over the development of Minaki Lodge and that his dealings and those of Minaki Inc. and Celestine were not at arm's length but were, instead, "entirely under the control and whim of Archer." Minaki Inc. and Celestine were therefore indistinguishable from Archer. The trial Judge then concluded that Celestine was an "owner" and that Parkland had priority over the proceeds.

On appeal, this decision was overturned by the Divisional Court, but the Court of Appeal affirmed the ruling of the trial Judge. It held that Celestine was an owner of Minaki Lodge, because of the "commercial unreasonableness of the overall course of conduct by Archer, Celestine and Minaki Inc . . . ." Several factors supported this conclusion, including the fact that no fire insurance was obtained. Also, funding was made to Minaki Inc. by Archer's other companies, but no payments had been made to Celestine for its mortgage. The Court agreed with the trial Judge that Celestine's corporate veil should be pierced, to ascertain the real motive of its interest in Minaki Lodge. The Court stated that the separate legal entity principle can be avoided, and the corporate veil lifted, if not doing so would yield a result "too flagrantly opposed to justice." As Archer exercised domination and control over Minaki Lodge through his companies, this was such a case. The acts of the companies were the acts of Archer and therefore Parkland had priority.

DISCUSSION QUESTIONS

Many businesspeople are surprised and react very negatively to a court's ability to ignore the fact of incorporation as happened here. What do you think? When, if ever, should a court have the power to "lift the corporate veil"?

Capacity

It was only in provinces using the registration system of incorporation where the capacity of the company to enter contracts was limited. That was more of a nuisance than anything else. Even in Nova Scotia (the only province still using the registration system), the legislation was changed so that all companies now have the capacity of a natural person. Under the articles of incorporation statutes, it is stated that a corporation has the capacity and the rights, powers, and privileges of a natural person, subject only to the provisions of the legislation.[7] The problem of capacity to contract still may arise when dealing with corporations created by special acts of the legislature or Parliament, where those acts limit their activities to specified areas. When dealing with such a corporation, it seems that unusual care should be taken to check that there is no restriction on its capacity. Some legislation states that it is possible to set down restrictions on what the corporation can do,[8] but outsiders dealing with that corporation would be affected only in the unlikely event that they had specific notice of the limitation.[9]

Most corporations have capacity of natural person

[7.] *Ibid.*, s. 16(2).

[8.] See, for example, *Canada Business Corporations Act*, R.S.C. 1985, c. C-44, s. 15(1).

[9.] *Ibid.*, s. 17.

The Role of Agents

Corporations must act
through agents

Since the corporate entity is a legal fiction, all of its activities must be carried out through the services of real people acting as agents. The principles of agency law set out in Chapter 11 are, therefore, extremely important when dealing with corporations. Directors and employees, from officers right down to clerks, may have actual or apparent authority to bind the corporation, depending on the nature of their jobs. Historically, a corporation could be protected from unauthorized action from such employees simply by filing with the incorporation documents a specific limitation on the actual authority of an agent. Today, these limitations on authority are no longer considered notice to the public, even when they are filed with the other incorporating documents.[10]

Filed documents no longer
notice of limited authority

FUNDING

mybuslawlab

www.pearsoned.ca/mybuslawlab

BC AB SK MB ON

An important attraction of the corporation is the ability to acquire capital from a large number of sources through the sale of shares. While the **share** gives the holder an interest in the corporation, that interest falls short of ownership. The corporation remains an independent personality, separate and apart from the shareholders or members who make it up. Owning shares gives the shareholder control of the corporation and, under certain circumstances, a right to the assets of the corporation upon dissolution.

Issued shares usually less
than authorized share capital

Registration and letters patent jurisdictions require that the authorized share capital be set out in the incorporation documents.[11] This sets an upper limit on the shares that can be sold. This limit is usually set quite high to avoid the problem of having to go back and amend the incorporating documents. It is difficult to justify this limitation, and the articles of incorporation jurisdictions, including British Columbia, no longer require a limitation on the authorized share capital.[12]

Par-Value Versus No-Par-Value Shares

Common practice to issue
no-par-value shares

The practice of issuing par-value shares is declining. Such practice involves each share being given a specific value, such as $1, at the time of issuance. This can be misleading, as the marketplace quickly sets a value on those shares that is not reflected in the stated par value. The more common practice in Canada and the United States is to not put a value on the share, making it a no-par-value share, and allowing the marketplace to determine the value. The articles of incorporation jurisdictions (except British Columbia) have abolished par-value shares.[13] Note that although the use of par-value shares is declining, there may still be some significant tax advantages to using them.[14]

---

10. *Ibid.*, s. 17.

11. *Companies Act, supra* note 3, s. 10(a).

12. See, for example, *Canada Business Corporations Act, supra* note 7, in which s. 6(1)(c) gives the incorporators discretion as to whether a maximum number of shares is set.

13. See, for example, *Canada Business Corporations Act, ibid.,* s. 24(1). British Columbia currently allows both par-value and no-par-value shares; *Business Corporations Act, supra* note 2, s. 52.

14. Janice Mucalov, "B.C.'s New Business Corporations Act Seen as Better than CBCA," *Lawyers Weekly* 23 No. 21, 3 October 2003.

Special Rights and Restrictions

The shares issued by a corporation are normally divided into different classes, usually called *common shares* and *special* or *preferred shares*. If there is only one class of shares, they will be common shares. If there are no preferred shares, the common shares must include the rights to vote at shareholders' meetings, to receive dividends declared by the corporation, and to receive the property of the corporation on its dissolution.[15]

Rights of common shares

The rights and restrictions associated with special shares can be designed to accomplish many diverse objectives. They usually give the shareholder preference when dividends are declared and are, therefore, called **preferred shares**. Usually, a preferred share will bear a promise to pay a specific dividend each year. This is not a debt, and the corporation is not obligated to declare a dividend, but once it does, the preferred shareholder has the right to collect first, before the common shareholders. These rights may be cumulative and, if they are, when there has been a failure to pay the promised dividend for a number of years, the preferred shareholder has a right to receive any back payments before the common shareholders get any dividends.

Usually, only common shareholders have the right to vote, but a preferred share usually gives the right to vote when the corporation fails to pay the promised dividend. There can be a right to vote, even without such a provision, when major changes that would materially affect the position of the preferred shareholder are proposed. For example, a proposal to change the rights or nature of the preferred share, or to sell the assets of the corporation, could not be adopted without allowing the preferred shareholders to vote.[16]

Different classes of shares can give some shareholders preference

Also, when a corporation is dissolved, preferred shareholders usually have the right to have those shares repaid before any funds are paid out to the holders of common shares.

Since a variety of rights and restrictions can be incorporated into preferred shares, depending on the interests of the parties, it is important that these matters be negotiated before the shares are issued. When a closely held corporation is involved, it is common to include a restriction on the transfer or sale of the shares, such as requiring the approval of the directors before the transfer or sale can take place. (Closely held and broadly held corporations are discussed below.)

 REDUCING RISK 12.2

It is relatively easy to incorporate a business. The process is now simplified to the extent that people can either do it themselves or purchase a simple off-the-shelf corporation, much like they can purchase a suit off the rack. But these approaches may result in a loss of some of the considerable flexibility that is available using the corporate form to carry on business. It is possible, by careful use of common shares, the creation of shares with special rights and restrictions, and shareholders' agreements, to cater to a great variety of different relationships and needs, giving different rights and obligations with unique advantages to the various players. In addition, through holding corporations, corporations working together, and even corporations in partnership, there is no limit to the creative solutions that can be designed to deal with a variety of business problems and needs. Businesspeople should be aware that, just as a personally tailored suit has advantages over one off the rack, paying a lawyer to custom design a corporation for their particular needs may well be worth the trouble and expense. Skimping to save a few dollars at the outset may cause expensive problems later on.

---

15. *Canada Business Corporations Act, supra* note 7, s. 24(3).

16. See s. 176 and s. 189 of the *Canada Business Corporations Act, ibid.*,which deal with class votes and extraordinary sales or leases of the corporation's assets, respectively.

Special shares used in estate planning

Special shares are used for other purposes, such as estate planning, when two classes of shares can be created: one with a right to vote and with some control in the affairs of the corporation, but no right to dividends or to receive money upon dissolution, and the other with a right to dividends, but no right to vote. Such a division allows the holder of the voting shares to maintain control of the operations of the corporation, but to surrender the income and the beneficial interests of the corporation to any heirs.

Borrowing

Corporation can borrow funds

The corporation can also borrow funds, thus accumulating debt. This can be done by borrowing large sums from a single creditor, such as a bank, which usually requires a mortgage on the property of the corporation. It can also be accomplished through the issuing of bonds or debentures, either secured or unsecured, to many different creditors. The result, in either case, is the creation of a debtor–creditor relationship and an obligation that must be repaid. When shares are involved, even preferred shares, there is no legal obligation to pay dividends, but a failure to repay a debt constitutes a breach of the corporation's legal obligation. The creditor can execute against security, bring an action and, once judgment is obtained, garnish or seize the assets of the corporation. If the corporation is unable to pay, bankruptcy will likely follow.

Corporation borrows funds by issuing bonds

Usually, the terms *bond* and *debenture* are used interchangeably, but in Canada a **bond** is normally secured by a mortgage, or a floating charge, on all assets of the corporation not already mortgaged or pledged. A **debenture** is more likely to be unsecured. The corporation typically makes a debt commitment to a trustee, who then issues shares in the indebtedness to individual bondholders. These bondholders are entitled to a portion of the repayment at a set rate of interest. They are free to sell such claims to others, sometimes at a premium or discount, depending on the market.

Shareholders are participants in the corporation, whereas bondholders are simply creditors. The corporation is in debt to the bondholder for the amount of the bond, but the corporation is not in debt to the shareholder for the price of the share. The bondholder can demand repayment and enforce that right in court, whereas a shareholder, even a preferred shareholder, has no similar right to demand payment of a dividend, or repayment of the cost of the share.

Bondholder has right to payment

Bondholder has no right to vote

On the other hand, while a shareholder can determine the operation of the corporation through the exercise of her voting power, a bondholder has no right to vote and cannot affect management decisions. In the event of a default, however, the bondholders usually have a right to take over the management of the corporation through the appointment of a receiver. This is similar to bankruptcy, but without the requirement of court involvement. While the corporation remains solvent, however, the shareholders retain control through their voting power, and the bondholders have only the right to be paid on a regular basis. From the investor's point of view, the choice among shares at one end, bonds at the other, and preferred shares in the middle, is likely to be simply a question of balancing risk and return. To calculate those risks, an understanding of the legal differences between these vehicles and of their different tax implications, is essential.

Most large corporations maintain a balance between common and preferred shares, and various types of debt instruments, such as large loans and secured and unsecured corporate bonds. To illustrate, suppose Bowman wanted to incorporate a small manufacturing business. There are several ways to transfer the assets of the business to the corporation. Bowman might incorporate a corporation that would acquire the manufacturing business and any property associated with it in return for all the shares of the corporation. A better alternative, however, might be to have the corporation purchase the manufacturing business as well as any property associated with it from Bowman, giving him a bond secured by a mortgage on the property as security for the repayment of the debt.

Bowman owns all the shares of the corporation in either case. However, in the second case, instead of simply owning shares in a corporation with significant assets, Bowman is a creditor of that corporation. Because the debt will be secured, he will be in a better position to get his money back if the corporation eventually runs into financial difficulties. This is similar to the situation in which Salomon found himself in Case Summary 12.1. Before decisions are made with respect to these options, careful consideration must be given to the various tax implications of the choices. Refer to Figure 12.2 for a summary of the funding of corporations.

mybuslawlab
www.pearsoned.ca/mybuslawlab

Closely Held and Broadly Held Corporations

Traditionally, company law statutes in various jurisdictions recognized a distinction between broadly held and closely held companies, which were usually called *public* and *private companies*, respectively. In recent years, statutory provisions relating to these two classes of corporation have received considerable attention and have been significantly modified. In general, a closely held corporation is one in which there are relatively few shareholders. There are restrictions on the sale of shares, which cannot be sold to the general public openly or on the stock market. Closely held corporations are usually (but not always!) small corporations that are used to operate a family business. They are usually managed by the shareholders themselves. The closely held corporation is much freer of government regulations and control than the broadly held corporation. The special requirements for broadly held corporations are found not only in the appropriate incorporation statutes, but also in the securities legislation of that jurisdiction.

Using Alberta as an example, corporations in that province that offer shares to the public and that have more than 15 shareholders are called distributing corporations.[17] Such corporations have to satisfy the most stringent legislative requirements. For example, section 160 of the Alberta *Business Corporations Act* requires them to file financial statements with the Alberta Securities Commission. They must have an audit committee (section 171). They must provide greater

Broadly held corporations more closely regulated

Figure 12.2 Funding of Corporations

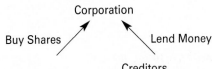

Shareholders
- buy shares from corporation
- common or preferred
- control corporation
- corporation not obligated to declare dividends
- share in liquidation of assets on winding up of corporation, after creditors paid

Creditors
- lend money to corporation
- secured or unsecured
- no control over management
- corporation has legal obligation to repay loans
- entitled to be paid before shareholders, on winding up of corporation

[17.] R.S.A. 2000, c. S-4.

access to corporate records (section 23). They cannot restrict the transfer of their shares, except to non-residents, or to enable the corporation to meet any requirement to allow them to obtain a business licence, to become a publisher of a Canadian newspaper, or to acquire shares in a financial intermediary (sections 48, 174). They must have at least three directors, two of whom must not be officers or employees of the corporation or its affiliates. A non-distributing corporation requires only one or more directors (section 101(2)). Legislative requirements for distributing corporations are found not only in the *Business Corporations Act*, but also in the securities legislation, the *Securities Act*.[18]

Non-distributing corporations with 15 or fewer shareholders have to comply with the least amount of government regulation and control. Non-distributing corporations with 16 or more shareholders that do not offer shares to the public do have to comply with more statutory requirements than those corporations with fewer than 16 shareholders, but not as much as distributing corporations.[19]

mybuslawlab
www.pearsoned.ca/mybuslawlab

BC AB SK MB ON

CORPORATE DIRECTORS, OFFICERS, AND SHAREHOLDERS

Directors (Managers)

WITHIN THE CORPORATION

Shareholders choose directors

The shareholders normally exercise control over a corporation through the election of directors at the annual meeting. Once the directors are elected, the shareholders have little real say in the operation of the corporation until the next election, but the expectation is that if they want to be re-elected, the directors will follow the wishes of the shareholders. Sometimes, a shareholders' vote will be held when decisions involving a fundamental change in the corporation are to be made or when required by the incorporating documents. Smaller (closely held) corporations are more often run like partnership. The shareholders are usually the managers as well as the directors, and they participate in all important decisions.

For a person to serve as a director, he must be an adult of sound mind, and cannot be a bankrupt,[20] or, in some jurisdictions, have been convicted of a crime involving fraud.[21] In most jurisdictions, the director no longer needs to be a shareholder[22] Because many corporations in Canada are foreign subsidiaries, usually a significant proportion of the directors must be resident in Canada.[23] British Columbia has eliminated the residency requirement for directors altogether.

---

18. *Business Corporations Act*, R.S.A. 2000, c. B-9, s. 1.

19. Such corporations must, for example, comply with s. 149 and s. 150 of the *Business Corporations Act, supra* note 16, regarding proxies and proxy solicitations, unless they are exempted by the Alberta Securities Commission.

20. See, for example, *ibid.*, s. 105(3) and (4). Note that the residency requirement for federal corporations was recently reduced from a majority to 25 percent.

21. See, for example, *Canada Business Corporations Act, supra* note 7, s. 105(2).

22. See, for example, *Business Corporations Act, supra*note 2, s. 124 (2) d.

23. See, for example, *Canada Business Corporations Act, supra* note 7, s. 105(1).

CASE SUMMARY 12.3

Fraud Disqualifies Director from Serving: *Reeves v. Hart*[24]

Hart was a director and the driving force of Sungold Entertainment Corp. (a publicly traded B.C. company) and Horsepower Broadcasting Network Inc. (a wholly owned subsidiary of Sungold). An application was brought by Reeves, another director of these companies, to have Hart removed as a director. This was opposed by Hart and the companies themselves. In 2002, Hart had been convicted of tax evasion, having relied on false documents overstating expenses and reducing taxable income. In British Columbia, a criminal conviction involving fraud disqualifies a person from serving as a director in a corporation registered in that province, unless the court exercises its discretion and orders otherwise. The Court found that the tax evasion conviction involved the submission of false documents, which satisfied the definition of fraud, and disqualified Hart from acting as a director of a B.C. company. Even though it was suggested that the reason for the application was that Reeves was disgruntled at having lost a valuable consulting contract with Sungold, and that Hart was the driving force behind the companies and his involvement was needed for them to succeed, the Court found that there was not sufficient reason to exercise its discretion and removed Hart as a director of the two companies.

SMALL BUSINESS PERSPECTIVE

This case illustrates the stringent qualifications that directors are required to not only meet, but retain. Are these standards too high? Should the disgruntled shareholder have been permitted to use these provisions for his own ulterior purposes?

A director owes a significant duty to the corporation to be careful. In common law, this duty was minimal, the director being liable only when there was some blatant or gross carelessness on his part. This standard has been significantly raised in most jurisdictions. The federal legislation, for example, now requires directors to exercise the care, diligence and skill of a "reasonably prudent person" when exercising their powers and discharging their duties.[25]

Director owes duty not to be negligent

Directors also owe a fiduciary duty to the corporation.[26] This duty requires the director to act in the best interests of the corporation, to be loyal, to avoid conflict of interest, and to otherwise act honestly and in good faith toward the corporation. Directors are not permitted to take personal advantage of opportunities that arise because of their positions as directors, nor can they start a business in competition with the corporation. Any gains made by directors from such dealings must be paid over to the corporation, but any losses must be borne by that director alone. When a director is personally involved in some transaction that the corporation may become involved in, the director must disclose that interest by making a declaration to the board of directors, avoid any involvement in the discussion of the matter and abstain from voting on it.[27]

Director owes fiduciary duty

[24.] 2003 BCSC 826, 35 B.L.R. (3d) 168.

[25.] *Canada Business Corporations Act, supra* note 7, s. 122(1)(b).

[26.] *Ibid.*, s. 122(1)(a).

[27.] *Ibid.*, s. 120.

A major problem associated with directors' liability is that they owe a fiduciary duty to the corporation itself, not to the shareholders. Only the corporation can sue the director when this duty is violated. Since the directors decide what the corporation does, a decision to sue a director must be made by the directors, and they are not likely to decide to sue themselves. In the *Wise* case discussed below, the Supreme Court clarified that the directors owe a fiduciary duty to the corporation only, and not to other stakeholders such as creditors or shareholders, even when the corporation is insolvent. The Court also made it clear that a duty of care is owed to creditors, and while that is less onerous than a fiduciary duty, a duty of care still imposes on directors a significant exposure to liability for negligence.

CASE SUMMARY 12.4

The Nature of a Director's Duty: *Peoples Department Stores Inc. (Trustee of) v. Wise*[28]

In 1992, Wise Stores Inc. ("Wise") purchased the shares of its rival, Peoples. Lionel, Ralph, and Harold Wise were the majority shareholders, officers, and directors of Wise. They became the sole directors of Peoples. Wise and Peoples were two large department store chains operating in Ontario and Atlantic Canada. For increased efficiency Wise and Peoples instituted a joint inventory and purchasing process. Soon after, both stores were forced into bankruptcy. The Trustee in Bankruptcy of Peoples, acting for its creditors, brought this action against the three Wise brothers. He claimed that, as directors of Peoples, the brothers had violated their fiduciary duty to Peoples, and to Peoples' creditors, by favouring the interests of Wise in the joint inventory and purchasing scheme.

The matter went to the Supreme Court of Canada, which made it clear that an honest and good faith attempt to solve a corporation's financial problems does not, if unsuccessful, qualify as a breach of fiduciary duty. The Court held the fiduciary duty of directors was owed only to the corporation, and not to its creditors. The fiduciary duty does not change when a corporation is in the nebulous "vicinity of insolvency." Directors owe their fiduciary obligations only to the corporation, not to the corporation's creditors or to any other stakeholder.

The Court also noted that this restriction in the scope of the directors' obligations did not apply to a duty of care and so would not protect them from a negligence action brought by creditors. The case is important because it differentiates between a fiduciary duty owed only to the corporation, and a duty of care which can also be owed to other stakeholders. The Court pointed out that the other stakeholders had options, including the right to bring an oppression action against the directors, or a derivative action on behalf of the corporation against the directors.

DISCUSSION QUESTIONS

Do you think that the fiduciary duty owed by a director should be limited to the corporation, or should it be extended to the shareholders or creditors? Is even the imposition of a fiduciary duty to the corporation setting too onerous a responsibility on the directors? Consider the problems that arise when a director is a director of both a parent and a subsidiary. To whom is the fiduciary duty owed? What should be done when the interests of the two corporations are in conflict?

---

28. *2004 SCC 68, [2004] 3 S.C.R. 461.*

In most circumstances, however, only the corporation can sue the director. To solve this problem, many jurisdictions give even minority shareholders the right to bring what is called a **derivative action** (in some provinces, a **representative action**) against the directors, or others, on behalf of the injured corporation.[29] This change, along with the change in the nature of the imposed duty to be careful, has significantly enhanced the peril associated with being a director. Refer to the MyBusLawLab for province-specific legislation.

Derivative or representative action

In addition to these general duties, statutes in all jurisdictions set out many specific responsibilities and liabilities to which directors are subject when they make specific prohibited decisions. For example, directors become personally liable if they allow shares to be sold for consideration that is less than the fair equivalent of the money that the corporation would have received if the share had been issued for money.[30] Directors will also be personally liable if they allow transactions that are not permitted by the legislation, such as the purchase of shares or the payment of dividends by the corporation, if there are reasonable grounds for believing that the corporation would, after carrying out the transaction, be unable to pay its liabilities as they become due, or if the value of its assets would then be less than the value of its liabilities.[31] Finally, directors may be liable if they contravene specific responsibilities as set out in the legislation, such as the calling of annual shareholders' meetings.[32]

Directors may face personal liability

Directors (and officers and others who are deemed to be insiders) are prohibited from using "insider knowledge" to their own advantage, or to the advantage of their friends or family. That is, directors who are aware of something about to happen that will materially affect the value of shares, bonds, or other assets of the corporation are prohibited from using that knowledge to their own advantage through dealing in these assets. There are strict disclosure requirements whenever an insider trades in the securities of the corporation. The misuse of insider information is prohibited by securities legislation, and an offender is subject to fines and imprisonment. The *Canada Business Corporations Act* also provides for personal civil liability of a director who commits insider trading.[33]

Directors are "insiders"

There are many other statutes that impose duties and responsibilities on directors. Directors of larger corporations, for example, face personal financial liability and even imprisonment if information is not provided to the Chief Statistician of Canada, as required by the *Corporations Returns Act.*[34]

EXTERNAL OBLIGATIONS

Various federal and provincial statues impose personal liability on the director primarily in three areas. Directors can be held personally liable when a corporation fails while owing workers unpaid wages.[35] Often, when a corporation

Director's statutory duty for
• wages

[29.] See, for example, *Canada Business Corporations Act, supra* note 7, s. 239.

[30.] *Ibid.,* s. 118(1).

[31.] *Ibid.,* s. 118(2).

[32.] *Ibid.,* s. 133(1).

[33.] *Ibid.,* s. 131. See *Tongue v. Vencap Equities Alberta Ltd.* (1996), 184 A.R. 368 (C.A.), in which the Court found the directors of a corporation personally liable for damages for breach of fiduciary duty and insider trading under the *Canada Business Corporations Act.*

[34.] R.S.C. 1985, c. C-43.

[35.] See, for example, s. 119 of the *Canada Business Corporations Act, supra* note 7, which makes directors of federal corporations liable for up to six months' wages payable to each employee of the corporation. For a discussion of two recent cases in which directors of corporations were found liable for unpaid wages, see Glenn Kauth, "Directors On Hook for Unpaid Wages and Benefits" *Law Times* (22 September 2008).

is in trouble, directors will resign rather than face this risk. Sometimes the corporation will agree to indemnify them, but if the corporation fails, such an agreement is useless. Insurance provides the best protection in these circumstances. Directors can also be held personally liable for breaches of employment standards legislation, as well as workers' compensation and occupational health and safety legislation in place in the particular jurisdiction. Refer to the MyBusLawLab for specifics.

• taxes

A second area of personal liability for directors involves unpaid taxes. Under federal income tax legislation, the directors are personally responsible if back taxes are left unpaid.[36] In many jurisdictions in Canada, if foreign firms wish to operate they must have local resident directors.[37] Local businesspeople are often expected to act as token directors, and are not actually expected to participate in the decision-making process of the corporation. Many take these positions not realizing their exposure. If the corporation fails, leaving unpaid taxes and other obligations, the personal liability can be ruinous.

CASE SUMMARY 12.5

When Are Directors Liable for Unpaid Taxes? *Axford v. Canada*[38]

Axford was the sole shareholder and director of a corporation. The corporation failed to remit to Revenue Canada income tax, GST, and source deductions of its employees. The corporation was assessed for these and the related interest and penalties. The corporation did not pay the required amount, so Revenue Canada assessed Axford for it. The Court held that Axford was involved in the corporation's affairs and knew of its financial difficulties. He was therefore under a positive duty to act when Revenue Canada demanded payment. Axford did not take any action, and thus did not exercise due diligence to prevent the corporation's failure to pay Revenue Canada. He was personally liable for the amount owed to Revenue Canada.

SMALL BUSINESS PERSPECTIVE

Do you agree with this outcome? Is there too much responsibility imposed on the directors of corporations? Has the separate legal entity principle been diluted too much?

• environment

The third area involves environmental regulation. Complicated statutes impose personal liability on directors for damages caused by the corporation to the environment.[39] Contamination of property, pollution of the air, unexpected spills, and the cost of cleanup are examples of potential sources of a director's

---

[36] This includes liability for the corporation's failure to remit any prescribed amounts under the *Income Tax Act*, R.S.C. 1985, c. 1 (5th Supp.), s. 227.1, and the *Excise Tax Act*, R.S.C. 1985, c. E-15, s. 323.

[37] *Canada Business Corporations Act, supra* note 7, s. 105 (3) and (4), discussed above in note 23.

[38] 2002, D.T.C. 2217, [2002] T.C.J. No. 597 (T.C.C.).

[39] See, for example, s. 280(1) of the *Canadian Environmental Protection Act, 1999*, S.C. 1999, c. 33, which states that when a corporation has committed an offence, any officer, director, or agent of the corporation who "directed, authorized, assented to, acquiesced in or participated in" the commission of the offence is also guilty of the offence and liable to the punishment provided for the offence.

personal liability. In addition to potential fines and imprisonment, the directors may also face being personally responsible for the actual damages caused, or the costs of cleanup, in a civil action.

Usually, directors can escape liability only when they can show that they acted with "due diligence."[40] What constitutes **due diligence** varies with the situation but, in general, directors must show that they kept themselves informed of what was required of the corporation and what the corporation was doing to comply, and that they did all that was reasonable to avoid the problem.

Individual liability has also been imposed on directors for offences under consumer protection legislation, the federal *Competition Act*, securities legislation, and provincial human rights codes. It is important to note that many of these statutes not only contemplate fines, but also provide for imprisonment in extreme situations. Both criminal and civil responsibilities may be imposed on the corporation itself, as well as on its directors and officers.

• other

It should also be remembered that when the commission of a tort, such as misrepresentation or deceit, is involved, a director may be held personally liable if he was the one who committed the wrong. The corporate structure sometimes does not provide protection to the person who actually commits the tort. The decisions on this issue have been inconsistent, but the following statement appears to accurately state the law:

> There will be circumstances in which the actions of a shareholder, officer, director or employee of a corporation may give rise to personal liability in tort despite the fact that the impugned acts were ones performed in the course of their duties to the corporation. Where those actions are themselves tortuous or exhibit a separate identity or interest from that of the corporation so as to make the act or conduct complained of their own, they may well attract personal liability. . . . [41]

The *Criminal Code* imposes a duty to take reasonable steps to prevent bodily harm in respect of workplace safety (section 217.1). A corporation can be found liable for criminal negligence if an employee, agent, or contractor is a party to an offence and the responsible "senior officer . . . departs markedly from the standard of care that could reasonably be expected" (section 22.1). (A "senior officer" includes a director, a chief executive officer, and a chief financial officer (section 2).) Corporations can be found guilty of a criminal offence requiring fault (section 22.2) when a senior officer, with the intent to benefit the organization, commits the offence, directs other representatives of the organization so that they commit the offence, or does not take all reasonable steps to stop a representative from committing the offence. Directors (as well as officers and employees) are, of course, liable for the crimes they commit. This would include breaching the duty set out in section 217.1.

Criminal liability

---

40. *Ibid.*, s. 283. Section 280.1(1) states that a director must take "all reasonable care" to ensure that the corporation complies with the legislation.

41. *Blacklaws v. Morrow* (2000), 261 A.R. 28 (C.A.), leave to appeal refused, [2000] S.C.C.A. No. 442, para. 41. For a case in which a director was found to be personally liable in tort, see *ADGA Systems International Ltd. v. Valcom Ltd.* (1999), 43 O.R. (3d) 101 (C.A.), leave to appeal refused, [1999] S.C.C.A. No. 124.

Officers and Senior Executives

CASE SUMMARY 12.6

Do Officers Owe a Fiduciary Duty to the Corporation?
Can. Aero v. O'Malley[42]

O'Malley (president and chief executive officer) and Zarzycki (executive vice-president) were senior management officers of Canaero, a wholly owned subsidiary of the U.S. company Canadian Aero Services Ltd. involved in topographical mapping and geophysical exploration.

When an opportunity to pursue a project in Guyana, financed through aid money from the Canadian government, came up, O'Malley and Zarzycki resigned from Canaero and incorporated their own company (Terra Surveys Ltd.) to divert the project from Canaero to Terra. O'Malley and Zarzycki had been involved in other projects for Canaero in the area and knew the local officials. They had been involved in the preparation work for the project for Canaero.

The Supreme Court of Canada found that these senior officers owed a fiduciary duty to Canaero. In the process of incorporating a rival company and diverting the Guyana project away from Canaero to their new company, they had violated that fiduciary duty. The Court held that this duty continued after they had left their position of employment. They were found liable for the damage caused. Note that the Court made it clear that the senior officers owed a fiduciary duty similar to that of a director of the company.

DISCUSSION QUESTIONS

Do you agree that the fiduciary duty owed by directors of a corporation should continue after they cease being directors of that corporation?

Similar duties owed by senior management

Although directors are legally responsible for management, in a large corporation they usually appoint a managing director or chief executive officer (CEO), who is given overall responsibility, along with a managing committee of the directors, to run the affairs of the corporation. The day-to-day operation of the corporation is assigned to others who report to the CEO. These officers may include a president, treasurer, secretary, and other senior executives, such as vice-presidents and managers, as deemed appropriate for the organization. In general, these officers and managers are in a fiduciary relationship to the corporation, similar to that of the directors. They owe the same types of general obligations, duties of care, and competence to the corporation as the directors, but may be held to an even higher standard. In the case of statutory obligations, they may have to pay any wages and taxes owing. They may be held personally liable for judgments against the corporation in human rights and consumer complaint actions, as well as costs for cleaning up any environmental damage caused by the corporation.[43] The legislation usually imposes the same obligations on officers as those imposed on directors. The *O'Malley* case (Case Summary 12.6 above)

---

42. [1974] S.C.R. 592.

43. For example, the personal liability described in s. 280(1) of the *Canadian Environmental Protection Act 1999, supra* note 39, extends not only to directors, but also to officers and agents of the corporation.

shows the nature of the fiduciary duty, as well as how that duty can continue even after the employment relationship has ceased.

Promoters

A **promoter** is someone who participates in the initial setting up of the corporation or who assists the corporation in making a public share offering. Provincial securities statutes control the sale of shares to the public, whether through the stock exchange or other means. A **securities commission** is established to prevent fraud and to encourage a free and efficient market in corporate shares and other securities. This requires the complete disclosure of as much information as possible. To accomplish this, a proper prospectus must be issued when shares are to be sold to the public. The purpose of the **prospectus** is to disclose all pertinent information of interest to investors about the corporation and its business operations. The corporation and the promoters are responsible to ensure full disclosure and that there is no misrepresentation in the prospectus. In addition to any civil liability, significant fines and jail sentences may be imposed when there is not full disclosure or when misrepresentations take place.

The securities commission is also charged with controlling other forms of abuse, including insider trading, when officers or people holding significant percentages of the shares of a corporation trade in those shares using their insider knowledge to anticipate a rise or fall in prices. The securities commission also controls abuses by providing for the licensing and regulation of all those involved in the selling and marketing of shares and other securities, including brokers, sales personnel, and the issuers of the shares (the corporations) themselves.

Whether promoters are officers of the corporation or not, they, like directors and other officers, owe a fiduciary duty to the corporation. This includes, for example, a duty to disclose any personal interest in deals in which the corporation is involved. When a promoter acquires property with the intention of incorporating a corporation and then selling that property to it, he has a duty to act in the best interests of the corporation. The promoter cannot sell the property to the corporation at an excessive profit, he must divulge the original price paid for the property, and he must not participate in the decision of the corporation to purchase the property from him.

www.pearsoned.ca/mybuslawlab

Promoters also owe duties

Disclosure required

Fiduciary duty

CASE SUMMARY 12.7

When Is a Promoter Personally Liable? *[1]080409 Ontario Ltd. v. Hunter*[44]

Garth Drabinsky incorporated 1080409 to purchase the subject property. He later decided to sell the property. He entered into an agreement with Hunter, but the purchase and sale agreement was in the name "Furama Investments." Furama was not incorporated. Hunter did not have sufficient funds, so the deal did not close. 1080409 later sold the property to a third party but at a lower price than Hunter had agreed to pay. 1080409 sued Hunter for the difference in net proceeds.

---

44. 2000 CanLII 22405 (Ont. S.C.).

The Court found that Hunter was personally liable, pursuant to section 21 of the Ontario *Business Corporations Act*, which provided in part that:

21(1) Except as provided in this section, a person who enters into an oral or written contract in the name of or on behalf of a corporation before it comes into existence is personally bound by the contract and is entitled to the benefits thereof.

21(4) If expressly so provided in the oral or written contract referred to in subsection (1), a person who purported to act in the name of or on behalf of the corporation before it came into existence is not in any event bound by the contract or entitled to the benefits thereof.

Hunter had signed the agreement on behalf of a corporation before it came into existence. He could have expressly provided in the purchase and sale agreement that he was not personally bound by the agreement, but he did not do so. Damages were assessed on the basis of what 1080409 would have received had the agreement been performed.

SMALL BUSINESS PERSPECTIVE

Should a businessperson enter into agreements prior to incorporating? If so, what should they do to minimize their potential liability?

REDUCING RISK 12.3

Promoters will often purchase property on behalf of a corporation before it has been incorporated and then have the corporation ratify the agreement after incorporation. Such ratification of pre-incorporation contracts is invalid in common law, since the corporation did not exist at the time the promoters were claiming to act on its behalf. Although this common law restriction against ratifying pre-incorporation contracts makes logical sense, it causes problems from a business point of view and many jurisdictions have made legislative changes permitting the later-incorporated corporation to ratify a pre-incorporation contract.[45] The result is that the contract is valid and binding on the corporation once it is so ratified. Of course, if the corporation does not ratify, or if a pre-incorporation contract is signed in a jurisdiction where the corporation cannot ratify, the promoter remains solely liable for any losses, since there was no authority to act. Businesspeople should try to avoid personal liability for pre-incorporation contracts. They may be able to do so by including a provision in the contract exempting themselves from any resulting liability.

Shareholders

Shareholder has few responsibilities

One of the main attractions of incorporation is that shareholders have few obligations to the corporation, or to other shareholders, other than to not use insider knowledge for their own purposes. Unlike directors, shareholders usually have no duty to act in the best interests of the corporation or other shareholders. They may have some obligations, if they hold enough shares to be classified as "insiders." The number of shares required to qualify as an insider varies from one

45. See, for example, *Canada Business Corporations Act, supra* note 7, s. 14.

jurisdiction to another.[46] Shareholders who have been classified as insiders have the same obligation as directors to not use insider information to their own benefit, or to the benefit of friends or relatives.

CASE SUMMARY 12.8

Can a Minor Shareholder Commence a Lawsuit on Behalf of the Corporation? *Richardson Greenshields of Canada Ltd. v. Kalmacoff*[47]

Two corporations with similar names were involved in this case, Security Home Mortgage Investment Inc. (Security Home) and Security Home Financing Ltd. (the Adviser). Security Home was controlled by a small group of individuals holding 85 percent of the common shares. That same group largely owned the shares in the Adviser, which had a contract to manage and run the operation of Security Home. A large number of preferred shares in Security Home had been sold on the open market through the agent Richardson Greenshields. Security Home ran into financial difficulty, but still renewed the management contract of the Adviser. This decision had to be approved by the preferred shareholders. Richardson Greenshields obtained enough proxies from this group to override the decision and terminate the management contract.

It was at this point that the basis of the complaint arose. Instead of hiring new management, the directors simply ended the contract with the Adviser and hired the same people to manage Security Home directly. In effect, the same people were doing exactly the same jobs they had been doing before, but now they were employed directly by Security Home instead of by the Adviser. In response to this, Richardson Greenshields bought 100 shares of Security Home on the open market and applied to the Court to bring a derivative action in the name of, and on behalf of, Security Home against its directors.

The question in this case was whether Richardson Greenshields had the right to bring such a derivative action, since it had acquired the shares after the conduct complained of. The Court of Appeal decided that the issues involved were significant, that it did not matter when Richardson Greenshields obtained the shares, and that, as a shareholder, it had the right to ask the Court for permission to commence a derivative action against the directors of the corporation. Permission was granted.

The Court's decision did not rule on the merits of the dispute; it simply authorized the action to proceed. The case does, however, illustrate some very important points. First, it shows how preferred shares can be set up with rights and obligations different from those of common shares and what the effects of those differences can be. It also illustrates how different corporate entities can be used and intermingled to accomplish different purposes, as was the case here with Security Home and the Adviser having essentially the same investors owning common shares in each. For our purposes, the most important point to note is the right of a dissatisfied shareholder to overcome the tyranny of the majority by bringing an action on behalf of the corporation against those who have, for their own ulterior purposes, made decisions not in the best interests of the corporation.

[46.] Section 131(1)(d) of the *Canada Business Corporations Act, supra* note 7, together with s. 40 of the *Canada Business Corporations Regulations*, 2001, S.O.R./2001–512, states that any person who beneficially owns, or exercises control or direction over, at least 10 percent of the outstanding voting shares of a corporation is considered an "insider."

[47.] (1995), 22 O.R. (3d) 577 (C.A.), leave to appeal refused, [1995] S.C.C.A. No. 260.

DISCUSSION QUESTIONS

Is this an abuse of the derivative action process? Remember that Richardson Greenshields purchased the shares after the offending conduct and did so with the sole object of getting itself into a position to sue the directors.

RIGHTS

Shareholder has right to see records and reports

Shareholders do have significant rights and remedies. Certain records must be kept at a designated corporate office and made available to the shareholders.[48] These records include

- the documents of incorporation
- lists of all the shareholders
- lists of transactions or changes in relationship to the shares
- lists of officers, directors, and debenture holders
- minutes of shareholders' meetings.

Some corporate records, including the minutes of directors' meetings and the actual financial records ("the books"), are not available to shareholders. Otherwise, such information could not be kept from competitors. Nonetheless, much important information is contained in documents that are accessible to anybody who holds a share in the corporation.

Shareholders are entitled to receive copies of annual financial statements of the corporation and the auditor's report, if any.[49] The financial statements of broadly held corporations must be audited.[50] An **auditor** is an unbiased outside accountant whose responsibility is to ensure that the financial statements use generally accepted accounting practices and are accurate.[51] The auditor's duty is to the shareholders, not to the directors, and the auditors have access to the corporation's books to ensure the accuracy of their conclusions.[52] Shareholders who have some doubts about the accuracy of these audited statements can have an inspector appointed to examine the auditing process.[53]

The shareholders also have considerable power to affect the decisions made by the corporation. An **annual general meeting** of shareholders must be held, at which the shareholders are given an opportunity to vote for the directors of the corporation, making the directors directly answerable to the shareholders for their actions. Advance notice of this meeting, including the appropriate financial statements, must be given to the shareholders. Any major changes that will affect the nature of the corporation must be placed before the shareholders to vote on before the decisions are implemented. If necessary, a special meeting can be called for this purpose.

[48.] *Canada Business Corporations Act, supra* note 7, ss. 20, 21, 138(4).

[49.] *Ibid.,* ss.159, 169(1).

[50.] *Ibid.,* s. 163.

[51.] *Ibid.,* s. 161.

[52.] *Ibid.,* s. 170.

[53.] *Ibid.,* Part XIX.

The incorporating documents or bylaws of the corporation may provide for the right of shareholders to vote in other situations as well. Shareholders at these meetings can put forward proposals concerning any matter for the decision of the other shareholders, but management may refuse to submit a proposal if it appears that it is self-serving or is, in some way, an abuse of the process. It must be remembered that each vote is based on the number of shares held. Thus, someone holding a majority of the shares will always be able to outvote minority shareholders.[54]

Shareholders have the right to vote

Shareholders can pass their right to vote at the annual general meeting to someone else, in the form of a **proxy**. Proxies can be very important when groups of shareholders band together to affect a particular result, or to determine which directors are elected at the annual general meeting. The rules for the creation and operation of proxies are quite strict because of the potential for abuse.[55] For example, for federal corporations, proxies (with some exceptions) cannot be solicited except by a circular in a form prescribed by regulation.[56] A proxy holder who fails to comply with the directions of the shareholder is liable to a fine of up to $5000 and/or imprisonment for up to six months.[57]

Proxy can be passed to someone else

The bylaws or articles set out how many votes each shareholder is entitled to, but this may vary with the type of shares held. Holders of **common shares** are usually entitled to one vote per share. **Preferred shareholders** usually cannot vote, unless the promised dividend has not been paid. A shareholder holding a significant portion of the shares can usually force the calling of an extra meeting,[58] while someone with fewer shares, if she has good reason, can apply to the court for the same purpose.[59] However, the majority shareholder is still protected, as a majority vote or greater is necessary to decide all matters once the meeting is held.

In many jurisdictions, shareholders have the right not to have their proportion of shares diluted by the sale of more shares to others. If there are 1000 shares outstanding and Pantaz has 500 of them, he owns 50 percent of the corporation. If the directors decide to issue 500 new shares and none are offered to Pantaz, his interest will be reduced to a one-third portion. In smaller corporations, this is usually avoided by including, in a separate shareholders' agreement, a provision requiring that a sufficient number of the new shares be offered to the existing shareholders first so that they may retain their proportionate share of the corporation. Such a right is called a *pre-emptive right*. In most jurisdictions in Canada, pre-emptive rights exist only when actually granted in the incorporating documents or shareholders' agreements.[60]

Pre-emptive rights entitle shareholder to be offered any new shares first

---

54. Most of the requirements regarding annual general meetings are set out in Part XII of the *Canada Business Corporations Act, ibid.* But see also s. 106 (3), requiring the election of directors by shareholders at the annual general meeting of the shareholders, and Part XV, dealing with fundamental changes, which must be approved by special resolution of the shareholders (i.e., by at least two-thirds of the votes cast). It should be noted that the amendments to the federal legislation in 2001 resulted in many changes to the rules governing annual general meetings. In particular, shareholder meetings for federal corporations may now be held by electronic means, and voting may be carried out by using telephonic or electronic communications facilities—see ss. 132 and 141.

55. The rules relating to proxies are set out in Part XIII of the *Canada Business Corporations Act, ibid.*

56. *Ibid.*, s. 150.

57. *Ibid.*, s. 152(4).

58. *Ibid.*; s. 143 states that the holders of not less than 5 percent of the issued shares may cause a meeting to be called.

59. *Ibid.*, s. 144.

60. *Ibid.*, s. 28.

CASE SUMMARY 12.9

Do Shareholders Owe a Fiduciary Duty to Anybody?
Agrium Inc. v. Hamilton[61]

Hamilton and Drever each held 50 percent of the shares of Flagstaff Fertilizers Ltd. They each sold 15 percent of the shares to Cominco Fertilizer Ltd. Hamilton, Drever, Flagstaff, and Cominco entered into a unanimous shareholders' agreement that included confidentiality provisions, requiring Hamilton and Drever not to disclose Flagstaff's confidential information, or to use it for any purpose. Hamilton entered into an employment contract with Flagstaff that included similar provisions. Besides Hamilton and Drever, the third director of Flagstaff was to be a representative of Cominco.

Drever left Flagstaff and a corporation wholly owned by Hamilton bought his shares. Spurrill became a director of Flagstaff and bought 5 percent of its shares from Hamilton. Stephens bought 9 percent of Hamilton's shares. Agrium was the successor to Cominco.

Hamilton advised Agrium that he wished to repurchase the shares of Flagstaff owned by Agrium. Negotiations were ongoing. Hamilton met with Coulman, the Agrium nominated director, and Yokley, vice-president of Agrium. He indicated that he wanted to buy Agrium's shares so that he could operate Flagstaff on his own. He said he had no intention of selling the corporation.

AgPro contacted Coulman about purchasing Flagstaff. Coulman referred AgPro to Hamilton. Flagstaff and AgPro entered into a confidentiality agreement, and Flagstaff disclosed confidential information to AgPro.

Hamilton then had discussions with United Grain Growers relating to a possible purchase of Flagstaff. Hamilton said at trial that he was not interested in selling Flagstaff to UGG at that time. Hamilton did enter into a confidentiality agreement with UGG and did provide it with confidential information about Flagstaff.

No one at Agrium was advised that Flagstaff had entered into confidentiality agreements with AgPro or UGG, or that Hamilton was considering selling the shares of Flagstaff to them. Agrium said that if it had known that there were parties interested in buying Flagstaff, it would not have sold its shares to Hamilton. The deal doing so closed on 31 December 1997. Hamilton said he was not serious about selling Flagstaff until 6 January 1998, when Agrium advised him that it was not going to continue Flagstaff's preferred status. Hamilton then became concerned about the profitability of Flagstaff.

The Court held that Hamilton, as a director and majority shareholder of Flagstaff, was not in a fiduciary relationship with Agrium, a minority shareholder. Agrium was very sophisticated and was aware that AgPro was interested in purchasing Flagstaff. Hamilton had not relinquished his self interest to that of Agrium's interest, and so there was no fiduciary relationship.

The Court also ruled that the knowledge that AgPro and UGG were interested in purchasing Flagstaff was not "specific confidential information." Hamilton was therefore not liable for insider trading. He was also not liable for fraudulent misrepresentation, as the statements he made were correct when he made them.

Agrium did succeed, however, on the basis that Hamilton's actions did constitute oppressive conduct, as he unfairly disregarded the interests of Agrium as a minority shareholder. It was reasonable for Agrium to expect that Hamilton would advise it if he was seriously considering selling Flagstaff. Agrium would expect that Hamilton would not

---

[61.] 2005 AB Q.B. 54, 44 Alta. L.R. (4th) 177.

be divulging confidential information about Flagstaff and that Agrium's director representative would be advised of the signing of confidentiality agreements. Hamilton treated Agrium differently than the other shareholders, as they were advised of what was going on. Hamilton's actions were therefore oppressive of Agrium. He was ordered to pay damages of $1.2 million, plus interest and costs, to Agrium.

DISCUSSION QUESTIONS

Should a shareholder owe a fiduciary obligation to the corporation or to other shareholders? What if she is a major shareholder?

These shareholder rights may seem significant, but to a minority shareholder such power may be an illusion. In large corporations, with great numbers of shares distributed, an individual shareholder's rights may be considerably diluted, and the only practical recourse may be to sell the shares. In small, closely held corporations, there is usually a restriction on the sale of shares. The "locked-in" shareholder may be unable to sell those shares and unable to influence the course of the corporation because of the overriding control exercised by the majority shareholder.

> Weak position of minority shareholders

SHAREHOLDER PROTECTIONS

To protect the shareholder from abuse in these circumstances, the statutes have provided several safeguards. The most important of these is the shareholder's right to sue the directors on behalf of the corporation when the directors have done something actionable. The right to a derivative, or representative, action exists in British Columbia, Nova Scotia, and those jurisdictions that use the articles of incorporation method of incorporation.[62]

To succeed in a derivative action, a shareholder must show that it is in the interests of the corporation that the action be brought. In the *Richardson Greenshields* case in Case Summary 12.8, the directors used a technicality to thwart the rights of the preferred shareholders to their detriment and that of the corporation. Richardson Greenshields, as a shareholder, was seeking permission of the Court to bring an action on behalf of the corporation against those directors who were unwilling to bring an action against themselves.[63]

> Derivative or representative action

In certain circumstances, the shareholder might be able to bring an **oppression action**. Under the federal legislation, current (or past) shareholders, directors, and officers, along with any other person (including a creditor) who, in the discretion of the court, is a proper person, may seek relief from the court on the basis of oppression or unfair prejudice.[64] For an example of an oppression action, the directors might arrange for the sale of shares just to weaken the voting position of a particular shareholder or, if the shareholder is also an employee, the directors might fire the shareholder to force the sale of the shares. (An oppression action was the basis of success in Case Summary 12.9.) In some jurisdictions, "complainants" have the right to go to court to seek an order for relief from

> Shareholders have right to relief from oppression

---

62. See, for example, *Canada Business Corporations Act, supra* note 7, s. 239.

63. See *McAskill v. TransAtlantic Petroleum Corp., (2002)*, 2002 AB Q.B. 1101, 332 A.R. 96, for a recent judicial review of the case law on derivative actions.

64. *Canada Business Corporations Act, supra* note 7, s. 238.

oppression if this type of abuse has taken place. The court may then make any order it thinks fit, including granting a restraining order, appointing a receiver or receiver-manager, appointing new directors, ordering compensation, or ordering liquidation or dissolution of the corporation.[65] The oppression action is becoming more common, due to the wide discretion it allows the courts in granting remedies to complainants.[66]

CASE SUMMARY 12.10

Oppression Remedy Available to Creditors as Well: *Piller Sausages & Delicatessens Limited v. Cobb International Corp.*[67]

Piller ordered a sterilizing machine from Cobb, which was never delivered. Piller had paid full price and sued when it was not delivered, obtaining judgment for $75 000 against Cobb. This was never paid. Kenneth Cobb, the sole shareholder and officer of Cobb, stripped the assets from Cobb by declaring dividends to another corporation of which he was sole shareholder, by having the corporation pay a management bonus directly to him, and by selling assets to a third corporation of which he was also the sole shareholder, without full payment. There was nothing left to satisfy the judgment. Piller brought this application for oppression against Mr. Cobb.

The Court held that this was an appropriate case for an oppression remedy. Oppression can take place when money is paid for an item that is not delivered and the money is not returned, when dividends are paid or shares redeemed when a corporation cannot pay its liabilities, or when the owner of a corporation diverts money from the corporation to himself, leaving the corporation without sufficient assets to meet its liabilities. Mr. Cobb had diverted assets for his personal benefit, stripping them from Cobb so that it couldn't pay the judgment. The Court found that this amounted to oppression against a creditor. It ordered Mr. Cobb to pay Piller $109 721 plus interest. The Court also said that for oppression to be present, it was not required that Mr. Cobb intend to divert the assets and leave the corporation in a position such that it could not pay the creditor, only that that was the effect.

DISCUSSION QUESTIONS

Do you agree with this outcome? Should a creditor be allowed to bring an oppression action? What if the object of transferring assets or paying other debts is to keep the corporation financially viable? Does the threat of an oppression action unduly fetter a corporation's ability to maneuver and deal with difficult financial situations?

Dissent provisions provide relief for shareholders

Sometimes, a minority shareholder is adversely affected by a decision that is beneficial to the corporation as a whole. In the past, there was no recourse. In many jurisdictions, however, the injured minority shareholder now has the right

---

[65] *Ibid.*, s. 241.

[66] For a case in which a creditor successfully used the oppression remedy, see *Bird v. Mitchell*, (2002), 30 B.L.R. (3d) 107 (Ont. S.C.J.). An employee was granted judgment using the oppression remedy in *Downtown Eatery (1993) Ltd. v. Ontario* (2001), 54 O.R. (3d) 161 (C.A.), leave to appeal refused, [2001] S.C.C.A. No. 397.

[67] (2003) 35 B.L.R. (3d) 193 (Ont. S.C.J.).

to **dissent and ask that her shares be sold**.[68] Such a procedure can be triggered when fundamental changes to the corporation adversely affect the shareholder. The **dissent and appraisal** remedy requires that an appraisal take place and the shareholder's shares be purchased by the corporation, at a fair price.

CASE SUMMARY 12.11

When Can Minority Shareholders Force the Corporation to Buy Back Their Shares? *Re 85956 Holdings Ltd. and Fayerman Brothers Ltd.*[69]

For several years, Sidney and Joseph Fayerman operated a merchandising business through Fayerman Brothers Ltd. Because of increased competition and the brothers' failing health, it was decided by the directors, and approved by the majority shareholders, not to purchase any more inventory but to simply sell off what the corporation had. The minority shareholders opposed this.

When the decision was made to continue the sell-off without replacing inventory, the minority shareholders asked that their shares be purchased at a fair value. The request was refused. This action was brought to force the share purchase at a fair price on the basis that the minority shareholders were dissenting. The Saskatchewan legislation, like many incorporation statutes, had a provision that when "a sale, lease, or exchange of all or substantially all the property of a corporation other than in the ordinary course of business of the corporation" takes place and a shareholder does not approve such a sale, the dissenting shareholder can force the purchase of his shares at a fair price. The problem in this case was whether the choice not to replace the inventory changed this from being a sale done in the ordinary course of business, thus triggering the dissent provision.

The Court held that a sale in the ordinary course of business required the replenishing of the inventory. Not to do so amounted to a sale of all, or substantially all, the assets of the corporation, and the dissent provisions were triggered. The Court found that the corporation was required to buy out the minority shareholders, paying a fair market price for the shares.

This case illustrates how the dissent provision works and under what circumstances a minority shareholder is entitled to this protection. It is interesting to note that the corporation retained its real estate holdings. Still, this was considered a liquidation of the assets of the corporation, and the minority shareholders were entitled to have their shares purchased by the corporation.

SMALL BUSINESS PERSPECTIVE

It is clear by the nature of the corporation that the majority shareholder has control. Do this right to dissent, and the right to bring an oppression action as discussed above, go too far in weakening this control and pandering to the position of minority shareholders who should have know the risks when they acquired their shares in the first place? Should majority shareholders restrict the sale of shares to others to maintain their control?

---

[68] See, for example, *Canada Business Corporations Act, supra* note 7, s. 190. This is a very significant shareholder power, but it is available only in limited circumstances, such as when a decision is being made to amend the articles of incorporation to restrict the issue or transfer of shares, or to restrict the type of business the corporation can carry on. It is also available when amalgamation with another corporation is involved, or when a significant portion of the assets of a corporation is going to be sold or leased.

[69] (1986), 25 D.L.R. (4th) 119 (Sask. C.A.).

DIVIDENDS

Shareholders have no legal right to force the payment of a dividend, although they can require payment if one has been declared by the directors. Their recourse is political; if the directors fail to declare a dividend when the shareholders expect one, they are likely to be voted out at the next shareholders' meeting. The shareholders, however, cannot go to court and sue for a dividend even when preferred shares, with the commitment to pay a specific dividend each year, are involved. Such preferred shareholders can force payment before any dividend is paid to the common shareholders (including, when the right is cumulative, the payment of any prior unpaid dividends). The rights associated with the shareholders' position are rights of control, information, and protection, but there is no corresponding right to a specific return on the funds invested. Many provisions are in place to protect the position of shareholders, but it is important to balance these rights against some important drawbacks. In rare circumstances, a shareholder may have the right to sue for oppression when there is an expectation of a regular income flow through dividends and that income flow is stopped.[70]

> **Shareholders have no right to dividends**

REDUCING RISK 12.4

Small, closely held corporations whose shareholders are also directors and managers of the corporation are often little more than incorporated partnerships. Often, the individuals will also be full-time employees of the corporation. When these individuals have a falling out, the problems can go far beyond what can be remedied, or even what has been anticipated in the legislation. An individual shareholder may lose not only her job as director and manager, but also her full-time employment, and she may not be able to sell her shares. In such circumstances, the importance of a properly drawn up *shareholder agreement* cannot be overemphasized. Such an agreement should include a provision whereby one shareholder must buy out the other if these types of events or other forms of dissatisfaction occur. Provisions relating to employment are often included in such agreements as well. Shareholder agreements are very important. They can be used to set out many important obligations between the parties, much as a partnership agreement does in a partnership relationship. Case Summary 12.12 illustrates the importance of a shareholders' agreement.

For an illustration of the concept of the corporate structure, see Figure 12.3.

Figure 12.3 Corporate Structure

Shareholders	Elect →	Board of Directors	Appoint →	Officers
• possibly subject to a shareholders' agreement • few obligations owed by shareholders to Corporation • liability limited to amount invested • many rights and remedies, but no right to be paid dividends		• responsible for management of Corporation • directors owe duties to Corporation, including fiduciary duty • personal liability if duties breached • due diligence is sometimes a defence		• appointed by Board of Directors to run the business • owe duties to Corporation, including fiduciary duty • personal liability if duties breached • due diligence is sometimes a defence

---

70. *Sutherland v. Birks* (2003), 65 O.R. (3d) 812; (2003), 174 O.A.C. 29 (Ont. C.A.). Note that the remedy in this case was the forced purchase of the shares of the minority shareholder by the corporation.

Shareholder Agreement Overrides Other Alternatives: *T.J. Whitty Investments Corp. v. TAGR Management Ltd.*[71]

Though the case is more complicated than stated here, essentially Whitty and Kinsman were shareholders of a corporation (TAGR) incorporated for the purposes of investment and the management of a family restaurant. Whitty went bankrupt and had to resign as a director of TAGR. In this action, he was bringing an application for an oppression remedy against Kinsman, whom he claimed had taken complete control of the family restaurant. The Court rejected his application, holding that a provision of the shareholders' agreement required such disputes to be arbitrated, not litigated.

There was a similar result in *Bird v. Marovino*,[72] in which a dispute arose between the parties with respect to one shareholder's right to purchase the shares of the other. Again, the application for an oppression remedy was refused because the shareholders' agreement required such disputes to be arbitrated. The shareholders' agreement provided a right of one shareholder to purchase the shares of another after they were independently evaluated. The claim of the applicant, Bird, was that the shares were undervalued because of the actions of the other party. Still, the Court held that the dispute resolution requirements in the shareholders' agreement prevailed and the matter had to be arbitrated rather than litigated.

SMALL BUSINESS PERSPECTIVE

Shareholders' agreements are very important for all corporations, including small, closely held corporations. In light of that, should the members of a family involved in an incorporation of the family business prepare a shareholders' agreement? If they do, is it necessary that each participant retain his or her own lawyer?

PROS AND CONS OF INCORPORATION

Advantages

There are several advantages associated with incorporation, most of which are derived from the concept of the separate legal personality of the corporation.

LIMITED LIABILITY

As illustrated in the *Salomon* case described in Case Summary 12.1, shareholders are not liable for the debts and other obligations of the corporation because the corporation, as a separate legal person, is responsible for its own wrongful conduct. When the corporation's assets are not enough to pay the unsatisfied creditors, they cannot turn to its shareholders for the difference. Shareholders can lose only what they have invested.

Liability of shareholder limited to investment

[71.] (2004), 47 B.L.R. (3d) 311 (Ont. S.C.J.).

[72.] 2005 CanLII 8682 (Ont. S.C.J.).

CASE SUMMARY 12.13

Is a Subsidiary Corporation a Separate Person? *Meditrust Healthcare Inc. v. Shoppers Drug Mart*[73]

Meditrust was a holding company that owned shares in several subsidiaries that were involved in selling prescription drugs through the mail. Meditrust alleged that Shoppers and other defendants were involved in a conspiracy to destroy Meditrust's mail-order prescription business and claimed substantial damages as a result.

The trial Court dismissed the claim of conspiracy on the basis that the holding company, which was a shareholder only, could not bring such a claim in its own right. The damages were suffered only by the subsidiary companies that were carrying on the business that the alleged conspiracy was intended to destroy. That decision was appealed. The Court of Appeal decided that Meditrust itself could claim compensation only for the damages it suffered (such as a loss of goodwill), and not for any damages suffered by the subsidiaries.

DISCUSSION QUESTIONS

The case emphasizes the separation between the shareholder and the corporation; a holding company is separate from its subsidiaries. Does this take the idea of separate legal entity too far?

Limited liability lost when guarantee given

This limited liability, although attractive and often the primary reason for choosing to incorporate, is often only an illusion. When dealing with a closely held corporation, banks and other major creditors will usually insist on a **personal guarantee** from the major shareholders or other principals, which effectively eliminates any advantage of limited liability for those asked to sign such a guarantee.

Liability of shareholder limited to investment

Still, limited liability will protect shareholders from unexpected corporate obligations, such as vicarious liability for torts committed by employees, or the failure to properly perform contractual obligations. Also, suppliers of materials usually do not obtain any personal commitment from shareholders, so they cannot seek compensation from them if the corporation becomes insolvent. For example, if a person operating a grocery business incorporates a corporation and borrows money from the bank for business purposes, that bank will probably insist on a personal guarantee from the shareholder. A supplier of groceries, however, would normally have no such personal commitment. If the corporation becomes insolvent, the shareholder will have to pay the bank because of the personal guarantee, but the shareholder will not be obligated to the supplier, who must look to the corporation for payment. This is because the contract for the goods supplied was with the corporation, rather than with the shareholder. If an employee of the corporation negligently injured a pedestrian while delivering groceries, the corporation would be vicariously liable for that injury, not the shareholder.

In rare cases, court will lift the corporate veil

Even this amount of limited liability is not certain. As the *Parkland* case discussed in Case Summary 12.2 illustrates, in rare cases the courts are willing to look behind the corporate veil and hold the principals liable for the obligations of the

---

73. (2001), 15 B.L.R. (3d) 221 (Ont. S.C.J.), aff'd (2002), 28 B.L.R. (3d) 163 (C.A.).

corporation. This is especially true when there is any taint of wrongdoing or avoidance of obligations that ought to be honoured.

TAXES

Although tax reforms have done away with many of the differences between the federal income taxes paid by sole proprietors, partners, and corporations, because the system is so complex, there still may be advantages available to the individual taxpayer through incorporation. At the very least, the shareholder can leave the funds in the corporation and use it as a vehicle of investment, thus deferring some taxes until a later date.[74] In addition, as many provinces have not followed the federal lead, there may still be significant provincial tax advantages to be gained through incorporation.

Tax advantages gained through incorporation

However, federal and provincial income tax laws are extremely complicated. It is possible that incorporation will backfire and that the process will lead to more income tax being payable rather than less. When losses are experienced, as is normally the case with a new business, the taxpayer is better off if the business is not incorporated so that these losses can be applied directly against personal income. Great care must be exercised in the process of tax planning for any business, and a prudent businessperson will seek expert advice in these circumstances.

SUCCESSION AND TRANSFERABILITY

Because a corporation is a separate legal entity and a mythical person, it does not die unless some specific steps are taken to end its existence. When a partner dies, the partnership will usually come to an end. The death of even a 100-percent shareholder will not affect the existence of the corporation, although the loss may have practical implications, especially when the shareholder is involved in the ongoing operation of the business. The share is simply an asset in the hands of the shareholder. Like any other asset, it therefore forms part of the deceased's estate and, in most cases, is simply distributed to the heirs.

Corporation does not die

Thus, when two people hold 50 percent each of the shares of a corporation and they are killed in an air crash, the corporation continues, and the shares would form part of the estates of the deceased. The heirs, therefore, would normally become the new shareholders. If the two people were carrying on business as partners, however, the partnership would automatically be dissolved.

When a partner leaves a partnership, the process is complex, often requiring the dissolution of the partnership. Shares in a corporation, however, usually can be transferred at will, without reference either to the other shareholders or to the corporate body. This free transferability of shares is one of the attractive features that led to the creation of the corporate entity in the first place. It provides an effective method for the contributors of capital to restrict their relationship with the corporation. When closely held corporations, which often have the same kinds of relationships as partnerships, are involved, this free transferability of shares is significantly restricted.

It is often said that a corporation cannot die, but actually there are several things that can cause a corporation to be dissolved.[75] The ultimate end for a

But can be dissolved

---

[74]. See Tim Kirby, "Tax Law: To Incorporate or Not to Incorporate, That is the Question" *LawNow* (September/October 2006).

[75]. See Part XVIII of the *Canada Business Corporations Act, supra* note 7, for the legislative provisions relating to the liquidation and dissolution of federal corporations.

corporation going through the bankruptcy process is dissolution by operation of law. Minority shareholders or creditors can bring an application to the court to have a corporation dissolved because of oppression or some other inappropriate conduct by the other shareholders or directors. The shareholders themselves can vote to bring the corporation to an end when they feel it is appropriate, filing articles of dissolution, or a statement of intent to dissolve, at the appropriate registry office. But the most common way is for the corporation simply to fail to file the required annual returns. After a year, the corporation will be considered inactive and removed from the registry. Such corporations can later be revived, or restored, by filing the missing returns, along with articles of revival and any other required documentation.

OBLIGATIONS OF THE PARTICIPANTS

No duty on shareholder in a corporation

Unlike partners, shareholders are generally free of any obligations or duties to the corporation or other shareholders. There is no fiduciary duty to act in the best interests of the corporation, or even to refrain from carrying on business in competition with the corporation.

The extent of this freedom of action can be illustrated by the activities of some environmental groups. They acquire a few shares in the large corporations they consider a threat to the environment, with the express purpose of using the special privileges available to shareholders (such as rights to information and to attend shareholders' meetings) in the battle against the polluting corporation. Even when the interests of the environmental group are diametrically opposed to, and interfere with, the profit-making ventures of the corporation and other shareholders, there is no obligation to act otherwise. Only when people acquire sufficient shares to be classed as insiders, or become directors or officers, or when an individual has a majority of the shares, are certain restrictions placed on shareholders' activities. These restrictions usually take the form of rules that prevent the shareholders from abusing their positions of power within the corporation and causing injury to other investors, usually through the misuse of information not available to the general public.

MANAGEMENT

Managers and shareholders separate

In a sole proprietorship, the business is controlled by the proprietor; in a partnership, each partner is entitled to participate in the business decisions of the partnership; in a corporation, however, it is common to separate the managers from the owners. The shareholders elect a board of directors that controls the business. The directors, in turn, can hire professional managers who have the expertise to make sound business decisions on behalf of the corporation. The shareholders do not have to devote time or attention to managing, but they can change the management, if they are unhappy with the decisions being made, by electing different people to the board of directors.

Disadvantages

A corporation is not always the best method of carrying on business. Many of the characteristics outlined above as advantages can just as easily be seen as drawbacks from another person's perspective.

It is helpful to compare incorporation with partnership to illustrate some of the disadvantages of incorporation. Partners who wish to change important aspects of their partnership arrangement need only reach an agreement to that effect. In the case of a corporation, however, the incorporating documents themselves may have to be altered, which is an involved and expensive procedure. A partner in a minority position may have considerable power. In a partnership, one partner can veto a proposal supported by 10 others. A minority shareholder in a corporation may be unable to alter unsatisfactory decisions and may not even be able to sell her shares.

Weak position of minority shareholders in corporations

 REDUCING RISK 12.5

Businesspeople usually assume that the best way for them to carry on their business is through incorporation. While that may in fact be the case, consideration should also be given to the alternatives. Sole proprietorship and partnership are the only real alternatives discussed in this text, although if the enterprise is not for profit or does not involve an ongoing business, there are other possibilities. For example, societies are used for non-profit activities, such as charities, clubs, and religious organizations, and when property is shared, cooperatives and joint tenancy arrangements might be appropriate alternatives.

Even the choice between partnership and incorporation is not always clear. The unlimited liability of a sole proprietorship or partnership can be overcome by appropriate insurance. The tax advantages of incorporation have, to a large extent, been eliminated, or extended to sole proprietorships and partnerships as well. The unique power of a single partner to veto the decisions of the other partners can be built into a corporation by a carefully drawn shareholder agreement. Many of the disadvantages that professionals experience because they are required to carry on their profession as partners can be overcome by creating a management corporation to manage the practice, or by creating a limited liability partnership.

The point is that there are many different options and many different combinations available to a businessperson when structuring the tools used to carry on the business. Expert advice should be sought and careful consideration given to the options earlier, rather than later, in the process.

In closely held corporations, the free transferability of shares is restricted, either through shareholder agreements or by limitations placed in the incorporating documents themselves. Often, shareholders are required to get approval of a sale of their shares, or offer their shares first to the other shareholders. As with partnerships, the reason people organize themselves into small, closely held corporations is often because of the individual skills each shareholder brings to the corporation. These shareholders are usually employees as well, and their contribution to the operation of the business is often vital to its success. Free transferability of shares in such circumstances might be a significant threat to the corporation, especially if the shareholder withdraws her services when the shares are sold.

A corporation is the most expensive way to operate a business. The initial incorporation process is costly, and the ongoing operation of a corporation involves more expense than that of sole proprietorships and partnerships. There are more formal record-keeping requirements and generally more government control exercised with a corporation.

Corporations more expensive than other forms of business

It is important to note as well that there are many variations on the corporate approach to business. Often, corporations are set up to merely hold shares in other corporations. Corporations may join other corporations or individuals in joint ventures or partnerships, usually for some major project or activity. Corporations may license others to use their products, software, or other forms of intellectual property, such as patents or copyrighted materials.

Corporation can be used to create a variety of business structures

It is also common to see small business enterprises that are part of a larger organization through franchising—business arrangements based on contracts of service and the supply of products between the larger and the smaller units. Fast-food restaurant chains are often set up this way. Many difficulties can arise in such relationships, and the changing nature of contract law and corporate responsibility is softening the normally narrow approach to these businesses. For example, statutes imposing good-faith requirements into business contracts put franchisees in a much more favourable position than they have formerly been.[76]

These statutes also impose consumer protection-like requirements on the franchisors. For example, when appropriate disclosure documents are not supplied to the franchisee within a stated period of time, that franchisee is entitled to rescind the contract with the return of any deposit paid.[77]

TERMINATION OF THE CORPORATION

Dissolution may be voluntary or involuntary

Corporations can be dissolved in several ways. Dissolution can take place either voluntarily or involuntarily, and the procedure can be induced internally, by the directors or shareholders, or externally, by the court or by the creditors. The process can be voluntary, by following the winding-up procedure found in the corporate law statutes or, in some jurisdictions, in a separate winding-up act.[78] If the corporation owns sufficient assets, it may be worthwhile to follow this process, but often it is not worth the expense.

Occasionally, a court will order a corporation to be dissolved when a minority shareholder has been unfairly treated. If there are more debts owing to the creditors than the corporation has assets to cover, the common procedure is bankruptcy, and the end result is usually the dissolution of the corporation. Under the current bankruptcy legislation, it is possible for the corporation to make a proposal to the creditors and, if accepted and followed, the corporation will continue.

One of the most common ways for corporations, especially small, closely held corporations, to come to an end is for the principals simply to neglect to file the annual return. A federal corporation must, for example, file an annual return within 60 days after the end of the corporation's taxation year.[79] If it fails to do so, a certificate of dissolution may be issued for it, one year later.[80]

---

[76] Alberta (*Franchises Act*, R.S.A. 2000, c. F-23) and Ontario (*Arthur Wishart Act (Franchise Disclosure), 2000*, S.O. 2000, c. 3) have enacted legislation governing franchising.

[77] See, for example, *Franchises Act, ibid.*, s. 13, and *Arthur Wishart Act (Franchise Disclosure), ibid.*, s. 6. For a relevant article, see Ben V. Hanuka, "When Can Prospective Franchisee Get a Refund?" *Lawyers Weekly* 23, No. 21, 3 October 2003.

[78] The liquidation and dissolution of federal corporations are dealt with in Part XVIII of the *Canada Business Corporations Act, supra* note 7.

[79] *Canada Business Corporations Act Regulations, 2001*, S.O.R./2001–512, s. 5.

[80] *Canada Business Corporations Act, supra* note 7, s. 212.

CASE SUMMARY 12.14

Does It Matter If a Corporation Is Dissolved? *602533 Ontario Inc. v. Shell Canada Ltd.*[81]

602533 made a claim against Shell with respect to the installation of allegedly defective underground tanks. The plaintiff was seeking damages "for breach of contract, misrepresentation, deceit, breach of warranty and negligent failure to warn and a declaration holding Shell responsible for any environmental damage caused by its conduct." Pangos had been operating the service station in question through the corporation for about five years, when it was discovered that the underground tanks were leaking. The corporation commenced the action against Shell in February 1990.

However, the corporation had been dissolved by operation of law for non-compliance under the *Corporations Tax Act* in 1988. This was unknown to Pangos and was not remedied by reinstating the corporation until 1996. The point made by Shell in its application to dismiss this action was that at the time the statement of claim was issued 602533 did not exist and so it could not have commenced the action. To further complicate matters, the limitation period within which an action against Shell must have been commenced expired before the corporation was revived.

The Court dismissed the action against Shell, and that decision was upheld on appeal. The corporation could not bring an action against Shell when it was dissolved, and although the revival of the corporation restored any rights that the corporation had when it was dissolved, that was subject to any rights that had been acquired by the other party during the dissolution period. The expiration of the limitation period was a right Shell had acquired after the corporation was dissolved and could not be overcome by the corporation's revival in 1996.[82] Note that a similar case in Alberta reached a different conclusion.[83]

The case shows how careful businesspeople must be to make sure they comply with government regulations. In this case, the consequence was dissolution of the corporation. Such a dissolved corporation no longer exists legally and thereby loses the right to bring an action on its own behalf. The case also shows that such a dissolved corporation can be resurrected by following the appropriate procedure, but sometimes even that process may not overcome the consequences of allowing the corporation to become dissolved in the first place.

SMALL BUSINESS PERSPECTIVE

Is this just playing with technicalities? Is the result inconsistent with the purpose of the legislation, which allows the restoration of the corporation by late filing of the appropriate documents? What steps should a businessperson take to ensure that all relevant laws are complied with?

[81.] (1998), 37 O.R. (3d) 504 (C.A.).

[82.] For a case in which an action commenced on behalf of a corporation that had been dissolved was declared a nullity even though the relevant limitation period had not expired, see *M.C.M. Contracting Ltd. v. Canada (Attorney General)*, [2002] Y.J. No. 108 (Y.T. S.C.).

[83.] *Associated Asbestos Services Ltd. v. Canadian Occidental Petroleum Ltd.*, [2003] 2 W.W.R. 680, 28 B.L.R. (3d) 232, (Alta. Q.B.), aff'd [2004] 9 W.W.R. 545, (2004), 43 B.L.R. (3d) 221, 346 A.R. 190, (C.A.).

Selling the shares or selling the assets

Often, when a corporation is to go out of business, a decision must be made whether to sell the shares of the corporation or to sell its assets. If its shares are sold, the corporation continues as before, but with new shareholders. The debts and other obligations continue, but problems may arise if the purchaser decides to make changes in wages and contracts with suppliers. Because the corporation continues, the contracts stay in place and continue to bind the corporation, even with new ownership.

When the corporation's assets are sold, on the other hand, the purchaser is not affected by the contractual or other obligations of the corporation selling those assets, unless those assets are encumbered. If the assets in question have been used to secure a debt, the secured creditor has first claim against the assets. Any purchaser of a business would be well advised to search the title of the assets for such liens and charges before entering into the transaction. As explained in Chapter 16, some provinces have bulk sales statutes in place to protect creditors from the sale of all, or substantially all, the assets of the debtor. Any debts or other obligations that have been incurred by the selling corporation could become liabilities of the purchaser of the assets if it does not pay the proceeds of the sale to the creditors. After the corporation's assets are sold and the corporation no longer has a business, the corporation can be wound up.

The process of distributing the assets upon winding up the corporation is set out in the various statutes and will not be dealt with here. It is important to note, however, that the directors have a considerable obligation not to allow any of the assets of the corporation to get into the hands of the shareholders until the creditors have been satisfied.

SUMMARY

The process of incorporation

- Corporations were created because of the need to finance costly projects
- A corporation is a fiction or a myth that has a separate status as a legal person from its shareholders
- Methods of incorporation in Canada are registration, letters patent, and articles of incorporation

Separate legal entity

- The corporation is a separate legal entity
- Shareholders own the shares of the corporation; the corporation owns the assets it buys
- Sometimes the courts "lift the corporate veil" and find directors or officers liable
- Shareholders are not liable for the debts of a corporation; they have limited liability so can lose only what they have invested
- Corporations have capacity of natural person, except for special statute corporations, whose capacity may be limited

Funding

- Funding may be derived from the selling of shares (which may be common shares or preferred shares with special rights and restrictions), or through borrowing (which can involve the sale of bonds or debentures, secured or unsecured)

- Shareholders are participants in the corporation, while lenders are creditors
- Broadly held corporations (many shareholders) have more stringent government controls and greater reporting requirements than closely held corporations (few shareholders)

Corporate directors, officers, and shareholders

Directors are elected by shareholders to manage the corporation
- Directors owe fiduciary duty and duty to be careful to the corporation
- Directors may be personally liable for decisions they make
- Directors, officers, employees, and the corporation itself may incur criminal liability
- Officers run the affairs of the corporation and owe it a fiduciary duty and a duty of care
- Promoters may be personally liable for pre-incorporation contracts
- Shareholders owe very few duties to the corporation or other shareholders unless they have sufficient shares to be classed as insiders
- Shareholders have significant rights and remedies
- Shareholders do not have a right to sue the directors when they act carelessly or wrongfully in carrying out their duties, as the duty of the directors is owed to the corporation, not to the shareholder
- Shareholders can bring a derivative or representative action against the directors on behalf of the corporation, they can commence an oppression action, or apply for a dissent and appraisal remedy
- Shareholders do not have a right to demand dividends

Pros and cons of incorporation

- There are several advantages, including limited liability, tax benefits, the ease of transferring shares, few ownership obligations, and the separation of ownership and management
- There are several disadvantages, including the cost of incorporating, the difficulty and cost of changing the incorporating documents, the cost of ongoing record-keeping, and the vulnerability of minority shareholders

Termination of the corporation

- Corporation can be dissolved many ways, some voluntary, some involuntary
- The dissolution of a corporation has legal consequences which may not be reversible even if corporation is revived
- The legal effect of selling a corporation's shares is different than that of selling the corporation's assets

---

QUESTIONS

1. What is meant by a corporation's having a separate legal identity?

2. Distinguish among companies and corporations that have been created by special acts of Parliament, by royal charter, by registration, by letters patent, and by filing articles of incorporation.

3. Explain the significance of the memorandum of association in a registration jurisdiction. Contrast it with articles of incorporation and articles of association.

4. What is a "society" and how does it compare to a corporation?

5. Explain how the liability of a shareholder is limited.

6. Explain under what circumstances a court will "lift the corporate veil."

7. What is the capacity of most corporations? What is the exception to this rule?

8. Why are the principles of agency law relevant to corporations?

9. Explain why the concept of a par-value share is misleading and why the use of such shares has declined.

10. What is meant by a "preferred" share? Contrast this with the "common" share. Explain why the term *preferred shares* is misleading.

11. Does a shareholder, whether preferred or common, have a right to a dividend? Explain.

12. What is the significant difference between a bondholder and a preferred shareholder, both of whom are entitled to a specified payment each year?

13. Distinguish between closely held and broadly held corporations and explain the differences in terms of the provisions in place in your jurisdiction.

14. Set out the nature of the duties owed by a director of a corporation. To whom are these duties owed? Who else in the corporate organization owes similar duties?

15. Explain why it is becoming increasingly difficult to get prominent individuals to serve as directors of Canadian corporations.

16. Who is usually responsible for running the affairs of the corporation?

17. How can a promoter avoid personal liability for pre-incorporation contracts?

18. Explain any duties shareholders assume. Summarize the rights of the shareholders in relationship to other shareholders, the management, and the directors of the corporation.

19. Explain what is meant by a "proxy" and why proxies can be so important at a corporation's annual general meeting.

20. Distinguish among a derivative action, dissent, and oppression. Explain when it would be appropriate to use each of them.

21. Explain the purpose of a shareholders' agreement and why it is important.

22. Explain how a personal guarantee reduces the limited liability of the principals of a closely held corporation.

23. Explain the advantages of free transferability of shares and how and why this right is often modified by shareholder agreement.

24. Set out and explain some of the disadvantages associated with the corporate method of carrying on business.

25. How can a corporation be terminated?

CASES AND DISCUSSION QUESTIONS

1. *E.M. Plastics & Electrical Products Ltd. v. Abby Signs Ltd.*, 2009 BCPC 0018.
E.M. sold goods to Abby but was not paid. E.M. sued Abby and Lardeur, "the controlling mind, sole officer, and director" of Abby. Abby did not dispute its liability, but was unable to pay the judgment. Lardeur claimed that E.M.'s contract was with Abby, not him.

Is this a case in which the Court would "pierce the corporate veil"? When would Lardeur be liable for the debts of Abby?

2. *Challenor v. Nucleus Financial Network Inc.*, 2004 CanLII 15949 (Ont. S.C.J.) aff'd 2005 CanLII 1067 (Ont. S.C.D.C.).
Challenor had a contract with, and provided consulting services to, Nucleus, as an independent contractor. She wasn't paid for her services, so she sued Nucleus and Tricaster Holdings Inc., which held the majority of shares in Nucleus. It was clear that Tricaster had provided financial support to Nucleus, acting as its "banker."

Assuming Nucleus does not have any resources, explain any arguments that would support the action against Tricaster and the likely outcome. In your answer, consider whether a partnership has been created between Tricaster and Network. Consider the nature of separate legal entity principle and whether a debtor ought to be able to hide behind it in this way.

3. *Blacklaws v. 470433 Alberta Ltd.*(2000), 7 B.L.R. (3d) 204, [2000] 11 W.W.R. 476, 84 Alta. L.R. (3d) 270, 187 D.L.R. (4th) 614 (C.A.), leave to appeal refused, [2000] S.C.C.A. No. 442, para. 41.
The Blacklaws purchased a timeshare interest in a golf resort operated and financed by Morrow through 470433, a corporation owned and controlled by him. The resort was generally inadequately financed, was poorly operated, and had serious sewage problems, which caused it to be closed down for two summers. The Blacklaws, along with other members, brought a class action suit against 470433 and against Morrow personally. Morrow managed the resort. He knew of the problems and failed to disclose them or provide adequate funds to correct them.

Explain the basis for any cause of action that might exist against Morrow and the likelihood of success.

4. *BCE Inc. v. 1976 Debentureholders*, 2008 SCC 69.
Bell Canada debentureholders opposed a buyout of BCE, a large Canadian telecommunications corporation, by a group headed by the Ontario Teachers Pension Plan Board. The buyout was financed in part by the assumption, by Bell Canada, a wholly owned subsidiary of BCE, of $30 billion of debt. This would reduce the value of the Bell Canada debentures by about 20 percent. The value of the BCE shares would, on the other hand, increase by about 40 percent as a result of the buyout. The debentureholders therefore opposed court approval of the buyout and claimed that they were entitled to relief under the oppression remedy. The Quebec Supreme Court approved the buyout, but the Court of Appeal allowed the debentureholders' appeal, and disallowed the buyout. The case went to the Supreme Court of Canada.

To whom do corporate directors owe a fiduciary duty? What should the directors do if the interests of the corporation and of particular stakeholders do not coincide? What remedies do these stakeholders have if they believe that they have not been treated fairly? Does the law require that business decisions be perfect, or they will be overturned by the courts if subsequent events showed that the decisions were not correct?

5. *Dilorenzo v. Canada*, 2002 FCA 466.

Dilorenzo immigrated to Canada from Italy. He started working in the construction industry at age 16. He had no formal education. He incorporated his business and was the sole director of the corporation. He stated that he had never been involved in the paperwork of the corporation, and that he hired accountants, lawyers, and office workers because of his lack of expertise. The corporation failed to remit GST to the federal government. Dilorenzo argued that he should not be personally liable for the GST, because he had shown due diligence in respect of the payment of the taxes.

Explain whether Dilorenzo should be found personally liable for the corporation's unpaid GST. Do you agree with that result?

6. *Montreal Trust Co. of Canada v. Call-Net Enterprises Inc.* (2002), 57 O.R. (3d) 775 (S.C.J.), aff'd (2004), 70 O.R. (3d) 90, (2003) B.L.R. (3d) 108 (C.A.).

Call-Net was in a proxy battle with one of its dissident shareholders, Crescendo. Call-Net entered into an agreement with its senior executives that said that a change in control would be deemed to have occurred if any person acquired the right to control or direct 35 percent or more of the combined voting power of the corporation in any manner. Crescendo accumulated proxies that, together with the shares it owned, were in excess of 35 percent of the voting shares. The meeting for which the proxies were obtained was not held, and the proxies were therefore not used. Some of the executives claimed that a change of control had occurred. Call-Net claimed that no such change had occurred.

Explain whether the executives were correct in their assertion that a change of control had occurred. Be sure to consider what a proxy is, and the power a proxy gives to the proxy holder. Should shareholders be allowed to give others a proxy to vote their shares?

7. *Salesco Limited v. Lee Paige*, 2007 CanLII 37463, (2007), 61 C.C.E.L. (3d) 279, (2007), 36 B.L.R. (4th) 229 (Ont. S.C.); *Capobianco v. Paige*, 2009 CanLII 29899 (Ont. S.C.)

C and P decided to buy their employer, Spray-Pak, which was owned by M. They used Salesco (of which P was both a director and officer) to do so. Z loaned $20 000 to Salesco. He received 20 percent of the shares in Salesco, while 40 percent of the shares were allocated to P and to C. Salesco obtained two-thirds of the shares of Spray-Pak. M continued to own the other one-third of the shares; he was also a director of the corporation. P was a director and also president of Spray-Pak. He wrote many cheques on Spray-Pak's bank account that benefited him personally, including one for $10 000 as a down payment on a house, and another for the purchase of a Jaguar. P, C, and M agreed that each of them would receive $2300 per week from Spray-Pak, and that Spray-Pak would pay M's personal and legal accounting bills. Spray-Pak experienced financial difficulties, so the payments to M were stopped. P and M then fired C so that the payments to M could resume. M was not providing services to Spray-Pak while C was. There was no just cause for firing C. Meetings of the shareholders and directors of Salesco were called. P, C, and Z were elected as directors. At a later meeting, C, Z, and M were elected as directors. M then started a lawsuit, asking for a declaration that P could not be removed as a director of Salesco and that Spray-Pak be wound up. C counterclaimed, asking for an injunction preventing depletion of Spray-Pak's assets.

P and M misrepresented Spray-Pak's financial situation to the CIBC, and effectively asked it to call in its loan to Spray-Pak, which it did. M incorporated New Spray-Pak and transferred 50 percent of its shares to P. New Spray-Pak acquired the CIBC's security in return for an assignment of Spray-Pak's debt and security. New Spray-Pak continued the business; the customers of Spray-Pak were not advised that they were now doing business with New Spray-Pak. C and Z were not advised of these developments. When they discovered what had happened, they began derivative actions on behalf of Spray-Pak and Salesco, with P, M, and New Spray-Pak as the defendants.

Should the derivative actions succeed? Were the actions of P and M oppressive or unfairly prejudicial? Did they unfairly disregard the interests of C, Z, Salesco, and Spray-Pak? Did P and M breach any fiduciary duties?

8. *Danylchuk v. Wolinsky*2007 MBCA 132, (2007), 37 B.L.R. (4th) 1, (2007), 225 Man. R. (2d) 2.

Danylchuk and other shareholders and creditors of Protos International Inc. ("the Respondents") brought an oppression action against Wolinsky and other directors of Protos ("the Appellants"). The Respondents claimed that the Appellants committed oppression by not having regular shareholders' meetings, by not providing timely financial statements, by using Protos as their personal bank account, by making unauthorized payments of personal expenses, by preferring the interests of some shareholders over the interest of others, and by disregarding the interests of some creditors to the advantage of others. The Appellants admitted the first two claims, but denied the others. They also claimed that they should not be found personally liable. The trial Judge held that the affidavit evidence supported the Respondents' claim that the conduct of the Appellants was oppressive, as it was unfairly prejudicial to, and unfairly disregarded, the interests of shareholders and creditors. The Court of Appeal upheld this ruling.

Given the finding of oppression, what is the appropriate remedy? Should the shareholders be given their original investments in Protos? Should the creditors be given the amount of their loans to Protos? There was no evidence that the oppression caused the failure of Protos.

9. *Robak Industries Ltd. v. Gardner*, 2007 BCCA 61, (2007), 28 B.L.R. (4th) 1.

Lepinski and Robak, his wholly owned holding company, sued the defendants for their wrongful conduct in managing a publicly traded corporation, Getty Copper Incorporated. Their claims included various torts, as well as a breach of fiduciary duty and a breach of duty of care, as Gardner was a director of Getty. Lepinski claimed that Gardner and others seized control of Getty by ousting Lepinski and by conspiring to do several acts, including insider trading, unauthorized withdrawal of funds from Getty, making defamatory statements, and taking steps in bad faith and contrary to the best interests of Getty.

Did the plaintiffs succeed in their claim, which was based on a decrease in value of the shares of Getty, which they owned? When would such an action succeed? What type of action should Lepinski and Robak have taken?

PEARSON
mybuslawlab

Be sure to visit the MyBusLawLab that accompanies this book at **www.pearsoned.ca/mybuslawlab.** You will find practice tests, a personalized study plan, province-specific material, and much more!

Chapter 13

Real, Personal, and Intellectual Property

This chapter focuses upon property rights and how they are protected in Canada. The various types of property, real, personal, and intellectual, are examined.

INTRODUCTION

While people usually think of property as a physical object, such as a boat, car, or land, "property" more correctly refers to the relationship existing between the item and the individual who owns it. When a person says he owns a boat, it is descriptive of the nature of the interest he has in the boat rather than the boat itself. This distinction must be kept in mind as we examine the nature of the different interests in property.

Ownership describes one interest in property

Although ownership or title is the highest form of property right to a particular item, other lesser forms of interest are also possible. In our legal system, ownership or title can be separate from possession. Thus, one person might be in possession of something that belongs to someone else.

Ownership and possession separated

Real property—land and buildings

The term "**real property**" refers to land and things permanently attached to the land, such as buildings. The essential characteristic of real property is that it is fixed and immovable. Personal property, on the other hand, is movable and can be divided into two categories. **Chattels** (or goods) are tangible personal property, consisting of movables that can be measured and weighed. An intangible right is a claim one person has against another, such as a claim for debt, and is called a *chose in action*, which is, in effect, a right to sue. Bonds, share certificates, and negotiable instruments are examples of choses in action.

Chose in action—intangible property

A special category of intangible personal property is now called **intellectual property**. **Copyright** gives an author control over the use and reproduction of his or her work; **patents** give an inventor the right to profit from his or her inventions; **trade-marks** protect the name or logo of a business; **industrial designs** protect the distinctive shape or design of an object; *confidential information* and **trade secrets** are further examples of intellectual property that can be protected contractually or by common law.

Intellectual property deals with ideas and creative work

This chapter will first focus on real property and then on tangible personal property (goods or chattels); it concludes with an examination of intangible personal property, specifically intellectual property.

REAL PROPERTY

Whether shelter is obtained through ownership, rental, or even squatting, the relationships created are governed by real property law. The following examination is necessarily abbreviated, but it will serve as an introduction to certain significant aspects of the law of real property. To understand this body of law, one must first acquaint oneself with unique concepts of ownership, estates in land, and rights to possession. We shall begin by examining interests in land and their transfer, followed by an examination of the landlord and tenant relationship.

Real property is land or anything attached to land

Interests in Land

The term *real property* includes land and anything affixed to it, such as buildings and chattels that are permanently attached. Students are often referred to the "carrot principle," which suggests the surface owner hold rights to everything beneath the surface, down to the center of the earth, as well as the airspace in the cone above that surface. Today, as far as the areas above and below the surface are concerned, only the portion that the owner can permanently use or occupy is now considered part of that property. Even to this space, an owner's rights will probably be restricted by local zoning regulations, which may limit the type or size of building that can be erected as well as the activity that can take place on that land.

Real property owners face restrictions on use

A landowner has no actionable complaint when an airplane flies over the property, but power lines or an overhanging building that permanently incur into this air space would give rise to a right to sue. As for the sub-surface rights, usually the Crown has retained the mineral rights, and the oil and gas rights. Property owners generally have no complaint when these rights are granted to others, and mine shafts or oil wells are developed under their property. In these cases, the property owner is entitled to compensation for surface disturbance, in the form of access roads, shafts, and so on, but not to a share of the profits coming from the minerals, oil, or gas. Mineral, oil, and gas rights are important topics with their own body of law and no attempt will be made to deal with them in this text.

Mineral rights may be separate from surface rights

Estates in Land

The current law of real property is rooted in the ancient feudal system of England, in which people held rather than owned their land. The king actually owned the land; the right to possession of it, called an **estate in land**, was granted on the basis of some obligation of service to the king. The original estates in land, which were numerous and based on the type of obligation owed to the king, have been reduced to a few significant types, known today as *estates in fee simple, life estates,* and *leasehold estates.*

FEE SIMPLE

Fee simple comparable with ownership

The greatest interest a person can have in land today (and what we think of as ownership) is an estate in **fee simple**. Although the Crown, federal or provincial, technically still owns the land, a fee simple estate gives the holder an infinite right to use the land or sell it, subject only to restrictions imposed by agreement or legislation. The "owner" of land is subject to government and municipal regulations with respect to what the property can be used for. The nature and description of the buildings that can be erected on it, and the health, sanitary, and appearance standards to be maintained, may also be prescribed. The property may even be expropriated under certain circumstances.

LIFE ESTATE

Life estate divides fee simple

Whereas a fee simple estate can be inherited, a **life estate** is more restrictive and cannot be willed to others. Both types of estate give exclusive possession of the property to the holder, but upon the death of the life tenant, the property reverts back to the original owner of the fee simple or that owner's heirs. This right to take back the property or **reversionary interest** may be transferred to a third party, who is then called the **remainderman**. The remainderman holds the right to the remainder of the fee simple after the death of the life tenant. Life estates are not particularly common in Canada and are usually used to ensure that some member of the family, such as a widow, is cared for to the end of her life. The holder of a life estate has special responsibilities and must pay for normal upkeep, pay fees and taxes, and not commit "waste"—that is, not do anything to harm the value of the reversionary interest, such as cut down trees or damage the house. The uncertainty associated with the life estate, and the difficulty in selling or otherwise dealing with the land in question, may make a life estate unattractive from a business point of view. Recently, however, life estates have been used to market accommodation for seniors.

Dower and homestead rights protect spouse

In many provinces, interests similar to life estates are created through the operation of law. **Dower rights** were intended to protect women who lost any individual claim to property when they married. Dower provided the wife a one-third interest in the husband's land as a matter of right, but this also interfered with the free transferability of property. Dower rights were also lost when the couple divorced. Because of these and other problems, dower rights have been modified or replaced by other statutory protections.[1] Today, these claims are protected in most provinces by **homestead rights**[2] or in family law statutes that give the spouse a claim to a substantial portion of all family assets in the case of marriage

---

1. *Dower Act*, R.S.A 2000, c. D-15.

2. *Homesteads Act, 1989*, S.S. 1989–90, c. H-5.1.

breakdown.[3] These family law considerations are beyond the scope of this text but can have a significant impact on property rights.

LEASEHOLD ESTATES

Fee simple estates and life estates are described as freehold estates because a person has exclusive possession of the property for an indeterminate time. **Leasehold estates** or leases are limited to a specific period of time, after which the property reverts back to the landowner. These leases may be short- or long-term (99 years) or may take the form of a periodic tenancy. With a periodic tenancy, there is no definite termination date; rather, the term is for some recurring unit of time (for example, month-to-month) that continues to be renewed until terminated by notice. For example, a person may rent an apartment on a month-to-month basis. The tenancy arrangement continues until the landlord or tenant notifies the other that it is to end. (Landlord and tenant law and will be discussed in a separate section of this chapter.)

Leasehold estates
determined by time

But may also be periodic

Lesser Interests in Land

Unlike freehold and leasehold, there are several lesser interests in land that do not convey the right to exclusive possession of the property. An **easement** gives a person the right to use a portion of another's land, usually for a particular purpose. The **right of way** is one of the most common forms of easement that allows people to cross another's land, usually to get to their own property or to reach another point of interest, such as a lake or the sea. The owner of the property cannot interfere with the right of the holder of an easement to cross his property, but it should also be noted that the person with the right of way cannot stop, park his car, or build some permanent structure on the property. The property that has the advantage of the right of way is called the **dominant tenement**, and the property subject to it is called the **servient tenement**. Another form of easement involves a permanent incursion onto the property, where, for example, someone has been given permission to have part of a building hang over onto the neighbour's property. **Statutory easements** give utilities or other bodies similar rights to run power lines or sewer lines across private property.

Easement gives right to use
of land—not possession

www.pearsoned.ca/mybuslawlab

BC   AB   SK   MB   ON

Other lesser interests include **licences**, where a person is given permission to use another's land. An example would be the invitation to the public to attend at a shopping mall. Licences can also be created by contract, as when a hotel rents a room for the night, but the rights created are not true interests in the property and do not run with the land.

Must be dominant and
servient tenement

Where use of land continues unabated over a long period of time, this can become a permanent enforceable right (in some provinces) as illustrated in the *Depew v. Wilkes* case described in Case Summary 13.1. Acquiring such a right over property through use is called an **easement acquired by prescription**. To prevent such an easement from arising, the landowner must periodically exercise some control over the portion of land in question, such as blocking off public access from time to time.[4]

Property rights may be
acquired
• by prescription

---

3. *Family Relations Act*, R.S.B.C. 1996, c. 128, s. 56.

4. See *Caldwell v. Elia*, [2000] O.J. No. 661 (C.A.), where the plaintiff made use of a gravel road, openly, for more than 20 years to access his cottage. The fact that another possible route existed was deemed irrelevant. The plaintiff had acquired a right to use it by prescription; thus the road could not now be closed off.

CASE SUMMARY 13.1

Rights Can Be Obtained by Use: *Depew v. Wilkes*[5]

The appellants, the Wilkeses, owners of cottages at Lake Erie, used a strip of land running between their respective properties and the beachfront for parking, a pier, and a water supply. The strip (Lot 13) was owned by the respondents, the Depews. Over the years, the appellants erected a number of structures on Lot 13 (including a pier, concrete high-water barriers, and a well) with permission from the owners. They also parked their cars on Lot 13 in front of their respective cottages. After decades of such uninterrupted use, further use was abruptly denied. The appellants claimed that they had acquired possessory title to parts of Lot 13 by way of adverse possession; alternatively, they claimed easements now gave them a right of use.

The claim of adverse possession failed. A claimant to possessory title "must have throughout the statutory period [10 years]: a) Actual possession; b) The intention of excluding the true owner from possession, and; c) To have effectively excluded the true owner from possession."[6] Here the owners were never excluded from using the roadway or pier.

On the other hand, prescriptive easements and easements based on the doctrine of equitable proprietary estoppel were established. For there to be an easement, there must be a dominant and servient tenement each owned by different parties, the easement must accommodate the dominant tenement, and the right over land must have been exercised not less than 20 years. All these requirements were made out; thus easements acquired by prescription (use) were established.

Further, since the respondents knew of their neighbours' making improvements (installing a pier and concrete barriers to protect the beach from erosion, for example) and knew of their expenditures of money year after year, and they acquiesced, the trial Judge found it would be unfair or inequitable to let the Depew family now demand that these improvements be taken down. Through acquiescence for 50 years, the Depews confirmed that approval would be given. Accordingly, easements by reason of equitable proprietary estoppel were deemed fair and were established.

DISCUSSION QUESTIONS

What steps could the Depew family have taken earlier that would have prevented the Court from finding easements by prescription? See the *Schwark* case for suggestions.[7]

• or by adverse possession

A right to actual possession of land can be gained in a similar manner. This is called acquiring possession through **adverse possession** and occurs when someone has had possession of land for a significant number of years in an open and notorious fashion, tolerated by the actual owner. The actual number of years needed varies with the jurisdiction. Several Canadian jurisdictions, specifically those using a land titles system, have abolished both the right to an easement by prescription and the right to acquire land by adverse possession. Refer to the MyBusLawLab for details.

---

5. [2000] O.J. No. 4303 (S.C.J.); appeal allowed as to fees payable (2002) 60 O.R. (3d) 499 (C.A.).

6. Quoted from *Masidon Investments Ltd. v. Ham* (1984), 45 O.R. (2d) 563 (C.A.), at page 567.

7. *Schwark v. Cutting*, [2008] O.J. No. 4997 (Sup. Ct. J.)

CASE SUMMARY 13.2

Mineral Claims—A Right in Property: *British Columbia v. Tener*[8]

Tener's predecessors in title obtained a right to the mineral claims on certain lands in British Columbia in 1937. These lands were later incorporated into a provincial park. The designation of the land as parkland prohibited the development of lands within the park, except where it would benefit the park. Tener, with others, applied for a permit to operate the mineral claims and was refused. They then applied for compensation for expropriation. This required the Supreme Court to determine the nature of the mineral rights that were owned.

The Court found that they were a profit à prendre. The Court decided that this was an interest in land giving them rights to minerals below the land and a right to interfere with the surface of the land as much as needed to extract the minerals. When the permit was denied, this was a form of expropriation for which they were entitled to compensation.

DISCUSSION QUESTIONS

If the mineral claim had been characterized by the courts as a licence, would the remedy have been the same?

Another important right is a *restrictive covenant*. When someone sells land to another, they can place restrictions on the use of that land that will bind all subsequent holders. These restrictive covenants are typically restrictions as to the type of buildings that can be put on the property relating to their height, shape, and style. Restrictive covenants may impose restrictions as to how the property may be used,[9] such as for residential, commercial, or light industrial use, and may even restrict whether children are allowed, (but such a provision may be challenged under human rights law).

> Restrictive covenant may bind future owners

Although these are lesser interests in land, they run with the land, meaning that they are tied to the property itself rather than to the owner of it; accordingly, they bind not only the original purchasers but also bind subsequent owners. They are better viewed as an interest in land rather than as a simple contract; the rule of privity of contract thus does not apply.

For restrictive covenants to bind subsequent owners of the property, they must be expressed as negative rather than positive obligations. Thus, a requirement that no building over three storey be constructed on the property is a negative covenant and will bind future owners. But requiring that a building be built within a certain time period imposes a positive obligation to do something and will bind only the initial purchaser. A **building scheme** involves placing the same restrictive covenants on all the properties in a large development. Building

> To bind future owners these covenants must be negative

---

8. [1985] 1 S.C.R. 533.

9. See *Goodman Rosen Inc. v. Sobeys Group Inc.*, [2003] N.S.J. No. 313 (C.A.), involving restrictive covenants. The court upheld a permanent injunction preventing the grocery store from opening a pharmacy where the lease said that premises were to be used only for purposes of "business of the retail sale of a complete line of food products, as well as general retail merchandising." Use of the premises for "professional services" as offered by a pharmacy did not fit within "general retail merchandising."

schemes take on many of the attributes of zoning bylaws because the developers have imposed basic rules governing the construction and use of property in the development, just as a municipality would normally do through zoning bylaws.

CASE SUMMARY 13.3

Positive Covenants Do Not Bind Future Owners: *Durham Condominium Corporation No. 123 v. Amberwood Investments Limited*[10]

WHDC Harbour Development Corporation subdivided land into two parcels, sold the first-phase portion to Amberwood, which in turn built a high-rise building and recreational facilities on that land. The agreement anticipated that WHDC would also build a high-rise, which would support those recreational facilities; in the meantime, WHDC would pay a portion of the facilities' operating expenses. This agreement was registered and contained a provision that the obligations were to run with the land. WHDC ran into financial difficulties, and the mortgagee sold the phase-two property to Durham pursuant to a power of sale in the mortgage. Durham refused to pay the interim expenses associated with the recreational facilities, thus Amberwood commenced this action to enforce that agreement. The Court held that since this was a positive obligation requiring Durham to make payments, such an obligation would not run with the land and would not bind a subsequent owner who had acquired ownership through a power of sale. This was the case even though the obligation was registered and stated it would run with the land.

SMALL BUSINESS PERSPECTIVE

Registering one's interests does not guarantee that those interests are adequately protected. If the claim itself is not an "interest" in land, registration will not cure the defect.

Tenancy in Common and Joint Tenancy

Owning property together may be joint or in common

When people own property together in a **tenancy in common**, they each have an undivided interest in the land, although they may be entitled to a different percentage of the proceeds on sale. The co-owners share the property, and if one dies, that person's heirs inherit his interest. People can also share ownership of property in a **joint tenancy** relationship, but here, if one dies, the others will be left with the whole property. In effect, the joint tenants own the entire property outright, and when one dies, the survivors continue to own the entire property. Where one joint owner of property dies, there is no inheritance, which avoids many of the problems encountered when property becomes part of the estate, such as probate fees and estate taxes. This is why joint tenancy is so attractive to couples holding property together.

Only joint ownership creates right of survivorship

Joint tenancy can be severed

Where property is owned jointly and one of the parties does not want the others to get his interest, it is possible to sever the joint tenancy. **Severance** must

---

[10] (2002), 58 O.R. (3d) 481 (C.A.).

take place before the death of the party seeking severance, and is accomplished by one of the parties acting toward the property in some way that is inconsistent with the joint tenancy continuing. Selling one's interest in the property to a third party, for instance, would sever the joint tenancy, creating a tenancy in common between the other party and that purchaser. But bequeathing the joint interest to someone else in a will does not work, since the will operates after death and after the rights of the survivor have been established. In some jurisdictions, legislation prevents registration of a transfer that would have the effect of severing a joint tenancy, unless that transfer is executed or consented to by all the joint tenants, or proof is submitted that a written notice of the intention to register such a transfer was served on all joint tenants.[11] Creditors can also bring applications to the court to partition or sever a joint tenancy so that the debtor's half of the property can be sold to pay the debt.

To avoid the creation of a joint tenancy, terms such as "held jointly" or "joint ownership" should not be used in the title document. When such words do not appear, the creation of a tenancy in common is presumed.

CASE SUMMARY 13.4

An Intention to Change a Joint Tenancy Is Not Good Enough: *Dunn Estate v. Dunn*[12]

Mr. and Mrs. Dunn owned their matrimonial home as joint tenants. During their marriage, Mr. Dunn had demanded the departure of Mrs. Dunn and his step-children several times, only to later reconcile. Prior to his death, the husband obtained a divorce and applied for division of the matrimonial home pursuant to the *Matrimonial Property Act*, but Mr. Dunn died before the property division was effected. The administrator of the estate, the public trustee, applied for division of the matrimonial property under the Act. The issue then arose as to whether the home formed part of the estate or whether it passed by survivorship to Mrs. Dunn.

The onus fell on the administrator to establish severance of the joint tenancy. Neither divorce nor commencement of a matrimonial property action suffices to effect severance. The deceased could have taken unilateral steps to sever the joint tenancy, but he did not do so. Nothing done by the wife, not even her leaving the home, constituted severance. The residence, therefore, passed to the wife by right of survivorship.

DISCUSSION QUESTIONS

This case highlights that to change a joint tenancy into a tenancy-in-common, positive action on the part of the co-tenants is required. An intention to sever may be suggested when one brings legal action to divide the property, but is this enough?

---

11. See, for example, s. 65 of Alberta's *Land Titles Act*, R.S.A 2000, c. L-4.

12. [1994], A.J. No. 42 (Q.B.).

REDUCING RISK 13.1

Shared property can be both a boon and a thorn in the side of the people who own it and those they deal with. Partners may find it efficient to own business property jointly so that if one dies the other acquires the whole property without having to deal with the estate and thus reducing taxes. Still, the consequences of this decision must be fully understood. If a joint owner dies, that property does not go to his estate and is not available to his heirs. This may be an appropriate result if planned for and other arrangements are made to provide for the family, but it may be a tragedy if the implications of joint ownership have not been fully appreciated.

www.pearsoned.ca/mybuslawlab

BC AB SK MB ON

Option gives right to purchase

Security given through mortgage or agreement for sale

Other Interests in Land

When an offer is made for the purchase of land, like other offers, it can be revoked at any point before acceptance. Such an offer can be made irrevocable when the offeree pays some additional consideration to keep the offer open for a specified period. This is called an **option agreement** and when land is involved, it conveys with it significant rights, giving the offeree a right to purchase the land at a specified price, which can, in turn, be sold to someone else. Leases often contain an option to purchase, which must be registered against the title to bind subsequent purchasers of the property. Registration is discussed below.

When a person purchases land, paying for it by a series of installments, this is secured by either a mortgage or less commonly by an **agreement for sale**. An agreement for sale is like a conditional sale of personal property, in the sense that title to the property does not transfer to the purchaser until the last payment is made. In the event of a default, the seller can reclaim the land that he has title to. In the interim, the agreement for sale bestows a significant interest in the property on the purchaser, including the right of possession. The agreement for sale also must be properly registered to protect the interest against subsequent claims against the property.

A more common way of financing the purchase of property is through a mortgage. The creditor lends the borrower money to make the purchase, and (depending on the jurisdiction) the title of the property is conveyed (transferred) to the moneylender as security, to be re-conveyed upon receipt of the last payment. Note that title doesn't actually transfer in all jurisdictions, for in jurisdictions using a land titles system of registration, title is held by the borrower and the mortgage appears as a security on the title. Mortgages are not restricted to financing the purchase of property but can be used to secure loans for any purpose. The subject of mortgages and foreclosures is broad and the rules vary by jurisdiction. Accordingly, reference to texts that focus on a particular jurisdiction is recommended.

Transfer and Registration of Interest in Land

www.pearsoned.ca/mybuslawlab

BC AB SK MB ON

The first stage in the purchase of property, commercial or residential, involves the creation of an **agreement of purchase and sale** (sometimes referred to as an interim agreement) between the vendor and purchaser. It is important to understand that this is the contract governing the transaction and great care must be taken in its creation. Unfortunately, prospective purchasers and vendors often don't secure legal representation until after the contract is signed. This may be too late!

All of the terms and special conditions must be properly set out in the interim agreement, which will govern the relationship between vendor and purchaser. If the purchaser wishes to avoid being bound until acceptable financing is arranged, or until his existing house is sold, or until the house passes a proper inspection, that must be carefully stated as a condition precedent in the contract. It will be too late to insist on it later. The purchaser's lawyer will search the title to ensure all is in order and at the appropriate time the transaction will "close"—at that point the property transfers from vendor to purchaser.[13]

Grants give title to property

Historically, land was transferred by grant. The document used to accomplish this transfer had to be under seal and was called a **deed of conveyance**, now shortened simply to *deed*. A problem with this system was that there was no way to keep track of the various deeds that would accumulate with respect to a particular property over the years. It was impossible to be certain that good title to the property had been transferred by the most current deed, without inspection of all the past documents. Two different solutions to this problem were developed, and either one or the other has been adopted in all Canadian jurisdictions.

Both systems require the registration of documents, but in the **registration system**, the rights of the parties are determined by the registered documents, rather than the process. The registry is merely a repository of documents that provides assurance to the parties that they will not be affected by any unregistered documents. The purchaser's lawyer must still "search the title" by examining the title documents and establishing a chain of valid deeds to determine whether the seller has good title. This usually means going back over the documents for a set period of time (40 years) to make sure no mistakes have been made. Anything before that period is presumed to be correct. Confusion may arise, however, since many interests in land may exist at the same time, all needing registration, including the fee simple, lease interests, easements, and judgments.

Registration system: registration imposed to assist ascertaining title

Land titles system: provincial government guarantees title

The western provinces, the territories, more recently New Brunswick and Nova Scotia,[14] and some areas of Ontario and Manitoba have taken the registry system one step further and adopted a **land titles system**, where the title to real property is guaranteed. In this system, once registration has taken place in a central registry a certificate of title is created and registered that is binding on all parties. The government guarantees that the information on that certificate of title is correct. This information sets out the declared owner of the property as well as any mortgages, easements, or other interests that might be held by others. The key to understanding this system is that the certificate of title determines the interest of the parties listed on it to the land specified.

For example, in Alberta the *Land Titles Act*[15] states that the **certificate of title** is conclusive evidence in any court that the person named on the certificate is the holder in fee simple of that property and that is the end to the matter. For this reason Mrs. Hill lost her home in the case discussed in Case Summary 13.5

---

13. See *535045 B.C. Ltd. v. 741662 Alberta Ltd.*, [2002] A.J. No. 1170 (Q.B.), where a commercial tenant's failure to pay rent was a material adverse change sufficient to justify termination of a purchase and sale contract. The contract contained a condition precedent to closing that "there shall have been no material adverse change to the condition or operation of the property from the condition and operation as at the date of acceptance of the offer."

14. For a good summary of recent developments, see Service Nova Scotia's Land Registration update, www.gov.ns.ca/snsmr/property/.

15. R.S.A. 2000, c. L-4, s. 62; see also British Columbia's *Land Title Act*, R.S.B.C. 1996, c. 250, s.23(2).

below. Both systems require registration, but in the registration system it is up to the parties to sort out the legal relationships derived from those registered documents, whereas in the land titles system the certificate of title determines the interests. The *Hill* case illustrates the difference between the land titles system and the system of land registry used in other parts of the country, where the validity of a forged document could be challenged and a person in Mrs. Hill's position would have retained her home. Prince Edward Island and Newfoundland and Labrador remain the only Canadian jurisdictions that have exclusively deed registry systems.

CASE SUMMARY 13.5

Certificate Guarantees Title: *Paramount Life Insurance Co. v. Hill*[16]

Mr. Hill had been turned down by Paramount Life Insurance Company when he tried to obtain a loan to be secured by a mortgage on the house that his wife owned. He then sold the property to his business partner and had his partner arrange for a loan with Paramount to be secured by a mortgage on the property. This mortgage was granted. The problem was that he had not obtained his wife's consent for the sale but had forged her signature on the documents. Neither the partner nor the Insurance Company knew this fact.

When Mr. Hill died, Paramount foreclosed, as it was no longer receiving mortgage payments. Mrs. Hill now discovered what her husband had done; she fought the foreclosure action claiming she was still entitled to the property because of the fraudulent sale. But because this happened in a land titles jurisdiction where title is guaranteed, and because the partner and Paramount were innocent of any wrongdoing, the Court found that the business partner had obtained good title to the property and that the mortgage granted was good. A certificate of title had been granted to the partner, which determines ownership against all other parties. Mrs. Hill was the victim of her husband's fraud and lost the property.

DISCUSSION QUESTIONS

Does the land titles system treat all parties fairly? Had Mrs. Hill done anything wrong or blameworthy?

Since governments guarantee title in a land titles system, parties who sustain a loss (through an omission, mistake, or misfeasance of the registrar, or who are deprived of their land by the registration of another person as owner) can bring an action against the registrar for damages. In Alberta, for example, every time land is transferred, assurance fees are paid and deposited into a fund. The party who suffers a loss (for example, Mrs. Hill, *supra*) can then bring an action against the registrar and any other party whose wrongful conduct caused the loss. The registrar can be found liable for any part of the judgment that remains unsatisfied, and recovery is then available out of the province's General Revenue Fund, where these assurance fees are pooled. Note, however, that the *Land Titles Act* requires that actions against the registrar be commenced within six years

---

16. [1986] A.J. No. 1111 (C.A.).

from when the deprivation took place or the cause of action arose.[17] Despite a government's "guarantee" of title, lawful owners may still be deprived of their title without adequate compensation, as Mrs. Hill discovered, if their actions against the registrar are not brought in time and thus are barred by statute.[18]

In both registry and land titles systems, great strides are being made to modernize the process using advanced data compilation technologies. Canada offers the world's first system of electronic registration for land titles documents, with more than half of all land-related documents being filed electronically. One very important change is in the process of filing the documents, which now can be done electronically in many jurisdictions, including British Columbia, Ontario, New Brunswick, and Nova Scotia.[19] Check the MyBusLawLab for details.

Electronic registration systems have advantages and disadvantages. One advantage is increased access to information. Searches can be conducted online, reducing the need to attend personally at a local registry or land titles office to complete a title search. Larger volumes of searches and registrations can be processed and physical storage requirements should be reduced with the reduction of paper. However, electronic systems can crash and fraud remains a serious threat. Title fraud may be simpler in a system that eliminates signatures, witnessing of documents, and paper itself.

REDUCING RISK 13.2

The purchase of real estate, be it residential or commercial, constitutes one of the most important transactions a person will be involved in. Both vendor and purchaser should have their own lawyer involved at an early stage. Remember that the purchase agreement ("interim agreement") is the contract governing the transaction and is binding on the parties. Great care should be taken with the terms of that contract; all conditions should be fully understood and carefully worded. The actual transfer documents that are completed later are just the execution of that contract.

Often it will be necessary to have the property surveyed to determine its proper boundaries. It is also important to have the buildings properly inspected by a competent independent professional so that any problems can be factored into the purchase price. In some jurisdictions, title insurance is recommended to protect mortgage lenders and consumers against fraud; but where a land titles system is used, the need for such insurance is minimal.

Condominiums and Cooperatives

Because traditional real property law did not recognize the difference between the land and the buildings affixed to it, it was incapable of handling the modern practice of creating ownership in suites stacked vertically in an apartment building or attached townhouses. All Canadian provinces have passed legislation allowing fee simple interest in individual units in a condominium structure. But because condominium ownership involves a combination of unit and common

my buslawlab
www.pearsoned.ca/mybuslawlab

Condominium legislation allows vertical title

---

17. *Land Titles Act*, R.S.A. 2000, c. L-4, S. 178.

18. See *Hill v. Alberta (Registrar, South Alberta Land Registration District)* [1993] A.J. No. 163 (C.A.), where the wife subsequently brought an action against the assurance fund seeking compensation. Unfortunately, the limitation period had expired, so no relief was available to her.

19. See British Columbia's *Land Titles Act*, R.S.B.C. (1996) c.406, Ontario's *Land Registration Reform Act*, R.S.O.1990, c. L-4, New Brunswick's *Land Titles Act*, S.N.B.1981, c. L-1.1, and Nova Scotia's *Land Registration Act*, S.N.S. 2001, c. 6.

Condominium interest involves some shared property

ownership, many unique rights and responsibilities apply. Although individuals may own their separate units, all common areas, such as the halls, reception areas, and laundry facilities are owned in common.

The condominium association is a corporate body and functions in a way similar to a company or society, holding regular meetings with each member (those owning units in the development) having a vote. Bylaws are passed that outline the rights and duties of members. Although these bylaws must conform with statutory requirements, they can still create hardship where rules are put in place that interfere with what would normally be considered a right of ownership, such as prohibitions on pets or children.

Rules must be obeyed and fees paid

Liens can be registered for non-payment of fees

The condominium association will levy a fee on each member to pay for such things as repairs, the cost of management, and other services. If these fees are not paid, the condominium corporation has a right to place a lien or caveat on the title of the member and force a sale, if necessary, to recover the funds.[20] When unexpected repairs occur, these fees or levies can be substantial. In British Columbia, there has been a particular problem with "leaky condos," the repair of which has required many condominium owners to pay levies sometimes in excess of $50 000, causing many to lose their homes. Each member of the condominium owns his or her own suite and the normal rules of real property apply; the suites can be sold, mortgaged, or rented, but the interest the member has in the common area goes with that conveyance and so do the responsibilities associated with it. The condominium structure is not limited to residential apartments but can be applied to commercial properties, townhouses, or even separate, physically unconnected units or vacation properties.

Apartments can be owned through cooperatives

A cooperative is a less common method of shared ownership. As with condominiums, cooperatives offer members shared amenities and individual entitlements. Members also cooperate in the administration of the project. Cooperatives may differ in their structure. The real property interest may be held in common, with leases granted in favour of the members. Alternatively, the entire property might be owned by a corporation, with individual units being leased to shareholders. In either case, the real property interest in all the suites and the common areas is held by the cooperative, and the members do not have title to the specific suite that they occupy.

The property may be covered by a blanket mortgage, since the title to the whole is placed in the cooperative. Members usually assume a portion of the mortgage obligation and a levy for operating expenses. Problems can develop if some members fail to contribute to the mortgage. This will affect everyone, even those who have paid their share. Accordingly, cooperative agreements often provide for a claim against a member's corporate interest in the event of a failure to contribute as agreed.[21]

There are some disadvantages to condominium and cooperative ownership, such as submission to the bylaws and the monthly fee, but there are also significant advantages. This form of ownership is the only viable alternative to renting an apartment. Although a monthly fee must be paid, which can change, there is no danger of a rent increase since the unit is owned by the member. Also, members can share facilities such as swimming pools and other recreational areas that

---

[20.] Ontario's *Condominium Act, 1998*, S.O. 1998, c. 19, grants condominium liens priority over every registered and unregistered encumbrance, even pre-existing encumbrances.

[21.] B. Ziff, *Principles of Property Law*, 3rd ed. (Toronto: Carswell, 2000), at 332.

normally would not be available to an individual homeowner. In condominiums or cooperatives, residents can be required to leave if they violate the bylaws. For example, buildings can be designated as adults-only or pet-free, and couples can be required to leave if they have pets or children (although such provisions may violate human rights legislation).

THE LANDLORD–TENANT RELATIONSHIP

Leasehold Estates

A leasehold estate lasts for a specific or determinable period of time, usually ending on a specified day or at the end of a specified period. It also may take the form of a **periodic tenancy** where the specific period (usually a month) is automatically renewed. Unlike a licence, which does not convey an exclusive right to the property, the lease gives the tenant the right to use the property to the exclusion of all others for the period of time stated in the lease agreement. If Jones were to rent a hotel room for a month, this would normally be a licence since the hotelkeeper has the right to come in the room, make the beds, clean the room, do any repairs, and even move Jones to another location if it is deemed appropriate. But if Jones were to lease an apartment for a month he would have the exclusive use of it and the landlord could not enter without permission unless some arrangement to do so had been set out in the lease agreement.

As with other business relationships, the general requirements of contract law apply to leasehold estates. Even though it is wise to put a lease in writing, one need not do so with a lease for three years or less. In most jurisdictions, however, leases over three years must be evidenced in writing to satisfy the *Statute of Frauds* or its equivalent.[22] The written evidence must specify the premises covered by the lease, the parties to it, the consideration or rent to be given by the tenant, the duration of the lease, and any other special provisions the parties may have agreed to. In the absence of written evidence, part performance, such as the occupation of the premises by the tenant, may satisfy this requirement.

Leases, like freehold estates, are interests that run with the land. Because leases are both contracts and estates in land, the absence of privity does not render the lease unenforceable. Accordingly, when a landlord sells the property, the prior lease binds the new owner. Also, if after the lease is made, the landlord mortgages the property and defaults, the creditor is subject to the lease arrangement; if the property is seized or resold, the lease must still be honoured. Many jurisdictions require long-term leases to be registered along with other claims affecting the title of the property.[23] Shorter-term leases, although not registered, are still enforceable by the tenant as against the new owner of the property.

As in other contracts, a landlord who contracts with an infant, a drunk, or a mentally incompetent person runs into all the problems associated with incapacity, as discussed in Chapter 7; the resulting contract may not be binding. Historically, frustration, as discussed in Chapter 9, did not apply to land.[24] Many jurisdictions have changed this with respect to residential tenancies so that if the

mybuslawlab
www.pearsoned.ca/mybuslawlab

BC AB SK MB ON

Tenant has right to exclusive possession during period of lease

Registration and writing requirements for leases

Leasehold interests run with the land

Terms of lease can modify obligations

Statutes apply frustration to some tenancies

---

22. *Statute of Frauds*, 1677 (29 Car. 2) c. 3, s. 4; see Ontario's *Statute of Frauds*, R.S.O. 1990, c. S.19, s. 3.

23. See, for example, Alberta's *Land Titles Act*, R.S.A. 2000, c. L-4, s. 95.

24. *Paradine v. Jane* (1647), Aleyn 26 (K.B.).

property is destroyed or damaged, rendering it unusable, the contract will be discharged by frustration and the tenant's obligation to pay rent will cease. In Ontario, for example, the *Residential Tenancies Act, 2006* states that the "doctrine of frustration of contract and the *Frustrated Contracts Act* apply with respect to tenancy agreements."[25]

Most jurisdictions have introduced special legislative provisions determining the rights and obligations of landlords and tenants in residential relationships. Commercial tenancy law has also been modified by statute to a lesser extent. This legislation varies from province to province, so reference to the MyBusLawLab for local detail is advised. What follow are statements concerning tenancies in general.

Types of Tenancies

Property may be sublet

Property may be leased for a specific period of time, such as for "one year" or "ending 5 September," or it may be a periodic tenancy with no set duration. When a lease has a set duration, it is a term lease, entitling the tenant to exclusive possession of the property for the specified period. Where the lease allows the tenant to *assign* the lease and she does so, all rights and claims in relationship to the property are given up to the new tenant. However, if the property is **sublet**, the tenant retains a reversionary interest, giving the tenant the right to retake possession at the expiration of the sublease. Usually, leases contain provisions allowing for such assignment or subletting with the permission of the landlord, "which shall not be unreasonably withheld." This gives the landlord some say in who takes possession of the property but does not allow unreasonable interference.

Periodic tenancy usually month to month

Notice period is one clear rental period

A periodic tenancy has no specific termination date; rather, it involves a specific lease period that is automatically renewed in the absence of notice to the contrary. The period involved can be weekly, monthly, or yearly, but the most common is the month-to-month tenancy. Without notice bringing the relationship to a close, a periodic tenancy will continue indefinitely. Notice to end the periodic tenancy must be given at least one clear period in advance (unless otherwise specified in the lease). Thus, in a month-to-month tenancy, notice must be given before the end of one month to take effect at the end of the next. If Jookie rents an apartment from Politichny in a month-to-month tenancy and pays her rent on the first of each month, the lease period ends at the end of the month. Notice to terminate must be given on or before the last day of the month to take effect at the end of the next month. If notice is given on the day the rent is paid to terminate at the end of that month it will not be effective because the lease period has already begun. This requirement has caused considerable problems and has thus been modified by statute with respect to residential tenancies in many jurisdictions.

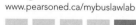

www.pearsoned.ca/mybuslawlab

BC AB SK MB **ON**

Obligations may be modified by statute

Rights and Obligations of the Parties

In common law, commercial and residential tenancies were treated the same way, but all provinces have passed statutes modifying these rules. These changes apply primarily to residential tenancies; reference to the specific legislation in effect in your jurisdiction is advised. The following comments apply primarily to commercial tenancies.

[25.] S.O. 2006, c. 17, s. 19.

It is important to remember that leasehold tenancies are based on contract and the following discussion relates to the rights and obligations of the parties where they have not been modified by unique terms set out in the lease. Normally a lease will set out a description of the premises—the parties, the rent to be paid, and the term of the lease. Other terms that are often included in commercial leases relate to what use the property can be put to and who is responsible for the payment of utilities, taxes, repairs, and insurance. In special situations, such as services or retail stores in shopping malls, provisions may prohibit the operation of a similar business close to the tenant. In the shopping mall situation, rent is sometimes fixed as a percentage of sales. Long-term commercial leases often include an option for the review of the rent at set periods or for its renewal.

Lease sets out rights of the parties

VACANT POSSESSION

The landowner has an obligation to ensure that the premises are vacant and ready for occupancy at the time the lease period is to start. A failure to deliver **vacant possession** is often caused by construction delays or an over-holding prior tenant, and compensation is normally based on how much it costs the tenant to find other accommodation in the interim.

Landowner must provide vacant premises

QUIET ENJOYMENT

A landlord is obligated to give a tenant **quiet enjoyment** of the premises. This does not mean that the tenant has to be happy or like the premises, only that the landlord must ensure that nothing happens to interfere with the tenant's use of the property. Tenants have the right to be protected against interference by the landlord or those claiming under the landlord. Where Labuda leases office space in a new building to Telzerow, but the construction is not complete, causing noise and vibration that interferes with Telzerow's business, this would be a breach of his right to quiet enjoyment of the lease. Where Telzerow's office is on the 10th floor and the elevator is not yet installed, where the entranceway is blocked by construction, or where the central heating is not yet working in the winter, a breach of quiet enjoyment occurs.[26]

Landlord must not interfere with the tenant's use of property

REPAIR OF PREMISES

The landlord has no general obligation to deliver premises that are clean or in good repair. The tenant takes the property the way it comes, and if he or she wants it in better condition, the cost is the responsibility of the tenant. Only when the premises are in such disrepair that it amounts to a breach of quiet enjoyment can the landlord be held responsible. In the example above, Telzerow would have no complaint if the premises were not painted or the carpet was threadbare when he moved in, unless a provision to provide better facilities were in the lease. But if the structure of the building were in such poor repair that it was no longer capable of supporting a wall or a floor and a resulting cave-in would make the office unusable, this would be a breach of the covenant of quiet enjoyment. Usually, the parties specify changes to these obligations in the lease agreement, but there are also many situations in which the courts will imply contractual obligations

No general obligation to repair

[26.] See *Truscan Property Corp. v. Beyond IT Solutions Inc.*, [2007] B.C.J. No. 316 (B.C.S.C.), where the tenants (defendants) were awarded $14 806 on the counterclaim for breach of a commercial lease. The landlord's failure to provide off-business-hours heating and air conditioning was a fundamental breach, going to the fitness of the premises for their intended use as a computer-skills instructional facility.

because of the circumstances. For example, when a tenant rents only part of a building, the court will assume that the landlord has an obligation to provide heat, unless otherwise stated in the lease. But when the tenant leases the entire building, that obligation may be assumed to fall on the tenant.

TERMINATION

Proper notice must be given for periodic tenancy

A lease that ends on a specific date, or is for a specified period of time, ends when specified, unless there is an agreement to extend it. But when a periodic tenancy is involved (for example, month-to-month), notice to terminate must be given.[27] If the tenant fails to leave after the lease has expired or after being given the appropriate notice, a **tenancy at sufferance** relationship is established. When this happens, the landlord is entitled to compensation; but if the normal rent payment is made and accepted, there is a danger of creating a periodic tenancy requiring more notice before the tenant can be ejected.

TENANTS' OBLIGATIONS

Tenant must pay rent

The tenant's primary obligation is to pay rent when due. In fact, a commercial landlord who accidentally charged a tenant lower rent than demanded by the lease was able to recover substantial back rent.[28] The obligation of paying the rent at the appropriate time is independent of any special obligations that the landlord may have agreed to in the lease contract, such as a duty to make repairs. As a result, when the landlord fails in his obligation to make repairs, the tenant cannot withhold rent until the repairs are made. In these circumstances, the tenant can ask the court for an order of **abatement** that will reduce the rent to be paid as compensation for the landlord's breach of the lease obligation.[29]

Tenants not responsible for normal wear and tear

The tenant has no obligation to repair normal wear and tear or even to make serious repairs when they occur, unless they are caused by waste (his or her own action). The landlord should be notified of any serious problems, but in common law, the landlord has no obligation to make these repairs unless failure to do so would interfere with the quiet enjoyment of the tenancy. If Telzerow rents an office from Labuda and the rug on the floor wears out over the years, Telzerow would be under no obligation to replace it. But neither would Labuda, since the landlord is not required to provide premises of any standard of fitness for the tenant. Of course, the landlord and tenant can agree otherwise, and in many lease agreements one of the parties assumes the responsibility for keeping the property in good repair.

When undue wear and tear takes place, a tenant does have an obligation to make repairs, because the premises have been used in a way not agreed to in the lease. The landlord may also be able to evict the tenant. If Telzerow rents premises from Labuda to be used as an office and instead it is used for manufacturing furniture, Labuda could demand payment for any excessive wear. Labuda can also and require Telzerow to vacate the premises, no matter how long the lease had left to run.

[27.] Landlords should err on the side of generosity in terminating commercial leases. Landlords may be required to show a legitimate business reason for terminating or not renewing a lease. See *Tannous (c.o.b. Tannous Produce) v. Ontario (Food Terminal Board)*, [2003] O.J. No. 2633 (S.C.J.).

[28.] See *Meadowvale Industrial Mall Ltd. v. Becquerel Laboratories Inc.*, [1999] O.J. No. 5199 (Sup. Ct. J.).

[29.] Under Ontario's *Tenant Protection Act*, a group of tenants may collectively apply for rent abatement, according to the decision in *Metropolitan Toronto Housing Authority v. Godwin*, [2002] O.J. No. 2514 (C.A.).

CASE SUMMARY 13.6

Tenant Responsible for Excessive Wear and Tear: *Horn Ventures International Inc. v. Horn Plastics Inc.*[30]

The plaintiffs owned and operated a custom mold injection business, manufacturing plastic components for the automotive, medical, and office equipment industries. They sold certain fixed assets to the defendant and sub-let the two premises used for operation of the mold injection business to the defendant. Four years later, the defendant gave notice it was vacating the premises. The lease required the tenant to leave the premises clean and in good repair. Instead, the defendant removed equipment not included in the agreement and damaged the premises in the process.

The plaintiffs thus sued for damages for breach of contract and damages for the cleanup and repair costs incurred at the end of a lease. After the defendant tenant left, the plaintiffs had to rent premises "as is" to a new tenant and could only negotiate a lower rent due to the disrepair of the premises. The Court determined that the premises had to be left in the same condition they were in when the tenant took possession, except for normal wear and tear. Videotape evidence documented that the premises were not maintained in good condition. As one witness testified, the premises were "left in a mess" and it "looked like a small hurricane had gone through it." Damages were assessed at $95 700. The further claim for lost rental income warranted damages of another $96 130. An additional award of $42 428 was granted as compensation for the equipment wrongfully taken, making the entire award against the tenant rather significant.

DISCUSSION QUESTIONS

Photographs taken of the premises certainly assisted the landlord in this case. From the tenant's perspective, when should photos be taken to have maximum effect?

A tenant's normal obligation to clean and repair is determined by the condition of the premises when occupied and the nature of the business carried on in the premises. A tenant is not responsible for normal wear and tear but will be responsible for consequential damage. For example, the tenant will not be responsible for a tile that blows off a roof, but will be responsible for any damage done to the premises when the hole caused by its loss is left open to the weather.[31]

When tenants attach something (a fixture) in such a way that it is clearly intended to become a permanent part of the building or will cause damage to remove it, they are not permitted to remove it when they leave.[32] If Telzerow installed modern wiring and added a staircase to the second floor of his rented

---

30. (1984), 47 O.R. (2d) 548 (H.C.J.).

31. See *Stellarbridge Management Ltd. v. Magna International (Canada) Inc.* (2004), 71 O.R. (3d) 263 (C.A.), leave to appeal to S.C.C. refused, [2004] S.C.C.A. No. 371, where the tenant vacated without doing any of the required restoration and repairs. It was held liable for costs of restoration and repair, subject to deductions for reasonable wear and tear. Damages for rent lost during construction were also awarded.

32. See *Farm Corp. v. Senari*, [1991] A.J. No. 468 (Q.B. Master), regarding fixtures. A modular home was bolted together over a developed basement, and a pre-fabricated barn was affixed to a concrete slab with screws and bolts. The mortgagee commenced foreclosure proceedings following default by the defendant mortgagors. The court decided that although it was possible to remove the barn and home, they were clearly fixtures, not chattels, and thus formed part of the security. The facts that the buildings were pre-finished and that they could be hauled away were not as significant as the fact that these buildings became affixed to the land, and a fully developed basement existed under the home.

Tenant can remove her fixtures before termination of lease

office, these fixtures would become permanent and he could not remove them when he left. Trade fixtures, on the other hand, such as shelving, display counters, machinery, decorative artwork, and signs can be taken away by the tenant who attached them. But they must be removed when the tenant leaves. If they are left by the tenant, they become part of the real property, and the tenant cannot come back later to recover them.

www.pearsoned.ca/mybuslawlab

BC AB SK MB **ON**

Landlord can sue for compensation when lease breached

Remedies

When the rent is not paid, the landlord can sue for the overdue rent. When some other breach occurs, the landlord may sue for damages and, in serious cases, may require the tenants to vacate the premises. This is called **forfeiture**, and when unpaid rent in a commercial lease is involved, no court order is needed and forfeiture may be accomplished by the landlord's simply changing the locks.[33] When the tenant is in breach of some other term of the lease, such as in the manner of use of the premises, the landlord must first give the tenant notice to end the breach and time to do so. When eviction is necessary, the services of law enforcement officers (such as sheriffs or civil enforcement bailiffs) must be obtained, which can be a costly and time-consuming process.[34] Residential tenancy statutes usually limit the availability of eviction as a remedy; landlords may be restricted to terminating a tenancy by giving a prescribed amount of notice or by seeking a court order. Refer to the legislation in effect in a particular jurisdiction for details.

When the landlord does retake the property for failure to pay rent prior to the end of the lease term, the tenant can pay the arrears and apply to the court to have the lease reinstated. This **relief against forfeiture** is an equitable principle. When the tenant abandons the premises, the landlord retains the right to payment of rent for the duration of the lease period. It should be noted that the landlord is normally not obligated to mitigate this loss, at least in commercial tenancies, by finding a new occupant for the premises until the expiration of the lease period.

Landlord can seize tenant's property when lease breached

The landlord of commercial premises also has the right to seize the tenant's property, and hold it until the rent is paid, or sell the tenant's property to pay the rent owing.[35] This is called **distress** or distraint. Written notice of distress is to be given the tenant, setting out the amount owing. Should the tenant deny the landlord access, a court order can be obtained. The landlord can either remove the tenant's property to a secure location, or separate and mark the property subject to distress. That property is then appraised and once the prescribed period (allowed the tenant to satisfy the indebtedness) expires, the property can be sold to satisfy the outstanding debt. Distraint often causes confusion, because the sale of property may result in the rent's being paid and the continuation of the lease.

---

[33] A commercial landlord's right of forfeiture is not absolute. Being an equitable remedy, it may be denied if the court determines the landlord acted on improper motives, such as seeking re-entry so as to extract a higher rent. See *Prime Restaurants of Canada Inc. v. Greeley Realty Holdings Ltd.*, [2003] O.J. No. 295 (S.C.J.), aff'd [2004] O.J. No. 3679 (C.A.).

[34] Note, however, that the landlord's options may be affected by the *Bankruptcy and Insolvency Act*, R.S.C. 1985, c. B-3 if the tenant faces bankruptcy. A stay of proceedings temporarily prevents creditors from seeking remedies against the tenant; thus the landlord would be delayed in terminating the tenancy, re-entering the premises, or distraining for rent.

[35] The right to distrain for rent, where denied by the tenant, can be remedied by the courts. See *1268227 Ontario Ltd. (c.o.b. Seamus O'Briens) v. 1178605 Ontario Inc.*, [2001] O.J. No. 3642, aff'd [2003] O.J. No. 2002 (C.A.). The tenant, while in default, fraudulently removed its property from the premises to defeat the landlord's right to rental arrears. The tenant was held liable for twice the value of the property removed, in accordance with the *Commercial Tenancies Act*, R.S.O. 1990, c. L.7, s. 50.

The landlord cannot treat the lease as ended and also distrain the tenant's property. This power to seize the tenant's property is usually significantly limited or eliminated in residential tenancy legislation.

The landlord can also seek contractual remedies in the form of damages when the lease is breached. This usually amounts to the rent due, but also may be compensation for the cost of repairs when damage is done to the premises.

Monetary compensation available for breach of lease

The courts will also issue an injunction when either tenant or landlord carries on some activity inconsistent with the terms of the lease. Thus, when a tenant uses the premises for a purpose different from that contemplated in the lease, the landlord can get an injunction to prevent the misuse of the property.

Also injunctions in some limited circumstances

The remedies available to the tenant for the landlord's breach of the lease are more limited. The tenant is generally entitled either to sue the landlord for compensation for any injury suffered because of the breach, or to seek an injunction. The tenant is not entitled to withhold rent to force the landlord's compliance with the lease obligations. But if the landlord's breach is significant enough to qualify as a breach of a major contractual term, the tenant may be entitled to treat the lease agreement as discharged and vacate the premises voluntarily, thus terminating the lease. For example, if the lease agreement requires the landlord to provide heat and water and those services are turned off, this would probably be a significant enough breach for the tenant to terminate the agreement. In any case, the tenant has the right to seek a court order, declaring the lease as ended or reducing the rent the tenant must pay, because of the landlord's breach.

Tenant has limited remedies

It is a principle of tort law that the occupier of property, including a tenant, is responsible for any injury caused to people using the property. The landlord may also be liable if the landlord is responsible for repairs under the lease and the tenant has notified the landlord but the repairs are not made. The landlord may also be responsible for injuries to the tenant or the tenant's employees when such repairs are not made and injury results.

Occupier's liability imposed on tenant

CASE SUMMARY 13.7

Tenant Responsible for Injury to Customer: *Barnett-Black v. Silad Investments Inc.*[36]

Silad leased a laundromat and paid a customer $27 000 when she was injured by a falling fluorescent light fixture. Silad sought contribution or indemnity from the landlord; the issue was whether the landlord was liable at all. Under Ontario's *Occupiers' Liability Act,* the occupier "includes, (a) a person who is in physical possession of premises, or (b) a person who has responsibility for and control over the condition of premises or the activities there carried on, or control over persons allowed to enter the premises." Because there was no provision in the lease making the landlord responsible for repairs, the Court held that the landlord was not an "occupier" with obligations under the *Act.* The tenant thus had no recourse to the landlord for the damages paid to the injured customer.

SMALL BUSINESS PERSPECTIVE

This case shows how important it is to specify in a lease agreement which party will be responsible for repairs, for that party will be an occupier and possibly liable to visitors injured on the premises.

---

36. [1990] O.J. No. 2008 (Gen. Div.).

> ## REDUCING RISK 13.3
>
> Businesses typically require physical space to carry on their activities. Whether it is office space, a manufacturing plant, or a warehouse, the space is usually leased rather than purchased outright. It is vitally important that the tenant understand the terms of the lease agreement. Legal advice should be sought to ensure that appropriate modifications are made to any standard form lease agreement before it is signed. Does the lease provide for the possibility that the
>
> facility needs of the business might change in the future? A common failing for tenants is to commit themselves for an extensive period without the flexibility to change as the business grows or declines. When entering into these commercial leases, legal advice should be sought to ensure that provisions are added or modified, providing for as much flexibility as possible.

www.pearsoned.ca/mybuslawlab

Residential tenancy rules modified by statute

Residential Tenancies

Most jurisdictions have introduced statutes that significantly modify the common law where the tenancy involves residential premises. Like consumer protection legislation, residential tenancy statutes alter the rights and obligations of the parties. Refer to the MyBusLawLab for details.

www.pearsoned.ca/mybuslawlab

PERSONAL PROPERTY

> ### CASE SUMMARY 13.8
>
> ### A Person's Ashes Are Property: *Mason v. Westside Cemeteries Ltd.*[37]
>
> Mr. Mason's mother died in 1970. She was cremated, and Mr. Mason, being uncertain about his future plans, asked the funeral home to look after the ashes. Several years later, his father died and was cremated. The same funeral home was asked to look after both urns pending further instructions.
>
> In 1979, arrangements were made to transfer the ashes to the defendant (carrying on business as Westminster Cemeteries), which was to bury the urns temporarily in common ground. Once the final resting place was decided upon in 1993, Mr. Mason approached Westminster Cemeteries to transfer the ashes. The ashes could not be found. Westminster had no record of them, and after an extensive search that included disinterring several crypts and examining the urns contained therein, it became clear that they would never be found.
>
> Mr. Mason sued, claiming that Westminster Cemeteries was a bailee, and the property had been lost due to its negligence. The action was successful. The Court determined that Westminster Cemeteries was indeed a bailee of the remains. Since the defendant was unable to return the urns to the plaintiff, it bore the onus of proving that the loss of the urns was not caused by any failure on its part to take reasonable care. Although it had kept careful records, it was clear that someone had made a mistake, and so, Westminster Cemeteries had failed in its duty as bailee and was liable for the loss. Mr. Mason had claimed $50 000 in damages, but the Judge had difficulty placing a value

---

37. [1996] O.J. No. 1387 (Gen. Div.).

> on human remains. The Court awarded only nominal damages for the loss of the remains, but the plaintiff was awarded $1000 damage for his mental suffering.
>
> ─────────────────────────
>
> *SMALL BUSINESS PERSPECTIVE*
>
> When entrusted to care for property that is not one's own, one becomes a bailee. Many businesses hold property on behalf of their customers, be it a restaurant holding garments in its coat check room; a boat shop storing customers' boats during the off-season, or a drycleaner holding clothing until pick-up. Bailment imposes special obligations upon the parties. Damages are available if these obligations are breached, even where the bailee is not paid for its services. It is thus particularly important to understand this body of personal property law if a business takes or holds possession of property belonging to others.

Chattels

Chattels are movables, such as electronic devices, clothes, animals, and motor vehicles. Even construction cranes, boats, and locomotives are chattels. Real property, on the other hand, is land and things fixed or attached to the land. A chattel can become part of the real property when it is attached to the land. "The test is whether the purpose of the attachment was (a) to enhance the land (which leads to the conclusion that a fixture exists); or (b) for the better use of the chattel as a chattel."[38]

This transformation from chattel to fixture can lead to conflict with respect to who has first claim to it. Assume Bowen buys and installs a hot water heater in his cottage. On installation, the item that was a chattel becomes a fixture. If Bowen later loses the cottage because he defaults on his mortgage payments, the mortgagee may have a claim to the hot water tank. If Bowen bought the water tank on credit, then two creditors may have conflicting claims, namely the mortgagee and the party that provided financing for the water tank. The *Personal Property Security Act*,[39] discussed in Chapter 16, aims to resolve such competing claims.

The owner of the land is free to remove a chattel that has become a fixture (severance) just as he or she was able to fix the chattel to the land in the first place. Difficulty arises when third parties, such as creditors or tenants, become involved and claim the property. Generally, when a chattel has been affixed to real property, it becomes part of that real property and cannot be removed. However, if a tenant of a commercial property attaches fixtures to enhance trade or carry on business, he or she has the right to remove those trade fixtures when leaving. In residential or commercial tenancies, non-trade fixtures attached for the comfort, convenience, or taste of the tenant, such as mirrors or paintings, can also be removed. Of course, when those fixtures have been incorporated into the property in such a way that they clearly are intended to stay or where their removal will cause damage, they must stay.

In any event, these fixtures can be removed only during the term of the tenancy. When the tenant moves out at the end of the tenancy and takes the mirrors, light fixtures, rugs, and display cases that had been installed by the tenant, the landlord has no complaint. But if the tenant comes back for them after

Chattels are movable things

www.pearsoned.ca/mybuslawlab

| BC | AB | SK | MB | ON |

Things fixed to the land become real property

Trade fixtures can be removed by tenant

─────────────────────────

38. B. Ziff, *Principles of Property Law*, 3rd ed. (Toronto: Carswell, 2000), at 106.

39. R.S.O. 1990, c. P.10; check MyBusLawLab for citations to similar legislation in other provinces.

the landlord has retaken possession, it is too late. Those fixtures have become part of the property of the landowner. Of course, any provisions in the lease to the contrary override these general provisions.

Finders Keepers

A finder gets good title against all but original owner

When a person finds a watch or ring in a park, he has the right to that item against everyone except a prior owner. If that finder were to hand it to the police or the lost-and-found centre and the rightful owner could not be found, that finder would be entitled to it. Only the rightful owner or someone having a proprietary interest in it, such as a secured creditor, could demand it from the finder. In *Thomas v. Canada (Attorney General)*[40], for example, the plaintiff inadvertently opened mail delivered to his address by mistake, and discovered $18 000 inside. The police were unable to discover the true owner. Canada Post claimed ownership, arguing this money remained its property as undeliverable mail. Canada Post's claim for ownership failed, thus the Attorney General was ordered to return the money to the plaintiff.

If the goods are found on private property, however, the owner of that property normally has a right to the item. If the finder is an employee of the occupier or owner of that property, the employer gets the item subject to the claim by the original owner. Only if the item is found on a public portion of that property, such as the public part of a restaurant, store, or shopping mall, will the finder have first claim. In *Trachuk v. Olinek*,[41] four oilfield workers dug up a bundle containing $75 000 when working on a well site. The farmer, who had a grazing lease on the land, claimed the money. The Court determined that the farmer was not in actual possession of the site, since a surface lease had been given the oil company. The finders thus had a better claim, and the money was directed to them. Here the "finders" were eventually the "keepers."

CASE SUMMARY 13.9

Where the Finder Was Not the Keeper: *Weitzner v. Herman*[42]

Mrs. Weitzner's husband died suddenly in a fire. She sold their home of 38 years to the Hermans, who had the house demolished. During demolition, the contractor found a fire extinguisher hidden in the basement crawlspace containing $130 000. Mr. Weitzner had operated a scrap business from the home, often taking cash but making no deposits in the bank. The Court found that he had put the money there. His sudden death prevented him from telling anyone about the hidden funds. The contractor had no claim to the money, since he was working for the Hermans and they had not given up any claim they had to the demolition materials. The Hermans were entitled to the funds against all except the original owner. As his heir, Mrs. Weitzner was entitled to all of the $130 000. "Finders keepers" is not always the case.

DISCUSSION QUESTIONS

Evidently "losers" are not always weepers. How about finders? When are they entitled to be keepers?

---

40. [2006] A.J. No. 1237 (Q.B.).

41. [1995] A.J. No. 1177 (Q.B.)

42. [2000] O.J. No. 906 (S.C.J.).

Note that whether it is the owner of the property where the goods are found, or the finder who eventually gets the goods, there is an obligation to exercise care in looking after them. This obligation is based on the law of bailment.

Bailment

A **bailment** exists when one person takes temporary possession of personal property owned by another. The owner giving up possession is called the **bailor** and the person acquiring possession is the **bailee**. Although chattels are usually involved, intangibles, such as bonds, share certificates, or negotiable instruments can also be the subjects of a bailment. "Bailments require a transfer of possession and a voluntary acceptance of the common law duty of safekeeping, while licenses amount to no more than a grant of permission to the user of the chattel to leave it upon the licensor's land on the understanding that neither possession shall be transferred, not responsibility for guarding the chattel accepted."[43] With bailment, the possession is to be only temporary, with the chattel to be returned at the end of the bailment period. Rentals of equipment; goods left for repair, storage, or transport; and simple borrowing of goods are examples of bailment.

> Bailment created by giving goods to bailee

Determining whether the goods have been *delivered* (possession temporarily transferred to and accepted by the bailee) is not as easy as it may seem. When a car is left in a parking lot and the keys are given to the attendant, a bailment has taken place because control and possession have been given to the car lot. But when a person drives onto a lot, parks the car, and takes the keys with her, there is no bailment. This is just a licence to use the parking space, and the control and possession of the car stay with the driver. During a bailment, the title to the goods remains with the bailor; only the possession goes to the bailee. Normally, a bailee cannot give the goods to someone else (a sub-bailment), unless there is permission to do so or where it is the custom of the industry, as might be the case where an automobile needing repairs is left with one mechanic who then transfers it to other specialists as needed.

When **fungibles**, such as timber, oil, and wheat, are placed in the care of a bailee, they can become indistinguishable from similar items being stored for others. In fact, the exact goods need not be returned, only goods of a similar quality and quantity. This situation is still a bailment and is treated under bailment law.

> With fungibles, the same goods need not be returned

The primary concern of bailment law is the liability of bailees for damage done to goods in their care. Bailees are responsible for any wilful, negligent, or fraudulent acts of themselves or their employees that cause injury or damage to the goods. In the past, the standard of care used in establishing that negligence varied with the type of bailment created. In recent years, the significance of the reward has declined considerably.

BAILMENT FOR VALUE

Bailments are either gratuitous or for value (or *reward*). **Bailment for value** involves a mutual benefit or consideration flowing between the parties. Usually, the relationship is commercial, and the bailor pays the bailee to repair, store, or transport the goods. But a bailment for value can also arise where a friend stores something, such as a piano, for another in exchange for the right to use it. The standard of care required in such circumstances is simply the ordinary standard

> Bailment for value—both parties receive benefit

---

43. N.E. Palmer, *Bailment*, 2d ed. (London: Law Book Co. Ltd., 1991), at 382.

for negligence—that is, the amount of care that would be expected from a prudent person looking after such goods in similar circumstances.[44]

Bailee has a duty to care for the goods

The amount of care that should be exercised will vary with both the value of the goods and their nature. More care would be expected where delicate or valuable items were involved, such as china or a rare violin, but where heavy-duty machines were being stored, the standard of care would be much lower.

CASE SUMMARY 13.10

Care Demanded from Bailee for Hire: *Spycher Estate v. J. L. Coulter Ltd.*[45]

The plaintiff purchased a mobile home. The price included transportation of the mobile home from Edmonton to the plaintiff's site in British Columbia. The defendant, an experienced trucker, was hired to transport this trailer. When the trucker discovered that problems might be encountered in crossing a narrow bridge en route, the defendant requested that the plaintiff meet him there. The parties met at the bridge, and the defendant insisted that the plaintiff sign a waiver; otherwise, the defendant would not proceed with crossing the bridge. A waiver was signed, purportedly excusing the defendant of "all responsibilities of damage done to trailer while transporting over Bailey bridge,..." The trailer had to be lifted and put on blocks so as to clear the bridge. During lifting, the winch line failed; the home fell and was severely damaged.

The Court of Appeal found that the defendant was a bailee for hire and, as such, he would be liable for any damage unless he could show that he was not negligent or had contracted out of his negligence. There were two problems with the waiver. First, no consideration was exchanged, so it was not a valid contract. Second, it did not specifically excuse negligence on the part of the carrier, and since the defendant drafted the waiver, it was to be narrowly construed against that party. Since the defendant failed to disprove negligence the Court found the defendant liable for the damage.

SMALL BUSINESS PERSPECTIVE

The case illustrates that the onus falls on the bailee to establish that it was not negligent. If the bailee fails to do so, it will be liable for any loss. A prudent bailee, wishing to minimize its risk, would retain a lawyer to draft its contracts, particularly the waiver. Furthermore, the bailee should point out the existence of the waiver and ensure the bailor is in agreement with it.

Care Required with Bailment for Value

Duty may be determined by contract or common practice

If the bailment is based on a commercial relationship, the provisions of the contract and industry practice will be taken into consideration in determining the standard of care required. In the *Spycher* case, the standard of care imposed on the defendant trucking corporation would be based on the customs and traditions of the industry. Often, when possession is given to the bailee and the subject matter is lost or damaged, only the bailee is in a position to determine what had

---

44. *Luider v. Nguyen*, [1994] A.J. No. 494 (Prov.Ct.).

45. [1982] A.J. No. 898 (C.A.).

happened. The onus is, therefore, reversed, and the bailee must prove that he was not negligent. Reversing the onus in this way is rarely done in our legal system, but since the bailee has the care of the goods, it is appropriate to require him to establish what happened. The onus to rebut a presumption of negligence was also imposed in the *Mason* case discussed in Case Summary 13.12.

Exemption Clauses

Contracts of bailment often contain exculpatory or exemption clauses, which limit the liability of the bailee. An example of such a clause is, "Goods left on the premises are entirely at the risk of the owner. The proprietor assumes no responsibility for any loss, whether caused by damage, loss, or theft of those goods." The parties are free to include such clauses, but as in the *Spycher* case, courts interpret them narrowly, since they favour one side. To be enforceable, such clauses must be clear and brought to the attention of the customer at the time they enter into the contract. Any, exemption clauses added to a contract after it is formed must be supported by new consideration, or they will not be enforceable.

Exculpatory clauses may limit liability

COMMON CARRIERS

A particularly onerous standard of care is imposed on innkeepers and "common carriers" (trucking and bus companies, railroads, airlines, and even pipelines). Common carriers must be distinguished from private companies or individuals that transport for a particular bailor. These private carriers are merely bailees for value and have the obligation of a reasonably prudent person in the circumstances. A common carrier offers general transport services to the public and undertakes the standard of an insurer. This means that if the goods are damaged or destroyed while in its care, the carrier is liable even when the damage was not caused by its negligence. But even a common carrier will not be liable when the damage was beyond its control, as when the goods deteriorate because of some inherent problem or because the packaging provided by the shipper is inadequate. If an animal dies in transit because of a previously contracted disease or goods are destroyed by spontaneous combustion, there is no liability. A common carrier is also not liable where the damage is caused by an act of war or "act of God," such as flood or earthquake. Most common carriers limit their liability by contract and include a term, such as "Not responsible for lost or stolen goods or damage over $500." Again, to be valid and binding on both parties, such a provision must be clearly brought to the attention of the shipper at the time the contract is entered into. Common carriers are usually controlled by statutory provisions regulating their industry.

Common carrier has duty of insurer

! REDUCING RISK 13.4

The law of bailment involves all those situations where one person's property is left in the care of another. From a business point of view, this affects not only service industries, such as restaurants and hotels, but also repairers, mechanics, and transporters of goods. A duty of care is owed to the owner of these goods. It is thus wise to both *insure* against loss and *limit liability* through the use of an exculpatory clause included in the service contract and specifically brought to the attention of the bailor. Furthermore, notices that risk remains with the bailor ("property left at own risk") should be posted where clearly visible on the bailee's premises.

INNKEEPERS' LIABILITY

Innkeeper has duty of an insurer

In common law, innkeepers are also treated like insurers, responsible for lost or stolen goods of a guest, unless it can be shown that they were lost because of some "act of God" or negligence on the part of the guest. To succeed, the guest must show that the establishment qualifies as an inn, offering both food and temporary lodging (transient-type accommodation).

Liability may be reduced by statute

Most jurisdictions have significantly reduced the innkeepers' liability by statute so that they are liable only when it can be proven that they or their employees were at fault. In most provinces, a copy of the appropriate section of the statute must be properly posted in the various rooms, otherwise the liability reverts to the higher common law standard (that of insurer). In Ontario, the innkeeper's common law liability has simply been reduced to $40.[46] Most statutes require the innkeeper to accept a guest's valuables and put them in a secure place, assuming liability for them. An innkeeper may have the option of refusing to receive the guest's property, but he must inform the guest at the time of refusal that safe custody cannot be offered. Refer to the MyBusLawLab, where the legislation applicable in various jurisdictions is identified and described.

GRATUITOUS BAILMENT

Gratuitous bailment

When bailee benefits, duty high

When bailor benefits, duty less

A gratuitous bailment occurs when only one side receives a benefit. Historically, when the bailee received the benefit (as when a friend borrows your car) the standard of care imposed was high, and liability would be imposed even when the bailee had been only slightly careless. On the other hand, when it was the bailor who received the benefit (as when the bailee stored golf clubs as a favour for a friend) the bailee would be liable only if there had been gross negligence. If the bailment was of mutual benefit, ordinary diligence applied. Presently, the courts seem to be moving toward imposing the ordinary tests for negligence for all gratuitous bailments, asking simply whether the bailee was careful enough considering all the circumstances. Thus, in *Gaudreau v. Belter*, where the bailee inadvertently left the garage door open overnight, and the bailor's golf clubs were stolen, the court indicated that gross negligence need not be shown. Ordinary negligence would suffice to impose liability in this gratuitous bailment.[47] (See Figure 13.2.)

Figure 13.2 Historical Level of Care Required of Bailee

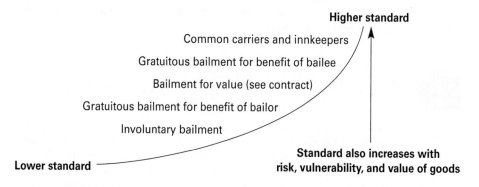

---

46. *Innkeepers Act*, R.S.O. 1990, c. I-1.7, s. 4.

47. [2001] A.J. No. 155 (Q.B.).

In a bailment action, unlike a normal negligence action, the onus of proof shifts to the bailee. Thus, once the bailment has been established and damage to the goods has been shown, a presumption of negligence arises, which the bailee must rebut to avoid liability. For example, in *Evans v. Northsite Security Services Ltd.*, the plaintiff placed his cell phone and camera in a bowl in the screening area at airport security as instructed and the items went missing. The presumption of negligence arose and since the defendant failed to explain how the items went missing, judgment was given to the plaintiff.[48]

INVOLUNTARY BAILMENT

When someone puts away a coat left behind in a restaurant or at a friend's house, or picks up a watch found on the sidewalk, an involuntary bailment has been created. Exercising control by putting away the coat or picking up the watch creates the bailment. You have no obligation until you pick up the item. As soon as you exercise that control, the obligations of a gratuitous bailee for the benefit of the bailor arise; now, there is a duty to take care of those goods. The responsibility as bailee is to keep the coat safe and return it to the bailor. Generally speaking, if the goods are returned to the wrong person or discarded, as in the *McCarthy* case below, the bailee is responsible. Although strict liability is not applied, the bailee is liable if his actions were negligent in the circumstances.

Involuntary bailment— duty low

CASE SUMMARY 13.11

Even Involuntary Bailees Have a Duty: *McCarthy v. Matthews*[49]

Mrs. McCarthy left the house, leaving all the furniture and appliances behind when she separated from her husband. No further mortgage payments were made. The subsequent foreclosure action led to the sale of the house. Mrs. McCarthy had, in the meantime, returned to the house to get the furniture and appliances, but the locks had been changed and she could not get in. The mortgagee ignored the realtor's advice to either store the goods or try to contact the previous owner. Instead, when the cleaning crew came to prepare the house for sale, the mortgagee simply told them to discard the items.

The Court held that the mortgagee was an involuntary bailee "and was therefore under duty to exercise that degree of diligence which men of common prudence generally exercised about their own affairs." When the mortgagee treated the property as abandoned, it had failed in its duty and was liable for Mrs. McCarthy's loss. Because Mrs. McCarthy failed to take the remaining goods (about half) when she had the chance, she was held contributorily negligent. Her damages were, therefore, reduced by one half.

SMALL BUSINESS PERSPECTIVE

This case demonstrates that while the duty owed by an involuntary bailee is minimal, if the bailee should treat that property with indifference, liability will be established.

---

48. [2002] N.W.T.J. No. 95 (Terr. Ct.).

49. [1987] B.C.J. No. 3163 (Prov. Ct.).

THE RIGHTS OF THE BAILEE AND BAILOR

Contract terms prevail

Except where modified by statute

The terms set out in the contract govern a bailment for value. Such provisions as the terms of payment, the requirement of insurance, and any exculpatory clauses are binding if they have been properly brought to the attention of the parties. An unpaid bailee has a common law right to a lien if he has repaired or otherwise worked on the goods, but there is no corresponding common law lien where the goods are just stored, as with a warehouse, or transported. Today, statutes give common carriers, repair persons, storage facilities, and other bailees for value the right to retain the goods until payment is arranged. This statutory lien includes a right to resell, after giving the bailor appropriate notice and an opportunity to reclaim the goods.[50] Refer to the MyBusLawLab for further detail as to the legislation in effect in your jurisdiction.

When it is the bailor who has not been paid (as when rent for tools used is unpaid), he can reclaim the goods and seek normal contractual remedies. Where no price has been agreed upon, the bailor is entitled to recover a reasonable payment on the basis of the principle of *quantum meruit.*

INTELLECTUAL PROPERTY

Although real and personal property may take physical forms and be tangible, the rights associated with such property are created by and protected by law. Similarly, the rights attached to intangible property are also defined and protected by law. Intellectual property law attempts to balance the protection of the product of a person's mental effort on the one side and the free flow of new and innovative ideas, which stimulate the advancement of the commercial environment, on the other. Its attention focuses both on defending the rights of individuals in relation to ideas, information, and other creative works, and on regulating how others use those products of the mind. These opposite interests often collide, especially now in the digital information age, with the explosion of computers, software, and internet technology.

Intellectual property must be contrasted to other forms of personal property. When a chattel is stolen or destroyed, it is no longer available for the use of the original owner. When an idea is taken and used by somebody else, or confidential information is wrongfully communicated to another, the idea or information does not change. It is still available to the original holder, although its value might be considerably diminished.

The expansion of internet information transmission, along with society's greater reliance on computers in general, has created pressure to enact more significant intellectual property laws. The development of law has not kept pace with this information and technological explosion. Existing laws, however, establish many rights and obligations, and changes are constantly being made by both Parliament and the courts.

Most legislation protecting intellectual property is federal, with copyright and patent legislation being exclusively granted to the federal government in the *Constitution Act, 1867.*[51] Other important federal statutes include the *Trade-marks*

[50.] The bailee must conduct the sale in a commercially reasonable way. See *Carr v. 1181607 Ontario Inc. (c.o.b. Elf Mini Storage),* [2002] O.J. No. 3250 (Sup. Ct. J.).

[51.] (U.K.), 30 & 31 Vict., c. 3, ss. 91(22)–(23), reprinted in R.S.C. 1985, App. II, No. 5. Specifically, see the *Copyright Act,* R.C.S. 1985, c. C-42 and the *Patents Act,* R.S.C. 1985, c. P-4.

Act and the *Industrial Design Act.*[52] Confidential information and trade secrets are protected by common law principles; passing-off actions provide remedies when parties misrepresent their products or services as those of another. These areas will also be discussed in this chapter.

CASE SUMMARY 13.12

Grad Students Shocked to Find Their Theses Marketed for Profit Online[53]

Canadian academics were angered to find their theses marketed online on Contentville.com, an American website. Graduate students submit copies of their work to the National Library of Canada when they complete their degrees. Amongst the forms students complete is one granting the Library permission to reproduce their work to facilitate scholarly research.

The Library contracted with UMI Dissertations Publishing to broaden the access to dissertations; UMI in turn made part of its catalogue available to Contentville. People wishing to purchase theses contacted Contentville and were turned over to UMI, which sent the requested copy to the buyer and collected the fee.

When possible violation of copyright was raised, Contentville agreed to remove Canadian dissertations and theses from their websites. Contentville conceded that Canadian academics had cause for concern since they were never given the opportunity to deny use of their material in this way. Subsequently, Theses Canada (part of Library and Archives Canada) launched the Theses Canada Portal, with over 45 000 electronic theses. To track further developments in this area, visit the Theses Canada Portal.[54]

Copyright

The *Copyright Act*[55] gives the owner of the copyright a monopoly over the use of the created work, prohibiting copying or reproduction of the work without permission. Only the actual work itself is protected, not the ideas or thought behind it. Thus, the actual expression of an idea in a book is protected, but someone else is free to express those same ideas in a different way.

The work is protected, not the idea

The federal government has the power to make law with respect to copyright. The *Copyright Act,* originally passed in 1928, underwent significant changes in 1997 and 2002.[56] These changes were required because of technological

---

[52.] R.S.C. 1985, c. T-13; R.S.C. 1985, c. I-9.

[53.] "Contentville Agrees to Take Down Canadian Academic Dissertations," *Lawyers Weekly* 20:16 (1 September 2000), (QL); National Library of Canada, News Release, "The National Library of Canada's Theses Canada" (19 September 2000).

[54.] Library and Archives Canada, Theses Canada Portal, online: www.collectionscanada.gc.ca/thesescanada/index-e.html.

[55.] R.S.C. 1985, c. C-42.

[56.] A comprehensive review of the *Copyright Act* was called for within five years of the 1997 major revision to copyright law. Bill C-11 came into effect in December 2002. It was the first to update Canada's copyright legislation in the internet era, and was prompted by certain companies' "streaming" broadcast programming over the internet. Bill C-60, introduced in June 2005, had its passage interrupted by a national election, as did Bill C-61 in 2008.

advances, including the ease of reproducing written, musical, visual, and computer works. Massive copying of books, sound recordings, and computer programs is now not only possible but common. This is particularly true on the internet—compression software and CD and DVD burners have made the wholesale copying of recorded music so widespread it has seriously affected the viability of the recorded music industry.

MATTERS COVERED

To be copyrightable, work must be original and the product of the author's skill

Only original work that is the product of an artist's or author's own work or skill is entitled to copyright protection. Note that it is the expression that has to be original, not the idea. Before the 1997 legislative amendments, only works that were somehow preserved, be it in writing or in some other manner, were subject to copyright. Now, a performer's performance is subject to copyright, whether fixed or not. There is also a separate copyright for a musical work (such as a song) and for the sound recording (such as the CD containing the song), so the owners of the separate copyrights may well differ.

The categories of copyrightable materials have been expanded to seven, as summarized by Table 13.1.

Table 13.1 Works Protected by the *Copyright Act*

Literary works	including tables, computer programs, and "literary compilations" such as poems, stories, and articles (books).
Dramatic works	such as shows (movies, videos, television, and theatre) and mime performances, including choreography and scenery
Musical works	musical compositions with or without words
Artistic works	such as paintings, drawings, charts, maps, plans, photos, engravings, sculptures, works of artistic craftsmanship, and architecture

In addition to these works, copyright protection has also been extended to

Performers' performances	including performances by actors, musicians, dancers, and singers
Sound recordings	including CDs, tapes, and other methods for reproducing sound
Communication signals	such as radio and TV created by a broadcaster

Note that there is considerable overlap, and someone's creative work might qualify for copyright protection in more than one of these categories.

When a collective work or compilation includes other works protected by copyright, one should exercise care when making a copy, electronic or on paper, of the collective work or compilation. For example, judges' decisions are compiled into collections such as the *Dominion Law Reports* published by Canada Law Book. The actual decision, being law, is not covered by copyright; to it the publisher adds headnotes and annotations. In the *CCH* case, the compilation was held to be original work subject to copyright; the service, operated by The Law Society of British Columbia, supplying photocopies of these annotated judgments to lawyers, was held to be a violation of the publisher's copyright.[57] This decision has since been varied by the Supreme Court of Canada,[58] which held that the Law Society of Upper Canada did not infringe copyright by providing single photocopies of cases to its members. Instead, this practice fell within the exception for "fair dealing" for the purpose of research or private study. In essence, the Court gave "fair dealing" a broad interpretation, holding that distribution of copies of case decisions to practising lawyers simply enabled them to conduct *research* on the law.

CASE SUMMARY 13.13

Digital Compilations: *Unauthorized Reproduction or not? Robertson v. Thompson Corp.*[59]

A freelance author whose articles were published by the *Globe and Mail* claimed a violation of her copyright when the *Globe* placed the articles in three databases, including Info Globe Online and CD-ROM. At the time Robertson submitted her articles to the *Globe*, it had not been contemplated that these would subsequently be included in CD-ROMs and electronic databases. In its decision, the Ontario Court of Appeal sought to strike a balance between the author's right to control and monetize the work, and the need to provide society with access to the work. "Excessive control by authors that limits creative innovation is not in the long-term best interests of society as a whole. At the same time, allowing powerful corporations to deprive authors of the fruits of their labour is unjust."[60]

Furthermore, the Court acknowledged the need for the *Copyright Act* to be media or technology neutral. In other words, copyright principles ought not to be affected by the medium of the work or the technology used.

The Supreme Court of Canada dismissed the appeal but allowed the cross appeal with regards to CD compilations. The CD compilations reproduced copies of the newspaper itself and thus the CD ROMs were simply a valid exercise of the *Globe and Mail's* right to reproduce its collective work. Essentially, media neutrality was recognized. Since the CD ROMs were simply a compendium of daily newspaper editions, the authors copyright was not infringed when the newspaper itself was reproduced digitally. But in Info Globe Online and CPI.Q, the originality of the freelance articles was reproduced, but the originality of the newspapers was not. The articles were decontextualized such that they were no longer presented in a manner that maintained their intimate connection with the rest of that newspaper. Accordingly, such reproduction violated the freelance authors' copyright as it was done without compensation and without obtaining their consent.

[57.] *CCH Canadian Ltd. v. Law, Society of Upper Canada*, [2002] 4 F.C. 213 (C.A.).

[58.] *CCH Canadian Ltd. v. Law Society of Upper Canada*, [2004] 1 S.C.R. 339.

[59.] [2006] S.C.J. No. 43.

[60.] *Robertson v. Thomson Corp.*, [2004] O.J. No. 4029 (C.A.)

Computer programs protected

The problem of whether computer programs are protected by copyright or patent law was solved by the 1988 amendment to the *Copyright Act* that now specifically provides copyright protection for computer software and hardware. A particular problem with computer programs is the difficulty in distinguishing between what constitutes the idea behind the software and its expression. Note that it is the expression of the idea, not the idea itself that is copyrightable. It is now settled that where one product has the same look and feel in its operation as the other, an infringement of copyright has taken place, even where the actual computer code is completely different. A specific statute, the *Integrated Circuit Topography Act*, has been enacted to protect the design of the integrated circuit expressed in the computer chip itself.[61] The actual three-dimensional design has to be registered, and the protection granted is for a period of 10 years.

CASE SUMMARY 13.14

Sharing Music: *What's all the Fuss About? BMG Canada Inc. v. John Doe*[62]

What is wrong with sharing music—or a movie? Technology has greatly facilitated the sharing of digital recordings. One need no longer lend a CD to a friend; people can now download music on the internet—often for free. However, the rights of the owners of the song recording may be violated.

Any audio source can be digitalized and then transferred over the internet. Through a process called *ripping*, copies of the digital information from the CD can be placed directly on a computer's hard drive. The file can then be compressed, copied, and emailed to another user. The compressed file can be converted back into a format that can be imprinted onto a recordable CD using a CD *burner* and played on a regular CD player. Napster was the first widely used peer-to-peer music sharing service. Napster Inc. set up a website that contained no music files. Instead, Napster allowed members to load the Napster file-sharing software, which, in turn, enabled users to search a database of files offered for sharing by other users. In other words, Napster only facilitated User A to get in touch with User B. User A could search for a song, find it on User B's computer, and download it directly from User B's computer. If User A had a CD burner, he could then record the file onto a blank CD and play it on a regular CD player. However, nothing ensured that a licence allowing copying had been first secured by User B from the owner of the sound recording.

In 1999, Napster Inc. was sued by several record labels who alleged that Napster was guilty of contributory and vicarious copyright infringement. An injunction was granted, ordering Napster.com to cease from engaging in or facilitating others in copying, downloading, uploading, transmitting, or distributing the plaintiffs' copyrighted materials without the permission of the copyright holder. Since Napster had no way of determining which files were subject to the plaintiffs' copyright, the order shut down Napster's site completely.[63]

Since then, other "peer-to-peer" (P2P) file-sharing software has emerged, designed to evade copyright laws. Users post songs onto the servers of their own computer, where

---

61. S.C.1990, c. 37.

62. [2005] F.C.A. 193.

63. K. Mills & T. Webb, "Napster: Innocent Sharing or Illegal Copying?" (December 2000/January 2001), *LawNow*, p. 17.

they can be shared with others. The users often hide behind pseudonyms, so the first obstacle to a copyright infringement action is identifying the defendants. In *BMG Canada Inc. v. John* Doe, Canada's major music proprietors brought an infringement action against 29 pseudonym users and sought to compel the internet service providers (ISPs) to disclose their identities. Although the Court dismissed the application due to evidentiary inadequacies and concerns regarding protection of privacy, it conceded that the defendants may have infringed copyright.

While downloading a song for private use may not infringe the law,[64] downloading for the purpose of sale, rental, distribution, communication by telecommunication, or performance in public is prohibited. Furthermore, it was possible that peer-to-peer users "authorized copying" (in violation of copyright) by putting songs into a shared directory on their computers, thus inviting and permitting others access to them.

Only the copyright holder has the right to *authorize* such communications. By making a song file available, User B would be authorizing its communication. It appears that the only way a user could stay within the law is by securing a licence from the copyright holder before making the files available for downloading. iTunes Music Store offers a pay service; royalties are presumably paid to those holding copyright.

DISCUSSION QUESTIONS

With technology constantly changing, it is likely that other similar services are bound to arise due to market demand. What must the entertainment industry do to adequately protect its interests?

Note that in April 2009, four owners of Pirate Bay, a torrent tracking website, were convicted in Sweden for promoting other people's infringements of copyright laws.[65] They were sentenced to one year in prison and payment of a fine equal to US$3.5 million. The damages were awarded to several entertainment companies, including Warner Bros, Sony Music Entertainment, EMI, and Columbia Pictures. The website facilitated file sharing of music, movies, and games. No copyright content was hosted on the Pirate Bay's web servers; instead the site hosts "torrent" links to TV, film, and music files held on its users' computers. The Pirate Bay site itself is still up and running pending appeal of the decision, but since the Pirate Bay moved most of its servers to the Netherlands, the site may keep running even if the Pirate Bay loses its appeal.

CREATION

In Canada, the creation of the work generates copyright protection automatically. There is no need to register or even publish the work. Still, registration may be wise, since it establishes when the copyright was created and the presumption that the person named in the registration is the owner of the copyright. Registration is now possible online with the Canadian Intellectual Property Office[66] (or by application sent by fax or mail). Although not specified in the Canadian legislation, there is a practice (following the provisions of the Universal Copyright Convention) of notification of copyright that generally takes the following form:

Copyright comes with creation of work

Registration ensures availability of remedies

Copyright © 2010 Pearson Education Canada Inc., Toronto, Ontario

---

64. *Supra* note 70, s. 80

65. See online http://news.bbc.co.uk/2/hi/technology/8003799.stm.

66. To register online go to www.cipo.ic.gc.ca. Fees for online registration were $50, and $65 (as of April 2009) for applications sent by fax or mail.

The United States and other countries that are parties to the copyright conventions discussed below recognize valid Canadian copyright, and so registration is not necessary. However, notification as set out above may be required; where the copyright is not registered, the remedies available for infringement may be significantly restricted.

International agreements establish common rules

For a person to obtain copyright protection in Canada, he or she must be a citizen or resident of Canada, or a citizen, subject, or resident of one of the countries that adhere to the *Berne Copyright Convention,* the *Universal Copyright Convention (UCC),* or *Rome Convention* (for sound recordings, performer's performances, and communication signals only). These international agreements set out common rules of conduct in matters concerning copyright. Persons whose country is a member of the World Trade Organization (WTO) can also secure copyright protection, and the federal minister can extend this protection to residents of other countries.

Increased international protection for copyright

Several countries do not have the same traditions of protection of artistic and literary works as in Western countries; the disregard for intellectual property protection in such countries has been a major stumbling block in the further development of trade relations. The Chinese government, amidst growing complaints that it was not doing enough to prevent illegal copying of DVDs and other media (often produced in other countries), has stepped up its intellectual property initiatives. It passed a series of copyright laws, and in March 2006, it established a Judicial Court of Intellectual Property to handle piracy and intellectual property cases.

OWNERSHIP

Copyright can be assigned

Copyright belongs to the person who created the work or to the employer where the work was created as part of employment, unless there is an agreement otherwise. Once copyright has been created, its owner can assign or license it, all or in part, to someone else. Courts will presume the copyright is held by the creator unless there is evidence to show otherwise. The owner of the copyright can assign it to someone else, but even then, the author will continue to have moral rights in the work. These moral rights allow the author to demand that his name continue to be associated with the work as its author, and that the new owner not distort, mutilate, or otherwise change the work in such a way as to degrade it and bring harm to the reputation of the author.

CASE SUMMARY 13.15

Injunctions Protect Moral Rights: *Pollock v. CFCN Productions Limited;*[67] *Snow v. The Eaton Centre Ltd.;*[68] *Patsalas v. National Ballet of Canada*[69]

The *Copyright Act* gives the author the right to restrain any distortion, mutilation or other modification of his work that would be prejudicial to his honour or reputation.[70] In the

---

[67] [1983] A.J. No. 772 (Q.B.).

[68] [1982] O.J. No. 3645 (H.C.J.).

[69] [1986] O.J. No. 1135 (H.C.J.).

[70] R.S., 1985, c. C-42, s. 28.2

Pollock case, the plaintiff, a playwright and recipient of the Governor General's Award, sought an interim injunction restraining CFCN Productions Limited from televising a movie made specifically for television based on Pollock's play *Blood Relations*. This play deals with the gruesome story of Lizzie Borden and the axe murder case of her father and stepmother in the United States. Pollock claimed that the screenplay, written by J. Barclay and filmed by CFCN, seriously distorted, violated, and mutilated Pollock's play to the extent that her reputation would be damaged if the film were televised. The injunction was granted.

In the *Snow* case, the plaintiff sculptor claimed that his naturalistic composition composed of 60 geese in flight had been made to look ridiculous by the addition of Christmas ribbons tied around their necks. He suggested "it is not unlike dangling earrings from the Venus de Milo." The Court agreed that the work had been distorted and modified in a prejudicial manner and ordered removal of the decorations. These cases illustrate that one must ensure that an author's moral rights are respected if one hopes to adapt or alter their work.

But an injunction will not necessarily be available if the author grants a license to others to perform his work and later claims irreparable harm if someone else is allowed to choreograph it. In the *Patsalas* case the Court concluded that if the Ballet proceeded to rehearse, stage, and produce Concerto as proposed, the Plaintiff would not suffer irreparable harm to his reputation. Thus an injunction stopping future performances was denied.

DISCUSSION QUESTIONS

When dealing with artistic works, how will the courts determine if a modification or performance causes the author of the work irreparable harm? (Note: See section 28.2 (2) of the *Copyright Act*).

In addition, the work may not be used in association with a product, service, cause, or institution that is prejudicial to the reputation of the author and without the author's permission. For example, Sarah McLachlan demanded that her song "I Will Remember You" be removed from a video that was put together for police-training purposes but which was later made available to the public. McLachlan claimed copyright infringement and asserted that permission would never have been granted because of the "exploitative nature" of the video. The film features aerial images of the Columbine High School in Littleton, Colorado, where two teenagers killed 13 other people and themselves. The song is played while images of the blood-splattered school library are depicted.[71]

Moral rights of the authors and artists have been incorporated into the *Copyright Act*. While the *Act* prohibits the assignment of moral rights, the author of the work can waive them. Provided the author has not waived these moral rights, the author can seek compensation even though someone else owns the copyright. Moral rights exist for the same length of time as copyright and can be passed to the author's heirs, even when those heirs do not inherit ownership of the copyright itself.

Copyright gives the owner control over the work. No one else can perform, copy, publish, broadcast, translate, or otherwise reproduce the work without the

Copyright can be assigned but moral rights are retained

Copyright holder has complete control over rights for author's life plus 50 years

---

[71] Herald News Services, "McLachlan Song on Columbine Tape: Singer Demands Removal," *Calgary Herald,* 28 April 2000, p. A7.

permission of the owner of the copyright.[81] This protection extends for the life of the author plus 50 years, with some exceptions, such as photographs and government publications, where the protection is limited to 50 years from the creation of the negative or document.[72] Then the work becomes part of the **public domain** and anyone can use it. Note that in the United States the protection period is now for life plus 70 years, which will provide added protection for Canadian works being used in the United States. Refer to the MyBusLawLab for further details regarding copyright.

Copyright infringement

Infringing copyright includes situations where a person tries to obtain a benefit from the sale, reproduction, distribution, performance, broadcast, or other commercial use of the work. Plagiarism (copying another's work and claiming its authorship) is also a violation of copyright. The moral rights of an author are infringed when someone else asserts authorship[73] or if the work is mutilated or modified in such a way that the reputation of the author is harmed. Regardless of who owns the copyright, where moral rights have been infringed, the author can seek an injunction or compensation.[74]

CASE SUMMARY 13.16

Students Are Entitled to Copyright Protection: *Boudreau v. Lin*[75]

Paul Boudreau was a part-time MBA student who was working for a high-tech firm. He wrote a paper for a course based on information gathered at his place of employment and incorporated suggestions from his professor. The professor and a colleague published the paper under a different title with only a few revisions, naming themselves as authors. Boudreau discovered his paper published in a casebook and brought an action for copyright infringement against the professor and the university. The Court found that the student was the author and holder of the copyright. The Court rejected the professor's claim that the student's name had been omitted in error. The university was deemed to have knowledge of the infringement, and thus shared liability with its employee. The removal of the student's name and changed title blocked the professor's claim of fair dealing. The inclusion of the paper in a casebook defeated the university's claim that it was for use in private study. Also, the author's moral rights were infringed, because they had interfered with the integrity of the work. The Court noted, "Plagiarism is a form of academic dishonesty which strikes at the heart of our educational system. It is not to be tolerated from the students, and the university has made this quite clear. It follows that it most certainly should not be tolerated from the professors, who should be sterling examples of intellectual rigour and honesty."

---

72. *Supra* note 70, ss. 6–10.

73. See *Dolmage v. Erskine*, [2003] O.J. No. 161 (Sup. Ct. J.), in which a contract lecturer prepared a case during a School of Business case preparation workshop. His moral rights were violated when the case was improperly attributed to others. Damages of $3000 were awarded.

74. *Supra* note 70, ss. 28.1, 34(2).

75. [1997] O.J. No. 3397 (Gen. Div.).

DISCUSSION QUESTIONS

In the academic environment it is not always clear who can claim copyright. This is especially true where university facilities and grants are involved. But in this case there was no doubt that others had taken credit for the student's work. So what steps should an author take who wishes to include, within his own work, the written work of another?

From a business perspective the *Boudreau* case raises a troubling issue, namely that of vicarious liability. If an employee infringes the copyright of a third party, will the employer be held vicariously liable? According to Justice Metivier "the University cannot stand idly by while its professors blatantly breach copyright laws. At the very least, the University is a passive participant. As employer of the professor—it is the duty of the University to set policies for the conduct of its employees and to accept responsibility for monitoring, or failing to monitor, the strict observation of these policies and, in this case, of copyright laws."[76]

Vicarious liability for copyright infringement

Case law both here and in the United States evidences that vicarious liability for infringement of copyright will be imposed.[77] In the case brought by MGM against Grokster Ltd., Justice Souter observed that a person "infringes vicariously by profiting from direct infringement while declining to exercise a right to stop or limit it."[78]

REDUCING RISK 13.5

Should employers implement a copyright policy? Will the existence of a policy relieve an employer from liability if its employees infringe copyright while at work?

In light of the fact that vicarious liability is a form of strict liability, even due diligence by the employer will not shield it from liability. So what is the point of implementing a copyright policy? Even if one's policy does not exempt you from your employees' copyright liability, it will help educate those in your enterprise about copyright. In doing so, the policy may lower the occurrences when copyright-protected material is used without permission.

EXCEPTIONS

There are a variety of exceptions and specific rules. Laws enacted by the federal government and decisions and reasons for decisions of federal courts and tribunals can be copied without permission and without a fee. Here the only condition is that due diligence be exercised in ensuring that the copy is accurate and is not represented as being an official version.

Legislation and case law can be copied without fee

Quotations from the work that are not extensive and are attributed to the author do not amount to an infringement of copyright. The *Copyright Act* specifically states that **fair dealing** for the purpose of research or private study, criticism or review, and news reporting does not infringe copyright.[79] But the line between

Exception for fair dealing

---

76. *Boudreau v. Lin*, [1997] O.J. No. 3397, at para. 52.

77. *Flag Works Inc. v. Sign Craft Digital (1978) Inc.*, [2007] A.J. No. 876 (Q.B.).

78. *Metro-Goldwyn-Mayer Studios Inc. v. Grokster, Ltd.*, 125 S.Ct. 2764, at 2776 (2005) (citing *Shapiro, Bernstein & Co. v. H.L. Green Co.*, 316 F.2d 304, 307 (C.A.2 1963)).

79. *Copyright Act*, R.S.C. 1985, c. C-42, ss. 29, 29.1, and 29.2.

fair dealing and infringement is a thin one. At a minimum, however, in the case of criticism, review, or news reporting, the user is required to give the source and the name of the author, performer, sound recording maker, or broadcaster. (Recall that in the *Boudreau* case summarized earlier in this chapter, the removal of the student's name was fatal to the professor's claim of fair dealing.)

Exception for educators

Certain categories of users are granted exceptions from the general requirements to seek permission or pay royalties for the privilege of copying or performing works. One category is non-profit educational institutions. For example, teachers may copy materials onto blackboards or flipcharts or incorporate materials into exam questions without infringing copyright. But if overhead projection slides are available on the market, these commercially produced alternatives are to be used. Educators can also record and keep for a limited period of time radio, newspaper, and television material.[80]

Further exceptions

Other categories of users to whom exceptions are granted are (1) libraries, archives, and museums, (2) persons with perceptual disabilities, and (3) people making private copies of commercially recorded music or sound recordings. People who have reading or hearing disabilities can make copies to help themselves access the material, for example, by converting the work to Braille. And, interestingly, anyone can make a recording of music tapes, records, and CDs for her own private use. Royalties are charged on blank tapes and other recording media to compensate artists and producers for this exception.

CASE SUMMARY 13.17

Canadian Private Copying Collective v. Red Coast Imports Inc.[81]

The Canadian Private Copying Collective sued Red Coast for failing to report and pay to the Collective private copying levies on account of the manufacture, importation into Canada, and sale of blank audio recording media. The Collective obtained an order requiring disclosure of certain information by affidavit, but despite repeated requests and several delays, the affidavit was not forthcoming. Eventually, the Collective obtained an order striking the defendant's statement of defence.

The defendant's appeal from this decision was dismissed. The Court conceded that striking out pleadings is a drastic remedy, but in light of the defendant's complete disregard for the process, it was warranted. The principal was still in default with an order that had been made six months earlier.

SMALL BUSINESS PERSPECTIVE

Can one simply ignore legal procedures or obstruct the same with numerous delays? The above decision evidences that one does so at one's own peril. Costs were also awarded against the defendant. In the end, the defendant "lost" without having its "day in court."

---

80. *Ibid.*, s. 29.4.

81. [2009] F.C.J. No. 62 (F.C.).

REMEDIES

The remedies normally available in a civil action, including an injunction, are available when a copyright is violated. Sometimes, an *interlocutory injunction* is given before the actual trial to prevent further damage. This is an interim measure, and a permanent injunction may or may not be granted at trial. Often, the effect of the interim remedy is so devastating to the offender that no further action need be taken. To obtain an interlocutory injunction, the plaintiff must establish a *prima facie* case (1) that there has been an infringement of copyright, (2) that if the injunction is not granted, irreparable harm will be suffered that could not properly be compensated for by an award of damages at the trial, and (3) that the **balance of convenience** is also in the plaintiff's favour. This refers to which side will suffer the greatest damage if the injunction is granted. Where the plaintiff seeks an order to stop the production and sales of a much larger operation, it will not be granted if the order would cause that business more damage than the plaintiff would suffer if the injunction were not granted.

Interlocutory injunctions may be granted before trial

Sometimes, a court will make an order, even before trial, that the offending material be seized. This is called an **Anton Piller order**. Typically, the application is made without notice to the offending party, because the evidence must be seized by surprise before the goods or relevant documentation can be hidden or destroyed. The court will only issue such an order where there is clear and compelling evidence of the infringement of copyright, the danger of significant damage to the plaintiff, and some indication that surprise is needed to protect the evidence. The seizure of the offending works before trial is now provided for in the *Copyright Act* itself.[82]

Anton Piller order provides for seizure of goods

One of the most important remedies is the **permanent injunction** prohibiting the production, sale, or distribution of any of the infringing products. If the defendants were unaware they were violating copyright, the only remedy under the *Copyright Act* is an injunction. This restriction does not apply, however, if at the date of infringement, the copyright was duly registered under the *Act*. Often sought together with an injunction is a **delivery up** order, directing the defendant to deliver all copies of the infringing items in its possession or control to the copyright owner.

Permanent injunction granted at trial

Delivery up order often sought

Where the infringement took place knowingly, damages or an accounting may be obtained. An award of *damages* is calculated to compensate the victim for the losses suffered, including the lost profits that would have been earned had the copyright not been infringed. An *accounting* is often given where it would be difficult to determine what actual damages have been suffered. This remedy requires that any profits made from the sale or rental of the offending product be paid over to the victim, even if this amount exceeds the damages suffered by the plaintiff. The court may also award *punitive damages* in cases of flagrant violation to punish the offender rather than simply to compensate the victim of the infringement. In any case, it must be noted that the limitation period in which an action should be commenced is three years. But if the plaintiff did not or could not have reasonably known of the infringement, that limitation period may be extended to three years running not from the date of infringement, but from the date the plaintiff discovered or ought reasonably to have discovered the infringement.[83]

Damages can compensate for loss

Accounting requires handing over profits

[82.] *Supra*note 70, s. 38.

[83.] *Ibid.*, s. 41(1)(b).

Punitive damages may be available to punish wrongdoer

Damages flowing from copyright infringement can be significant. Consider the case recently commenced by Viacom and Paramount Pictures as against YouTube and Google,[84] where the plaintiffs are seeking damages in excess of US$1billion. The plaintiffs allege that YouTube has harnessed technology to infringe the copyright of writers, composers and performers on a vast scale, without payment or permission. The plaintiffs identified more than 150 000 unauthorized clips of their copyrighted programming on YouTube that had been viewed an astounding 1.5 billion times.

Statutory damages now available

The Copyright Act now provides a copyright owner with three new remedies. The first, **statutory damages**, enables a court to award damages that it "considers just" in the circumstances, with a general limit of between $500 and $20 000. This remedy was introduced to alleviate difficulties encountered in providing the exact losses to the plaintiff or the net gain reaped by the wrongdoer.

Injunctions prevent repeated infringements

The second addition is a wide or **enhanced injunction**. It allows the court to order a wrongdoer to refrain from future infringements of copyright in other works owned by the plaintiff copyright owner. It even applies to works later acquired by that plaintiff. This remedy saves the plaintiff the time and expense of future litigation and can be obtained if the plaintiff shows it is likely the wrongdoer will engage in such future infringements.

Third, **summary procedures** are more expedient and less expensive than full court actions, since the court can make a decision based on affidavit evidence.

Fine and imprisonment available for infringement

Criminal Code *may apply*

In addition to these civil remedies, the *Copyright Act* provides for penalties of up to a million dollars in fines and five years in jail for the most serious cases. The provisions set out in the *Criminal Code,* such as those sections prohibiting theft and fraud, may also apply to infringement of copyright cases.[85]

CASE SUMMARY 13.18

Cracking Down on Unauthorized Copying: *Canadian Reprography Collective v. Copy Ink Inc.;*[86] *SOCAN v. Maple Leaf Sports and Entertainment Ltd.*[87]

In April 1994, CANCOPY secured a civil judgment against a photocopy shop located near the University of Toronto. The Court found that the copy shop was deliberately making copies of a textbook for resale. The text, *Computer Organization,* was priced at $88.26 by the university bookstore. Copy Ink was selling illicit copies of this McGraw-Hill Ryerson text to students at a bargain price of $20. It was also taking orders for other textbooks, and copying them without prior permission from the copyright owners. Damages in the sum of $133 000 were awarded to CANCOPY and publisher McGraw-Hill Ryerson. Evidence in this case was secured by search and seizure. It is rare for a court to award a search and seizure order in a civil, as opposed to criminal, action. In fact, this was the first such order secured by CANCOPY, and it enabled the police and CANCOPY officials to find the necessary evidence.

---

84. *Viacom International Inc. v. YouTube, Inc.,* (S.D. NY., filed 13/3/2007).

85. *Criminal Code,* R.S.C. 1985, c. C-46.

86. [1994] O.J. No. 1003 (Gen. Div.).

87. [2008] F.C.J. No. 1384 (F.C.).

In the Maple Leaf case, SOCAN alleged that the defendant (operator of Air Canada Centre (ACC), a large sports arena used for indoor sports events as well as public concerts and other shows) authorized or permitted a large number of unlicensed musical performances at the ACC over the past ten years. At discoveries, the plaintiff asked the latter to give the detail of all performances which had been put in issue by the pleadings, including names of performers and works performed. Over that decade, employees working at ACC (stage hands, ushers, security agents, salespersons, etc.) would have had occasion to notice who was performing and what musical works were being performed. When the plaintiff asked the defendant for the names and contact particulars, the defendant outright refused to divulge that information.

The Court found that had the defendant been asked to interview all 2400 employees itself, such a direction could have been viewed too onerous. But the defendant's refusal to allow the plaintiff to engage in such an inquiry amounted to an obstruction, frustrating the plaintiff's ability to collect material evidence. Accordingly, the Court ordered Maple Leaf's representative on discovery to provide "the name of the performer(s) and songs performed in all concerts at issue where such information can be obtained by diligent inquiry of all of MLSE's present and former employees who might reasonably be expected to have such knowledge."

SMALL BUSINESS PERSPECTIVE

The Courts appear ready to provide parties with tools to assist them with collection of evidence. Costs can also be used to further penalize those who obstruct legal procedures. In light of the above, what should a party do if it comes to light that copyright has been infringed, be it unintentionally or unknowingly, by one's staff?

It is important to understand that the unauthorized copying of artwork, photographs, computer programs, compact discs, videotapes, or even designs on clothing can result in a criminal conviction as well as copyright infringement even though the original is unaffected. In *R. v. Chen*, for example, the accused was sentenced to 12 months' imprisonment and fined for selling clothing that replicated brand names. She sold the clothes from her home at 10 percent of the price demanded for the genuine merchandise.[88]

THE COPYRIGHT BOARD

The *Copyright Act* establishes a Copyright Board with broad powers to handle disputes between individuals and otherwise supervise and regulate the industry. It arbitrates tariffs if there is a disagreement between a licensing body and another party; it sets levies on blank audio recording devices (cassettes, CDs, and so on); and it reviews and approves fees for public performance or telecommunication of sound recordings. Tariffs are set fees that users must pay for using certain copyright material. Cable companies pay tariffs for permission to transmit programs. Royalties are sums paid as commission for sales of a work or permission to use it. Royalties are paid to musicians when radio stations play their songs. Several collective societies have been created to represent the owners of copyright in licensing arrangements with others and to assist in the collection of tariffs and

---

88. [2004] B.C.J. No. 2072 (Prov. Ct.).

royalties. A collective may also commence a civil action on behalf of a member seeking compensation for copyright infringement. SOCAN (Society of Composers, Authors and Music Publishers of Canada) performs this service in the music industry. Access Copyright (Canadian Copyright Licensing Agency, formerly CANCOPY) serves a similar function in the literary field. Refer to the MyBusLawLab for further information concerning the Copyright Board and copyright collective societies.

Patents

Must be original invention to be patentable

A patent is a government-granted monopoly, giving only the inventor the right to produce, sell, or otherwise profit from a specific invention. Unlike copyright, patent protection extends to the *physical embodiment* of the idea or concept. To qualify, the invention must be new, in the sense that no one else has been given a patent for it and that it has not been disclosed to the public in Canada or elsewhere more than a year prior to application. This includes disclosure in an academic paper. The invention must also be the original work of the inventor. Thus, a person could not take an invention found in another country and patent it in Canada as his own. The invention must be unique and distinguishable from other products. It must be a development or improvement that would not have been obvious to others in the technology involved. It must have some utility or perform some useful function. It must also be possible to construct and use it on the basis of the information supplied to the patent office.

CASE SUMMARY 13.19

Selling Product Was Fatal to Patent: *Baker Petrolite Corp. v. Canwell Enviro-Industries Ltd.*[89]

Canwell Enviro-Industries developed a chemical formula to sweeten the sour smell associated with "sour gas" natural-gas wells. It started selling the product (W-3053) on 10 December 1987. The following year, on 23 December 1988, it made an application for a patent on the process in the United States, followed by an application for one in Canada on 19 December 1989. This application was opposed by Baker Petrolite, which had developed a similar product. The Federal Court of Appeal held that Canwell was not entitled to a patent because of disclosure more than a year before the application for the patent. Canwell had not actually disclosed the formula itself; however, the Court reasoned that if a person with the appropriate skills could, by analyzing the product, determine its active components and develop a similar product, then making the product available to the public amounted to disclosure. Thus a patent could not be given.

You cannot patent a scientific principle or abstract theory, such as Newton's discovery of gravity;[100] nor can you patent obvious improvements to other products, inventions designed for illegal purposes, things that cannot work, and things

---

[89] [2003] 1 F.C. 49 (C.A.).

[90] *Patent Act*, R.S.C. 1985, c. P-4, s. 27(8).

generally covered by copyright law. But a non-obvious improvement on an already existing invention is patentable. It is clear that lower forms of life such as plants and bacteria are patentable, but what about higher forms of life?

Theories, concepts, or obvious improvements are not patentable

---

CASE SUMMARY 13.20

Mice? Untested Drugs? What Is Patentable? *Harvard College v. Canada (Commissioner of Patents);*[91] *Apotex v. Wellcome Foundation*[92]

Does a genetically altered mouse fall within the *Patent Act* definition of an "invention"? Scientists injected an oncogene into the embryo of the mouse, thereby creating a mouse that was susceptible to cancer. Harvard College sought patent protection, fearing others might buy an oncomouse and breed it, undermining its market among cancer researchers. The Federal Court of Appeal surprised many when it declared that higher life forms were patentable. For a patent to be available, the legislation requires that the subject matter be a non-naturally occurring composition of matter, arising from the application of inventiveness or ingenuity. Arguably, "oncomouse" is not merely the product of the laws of nature. The Supreme Court of Canada held otherwise. The Court stated that the patentability of higher life forms should be left to Parliament. So unless the *Patent Act* is amended, higher life forms cannot be patented in Canada.

In June 2006, the patent office published an office practice notice regarding the patentability of fertilized eggs, stems cells, organs, and tissues. Animals at any stage of development, from fertilized eggs on, are higher life forms and are thus not patentable subject matter under section 2 of the Patent Act.

> Totipotent stem cells, which have the same potential as fertilized eggs to develop into an entire animal, are considered to be equivalents of fertilized eggs and are thus higher life forms and are not patentable subject matter. Embryonic, multipotent and pluripotent stem cells, which do not have the potential to develop into an entire animal, are patentable subject matter . . . . Organs and tissues are not compositions of matter for the purposes of the definition of invention under section 2 of the Patent Act and are therefore not patentable subject matter.[93]

What about drugs, the effectiveness of which has not yet been tested? In *Apotex v. Wellcome Foundation*, the Supreme Court articulated the doctrine of "sound prediction," which allows a patentee to claim subject matter not made or tested in certain circumstances. Notably, there must be a factual basis for the prediction, and a sound line of reasoning from which the desired result can be inferred from the factual basis. Proper disclosure is likewise required.

---

91. [2000] 4 F.C.R. No. A334–98 (F.C.A.); overturned on appeal, [2002], 4 S.C.R. 45.

92. [2002] 4 S.C.R. 153.

93. Canadian Intellectual Property Office, online: www.cipo.ic.gc.ca/eic/site/cipointernet-internetopic. nsf/eng/wr00295.html, accessed 19 April 2009.

The main issue in this case was whether there was really an "invention." The drug AZT was a compound initially developed in 1964 to combat cancer. In 1985, scientists presented a sound prediction (educated guess?) in the patent application that AZT would be useful in treating AIDS. The Court held that as long as the "guess" is subsequently demonstrated to work, it will be deemed to have been an invention at the time the patent application was made.

DISCUSSION QUESTIONS

Can you think of other inventions or products where an application for a patent might be challenged?

What can and cannot be patented

In Canada, as a general rule, computer programs cannot be patented and are now covered by copyright legislation, but such patents have been granted in the United States and may be available in limited situations in Canada in the future. In the United States, it is possible to patent business methods (BMPs), which create a patent monopoly on a particular process or model of carrying on business. In Canada there is no right to patent methods of carrying on business as yet, but Canadian firms doing business in the United States or even selling products there could be sued for patent infringement for their business practices taking place in Canada. U.S. patents have been issued for business methods including distribution models, inventory management, service delivery models, training methods, financial models, and models for sharing information.

CREATION

Patent must be applied for and registered

Unlike copyright, the patent must be registered before conferring rights on the inventor, and so it is vital that a patent be applied for right away. If someone else beats you to it, you will not only lose the right to patent but also be prevented from producing or otherwise using or profiting from the invention. Employers are entitled to patent the inventions of their employees, and the holder of a patent can assign that patent to others. Joint patents can be obtained when several people have worked on the same invention.

The process of obtaining a patent is complex, requiring that patent records be searched to see if a patent already exists, and then submitting an application with supporting documentation and the prescribed fee to the appropriate patent office. These documents include a petition, specifications, claims statements, an abstract, and a drawing that set out not only what the invention is supposed to do, but also enough information so that someone looking at them could build and use the item. The patent office then assigns an examiner, who may require further submissions from the applicant, and when all conditions have been met, the patent will be granted. If there are opposing applications, the patent will be granted to the person who first made an application. This process is usually handled by a registered patent agent with both legal and engineering training, and may take two or three years to complete.

Date of application in own country determines priority

Pursuant to international agreements, once a Canadian patent has been granted, application can be made for patents in other jurisdictions, but priority in those countries will be based on when the application was first made in Canada. The reverse is also true, and the Canadian patent office will grant a patent to a foreign applicant who applies in his or her own country before the Canadian applicant applies here. There is a limited period of time after obtaining the Canadian patent to make an application for a foreign patent, and so this should be done without delay. (For further information, go to the MyBusLawLab, where numerous external links on this topic can be accessed.)

Once the patent has been issued, the patent number should be put on the manufactured item to which it applies. The use of "patent pending" has no legal effect but the phrase is put on goods to warn that a patent has been applied for. A patent gives its holder a monopoly for a maximum period of 20 years from the date of application, but it requires that the inventor publicly disclose how to make the item in documents that are open to public inspection. Secrecy is surrendered in exchange for the 20-year protection, the idea being that others will be stimulated to produce new inventions because of the disclosure of that information. The granting of the patent gives the patent holder exclusive rights to manufacture, sell, and profit from the invention for those 20 years. A patent will even protect someone who merely develops a variation of the product, providing that variation satisfies the three basic criteria for patentability, namely: (1) it must be new and original; (2) it must be useful, functional, and operational; and (3) it must be inventive, displaying ingenuity on the inventor's part.

Because a patent protects the idea rather than its expression, another person would not be able to produce a simple variation of the product without breaching the patent. An infringement of patent may take place by an unauthorized person's manufacturing, importing, selling, or otherwise dealing with or using the invention. The patent holder is entitled to the same remedies that would be available in any civil action, including injunction, damages, and accounting, as discussed above under the heading of copyright.

Patent grants monopoly for 20 years but requires disclosure

CASE SUMMARY 13.21

How Far Should Patent Protection Go? *Monsanto Canada Inc. v. Schmeiser*[94]

Using genetic engineering, Monsanto developed a specific strain of canola seed that was resistant to Roundup, a herbicide also produced by Monsanto. Farmers planting "Roundup Ready Canola" would also use Roundup, which would kill all other plant forms, leaving the modified canola plants unscathed. Monsanto licensed farmers to use its Roundup Ready Canola for a fee of $15 per acre, and licencees agreed to purchase new seeds every year and not plant seeds from last year's crop.

Mr. Schmeiser did not purchase Roundup Ready Canola but noticed that some of his crop was resistant to Roundup. He collected seeds from that section and planted them the next year, giving his entire crop this resistance to Roundup. Through tests on the canola crop grown on Schmeiser's farm (likely through illegally obtained samples), Monsanto determined that his plants contained the genetically engineered genes it had developed and sued him for patent infringement. Even though Schmeiser used seeds from plants growing on his field, the Federal Court of Appeal held that he was infringing on the Monsanto patent and ordered an injunction and damages. It didn't matter how the Roundup Ready Canola had originally gotten on his property or even whether he actually used the herbicide Roundup to take advantage of it.

---

94. [2003] 2 F.C. 165 (C.A.); appeal allowed in part, [2004] 1 S.C.R. 902.

> Schmeiser appealed to the Supreme Court of Canada, but was only partially successful. While the Supreme Court confirmed that the farmer, by collecting, saving, and planting the seeds, infringed the *Patent Act,* it also found that the trial judge erred by awarding an amount for improper profits (as Schmeiser did not make any greater profit as a result of planting Roundup Ready, rather than ordinary, canola). In essence, the Court confirmed that one can patent genetically altered plant forms. It also warned plaintiffs that if an accounting for improper profits is sought as the remedy, an award will only be made if improper profits are actually made.

Note that the *Monsanto* decision significantly expands the concept of patent infringement. Whereas in the *Harvard College* case regarding the "oncomouse" (Case Summary 13.25) the Supreme Court held that higher life forms were not patentable, in *Monsanto* the Court held that the unlicensed cultivation of plants containing a patented gene infringed the patent. Thus, so long as the gene or cell is patented, use of the organism in which the gene or cell is contained can constitute violation of the patent.

Often, the holder of the patent does not have the resources to manufacture or otherwise exploit the invention and will license its manufacture to another company. Where an important invention is involved, there is provision for compulsory licences to be granted with the payment of royalties, even over the objections of the inventor.

A 1987 amendment to the *Patent Act* gave drug manufacturers more control over the production and sale of their products. This was aimed at preventing competitors from capitalizing on the research and development of those manufacturers and producing much cheaper "generic drugs." A Patented Medicine Prices Review Board was also established with broad powers, including the power to reduce the sale of patented medicines. Pharmaceuticals obtained increased patent protection, with exclusive control extended to 20 years.[95] But in 2005, Bill C-9 (known as the Jean Chrétien Pledge to Africa (JCPA)) came into force. It facilitates access to pharmaceuticals in the developing world, in order to address public health problems, especially those resulting from HIV/AIDS, tuberculosis, malaria, and other epidemics.[96] In September 2007, Apotex Inc., a generic drug manufacturer,was granted authorization under Canada's Access to Medicines Regime to manufacture a pharmaceutical product used in the treatment of HIV/AIDS for export to Rwanda.[97] See links on the MyBusLawLab for further details.

[95.] *Patent Act Amendments,* R.S.C. 1985 (3d Supp.), c. 33.

[96.] *An Act to Amend the Patent Act,* S.C. 2005, c. 18

[97.] For information on Canada's Access to Medicines Regime, see online http://camr-rcam.hc-sc.gc.ca/index_e.html.

REDUCING RISK 13.6

A business should take great care to protect its intellectual property. Whether a process or product is developed by an independent contractor, a consultant, or an employee, a provision in the contract creating that relationship should designate who is entitled to the patent, copyright, or other form of intellectual property developed. Otherwise, when the relationship ends it is quite possible to find that process being given to and used by a competitor.

Equally important is the need to ensure that one is not infringing the copyright or patent held by another. Research in Motion (RIM) agreed to pay US$612.5 million to settle its Blackberry patent dispute with NTP.[98] The U.S. Court of Appeal for the Federal Circuit had earlier declared that RIM infringed upon U.S. patents owned by NTP. The finding shocked many, as patent law historically has not stretched across borders. RIM located its equipment and performed its activities in Canada; nonetheless, U.S. patent law was applied. The case leads Canadian businesses to ask: To what degree are Canadian companies exposed to liability if ecommerce or business method patents issued in the United States are infringed? Could one be infringing a foreign patent if serving a foreign customer over the internet?[99]

Trade-marks

A *trade-mark* is any term, symbol, design, or combination of these that identifies a business service or product and distinguishes it from a competitor. Registered trade-marks are protected by the federal *Trade-marks Act*.[100] Examples of protected trade-marks are such words as "Kodak" and "Xerox"; symbols such as the arm and hammer used on that company's baking soda box; combinations of words and symbols, such as the apple logo on computers; and even the distinctive design of a product's container, such as the Coca-Cola bottle. Trade-marks also include the special marks used by some organizations, such as the Canadian Standards Association, to indicate quality or certification.

A business may be worth more than the total of its *tangible* assets. Its reputation, ongoing relations with customers, and product identification, collectively known as its **goodwill**, also have value. The name and trade-marks associated with the business largely embody that goodwill. The object of trade-marks is to protect the value of the goodwill and prevent other parties from misleading the public by using the trade-mark words or symbols for their own purposes. Ultimately, businesses seek to prevent the trade-mark's value from being diminished through association with inferior products.

For a trade-mark to be protected under the *Act*, it must be registered. As part of the registration process, it is published in the *Trade-mark Journal*, and if any parties believe that it does not qualify, they can oppose the registration. Once registered, the trade-mark gives its owner an exclusive right to use it throughout Canada for 15 years (renewable). The registration also establishes a presumption of ownership so that in an action for infringement, a defendant claiming otherwise must

my buslawlab
www.pearsoned.ca/mybuslawlab

Symbols or designs of business protected as trade-marks

Purpose to protect consumer deception

Registration protects trade-mark

---

98. See www.rim.com/news/press/2006/pr-03_03_2006.shtml.

99. James Longwell, "Court Applies American Patent Law to Canadian Business," *Lawyers Weekly,* Vol. 24 No. 37, 11 February 2005.

100. R.S.C. 1985, c. T-13.

produce strong evidence to that effect. (Using a trade-mark for a certain length of time can establish your ownership through common law, but use of an unregistered trade-mark can lead to lengthy litigation.)

Trade-marks must be distinctive

A trade-mark can be any word, design, symbol, or packaging that distinctively identifies a business or product. It cannot be obscene or scandalous or just a sound[101] or colour, although a colour may be part of the trade-mark. Nor can it be anything that resembles the insignia, crests, or other symbols of royalty, the government, or government agencies (such as the RCMP), service organizations (such as the Red Cross), or even names, portraits, or signatures of individuals (without their consent). There is also a prohibition against using any marks, symbols, or designs that resemble a well-known one, which would cause confusion with the products or services of that other body.

Injunctions available against imitators

So what about "knock-offs"? Who's to stop one from imitating another's product? Evidently, it is up to the party aggrieved by the imitator to take legal action. See, for example, *Hermes Canada Inc. v. Park (c.o.b. Henry High Class Kelly Retail Store).*[102] Hermes was in the process of applying for a trade-mark for its bags when it discovered a store selling imitation Hermes-style purses. Hermes was successful in obtaining an injunction in this passing-off situation.

CASE SUMMARY 13.22

Louis Vuitton Fights Back: *Louis Vuitton Malletier S.A. v. 486353 B.C. Ltd. (c.o.b. Wynnie Lee Fashion);*[103] *Louis Vuitton Malletier S.A. v. Lin*[104]

Parties holding designer trademarks are taking vendors of "knock-offs" to court—with success. In the action against Winnie Lee Fashion, the defendants sold counterfeit items bearing the Louis Vuitton trade-marks without authority. Although there was no solid evidence linking Lee directly to the counterfeit operations, Lee knew she was selling counterfeit items as of August 2006. Since these activities took place over a short period of time, the plaintiffs were award was modest—$58 000 in nominal damages and $25 000 in exemplary and punitive damages.

But in the action against Lin, the Court found that the defendants knowingly and willingly imported and sold counterfeit items bearing Louis Vuitton trade-marks, without the plaintiffs' authorization. Here the plaintiffs were awarded $40 000 for infringement of copyright, $87 000 for infringement of their trade-marks, and $100 000 in punitive damages.

SMALL BUSINESS PERSPECTIVE

In light of designers' increased propensity to sue, does it make sense to check the Trade-marks Database before handling products that look suspiciously like designer products? The Canadian Trade-marks Database can be accessed online at http://www.ic.gc.ca/app/opic-cipo/trdmrks/srch/tmSrch.do?lang=eng.

---

101. While other jurisdictions are allowing registration of sounds as trade-marks, it appears that such marks are not currently registrable in Canada.

102. [2004] B.C.J. No. 2660 (S.C.)

103. [2008] B.C.J. No. 2276 (B.C.S.C.).

104. [2007] F.C.J. No. 1528 (F.C.).

Normally, simple surnames cannot be registered, and so people can use their own surnames in their business without fear of violation. Only where the name has become associated with another product (such as McDonald's hamburgers, Campbell's soup or Louis Vuitton handbags), will the applicant run into problems. Traditionally, a word that is descriptive of what the product is used for, such as "food" or "cleaner," can't constitute the trade-mark because it does not distinguish the product. This can cause great difficulty with domain names on the internet, which have to have that characteristic to assist the browser. Also, a trade-mark can't be a functional aspect of the design of the product. For example, the studs on the tops of LEGO blocks are functional in that they are used to connect one block to another. Because they were functional rather than a distinctive mark, the Supreme Court of Canada refused to recognize them as an unregistered trade-mark.[105] LEGO's manufacturer had held a patent for LEGO construction sets. Those patents expired and Ritvik, a Canadian toy manufacturer, began selling toy bricks (Micro Mega Blocks) that were interchangeable with LEGO's product. Justice Lebel clarified that "despite its connection with a product, a mark must not be confused with the product—it is something else, a symbol of a connection between a source of a product and the product itself."[106] One cannot trade-mark the product itself; to do so would be akin to granting a perpetual patent.

Surnames may not qualify as trade-marks

Trade-marks can lose their status through common use. Aspirin, trampoline, kleenex, and linoleum are examples of terms that have lost their unique status because people use them to describe the general type of product. Trade names are names under which one conducts business. A trade name can be registered as a trade-mark only if it is used as a trade-mark, such as where business products or services become associated with that name.

Trade-mark lost through common usage

Applying for trade-mark registration is a complicated process requiring the services of an expert, and once registered, a trade-mark must be used. Failure to do so can result in the loss of the trade-mark through abandonment. Also, whenever the trade-mark appears, it should be marked with the symbol "®" (indicating that the trade-mark has been registered). An unregistered trade-mark can be marked with "TM."

Registration and use of trade-mark

The object of trade-mark protection is to preserve the value of the goodwill associated with it by preventing others from using the mark to mislead others into thinking they are dealing with the owner of the trade-mark when they are not. To enforce that right, the plaintiff must show not only that she is the owner of the trade-mark, but also that the public would likely be confused by the wrongful use of the trade-mark, causing damage to the plaintiff.

RESTRICTIONS

If the action to protect a trade-mark is successful, the types of civil remedies available are the standard ones discussed under copyrights and patents. A very effective remedy in the appropriate circumstances is an order giving the owner of the trade-mark custody of the offending goods. An action can be brought in the Federal Court when the infringed trade-mark has been properly registered under the *Act,* but it may be more effective to bring the matter before the appropriate

Remedies same as copyright infringement

---

[105]. A purely functional design cannot be the basis of a trade-mark. See *Kirkbi AG v. Ritvik Holdings Inc.,* [2005] 3 S.C.R. 302.

[106]. *Ibid.*

provincial court. Such courts are not limited to enforcing the statute (as is the Federal Court) but may rely on common law principles as well.

CASE SUMMARY 13.23

Don't Put Barbie on the Bar-B: *Mattel, Inc. v. 3894207 Canada Inc.*[107]

When can a party "use" a famous mark and "get away with it"? Shouldn't the party who developed the goodwill be entitled to protect it? These were some of the issues raised when certain Canadian companies used marks that already enjoyed a reputation.

The company 3894207 Canada Inc., having used "Barbie's" to identify its barbeque restaurant and catering business since 1992, applied to register the "Barbie's" trademark. Mattel opposed the application, claiming that the public would be confused. The opposition was overruled; it was held that there was no reasonable likelihood of confusion between the wares of the parties. Mattel's wares were dolls and doll accessories, marketed toward pre-teen girls; the applicant, on the other hand, was in the restaurant business, serving an adult market.

In determining whether trade-marks are confusing, the *Trade-marks Act* directs the court to have regard to all the surrounding circumstances including the nature of the wares, services, or business.[108] The Federal Court of Appeal held that the mere possibility of confusion was not sufficient to block an application. Risk of confusion, or the lack thereof, was also raised in the *Veuve Clicquot Ponsardin* action, where a champagne manufacturer opposed use of the "Clicquot" mark by a clothing retailer. On 18 October 2005, the Supreme Court heard both trade-mark appeals[109]—it decided in favour of the BBQ restaurant and the Canadian clothing retailer. Confusion in the marketplace was not established by those holding the famous marks, especially as the wares, services, and ultimate consumers were very different. In light of these decisions, what factors should parties consider before using a famous mark to promote their own business?

Common law passing-off action gives similar protection

In addition to the federal *Trade-marks Act,* this area is also covered by common law in the form of a passing-off action. A *passing-off* action is founded in tort and prevents a person from misleading the public into thinking it is dealing with some other business or person when it is not. The court can order compensation be paid or that the offending conduct stop. This remedy is available even when an unregistered trade-mark is involved.

Public must have been misled

For a passing-off action to succeed, it is necessary to establish that the public was likely to be misled. The plaintiff must show that its mark, name, or other feature associated with its business was used by the offending party in association with its own operation, causing confusion in the minds of the public. It would be an actionable passing-off for an independent hamburger stand operator to put golden arches in front of his place of business so that people would assume it was

---

[107.] [2005] F.C.J. No. 64; aff'd [2006] S.C.J. No. 23.

[108.] R.S.C., 1985, c. T-13, s. 6(5).

[109.] *Veuve Clicquot Ponsardin v. Boutique Clicquot Ltee*, 2004 F.C.A. 164; aff'd [2006] S.C.J. No. 22.

part of the McDonald's chain. But if a person were to use an attractive logo developed by someone else but not yet registered or used in association with any business, a passing-off action would not succeed because the logo had not become associated with any business and, therefore, the public could not be misled. Finally, the onus is on the plaintiff to establish actual or potential damage was caused.

Note, however, that if the defendant has registered a trade-mark, it may operate as a complete defence to a passing-off action.[110]

CASE SUMMARY 13.24

Disney's No Mickey Mouse: *Walt Disney Productions v. Triple Five Corp.*[111]

What's in a name? Plenty, if that name is Fantasyland. Walt Disney Productions did not take kindly to the use of that name by the owners of West Edmonton Mall. Disney brought a passing-off action and secured a permanent injunction prohibiting the use of "Fantasyland" as the name of the amusement park.

Disney coined the name "Fantasyland," and since 1955 used it in its operations and advertising for Disneyland and Disneyworld. In 1983, Disney reopened its rebuilt Fantasyland in California. Coincidentally, West Edmonton Mall opened its amusement area and in its advertising described Fantasyland as an "indoor Disneyland." This advertisement prompted an immediate response from Disney, which claimed exclusive rights to use of the names Disneyland and Fantasyland. West Edmonton Mall discontinued reference to Disneyland in its advertising but continued to use Fantasyland as the name of the amusement park.

At the trial, evidence of public association of the name Fantasyland with Disney was adduced. A goodwill or reputation, linking Disney with Fantasyland in the mind of the public, was established. Disney also established misrepresentation by the mall owners, likely to lead the public to believe that the mall amusement park was that of Disney or authorized by Disney. The court then proceeded to presume damages.

The mall owners appealed. They argued that the tort of passing-off involved deliberate misrepresentation and the appellants did not intend to mislead. They challenged whether the public was actually misled. The appellants also argued that the trial judge erred in presuming damage had been or was likely to be sustained. Surveys conducted in malls across Canada suggested that, in Alberta at least, the majority of the public did associate Fantasyland with West Edmonton Mall. Elsewhere, the majority associated Fantasyland with Disney.

The appellate court held that the law of passing-off does not require proof of actual confusion; likelihood of confusion or deception resulting from misrepresentation is sufficient. Also, passing-off does not require proof of any intent to deceive or misrepresent. The fact that some Albertans linked the name Fantasyland with West Edmonton Mall was enough evidence of some actual damage to the goodwill of Disney. Accordingly, the appeal was dismissed. The amusement park at West Edmonton Mall is now named Galaxyland.

---

110. *Molson Canada v. Oland Breweries Ltd.* (2002), 59 O.R. (3d) 607 (C.A.).

111. [1992] A.J. No. 571 (Q.B.) upheld on appeal [1994] A.J. No. 196 (C.A.), leave to appeal to S.C.C. refused, [1994] S.C.C.A. No. 204.

> Disney next brought a passing-off action against Fantasyland Hotel Inc. for use of the name "Fantasyland Hotel" in connection with the hotel located at West Edmonton Mall.[112] This action failed. While having goodwill and a reputation in the word "Fantasyland" in the context of amusement parks, Disney failed to establish the same in the context of hotels. Disney does not operate a "Fantasyland" hotel.
>
> Matters did not end there, however. Fantasyland Holdings Inc. "applied to register the mark FANTASYLAND HOTEL for use in association with novelty items and hotel and restaurant services." Naturally, Disney opposed the trade-mark application. But Disney had never registered "Fantasyland" as a trade-mark in Canada; consequently, Disney failed to block those determined to have a "Fantasyland" presence in Alberta.[113]

Industrial Designs

Industrial Design Act—artistic designs must be registered to have protection

Through registration under the federal *Industrial Design Act*,[114] one can protect a unique design, shape, or pattern that distinguishes a manufactured article, such as the Coca-Cola bottle. Registration is particularly important, for unlike trademark and copyright protection, there is no legal protection against imitation unless an industrial design is registered. Registration must take place within one year of the design being published and items (or their labels or packaging) should be marked with the capital letter "D" enclosed in a circle, followed by the proprietor's name or an abbreviation thereof. Damages are available for infringement if the design is marked; otherwise, only an injunction forbidding others from using the design is available. The *Act* gives the proprietor protection for a period of up to 10 years, but unless a maintenance fee is paid within 5 years from the date of registration, the protection expires after 5 years.

The *Act* is intended to protect attractive and distinctive patterns or shapes as opposed to useful ones. For example, in the *Bench Made Furniture* case, a uniquely designed sofa was protected by an industrial design registration.[115]

As with copyrights, patents, and trade-marks, the product involved must be original and not a copy of some product already on the market. Industrial designs can also be assigned to others, or licences allowing usage can be granted, typically for a fee.

[112.] *Walt Disney Productions v. Fantasyland Hotel Inc.*, [1994] A.J. No. 484 (Q.B.); aff'd [1996] A.J. No. 415 (C.A.).

[113.] *Walt Disney Productions v. Fantasyland Holdings Inc.* (1997), C.P.R. (3d) 356 (T.M.Opp.Bd.); aff'd [1999] 1 F.C. 531 (Fed. T.D.); aff'd (2000), 4 C.P.R. (4th) 370 (Fed.C.A.).

[114.] R.S.C. 1985, c. I-9.

[115.] *Cimon Ltd. v. Benchmade Furniture Corp.* (1965), 1 Ex. C.R. 811.

REDUCING RISK 13.7

Intellectual property is fast becoming the most important asset of many businesses, yet many businesses fail to properly protect or exploit these assets. The right to use such resources can also be abused. A party who recognizes the value a name, a domain name, a logo, or a concept might have for an established business might be tempted to register it himself if he discovers that registration has been overlooked. He may then attempt to sell the rights to use the name, domain name, logo, or concept back to the business, for a price. A business's exclusive right to a logo can also be lost through lack of use or not exercising proper control over its use. It is vital that businesses turn their attention to their intellectual property resources, determining the extent of those resources and taking steps to protect and benefit from them.

Confidential Information

Confidential information is given in circumstances where it is clear that the information is intended to remain confidential and not be disclosed. In business, it may be necessary that confidences be kept by insiders, such as managers, investors, and employees, as well as outsiders, such as contractors, consultants, and suppliers. The disclosure of confidential information can prove as devastating to a company as interference with other forms of intellectual property, and so, its protection is a vital concern of business. For information to be confidential it must not be generally known and not already disclosed to others.

In fiduciary and other trust relationships, there is a common law duty not to disclose such information or to use it for personal benefit. Such a duty usually arises because of a special relationship such as between principal and agent, between partners, between employer and employee or contractor,[116] between business and consultant, or between officers and their corporation. The duty not to disclose or misuse confidential information is not restricted to fiduciary relationships. It can also arise in other situations, for example pursuant to express or implied contracts between the parties, as was the situation in Case Summary 13.29.

www.pearsoned.ca/mybuslawlab

Duty to keep confidence

Duty may arise due to parties' relationship

CASE SUMMARY 13.25

A Drink by Any Other Name: *Cadbury Schweppes Inc. v. FBI Foods Ltd.*[117]

Caesar Canning contracted to produce Clamato juice for Duffy-Mott in Canada and retained FBI Foods to produce the product in parts of Canada where it did not operate. The contract with Duffy-Mott included a promise not to produce a similar product for five years after the agreement was terminated. Duffy-Mott provided a recipe to Caesar Canning and FBI Foods for the juice and certain pre-packaged herbs and spices needed to produce the unique flavour.

---

116. *Gertz v. Meda Ltd.*, [2002] O.J. No. 24 (Sup. Ct. J.) involves the duties of an employee. In this case, the information in question was found not to be confidential, no fiduciary duty was found to exist, and since no confidentiality agreement existed, no liability was imposed.

117. [1999] 1 S.C.R. 142.

Cadbury Schweppes bought out Duffy-Mott and terminated the agreement with Caesar Canning. Caesar Canning and FBI Foods developed a replacement product called Caesar Cocktail, which copied the Clamato juice recipe. "It is beyond doubt that without the formula and process information about Clamato, Mr. Nichlason could not have developed Caesar Cocktail personally. He did not have the necessary skills." Even though the companies could have developed their own product within the 12 months' notice they were given, they chose instead to copy the Clamato recipe. The Court found that the information in question was confidential, that it had been communicated in confidence, and that the party to whom it was communicated had misused it. These three elements established that a breach of confidence had taken place.

The Supreme Court of Canada, however, decided that given the long delay (11 years) had transpired between the infringement and the legal action) and the relative unimportance of the confidential information, an award of damages (based on 12 months' production) was a more appropriate remedy than the permanent injunction ordered by the lower court.

DISCUSSION QUESTIONS

This case illustrates what constitutes a breach of confidential information. The information was given in a manner that indicated it was intended to remain confidential so an obligation to keep it confidential arose.

One of the most significant legal settlements in Canada arose out of such a duty by LAC Minerals Ltd. not to use information obtained in confidence from International Corona Resources Ltd. Essentially, Corona had obtained land claims in the Hemlo district of northwestern Ontario. Representatives of LAC entered into discussions with representatives of Corona with the prospect of a joint venture or partnership. In the process, information was given in confidence to LAC to the effect that Corona did not own the surrounding gold claims but was in the process of negotiating for them. When negotiations broke down between LAC and Corona, LAC independently purchased the surrounding claims and made huge profits from the resulting mines. The Court held that LAC violated its duty (which arose as a result of the special circumstances in which it was obtained) not to disclose or use the information for its own benefit. A trust relationship had been established; the information gained because of it was intended to remain confidential. When the information was used for LAC's gain at Corona's expense, the duty of confidentiality was breached.[118] In both the *LAC Minerals* case and the *Cadbury* case described in Case Summary 13.29, the courts found that the duty to keep information confidential arose when information was disclosed in circumstances that showed it was to remain confidential. The unauthorized use of that information was a breach of that duty of confidentiality.

TRADE SECRETS

Duty of confidentiality covers trade secrets as well

A *trade secret* is a particular kind of confidential information that gives a businessperson a competitive advantage. Customer lists, formulas or processes, patterns, jigs, and other unique features unknown to competitors are trade

---

[118.] *LAC Minerals Ltd. v. International Corona Resources Ltd.*, [1989] 2 S.C.R. 574.

secrets. Successful actions for the wrongful disclosure of trade secrets have been brought in such varied matters as recipes for fried chicken and soft drinks, formulas for rat poison, methods to flavour mouthwash, processes for making orchestral cymbals, and even the techniques prescribed in a seminar to help people quit smoking. A trade secret has the additional requirement that it be valuable to the business and not readily available to any other user or manufacturer. Customer lists available through government publication cannot be classed as trade secrets, nor can a process involved in the manufacturing of a product that is plainly discoverable simply by examining or disassembling the product.

It is the conveying of the private information that is wrongful. There is no proprietary right in the idea or information itself. If Deng operated a company manufacturing tiddlywinks and had a secret process by which they could be produced more cost-effectively, which he failed to patent, and one of Deng's employees were to give that information to a competitor, it would be a wrongful disclosure of a trade secret. But if the competitor were to develop the same or a similar procedure independently, Deng would have no complaint, since he has no proprietary right in the idea or process.

While an employee may be required, either expressly in the employment contract or by implication, not to disclose trade secrets and confidential information that he or she acquires in the process of employment, the employee can use the general skills and knowledge he or she gains on the job in another employment situation.[119] An employee working in a guitar-manufacturing factory who acquires the skills of a luthier would not be expected to refrain from using any of those skills if he or she were to work for another manufacturer. However, specific processes or jigs used to make guitars might qualify as a trade secret. It is sometimes difficult to draw the line, and in such circumstances it would be wise for the first manufacturer to include a *restrictive covenant* in the employment contract (a non-competition clause).

Employers should impose covenant not to disclose trade secrets or confidential information

Although the courts are reluctant to enforce such covenants against employees, if the covenant is reasonable, and limited to an appropriate time and area, it may be enforceable. Some employees may refrain from seeking subsequent employment with a competitor. In any case, it is good policy to specifically include in the employment contract prohibitions and consequences dealing with the disclosure of confidential information and other forms of intellectual property of the employer. Consultants and independent contractors should also be required to sign such an agreement. The owner of secret information can best maintain its confidentiality by informing the employee or other confidant that he or she is in a position of confidence and is expected to keep the information private.

Employees, consultants, and contractors should sign non-disclosure agreements

Specify what is confidential

A person cannot be accused of wrongful disclosure of information if it has been widely distributed and is no longer confidential. While Canada's law related to trade secrets is founded on common law and equity, in some parts of the United States statutes have been passed to govern this area. Whenever foreign jurisdictions are involved, care should be taken to be aware of and comply with the appropriate statutes.

REMEDIES

Where someone wrongfully discloses information causing harm, the remedies of injunction, damages, and accounting may be available. The court, however, is

---

[119.] *Gertz v. Meda Ltd.*, [2002] O.J. No. 24 (Sup. Ct. J.).

Non-disclosure provisions in employment contracts

reluctant to grant an injunction that will prevent an employee from earning a living, unless it is clear that the injunction is necessary to prevent the disclosure of confidential information. This usually happens when the employee goes to work for a competitor. Damages or an accounting are also available when confidences have been breached in this way. Even punitive damages have been awarded.

Contract and tort law may be used to give increased protection to the various forms of intellectual property. Non-disclosure provisions in employment and service agreements will provide grounds for remedies such as dismissal, damages, accounting, or an injunction in the event of breach. While it may not be worth the trouble to seek damages from an employee, when the employee has been enticed away or persuaded to disclose the information to a rival business, the employer can sue the competitor for the tort of inducing breach of contract. To succeed in such an action, the plaintiff is not required to establish malice on the part of the defendant, but it must be clear that the interference was intentional (see Chapter 4).

Suing for inducing breach of contract

The confidant who uses the information personally, and possibly the recipient who induces its disclosure, can be sued if confidential information is disclosed or used to the detriment of the owner.

REDUCING RISK 13.8

When a business has trade secrets and other forms of confidential information to protect, it should impress upon its employees and those with whom they do business the importance of keeping information confidential. The company should reiterate that duty to keep material confidential in its written contracts with such parties. It may require recipients to sign a non-disclosure statement identifying just what is to be kept confidential. If marking documents "Confidential," it should not to take this too far or the notification loses its effect. It is also important to remind employees of their obligations with respect to confidentiality when their employment comes to an end.

SUMMARY

Real property

- Land and things attached to it
- Estates in land—grant right to exclusive use of the land
- Fee simple estate—closest concept to complete ownership of the land
- Life estate—right to the land for life; reversionary interest or remainder is held by others
- Leasehold estate—right to the land for a specific period, either for a fixed term or renewable periodic term
- Lesser interests—easements, rights of way, licences, *profità prendre*, restrictive covenants and building schemes, option agreements, agreements for sale, and mortgages
- Joint tenancy—when one of the parties dies, the others take the whole property by right of survivorship
- Tenancy in common—a form of co-ownership where separate interests remain apart
- Land registry system—depository of documents that affect title
- Land titles system—Torrens system—government provides a certificate of title that is conclusive proof of the interests affecting the title of the land

- Condominiums—owners have fee simple estate in individual units and own common areas in common
- Cooperatives—ownership of individual units and common areas is held by the cooperative

Leasehold estates

- Leasehold estates, or leases, involve landlord and tenant relationships
- Commercial tenancies are governed primarily by common law, with the rights of the parties set out in the lease
- Residential tenancies have been significantly modified by statute
- Notice must be given by the landlord to increase rent or terminate a lease
- Parties have limited obligations to repair, to pay security deposits

Personal property

- Chattels—tangible, movable property
- Chose in action—intangible property; one may have to sue to realize this property
- Fixtures—chattels that have become fixed to real property
- Trade or tenant fixtures can be removed when the tenant leaves, if this can be done without damage
- Bailment—placing property, owned by one person, temporarily in the possession of another
- A duty to look after that property is imposed on the bailee; nature of the duty depends on contractual terms
- Where no bailment contract exists, extent of duty may depend on several factors, including who benefits from the bailment

Intellectual property

- Protected by both federal legislation and common law
- Comparison of the Five Main Types:

Type	Copyright	Trade-marks	Patents	Industrial Designs	Confidential Information
What is protected	Original works	Marks used to differentiate	Inventions	Shapes and patterns	Trade secrets and other private information
Registration required	No	Recommended	Yes	Yes	N/A
Length of protection	Life of author plus 50 years	Renewable, so long as being used	20 years	20 years	Indefinitely, if secrecy maintained

- Copyright—
  - Protects literary, artistic, dramatic, and musical works, as well as performers' performances, sound recordings, and communication signals, from being copied or used by unauthorized parties
  - Generally lasts for the author's life and to the end of the calendar year, plus 50 years
  - Producing the work creates the copyright

- Registration ensures international protection
- Remedies include injunctions, Anton Piller orders, damages, and accounting of profits
- Patents—registration gives international monopoly protection on the use of an invention for 20 years
- Trade-marks—registration protects certain terms, symbols, and designs associated with a business or product; prevents deception of consumer, and protects goodwill. Passing-off action may provide similar protection
- Industrial designs—visual appeal of an object is protected by federal legislation
- Confidential information—
  - Trade secrets and other private or sensitive information can be protected contractually
  - In common law, an employee or associate under a fiduciary obligation is prohibited from disclosing confidential information including trade secrets
  - Damages or an injunction may be awarded when such confidences are breached

---

QUESTIONS

1. How does personal property become real property? Discuss why a determination of when this has happened may be important.

2. What is a fixture? Under what circumstances can someone other than the owner of real property, such as a tenant, remove fixtures?

3. What interest in land does the purchaser get when he or she buys a house?

4. What is meant by a fee simple estate in land?

5. Explain the rights and obligations of reversion and remainder when discussing a life estate.

6. Contrast life estates and leasehold estates.

7. What is meant by an easement? Give examples and explain why an easement is called a lesser interest in land.

8. Explain the significance of dominant and servient tenements when dealing with easements.

9. What is meant by a restrictive covenant? Under what circumstances will such a covenant be binding on subsequent landowners? How does this relate to a building scheme?

10. Contrast a tenancy in common with a joint tenancy and indicate how one can be changed to another. Why is the distinction important?

11. How can failure to properly register a mortgage or deed affect the initial parties to an instrument in a registration jurisdiction? What happens when an innocent third party becomes involved?

12. How are rights under a lease different from the rights of a resident created under a licence agreement?

13. Under what circumstances must a leasehold interest be evidenced in writing? Why?

14. What is a periodic tenancy? What special problems come into play with periodic tenancies that are not present with term leases?

15. Explain what is meant by a landlord's obligation to ensure a tenant's "quiet enjoyment"?

16. Explain what is meant by the saying "finders keepers" in terms of who is entitled to property that has been found.

17. Discuss the different ways in which a bailment may be created. What duty is imposed on a gratuitous bailee? What duty is imposed on a bailee for value?

18. Distinguish between the obligation placed on a bailee for value and that imposed on a common carrier or innkeeper.

19. What two principles does the law of intellectual property try to balance?

20. Explain how a copyright is obtained and the qualifications that must be met to obtain such protection.

21. Summarize the nature of the protection given to the holder of a copyright and indicate what remedies are available to enforce such rights.

22. Discuss under what circumstances an Anton Piller order would be given and indicate how this remedy might be more valuable than other remedies that might be available.

23. What is the purpose of patent law, and why is registration required for protection?

24. What kinds of things are protected by the trade-mark legislation, and how is that protection obtained or lost?

25. What type of protection extends to industrial designs? How is this protection obtained?

26. How does the duty of confidentiality arise, and what protection or remedies are available to the confider?

27. Indicate how criminal law, tort law, and contract law can be used to protect intellectual property. How effective are such alternatives?

CASES AND DISCUSSION QUESTIONS

1. *Re Ramsay and Heselmann* (1983), 148 D.L.R. (3d) 764 (Ont. H. C. of J.).
The appellant was the owner of a property consisting of 12 furnished rooms, one of which was rented to the respondent. Rent was paid weekly. The respondent failed to make proper payments, and the appellant seized her clothing and personal effects as security for the non-payment of rent. (The *Innkeepers Act* allows an innkeeper or boarding house-keeper to seize goods in this way. The *Landlord and Tenant Act* [R.S.O. 1980, c. 232] does not allow a landlord a similar right.)

The respondent brought this action, applying for a declaration that her goods and personal effects had been wrongfully seized. How will the Court determine if there was a tenancy or licence to use the premises? What further information is required before one can predict the outcome of this case?

2. *Pacific Center Ltd. v. Micro Base Development Corp.* (1990), 43 B.C.L.R. (2d) 77 (B.C. S.C.).

Pacific Center, as landlord, and Micro Base, the tenant, entered into a five-year lease agreement, commencing 1 July 1986. Edmonds, a shareholder in Micro Base, essentially guaranteed the lease, signing an indemnity agreement. Micro Base occupied the leased space until 1 June 1987, at which time the defendant company abandoned the premises. Micro Base clearly repudiated the lease. The landlord notified the tenant that it was exercising its right to enter the leased premises and re-let the premises on behalf of the tenant. The rent received from a new sub-tenant would be applied against the rent payable by Micro Base for the remainder of the term. The landlord also exercised its remedy of distress, recovering close to $700 from the sale of the tenant's goods. The landlord managed to find a new tenant, Horton Technologies Ltd., to lease the premises, for a term of five years. However, that term extended beyond the term of the Micro Base lease.

Unfortunately, Horton abandoned the premises within two years; a new tenant was then found. Pacific now claims damages against Micro Base and Edmonds for the rent payable over the five-year term of its lease, less sums received from the subtenants.

Explain the rights and remedies available to each party. Was the Micro Base lease terminated, thus preventing the landlord from suing for further rent, when the Horton lease was entered into? Is it significant that the term of the Horton lease was longer than that granted to Micro Base?

3. *Letourneau v. Otto Mobiles Edmonton (1984) Ltd.*, [2002] A.J. No. 825 (Q.B.).

Letourneau's trailer was in need of repair, so he took it to Otto Mobiles and was directed to park the trailer in the adjacent parking lot. Otto Mobiles agreed to repair the trailer the following day. Overnight, the trailer was stolen. Letourneau sued Otto Mobiles for damages, alleging a bailment existed that was negligently breached. The defendant denied liability, relying on a waiver that was contained in a previous work order signed by Letourneau. No work order for the requested service on the trailer was created on this occasion.

Identify the issues. If a bailment does exist, what duty of care arises? What weight will be given to the waiver? Explain the likely outcome of this case.

4. *Thurston Hayes Developments Ltd. v. Horn Abbott, Ltd.* (1985), 6 C.I.P.R. 75 (F.C.A.).

The plaintiff was the developer of the board game "Trivial Pursuit," which had been on the market successfully for several years. The defendants brought out a new board game with the same approach but which involved a different subject matter and called it "Sexual Pursuit." The board used was essentially the same, the box the game came in was similar, and the games were even played the same way.

Explain the nature of the complaint the plaintiff has. What legal action can be taken to protect its rights? To avoid situations like this, what steps should be taken by parties who develop a product?

5. *Ciba-Geigy Canada Ltd. v. Apotex Inc.*, **[1992] 3 S.C.R. 120.**

Ciba-Geigy had the right to manufacture in Canada the product metoprolol, a drug used for treating hypertension and angina. Under the *Patent Act* then in place, other manufacturers could acquire a licence and manufacture and sell the product in Canada. These versions are known as generic drugs. Apotex and Novopharm both obtained licences and, in the process, produced a drug with the same appearance as that produced by Ciba-Geigy. They used the same shape, size, and colour. Even the dosages were the same. In fact, these drugs were interchangeable with the original product.

Given that these companies have the right to produce generic drugs that are similar and useable for the same purpose, is there any complaint Ciba-Geigy can use against these imitators? Would your answer be affected by the fact that only doctors and pharmacists are aware of the differences and the ultimate consumer would not notice the difference?

6. *Mars Canada Inc. v. M&M Meat Shops Ltd.* **[2008] O.J. No. 511.**

Mars, the manufacturer of M&M candies, had held its trademark in Canada since the 1950s. M&M Meats operated a retail chain across Canada selling specialty foods including desserts. In 1991, M&M Meats applied to register a new logo with just the letters M&M. Mars opposed the application largely because M&M Meats had dropped the words "Meat Shops" from its logo. Eventually, the parties reached an agreement under which Mars agreed to withdraw opposition in exchange for M&M Meats' promise not to use marks in association with candy or toys and not to use letters in a style similar to that used by Mars for M&M candies. Subsequent amendments to the agreement resulted in M&M Meats' agreeing to restrict the sale of ice cream and baked goods to company-owned or franchised stores trading under the name M&M Meat Shops. M&M Meats entered into an arrangement with Mac's Convenience stores in 2001, whereby Mac's became M&M Meats' franchisee. When Mars learned of the arrangement, it took the position that the sale of M&M Meats' ice cream and dessert products in Mac's stores breached the agreement between Mars and M&M Meats.

Should M&M Meats be allowed to continue selling its ice cream and baked goods through Mac's outlets? In each Mac's franchise, M&M Meat Shops had separate signs, counters, displays, fixtures, and equipment. Does this additional information have any impact on your opinion?

PEARSON
mybuslawlab™

Be sure to visit the MyBusLawLab that accompanies this book at **www.pearsoned.ca/mybuslawlab.** You will find practice tests, a personalized study plan, province-specific material, and much more!

Chapter 14

Information Technology and the Internet

CHAPTER OBJECTIVES

1. Describe how existing laws are being applied to regulate the internet
2. Identify three torts that are often committed online
3. Identify the legislation applicable to internet transactions
4. Explain the significance of clicking "I Accept" upon formation of contracts online
5. List the requirements imposed by legislation on internet sales contracts
6. Identify several crimes commonly committed over the internet
7. Describe the recurring problems with ascertaining jurisdiction over issues arising in cyberspace
8. Outline the security and privacy concerns arising in the workplace as a result of computer use
9. List steps that businesses should take to protect intellectual property in the online environment

The increasing amount of information transmitted over the internet, along with society's greater reliance on computers in general, has created pressure to enact a variety of laws. On the one hand, there is pressure to enact laws to protect the rights of those creating software and applications; on the other hand, there are demands to create laws to protect the privacy of computer users. The development of law has not kept pace with the demands of the information and technological explosion. Existing laws, however, establish many rights and obligations, and changes are constantly being made by both Parliament and the courts.

INFORMATION TECHNOLOGY AND THE INTERNET

The internet has established an attractive new medium for business that is international in scope and almost unlimited in its potential. Laws and regulatory processes are working hard to catch up with an area that has been marked by phenomenal growth. Initially, it was argued that the internet should be left unfettered by laws and regulation so that it might be free to realize its vast potential, but abuses have created considerable demand for imposing some formal controls. As stated by Justice Blair in the *Barrick Gold* case, "The Internet represents a communications revolution. It makes instantaneous global communication available cheaply to anyone with a computer and an Internet connection. It enables individuals, institutions, and companies to communicate with a potentially vast global audience. It is a medium which does not respect geographical boundaries. Concomitant with the utopian possibility of creating virtual communities, enabling aspects of identity to be explored, and heralding a new and global age of free speech and democracy, the Internet is also potentially a medium of virtually limitless international defamation."[1]

Canada's Chief Justice Beverley McLachlin remarked that the "new technologies of the computer are far ahead of the law. They are, quite literally, 'outside' the law. If we are to use these modern 'outlaws' with confidence and safety and realize their enormous potential for increasing world prosperity, we must find ways to bring them within the protective regulatory umbrella of the law." She continued, saying that combating computer fraud and hacking requires countries to coordinate their legal approaches: "There is but one alternative—international co-operation backed up by international law."[2]

Formal regulation of the internet required

Creating laws to regulate the internet presents some unique challenges. One of the greatest problems relates to jurisdiction. For example, the location of the parties typically impacts where a contract was made and whose laws apply to that contract. The internet has blurred those markers. Another difficulty with online transactions is that often the identity of the person or business being dealt with is uncertain. Also, the devices to protect consumers from unscrupulous business dealings are inadequate. The internet provides access to a wealth of information, so another important issue is how to protect the rights to that information. Because the technology has the means to store and replicate data, questions of privacy and security are also pressing.

Regulation poses unique challenges

Existing laws go a long way to establish rights and obligations for the parties doing business online, but the protection and enforcement of those rights can be an insurmountable problem. Referring to the need to regulate the internet, Chief Justice McLachlin affirmed: "People can get hurt, without legal recourse. Business transactions may fail, without remedy. Ultimate uncertainty, the great threat to economic development—looms in prospect."[3] Internet liability, an area described by the Supreme Court of Canada as "a vast field where the legal harvest is only beginning to ripen,"[4] will be explored in this chapter. Issues related to electronic commerce and consumer protection online will also be examined. Privacy issues, including email monitoring in the workplace and other employment issues, will be addressed. The internet has also impacted intellectual property. Is greater regulation of the internet looming? Although difficult, it appears necessary.

Lack of enforcement a major problem

---

[1] *Barrick Gold Corp. v. Lopehandia* (2004), 71 O.R. (3d) 416 at p. 416, per Blair J.A.

[2] Cristin Schmitz, "McLachlin Calls for Regulation of the Internet," *Lawyers Weekly* 20:2 (12 May 2000), (QL).

[3] *Ibid.*

[4] *Society of Composers, Authors and Music Publishers of Canada v. Canadian Association of Internet Providers*, [2004] 2 S.C.R. 427.

Implications for Tort Law

DEFAMATION

Many concerns related to the internet can be examined in the context of topics already discussed in the text and applied to this new medium of communication. Because the internet provides direct and inexpensive access to a massive audience, torts that involve the communicating of statements such as deceit, negligent misstatement, and defamation[5] are primary concerns. Contributing to the problem is the absence of an intervener (editor or publisher) to monitor the communication; people can say whatever they want, however they want to say it. The communication may be individual-to-individual (email) or published on a broader scale, such as in chat rooms, through Facebook, or posted on websites generally.

Defamation on the internet—is it libel or slander?

Where the communication is found to be defamatory, the first question to be determined is which rules will apply. Is defamation over the internet libel or slander? As is evident from the *Bahlieda* case,[6] even answering this question is complex. Placing material on the internet, via a website, where it may be accessed by a large audience, has been likened to broadcasting information on television or radio. The Ontario Court of Appeal, however, held that a genuine issue for trial did exist with respect to whether material placed on a website and made available through the internet is "broadcast." That issue is significant because if communication over the web qualifies as broadcasting, provincial legislation concerning libel rather than slander may apply. One might ask, should the size of the audience make a difference? If the communication is between two individuals, as in an email message, will a defamatory message be considered libel or slander? A definitive answer to these questions is still not available.

ISP can be forced to disclose source

ISP will be liable only where it fails to remove after notification

Another problem relates to whom an injured party can sue. If the author is known and lives in the same jurisdiction there is little difficulty, but where the author is unknown, uses a false name, or resides in another jurisdiction with different rules, where does one sue? If one doesn't have access to the author, can one sue the service provider (ISP) or website operator for defamation? What happens where an offensive email is intercepted and sent to others? It is now clear that an ISP can be forced to disclose the sources of such material,[7] but even that may not be helpful where they are in a different jurisdiction or without resources. It is likely that these intermediaries will be liable for the defamation only if they encouraged the offending behaviour, or if they knew or ought to have known of it and failed to remove it after notification.[8]

[5.] See *Hay v. Partridge*, [2004] Nu.J. No. 9 (Ct. J.), where two staff at a correctional facility were sued by their supervisor for defamation, over a newsletter circulated and posted to the internet. Use of the internet was considered an aggravating factor, thus both general and aggravated damages were awarded.

[6.] See *Bahlieda v. Santa* (2003), 68 O.R. (3d) 115 (C.A.).

[7.] *Irwin Toy Ltd. v. Doe* (2000), 12 C.P.C. (5th) 103 (Ont. S.C.). But see *BMG Canada Inc. v. John Doe*, [2005] F.C.A. 193, where the plaintiff sought an equitable "bill of discovery" (a form of pre-action discovery) to compel an ISP to assist by providing information, namely the identities of the file sharers downloading music. That request was denied. The court rationalized that there could be no disclosure of a document that did not exist—there was no actual document listing the file sharer's identities and the pseudonyms they used for their IP addresses.

[8.] See *Society of Composers, Authors and Music Publishers of Canada v. Canadian Association of Internet Providers*, [2004] 2 S.C.R. 427. This case was concerned with copyright law, but the ISPs argued that they should be likened to a postal service and should not be liable for material transmitted by them. The Supreme Court of Canada accepted this position. It appears that ISPs will not be held liable for torts committed over the internet so long as their activities are restricted to the transmission of information.

CASE SUMMARY 14.1

When Will a Court Hear a Case Involving Defamation on the Internet? *Dow Jones v. Gutnick;*[9] *Young v. New Haven Advocate;*[10] *Bangoura v. Washington Post;*[11] *Burke v. NYP Holdings, Inc.*[12]

Two foreign cases illustrate the problems when dealing with defamation over the internet. In the *Dow Jones* case, Gutnick sued in Australia, where he resided, for defamation in an article published by Dow Jones over the internet, originating in New Jersey. The High Court agreed with Gutnick that since the article was read and the damage to his reputation was done in Australia, Australia was the appropriate place to sue. But in *Young v. New Haven Advocate*, a U.S. appeal court decided essentially the opposite. Young, a prison warden residing and working in Virginia, brought an action in that state against the *New Haven Advocate* for publishing a defamatory article over the internet, originating in Connecticut. The Court held that the fact that the defamed person lived and worked in Virginia and his reputation was damaged there was not enough. There also had to be some evidence that the offending party did something to focus on Virginia readers (targeting), and since this wasn't proven, the Court declined to take jurisdiction.

Courts in Canada appear to be following the *Gutnick* rationale by focusing on the connections with the jurisdiction rather than on whether readers in a jurisdiction were targeted. In the *Bangoura* case, the *Washington Post* published articles online, alleging that Bangoura's colleagues accused him of financial improprieties and harassment during his posting with the U.N. in the Ivory Coast. Bangoura later moved to Ontario and commenced an action there—more than six years after the publication of the articles. Because the connection between Ontario and the plaintiff's claim was minimal at best, the Ontario courts refused to assume jurisdiction

However, in *Burke v. NYP Holdings, Inc.*, the general manager of the Vancouver Canucks was able to pursue a defamation action against the *New York Post* in British Columbia. Burke established a real and substantial connection within British Columbia. Although the *New York Post* published the article on its American website, the material was read in British Columbia and that was where Burke claimed to have suffered damage to his reputation.

The key to a court assuming jurisdiction is evidently the number and strength of the connecting factors between the cause of action and the jurisdiction.

---

9. [2002] H.C.A. 56 (H.C.A.).

10. 315 F.3d 256 (4th Cir. 2002).

11. [2005] O.J. No. 3849 (C.A.).

12. [2005] B.C.J. No. 1993 (S.C.).

Where several connecting factors exist, Canadian courts thus appear willing to assume jurisdiction. In the *Warman v. Fromm* case,[13] the defendants admitted to posting defamatory articles on different websites hosted by servers in United States and reposted material to other sites by way of email sent to a large distribution list. The Court awarded the plaintiff $20 000 in general damages and $10 000 in aggravated damages. The mode and extent of publication, absence of retraction or apology, and malicious conduct and motive of Fromm impacted the award of damages.

When determining damages, the size of the audience has been regarded as relevant, as in *Ross v. Holley*.[14] Holley emailed statements about an archeologist, accusing her of grave robbing. Ross was awarded general ($75 000) and aggravated damages ($50 000) as Holley urged recipients to republish. Similarly, in *Barrick Gold Corp. v. Lopehandia*,[15] the defendant made hundreds of internet postings accusing Barrick of fraud, tax evasion, money laundering, and genocide. On appeal, Barrick was awarded $75 000 in general damages, $50 000 in punitive damages, and a permanent injunction. The Court considered the internet's unique ability to cause instantaneous and irreparable harm.

NUISANCE

Current tort law likely to adapt to new technology

Although the courts have been reluctant to create new categories of torts, they have been willing to provide remedies where an already established type of tort is committed in some new way. For example, in the case of *Motherwell v. Motherwell*,[16] the Alberta Court found that a nuisance had been committed even though the interference was perpetrated from a distance over the telephone. It is likely that the same will hold true for the internet and that courts will be willing to expand existing tort law to encompass these new technologies.

NEGLIGENCE AND MISREPRESENTATION

Disclaimers may help protect business

While defamation may be the obvious concern for regulators, there are many other ways that users can be injured by improper communications over the internet. Where careless recommendations, advice, or tips are given, injury can result. It is likely that the adage "buyer beware" is even more applicable to internet resources, and consumers will have to use a healthy dose of skepticism and seek additional opinions before relying on the information obtained there. The principles of misrepresentation and negligent misstatement will apply to the internet just like any other form of communication, but the problems of jurisdiction and whom to sue may pose obstacles. From a business point of view, professionals dispensing information should include disclaimers, specific instructions for use, and restrictions. Liability may be avoided by establishing a process for creating a contract that lists restrictions and disclaimers. People using the information should be required to indicate their agreement with the instructions and restrictions. Still, there will be an expectation that the information will be accurate and kept reasonably current, and where injury is caused by outdated or inaccurate information, liability may still be imposed.

---

13. [2007] O.J. No. 4754 (Ont. S.C.).

14. [2004] O.J. No. 4643 (Sup. Ct. J.).

15. (2004), 71 O.R. (3d) 416 (C.A.).

16. (1976), 1 A.R. 47, 73 D.L.R. (3d) 62 (C.A.).

CASE SUMMARY 14.2

Misrepresentation over the Internet: *Ness v. Cunningham (c.o.b. Lynn Creek Lodge)*[17]

The plaintiff learned over the internet of the defendant, a residential centre for therapy of eating disorders. She was later faxed further information about the Lynn Creek Lodge for Holistic Therapy, including representations that a team of psychologists, art therapists, and holistic and Chinese medicine doctors would be addressing patient needs. Relying on this information, she enrolled and paid the $5000 fee. As it turned out, none of the people involved in her treatment were qualified as therapists and most of the 14 retreats did not materialize. The Court held that the internet information and faxed materials contained serious misstatements of fact. These misrepresentations were either made dishonestly or recklessly, to induce Ness to enroll in the program. The tort of deceit was established, for which damages were awarded.

SMALL BUSINESS PERSPECTIVE

Advertising a product over the internet enables one to reach a huge market, but the potential for liability to a great number of consumers must also be considered. Misleading claims must be avoided and any disclaimers should be clear and visible. Overstating one's product should be tempered with caution.

PRODUCT LIABILITY

Companies that sell their products over the internet will still be held liable under the law of contract or negligence if that product causes injury. If the purchaser is the injured party, he can sue the seller in contract. If someone else is injured, a negligence action against the manufacturer may be appropriate, unless consumer protection legislation has been passed allowing non-purchasers to sue sellers or manufacturers for breach of contract. The problem with internet transactions is again determining jurisdiction. From the sellers' perspective, the issue of whose laws apply to the contract is even more important. Unless the seller wants to become familiar with the laws (especially the consumer protection laws) of each state where purchasers may reside, provisions must first be included in the standard form of contract used, limiting its liability and indicating whose laws apply.

> Injured party can sue for negligence

> Product liability rules will apply to internet purchases

> Problem will be where goods are sold and manufactured

Internet Transactions

Most internet transactions involve contracts, and their validity should not be affected by the fact that they were made over the internet. The *Uniform Electronic Commerce Act* (*UECA*),[18] a model statute created by the Uniform Law Conference of Canada, has largely been adopted in whole or in part by every legislative body

mybuslawlab
www.pearsoned.ca/mybuslawlab

---

17. [2003] B.C.J. No. 957 (Prov. Ct.).

18. *Uniform Electronic Commerce Act* (*UECA*), http://www.ulcc.ca/en/poam2/index.cfm?sec=1999&sub=1999ia

in Canada, except for the Northwest Territories.[19] The *UECA* clearly states that an offer may be made and accepted electronically.[20] But internet transactions do create some special problems. An advertisement is normally just an invitation to treat, but if the terms are clear, certain, complete, and are communicated to the offeree, and provision is made for the web surfer to click on a button on the screen to actively accept those terms and make the purchase, it will likely qualify as an offer. If the retailer wants the advertisement to remain an invitation, it must demonstrate clearly in the advertisement that it is merely an invitation to treat. It might want to do this to retain control over the process, or to make the website more passive to avoid being found to be carrying on business in a particular jurisdiction and being subject to that jurisdiction's law.

CONSENSUS

Clicking "I Accept" button accepts terms

Internet ad with "click-wrap" may be offer

An offer accepted on a website or by email will also be effective so long as the basic requirements of acceptance are met. A purchaser of a product, whether in a store or online, will be bound only by those terms of the agreement of which he has notice. When purchasing software in a store, it is common to find the actual product sealed in shrink-wrap, which when opened indicates acceptance of the terms set out on the package itself. When people buy software over the internet, or the licence to use it, the purchasers are usually required to indicate that they have read and accepted the seller's terms and conditions before accepting. Clicking the "I Accept" button is the equivalent of removing the shrink-wrap. This is called "click-wrap," and the contract is binding as soon as that button is clicked.[21]

When a product has been ordered, there is now a binding contract and it remains for delivery to be made by the supplier. Where software is involved, it is usually downloaded as soon as the "I Accept" button is clicked. Unlike other products, software is usually provided in the form of a licence rather than a purchase. This gives the customer a limited right of use and by following this process the seller has a remedy if the purchaser produces unauthorized copies or otherwise misuses the product. The buyer must take care to read these terms and understand them before accepting.

Form of assent and reasonableness of terms affect enforceability of electronic contracts

Two issues seem particularly important when the courts are examining whether to enforce an online contract. One is the form of assent. Did the offeree really know and accept the terms? In *Ticketmaster Corp. v. Tickets.com, Inc.,*[22] the Court held that the terms and conditions were unenforceable as the user was not required to click "I Agree" or otherwise confirm that the customer read the terms. In *Canadian Real Estate Association v. Sutton,*[23] users of a website were not required to click on an "I Agree" icon to agree to the terms of use of the website. The court

---

[19] Alberta: *Electronic Transactions Act*, S.A. 2001, c. E-5.5; British Columbia: *Electronic Transactions Act*, S.B.C. 2001, c.10; Manitoba: *Electronic Commerce and Information Act*, C.C.S.M. c. E55; New Brunswick: *Electronic Transactions Act*, S.N.B. 2001, c. E-5.5; Newfoundland and Labrador: *Electronic Commerce Act*, S.N.L. 2001, c. E-5.2; Nova Scotia: *Electronic Commerce Act*, S.N.S. 2000, c. 26; Ontario: *Electronic Commerce Act, 2000*,S.O. 2000c. 17; P.E.I.: *Electronic Commerce Act*, R.S.P.E.I. 1998, c. E-4.1;Saskatchewan: *Electronic Information and Documents Act, 2000*,S.S.2000, c. E-7.22; Yukon: *Electronic Commerce Act*, R.S.Y. 2002, c.66; Nunavut: *Electronic Commerce Act*, S.Nu.2004, c.7.

[20] *Uniform Electronic Commerce Act*, s. 20, http://www.ulcc.ca/en/us/index.cfm?sec=1&sub=1u1 (Accessed October 24, 2008)

[21] The first landmark decision in this area was *Rudder v. Microsoft Corp.*, [1999] O.J. No. 3778 (Sup. Ct. J.), in which an Ontario court upheld the validity of a "click-wrap agreement."

[22] *(C.D. Cal. 2000)*, www.internetlibrary.com/cases/lib_case25.cfm.

[23] [2003] J.Q. no 3606.

nonetheless granted an injunction preventing Sutton from violating the terms of use. This decision suggests that conduct—using a website with knowledge of the terms of use—may constitute acceptance of these terms. The result is a binding contract. The reasonableness of the actual terms is the second consideration. Several courts have refused to enforce electronic contracts where the terms have been found to be unreasonable. For example, in *Mendoza v. America Online*[24] the court refused to enforce AOL's online forum-selection clause. The court noted that "it would be unfair and unreasonable because the clause in question was not negotiated at arm's length, was contained in a standard form contract, and was not readily identifiable by the plaintiff due to the small text and location of the clause at the conclusion of the agreement."

Another problem relates to the application of the postbox rule. As detailed in Chapter 6, if it is appropriate to answer by mail, an acceptance is effective when and where posted. This is an exception to the rule that an acceptance has to be received to be effective. The courts have not been willing to extend this exception to instantaneous forms of communication such as telephone, telex, and fax. The Ontario Court of Appeal reviewed the application of the "instantaneous communication" rule in *Eastern Power Ltd. v. Azienda Communicale Energia and Ambiente,*[25] where communication of acceptance was sent by fax. The Court held that where acceptance is made using instantaneous communication, the contract is formed when and where the acceptance is received. But what of email and web-based communications where there can be some delay before transmission or reading? What if the offeror receives the email on his Blackberry device while travelling abroad? What if the email is received on 1 December, but the offeror does not read it until 15 December? Determining where and when internet transactions are created is made more difficult (a) because email involves asynchronous communication, and (b) because email is mobile—it can be received at multiple locations. Recent statutes in various jurisdictions provide that such communication will be effective when it reaches the information system of the recipient, even though there may be some time before it is actually read.

Postbox rule will likely not apply to online communications

CAPACITY

It is also not possible when using online communications to determine the capacity of the person with whom you are dealing. A business may not even be incorporated as claimed. Children and people with limited mental faculties often have access to computers and the internet. For this reason it is particularly important that buyers beware and sellers include appropriate restrictions and disclaimers. Any business engaged in internet transactions with parties in the United States ought to be aware of the *Children's Online Privacy Protection Act.*[26] This U.S. law includes restrictions on marketing to children under 13 years of age.

Difficult to be sure whom you are dealing with over the internet

WRITING

Another problem arises in those few contracts needing a written record or signature. Requiring a written record is of course always a good policy, and, while electronic records can be easily altered, sophisticated methods have been created to

Statutes to make electronic document equivalent to written ones

---

24. (Cal. Sup. Ct. 25 September 2000), upheld on appeal 90 Cal. App. 4th 1 (Cal. App. Ct. 21 June 2001).

25. *[1999] O.J. No. 3275, 178 D.L.R. (4*th*) 409 (C.A.).*

26. 15 U.S.C. 6501.

ensure the authenticity of electronic signatures and evidence. Many jurisdictions have passed legislation making electronic communication the equivalent to written documents, and some have adopted processes for providing electronic identification. Many land registries have created computer databases of their registration system that now allow lawyers to transfer properties and register interests online. Saskatchewan has adjusted the fees charged to reflect the replacement of the former labour-intensive system with a less costly electronic one.

In many jurisdictions, however, it is still necessary to print a document, sign it, and return it to the other party to provide the required evidence in writing. The *Statute of Frauds* survives today in certain common law provinces, and some provincial *Sales of Goods Acts* similarly contain writing requirements. Furthermore, provincial consumer protection acts that comply with the *Internet Sales Contract Harmonization Template*, require that consumers be provided certain information in writing or in an easily-printed format. A broad and liberal interpretation of the words "writing" and "written" may alleviate this problem. Judges have tried to accommodate new technology and have recognized electronic writings as a matter of common law. Whether a particular document constitutes a "writing" is determined not by the medium of communication, but by whether the document meets the *purpose* for which the writing is required. Each Canadian common-law province's e-commerce statute allows for electronic records to substitute writing requirements as long as "the information is accessible so as to be usable for subsequent reference."[27] The basic function of writing is to provide a durable record of information. To be accessible for subsequent reference, the information must be understandable and available, conditions that are generally satisfied by email communications.

The federal *Personal Information Protection and Electronic Documents Act*[28] sets out a definition of an electronic signature and how it may be used in federal government documents; it may well become the model for similar legislation recognizing electronic or digital signatures in the provinces.[29]

E-Commerce Legislation

E-commerce legislation (in common law provinces) specifies how the time and place of formation of electronic contracts, including contracts negotiated via email, are to be determined. Ontario's *Electronic Commerce Act, 2000*[30] splits the risks of failed communications between the parties. It does so by prescribing a time when the message is deemed to be sent and by creating a presumption of reception. Under this *Act*, electronic information is deemed "sent" when it enters an information system that lies outside the sender's control. The message is presumed to have been "received" when it enters the addressee's information system, such that it can be retrieved and processed. If the addressee has not designated or does not use the information system for the purpose of receiving such information, then the receipt only occurs when the addressee becomes aware of the information in the addressee's information system.[31]

---

27. See, for example, *Electronic Transactions Act*, R.S.A. 2000, c. E5.5, s.11.

28. S.C. 2000, c.5.

29. Michael Geist, *Internet Law in Canada,* 3rd ed. (Toronto: Captus Press, 2002) at 652.

30. S.O. 2000, c.17.

31. S.O. 2000, c.17, s. 22.

The Ontario *Act* deems electronic information sent in the context of an electronic transaction to have been sent from the sender's place of business and to have been received at the addressee's place of business. Accordingly, the actual physical location of the computer or the person receiving the information becomes irrelevant to the place of contract formation.

It remains open to the parties to agree to modify any rule pertaining to electronic information. The retailer or other business person can specify in the offer or website advertisement that an acceptance will not be effective until actually received, no matter what form of communication is used. The parties can also agree as to which jurisdiction's laws shall apply to the transaction.[32] Such a *forum selection* clause was upheld in *Rudder v. Microsoft Corp.*[33] If a forum is not specifically selected, the contract is formed and is governed by the laws of the jurisdiction where the acceptance is received.

The provincial and territorial variants of *UECA* contain provisions validating electronic documents and signatures. In effect, such statutes "strengthen confidence in ecommerce by, among other things, ensuring that electronic contracts, documents, and signatures have the same legal effect as those signed on paper, and setting up rules for automated transactions and for correcting computer-generated errors."[34] For example, the Ontario *Electronic Commerce Act*[35] recognizes electronic signatures for all documents except wills and negotiable instruments.

Sale of Goods and Consumer Protection

Canadian contract law and consumer protection statutes can offer some protection, but deceitful practices and fraud are ongoing concerns for those transacting business on the internet. The internet is perilous even for those who are careful. Money should never be sent without independent verification that the goods are shipped. Services provided by PayPal and third-party guarantors try to ensure the validity of these transactions, but it is surprising how clever unscrupulous sellers can be in getting around these protections. It is doubtful whether statutory intervention or other forms of government regulation will ever completely prevent such abuses.

Internet marketing is a leading global issue, with a number of jurisdictions (United States, Australia, AND Europe) passing legislation against **spam** (which is unsolicited bulk email). Further, there are cases arising worldwide dealing with "pop-up ads" and paid search results on search engines. Canada's Task Force on Spam has also recommended anti-spam legislation with tough penalties. Links to its report can be accessed through the MyBusLawLab.[36]

Amendments to provincial and territorial legislation have facilitated the sale of goods online and protect both buyers and sellers. As stated above, the provincial and territorial variants of the *Uniform Electronic Commerce Act* validate internet transactions and legitimize such things as electronic signatures and computer-to-

www.pearsoned.ca/mybuslawlab

Current law will apply to online transactions

---

32. S.O.2000, c.17, s. 22.

33. *Supra*, no. 23.

34. "Law Aims to Strengthen E-Commerce Opportunities," *Lawyers Weekly* 20:8 (23 June 2000), (QL).

35. S.O. 2000, c.17.

36. *Stopping Spam: Creating a Stronger, Safer Internet*, http://www.ic.gc.ca/epic/site/ecic-ceac.nsf/en/h_gv00317e.html (Accessed October 23, 2008).

computer transactions. Generally, the provincial *Sale of Goods Act*s and consumer transaction statutes discussed in Chapter 15 apply to electronic transactions as well. The *International Sale of Goods Contracts ConventionAct*,[37] as well as the provincial and territorial counterparts,[38] may also come into play when transactions cross national borders. Consumer protection legislation in several jurisdictions imposes restrictions on mail-order transactions; these restrictions are being extended to internet transactions as well.

The *2001 Internet Sales Contract Harmonization Template*[39] has been implemented by Manitoba, Alberta, Nova Scotia, Ontario, British Columbia, and Quebec.[40] New formalities for online and other distance sellers have thus been imposed. Merchants must disclose specific information items prominently, bringing them expressly to the consumer's attention. The consumer must be able to print and retain this information. The Ontario *Consumer Protection Act, 2002,* for example, and the *Regulation* under that *Act,* require that the supplier disclose to the consumer (before the consumer enters into an internet agreement) detailed information including:

1. The name of the supplier and, if different, the name under which the supplier carries on business.

2. The telephone number of the supplier, the address of the premises from which the supplier conducts business, and information respecting other ways, if any, in which the supplier can be contacted by the consumer, such as the fax number and email address of the supplier.

3. A fair and accurate description of the goods and services proposed to be supplied to the consumer, including the technical requirements, if any, related to the use of the goods or services.

4. An itemized list of the prices at which the goods and services are proposed to be supplied to the consumer, including taxes and shipping charges.

5. A description of each additional charge that applies or may apply, such as customs duties or brokerage fees, and the amount of the charge if the supplier can reasonably determine it.[41]

Consumers must also be notified of any cancellation, return, exchange, or refund conditions. The merchant must further give the consumer an express opportunity to accept or decline the proposal, such as by clicking on an "I Accept" icon, which when clicked would send an email back to the merchant. Finally, the merchant must send a copy of the contract to the consumer within a set time

---

[37.] S.C. 1991, c. 13.

[38.] See the MyBusLawLab for a full listing. An example of a provincial statute is Ontario's *International Sale of Goods Act,* R.S.O. 1990, c. I.10.

[39.] Canada's Office of Consumer Affairs, http://www.ic.gc.ca/epic/site/oca-bc.nsf/en/ca01642e.html (Accessed 23 October 2008)

[40.] *Consumer Protection Act,* C.C.S.M. c. c200; *Internet Agreements Regulation,* Man. Reg. 176/2000; *Fair Trading Act,* R.S.A. 2000, c. F-2; *Internet Sales Contract Regulation,* Alta. Reg. 81/2001; *Consumer Protection Act,* R.S.N.S. 1989, c. 92; *Internet Sales Contract Regulations,* N.S. Reg. 91/2002; *Consumer Protection Act, 2002,* S.O. 2002, c. 30, Sch. A; O.Reg 17/05; *Business Practices and Consumer Protection Act,* S.B.C. 2004, c. 2; *Consumer Contracts Regulations,* B.C. Reg. 272/2004; *Consumer Protection Act,* R.S.Q. c. P-40.1.

[41.] Refer to the *Regulation* for a full list of the disclosures required: *Consumer Protection Act, 2002,*S.O. 2002, c. 30, Sch. A; General, O.Reg. 17/05, art. 32.

(typically 15 days). Consumers have the right to cancel contracts if the above information requirements are not met. A right to cancel also arises if the merchant fails to begin performing its principal obligation within a prescribed time frame.

Additional consumer protection legislation to guard against technology misuse is required, especially in light of cases such as the Sony "rootkit" incident.[42] This controversy resulted in thousands of Canadians having their personal computers made vulnerable to hackers because of copy-protection inserted into certain CDs. Millions of audio CDs were recalled after the security risk was discovered.

Provincial securities regulations will also apply to trades on the internet, but amendments will likely be enacted to apply special provisions to electronic trading. The internet seems to attract an unusual number of frauds and get-rich-quick schemes, and so it will be a considerable challenge for government regulators to develop effective methods of controlling these abuses.

Securities laws need to adapt to new technologies

Electronic Money

Negotiable instruments cannot be created or transferred online since their essential nature is a unique written document. There are, however, electronic substitutes. Credit and debit cards have largely replaced the use of negotiable instruments in both commercial and consumer transactions. Access and stored-value cards, which have value embedded in a chip on the card and reduced as it is used, are also available in some areas. Many credit card transactions and most debit cards no longer require a signature, substituting the PIN (personal identification number) as the essential element of identification. A key electronic substitute involves utilizing the services of a third party internet business. The most notable is PayPal, managing over 100 million accounts.[43] These internet businesses are designed to allow efficient exchange of money between internet users and merchants. PayPal, for example, considers itself to be an "electronic money transmitter"; since it is not subject to regular banking regulations, users' rights and safeguards are not as well protected.

Credit cards, debit cards, and other forms of electronic money replacing negotiable instruments

While automated banking machines and credit, debit, and access cards have made life more convenient, they have also provided ample opportunity for criminals to gain illegal access to our funds. Many jurisdictions have passed consumer protection legislation limiting a cardholder's liability, placing most of the responsibility for credit card loss on the banks. With clever new schemes appearing daily, we must use extra caution in protecting our PIN and other personal information, for it is clear that the cost of these losses will be passed on to the bank's customers in one way or another. The issue of fraud relating to electronic funds is a serious one that affects consumers and businesses alike. As the incidents increase in frequency and magnitude, everyone must take precautions.

Criminal Activity and Other Abuses

In addition to the problems related to the fraudulent uses of electronic technologies and the outright piracy of computer programs, businesses must contend with computer viruses that interfere with the operation of programs and corrupt or destroy data. Hackers can steal telephone services and access confidential or secret information through misuse of the telecommunications

Criminal offences proliferate on internet

---

42. See online: en.wikipedia.org/wiki/2005_Sony_CD_copy_protection_controversy.

43. See online: http://en.wikipedia.org/wiki/PayPal.

systems and computers of other businesses. This has become particularly easy with the growing use of wireless networks. Outright piracy of computer programs, tapes, and videos is already a huge problem. Other common internet and computer offences include pornography, theft, gambling,[44] criminal defamation and harassment, pedophilia,[45] hate literature,[46] and other human rights violations.

General *Criminal Code* provisions such as theft and fraud, specialized provisions prohibiting the unauthorized use of computers (section 342.1), mischief relating to computer data (section 430 (1.1)) and the specific offences included in the *Copyright Act*[47] and *Trade-marks Act*[48] are used to deal with these problems. Also, sections 183 and 184 of the *Criminal Code* prohibiting the interception of private communications apply to the internet as well as to more traditional methods of communication. But relying on criminal prosecution is not a very reliable way to protect a business from these activities. Matters are made worse by the international nature of the internet and other forms of electronic communication and data transfer, which requires international cooperation to prosecute. It is hoped that the recommendations made in a recent international treaty on cybercrime now being implemented in various jurisdictions will eventually lead to much greater control and regulation of electronic communication.[49]

CASE SUMMARY 14.3

Be Careful as to What You Promote or Counsel: *R. v. Hamilton*[50]

In this Alberta case, the accused sent "teaser" emails on the internet to more than 300 people, advertising "Top Secret Files" and software that could be used to generate "valid" credit card numbers. The accused made at least 20 sales of files, including instructions on how to make bombs and how to break into a house. The accused was charged with multiple counts of counselling indictable offences that were not committed. The trial Judge acquitted the accused on the basis of a lack of *mens rea*, or culpable intent. The Supreme Court of Canada allowed the appeal with respect to one count of counselling fraud and ordered a new trial. It held that the trial Judge confused motive with intent. The

---

44. See Javad Heydary, "Online Gambling Is Still an Uncertain Area of the Law in Canada," *Lawyers Weekly* 25:37 (10 February 2006), (QL).

45. In *R. v. Legare*, [2006] A.J. No. 371 (Q.B.), the accused (a 32-year old man, presenting himself as a 17-year-old) engaged in explicit sexual conversation with a 12-year-old girl using electronic "chat" and the telephone. While the actions were despicable, the court found that no crime had been committed.

46. See *Warman v. Kulbashian*, [2006] C.H.R.D. No. 3 (CHRT), regarding communication of hate messages over the internet. Also see *Citron v. Zundel*, online: www.chrc-ccdp.ca/media_room/news_releases-en.asp?highlights+1&id=232. Also see online: www.chrt-tcdp.gc.ca/search/view_html.asp?doid+252&lg+_e&isruling+0.

47. R.S.C. 1985, c. C-42.

48. R.S.C. 1985, c. T-13.

49. Cristin Schmitz, "Government Plans Massive Expansion of 'Lawful Access,'" *Lawyers Weekly* 22:18 (13 September 2002), (QL). Note: Canada was the first non-European country to sign the Council of Europe's Cybercrime Treaty Protocol (focusing on internet hate). This protocol is a side agreement to the larger COE Cybercrime Treaty. For a summary of the treaty and links to the conventions, see the MyBusLawLab.

50. [2005] 2 S.C.R. 432.

accused may have been motivated by a desire to make money; nonetheless, that doesn't mean he didn't knowingly counsel commission of an offence. Knowingly counselling others to commit a crime is all that is required to show guilty intent.

The authorities are to be commended for several successful prosecutions, extending from hackers such as the infamous cybervandal "Mafia Boy" to recent pedophilia and child pornography convictions.[51] But law-enforcement agencies are overwhelmed, and businesses cannot count on help from that quarter for effective prevention. Civil litigation is often not much more attractive. Although the person bringing the action is in control of the process, there are many inherent disadvantages. For example, determining the identity of perpetrators is often impossible, and even then they usually have limited resources, making a civil action a waste of time and money.

Usually, the best solution is a defensive one. Internet technology continues to outstrip the law, and businesses must take active steps to protect their data and their communications. Effective security is vital, but this measure must go further than simply changing passwords frequently. With the common use of wireless networking, it is now a simple matter to access others' wireless networks from the car—either for a sinister purpose with respect to a particular target, or simply to get a free ride onto the internet. The solution requires encryption of data and the use of special software to protect against viruses and hackers; these programs also require constant updating. There is an ongoing contest between the hackers and those creating viruses, worms, and other destructive devices on the one side and those trying to develop effective defences on the other.

> Encryption of data and other defences best protection

Jurisdiction

Jurisdiction with respect to the internet is an important area of concern, and the body of existing rules (referred to as the "**conflict of laws**") may require modification to effectively handle these disputes. The problem is to determine which court will have the right to hear a case when the parties reside in different jurisdictions. When a retail business advertises or offers a product or service over the internet, does it face the risk of being sued or prosecuted in every area that the internet message is seen? Is it subject to the variations of tort, contract, criminal, or consumer protection law in all of those jurisdictions? Web messages go into every jurisdiction in the world, but it is now generally accepted that there has to be something more than information delivery or mere advertising to give a particular court jurisdiction to hear a complaint. A passive website will usually not create a problem in any particular jurisdiction where it is read.[52] There must be a special link or connection or *degree of interactivity* to have a local court take jurisdiction. Without that special connection, the courts in a particular province may refuse to hear a case.

> Special link or connection needed to give court jurisdiction

---

[51]. See, for example, online: www.ctv.ca/servlet/ArticleNews/story/CTVNews/1116014216117_17/?hub=TopStories.

[52]. The leading and most cited case in this area is *Braintech, Inc. v. Kostiuk* (1999), 171 D.L.R. (4th) 46 (B.C.C.A.), leave to appeal to S.C.C. refused, [1999] S.C.C.A. No. 236, which involved the refusal of the B.C. Court of Appeal to enforce a Texas judgment for internet defamation. This was the first Canadian appellate decision to address the issue of internet jurisdiction. In it, the court adopted the "passive versus active" test.

CASE SUMMARY 14.4

Canadian Court Had No Jurisdiction: *DesJean v. Intermix Media, Inc.*[53]

Lack of any "real or substantial connection" to the jurisdiction may well doom a claim. An action was commenced against the defendant, a publicly traded Delaware corporation with its principal offices in Los Angeles. The plaintiff alleged that the defendant violated the provisions of the *Competition Act* by bundling "spyware" or "adware" with the free software that it offered on various websites, without disclosing the bundling to consumers. The spyware would infect the consumer's computers when they downloaded the free screensavers. Desjean alleged that Intermix thus engaged in deceptive, fraudulent, and illegal practices, and false advertising in the distribution of spyware and adware. Intermix enabled third parties to expose consumers to all sorts of schemes, causing their computers to come to a halt or crash altogether.

Intermix challenged the jurisdiction of the Federal Court to hear the action. Evidence was submitted establishing that Intermix did not have any offices in Canada, did not have nor ever had any employees in Canada, had no bank accounts in Canada, nor did it pay taxes to either the federal government or any provincial government. Intermix was not registered as doing business in any Canadian jurisdiction. Furthermore, Intermix did not engage in direct advertising, marketing, or solicitation directed at the Canadian market. Intermix's websites did not target Canadian consumers in any specific way. They contained no specific references to Canada, no specialized content for a Canadian audience, and no French language content. Intermix also had no servers in Canada; MyCoolScreen.com was hosted on a server located in California. Further, before downloading Intermix applications, consumer's accepted the licence agreement, which contained a jurisdiction and choice-of-law clause providing that the laws of the State of California would govern the agreement.

Earlier case law identified eight factors which courts should look to when dealing determining jurisdiction:

1. The connection between the forum and the plaintiff's claim;
2. The connection between the forum and the defendant;
3. Unfairness to the defendant in assuming jurisdiction;
4. Unfairness to the plaintiff in not assuming jurisdiction;
5. Involvement of other parties to the suit;
6. The court's willingness to recognize and enforce an extra-provincial judgment rendered on the same jurisdictional basis;
7. Whether the case is interprovincial or international in nature; and
8. Comity and the standards of jurisdiction, recognition, and enforcement prevailing elsewhere.

The application of these factors clearly indicated that the connection between the forum and the defendant or subject matter was not substantial enough to warrant the Federal Court's intervention. The action was thus dismissed.

[53.] [2007] 4 F.C.R. 151;

SMALL BUSINESS PERSPECTIVE

When doing business over the internet, it is prudent to insert a forum selection clause into any electronic contract. But the above case demonstrates that this clause will be just one of the factors considered when a court jurisdiction to hear a case is challenged. There must be some special or unique connection to a particular jurisdiction before the court will have the authority to hear the case.[54]

A Canadian may be prosecuted for an activity that is against the law in one jurisdiction but perfectly acceptable in another. These cases often involve moral issues, such as gambling and the distribution of pornography, where different community standards contribute to variation in laws. The borderless nature of the internet, blurring international boundaries, only complicates compliance with law. It is no longer sufficient to simply follow the rules of one's own jurisdiction. A business must also consider where it is "doing business" and ascertain the laws that apply in all those jurisdictions. Some countries even try to attract business by making themselves a safe haven for questionable activities. International efforts to rationalize this area are underway, but it is unlikely that universal rules will be developed that will be acceptable to all of the various players.

Safe havens provide protection for internet

Exacerbating the problem of establishing jurisdiction is the fact that the origin of the service provider or the business is not always obvious. Furthermore, it is also complicated to take a judgment obtained in one jurisdiction and enforce it in another (specifically where the offender resides or may have assets). Treaties often allow for the enforcement of one court's orders in another jurisdiction, but generally, as a prerequisite, the conduct complained of must be actionable in both areas. Offshore gambling[55] over the internet exemplifies the problem with respect to jurisdiction. Is the activity happening in this country or where the operators reside? Where the bet is made? While the activity may be criminal in Canada it is usually permitted in the jurisdiction where the operators reside, making enforcement of Canadian laws and extradition impossible.

To avoid battles over jurisdiction, the parties should make their own rules, specifying in their contract what law is to apply. Where business is solicited, disclaimers should be included similar to product warranties, such as: "Void where prohibited by law," or "Only available to residents of Canada." If a website is created to do business in another jurisdiction, the law of that jurisdiction will likely apply to the transactions unless it is clearly stated otherwise in the contract. But even with that precaution, if the content of the website offends the laws of that other jurisdiction, prosecution may follow. A sophisticated business will take proactive steps to anticipate and provide for these contingencies before they

---

[54.] Turn to the MyBusLawLab, where several cases dealing with jurisdictional issues are compared and contrasted.

[55.] One example of how this issue may be addressed, at least in part, is evidenced by a private member's bill introduced in Ontario (Bill C-60). *An Act to Amend the Consumer Protection Act, 2002 to Regulate the Promotion and Advertising of Internet Gaming in Ontario*, would have prohibited advertising of unregulated internet gambling. See online: "http://www.ontla.on.ca/web/bills/bills_detail.do?locale=en&BillID=354&isCurrent=false&detailPage=bills_detail_the_bill" Now see the amended *Consumer Protection Act*, 2002, S.O. 2002, c. 30, Sch. A, s. 13.1.

happen: "The nightmare of costly and difficult multi-jurisdictional conflict of laws disputes demands a creative solution, particularly for the mid-size to small business person or individual."[56]

REDUCING RISK 14.1

A business that offers over the internet some services or products, the legality of which is at all questionable, should offer them only in jurisdictions where they are permitted. It is also prudent to declare which jurisdiction's law applies to the transaction. It makes sense to establish the contracting process such that the contract is actually formed in the jurisdiction where the business is located. Care should also be taken to include appropriate disclaimers of liability in the contracts. Another key is to preclude any degree of interactivity in those prohibited jurisdictions. Still, if the material is perceived as offensive, some localities may try to prosecute; thus insurance, if available to cover such a risk, may be a wise investment.

Trading in securities closely controlled in whatever form

The selling of securities also poses particular problems when done online. Securities regulations control abuses such as insider trading, fraud, and other unfair practices, and strictly control the flow of information requiring complete disclosure by the parties. Trading in securities over the internet is subject to all of the normal restrictions and regulations imposed for any sale of securities in Canada. Any parties making offerings over the internet must comply not only with the rules of where they reside but also those in place where the other party resides.

www.pearsoned.ca/mybuslawlab

BC **AB** SK MB ON

Voluntary protection of privacy has failed

Private data often sold for profit

Privacy

The introduction of computers has only heightened concerns over privacy and confidentiality. Modern businesses are particularly vulnerable as information becomes much easier to access, accumulate, and sort. Internet transactions usually require the exchange of private information, and the misuse or resale of this information without consent is a growing concern. The hope of self-regulation in this area was misplaced. It is clear that as the value of intercepted, confidential data taken from stored computer files or from online communications increases, so too does the temptation to acquire that data in any way possible.[57] The data can reveal a person's browsing and buying habits as well as other personal information. It is now reluctantly acknowledged that increased business and consumer protection is needed.

Many users don't realize that information from electronic mail and other internet communications can easily be intercepted, made public, or redirected to competitors or others who might misuse it. In the past there was some anonymity

---

[56.] Victoria Carrington, "Internet Needs Fast, Fair Dispute Resolution Process," *Lawyers Weekly* 20:27 (17 November 2000), (QL).

[57.] For a civil case involving a privacy transgression, note *Autosurvey Inc. v. Prevost,* [2005] O.J. No. 4291 (Sup. Ct. J.). The plaintiff was suing a former business partner over misappropriation of intellectual property and business opportunities. The plaintiff, however, in anticipation of a hearing, infiltrated the defendant's computer server, copied documents, and then deleted computer logs to hide the infiltration. A permanent stay of the civil action was granted to compensate the defendants for the unauthorized, invasive access and download.

in the vast amounts of data collected, but today this information can be sorted and arranged in such a way that individuals with specific buying habits can be identified and targeted by advertisers, charities, and others seeking to do business with them. It is common for this gathered data to be sold without the subjects' being aware or giving consent. The ISP or business being dealt with may use the information to provide better service, but it is just as likely that it will get into the hands of entrepreneurs who inundate users with spam and pop-ups. Protecting privacy is an immense challenge, and computer users ought to refrain from giving out their private information online. Encryption of the information or data communicated is advisable, but even then there is no guarantee that it will be secure from a motivated hacker. This area is now regulated by the *Personal Information Protection and Electronic Documents Act (PIPEDA)*,[58] which applies to all jurisdictions in Canada except where the provinces have passed "substantially similar" legislation. This gives each province a choice of having the federal legislation apply or passing its own statute. Quebec has had a privacy act in place since 1994. Ontario's draft legislation did not get passed, though Ontario did pass health privacy legislation. Current legislation deemed substantially similar ("dss") to *PIPEDA* is as follows:

Some provinces have passed privacy legislation

- Quebec's *An Act Respecting the Protection of Personal Information in the Private Sector* dss December 2003
- B.C.'s *Personal Information Protection Act* dss October 2004
- Alberta's *Personal Information Protection Act* dss October 2004
- Ontario's *Personal Health Information Protection Act* dss to Part I November 2005.[59]

Various provinces have also passed health privacy laws, including Alberta, Manitoba, Quebec, Saskatchewan, and, as mentioned, Ontario.

Federal statute protects privacy

The federal legislation provides that:

4.1.3 An organization is responsible for personal information in its possession or custody, including information that has been transferred to a third party for processing. The organization shall use contractual or other means to provide a comparable level of protection while the information is being processed by a third party.

The *Act* was implemented in three stages, and by 1 January 2004 it applied to all organizations that disclose personal information in connection with commercial activities. The rules are there, but governments still face the seemingly insurmountable challenge of enforcing these new regulations because of the borderless nature of the internet. Self-regulation remains important, as does the creation and implementation of international treaties.

As mentioned above, a particular problem relating to privacy is the unauthorized interception of communications between individuals. This is now a criminal offence in Canada.[60] Encryption helps, but is no guarantee. Links connecting internet sites are commonplace but are sometimes misused to redirect customers from one website to a competitor's. Sometimes, embedded software devices called "cookies" that trace a user's internet activities are misused, giving others the

Computer data vulnerable

[58.] S.C. 2000, c. 5.

[59.] Online: www.privcom.gc.ca/legislation/ss_index_e.asp.

[60.] *Criminal Code*, R.S.C. 1985, c. C-46, s. 184.

capacity to read private information. This information can be used by the ISP to provide more efficient service and by retailers for marketing purposes, or it can be used to incriminate a person who has been downloading and inappropriately using websites. Users should remember that the information stored in computers is traceable, and even when information is deleted, someone with the appropriate expertise can readily recover it. Eventually, it is likely that regulations will require notice and consent before such private information can be gathered, as well as disclosure of how it will be used and the right to check its accuracy. Again, the problem will be enforcement.[61]

Employment

Business must develop programs to control employee conduct on computers

Employers are particularly vulnerable to the misuse of their computer resources by employees. Employees can tamper with company data directly, and they can also expose the employer to criminal and civil liability as they use company equipment in their dealings with outsiders. The challenge is to curb employee misconduct and monitor the use of computers in the workplace without running afoul of privacy laws.[62]

The employer will be responsible for data transmissions that result in intentional or careless violations of intellectual property rights, privacy rights, or even the criminal law in local or foreign jurisdictions. The employer must be concerned with the security of not only their own information but also that of their customers and others.

Employee's use of computers can expose employers to risk

Businesses may find themselves linked to criminal activities through the actions of their employees. Employees who use company computers to carry on improper activities can bring civil and criminal liability to the company. To avoid such liability, the company must take active steps to establish a comprehensive communications systems policy. The use of computers may have to be monitored, and employees must be taught what they can and cannot do on their computers. In addition, active measures must be taken to protect the business from this kind of attack by outsiders or disgruntled former employees.

The ease of communicating by email can lead to casualness and carelessness; employees often don't realize that their messages may be defamatory, reveal private or confidential information, or eventually be used to create a digital trail that would expose illegal activity. The circulation of confidential, hateful, discriminatory, or defamatory material, or the practice of using company computers to harass other employees, will also put the employer at risk. A message intended for one person may in error be sent to another, or upon receipt could be intentionally reproduced and broadly distributed, greatly increasing the potential for damage. Often these messages are sent anonymously, but they can be easily traced back to the employer's computer. Emails are deceptive; they are not nearly as private as they appear. They are susceptible to unauthorized access, and unlike

---

61. Key privacy issues recently addressed include workplace privacy, trans-border data flow, online data brokers, national identity cards, passenger information, "lawful access" proposals, video surveillance, the *Public Safety Act*, the *Anti-Terrorism Act*, Canada Post's change of address service, the Canadian Firearms Program, and mail opening by Customs officials. See online: www.privcom.gc.ca/keyIssues/index_e.asp.

62. For a fact sheet from the Privacy Commissioner on Privacy in the Workplace, see online: www.privcom.gc.ca/fs-fi/02_05_d_17_e.asp. See also Commissioner's Findings in *PIPEDA* Case Summary #279, in which webcams were used to monitor employee performance. The employee's complaint was found to be well-founded, online: www.privcom.gc.ca/cf-dc/2004/cf-dc_040726_e.asp.

paper, which can be destroyed, the evidence remains in the computer even after it has been erased.

Employees—sometimes with the company's blessing—may also photocopy copyrighted material without permission or use pirated software.

Monitoring employees' email and their internet use can be effective, but it also raises privacy concerns; the employer should advise employees that these activities are being monitored.[63] Such notification may eliminate any expectation of privacy and will encourage employees to use discretion. But to protect itself, the company must show that steps have been taken to prevent these abuses; a comprehensive company policy and education program with respect to electronic communications, confidentiality, and data storage is evidently a necessity.

Employers should inform employees of surveillance

Employer must have a viable electronic communication and data policy in place

---

CASE SUMMARY 14.5

Collecting Information Secretly: Re: *Parkland Regional Library Review No. 3016*[64]

An information technology employee made a complaint under the Freedom of Information and Protection of Privacy Act[65] when the Parkland Regional Library installed keystroke logging on his computer without his knowledge. The Library tried to justify its actions based on concerns over the employee's productivity. Parkland Regional Library was found not to have the authority to collect the employee's personal information in this way, particularly as less intrusive means were available for collecting management information.

SMALL BUSINESS PERSPECTIVE

So what steps should an employer take to balance privacy concerns with the need to minimize liability arising from misuse of computers?

In Canada, the legality of monitoring email in the context of employment is circumscribed by judicial interpretations of section 8 of the *Charter of Rights and Freedoms*, as well as the pertinent sections of the *Personal Information Protection and Electronic Documents Act* and provincial legislation that is "substantially similar" to *PIPEDA*. Although employers have many legitimate reasons to monitor email, employees and the general public are justifiably concerned that allowing monitoring would lead to abuses that undermine privacy rights. The courts and legislatures have tried to be responsive to both sides.

Section 32 of the *Charter* states that the *Charter* applies to government action—so why should employers in private industry be concerned about safeguards against unreasonable search and seizure? The answer lies in case law. A number of Supreme Court decisions have left room for the *Charter* to impact private disputes

---

63. While such notification is recommended at a minimum, it may not be sufficient. According to the Privacy Commissioner, it is questionable whether advising someone that there is no expectation of privacy constitutes consent. See the "Privacy in the Workplace Fact Sheet", online: http://www.privcom .gc.ca/fs-fi/02_05_d_17_e.asp.

64. (24 June 2005), OIPC Order F2005–003 (Alberta).

65. R.S.A. 2000, c. F-25.

indirectly. For example, in *RWDSU v. Dolphin Delivery Ltd.*[66] the Court held that although the *Charter* does not apply to disputes between private parties, the courts ought to apply and develop principles of common law *in a manner consistent with the values enshrined in the Constitution.*

Whereas there had long been no common law right of privacy in Canada, the courts now recognize that the tort of invasion of privacy exists at common law. The first case to acknowledge this tort was *Saccone v. Orr*, where the defendant taped a telephone conversation and then broadcast it publicly without obtaining prior consent or authorization. Subsequent decisions have confirmed this common law right of privacy.[67] In *Somwar v. McDonalds*,[68] the Court recognized invasion of privacy as a tort in its own right, pointing to the inadequacy of traditional torts to protect individuals from unauthorized access to personal information. This expansion of tort law demonstrates that the common law is in fact developing in conformity with the *values enshrined in the Constitution.*

Before an employer engages in monitoring email, it should also consider the *Criminal Code* prohibition relating to interception of private communications. Section 184(1)[69] stipulates: "Every one who, by means of any electro-magnetic, acoustic, mechanical or other device, wilfully intercepts a private communication is guilty of an indictable offence and liable to imprisonment for a term not exceeding five years." Whether a communication is "private" depends on the expectation of privacy associated with the nature of the communication. If individuals are told over the phone, for example, that the conversation is being taped, then no reasonable expectation of privacy exists. Without such a caution, telephone conversations are private communications. Similarly, if those exchanging emails are not cautioned that their exchange is being monitored, an expectation of privacy may well arise. However, subsection (1) does not apply to "(*a*) a person who has the consent to intercept, express or implied, of the originator of the private communication or of the person intended by the originator thereof to receive it." Even though Criminal charges are not likely to be brought against an employer, a prudent employer would secure employee consent prior to monitoring to avoid such a risk.

Furthermore, employers must consider the impact of *PIPEDA* before monitoring employee email. This *Act* applies to all private sector organizations that collect, use or disclose personal information in the course of carrying out a commercial activity. "Personal information" includes "information about an identifiable individual,"[70] and this broad definition likely includes information that would be gleaned from monitoring email, especially personal email. Thus employers must act in accordance with Part One of *PIPEDA* and with the ten privacy principles enunciated in Schedule I. Alberta and British Columbia each have

---

66. [1986] 2 S.C.R. 573 at 593ff and 603.

67. *Provincial Partitions Inc.* v. *Ashcor Implant Structures Ltd.*, [1993] O.J. No. 4685, 50 C.P.R. (3rd) 497 (Gen.Div.); *Lipiec* v. *Borsa*, [1996] O.J. No. 3819, 31 C.C.L.T. (2d) 294 (Gen. Div.), recognizing intentional Invasion of privacy as actionable; *Dyne Holdings Ltd.* v. *Royal Insurance Co. of Canada*, [1996] P.E.I.J. No. 28, 135 D.L.R. (4th) 142 (S.C. (A.D.)); *Tran* v. *Financial Debt Recovery Ltd.*, [2000] O.J. No. 4293, 193 D.L.R. (4th) 168 (S.C.J.),

68. *Somwar* v. *McDonald's Restaurants of Canada Ltd.*, [2006] O.J. No. 64, 79 O.R. (3rd) 172 (S.C.J.)

69. *Criminal Code*, R.S.C. 1985, c. C-46.

70. *Personal Information Protection and Electronic Documents Act*, S.C. 2000, c. 5, s. 2.

legislation that is "substantially similar" to *PIPEDA* and so in those province, privacy is protected by these *Personal Information Protection Acts.*[71]

Besides privacy concerns, another consideration that employers may want to factor into their decision making is employee autonomy. Employers may want to attract creative, independent workers who espouse life-long learning. If employees feel overly-monitored, this may impact productivity and quality of work. On the other hand, employers do have justifiable concerns—they want to ensure employees are being productive (not just surfing online on personal tasks). Avoiding any vicarious liability that may arise as a consequence of computer misuse is also a serious concern.

CASE SUMMARY 14.6

Sexual Harassment via Email Leads to Dismissals: *Di Vito v. MacDonald Dettwiler & Associates Ltd.*[72]

In this action, the central issue was whether the employer (MDA) fired the plaintiffs for cause. The events precipitating the dismissals originated with an email message composed by an MDA employee. The email message was based on a monologue performed by the controversial comedian Andrew Dice Clay, describing, in a derogatory fashion, sexual acts with an obese woman. The monologue had been personalized and altered, so that it appeared to refer to a specific female employee of MDA who suffered from a serious weight problem. Mr. Di Vito received that email and promptly sent it on to his co-plaintiff, Mr. Mathers, and another employee. One month later, Mathers asked Di Vito to resend the subject email. Mathers printed a hard copy, gave it to a former MDA employee, and then emailed it to several other co-workers. Someone then posted a copy of the "joke" on one of the office bulletin boards.

This was brought to the attention of the Supervisor, who saw that it had been sent from the Repair Department to the Service Desk where Di Vito worked. The Supervisor summoned Di Vito into his office and asked him whether he knew anything about the distribution of the material. Di Vito admitted that he had received the message and forwarded it to several other employees including, recently, Mathers. Mathers was questioned but he failed to completely disclose how far the message was disseminated.

When questioned whether they had disclosed everything that they knew about the circulation of the offensive material, both plaintiffs replied that they had. This was untrue. The Court determined that circulating the email, while wrong, was not in itself sufficient grounds for a summary dismissal. But later lying about how far and to whom the email was forwarded gave the employer cause for dismissal.

SMALL BUSINESS PERSPECTIVE

One concern is that employees may waste time at work on personal email. A greater concern surrounds the content of these communications, as the employer may be held vicariously liable for defamation, harassment, racist comments, or other human rights violations perpetrated by email originating in the workplace.

[71.] *Personal Information Protection Act,* S.A. 2003, c. P-6.5; *Personal Information Protection Act,* S.B.C. 2003 c. 63.

[72.] (1996), 21 C.C.E.L. (2d) 137 (B.C.S.C.).

Employment contracts, by their very nature, create a relationship of subordination. The employer is entitled to exercise direction and control over their employees. Reprimanding an employee who wastes inordinate amounts of time on personal email or surfing on the web would be within an employer's rights. Despite the trend in Canada towards protecting privacy rights, a review of recent case law reveals that employers do have the right to discipline employees for using the employer's computer system to access inappropriate content. The decisions have largely focused on whether, in the circumstances, the employee had a reasonable expectation of privacy. Factors such as whether the employer had an email policy in place, whether the employer had created a permissive culture by turning a blind eye to computer misuse, whether employees were using laptops at home rather than at the workplace, whether the email was sent during "off hours," are all relevant when assessing whether the employee should have been able to expect privacy. But where an employer has a well known policy concerning inappropriate email usage, a limited expectation of privacy exists.

As to what sanctions are appropriate for computer misuse, "the penalty must fit the crime." For minor infractions, a reprimand may suffice, whereas graver infractions may warrant dismissal. The content of the email is an important factor. A more serious penalty is justified where the material is more offensive.

REDUCING RISK 14.2

As in other circumstances, employers can be liable when their employees misuse the internet. This may involve not only internet activities at work, but also the use of their own computers at home using company email services. The misuse can range from defamation and harassment of other workers and outsiders to downloading child pornography. The employer should have a clear and comprehensive policy prohibiting such use of company resources. The policy should include educating employees with respect to the rules, and notifying them that their use of company resources may be subject to monitoring by the employer.

Intellectual Property Online

Current copyright and trade-mark law applies to the internet

The internet and other forms of electronic communication and information manipulation have had a significant impact in the area of copyright, trade-marks, and confidential information. Canadian copyright law specifically protects computer software and also protects original works including those published on the internet.[73] Trade-mark law will apply to domain names and website logos. Again, it is one thing to have these laws and another thing to enforce them. A business must do all it can to protect its own interests. Where software products are involved, contractual terms including limitations on use must be clearly specified and acknowledged before downloading, or clearly indicated on the packaging with clear notification that breaking the seal commits the purchaser to those terms. Domain names should be acquired and trade-marks registered. Registration of copyright, although not required in Canada, is recommended to provide protection internationally and to establish a proprietary interest in work produced.

[73.] But are those protections adequate? See "Commentary: Are Canada's Copyright Laws Too Antiquated for the Digital Marketplace?" *Lawyers Weekly* 24:28 (29 April 2005), (QL).

REDUCING RISK 14.3

As technology advances, it has become much easier to copy materials and more difficult to enforce copyright law. Microsoft decided to take the fight into its own hands. It tackled piracy by introducing Windows Genuine Advantage (WGA) and Office Genuine Advantage (OGA), which pesters users of pirated versions of Windows software by sending out reminders every couple hours and turning screens black, presumably until users relent and buy legitimate copies. The consumer backlash was immediate. People fumed about what they perceived as an invasion of privacy.[74]

This fight demonstrates that protecting one's copyright does not win friends. A cost–benefit analysis must precede any decision to stand up for one's rights. Greater regulation is required, but in the meantime, a business may be forced to take action itself, using encryption, watermarks, and other devices to protect its intellectual property.

COPYRIGHT AND FILE SHARING

Copyright law provides the owner of electronic material with the legal right not only to prevent unauthorized copying, but also to rent it and otherwise control its use. While the misuse of software causes difficulty, a much greater problem is the unauthorized copying of music, movies, and the written word found online. The ease of reproducing information has led to massive illegal copying and to dramatic legal steps being taken to stop the process. The ease of downloading free music may have been a boon to music lovers, but it came at a great expense to the producers and musicians. The Napster trial and other high-profile cases have shown that the courts will not tolerate such abuse. The problem, however, continues, with vast amounts of music still being improperly copied. As soon as one website is shut down, another is created, utilizing different technology.

> Copying music is a massive problem that has resulted in serious litigation

CASE SUMMARY 14.7

Downloading Music—The Battles Continue: *Canada (Canadian Private Copying Collective) v. Canadian Storage Media Alliance;*[75] *Apple Canada Inc. v. Canadian Private Copying Collective*[76]

In a landmark decision, the Copyright Board of Canada held that peer-to-peer downloading of music is lawful in Canada under certain circumstances, but it also held that the blank media levy should apply to MP3 players (such as the Apple iPod). This decision would have meant that, just as a levy is imposed on blank cassette tapes, a levy should be imposed on the sale of MP3 players. Blank media levies are collected by the Canadian Private Copying Collective and distributed to various rights holders (such as SOCAN) to benefit recording artists and musicians.

---

74. "Microsoft Goes Black, Making Chinese See Red" by Cara Anna, http://www.realclearmarkets.com/news/ap/finance_business/2008/Oct/28/microsoft_goes_black__making_chinese_see_red.html (Accessed October 28, 2008.

75. [2005] 2 F.C.R. 654 (F.C.A.), leave to appeal to S.C.C. refused, [2005] S.C.C.A. No. 74. See also Henry Lue, "Private Copying Provisions Upheld by Federal Court of Appeal," *Lawyers Weekly* 24:36 (4 February 2005), (QL).

76. [2008] F.C.J. No. 5, (F.C.A.).

The case was appealed, however, to the Federal Court of Appeal. The legality of the private copying system was upheld, so sharing music online can be done legally in Canada. But what surprised many was the decision that the embedded memory in an MP3 player does *not* fall within the definition of "blank audio recording medium." In so doing, the Court affirmed that the iPod would not be subject to the private copying levy.

The Canadian Private Copying Collective continued the battle by filing a proposed tariff for 2008 and 2009 pursuant to s. 83(8) of the *Copyright Act*, seeking the right to collect a tariff on digital audio recorders. Apple objected. When the matter finally came before the Court, Apple was successful. The Court held that the Copyright Board erred in law when it concluded that it had legal authority to certify the tariff proposed for 2008 and 2009 on digital recorders.

Accordingly, levies are payable to artists when blank tapes are purchased, but not when MP3 players are purchased.

Similar issues exist with illegally copied movies, games, and other forms of entertainment. The video games industry, worth tens of billions of dollars annually, is an enormous area in entertainment. It is not surprising that it is also facing significant legal liability.[77]

In Canada, software is protected primarily under copyright legislation, although there are many situations where patent law will apply to software embedded in a particular invention or application. There is also a unique Canadian statute protecting the design of an integrated circuit embodied in a computer chip.[78] But most disputes with respect to intellectual property and the internet involve copyright and trade-mark legislation.

Trade-marks

Viewing a website is no violation but downloading information from it may be

A major area of confrontation involves the use of trade-marks on the internet. Brand names and company logos are important company assets and have become even more important as they continually flash across a computer screen. Keeping them in the conscious or subconscious mind of the web browser is a key marketing tool. These assets are protected by trade-mark, and unauthorized use of a name or mark is against the law. The posting of material on a website invites viewing, and so merely accessing such sites does not violate the trade-mark. Communication by itself is not an infringement, but when the viewer downloads the visual or sound sequence and prints it, creates a link, or otherwise *uses* it to enhance his or her own website without permission, an actionable infringement has taken place. While people thought the freewheeling nature of the internet allowed them to use information in any way they wanted, it is now clear that the traditional rules of trade-mark and copyright law apply. As always, the problem is with enforcement.

[77.] See Chris Bennett, "Video Games Create a Whole New World of Legal Liabilities," *Lawyers Weekly* 25:27 (18 November 2005), (QL); and Denis Sloan, "Online Gaming Superheroes May Not Have Immunity to Copyright," *Lawyers Weekly* 25:12 (22 July 2005), (QL).

[78.] *Integrated Circuit Topography Act*, S.C. 1990, c. 37.

CASE SUMMARY 14.8

Infringement Requires Use of Trade-mark: *Pro-C Ltd. v. Computer City Inc.*[79]

To infringe a trade-mark the violator must somehow use it, not merely display it on a website. At trial, the plaintiff ("Pro-C") recovered judgment for $450 000 as general damages and $750 000 as punitive damages for trade-mark infringement by the defendant, Computer City, Inc. The plaintiff's trade-mark "Wingen" covering its software product, was registered in both Canada and the United States. Subsequently, despite being aware of Pro-C's trademark, Computer City developed a line of computers named "Wingen". These computers were not sold in Canada. Problems nonetheless arose.

Pro-C used the trade-mark as the name of its website (www.wingen.com) and when Computer City's American customers sought information on Wingen computers, they mistakenly arrived at Pro-C's website. Pro-C alleged that their site was so overwhelmed that it could not service its own customers and its business was ruined.

Computer City appealed. The appeal decision turned on the definition of "use" found in section 4 of the *Trade-marks Act*: "A trade-mark is deemed to be used in association with wares if, at the time of the transfer of the property in or possession of the wares, in the normal course of trade, it is marked on the wares themselves . . . " For there to be an infringement of trade-mark, there had to be use of that mark. The Court of Appeal found that the alleged violator, Computer City, had not *used* the trade-mark. Computer City sold computers (named Wingen) in the United States, and had its own passive website, which it used to advertise products but not sell them. Because customers could not buy wares (or have property transferred) by accessing Computer City's website, the Court determined that simply displaying a trade-mark was not *use* of the trade-mark in Canada. The award of damages for trade-mark infringement was thus set aside.

SMALL BUSINESS PERSPECTIVE

Doing a trade-mark search before launching a product and investing in promoting it, is a wise move—especially when one considers the cost of defending a trade-mark infringement action or the alternative, the cost of re-branding one's own product, after an infringement claim is launched.

The ease with which people can transfer material from one website to another—or link to other websites, even bypassing that website's homepage—is also a cause for concern. Information on the linked site may be connected, in the viewer's mind, to the host site. This was the problem addressed by the Federal Court in the *Imax Corp. v. Showmax* case below.

[79.] (2001), 55 O.R. (3d) 577 (C.A.), leave to appeal to S.C.C. refused, [2002] S.C.C.A. No. 5.

Another Showstopper: *Imax Corp. v. Showmax Inc.*[80]

Imax Corp. applied for an interlocutory injunction for trade-mark infringement against Showmax Inc., a company based in Montreal that opened a large-format motion picture theatre. Showmax promoted its grand opening on banners, in magazines, and on its website. The website used a framing device to show multiple windows on its homepage. One of the windows linked browsers to the Old Port of Montreal website, which, in turn, contained information and advertising regarding the Imax theatre at the Old Port of Montreal. The plaintiff argued that the arrangement of framing and linking could cause confusion; viewers might think that Imax was responsible for or was connected with Showmax. The Federal Court of Canada agreed.

This evidence of confusion was sufficient to lead to the loss of "name, goodwill, and reputation." The Judge concluded that this was a serious issue with the possibility of irreparable harm, and therefore granted the interlocutory injunction. This case illustrates that laws governing copyright and trade-mark infringement will be applied to internet communications. It also illustrates how an injunction—and particularly an interlocutory injunction, which is granted before the actual trial—can be an important remedy when such an infringement takes place.

SMALL BUSINESS PERSPECTIVE

If a business decides to have a presence on the internet, it is evident that steps must be taken to ensure that their links and frames do not mislead browsers as to the source of the information. Intellectual property and the rights to it will be further developed and explored in Chapter 13.

DOMAIN NAMES

The granting of domain names has led to considerable conflict.[81] Like a trademark, a domain name identifies the user, but because of their descriptive nature, domain names have been subject to considerable abuse. Because of the worldwide nature of the internet, each domain name can be used only once. This has led to numerous conflicts over the acquisition and use of the same or a similar name. To make matters worse, cybersquatters (users who buy up certain names just to sell them to others) have tied up domain names that a browser would associate with well-known companies. For example, shortly after Vancouver was granted the 2010 Olympic Games, several domain names (including www.2010-wintergames.com and www.Vancouver2010-Olympicgames.com) were registered and put up for sale on eBay. The Vancouver Olympic officials take the position, which is supported by current trade-mark law, that anyone acquiring these domain names will not be able to use them because the use of any name that can be confused with

---

[80.] (2000), 182 F.T.R. 180 (T.D.).

[81.] For interest, see John McKeown, "Cases Demonstrate Importance of Quickly Securing Domain Names," *Lawyers Weekly* 25:37 (10 February 2006) (QL).

registered Olympic domain names is actionable. The Vancouver Organizing Committee and the Canadian Olympic Committee have also commenced legal proceedings against J. Darren Carlson over his unauthorized registration of the domain names *vancouver2010.org, vancouver2010.net, vancouverwhistler 2010. com,* and *vancouverwhistler2010.net.*[82] It is important to remember that the registration of domain names and their use on the internet will not overrule trade-mark law. In other words, where trade-marks are infringed, it will be no defence to show one registered a domain name. This is another example of the internet's being subject to general legal principles and statutes.

Domain name disputes often solved by trade-mark law

REDUCING RISK 14.4

Private companies, such as Network Solutions Inc.,[83] have been given the responsibility of issuing domain names to applicants on a first-come, first-served basis. To facilitate browsing, these names should be closely related to the product or service provided, with the attendant danger that competitors will acquire the name or a similar one first, and will divert browsers to their own site. As one of the first things done in establishing a business, it is wise to apply not only for trade-mark registration but also for all variations of domain names that are likely to be associated with one's service, product, or website.

Controls have been introduced to try to stop this kind of abuse. A person wishing to claim a particular domain name or web address applies to the Domain Name Registry operated by the Canadian Internet Registration Authority (CIRA), which for a small annual fee will issue the name if it is available. If someone else already owns it, the parties can negotiate its purchase; an alternative is to bring an application to reverse the original registration on the basis that this new claimant has a better right to the name. Dispute-resolution mechanisms are now in place to resolve these conflicts, and a name issued to one party can be rescinded on the basis that the registration was improper because of bad faith. The CIRA, which handles such disputes in Canada, defines bad faith as obtaining the name to resell at a profit, to prevent someone who has a greater right from using it, or to disrupt another's business.[84]

Issued domain name may be reversed because of bad faith

---

82. For news releases on this issue from the Vancouver Organizing Committee, see online: http://www. vancouver2010.com/en/news/news-releases/-/35838/32566/g1w77a/lawsuit-against-jon-carlson-re.html (Accessed 22 April 2009).

83. Network Solutions was acquired by VeriSign, Inc. for nearly $15 billion, in 2000.

84. John C. Cotter, "CIRA Cybersquatting Dispute Resolution on the Way," *The Lawyers Weekly* 21:29 (30 November 2001), (QL). Note that in 2002, CIRA announced the institution of the CIRA Dispute Resolution Policy (CDRP), the purpose of which is to give trade-mark and trade name holders a mechanism for dealing with bad faith registrations of dot-ca domain names. The policy is similar to the Uniform Dispute Resolution Policy (UDRP) for dot-com domain name disputes, but with some differences. For the CIRA, online: www.cira.ca, and for the dispute resolution policy, online: www.cira.ca/en/cat_Dpr.html.

CASE SUMMARY 14.10

Title: *Google Inc. v. Fraser*[85]

This dispute was resolved under the CIRA Domain Name Dispute Resolution Policy. Google Inc. announced its "froogle" services and "froogle.com" website in December 2002. Coincidentally, the very next day, Fraser registered the domain name "froogle.ca". It was not until months later that Fraser activated a froogle.ca website containing recipes. Nonetheless, she claimed that her domain name had nothing to do with Google's activities. Google Inc. contacted Fraser, advising that legal action would be taken; it alleged bad faith on Fraser's part in registering the domain name. Fraser retorted that she had acted in good faith, but that she was willing to sell the domain name to Google Inc. for $25 000. By requesting money from the complainant for the transfer of the registration, it was inferred that the purpose of registering the domain name in the first place was to extort monies from Google Inc. Bad faith was established. Consequently, the domain name was directed to be transferred to the complainant.

SMALL BUSINESS PERSPECTIVE

It is becoming increasingly important to secure appropriate domain names in a timely fashion. Failure to act quickly may mean that one will have to bring costly legal proceedings alleging "passing off" or "bad faith" by those deliberately registering confusingly similar domain names, to protect one's presence in the marketplace.

The Internet Corporation for Assigned Names and Numbers (ICANN) is the U.S. organization comparable to CIRA. In June 2008, ICANN overwhelmingly approved new guidelines to loosen restrictions on internet names, a move that could allow thousands of variations of suffixes beyond the basic .com or .ca. Under the new rules, ICANN would allow any string of letters to be used in a domain name. The preliminary guidelines were issued in October 2008, for the introduction of hundreds, perhaps thousands, of alternatives to ".com" in the first sweeping changes to the network's 25-year-old address system. It remains to be seen whether these new rules reduce cybersquatting or provide cybersquatters with greater opportunities to profit.

The *Personal Information Protection and Electronic Documents Act* (PIPEDA) necessitated that CIRA introduce a new privacy policy in 2008, protecting the rights of domain name registrants. Under the new policy, the personal information of individual (as opposed to corporate) domain name registrants, including registrant name, home address, phone number, and email address, is now protected; it was previously available through an internet search called "Whois." Exceptions, however, do exist, allowing contact information to be disclosed in situations arising from child endangerment offenses, intellectual property disputes (e.g. cybersquatting), threats to the internet, and identity theft. These rules attempt to strike a balance between privacy and disclosure, but trade-mark holders may find these new rules an obstacle, making it more difficult to effectively protect intellectual property rights.

[85.] (2005), 42 C.P.R. (4TH) 560 (CIRA).

Regulation

Since the tragic events of 11 September 2001, and with the resultant fixation with security, it is clear that the freewheeling, unregulated nature of the internet will no longer be tolerated. Unfortunately, there is both an upside and a downside to all freedoms. Actions taken to buttress security often result in rights to privacy being drastically curtailed; internet communications appear to be a primary target. Furthermore, complaints about unreliable medical, financial, and other advice, coupled with outrages over online frauds and scams, make it impossible for governments to resist intervening. The proliferation of spam[86] and invasions by various worms and viruses continue to do untold damage.[87]

More regulation coming

Governments, of course, also realize the attraction of collecting fees and taxes. Certainly, federal and provincial taxes, including sales taxes (PST), and the goods and services tax (GST) or Harmonized Sales Tax (HST), will be payable on products, services, and information sold on the internet, and income tax will be payable by companies residing and doing business in Canada.[88] But it is difficult to determine residency and to trace the origin of products. Canadian products can be sold from other countries to avoid taxes. Goods delivered to Canadian customers are subject to taxes and duties as they enter the country, but it is difficult to exercise such control when software or services are downloaded from the internet. Canadian content rules, generally administered by the Canadian Radio-television and Telecommunications Commission (CRTC), have been temporarily set aside with regard to the internet, largely because it is impossible to enforce them.[89] In some areas, such as gaming and lotteries, federal and provincial regulations are applied and both the originator of the contest and the ISP will be held liable if it is found to infringe these regulations. These services are, however, usually provided by companies operating from offshore locations, making enforcement extremely difficult. Although there are several examples of statutes that apply to companies doing business on the internet, many internet transactions and communications remain unregulated.

Difficult to enforce such regulations

Another major problem is determining who is subject to these controls and who can be held responsible for violations. An internet-based business can involve many players—including the retailer or business providing the service, the website developers and operators, the ISPs, and even the advertisers, product manufacturers, and deliverers. The *Nexx Online* case[90] serves as an example of an ISP responding to non-legal pressure. A home furnishing company attempted to advertise by sending out bulk emails (spam). This practice was thwarted when its ISP deactivated the

ISP may be responsible to stop abuses

[86.] The Messaging Anti-Abuse Working Group (MAAWG), a global body working to measure and reduce spam, reported in March 2006, that it estimates that 80 percent of all internet traffic today is comprised of abusive email. See online: www.maawg.org/home.

[87.] Recent controversies suggest a heightened need for internet governance. For example, VeriSign, a provider of security and telecom services, introduced a "Site Finder" service in 2003. However, it redirected browsers to a search service if they tried to go to a non-existent dot-com or dot-net site. After warnings from ICANN, VeriSign shut down the service but then sued ICANN (claiming ICANN had overstepped its authority). The parties settled, but the settlement has been subject to significant criticism. The extent of ICANN's authority remains in question. See online: http://en.wikipedia.org/wiki/Verisign and http://en.wikipedia.org/wiki/ICANN.

[88.] Existing tax laws apply to business conducted over the internet. For further details, see the following from the Canada Revenue Agency, online: http://www.cra-arc.gc.ca/tx/bsnss/tpcs/cmm/menu-eng.html.

[89.] Online: www.crtc.gc.ca/ENG/NEWS/RELEASES/1999/R990517.htm.

[90.] *1267623 Ontario Inc. v. Nexx Online* (1999), 45 O.R. (3d) 40 (Sup. Ct. J.).

company's website after receiving complaints from other users who received the unsolicited emails. When the home furnishing company, claiming irreparable harm, sought an injunction to force the ISP to reinstate the service, the court refused. It found that the ISP had included a term in the contract restricting this kind of activity. When, after notification, the home furnishing company refused to stop, the ISP acted within its rights by discontinuing the company's account. It will likely take a combination of government regulation, the application of traditional law, and this kind of self-regulation by the major players to finally strike the appropriate balance in these new and challenging areas of electronic communication.

DISPUTE RESOLUTION

It has been suggested that the problems with monitoring the internet make it a prime area for the use of alternative dispute resolution mechanisms, thereby avoiding the bureaucratic red tape that would come with government regulatory bodies. Independent dispute resolution processes have already been used with success. For example, the National Arbitration Forum has been very effective in handling internet domain-name disputes. Also, negotiation and mediation services such as eResolution or Cybersettle.com are now available online offering the same savings in time and money that have characterized the alternative forms discussed in Chapter 3. So far these online services have dealt mostly with domain-name disputes, but they will likely expand to handle other disputes arising from the use of the internet.

ADR used to settle internet disputes

REGULATORY TRENDS

Web users often do impose sanctions on each other and report offenders to ISPs or groups who patrol illegal activities on the net. This is one aspect of "netiquette" and is a form of self-regulation utilized by applications such as Usenet (which distributes news posted by users, but also enables users to request the automated removal of a posting). Another example of self-regulation is the code of ethics and standards of practice established by the Canadian Direct Marketing Association, with which its members must comply.

It is clear that a substantial amount of business is now being done online and that this will continue to increase. Complete self-regulation is a failed dream, and governments will continue to impose ever more effective regulations. There will be more comprehensive international treaties, leading to a more unified approach to law creation and enforcement. To avoid pitfalls that could be disadvantageous, businesspeople need to understand the law with respect to electronic commerce and internet communication.

It would be even more advantageous if one could anticipate where the law would likely be going!

SUMMARY

Information technology and the internet

- Voluntary compliance falls short and more regulation of the internet is needed
- Determining jurisdiction is a problem. Courts need some special local connection
- Enforcement out of jurisdiction is also problematic
- Problems posed with respect to identifying source of defamation and other torts
- Existing laws concerning product liability and consumer protection will also apply
- Internet users are particularly vulnerable to scams and fraud
- Current criminal law applies; may be difficult to enforce
- Self protection is safest defence, including encryption, supervision of employees, and security
- Federal and some provincial protection of privacy statutes as well as some provincial electronic commerce acts now in place
- ADR is used to solve domain-name disputes
- Employers should notify if monitoring employee email and computer use
- Current copyright and other intellectual property statutes apply to internet
- Use of domain names often conflict with trade-mark law; trade-marks may prevail

QUESTIONS

1. Why has it become necessary to regulate the internet?

2. What are some of the problems related to enforcing the law when the medium for transmitting information is the internet?

3. How does the current law of tort, contract, consumer protection, and intellectual property affect internet communications?

4. Explain the role played by private bodies and ADR in regulating the use of the internet.

5. How are disputes between different domain-name claimants resolved?

6. How does federal and provincial legislation contribute to the increase of security on the internet?

7. List the concerns for employers arising from computer misuse by employees in the workplace. What steps can employers take to minimize the risk of vicarious liability?

8. Explain the problems created by the internet with respect to jurisdiction and what factors courts now use to determine whether they will hear a case.

9. What steps should a company take to protect itself and its data from internal and external threats?

10. Identify the potential problems that may arise if an employer installs webcams on the computers used in the workplace.

CASES AND DISCUSSION QUESTIONS

1. *Allen v. Toronto Star Newspapers Ltd.* (1997), 152 D.L.R. (4th) 518 (Ont. Gen. Div.).
Jim Allen, a photographer, took a photograph of Sheila Copps, MP, wearing leathers and sitting on a motorcycle. It was used on the cover of *Saturday Night* magazine, which had employed Allen to take the picture. Allen sold the picture on two other occasions. It became a matter of some controversy. The *Toronto Star,* without the photographer's permission, published the picture, including the cover, in its newspaper as part of a news story. No objections were raised by *Saturday Night* magazine.

What options are available to Jim Allen? What defences are available to the *Toronto Star*?

2. *R. v. Weir* (1998), 59 Alta. L.R. (3d) 319.
Mr. Weir had a computer and was communicating on the internet. His ISP was doing some repair work requiring it to access his email and in the process discovered what it took to be child pornography as an attachment to a particular email message. It notified the police, who obtained a warrant and at his residence confiscated computer equipment and disks containing the original email and other material they assessed to be child pornography. Mr. Weir was charged, and in his defence he claimed that the ISP had no right to intercept his private email. Therefore, the warrant was wrongly obtained and the evidence should be thrown out.

There is no question that this right to privacy exists with respect to first-class surface mail, but should it be extended to email? What do you think?

3. *Black v. Molson Canada* (2002), 60 O.R. (3d) 457 (Ont. S.C.J.).
Black obtained the use of the domain name *Canadian.biz* through proper registration with the intention of using it with respect to a website catering to Canadian businesses and entrepreneurs. This site was not yet established as it awaited resolution of the dispute over who had the right to the use of this domain name. Molson, which produces a product called "Molson Canadian," claimed the exclusive right to the use of the domain name on the basis that it was identical to its trade-mark. The brewer demanded its transfer from Black, and when he refused, Molson complained to the National Arbitration Forum, the body that dealt with these kinds of issues. The Forum agreed with Molson, concluding that the name had been registered in bad faith by Black, who had no legitimate claim to its use, and ordered its transfer to Molson. Black brought this application to the Court to have that decision overturned.

Who do you think should be entitled to use this domain name?

PEARSON
mybuslawlab™

Chapter 15

Sales and Consumer Protection

CHAPTER OBJECTIVES

1. Describe the scope of the *Sale of Goods Act*

2. Explain the relationship between title and risk and outline the rules for determining who has title

3. Examine the rights and obligations of buyers and sellers

4. Describe the remedies of buyers and sellers upon default

5. Explain what consumer protection legislation is and why it exists

6. Review the *Competition Act* and other federal consumer protection legislation

7. Review the areas of consumer protection covered by provincial legislation

8. Identify the main forms of negotiable instruments and explain their basic characteristics

The preceding four chapters were devoted to a general examination of the law of contracts as developed primarily by the courts and embodied in case law. There are, however, several important areas where legislation has been enacted that profoundly affect the contractual relationship. This chapter is devoted to an examination of sale of goods legislation and various consumer protection provisions. The topics covered in this and the following chapter fall primarily within provincial jurisdiction, resulting in various statutes with considerable provincial variation. In the United States this potential conflict of laws between states is largely overcome by each state's adopting the unified commercial code. Consequently, there are only minor state variations. The Uniform Law Conference of Canada has recommended a modernization of sale of goods legislation and the introduction of other uniform legislative initiatives.[1]

[1.] See the Uniform Law Conference of Canada's "Commercial Law Strategy," online: www.ulcc.ca/en/cls/index.cfm?sec=2.

THE SALE OF GOODS

Scope of the *Sale of Goods Act*

Sale of Goods Act implies terms into contract

The *Sale of Goods Act* is essentially a summation and codification by the British Parliament of the case law in place in the nineteenth century. This statute was adopted with only minor variations by every common law province in Canada. Refer to the MyBusLawLab, where the various provincial *Sale of Goods Acts* are linked and described.

www.pearsoned.ca/mybuslawlab

BC AB SK MB ON

The primary purpose of the *Act* is to imply the terms that the parties to sale of goods transactions often leave out. For example, the parties may fail to specify a date for payment or time of delivery, and the *Act* will imply the missing terms into the contract. Note that the *Act* provides only missing terms, and so the stated intention of the parties will override the provisions of the *Act*. The *Sale of Goods Act* is not restricted to retail and consumer transactions; rather, it applies to all situations where goods are bought and sold. Even significant commercial transactions involving large machinery such as railway locomotives or earth-moving equipment are governed by this *Act*.

All other contract rules must be complied with

It must be emphasized that the normal contract rules apply to sale of goods transactions except where overridden by the *Sale of Goods Act*. Thus, offer and acceptance, as well as consideration, capacity, legality, and intention must be present for the contract to be formed. Also, the rules with respect to mistake, misrepresentation, privity, and breach apply to the contract.

GOODS AND SERVICES

Act applies only to sale of goods

The *Sale of Goods Act* affects only those contracts involving goods. Goods are tangible items, such as watches, televisions, books, and so on. The term "goods" does not include real estate but does include crops still growing on land. Buildings and building materials are subject to the *Sale of Goods Act* until they become attached to the land. They are then treated as part of the real property and are not subject to the *Act*, unless the contract itself provides for the building to be severed from the land before the sale or under the contract of sale. Contracts for intangibles, such as services or the exchange of negotiable instruments, stocks, bonds and other documents representing rights or claims (referred to as *choses in action*), are not covered by the *Act*.

Transactions involving both goods and services can pose a problem. When a lawyer drafts a will, or an artist paints a portrait, the client gets a physical item, the will or portrait, but the main component of the transaction is the service provided. The *Sale of Goods Act* will therefore not apply.[2] Note that if the client were to then resell the portrait, the *Act* would apply. Sometimes, the service and sale of goods components of a transaction can be separated, as when parts are installed to repair an automobile. The *Sale of Goods Act* will apply to the goods portion of that contract.

When only services are involved, the court may still be willing to imply terms, such as the requirement of a certain level of quality, even though the *Sale of Goods Act* does not apply. For example, in *Borek v. Hooper*,[3] Borek commissioned a large

---

[2.] In cases in which both goods and services are provided, the court must determine if the essence of the contract was the materials or the work provided. See *Keillian West Ltd. v. Sportspace Enterprises Ltd.* (1982), 40 A.R. 586 (Q.B.), in which the Court decided that a contract for the printing of 20 000 copies of 44-page programs was a contract for goods, not services, and was, therefore, subject to the *Act*.

[3.] (1994), 114 D.L.R. (4th) 570 (Ont. Div. Ct.).

painting from Hooper, an artist. When the painting showed serious problems of discolouration and surface deterioration, Borek sued for breach of warranty as to quality under the *Sale of Goods Act*. The appeal court held that the *Act* did not cover this transaction, as it did not involve a sale of goods, but of work, labour, and materials. The court did, however, recognize a similar provision implied into the contract by the common law, in that there was a warranty with respect to quality and fitness for purpose. The case was thus sent back to the trial court for a proper assessment of damages.

CASE SUMMARY 15.1

Has There Been a Sale of Contaminated Goods? *Gee v. White Spot Ltd.* and *Pan v. White Spot Ltd.*;[4] *ter Neuzen v. Korn*[5]

In July 1985, Gee suffered botulism poisoning from food obtained at the White Spot restaurant. He sued. The Judge decided that, since the primary purpose of the transaction was to obtain the food (a chattel), the service component being incidental, the *Sale of Goods Act* applied to the purchase. Section 18(b) of the *Act* required the goods to be of merchantable quality, meaning that they had to be fit for their normal purpose; in this case, fit for human consumption. Section 18(a) required that when the skill of the seller is relied on, and it is in the normal course of the business to supply the goods, those goods have to be fit for the purpose for which they are purchased. The Judge found that the goods failed both of these tests and Gee was successful in his action, the contract of purchase having been breached.

In contrast, consider the facts in *ter Neuzen v. Korn*. In this case, the Court ruled that a patient who contracted an HIV infection from an artificial insemination program could not rely on the *Sale of Goods Act*, as the contract was mainly for the sale of services, not goods. The Court also held that there was not a common law warranty of fitness and merchantability applicable to the contract, which involved the provision of a donor's semen.

DISCUSSION QUESTIONS

Based on these precedents, how would the courts characterize cosmetic services, such as botox injections? What if the sample of botox itself was defective or contaminated? Would the *Sale of Goods Act* apply?

TRANSFER OF GOODS

The *Sale of Goods Act* applies only when it can be demonstrated that the parties intended that the actual possession and property of the goods would transfer to the buyer.

Goods must be transferred

When goods are used to secure a loan with no intention that they actually be transferred, the *Sale of Goods Act* will not apply even though a **bill of sale** may have been used to create the credit relationship. However, when the goods used as security actually do change hands, as in a conditional sale, the *Act* will apply. These secured transactions will be discussed in Chapter 16.

---

4. (1986), 32 D.L.R. (4th) 238 (B.C.S.C.).

5. [1995] 3 S.C.R. 674.

MONETARY CONSIDERATION

Act does not apply to barter

It is also necessary that the sale involve the actual payment of some money. The *Act* will not apply to traded goods unless some money is also exchanged.

REQUIREMENT OF WRITING

Some provinces require evidence in writing

Despite the trend to move away from the *Statute of Frauds*, some jurisdictions still require in their *Sale of Goods Acts* that sales of goods sold over a specified amount[6] must be evidenced in writing for the contract to be enforceable. Part performance, when some of the goods have been accepted by the buyer, will likewise make the contract enforceable. Giving something in earnest (anything of value) will also make the contract binding. Other provinces, including British Columbia, New Brunswick, Ontario, and Manitoba, have eliminated any writing requirement in sale of goods transactions, although British Columbia, in its *Consumer Protection Act*, still requires that there be a written contract for direct sales of consumer goods.

www.pearsoned.ca/mybuslawlab

BC AB SK MB ON

Distinction between sale and agreement to sell

Normally risk follows title

Title and Risk

When the title (the property interest in the goods) does not transfer immediately upon the sale agreement's being concluded, it is called an **agreement to sell**. The *Sale of Goods Act* also applies to this future transfer of goods. Determining who has title, at any given time, is important because, under the *Sale of Goods Act*, whoever has the title bears the risk of damage or destruction to the goods—unless the parties have agreed otherwise.

Four common methods are sometimes used to override this provision of the *Act*.

1. **C.I.F. contracts (cost, insurance, and freight)**. In this type of contract it doesn't matter when title transfers, because one of the parties has been designated as being responsible for paying the costs involved in the shipping of those goods as well as arranging insurance, in the process assuming the risk if anything goes wrong.

2. **F.O.B. contracts (free on board)**. With F.O.B. contracts, the parties have agreed that the seller will bear the risk until a specified point in the transport process. For example, if the goods are to be delivered F.O.B. the loading dock at the seller's place of business, the buyer assumes the risk at that point.

3. **C.O.D. contracts (cash on delivery)**. This type of contract entitles the seller to maintain the proprietary rights (or title) as well as control over the possession of those goods, until they are delivered to the buyer's premises and paid for. The risk stays with the seller until delivery at the specified location is complete.

4. **Bills of lading**. Bills of lading are also often used by the seller to maintain control over the goods during shipment. A bill of lading is a document given by the transporter (or carrier) of the goods to the shipper as a form of receipt. The seller can maintain control (and the risk) with respect to those goods by naming itself as the party entitled to receive delivery of the goods at their destination.

[6.] The relevant dollar amount is $50 in Alberta, Saskatchewan, Newfoundland and Labrador, Nunavut, and the N.W.T., $40 in Nova Scotia, and $30 in P.E.I. In the Yukon, the amount is $1000!

REDUCING RISK 15.1

There are many opportunities to exercise control over the various legal aspects of business transactions, such as who bears the risk and when title transfers. While there have been many restrictions imposed when consumers are involved, it is still important to understand what options you can exercise to reduce the risk you face in both consumer and commercial transactions.

TRANSFER OF TITLE

Who has title can not only can determine who bears the risk, but it will also affect which remedies are available in the event of a breach. If title is transferred, the seller can sue for the entire price; otherwise, only damages for breach of contract are available. Who has title can also determine who has first claim to the goods in the event of default or bankruptcy. The rules for determining who has title as found in the *Sale of Goods Act* are set out below.[7]

Remedy may depend on who has title

Rules for determining title

Rule 1

When there is an unconditional contract for the sale of specific goods in a deliverable state, the property in the goods passes to the buyer when the contract is made and it is immaterial whether the time of payment or the time of delivery or both are postponed.

Unconditional contract—title transfers immediately

If the goods are identified and nothing more has to be done to them, the buyer gets title at the point of contracting to purchase. Thus, if Cristina decides to buy a used car, sold "as is" by Mills, and Cristina says, "I'll pay you $15 000 for this Toyota and not a dollar more," title would transfer as soon as Cristina's offer was accepted even though she might take delivery and pay at a later date. Were the car vandalized while parked on the street overnight, before the buyer picked it up, the loss would be the buyer's.

Rule 2

When there is a contract for the sale of specific goods and the seller is bound to do something to the goods for the purpose of putting them into a deliverable state, the property does not pass until such thing is done and the buyer has notice thereof.

Seller required to do something to put goods in deliverable state—title transfers when task completed and notice is given

If some repair or work has to be done on the car in the above example, title and risk would pass to the buyer only after the repair was done and the buyer was notified the goods were ready. If the car was vandalized or otherwise damaged before the notice, the loss would be the seller's, as was the case in *Kovacs v. Holtom*.[8]

Notice required if repairs are needed

Rule 3

When there is a contract for the sale of specific goods in a deliverable state, but the seller is bound to weigh, measure, test or do some other act or thing with reference to the goods for the purpose of ascertaining the price, the property does not pass until the act or thing is done and the buyer has notice thereof.

Seller required to ascertain price—title transferred when purchaser notified

---

[7.] These provisions are taken from s. 19 of the *Ontario Sale of Goods Act*, R.S.O. 1990, c. S.1. Every province has a similar act, although the wording of the provisions may vary. Refer to the MyBusLawLab, where these statutes are identified and linked.

[8.] See *Kovacs v. Holtom*, [1997] A.J. No. 775 (Prov. Ct.), in which the Court applied Rule 2 with respect to a car that was destroyed prior to the completion of its restoration and delivery.

If Schmidt bought a truckload of potatoes from Naslund, title would not pass until they had been weighed to determine the price and Schmidt had been notified.

Rule 4

Goods delivered subject to buyer's approval—title passes when approval by acceptance is signified or a reasonable time has passed

When goods are delivered to the buyer on approval or on "sale or return" or other similar terms, the property in them passes to the buyer

(i) when the buyer signifies approval or acceptance to the seller or does any other act adopting the transaction, or

(ii) if the buyer does not signify approval or acceptance to the seller but retains the goods without giving notice of rejection, then if a time has been fixed for the return of the goods, on the expiration of that time, and, if no time has been fixed, on the expiration of a reasonable time, and what is a reasonable time is a question of fact.

This rule covers situations in which goods are taken by the buyer to test for a trial period before deciding to keep them. To modify our earlier example, if Mills had allowed Cristina to take the car home for two days, to test drive it and have it inspected by a mechanic, title and risk would not transfer to Cristina until the expiration of those two days unless Cristina notified Mills before that time that she was happy with the car. Title would pass earlier if Cristina resold the car or had repairs done on the car.

Rule 5

When goods are not manufactured or identifiable as goods in question, title passes upon unconditional appropriation and assent

(i) When there is a contract for the sale of unascertained or future goods by description and goods of that description and in a deliverable state are unconditionally appropriated to the contract, either by the seller with the assent of the buyer, or by the buyer with the assent of the seller, the property in the goods thereupon passes to the buyer, and such assent may be express or implied and may be given either before or after the appropriation is made.

(ii) When, in pursuance of the contract, the seller delivers the goods to the buyer or to a carrier or other bailee (whether named by the buyer or not), for the purpose of transmission to the buyer and does not reserve the right of disposal, the seller shall be deemed to have unconditionally appropriated the goods to the contract.

The goods covered by Rule 5 are those that have not been manufactured at the time the contract was entered into or that exist but have not yet been separated out and identified as the particular goods to be used in a given transaction. If one purchases a specific model of a car from a dealer, title does not pass until the specific vehicle is selected from the several like it on the lot. Rule 5 would apply because no specific car has yet been appropriated to the contract at the time of the sale. Rule 5 would also apply when a buyer orders a new car that has not yet been manufactured.

Only when the goods have been manufactured or separated out and unconditionally committed to the buyer with the buyer's assent does title pass. While notice to the buyer that the goods are ready may be the most common method of satisfying the assent or approval provision, assent is often implied from the circumstances. Thus, if a person were to leave her car with a dealer for the installation of a new stereo system, she will be taken to have assented to the selection of the stereo when it is installed, since she left her car there for that purpose.

It must always be remembered that the parties can specify a contrary intention in the contract, overriding these rules with respect to title and risk. Great care should be used in examining the terms of the contract to determine whether this has been done.

CASE SUMMARY 15.2

Did Property in the Fire Truck Pass? *In the Matter of the Bankruptcy of Anderson's Engineering Ltd.*[9]

Anderson's contracted with Online to build and deliver a fire truck. Online paid Anderson's two advances toward the total purchase price of fire truck. Anderson's viewed these billings as advances against the full contract price, consistent with Anderson's procedure on other contracts and with industry practice. Anderson's made an assignment into bankruptcy before the work on fire truck was complete, and listed the chassis and pump that were to be part of the fire truck as assets owned at the time of the bankruptcy. Online claimed ownership of the chassis and pump, the cumulative value of which was approximately equal to the amount paid in advances. An application was brought to determine whether Online's claim to a property interest in these assets was defeated on the grounds that property did not pass to it prior to bankruptcy.

DISCUSSION QUESTIONS

Which provisions of the *Sale of Goods Act* are relevant to Online's claim? Are the chassis and pump "specific goods," "unascertained goods," or "future goods by description"? Was that distinction relevant to the Court's decision? Was the fire truck in a "deliverable state"? Would it matter if there was evidence that the parties intended that the chassis and pump were to become Online's property after the advances were paid?

Rights and Obligations of the Parties

The *Sale of Goods Act* implies both conditions and warranties into the contract. The difference is important. An implied warranty is a minor term. A breach of warranty does not discharge the victim from the rest of his contractual obligations. On the other hand, a breach of an implied condition allows the victim to treat the contract as ended. But a breach of a condition does not always bring a contract to an end. The victim of a breach of a condition has the option to ignore it or to treat it as a breach of warranty. By accepting the goods, the victim of a breach may also lose the right to have a contract discharged by a breach of condition.

The buyer of a television set, for example, would be entitled to return the set and demand a refund if it were specified as a condition of the contract that the television had a remote control device and he did not discover until he got it home that his set did not have one. However, if he assembled the TV knowing that there was no remote and watched it over the weekend, he would be deemed to have accepted the goods. He could not return the set, but he could still sue for damages for the reduction in value.[10] It should also be noted that while the parties

Conditions and warranties under *Sale of Goods Act*

Acceptance causes victims of breach to lose right of discharge

---

9. (2002), 33 C.B.R. (4th) 1, (2002), 26 B.L.R. (3d) 62 (B.C.S.C.).

10. In *Saville v. Sher-Ell Equipment Sales Ltd.* (1980), 25 A.R. 550 (Q.B.), the buyer who used the defective equipment he had purchased, instead of returning it promptly, lost the right to treat the contract as discharged. He was limited to the remedy of damages.

are free to designate a term as a condition or warranty, the court retains the right to make the final determination.

Contracting parties often try to limit their liability as much as possible, and sometimes they try to contract out of all obligations and responsibilities. The Supreme Court of Canada, in *Hunter Engineering*, has made it clear that a properly worded exemption clause can overcome even a **fundamental breach**—particularly where sophisticated businesspeople are involved on both side

Manufacturers and retailers often try to override the implied conditions and warranties set out in the *Act*, especially in the areas related to fitness and quality. They do this in "warranties" that include exemption clauses attempting to limit their liability. If such clauses are carefully worded, they can override the provisions of the *Act* unless prohibited by statute. In the *Hunter Engineering* case, discussed in Case Summary 15.4 below, the exemption clause was effective with respect to Allis Chalmers but not with respect to Hunter Engineering, which had failed to exclude the implied conditions of the statute. Several provinces have enacted legislation prohibiting the seller from excluding or limiting these provisions relating to fitness and quality in consumer sales transactions. Others will allow parties to a sales contract to exclude any implied terms. Refer to the MyBusLawLab for details as to the law in a particular jurisdiction.

> **Parties may be free to contract out**

> **Seller must convey good title**
> **• and quiet possession**

RIGHT TO CONVEY CLEAR TITLE

The *Sale of Goods Act* implies several terms into sales agreements that cover a seller's right to sell goods to a buyer. Section 13(a) of the Ontario *Sale of Goods Act* makes it a condition that the seller has the right to sell the goods, or will have the right at the time title is to be transferred. Thus, Mills breaches a condition of the contract if he cannot deliver good title at delivery. Cristina would then be free from any further obligation under the contract.

Section 13(b) requires that the seller provide **quiet possession** of the goods as a warranty of the contract. This means that the goods must be delivered in such a condition that they can be used and enjoyed by the buyer in the way they were intended, free from any interference. If the car sold to Cristina was subsequently seized by one of Mills' creditors, this would constitute a breach of the covenant of quiet possession.

> **• and goods free from charge or encumbrance**

Section 13(c) of the *Act* specifies that it shall be an implied warranty of the contract that the goods shall be free from any charge or encumbrance that has not been disclosed to the buyer. Such a **lien** gives the lien holder (a secured creditor) the right to retake the goods if not paid. The presence of such a lien without telling the buyer would be a breach of warranty under section 13(c) of the *Act*. (Secured transactions will be discussed in Chapter 16.) The buyer would be well advised to conduct a title search at the appropriate registry office before buying. But even if a search is not done, section 13(c) gives the buyer the right to claim against the seller for any losses if a lien is in fact present—assuming he can still locate the seller!

> **Goods must match description**

GOODS MUST MATCH DESCRIPTION

Goods sold on the internet, by catalogue, by mail order, or through other forms of distance shopping, usually with a picture and accompanying text, are being sold by description. Section 14 of the Ontario *Sale of Goods Act* provides that when goods are sold by description there will be an implied condition that the goods delivered must match that description. If Afsari ordered an iPod pictured as "60

GB with video" on the internet and what was delivered was a 30 GB iPod, there has been a breach of the implied condition that the goods match the description, as there was when an odometer in a used car had been tampered with.[11]

In fact, today the sale of any manufactured good is a sale by description, one item being indistinguishable from another of the same model. When we buy, we are relying on the manufacturer's description, whether that description is found on the box, a specification sheet, a brochure, a catalogue or the internet. All goods delivered must match that description.[12]

> Most sales of manufactured goods are by description

> Goods bought must match the description or picture provided

GOODS MUST BE OF MERCHANTABLE QUALITY AND FIT FOR PURPOSE

The *Sale of Goods Act* applies to both small and large transactions, whether they are consumer or commercial in nature. But the parties can contract out of its provisions if they wish. Even the principle of fundamental breach can be overcome by a very carefully and specifically worded exemption clause.

The *Sale of Goods Act* requires, as a condition, that when goods are sold by description they must be of **merchantable quality** (section 15 of the Ontario *Act*). This means that the goods must be free of any defect that would have persuaded the buyer not to purchase them at the agreed-upon price if the buyer had known of the defect at the outset.[13] If a sample has been inspected, the defect must not have been readily apparent upon examination. Because of the broader approach taken today as to what constitutes goods sold by description, this provision has become much more important, covering virtually all sales of mass-produced goods.

> Goods must be of merchantable quality

CASE SUMMARY 15.3

Suppliers of Defective Gears Fail to Protect Themselves: *Hunter Engineering Co. v. Syncrude Canada Ltd.*[14]

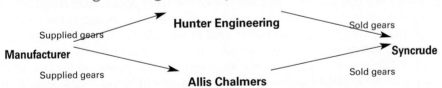

As part of its tar sands extraction project, Syncrude operated a large conveyor belt to carry sand over long distances. Syncrude ordered a number of gearboxes for this system from two different companies. Both companies, Hunter Engineering and Allis Chalmers, obtained the gears from the same manufacturer. All of the gears were made according to

---

11. (2000), 194 Sask. R. 249 (Q.B.).

12. See *Coast Hotels Limited v. Royal Doulton Canada Ltd.* (2000), 76 B.C.L.R. (3d) 341 (S.C.), in which the substitution of the word "Capital" for "Royal Doulton" on tableware resulted in the goods provided not corresponding with the description.

13. See *Eggen Seed Farms Ltd. v. Alberta Wheat Pool* (1997), 205 A.R. 77 (Q.B.), in which the Court held that the sale of contaminated fertilizer was a breach of the implied condition of merchantable quality. Because the buyer had accepted the goods, it was only entitled to damages for breach of warranty. In *Satara Farms Inc. v. Parrish & Heimbecker, Ltd.* (2006), 280 Sask. R. 44, four farmers were successful in a claim relating to defective ostrich feed as the manufacturer and distributor were liable for breach of the implied conditions of fitness for purpose and merchantable quality.

14. [1989] 1 S.C.R. 426.

the same design and specifications. After several gears failed, it was determined that all would have to be repaired. Syncrude sued both companies. Both companies claimed that they were protected by clauses in their contracts limiting their responsibility to a specific period of time that had expired. Although the *Sale of Goods Act* applied, requiring the goods to be fit for their intended purpose, the Court had to determine whether the exemption clauses contained in the contracts overrode the operation of the *Act*.

The Hunter Engineering contract did have a clause limiting its liability, but it failed to include a clause exempting the operation of the *Sale of Goods Act* provisions which, still being in force, imposed liability on it. The Allis Chalmers contract specifically excluded all statutory warranties or conditions, and so there was no liability. It was also argued that if the breach were fundamental, this exemption clause could not stand. But the Supreme Court of Canada held that even in the face of such a fundamental breach, it was still possible for the parties to exempt themselves from liability, as Allis Chalmers had effectively done in this case. (Fundamental breach is discussed in more detail in Chapter 9.)

SMALL BUSINESS PERSPECTIVE

Is knowledge of case law important when deciding how to word exemption clauses? Is it worth the expense to have contracts prepared, or at least reviewed, by one's lawyer?

Goods must be suitable for purpose of purchase when sales person relied upon

Sometimes a buyer with a particular need will rely on a seller's recommendation as to what product to use. In these circumstances, there is an implied condition that the goods will be reasonably fit for that purpose. The requirement of fitness applies not only when the goods are being used for some unique purpose, but also when they are being used normally. (This is the section applied in the *Hunter Engineering* case discussed in Case Summary 15.3.)

This protection does not apply when the goods are purchased by trade name in such a way that it is clear that the skill of the seller is not being relied on,[15] or when it is not in the normal course of the seller's business to supply the goods.

If Florio were to buy a particular kind of paint from McGregor's paint company after asking if it were suitable for concrete and later found that the paint peeled, Florio would be able to sue McGregor for compensation because of the breach of the implied condition that the goods would be reasonably suitable for their intended purpose. However, if he bought it by trade name, disregarding any recommendations from the sales staff, he would have only himself to blame.[16]

In British Columbia, goods leased or sold must be durable

In British Columbia this protection has been extended to leased goods and a provision has been added that the goods be "durable for a reasonable period of time."[17] While these provisions do not relieve the buyer of the obligation to be cautious, they do provide for a certain minimum level of protection and quality.

The provisions related to fitness and quality apply in most sale of goods situations.[18] The principle of *caveat emptor* also applies to these situations. The end

[15] *Baldry v. Marshall*, [1925] 1 K.B. 260 (C.A.).

[16] For a case in which the Court held that a paint manufacturer breached the implied condition that the paint supplied to the buyer was reasonably fit for its intended purpose, see *McCready Products Ltd. v. Sherwin-Williams Co. of Canada Ltd.* (1985), 61 A.R. 234 (C.A.), aff'g on this point (1984), 53 A.R. 304 (Q.B.).

[17] *Sale of Goods Act*, R.S.B.C. 1996 c. 410, s. 18(c).

[18] For a good discussion of the implied conditions of fitness and quality, see *Gill v. Kittler* (1983), 44 A.R. 321 (Q.B.).

result is that while the buyer is required to be careful when buying goods, she still has the right to expect a certain level of quality and protection when such care has been shown. Courts have found sellers liable for breach of the implied condition that the goods will be reasonably fit for their purpose in cases involving the sale of a sandwich that contained a piece of wood,[19] a truck that was plagued by constant breakdowns,[20] and a laptop computer that frequently broke down.[21]

Many argue that people don't take enough responsibility for themselves. Have we shifted too much of this responsibility to merchants and manufacturers? Or is it appropriate to force vendors to stand behind their products?

Other examples in which the warranties of fitness or merchantable quality were breached include a vendor of herbicides held liable when the herbicide failed to be effective,[22] a contractor found liable when the sauna heaters it installed were not reasonably fit for the known purpose,[23] a manufacturer of a forklift tractor held liable because the equipment sold never functioned properly,[24] and a farm dealership found liable because a tractor had mechanical problems.[25]

GOODS MUST MATCH SAMPLE

The *Sale of Goods Act* uses a similar approach for the purchase of goods after examining a sample. There is an implied condition that the bulk of the goods must match the sample provided and be free of any hidden defects. For example, if the load of bricks Tsang bought from Cashin after first inspecting a sample brick looked fine, but in fact had not been baked properly and disintegrated after being used in Tsang's building, the bricks would be of unmerchantable quality, a breach of an implied condition of the contract.

OTHER IMPLIED TERMS

There are several other terms that are implied by the *Sale of Goods Act* unless otherwise specified by the parties. Where no price is stated, a reasonable price must be paid for goods. Delivery must take place within a reasonable time, and payment is due upon delivery. The time of payment will be treated as a warranty, unless the parties state time is of the essence. Whether the time of delivery will be treated as a condition or a warranty will be implied from the conduct of the parties. When bulk goods, such as grains, lumber and ore are involved, if significantly too little or too much is delivered the buyer is free to either reject the goods or keep them and pay for them at the contracted rate. The provisions affecting delivery, place, time, and quantity of the goods are usually made conditions by the parties.

Goods must match sample
and be free of hidden
defects

www.pearsoned.ca/mybuslawlab

Where price omitted—
reasonable price

Time, payment and place for
delivery implied terms

19. *Coote v. Hudson's Bay Company* (1977), 6 A.R. 59 (Dist. Ct.).

20. *Rosseway v. Canadian Kenworth Ltd.* (1978), 11 A.R. 91 (Dist. Ct.).

21. *Gadd v. London Drugs Ltd.* (1991), 123 A.R. 335 (Prov. Ct.).

22. *Caners v. Eli Lilly Canada Inc.* (1996), 110 Man. R. (2d) 95 (C.A.).

23. *Young Men's Christian Association of Hamilton-Burlington v. 331783 Ontario Ltd.*, [2001] O.J. No. 4152 (Sup. Ct. J.), aff'd [2003] O.J. No. 2201 (C.A.).

24. *Champs Food System Ltd. v. de Koning Manufacturing*, [2004] M.J. No. 174 (C.A.).

25. 2006 AB P.C. 127, [2006] A.W.L.D. 2311.

SALES MADE ONLINE

Many sale of goods transactions are now conducted online, and parties to such transactions are still required to comply with the terms of the *Sales of Goods Act* in place in the jurisdiction that covers the transaction. These *Sales of Goods Acts* vary, and in many jurisdictions it is still possible for the parties to agree to override even the requirements with respect to fitness and quality. Where sellers can, it is normal practice for them to include terms (interestingly, often called "warranties") that override or otherwise limit these provisions. Consumers should be extremely careful to look for such provisions and understand their effect. Some sellers may fail to make those exemptions clear to the buyer by burying them at the end of the site or in pages that most buyers skim or neglect to read at all. Generally, online retailers are required to take reasonable measures to draw such terms to the attention of the other party, and if they fail to do so, these terms do not bind the buyer. But if retailers do direct buyers to these terms and the buyer fails to read them, the buyer will typically be bound.[26]

CASE SUMMARY 15.4

Performance Required Within a Reasonable Time: *Dansway International Transport Ltd. v. Lesway and Sons Ltd.*[27]

Dansway bought two trailers from Lesway, paying a $2000 deposit on the $100 000 purchase price on 16 July 1998. Nothing had been said as to the time of delivery or whether the time for delivery and payment were important. Dansway claimed to have said that payment had to wait for an insurance settlement, but Lesway said it had thought that the deal was to go through within one week. Lesway claimed to have sent notification of termination on 29 July 1998, but Dansway denied receiving it and continued arranging financing. On 27 August Dansway tried to complete the deal, but Lesway told it of the termination and returned its deposit.

Dansway sued. The Judge determined that since neither party had either stated that time was important or specified a time for performance, there was an implied term that performance had to be within a reasonable time. What constituted a reasonable time depended on the circumstances. In this case, a reasonable time would be one month. In any event, the party wishing to terminate the contract had to serve notice on the other that performance was required or that the contract would be considered at an end. Since this wasn't done, the seller was in breach of the contract. Damages were awarded accordingly.

SMALL BUSINESS PERSPECTIVE

If performance of a contract doesn't proceed as expected, parties may grow dissatisfied and attempt to cancel the deal. Can such situations be avoided? If a party feels a need to terminate a contract, what should that party do first?

---

26. See *Kanitz v. Rogers Cable Inc.* (2002), 58 O.R. (3d) 299 (Sup. Ct. J.), in which the Court held that adequate notice of changes to an online agreement was given and that the customers were therefore bound by the amended terms of the online agreement. This result is consistent with general contract law and non-internet cases.

27. [2001] O.J. No. 4594 (Sup. Ct. J.).

Remedies on Default

SELLER'S REMEDIES

When the buyer defaults, the seller has an unpaid **seller's lien** against the goods. This gives the seller the right to retain the goods until appropriate payment has been made, even though title may have transferred.

Similarly, if the goods are en route to the buyer, and the buyer defaults, the seller has the right to intercept the goods and retake possession from the transporter, as long as the goods have not yet reached the buyer. This is referred to as the seller's right of **stoppage in transit**. Reference to the specific provincial legislation is necessary to ascertain when this right arises. (See MyBusLawLab for details.) The *Bankruptcy and Insolvency Act* [28] also allows a seller of goods to recover those goods even after they are delivered to the buyer if, within 30 days of delivery, the buyer has become bankrupt or a receiver has been appointed and, of course, provided the buyer, receiver or trustee still has them. This gives the seller priority over the bankrupt's other creditors.

When the seller exercises this power to retake the goods sold and, after appropriate notice, remains unpaid, the goods can be sold to recover the loss. Such notice of resale is not required when perishable goods are involved.

In the event of a breach of contract, the seller retains all of the normal remedies that were discussed in the previous chapter. He has the right to sue for the price of the goods when title has passed to the buyer. In such a case, if the buyer refuses to accept delivery of the goods, she is rejecting her own goods and may still be required to pay the purchase price. If the time specified for payment passes, the seller can sue for the purchase price even if title has not yet passed to the buyer. Buyers would be wise to refuse delivery only when the seller has breached a condition of the contract. Otherwise, by refusing delivery, the buyer takes the risk of not getting the goods but still being required to pay full price for them. But the seller must be careful and do nothing inconsistent with his continued willingness to perform. If he tries to sell the goods to someone else, for example, he will no longer be able to sue for the whole price, just for what he has lost on the sale.

The seller may be able to claim for damages for breach of contract even in situations in which it is not possible to claim the purchase price of the goods. These losses will normally include the costs involved in restocking and resale. When the goods are resold at a lower price, that loss will be included as well. The seller also has an obligation to mitigate losses, which usually requires the seller to take steps to resell the goods immediately. When a deposit is involved, the seller can keep the deposit. This is not the case when the prepayment is a down payment only. In fact, it may well not be worth the effort to sue for damages if it is not possible to sue for the actual price of the goods.

BUYER'S REMEDIES

The remedies available to the buyer if the seller defaults are those provided by general contract law. Where misrepresentation is involved, the buyer may be able to rescind the contract or seek damages when there has been fraud or negligence. When a condition of the contract is breached, the buyer may refuse to perform or

Right of stoppage in transit

Seller protected in case of bankruptcy

Seller can sue for price in cases of default or refusal of delivery once title has passed

---

28. R.S.C. 1985, c. B-3, s. 81.1.

Buyer's remedies those of contract law

demand return of any money paid. If only a warranty is breached, the buyer must go through with the deal, subject to a right for damages. The damages will usually be based on the difference between what the buyer had agreed to pay for the goods and the cost of obtaining the goods from another source. But when there are additional losses suffered because of the delay in obtaining the goods or the defect involved, the buyer will be able to claim them as well.

If title has passed, the buyer may lose his right to discharge the contract in the event of a breach of condition. The damages usually are determined by what it costs to bring the goods up to the specifications in the original contract or by their reduction in value because of the breach.[29] When defective goods have caused physical injury or damage to other property, those damages are also recoverable, provided they were reasonably within the contemplation of the parties at the time the contract was entered into.[30] Thus, people who suffer food poisoning because of poor-quality food at a restaurant can seek compensation for their injuries under the *Sale of Goods Act* provisions, and those damages can be substantial. When unique goods are involved, the buyer may also be able to claim a remedy of specific performance and force the seller to go through with the sale rather than pay damages in compensation.

Extent of damages depends on circumstances

Finally, it should be mentioned that every Canadian jurisdiction (federal, provincial, and territorial) has now enacted an international sale of goods act.[31] Refer to the links on the MyBusLawLab to review these statutes.[32] A great deal of trading today is done in the international arena, and these statutes are intended to bring the same kind of structure and certainty to import and export dealings as the *Sale of Goods Act* provides domestically.

Additionally, the federal government is a signatory to the U.N. *Convention on the International Sales of Goods (CISG)*, which governs trade between Canada and the United States as well as 60 other signatory states. Oddly, many North American legal practitioners are wary of resorting to the *CISG* (adopted by the United States in 1988 and in Canada in 1992), so there is little case law interpreting it. Apparently, legal practitioners prefer the "devil they know" and opt to insert choice of law provisions into contracts to avoid having "uncertain" law applied to their contracts.

! REDUCING RISK 15.2

Businesspeople should always be aware of the operation of the *Sale of Goods Act*, especially the provisions related to fitness and quality. Even in large commercial transactions, it is important to specify the nature and limits of the obligations of the parties to avoid unwanted terms from being implied into the contract. As seen in the *Hunter* *Engineering* case (Case Summary 15.4), the failure of one supplier to exclude the operation of the *Sale of Goods Act* made that supplier responsible for substantial damages. Whether buyer or seller, it is important to keep the *Sale of Goods Act* in mind whenever goods are being transferred for money.

[29.] See *A.C. Neilsen Co. of Canada v. Kiosk Design Inc.*, [2003] O.J. No. 4647 (Sup. Ct. J.) for a case in which only nominal damages were awarded after a seller acted promptly to address concerns.

[30.] *Hadley v. Baxendale* (1854), 156 E.R. 145 (Ex. Ct.).

[31.] In Alberta, for example, the *International Conventions Implementation Act*, S.A. 1990, c. 1–6.8., now cited as R.S.A. 2000, c. I-6.

[32.] All of the following have enacted legislation based on the Uniform Law Conference of Canada's *International Sale of Goods Act*: British Columbia (1990, 1992), Alberta (1990), Saskatchewan (1991), Manitoba (1989), Ontario (1988), Quebec (similar act, 1991), New Brunswick (1989), P.E.I. (1988), Nova Scotia (1988), Newfoundland (1989), Yukon (1992), N.W.T. (1988), Nunavut (2006), and Canada (1991).

CONSUMER PROTECTION

Freedom of contract has been significantly affected by legislation in the context of consumer transactions. **Consumer transactions** involve goods or services purchased by individuals for personal use and not for resale or for business purposes.

Consumer protection legislation imposes standards and responsibilities on manufacturers and suppliers of goods and services. It controls the use and disclosure of information and advertising. It controls the safety and quality of the goods sold. This legislation also controls unethical or otherwise unacceptable business practices. The rest of this chapter will examine this area and consider the regulatory bodies created to enforce the legislation. There are both federal and provincial statutes involved, with considerable variety among provincial jurisdictions. Once again, refer to the MyBusLawLab for details pertaining to a particular jurisdiction. Depending on the jurisdiction, the legislation may be contained in one statute or several.[33] Although there has been some limited form of consumer protection in our law for centuries, modern statutes have significantly expanded and modified the law in this area. Until recently, the common contractual themes of *caveat emptor* and freedom of contract dominated consumer transactions. But because of the vulnerability of consumers to abuse and their weakened bargaining position given modern business practices, limits have been placed on those principles.

www.pearsoned.ca/mybuslawlab

Consumer transaction involves purchases for personal consumption rather than business use

Statutes prevent abuse

CASE SUMMARY 15.5

Parked Truck Goes Up in Flames: *Prebushewski v. Dodge City Auto (1984) Ltd.*[34]

Fourteen months after the Plaintiff purchased a new truck, it was destroyed by fire. An investigation determined that a defect in the daytime running light module had caused it to short-circuit, leading to the fire. Both Dodge City and Chrysler refused to assist the Plaintiff, even though she had purchased an extended warranty. They simply referred her to her insurer. The insurance settlement did not cover the amount still owing on the Plaintiff's bank loan, so she commenced an action under the *Consumer Protection Act* (*CPA*).

The trial Judge had no difficulty in finding that the module was not durable for a reasonable period, in breach of section 48 of the *CPA*:

> Where a consumer product is sold by a retail seller, the following warranties are deemed to be given...
>
> (g) that the product and all its components are to be durable for a reasonable period.

---

33. Ontario and British Columbia have each consolidated a collection of consumer protection laws into a single statute. Ontario's *Consumer Protection Act*, 2002, S.O. 2002, c. 30, Sch. A, was proclaimed in force on 30 July 2005. British Columbia's *Business Practices and Consumer Protection Act*, S.B.C. 2004, c. 2, is notable for creating the Business Practices and Consumer Protection Authority. This not-for-profit organization operates at arm's length from the government and has been responsible for overseeing business practices and consumer protection in British Columbia since July 2004. See http://www.bpcpa.ca/.

34. [2005] 1 S.C.R. 649.

> Pursuant to the legislation, the manufacturer is also bound by these statutory warranties. The CPA remedies for a substantial breach enable the purchaser to reject the product and recover the price, which the Judge awarded (less $5000 for usage). The Judge also awarded bank interest charges, $560 for property destroyed by the fire and $25 000 in exemplary damages.
>
> The Supreme Court of Canada affirmed the award since Chrysler willfully violated the *CPA*. Chrysler knew about the defective module, but had "made a business decision to neither advise its customers of the problem nor to recall the vehicles to replace the modules.... Chrysler was not prepared to spend $250 million even though it knew what the defective module might do."
>
> ---
>
> *SMALL BUSINESS PERSPECTIVE*
>
> The Supreme Court held that, since Chrysler's conduct was voluntary, intentional, and deliberate, an award of exemplary damages was justified. The *Consumer Protection Act* purposely sets a low threshold for exemplary damages so that protection for consumers is enhanced. Do you think this is appropriate? Without such a legislative provision, might manufacturers be tempted to maintain secrecy despite risks to consumers?

Federal Legislation

Federal department enforces statutes, educates, and protects consumers

Although the most dramatic developments in consumer protection legislation have taken place provincially in recent years, there are some significant and effective federal statutes as well. Industry Canada was established under the *Department of Industry Act*.[35] Industry Canada, through its various offices, such as Consumer Affairs, the Competition Bureau, and the Office of the Superintendent of Bankruptcy, regulates the various areas of concern. The mission of Industry Canada is to foster a growing, competitive, knowledge-based Canadian economy. Its mandate includes three strategic objectives—a fair, efficient, and competitive marketplace; an innovative economy; and competitive industry and sustainable communities. Product safety is now overseen by Health Canada, which was established under the *Department of Health Act*.[36] Information about these and other consumer-oriented agencies can be found in the *Canadian Consumer Handbook*, discussed below.

THE COMPETITION

The mission of the Competition Bureau "is to protect and promote competitive markets and enable informed consumer choice in Canada."[37] The Competition Bureau is an independent law enforcement agency that administers and enforces the *Competition Act*.[38] This legislation can be characterized as a criminal statute that has as its objective the maintenance and encouragement of competition in

---

[35] S.C. 1995, c. 1.

[36] S.C. 1996, c. 8.

[37] See the website for the Competition Bureau, at: www.competitionbureau.gc.ca/eic/site/cb-bc.nsf/eng/home.

[38] R.S.C. 1985, c. C-34.

Canada so that Canadians can benefit from product choice, competitive prices, and quality services. Hearings pursuant to the *Competition Act* are conducted before the Competition Tribunal, which functions much like a court, prosecuting violations and imposing fines and imprisonment for up to five years on those who are found guilty of violations.

One purpose of the *Competition Act* is to control mergers. Mergers are no longer treated as inherently bad; the Competition Tribunal just reviews them to determine whether they will have the effect of substantially limiting or lessening competition. The Tribunal must weigh different factors. It will tolerate some lessening of competition if it is justified by the efficiency gained. A **horizontal merger** takes place when one competitor buys another. A vertical merger involves the merger of a supplier and retailer. The danger of this is that the supplier may squeeze out the competition by favouring its own retailer, as explained below. A **conglomerate merger** involves companies not in direct competition. The Tribunal will look to determine if the overall effect is to unduly limit competition.

The "efficiency defence"[39] has recently been successfully raised, for example, in the merger of Superior Propane Inc. and ICG Propane Inc.[40] Acknowledging that the merger would lessen competition, the Tribunal nonetheless approved it because of increased efficiencies of cost savings, improved customer service, and improved position in the overall energy market. These efficiencies were quantified at $29.2 million, while the anti-competitive economic effects were calculated to be $6 million. The decision surprised many. Even mergers that will lead to price increases may pass the merger-review provisions of the *Competition Act* if the efficiencies gained exceed the anti-competitive effects.

The *Competition Act* criminalizes some anti-competitive practices, including conspiracy to unduly lessen competition (for example, price fixing among suppliers); bid rigging (for example, a group of bidders agreeing in advance who will bid lowest); discriminatory and predatory pricing (for example, using loss leaders to drive competitors out of business); price maintenance and refusal to supply; and certain misleading advertising and deceptive marketing practices (including deceptive notices of winning a prize, pyramid selling, and double ticketing). Criminal prosecutions must be proven beyond a reasonable doubt. Upon conviction, penalties include fines, imprisonment, and injunctions ordering the offender to cease-and-desist its anti-competitive behavior.

Some practices are subject to civil, as opposed to criminal, sanctions, including refusal to deal (for example, substantially affecting a business by refusing to supply product on the usual terms); consignment selling; tied selling, exclusive dealing, and market restriction (for example, inducing a buyer to purchase a second product as a condition of supplying a particular product, requiring a customer to deal only or mostly in certain products, or requiring a customer to sell specific products in a defined market); delivered pricing (for example, bait-and-switch selling, selling above the advertised price, or advertising a "bargain price" which is actually the original price); abuse of dominant position; and merger review.

In June 2002, the *Competition Act* was amended to create a new right of "private access." This enabled private persons or businesses to seek a legal remedy against another's anti-competitive conduct. This was a substantial change. Previously, the Commissioner of Competition had an "enforcement monopoly" over civil

Competition Act controls abuses in free market

Mergers controlled

Abusive trade practices prohibited

Undue restriction of competition prohibited

---

[39]. *Ibid.* s. 96.

[40]. *Canada (Commissioner of Competition) v. Superior Propane Inc.*, 2003 FCA 53, [2003] 3 F.C. 529.

provisions of the *Competition Act*. Now, competitors can apply for remedies if confronted with a refusal to deal. Suppliers may thus be required to supply product to would-be distributors and customers. Cease-and-desist type orders can also be obtained to counter exclusive dealing, tied selling, and market restriction when such practices have resulted, or are likely to result, in a lessening of competition.

It is conceivable that this extension of remedies to those most affected by the anti-competitive practices may lead to greater enforcement of the *Competition Act*. The Competition Bureau may thus focus on business practices that affect the public generally. For example, on 6 March 2009, the Competition Bureau announced that Moores Clothing for Men had agreed to amend its advertising regarding a two-for-one suit sale.[41] The advertising did not disclose that the sale applied only to select designer suits, contrary to the misleading representations provisions of the *Competition Act*. Moores agreed to "prominently disclose" that the sale applied only to select designer suits.

Misleading representations stopped

On 26 March 2009, the Competition Bureau announced that The Brick Warehouse LP had agreed to cancel all advertising related to a national mail-in rebate promotion.[42] The Brick advertised an $80 mail-in rebate, implying that consumers would receive a cash rebate. Consumers were instead sent a Brick gift certificate. This too was contrary to the misleading representations provisions of the *Competition Act*. The Brick agreed to provide consumers who made a purchase under the promotion with an $80 rebate cheque, rather than a Brick gift certificate.[43]

The primary purpose of the *Competition Act* is to ensure the proper operation of the free-market system. To accomplish that purpose, provisions are included that prohibit any attempt to unduly restrain competition.[44] The key here is "unduly." As a result, it is clear that not all agreements restricting competition will be illegal or in violation of the *Act*. Cynically, one might state that "Not all attempts to lessen competition are prohibited—just those that are successful!" Thus, if two merchants agree not to sell specific goods in the other's area and they are the only source of those goods, this would likely violate the *Act* as an agreement that unduly restricts competition. On the other hand, if competition is not lessened because customers still have alternative sources, then a violation of the *Act* may not have occurred.

---

[41]. "Moores Clarifies Advertising to Resolve Competition Bureau Concerns," 6 March 2009, www.competitionbureau.gc.ca/eic/site/cb-bc.nsf/eng/03016.html.

[42]. "Furniture Chain Cancels Rebate Promotion to Resolve Competition Bureau Concerns," 29 March 2009, www.competitionbureau.gc.ca/eic/site/cb-bc.nsf/eng/03032.html.

[43]. The Competition Bureau set up a special research group to investigate consumer rebates. See "Competition Watchdog to Warn About Misleading Rebate Offers: Report" CBC News, 8 December 2008, www.cbc.ca/canada/manitoba/story/2008/12/08/competition-bureau.html. The Bureau has issued a Draft Information Bulletin on Consumer Rebate Promotions, www.competitionbureau.gc.ca/eic/site/cb-bc.nsf/eng/03033.html. The Bureau is seeking comments from the public on this Draft Information Bulletin, www.competitionbureau.gc.ca/eic/site/cb-bc.nsf/eng/03037.html.

[44]. See s. 45(1) of the *Competition Act, supra* note 38.

CASE SUMMARY 15.6

Conspiracy to Fix Prices Not a Violation: *R. v. Clarke Transport Canada Inc.*[45]

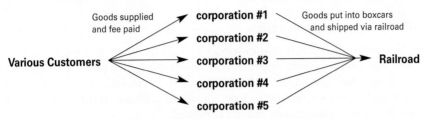

The five corporations agree to fix price charged to customers

Five corporations were involved in providing services to forward freight by pool car. They paid a set price per boxcar and charged their customers a fee based on the weight of the commodities they wanted shipped. Representatives of these five corporations attempted to keep prices high by agreeing not to compete amongst themselves or to undercut each other's prices. This apparently was a clear case of price maintenance or price fixing. The Court, however, found the corporations not guilty of charges laid under the *Competition Act*, because customers could still choose to use another mode of transportation. The Crown thus failed to show that the conspiracy *unduly* limited competition.

DISCUSSION QUESTIONS

Does this interpretation make it too difficult to prosecute those engaged in price maintenance practices? Would the result of this case be different under the amendments to the *Competition Act* discussed below?

On 12 March 2009, the *Budget Implementation Act, 2009*[46] received Royal Assent. It contained amendments to the *Competition Act*. These amendments address topics such as price fixing, bid rigging, agreements between competitors, misleading advertising, and mergers and acquisitions. Fines were increased to as much as $25 million and jail sentences were increased to as long as 14 years. The conspiracy section of the legislation was toughened so that it is now an indictable office to conspire with a competitor to fix prices, allocate sales, territories, customers, or markets and fix production and supply. It is now assumed that an agreement among competitors automatically impacts competition. That means that existing agreements may be caught by the legislative changes. On the other hand, criminal provisions relating to price discrimination, promotional allowance, and predatory pricing provisions were repealed.

At the time of the writing of this chapter, regulations to implement the amendments to the *Act* had not yet been published. The Competition Bureau had just published its draft merger review process guidelines.[47] These were open for

Effect of recent amendments unclear

---

45. (1995), 130 D.L.R. (4th) 500 (Ont. Gen. Div.).

46. S.C. 2009, c. 2.

47. "Draft Merger Review Process Guidelines Issued for Comment," www.competitionbureau.gc.ca/eic/site/cb-bc.nsf/eng/03029.html.

public comment for 60 days. Furthermore, the amendments did not undergo the usual parliamentary scrutiny. It is therefore difficult to predict what the results of the amendments will be. On 23 March 2009, Suncor Energy Inc. and Petro-Canada announced a merger that would create a corporation worth $43 billion.[48] This merger will provide the first test of how effective the amendments will be in protecting competition in Canada.

OTHER FEDERAL LEGISLATION

The Competition Bureau also enforces and administers several other federal statutes that have a consumer protection aspect to them. The *Consumer Packaging and Labelling Act,*[49] the *Precious Metals Marking Act,*[50] and the *Textile Labelling Act*[51] are criminal statutes intended to force proper disclosure of information to help consumers make comparisons among products.

Food and Drugs Act carries strict penalties

There are several statutes, both federal and provincial, designed to protect the consumer from dangerous products. The federal *Food and Drugs Act*[52] is intended primarily to control the sale of food, drugs, and cosmetics unfit for consumption or use. The legislation also prohibits misleading or deceptive claims associated with the sale, labelling, and advertising of these products. Several categories of drugs are created. Unsafe drugs, such as thalidomide, are prohibited from sale in Canada. Under the *Controlled Drugs and Substances Act,*[53] certain *dangerous drugs* that are useful are allowed to be sold under controlled conditions. The *Act* makes it an offence to traffic in certain *controlled drugs,* such as amphetamines and steroids. Strong and effective enforcement provisions are included.

Hazardous products controlled

Another federal act, the *Hazardous Products Act,*[54] similarly controls the manufacture, import, and sale of products that are inherently dangerous. Some particularly dangerous products, such as inflammable clothing or dangerous toys, are prohibited from sale in Canada, while the sale of other potentially dangerous products is allowed provided that they comply with the enacted regulations. Examples of the latter are such products as cradles, cribs, carpets, kettles, toys, and pacifiers. The *Act* also contains important inspection, analysis, and enforcement provisions. Some hazardous products are covered by their own legislation, such as the *Explosives Act,*[55] the *Pest Control Products Act,*[56] the *Motor Vehicle Safety Act,*[57] and the *Organic Products Regulation.*[58]

Of course, consumers injured by dangerous products retain their common law right to seek compensation from the seller or manufacturer. This may be done in the form of a contract action (usually under the fitness and quality provision under

---

48. "Suncor, Petro-Canada Announce Merger" CBC News, 23 March 2009, www.cbc.ca/money/story/2009/03/23/suncor-petro-canada-merge.html.

49. R.S.C. 1985, c. C-38.

50. R.S.C. 1985, c. P-19.

51. R.S.C. 1985, c. T-10.

52. *R.S.C. 1985, c. F-27.*

53. S.C. 1996, c. 19.

54. *R.S.C. 1985, c. H-3.*

55. R.S.C. 1985, c. E-17.

56. S.C. 2002, c. 28.

57. S.C. 1993, c.16.

58. S.O.R./2006-338 enacted pursuant to the Canada *Agricultural Products Act,* R.S.C. 1985, c. 20 (4th Supp.), c. 0.4.

the *Sale of Goods Act* or the consumer protection legislation). It can also be done in tort, suing for negligence as illustrated by the *Donoghue v. Stevenson* case discussed in Chapter 5. In that case, the plaintiff consumed a ginger beer purchased for her by her friend that was contaminated by a decomposed snail. She sued the manufacturer for negligence. With the advent of consumer protection legislation, the manufacturer would be in a more precarious position today.

REDUCING RISK 15.3

It is important for businesspeople dealing with the public to keep up with statutory changes in the area of consumer protection, including those within federal jurisdiction. The enforcement sections of consumer protection legislation have become stronger, and abusive practices that may have gone unchallenged in the past are now much more likely to result in bad publicity, censure, fines, or even the loss of a business licence.

Provincial Legislation

RESPONSIBILITY FOR GOODS

When products are defective, causing injury or loss, consumers have recourse in either contract or negligence. As we learned in Chapter 5, the problem with suing in negligence is that there must be a failure on the defendant's part to live up to a demonstrated standard of care. This carelessness is often difficult to prove. Another problem is that often only the manufacturer can be sued, since the wholesalers and retailers don't deal with, or even inspect, the prepackaged goods they sell. An action based on contract law is much simpler, since the consumer need only show that the product delivered was defective and caused loss or injury. But, because of the principle of privity, any action for breach of contract is limited to the actual purchaser suing the merchant that sold the defective product. Also, the contracts involved usually include exemption clauses that attempt to significantly limit the responsibilities of the seller. There are several examples of statutes that overcome these problems.

The sections of the *Sale of Goods Act* requiring the delivery of good title, that goods correspond to the description and sample, and that the goods supplied be fit and of merchantable quality, have one serious drawback. In commercial transactions, these can be overridden by properly drafted exemption clauses. Many provinces in Canada have therefore enacted legislation removing the right to override these provisions in consumer transactions. Some do this in their *Sale of Goods Acts*, while others provide similar protection in separate statutes. Some jurisdictions require these goods to be "durable", while some have also extended the protection to leased goods. Again, refer to the MyBusLawLab for specific details for each jurisdiction.[59]

mybuslawlab
www.pearsoned.ca/mybuslawlab

BC AB SK MB ON

Statutes overcome problems in contract and tort

Effect of exemption clauses limited by statute

---

59. Different provinces take different approaches. For example, the B.C. *Sale of Goods Act* prevents the exclusion of such implied terms. The *Consumer Protection Acts* of the Northwest Territories, the Yukon, Manitoba, and Nova Scotia imply similar warranties and conditions and then remove the right to override them. The Ontario *Consumer Protection Act, 2002, supra* note 33, refers to the Ontario sale of goods legislation, and then prevents exclusion of the implied provisions. (See section 9.) In Alberta, however, merchants can rely on exemption clauses to relieve themselves of the obligation to deliver quality goods to the buyer pursuant to s. 54 of Alberta's *Sale of Goods Act*, R.S.A. 2000, c. S-2.

Manufacturers usually include a "warranty" with their products stating the extent of their responsibility for fitness and quality. These are in fact exemption clauses that attempt to limit the liability of the manufacturer and retailer for the product. With the recent legislative changes, manufacturers and retailers may not be able to rely on such exemption clauses to relieve themselves of the obligation to deliver fit and quality goods to the consumer. Purchasers can now sue for breach of contract and receive significant compensation for their losses when products are unfit, even after the expiration of a stated warranty period. This also may apply to online consumer transactions depending on the legislation in place in the particular jurisdiction.

If Joyce bought a new vehicle for family use from Ace Dealership and the engine seized three days after the expiration of the three-year warranty period, Ace would not be allowed to claim that the stated warranty had expired and refuse to fix it. The three-year warranty is an exemption clause that is void in a consumer transaction. The vehicle must be of merchantable quality. Since most people would expect a transmission in a modern car to last longer than three years, it is likely that Ace would be required to be responsible for its product and make (or pay for) the repairs in these circumstances.

As mentioned, there are several advantages to suing in contract—as is the case when proceeding under the *Sale of Goods Act*—rather than basing a lawsuit upon tort law. The plaintiff does not need to prove that the defendants failed in their duty of care. The damages awarded in breach of contract cases (like in cases based on negligence) can go far beyond a refund of the purchase price. This was the case in *Gee v. White Spot*, discussed above. However, the principle of privity can pose a significant obstacle to suing in contract, since only the parties to an agreement can sue for breach. In the case of *Donoghue v. Stevenson* discussed in Chapter 5, Donoghue consumed a contaminated bottle of ginger beer given to her by a friend. She could not sue the seller for breach, not being "privy" to the contract. She had to sue the manufacturer for negligence instead.

Privity problem overcome by statute

Some provinces have extended the requirements of fitness and quality discussed above to anyone the seller could reasonably foresee might use the product. Through their consumer protection statutes, others have eliminated privity as a defence when warranties of fitness are implied. The result in those jurisdictions is that anyone injured or suffering a loss because of a defective product can sue the seller or manufacturer for breach of the implied conditions, whether he is the purchaser or not.

CASE SUMMARY 15.7

Defective Bottle Cap Causes Injury: *Morse v. Cott Beverages West Ltd.*[60]

Morse sustained a serious eye injury when she used a nutcracker to remove a difficult bottle cap, which exploded in the process. She sued, relying on Saskatchewan's *Consumer Products Warranties Act*, claiming that the manufacturer's poor quality control

---

60. (2001), 215 Sask. R. 47 (Q.B.).

caused the accident. The corporation's records showed that on the day the subject bottle was manufactured, more than half of the bottles produced required a pressure greater than that recommended. The Judge therefore concluded that the caps were defective because they were too tight. He awarded damages to Morse, including punitive damages because the corporation, given its own test results, had wilfully jeopardized the safety of the public by distributing a dangerous product.

Note that the *Act* imposed contractual obligations with respect to fitness and quality, eliminating the need to prove negligence. It also removed the barrier of privity of contract, allowing the consumer to sue the manufacturer in contract.[61]

DISCUSSION QUESTIONS

Is it justifiable to facilitate the consumer's ability to sue in this fashion?

The right to sue for breach is extended by these statutes beyond the original parties to the contract, making the seller liable even when there is no indication of fault on its part. The courts have also shown a willingness to get around the privity problem. In *Murray v. Sperry Rand Corp.*,[62] the manufacturer was found liable to the consumer in contract even though the purchase was made from a retailer. Because false claims were included in the advertising brochures produced by the manufacturer, the Court found that there was a subsidiary, or collateral, contract between the manufacturer and the consumer that allowed the consumer to sue the manufacturer directly in contract. This is consistent with the tendency of the courts to abandon the privity principle.

It should be mentioned, however, that although exemption clauses in warranties will not protect the seller in consumer transactions, they might still be effective in limiting the liability of the manufacturer, depending on the nature of the contract and the legislation in place in the particular jurisdiction.

Privity problem overcome by the courts

REDUCING RISK 15.4

Most salespeople don't understand the merchant's liability beyond the manufacturer's limited warranty included with the product sold. It is important, however, for merchants to understand their potential liability for defective products. As consumers become more aware of their rights and become more aggressive in enforcing them, a merchant's very existence may depend upon whether appropriate steps were taken to eliminate or reduce such potential liability.

Some useful products, by their very nature, are hazardous. The obligation of the manufacturer and seller of such products is to make them as safe as possible, to warn the potential user of the dangers, and to provide information on their proper use. An injured consumer can successfully sue in contract or negligence when these steps are not followed. Except when the danger is obvious, a warning

Duty to warn when product hazardous

---

61. This legislation has been replaced by the Consumer Protection Act, S.S. 1996, c. C-30.1, which likewise augments the buyer's ability to sue the retailer and manufacturer.

62. (1979), 23 O.R. (2d) 456 (H.C.).

incorporated into the product label must alert the consumer to the hazards associated with the product. If the warning is inadequate, the manufacturer and seller may be liable for the injuries that result. Even when such dangers are obvious, as with a sharp knife, the practice is growing for manufacturers to include such a warning, out of an abundance of caution. Federal legislation dealing with the merchandising of dangerous products was covered earlier in this chapter.

UNACCEPTABLE BUSINESS PRACTICES

False or Exaggerated Claims

Another major thrust of consumer protection legislation is to prohibit or control certain unacceptable business practices such as making misleading or false statements to persuade people to buy a product. Under the common law, these statements normally do not form part of the contract and generally are dismissed as mere advertising puffs, leaving the purchaser with little recourse. Further, contracts of sale often contain clauses stating that there are no representations other than those contained in the written document, making any false or misleading claims by salespeople not actionable unless they are actually included in the contract itself. Today these statements are controlled by statute, with most provinces incorporating them into the contract and making any attempt to override them void. As a result, when a salesperson makes a false or exaggerated claim, or one is included in an advertisement, it becomes a term of the contract and is actionable as a breach if it proves incorrect or is not honoured. If Mrs. Holberg, the purchaser of a used car from Affleck's Fine Car Co., was informed by the salesperson that the car had been driven "only to church on Sundays," that statement would, under these provisions, be incorporated into the contract, even if it were not contained in the written document. If Mrs. Holberg could convince the court that a false statement had been made, she could successfully sue for breach of contract when the statement proved false. The actual statutes used to accomplish this vary considerably from province to province. Greater detail as to the specific legislation and relevant case law is found in the MyBusLawLab.

Typically, this type of statute lists several different kinds of misleading and deceptive statements which are deemed to be unfair practices. For example, taking advantage of a consumer and exerting undue pressure on a consumer are deemed to be unfair practices in Alberta.[64] In addition to the penalties imposed by governments for violations, the consumer is given the right to have the contract rescinded or specifically performed, or to sue for damages. Any attempt to override these provisions, or to declare in a contract that there are no other representations other than what appears on the written document, will be void, leaving the purchaser free to sue. This is true even when the parties involved have been relatively innocent, for negligence or fraud on the seller's part need not be shown. Innocent but misleading statements may still qualify as deceptive practices under the relevant legislation.

The government department involved is typically given considerable powers to investigate complaints and to deal with complaints against offending merchandisers, including the powers to impose fines, to suspend licences and, in some provinces, to pursue a civil action on behalf of the consumer.

Perhaps the most effective provisions controlling misleading advertising and other deceptive business practices are contained in the federal *Competition Act,*

Legislation incorporates misleading statements into contract

Unfair practices identified in statute

Government bodies have been given significant powers

---

64. An example of legislation of this type is the *Fair Trading Act*, R.S.A. 2000, c. F-2.

which was discussed above. The common law provisions concerning false and misleading claims in consumer transactions have been considerably strengthened by these statutory provisions.

CASE SUMMARY 15.8

B.C. Act Controls Frauds Against U.S. Residents: *Director of Trade Practices v. Ideal Credit Referral Services Ltd. et al.*[65]

Ideal was a B.C. company directing misleading advertising to customers in the United States. It claimed it would loan even to those with a bad credit rating. The advertising included such phrases as "Good or Bad Credit!", "Bankruptcies O.K.!", and "Guaranteed Results!" To apply, customers had to pay a non-refundable $300 "processing fee." Ideal did a credit check, refused the application and kept the balance of the $300. The Director of Trade Practices applied for a declaration that this was a "deceptive or unconscionable act" and for an injunction. Ideal claimed that the B.C. *Act* did not apply, since its customers were in the United States, The Court of Appeal held that the *Act* prohibited deceptive and misleading practices that took place in British Columbia no matter where the victim was located. The *Act* was meant to control unethical business practices within the province.

DISCUSSION QUESTIONS

Is this an extraterritorial application of provincial law? Should the provisions of the statute be limited to the protection of B.C. residents? Is this too much of an interference in the operation of a free-market system?

Note that in *Robson v. Daimler Chrysler Corp.*,[66] the shoe was on the other foot; the customers were in British Columbia and the car manufacturers were in the United States. The B.C. *Trade Practice Act* was found to apply nonetheless. The customers alleged that the supplier engaged in deceptive acts or practices with respect to consumer transactions by failing to disclose that the paint finishes on the vehicles sold in British Columbia were defective. It was not essential that the alleged deceptive practices or acts took place within the province.

Unconscionable transactions or unfair bargains controlled

Unconscionable Transactions

Consumers sometimes are taken advantage of because of some vulnerability, such as desperation, poverty, lack of sophistication, or intellectual weakness. To prevent unscrupulous merchants from taking advantage of such vulnerable individuals, legislation has been enacted, either in separate acts (e.g., *Unconscionable Transactions Act*) or included in other statutes. Refer to the MyBusLawLab to identify the relevant legislation for a particular jurisdiction.

In some provinces, this legislation is restricted to situations involving the borrowing of money. For a transaction to be found unconscionable when money

---

65. (1997), 145 D.L.R. (4th) 20 (B.C.C.A.).

66. (2002), 2 B.C.L.R. (4th) 1 (C.A.).

is loaned, the actual cost of borrowing must be excessive in the circumstances. If the risk justifies the high rate of interest, it is not an unconscionable transaction, even when the consumer is of weak intellect or in desperate straits. When unconscionability is demonstrated, the courts can set the contract aside, modify its terms or order the return of money paid.

CASE SUMMARY 15.9

Aged Homeowner Protected from Unscrupulous Salesperson: *Dominion Home Improvements Ltd. v. Knuude*[67]

A door-to-door salesperson using intense tactics persuaded Knuude, an 80-year-old homeowner, to purchase a number of home improvements that she didn't need. After four hours of extremely high-pressured selling, including a refusal to leave unless the contract was signed, Knuude agreed to have the renovations done. She signed a $300 cheque as a deposit, but stopped payment on it immediately after the salesperson left.

The next day, workers from the company came to do the work. Knuude insisted that they leave. This brought back the salesperson who, by devious means, persuaded Knuude to reinstate the contract. The work was done. Knuude refused to pay. The company sued for the money owed under the contract.

The Judge determined that the contract was not binding on Knuude as it was fraudulent and unconscionable, and did not conform to the requirements set out in the provincial consumer protection legislation. This kind of unscrupulous business practice has led to the increase in consumer protection legislation.

DISCUSSION QUESTIONS

Has such legislation gone too far? Should consumers assume more responsibility for their own mistakes? Are there occasions when protection is necessary?

Some statutes do not limit unconscionability to loan transactions

In several other provinces, the legislation goes further, extending the concept of unconscionability beyond loan transactions to also cover unacceptable business practices. In these provinces, the courts can look at factors such as physical infirmity, illiteracy, inability to understand the language of an agreement, undue influence, a price that grossly exceeds the value of the goods, and the lack of reasonable benefit to the consumer, in establishing unconscionability. Remedies such as rescission, damages, and punitive damages are available. In some provinces, the government agency may assist in, or even initiate, an action on behalf of the consumer. In addition to these legislative provisions, the common law doctrine of **Common law developments** unconscionability in contract law, as discussed in Chapter 8, has become much more accepted. It can also be applied in these consumer situations. In Case Summary 15.9, Knuude was able to escape her contractual obligations because she was taken advantage of and unreasonably pressured by the salesperson. The key to unconscionability is that there must be an inequality of bargaining power.

---

67. (1986), 20 C.L.R. 192 (Ont. Dist. Ct.).

According to Lord Denning, this inequality exists when a person "who, without independent advice, enters into a contract upon terms that are very unfair... when his bargaining power is grievously impaired by reason of his own needs or desires, or [ignorance]... coupled with undue influences or pressures brought to bear on him...."[68] This was certainly the situation with Knuude; however, McHugh v. Forbes (1991), 4 O.R. (3d) 374 (C.A.), the terms of the agreement were not unreasonable. Therefore, although there was pressure and desperation, there was no unconscionability.[69]

Gift Cards

Gift cards are increasingly popular in North America; there are now $80 billion of gift card sales annually in North America.[70] Gift cards do not involve credit. The purchaser pays in advance to "load" a card, which can then be used up to the amount that has been loaded onto the card. The key issues involving gift cards relate to expiry dates and fees. A monthly fee could, for example, eventually consume the entire value of the card.

Because of the increasing popularity of gift cards and the corresponding increase in consumer complaints, governments have begun to introduce laws to deal specifically with gift cards. In Alberta, for example, the *Fair Trading Act*[71] contains general provisions that could be used with respect to gift cards. Section 6(4)(a) indicates that it is an unfair practice for suppliers to do or say anything that might reasonably deceive or mislead a consumer. Section 7(3) entitles consumers to recover the amount by which the consumer's payment under the consumer transaction exceeds the value of the goods or services to the consumer.

Nevertheless, the *Gift Card Regulation*[72] came into force on 1 November 2008. It stipulates that gift cards may not have expiry dates, that only certain fees can be charged with respect to gift cards and that certain activities (such as refusing to accept a gift card as partial payment on a purchase) are unfair practices under the *Fair Trading Act*. It is likely that most jurisdictions will introduce similar provisions to protect consumer interests if the use of gift cards continues to grow.

CONTROLLED BUSINESS PRACTICES

Consumer protection legislation also places controls on several specific kinds of business activities. All provinces restrict **door-to-door** sales, also known as **direct sales**. The main method of doing this is by imposing a **cooling-off period**, which allows a purchaser a given period of time to change his mind and to rescind the contract. Some jurisdictions also require the disclosure of certain information and that the contract be in writing, and provide for an extended cooling-off period. Check the MyBusLawLab for specific details.

Other types of potentially abusive business activities prohibited or controlled in various jurisdictions are unsolicited goods and services or credit cards, discounted

Laws governing gift cards becoming more common

mybuslawlab
www.pearsoned.ca/mybuslawlab

Door-to-door sales controlled

Other activities controlled including referral selling

---

68. *Lloyd's Bank Ltd. v. Bundy*, [1975] Q.B. 326 (C.A.).

69. For an article explaining unequal bargaining power, unconscionability, and Canadian legislation dealing with unconscionable contracts, see Donald Manderscheid Q.C., "The Right to a Fair Bargain", *LawNow* (May/June 2008).

70. For a good article on the subject of gift cards, the need for legislation to protect consumers, and a review of some of the existing legislation, see Peter Bowal, "Playing Your Cards Right", *LawNow* (March/April 2008).

71. *Supra* note 67.

72. Alta. Reg. 146/2008.

income tax returns, pre-arranged funeral services, inappropriate debt collection activities, prepaid contracting, time-share contracts, and referral selling. **Referral selling** involves a purchaser supplying a seller with a list of friends or acquaintances. When sales are made to any of those people, the purchaser is given a benefit, such as a reduction of the purchase price.

Methods of Control

Controlling these unacceptable activities through legislation is accomplished by several methods. One method involves requiring that the party supplying these goods and services be licensed. This gives the government an effective control mechanism, as licences can be suspended or revoked. Legislation may also impose fines or imprisonment in the event of abusive behaviour. In addition to the powers to investigate, to seize records and to impose penalties for violations, government bodies are often given the power to initiate actions on behalf of victimized consumers, or to help them start their own actions.

www.pearsoned.ca/mybuslawlab

True cost of borrowing must be disclosed

LOAN TRANSACTIONS

In addition to unconscionable transactions legislation, every province has enacted legislation requiring that the true cost of borrowing be disclosed, thus prohibiting excessive rates of interest and costs in loan transactions. The federal *Interest Act*[73] has similar requirements. The *Criminal Code*[74] also prohibits the charging of excessive rates of interest.

CASE SUMMARY 15.10

Proper Disclosure of Interest Rates Required: *Elcano Acceptance Ltd. v. Richmond, Richmond, Stambler & Mills*[75]

Elcano retained the services of the defendant law firm to draft promissory notes on its behalf, for use in its business. These notes stated interest was to be calculated at the rate of 2 percent per month. Section 4 of the *Interest Act* provided that in any contract for which interest is payable, interest must be stated as an annual rate; otherwise, it is not permissible to collect more than 5 percent interest. Because of this oversight, Elcano was not able to collect the interest due and payable from its customers pursuant to its promissory notes. It sued the law firm alleging negligence, and won.

---

[73]. R.S.C. 1985, c. I-15.

[74]. R.S.C. 1985, c. C-46, s. 347.

[75]. (1991), 3 O.R. (3d) 123 (C.A.).

> **CASE SUMMARY 15.11**
>
> ## Excessive Interest Costly for All Concerned: *Garland v. Consumers' Gas Co.*[76]
>
> In a stunning class action suit, Garland brought an action on behalf of over 500 000 customers of Consumers' (now Enbridge Gas Distribution Inc.). He demonstrated that the 5 percent late payment penalties charged on unpaid accounts constituted a criminal rate of interest. Garland established that when a late payment penalty was charged, and the actual bill and late payment were paid within 38 days, the actual annual interest rate was over 60 percent, contrary to section 347 of the *Criminal Code*.
>
> The case went to the Supreme Court of Canada—twice! In the first instance, the Court found that the late payment penalties were collected in contravention of the *Criminal Code* and, as a matter of public policy, criminals should not be permitted to keep the proceeds of their crime. The Court thus ordered Consumers' to repay the late payment penalties collected from the representative class in excess of the interest limit stipulated by the *Criminal Code*.
>
> The issue of restitution brought the matter back to the Supreme Court. It decided that, although late payment penalties had been collected since 1981, only those penalties imposed after the class action was commenced (in 1994) had to be repaid. Prior to 1994, reliance on the Ontario Energy Board's orders gave Consumers' juristic reason for the enrichment; but once Garland's action was commenced, Consumers' was put on notice that it was violating the *Criminal Code*. Collecting excessive interest from that point constituted unjust enrichment.
>
> ### DISCUSSION QUESTIONS
> **Consider other situations where consumers must pay late payment penalties. Should it be left to consumers to challenge these in court?**

Legislative provisions aim to prevent the practice of hiding excessive interest rates in the payment of a bonus or through some other form of subterfuge. Statutes demand that all this information be fully disclosed to the borrower at the outset. They usually prohibit misleading information in advertisements about the cost of borrowing, require the cost of borrowing to be stated in a standard format and require moneylenders to be registered, which makes them subject to suspension by the governing body for misbehaviour or incompetence.

The payday loan industry has come under attack recently, particularly in British Columbia and Manitoba. In response to public pressure, Manitoba amended the *Consumer Protection Act*[77] by adding Part XVIII, dealing with "Payday Loans." Among other things, these provisions require the Public Utilities Board to hold hearings when it is setting the maximum interest rates that may be charged for payday loans. The *Payday Loans Regulation*[78] allows for the licensing of payday lenders. Because of this statutory framework, Manitoba was the first province to receive

---

76. [2002] S.C.C.A. No. 53; [2004] 1 S.C.R. 629.

77. C.C.S.M. c. C200.

78. Man. Reg. 99/2007.

designation under s. 347.1 of the *Criminal Code*, allowing it to regulate the rates that can be charged for payday loans.[79] Other provinces are likely to follow this lead; refer to the MyBusLawLab for specific provincial provisions.

CASE SUMMARY 15.12

Court Refuses to Enforce Payday Loans Where Interest Is Usurious: *Consolidated Financial Corp. v. Forde*[80]

Consolidated's lawyer, who also represented Consolidated's related company, Intercapital, sought to enforce numerous unpaid loan cases, including loans to Forde, Gentile and 78 other debtors. These "payday loans" were challenged by the debtors on the basis that the effective rate of interest was usurious (excessive) and contrary to section 347 of the *Criminal Code*.

The loans were generally for 14 days. The stated interest was 47 percent per annum. Upon default, a $180 fee would be imposed, as "liquidated damages" (a supposed estimate of the damages) but, in essence, it constituted a penalty. Evidence was given that the lender also inflated the principal. A "fee" of some sort may have been subsumed into the principal, disguising the true amount advanced. If Gentile was advanced $500, but the loan stipulated that $620 was to be repaid in 14 days, on the 15th day, $806.95 was owing (once liquidated damages were included), bringing the effective rate of interest ($306.95 for 15 days) to 1500 percent per annum!

The Court decided *not* to assist Consolidated in the collection of *any* of its contractual debts. Instead, it ordered that no further action by Consolidated or Intercapital on this form of loan agreement could proceed, until the higher court (B.C.S.C.) ruled on the enforceability of this type of contract.

SMALL BUSINESS PERSPECTIVE

The B.C. Supreme Court was already considering the enforceability of these payday loans. Until the superior court rules on this issue, all other collection actions by the lenders are stayed. If denied access to the courts to enforce these debts, will payday lenders survive?

The "unconscionability" of the transaction has an impact on the severity of the penalty imposed by the courts. When it is shown that the parties' bargaining positions were relatively equal and that each had independent advice, the reduction in the eventual interest deemed payable may be less. In the *Transport North American Express* case,[81] in which the parties' bargaining positions were relatively equal and each had legal representation, the Supreme Court of Canada refused to enforce the illegal rate of interest agreed upon. Instead, it imposed interest at 60 percent, the highest rate possible to comply with section 347 of the *Criminal Code*. The rationale expressed for the decision was that if the borrower had been

---

[79.] See *Order Designating Manitoba for the Purposes of the Criminal Interest Rate Provisions of the Criminal Code*, S.O.R./2008-212.

[80.] 2005 BCPC 0209.

[81.] *Transport North American Express Inc. v. New Solutions Financial Corp.*, [2004] 1 S.C.R. 249.

relieved of paying a commercially appropriate rate of interest, it would enjoy a windfall. Partial enforcement of the loan was more likely since the parties stood on equal bargaining positions.

But when the borrower is less sophisticated and the transaction smacks of unconscionability, the court may refuse to enforce the indebtedness in its entirety.[82]

DEBT-COLLECTION PROCESSES

Unpaid creditors often turn to debt collection agencies to assist in the collection process. The actual debts owed are usually assigned to these agencies for a fee. The practices used by such agencies are sometimes abusive, so legislation has been enacted to control their activities. Common law remedies for abusive debt collection practices, such as defamation, assault and battery, trespass and even false imprisonment, are usually ineffective. The legislation enacted requires these agencies to be licensed, adding the threat of a suspended or revoked licence in the event of infractions. These statutes set out specific unacceptable collection practices, such as excessive phone calls, calls at unreasonable hours, collect calls, threats of legal action with no foundation, issuing letters of collection that resemble official court documents, making deceptive or misleading statements, communicating with employers, friends or relatives, and putting pressure on innocent relatives to pay the debt.

Some provinces require that debt-collection agencies use only previously approved form letters in their demands for payment. In British Columbia, a collector must not communicate with a debtor, a member of the debtor's family or household, a relative, neighbour, friend, or acquaintance of the debtor, or the debtor's employer in a manner or with a frequency as to constitute harassment. Any use of undue, excessive or unreasonable pressure constitutes harassment.[83] The punishment for a party engaged in such activities may range from the loss of its licence to prosecution and a fine. Some provinces give debtors the right to civil action for any damages suffered because of the abusive practices. The threat of criminal prosecution to pressure a debtor to pay is a violation of the *Criminal Code*[84] and can result in prosecution for extortion against the person making the threat.

Legislation to control credit-reporting agencies is also in place. While providing a valuable service to the lender, these businesses sometimes cause great harm to the borrower through carelessness or indifference. The relevant statutes usually require such bodies to be registered, limit the type of information that they can disclose, make it an offence for them to knowingly include false information in a credit file, give the individual the right to inspect the file and to correct or remove erroneous information, and, in some jurisdictions, prohibit an agency from making any report to a lender without the written permission of the borrower. Refer to the MyBusLawLab for details of the legislation in place in specific jurisdictions.

mybuslawlab
www.pearsoned.ca/mybuslawlab

BC **AB** SK MB ON

Abusive debt collection practices controlled

Credit reporting practices controlled

[82.] See *C.A.P.S. International Inc. v. Kotello* (2002), 164 Man. R. (2d) 202 (Q.B.), or *Direct Advances (Spruce) Ltd. v. Halgren*, 2003 ABPC 136, in which the Courts refused to enforce any part of the contract due to violation of s. 347 of the *Criminal Code*. In each case, the Court refused to sever the illegal interest clause and enforce the principal indebtedness due to the unconscionability of the loans. But in *Milani v. Banks* (1997), 32 O.R. (3d) 557 (C.A.), the Court ordered the debtor to repay the amount she received and interest at the rate normally charged litigants on money due.

[83.] *Business Practices and Consumer Protection Act*, *supra* note 33, s. 114.

[84.] *Criminal Code*, *supra* note 79, s. 346.

BC **AB** SK MB ON

Government agencies enforce statutes

Government agencies educate and publicize

Private agencies also provide helpful information and services

CONSUMER SERVICE BODIES

In most jurisdictions, government departments have been empowered to implement and enforce these consumer protection statutes. The authority given to such departments usually includes the right to hear and investigate complaints, seize records, search premises, suspend licences, impose fines, or some other corrective action, and initiate civil actions on behalf of the consumer.

In some jurisdictions, these bodies have become clearing houses of consumer information, with a mandate to collect and disseminate that information to the public. Consumer bureaus can collect information on dangerous products, consumer business scams, or unacceptable practices. They may get involved in advertising to educate the consumer.[85]

Representatives of the federal government and of each of the provinces and territories belong to the Consumer Measures Committee (CMC). The aim of the CMC is to provide, through national cooperation, an improved marketplace for Canadian consumers. To create public awareness, the CMC has published an electronic version of the *Canadian Consumer Handbook*.[86] This publication provides advice and information on a wide range of consumer issues. It includes a Canada-wide directory of names, addresses, and telephone numbers for contacts in government, business, and consumer associations.

Private organizations, such as the Better Business Bureau ("BBB"), are also designed to be clearinghouses for such information. It must be remembered, however, that the BBB is supported and sustained by the business community. It thus has a vested interest in serving that community. The theory is that it is in the best interests of the business community to maintain high standards by weeding out disreputable businesses. The BBB and similar organizations serve that function for members of the business community who join them. Specialized bodies have also been set up to deal with disputes in unique industries. In particular, there are several organizations that are available to arbitrate disputes arising from the sale and repair of automobiles in Canada. The Canadian Motor Vehicle Arbitration Plan (CAMVAP) is a prime example.[87]

REDUCING RISK 15.5

For businesspeople, it is important to understand that the operation of the consumer protection legislation has shifted the balance. The old principle of *caveat emptor* required the consumers of products or services to be careful in their dealings. Now that principle is often downplayed. Instead, responsibility has shifted to the merchant to exercise care. But, even though these consumer protection statutes may *seem* strong, they will be ineffective if they are poorly enforced. Still, merchants must be aware that the nature of their responsibility has changed and has become much more onerous.

---

85. See, for example, services provided by the government of Alberta, at www.servicealberta.gov.ab.ca/Consumer_Info.cfm, www.servicealberta.gov.ab.ca/548.cfm, and www.servicealberta.gov.ab.ca/ConsumerTipsheets.cfm

86. Available online at www.ic.gc.ca/eic/site/oca-bc.nsf/eng/h_ca02058.html.

87. Check CAMVAP online at www.camvap.ca/.

NEGOTIABLE INSTRUMENTS

Negotiable instruments are often associated with consumer and commercial transactions. They take many different forms, but are primarily *cheques, bills of exchange* (sometimes called drafts) and *promissory notes,* as set out in the federal *Bills of Exchange Act.*[88] The most familiar form of negotiable instruments is the cheque (see Figure 15.1), which is an order made by the drawer to his bank to pay funds to a third party called the *payee;* these funds must be paid as soon as the cheque is presented for payment (on demand).

Negotiable instruments are controlled by federal statute. They include
• cheques

Figure 15.1 Cheque

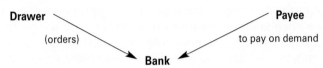

The drawer physically hands the cheque to the payee, who later presents it to the bank.

A bill of exchange or draft (see Figure 15.2) is similar to a cheque, but with two important differences. There are three parties involved, and the *drawer* orders the *drawee* to pay the *payee* a certain sum of money. But with the bill of exchange, the drawee need not be a bank, and the instrument may be made payable at some future time. (A cheque is defined as a "bill of exchange drawn on a bank, payable on demand.") The cheque is much more common today than the bill of exchange, especially in consumer dealings. Bills of exchange are used in sophisticated financial transactions.

Figure 15.2 Bills of Exchange

• bills of exchange

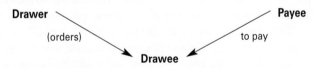

The drawer physically hands the instrument to the payee, who then presents it to the drawee for payment or acceptance.

With these kinds of instruments, the drawer retains the power to countermand even after he has given the cheque or bill of exchange to the payee. To overcome this problem, the payee will often take the instrument directly to the drawee to determine if the latter will honour it. If the drawee "accepts" the instrument, a direct obligation is created on the drawee to pay the payee, ensuring payment. Having a cheque certified has a similar result.

A **promissory note** (see Figure 15.3) involves only two parties. The *maker* promises to pay a certain sum to the *payee* at a specified future date or on demand. Because of their nature, promissory notes are always associated with a creditor–debtor relationship.

• promissory notes

Cheques are used primarily as a convenient means of transferring funds. To a considerable extent, their use has been replaced by tools associated with electronic banking, such as debit cards and credit cards. Cheques are still common,

[88]. R.S.C. 1985, c. B-4.

Figure 15.3 Promissory Note

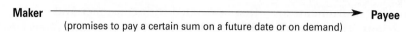

Maker ⟶ **Payee**

(promises to pay a certain sum on a future date or on demand)

The maker hands the note to the payee, who later presents it to the maker for payment.

however, and students should be familiar with their unique qualities. Often sellers will require payment by certified cheque, which is extremely secure, as payment is in effect guaranteed by the bank. Once the cheque has been transferred to the payee, the bank will no longer honour an order to stop payment. Instead of certifying a cheque, many banks now issue a bank draft in the name of the payee. It will be given by the customer to the payee at the appropriate time. Another common practice when goods are bought on credit is to give the creditor a series of post-dated cheques that are subsequently deposited on the appropriate dates. Negotiable instruments are also regularly used to bolster secured transactions, which will be discussed in Chapter 16.

CASE SUMMARY 15.13

A Certified Cheque Is Like Cash: *Centrac Inc. v. Canadian Imperial Bank of Commerce*[89]

Officeplus paid for office furniture purchased from Centrac with a $48 000 certified cheque. The CIBC had certified the cheque on the strength of the deposit of another cheque for $76 000. Upon learning that the $76 000 cheque would not be honoured, the CIBC stopped payment on the $48 000 cheque and phoned Centrac to inform it of having done so. The cheque was dishonoured when Centrac presented it for payment. Centrac sued the CIBC. The Court held that after the CIBC had certified the cheque, it was considered equivalent to cash. "Once certification was made, any attempt made by the bank to avoid payment was too late." The CIBC could not hide behind its failure to check the validity of the $76 000 cheque. It had committed to honour the certified cheque, and was required to do so.

REDUCING RISK 15.6

Negotiable instruments can be very dangerous to those who make and endorse them. Great care should be taken in their use. People often think that, if they write a cheque and something goes wrong, they can simply stop payment. This is often not possible, since once that cheque gets into the hands of an innocent third party—even if it is the payee's bank—one will likely have to honour the instrument. The same holds true with respect to the liability of the endorser.

---

89. (1994), 21 O.R. (3d) 161 (C.A.).

CASE SUMMARY 15.14

Are Money Orders Bills of Exchange? *Bendix Foreign Exchange Corp. v. Integrated Payment Systems Canada Inc.*[90]

Sidhu operated as an agent for IPS, selling money orders. His obligation was to collect the face value of each money order sold, and not to use money orders to pay his debts. He purchased foreign currency from Bendix. He paid for this purchase with money orders. Bendix wired $46 000 to a bank in India. When IPS discovered that the money orders had been stolen by Sidhu, it refused to honour them. Bendix sued to recover the funds. IPS asked for summary judgment, an order dismissing the action.

Bendix argued that the money orders were bills of exchange and that, as it was a holder in due course, it was entitled to payment. The Court disagreed, holding that the money orders were not bills of exchange, as they stated that they were payable only if certain conditions were satisfied. One of these conditions was that the money orders must not have been stolen. Bendix was therefore not entitled to payment and its action was dismissed.

Bendix appealed, and the Court of Appeal set aside the summary judgment.[91] It said that a judicial definition of a money order would best be decided by a trial court. Accordingly, it ordered that Bendix's action proceed to trial.

SMALL BUSINESS PERSPECTIVE

Money orders are commonly used in consumer transactions. Like certified cheques, they are considered equivalent to cash. What will be the effect if a court rules that money orders are not bills of exchange?

This unique transferability of negotiable instruments also makes their use particularly attractive when used with secured transactions. When a negotiable instrument such as a promissory note or cheque is transferred (negotiated) to some innocent third party, the latter can enforce that instrument despite any difficulties that arise under the original transaction (short of forgery or alteration of the instrument). As was discussed in Chapter 8, when a benefit under a contract is assigned, the assignee can be in no better position than the person assigning that right. Thus any defence that the original contracting party has against the person assigning those contractual rights can also be used against the assignee. On the other hand, when a negotiable instrument is signed and passes into the hands of an innocent third party—called a **holder in due course**—the signee almost certainly will be required to honour it.

Stop payment order may not protect drawer

To qualify as a holder in due course, the person receiving the negotiable instrument (whether it is a cheque or a promissory note) must be innocent in that she must have had no knowledge of the problems with the original transaction. There must also be no indication of alteration or irregularity on the instrument itself. Consideration must have been given for the instrument by someone during

Holder in due course can enforce negotiable instrument independent of problems

---

90. [2004] O.J. No. 4455 (Sup.Ct.).

91. [2005] O.J. No. 2241 (C.A.).

the process, and she must have otherwise received the instrument in good faith. For the instrument to be negotiable, it must meet several requirements, including that it be an unconditional promise to pay a specific amount at some future date or on demand.

REDUCING RISK 15.7

People often write cheques, or sign promissory notes, as simply one aspect of the transactions in which they are involved. If they think about a deal going sour at all, they assume that they can either stop payment on the cheque they wrote, or simply not pay the promissory note they signed. But negotiable instruments are much more dangerous than simple contractual obligations. If they are negotiated to a third party (as they are designed to be), and that third party qualifies as a holder in due course, the instruments can be enforced despite any problems with the original transaction. It is wise, therefore, to understand that, when you write a cheque, or sign a promissory note, you could very likely be called on to pay, independent of the transaction for which the cheque or promissory note was given. Even the bank of the payee where the cheque is deposited can be a holder in due course and force you to pay, despite any stop-payment order you may have given.

Endorser can be liable for payment

Another important feature of negotiable instruments involves the need for free transferability. As the instruments transfer from holder to holder, others not party to the original instrument will be required to sign or endorse the back of the instrument. There are several different forms of endorsement, but the usual purpose of an endorsement is for the endorser to add its credit to the instrument. This means that if the instrument is not honoured when it is presented for collection, the holder can then turn to the endorser for payment, provided that the holder gave proper notice of dishonour to that endorser immediately after payment was refused.

Promissory notes often part of loan transaction

In most credit transactions, debtors are required to sign *promissory notes* as part of the process. This may seem redundant, given the commitment to pay in the primary contract, but remember that promissory notes provide a great deal of flexibility, making them much more attractive to third parties to whom the creditor may wish to assign the proceeds of the transaction. Merchants supplying goods or services on credit will often assign the debt to a finance company. With the promissory note, the finance company becomes a holder in due course, able to enforce the promissory note independent of any problems that might arise from the original transaction, or with the product sold.

Advantages reduced in consumer transactions

Pursuant to the *Bills of Exchange Act*,[92] any negotiable instrument used to advance credit in a consumer transaction must be marked "Consumer Purchase." This is notice to any third party that the instrument does not convey the usual rights, and that a holder in due course would in fact be subject to the same defences that the drawer would have against the original payee. Thus, most of the advantages of being a holder in due course are lost. This applies only to consumer transactions, however, and when negotiable instruments are used in business transactions, the advantages of being a holder in due course still exist.

[92.] R.S.C. 1985, c. B-4, Part V.

SUMMARY

Sale of Goods Act

- Implies certain terms into a contract unless the parties have agreed otherwise
- Applies only when goods are being sold
- Except where there is agreement otherwise, risk follows title, and the *Act* supplies five rules to determine when title is transferred
- Seller must convey good title and quiet possession
- Goods must be free of any lien or charge
- Goods must be fit for communicated purpose and be of merchantable quality
- Goods must match the sample or description
- In the event of a default, where the goods are not yet in the hands of the purchaser, the seller has an unpaid seller's lien and has the right of *stoppage in transit*

Consumer protection

- The federal *Competition Act* controls practices that unduly lessen competition
- The federal *Food and Drug Act* and *Hazardous Products Act* control dangerous products
- Many other federal statutes protect customers
- Various provincial statutes require that goods be of acceptable quality
- A number of other statutes are in place to protect consumers, including consumer protection acts, trade practices acts, and unconscionable transactions acts—check the MyBusLawLab for details
- These statutes control unacceptable business practices, such as misrepresentation and other forms of misleading advertising, unconscionable transactions (that is, when a merchant takes advantage of a weak-willed or otherwise unequal customer), and specific activities, such as door-to-door and referral selling
- Moneylenders are required to disclose the true cost of borrowing to their customers
- Abusive debt collection practices are restricted

Negotiable instruments

- Negotiable instruments are cheques, bills of exchange, and promissory notes
- They are freely transferable without notice to the maker/drawer
- Holders in due course may be in a better position to enforce the negotiable instrument than the original parties
- An endorser is liable on default by the original drawer/maker only if properly notified of default

---

QUESTIONS

1. Explain the purpose of the *Sale of Goods Act* in relation to the obligations of the parties to a sale of goods transaction.
2. What three conditions must be met before the *Sale of Goods Act* applies to a transaction?
3. What is the distinction between a sale and an agreement to sell? What is the significance of that distinction?
4. When does the risk transfer to the buyer in a sale of goods transaction? Explain the exceptions to this general rule.

5. What is a bill of lading? How can it affect who bears the risk in a sale of goods transaction?

6. Indicate when title transfers in the following situations:

   a. when the contract for sale is unconditional and the goods involved are in a deliverable state at the time the purchase is made

   b. when the subject of the contract involves specific goods to which the seller is obligated to do something, such as repair, clean, or modify to get them into a deliverable state

   c. when the contract for sale involves specific, identified goods, which must be weighed or measured before being given to the buyer

   d. when the goods are delivered to the buyer on approval

   e. when goods purchased by description have not been selected, separated out, or manufactured at the time the sales contract is entered into.

7. The *Sale of Goods Act* imposes terms relating to goods matching samples or descriptions and meeting standards of fitness, quality and title. Explain the nature of these implied terms and their effect on the parties. Indicate which terms are conditions and which are warranties. Explain the significance of the distinction.

8. Explain what merchantable quality means.

9. Explain the effect of an exemption clause included in a contract that is inconsistent with the terms set out in the *Sale of Goods Act*.

10. Explain the rights of the seller when the buyer of goods:

    a. becomes insolvent

    b. defaults on the contract of sale while the goods are still in the hands of the seller

    c. defaults after the goods have been given to a third party to deliver but before they are received by the buyer

    d. where the buyer becomes bankrupt after the goods have been delivered.

11. Explain why a seller of goods might be less likely to sue for damages than for price.

12. Under what circumstances may a buyer refuse delivery of goods?

13. The *Sale of Goods Act* in each province implies certain terms into contracts of sale relating to the fitness and quality of the product. Some Canadian jurisdictions make these provisions mandatory in consumer transactions. Explain the situation in your jurisdiction.

14. Describe the practices controlled by the *Competition Act* and explain how that control is accomplished.

15. How does the concept of privity of contract limit the effectiveness of many consumer protection provisions? How have some jurisdictions overcome this problem?

16. What common law provisions are available to protect consumers from unscrupulous business practices?

17. Describe the methods outlined in federal and provincial consumer protection statutes to control businesses with a tendency to abusive practices. Discuss the effectiveness of these tactics.

18. Identify the legislation in effect in your jurisdiction that offers relief to victims of unconscionable transactions.

19. What statutory provisions have been introduced throughout Canada to control door-to-door selling, referral selling, and other potentially abusive practices?

20. What services are provided to consumers through organizations set up by the federal and provincial governments? Discuss whether these services are adequate.

21. Distinguish among a cheque, a bill of exchange, and a promissory note.

22. Explain how the position of a holder in due course compares to the position of an assignee of contractual rights.

23. Explain the nature of an endorsement and its significance on a negotiable instrument.

CASES AND DISCUSSION QUESTIONS

1. *Whiteway v. O'Halloran*, (2007), [2008] 271 Nfld. & P.E.I.R. 239 (P.E.I.S.C. (A.D.)).
The Buyer purchased a rebuilt diesel engine from the Seller, who operated a marine engine service. The parties agreed that the price was $10 500, which included a "50/50 Warranty" for one season. This meant that the parties would share the cost of any repairs on a 50/50 basis if there was a problem with the engine. The parties then renegotiated the agreement. The price was $8500. The Seller said that the agreement did not include a warranty; the Buyer said that it did, as the Seller guaranteed his work. The Seller's invoice indicated "No warranty". The Buyer used the engine for the remainder of the lobster fishing season. On the commencement of the next lobster fishing season, the Buyer experienced problems with the engine. He was advised that his only option was to acquire a new engine.

Which provision of the *Sale of Goods Act* would the buyer rely on in his action? How would the damages be calculated if the Buyer's evidence was accepted by the Court?

2. *Canadian Barter System v. Pemset Food Services Ltd.* (2007), 213 Man. R. (2d) 154.
The Seller agreed to transfer ownership of three pieces of restaurant equipment to the Buyer to settle a prior account. One piece of equipment was an oven that could not be picked up on the agreed date because it would not fit through door of the premises. The parties agreed to leave the oven on the premises until the new owner commenced demolition of the building. The Seller informed the Buyer of the date of the demolition. The Buyer alleged that the oven had been damaged at some point during the demolition, but he nonetheless made arrangements for the removal of the oven. The oven was destroyed during the removal process. The Buyer brought an action against the Seller for damages for breach of contract.

Would the action succeed if the agreement indicated that the Buyer was to assume title when he assumed the risk of delivery? When did this occur?

3. *Ziegler v. East Alta Organic Farms Incorporated*, 2006 ABQB 52.
The Buyer purchased a boiler from the Seller. It was installed in the Buyer's greenhouse. The Buyer claims that the boiler was defective, as it wasted above average amounts of coal and did not heat the greenhouse to a temperature in accordance with the Buyer's expectations and the boiler's specification. The Seller denied making any representation as to the capacity of the boiler or giving any performance warranty. The Seller advised the Buyer that he could return the boiler for a refund. The Buyer chose not to return the boiler because of the cost of doing so. He instead repaired the boiler.

Which sections of the *Sale of Goods Act* could the Buyer raise in his action? What would the result of the action be if the Court found that the boiler did serve the purpose of a supplementary heat source, that the Seller did not make a representation as to fuel economy and that the boiler was reasonably fit for the purpose of fuel economy?

4. *Maritime Travel Inc. v. Go Travel Direct.Com Inc.* (2008), 265 N.S.R. (2d) 369 (S.C.).
Maritime was an established travel agency, while Go was a new direct-sales tour operator. Go ran a newspaper advertisement on 8 January 2004 which compared the parties' prices for a specific resort, with Go's price being $360 per person less. The disclaimer noted that the comparison was based on prices available on 6 January 2004. The advertisement also contained the words "No travel agent. No comission" *[sic]* and stated that Go "offer[ed] vacations for less by eliminating the travel agent middleman." Maritime brought an action against Go under the *Competition Act*, alleging that the advertisement was false or misleading.

Was the action successful? What was the general impression left by the advertisement? Was it relevant that Go dropped its price for four days only and for the sole purpose of running the advertisement? That the disclaimer was in small print? That Maritime was matching Go's prices at the relevant time? If the action was successful, how would the damage award be calculated? Note that the *Competition Act* states that recovery is limited to losses suffered as a result of false or misleading advertisements.

5. *De Wolf v. Bell ExpressVu Inc.* (2008), 298 D.L.R. (4th) 526 (Ont. S.C.).
The Plaintiff was charged interest and an administration fee when he was late in paying his account with the Defendant for satellite TV service. He sued, alleging that the charges were illegal under the *Criminal Code*, because they amounted to an excessive rate of interest. Section 347 of the *Criminal Code* states that it is illegal to enter into an agreement for, or to receive, interest at a rate exceeding 60 per cent per year. The Defendant countered that its administration fee was not illegal interest, but lawful liquidated damages, as it was a genuine pre-estimate of the costs it incurs in recovering delinquent accounts.

Did the Court rule that the administration fee was illegal interest or liquidated damages? What if the Court found that the administration fee was an agreement or arrangement on the part of the Defendant to extend credit, because its standard contract allowed for uninterrupted service until day 75 of its payment cycle, even if the customer's payment was overdue? Note that this action was certified as a class action on behalf of all of the Defendant's subscribers.

Be sure to visit the MyBusLawLab that accompanies this book at **www.pearsoned.ca/mybuslawlab.** You will find practice tests, a personalized study plan, province-specific material, and much more!

Chapter 16

Priority of Creditors

CHAPTER OBJECTIVES

1. Outline the process of securing debt, using personal property, guarantees, and other forms of security

2. Review other laws related to creditors

3. Review an introduction to bankruptcy

4. Explain the process of bankruptcy and describe alternatives

5. Distinguish the priorities among creditors in a bankruptcy

6. Describe the bankruptcy offences

7. Explain the situation after discharge from bankruptcy

A considerable industry has developed around the practices of lending money and granting credit. This chapter will examine the various methods that have been developed to ensure that money owed is paid and the legislation that has been created to control such transactions. Federal bankruptcy and insolvency legislation will also be examined. Other than this federal statute, creditors' rights are generally a matter of provincial jurisdiction. The common principles embodied in the relevant provincial statutes will be the primary area of concentration in this chapter.

METHODS OF SECURING DEBT

When a debtor borrows money, or is extended credit, the creditor is at risk that the debtor cannot, or will not, pay the debt. Usually, the creditor requires the debtor to take steps to reduce this risk by ensuring that the creditor will be paid first, before other creditors, even in the event of bankruptcy or insolvency. Several methods have been developed to provide the creditor with this protection. When the creditor is successful in ensuring her **priority** over other creditors, she is said to be a *secured creditor*.

 mybuslawlab
www.pearsoned.ca/mybuslawlab

Security helps ensure creditor is paid

Personal Property

Real property includes land and anything attached to the land

Both real property and personal property have been used as security. *Real property* includes land, buildings attached to the land, and fixtures, that is, items attached to the land or to **fixtures** attached to the land. **Mortgages**, the most common method of using real property as security, were briefly discussed in Chapter 13.

Personal property can also be used as security

Personal property is also used extensively to secure debt. **Personal property** can be divided into *chattels*, which are tangible, movable things, and *choses in action*, which are intangible rights that are legally enforceable claims. Cheques and promissory notes are examples of choses in action.[1] For a chose in action, the relevant document merely represents an obligation that can be legally enforced. Although a chose in action is often used to secure debt, it is much more common to take real property or chattels as security.

When a pawnbroker lends money, the borrower leaves an item, like a watch or a ring, with the pawnbroker, who holds the item until the loan is repaid. The borrower (debtor) still owns the item. The pawnbroker (creditor) only gains the right to sell the item if the borrower does not repay the loan. This type of transaction is referred to as a **pledge.**

Personal property security involves right to take possession upon default

In most situations, however, the debtor needs the use of the goods used as security. When, for example, you borrow money to buy a new car, the assumption is that you will have the use of the car while you are repaying the loan. In such cases, the security of the creditor is the right to take the car and sell it if you fail to repay the loan. In the past, the creditor assumed ownership of the goods used as security, while the debtor had possession of the goods. In the event of default, the creditor would simply take possession of the goods based on this ownership. Under modern legislation, the creditor usually does not actually assume ownership of the goods, but the effect is the same. The creditor has first claim to the goods in the event of a default by the debtor. Note that a default may occur not only when a payment is missed, but also when the debtor fails to meet any obligation (such as maintaining sufficient insurance coverage) that increases the creditor's risk, or that threatens the value of the assets used as security.

CASE SUMMARY 16.1

Is a Fishing Licence "Property"? *Saulnier v. Royal Bank of Canada*[2]

Saulnier held four fishing licences. He and his company signed a General Security Agreement with RBC. Saulnier also signed a guarantee for the debts of his company. The GSA gave RBC a security interest in "all present and after acquired personal property including . . . Intangibles . . . " "Intangibles" was to be interpreted according to its definition in the *Personal Property Security Act (PPSA)*. Saulnier made an assignment in bankruptcy. The Receiver for RBC and the Trustee in Bankruptcy agreed to sell the four licences, but Saulnier refused to sign the necessary documents. He argued that the fishing licences were not "property" available to a Trustee in Bankruptcy or to a creditor

---

[1.] For a case that held that taxi licences were "property" that could be used to secure a loan under the *PPSA,* see *Re Foster*(1992),8 O.R. (3d) 514 (Ont. Gen. Div.). For a case that held that seismic data was "property", see *Re Gauntlet Energy Corp.* (2003), [2004] 336 A.R. 302 (Q.B.).

[2.] [2008] 3 S.C.R. 166.

under the *PPSA*; they were just a privilege to do what would otherwise be illegal. The trial Judge and the Court of Appeal both ruled that the Trustee in Bankruptcy was entitled to direct Saulnier to sign the required documents.

The Supreme Court of Canada held that fishing licences are indeed "property." They are a "major commercial asset" that gives the holder "a right to engage in an exclusive fishery under the conditions imposed by the licence, and a proprietary right in the fish harvested and the earnings from their sale." The Court referred to the *PPSA* and the *Bankruptcy and Insolvency Act* as "largely commercial instruments which should be interpreted in a way best suited to enable them to accomplish their respective commercial purposes."

This case illustrates the flexibility of the PPSA in allowing something unique as a fishing licence to be used as security for the purposes of the legislation.

SMALL BUSINESS PERSPECTIVE

Choses in action are rights to intangible property, such as stocks, bonds, patents, copyrights, and even funds deposited in a bank account. Can a business use such rights as security when obtaining credit? If so, can the rights be taken by the creditor upon default by the business?

THE TRADITIONAL APPROACH

Historically, conditional sales agreements, chattel mortgages, and assignments of accounts receivables were the common methods of using personal property as security. A conditional sale involves a two-step process. First, possession of the goods is given to the buyer. The seller, who is also the creditor, retains the title (that is, ownership) as security. Second, after the final payment is made, title to the goods is conveyed to the buyer. It should be noted that the *Sale of Goods Act* applies to conditional sales even though the sale takes place over a protracted period of time.[3]

Conditional seller retains title until last payment

A chattel mortgage differs from a conditional sale in that the creditor is not the seller of the goods. Typically, the debtor approaches a bank to borrow money. The bank requires the debtor to secure the loan, by transferring the title of some good (such as a car or a boat) to the creditor as "collateral security." Throughout the duration of the loan transaction, chattel mortgages, like conditional sales, involve the creditor's having title to the goods as security, while the debtor has possession of the goods. With a chattel mortgage, when the last payment is made, title of the goods is returned to the debtor. Even though a *bill of sale* is often used to create the security, since no actual sale is contemplated, the *Sale of Goods Act* does not apply to a chattel mortgage transaction.

Chattel mortgage involves transfer of title to goods to secure loan

The assignment of book accounts involves using a chose in action as security, rather than goods. Often, a business will have few tangible assets, but will have considerable funds owed to it for goods or services provided to customers. These claims are called **accounts receivable**. If the debtor assigns her accounts receivable, and then defaults, the creditor has the right to intercept the payment of the accounts receivable. The loan is thereby secured.

Accounts receivable can be used as security for a loan

[3.] See, for example, the *Sale of Goods Act*, R.S.S. 1978, c. S-1, which states, in s. 2(1)(c), that a contract of sale includes an agreement to sell, and then defines, in s. 3(4), an "agreement to sell" as a contract in which the transfer of property to goods is to take place at a future time or is subject to some conditions to be fulfilled in the future.

Leases are also a common method of creating a secured relationship between a creditor and a debtor. The most common type of lease is an **operating lease**, in which goods are simply rented to the lessee to use during the lease period, after which the goods are returned to the lessor. Today a **lease to purchase** is being used more frequently. A lease to purchase involves, essentially, a credit purchase. Title to the goods will be transferred to the lessee at the end of the lease period, with the lease simply providing security. In both an operating lease and a lease to purchase, possession of the goods goes to the lessee, while the title to the goods remains with the lessor, providing the lessor with security for the transaction.

Lease to purchase also provides security to creditor

When the manufacturer or the supplier of goods leases them to the lessee using a lease to purchase, the transaction is much like a conditional sale. The lessee can make claims against the manufacturer or the supplier for the quality and fitness of the goods supplied. But when the goods are sold to a financial institution and then leased to the lessee, the relationship is more like a chattel mortgage, as there is only a financial arrangement between the lessee and the financial institution. The lessee has to deal with the manufacturer or the supplier with respect to problems relating to the goods themselves. This may be difficult because of the lack of a contract with them.

Personal property security acts now in place

In the past, separate statutes with different provisions governed the various ways of using personal property as security. To further confuse things, when other forms of personal property such as negotiable instruments, shares, or bonds were used as security, there was no legislation at all. Today, personal property security acts are in place in most jurisdictions and govern all situations where personal property is used as security.

THE PERSONAL PROPERTY SECURITY ACT

PPSA creates common process for using personal property as security

The *Personal Property Security Act* (*PPSA*) is now used in all jurisdictions in Canada. It creates a unified approach toward the use of personal property as security. (The details of the provincial statutes, however, do vary significantly, so businesspeople must be familiar with the legislation of their province.) As a result, the *PPSA* is more complicated than legislation used previously, but because it uses one set of rules and a common approach to cover both tangible and intangible forms of personal property and the various ways that security can be taken, its application is simpler. A secured transaction is still created by contract in the traditional forms of conditional sales, chattel mortgages, and assignments of accounts receivable, but other forms, such as leases, can also be used, depending on the property used as security. The formal requirements and procedures for all these types of securities are now the same. As well, the *PPSA* allows other, less common, forms of personal property, such as licences, shares, bonds, and even intellectual property (including copyright, patents, and trade-marks), to be used as security and to be treated in a uniform way. The *PPSA* provides for some or all of the assets of a particular debtor to be used as security. It also provides rules to determine the ranking of various claims when several secured creditors have claims against those assets.

The right to take possession of the goods used as security even when they get into the hands of an innocent purchaser is the essential nature of a secured transaction. Thus, when Lee purchases his car under a conditional sale agreement and then defaults, the creditor must have the right to retake the car even if it has been resold, or if Lee has become bankrupt. In the past, this was accomplished by the creditor's retaining title to the goods and retaking them in the event of default. To protect an innocent third party who might be misled by the debtor having possession of the goods, the secured creditor was required to register his secured claim against the goods at the designated government agency. A would-be purchaser, or a potential creditor wanting to use the goods as security, could search the title to the goods and would be forewarned of the prior claim of the secured creditor. Under the *PPSA*, the process is a little more involved but it accomplishes the same purpose.

Registration protects secured creditors and others

CASE SUMMARY 16.2

Keep Your *PPSA* Registrations Current! *Royal Bank of Canada v. Wells Fargo*[4]

Meerford Inc. was incorporated in March 2000. It changed its name to Harrison Western Canadian Inc. in December 2000, then to 873052 Alberta Ltd. on 6 July 2004, and finally to Head West Energy Inc. on 8 July 2004. Head West and 876652 Alberta Ltd., a related corporation, entered into two lease agreements with Wells Fargo. Head West alone entered into a third lease with Wells Fargo. Wells Fargo registered its interest in one lease on 23 April 2004 and in the other two on 10 May 2004. Wells Fargo did not amend its registrations to reflect the name change on 8 July 2004 until 18 October 2005. RBC registered a General Security Agreement against Head West on 4 November 2004. Head West became insolvent. The Receiver sold the property. RBC and Wells Fargo both claimed the proceeds of the sale.

The *PPSA* provides that a secured party must amend its registrations within 15 days of having knowledge of the debtor's name change. Wells Fargo said that it first learned of the change of name to Head West on 18 October 2005, when it learned of the appointment of the Receiver.

The trial Judge ruled that Wells Fargo had knowledge (actual and constructive) of the name change prior to RBC's registration on 4 November 2004, as a result of receiving correspondence, credit statements, and credit applications which advised of the name change. The Court of Appeal agreed. RBC therefore had priority to the sale proceeds.

This case illustrates the effect of the perfection of a security under the *PPSA* (and of maintaining perfection). It also demonstrates the unforgiving nature of the *PPSA* and how even minor mistakes can have a dramatic effect on the validity of a claim. Note that the result of this case may not have been the same in other jurisdictions, as the provincial *PPSA*s (and their related case law) are different from one another in many respects. For example, the courts of the various provinces are divided as to whether a misspelled debtor name on a *PPSA* registration invalidates that registration.[5]

DISCUSSION QUESTIONS

Should registration under the *PPSA* have to be perfect to be effective, or should it be possible for an incorrect registration to be valid in certain circumstances? If the latter is the law, what does this mean for someone searching the personal property registry?

---

4. (2008), [2009] 440 Alta. R. 385, (2008), 48 C.B.R. (5th) 15 (C.A.).

5. See, for example, *Stevenson v. GMAC Leaseco Ltd.* (2003), 257 N.B.R. (2d) 141 (C.A.), in which the Court held that in cases where the inclusion of a serial number is mandatory, a seriously misleading error in either the name of the debtor, or in the serial number renders the registration invalid. In Ontario, however, if a serial number is correctly stated on a registration form, a misspelled name will not invalidate the registration, as Ontario has a "dual search requirement" requiring debtors to search both the name of the debtor and the serial number of the goods.

Creating a Secured Relationship

The method of creating a secured relationship under the *PPSA* is unique. There are three stages. First, the parties must enter into the contractual agreement. Second, the secured interest must attach to the collateral that has been identified to provide the security. Third, the secured interest must be perfected.

Contract must be a security agreement

The parties must have entered into a contract that created a secured relationship. While the *PPSA* may deem some relationships to be secured, it does not create security agreements. In a recent case,[6] a lender claimed that it had a perfected security interest in the "capital account" of the borrower, a lawyer in a law firm. The Court ruled that the documents obtained (a loan agreement and a comfort letter from the law firm) did not contain the language required by the *PPSA*. Regardless of the lender's intention, the Court would not accept the lender's claim that a security interest had been taken, in the absence of appropriate documentation.

Security must attach to collateral

Assuming there is a security agreement in place, **attachment** takes place when the debtor receives some value under the contract. That is, if a person borrowing funds uses his car as collateral security for the loan, that security attaches to the car only when the bank makes the money available to the debtor pursuant to the agreement. Attachment gives the creditor a claim against the security in the event of default by the debtor. This is normally a right to take possession, if so stated in the contract. It is important to remember that the obligations and the remedies of the parties must be set out in the contract. The purpose of the *PPSA* is to give effect to the contractual obligations entered into by the parties.

Provisions of contract prevail

It is vital to understand that attachment gives the creditor rights against the debtor only. To protect the creditor's claim if the goods are sold, or if another creditor becomes involved, the secured transaction must not only be attached, it must also be perfected. This **perfection** can be accomplished in one of two ways.

Perfection required to prevail against outsiders

Perfection through registration

The first way perfection occurs is by the registration of the security obligation at the appropriate government agency, as was the case under the old system. This process has been simplified so that the actual contractual documents no longer have to be filed. A single form (a financing statement) is now used to provide notice of the security arrangement. There are some provincial variations but, in general, a financing statement requires the complete name and address of the parties, the type and description (including the serial number) of the security used, and the date and time of registration. When a motor vehicle is used as security, its year, make, model and vehicle identification number must also be set out. There may also be specific requirements when consumer goods are involved.

Perfection through possession

The second, and less common, way of perfecting a secured transaction is for the creditor to obtain physical possession of the collateral used. Whether possession or registration is used depends on the nature of the security. When promissory notes or shares are involved, there is no need for the debtor to keep them, and perfection by possession is appropriate. Note that the original note or certificate must be taken into possession, not a photocopy. When tangible property is involved, such as a car, a truck, or equipment that is required for use by the debtor, registration is the more appropriate process. The purpose of registration is to ensure that others are alerted that the goods have been used as security and that the debtor is not in a position to deal with them. When perfection by possession is involved, this is not necessary, since the goods are not in the possession of the debtor and third parties cannot be misled with respect to them.

---

6. *Re Hupfer*, 2003 ABQB 267.

Priority of Secured Creditors

If more than one security interest is perfected by registering different financing statements against the same collateral, the priority of those secured parties is generally determined by the date registration takes place. But this is not always the case. For example, sometimes a merchant will secure a loan by granting a security on all of her assets, including after-acquired assets. This can cause a problem if a supplier of goods also claims a security interest in the future acquired goods. The secured creditor selling those goods will have priority with respect to them providing that his security interest is registered within a specified time (for example, 15 days in Nova Scotia). This is called a **purchase money security interest**, or PMSI. A PMSI will prevail over a general security agreement covering all of a merchant's assets, if it is registered within the specified time period.

First to perfect usually prevails

But PMSIs are an exception

Similarly, if customers purchase goods from that merchant in the normal course of business, the goods will normally be free of any secured interest of the creditor. If you purchase a car from a dealership, you would get good title even though the assets of the dealership had been used to secure a general loan to operate the business. Since the creditor knows that the inventory will be sold in the normal course of business, an innocent buyer will not be affected by that security.

and buyers in the normal course of business are not bound

REDUCING RISK 16.1

For a creditor, it is vitally important that a security interest be properly perfected. Legislation in most jurisdictions has registration requirements that must be carefully followed, including the exact recording of serial numbers and names. Sometimes errors in registration can be corrected, but not if the interests of other parties have been affected. Creditors usually register their security interest first, before advancing their credit. Although perfection takes place when that credit is actually advanced (the point of attachment), it takes place immediately. There are not, therefore, any problems with intervening interests arising, or with subsequent errors that affect the validity of the perfection taking place.

CASE SUMMARY 16.3

When Possession Takes Priority Over Registration: *Royal Bank of Canada v. Steinhubl's Masonry Ltd.*[7]

The Bank took a security interest in all of the undertakings and goods (including equipment) of Pro Masonry Construction Ltd. Pro Masonry then gave Steinhubl's a forklift to secure a debt. Pro Masonry subsequently went out of business, without paying its debts. Both the Bank and Steinhubl's claimed priority over the forklift.

The Court held that the forklift was a "motor vehicle" as defined by the *Personal Property Security Regulations*. As the Bank's financing statement did not describe the forklift by serial number, its security interest did not get the maximum priority available for serial-numbered goods. Steinhubl's had perfected its security interest by taking possession of the forklift. It therefore had priority over the Bank's limited interest.

The Bank's problem was that the *PPSA* required the registration of motor vehicles to include the serial number. At the time it registered its interest pursuant to the general

---

7. (2003), 237 Sask. R. 297 (Q.B.).

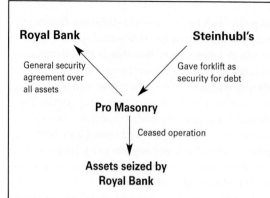

security agreement with Pro Masonry, the Bank did not know the serial number of the forklift.

DISCUSSION QUESTIONS

What else could the Bank have done? The effect is that a creditor in this type of situation gets priority over some, but not all, future acquired property, even though it had done everything it could to secure its position at the time of registration. Is this result consistent with the philosophy behind the *PPSA* and its objectives?

Rights and Remedies Upon Default

Upon default, creditor can take possession and sell collateral

In the event of a default by the debtor, the creditor has recourse as set out in the contract and as provided in the *PPSA*. This usually involves taking possession of the goods and selling them to recover the amount owed. In doing so, the creditor not only must comply with the contract, but also must not otherwise violate the law in the process.

Bailiff seizes goods

Usually, when taking possession of goods, the creditor must hire a bailiff, who can go onto the debtor's property and seize the goods. The relevant legislation usually requires that the bailiff not use force when seizing property. (At least one province, however, allows bailiffs to use reasonable force when entering premises other than the debtor's residence.[8]) If the debtor won't allow a bailiff access to the premises, then the bailiff can apply for a court order. If such an order is not obeyed, then the debtor may be guilty of contempt of court. The police will assist a bailiff only when required to by court order, or when the bailiff has reasonable grounds to believe that an attempt to seize is likely to lead to a serious breach of the peace.

Creditor must take reasonable care of goods in possession

Note that some provinces will not permit the creditor to take possession of the collateral without a court order, when consumer goods are involved and a significant amount of the debt has been paid. With respect to goods (consumer or commercial) that the creditor has taken possession of, the creditor must take "commercially reasonable" care to protect the goods and keep them in good repair. If the goods require repairs to sell them, such "commercially reasonable" expenses will be added to the amount the debtor owes.

[8.] See *Civil Enforcement Act*, R.S.A. 2000, c. C-15, s. 13(2).

Before a sale of the goods can take place, interested parties (usually the debtor and other creditors) must be given a chance to redeem the goods by paying any money owing. Notice must be given setting out a description of the goods and the amount owing, that the party receiving the notice has the **right to redeem**, and that failure to do so will result in the sale of the goods. The notice should also declare, when appropriate, that the debtor will be liable for any shortfall between the amount owing plus expenses, and the amount realized from the sale. Sometimes only the missed payments plus expenses need be paid, but there is often an acceleration clause requiring that the entire debt plus expenses be paid to redeem the goods. Some provinces prohibit such acceleration clauses.

Right to redeem

Debtor must be given notice and opportunity to redeem

After possession of the goods has been taken, and the notice period has expired, the goods are usually sold, by private or public sale, to satisfy the debt. Under the *PPSA*, the method chosen must be commercially reasonable.

Sale—goods taken into possession can be sold to satisfy debt

If the proceeds from the sale do not cover the debt, additional costs, and interest, the debtor will usually have to make up the difference. Thus, not only may the debtor lose his collateral, but he may also still owe the creditor a considerable amount of money to pay for the shortfall. In several jurisdictions, this right to sue for a deficiency is lost as soon as the creditor chooses to take possession of the goods. In some provinces, this rule applies only when consumer goods are involved. For example, in British Columbia, if Jones defaulted on a consumer car loan owing $15 000, and only $10 000 was realized from the sale of that car after the creditor took possession of it, the creditor would lose not only the $5000 shortfall on the loan but also any costs and interest incurred.[9]

Debtor may be liable for deficiency

Because this was a consumer loan in British Columbia, the creditor exhausted her remedies against Jones when she took possession of the car. The creditor must therefore take great care in these circumstances to balance the risks of suing (and possibly getting nothing), against taking possession of the collateral (and getting at least something). The creditor can also lose the right to a deficiency by failing to properly look after the goods, or by failing to get a fair price because of an improvident sale.

Creditor must consider alternatives

REDUCING RISK 16.2

When a debtor defaults, creditors are often quick to seize property used as security. In some jurisdictions, however, this might prevent the creditor from pursuing other, more effective, remedies. Even in those jurisdictions in which it is possible to sue for a shortfall after the goods have been sold, that right may be lost if the goods are not properly cared for and sold in a commercially reasonable manner. On the other hand, if the debtor defaulted on the original debt, it is likely that any attempt to sue and seize other assets will not result in a significant recovery. Another issue involves the question of whether the debtor can be rehabilitated and kept as a good customer. All of these factors should be carefully considered before deciding to take possession of the collateral. Just because you have the legal right to do something doesn't mean it is always a good idea for you to do it.

[9.] *Personal Property Security Act*, R.S.B.C. 1996, c. 359, s. 67.

Debtor entitled to surplus

Note that, in all jurisdictions, when there is a surplus from the sale, the debtor is entitled to that surplus. In the example above, if the car were sold for $20 000, and costs and interest brought the entire debt up to $17 000, Jones would be entitled to the $3000 surplus from the sale.

Option to retain the collateral

In some jurisdictions, instead of taking possession and selling the goods, the creditor can take the goods and simply keep them, in full satisfaction of the debt. This ends any claim the debtor may have to a surplus and any claim the creditor may have to a deficiency. Notice must be given to all interested parties. If someone files an objection, the goods must be sold in the usual way.

CASE SUMMARY 16.4

If You Elect to Keep the Goods, You Can't Sue: *241301 Alberta Ltd. v. 482176 B.C. Ltd.*[10]

241301 Alberta Ltd. (241) loaned money to one of the defendants, 765918 Alberta Ltd. (765). The loan was to enable 765 to buy equipment and set up a restaurant. The restaurant had only operated for two months when 241 gave notice of its intention to enforce its security on the restaurant's assets. 241 then appointed a receiver for 765, without providing notice. 241 took possession of the assets of the restaurant and operated it for 10 months. It then sold the assets, and sued for the deficiency.

The Court dismissed 241's action. It held that 241 breached the *PPSA* by failing to provide notice of the receivership to 765. The notice it gave of its intention to enforce its security was not sufficient to comply with the legislative requirements. The Court also ruled that, because 241 used the assets to operate the restaurant for 10 months before selling them, there was no deficiency owing. 241 had elected to take the collateral in full satisfaction of the debt. The *PPSA* specifically states that if such an election is made, a deficiency judgment may not be obtained.

SMALL BUSINESS PERSPECTIVE

This case illustrates how important it is to understand and to follow the procedures set out in the *PPSA*. Would 241 have used the assets to operate the restaurant if it knew that doing so would prevent it from obtaining a deficiency judgment? The provisions of the *PPSA* are designed to protect both the rights of the debtor and the rights of the secured creditor. How can creditors (such as merchants who take security interests from their customers) ensure that they are in compliance with the legislation, so that they can realize the benefits of the legislation, rather than suffer its penalties?

The procedures under the *PPSA* may appear very cumbersome, and the legislation itself is very complex, but in actual practice the process outlined by the *PPSA* works quite well. When a person borrows money from a credit union using a car as security, attachment takes place once the contract has been entered into and the moneys have been advanced. Perfection takes place when the credit union files the financing statement with the appropriate registry. A buyer or subsequent creditor interested in the car would search the registry and, finding the

---

10. (2003), 341 A.R. 172 (Q.B.).

registered security against the vehicle, would be forewarned to avoid any dealings with the car. If the car is purchased, and a default takes place, the credit union can recover the vehicle even from the innocent third party. This is the essence of the creditor's security. Once there is a default, the credit union has the option of either pursuing its normal breach-of-contract remedies, or taking possession of the vehicle and selling it. If it chooses the latter option, it must follow the proper procedures.

Guarantees

Another method creditors use to ensure the repayment of a debt is the guarantee. When corporations are involved, the use of guarantees is very common as a means of circumventing the limited liability characteristic of incorporation, making the principals of a corporation ultimately responsible for loans and other obligations. In consumer transactions, guarantees are used to make another, more substantial, debtor liable to pay a loan or other debt. Guarantors ensure that the debt will be paid even when the debtor defaults. When Der borrows $5000 from the bank with his mother as a guarantor, and then fails to pay, his mother is responsible to repay the $5000 debt.

Guarantor must pay when debtor defaults

A guarantee involves a secondary, or conditional, obligation that arises only in the event of a default. When a person agrees to be directly responsible for paying the debt of another, the obligation is not secondary, but primary, with the debtors sharing the responsibility. This is referred to as an *indemnity*.

The distinction between a guarantee and an indemnity, although subtle, can be important. As discussed in Chapter 7, the *Statute of Frauds* requires that some agreements must be evidenced in writing to be enforceable. In most provinces, only guarantees must be evidenced in writing, but in British Columbia both guarantees and indemnities must be evidenced in writing.[11]

Evidence in writing of guarantee required

In Alberta, a guarantor must appear before a notary public, acknowledge that he signed the guarantee, and sign a certificate.[12]

Since a guarantee is a separate contract, all of the elements of a contract must be present. Consideration can sometimes be a problem. Because the creditor would not advance funds without the guarantee, the advancement of those funds amounts to consideration supporting the guarantee. When the guarantee is given after default on a loan, the consideration is the creditor's refraining from suing the debtor.

Elements of a contract must be present.

When a guarantee is given after the funds are advanced, there can be a serious problem. If Kotsalis borrows money from the Business Bank, and the loans officer fails to obtain a guarantee as required by bank policy, he will face difficulties if he tries to get it later. Since the funds have already been advanced, there is no consideration to support the subsequent guarantee. To avoid any problem with consideration, lending institutions usually require that all guarantees be placed under seal. As discussed in Chapter 6, when a seal is present, consideration is conclusively presumed.

Guarantees often given under seal

11. *Law and Equity Act*, R.S.B.C. 1996, c. 253, s. 59.

12. *Guarantees Acknowledgement Act*, R.S.A. 2000, c. G-11.

REDUCING RISK 16.3

People are often persuaded to sign a guarantee thinking that it is just a formality, and that no serious obligations are incurred, since the primary debtor will pay the debt. This is a dangerous assumption to make! Whether in business, or in your personal affairs, you should never sign a guarantee without first carefully weighing the risks. The creditor is insisting on a guarantee because she doesn't have confidence that the debt will be paid by the primary debtor. She wants someone else to also be responsible. You are adding your credit to the transaction, and there is a good chance that you will be required to honour your commitment. Many bankruptcies result from people signing guarantees without realizing the risks they may face.

RIGHTS AND OBLIGATIONS OF THE PARTIES

Creditor should ensure guarantor understands guarantee

The creditor has significant duties to protect the interests of the guarantor. At the outset, the creditor should make sure that the guarantor understands the full nature of the guarantee he is signing. Guarantors often escape their obligation by claiming misrepresentation, *non est factum,* or undue influence. When in doubt, the creditor should insist that the guarantor obtain independent legal advice.

CASE SUMMARY 16.5

Guarantor Released Because of Material Changes: *Toronto-Dominion Bank v. Duffett*[13]

Duffett gave five guarantees to the Bank in support of three mortgages between two companies and various lending institutions who were predecessors in title to the Bank. The mortgagors defaulted and the Bank demanded that Duffett pay the deficiency after the properties were sold.

The Court held that Duffett was not liable for the deficiency. Over the years, the Bank had made numerous material alterations to the mortgages, including increasing the interest rates, extending the amortization periods of the mortgages, increasing the monthly payments, and permitting a tax liability to accumulate on the properties. The Court concluded: "The Plaintiff made numerous material alterations to the mortgage contracts between 1988 and 1998 of which the Defendant had no notice or knowledge and to which he did not consent. The guarantees were no longer valid and enforceable against the Defendant and he is discharged from any liability to the Plaintiff."

DISCUSSION QUESTIONS

Why should guarantors be treated with such deference when their involvement persuaded the creditor to loan money to the debtor? Why should the creditor be responsible to protect the interests of the guarantor? And, if it is important for the creditor to protect the position of the guarantor, should we allow this to be changed by a one-sided exemption clause included in the guarantee agreement itself?

---

13. (2004), 234 Nfld. & P.E.I.R. 223 (Nfld. S.C.T.D.).

The creditor should also avoid any subsequent dealings that may weaken the position of the guarantor. Any substantial change in the nature of the contract between the creditor and debtor without the guarantor's consent will relieve the guarantor of any obligation. If the creditor advances more funds, or even extends the terms of repayment at a higher interest rate, without the consent of the guarantor, the guarantor will usually be discharged from the guarantee. This was the result in the *Duffett* case. Note that a creditor's simply deciding not to sue, and giving the debtor more time to pay, will not be considered a substantial change. Such actions will therefore not discharge the guarantee. In any subsequent dealings with the debtor independent of the guarantor, the creditor should obtain the consent of the guarantor to any material change. The effect will then be that the guarantor will continue to be bound by the original guarantee.[14]

> Creditors must not weaken the position of the guarantor
>
> Significant changes may release guarantor
>
> Creditor should obtain consent of guarantor

A guarantor is also released from her obligation when other forms of security, such as chattel mortgages, are released. For example, if Kotsalis obtained a loan from the Business Bank, with the Bank taking a guarantee from Bruno and a chattel mortgage against Kotsalis's car as security, such an arrangement would cease to be binding on Bruno if the Bank subsequently allowed Kotsalis to sell the car without Bruno's consent.

> Releasing security may release guarantor

The withholding of important information from the guarantor by the creditor may also be enough to discharge the guarantee. The information withheld must be of some substantial and unusual nature, not simply the usual kind of information that would pass between business associates. A creditor is obligated, for example, to advise a guarantor of a priority agreement which reduced the assets available in the event of a default.[15]

> Withholding information may release guarantor

Because the basic rights and obligations of the creditor and the guarantor are determined by contract, they can be modified by contract as well. It is common for creditors to include provisions that attempt to exempt the creditor from the basic obligations discussed above. Like all exemption clauses, exemption clauses in guarantees are interpreted by the courts very carefully. It is becoming common for a guarantee to contain clauses creating a **continuing guarantee**, allowing the creditor to continue to advance funds up to a pre-set limit without affecting the obligation of the guarantor to pay in the event of default. Clauses that allow the creditor to discharge and otherwise deal with security, and to otherwise change the terms of the agreement (including changing terms of repayment and increasing interest rates), are now often included in guarantees. These clauses can be effective if they are carefully worded. They then significantly limit the protection normally enjoyed by a guarantor.

> Contract can modify rights and obligations

When a default occurs, the creditor is not required to demand payment from the debtor, or to take steps to seize any other security, before seeking payment from the guarantor, unless that has been agreed to in the contract. A guarantor who pays the debt is *subrogated* to the rights of the creditor, which means, in effect, that the guarantor steps into the creditor's shoes. Any remedy or right available to the creditor after payment is assumed by the guarantor, including the right to seize a chattel used as security for the debt, or to sue the debtor and take advantage of the processes available to assist in collecting the debt.

> Guarantor assumes rights of creditor upon payment

---

14. For a case in which the Court held that a guarantee was clear in stating that a renewal agreement did not require the explicit approval of the guarantor, see *A.G.F. Trust Co. v. Muhammad* (2005), 73 O.R. (3d) 767 (C.A.), leave to appeal to S.C.C. refused, [2005] S.C.C.A. No. 139.

15 (2004), 47 B.L.R. (3d) 39, (2004), 29 B.C.L.R. (4th) 18 (C.A.).

CASE SUMMARY 16.6

Failure to Register Security Releases Guarantor: *First City Capital Ltd. v. Hall*[16]

First City leased word-processing equipment to Karsha Holdings Ltd., whose principals, Hall and deHaan, signed personal guarantees for the indebtedness. Karsha also owed money to the Royal Bank that was secured against the assets of the corporation. When Karsha defaulted, the Royal Bank, which had perfected its security, was entitled to the word-processing equipment because First City had failed to perfect its security. First City sued Hall on the personal guarantee for payment.

First City had an obligation to the guarantor to ensure that the security was perfected. Its failure to do so relieved Hall of any liability on the guarantee. Note that the Court found that a provision in the contract stating that the guarantee would be enforceable ("notwithstanding that the lease or any other arrangements shall be void or voidable against the lessee... including... by reason... of... failure by any person to file any document or take any other action to make the lease... enforceable") did not apply, since the failure to register did not make those leases void or voidable, just ineffective against third parties.

A similar case in Newfoundland had the opposite result. There, the Bank also failed to perfect its security but the clause in the guarantee stated that the Bank may "abstain from perfecting securities... as the Bank sees fit." The Court held that this term effectively covered the situation, and that the guarantee remained binding despite the Bank's failure to perfect.[17]

DISCUSSION QUESTIONS

These cases illustrate not only the operation of a guarantee, but also the obligations placed on the creditor to preserve and protect the position of the guarantor by doing nothing to weaken it. They also show that carefully worded provisions in the guarantee may change that obligation, and how such provisions are strictly interpreted in favour of the guarantor.

Finally, these cases raise the same question as the *Duffett* case discussed in Case Summary 16.5. Why should the creditor have any obligation to the guarantor? He has guaranteed payment; why shouldn't the creditor be able to choose from whom it seeks payment? And, if the responsibility of the creditor is justified, why should an exemption clause in a one-sided contract change that obligation?

---

16. (1993), 11 O.R. (3d) 792 (C.A.).

17. *Bank of Montreal v. Mercer* (2000), 193 Nfld. & P.E.I.R. 88 (Nfld. S.C.T.D.).

In addition, any defences that are available to the debtor are also available to the guarantor. If breach of contract, fraud, or misrepresentation on the part of the creditor has barred an action against the debtor, it also bars an action against the guarantor. Note, however, that if the reason the guarantee was required was because of the infancy of the debtor, or some other factor known to all parties at the time of the guarantee, the guarantor will normally not be allowed to use that reason as a defence against the creditor.

Defences of debtor are available to guarantor

Other Forms of Security

THE BANK ACT[18]

This federal statute predates the passage of the *PPSAs*. It allows banks flexibility in what they can take as security. Under the *Bank Act,* growing crops, inventories, and goods in the process of manufacture can be taken as security by the banks, despite the fact that the nature of the goods changes in the process. For this type of security, it must be possible to sell the collateral during the course of business without affecting the nature of the security. Sections 426 and 427 of the *Bank Act* allow this to happen.

Anticipated crops can be used as security

As can inventory and goods in process of manufacture

The *Bank Act* is still an important federal statute, but under the provincial *PPSAs*, other lenders now have similar flexibility. There is therefore now more potential conflict between the *Bank Act* and the provincial legislation. Businesspeople must now learn two sets of rules. For example, under the *Bank Act,* security must be registered with the Bank of Canada, creating duplication and confusion. This confusion is compounded because the *Bank Act* enables the banks to continue to use the usual types of secured transactions available to other lenders, such as chattel mortgages, real property mortgages, assignment of debts, guarantees and so on.

Conflict and confusion between *Bank Act* and *PPSA*

FLOATING CHARGES

Floating charges are used by creditors when dealing with corporations that must be free to buy and sell, without interference, the assets used as security for the loan. When a corporation borrows funds, it may issue bonds or debentures. In Canada, bonds are usually secured by a floating charge. In effect, they involve a mortgage of corporate assets. Debentures are usually unsecured. Bonds and debentures are commonly sold on the open market.

Bonds usually secured by floating charge

When a bond is issued, the security granted often takes the form of a **floating charge** against the general assets of the corporation, including inventory and the goods in the process of manufacturing. This allows the corporation to continue to deal with those goods, buying and selling in the normal course of business, unaffected by the floating charge. Customers, for example, take the goods they buy free and clear of the floating charge. It is only upon default, or some other specified event (such as the payment of unauthorized dividends or the sale of a valuable asset), that the floating charge crystallizes, by descending, attaching to the specific goods, and becoming a fixed charge. The advantage of a floating charge is that it does not interfere with the ongoing business, while still providing a priority over unsecured creditors. Because the various *PPSAs* now allow inventory

Floating charge provides priority, but allows business to continue

---

18. S.C. 1991, c. 46.

and other changing assets to be used as security, the floating charge is of diminishing importance. It is, however, still a common aspect of corporate financing.

BUILDERS' LIENS

Builders' liens were created to overcome a problem in the construction industry. The suppliers of goods and services (such as merchants selling building supplies, or electricians wiring a house) often dealt with a general contractor, rather than with the owner of the land or building that was to be enhanced by their goods and services. If they were not paid, their recourse was limited to the contractor. They had no claim against the owner, or the land or building that was enhanced. Statutes in all provinces—variously called *Builders' Lien Act, Construction Lien Act,* or *Mechanics' Lien Act*—now give these suppliers of materials and work a claim for payment against the actual land and buildings enhanced by their goods and services. Once the goods or services are provided, the suppliers and workers can register a lien, giving them a claim against the land and buildings. This puts considerable pressure on the owner of the property to ensure that they are paid. The effect of the legislation is to prevent the owner of property from unjustly benefiting from the goods and services that enhance the value of the property, without paying for them.

Under the various acts, the owner of the property retains a percentage of what she would otherwise pay to the general contractor. This is the **holdback**, which in most provinces is set at 10 percent. After a relatively short period of time, within which any liens must be registered, the owner checks the land registry and, if there are no liens registered, pays out the holdback to the general contractor. If liens have been filed, the amount of the lien is retained and made available to the lien claimants. The owner's obligation is usually limited to the amount of the holdback, even when the total claimed in the liens exceeds that amount. In such a case, the lien claimants will get a proportional share of the amount held back, based on what they are owed.

This requirement of holdback applies to anyone in the construction chain. Thus, the general contractor in turn must hold back from the payment to subcontractors to cover claims by their employees or suppliers of goods and services. The times, percentages and amounts vary from jurisdiction to jurisdiction, but the general approach is the same. This system provides a form of security to those supplying material and work in the construction industry. In most jurisdictions, similar liens are created by statute against property stored in a warehouse and for maintenance people working on vehicles, machinery and other goods.[19]

NEGOTIABLE INSTRUMENTS

Negotiable instruments in the form of cheques, bills of exchange, and promissory notes are often associated with secured transactions. For example, debtors are usually required to sign promissory notes in credit transactions. Negotiable instruments were discussed in Chapter 15.

[19.] See, for example, Alberta's *Garage Keepers' Lien Act*, R.S.A. 2000, c. G-2, *Possessory Lien Act*, R.S.A. 2000, c. P-19, *Warehousemen's Lien Act*, R.S.A. 2000, c. W-2, and *Woodmen's Lien Act*, R.S.A. 2000, c.W-14; *Saskatchewan's Threshers' Lien Act*, R.S.S. 1978, c. T-13; and British Columbia's *Tugboat Worker Lien Act*, R.S.B.C. 1996, c. 466.

Marginal notes:
Suppliers of goods and services can file lien

Holdback fulfills obligation of owner

All in chain must hold back

LETTERS OF CREDIT

Similarly to negotiable instruments, the **letter of credit** is used in commercial relationships, especially in international trade. The letter of credit is a commitment by the importer's bank that the price stated will be paid upon presentation of appropriate documentation confirming delivery. This provides assurance to the exporter, from the financial institution, that he will be paid. This letter of credit is normally delivered to the exporter by the importer. Upon delivery of the goods, the exporter submits the appropriate documentation (relating to shipment, insurance, customs declarations and so on) to the importer's bank and receives payment.

Sometimes, especially when the importer's bank is in a foreign country, the exporter will require that a bank he has confidence in, usually in his own country, become involved as a confirming bank. The importer's bank and the exporter's bank communicate with each other, and both commit to honour the letter of credit upon receiving the appropriate documentation. The confirming bank plays a role similar to endorsing a negotiable instrument in that it adds its commitment to honour the letter of credit. The exporter then simply submits the appropriate documents indicating performance to his bank and receives payment. In effect, the two traders choose banks that they trust to hold and transfer the funds. The effect is quite similar to that of a bank draft, but this process is often more convenient and more flexible.

Letters of credit are used primarily in international trade, but as they are very flexible, it is not uncommon to find them being used in domestic business transactions as well. Letters of credit are also used in other ways. They can, for example, guarantee, in effect, that one party to a contract will properly perform. If there is a breach, the victim has recourse to the bank that has issued the letter of credit. This is referred to as a **standby letter of credit**.

> *Letters of credit used in international trade*

> *Role of confirming bank*

> *Also used in domestic transactions*

Related Laws

BULK SALES

Other legislation has been enacted to protect creditors against frauds committed by debtors. Most provinces formerly had a bulk sales act in place, but Ontario is now the only province to have such legislation.[20] It is designed to prevent merchants from selling all, or almost all, of their business's assets before a creditor can take action to stop them. Creditors expect a business to sell inventory in the normal course of operations, but when all, or most, of the inventory, equipment, or other assets needed for the ongoing operation is sold, that is an indication that the merchant is going out of business. The *Bulk Sales Act* operates in these circumstances to protect the creditors. The purchaser must obtain a list of creditors, notify them of the sale and pay the proceeds directly to them, if they so wish. Great care must be taken to comply with the legislative requirements. Failure to comply will make the sale void as against the creditors, requiring the purchaser to account to the creditors for the value of the goods.

mybuslawlab
www.pearsoned.ca/mybuslawlab

> *Creditors protected when merchant sells bulk of business*

---

20. *Bulk Sales Act*, R.S.O. 1990, c. B.14.

LANDLORD'S RIGHT TO DISTRAIN FOR RENT

Landlord has right to distrain

When a tenant fails to pay rent on a leased property, an ancient common law right called *distress* is available to the landlord of the property. The landlord has the right to seize and hold the tenant's assets that are on the rented premises and, eventually, to sell them to pay for the rent owed. There are several restrictions on the right of distraint, and many procedural requirements that must be carefully complied with, especially with respect to residential tenancies. The nature of residential and commercial tenancies, and the rights of the parties, were discussed in Chapter 13.

CASE SUMMARY 16.7

A Transfer of a Home to a Spouse for "Natural Love and Affection" Can Be Fraudulent! *Pilot Insurance Co. v. Foulidis*[21]

Foulidis bought an insurance policy from Pilot. His wife was injured in a car accident. Pilot made payments to her. Pilot then discovered that Workers' Compensation benefits had been paid to the wife. It demanded partial reimbursement for the amounts it had paid. After Pilot sued the wife, she transferred her share of the matrimonial home to her husband, for $2 and "natural love and affection." Pilot obtained judgment against the wife and then sued her husband, claiming that the conveyance of the property was made to prevent it from collecting its judgment. The husband claimed that the transfer was made to facilitate the acceptance of an offer from a third party and to effect the sale of the home to the third party. Seventeen months after selling the home to the third party, Foulidis gave half of the proceeds from the sale to his wife.

The trial Court ruled that the transfer of the wife's share of the home was made with fraudulent intent and therefore contravened the *Fraudulent Conveyances Act*. The Court of Appeal agreed and ordered the husband to pay the proceeds of the sale to Pilot:

> John Foulidis accepted a voluntary conveyance of property in fraudulent circumstances. He had knowledge of the true nature of the conveyance. He cannot, with impunity, sell the property and give to the debtor that part of the sale proceeds attributable to the debtor's ownership when the conveyance was fraudulent. To permit such a result would undermine the purpose of the *Fraudulent Conveyances Act* and the *Assignments and Preferences Act*.

DISCUSSION QUESTIONS

This case illustrates the danger of ignoring legislation regarding fraudulent transfers and preferences. Many married couples own their homes together, as joint tenants. If one of the spouses has a judgment entered against him or her, the creditor may be able to obtain a court order requiring the joint tenancy to be severed, so that the debtor's half of the property can be sold to pay the debt. Is this a fair result? Should spouses be exempt from fraudulent transfers and preferences legislation?

---

21. (2005), 199 O.A.C. 391, (2005), 256 D.L.R. (4th) 360.

FRAUDULENT TRANSFERS AND PREFERENCES

Sometimes, desperate debtors are tempted to hide property, or otherwise protect it, from the claims of creditors. Giving or selling property to a friend or relative to avoid the debt is a fraudulent transfer. Such a transaction is void. The creditor can seek out the fraudulently transferred property and get it back from the current owner. If the transfer is a valid arm's-length sale at a fair price to an innocent third party (a **bona fide purchaser for value**), the transaction is valid and cannot be reversed.

Fraudulent conveyances void

Sometimes, a debtor will seek an advantage by paying one creditor in preference to another. This is also a prohibited transaction, called a **fraudulent preference**. Fraudulent preferences can also be reversed.

Fraudulent preferences void

Legislation embodying these provisions varies from province to province; the statutes are variously called *Assignment and Preferences Act, Fraudulent Conveyances Act,* and *Fraudulent Preferences Act.* This sort of legislation is designed primarily to prevent debtors from unfairly making payments or transferring property in such a way as to keep the money or property away from the creditors.See Section 3 of the Saskatchewan *Fraudulent Preferences Act,* for example.[22]

The federal *Bankruptcy and Insolvency Act* discussed below also has provisions prohibiting settlements (transfers for nominal, or no, consideration) and fraudulent preferences. These provisions apply uniformly throughout Canada. While the general intent of the provisions in the bankruptcy legislation is the same as that of the provincial statutes, it should be noted that the wording used in the bankruptcy legislation is quite different than that found in the provincial statutes.

Similar restrictions in bankruptcy legislation

REDUCING RISK 16.4

Businesspeople are sometimes so focused on closing a deal that they miss complying with related statutory requirements. This can come back later to haunt them. In Ontario, where there is a bulk sales statute in place, businesspeople must take great care to comply with it whenever the sale of a significant portion of a business's assets is involved. Failure to do so can result in having to pay twice. Similarly, whenever dealing with an insolvent debtor, creditors must take care to comply with fraudulent conveyance, fraudulent preference, and other legislation that may affect the validity of the transaction.

BANKRUPTCY

Introduction

As discussed above, debtors will often find themselves in a position where they cannot repay their debts. For that reason, wise creditors take steps at the outset of a relationship to ensure repayment. They may take an asset belonging to the debtor as security, or get someone else, such as a guarantor, to also be responsible for the debt.

Creditors may take security

Unpaid unsecured creditors have all of the usual remedies available when someone breaches a legal obligation, including the right to proceed to a civil judgment. A judgment creditor can seize the debtor's assets and sell them to

Unsecured creditors can sue and try to collect

[22.] R.S.S. 1978, c. F-21.

recover the judgment, or she can garnishee wages and other debts, as discussed in Chapter 3. Such action is often ineffective. There may be many creditors with claims outstanding. Secured creditors will have priority with respect to any secured asset that they might claim. The debtor may have limited resources with which to pay. Furthermore, in such a situation, the debtor may choose to declare bankruptcy, or may be forced into bankruptcy.

But debtor may declare bankruptcy

Purposes of bankruptcy are to protect creditors and to rehabilitate debtor

The *Bankruptcy and Insolvency Act*[23] (*BIA*) is a federal statute that is uniformly applicable throughout Canada. It has two purposes. The first is to preserve as many of the debtor's assets as possible for the benefit of the creditors. The second is to rehabilitate the debtor by forgiving the unpaid debt, thus removing an insurmountable burden, and restoring the debtor as a productive member of society.

The previous edition of this textbook noted that Bill C-55, which provided a comprehensive insolvency reform, had received Royal Assent on 25 November 2005. When the textbook was written, in November 2006, the Bill (actually S.C. 2005, c. 47) had not yet been proclaimed. Its provisions were therefore not discussed.

Bill C-62 contained amendments to c. 47. It was passed by the House of Commons, but not the Senate. Bill C-12 was then introduced. It was passed by the House of Commons and the Senate. It received Royal Assent in December 2007 (S.C. 2007 c. 36).

Some of insolvency reform now in force

Some of the provisions of c. 47 and c. 36 came into force in July 2008. For example, the *Wage Earner Protection Program Act*[24] and its regulations were proclaimed in force as of 7 July 2008; it was subsequently amended by Bill C-10, which came into force on 10 March 2009. (The amendments were retroactive to 27 January 2009.)

On 8 December 2008, the Canadian Association of Insolvency and Restructuring Professionals, in Bulletin 08-14,[25] indicated that "the remaining insolvency amendments will not come into force in January 2009, as previously anticipated . . . " The Office of the Superintendent of Bankruptcy discussed, on its website, the changes set out in c. 47 and c. 36. It provided a "Summary of Key Provisions of the BIA in Force as of July, 2008."[26] This was last modified on March 17, 2009. This edition of the textbook will discuss only the provisions of c. 47 and c. 36 that were in force in June 2009, as indicated by the updated Summary.

Bankruptcy involves transfer of assets to Trustee

People are often confused by the terms used to describe bankruptcy. **Insolvency** simply means that a person is unable to pay his debts as they become due. **Bankruptcy**, on the other hand, is the process by which a debtor's assets are transferred to a Trustee in Bankruptcy, who then deals with them for the benefit of the creditors. When the debtor makes the transfer voluntarily it is called an **assignment in bankruptcy**. Bankruptcy can be forced on the debtor, by a creditor obtaining a **bankruptcy order** from the court. The *BIA* does not apply to banks, insurance companies, trust companies, loan companies, or railways. Farmers

---

[23] R.S.C. 1985, c. B-3.

[24] S.C. 2005, c. 47, s. 1.

[25] See Bulletin 08-14, online: www.cairp.ca/english/communications_advo/doc/BUL08-14.doc.

[26] See "Summary of Legislative Changes," www.ic.gc.ca/eic/site/bsf-osb.nsf/eng/br01782.html.

and fishers cannot be forced into bankruptcy, but they can make a voluntary assignment.

The government official responsible for bankruptcy for all of Canada is the Superintendent of Bankruptcy. The Superintendent, in turn, appoints Official Receivers for the bankruptcy districts throughout the country (there must be at least one in each province). A **Trustee in Bankruptcy** is a licensed private professional who, for a fee, assists the debtor in the bankruptcy process—administering the bankrupt's estate for the benefit of the creditors, filing various documents with the Official Receiver, and otherwise shepherding the bankrupt through the process from initiation to discharge. A Trustee serves the same purpose when a proposal is involved. A Trustee is called an Administrator when dealing with consumer proposals. The courts become involved when a bankruptcy order is requested and when other types of disputes arise. The superior trial court of each province and territory is designated as a bankruptcy court for the purposes of the *BIA*. Although these are courts of the provinces or territories, they have a national jurisdiction when administering the *BIA* and related legislation, because these are federal statutes.

> **Superintendent of Bankruptcy responsible**
>
> **Superintendent appoints Official Receivers**
>
> **Trustees in Bankruptcy administer process**

CASE SUMMARY 16.8

No Act of Bankruptcy, No Bankruptcy! *American Bullion Minerals Ltd. (Re)*[27]

The Court granted the petition of the controlling shareholder of ABML, bcMetals Corporation (bcM), asking for a bankruptcy order for ABML. The minority shareholders of ABML applied for an order annulling the bankruptcy. They claimed that bcM made a number of misrepresentations when it petitioned ABML into bankruptcy, that the sole director of ABML failed to oppose the petition or alert ABML shareholders of it, and that bcM petitioned ABML into bankruptcy to facilitate bcM's acquisition of ABML's interest in mineral claims without compensating ABML's minority shareholders.

The Court found that the petition, the affidavit in support, and the submissions of counsel did not inform the Court of the real relationship between ABML and bcM, fully disclose the circumstances of some of the liabilities of ABML, or provide any information relevant to some of its liabilities. The Court found that bcM was the only creditor of ABML, and that bcM could not prove that there were special circumstances that warranted a bankruptcy order. Also, there was no evidence that ABML had committed an act of bankruptcy. The Court concluded that if the bankruptcy Court had been fully informed, it would not have made the bankruptcy order. The bankruptcy was therefore annulled.

DISCUSSION QUESTIONS

A creditor must prove that the debtor has committed an act of bankruptcy, or the petition will be refused. In such a case, the creditor may be liable for any losses suffered by the debtor. In the ABML case, what remedy may the minority shareholders be able to seek?

---

[27]. (2008), 43 C.B.R. (5th) 210 (B.C.S.C.).

Bankruptcy can be forced by creditors

If creditor owed more than $1000 and debtor committed an act of bankruptcy

The Process

In an involuntary bankruptcy, a creditor petitions the court to force the debtor into bankruptcy. In granting the petition, the court makes a bankruptcy order. This results in a statutory assignment of the debtor's assets to the Trustee in Bankruptcy, ensuring that the assets will be preserved and distributed fairly, so that the creditors will recover as much as possible of what they are owed.

To obtain a bankruptcy order, the creditor must specify in the petition that the debtor owes more than $1000 in debt and has committed an act of bankruptcy during the previous six months. Significant acts of bankruptcy include the voluntary assignment of assets to a trustee in bankruptcy, fraudulent transfers of money or assets to keep them out of the hands of the trustee, the giving of a fraudulent preference to one of the creditors, an attempt to leave the jurisdiction without paying debts, and general insolvency. It is usually the failure to pay debts as they become due that is the specified act of bankruptcy. A sworn affidavit must also be filed with the Registrar in Bankruptcy in the district in which the debtor is located, verifying the facts alleged in the petition. If the debtor opposes the petition, as is often the case, a hearing before a Judge will take place. If she is satisfied, the Judge can issue a bankruptcy order, designating a Trustee in Bankruptcy (normally chosen by the creditors) to receive the assets of the bankrupt. When the petition is unopposed, the hearing can be held before the Registrar.

Creditor must be careful when petitioning

Petitioning a debtor into bankruptcy is an involved process, normally requiring the assistance of a lawyer. Caution should be exercised before using this approach. Great damage can be done to the business and reputation of the debtor. If the application is refused, the creditor may be liable to pay compensation for the losses incurred by the debtor. See Figure 16.1 for an illustration of the bankruptcy order process.

Bankruptcy can be voluntary by debtor

In a **voluntary assignment in bankruptcy**, the debtor must make an "assignment for the general benefit of his creditors," using the prescribed form. The debtor must also prepare a "statement of affairs," summarizing his property and listing all of his creditors, showing the amounts and nature of their claims (whether they are secured, preferred, or unsecured). These documents are filed with the Official Receiver, who then appoints a Trustee in Bankruptcy. The Trustee will receive the debtor's assets and administer the estate. In practice, debtors will first seek out a Trustee in Bankruptcy, who will counsel them, advising of the various alternatives and, if appropriate, assisting them in the preparation of the documents and their filing with the Official Receiver. When larger estates are involved, the debtor will usually also involve the services of a lawyer. The voluntary assignment process is illustrated in Figure 16.2.

Exempt property is protected

It should be noted that not all of the debtor's property is transferred to the Trustee in Bankruptcy. The exempt property is determined by the provincial legislation, so it varies from province to province. It usually includes medical and

Figure 16.1 Bankruptcy Order Process

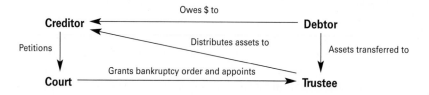

Figure 16.2 Voluntary Assignment

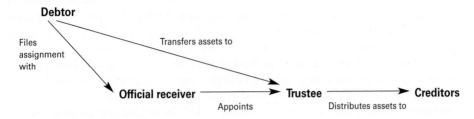

dental aids, food, clothing, furniture and appliances, and tools and other items used to earn an income, up to a limited value. A vehicle of limited value and a personal residence where the debtor has a limited equity may also be protected. The Trustee will not take property of little value, or property that she considers to be worth less than what it will cost to liquidate.

The Trustee in Bankruptcy holds the debtor's property in trust for the creditors. She therefore owes them a duty to preserve the property and to sell it for as much as is reasonably possible. The debtor must cooperate with the Trustee, disclosing all assets, documentation and tax receipts. Often a meeting of the creditors will take place. The debtor must attend, answering the creditors' questions, and otherwise cooperating in the process. The creditors may ask to appoint up to five Inspectors to supervise the Trustee and the process, to ensure their interests are protected. The debtor may also be required to meet with, and answer the questions of, the Official Receiver.

> Trustee holds property in trust for creditors

Alternatives to Bankruptcy

The debtor should, of course, do all he can to avoid bankruptcy. If he becomes bankrupt, he will lose most of his property. He will also find it difficult in the future to conduct business, or to make personal credit purchases, due to a poor credit rating. A personal bankruptcy will remain on an individual's credit record for about six years. Even after that period of time, it will be obvious to a credit grantor that there must have been serious financial problems, because of the lack of credit transactions during that six-year period. If a corporation becomes bankrupt, it will not be discharged and will therefore not survive.

> Debtor should try to avoid bankruptcy

For a debtor who is having financial problems, the first step should be to talk to the creditors involved, to try to make alternative arrangements for paying the debt. Creditors are usually quite responsive to reasonable arrangements for avoiding both commercial and personal bankruptcies. They will often get much less if bankruptcy is forced. There are also many tangible and intangible advantages for creditors to keep their debtor as a functioning customer. Another option, especially when significant credit card debt is involved, is to obtain a consolidation loan from a bank or other lending institution. A consolidation loan enables the debtor to consolidate the various debts he owes. There will then be only one creditor, and a more manageable payment schedule, often at a lower rate of interest. Individual creditors will sometimes agree to take less to pay off the debt. They realize that they will be better off accepting less, rather than risking getting nothing by continuing to demand full payment and thus forcing bankruptcy.

> There are several possible informal solutions

If these informal negotiations fail, the *BIA* still provides for an alternative to bankruptcy. Two separate procedures are involved; both allow the debtor to reorganize her affairs and make proposals for partial payment that will satisfy her

> Debtors can make proposal and avoid bankruptcy

Division I proposals for corporations and people with debts over $75 000

creditors sufficiently to avoid actual bankruptcy. **Division I proposals** usually involve commercial debtors in the form of corporations or individual debtors with significant claims against them (more than $75 000). The process is started by filing, with the Official Receiver, a proposal, or a notice of intention to file a proposal. The filing should be done with the help of a professional licensed to provide these services (a Trustee in Bankruptcy). Within 10 days of filing a notice of intention, a statement of projected cash flow must also be filed, followed within 30 days by the filing of the proposal itself (although this time limit may be extended). A meeting with the creditors is then held and the proposal is discussed and voted upon. For the proposal to be approved, two-thirds of the unsecured creditors by value and a majority by number, must vote to accept it. (Note that they may be divided into classes of creditors and then vote within that class.) The same approach applies to each class of secured creditors to which the proposal was made. The court also must approve the proposal.

If proposal rejected, debtor into bankruptcy

If the unsecured creditors approve the proposal, all of them are bound by it. If the unsecured creditors (or the court) reject the proposal, the debtor is deemed to have made an assignment in bankruptcy from the day of the meeting of the creditors. Normal bankruptcy procedures will follow. Secured creditors whose class gave its approval are also bound by the proposal. Secured creditors not included in the proposal, or whose class rejected the proposal, can still realize on their security.

Proposals are flexible and they stay proceedings

Division I proposals are very flexible. They may include anything from arranging to reduce the debt, to devising a new payment structure, to helping the creditors wind up the corporation. An important effect of starting this process by filing a proposal, or a notice of intention, is that creditors, including secured creditors who have been included in the proposal process, are prevented from taking action against the debtor or her assets until the vote takes place, at least two months later. In effect, the insolvent debtor is protected from the creditors. If the proposal is accepted, that protection continues.

CASE SUMMARY 16.9

Proposal Abused: *Janodee Investments Ltd. v. Pellegrini*[28]

Pellegrini had two mortgages on his home. When he defaulted on them, the mortgagees/creditors proceeded to judgment and obtained an order to take possession of the house. Before the order could be enforced, Pellegrini served notice of intention to make a proposal under the *BIA*. Normally, such a notice would result in a stay of proceedings, delaying enforcement of the order. However, in this case the Court held that Pellegrini was using the notice as a delaying tactic. He had no serious intention of reordering his affairs. No other secured creditors were involved, and the mortgagees would not be responsive to such a proposal in any event.

This case is instructive in that it shows not only the normal operation of a proposal, but also how such a proposal can be abused. In this case, the Court refused to order the stay, thus preventing such abuse. The difficulty with the operation of such proposals—as well as with the whole bankruptcy process—is that it interferes with the creditors' rights

---

28. (2001), 25 C.B.R. (4th) 47 (Ont. S.C.J.).

> to proceed against the debtor and enforce full payment in a timely manner. The justification for this is that, in the long run, the creditors get more and that, after discharge, the bankrupt is able to carry on without overwhelming debt. But, in fact, many creditors get very little or nothing and are barred from further proceedings after discharge.
>
> ---
>
> *SMALL BUSINESS PERSPECTIVE*
>
> Does the Division 1 proposal process in the *BIA* provide too much protection for insolvent people and businesses, at the expense of legitimate creditors?

Consumer debtors with less than $75 000 in claims against them (excluding a mortgage on their home) are similarly protected when they make a consumer proposal under Division II of Part III of the *BIA*. The insolvent debtor must hire an Administrator (a Trustee in Bankruptcy or a person appointed to administer consumer proposals). The Administrator examines the debtor's finances, prepares the consumer proposal and any reports required, provides counselling for the debtor, and files the consumer proposal. This is a simpler process than filing a Division I proposal. No actual meeting is required unless demanded by the creditors. If the creditors reject a consumer proposal, the debtor is not automatically bankrupt. A consumer proposal must contain a commitment by the debtor that the performance of the consumer proposal will be completed within five years. Payments under a consumer proposal are paid to the Administrator, who distributes the funds to the creditors.

Consumer proposals available for people with debts less than $75 000

As long as the debtor complies with the obligations in the consumer proposal, acts honestly and participates in any mandatory counselling required, action cannot be taken against him by unsecured creditors. Even those supplying ongoing services, such as public utilities and landlords, must continue supplying them. But if the debtor defaults on his commitments, the consumer proposal is annulled, and the debtor may face the normal bankruptcy procedures. Court approval of Division II proposals is not required.

Consumer proposals stop all legal actions by unsecured creditors

For both Division I proposals and consumer proposals, if a proposal is accepted and then properly performed, a certificate is issued and the debtor's obligation is complete with respect to those matters covered by the proposal. There are some matters that cannot be included in a proposal, just as some types of obligations cannot be discharged though bankruptcy. These will be discussed below. If a secured debt was not included in the proposal, then that obligation remains and is not affected by the completed performance of the proposal or the certificate issued.

Secured debts not affected if not in proposal

In some provinces, individual debtors may also utilize Part X of the *BIA*, Orderly Payment of Debts (OPD). If the amount the debtor owes is less than $1000, or if the debtor obtains the consent of the creditors, he can apply to the court for a consolidation order. He must provide an affidavit, setting out his relevant financial and personal situation. The application will be approved, unless a creditor objects to it. If there is an objection, there will be a hearing in front of the Clerk of the Court to determine the validity of the objection.

Orderly payment of debt program available in some provinces

A consolidation order requires the debtor to make the stipulated payments into court, such that all of his debts will be paid in full within three years, unless the creditors consent to a longer period. Such an order acts as a stay with respect to the debts covered by the order, except for secured debts. If the debtor defaults, the creditors can enforce the consolidation order like any other court order, subject to the court's approval. The OPD program is administered by various public and private agencies in the provinces where it is available. In Alberta, for example, Money Mentors (the successor to Credit Counselling Services of Alberta Ltd.) administers the OPD program.[29]

Large corporations can ask court for bankruptcy protection

For corporations owing more than $5 million, there is an alternative process available that enables them to restructure their affairs and avoid bankruptcy. This alternative is available under the *Companies' Creditors Arrangement Act (CCAA)*.[30] This is a federal statute providing protection to debtors with some advantages over the *BIA*. The attraction of the *CCAA* is in the protection given to debtors, from their creditors. This may provide more flexibility to the debtor corporation in its restructuring efforts, as it will be protected from its creditors, both secured and unsecured, for a longer period of time. A judge will often combine the flexibility provided under the *CCAA* with the power under section 47 of the *BIA* to appoint an interim receiver to supervise the restructuring process. Many corporations have filed for bankruptcy protection under the *CCAA* in recent years, including Air Canada and Nortel Networks Corp.

Commercial and consumer proposals under the *BIA*, consolidation orders in the OPD program, and arrangements under the *CCAA* all enable a debtor to avoid the bankruptcy process. Bankruptcy will occur, however, if the creditors reject a proposal, or if the debtor defaults on his obligations under a proposal. Business students should be aware of bankruptcy and its alternatives, from both a consumer and a commercial perspective. Consumer bankruptcies are much more numerous than commercial bankruptcies. Any business dealing with the public must therefore factor this risk into its business considerations. Commercial bankruptcies may be less common than consumer bankruptcies, but they generally involve much more money and have a greater impact on the businesses with which the debtor is dealing. Even very high-profile businesses (General Motors Corp.) are facing bankruptcy or restructuring in these difficult economic times. A businessperson ignores these risks at his peril.

REDUCING RISK 16.5

Bankruptcy is a very serious and drastic step. Both creditors and debtors should do all they can to avoid it. Often negotiation between the parties, perhaps with a mediator, will result in an acceptable alternative. The creditors get more than they would get by forcing bankruptcy, and a valued customer is preserved. If these informal steps fail, and proposals are presented, they should be treated seriously. Bankruptcy should be used only as a last resort.

Priority Among Creditors

Trustee holds property in trust for creditors

Once the Trustee in Bankruptcy has been given the property of a bankrupt debtor (referred to as the bankrupt's "**estate**"), she holds those assets in trust for the benefit of the creditors. The Trustee has the right and responsibility to lease, repair, receive rents or otherwise deal with those assets to preserve their value. The Trustee will eventually sell the assets and distribute the proceeds fairly to the creditors.

---

29. See Money Mentors, online: www.moneymentors.ca/home.html.

30. R.S.C.1985, c. C-36.

Each of the creditors must establish the validity of his claim by filing a **proof of claim** with the Trustee. This document sets out the nature of the debt, how much remains owing, and any claims the debtor might have in return. An important function of the Trustee is to evaluate the claims of the creditors. If they are accepted as valid, they will form part of the body of claims against the estate. Some claims of questionable legitimacy may be rejected by the Trustee. The affected creditors have the right to challenge the Trustee's decision by making application to the bankruptcy court. Mediation is often employed to resolve these and other disputes.

The *BIA* allows a supplier of goods to demand the return of those goods upon learning of the bankruptcy. The supplier must make his written demand for repossession within 30 days of delivery of those goods, and the debtor (or the Trustee) must still have possession of them. Even suppliers of goods that become commingled and lose their identity, such as crops, produce, and fish, have a prior claim. Such suppliers become secured creditors with respect to the value of those goods, provided that the goods were delivered within 15 days preceding the bankruptcy and their claims are filed within 30 days after.

Secured creditors retain their priority position, having a prior claim to at least the value of the property used as security. Most creditors are prevented from taking any further independent action once the assignment or bankruptcy order has been made. (Note that this stay does not apply to criminal prosecutions or matrimonial disputes, which can continue.) A secured creditor, on the other hand, retains a right to take possession of, or otherwise proceed against, the property used as security, without waiting, unless the court orders otherwise. A secured creditor can choose to file a proof of claim for all of what she is owed, giving up any claim for the secured property. She will then be treated as an unsecured creditor for the entire amount. This tactic may be attractive when there is little value in the property, when the property is of such a nature that it would be difficult to sell, or when there are considerable resources in the estate. Otherwise, a secured creditor can, on the basis of a filed proof of claim, take possession of the secured property and sell it. She then becomes an unsecured creditor against the estate for any shortfall. If there is sufficient value in the property, the Trustee may simply pay the secured creditor's claim, retaining that property for the benefit of the other creditors. The Trustee can also serve notice on the secured creditor, requiring her to place a value on the property and deal with it on the basis of that value or, if the Trustee is dissatisfied with the value provided, require the creditor to sell the property.

After the secured creditors have received what they are entitled to, the Trustee distributes the remaining assets, or the proceeds from the sales of those assets, to the other creditors. Preferred creditors are paid first, pursuant to section 136 of the *BIA*. This section indicates that the following are to be paid, in this order: funeral expenses, costs associated with the bankruptcy process, claims for arrears in wages for a limited amount and time period, arrears in maintenance or alimony, municipal taxes, arrears in rent for a limited period, some direct costs incurred by creditors in the execution process, amounts owed for workers' compensation, employment insurance, and income tax that should have been deducted from salaries, and other claims of the Crown. Unsecured creditors, usually suppliers of goods and services, are paid only after all of these obligations have been satisfied. The unsecured creditors will receive a share on a pro rata basis (a share of the remaining estate determined by the percentage of overall claims their particular claim represents).

Government sometimes has priority over secured creditors

The federal government has passed legislation that gives it priority over all other creditors, including secured creditors, in certain situations. Examples include section 224 of the *Income Tax Act*[31] and section 317 of the *Excise Tax Act*.[32] These sections essentially create a trust, in situations where there are unremitted source deductions or GST. This gives the government a "super priority." When a Requirement to Pay (the equivalent of a Garnishee Summons) is served by the government on debtors of the tax debtor, any amount that is owed, and which would normally be paid to the tax debtor, becomes the property of the government. It never becomes the property of the tax debtor and is therefore not available to its creditors. The courts have held that this gives the government priority over secured creditors of the tax debtor in the case of a bankruptcy of the tax debtor.[33]

Offences

As discussed above, debtors often attempt to keep their property out of the hands of creditors by transferring it to friends or relatives. Debtors also sometimes try to pay one creditor and not others. **Fraudulent transfers** and *preferences* often take place in bankruptcy situations. The Trustee in Bankruptcy can reverse such transactions.

CASE SUMMARY 16.10

Transferring House to Wife Prohibited: *Re Fancy*[34]

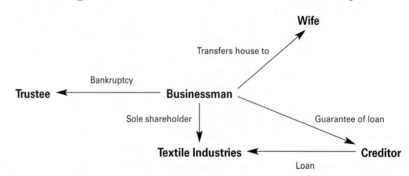

A successful businessman guaranteed the debts of his corporation, Textile Industries, making him personally responsible if it ran into financial difficulties. An action against the corporation resulted in a judgment, causing the corporation to fail and forcing him into bankruptcy. Shortly before his bankruptcy, he transferred his interest in the matrimonial home to his wife. At the time of the transfer, it was clear that the litigation would go to trial and that he was facing substantial losses.

The Court reversed the transfer, determining that the transfer of the house to the wife amounted to a prohibited settlement under the provisions of the *BIA*. A settlement

---

31. R.S.C. 1985, c. 1 (5th Supp.).

32. R.S.C. 1985, c. E-15.

33. See, for example, *Bank of Montreal v. Canada (Attorney General)* (2003), 66 O.R. (3d) 161 (C.A.).

34. (1984), 46 O.R. (2d) 153 (H.C.J.).

can occur when a person transfers property to another to preserve some benefit for himself, which is exactly what was done in this case.

SMALL BUSINESS PERSPECTIVE

Would the result have been the same if the businessman had transferred his interest in the home to his wife before he incorporated his business?

Settlements involve the transfer of assets for nominal or no consideration. A settlement is void if it took place within one year of bankruptcy. This period can be extended to up to five years, if it can be proven that, at the time of the settlement, the bankrupt knew that he was insolvent.

Settlements prohibited

A payment made in preference to one creditor over the others is also void. The Trustee can force the return of those funds so that they can be fairly distributed to all of the creditors. This is the situation in the *Speedy Roofing* case discussed in Case Summary 16.11. There is a presumption that a payment was made to create a preference if it was made within three months of the bankruptcy. Such payments can be challenged even if they were made earlier than that, if it can be shown that the debtor was attempting to avoid other creditors.

Fraudulent preferences prohibited

CASE SUMMARY 16.11

Preferring One Creditor Prohibited: *Re Speedy Roofing Ltd.*[35]

Roofmart supplied materials to Speedy Roofing. As Speedy Roofing was not paying its account, mortgages were given to Roofmart as security for the debt. The mortgages were on the homes of Pompeo and Gaggi, the wives of the principal shareholders of Speedy Roofing. Shortly before the Royal Bank, another creditor, forced it into bankruptcy, Speedy Roofing paid Roofmart $80 000 to discharge the mortgages. The Court

---

[35.] (1987), 62 O.R. (2d) 312 (H.C.J.), aff'd (1990), 74 O.R. (2d) 633 (C.A.).

had to determine whether that payment was a fraudulent preference and therefore prohibited under the *BIA*. Since the payment was made within three months of the bankruptcy, it amounted to a fraudulent preference. The Court ordered Roofmart to repay the $80 000 it received from Speedy Roofing to the Trustee in Bankruptcy.

SMALL BUSINESS PERSPECTIVE

A debtor cannot choose to pay one creditor over another, or transfer property to a creditor, to escape a debt. Do you agree with this policy? Should the debtor be able to choose which creditors will be paid and which will not be paid? If a debtor chooses to pay money owed to one creditor, should the other creditors be able to complain even if a legitimate debt has been properly paid?

Bankrupt has many duties, including swearing affidavit about financial information

At the beginning of the bankruptcy process, the debtor is required to file an affidavit setting out all of his debt, creditors, and assets. He must provide a summary of all of the transactions that have taken place regarding these assets over the last year (or longer if so ordered). He must disclose any settlements he has made during the previous five years. A bankrupt also has an obligation to cooperate with the Trustee by disclosing all relevant information and answering any relevant questions. The bankrupt can also be required to attend before the Official Receiver, or the court, to answer questions about how he got into financial trouble, as well as questions regarding his debts, creditors, and assets, and what he has done with them. The bankrupt has many other duties, including transferring his assets to the Trustee, delivering his credit cards, records, and documents to the Trustee, and keeping the Trustee advised of his address. The bankrupt must "generally do all such acts and things in relation to his property and the distribution of the proceeds among his creditors as may be reasonably required by the trustee, or may be prescribed by the General Rules, or may be directed by the court. ..."[36]

In addition to settlements, fraudulent preferences, and a failure to fulfill the duties of a bankrupt, the *BIA* sets out several other bankruptcy offences for which a bankrupt may be punished, including refusing to answer questions truthfully, hiding, falsifying or destroying records, failing to keep proper records, and hiding or concealing property. If a bankrupt is convicted of a bankruptcy offence, he may be fined up to $10 000 and/or be imprisoned for up to three years.[37]

Once the assets have been transferred to a Trustee by voluntary assignment, or through a bankruptcy order, the debtor is a bankrupt. A bankrupt is subject to several restrictions. If he is involved in any business transaction, or borrows more than $500, he must disclose his status. He cannot be a director of a corporation.[38] He may also be restricted from carrying on some professions, such as accounting, depending on the particular rules of the professional body in question.[39]

[35.] *Bankruptcy and Insolvency Act, supra* note 30, s. 158 (o).

[36.] *Ibid.*, s. 198.

[37.] See, for example, *Canada Business Corporations Act*, R.S.C. 1985, c. C-44, s. 105.

[38.] See, for example, Rule 601.1 of the "Rules of Professional Conduct" of the Institute of Chartered Accountants of Alberta, www.albertacas.ca/Libraries/Rules/Rules_of_Professional_Conduct_2006-newlogo-pol.pdf.

[39.] *McAfee v. Westmore* (1988), 49 D.L.R. (4th) 401 (B.C.C.A.).

Once the bankruptcy process is completed and the estate has been distributed, the bankrupt may apply to the court to be discharged. This application is automatic, after nine months, for an individual involved in his first bankruptcy, unless a creditor or the Trustee opposes the discharge. If someone opposes a first-time bankruptcy, or if the bankrupt has been bankrupt before, the matter will be heard by a court. An application for a discharge from bankruptcy may be granted unconditionally, it may be granted subject to certain conditions, or it may be denied.

A lawyer became bankrupt when a business in which he was involved failed. He maintained a very high lifestyle while going through the bankruptcy process. He was looking forward to a reasonable income after his discharge, as well. He had not made any payments to the Trustee. Given these circumstances, the Court ordered that his discharge be conditional on him paying a significant amount to his creditors.[40] A court has the discretion to place such conditions on the discharge of a bankrupt.

On the other hand, the same Court dealt with another lawyer in a different manner. He was 53 years old when he ran into financial difficulties. He did all he could to repay his creditors, including significantly reducing his lifestyle. It was only after his honest efforts failed, through no fault of his own, that he was forced to make an assignment in bankruptcy. In this case, the Court had no hesitation in finding that the bankrupt was entitled to an unconditional discharge and a fresh start, even though his assets were not sufficient to pay back 50 cents on the dollar. In reaching this conclusion, the Court considered the bankrupt's honesty, his struggle for nine years to pay back his creditors, and his need to be free to prepare for his retirement.[41]

But discharge may be unconditional, depending on circumstances

These two cases illustrate the power of the bankruptcy court to place significant conditions on a discharge and the factors that might affect such a decision. Debtors who commit bankruptcy offences will normally not be unconditionally discharged; they may even be imprisoned. The court will also be reluctant to unconditionally discharge bankrupts who have not fulfilled their duties or whose behaviour has not been reasonable. As shown by the *McAfee* case, in such cases the court can grant a conditional discharge, putting conditions or restrictions on the bankrupt. Justice Estey commented on the purpose of the bankruptcy process as follows: "The purpose and object of the *Bankruptcy Act* [now the *BIA*] is to equitably distribute the assets of the debtor and to permit his rehabilitation as a citizen, unfettered by past debts. The discharge, however, is not a matter of right, and the provisions of Sections 142 and 143 [now ss. 172 and 173 of the *BIA*] plainly indicate that in certain cases the debtor should suffer a period of probation."[42]

Unconditional discharge not granted if bankruptcy offence committed

---

[40] Re Irwin (1994), 112 D.L.R. (4th) 164 (B.C.C.A.).

[41] *Industrial Acceptance Corp. v. Lalonde*, [1952] 2 S.C.R. 109, at 120.

[42] *Bankruptcy and Insolvency Act, supra* note 30, s. 178. This was changed from 10 years on 7 July 2008, when some of the provisions of the recent amendments to the *BIA* came into force. Also, the period before which an application may be made to request a discharge on the basis of hardship was reduced from 10 years to 5 years.

REDUCING RISK 16.6

Debtors sometimes use bankruptcy as a convenient way to avoid paying their debts. Some even declare bankruptcy several times. While this is obviously an abuse of the process,, merchants and other creditors must be ever-vigilant to avoid doing business with such people. Use of credit checks can be a great help, even when goods or services are being supplied. On the other hand, debtors who are tempted to abuse the process should realize that, as a rule, committing a bankruptcy offence will likely result in fines and/or imprisonment. Furthermore, the courts will generally not grant an unconditional discharge when faced with abuses such as the debtor failing to cooperate with officials, trying to hide assets, or otherwise abusing the process.

After Discharge

Effect of absolute discharge is to end most debts

During the bankruptcy process, the bankrupt is required to continue to make regular payments (surplus income payments) to the Trustee to be distributed to the creditors. Any windfall she receives, such as an inheritance or a lottery win, will go to the Trustee for distribution. That all changes upon discharge from bankruptcy (assuming that the discharge is unconditional). When discharged, the debtor is freed from most previous claims by creditors and is in a position to start over. Any assets subsequently obtained by the discharged bankrupt are hers to do with as she wishes. Unpaid creditors cannot claim against them. Pursuant to the *BIA,* some obligations do survive discharge, such as fines, alimony and maintenance payments, and some civil damage awards. Student loans also survive bankruptcy. They are payable for up to seven years after the debtor ceases to be a student.[43]

Corporations not discharged after bankruptcy

Corporations may use proposals and arrangements to avoid bankruptcy

The discussion above focused primarily on the bankruptcy of an individual. The primary difference with a bankruptcy of a corporation is that there will not be a discharge after the bankruptcy unless the corporation has been able to repay all of the money owing. That, of course, is highly unlikely, there being very little likelihood of a bankruptcy in the first place in those circumstances. A Division II consumer proposal under the *BIA* is not available to a corporation, but corporations often try to restructure using Division I commercial proposals. Larger corporations also often restructure using the *CCAA.* If a corporation's proposal is approved, or if it reaches an arrangement with its creditors, and it properly fulfills its obligations, the corporation will be free to carry on its business, avoiding bankruptcy altogether. The obligations of the debtor to supply appropriate information and documents apply to corporations as well. A corporation must provide someone who is familiar with the situation to answer the questions that would otherwise have been put to an individual debtor by the Trustee, the creditors in a creditor meeting, the Official Receiver or the court.

Directors of corporations owe creditors a duty of care

Receivers may be appointed by creditors pursuant to security agreement

A corporation will often face dissolution after the bankruptcy process, although this is usually not worth the trouble. Still, disgruntled shareholders and creditors may have further rights under winding-up acts, or the various business corporations' legislation in place at both the provincial and federal levels. They also may have claims against the directors and other officers of the corporation under those statutes. In this regard, the Supreme Court of Canada recently held that, in certain circumstances, directors owe a duty of care to creditors of the corporation, but that the duty does not give rise to a fiduciary duty. The directors owe a fiduciary duty to the corporation only.[44]

---

43. *Peoples Department Stores Inc. (Trustee of) v. Wise,* [2004] 3 S.C.R. 461.

44. See, for example, *Royal Bank of Canada v. W. Got and Associates Electric Ltd.,* [1999] 3 S.C.R. 408.

Corporations that go into receivership are usually not involved in bankruptcy at all. When a creditor lends a corporation significant funds, the security agreement usually gives the creditor the right, in the event of default or some other triggering event, to appoint a receiver to take possession of the assets given as security, without the necessity of going through the bankruptcy procedure. Such an assignment of assets to a receiver is not a bankruptcy, but the effect can be every bit as devastating to the business. Some of the rights and responsibilities of receivers are set out in Part XI of the *BIA*. A secured creditor must give the debtor reasonable notice before the appointment of a receiver, or taking possession of the goods used as security. Whether the receiver is appointed by the creditor directly, or it obtains a court order allowing the appointment, failure to give reasonable notice can be devastating to the debtor. This will result in significant liability to the creditor when it is improperly done.[45]

It must be remembered that there are two main purposes of the *BIA* and the other legislation discussed in this section. The first is to ensure that the creditors realize as much of the amount owed as possible. The second is to facilitate the rehabilitation of the debtor. We will continue to see legislative changes as the debate over the proper balance of these two objectives continues.

SUMMARY

Methods of securing debt—personal property

- Real and personal property may be used as security, giving creditor some assurance that she will be paid even when other creditors are not
- In a conditional sale, the debtor has possession of the goods, while the seller retains title until final payment is made
- In a chattel mortgage, the debtor has possession of the goods but gives title to the creditor until final payment is made
- Assignment of book accounts gives creditor right to intercept payments upon default

Personal Property Security Act

- *PPSA* allows both tangible and intangible forms of personal property to be used as security
- The security must first attach to the collateral, but priority is established through perfection, either by registration or by taking possession of the collateral
- Priority is usually determined by date of registration, but PMSIs and sales in normal course of business are exceptions
- In the event of default, the creditor can take possession of the goods and sell them. Creditor can usually sue for deficiency, but sometimes must make election to take possession or sue
- Debtor has the right to be notified of sale and to redeem the property

Guarantees

- A guarantee is a contingent liability in which someone agrees to be responsible when a debtor fails to pay; an indemnity involves co-responsibility for the debt
- Creditor must protect interests of guarantor, but this protection can be limited by the terms of the guarantee
- If a guarantor is required to pay the creditor, he steps into the shoes of the creditor and can seek repayment from the debtor
- The guarantor usually has the same defences as the debtor

Other forms of security

- *Bank Act* security enables growing crops and goods being manufactured to be used as security
- Floating charges used by creditors of corporations allow inventory to be free of floating charge until it crystallizes
- Builders' liens protect contractors and subcontractors by enabling them to file a lien against the land and by forcing the owner to hold back a portion of what is paid
- Certified cheques, bank drafts, bills of exchange, and promissory notes are often used in credit transactions
- Letters of credit are used to secure credit in international trade

Related laws

- Bulk sales acts protect unsecured creditors from sale of all assets of business
- Fraudulent transfers and preferences are void

Bankruptcy—introduction

- Two main objectives of bankruptcy legislation are to protect creditors and to enable rehabilitation of the bankrupt

The process of bankruptcy

- Bankruptcy can take place voluntarily through assignment, or involuntarily through a bankruptcy order
- Involves the transfer of the debtor's non-exempt assets to a Trustee in Bankruptcy, who sells the assets and distributes the proceeds to the creditors

Alternatives to bankruptcy

- Debtors should try to avoid bankruptcy through informal negotiations
- Division I proposal is used to protect commercial debtors and individuals with significant debts from action by creditors, until the proposal is accepted or rejected
- Division II proposal is used to protect consumers with debts less than $75 000
- The Orderly Payment of Debts program gives individuals protection so they can avoid bankruptcy, if they pay off their debts within three years
- Large corporations can ask courts for protection from creditors under the *Companies' Creditors Arrangements Act*

Priority among creditors in bankruptcy

- Creditors must file proof of claim with Trustee
- Assets go first to secured creditors, then to preferred creditors, and then to unsecured creditors
- Suppliers of goods can reclaim them if make demand within time limits

Bankruptcy offences

- Fraudulent transfers and preferences may be reversed by Trustee
- Bankrupt has many duties; if she fails to fulfill them or commits another bankruptcy offence, she can be fined and/or imprisoned
- Once process is complete, bankrupt can apply for discharge; discharge is automatic for first-time bankrupt unless an objection is made
- Discharge may be granted unconditionally, subject to conditions, or denied

After discharge from bankruptcy

- Absolute discharge relieves responsibility for most prior debts
- A corporation will not survive bankruptcy, but it can make a *BIA* Division II proposal, or a *CCAA* arrangement
- Receivership involves a receiver taking possession of the secured assets

---

QUESTIONS

1. Distinguish between the following:

   a. Real property and personal property

   b. Choses in action and chattels

   c. A chattel mortgage and a conditional sale

   d. A chattel mortgage and a mortgage on real estate

2. What kinds of property can be used as collateral under the *PPSA*?

3. What are the advantages of using a personal property security act to govern all transactions involving the use of personal property as security?

4. What significant problem associated with the practice of taking goods as security is alleviated by the registration requirements introduced by legislation? Describe the resulting obligations on all parties.

5. Distinguish among security agreement, attachment, and perfection. Explain the significance of each of them and how each is accomplished.

6. How is the priority of secured parties determined? What are two exceptions to this general approach?

7. What are the rights of a secured party when there is a default by the debtor? What determines the limitations of those rights?

8. What obligations are imposed on a secured creditor who takes possession of goods used as security, after a debtor defaults?

9. Explain the rights of a debtor after she has defaulted and the secured party has taken possession of the collateral.

10. "The debtor is always liable to the creditor for any deficiency after the goods used as security have been sold." True or false? Explain your answer.

11. What is the difference between a guarantee and an indemnity? Why is the distinction important?

12. What duties does the creditor owe the guarantor before and after the guarantee is given?

13. If the debtor defaults, what steps does the creditor have to take before she is entitled to demand payment from the guarantor? If the guarantor pays the creditor, what rights does she have against the debtor?

14. What is the main advantage of the provisions of the *Bank Act* that allow the banks to take security for the loans they grant? Why may these provisions cause confusion?

15. What happens upon default when a floating charge has been used to secure a debt? What is the main advantage of using floating charges?

16. What significant difficulty facing suppliers of goods and services in the construction industry is overcome by the creation of the builders' lien? How can suppliers protect themselves? Explain the role of the holdback.

17. Who is "a holder in due course"? Why should buyers be careful when writing a cheque or signing a promissory note when entering into a business transaction? Does this concern apply to consumer transactions?

18. Explain the nature and use of a letter of credit. Distinguish between a standby letter of credit and a normal letter of credit.

19. How does the *Bulk Sales Act* protect creditors when a business is selling all, or almost all, of its assets?

20. Explain the difference between a fraudulent transfer and a fraudulent preference. What is the legal effect of both of these types of transactions?

21. Define the objectives of bankruptcy legislation.

22. Distinguish between bankruptcy and insolvency.

23. Distinguish between an assignment in bankruptcy and a bankruptcy order. Explain the process involved in each case.

24. Explain the role of the Trustee in the bankruptcy process.

25. Discuss the informal options that are available to debtors who are experiencing financial difficulties.

26. Distinguish between Division I and Division II proposals. Explain the advantages of making a proposal.

27. "A consolidation order under the Orderly Payment of Debts program requires the debtor to pay her debts in full." True or false? Explain your answer.

28. What legislation is used by large corporations to obtain bankruptcy protection? What is the main advantage of using this legislation?

29. Who files a proof of claim? What is its purpose? Who evaluates the validity of a filed proof of claim?

30. Describe the order of distribution of the assets, and the proceeds from the sale of assets of the bankrupt. How does a "super priority" affect the order of distribution?

31. How are fraudulent transfers and fraudulent preferences dealt with by the *BIA*?

32. What are the duties of a debtor in the bankruptcy process?

33. Explain what is meant by a bankruptcy offence and the possible consequences of committing one.

34. What restrictions are bankrupts subject to?

35. "An application for discharge by a first-time bankrupt will automatically be granted." True or false? Explain your answer.

36. What factors will a court consider when determining what conditions, if any, to place on a discharge from bankruptcy?

37. What changes for a bankrupt after an absolute discharge?

38. Why is it unlikely that there will not be a discharge after the bankruptcy of a corporation?

39. What can a corporation in financial difficulty do to avoid bankruptcy?

40. When could a creditor who has appointed a receiver to take possession of a debtor's assets face liability for making the appointment?

CASES AND DISCUSSION QUESTIONS

1. *Ontario Wilderness Outposts Inc. v. Nishnawbe Aski Development Fund*, [2006] O.J. No. 892 (Sup. Ct. J.).

The operator of two tourist operations built four cabins on Crown land, pursuant to Land Use Permits issued by the government. NADF lent the operator funds, taking the cabins as security. The security agreement was properly registered under the *PPSA*. The operator defaulted and NADF wanted to take possession of the cabins. The *PPSA* applied to security interests in personal property, but not to security interests in real property.

Were the cabins subject to a security interest in favour of NADF? What if the evidence showed that the cabins were not affixed to the land and could be moved with little or no damage? If the cabins were affixed to the land, would it have been possible for NADF to take them as security for the loan? How?

2. *Harder (Trustee of) v. Alberta (Treasury Branches)* (2004), 356 A.R. 320 (Q.B.).

Harder borrowed funds from the Treasury Branches (ATB) to purchase a trailer. ATB registered the security agreement pursuant to the *PPSA*, but there was a mistake in the serial number of the trailer in the registration. Harder made an assignment in bankruptcy. The Trustee in Bankruptcy did a serial number search, which did not reveal the security interest of ATB. The Trustee also did a debtor search for Harder, which did reveal the security interest. The Trustee disallowed the claim of ATB as a secured creditor on the grounds that its registration did not create a valid security interest.

Should the Court allow ATB's claim, on the basis that the Trustee had knowledge of the security interest and the mistake in registration was therefore not seriously misleading? Should an incorrect serial number in a registration of a security interest invalidate the registration when the inclusion of a serial number is required by the legislation? What is the law in your province?

3. *Transamerica Commercial Finance Corp. Canada v. Northgate RV Sales Ltd.* (2006), 31 C.B.R. (5th) 144 (B.C.S.C.).

T provided inventory financing to M. U. Ltd., which sold recreational vehicles. Mr. and Mrs. M were directors, officers and shareholders of M. U. Under a Dealer Finance Agreement, M. U. needed T's approval before buying goods from a supplier. T would pay the supplier, take security over the goods and sell them to M. U. Mr. and Mrs. M both signed personal guarantees of the indebtedness of M. U. to T. T then consented to an assignment of M. U.'s inventory and indebtedness to Northgate. M. U. was to remain liable to T for the indebtedness. Mr. M was a director and President of Northgate. Mrs. M was neither an officer nor a director of Northgate. Three years later, T made a demand on Northgate. It also demanded payment from M. U., and Mr. and Mrs. M, pursuant to their guarantees. The amount outstanding was $283 062.62.

The Court granted judgment against Northgate, M. U., and Mr. M. Should Mrs. M be liable to pay the indebtedness pursuant to her guarantee? What could T have done to ensure that she would have been liable?

4. *430872 B.C. Ltd. v. New Home Warranty of British Columbia (Trustee of)*, [2004] B.C.J. No. 612 (C.A.).

NHW provided warranties to builders of new homes. 430872 registered for the warranty. Its bank issued a letter of credit to NHW, which later went into bankruptcy. The creditors of NHW wanted to draw on the letter of credit, as the bank was obligated to pay upon demand. 430872 argued that the letter of credit should be returned to it, as it had not breached the terms of its contract with NHW.

Should the creditors be allowed to draw on the letter of credit? What if the Court found that the letter of credit was a standby letter of credit?

5. *Keith G. Collins Ltd., as Trustee of the Estate of Coderre, a Bankrupt v. MBNA Canada Bank,*(2006), 209 Man. R. (2d) 154 (Q.B.).

C's sole proprietorship ran into financial problems. He approached RBC to obtain a loan, secured by a mortgage on his home, to consolidate his debts. RBC approved the financing on condition that the debts to MBNA and CT Bank be paid from the loan proceeds. The consolidation reduced C's monthly payments and the interest rate he would pay. When C applied for the consolidation loan, he was expecting a GST refund of $10 000. After the loan was approved, he was advised that instead of being entitled to a refund, he owed an additional $2500. He then made an assignment in bankruptcy. The Trustee in Bankruptcy claimed that the payments to MBNA and CT Bank were fraudulent preferences, as the payments preferred them over the other creditors, and that the money therefore had to be paid to the Trustee.

Should MBNA and CT Bank be ordered to pay the money to the Trustee? What if they can prove that C's intention in making the payments to them was not to give them a preference over other creditors, but to avoid bankruptcy and remain in business?

6. *Bank of Montreal v. Canada (Attorney General)* (2003), 66 O.R. (3d) 161 (C.A.).

The Bank was a secured creditor of the debtor, Vita Pharm. Canada Customs sent a notice to pay GST to the debtors of Vita Pharm. On 22 February 2001, the Bank applied for a bankruptcy order against Vita Pharm. On 23 February, Canada Customs sent another notice to pay GST to the debtors. On 8 March, Vita Pharm was declared bankrupt.

Should the notices to pay issued by Canada Customs take priority over the Bank's secured claim? In light of the "super priority" of the government in certain situations, what will lenders do to ensure that they will be repaid? What effect will this have on the availability of credit, especially to small business?

7. *Re Walterhouse (Bankrupt)* (2002), 318 A.R. 394 (Q.B.).

W made an assignment in bankruptcy in 1996, and received an absolute discharge in 1997. In 2000, he filed a consumer proposal, but he defaulted on it and it was cancelled. While under the protection of the proposal, he obtained $600 credit. He filed a second assignment in 2001. When he was examined by the Official Receiver, he said that he went into bankruptcy because credit was too easy to get. The Official Receiver opposed W's application for discharge, for several reasons. Registrar Funduk (the Registrar) ordered W to pay an income tax refund to the estate. If he did so, then he would be discharged, but not for 25 years! W appealed.

The Court reviewed several cases in which the Registrar imposed lengthy suspensions on bankrupts who had been absolutely discharged on a previous bankruptcy less than ten years before. In each of these cases, the Registrar imposed a lengthy suspension of the discharge, making statements such as "Recidivist bankrupts are not rehabilitated with a figurative slap on the wrist with a wet noodle." The Court held that a suspension of 25 years is "very much too long." It noted that a long suspension is really a refusal of a discharge, and that if the circumstances justify refusal, then the discharge should be refused. The Court therefore ordered W to make certain cash payments and the discharge would then be suspended for five years, which the Court suggested was the maximum period of time a discharge should be suspended.

Do you believe that the bankruptcy legislation is too lenient on debtors, and that the Registrar's approach is appropriate? Is the Court's guideline of a maximum five-year suspension of a discharge reasonable? Should the *BIA* be amended, by placing more restrictions on defaulting debtors, and by assessing them stiffer penalties?

8. *Re Coates,* [2006] A.J. No. 300 (Q.B.).

The Alberta government paid Albertans a non-taxable, one-time bonus, the Alberta 2005 Resource Rebate. The government amended the *Alberta Personal Income Tax Act* to state that Albertans had overpaid their income taxes, that the Rebate was not subject to garnishment or attachment, and that the Rebate was exempt from execution or seizure. C went into bankruptcy. The Trustee asked the Court if the Rebate owed to C was exempt, or whether it formed part of her estate and was therefore available to C's creditors.

Is the Rebate "income" under the *BIA*? Is it exempt? Are other "windfalls" exempt from distribution under the *BIA*?

9. *Re Insley* (2007), 308 Sask. R. 136 (Q.B.).

Insley attended medical school for four years. Her education was financed almost entirely by government student loans of $55 244, and a RBC line of credit of $193 475. Upon graduation, she enrolled in a two-year residency program, for which she was paid a net monthly income of $3465. After finishing her residency and passing the required exams, she hoped to work as a doctor at an estimated annual gross salary of $200 000.

Insley admitted that the line of credit was used to finance her education, that she overspent, and that she could have spent her loans more appropriately. For example, she purchased a Mercedes Benz automobile, went on vacations, and purchased an expensive dog just one month before making an assignment in bankruptcy. When she applied for a discharge from bankruptcy, the RBC requested a conditional discharge, requiring her to repay the full amount owed to it. Insley's assets were $23 500, while the unsecured claims against her were $258 224.

Should Insley, as a first time bankrupt, be granted an absolute discharge? If not, what conditions should be imposed on her? Why didn't the government, which had granted her the student loan, oppose her application for discharge from bankruptcy?

PEARSON
mybuslawlab™

Be sure to visit the MyBusLawLab that accompanies this book at **www.pearsoned.ca/mybuslawlab.** You will find practice tests, a personalized study plan, province-specific material, and much more!

Glossary

A

ab initio from the beginning; an agreement is void *ab initio* if it has at no time been legally valid

abatement a court order to reduce the rent to be paid to compensate for breach of lease by landlord

absolute privilege exemption from liability for defamatory statements made in some settings (such as legislatures and courts), without reference to the speaker's motives or the truth or falsity of the statement

abuse of power action by a tribunal beyond the jurisdiction set out in the legislation governing it, or making an unreasonable decision

acceleration clause a contractual term that comes into effect when there is a failure to make an instalment payment and which requires that the entire debt plus expenses be paid

acceptance agreement by one party to the terms of the offer made by another

accord agreement by both parties on some change in the contract

accord and satisfaction agreement to end a contract, with extra consideration to be supplied by the party benefiting from the discharge

accounting court-ordered determination of the injuries suffered; agent must pay over money or property collected on behalf of principal; court order that any profits made from wrongdoing be paid over to victim

accounts receivable funds owed to a business for goods or services provided to customers

actual authority authority given to agent expressly or by implication

adjusters employees or representatives of the insurance corporation charged with investigating and settling insurance claims against the corporation after the insured-against event takes place

administrative law the rules and regulations governing the function and powers of executive branch

administrative tribunals government decision makers (committees, commissions, tribunals, or individuals) who act with quasi-judicial powers

adverse possession a right to actual possession, which can be acquired by non-contested use of the land

affidavit a written statement made by a witness out of court, but under oath

affirmative action programs intended to correct racial, gender, or other imbalances in the workplace

agency the service an agent performs on behalf of a principal

agency agreement an agreement creating an agency relationship between principal and agent

agency by necessity consent to act as an agent, which is implied when there is an urgent reason

agency shop *see* **Rand formula**

agent person representing and acting on behalf of a principal in dealings with third parties

agreement for sale an agreement where title will be transferred at some time in the future, typically once the property is fully paid for; an agreement that grants possession of property to the purchaser pending full payment of the price

agreement of purchase and sale first stage in the purchase of real property; also referred to as an interim agreement between vendor and purchaser

agreement to sell an agreement that title will be transferred at some time in the future

annual general meeting a meeting where shareholders elect directors and vote on other important resolutions

anticipatory breach repudiation of contract before performance is due

Anton Piller order court order to seize offending material before trial

apparent authority authority as suggested to third party by conduct of principal; may exist even when there is no actual authority

appeal a formal process whereby a higher court will reexamine a decision made by a lower court

appearance document filed by the defendant indicating that the action will be disputed

arbitration submission of parties in a dispute to having an arbitrator make a binding decision on their claims

arbitrator a panel or other third party that has been given the authority to make a binding decision on a dispute between parties

articles of association internal regulations setting out the procedures for governing a corporation in a registration jurisdiction

articles of incorporation a method of incorporating based on a U.S. approach

and used in some jurisdictions in Canada

assault a verbal or physical threat; an action that makes a person fear physical interference

assignment the transfer of rights under a contract to another party

assignment in bankruptcy the voluntary transfer of a debtor's assets to a Trustee in Bankruptcy so that they can be administered for the benefit of the creditors

attachment under the *PPSA*, the situation in which value has been given pursuant to the contract, giving the creditor a claim against the assets used as security if there is a default by the debtor

attachment of debt court order that monies owed to the judgment debtor (defendant) be intercepted and paid to the judgment creditor (plaintiff)

auditor party responsible for ensuring that financial statements for an organization are properly done

authority the right or power to act or to make a decision

B

bailee person acquiring possession of personal property in a bailment

bailment temporary possession by one person of chattels owned by another

bailment for value bailment involving a mutual benefit or consideration flowing between the parties

bailor the owner giving up possession of property in a bailment

balance of convenience determination of who will suffer the greatest injury if the damage were allowed to continue

bankrupt a person who has made an assignment in bankruptcy or been forced into bankruptcy through a court order obtained by a creditor, and who has not been discharged from bankruptcy

bankruptcy process by which an insolvent person voluntarily or involuntarily transfers assets to a trustee for distribution to creditors

bankruptcy order a statutory assignment of a debtor's assets to a Trustee in Bankruptcy

bargaining agent a body certified to act on behalf of a group of employees or employers

bargaining unit group of employees who have been certified

battery unwelcome physical contact; non-consensual physical interference with one's body

bias prejudice against or partiality towards one party, for example, based on a decision maker's personal interest in the decision

bilateral contract a contract in which there is an exchange of promises: both parties assume an obligation

bilateral discharge agreement by both sides to terminate the contract or to disregard a term of the contract

bill the form in which legislation is introduced into Parliament or legislature

bill of exchange a negotiable instrument by which the drawer directs the drawee to pay out money to the payee; drawee need not be a bank, and the instrument may be made payable in the future

bill of lading a receipt for goods in the care of the shipper, accompanied by an undertaking to move the goods or deliver identical goods to a designated place

bill of sale a written agreement which conveys title from seller to buyer

bona fide purchaser for value innocent third party who has paid a fair price for goods under claim by creditor

bond a share interest in the indebtedness of a corporation; often used synonymously with debenture, though a bond is normally secured against specific assets, while a debenture is likely not

book accounts accounts receivable that can be used as security for a loan

breach of contract failure to live up to conditions of a contract

breach of trust misuse of property held in trust for another by a trustee

broadly held corporations corporations that are publicly traded on the stock market; also called distributing corporations in some jurisdictions

brokers agents retained by the insured to ascertain their insurance needs and secure the necessary coverage

builder's risk policy insurance against liability and other forms of loss taking place during the construction process

building scheme set of restrictions placed on all the properties in a large development

business interruption insurance a form of insurance that compensates the insured for continuing expenses incurred while the business is not earning income

"but for" test a test for causation used in negligence actions to determine whether the injury would have occurred had it not been for the act of the defendant

C

Canadian Charter of Rights and Freedoms a document entrenched in the Canadian Constitution in 1982 listing and guaranteeing fundamental rights and freedoms

canon or church law legal system of the Catholic Church, from which common law drew principles relating to families and estates

capacity the freedom to enter into a contract, which is sometimes limited by law, as is the case, for example, with minors, the insane, the intoxicated, aliens, bankrupts, and Indians.

causation determining whether the act actually caused the injury

caveat emptor "let the buyer beware"; principle that purchaser must examine, judge, and test for herself

certificate of title conclusive evidence as to the ownership of a property

certified cheque means of transferring funds by cheque where payment is, in effect, guaranteed by the bank

certiorari a court order overturning a decision and making it null and void

applications interim applications and questions that are brought before a judge (before the actual trial) for a ruling

champerty an agreement to allow a third party to share in the proceeds of a litigated claim; a sale of the right to sue. Generally, champerty is discouraged

chattel mortgage a loan for which a creditor provides credit to the debtor, securing the loan by taking title of a good such as a car

chattels tangible, movable personal property that can be measured and weighed; also known as goods

check-off provision provision in collective agreement whereby employees agree to have employer deduct union dues from payroll

cheque a negotiable instrument consisting of a bill of exchange drawn on a bank, payable on demand

chose in action the thing or benefit that is transferred in an assignment; intangible personal property, such as a claim or the right to sue

C.I.F. contracts (cost, insurance, and freight) sales contracts in which one of the parties has been designated as being responsible for paying the costs involved in the shipping of those goods as well as arranging insurance

circumstantial evidence facts or evidence that lead one to infer the existence of other facts

civil law legal system the legal system used in most of Europe based on a central code, which is a list of rules stated as broad principles of law that judges apply to the cases that come before them

civil litigation the process of one party's suing another in a private action, conducted in a trial court

clean hands absence of wrongdoing on the part of a person seeking an equitable remedy

closed shop workplace where only workers who are already members of the union can be hired

closely held corporations corporations in which there are relatively few shareholders; referred to as "non-distributing corporations" in some jurisdictions

C.O.D. contracts (cash on delivery) sales contracts in which the seller maintains the proprietary rights or title as well as control over the possession of those goods until they are delivered to the buyer's premises and paid for

code of conduct a formal statement that sets out the values and standards of business practices of an organization

co-insurance clauses requirements that the insured bear some risk

collateral goods or property used to secure a debt

collateral contract a separate contractual obligation that can stand alone, independent of the written contract

common law legal system the legal system developed in England based on judges applying the customs and traditions of the people and then following each other's decisions

common law courts the three historical English courts (Court of Common Pleas, the Court of King's Bench, and the Exchequer Court), where in theory law was discovered in the customs and traditions of the people

common shares shares to which no preferential rights or privileges attach

comprehensive policy property insurance covering all losses not specifically excluded

conciliator a neutral third party who facilitates discussion between parties to a dispute to encourage and assist their coming to an agreement; also known as a mediator

conditional sale sale in which the seller provides credit to the purchaser, holding title until the goods are paid for

conditions major terms of a contract

condition precedent condition under which the obligations of a contract will begin; also called "subject to" clause

condition subsequent condition under which the obligations of a contract will end

Confederation the process that united the British colonies in North America as the Dominion of Canada in 1867

confidential information private information, the disclosure of which would be injurious to a business; a type of intellectual property

confirmed letter of credit a document, ratified by the lender, that secures or guarantees the financial aspects of a trade transaction

conflict of laws rules used to resolve questions as to which jurisdiction's laws are to be applied to a particular issue; includes paramountcy, a principle that if there is overlapping jurisdiction, federal law prevails and provincial law goes into abeyance; also, the area of law dealing with disputes with parties in other jurisdictions

conglomerate merger a merger of companies not in direct competition

consensus factor in validity of a contract: both parties must objectively know and agree to its terms

consent permission or assent to conduct that would otherwise constitute a tort such as assault and battery; can be expressed or implied; an informed consent constitutes a defence to torts such as assault and battery

consideration the price one is willing to pay for the promise set out in the offer

conspiracy to injure coordinated action of two or more persons using illegal methods to harm the business or other interests of another

construction approach in situations of fundamental breach, a way to ascertain the meaning of a written contract; a finding by a court, after carefully examining the wording, that an exemption clause does not limit liability

constructive dismissal unilaterally demoting or changing the duties of an employee, contrary to what was agreed to in the employment contract; conduct that essentially terminates a pre-existing contractual relationship, which could be treated as dismissal

constructive trust a trust inferred by the courts to benefit a third party to a contract

consumer transactions purchases by individuals of goods or services for personal use and not for resale or for business purposes

contingency fee a fee paid to a lawyer that is based on a percentage of the sum recovered by the client

continuing guarantee a provision in a guarantee allowing the creditor to advance further funds without affecting the obligation of the guarantor to pay in the event of default

continuing trespass permanent incursion onto the property of another

contract a voluntary exchange of promises creating obligations that, if defaulted on, can be enforced and remedied in the courts

contra proferentum rule rule interpreting ambiguities in an insurance policy in favour of the insured

contributory negligence a failure to take reasonable care, which contributes to the injury complained of

control test test of whether an employment relationship exists based on whether the person being paid for work is told how, when, and where to do it

conversion intentional appropriation of the goods of another person

cooling-off period a statutorily defined period during which purchasers in door-to-door sales may change their minds and rescind a contract

cooperative company composed of members holding shares in it; method of acquiring residential accommodation

copyright control over the use and reproduction of the expression of creative work; type of intellectual property

corporate myth a corporation is a legal fiction

corporation a business organization that is a separate legal entity from its shareholders

counterclaim a statement of claim by the defendant alleging that the plaintiff is responsible for the losses suffered and claiming back against the plaintiff for those losses

counteroffer a new offer, proposal of which rejects and terminates the offer available until then

Court of Chancery court developed as a supplement to the common law courts; sometimes referred to as the Court of Equity

crimes wrongs that affect society as a whole and are punishable by the state

crumbling skull rule principle of torts that the defendant is not responsible for an inevitable loss by plaintiff; used in conjunction with thin skull rule

D

damages monetary compensation to victim

debenture an acknowledgment of debts by a corporation normally involving more than one creditor; often used interchangeably with bond, but whereas a bond is typically secured against a specific asset, a debenture may be unsecured or secured by a floating charge against inventory

deceit the fraudulent and intentional misleading of another person, causing injury

declaration official statement by the court on the law applicable to a particular case, as an outcome of a trial

declaratory judgment declaration by the court as to what the law is in any matter brought before it

deed of conveyance document transferring an interest in property

deeds of settlement contracts used historically for setting up a company

defamation a false statement published to a person's detriment

delegation entrusting someone else to act in one's place; an agent normally cannot turn his responsibilities over to someone else

delivery up order directing the defendant to deliver all copies of the infringing items in his or her possession or control to the copyright owner

deposit money prepaid with the provision that the funds are to be forfeited in the event of a breach

detinue wrongful retention of goods legally obtained but subsequently not returned in response to a proper request

deregulation the dissolution of agencies created to monitor and enforce certain standards; corporations are encouraged to self-regulate

derivative action a lawsuit where certain shareholders are given the right to launch a civil action against the directors on behalf of an injured company; sometimes called representative action

devolution of powers the process of transferring power from one level of government to another

digital watermarks a method of ensuring the authenticity of a website

direct sales sales made to consumers at their dwellings or places of business; also known as door-to-door sales

disbursements out-of-pocket costs incurred by the lawyer on the client's behalf

discharge by agreement agreement by parties that a contract is ended

discovery pre-trial disclosure of information, consisting of discovery of documents (records) and examination for discovery

discovery of documents (records) pre-trial inspection of any document that is held by the other party and may be used as evidence

dissent and appraisal right of minority shareholders who are adversely affected by major changes to indicate their opposition and force the company to buy back their shares at a fair price

distinguishing the facts the process judges use to decide which case is the binding precedent; involves comparing the facts relevant to the issues being determined

distress seizure by landlord of any property left by tenant and holding of it until the rent is paid or sale of it to pay rent owing

dividends payments to shareholders out of company profits

Division I proposals an alternative to bankruptcy, created by the *Bankruptcy and Insolvency Act*, whereby the debtor secures some time to reorganize his or her affairs and make a proposal for partial payment that will satisfy its creditors; if the creditors reject the proposal, the insolvent debtor is deemed to have made an assignment in bankruptcy from the day of the meeting of the creditors, and the normal bankruptcy procedures follow

dominant property property that has the advantage of an easement

door-to-door sales same as direct sales

dower rights protection of the rights of spouse in certain matrimonial property; have been modified or abolished in most jurisdictions

down payment an initial payment that must be returned to the purchaser in the event of a breach

drawee person or institution ordered to pay out the amount indicated on the negotiable instrument

drawer person creating the negotiable instrument

due diligence doing everything reasonable to avoid a problem leading to legal liability

duress force or pressure to enter into a contract

duty in a negligence action an obligation to live up to a reasonable standard

duty counsel court-appointed lawyers who assist individuals who are not represented by a lawyer; duty counsel may be available in criminal, family, or immigration courts

duty of care an obligation to take steps to avoid foreseeable harm; an essential element for establishing liability in the tort of negligence

E

easement the right of a person other than the owner to use a portion of private property

easement acquired by prescription a right to the use of land, acquired through free use of that land without interference over a number of years

electronic commerce retail selling using the Internet

employee a person working for another who is told what to do and how to do it

employers' organizations bargaining agents representing groups of employers

employment equity correction of employment situations where there has been a tradition of racial or gender imbalance

encryption coding technological innovations to protect privacy and security on the Internet

endorser person who signs the back of a cheque usually assuming the obligation to pay it if the drawee or maker defaults

enduring power of attorney the power to act as the donor's trustee or representative following the donor's lack of capacity

enhanced injunction a new remedy allowing a court to order a wrongdoer to refrain from future infringements of copyright in other works owned by the plaintiff copyright owner

equality rights basic rights, enumerated in the *Canadian Charter of Rights and Freedoms*, including the right not to be discriminated against on the basis of grounds such as gender, age, religion, race, or colour, and the guarantee of equal benefit of and protection by the law

equitable estoppel the principle that when a gratuitous promise to do something in the future causes a person to incur an expense, the promisor may be held liable for those expenses if he fails to live up to the promise; also known as promissory estoppel

equity legal principles developed in Courts of Chancery to relieve the harshness of the common law; and value left in an asset after subtracting what the owner owes

equity of redemption an interest in land retained by the mortgagor even after default

error of fact a decision maker's making an incorrect conclusion with respect to the facts in the matter in dispute

error of law a decision maker's incorrectly stating the legal interpretation or effect of the statute or common law

errors and omissions insurance insurance to protect holder should the holder cause injury by negligence

estate all the property the owner has power to dispose of, less any related debt; also an interest in land

estate in land right to uninterrupted possession of land for a time. The amount of time is determined by the nature of the estate

estoppel an equitable remedy that stops a party from trying to establish a position or deny something that, if allowed, would create an injustice

ethics a system of moral principles governing the appropriate conduct for an individual or a group

evidence in writing any document that provides information or proof

examination for discovery a pre-trial meeting in which lawyers from opposing sides question the plaintiff and defendant in a civil suit under oath—their responses can be entered as evidence; a method of making all relevant information known to both sides before trial

examination in aid of execution (examination in aid of enforcement) court-ordered review of judgment debtor's finances to arrange for payment of the judgment

executed contract a fully performed contract; a contract at the stage when both parties have performed or fulfilled their obligations

executive branch part of government comprised of the Queen acting through the prime minister, cabinet, deputy ministers and government departments and officials; also known as the Crown

executory contract a contract yet to be performed; a contract at the stage when an agreement has been made but before performance is due

exemplary damages damages in excess of plaintiff's actual losses, intended to punish the wrongdoer for outrageous or extreme behaviour; also known as punitive damages

exemption clause an attempt to limit liability under an agreement (also exclusion or exculpatory clause)

express authority the authority of the agent as actually stated by the principal

express contract contract in which the parties have expressly stated their agreement, either verbally or in writing

F

fair comment defence available when defamatory statements are made about public figures or work put before the public

fair dealing use of copyrighted material (as permitted under Canadian law) for the purpose of research or private study, criticism or review, or news reporting

fair hearing a hearing conducted in accordance with the rules of procedural fairness; person affected negatively by a decision has a right to receive proper and timely notice of all the matters affecting the case and be given a chance to put forward her side

false imprisonment holding people against their will and without lawful authority

fee simple highest interest in land, equivalent to ownership; an estate granting possession for an infinite time

fidelity bond employer's insurance against an employee's wrongful conduct

fiduciary duty a duty to act in the best interests of another; such duty may arise between directors and officers and the corporation they serve, between business associates including senior employees and their employer, between agents and their principals, and between partners

fixed fee a predetermined fee paid to a lawyer for completing a specific task

fixture a thing attached to land or to a building or to another fixture attached to the land

floating charge a security not fixed on any particular assets until default or some other specified event

force majeure **clause** contract term anticipating some catastrophic event usually exempting liability when such an event interferes with performance of the contract

foreclosure court process ending the mortgagor's right to redeem

forfeiture requirement by the landlord that the tenant who breached the lease vacate the property

forfeiture rule principle that a criminal should not be permitted to profit from a crime

formal contract an agreement under seal

franchising arrangements based on contracts of service and the supply of products between larger and smaller units of one organization

fraud the tort of intentionally or recklessly misleading another person, or making statements without belief in their truth

fraudulent misrepresentation misleading (false) words said knowingly, without belief in their truth, or recklessly, causing injury

fraudulent preference a debtor's payment of money to one creditor to give that creditor preference over the other creditors

fraudulent transfer a debtor's transfer of property in an attempt to keep it out of the hands of creditors; not a valid sale at a fair price to an innocent third party

F.O.B. contracts (free on board) sales contracts in which the parties have agreed that the seller will bear the risk until a specified point in the transport process

frustration interference with a contract by some outside, unforeseen event that makes performance impossible or essentially different in nature

full disclosure obligation to reveal all details of a transaction

fundamental breach breach of a fundamental aspect of the contract that is not covered by an exclusion clause; a breach that goes to the very root of the contract

fundamental freedoms basic rights, enumerated in the *Canadian Charter of Rights and Freedoms*, including freedom of conscience and religion, of thought and belief, of opinion and expression, and of assembly and association

fungibles goods being of such a nature that one part or quantity may be replaced by another equal part or quantity of similar quality

G

garnishment court orders that monies owed to the judgment debtor by third parties be paid into court and applied towards judgment debts; a portion of the defendant's wages may be so directed to payment of the judgment

general damages compensation for future pecuniary losses and incalculable losses such as pain and suffering

good faith the decision maker must act with honesty and integrity

goodwill a business's reputation and ongoing relations with customers and product identification

goods tangible, movable personal property that can be measured and weighed; also known as chattels

gratuitous promise a one-sided agreement that the courts will not enforce

grievance process procedure for settling disputes arising under a collective agreement

guarantee a written commitment whereby a guarantor agrees to pay a debt if the debtor does not

guarantor person assuming obligation to pay if the debtor does not

H

habeas corpus a court order to bring an arrested person before a judge to determine if that person is being improperly detained

holdback a specified percentage that a person owing funds on a construction contract must retain for a specified period to protect against claims made by the suppliers of goods and services

holder in due course an innocent third party entitled to collect on a negotiable instrument despite any claims of the original parties

holding corporation a corporation that owns shares in other corporations

homestead rights rights giving a spouse a claim to a substantial portion of family property

horizontal merger a merger in which one competitor buys out another

I

illegal consideration a promise to commit an unlawful act or to do something against public policy, which is not valid consideration and will not be enforced by a court

illegal contract one that is void because it involves the performance of an unlawful act

implied authority the authority of the agent as implied from surrounding circumstances, such as the position or title given (by the principal) to the agent

implied contract an agreement inferred from the conduct of the parties

in camera hearings part of trial proceedings closed to the public

in good faith characteristic of bargaining that makes every reasonable effort to reach an agreement

indemnity a primary obligation of a third party to pay a debt along with the debtor

independent contractor a person working for himself who contracts to provide specific services to another

inducing breach of contract encouraging someone to break her contract with another

industrial design unique shapes or patterns that distinguish manufactured articles; type of intellectual property

infant a person under the age of majority

injunction court order to stop offending conduct

injurious falsehood defamation with respect to another's product or business; also known as product defamation or trade slander

innocent misrepresentation a false statement made honestly and without carelessness by a person who believed it to be true

innuendo an implied statement that is detrimental to another

insanity when a person cannot understand the nature or consequences of his acts

insider knowledge information that affects share pricing that is not publicly known; directors, officers, and large shareholders, amongst others, cannot profit by improperly using confidential knowledge about the company

insolvency inability of a person to pay her debts as they become due

insurable interest a real and substantial interest in specific property or in someone's life

insurance agents person acting on behalf of insurer to handle policies

intellectual property personal property in the form of ideas and creative work

intention desire or aim; parties must objectively intend an agreement to be legally binding; must intend to assume the obligations of the agreement

intentional infliction of mental suffering a tort constituted by harassment or prank causing nervous shock

interest dispute disagreement about the terms to be included in a new collective agreement

interference with economic relations a tort consisting of unlawful competitive practices such as inducing breach of contract

interim agreement binding contract that will subsequently be put into a more formal document

interlocutory injunction court order issued before a trial to stop an ongoing injury

interpretation statutes statute terms that direct the court to interpret legislation in specific ways

intimidation a threat to perform an illegal act, used to force a party to act against its own interest

intra vires within one's jurisdiction or scope of power

invitation to treat invitation to engage in the bargaining process

invitee a person coming on a property for a business purpose

involuntary assignment assignment of rights that takes place involuntarily, as in the cases of death and bankruptcy

issue estoppel principle preventing an issue from being litigated again on grounds that it has already been determined in an earlier trial or hearing

J

joint liability liability under which all parties must be sued together; partners may face joint liability for debts of the firm

joint tenancy shared property ownership with right of survivorship

joint venture the collaboration of several businesses to accomplish a major project

judicial branch part of government comprised of courts and officers of the court

judicial review power held by the courts to review decisions made by administrative decision makers

judgment creditor person to whom court awards damages or costs

judgment debtor person ordered by court to pay damages or costs

jurisdiction legal authority and scope of power; the Constitution Act (1867) delegated responsibility for matters to federal or provincial governments, thus giving them distinct jurisdiction to create laws in those areas

jurisdictional dispute a disagreement over who has authority; in the labour

context, a dispute between two unions over which one should represent a group of employees, or over which union members ought to do a particular job

just cause valid reason to dismiss an employee without notice

justification the truth of a statement, applied as a defence to a defamation action

L

laches undue delay; neglect, or omission to assert a right or claim

land titles system registration system that guarantees title to real property

last clear chance doctrine largely outdated principle of torts that the last person capable of avoiding an accident is wholly responsible

law the body of rules that can be enforced by the courts or by other government agencies

law of equity the system of law developed by the Court of Chancery

law merchant laws developed by the merchant guilds and source of common law relating to negotiable instruments such as cheques and promissory notes

law society self-governing body whose mandate involves regulating the legal profession, in the public interest; law societies set, and enforce, ethical and professional standards for lawyers

lease a secured arrangement whereby possession of the goods goes to the lessee, while the title to the goods remains with the lessor

lease to purchase a lease in which title to the goods is transferred to the lessee at the end of the lease period

leasehold estate an interest in land which grants the tenant exclusive possession until a specific date

legal advice the giving of an opinion by a lawyer regarding the substance or procedure of the law

legal aid the provision of legal services to persons in financial need

legal representation a lawyer who has the authority to represent a person in court proceedings or in other legal matters

legal rights basic rights, enumerated in the *Canadian Charter of Rights and Freedoms*, such as the right to life, liberty, and security of the person; and security against unreasonable search and seizure, or arbitrary imprisonment or detention

legality one of the elements of a valid contract; the object and consideration of the contract must be legal and not against public policy

legislation laws passed by Parliament or provincial legislatures; also referred to as statutes

legislative branch part of government comprised of Parliament and legislatures

letter of credit commitment by the importer's bank that the price stated will be paid upon presentation of documentation confirming delivery

letters patent a method of incorporating used in some jurisdictions in Canada whereby the government grants recognition to the company as a separate legal entity

liability the situation of being potentially or actually subject to some obligation

liability insurance insurance covering loss caused by the negligence of oneself or one's employees

libel the written or more permanent form of a defamatory statement

licence a non-exclusive right to use property; revocable permission to use another's land

licensee a person on a property with permission but for a non-business purpose

lien a claim registered against property, such as a mortgage; charge giving the creditor the right to retain what is in his possession until his demands for payment are satisfied

life estate an interest in land ending at death

limitation periods rules requiring that legal action be undertaken within a specified time from when the offending conduct occurs

limited liability liability is restricted to capital contributed; shareholders are shielded from liability for the corporation's debts

limited partnership a partnership with general and limited partners; limited partners are liable only to the extent of their investment

liquidated damages a remedy requiring party responsible for a breach to pay an amount specified in the contract

lockout an action in which the employer prevents employees from working

M

maintenance of membership requirement in collective agreement that union members pay dues and maintain their membership, though new employees need not join the union

malicious prosecution a tort action based on criminal or quasi-criminal prosecution motivated by ill will towards the accused and lacking reasonable evidential grounds for proceeding

mandatory retirement forced retirement from employment generally at 65 years

mandamus a court order directing that a specific act be performed

mediation a discussion, between the parties to a dispute, that is facilitated by a mediator in an effort to encourage and assist them in coming to an agreement

mediator a neutral third party who facilitates discussion between parties to a dispute to encourage and assist their coming to an agreement; also known as a conciliator

memorandum of association constitution of a corporation in a registration jurisdiction

merchantable quality freedom of goods from defects that, if known, would impact the price

minor a person under the age of majority

misfeasance wrongful conduct

misrepresentation a false statement of fact that persuades someone to enter into a contract or take some other action

mistake an error about some aspect of a contract that destroys consensus

mitigate lessen a loss, for example, by victims of a breach, who have a duty to take all reasonable steps to minimize losses suffered

moral rights author's right to prohibit others, including any new owner of a creative work, from distorting or degrading it

mortgage means of securing loans; title of property is held by the money-lender as security in some jurisdictions; in other jurisdictions, a mortgage is simply a charge against title

N

necessaries the essential goods or services required to function in society, such as food, clothing, and shelter

negligence an unintentional careless act that results in injury to another

negligent statements failure to live up to a duty not to communicate misleading words causing economic loss

negotiable instruments substitutes for money that bestow unique benefits; vehicles for conveniently transferring funds or advancing credit

negotiation direct communication between the parties to a dispute in an effort to resolve the problems without third-party intervention; transferring negotiable instruments to third parties

netiquette a code of conduct for on-line activities

"no fault" programs insurance program compensating people for their injuries whether they were at fault or not

non est factum "it is not my act"—grounds for court to declare a contract void because a party is unaware of the nature of the contract

non-disclosure silence constitutes misrepresentation only when there is a duty to disclose

nonfeasance failure to act; such failure is actionable in tort only where there is a specific duty to act, as with a guardian, parent, or lifeguard

non-pecuniary damages damages based on non-monetary factors such as pain and suffering

non-profit society separate legal entity with different rules for incorporation than corporations

novation creation of a new contract through the substitution of a third party for one of the original parties to a contract, by the consent of all

O

offer a tentative promise to do something if another party consents to do what the first party requests

offer to settle a formal offer by either party to modify or compromise its claim to settle the matter before trial, refusal of which offer may affect costs

operating lease a lease in which the goods are returned to the lessor at the end of the lease period

oppression action action against the directors who have allegedly offended the rights of creditors or minority shareholders

option agreement a subsidiary contract creating an obligation to hold an offer open for acceptance until the expiration of a specified time

order absolute final order of foreclosure ending the right to redeem

order nisi an order establishing the time limit within which the mortgagor can redeem his interest

organization test test of whether or not a service-provider is an employee and part of employer's organization

P

par value a share with a stated value at issuance (most shares are now no-parvalue)

paramountcy principle that when a matter is addressed by both valid federal and provincial legislation and there is a conflict, the federal legislation takes precedence

parliamentary supremacy principle that the primary law-making body is Parliament or the provincial legislatures in their respective jurisdictions,

and that statutes take priority over the common law

parol contract a simple contract that may be verbal or written but is not under seal

parol evidence rule principle that courts will not permit outside evidence to contradict clear wording of a contract

partially executed contract a contract at the stage when one party has performed and the other has not

partnership ownership and responsibilities of a business shared by two or more people, with a view towards profit

party and party costs court costs determined by a tariff establishing what opposing parties in a civil action ought to pay

passing-off the tort of misleading the public about the identity of a business or product

past consideration something completed before an agreement is made; it is not valid consideration

patent government-granted monopoly prohibiting anyone but the inventor from profiting from the invention; gives inventors the right to profit from their inventions

pay equity principle or statute requiring equal pay for work of equal value

pay in lieu of notice an amount paid to a dismissed employee rather than notice to terminate

payee the person designated on the instrument to receive the money to be paid out

perfection protection of a secured creditor's claim, either by registering the secured obligation or by taking possession of the collateral

performance completion by both parties of the terms of a contract

periodic tenancy automatically renewing tenancy with no specific termination date

permanent injunction court order prohibiting offending conduct

personal guarantee a guarantee of payment for another's obligation

personal property tangible, movable goods (chattels) and intangible claims (choses in action); also known as personalty

picketing job action during a legal strike when employees circulate at the periphery of the jobsite to persuade others not to do business with struck employer

pleadings the documents used to initiate a civil action, including the statement of claim, the statement of defence and counterclaim, and any clarification associated with them

pledge an item that a creditor (such as a pawnbroker) takes possession of as security and holds until repayment

postbox rule principle that mailed acceptance is effective when and where it is dropped into a mailbox

power of attorney an agency agreement in writing and under seal

precedent an earlier court decision; in a common law system, judges are required to follow a decision made in a higher court in the same jurisdiction

preferred creditors creditors who, by legislation, must be paid before other unsecured creditors

preferred shareholders holder of preferred shares who may have a right to vote arising if dividends are not paid

preferred shares shares giving the shareholder preference over other classes of shares; that preference often pertains to payment of dividends

prerogative writs the remedies the court may apply if it finds that an administrator has acted beyond its jurisdiction, made an unreasonable decision, or not followed the rules of natural justice

prima facie case a judicial finding that circumstantial evidence establishes a case "on the face of it"

principles of fundamental justice principles set by tradition and convention that protect the right to a fair hearing by an impartial decision maker acting in good faith to implement a valid law

priority when there are two or more creditors, the one entitled to be paid first has priority; for example, a registered lien usually has first claim (over other interests) to goods used as security

privacy the right to be let alone, to protect private personal information, and to be free of physical intrusion, surveillance, and misuse of an image or name

private law the rules that govern our personal, social, and business relations, which are enforced by one person's suing another in a private or civil action

private nuisance the use of property in such a way that it interferes with a neighbour's enjoyment of his or hers

privative clause terms in a statute that attempt to restrict the right of judicial review

privity of contract principle that contract terms apply only to the actual parties to the contract

probate courts specialized courts dealing with wills and estates; also known as surrogate courts

procedural fairness rules of natural justice that a hearing must follow

procedural law law determining how the substantive laws will be enforced,

for example, the rules governing arrest and criminal investigation, pre-trial and court processes in both criminal and civil cases

product defamation defamation with respect to another's product; also known as injurious falsehood or trade slander

product liability manufacturers owe a duty when users are injured by their products

professional associations organizations for professionals that are set up under provincial legislation; they have extensive power to regulate educational and professional qualifications and standards of behaviour and to establish methods of disciplining members for wrongful conduct or incompetence

professional liability liability owed by persons failing to live up to the standard expected of a reasonable member of a group with special expertise

professional liability insurance specialty insurance for lawyers, doctors, and other professionals designed to cover risks occurring in their practices

profit à prendre contracts to take resources off the land

prohibition an order not to proceed with a hearing or other administrative process

promissory estoppel principle that when a gratuitous promise to do something in the future causes a person to incur an expense, the promisor may be held liable for those expenses if she fails to live up to the promise; also known as equitable estoppel

promissory note a promise to pay the amount stated on the instrument

promoter a person who participates in the initial setting up of a corporation or who assists the corporation in making a public share offering

proof of claim document filed with the Trustee in Bankruptcy establishing validity of a creditor's claim

prospectus public document disclosing relevant information about a corporation

proxy shareholders' designation of another person to vote on their behalf at an annual general meeting

public domain category of works that are no longer copyrighted and may be used by anyone

public interest responsible journalism defence a defence to defamation, excusing incorrect statements on matters of public interest, where conclusions were reached following responsible investigation

public law the public good; law concerning the government and individuals' relationship with it, including

criminal law and the regulations created by government agencies

public nuisance unreasonable interference with public property

public policy the public good; some acts, although not illegal, will not be enforced by the courts because they are socially distasteful (against public policy)

punitive damages damages in excess of plaintiff's actual losses, intended to punish the wrongdoer for outrageous or extreme behaviour; also known as exemplary damages

purchase money security interest (PMSI) a security interest on specific goods that has priority over a general security agreement provided it is registered within a specified time

Q

qualified privilege exemption from liability for defamatory statements made pursuant to a duty or special interest, so long as the statement was made honestly and without malice, and was circulated only to those having a right to know

quantum meruit "as much as is deserved"; reasonable price paid for requested services; sometimes called a quasi-contract

quasi-contract contractual relationship involving a request for goods and services where there is no agreement on price before the service is performed; courts impose obligation to pay a reasonable price; also known as *quantum meruit*

quiet enjoyment an obligation that the lessor or anyone claiming through the lessor will not interfere with the tenant's use of the property

quiet possession a condition that the seller, or anyone claiming through the seller, will not interfere with the buyer's use and enjoyment of the property

R

Rand formula option in collective agreement enabling employees to retain the right not to join the union, though they are still required to pay union dues; also known as agency shop

ratification majority agrees with terms of collective bargain; principal confirms a contract entered into by his or her agent

real property land, buildings attached to the land, and items called fixtures, that is, items which are attached to the land or to a building or to another fixture attached to the land

reasonable foreseeability test test of whether a duty of care is owed, based on what a person should have anticipated would be the consequences of his or her action

reasonable notice length of notice to be given an employee to terminate an employment contract of indefinite term; determined with reference to length of service and nature of employee's position amongst other factors

reasonable person test in a negligence action, the judicial standard of socially acceptable behaviour; standard to determine the existence of apparent authority of an agent

receivership proceeding in which a receiver is appointed for an insolvent corporation, partnership, or individual to take possession of its assets for ultimate sale and distribution to creditors

recognition dispute dispute arising between a union and employer while union is being organized

rectification correction, by the court, of the wording of a mistake in the contract

referral selling a type of sales practice in which the purchaser supplies a seller with a list of friends or acquaintances and receives a benefit when sales are made to those people

registration a legislated requirement for incorporating a company in some jurisdictions in Canada

registration system a means of registering and tracking property deeds

regulations supplementary rules passed under the authority of a statute and having the status of law

regulators government agencies including ministries, departments, boards, commissions, agencies, tribunals, and individual bureaucrats at the federal, provincial, and municipal levels

relief against forfeiture equitable principle that when a landlord retakes a property for failure to pay rent prior to the end of the lease term, the tenant can pay the arrears and apply in the court to have the lease reinstated

remainderman third party with the right to the remainder of the fee simple after the death of a life tenant

remoteness test determining whether the damages were too far removed from the original negligent act; a breaching party is only responsible for reasonably expected losses

representative action a lawsuit where certain shareholders are given the right to launch a civil action against the directors on behalf of an injured company; sometimes called a derivative action

repudiation an indication by one party to the other that there will be a failure

to honour the contract (expression can be expressed or implied)

res ipsa loquitur principle of establishing negligence based on facts that "speak for themselves"; this no longer applies in Canadian tort law

rescission returning of the parties to the position they were in before the contract

restrictive covenant in property law, a condition imposed by the seller as to what the purchaser can use the land for; in employment law, a commitment not to work in a certain geographical area for a designated period of time

retainer a deposit paid by a client to a lawyer before the lawyer commences work on behalf of the client

reverse discrimination prejudice or bias exercised against a person or class for purpose of correcting a pattern of discrimination against another person or class

reversionary interest right of original owner to retake possession of property upon death of life tenant

revocation withdrawal of an offer before acceptance (must be communicated to the offeree)

right of salvage an insurer's right after paying the insured to sell damaged or recovered goods to recover losses

right of way type of easement that allows the crossing of another's land

right to redeem after a creditor has taken possession of collateral, the right of the debtor to reclaim it on payment of any money owing

rights dispute disagreement about the meaning of a term in a collective agreement

riparian rights common law right given to people living near rivers and streams to have the water come to them in undiminished quantity and quality

risk potential loss due to destruction or damage to goods, injury, or other eventuality

Roman civil law law of the Roman Empire, from which the common law drew its concepts of property and possessions

royal assent the final approval of the representative of the British Crown, by which a bill becomes law in Canada

rule of law unwritten convention inherited from Britain that recognizes that although Parliament is supreme and can create any law considered appropriate, citizens are protected from the arbitrary actions of the government

rules of evidence rules governing the kind of evidence that will be accepted by the courts

rules of natural justice basic standards of procedural fairness

S

sale a transaction in which the seller transfers possession and property to a buyer, for valuable consideration

salvage that portion of goods or property which has been saved or remains after a casualty such as fire or other loss

satisfaction a substitute in consideration accepted by both parties

secondary picketing picketing by striking employees not just of their own workplace but also of other locations where the employer carries on business

secured creditor a creditor who has claim on property of the debtor, giving priority over other creditors

secured transaction collateral right to debt giving the creditor the right to take back the goods or intercept the debt owing used as security in the event of a default

securities commission provincial agency that serves as watchdog on stock market

seizure court authorizes property of the defendant to be seized and sold to satisfy the judgment

self-defence the right to respond to an assault with as much force as is reasonable in the circumstances

self-induced frustration frustration arising when one of the parties to a contract causes or fails to prevent a frustrating event; treated as a breach of contract

seller's lien seller who holds the goods has a lien against defaulting purchaser

sentencing circles meetings to suggest sentences in cases involving Aboriginal offenders and victims

separate legal entity a corporation exists separately from the people who created it

service contract an agreement to perform a beneficial service

servient property the property subject to an easement

settlement transfer of assets where nominal or no consideration is involved

several liability liability under which each partner can be sued separately

severance owner's removal of chattel he or she has affixed; separation or division of joint ownership; action by one of the co-owners that is inconsistent with joint tenancy

share the means of acquiring funds from a large number of sources to run a corporation; an interest in a corporation held by an investor

shared mistake the same mistake made by both parties to a contract

shareholder agreement protects the rights of shareholders in relations with the corporation

simple contract written or verbal contract not under seal, also called a parol contract

site audit the process of examining a site to determine its state of environmental contamination

slander spoken defamation

sole proprietorship an individual carrying on business alone

solicitor and client costs costs based on what a lawyer ought to actually charge his client

sophisticated client a person who understands and appreciates the importance of the law and the role of a lawyer in making good decisions

spam unsolicited email sent in bulk

special damages monetary compensation awarded by court to cover actual expenses and calculable pre-trial losses

specific performance order by a court to a breaching party that it live up to the terms of an agreement

standard form contract contract with fixed terms prepared by a business

standby letter of credit commitment by the importer's bank that the price stated will be paid upon presentation of documentation confirming delivery; used as a guarantee

stare decisis a principle by which judges are required to follow the decision made in a similar case in a higher court

statement of claim the document setting out the nature of complaint and facts alleged forming the basis of the action

statement of defence response by the defendant to a statement of claim

statutes law in the form of legislation passed by Parliament

statutory assignment an assignment that meets certain qualifications and under which the assignee can enforce a claim directly without involving the assignor

statutory damages a new remedy enabling a court to award damages that it "considers just" in the circumstances

statutory easements easements giving utilities or other bodies rights to run power or sewer lines across private property

stoppage in transit seller's right to stop the shipment during transit in event of default

strict liability liability even in the absence of fault

strike withdrawal of services by employees

"subject to" clause term making a contract conditional on future events

sublet lease executed by lessee of land or premises to a third party for a shorter term than that which the lessee holds

subrogation the right of insurer upon payment to take over the rights of the insured in relation to whoever caused the injury

substantial performance performance of a contract in all but a minor aspect of it

substantive law law establishing both the rights an individual has in society and also the limits on her conduct

suing on the covenant creditor can sue for breach of contract

summary procedures an arrangement allowing a court to make a decision based on affidavit evidence

surety bond insurance arranged in case a party to a contract fails to perform

surrogate courts specialized courts dealing with wills and estates; also known as probate courts

T

tenancy at sufferance situation in which tenant fails to leave after lease has expired and owes compensation to the landlord

tenancy at will an interest that allows the party in possession to remain on the property at the pleasure of the grantor, without creating any durable right

tenancy in common ownership of land by two or more people with equal undivided interests in it

tender of performance an unsuccessful (because it is rejected or prevented by the other party) attempt by one of the parties to a contract to perform its obligations under the contract

thin skull rule principle of torts that we take our victims as we find them, even those with unique physical or mental conditions

tort an action that causes harm or injury to another person

trade secret confidential information that gives a business competitive advantage

trade slander defamation with respect to another's product or business; also known as injurious falsehood or product defamation

trade-mark any term, symbol, design, or combination of these that identifies a business service or product and distinguishes it from a competitor

trespasser one who intentionally and without consent or privilege enters another's property

trespass to chattels direct intentional interference causing damage to the goods of another

trespass to person intentional physical interference with another person; also known as assault and battery

trust provision in equity whereby one person transfers property to a second person obligated to use it to the benefit of a third

Trustee in Bankruptcy the licensed professional appointed to administer the estate of a bankrupt for the benefit of the creditors

truth accuracy of a statement, applied as a defence to a defamation action; also known as the defence of justification

U

ultra vires beyond the jurisdiction, power, or authority of a decision maker

umbrella liability a package of several kinds of insurance

unconscionable transaction equitable principle allowing courts to set aside a contract in which a party in a superior bargaining position took advantage of the other party, and the consideration was grossly unfair

undisclosed principal a principal whose identity is concealed from the third parties with whom the agent is dealing; the rights and obligations of the parties depend on whether the agent makes it clear that he is representing an undisclosed principal rather than operating on his own behalf

undue influence pressure from a dominant, trusted person that makes it impossible for a party to bargain the terms of a contract freely

unenforceable contract an otherwise binding contract that the courts will not enforce, such as a contract that does not satisfy the *Statute of Frauds*

unilateral contract a contract formed when one party performs what has been requested by the other party; there is a promise followed by an act, but not an exchange of promises

unilateral discharge non-binding agreement to discharge that only benefits one of the parties

unilateral mistake a mistake made by only one of the parties about the terms of a contract

union shop workplace where new employees must join the union

unjust enrichment a windfall that one party to a contract stands to make at the expense of the other

unlimited liability the liability of the business owner or partners for all debts incurred by the business to the extent of their personal resources

utmost good faith another term for fiduciary duty

V

vacant possession an obligation to deliver possession of vacant premises to the tenant at the beginning of the lease period

valid contract an agreement legally binding on both parties

vertical merger a merger of a supplier and a retailer

vicarious liability liability of an employer for injuries caused by employees while carrying out their employment duties

vicarious performance performance by another qualified person of the obligations under a contract

void contract an agreement that is not legally binding because an essential ingredient is missing

voidable contract an agreement that has legal effect but that one of the parties has the option to end

volenti non fit injuria defence in torts based on the plaintiff's voluntarily assuming a clear legal risk

voluntary assignment in bankruptcy an assignment of assets to a Trustee in Bankruptcy for the benefit of creditors, made voluntarily by a debtor

W

warranties minor terms of a contract

without prejudice words that, when used during negotiation, are a declaration that concessions, compromises, and admissions made by a party cannot be used against that party in subsequent litigation

work to rule job action in which employees perform no more than is minimally required, so as to pressure an employer

work stoppages strikes (initiated by employees) and lockouts (initiated by employers)

writ of summons the written judicial order by which legal actions are commenced in some jurisdictions

wrongful dismissal dismissal without reasonable cause or notice

Tables of Statutes

Tables of Cases

Notes: The page numbers given at the end of each case in parentheses refer to pages of this book. Numbered companies are listed at the beginning.

Index